Music Innovators

Music Innovators

Volume 3
N–Z
Appendixes
Indexes

SALEM PRESS
A Division of EBSCO Information Services
Ipswich, Massachusetts

GREY HOUSE PUBLISHING

Cover photo: John Lennon by photographer Bob Gruen

Music Innovators, 2016, published by Grey House Publishing, Inc., Amenia, NY, under exclusive license from EBSCO Information Services, Inc. Majority of the content originally appeared as articles in various issues of *Current Biography* magazine, published by H. W. Wilson. New profiles and other materials have been added to this work.

∞ The paper used in these volumes conforms to the American National Standard for Permanence of Paper for Printed Library Materials, Z39.48 1992 (R2009).

Publisher's Cataloging-In-Publication Data

Names: Salem Press.
Title: Music innovators / the editors of Salem Press.
Description: Ipswich, Massachusetts : Salem Press, a division of EBSCO Information Services, Inc. ; Amenia, NY : Grey House Publishing, [2016] | Includes bibliographical references and index.
Identifiers: ISBN 978-1-61925-896-9 (set) | ISBN 978-1-68217-207-0 (v.1) | ISBN 978-1-68217-208-7 (v.2) | ISBN 978-1-68217-209-4 (v.3)
Subjects: LCSH: Musicians--Biography. | Music--History--20th century. | Music--History--21st century.
Classification: LCC ML394 .M87 2016 | DDC 780.092/2--dc23

PRINTED IN THE UNITED STATES OF AMERICA

Contents

VOLUME 1

VOLUME 2

VOLUME 3

Appendixes

Indexes

KEY TO ABBREVIATIONS USED IN FURTHER READING

Ag	August
Ap	April
A.P.	Associate Press
D	December
ed	edited, edition, editor
F	February
il	illustrated
J	Journal
Ja	January
Je	June
Jl	July
mag	magazine
Mr	March
My	May
N	November
nd	no date
no	number
O	October
p	page
pam	pamphlet
por	portrait, -s
S	September
sup	supplement
tr	translated, translation, translator
v	volume
w	weekly

Music Innovators

Nas (nahz)

Rap musician; actor

Born: Sep. 14, 1973; Queens, New York
Primary Field: Rap
Group Affiliation: The Firm

Introduction

Since his recording debut, in the early 1990s, Nas has risen to become one of the most influential and respected rappers in the industry. Though he has often struggled to reach the bar he set for himself with his first solo album, Illmatic *(1994), the Queens, New York, rapper has since released some of the genre's most heralded albums of recent memory, including* It Was Written *(1996),* God's Son *(2002),* Street's Disciple *(2004), and his untitled 2008 recording. In 2006 the cable channel MTV ranked Nas number five on its list of the "10 Greatest MCs of all time," and the Grammy Award–nominated rapper Slick Rick provided a testimonial for the MTV Web site, saying, "[Nas] comes with emotions, he speaks on positivity. . . . There aren't too many rappers who can compete with him."*

Early Life

The older of two boys, Nas was born Nasir bin Olu Dara Jones on September 14, 1973 in Long Island City, Queens, New York. ("Nasir" is an Arabic name meaning "helper" or "protector," while "bin" means *"son* of.") Nas hails from a long line of musicians. Nas's father, the jazz musician Olu Dara, fostered his interest in music early on. "If it wasn't for my pops makin' music, I wouldn't be makin' music," Nas told Shawn Edwards for the Kansas City, Missouri, *Pitch Weekly* (June 6, 2002). "He brought me onstage when I was about four or five.... So I've always had an understanding of the power of words and what my voice represents." His father, a cornetist and trumpeter, performed with Art Blakey's Jazz Messengers during the 1970s. Olu Dara's father and grandfather were both singers, and his great-uncles were members of the Rabbit Foot Company minstrel and variety troupe, alongside the legendary blues singers Ma Rainey and Bessie Smith. Dara was born Charles Jones III in Natchez, Mississippi, and adopted his current name, which means "God is good" in the West African language of Yoruba, when he was 23. Dara, who has performed on Nas's albums, leads the Okra Orchestra and Natchezsippi Dance Band.

Nas grew up in Long Island City's Queensbridge Houses, the largest public-housing development in the United States. Dara exposed his son to music at a young age. Nas's parents divorced when he was 12 years old, and he and his brother, Jabarinow known in hip-hop circles as Jungle—lived with their mother, Fannie Ann Jones, who worked for the U.S. Postal Service. In the 1980s Nas developed a passion for the hip-hop music of the era. The Queensbridge Houses complex is known as a hotbed for hip-hop talent, producing such legends as Marley Marl and MC Shan as well as Nas. Although Nas hoped ultimately to get into the music business, he noticed his peers making quick money on the streets by selling drugs, and for that and other reasons, he decided to drop out of school in the ninth grade (some sources say eighth grade). "If it was up to me, I would have gone to college, but school wasn't what I wanted it to be. I hate to sound corny, but there's a problem between a lot of teachers and black boys. They don't understand our attitudes at an early age. They treat us like violent animals and throw us in special classes where we can't develop ourselves as people," Nas told Cheo Hodari Coker for the *Los Angeles Times* (August 11, 1996). "But even if you get through that, you still have to deal with society. As a young black man, sometimes you think the whole world is against you, and ignorant people—some teachers especially—will feed that to you. You need people feeding you motivation." When he was 18 his hustling days came to an abrupt end, after his best friend, William "Ill Will" Graham, was murdered. Graham's death convinced Nas that "there was no love on the street," as he recalled to Coker. "At that moment, I knew either I was going down or music was going to save me. I believe God came to me through the music, and he came right on time." (Nas, who has a tattoo dedicated to his friend on his left arm, later named his recording label Ill Will.)

Life's Work

Nas's first recorded work came in 1991, on the hip-hop group Main Source's debut album, *Breaking Atoms*; then known as Nasty Nas, he performed a verse on the track "Live at the Barbecue." MC Serch, formerly of the hip-hop group 3rd Bass, approached Nas soon afterward about contributing to the soundtrack for the 1992 film *Zebrahead.* For that album Nas recorded his first solo song, "Halftime." Serch, impressed with Nas, featured the young rapper on "Back to the Grill" on his solo album *Return of the Product,* released in 1992. Nas soon caught the attention of executives at Columbia Records and was signed to the label that same year.

Nas's debut album, *Illmatic,* was released in 1994. Named in honor of his slain friend, the album featured songs including "N.Y. State of Mind," in which Nas raps over a jazzy piano loop about life in his tough neighborhood, and the QTip-produced "One Love," written as a series of letters to friends in prison: "So stay civilized, time flies / Though incarcerated your mind (dies) / I hate it when your mum cries / It kinda wants to make me murder . . ." Nas's father made an appearance, playing trumpet at the end of the track "Life's a Bi**h." The album received rave reviews. The *Source* awarded *Illmatic* five (out of five) microphones, an extremely rare rating from the magazine for any album, even more so for a debut record. The magazine's reviewer Shortie wrote (April 1994), "I must maintain that this is one of the best hip-hop albums I have ever heard. . . . Your mind races to keep up with Nas's [lyrics], while your body dips to the beat." Giving the album four out of five stars in *Rolling Stone* (1994, on-line), Toure declared Nasa new member of "the elite group of MCs" with "sharp articulation, finely detailed lyrics and a controlled tone reminiscent of [the rapper] Rakim." Toure also wrote that the album is "like a rose stretching up between cracks in the sidewalk, calling attention to its beauty, calling attention to the lack of it everywhere else."

In spite of its critical praise, the album failed to achieve substantial commercial success. After peaking at number 12 on the *Billboard* 200 chart in May and selling 59,000 copies in its first week, *Illmatic's* sales soon dropped. It was not until two years later, in January 1996, that sales of the album rose to more than 500,000 copies, and it was certified gold by the Recording Industry Association of America (RIAA). (At the time of the album's release, the rap scene was dominated by West Coast artists and G-funk, a highly synthesized style of hip-hop that uses funk music and slow beats. In retrospect, many music critics have acknowledged that *Illmatic* both redefined and led the resurgence of East Coast hip-hop, placing a renewed focus on lyricism and vocal delivery.) *Illmatic* has since become one of the most popular hip-hop albums in history and is often cited as one of the most influential.

Nas's sophomore album, *It Was Written* (1996), shot to the top of the *Billboard* charts, selling more than three million copies, and was certified platinum. The album's hit single, "If I Ruled the World (Imagine That)," featured vocals by the future Grammy Award-winner Lauryn Hill, then a member of the acclaimed hip-hop group the Fugees. The album received mixed reviews, however. Dimitri Ehrlich gave the album an A- in *Entertainment Weekly* (July 26, 1996, on-line), writing, "Nas' delivery on *It Was Written* is disjointed, but his concerns are straightforward. On 'Street Dreams' he details how coke has ravaged his neighborhood, and on 'Black Girl Lost' he sympathizes with the struggle of African-American women without sounding self-consciously PC. Humor disguises the grim subject matter while Nas' eye for minutiae lends credibility and urgency to his hip-hop short stories." In *Rolling Stone* (September 19, 1996, online), Mark Coleman wrote, "Gang Starr's DJ Premier lays down a spooky, jazz-fusion groove on 'I Gave You Power,' and this time, Nas responds with a mind-blowing sustained metaphor, speaking as the voice of a gun. This extraordinary view of casual violence measures the exact dimensions of a vicious circle: 'I might have took your first child, scarred your life,

Affiliation: Rapper Feud

Nas is also well-known for his longtime feud with the Brooklyn, New York-born rapper Jay-Z. Following the 1997 murder of the famed New York City rapper Notorious B.I.G. (also known as Biggie Smalls), Nas and Jay'Z became rivals for the unofficial title of New York's top rapper. For years the two included on their albums insults targeted at each other. Their feud ended in 2005, much to the surprise of their fans, and Nas signed with Jay-Z's label Def Jam Recordings the following year. Later acknowledging his respect for Nas, Jay-Z told Toure for BET News, as quoted in the *Washington Afro-American* (March 17, 2006), *"[Illmatic]* was a great album. It was one of the. most important albums in hip-hop history."

crippled your style / I gave you power / I made you buck wild."' Despite such praise Coleman awarded the album only two out of five stars, lamenting, *"It Was Written* proves that [Nas] . . . possesses a phenomenal way with words and some savvy musical sense. It's a pity that he doesn't put his verbal dexterity and powers of observation to better use."

Nas next became a member of the ill-fated group the Firm, with the rappers AZ, Foxy Brown, and Nature. Signed to Dr. Dre's Aftermath Entertainment label, the Firm released a self-titled 1997 album so critically and commercially disappointing that the group promptly split up. Two years later Nas released *I Am ...* , his third studio album, which debuted at the top spot on the *Billboard* charts, selling more than 470,000 copies in its first week. The album was later certified platinum twice over. Although criticized for its commercial nature, it received generally good reviews. Later in

1999 Nas released *Nostradamus,* the rapper's first album under his newly established Ill Will Records imprint. Regarded as one of his most unpopular albums, *Nostradamus* was generally panned as uninspired and cliched. His next release, *Stillmatic* (2001), fared much better. Though a number of critics felt that Nas was still not performing up to his potential, he received another five microphones from the *Source.* Rating the album a seven out of 10, Alex Needham wrote for *NME* (January 11, 2002, on-line), "Lyrically, Nas is pretty much back on form." Within a year *Stillmatic* had sold more than 1.7 million copies.

In 2001 the rivalry between Jay-Z and Nas, which had been brewing throughout the late 1990s following Jay-Z's unauthorized sampling of Nas's "The World Is Yours" on his 1996 song "Dead Presidents," escalated with the release of Jay-Z's *Blueprint.* On the album's song "Takeover," Jay-Z ridicules Nas for being unable to record an album that lives up to his debut *(Illmatic)* and questions Nas's "street cred." The song sparked a series of back-and-forth "diss" songs, including Nas's "Ether" on *Stillmatic,* Jay-Z's "Blueprint 2" on *The Blueprint 2: The Gift & the Curse* (2002), and radio freestyles from both rappers. The highly publicized feud gradually cooled off and was declared officially over when, on October 27, 2005, Jay-Z invited Nas to perform a few songs with him during a concert in East Rutherford, New Jersey. The following year Nas left Columbia Records to sign with Jay-Z's Def Jam Recordings. Referring to the feud between the rappers Tupac Shakur and Notorious B.I.G., which ended with both men murdered in 1996 and 1997, respectively, Jay-Z told Steve Jones for *USA Today* (January 25, 2006), "Everybody talks about Big and Pac and how that ended. [Nas and I] talked about showing a different side and what it would mean to the culture of hip-hop. It was bigger than just us and our trivial little beefs." Nas told Gail Mitchell for *Billboard* (February 4, 2006), "It was time for [the feud] to go in a direction that benefits the people who live for and love hip-hop; Our whole point is to move hip-hop to a much bigger level."

Nas's mother died of breast cancer in 2002. "That really pushed me forward," the rapper told Mike Osegueda for the *Fresno (California) Bee* (November 12, 2004). "Losing her was a thing that really made me look around and really not want to take another day for granted." His 2002 release, *God's Son,* reflected Nas's more emotionally open, mature side. Many of the songs refer to his mother, and the track "Dance" was written for her: ''I'm thankful, to ever know a women so real / I pray when I marry my wife'll have one of your skills / But mom you could never be replaced / I'd give my life up / Just to see you one more day / To have . . . / One more dance with you mama."

The singles from *God's Son* enjoyed substantial commercial success. "I Can," a song set to the melody of Beethoven's "Fur Elise," warns children of the dangers of drugs, sexual exploitation, gangs, and racism. In "Made You Look," which features samples from the Incredible Bongo Band's cover of "Apache," Nas boasts about his rapping prowess; in the chorus he raps,

"They shootin'!-Aw made you look / You a slave to a page in my rhyme book / Gettin' big money, playboy your time's up / Where them gangstas at? / Where them dimes at?" Ethan Brown reviewed *God's Son* positively for *New York* magazine (December 16, 2002), writing, "Here, Nas is so fierce, so plainspoken, so lean with words, that he demolishes not just the oeuvre of our ruling rappers . . . and recalls the music's lyrical champs like Rakim, he even brings to mind hip-hop progenitors like Muhammad Ali in the 'Rumble in the Jungle' era."

Nas collaborated with his father, Olu Dara, for the first single from his two-disc release *Street's Disciple* (2004). The bluesy "Bridging the Gap" features Dara singing the song's hook while Nas raps about the foundations of black music. Nas reflected on the history of black music, rapping, "The blues came from gospel, gospel from blues / Slaves are harmonizin' them ahs and oohs / Old school, new school, know school rules / All these years I been voicin' my blues / I'm a artist from the start, Hip Hop guided my heart." Nas has said that he considers "Bridging the Gap" his greatest song. In 2006 Nas released his eighth studio album, *Hip-Hop Is Dead,* on the Def Jam label. His first single, the album's title track, criticizes the influx of rap artists ignorant of hip-hop's roots as well as the commercialization of the genre. When asked about the title of his album and first single, Nas told Ryan Dombal for *Pitchfork* (December 6, 2006, on-line), "To me, hip-hop's been dead for years . . . . With that being said, then, the object of the game now is to make money off of exploiting it. That's what it's all about-get this money. That's basically what I'm saying." Produced by Dr. Dre, Kanye West, and will.i.am, the album received favorable reviews.

Nas's most recent solo album, *Untitled,* sparked controversy even before it reached stores, when news spread that Nas was planning to title the album "Nigger." Several public figures and organizations, including the NAACP, publicly condemned the rapper for using a term so hurtful and derogatory to the African-American population. Nas said in response that he merely wanted the title to reflect the album's content, which focuses largely on the plight of black men in America. Even so, the rapper abandoned the title before the record's release, in July 2008; the record is untitled. "It got to the point where people were too concerned about the title," Nas told Joseph Barracato for the *New York Post* (July 13, 2008). "I didn't want them to miss the messages in it. But to be honest, I really believe my fans will always know what the real title of this album is and what to call it." Despite the controversy, or perhaps because of it, the album sold 186,600 copies in its first week.

Personal Life

An avid reader, Nas enjoys writing short stories; he also paints. In 1998 he made his acting debut, starring alongside the rapper DMX in Hype Williams's urban film drama *Belly.* (Nas also helped write the script.) While the film was praised for its visual style, it suffered from a weak plot. Nas also had starring roles in the 2001 action film *Ticker,* which co-starred Steven Seagal, Tom Sizemore, and Dennis Hopper, and the 2001 drama *Sacred Is the Flesh,* which Nas also co-wrote. It was rumored that he was to portray the rapper Kool G. Rap in "Vapors," a biographical film about the legendary Juice Crew hip-hop group. As of late 2009 financing for the film had not materialized. Nas has said that he enjoys acting and hopes to get the opportunity to do more of it.

Nas married the R&B singer Kelis (Rogers) in a small ceremony in Atlanta, Georgia, on July 28, 2003. In April 2009, when Kelis was seven months pregnant with the couple's first child, she filed for divorce. Citing irreconcilable differences, she took Nas to court to receive monetary support. Their son, Knight, was born on July 22, 2009. The following day a judge ordered Nas to pay his ex-wife nearly $40,000 per month in spousal and child support. Nas has a 15-year-old daughter, Destiny, from a previous relationship with Carmen Bryan, His next album, "Distant Relatives," a collaboration with the reggae artist and producer Damian Marley, was to be released in late 2009.

Further Reading

defjam.com; (Kansas City, Missouri) *Pitch Weekly* Music June 6, 2002;

Los Angeles Times p62 Aug. 11, 1996, E p51 Dec. 5, 2004;

(Minneapolis, Minnesota) *Star Tribune* E p1 Sep. 5, 2008;

New York Times II p42 Oct. 6, 1996, II p35 Dec. 5, 2004;

Nelly

Rapper

Born: November 2, 1978; Austin, Texas
Primary Field: Rapper
Group Affiliation: "Country Grammar"

Introduction

"This is undeniable: Nelly is a gifted, witty MC in possession of one of the catchiest rhyme flows to ever hit the pop charts," Rob Marriott wrote for Rolling Stone *(July 2, 2002, on-line). Nelly's first album,* Country Grammar *(2000), which features the Midwest flavor of his native St. Louis and the hit singles "Country Grammar," "Ride Wit Me," and "E.I.," rose to number one on the Billboard album charts and sold more than eight million copies, in the process making Nelly a rap icon and putting St. Louis on the hip-hop map. He followed up that success with the album Nellyville, which also went to number one, as did its singles "Hot in Herre" and "Dilemma." "I don't sound like anyone," Nelly told a writer for* Jet *(July 30, 2001). "I've got a style that's all my own. I'm rappin' the blues. I like to think of my music as a jazz form of hip hop." Nelly was nominated for two Grammy Awards each in 2001 and 2002 and has won a number of honors, including an American Music Award for favorite rap/hip-hop artist in 2002.*

Early Life

Nelly was born Cornell Haynes Jr. in Austin, Texas, on November 2, 1978. His father was in the United States Air Force, and the family moved often—at one point living in Spain—as Nelly was growing up. After they moved to St. Louis, Missouri, Nelly's parents divorced. Nelly then found himself "moving around amongst friends and family, and . . . just always on the go," as he told a reporter for MTV, as quoted on the Web site *NellyHQ.com.* A talented baseball player as a teenager, Nelly attended the training camps of the Atlanta Braves and the Pittsburgh Pirates before deciding to pursue a career in music. During this time, Nelly, who did not graduate from high school, worked jobs at McDonald's and the United Parcel Service. In 1993 he formed the St. Lunatics, a rap group that included his high-school friends Robert "Kyjuan" Cleveland, Tohri "Murphy Lee" Harper, Ali "Big Lee" Jones, Corey "Slow Down" Edwards, and Lavell "City Spud" Webb, Nelly's younger half-brother. The group achieved a measure of success in 1996 with the single "Gimme What Ya Got," which sold nearly 10,000 copies and was a hit in the St. Louis area. Nelly told MTV, "Well my man Big Lee's the oldest. He went away to college. And me, Kyjuan, and City Spud, my little brother, Murphy Lee, Kyjuan's little brother, we were back at home and, so to speak, rapping for the 'hood. My man Big Lee came home with a new outlook. He helped motivate us a little bit, like, 'Yo, we should try to do it this way. We should try to listen to what St. Louis is doing. Just listen to the other groups and just differentiate ourselves from all that.' That's what we did. We just took time and kept planting it, kept planting it, kept working in the studio for years in a row. I'm talking 'bout every day was a studio day. Even if we was just dropping by, grabbing a beat, or whatever, I [was in] the studio every day for three years. We just really pressed hard, man. It took hard work to get here." When asked by the MTV reporter about the group's relationship with their hometown, Nelly responded, "St. Louis is our foundation. No matter what we do right now, we always can fall back on the Lou', 'cause they've been loving us. They've been holding us up for so long. Any time we go down, they can give us that boost to come back up, and I think everybody needs that. Lock down home first, 'cause that's very important, we think." Nelly explained that because of its central location in the U.S., St. Louis absorbs the rap and hip-hop styles of both the East and West Coasts, in addition to southern and midwestern musical influences. "I listen to everybody from 2Pac [Shakur], Biggie [Smalls] . . . Nelly told MTV. "When you say L.L. [Cool J], man, you know that's a big influence right there. Snoop [Dogg], Goodie M.O.B, Outkast. We just pump it all right there. If it's hot, it's definitely in St. Louis."

Life's Work

In 1999 Nelly signed a solo deal with Universal Records. "Well, it wasn't my idea, it was a group idea," the rapper told MTV. "We sat down, and I want to tell everybody that it's not Nelly and The St. Lunatics, it's Nelly from The St. Lunatics, 'cause I'm still in the group, always will be in the group, started in the group, and I ain't never leaving the group. But it was something we all decided on." The St. Lunatics were having trouble acquiring a record deal and thought that Nelly, with his

Affiliation: "Country Grammar"

In May 2000 Nelly released the single "Country Grammar," which reached number one on the *Billboard* rap singles chart—a spot it occupied for four weeks. The song featured the catchy refrain "down, down, baby," which was taken from a children's song, and the words "shimmy, shimmy ko-ko bop," borrowed from an old song by Little Anthony and the Imperials. "Country Grammar" was played often on the radio and could be heard blasting from cars and clubs in cities nationwide. In June Nelly's debut album, also titled *Country Grammar,* appeared. When asked by the MTV reporter about the meaning of the title, Nelly said, "I'm basically representing for everybody [in the] Midwest, South . . . everybody with that slur on their English, or everybody with that pronunciation that sounds a little off." For the album, in a smooth, sing-song style, Nelly took on such typical rap themes as crime, on the song "Greed, Hate, Envy," and sex, on the track "Thicky Thick Girl." The song "Batter Up" exemplifies bravado and male posturing, and in "Ride Wit Me" Nelly rapped breezily about an intoxicated spin in a Mercedes Benz. In a review of the album for VH1, which appears on the Web site *cdnow.com,* a critic commented, "Not only does [Nelly] deserve to take his place as the leading exponent of Midwest rap thanks to his spicy rhymes, innovative country slanguage, and diverse street dreams, but Nelly proves the true strength of 'outer borough' hip-hop with every track. . . . Nelly raps with a knowledge that he has nothing to lose. And that degree of street and craft passion soars high," as Nelly injects "strong doses of dirty Mississippi blues and earthy jazz rhythms into his jangly, bounce-driven rhymology."

By September 2000 *Country Grammar* had sold more than three million copies and reached number one on the *Billboard* album charts, where it stayed for several weeks, supplanting the rapper Eminem's album *The Marshall Mathers LP.* Nelly performed "Country Grammar" at the MTV Video Music Awards, and the video for the song topped MTV's listing of Top 20 videos. In December Nelly's "E.I.," a party anthem with the infectious arms-in-the-air refrain "Ohhh! Ohhh!," became the second cut from *Country Grammar* to reach the Top 10. In 2000 Nelly was named the world's best-selling new artist at the World Music Awards ceremony in Monaco. He was nominated the following year for Grammy Awards for best rap solo performance, for the song "Country Grammar," and for best rap album. That same year he won a Blockbuster Entertainment Award for favorite new male artist; a Black Entertainment Television (BET) Award for best new artist; an MTV Video Music Award for best rap video for "Ride Wit Me," which was also nominated for best male video and a viewer's choice award; two *Source* Awards, for album of the year and new artist of the year; and a Soul Train Music Award for best rhythm & blues/soul or rap new artist. Nelly's popularity earned him a spot alongside Aerosmith, Britney Spears, and 'N Sync as a performer at the 2001 Super Bowl halftime show, and Nelly could be heard singing with other famous performers on the All-Star Tribute benefit single "What's Going On," an updated version of a classic Marvin Gaye song, the proceeds from which were donated to the fight against AIDS and to the United Way's September 11th Fund, which was set up in the wake of the September 11, 2001 terrorist attacks. By the end of 2001, *Country Grammar* had sold more than eight million copies.

charisma and rhyming skills, might be able to achieve success more easily by himself and then be in a position to assist the others. In an article on the *Teen People* Web site, Nelly is quoted as saying, "I don't necessarily feel like a solo artist. . . . I'm just the key in the door for the rest of the St. Lunatics. I'm the first to release an album. But we're all family. We came up together from nothing. So it's St. Lunatics for life."

After achieving success as a solo artist, Nelly helped the St. Lunatics acquire their own record deal, then joined them to record the album *Free City* (2001). The title expressed the group's desire to see Nelly's younger brother and bandmate City Spud, who raps on and produced the Nelly hit "Ride Wit Me," freed from prison, where he is serving time on charges of armed robbery. *Free City,* which features the hit single "Midwest Swing," debuted at number three on the *Billboard* 200 albums chart and quickly sold more than a million copies. (Jason Epperson, who produced most of *Country Grammar,* produced most of *Free City* as well.) In a review of *Free City* posted on the Web site *dotmusic.com,* John Mulvey pronounced the record to be almost as good as Nelly's *Country Grammar* and praised the atmosphere of fun that resulted from its celebration of cars, girls, and partying. "There's something improbably good-natured about these low-slung grooves," Mulvey wrote.

In January 2002 Nelly was in the Top 10 again, with the song "#1," which he contributed to the soundtrack for the movie *Training Day* (2001) and later included on his second album. In June 2002 Nelly's single "Hot in Herre" went to number one on the *Billboard* Hot 100 chart. (Nelly added the extra "r" to the title "Hot in Herre" to emphasize the way in which fellow natives of St. Louis and the Midwest pronounce certain words—another example of the "country grammar" he celebrated on his first album.) The August 5, 2002 issue of *Jet* estimated the song's radio audience during one record-setting week at 163.1 million people. That same month his second album, *Nellyville,* was released. "Nelly's music moves forward in funk-rooted blips and starts, embellished with high vocal whoops, asides, and exclamations that function as hooks," Tom Sinclair wrote in a review of *Nellyville* for *Entertainment Weekly* (June 28-July 5, 2002, on-line). "He works with a variety of producers (including young St. Louis native Jason 'Jay E' Epperson and, on 'Hot in Herre,' the Neptunes), rapping with an easy confidence and a steady, steamrolling flow. . . . Nelly offers some words of advice to his rivals: 'If what you got ain't hot, then check your flame/If what you're spittin' ain't hittin', then check your aim.' On the evidence of *Nellyville,* our man seems to be in control of his flame and on top of his game as he takes aim at the pop charts once again. If you like your rap loose and funny, Nelly's the man for you." Sinclair also praised the album's nods to older works, including the music of the go-go pioneer Chuck Brown. While most other reviews of the album were positive, some critics qualified their praise. "It's a solid dance record, peppered with clever punch lines and very likable, yet it fails to capture the imagination," Rob Marriott wrote. "Outside of 'Pimp Juice,' the album sounds weighed down by the commercial pressures of going multiplatinum the last time out. After five tracks, one cannot help but wonder what might have been had Nelly not gotten so pop so quickly." Other songs on the album include "Splurge," in which Nelly sang about the benefits of success; the title track, for which he imagined a fictional city where marijuana is legal, everyone is rich, and children are given cars and diamonds; and "Work It," for which Justin Timberlake of the group 'N Sync joined Nelly. Cedric "The Entertainer," a St. Louis comedian and actor who was one of the stars of the Spike Lee movie *The Original Kings of Comedy* (2000), is featured in several humorous segments on *Nellyville.*

July 2002 found "Hot in Herre" at the top of three *Billboard* charts: those for Hot R&B/Hip-Hop Singles and Tracks, Hot Rap Tracks, and the Hot 100. In addition, Nelly's song "Dilemma," which is also on *Nellyville* and features Kelly Rowland from the music group Destiny's Child, was the fastest- climbing song on the *Billboard* Hot 100 chart and reached number one in August 2002, bumping "Hot in Herre" to number two. *Nellyville* topped the *Billboard* 200 albums chart and the Hot R&B/Hip-Hop Albums chart, selling more than 700,000 copies in its first week alone and eclipsing Eminem's 2002 CD, *The Eminem Show.* A month after its release, *Nellyville* had sold nearly two million copies. In 2002 Nelly was again nominated for two Grammy Awards, for best rap solo performance for "Ride Wit Me" and best rap/sung collaboration for "Where the Party At," a song by the Atlanta-based soul-music quartet Jagged Edge, which features a performance by Nelly and entered *Billboard* Top 10 lists in the second half of 2001.

Personal Life

Nelly sang with 'N Sync on their hit song "Girlfriend." He made his big-screen debut in the independent movie *Snipes* (2001), a drama in which he played a hip-hop star who is kidnapped. As of July 2002 Nelly was in talks with Paramount Network Television concerning a possible starring role in a new television sitcom. Nelly has appeared on the late-night Fox comedy show *Mad TV.* He helps the St. Louis community in a variety of ways, which include running a nonprofit foundation called 4Sho4Kids; that organization sponsors programs and events, such as basketball games and literacy drives, donates goods to schools, and assists children affected by drug addiction and Down syndrome. The rapper also runs his own clothing line, Vokal.

Further Reading

Billboard.com
Entertainment Weekly (on-line) June 28-July 5, 2002
Jet p32+ July 30, 2001, with photos
mtv.com
NellyHQ.com
rockonthenet.com
Rolling Stone (on-line) July 2, 2002

WILLIE NELSON

Singer; musician; composer

Born: Apr. 30, 1933; Abbott, Texas
Primary Field: Country
Group Affiliation: Outlaws; solo performer

INTRODUCTION

Perhaps not since the late Hank Williams has there been as distinctive and renovative an artist in country music as the composer and performer Willie Nelson, who created the "Austin sound" and is worshiped by his fans as the "King of Country Music." In the 1960's, such Nelson compositions as "Crazy" and "Night Life" became country standards—as recorded by other singers. But since 1972, when Nelson left Nashville, Tennessee, the country music capital, to strike out on his own, he has become, in the words of John Rockwell of the New York Times *(August 8, 1975), "the acknowledged leader of country music's 'left wing,' working to cleanse Nashville of stale excesses by bringing it up to the present and back to its. own folkish roots." Nelson has attracted an entirely new audience—the young aficionados of rock 'n' roll, who had been intimidated by the "redneck" image of country music. As a result, his recordings sell by the millions, his concerts are routinely sold out, and his annual Fourth of July "picnics" attract as many as 100,000 fans. As Mick Martin observed in the September 15, 1978 edition of the Sacramento Union, "The magic of Willie Nelson transcends all boundaries and prejudices."*

Willie Nelson.

EARLY LIFE

Willie Nelson was born on April 30, 1933 during the depths of the Great Depression, in the small Texas farming community of Abbott, some sixty miles south of Fort Worth. (Some sources give Fort Worth as his birthplace and March as the month of his birth.) When Willie was a small boy, his mother went off to find a job, never to return, and his father, Ira D. Nelson, eventually remarried and opened Willie's Pool Hall in Austin, Texas, which he ran until his death in late 1978. Willie and his older sister, Bobbie were raised by their grandparents and aunts in Abbott, where he helped to earn his keep by picking cotton after school. His grandfather, a blacksmith by trade and a devoted amateur musician, gave him his first guitar and rudimentary musical instruction—the only training Nelson ever received. By the time he was ten, Willie was playing at local dances, along with Bobbie, who had taken up the piano, and who is still a member of her brother's band. At thirteen he had his own musical group.

"I have no negative memories about growing up," Nelson told Pete Axthelm of *Newsweek* (August 14, 1978). "It was being grown up that started to be a problem." In 1950 he dropped out of high school and left Abbott to join the Air Force. Discharged for medical reasons after eight months, he went to Waco, Texas where, intent on a career in agriculture, he briefly studied at Baylor University. About that time he married a sixteen-year-old Cherokee Indian waitress named Martha Matthews, by whom he had a daughter, Lana. But that stormy marriage· eventually broke up. Meanwhile, between doing odd jobs, such as working as a janitor and as a door-to-door salesman of Bibles, encyclopedias, vacuum cleaners, and sewing machines, Nelson wrote songs and performed on the Jacksboro strip outside Fort

Worth at rowdy bars and at honky-tonks with names like County Dump and Bloody Bucket, where the performers had to be shielded from flying cans and bottles by chicken wire fences. For a time he taught at a Baptist Sunday school—until its officials objected to his performances in honky-tonks. He also tried his luck in Oregon but had to content himself with a job as a plumber's helper. In the late 1950's he worked as a disk jockey for radio stations in Houston, San Antonio, and Fort Worth, and it was during those years that his music began to attract attention.

Life's Work

Nelson sold his first song, "Family Bible," for $50 just to feed his family. Like many of his later compositions, it was destined to become a country classic. In 1959 he wrote "Night Life," a song that was eventually recorded by more than seventy artists and sold over 30,000,000 copies. In 1961 Nelson sold the copyright to "Night Life" to three Houston businessmen for $150, bought a second-hand Buick, and left Fort Worth for Nashville, hoping to become a country music star.

In Nashville, Nelson married again, this time singer Shirley Collie, and that union, although also turbulent, lasted nearly a decade. While performing at Tootsie's Bar, a hangout for aspiring songwriters, Nelson came to the attention of singer Hank Cochran, who signed him up with Pamper Publishing, of which Ray Price, a leading Nashville vocalist and bandleader, was part-owner. Price soon hired Nelson as bass guitarist in his band, and by adopting "Night Life" as his theme, became one of a number of country stars who in the early 1960's scored a major success with a Willie Nelson song. Patsy Kline, one of Nashville's leading female performers, made Nelson's "Crazy" a big hit of 1961, and Faron Young did the same thing with "Hello Walls." Another Nelson classic, "Funny How Time Slips Away," written in 1961, has been recorded more than eighty times.

In the late 1960's a hog-raising venture that Nelson had started on a farm near Nashville failed, just about the time that his second marriage began to break up. Then, toward the end of 1969, his house in Nashville burned to the ground, and all he was able to salvage was a sack of marijuana and an old guitar. The event was a watershed in Nelson's life. In the words of Pete Axthelm of *Newsweek*, "In 1970 Willie surveyed the ashes of his Nashville house, his two marriages, and his dozen or so flop albums—and decided to go home to Texas." He moved to Austin and worked on *Yesterday's Wine*, his last album produced in Nashville. Released in 1971, it became the first country music "concept album": a style long familiar to the world of rock music, in which the lyrics and music in each song are part of an overall theme or story. Nelson considered it the finest of his Nashville creations, and when it failed to sell, like his previous albums, it fortified his determination to abandon Nashville.

At the time that Nelson moved to Austin, its Armadillo World Headquarters had already begun to acquire a reputation as the refuge for Nashville expatriates dissatisfied with the ·country music mainstream. Those musicians, who came to be known as "outlaws," were country music's "counter-culture," rejecting the conservative image of Nashville for the dress, hairstyles, and taste for drugs associated with rock music. Nelson soon was in the vanguard of the "progressive country" movement in Texas. After he bought a second-hand Greyhound bus, he and his band toured dance halls and country fairs throughout the South and Southwest, where they became increasingly popular. On July 4, 1973 he staged the first of several annual country music festivals in Dripping Springs, Texas that featured such other prominent "outlaws" as Kris Kristofferson, Billy Joe Shaver, and Waylon Jennings, in addition to more traditional country stars. The audience was no less an unusual blend of the "red-neck" and the radical "hippie" contingents of country music. In recent years the more radical elements have tended to predominate at those festivals.

With the failure of Yesterday's Wine, Nelson decided to leave RCA. In 1973 he signed with Atlantic Records of New York City after receiving encouragement from its vice-president, Jerry Wexler. That year Wexler produced Nelson's *Shotgun Willie* album, described by Al Reinert as "the first album to catch any of the flavor of Nelson's live performance sound." It was also the first of Nelson's albums to succeed commercially. Within six months, its total sales outnumbered those of all his previous albums combined, and in November 1973 the Nashville Songwriters Association elected Nelson to its Hall of Fame.

In the spring of 1974 the album *Phases and Stages*, another joint effort of Nelson and Wexler, was released and it also became a major financial and critical success. The second of Nelson's concept albums, it depicted the collapse of a marriage from the viewpoint of both the wife and the husband. "Unlike most concept albums, this one never forces the idea or relies on gimmicks,"

Loraine Alterman wrote in the *New York Times* (May 19, 1974). "Both the music and lyrics Nelson has written touch us directly because of their genuine concern for the situation that in one form or another strikes many people." The album sold over 400,000 copies, and one of its numbers, "Bloody Mary Mornings," became very popular as a single.

After Atlantic phased out its country music line, Nelson formed his own company, Lone Star Records, and signed a distribution agreement with Columbia Records. His album *Red Headed Stranger*, released in mid-1975, continued the "concept" approach and was even more personal in its content than its predecessors. It was intended, according to Nelson, as a combination of original compositions and "old songs [he] always liked and wanted to go into the studio and record." John Rockwell wrote in the *New York Times* (August 8, 1975): "What Mr. Nelson has done . . . is to keep the music naturally simple and to link the songs with short recurrent refrains and flashbacks to earlier material. The result is somewhat like Kurt Weill did in his collaboration with Bertolt Brecht, although, of course, the actual idioms are very different." *Red Headed Stranger* told the story of a wandering preacher and the lessons he learned in his travels. One of its selections, "Blue Eyes Crying in the Rain," brought Nelson-who had received five previous Grammy nominations—the 1976 Grammy Award for the best country performance on a single. The album eventually "went platinum," that is, it sold more than 1,000,000 copies. Universal Pictures has indicated an interest in developing its theme into a motion picture.

In his home state, Nelson has become almost a cult figure. The Texas state legislature unanimously declared July 4, 1975 "Willie Nelson Day." By 1976, "Williemania" was in full swing. Seven Nelson albums appeared that year on the charts of *Billboard* magazine, which named *The Sound in Your Mind* the country album of the year. He recorded *Wanted: The Outlaws with Waylon Jennings*, another progressive country musician who benefited from the Austin renaissance. A collection of duets and solos, it sold even more swiftly than *Red Headed Stranger*. Among other honors, Nelson and Jennings won the 1976 Country Music Association award for album of the year, and their "Good Hearted Woman" was named single of the year.

Among Nelson's recent albums are *Troublemaker* (Columbia, 1976); *To Lefty from Willie* (Columbia, 1977), dedicated to the late singer-composer Lefty Frizzell: Waylon and Willie [RCA, 1978); *Willie and Family Live* (Columbia, 1978): and *One for the Road* (Paradise, 1979), with Leon Russell. *Stardust* (Columbia, 1978), his own favorite and perhaps his most unusual album, consists of a series of venerable pop standards by such masters as Irving Berlin, George Gershwin, Duke Ellington, Kurt Weill, and Hoagy Carmichael, performed in Nelson's inimitable country blues manner. Carl Arrington of the *New York Post* (May 5, 1978) cited Nelson's "clear and variable country baritone" and commented, "Willie's phrasing is distinct from . the styles of . most other country artists. He leaves off the twang and paces his vocals behind the beat in a fashion that resembles that of one of his idols, Frank Sinatra."

Nelson's television credits include performances on such programs as the variety show *Austin City Limits*, presented on PBS-TV in March 1975. He maintains a grueling concert schedule, spending as many as 250 days a year on the road. In September 1978 he gave a performance on the White House lawn for the National Association for Stock Car Auto Racing. Although President Jimmy Carter was detained at the time by Middle East negotiations at Camp David, Nelson sang some impromptu duets with First Lady Rosalynn Carter, who, like the President, is a Nelson fan of long standing. In May 1979 Nelson presented Carter with a special Country Music Association award.

Nelson's acting debut was in the 1979 film, *The Electric Horseman*, followed by appearances in *Honeysuckle Rose*, *Thief*, and *Barbarosa*. He played the role of Red Loon in *Coming Out of the Ice* in 1982 and starred in *Songwriter* two years later. He portrayed the lead role in the 1986 film version of his album *Red Headed Stranger*. Other movies that Nelson acted in include *Wag the Dog*, *Gone Fishin'* (as Billy 'Catch' Pooler), the 1986 television movie *Stagecoach* (with Johnny Cash), *Half Baked*, *Beerfest*, *The Dukes of Hazzard*, *Surfer, Dude* and *Swing Vote*.

During the 1980s, Nelson recorded a series of hit singles including "Midnight Rider," a 1980 cover of the Allman Brothers song which Nelson recorded for *The Electric Horseman*, the soundtrack "On the Road Again" from the movie *Honeysuckle Rose*, and a duet with Julio Iglesias titled "To All the Girls I've Loved Before." In 1982, *Pancho & Lefty*, a duet album with Merle Haggard was released. During the recording sessions of *Pancho and Lefty*, session guitarist Johnny Christopher and co-writer of "Always on My Mind," tried to pitch the song to an uninterested Haggard. Instead, Nelson recorded it. The single of the song won

Affiliation: Abandoning Nashville

Nelson's own efforts to record his songs proved disappointing. A few early successes, such as the 1962 hit "Touch Me," which reached the top ten, and "Willingly," which he sang with his wife, Shirley, were followed by a number of RCA albums that failed to sell. "My music was not exactly what you'd call country music," Nelson explained to Wayne Robins of *Newsday* (January 22, 1975). ". . . We were just doing too many new things for the country audiences to accept right away." Nashville in the 1960's was a poor environment for the unorthodox, since it had become the leading regional recording center outside of New York and Los Angeles, and albums were being ground out on an assembly line formula. In competition with the new "studio sound" of florid orchestral arrangements and diluted rhythms, the free-wheeling, honky-tonk spirit of Nelson's music could not have been more out of place.

Nor were Nashville's production methods suited to Willie Nelson's material and style. Performers were expected to work with musicians hired by the studio. "You'd walk into the studio and they'd put six guys behind you who'd never seen your music before," Nelson explained to Al Reinert in the *New York Times Magazine* (March 26, 1978). Nelson preferred working with his own band comprised of musicians whom he had known for years. But as Nelson told Wayne Robins, "It just wasn't an accepted thing to make records with members of your own band." Thus hampered by a system that would not accommodate his special musical personality, Nelson found only a limited audience during his years in Nashville.

Yet those years were not without their rewards. Nelson received substantial royalties from his songs; he was one of the few country musicians able to make frequent appearances in Las Vegas; and the Grand Ole Opry, the nation's blue-ribbon showcase for country music talent, made him a company member in 1964. He also appeared regularly on Ernest Tubb's syndicated country music television show, often singing the sacred song featured on the program. In 1967 Nelson introduced audiences to Charlie Pride, country music's first black singer, whose career skyrocketed while Nelson's was still foundering in Nashville.

three awards during the 25th Annual Grammy Awards: Song of the Year, Best Country Song and Best Male Country Vocal Performance. The single was certified platinum; while the album of the same name was certified quadruple-platinum.

Also in the 1980s, two collaborations with Waylon Jennings were released: *WWII* in 1982, and *Take it to the Limit*, another collaboration with Waylon Jennings was released in 1983. In the mid-1980s, Nelson, Jennings, Kristofferson, and Johnny Cash formed The Highwaymen, who achieved platinum record sales and toured the world. Meanwhile, he became more involved with charity work, such as singing on *We Are the World* in 1984. In 1985, Nelson had another success with *Half Nelson*, a compilation album of duets with a range of artists such as Ray Charles and Neil Young. In 1980, Nelson performed on the south lawn of the White House. The concert of September 13 featured First Lady Rosalynn Carter and Nelson in a duet of Ray Wylie Hubbard's "Up Against the Wall Redneck Mother." Nelson frequently visited the White House, where according to the biography by Joe Nick Patoski, *Willie Nelson: An Epic Life*, where he smoked marijuana on the White House roof.

During the 1990s and 2000s, Nelson toured continuously, recording several albums including 1998's critically acclaimed *Teatro*, and performed and recorded with other acts including Phish, Johnny Cash, and Toby Keith. His duet with Keith, "Beer for My Horses," was released as a single and topped the *Billboard* Hot Country Songs charts for six consecutive weeks in 2003, while the accompanying video won an award for "Best Video" at the 2004 Academy of Country Music Awards. A USA Network television special celebrated Nelson's 70th birthday, and Nelson released *The Essential Willie Nelson* as part of the celebration. Nelson also appeared on Ringo Starr's 2003 album, *Ringo Rama*, as a guest vocal on "Write One for Me."

In 2005, a live performance of the Johnny Cash song "Busted" with Ray Charles was released on Charles' duets album *Genius & Friends*. Nelson's 2007 performance with jazz trumpeter Wynton Marsalis at the Lincoln Center, was released as the live album *Two Men with the Blues* in 2008; reaching number one in *Billboard's* Top Jazz Albums and number twenty on the

Billboard 200. The same year, Nelson recorded his first album with Buddy Cannon as the producer, *Moment of Forever*. Cannon acquainted Nelson earlier, during the production of his collaboration with Kenny Chesney on the duet "That Lucky Old Sun," for Chesney's album of the same name. In 2009 Nelson and Marsalis joined with Norah Jones in a tribute concert to Ray Charles, which resulted in the *Here We Go Again: Celebrating the Genius of Ray Charles* album, released in 2011.

In 2010, Nelson released *Country Music*, a compilation of standards produced by T-Bone Burnett. The album peaked number four in *Billboard's* Top Country Albums, and twenty on the *Billboard* 200. It was nominated for *Best Americana Album* at the 2011 Grammy Awards. In February 2012, Legacy Recordings signed a deal with Nelson that included the release of new material. Nelson's first release for the Legacy Recordings was *Heroes* and included guest appearances by his sons Lukas and Micah of the band Insects vs Robots, Ray Price, Merle Haggard, Snoop Dogg, Kris Kristofferson, Jamey Johnson, Billy Joe Shaver and Sheryl Crow. The album reached number four on *Billboard's* Top Country Albums. His 2013 release *To All the Girls...*, a collection of duets with all female partners, featured among others Dolly Parton, Loretta Lynn, Rosanne Cash, Sheryl Crow, Mavis Staples, Norah Jones, Emmylou Harris, Carrie Underwood and Miranda Lambert. The album entered *Billboard's* Top Country Albums at number two, marking his highest position on the chart since the release of his 1989 *A Horse Called Music*, and extending his record to a total of forty-six top ten albums on the country charts. Nelson scored as well his second top ten album on the *Billboard* 200, with the release entering at number nine.

His following release was *Band of Brothers*, in 2014, the first Nelson album to feature the most newly self-penned songs since 1996's *Spirit*. Upon its release, it topped *Billboard's* Top Country albums chart, the first time since 1986's *The Promiseland*, the last Nelson album to top it. The release reached number five on the *Billboard* 200, Nelson's highest position on the chart since 1982's *Always On My Mind*. In December 2014, a duet with Rhonda Vincent, "Only Me," topped *Bluegrass Unlimited's* National Airplay chart. In June 2015, his collaboration with Haggard *Django and Jimmie* topped *Billboard's* Top Country albums chart and reached number seven on the *Billboard* 200.

Nelson is widely recognized as an American icon. He was inducted into the Country Music Hall of Fame in 1993, and he received the Kennedy Center Honors in 1998. In 2011, Nelson was inducted to the National Agricultural Hall of Fame, for his labor in Farm Aid and other fund raisers to benefit farmers. In 2015 Nelson won the Gershwin Prize, the lifetime award of the Library of Congress. He was included by *Rolling Stone* on its *100 Greatest Singers* and *100 Greatest Guitarists* lists.

Personal Life

Willie Nelson was described by Stephanie Mansfield in the Washington *Post* (April 25, 1978) as "a five-foot-eight-inch . . . Gabby Hayes look-alike with a fondness for baggy jeans, green and yellow imitation Adidas, worn T-shirts and shoulder-length strawberry hair tied Tonto fashion with a faded bandana." Nelson has real estate holdings in Texas and owns controlling interest in a record label and a music publishing company. He is an enthusiastic reader of Edgar Cayce and Kahlil Gibran, and an avid jogger. Generally soft-spoken and self-possessed, Willie Nelson is also known for a quick temper that can be set off by such inanimate adversaries as locked doors and intrusive telephones. His broad, winning smile has been characterized as "beatific," "radiant," and "straight out of Huckleberry Finn."

Nelson lives in Maui, Hawaii, in a largely self-sustaining community where all the homes use only solar power. Neighbors include Kris Kristofferson, Woody Harrelson, and Owen Wilson. Nelson also owns a ranch near Austin, Texas. He has married four times and fathered seven children.

Further Reading

N Y Sunday News Mag p5+ F 4 '79 por
NY Times Mag p20+ Mr 26 '78 pors
Newsweek 92:52+ Ag 14 '78 pors
Time 110:86+ S 19 '77 por, 112:81+ S 18 '78 pors
Brown, Len and Friedrich, Gary. *Encyclopedia of Country and Western Music (1971)*
Illustrated Encyclopedia of Country Music (1977)
Malone, Bill C. and McCulloh, Judith, eds. *Stars of Country Music (1975)*
Shestack, Melvin. *Country Music Encyclopedia (1974)*
Stambler, I. and Landon, G. *Encyclopedia of Folk, Country and Western Music (1969)*
Who's Who in America, 1978-79
Nelson, Susie. *Hear Worn Memories: a Daughter's Personal Biography of Willie Nelson (1987)*

Neptunes

Music production team; singer-songwriters

Chad Hugo
Record producer; singer; songwriter
Born: 1974-

Pharrell Williams
Record producer; singer
Born: Apr. 5, 1973; Virginia Beach, Virginia

Primary Field: Digital audio
Group Affiliation: Neptunes

Introduction

Pharrell Williams and Chad Hugo, the Grammy Award-winning production team known as the Neptunes, began their ascent to the heights of the music world in the late 1990s. Working with the biggest stars in hip-hop, pop, and R&B-Jay-Z, Nelly, Whitney Houston, Prince, Mary J. Blige, Beyonce Knowles, and Britney Spears, to name only a few—the Neptunes have produced close to 20 platinum singles ("platinum" denoting sales of more than one million units) and are one of the most in-demand production teams in the music industry. Among the hit songs the Neptunes have produced, many of which have won or been nominated for awards, are Justin Timberlake's "Rock Your Body," Nelly's "Hot in Herre," and Snoop Dogg's "Beautiful."

Early Lives

The oldest of three sons, Pharrell Williams was born on April 5, 1973 in Virginia Beach, Virginia, to Pharoah and Carolyn Williams. His father worked as a handyman; his mother was a schoolteacher. Williams, an African-American, has recalled that when he was 11 years old, wishing to emulate the then-popular television personality Mr. T, he had his father cut his hair into a mohawk. "Going to school with that haircut taught me a lot of humility," he commented, in answer to a reader's question in *Blender* (April 2004). Williams and Chad Hugo, a Filipino-American who was born in 1974, met while attending separate junior high schools. Their musical interests brought them together: Williams played drums, rhymed, and rapped, and Hugo played saxophone in a special music program, run by their Virginia Beach school system, that focused on improvisational skills. In an interview for *Rhythm Nation* posted on the Web site hip-hop-network.com, Williams recalled that nearly every day he and Hugo "would go over to Chad's house and play [music] equipment [including a cheap Casio keyboard] and just come up with beats and ideas and tracks." The two formed a band, choosing the name Neptunes, after Neptune, the Roman god of the sea, in part because they wanted their music to flow freely and widely over the earth, like water. In addition, Hugo told Scott Paulson-Bryant for *America* magazine, as quoted on startrakmusic.com, he and Williams sought an "alternative name that didn't box us into one style. We didn't want to be typical, we wanted to be like old school bands like Earth, Wind and Fire."

Williams and Hugo were greatly influenced by such standout hip-hop groups of the late 1980s and 1990s as the Native Tongues, De La Soul, the Jungle Brothers, and A Tribe Called Quest, all of whom drew upon a wide variety of musical genres and were known for positive, Afrocentric, socially conscious lyrics highlighted by jazz-inflected beats. Referring to those groups specifically, Hugo told Jim Macnie for the VH1 Web site, "That whole movement's rhyme scheme was different [from most other music of that time]; the loops they sampled were wild. The chords really touched me, man. . . . Hearing those jazz chords . . . I don't want to get technical on you, but [they] hit me hard. They're not your typical A-C-G chords. Sonically, it was crazy." Hugo also told Macnie that in his opinion the most innovative hip-hop albums include A Tribe Called Quest's *The Low End Theory,* Dr. Dre's *The Chronic,* and many of the disks produced by Timbaland. Regarding the music that inspired him early on, Williams told Paulson Bryant that his favorite parts of Michael Jackson's songs were those in which the keys changed, or the chords flowed toward a bridge. "I didn't know what that was, but it was what got me," he said. As evidenced by the sounds they create, the Neptunes' musical taste is not limited to rap and hip-hop. The men have also named as musical influences such diverse artists or groups as Stevie Wonder, AC/DC, Queen, America, and Steely Dan.

Lives' Work

Hugo and Williams both attended Princess Anne High School, in Virginia Beach, and played together in the school band. (Hugo later attended a college, but readily available sources do not reveal which one or how long he studied there.) In 1992, while still secondary-school students, the two friends sold their first song, "Rump Shakur," to the rap duo Wreckx-N-Effects, who performed it. The track sold more than 500,000 copies and thus became Williams and Hugo's first gold single. Although Hugo told Bernard that in Virginia Beach "there is no music scene," the highly regarded producer Teddy Riley worked out of the city. Riley's production studios were located across the street from Williams and Hugo's high school. During a talent show at the school, Riley "discovered" the young beatmasters (who earlier, hoping to land a record deal, had unsuccessfully stalked him) and invited them to work with him. Along with Riley, in 1994 Hugo and Williams helped to produce Blackstreet's debut album and later did the same for the groups S.W.V. and Total. In 1997 Williams and Hugo produced a track on the rapper Mase's successful album *Harlem World* and helped produce rap albums by Jay-Z and MC Lyte.

In 1998 Hugo and Williams ended their apprenticeship. with Riley and struck out on their own. They registered a hit with the single "Superthug," by the rapper Noreaga (now known as N.O.R.E.), from his debut solo album, *N.O.R.E.* In "Superthug" Noreaga included the Neptunes' name in his lyrics. "We didn't ask [Noreaga] to do that, that's hot," Hugo told Bernard, while .discussing the Neptunes' strong relationship with the rapper. "Ever since then, we sorta took off." Drawing a comparison to the award-winning California-based rapper/producer team of Snoop Dogg and Dr. Dre and their ability to turn out popular tracks consistently, Noreaga said of the Neptunes, as quoted by Bernard, "It's almost like Snoop and Dre, when I get with the Neptunes, it's a wrap."

The Neptunes' early rap-production successes, many of which were party-themed tracks, included Ol' Dirty Bastard's "Got My Money" (1999), Mystikal's "Shake Ya Ass" (2000), and Jay-Z's "I Want to Love U" (2001). While the duo continued to produce hit songs for some of the biggest names in rap and hip-hop, including L.L. Cool J ("Luv U Better"), Busta Rhymes ("Pass the Courvoisier"), and Nelly ("Hot in Herre"), in 2001 the Neptunes also began producing songs for mainstream pop performers such as 'N Sync ("Girlfriend"). Also that year the pop icon Britney Spears performed her Neptunes-produced hit "I'm a Slave 4U" at the MTV Video Music Awards ceremony, thereby affirming Hugo and Williams's growing prominence within the music industry. In regard to working with artists as different as Busta Rhymes and Britney Spears, Hugo told Ware, "As producers, you have the power to work with anybody every which way. We try to switch sounds with different people. . . . It's our way of being the Wizard of Oz. We run [expletive] from where you can't see us, switching up the styles. Ultimately I'd like it to be where you could turn on any station-rock, R&B, country—and know that the Neptunes did a lot, but not know [specifically] what the Neptunes did."

The Neptunes' artistic process has evolved. When they were younger, Williams and Hugo would listen to certain loops or repeated sections of already-produced songs and then, inspired by what they had heard, turn off the music and mix new sounds of their own. Now Williams and Hugo often listen to samples of songs and try to determine what is missing in them that might have made the tracks better, as Williams said in an interview posted on the VH1 Web site. Hugo concentrates mainly on the backdrop of productions-the beats, samples, and rhythms-while Williams excels at songwriting and possesses a falsetto singing voice that some critics have compared to that of Curtis Mayfield. Hugo told Paulson-Bryant that Williams is a "brilliant songwriter who can take the skeleton of a beat and put a great song on it." When Paulson-Bryant asked him about the Neptunes' collaborations with other musicians, Williams responded, "Artists are like vessels for us [producers] to use . . . I don't put something out if I feel like something is already out there like it. I strive for everything to be different. . . .. I want to give [both the artist and the eventual listener] what I think is missing." Hugo told an interviewer for the music Web site rwdmag.com that his favorite piece of studio equipment is the computer: "Everything can be. done on the computer, it has sped up the process, with a computer we can knock out 6 songs a day."

In 2001 Williams and Hugo recruited the talents of a high-school friend of theirs, the performer Sheldon Haley, better known as Shay, and along with him created a kind of musical alter-ego for the Neptunes: an alternative hip-hop and rock group called N.E.R.D. (an acronym for "No One Ever Really Dies"). "We weren't really nerds," Hugo told Bernard. "Pharrell got kicked outta band [in high school] a couple times, I got kicked outta my college band for quitting practice, and stole my first equipment. During a [school] pageant I stole a computer because I didn't have one." On the N.E.R.D. Web site, however, the men wrote, "We call ourselves

N*E*R*D because we have a different view of life. . . . If you ever listen to a nerd speak about their experiences in high school, they tell an ill ['interesting' or 'cool'] story. They have an ill perspective because of [what] they've been through.... I don't mind being called a nerd. We are the people who are proud of being smart, being witty and being clever when everyone else doesn't understand. That's what we do, that's the flag we're raising and waving."

Using electronic samplers and music computer software, the trio recorded tracks in the studio for their first album, *In Search Of. . .* , which was released in the United Kingdom in 2001. Williams and Hugo, however, feeling dissatisfied with the disk, re-recorded all the songs on *In Search Of. . .* , this time using live instrumentation, much of it performed by the band Spymob (which has been associated with the Neptunes' Star Trak label). "From the start, we wanted to distinguish what we did [as N.E.R.D.] ... from what we did as the Neptunes," Hugo told Tony Ware. "People expect the Neptunes to have a drum machine/keyboard sound. We didn't want *N.E.R.D.* to be the Neptunes Project.'" Reviewing *In Search Of. . .* for *Entertainment Weekly* (March 15, 2002), David Browne wrote that the album had a "crackling vigor . . . and its mélange of genres makes for music unlike anything else around. Tracks like 'Am I High' and 'Things Are Getting Better' pull together jazz-fusion funk, rapping, and slippery soul harmonies into a cogent, kinetic whole." Though Browne qualified his praise, complaining that parts of the album are "ugly, musically and lyrically," he concluded that *In Search Of*. .. reveals the Neptunes' "real need to stretch out, to see what other musical possibilities are out there. Pop needs to be shaken up, and these extra-loose cannons may be just the ones to do it." Stephen Thomas Erlewine wrote for *All Music Guide* that despite its flaws *In Search Of*. .. is a mostly "lively affair" that provides "genuine musical thrills. Although, be forewarned-it's easy to overrate this record simply because it deviates from the norm at a time when nobody deviates from the norm or has deviated from the norm in years. With better lyrics and a little less smirking hipsterism, it could have been the record it was intended to be, but as it stands it's still a pretty terrific listen and one of the most adventurous, intriguing hip-hop albums in a long, long time." The album's tracks "Lapdance" and "Rock Star" climbed onto *Billboard's* singles chart. While not as successful commercially as many of the Neptunes' other projects, *In Search Of*. .. achieved gold status.

By the time *In Search Of*. .. was released, Williams and Hugo had become as much in demand as producers of rap and hip-hop as Dr. Dre and Timbaland. Also during that period, five Neptunes-produced songs were on *Billboard's* Hot 100 chart: 'N Sync's "Girlfriend"; Usher's "U Don't Have to Call"; Fabolous's "Young'n (Holla Back)"; Busta Rhymes's "Pass the Courvoisier Part II" (with P. Diddy and Pharrell Williams); and Mystikal's "Bouncin' Back (Bumpin' Me Against the Wall)." Also in 2002 N.E.R.D. went on tour with Spymob.

In the same year the Neptunes signed an agreement that established their own record label, Star Trak Entertainment, and placed it under the wing of the record mogul Antonio Reid at Arista Records. (Reid later resigned from Arista.) Headed by the Neptunes and their manager, Rob Walker, Star Trak produces artists signed to Star Trak or Arista and signs and develops new talent. They have recruited to their label their fellow Virginians Fam-Lay, a rapper, and the rap duo Clipse (Malice and Pusha T). Clipse's album *Lord Willin'* (2002) debuted in the Top 10 on *Billboard's* album chart and has sold close to one million copies. In a review of *Lord Willin'* for *Rolling Stone* (September 5, 2002), Kathryn McGuire wrote, "[Clipse's] verses roll out with an infectious strut, but it's the beats backing them up, courtesy of hip-hop superproducers ... the Neptunes, that elevate Malice and Pusha T's cocky gangsterisms to radio-hit heights." Clipse's second album, *Hell Hath No Fury,* will be released in 2004. Another Star Trak-signed talent, the R&B singer Kelis, has achieved a degree of fame with her highly acclaimed, Neptunes-produced debut album, *Kaleidoscope* (1999), and the Neptunes-produced song "Milkshake," which was listed in the Top 10 on several *Billboard* charts in late 2003 and early 2004. Others who record on the Neptunes' Star Trak label are the rock group High Speed Scene and the rapper Rosco P. Coldchain.

In 2003 the Neptunes released *The Neptunes Present . . . Clones,* which topped *Billboard's* album chart and sold more than 250,000 units during its first week in stores; it later achieved platinum status. The disk's single "Frontin'," for which Williams sang and Jay-Z rapped, debuted at number one on music charts in August 2003. Featured on *Clones* are such music stars as Ludacris, Dirt McGirt (the erstwhile Ol' Dirty Bastard), and Snoop Dogg. In *Rolling Stone* (September 4, 2003), Kelefa Sanneh wrote, "With appearances from most of the big-name rappers and wall-to-wall Neptunes beats,

Affiliation: Digital Audio

Terry Sawyer, writing for the Web site popmatters.com, summed up the Neptunes' musical prowess and their wide appeal: "Once the Neptunes have laid their hands on a song, it's indisputably their own. You can recognize a Neptunes track by the way that the song's bones are lifted to the surface and pounded out like a giant's footfalls. The beats are simple, tactile and instantly demand a head nod, an ass shake, and an almost demonic surrender." Sasha Frere-Jones, in the *Village Voice* (February 18, 2003), described the Neptunes as the "first important producers of the 21st century, happy children of the loud, brassy world of digital audio. It's not just how their beats return again and again, deathlessly big like a can-crushing machine. . . . They have come—grind grind—to pump you up.... They are the first of a new cognitive class, working without a genre or a map." In 2003 Hugo and Williams released the compilation album *The Neptunes Present . . . Clones,* which features tracks with an array of top hip-hop performers and made its debut at number one on several of *Billboard* magazine's album charts. *Clones* has since achieved platinum status. Under the name of their alter-ego band N.E.R.D., Hugo and Williams released the albums *In Search Of. . .* (2002) and *Fly or Die* (2004). Referring, respectively, to a hip-hop group that became hugely popular in the early 1990s and a legendary funk/soul group whose heyday was in the 1970s, Hugo told Tony Ware for the Web site creativeloafing.com (July 17, 2002) that he and Williams started out trying to be "the R&B version of A Tribe Called Quest . . . the new wave Earth, Wind & Fire with turntables and drum machines." The Neptunes are nurturing future recording artists through their own record label, Star Trak Entertainment, which is an imprint of Arista Records. Hugo told Adam Bernard for reactmag.com, "Being a producer you get to kinda provide a backdrop to bring out whatever's in that artist, and you pick up things, like different opinions, it's like gain' to school. Every artist teaching you something in some way, indirectly." As posted on the Web site hip-hopnetwork.com, Williams told the publication *Rhythm Nation,* "Being a Neptune is all about exploring and discovering and that's no matter what it is that you do-we just happen to be producers . . . whatever it is that you do in your life be prepared to explore and discover, because if you're not, then you're sort of just running across stagnant territory, you're doing a disservice to your soul, your soul is here to learn." In addition to a number of other nominations and honors, in February 2004 the Neptunes won the Grammy Award for producer of the year.

this should be the world's greatest hip-hop compilation-and much of the time it is." Oliver Wang, in *LA Weekly* (November 21-27, 2003), dubbed the Neptunes "hip-hop's new wave apostles," whose "sonic playfulness has helped them all but make the rest of today's hip-hop, R&B and pop production indistinguishable. . . . So why isn't their new *Clones* album better than it is?" After describing the track "Light Your Ass on Fire" as "all lit up in screaming sirens and jangling guitar hooks," Wang wrote, "But Vanessa Marquez's painfully thin 'Good Girl' isn't even demo good, and N.O.R.E.'s 'Put 'Em Up' seems destined for strip clubs only.... The balance of *Clones* still gets a passing grade, but whatever the album boasts in competence it still lacks in adventure." In 2004 the Soul Train Music Awards honored *Clones* as best R&B/soul album by a group, band, or duo.

Fly or Die (2004), the second N.E.R.D. album, quickly jumped to a spot in the Top 10 on *Billboard's* album chart. For *Fly or Die* Hugo and Williams handled more of the instrumentation while blending aspects of rock, rap, soul, and hip-hop. According to a biography of N.E.R.D. on artistdirect.com, *Fly or Die* reaffirms that the group is "unrelenting in their knack for the absurd." For example, artistdirect.com continued, the video for the album's first single, "She Wants to Move," shows the N.E.R.D. trio in the "derriere" of an imaginary space vessel shaped like a woman's body. David Browne, in *Entertainment Weekly* (April2, 2004), opined that *Fly or Die* is "craftier and more multilayered" than N.E.R.D.'s first album, and described it as a "set of clever, complex, studio-crafted pop—complete with musicianly, smooth jazz licks—that doesn't owe allegiance to any one genre." Hugo, Williams, and Shay are not afraid, Browne wrote, "to thrash a melody one minute, caress it with suave harmonies the next, toss in fusion jazz piano, and set it all to beats (with real drums) that truly swing." In a review for Amazon.com, Aidin Vaziri wrote that *Fly or Die* revealed the influence of "Duran Duran's silk-spun new wave classics and the Beatles' strapping psychedelic epics," and praised the album as a "bustling, bumping disc highlighted by rowdy tracks like 'She Wants to Move' and 'Jump.' . . . The nu-metal crunch of the last album gives way to a more suitable '70s vibe, making the band sound like an unholy cross between Sly & The Family Stone and E.L.O.-as filtered through A Tribe Called Quest. That's a good thing." In conjunction with the release of *Fly or Die,* N.E.R.D. appeared as the guest band on *Saturday Night Live* and toured the country for two months.

In the VH1interview Hugo called the Neptunes' remix of Sade's popular song "By Your Side" their most drastic overhaul of an existing song. In 2002 it was nominated for a Grammy Award. Williams collaborated with Sean "Puffy" Combs, also known as P. Diddy, and Lenny Kravitz to create the song "Lose Your Soul." Among the other big-name artists or groups the Neptunes have worked with or have plans to produce are Alicia Keyes, Nelly Furtado, Counting Crows, No Doubt, Babyface, Lil' Kim, Bow Wow, Janet Jackson, Kid Rock, Toni Braxton, and Moby. Referring to the number and variety of their collaborations, Hugo told Joseph Patel for the MTV Web site, "Sometimes I find myself in the studio doing a song and I don't know who it's for."

In 2002 Hugo, having won praise for such songs as "Cross the .Border," "Danger (Been So Long)," and "I Just Wanna Love U (Give it 2 Me)," shared with Dr. Ore the American Society of Composers, Authors and Publishers (ASCAP) award for songwriter of the year. In 2003 both the Neptunes and N.E.R.D. received *Vibe* Award nominations. With another three nominations in his own name, Williams led all performers at that year's *Vibe* Awards. Both Usher and Nelly won Grammy Awards in 2003 for Neptunes-produced songs ("U Don't Have to Call" and "Hot in Herre," respectively). As songwriters, Hugo and Williams were both nominated for Grammy Awards in 2004 for the songs "Beautiful written with Calvin Broadus (known as Snoop Dogg), and "Excuse Me Miss," written with Shawn Carter (known as Jay-Z). As a singer, Williams (who tied with Jay-Z, Beyonce, and Outkast as the individuals with the highest total number of nominations—six) also received two nominations for best rap/sung collaboration for the songs "Frontin'" and "Beautiful." Hugo received two individual nominations and three as a member of the Neptunes. The Neptunes earned the 2004 Grammy Award for producer of the year.

Williams told an MTV interviewer that he avoids basking in his own success. "You can't pay attention to that," he said. "That's cancerous. 'Cause then you start believing it and your [expletive] gets weak. You gotta always think, 'There's more to do.' You can't ever look over your shoulder and be like, 'You know what I did?' 'cause you didn't do it—you just did what every other artist did and the people [the fans] embraced it and made it what it was. It was the people."

Because Williams sings the hooks, or repeated themes, on a number of the tracks that the Neptunes have produced, he has appeared in several music videos; his image has appeared significantly more often than Hugo's in magazines and elsewhere. "We do what we do to make music," Hugo, who is married with two children, told an interviewer for rwdmag.com. "I would like to be out there more, but that is not my main thing. Pharrell does what he has to do and it's all good between us. I don't sing hooks; I'm more about production, so I can't expect to be in every video. I also have a family which I'm trying to see as much as possible which is why I'm rarely [in the limelight]. We are two individuals-that's what makes us the Neptunes." Williams told MTV, "I love making music . . . I love playing. The keyboard is my journal."

Personal Lives

In 2003 Williams designed a limited-edition athletic shoe for Nike as part of a series the company commissioned from various artists. All proceeds from sales of the shoe will be donated to Goodwill's Good Books Program, which provides free books to children. Williams launched his own clothing line, BBC, or Billionaire Boys Club, in the summer of 2004. In his leisure time, Williams enjoys skateboarding. He and Hugo can be seen moving to their own music in the video for their recent single "She Wants to Move."

Further Reading

Blender p52 Apr. 2004, with photo

Entertainment Weekly p44+ Mar. 26, 2004, with photos, p62 Apr. 2, 2004, with photo

MTV Web site; n-e-r-d.com

New York Times Magazine p50+ Feb. 8, 2004, with photos

startrakmusic.com

VH1 Web site

Yannick Nézet-Séguin (YAH-nik nay-ZAY say-GHEN)

Orchestra conductor

Born: 1975; Montreal, Canada
Primary Field: Symphonic repertoire and opera
Group Affiliation: Philadelphia Orchestra; Rotterdam Philharmonic; Montreal's Orchestre Metropolitain

Introduction

"Though a diminutive figure," the music maestro Yannick Nézet-Séguin "exudes charisma on the podium," Anthony Tommasini wrote for the New York Times *(August 6, 2009). "He has striking musical ideas and communicates with his players through gestures that blend kinetic animation with elegant precision." Since June 2010 Nézet-Séguin—a Canadian-born conductor of symphonic repertoire and opera—has been the music director designate of the Philadelphia Orchestra, whose previous leaders have included the luminaries Eugene Ormandy, Riccardo Muti, and Leopold Stokowski. He also serves as music director of the Rotterdam Philharmonic, of the Netherlands; artistic director and principal conductor of the Orchestre Metropolitain in Montreal, Canada; and principal guest conductor of the London Philharmonic Orchestra, in England.*

Early Life

Yannick Nézet-Séguin was born in Montreal, Canada, in 1975. His last name combines the maiden name of his mother, Claudine Nézet, and the surname of his father; Serge Séguin. His parents both taught education at the Universite du Quebec a Montreal; he has two sisters, Sylviane and Isabelle, who are also teachers. When he was five years old, Nézet-Séguin began to take piano lessons with Jeanne-d'Arc Lebrun-Lussier, and by the age of 10, he had decided that he wanted to become a conductor. He was inspired after attending concerts by the Swiss conductor Charles Dutoit, who was maestro of l'Orchestre Symphonique de Montreal at the time. "I became fascinated by it and began to wave a stick with recordings," he recalled to Steve Smith for *Time Out New York* (September 9, 2010). "Dutoit would introduce pieces and be very accessible, and that had a big impact on me as a little boy," he told Robert Everett-Green for the Toronto, Canada, *Globe and Mail* (February 4, 2008). "If it had not been for this, I would maybe never have been a conductor."

During his youth Nézet-Séguin attended the Conservatoire de Musique du Quebec, in Montreal, where he studied piano, composition, chamber music, and conducting. "My main conducting teacher was actually my piano teacher"—Anisia Campos—"because a conductor is also an interpreter," he recalled to Everett-Green. "She was a very old-school teacher, very strict and demanding. She wouldn't allow any compromise in my piano study just because I wanted to be a conductor. I remember some years, I was really angry with her, because she wanted to develop some aspect of my playing that I considered very superficial. But I'm so grateful now. I couldn't have wished for a better teacher." He learned from her, as he was quoted as saying by the *Australian* (January 25, 2001, online), that "the best way to develop as a conductor is to become a better musician." For two summers when he was a teenager, Nézet-Séguin also studied choral conducting at Westminster Choir College, in Princeton, New Jersey. "I learned early in Princeton that everything you do has an impact on the sound," he explained to Matthew Gurewitsch for the *New York Times* (August 2, 2009). "I do move a lot. But I try never to be calculating or self-conscious about what I do. Maybe I just conduct big because of my small stature." When he was 19 years old, he became music director of the Choeur Polyphonique de Montreal, for which he had been singing since he was a child.

Life's Work

In the 1990s Nézet-Séguin furthered his education through master classes with figures including the preeminent Italian conductor Carlo Maria Giulini, who died in 2005. "[Giulini] remains completely special for me," Nézet-Séguin said in the interview with Tom Service. "He used to say that conductors were 'luggage and transit.' That was their function: the composers need their masterpieces to be carried and brought to people, so that's what we're doing. It's about not taking yourself too seriously." "Young as I was, he treated me almost as a colleague," he told Matthew Gurewitsch, "always putting my questions back into my own hands. Giulini always said that gesture must be the extension of your thought. When something goes wrong, it's because you don't have a clear idea. When the idea is simply the extension of your thought, the gestures will be clear and immediate." Nézet-Séguin was named chorus master and assistant conductor of the Opera de Montreal in 1998. Two years later, when he was 25, he received the Virginia-Parker Award, given annually to a Canadian classical musician or conductor under the age of 32. That honor brought him a great deal of attention, and in the same year the Orchestre Metropolitain appointed him as its principal conductor and artistic director. In 2004 Nézet-Séguin made his European conducting debut, with the Orchestra National du Capitole de Toulouse, based in France. Around the same time he began a five-year tenure as the principal guest conductor of the Victoria Symphony, in Canada. From 2005 to 2007 he served as a guest conductor of the Rotterdam Philharmonic Orchestra, and in 2008 he replaced Valery Gergiev as its principal conductor. "I never imagined I was a real candidate," he admitted to Everett-Green. "Maybe that's what got me the job, because I didn't act like someone who wanted the job. I just worked the way I always do." Also in 2008 Nézet-Séguin was appointed as principal guest conductor of the London Philharmonic and led the Philadelphia Orchestra for the first time, conducting Tchaikovsky's Symphony no. 6 and Rachmaninoff's Piano Concerto no. 2, with Andre Watts as soloist.

In 2009 Nézet-Séguin made his well-received New York Metropolitan Opera debut, with Richard Eyre's revival of Georges Bizet's *Carmen.* Anthony Tommasini wrote in a review of the performance for the *New York Times* (January 2, 2010), "The singers benefited immensely from the work of the rising 34-year-old Canadian conductor Yannick Nézet-Séguin ... who led a bracing, fleet and fresh account of the score, although he started the rousing prelude at a breakneck, frenetic tempo." The following year Nézet-Séguin conducted Nicholas Hytner's production of Giuseppe Verdi's *Don Carlo.* "Few Verdi singers know how to shape a recitative so eloquently-palpably aided by Nézet-Séguin ...," the music critic David Patrick Stearns wrote for the *Philadelphia Inquirer* (November 24, 2010). "He found inner voices in the orchestra that propel the action; blends brought new coloristic dimensions to even the most familiar passages; climaxes were masterfully built but never forced."

In June 2010 Nézet-Séguin, at 35, was selected as the eighth music director of the Philadelphia Orchestra; he signed a seven-year contract and will officially assume the position in the 2012–13 season. Nézet-Séguin has said that he felt a connection with the orchestra right away. "In every orchestra it's an average of very dedicated people and some who are worn down by the years," he explained to Marcia Adair for the *Los Angeles Times* (August 1, 2010). "In this orchestra I felt that it was so easy to get roughly everyone involved. It's my role to awaken the fire and joy of music making. Maybe for some people it's strange; for me that's why it clicked." Blair Bollinger, the bass trombone player who headed the orchestra's Conductor Search Committee, said to Adair, "Right from the first rehearsal the orchestra really responded to him. He has a fantastically clear technique, which makes it very comfortable." The choral conductor and tuba player Alain Cazes said to Robert Everett-Green for the *Globe and Mail*

Affiliation: Fulfilling a Dream

Since he was a child, Nézet-Séguin-perhaps the most celebrated conductor to have emerged from Canada—has wanted to lead orchestras. "The funny thing is that when you're that young, you dream of something without really knowing what it implies," he told Tom Service for the London *Guardian* (October 15, 2009). "But, on my way to becoming a conductor, I haven't had many surprises. I had a dream, and that dream has come true, and there is something normal about it, in a way." Nézet-Séguin formed a close relationship with the legendary maestro Carlo Maria Giulini, attending by invitation all of the older man's rehearsals and concerts in 1997 and 1998, before assuming the Montreal Metropolitain's leadership in 2000, at age 25. He made his .European conducting debut four years later. He has guest-conducted orchestras around the world, including the Toronto Symphony; the philharmonic orchestras of Berlin, Germany, Vienna, Austria, and Stockholm, Sweden; the Mozarteum Orchestra of Salzburg, in Austria; the Vancouver Symphony, in Canada; the Orchestre National de France; and the Chamber Orchestra of Europe. In the United States he has conducted in Boston, Massachusetts; New York; Washington, D.C.; and Los Angeles, California, among other cities. "When I'm on the podium, it feels natural, like I belong there," Nézet-Séguin said to Steven Mazey for the *Ottawa (Canada) Citizen* (February 20, 2010). "But off the podium, I of course have this fear that it could all end tomorrow. . . . I am always reminding myself how lucky I am to be here."

(October 30, 2010), "[Nézet-Séguin] has the ability to transfer his passion to the orchestra.... He's a great communicator. His requirements become our requirements. And he's always polite and respectful." Everett-Green wrote that Nézet-Séguin "describes himself as a risk-taker, willing to follow the impulse of the moment in performance even if it means colouring over the lines a little." After his appointment was announced, Nézet-Séguin attended a Philadelphia Phillies baseball game at Citizens Bank Park, where he conducted tens of thousands of fans in a seventh-inning-stretch rendition of the song "Take Me Out to the Ball Game."

Nézet-Séguin has said that the offer to lead the Philadelphia Orchestra came much sooner than he thought it would. "I was expecting to have to meet the orchestra for a third, fourth or fifth visit," he said in the October 30, 2010 interview with Everett-Green. "I was expecting that one of the big five American orchestras would be somewhat cold, or playing their usual stuff very professionally. But there was something extremely available about those musicians, and I responded very strongly to that." While the Philadelphia Orchestra has been struggling financially, many hope that Nézet-Séguin will help reverse the company's fortunes, Toward that end the conductor has added a week of performances to the three weeks he had already scheduled for the 2011-12 season in Philadelphia, where his appearances have proven to be highly popular.

In addition to his upcoming post with the Philadelphia Orchestra, Nézet-Séguin continues to serve as music director of the Rotterdam Philharmonic and principal guest conductor of the London Philharmonic. He also plans to maintain his post as artistic director and principal conductor of Montreal's Orchestre Metropolitain. "As I'm going on with this career, I realize every day that I need my place in Montreal, my hometown, because I love the city," he said in the interview with Steven Mazey. "It helps me settle down. Whenever I get back to the Orchestre Metropolitain, I feel it is rewarding musically, and I think we are still growing together. If that were not the case, I would say that it's time to move on." He added, "To do five or six concerts a season with this orchestra in which I have been growing for the past 10 years is not a lot to ask."

Nézet-Séguin has received numerous honors, including a Royal Philharmonic Society Award (2009) and a National Arts Centre Award (2010), the latter of which was presented as part of the Governor-General's Performing Arts Awards and included a commemorative medallion and $25,000. In April 2011 he was granted an "Honoris causa Doctorate" by the Universite du Quebec a Montreal, "to acknowledge his radiating international musical career and for his relentless endeavour towards promoting classical music." He has made a series of critically acclaimed live recordings, notable among them a 2007 CD of Bruckner's Seventh Symphony and a 2011 disc of Berlioz's *Symphonie Fantastique.*

Personal Life

In 2012 Nézet-Séguin will conduct for the first time at the Royal Opera House in London's Covent Garden; he will also officially become the new musical director of the Philadelphia Orchestra. His contract with the London Philharmonic Orchestra extends to 2014, and his contracts with the Orchestra Metropolitain and the Rotterdam Philharmonic will be in effect until 2015. "For me it's a question of enjoying as much as possible whatever I'm doing, wherever I am," Nézet-Séguin told Steve Smith, after being asked about his professional goals. "I'm privileged that my career is now leading to the main cities and the most wonderful opera houses and orchestras. But I've decided not to project myself and say, 'Okay, after this I would like to be there.'" Nézet-Séguin has said that in the future he will cut back on his appearances as a guest conductor. His primary goal, he told Smith, is "to remain as happy as I am-and for the rest, I'll trust life."

Further Reading

Los Angeles Times E p10 Aug, 1, 2010
New York Times (on-line) Aug. 2, 2009
Ottawa (Canada) Citizen G p1 Feb. 20, 2010
Philadelphia Inquirer D p1 July 19, 2010
(Toronto, Canada) *Globe and Mail* R p1 Feb. 4, 2008

Marni Nixon

Singer; dubber; actress; educator

Born: Feb. 22, 1930; Altadena, California
Primary Field: Cinema
Group Affiliation: Independent contractor; soloist

Introduction

Although her name and face are not familiar to most filmgoers, the voice of Marni Nixon is well known among fans of movie musicals and their soundtrack albums. A classically trained soprano and violinist, Nixon provided the singing voices of Deborah Kerr, in the role of the very proper British governess Anna Leonowens, in The King and I *(1956); Natalie Wood, as the Puerto Rican American teenager Maria, in* West Side Story *(1961); and Audrey Hepburn, as the Cockney flower-seller turned grand dame Eliza Doolittle, in* My Fair Lady *(1964)—three of the most famous characters and movie musicals in cinema history, Labeled "Hollywood's vocal doppelganger of choice" by Sam Sutherland, writing for Amazon.com, and "the queen of the dubbers" by the musicologist and musical-theater historian Kurt Gänzl, Nixon has perfect pitch, extraordinary skill at sight-reading musical scores, and the ability to mimic perfectly actresses' voices and enunciation and their characters' accented English. Because of the secrecy about her roles that her contracts obligated her to maintain, however, her name never appeared among the credits that moviegoers saw, and she has received no royalties for most of her work as a Hollywood dubber, or ghost singer. Despite her success in that field, she became disenchanted with the film industry and left to pursue a singing career as a soloist.*

Early Life

Of Scottish and German descent, Nixon was born Margaret Nixon McEathron to Charles Nixon McEathron and Margaret Elsa (Wittke) McEathron on February 22, 1930 in Altadena, California, a suburb of Los Angeles. Her mother nicknamed her Marni, by combining parts of her first and middle names. Nixon has two older sisters, Donyll and Adair, and a younger sister, Ariel (called Midge). Her father was a talented singer, and during the early years of her parents' marriage, he toured with trios and quartets. His wife encouraged him to continue his career in singing, but he disliked constant traveling and decided to take a job, in 1927, with the General Motors Co. in Los Angeles. Nixon has been singing since she was a baby; her parents told her that for a few weeks when she was about one and a half years old, she used to wake up after midnight and sing in her crib until she fell back to sleep. At the age of four, she saw a performance by Karl Moldrem's Hollywood Baby Orchestra (whose members were as young as two); afterward, at her request, her parents bought her a child-size violin. After only four violin lessons she joined Moldrem's orchestra. Moldrem soon found that she had perfect pitch, and he would often ask her to sing to provide examples for the other children. As a five-and-a-half-year-old violinist, Nixon joined the City Schools Youth Orchestra, in Altadena, with which her older sisters played. Her mother, father, and younger sister also played instruments, and the whole family would give concerts for neighbors on a platform built for that purpose in their living room. "Life in our household was strict," Nixon wrote in her memoir. "Mother ruled the roost with her Germanic perfectionism and our achievement was glorified." She also wrote that once, after she had accidentally lost her way while walking home from kindergarten, her mother screamed at her, "Either you're perfect, Marni, or you're nothing!"

Nixon made her debut on the silver screen in 1937, in a feature film whose script called for a young, red-headed violinist to play in the background. For the next decade she appeared in minor roles or as an extra in more than 50 films, including *The Great Waltz* (1938), *The Grapes of Wrath* (1940), *Babes on Broadway* (1942), *The Bachelor and the Bobby-Soxer* (1947), and *In the Good Old Summertime* (1949). She also had a recurring role as Angelica Abernathy in several of the. "Lum and Abner" films of the 1940s (spin-offs from the radio series originated by Chester Lauck and Norris Goff, whose characters were named Columbus "Lum" Edwards and Abner Peabody, respectively), starting with *The Bashful Bachelor* in 1942. By that time Nixon had been taking singing lessons for years; the money she earned from her jobs in cinema and from babysitting helped pay for them. Her parents paid the balance, and once, when they had no extra money, her mother sold her diamond engagement ring so that Nixon could continue with her lessons.

In 1946 Nixon placed second in a singing competition judged by the celebrated choral director Roger Wagner (one of several competitions in which she placed at or near the top). At Wagner's invitation she joined his newly formed Los Angeles Concert Youth Chorus. The following year, now named the Los Angeles Concert Chorale—commonly referred to as .the Roger Wagner Chorale—it turned professional. The group performed regularly with the Los Angeles Philharmonic Orchestra. Nixon became close friends with another chorus member, the future opera star Marilyn Horne (who later wrote the foreword to Nixon's memoir).

While a student at Susan Miller Dorsey High School, in Los Angeles, Nixon worked as a messenger girl at MGM Studios, delivering mail and giving guided tours. In 1947 she graduated from high school and entered Los Angeles City College, where she majored in music (but did not earn a degree). (Bennington College, in Vermont, had accepted her, but her mother had refused to let her enroll there.) One of her professors, Hugo Strelitzer, expanded her knowledge of opera and introduced her to leider, or art songs, written by 16th- and 17th-century French and Italian composers and 19th-century German composers. She took piano lessons with Leonard Stein, a teacher recommended by Strelitzer, but soon quit because she disliked practicing. "Now when my students and I anguish that I'm not a better pianist, I could kick myself for being so foolhardy and arrogant," she wrote in her memoir. "I should have taken the time to learn to play well."

Also in 1947 Nixon sang at the Hollywood Bowl in a performance of Carl Orff's *Carmina Burana,* with Leopold Stokowski conducting the Philadelphia Orchestra, and she participated in a performance of Mozart's Requiem with the Los Angeles Philharmonic, under the direction of Alfred Wallenstein. That year she won her first leading stage role, as the title character in a new musical, *Oh, Susanna,* mounted at the Pasadena Playhouse, in California. In addition, she took on her first ghosting job, as the singing voice of the child star Margaret O'Brien in *Big City* (1948). She dubbed for O'Brien again in *The Secret Garden* (1949). In1948 she appeared in a production of Richard Strauss's opera *Elektra,* and around that time she debuted on CBS radio, singing a medley of songs by Jerome Kern on a program called *Tomorrow Calling.* Years later she recorded the album *Marni Nixon Sings Classic Kern* (1988).

Life's Work

Meanwhile, Nixon had become involved in musical activities in college. Her performances on campus and ability to sight-read complex scores led the composer

Affiliation: Reclaiming Her Voice

"It got so I'd lent my voice to so many others that I felt it no longer belonged to me. It was eerie, I had lost part of myself," she told Albin Krebs and Robert Thomas for the *New York Times* (March 26, 1981). In a rare return to dubbing, she provided the singing voice for Grandmother Fa in the Disney animated feature *Mulan* (1998). Now 79, Nixon has worked virtually nonstop since early childhood. As a youngster she appeared in bit parts or as an extra in dozens of films and performed with local orchestras and choral groups. She has sung in operas by composers including Richard Strauss, Arnold Schoenberg, and Francis Poulenc, performing for radio and TV programs and with such companies as the Seattle Opera, in Washington State, and the San Francisco Opera and the Los Angeles Opera, in California. She has appeared in concert under such esteemed orchestra conductors as Leopold Stokowski, Bruno Walter, Otto Klemperer, and Zubin Mehta and such composer/conductors as Igor Stravinsky, William Walton, and Leonard Bernstein. She has appeared in singing and nonsinging roles on and Off-Broadway, in regional theater, and on TV; as the host of the Seattle children's TV series *Boomerang,* she won four local Emmy Awards. As a soloist or with others, Nixon has recorded two dozen albums, among them *Walt Disney's Story and Songs from Mary Poppins* (1964), Marni *Nixon: Songs of Love and Parting* (1974), and Marni Nixon *Sings Gershwin* (1993). She was twice nominated for a Grammy Award, in the category of best classical performance-vocal soloist, for her albums *The Cabaret Songs of Arnold Schoenberg and Nine Early Songs* (1975) and *Aaron Copland: Eight Poems of Emily Dickinson* (1986). Her voice has also been heard on many radio and TV commercials. For four decades she has worked as a vocal and dialect coach, both privately and as a member of the faculty of several schools, and she has conducted many master classes. Her memoir, *I Could Have Sung All Night,* written with Stephen Cole, was published in 2006. In 2007 she was a co-winner of the VERA (Voice Education Research Awareness) Award, from the Voice Foundation, for her "contribution to the field of voice communication."

Ernst Krenek to recruit her to sing one of his pieces at a chamber-music series at the college in 1948. Krenek was among many Jewish artists, musicians, writers, and others who had emigrated from European nations in the 1930s to escape the Nazis and had settled in Southern California, and thanks to him, Nixon began to attend informal concerts, called "Evenings on the Roof," at which she met other talented emigres as well as native-born American musicians. Her participation in a performance of Stravinsky's cantata *Les Noces* at one of those concerts led to her professional and personal association with Stravinsky and his wife; to prepare for studio recordings of works by the composer, she often rehearsed in the Stravinskys' home.

On May 22, 1950 Nixon married the Austrian-born emigre and composer Ernest Gold, whose credits include the scores for the films *The Defiant Ones, On the Beach, Exodus,* and *It's a Mad, Mad, Mad, Mad World.* Later that year Nixon, whose greatest ambition had been to become a great opera singer, "made a major professional mistake," as she wrote in her memoir: after she auditioned for the New York City Opera's forthcoming production of Mozart's *The Magic Flute,* she turned down the role that she was offered-that of the Queen of the Night—because she regarded it as "totally pyrotechnic." "In retrospect," she wrote, "I realize that if I had accepted the role it might have led to others in the company and I probably would have come to New York and based my career on the East Coast, which might have afforded me more opportunities in the opera world."

Nixon gave birth to her first child in 1951 and her second in 1953. Juggling her career with her responsibilities as a homemaker, she continued to perform in "Evenings on the Roof" concerts and with the Roger Wagner Chorale. In a job that required her to mimic Marilyn Monroe's "breathy, sexy sound," in her words, she dubbed the second half of the line "But square cut or pear shape, these rocks don't lose their shape" in the song "Diamonds Are a Girl's Best Friend," from *Gentlemen Prefer Blondes* (1953); the notes accompanying those words were too high for Monroe, who starred in the film.

In 1955 Nixon landed her first major ghosting job, for the film version of the Richard Rodgers and Oscar Hammerstein musical *The King and I,* originally staged in 1951 with Gertrude Lawrence as Anna. (Nixon replaced a dubber, not named in her memoir, who had suddenly died.) The contracts offered to her by the film studio now known as 20th Century Fox and with Capitol Records, which later released the film's soundtrack, specified that she would receive a single payment but no royalties and no credits, either in the film or on the record jacket. "I was torn," she recalled in her memoir, "but the studio had made the choice very clear: either I do the job anonymously, with no credit at all, or walk away." Eager to work on such a high-profile project, as well as with the actress Deborah Kerr, Nixon signed the contracts. The recording process involved extremely close cooperation between Kerr and Nixon. "Whenever there was a song to be sung in a scene, I would get up and stand next to [Kerr] and watch her while she sang and she would watch me while I sang," Nixon told Jeff Lunden for the National Public Radio program *Weekend Edition Sunday* (September 3, 2006, on-line). "After we recorded that song, she would have to go to the filming of it and mouth to that performance. So she had to be very aware of what she was going to do and how she was going to sing the song ahead of time." "The challenge [for me] was singing in a voice that was consistent with the sound of [Kerr's] speaking voice," Nixon told Frank Magiera for the Worcester, Massachusetts, *Telegram & Gazette* (July 10, 1997). "You must imagine the conformation of the resonance that you hear coming out of [singers'] mouths; how to manufacture that within your own vocalism and not destroy yourself and still incorporate that as part of your own voice."

Studio executives ordered Nixon to keep her role in *The King and I* a secret. Though dubbing was a well-known practice within the film industry, many moviegoers were unaware of it. "Nowadays people accept stuntmen, doubles, all that," Nixon told a Minneapolis, Minnesota, *Star Tribune* (February 17, 2008) reporter. "But in those days, it was considered a detriment if people found out." Kerr, bound by no such constraints, revealed Nixon's role to reporters. "The first interview she gave with [the *New York Post]* columnist Earl Wilson was headlined 'Deborah Tells a Secret,'" Nixon told Frank Rizzo for the *Hartford (Connecticut) Courant* (July 5, 1997). "Of course, she said I just did the high notes, but she did mention me by name and said that I was dubbing her voice." In a representative, highly enthusiastic review of *The King and I* for the *New York Times* (June 29, 1956), Bosley Crowther wrote, "The voice of Marni Nixon adds a thrilling lyricism to [Kerr's] songs." Nixon dubbed Kerr's singing voice again in the romantic drama *An Affair to Remember* (1957), co-starring Cary Grant, in which Kerr played a lounge singer. Although Nixon received neither screen credit nor royalties, her name appeared on the back cover of the soundtrack album to that motion picture. In 1960, in her first appearance on screen as an adult, Nixon sang in the chorus in the film version of Cole Porter and Abe Burrows's 1953 stage musical, *Can-Can.*

Nixon was recruited to dub the singing voice of Natalie Wood in the film version of the theatrical musical *West Side Story* (1961), with music by Leonard Bernstein and lyrics by Stephen Sondheim, based on ideas of the choreographer Jerome Robbins and Shakespeare's *Romeo and Juliet.* Wood, who played the female lead, Maria (a role originated on the stage in 1957 by Carol Lawrence), worked on the project without knowing that her songs would be dubbed; indeed, according to Nixon, the film crew led Wood to believe that her own singing would be heard by moviegoers. After the shooting Nixon had to synchronize her singing precisely to the movements of Wood's lips and her facial expressions in the songs "Tonight" (and the "Tonight" quintet), "I Feel Pretty," "One Hand, One Heart," "Somewhere," and "I Have a Love." "That's a much more difficult process" than the one she and Kerr had used, she told the *Star Tribune* interviewer. Although Nixon was again sworn to secrecy, and her name did not appear among the credits in the film, she instructed her new agent to fight for her fair share of the royalties from the soundtrack album. That battle ended when Leonard Bernstein agreed to give to Nixon a quarter of one percent of his own royalties—"not a negligible amount," in Nixon's words: the album remained on the *Billboard* pop chart for 198 weeks—in the top spot for 54—and by 1986 it had sold more than three million copies. It also won the 1961 Grammy Award in the category "best soundtrack album-original cast." (Bernstein and Nixon's agreement applied only to long-playing records; Nixon has received no royalties from sales of the *West Side Story* CD.) Nixon's third child was born in 1962.

For *My Fair Lady,* her next major feature film, Nixon dubbed the singing of Audrey Hepburn. Julie Andrews, who had played the lead when Alan Jay Lerner and Frederick Loewe's *My Fair Lady* opened on Broadway, in 1956, had not yet appeared on the big screen, and the producers of the film wanted the name of a female superstar on movie marquees.) Hepburn had demonstrated her ability to sing in the films *Funny Face* (1957) and *Breakfast at Tiffany's* (1961), but the role of Eliza Doolittle required a voice more powerful and higher-pitched than hers. "Audrey, of course, wanted to do it all," Nixon wrote in her memoir, "but realized that I might have to supplement some of the higher notes and sing some of the longer-lined, more lyrical phrases." When Hepburn learned that all but one of the songs would be recorded in Nixon's voice, Nixon told Frank Rizzo, "she stomped out of the studio without saying a word. The next day she came back and apologized for her 'wicked' behavior." The knowledge that her singing was dubbed led to much criticism of Hepburn immediately after the release *of My Fair Lady,* at the end of 1964; the movie won eight Oscars (including one for the male lead, Rex Harrison) and many others awards, but Hepburn earned none. Earlier that year Nixon had provided the singing voices for the trio of animated geese in the "Jolly Holiday" sequence in the film *Mary Poppins* (in which Julie Andrews starred and for which she earned the Academy Award for best actress). In *The Sound of Music* (1965), in which Andrews also starred, Nixon was cast in the small part of a nun, Sister Sophia.

Later in the 1960s Nixon performed with the celebrated showman and pianist Liberace in Las Vegas, Nevada, and toured with the Danish-born pianist and comedian Victor Borge. In 1971, two years after her divorce from Gold, Nixon remarried and moved to Seattle to sing with the Seattle Opera. She appeared in productions mounted in local theaters and also gave concerts. During the late 1970s and early 1980s, Nixon hosted *Boomerang,* a local children's program for the Seattle TV channel KOMO 4. After the show's cancellation, reruns of its 169 episodes aired on local television for 25 years. Nixon earned four Northwest Chapter Emmy Awards for her work on the series.

In the early 1980s Nixon moved to New York City. In 1983 she starred alongside the singers Margaret Whiting and Cissy Houston in the Off-Broadway musical *Taking My Turn,* for which she earned a 1984 Drama Desk Award for outstanding featured actress in a musical. On Broadway she originated the roles of Sadie McKibben in *Opal* (1992) and Aunt Kate in *James Joyce's The Dead* (1999-2000). She also appeared in Broadway revivals of *Follies* (2001) and *Nine* (2003). In 2007 she appeared as Professor Henry Higgins's mother, a nonsinging role, in a concert performance of *My Fair Lady* with the New York Philharmonic at Lincoln Center, in New York City.

Personal Life

Earlier, Nixon underwent treatment for breast cancer in 1985 and again in 2000, after a recurrence. She has been married to her third husband, the jazz flutist Al Block, since 1983. Her second marriage, to Lajos Frederick Fenster, a physician, ended in divorce in 1975 after four years. From her first marriage she has one son, Andrew Gold, a musician and producer; two daughters—Martha Gold Carr, a psychologist, and Melani Gold Friedman, a singer and songwriter; and six grandchildren.

Since 1999 Nixon has given many performances of her one-woman show, *Marni Nixon: The Voice of Hollywood.* "I show some stills from the films I dubbed, tell some stories, sing a few things and answer questions about my life," she told Frank]. Prial for the *New York Times* (March 6, 2007). "People always love to ask me questions. And why not? I've had a really fantastic life."

Further Reading

AllMusicGuide.com
New York Times E p3 Mar. 6, 2007
Opera News p42+ Apr. 2004, p30+ Oct. 2004
Philadelphia Inquirer H p1 Mar. 9, 2008; *Playbill* (online) Jan. 4, 2000
Time p81+ Feb. 7 1964;
Nixon, Marni, with Stephen Cole. *I Could Have Sung All Night,* 2006

Ted Nugent

Musician, hunting advocate, radio and television host, magazine publisher, writer

Born: Dec. 13, 1948; Detroit, Michigan
Primary Field: Rock and Roll, Blues
Group Affiliation: Amboy Dukes, Solo artist

Introduction

From his octane-fueled music career, first as the lead guitarist for the Amboy Dukes, then as a solo artist, to his passion for hunting and the outdoors, Ted Nugent has spent his professional life pushing the limits. His propensity for performing on stage either while wearing a loincloth or only animal pelts and his well-publicized right-wing positions on such hot-button topics as gun control, abortion, and the death penalty have earned Nugent the nickname "Motor City Madman"-a reference to Detroit, Michigan, Nugent's hometown, which is the historical home of the automobile industry. They have also earned him a reputation as a colorful, unrepentant extremist. After landing a smash hit with the song "Journey to the Center of the Mind" with the Amboy Dukes in the late 1960s, Nugent split from the band and pursued a solo career. During the 1970s and 1980s, he recorded several more highly successful singles, including the now-classic "Wango Tango" and "Cat Scratch Fever." All told, Nugent has sold more than 30 million albums and is one of the top-grossing live musical acts of all time.

Early Life

Ted Nugent was born on December 13, 1948 in Detroit, Michigan. According to some sources, he first picked up a bow and arrow, supplied by his father, when he was five years old. When he was nine he began learning to play the guitar. He has traced his passion for hunting and the outdoors to about that time. "My first kill ever was with a Whammo slingshot," Nugent told Steve Miller for the *Washington Times* (May 2002). "I was 10 years old, and it was in a park near Redford Township in Michigan. I killed [a wild turkey] with a marble, and I took it home, and my mom and dad showed me how to dress it and cook it. There was definitely some cause and effect there." By the time he was a teenager, Nugent had formed his first rock band, the Royal Highboys. Soon afterward he formed the Lourds, with whom he won a Battle of the Bands contest, finishing the performance by playing a guitar solo atop the judges' table. Following that victory the Lourds became an opening act for such well-known groups as the Supremes and the Beau Brummels. However, hunting was the source of Nugent's greatest pleasure. "The family took annual fall excursions [to northern Michigan] for an extended weekend along the Titabawasee River. . . ," he wrote in an editorial for huntingdigest.com. "Dad and I rambled around the Ogemaw State Forest, bows in hand, for absolutely thrilling adventure. He didn't push me by any means, but rather just exposed me to the thrill of the wild and taught me a little along the way."

Life's Work

In 1967 Nugent formed the Amboy Dukes, a Detroit-based version of a band he had led during the two years he and his family had lived in Chicago. Made up of Nugent, the former Lourds vocalist John Drake, Bill White on bass, Steve Farmer on rhythm guitarist, and Dave Palmer on drums, the Amboy Dukes released an eponymous debut album that year. The band quickly became a fixture in Detroit's club scene. Infused with a strong work ethic and a rough-and-tumble attitude, the Amboy Dukes were examples of the fast and furious Motor City sound that was becoming popular in the late 1960s. Such bands as the Stooges, MC5, and Mitch Ryder and the Detroit Wheels took conventional rock music and intensified it, creating a sound that made the Motor City distinct from other burgeoning music centers in the U.S. Nugent himself became known for his idiosyncratic diction.

In 1968 the Amboy Dukes released a hit single, "Journey to the Center of the Mind," the title track from the group's second album. Many people assumed that the song was about drug use, although the lyrics contain no references to artificial stimulants. Nugent, who maintains a rigid anti-drug stance, told Allan Varda for *Psychedelic Psounds* (February 24, 1988, on-line), "When we put out 'Journey to the Center of the Mind' . . . it had that [image of a] pipe collection on the front cover and I didn't have the faintest idea what those pipes were all about! Everybody else was getting stoned and trying every drug known to mankind. I was meeting women, playing rock and roll. I didn't have the faintest idea about dope. I didn't know anything about this cosmic inner probe. I thought 'Journey to the Center of the Mind' meant look inside yourself, use your head, and move forward in life." He also told Varda, "I watched incredible musicians fumble, drool, and not be able to tune their instruments [because of drug or alcohol use]. It was easier to say no than to say, 'Hey, gosh, that's for me.' I've also seen my fellow musicians die. It was so obvious. The same reason you don't run across certain highways during peak rush hours." Nugent has maintained that he was never troubled about his lack of popularity with people in the music scene, some of whom ridiculed him because of his disapproval of drugs.

During the last years of the 1960s and the early 1970s, the Amboy Dukes released a series of well received albums, including *Migration* (1969) and *Marriage on the Rocks* (1970). At the same time, Nugent was growing increasingly irritated by his bandmates' attitudes and their continued drug use. He fired Drake and Palmer, and afterward the band's lineups changed often. Renamed Ted Nugent & the Amboy Dukes, the group released the albums *Call of the Wild* (1973) and *Tooth, Fang & Claw* (1974), but Nugent found that managing the band was becoming intolerably stressful. "I was so upset internally with the amount of effort I was putting out with the constant human battering I was doing with the musicians," he recalled to Varda. "I was bailing [a band member] out of jail in Montgomery, Alabama for breaking into a Coke machine. Or getting someone else out of jail because he got caught with a joint. . . . I also acted as a road manager. I used to book the band. I used to maintain all the equipment. I used to change the oil in the cars. I used to drive the truck and set it up. I handled all the hotels. I kept all the ledger books. I did everything . . . . So for the first time in my life I took a year off."

Nugent now focused his attention on carving out a solo career. After spending some time hunting deer in Colorado, he returned to the recording studio and soon released his first solo album, *Ted Nugent* (1975), to which Derek St. Holmes contributed rhythm guitar and vocals. In the *All Music Guide* (on-line), Greg Prato called the album "a prime slice of testosterone-heavy, raging, unapologetic rock & roll." Offering such classics as "Hey Baby," "Just What the Doctor Ordered," and "Motor City Madhouse," the album achieved platinum status (with more than one million copies sold).

With the then-unknown singer Meat Loaf replacing St. Holmes during the latter's brief absence, the band next released *Free-for-All* (1976). Popular singles from that album included "Hammerdown" and "Turn it Up." St. Holmes traveled with the band on its subsequent tour and collaborated on its follow-up album, *Cat Scratch Fever* (1977). Featuring the tracks "Cat Scratch Fever" and "Dog Eat Dog," songs that are still ranked among Nugent's best, the album proved to be Nugent's breakthrough effort, selling more than two million copies. "For sheer jubilant ferocity in recent hard rock," Ken Tucker wrote for *Rolling Stone* (July 28, 1977, on-line), "Ted Nugent has only himself to top, and he does it on Cat Scratch Fever." Tucker described Nugent's guitar playing as an "amalgam of innumerable heavy-metal quotations raised to fascination by the speed and cunning with which he runs through them."

Nugent's live album *Double Live Gonzo* (1978) sold extremely well. "As exciting as they were, Ted Nugent's first three albums lacked the sonic punch in the gut of his outrageous live performances, something readily proved by 1978's classic *Double Live Gonzo*," Ed Rivadavia wrote for the *All Music Guide* (on-line).

On the band's extensive tours, Nugent's unrestrained stage shows made him the number-one-grossing musical act in 1977, 1978, and 1979. His subsequent recordings included *Scream Dream* (1980), *Intensities in 10 Cities* (1981), and *If You Can' t Lick 'Em . . . Lick 'Em* (1988). These albums contained some of Nugent's most famous songs, including "Wango Tango," "Spread Your Wings," and "Terminus Eldorado."

In 1990 Nugent, along with the former Styx guitarist Tommy Shaw and Night Ranger bassist Jack Blades, formed *Damn Yankees*. A supergroup designed to challenge some of the "disposable" pop metal acts of that era, the musicians released their debut album, *Damn Yankees,* in 1990. Propelled by the success of the first single, the ballad "High Enough," the record climbed to number 13 on Billboard magazine's album charts and achieved platinum status. The group's second effort, *Don't Tread* (1992), did not fare as well, and *Damn Yankees* disbanded in 1993. Nugent resumed his solo career with *Spirit of the Wild* (1995), an album that celebrated his passion for hunting and the wilderness. Critics praised the record as a restrained and mature effort. "Spirit of the Wild" ranks as one of Ted Nugent's finest moments because it cuts away the filler and keeps the wildman's tendency for indulgence in check," Stephen Thomas Erlewine wrote for the *All Music Guide* (online). In 1996 Nugent released Motor City Madness.

In the late 1990s Nugent continued to tour extensively, averaging more than 100 shows a year. In 2000 he performed on a tour with the legendary rock band Kiss, which became the top-grossing concert act of the year. Nugent's live album *Full Bluntal Nugity* (2001) is a 12-track recording of a show Nugent played on New Year's Eve 2000 in Detroit. In 2002 he released *Craveman*, his first studio album in seven years. He told Benfer, "I crave the American dream. The American dream is about optimal partying. Not puking and dying-that's not a party. . . . My point is that *Craveman* . . . is a huge shout from the top of the top mountain. Mankind: A quality of life upgrade is available to each and every one of you . . . which means no drugs, no alcohol, no fast food-unless, of course, it's a mallard." The record received positive reviews. "Ted Nugent-gonzo guitarist, unabashed American patriot, shameless meat-eater/hunter [has] cranked

Affiliation: Hunter, Outdoorsman, Activist

Nugent is also an avid hunter and outdoorsman. He is the editor and publisher of Ted Nugent Adventure Outdoors magazine, the president of Ted Nugent United Sportsmen of America, and the founder of Ted Nugent's Kamp for Kids, and in all those capacities, he advocates hunting as both a way to commune with nature and a purer, healthier source of meat than the processed products derived from domesticated livestock. His outspoken views of those subjects have drawn criticism from animal-rights activists. Nugent has dismissed their arguments and has maintained that, far from simply killing animals and drawing resources from the land, he works harder than most environmentalists to preserve the natural world. "We have the figures back," he told Amy Benfer for *Salon* (June 11, 2002, on-line), "and they say that by the spring of '99, my Kamp for Kids and other hunting, sporting and conservation groups were responsible for planting over 10 million trees. So I'd like to ask my critics: How many trees have you planted? How many acres of wildlife habitat have you restored?"

In addition to his Kamp for Kids-which provides archery instruction, gun-safety lessons, and other hunting-related activities for youngsters Nugent sponsors the organizations Hunters for the Hungry, which encourages hunters to provide surplus meat for the needy; Sunrize Safaris, which offers individuals the chance to hunt and camp with Nugent as their guide; and Hunt of a Lifetime, which gives terminally ill children the chance to hunt in the U.S. and overseas.

He has also supported many local and national law-enforcement organizations and has long been a vocal critic of drug and alcohol abuse, serving as a national anti-drugs spokesman and working with programs dedicated to keeping young people sober and drug free. For his charitable work and efforts within his community and in the outdoors, Nugent was honored on the floor of the U.S. Senate in 1994 and named Michigan conservationist of the year in 1999. "Some people with small minds call me an extremist," he wrote in an essay for chicagoscene.com (July 2001). "It is weird, extremely weird, to be given such a compliment by such an obviously uncomplimentary source. After all, when those who do nothing in the face of disaster condemn our progressive activism, it is living proof that we are on a True North track. Compared to my apathetic, lame critics, I am extremely proud to be an extremist."

out a sure-to-become-classic with *Craveman*," Michael Paoletta wrote for *Billboard* (October 5, 2002, online). "The album is full bluntal nugity: over-the-top, sex-fueled lyrics and anthemic compositions featuring bluesy undercurrents that have guitars roaring with rock' n 'roll fury."

While pursuing his musical career, Nugent has always made time for his other passions. Among them are the Ted Nugent Kamp for Kids; founded in 1990, the camp teaches children hunting and survival skills and wildlife conservation, in classes ranging from archery to compass reading to first aid. (Nugent is a certified hunting-safety instructor and an International Bowhunter Education Foundation instructor.) In 1989 Nugent established Hunters for the Hungry, which encourages hunters and meat processors to distribute game meat to people without enough to eat. To date, the organization has helped to deliver more than one million pounds of meat to the needy. Nugent himself is often on hand at soup kitchens, serving such dishes as venison stew. In 1994 his efforts in education and conservation led then-governor John Engler of Michigan to appoint him to the state's International Year of the Family council. Nugent has also served as director of the state's Hunting and Fishing Heritage Task Force and as an appointee to the Michigan State Parks Foundation. He has been honored as Michigan's Recreation and Parks Association man of the year.

Gun control is chief among the topics about which Nugent is outspoken. A member of the board of directors of the National Rifle Association, he staunchly supports the view that the Second Amendment of the U.S. Constitution, which reads, "A well-regulated militia being necessary to the security of a free State, the right of the people to keep and bear arms shall not be infringed," means that even in the absence of a militia, people have the right to bear arms. He believes that most Americans are more "pro-gun" than they might admit. "Even those that claim to be against gun ownership . . . have made a big deal out of wishing for more law enforcement personnel on the streets of America," he said in an online chat on the ABC News Web site (August 3, 2000), "when in fact, in those jurisdictions where law abiding citizens have a higher rate of concealed weapons permits, they have for all practical purposes performed the very duties in stopping and deterring crime that armed law enforcement personnel have."

In response to animal-rights activists who have painted him as a bloodthirsty butcher, Nugent has insisted that he is interested in the overall ecology of the world. He and his family raise many animals and plant trees on their land. "In 2002, it is irrefutably documented that there are more deer, more turkey, more Canadian geese, more mountain lion, more bear than ever in recorded history in North America," he told Benfer. (Many scientists would dispute that assertion.) He continued, "There's not a farmer in America that if approached by a reasonably groomed, decent, courteous family wouldn't be pleased as punch to have you come in and help reduce the damned deer population! Or the mountain lion, or the elk-there's more elk, there's more moose, there's more buffalo than in over 150 years." "I don't even want to hear about animals being equal to human beings," he told Steve Walters for the Fort Lauderdale, Florida, *Sun-Sentinel* (March 13, 1993). "I don't even want to hear their rhetoric and their lies. I have on file with law enforcement agencies threats to kill my [four] children because we eat pheasants. They want to kill me, they want to take our lives because I hunt. We're talking evil, out-of-whack scum who have completely lost respect for life itself." He has also drawn fire from a number of animal-rights celebrities, among them the former Beatle Paul McCartney. "When McCartney says he won't eat anything with a face, I ask 'What are you saying to millions of Americans barbecuing chicken on the Fourth of July?' I think Paul should just shut up and sing. . . . I'm proud to be a hunter because it's as pure a function as giving birth. There's this vicious misrepresentation of hunting, a lie repeated so often people believe it: That I weigh 350 pounds, inbred, shooting Bambi and stop signs and the occasional nephew in the leg. Hunters are mothers and fathers . . . we understand how we fit in."

In 1990 Nugent published his first book, *Bloodtrails: The Truth about Bowhunting.* His second, the essay collection *God, Guns, & Rock 'N' Roll* (2000), offers autobiographical material along with discussions of social and political issues. The title of the book refers to what Nugent considers to be his greatest influences. "I'm 52 years clean and sober and I attribute that discipline in my life to the fact that I've been surrounded for 52 years by God, lots of guns and outrageous rock and roll," he told Geoff Metcalf for *Metcalf's* Web site. "It has been a good regimen for me. My parents raised me in a very loving, very disciplined-there's the key word-a disciplined environment to teach me self-discipline. And, as a hunter, I can't deny the incredible gifts of the Creator." *God, Guns, & Rock 'N' Roll* landed on the *New York Times* best-seller list, where it remained for several weeks. Nugent wrote his third book, *Kill It and Grill It: A Guide to Preparing and Cooking Wild Game and Fish* (2002), with his wife, Shemane. In addition to some of Nugent's exotic recipes (sweet-and-sticky rabbit, big-game meat cakes, and wild-boar chops, for example), it offers hunting stories and tips for inexperienced hunters and trappers. Nugent dedicated the book to "the great American families who celebrate hands-on environmental awareness in the grand and honorable culture of hunting, fishing, and trapping, thereby guaranteeing balanced biodiversity." In the book Nugent also explains why a diet of meat that one has killed oneself is better for health than meat sold in stores. "Pure, perfect-quality protein is available to everyone who wants to flex their natural instinct to be self-sufficient, independent, more honestly in tune with the source of their sustenance," he told Benfer. "There's plenty of critters to go around, plenty of land to go around. . . Kill 'em and grill 'em! That's not just a clever title. I really mean it! If you want your body to be healthier, get off the salmonella, e-coli, mad cow, assembly-line toxic hell train! . . . What I do is pure." Articles by Nugent have appeared in many publications, including his magazine, *Ted Nugent Adventure Outdoors*.

Nugent has mentioned that he is considering running for governor of Michigan in 2010. He has served as a national spokesman for the conservative radio talk-show host Rush Limbaugh and such organizations as Mothers Against Drunk Driving, Big Brothers/Big Sisters, and the Drug Abuse Resistance Education law-enforcement program. He hosts the *Ted Nugent Morning Show* on WWBR in Detroit. In 2004 he joined the ranks of reality-TV personalities with *Surviving Nugent,* a VH1 series in which a dozen contestants competed against one another in wilderness activities on Nugent's Texas ranch. "One critic dubbed the series 'plain awful,'" Tony Allen-Mills reported in the London *Sunday Times* (May 16, 2004); the show was canceled after one season. Nevertheless, Nugent was hired to star in another reality show, *Wanted: Ted or Alive.* Scheduled to premiere on November 5, 2005 on the Outdoor Life Network, the show puts five "city slickers" in the wilderness and presents them with challenges, such as killing and skinning a boar.

Personal Life

Nugent lives and often hunts on his 800-acre ranch in Jackson, Michigan. He opens the ranch each year to a few select hunters and accompanies them in the wild. He has two sons and two daughters. The children from his first marriage, which ended in divorce in 1976 after six years, are Toby and Sasha. The children from his union with his second wife, the former Shemane Deziel, whom he married in 1989, are Starr and Rocco. Shemane, a certified fitness instructor, helps her husband to write, edit, and produce Ted Nugent's *Spirit of the Wild* television series for the Public Broadcasting System and writes for *Ted Nugent Adventure Outdoors* magazine. His younger son's school once named him father of the year. "I always stop working in September," he told an Associated Press reporter (December 26, 1986), "because as a father I want to be more than a visitor." He hunts with his children and stresses to other parents the importance of getting their children involved in wildlife education or other activities that foster parent-child interactions and communication. In an essay on his official Web site, Nugent wrote, "If your kid spends more than 30 minutes a day in front of the TV set, watching programs or playing zombie inducing video games, you are asking for trouble. If you can't remember the last Saturday you took the family to a wild place, early and long, you are asking for trouble. If you can't talk with your kids because they have headphones glued to their ears, you are out of their loop, and may I dare say, a failing parent."

In an interview in 2000 with Classic Rock Revisited (on-line), Nugent said, "The reason I'm able to [accomplish what I have is that] my wife, Shemane, my four wonderful children, and the people I surround myself with, are working hard, playing hard, American families. We put our heart and soul into everything."

Further Reading

Chicago Tribune 0 p1+ July 29, 1994, with photos
Field ET Stream p589 July 2003
Orange County (New Jersey) Register F p2 May 4, 1994, with photo; *People* p604+ Jan. 10, 1994, with photo
Salon (on-line) June 11, 2002, with photo
tnugent.com
Nugent, Ted. *God, Guns, ET Rock 'N' Roll,* 2000

Mark O'Connor

Violinist and composer

Born: August 5, 1961; Seattle, Washington
Primary Field: Multiple genres, including bluegrass
Group Affiliation: Sideman and solo artist

Introduction

In a career spanning more than forty years, Mark O'Connor has demonstrated time and again that versatility and virtuosity can peacefully coexist in the same musician. Equally adept at a number of string instruments but best known for his work as a violinist, the award-winning musician and composer is known for his ability to play country, bluegrass, jazz, classical, and folk music with both dexterity and improvisation. He has also branched out from his roles as a performer and composer to begin work on a massive project: teaching others how to play their instruments through a method that he developed, which employs the improvisational skills honed by playing American music, rather than through more traditional, rote memorization methods. ''The biggest part .of the last decade as far as my career was about my performances, my playing, my music," he told Randy Lewis for the Los Angeles Times *(15 Mar. 2009). "Now in my life it's more about what this music means to other musicians. It's becoming less about my performances as an artist and maybe more about being in a leadership position to steer in new ideas and bring new material for people to try out. It's a really, really gratifying development."*

Early Life

Mark O'Connor was born in Seattle, Washington, on August 5, 1961. His paternal ancestors had settled in Seattle in the late nineteenth century. His maternal ancestors had come to the Americas far earlier, in 1608, and traveled across the country until World War I, when his Memphis-born grandmother moved to Seattle. "So the journey west, both branches of my family took it, just like so many people," O'Connor told Martin Steinberg for the Associated Press (15 Mar. 2009). "And it was this journey out of our cities, towns, into whatever it was to get more land, just to get more breathing room or to get away from something. A lot of this movement was our cultural backdrop to make the music that we [Americans) have."

O'Connor came to music early, when his mother—a classical music lover who died when he was just twenty—bought him a guitar at age three. Two years later she found him a classical guitar instructor who taught him how to read music. By the age of nine or ten he was competing in classical guitar competitions, including a contest held at the University of Washington, at which he competed against college-aged students and won second prize. During this period he became interested in the violin after seeing violinists and fiddlers performing on his local PBS television affiliate. He recalled to Peter Anick for *Fiddler Magazine* (21 Aug. 2010), "For three years, I begged them for a fiddle. They thought I was a little bit fickle and wasn't completely serious about my request. And it wasn't until I was trying to construct one out of cardboard around age ten, attempting to put my old set of guitar strings on it, that convinced my mother. It folded up on me and I ended up crying about it. So I finally got one at eleven."

It was clear from the start that O'Connor had an innate connection with the instrument. His mother began to take him on trips where he could hone his fiddling skills. His father, an alcoholic laborer whom O'Connor has described as somewhat domineering, approved of these trips because O'Connor usually won or earned money on them. "If it weren't for my musical talent, I would have been his slave, no doubt," he told Steinberg.

O'Connor's first lessons as a student of the fiddle were with Barbara Lamb, who had a musical background that included classical, bluegrass, and old-time fiddling. He then worked under John Burke, who sparked the improvisation and ingenuity he would later more fully develop under Stephane Grappelli, the noted French jazz violinist considered by many music fans to be one of the instrument's greatest improvisers. Perhaps most significantly, he began taking lessons with the legendary Benny Thomasson, a champion fiddler who had won competitions for two decades in Texas. Thomasson lived two hours away from O'Connor's boyhood home in Seattle, so Thomasson and the O'Connors developed a unique arrangement. O'Connor explained to Anick, "My mother would drive me down to his house and my lesson would literally last an entire weekend. These excursions took place every other weekend. So I would learn from him hours and hours a day on a Saturday and half of Sunday, then come back home in order to go to school the next day. And we kept up that schedule more or less for a good three years."

O'Connor studied under Thomasson until he was fourteen years old. During that time he worked on about four or five songs per weekend. At the end of those three years, O'Connor had learned some 250 songs from the Texas fiddle master, as well as perfecting the style of Texas fiddling itself. He also competed in contests all over the country, at which he played about fifty of the tunes he had learned from Thomasson. Although he now claims to have lost about 75 percent of the contests he entered, O'Connor is remembered by many music fans as being the young winner of the Grand Master Fiddler Championship, which he won in 1975 at age thirteen. O'Connor beat numerous fiddling legends in that contest, including James "Texas Shorty" Chancellor, Lewis Franklin, and J. T. Perkins. According to his official website, he remains the only musician ever to win 'national championships on bluegrass guitar, fiddle, and mandolin.

Life's Work

O'Connor began .a career as a session -musician on: country music records in Nashville, Tennessee, shortly after graduating from high school. Unfortunately;- when he arrived in the early 1980s, Nashville musk executives were trending against what were considered "old time" country instruments, such as steel guitars and fiddles. 'Buddy Spicher, one of the great session players of the '60s and '70s, told me, 'Kid, you came to town at the wrong time—all the work has dried up,"' O'Connor recalled to Lewis. "But I had an idea that I could prove that a fiddle could play alongside a *DX7* [synthesizer], a rock guitar, or a· Fender Rhodes [electric piano]. I've been cross-pollinating for my entire career."

O'Connor's idea paid off: Over the next two decades, he had tremendous success as an in-demand session musician, or sideman. He has played on more than five hundred albums and has worked with such diverse musicians as Dolly Parton, Paul Simon, James Taylor, and Randy Travis, among others. From .1991 to 1996 the Country Music Association named him its musician of the year. He was also a member of several bands during this period. O'Connor joined the David Crisman Quintet, an acoustic string band, as a guitarist at the age of seventeen. Two years later, at nineteen, he served as a violinist and guitarist for the Dregs, a rock-fusion instrumental band of the 1980s. Also in the 1980s, he joined Strength in Numbers, an acoustic band with Sam Bush on fiddle and mandolin, Jerry Douglas on dobra, Bela Fleck on guitar and banjo, Edgar Meyer on bass; and O'Connor himself on fiddle, guitar, and mandolin. He then joined a pair of celebrated country bands, the American Music Shop house band and New Nashville Cats, in 1989 and 1990: O'Connor's solo albums met with critical and commercial success as well. *The Fiddle Concerto* (1995) hit number six on the classical Billboard charts, *Liberty!* (1997) reached number eight on the same charts, and *Midnight on the Water* bested both of its predecessors, topping out at number five. O'Connor won Grammy Awards for his work with New Nashville Cats in 1992 and in 1996 released the chart-topping classical album *Appalachia-Waltz,* a collaboration with cellist Yo-Yo Ma. In interviews O'Connor has expressed his belief that his success in so many styles of music is directly linked to his student days working under Thomasson.. He told Anick, ''The; theme and variations concept of Texas fiddling really is a very nice interesting musical bridge to other styles of music—jazz arid classical, for instance.

Affiliation: Teaching

In order to develop this national style of American music further, O'Connor aids emerging musicians by teaching at music programs at such prestigious institutions as the Aspen Summer Festival, Berklee College of Music, the Cleveland Institute of Music, the Juilliard School, Harvard University, Rice University, the University of Maryland, the University of Texas, and Tanglewood, among others. He also established the Mark O'Connor String Camp, which is held each summer; in 2013, it was held in Charleston, South Carolina. Most musical historians agree that O'Connor is not inventing a new approach to music but rather returning to an approach that had been employed by many musicians throughout the years. O'Connor, who concurs with that opinion, noted in the *Chicago Tribune* (2 Mar. 2010), "The music that we enjoy today is there simply because there were people who created musical styles that also ignored boundaries. People from Chuck Berry and Little Richard to Elvis Presley and Louis Armstrong to Jimmie Rodgers to Bob Wills to Bill Monroe. These guys were boundary-defiers."

In the fall of 2009 O'Connor introduced the O'Connor Violin Method, which breaks with the traditional, rote-memorization European and Japanese approaches to learning the instrument and instead promotes a more improvisational method that employs American music. The method is considered by many music teachers to be a revolutionary approach that helps to fill a gap in musical instruction. O'Connor explained in an interview with the *Huffington Post* (7 July 2013), "I think a complete and holistic music education is best for young students in today's challenging environments. That means that a music method book must join the technical with the creative. . . . Learning by rote, acquiring great technique, and using one's memory are all important, [but] I feel that it is an incomplete methodology if we continue to learn technically without learning to be musically creative."

Although he made excellent money as a session musician and enjoyed working with· his various bands and as a solo artist, O'Connor spent much of his spare. time writing and recording themes that were unconnected to the work he was doing with others. These themes; which he had begun working on in the early 1990s, would eventually evolve into. his first forays· into composing classical music infused with a wholly American style, combing bluegrass, classical, country, folk, and jazz. 'When I started this I really thought . . . I was going to write it for posterity. So I came from a lucrative session career where I made enough money to buy- a very nice home and I quit my career -cold turkey," O'Connor explained to Steinberg. "I- just canceled everything. I said, 'That's it,' and I walked away—to a lot of people's dismay."

His first orchestral composition would eventually become his *Fiddle Concerto,* which he recorded in 1995 and has performed in concert more than two hundred times. By mid-2013, O'Connor had written more than forty classical works, including pieces for small musical ensembles and violin concertos. Most notably, he composed his *Americana Symphony,* which he completed in 2006 and released as an album in 2009. This masterwork drew heavily from both his varied musical influences· and his personal family history in the United States, which he believes reflects the larger themes of average Americans living through the country's history. "I want to use jazz and blues and other vernacular music as the language on which classical compositions are built," O'Connor told Lewis. "It's the same thing [Astor] Piazzolla did in his native Argentina, what [Bela] Bartok did in Hungary, and what Tan Dun is doing in China. It's not a new concept. It's just new in American classical circles. It's so funny-it reveals some people's idea that our cultural musical heritage is somehow not important enough."

Personal Life

Although O'Connor spends much of his time on the road, teaching or performing either solo or as part of an ensemble, he maintains a home in New York City as well as a country home in Pennsylvania. He lives with his partner, fellow string player Sadie Rose deWall, and their daughter, Autumn Rose O'Connor, who was born in 2010. He also has a son, Forrest, who in 2010 graduated from Harvard University, where he studied musicology and music composition. O'Connor was married to Forrest's mother, a former concert flutist named Suzanne, from 1987 to 1991.

While at home in New York, O'Connor tends to stay up very late working. He often works on his YouTube channel playlist and then goes out and has lunch and tea before returning to his apartment to work on new compositions or his method. He enjoys walking in Central Park, visiting famed jazz clubs such as Dizzy's and the Blue Note, and holding jam sessions with friends. Although he does not keep a traditional work schedule, O'Connor finds his routine tremendously helpful in his creative processes, particularly in perfecting his method. "The work it takes is incalculable," he noted in an interview with Sarah Harrison Smith for the *New York Times* (5 Jan. 2013). "I want to give stature to American string music and its history, culture, creativity; the social aspects and the power of its being a vehicle for political change. That really hasn't been researched before."

Further Reading

Anick, Peter. "Mark O'Connor: On Learning, Playing, and Teaching Strings, American Style." *Fiddler Magazine.* Fiddler Magazine, 21 Aug. 2010. Web. 7 July 2013.

Harrison Smith, Sarah. "The Fiddler in the Cave." *New York Times.* New York Times, 5 Jan. 2013. Web. 7 July 2013.

Lewis, Randy. "Mark O'Connor, Genre Fiddler." *Los Angeles Times.* Los Angeles Times, 15 Mar. 2009. Web. 7 July 2013.

"Mark O'Connor: Violinist and Former Child Prodigy Celebrates Forty Years of Music." *Huffington Post.* Buffington Post, 9 June 2013. Web. 7 July 2013.

Steinberg, Martin. "First Symphony by Mark O'Connor Manifests the Fiddler's Destiny." *Seattle Times.* Seattle Times, 15 Mar. 2009. Web. 7 July 2013.

Omarion

Singer

Born: Nov. 12, 1984; Inglewood, California
Primary Field: Rhythm and blues
Group Affiliation: B2K

Introduction

"Coming from a boy group and a young genre, it's hard to make the transition into adulthood and still be respected," Omarion, a Grammy Award–nominated R&B musician and former member of the boy band B2K, explained to Cori Bolger for the Jackson, Mississippi, Clarion-Ledger *(August 25, 2005). "Now that I'm coming into my manhood, I can have control of my career and destiny. It doesn't rely on other people and I can go where I want to, physically, spiritually and mentally. It's a lot of responsibility, but nothing I can't bear." Like Justin Timberlake, formerly of the group 'N Sync, Omarion has successfully made the often difficult transition from instant boy-band stardom to a career as a solo performer; his extreme versatility as a singer, dancer, songwriter, and, recently, record producer has inspired comparisons to the likes of the pop superstar Michael Jackson.*

Early Life

The oldest of the seven children of Leslie Burrell and Trent Grandberry, the singer was born Omari Ishmael Grandberry on November 12, 1984 in Inglewood, California. "Omari," a name of Swahili origin, means "God the highest"; the suffix "ion" in his stage name was inspired, according to some sources, by "eon"-meaning, as the singer defines it, "forever." Omarion's mother, a hairstylist, raised him and his siblings by herself; she encouraged him when he was very young to pursue a life in the entertainment business. Little is known of his father; it has been reported that he introduced his son early on to the music of Marvin Gaye and the group Earth, Wind and Fire. Omarion started performing at the age of five, appearing in local theater and in nationally televised commercials for McDonald's and Kellogg's Corn Pops cereal. He said to Margena A. Christian for *Jet* (May 9, 2005), "I was like the only Black kid to have a Pops commercial." He became a music performer at a young age as well. As he recalled to Alicia Quarles for Associated Press Online (March 15, 2007), he was already part of a rap group, the Wild Kingdom, when his mother told him, '"Omari, you might want to sing.' I said, 'Why?' She said, 'Because you know singers get all the women.' I was like, 'Okay.' It stuck with me."

Even as he pursued performing opportunities, Omarion became involved in the gang activity that was ubiquitous in Inglewood, joining a gang called the Under Age Criminals. "A lot of people don't really expect [gang activity] to come from a person like me, because I'm a singer," he explained to Corey Levitan for the *(Torrance, California) Daily Breeze* (March 18, 2005). "But at the same time, Inglewood is Inglewood, just like any 'hood. Gangs are a popular thing here. It's pretty tough and if you don't belong, you pretty much can get hurt in the line of crossfire. . . . When I look back on it now, I think, 'Dang, I was doing a lot of crazy stuff when I was younger. I really could have got hurt.'"

Life's Work

Music helped to steer Omarion away from petty theft and other crime. His older half-brother, Marques Houston, had been performing in the teen group Immature (now known as IMX) for years when he introduced Omarion to the group's manager, Christopher Stokes. In the late 1990s, during the height of the popularity of boy bands, Stokes helped form a new band, consisting of Omarion, his cousin Jarell "J-Boog" Houston, Dreux Pierre "Lil' Fizz" Frederic, and De'Mario Monte "Raz-B" Thornton. The band, initially called Y2K to parallel the worldwide anticipation of the new millennium, instead chose the name B2K, which means "Boys of the New Millennium." In early 2001 the group performed in Los Angeles, California, in front of executives at Epic Records, who instantly felt that B2K had the potential to become as popular as the highly successful act Boyz II Men. Max Gousse, a vice president at Epic, told Nekesa Mumbi Moody for the Dubuque, Iowa, *Telegraph Herald* (February 16, 2003) about the members of B2K, "They're all perfectionists and they each serve a purpose in the group."

Omarion's talents as lead singer and dancer contributed greatly to the foursome's immediate success. B2K's first single, the dance number "Uh Huh," reached the top spot on the singles chart not long after its release, in late 2001. On March 12, 2002 Epic released the group's eponymous debut album to critical acclaim. Jason Birchmeier wrote for the All Music Guide Web site, "Epic Records definitely did its homework before unleashing B2K into the pop market. The boy band of clean-cut and suave young black men is everything a marketing department dreams about: attractive teens-becoming-men who make the girls melt with a little bit of a rugged, tough-guy attitude and flashy clothes." The album, whose highlights included the hit singles "Gats ta Be," "Understanding," and "Why I Love You," went on to achieve gold status in sales. The same month that the album was released, hype surrounding the band resulted in approximately 1,000 fans' storming a record store in a Concord, California, shopping mall during a B2K autograph-signing session, which forced police to close down the mall temporarily. Other, similar incidents included one at a show at the New York venue Planet Hollywood, where unruly fans had to be physically restrained in order for the group to perform. Such fan frenzy attended the group's aptly titled Scream and Scream 2 tours, which saw near-riots among those awaiting the band. In the summer of 2002, B2K toured Europe as an opening act for the group Destiny's Child. On December 10, 2002 B2K released the follow-up to their debut, *Pandemonium,* which included the singles "Bump, Bump, Bump," "Girlfriend," and "What a Girl Wants." Despite mixed reviews, the album achieved platinum status, selling over a million copies. Between the two albums B2K released a remix collection and a Christmas EP, titled *Santa Hooked Me Up.* By year's end, B2K had received a number of awards, including BET's Viewer's Choice Award, a *Billboard* Music Award for the single "Uh Huh," and the Best Group Award from the editors of *Vibe* magazine.

In 2003 B2K embarked on a third successful Scream tour and starred together in the critically panned movie *You Got Served,* about competing crews of hip-hop dancers in Los Angeles. Later that year disagreements among the group's members, among other factors, led to B2K's dissolution. Their final performance together was at a December 2003 concert in Washington, D.C., after which Omarion was briefly hospitalized with head and back pain. The breakup was underscored when Omarion was the only group member to show up for a Philadelphia, Pennsylvania, concert, which unexpectedly became the scene of his solo debut. He explained to Margena A. Christian for *Jet* (January 26, 2004), "It is true that B2K broke up but it's not about me leaving or them leaving. It's about us growing up and wanting to do our own thing. We have been together since we were 14 years old. The guys are like my brothers and I love them and only wish the best for them in everything they do, but the time was coming that we were all more focused on our solo projects than we were in the group." While several of B2K's members accused Stokes (who wrote and directed *You Got Served)* of cheating them of money earned during the Scream 3 tour, Omarion disputed those claims, saying to Christian that he had received "plenty of money." With Stokes continuing to serve as his manager, Omarion began working on his solo material. On February 22, 2005 he released his debut effort, 0, which featured his collaborations with the noted producers the Neptunes and Rodney Jenkins. The album entered the *Billboard* album chart at the top spot; it was released concurrently with his same-titled autobiography, published by Pocket Books, in which he gave an intimate account of his growing up in Inglewood and escaping a life of crime through music. Despite entering the charts at number one, the album went on to have comparatively modest sales; that surprised many, as 0 featured a number of singles that scored high on the charts, including "Never Gonna Let You Go (She's a Keepa)," with Big Boi of the group Outkast, which was included on the soundtrack of the romantic film comedy *Hitch.* Reviewers criticized Omarion's ostensible transformation from innocent boy-band member to "bad boy." They were silenced later that year, however, when *0* garnered a Grammy Award nomination for best contemporary R&B album. The singer was also featured on the rapper Bow Wow's hit song "Let Me Hold You," which reached the number-four spot on the *Billboard* 100 chart, making it Omarion's first top-10 single as a solo performer.

A controversy surrounding Omarion arose in the summer of 2005, when the singer was touring in London, England. Following the terrorist bombings that occurred in that city on July 7, a press release purporting to be from Omarion's publicist asked the singer's fans to pray for his safe return to the U.S., while making no mention of the more than 50 people killed or hundreds injured in the attacks. Though a statement on Omarion's Web site denied any connection between the singer and the press release, the episode temporarily marred his reputation. In December 2006, after months of heavy touring, Omarion released his second album, *21,* named to reflect his transition from boyhood to manhood. The record, which entered the *Billboard* chart at number one, drew immediate comparisons to Janet Jackson's album *Control* and Stevie Wonder's *For Once in My Life,* as it was considered to be a breakthrough project for the performer. Omarion had a lot more creative control in the making of the album than he had had with *0.* "It played out wonderfully," he told Richard Harrington. "It was, 'Yes, I want to do this record. . . . No, I don't really like this, let's try something else,' and not having everybody look at you with a raised eyebrow, like, 'He doesn't really know what he's talking about.' But I've been doing this since I was 15, and, for me, it was good to be able to make a suggestion or to have a comment or a question and not be overlooked; when I was a little younger, if I said something, they might not have taken it as seriously or into consideration." He added to Alicia Quarles, "For this album it was definitely a more mature side of me. Not just with the topics or the writing, but just my image as well. If you look at the front cover of the CD . . . there is a real grown-up feel. That

Affiliation: Boy Bands

Dancing, in particular, is "very important to my career," as Omarion noted to Richard Harrington for the *Washington Post* (December 29, 2006). "That was something Michael Jackson had: the ability to excite people differently than the next person could. He could just move his arm, and it was 'Wow!' I want to be able to excite people in that way and have them say, 'I wonder what Omarion's going to do next,' because it challenges me. At the same time, it makes my whole entertainment spontaneous."

As the lead singer of the hip-hop/R&B quartet B2K, Omarion anchored the group's eponymous 2001 debut album and their sophomore effort, *Pandemonium* (2003). Omarion's solo albums, *0* (2005) and *21* (2006), each received critical acclaim and reached the top spot on the *Billboard* chart, making the singer one of few to have achieved back-to-back number-one debuts on both the Hot 100 and the R&B charts. The latter album also featured two hit singles, "Entourage" and the Timbaland-produced "Ice Box." *Face Off,* Omarion's collaboration with the rapper Bow Wow, reached stores in December 2007. In addition to his musical endeavors, Omarion has ventured into acting, with roles in the movies *You Got Served* (2004), *Fat Albert* (2004), *Feel the Noise* (2007), and *Somebody Help Me* (2007). In 2005 he had a recurring role in the UPN TV series *Cuts,* about a family-run barbershop. He explained to Bolger in 2005: "I don't want to be 35 and a 100-millionaire like Jay-Z and Puffy. I want to learn the game now and soak it up and by 23 make a lot of money." He added, "I want to be somebody who hangs tough in the industry. I want to own teams and have the Omarion shoe one day. I want to be an entrepreneur."

is the image I was looking for." Harvey Mason Jr. and Damon Thomas, known collectively as the Underdogs, served as the main producers of the album, which also featured the production work of Pharrell Williams and behind-the-scenes help from Timbaland, who produced the album's biggest hit to date, "Ice Box." *21* received generally favorable reviews for its eclectic mix of dance tracks (including "Entourage") and slow songs (such as "Just Can't Let You Go"). Omarion said to Harrington, "There's still ... a lot of things business-wise, that I want to do that I haven't been able to do yet. I feel good, and I feel really, really blessed to have had longevity in the industry as long as I have. But I can't ever stop staying hungry because there's always something new, something fresh, always something somebody else is doing, so I'm constantly thinking of creative stuff."

Omarion's long-awaited collaborative album with the rapper Bow Wow, titled *Face Off,* appeared on December 11, 2007. The album did not meet commercial expectations but received generally favorable reviews, with Simon Vozick Levinson writing for *Entertainment Weekly* (December 7, 2007, on-line), "The formerly pint-size MC (Bow Wow, ne Lil') and the ex-boy-band singer (Omarion, late of B2K) made an adorable pair on Bow's 2005 puppy-love ode 'Let Me Hold You.' With *Face Off,* they united again to serenade lady fans-this time with a whole album of raunchier tunes—and their charm proves undeniable. Neither dude will likely be recognized as a world-class vocalist on his own. But together, Bow (he of quicksilver flow) and 0 (he of slender harmonies) are urban-pop Wonder Twins." Gail Mitchell added for *Billboard* (on-line), "A couple of tracks sound derivative, but for the most part fans of the duo will embrace this album as well as the twosome's maturing sound." In the summer of 2008, Omarion announced that his as-yet untitled third studio album would be released on Timbaland's record label, Mosley Music Group.

The fall of 2007 also brought the releases of two films featuring Omarion: *Feel the Noise,* in which he portrayed a young man from the South Bronx who dreams of success as a rapper, and the horror film *Somebody Help Me,* directed by Christopher Stokes, in which the singer starred alongside his best friend and frequent collaborator, Marques Houston. A sequel to *You Got Served* is planned.

Personal Life

With Houston and Stokes, Omarion founded a production company, the Franchise Boys. His hobbies include playing basketball, football, and video games and watching movies. Omari is currently single. Rumors have linked him romantically to the pop star Rihanna.

Further Reading

Ask Men Official Web site; Associated Press Online Mar. 15, 2007;

(Jackson, Mississippi) *Clarion-Ledger* F p17 Aug. 25, 2005; *Jet* p58+ Oct. 21, 2002, p56+ Jan. 26, 2004, p56 May 9, 2005;

St. Louis Post-Dispatch p4+ July 24, 2003; (Torrance, California) *Daily Breeze* K p16 Mar. 18, 2005; *Washington Post* T p6+ Dec. 29, 2006

Rita Ora

Singer-songwriter

Born: November 26, 1990; Pristina, Kosovo
Primary Field: Pop
Group Affiliation: Solo artist

Introduction

Rita Ora, who sports peroxide blond hair, is a British singer-songwriter and actor of Kosovar Albanian descent. Signed by rapper Jay-Z to his Roc Nation Records when she was only eighteen years old, she waited four years to release her first studio album, Ora *(2012). The album hit number one on the UK charts—as did her first three singles—and went platinum in the United Kingdom. Though she was only twenty-two years old when she released* Ora*, the album was the culmination of years of work for the singer.*

Early Life

Born Rita Sahatçiu on November 26, 1990, in the city of Pristina, then in the former state of Yugoslavia and now in Kosovo, Ora began singing at the age of six, and by fourteen she had already appeared in a major motion picture. Her paternal grandfather was the well-known Yugoslavian film director Besim Sahatçiu, and she is named after his favorite film star, Rita Hayworth. Ora's family long held ties to intellectuals and artists in their hometown, but in the early 1990s, ethnic Kosovar Albanians like the Sahatçius were being oppressed by the Serbian majority, and more than eight hundred thousand ethnic Albanians fled their homes in Kosovo during this time.

In 1991, when Ora was just one year old, Ora's family—her father, Besnik; her mother, Vera; and her older sister, Elena—moved to London, England, where they settled in a oneroom flat in Earls Court. The family spoke Albanian in the house and worked to overcome the stigma of being refugees. Eventually, Ora's mother, a doctor in her native country who had been working as a waitress, learned English and found a job as a psychiatrist. Ora's younger brother Don was born in 1998, the same year that the family moved to a larger flat in Kensal Rise and Besnik opened a pub called the Queens Arms at Kilburn. The year 1998 was also when war broke out among the splintering factions of the former Yugoslavia, and Ora recalls her parents worrying about relatives back home. "I couldn't figure it out. All the arguments, all the tension—I knew it was coming from something," she told Ed Caesar for *British GQ magazine* (1 Aug. 2013).

Growing up, Ora delighted in perusing her parents' record collection and idolized Canadian songstress Celine Dion. Ora won a place at the Sylvia Young Theatre School, a performing-arts school in London, when she was eleven. Around that time—and with Rita's future stage career in mind-her father decided to add "Ora" to the family surname, making it easier to pronounce. When Ora was fifteen, her mother was diagnosed with breast cancer, and Ora stopped going to school. Her mother soon recovered—and her older sister, Elena, prodded Ora to return to class—but the experience left an impression on Ora. "My mum had always been one of those free-spirited women and her being ill was really confusing for me," she told Mills. "I couldn't understand why my mum wasn't a superhero, why she wasn't, you know, unbreakable. I'd sit around the house for days. I was really down."

When Ora was not in class or working at her dad's pub or at a shoe store, she was hustling to be recognized as a singer. She performed in clubs, bars, and even in a few musicals, though she admitted to Mills that musical theater is not her style. Navigating both gigs and school was taking its toll, however. "It was a really weird time in my life but it was also amazing because I had to grow up fast," Ora told Lauren Nostro for *Complex* magazine (23 Apr. 2012).

In 2004, at the age of fourteen, she was cast as an Albanian youngster in the British film *Spivs*, an experience she told Nostro was "good fun." The same year, Ora landed a production deal with Swedish record producer Martin Terefe. The deal was not a lot of money, Ora told Nostro, and the stipulations of the contract were loose. "I used to go there after school and just sit there, work with him and just kind of get the vibe of it," she recalled to Nostro. In 2007, Terefe was working with British R&B star Craig David, and he asked Ora to complete a demo for David's new record. Terefe and David liked Ora's take so much that they kept her on the song "Awkward," Ora's first official appearance on a record. She also appeared on David's next album *Greatest Hits* (2008), on a single called "Where's Your Love," featuring rapper Tinchy Stryder.

Life's Work

After two years, Ora felt that the partnership with Terefe had run its course and elected not to extend her contract. She was only sixteen but felt the pressure to jump-start her career. She auditioned for *Eurovision: Your Country Needs You!*, a BBC program looking for a British vocalist to compete in the 2009 Eurovision Song Contest. It was not how Ora wanted to start her career, but she took the opportunity anyway. "I just felt like I didn't know what was going to happen to me," she told Nostro, "so I thought that was my last chance." At the audition Ora sang for judges, including Andrew Lloyd Weber, the composer of *Cats* and *The Phantom of the Opera*, but, as she relayed to Mills, as soon as she entered the room she had a bad feeling. "Right from the start I was, like, 'What am I doing here?'" she recalled. Without waiting for feedback, Ora walked out of the audition immediately after finishing her song. The judges were shocked and even tried calling her agent to bring her back, but Ora refused to return. The same year, as she told Mills, she was walking down Kensington High Street in London when she received an incoming international call on her cell phone. She thought it was her grandmother, but instead it was someone at Roc Nation, the record label owned by Jay-Z.

Ora's brief professional relationship with Terefe had put her on the radar of record-label talent scouts, including an A&R at Universal named Brynee. Brynee contacted Jay Brown, the cofounder (along with Jay-Z and Ty Ty Smith) and president of Roc Nation Records, on Ora's behalf. Meanwhile, Ora received offers from labels such as Universal and Island Records, but no deal seemed imminent. She sent Brown a rough demo of a song she composed called "I'll Be Waiting," which she recorded using the Apple software GarageBand. Two days later, she received a call from Roc Nation; Brown offered to fly her to New York City for a meeting. As soon as she got off the plane, the representatives from Roc took her to a club where Rocawear, a clothing manufacturer that is also owned by Jay-Z, was having a Christmas party. She met Brown, Smith, and—unexpectedly—Jay-Z himself. "I'm happy I didn't know," Ora told Nostro of the encounter, "because if I knew, I would've freaked out."

The group took Ora to Hoc the Mic, Jay-Z's recording studio in Manhattan, and played some of her songs. Jay-Z offered to sign her on the spot. The eighteen-year-old Ora was excited but also restless to make it big. "I got signed and I was like 'Cool, Oprah next week,'" she recalled to Nostro. "But obviously not. I knew I was going to record the album or whatever but I was so eager to put everything out that I didn't think about the long run." Jay-Z advised her to be patient and told her to take her time recording her first album. "They told me to go find myself and do what I do," she said. The process ultimately took much longer than Ora had anticipated. Roc Nation sent her on an exhausting tour in the United States and, in 2008, she recorded an album, only to scrap the entire project. During this time, she wrote songs with singer and rapper Drake, who asked Ora to appear in the music video for his single "Over" in 2010. In 2012, Ora met DJ Fresh, who was looking for a vocalist for a single. Ora, who was putting the finishing touches on her debut album, jumped at the chance. The turnaround was quick—"We did it and the next week it was on the radio," she told Nostro. The song, "Hot Right Now," was released in February 2012 and quickly became the number-one song on the UK singles chart.

Affiliation: Pop Music

In March 2014, Ora released the lead single from her second album, "I Will Never Let You Down," which was produced by the successful Scottish DJ Calvin Harris. The song also rose to number one on the UK charts, making Ora the second British female solo artist to have four singles reach the number-one ranking on the UK charts after pop star Geri Halliwell A superstar in the United Kingdom, Ora continues to establish herself alongside similar pop artists in the United States. "I kinda think, when your ball is rolling, you don't stop it," Ora told Simon Mills for the *London Evening Standard* (1 Feb. 2013). "You keep it rolling. You have to make yourself . . . unforgettable."

Alongside Jay-Z, Ora officially released her first US solo single "How We Do (Party)" at New York City's Z100 radio station in February 2012. Ora told Nostro that after the release she cried with relief and happiness. The song, which samples the 1993 song "Party & Bulls——" by the late rapper Notorious B.I.G. (then known as Biggie Smalls), became a summer anthem. It also hit number one in Britain, just after her first UK single "R.I.P.," featuring English rapper Tinie Tempah, did the same. Ora became the first artist of 2012 to have three consecutive number-one hits in the United Kingdom.

Drake had written "R.I.P." for Barbados-born H & B singer Rihanna, but she turned it down. When Ora heard "R.I.P." she knew she had to record it. "It was such a hanger that I was like, 'I don't care who it's been through, I want that song. And I will own it,'" Ora recalled to Nostro. Ora said the song is about a young woman taking ownership of herself. The video, which "oozes confidence," Ora told Nostro, garnered 2.5 million hits on YouTube in the two days after it was posted.

Incidentally, Ora bears a striking resemblance to Rihanna and has been accused of being a Rihanna-copycat since the beginning of her career. Some critics have been unable to resist the comparison when reviewing Ora's music. In fact, though a commercial success, *Ora* was not a critical favorite. Michael Cragg wrote in a review of the album for the *Guardian* (30 Aug. 2012) that *Ora* feels "more like a collection of other people's songs than a cohesive album." Ryan Copsey's review for *Digital Spy* (28 Aug. 2012) was more positive, and he acknowledged the less-than-flattering Rihanna comparison.

"She rarely colors outside the lines," he wrote, "but when she does—in the case of gentle ballad 'Hello, Hi, Goodbye'—it points to an artist with brighter prospects than a sub-par Rihanna."

Ora's second US single was "Radioactive," written by the Australian singer-songwriter Sia Furler, better known simply as Sia. Best known for her appearance on DJ David Guetta's 2011 hit "Titanium," Sia has collaborated with everyone from Beck to Beyoncé. Long before working with her, Ora counted Sia as one of her musical idols.

Ora's third single, the empowering anthem "Shine Ya Light," also performed well in the United Kingdom, though it did not rise to number one. Ora shot the video in her hometown of Pristina, Kosovo, where her extended family still lives. "The whole country was outside," she told Caesar of her arrival. "I got off the plane, it was like millions of heads. I couldn't see the floor." The moment was captured at the beginning of the video. When she walked on stage, the fans were chanting her name. "It was the most surrealest [sic] experience I've ever felt. It was more than a music video. [It] was a moment in our history as Kosovo, it was a moment for people to see us: how we live, our landscape."

Personal Life

Ora made a cameo appearance in the 2013 movie *Fast and the Furious 6* and was cast as Christian Grey's sister in the film adaptation of the 2011 erotic novel *Fifty Shades of Grey*. The role, for which Ora had to perfect an American accent, was hard-won: It took her eight callbacks to secure the part. The film is scheduled for a 2015 release.

Ora briefly dated Scottish DJ Calvin Harris, with whom she collaborated on "I Will Never Let You Down," but the couple parted in June 2014. In August, Ora said that Harris would not allow her to perform the song live for the Teen Choice Awards. Also in 2014, Ora teamed with Australian rapper Iggy Azalea on the song "Black Widow," for which the pair made a music video that pays homage to Quentin Tarantino's Kill Bill films (2003–4). Ora lives in London.

Further Reading

Caesar, Ed. "The Golden Ora." *British GQ*. Condé Nast, 1 Aug. 2013. Web. 18 Aug. 2014.

Gannon, Emma. "The Improbable Rise of Rita Ora: A Guide for the Modern-Day Celebrity." *Daily Beast*. Daily Beast, 5 May 2014. Web. 18 Aug. 2014.

Godwin, Richard. "Elevating Rita." *Vogue* UK. Condé Nast, 20 Dec. 2012, Web. 18 Aug. 2014.

Mills, Simon. "Rita Ora: 'You Have to Make Yourself... Unforgettable.'" *London Evening Standard*. London Evening Standard, 1 Feb. 2013. Web. 18 Aug. 2014.

Nostro, Lauren. "Who Is Rita Ora?" *Complex*. Complex Media, 23 Apr. 2012. Web. 18 Aug. 2014.

OutKast

Rap duo

Andre 3000
Rapper; songwriter
Born: May 27, 1975; Atlanta, Georgia

Big Boi
Rapper; songwriter
Born: Feb. 1, 1975; Savannah, Georgia

Primary Field: Rap
Group Affiliation: OutKast

Introduction

During the Democratic presidential campaign in 2003 and 2004, two of the nominees courting young voters posed as fans of the ultra-cool hip-hop group OutKast: Howard Dean, the former governor of Vermont, sought to impress potential supporters with his rendition of the duo's 2001 hit "Ms. Jackson," while General Wesley K. Clark publicly mentioned a rumored OutKast split and demonstrated his hip-hop knowledge by quoting the line "I can shake it like a Polaroid picture!" from the OutKast song "Hey Ya!" Since the release of their first album, Southernplayalisticadillacmuzik *(1994), when they were still in high school,*

Early Lives

The only child of Lawrence Walker, a collections agent, and Sharon Benjamin-Hodo, a real estate agent, Andre Lauren Benjamin was born on May 27, 1975 in Atlanta, Georgia. Andre was raised by his mother, with whom he moved frequently in southwestern Atlanta until, at the age of 15, he went to live with his father. Andre's partner, Antwan Andre Patton, was born on February 1, 1975 in Savannah, Georgia, the oldest of the five children of Rowena Patton, a retail supervisor, and Tony Kearse, a marine-corps sergeant. The rappers met as students at Tri-Cities High, a performing arts school in suburban Atlanta, when they ran into each other at a mall. Their shared fashion sense drew them together. "We were preps," Big Boi told a reporter for *People* (February 16, 2004). "We wore loafers, argyle socks and V-neck sweaters with T-shirts. We were new to the school and we didn't know anybody." Andre and Big Boi also shared a love of rap, and they decided to try to make some of their own. "We were in my living room one day watching videos," Big Boi recalled to Rob Brunner, "and we was like, 'Man, we can do that [expletive].' From that day forward we formed a group." At that time, Big Boi has said, he aimed to become either a child psychologist or a football player; Andre was interested in architecture but disliked math.

Lives' Work

Initially calling themselves 2 Shades Deep, Andre and Big Boi soon met Rico Wade, who worked in a beauty-supply shop and headed the Organized Noize rap-production group. Wade impressed the duo with his originality and helped them conceive a sound that was quintessentially southern—emphasizing laid-back beats and southern drawls—rather than being an imitation of the two dominant rap styles of the time, West Coast and East Coast. The three began hanging out in Wade's basement at all hours, writing rhymes, toying with beats, and experimenting with their sound. In 1993 they landed an audition with the president of LaFace Records, Antonio "L.A." Reid (who is currently the chairman of the Island Def Jam Music Group). "They were a little shy, a little nervous," Reid told Brunner. "They were good, but they weren't ready yet. So they auditioned again. I told them, 'You're much closer, but still not yet.' Then I got home and thought, Am I out of my mind? These guys are incredible."

Changing their name to OutKast, Big Boi and Andre released their first single, "Players' Ball," on the album *LaFace Family Christmas* (1993). The bouncy rap number was somewhat out of place among the Christmas songs, performed by such R&B artists as TLC and Usher, but it nevertheless found its way onto radio and television (the video for the song was directed by Sean "Puffy" Combs, now known as P. Diddy) and reached the top position on the *Billboard* Hot Rap Singles chart. By then, having become consumed with making music, both Big Boi and Andre considered dropping out of high school. Andre did so but later returned, completing his high-school education in 1996. Big Boi, who had reportedly maintained a 3.68 grade-point average, decided to continue working toward his diploma. He graduated from high school in 1994.

Meanwhile, OutKast's first album, *Southernplayalisticadillacmuzik,* was released in 1994; within a year, it had gone platinum. The title seemed to be a play on the rapid-fire utterances of Andre and Big Boi, who somehow sounded laidback and casual despite the speed of their vocals. Though the young rappers' lyrics tended to reflect the hip-hop "playa" cliché, presenting them as perennial ladies' men and hard partyers, musically the album was groundbreaking, and its blending of funky beats, catchy vocal hooks, aspects of 1970s soul music, and live instrumentation became a prototype for southern rap. At the *Source* rap awards in 1995, OutKast was named best new rap group.

In 1996 OutKast issued *ATLiens,* whose title refers to their Atlantan roots, which the duo felt made them aliens in the East Coast/West Coast world of rap. The album revealed more of the rappers' idiosyncrasies and signaled their movement from safer, laid-back grooves toward choppier, propulsive rhythms. The production was more experimental as well, much of it drenched in spacey reverb and peppered with dub-reggae flavors as well as even more live instrumentation. In their lyrics, OutKast turned away from the "playa" themes of their first album to focus on more serious topics, such as black identity and, on "Decatur Psalm," the poverty and violence that pervade many African American communities and the inadequate education provided in many of their schools. "When you're 17 and 18," Andre told Cheo Hodari Coker for the *Los Angeles Times* (December 22, 1996), "you think you can smoke and drink all day and sleep around. You feel invincible. Then there comes a time where you have to [rise] up and do something else with yourself. On our first album, we were determined to smoke herb until the world ended. Now, I've stopped smoking and drinking, and I'm trying to live up to my abilities, and take life much more seriously." The song "Elevators (Me and You)" topped the *Billboard* Hot Rap Singles and Hot R&B Singles Sales charts and made it to the Top 40, while *ATLiens* shot to number one on the *Billboard* Top R&B Albums chart and went double platinum. In the *Washington Post* (October 11, 1996), Richard Harrington, echoing the sentiments of many reviewers, called it "proof (if any were needed) that hip-hop innovation isn't just an East-West thang."

With *Aquemini* (1998), OutKast continued in the vein of their previous effort, splicing together laid-back grooves with more futuristic sounds and showing further interest in social issues. The album also features guest performances by the funk guru George Clinton as well as the hip-hop vocalists Cee-Lo, Witchdoctor, Raekwon, and Erykah Badu, among others. Critics hailed the recording as OutKast's most fully realized up to that time and one of the best of the 1990s. *"Aquemini* fulfills all its ambitions, covering more than enough territory to qualify it as a virtuosic masterpiece, and a landmark hip-hop album," Steve Huey wrote for the All Music Guide Web site. A reviewer for Source, as excerpted on Amazon.com, gushed, "It possesses an uncanny blend of sonic beauty, poignant lyricism and spirituality that compels without commanding. The record offers a rich blend of potent beats—tight snares, booming kicks and cool rimshots—and a diverse tapestry of various musical textures." Within a couple of months, *Aquemini* went platinum (and later, double platinum).

In January 1999 "Rosa Parks," one of the tracks on *Aquemini,* was nominated for a Grammy Award for best rap performance by a duo or group. (It did not win.) A few months later the real Rosa Parks sued OutKast. Parks, the legendary civil rights figure whose refusal to give up her seat to a white man on a segregated public bus in Montgomery, Alabama, in 1955 was crucial in the emerging civil rights movement, claimed that her name had been used without her permission and exploited for financial gain. She also declared that the song defamed her, because, although her name is not in the lyrics, the title and veiled references to her automatically linked her to the profanity and sexual vulgarities in the words. OutKast claimed that the song was about the rap industry; the words in the repeating hook, or chorus, as quoted on the Lyrics A-Z Universe Web site, are "Ah ha, hush that fuss / Everybody move to the back of the bus / Do you wanna bump and slump with us / We the type of people make the club get crunk [intoxicated]." U.S. district judge Barbara Hackett dismissed the suit in 1999; in 2003 it was reinstated by the U.S. Court of Appeals for the Sixth Circuit, in Cincinnati, Ohio. That year the U.S. Supreme Court, which had been asked to intervene in the case, declined to do so, thus returning it to a lower federal court. A decision has yet to be reached.

In 2000 Big Boi and Andre unveiled *Stankonia,* a meandering, 24-track album that gave free rein to their

Affiliation: Eclecticism

OutKast's members—Big Boi (Antwan Patton) and Andre 3000 (Andre Benjamin, also called Dre)—have dazzled the music-buying public and professional critics. Their first album and each of their next five have sold more than a million copies each, thus reaching platinum or even multi-platinum status; their most recent recording, *Speakerboxxx/The Love Below* (2003), sold more than eight million copies in the U.S. in less than six months. What makes these numbers especially remarkable is that OutKast is far from the typical pop group: Andre and Big Boi have achieved success not by adhering to musical conventions but by breaking them, forging a genre-busting brand of hip-hop that celebrates eccentricity and, in the words of the hip-hop superstar LL Cool J, makes fans feel that "it's okay to be yourself and give(s) them a feeling of being free," as quoted by Chris Campion in the London *Observer* (February 22, 2004).

OutKast is the product of a strange musical alchemy, as its masterminds, though old friends, could scarcely be more different. The lanky Andre is the mercurial artist, always searching for different forms of personal expression and attracting attention with his flashy ensembles, which incorporate such seemingly disparate elements as billowing ascots, hot-pink silk shirts, plaid or sequined pants, and feather boas. Big Boi, widely considered the practical glue behind the duo, exudes a tough, no-nonsense persona and favors more typical hip-hop attire: diamond-encrusted jewelry, Phat Farm sweat suits, and sports jerseys, to name a few favorite items. But Big Boi and Andre share an important trait: eclectic taste in music. "I consider me and Dre to be funkateers, man," Big Boi told Campion. "Growing up, we listened to everything and I think that gives us the ability to make a free-flowing type of music. It doesn't matter whether it's country, reggae or rock and roll." "We wanted to revive [music]," Andre told Rob Brunner for *Entertainment Weekly* (November 10, 2000), "kind of like church: a hip-hop Holy Ghost. We're in the age of keeping it real, but what we're trying to do is to keep it surreal. Real has gotten really boring."

experimental impulses and—somewhat paradoxically—made them pop superstars. Created largely from a series of improvisational sessions, *Stankonia* is an album of extremes. It contains some of OutKast's most head-bobbing songs—such as "B.O.B." and "Gasoline Dreams"—as well as some of their most abstract and offbeat pieces. "In rap there's nothing new under the sun," Andre told a reporter for *Newsweek* (October 30, 2000). "But I think it's the way you say it and how you approach it. People are afraid to step out. There's a formula to making music now, and no one really has the courage to do their own thing." OutKast's courageousness paid off for them, as *Stankonia* became a huge commercial and critical success. In *Entertainment Weekly* (November 3, 2000), Ken Tucker praised OutKast for being "endlessly good humored and imaginative even when dealing with the most grim and mind-deadening facets of ghetto life," and he asserted that the album "reeks of artful ambition rendered with impeccable skill." Hua Hsu, in a review for Amazon.com (which included *Stankonia* on its list of best albums of 2000), wrote, "At a time when the hip-hop 'album' seems to be sadly declining in significance, Atlanta's finest deliver a classic package of space-case imagery, curbside poetry, and delicious experimental funk. ... While *Stankonia* certainly isn't an 'easy' album, its ambition and vision easily rank it among hip-hop's greatest in some time." *Stankonia* went quadruple platinum, peaked at number two on the *Billboard* album chart, and won a Grammy Award for best rap album. The hit song "Ms. Jackson," a farcical apology to a girlfriend's mother, topped the *Billboard* Hot 100, the R&B/Hip-Hop Singles Sales chart, and the Hot Rap Singles chart, and made it into *Billboard's* Top 40.

Late in 2001 OutKast released the hits collection *Big Boi & Dre Present OutKast,* which also presented three new songs; one of those, "The Whole World," won a Grammy Award for best rap performance by a duo or group. The album went platinum and peaked at number 18 on the *Billboard* album chart. Around this time, following extensive touring in support of *Stankonia,* Andre began to show signs of burnout. "It got to a point where I would be onstage going through the motions while performing every night," he told Joe Silva for *Remix* (August 1, 2003). "I was totally distant from what I was doing. It was like I was watching myself. There was no passion in it at all." After the tour Andre began to focus on playing guitar, resolving to become proficient in time to play one onstage for the next tour. Soon the guitar became a new songwriting tool for him, helping to spur his creativity. (He has also taken saxophone lessons.) With a wealth of new material, Andre wanted to release a solo album, but both his manager and Big Boi were against it. One argument they offered was that fans would be eagerly anticipating a new release by OutKast following the group's Grammy Award for *Stankonia,* and a solo album would detract from that momentum. Andre was not deterred and even asserted that he would give the music away for free if need be. In response, Big Boi undertook and soon completed his own solo project. "[Big Boi's] was scheduled to come out in February, and mine was scheduled to come out this summer [in 2003]," Andre told Silva. "But I said that it's so close of a release, why don't we just put them together? And to him, that was really the best thing that I could have said because no one really wants to go out there and do it by themselves."

The result, which appeared after several postponed release dates, was the two-disk album *Speakerboxxx/ The Love Below* (2003), which is essentially a joint packaging of two not-quite-solo projects. (Andre co-wrote four tracks on Big Boi's *Speakerboxxx;* Big Boi co-wrote and guest rapped once on *The Love Below.)* Anchored in heavy beats, Big Boi's contribution is the more traditional, but as Stephen Thomas Erlewine wrote for the All Music Guide Web site, "it's clear that Boi is ignoring boundaries.... [His tracks are] grounded firmly within hip-hop, but the beats bend against the grain and the arrangements are overflowing with ideas and thrilling, unpredictable juxtapositions, such as how 'Bowtie' swings like big-band jazz filtered through George Clinton, how 'The Way You Move' offsets its hard-driving verses with seductive choruses, or how 'The Rooster' cheerfully rides a threatening minor-key mariachi groove, salted by slippery horns and loose-limbed wah-wah guitars." On *The Love Below* Andre did more singing—mainly in a Prince-like high falsetto—than rapping. His songs could as easily be classified as funk or soul as labeled hip-hop, and he even incorporated a liberal sprinkling of lounge music. Experimentation—and what some critics saw as self-indulgence—is rampant, as evidenced by the accelerated drum-and-bass rendition of Richard Rodgers and Oscar Hammerstein's "My Favorite Things" and odd numbers such as "God (Interlude)."

With the number-one singles "I Like the Way You Move" (Big Boi) and "Hey Ya!" (Andre), *Speakerboxxx/ The Love Below* was a smashing success. It reached the top positions on the *Billboard* ZOO album chart and the *Billboard* R&B/Hip-Hop Albums chart. Critical reaction was generally positive, although some reviewers felt that, taken separately, the OutKast duo amounted to less than the sum of their parts. *"Speakerboxxx* is solid but ultimately [only] decent," Baz Dreisinger wrote for Salon.com. *"The Love Below* often bears the mark of an artist who's been trapped in the studio too long. Like an ivory-tower academic, Andre occasionally forgets that an audience hopes to understand what he's getting at." On the other hand, Will Hermes, writing for *Entertainment Weekly* (September 19, 2003), asserted that the two disks, "if released separately, would each be a candidate for Hip-Hop Record of the Year. Packaged together, they make a twofer whose ambition flies so far beyond that of anyone doing rap right now (or pop, or rock, or R&B), awards shows may need to create a special category for it." In December 2003 *Rolling Stone* named "Hey Ya!" the best single and video of the year, *Speakerboxxx/The Love Below* the best album of the year, and OutKast the artist of the year and best hip-hop artist. *Rolling Stone* readers agreed, picking "Hey Ya!" as the best single and best video and OutKast as the best hip-hop artist. In February 2004 OutKast won three Grammy Awards, for album of the year, best rap album, and best urban/alternative performance ("Hey Ya!").

Personal Lives

Andre has a son named Seven Sirius from a now-ended relationship with the R&B artist Erykah Badu. In *Time* (September 29, 2003), Josh Tyrangiel suggested that Andre might be in the process of toning down his famously ostentatious appearance and also noted that the rapper had expressed interest in enrolling at Oxford University. At the Grammy ceremonies in 2004, however, Andre showed up in one of his most flamboyant costumes, wearing a leaf-green, fringed outfit made of buckskin-like material to perform, along with a group of similarly clad female dancers, a rendition of "Hey Ya!" The performance angered many Native American groups, including the National Congress of American Indians and the National Indian Gaming Association, who accused Andre and, by association, the Grammy Academy, of making a mockery of American Indian ceremonies. Andre, who lives in Los Angeles and has taken acting classes at the University of Southern California (USC), appeared as the character Silk Brown in the film *Hollywood Homicide* (2003) and will appear in *Be Cool,* the sequel to *Get Shorty* (1995), scheduled for release in 2004. He also plans to play one of his idols, Jimi Hendrix, in a biopic to be directed by the Hughes Brothers.

Big Boi, who is single, has referred to himself as a "soccer dad," according to *People* (February 16, 2004); he lives in Fayetteville, Georgia, with his three children-a daughter, Jordan, and sons Bamboo and Cross, who were eight, four, and three, respectively, in early 2004. He is an avid pit-bull breeder and owns the lucrative Pitfall Kennels, known for breeding "rare blue pits," which have grayish-blue coats and light-blue eyes. Other OutKast-related businesses include Aquemini Records, an OutKast clothing line, and several Atlanta apartment complexes. Rumors about an impending OutKast breakup have been circulating since before the release of *Speakerboxxx/The Love Below,* but Andre (who has repeatedly expressed discontent with making music) and Big Boi have insisted that the group will be together for years to come. Their next album, Andre told Chris Campion, will be a soundtrack for an HBO movie that is "a period piece not an OutKast biography."

Further Reading

All Music Guide Web site

Entertainment Weekly p81 Nov. 3, 2000, p36+ Nov. 10, 2000, with photos, p83+ Sep. 19, 2003

Los Angeles Times Calendar p78 Dec. 22, 1996

Newsweek p88 Oct. 30, 2000

People p87 Feb. 16, 2004

Remix p8+ Aug. 1, 2003

Dolly Parton

Singer; songwriter

Born: January 19, 1946; Sevierville, Tennessee
Primary Field: Country music artist
Group Affiliation: Gypsy Fever

Introduction

Sassy, flashy Dolly Parton, the leading lady of country music, has "crossed over" to become, in the inflated language of show business, a pop-rock megastar. The song-writing Tennessee mountain soprano came to prominence in Nashville in the late 1960's as the protégé of the legendary Porter Wagoner; struck out on her own in 1974, and in each of the following two years was chosen Best Female Singer by the Country Music Association; and in 1977 moved with éclat into the mainstream of popular music with her new, rockish backup band, Gypsy Fever. The dimpled Miss Parton, who accentuates her pretty face and buxom figure with flamboyant coiffures, heavy make-up, and come-hither clothes, carries off her painted-woman gimmickry with the innocence of a backwoods girl who has finally come into glad rags, and when she chirps out her down-home hit songs—such as the aggressive "Jolene" and the tender "I Will Always Love You" and "Love Is Like a Butterfly"—in her high, often tremulous, childlike voice, her sincerity, warmth, and homespun good spirits reach the hearts of good old boys and city slickers alike. Miss Parton, who often accompanies herself on the guitar or banjo, publishes her music through her own Nashville company, Owepar Inc., and records her songs on the RCA label.

Dolly Parton.

Early Life

Of mixed Dutch, Irish, and Cherokee Indian ancestry, Dolly Rebecca Parton was born on January 19, 1946 in a two-room wooden shack in Locust Ridge, near Sevierville, Tennessee, in the foothills of the Great Smoky Mountains. As the fourth of twelve children of Robert

Lee Parton, a struggling dirt farmer and laborer, and Avie Lee (Owens) Parton, a preacher's daughter, she helped raise her younger brothers and sisters. "We had absolutely nothin'," she reminisced when interviewed by Cynthia Heimel for an article in the *Soho Weekly News* (May 17, 1977). "We wore rags. . . . For make-up we used merthiolate and mercurochrome . . . and we used to use flour for powder. I was fascinated even then with make-up and stuff. Course they never allowed us to wear lipstick. My daddy would whip me . . . but the whippin' was worth it for a few days with a red mouth."

But Miss Parton is quick to add that she "had the best mama and daddy in the world" and that she and her brothers and sisters had "fun . . . love . . . music—all my people was musical." Her first love was gospel music, as she told Chris Chase when Miss Chase interviewed her for an article in the *New York Times Magazine* (May 9, 1976): "Where we lived was so far back in the mountains, there was only relatives and close friends went to our little church. And my granddaddy [Reverend Owens] being the preacher, we didn't feel ashamed to sing and play our gittars. We believed in makin' a joyful noise unto the Lord."

The Reverend Owens "preached hell so hot you could feel the heat," as Miss Parton recounts in one of her songs, Much of her inspiration in songwriting comes from her roots. "Coat of Many Colors," for example, is about a coat her mother pieced together for Dolly out of remnants, and there is an overall evocation of her childhood years in "In the Good Old Days (When Times Were Bad)" and "My Tennessee Mountain Home." Even before she could recite the alphabet Dolly was creating songs, the lyrics of which her mother would transcribe until Dolly herself learned to write. (She never did learn to write, or read, music.) Her first musical instrument was, as she describes it, "a busted-up mandolin" that she began picking when she was six. Her uncle Bill Owens, a band musician, gave her a guitar when she was eight, and three years later Owens obtained some radio bookings for her in Knoxville, Tennessee. Owens collaborated with her on the first song she recorded, "Puppy Love," released by Gold Band, a small company in Lake Charles, Louisiana.

In high school Dolly Parton played the snare drum in the marching band. The day after her graduation, in 1964, she took a bus to Nashville, Tennessee, the country music capital, where her uncle Bill was living with his family. She stayed with the Owenses until she was able to afford her own apartment, after signing contracts with Monument Records and Combine Music.

Life's Work

Recognizing that her voice was "so strange, and still is," Dolly Parton remembers that when she signed with Monument Records the people selecting her music there thought of her as "someone who sounded like she was twelve." "They thought I had potential—but not in country music," Miss Parton recounts. "They felt it wouldn't be commercial for me to try and sell a song with hard lyrics, that it would sound funny for someone who sounded like she was twelve to be singing about a marriage that went bad. So I started cutting rockabilly, a blend of country and rock. But I soon learned that when you ride the fence you just kind of sit there. I wasn't writing much or choosing any of my own material. I needed to do both."

Having persuaded Monument to let her record country songs, she came up with the BMI awardwinning "Put It Off Until Tomorrow," written in collaboration with her uncle, and the following year she had two successful singles, "Dumb Blonde" and "Something Fishy." Her first big breakthrough came when, in 1967, she joined Porter Wagoner's band, the Wagon Masters, replacing Norma Jean, who was leaving to get married. She sang with the heavily booked Wagoner band for seven years, playing road dates and gaining national television exposure on the syndicated *Porter Wagoner Show.* While with the band she wrote songs and made records with Wagoner, who used his influence at RCA Records to move her to that label. For several years after she left the band, Wagoner continued to produce and arrange for her, and together they own the Owepar Publishing Company, on "Music Row" in Nashville.

In his book *The Nashville Sound* (1970), Paul Hemphill described Dolly Parton as a "petite blonde of incredible vanilla-ice-cream beauty" when she was singing at the Grand Ole Opry, the Carnegie Hall of country music, in Nashville, and he called her vocalizing, along with the playing of the Wagon Masters, "gut-country music at its purest." For her singing with Wagoner and his band, Miss Parton shared in the Country Music Association's Vocal Group of the Year award in 1968 and Vocal Duo of the Year awards in 1970 and 1971. In 1971 she also placed in the top five in all the trade papers in the Best Female Vocalist category, was named Best Female Songwriter by *Billboard*, and won citations from Broadcast Music Incorporated (BMI) for her songs "Joshua" and "Daddy Was an Old Time Preacher Man."

In August 1974 Dolly Parton struck out on her own, going on the road with her Travelin' Family Band, composed of two of her brothers, two of her sisters, an uncle, and a cousin. One of the first stops in her new itinerary was the Felt Forum in New York City, an engagement covered by John Rockwell for the *New York Times* (September 16, 1974). "She is an impressive artist," Rockwell wrote. "Her visual trademark is not far from that of Diamond Lil: a mountainous, curlicued bleached-blonde wig, lots of make-up, and outfits that accentuate

Affiliation: Gypsy Fever

In her quest for a wider audience, Dolly Parton in the fall of 1976 replaced her Nashville-based manager with the Hollywood firm of Katz, Gallin and Cleary, which also manages Olivia Newton-John, Cher, Tony Orlando and Dawn, the Osmonds, and Mac Davis. Also, she formed a new backup group, Gypsy Fever, consisting of eight crack Nashville musicians experienced in pop and rock as well as country music. Before going on the road with her new group, Miss Parton gave her vocal chords a long rest, including two weeks of total silence, on the advice of her otolaryngologists, to assuage the swelling of nodes on her vocal chords, a chronic problem.

In January 1977 Dolly Parton began touring with Gypsy Fever, doing one-night stands in places like Peoria, Illinois and Battle Creek, Michigan, perfecting her new act for the big time. As usual, she traveled in her own bus, a home-and-studio-on-wheels equipped with reel to-reel tape deck, cassette player, color television, refrigerator, two bathrooms, a closet for twenty costumes and four wigs, and sleeping accommodations for eleven.

Jean Vallely, a correspondent for *Time* (April 18, 1977), who stopped in on the tour shortly before it returned to Nashville, reported: "A Dolly Parton concert is a treat, like a hot-fudge sundae after a month of dieting. As the lights come up the band tears into Jackie Wilson's old rhythm and blues specialty 'Higher and Higher/ . . . [Dolly] leaps onstage and takes 'Higher and Higher' even higher. Those who have never seen Dolly gasp. That mountain of a teased blond wig and the hot-pink, jeweled jumpsuit are spectacular. Only five feet tall, she totters atop five inch gold heels. Swinging into 'All I Can Do' she catches the eyes of the people in the front rows and plays to them, talking, teasing. Next Gomes 'Jolene' . . . 'about a woman who tried to steal my man. . . .' By now Dolly is ready for 'Light of a Clear Blue Morning,' the declaration of artistic independence that leads off her latest RCA album, *New Harvest, First Gathering.*" Three weeks after Vallely's report in *Time, New Harvest, First Gathering* was number one on the country charts and was rising rapidly up the pop charts.

In their invasion of the rock world, Dolly Parton and Gypsy Fever first conquered the Roxy on Sunset Strip in Los Angeles, the Boarding House in San Francisco, and, with Mac Davis, the Anaheim Convention Center. From California they traveled to New York City, where they began a three-day engagement at the Bottom Line, the Greenwich Village nightclub that is; the hallowed ground of the current East Coast rock establishment, on May 12, 1977.

Dolly Parton's opening at the Bottom Line was, in the words of the reviewer for the *New York Times* (May 14, 1977), "a triumph": "The packed crowd [which included such luminaries as Mick Jagger, Bruce Springsteen, Candice Bergen, Phoebe Snow, Berry Berenson, Olivia Newton-John, Robert Duvall, John Belushi, Patti Smith, Andy Warhol, and Barbara Cook] cheered on Miss Parton supportively from the moment she swept onto the stage, and rewarded her with an idolatrous ovation at the end." Reviewing the Bottom Line gig in the *Soho Weekly News* (May 19, 1977), Cynthia Heimel described Miss Parton's voice as "strong, sweet, and exuberant," and Carl Arrington of the New York *Post* (May 14, 1977) observed that "with fans and media people gobbling up seats, she's been the hottest ticket in town."

In an interview with Arrington, Miss Parton said: "I feel like a bird with new wings. . . . It's been exciting to see that I can touch all kinds of different people with my music." Among the "kinds," she noted, was an especially loyal following in the homosexual community. "I guess a lot of my popularity with gays is my gaudy, flashy appearance. And they like to have a good time." Following the Bottom Line engagement, Dolly Parton and Gypsy Fever crossed the Atlantic to give concerts in Great Britain, Germany, Holland, and Belgium.

her quite astonishing hourglass figure. But Miss Parton is no artificial dumb blonde. Her thin little soprano and girlish way of talking suggest something childlike, but one quickly realizes both that it is genuine and that she is a striking talent. . . . Many country singers have [real rural] backgrounds like [hers]. Miss Parton stands apart for the sheer quality of her songs. The words . . . toe the line between the banal and the basic, but in her case honesty and an almost fervent sincerity win out."

At a performance by Miss Parton and her band the following year in Stanhope, New Jersey, Rockwell found Miss Parton "more quintessentially country than ever," as he reported in the *New York Times* (August 4, 1975): "Her poetry has such a range of emotion and such a truth to it that—as always happens with the best art—the very specificity of her imagery becomes universal. Her music is often colored by the modalities and rhythmic abnormalities of old English folk songs, and she nearly always manages to shape her best songs into something unusual without courting gimmickry. Even when she indulges in all-out sentimentality, as in . . . 'Me and Little Andy,' about a child who is abandoned by her drunken father and goes to heaven with her puppy, Miss Parton . . . performs . . . in a way that quiets cynicism."

At the time of the Stanhope concert Miss Parton told Jan Hodenfield of the New York *Post* (August 6, 1975): "I want to be known as a great writer. . . . I like to describe my writing as being simply complicated. It's got enough depth to be appreciated and enough simplicity to be understood. . . . It's a part of me as long as I remember, a way to describe my feelings, . . . my memories. . . . Some of them bother me, so it's almost like going to a psychiatrist if I can write a song about my problem—then I can share it with the world and it never bothers me anymore." In addition to the Country Music Association's 1975 and 1976 Best Female Vocalist of the Year awards, Dolly Parton won the 1975 Best Female Vocalist designations of *Cash Box, Record World,* and *Billboard*, as well as *Billboard's* 1975 citation for Best Female Singles Artist.

When preparing an article on Dolly Parton for the *New York Times* (May 9, 1976), Chris Chase traveled to East Burke High School outside of Hickory, North Carolina when Dolly and the Travelin' Family Band were playing in the auditorium there, sharing the bill with Merle Haggard. "Her voice is an amazement . . . ," Miss Chase wrote of Miss Parton. "In 'Love Is Like a Butterfly' Dolly's work is as sheer and delicate as a butterfly's wings . . . while in 'Travelin' Man' she hoots and hollers and drives and mocks. . . . Her voice can quiver. . . . twang . . . throb . . . lift .... It takes an octave jump with foolish ease, and it is almost always true and sweet. . . . She ends the session with a rocking version of 'The Seeker' [and] sends you home feeling good."

As her popularity zoomed in 1976, Dolly Parton made guest appearances on *Today, Hee Haw, Dinah!, Merv Griffin, the Tonight Show Starring Johnny Carson,* and other television shows, and in Norman Lear's soap opera spoof, *Mary Hartman, Mary Hartman.* Loretta Haggers, played by Mary Kay Place, became a country singer with dreams of going to Nashville and buying "Dolly Parton outfits." (Later Dolly sang backup for Miss Place's debut LP, *Tonite! At the Capri Lounge: Loretta Haggars*.) In the 1976-77 television season Miss Parton essayed her own syndicated television show, *Dolly*, but, as she concedes, "didn't have the time to make it right."

Miss Parton's album *Bargain Store* was followed by *All I Can Do*, which included the songs "When the Sun Goes Down Tomorrow," "Shattered Image," "I'm a Drifter," and "Falling Out of Love with Me." The last mentioned "hurtin' " song ("I left while love was still alive/ It was dying and I'd rather/ I didn't have to watch it die") is generally acknowledged to be one of her most hauntingly beautiful creations. 1977's *Here You Come Again,* became her first million-seller, topping the country album chart and reaching No. 20 on the pop chart; the Barry Mann-Cynthia Weil-penned title track topped the country singles chart, and became Parton's first top-ten single on the pop chart (#3). A second single, the double A-sided "Two Doors Down"/"It's All Wrong, But It's All Right" topped the country chart and crossed over to the pop top twenty. In 1978, Parton won a Grammy Award for Best Female Country Vocal Performance for her *Here You Come Again* album.

Robert Windeler in *People* (April 4, 1977) described Dolly Parton's voice as "shivery, crystalline." Over 400 of Dolly's songs have been recorded, and "thousands and thousands and thousands" more, by her own estimation, fill trunks and boxes in her home. She writes, or rather, sings into a tape recorder, up to twenty sets of lyrics daily. A secretary writes out the lyrics, which are set to written music by a lead sheet service. "I have no set pattern while writing," she says. "A strange feeling usually comes over me; almost like being in a trance. I know what's going on, but I'm totally separated from it. When you're talented I think much of the inspiration is spiritual—from God." While she "ain't much for church," Dolly says that she reads the Bible and prays regularly. "I guess I'm sort of a vanilla sinner—too bad to be real good and too good to be bad."

For the remainder of the 1970s and into the early 1980s, many of her subsequent singles charted on both charts simultaneously. Her albums during this period were developed specifically for pop-crossover success. "9 to 5," the theme song to the 1980 feature film *9 to 5* she starred in along with Jane Fonda and Lily Tomlin, not only reached No. 1 on the country chart, but also, in February 1981, reached No. 1 on the pop and the adult-contemporary charts, giving her a triple No. 1 hit. Parton became one of the few female country singers to have a No. 1 single on the country and pop charts simultaneously. It also received a nomination for an Academy Award for Best Original Song. Her singles continued to appear consistently in the country Top 10: between 1981 and 1985, she had 12 Top 10 hits; half of them hit No. 1. She continued to make inroads on the pop chart as well. A re-recorded version of "I Will Always Love You" from the feature film, *The Best Little Whorehouse in Texas* (1982) scraped the Top 50 that year and her duet with Kenny Rogers, "Islands in the Stream" (written by the Bee Gees and produced by Barry Gibb), spent two weeks at No. 1 in 1983.

Along with Emmylou Harris and Linda Ronstadt, she released *Trio* (1987) to critical acclaim. The album revitalized Parton's music career, spending five weeks at No. 1 on Billboard's Country Albums chart, and also reached the top-ten on Billboard's Top-200 Albums chart. It sold several million copies and producing four Top 10 country hits including Phil Spector's "To Know Him Is to Love Him," which went to No. 1. "Trio" won the Grammy Award for Best Country Performance by a Duo or Group with Vocal and was nominated for a Grammy Award for Album of the Year. After a further attempt at pop success with "Rainbow" (1987), including the single "The River Unbroken," Parton focused on recording country material. "White Limozeen" (1989) produced two No. 1 hits in "Why'd You Come in Here Lookin' Like That" and "Yellow Roses." Although it looked like Parton's career had been revived, it was actually just a brief revival before contemporary country music came on in the early 1990s and moved most veteran artists off the chart.

A duet with Ricky Van Shelton, "Rockin' Years" (1991), reached No. 1, though Parton's greatest commercial fortune of the decade came when Whitney Houston recorded "I Will Always Love You" for the soundtrack of the feature film *The Bodyguard* (1992); both the single and the album were massively successful. Parton's soundtrack album from the 1992 film, *Straight Talk,* however, was less successful. But her 1993 album *Slow Dancing with the Moon* won critical acclaim, and did well on the charts, reaching No. 4 on the country albums chart, and No. 16 on the *Billboard* 200 album chart. She recorded "The Day I Fall in Love" as a duet with James Ingram for the feature film *Beethoven's 2nd* (1993). The songwriters (Sager, Ingram, and Clif Mangess) were nominated for an Academy Award for Best Original Song and Parton and Ingram performed the song on the awards telecast. Similar to her earlier collaborative album with Harris and Ronstadt, Parton released "Honky Tonk Angels" in the fall of 1993 with Loretta Lynn and Tammy Wynette. It was certified as a gold album by the Recording Industry Association of America and helped revive both Wynette's and Lynn's careers.

Parton's recorded music during the mid-to late 1990s remained steady, though somewhat eclectic. Her 1998 country-rock album *Hungry Again* was made up entirely of her own compositions. Although neither of the album's two singles, "(Why Don't More Women Sing) Honky Tonk Songs" and "Salt in my Tears," charted, videos for both songs received significant airplay on CMT. A second and more contemporary collaboration with Harris and Ronstadt, *Trio II,* was released in early 1999. Its cover of Neil Young's song "After the Gold Rush" won a Grammy Award for Best Country Collaboration with Vocals. Parton was also inducted into the Country Music Hall of Fame in 1999.

Parton earned her second Academy Award nomination for Best Original Song for "Travelin' Thru," which she wrote specifically for the feature film *Transamerica* (2005). Due to the song's (and film's) uncritical acceptance of a transgender woman, Parton received death threats. She returned to No. 1 on the country chart later in 2005 by lending her distinctive harmonies to the Brad Paisley ballad, "When I Get Where I'm Goin'."

The music-competition reality-television show *American Idol* (since 2002) has weekly themes and the April 1–2, 2008, episodes' theme was "Dolly Parton Songs" with the nine then-remaining contestants each singing a Parton composition. Parton participated as a "guest mentor" to the contestants and also performed "Jesus and Gravity" (from *Backwoods Barbie* and released as a single in March 2008) receiving a standing ovation from the studio audience.

In September 2007, Parton released her first single from her own record company, Dolly Records, titled, "Better Get to Livin'," which eventually peaked at No. 48 on *Billboard's* Hot Country Songs chart. It was followed by the studio album *Backwoods Barbie,* which was released on February 26, 2008, and reached No. 2 on the country chart. The album's debut at No. 17 on the all-genre *Billboard* 200 albums chart was the highest in her career. *Backwoods Barbie* produced four additional singles, including the title track, written as part of her score for *9 to 5: The Musical,* an adaptation of her feature film *9 to 5*. After the sudden death of Michael Jackson, whom Parton knew personally, she released a video in which she somberly told of her feelings on Jackson and his death.

On October 27, 2009, Parton released a four-CD box set, "Dolly," which featured 99 songs and spanned most of her career. She released her second live DVD and album, *Live From London* in October 2009, which was filmed during her sold out 2008 concerts at London's The O2 Arena.

In 2013, Parton and Kenny Rogers reunited for the title song of his album *You Can't Make Old Friends*. For their performance, they were nominated at the 2014 Grammy Awards for Grammy Award for Best Country Duo/Group Performance.In 2014, Parton embarked on the Blue Smoke World Tour in support of her forty-second studio album, *Blue Smoke*. The album was first released in Australia & New Zealand on January 31 to coincide with tour dates there in February, and reached the top 10 in both countries. It was released in the US on May 13, and debuted at No. 6 on the *Billboard* 200 chart, making it her first top 10 album and her highest-charting solo album ever; it also reached the No. 2 position on the US country chart. The album was released in Europe on June 9, and reached No. 2 on the UK album chart. On June 29, 2014, Parton performed for the first time at the UK Glastonbury Festival performing songs such as "Jolene," "9 to 5"and "Coat of Many Colors" to a crowd of over 180,000.

Parton is the most honored female country performer of all time. Achieving 25 RIAA certified gold, platinum, and multi-platinum awards, she has had 25 songs reach No. 1 on the Billboard Country charts, a record for a female artist. She has 41 career top 10 country albums, a record for any artist, and she has 110 career charted singles over the past 40 years. All-inclusive sales of singles, albums, hits collections, and digital downloads during her career have topped 100 million worldwide. She has garnered eight Grammy Awards, two Academy Award nominations, ten Country Music Association Awards, seven Academy of Country Music Awards, three American Music Awards, and is one of only seven female artists to win the Country Music Association's Entertainer of the Year Award. Parton has received 46 Grammy nominations, tying her with Bruce Springsteen for the most Grammy nominations and placing her in tenth place overall. In 1999, she was inducted into the Country Music Hall of Fame. She has composed over 3,000 songs, the best known of which include "I Will Always Love You" (a two-time U.S. country chart-topper for Parton, as well as an international pop hit for Whitney Houston), "Jolene," "Coat of Many Colors," "9 to 5," and "My Tennessee Mountain Home." Parton is also one of the few to have received at least one nomination from the Academy Awards, Grammy Awards, Tony Awards, and Emmy Awards.

Personal Life

Dolly Parton's own hair, shoulder length and naturally brown, is bleached and combed up over the front of her wig. "I enjoy the way I look, but it's like a joke . . . ," she told Cynthia Heimel in the *Soho Weekly News* article. "I like to kid the audience about it. . . . They know I'm going to come out with every spangled thing I can get on. . . . It's a joke that we share." In further explanation of her "outrageous" appearance and her attitude in general, she says: "I think I live in a fairy tale, and I think that's why I stay so happy. Cause I don't have to see all the ugly things. Even though I know they exist, I know how to get away from them. I don't have to dwell on my sorrow or anybody else's." Miss Parton can be hard-headed when necessary, and people who are close to her agree that she is "no dumb blonde" but a realistic woman of "quick intelligence."

Dolly Parton and Carl Dean, owner of an asphalt paving company, were married on May 30, 1966. They live in a twenty-three-room mansion on 200 acres just outside of Nashville. Dolly's teen-aged sister Rachel lives with them, and four of her other siblings were raised at Tara, as the estate, or farm, is called. Most of her close relatives live nearby, and a trailer home is maintained at Tara to house her parents when they visit. "Behind all this gaudiness I'm made up of real stuff," Dolly says. Beyond "becoming more and more successful" at what she is doing, her biggest dream is "to touch people's lives enough to lead them in a certain direction."

Miss Parton and her husband raise Hereford cattle, as well as two hounds and two peacocks. A maid does the housekeeping, but Dolly likes to cook on occasion. Away so much of the time, she does not do much socializing among other country artists, preferring to stay close to home. "I don't want to leave the country," she says, "but to take it with me wherever I go."

Further Reading

Biog N 2:613 My '75 por
Esquire 87:62+ Mr '77 por
N Y *Post* p43 Ag 6 '75; P31 My 14 '77 por
N Y Times Mag pl7+ My 9 '76 pors
Newsday II p3 My 29 '77 por
People 7:77+ Ap 4 '77 pors
Soho Weekly News pl6+ My 19 '77 pors
Time 109:72+ Ap 18 '77 pors
Who's Who in America, 1978-77
Nash, Alanna. *Dolly: The Biography* (2002)
Miller, Stephen. *Smart Blonde—Dolly Parton* (2008)

Sandi Patty

Christian singer

Born: July 12, 1957, Oklahoma City, Oklahoma
Primary Field: Christian music
Group Affiliation: Solo performer

Introduction

Sandi Patty has sold more than 11 million records over the course of the last two decades and sung at the inaugural galas of three U.S. presidents: George H. W. Bush (in 1989), Bill Clinton (1997), and George W. Bush (2001). The recipient of five Grammy Awards, four Billboard Awards, and 39 Dove Awards (given by the Gospel Music Association), she is one of the most honored female vocalists in the history of contemporary Christian music. The singer, who has also been known professionally as Sandi Patti (the latter spelling appears on several of her albums), is sometimes called the "First Lady of Inspirational Music" or simply the "Voice" by the gospel-music press. Thanks in part to her frequent appearances on the Tonight Show *and various other television programs, Patty has become popular with mainstream audiences, in addition to her devoted Christian-music fans. By her own account, she feels a special responsibility when performing for non-Christian listeners. "Someone like Johnny Carson [then host of the* Tonight Show*] is very aware that I am a Christian artist," Patty told Holly G. Miller for the* Saturday Evening Post *(December 1986). "So it becomes more than my name at stake when I encounter him. It's the name of Christianity, and as we know, so many things have given that a negative connotation. It's a challenge to present who I am in the light of being a Christian and to leave a positive feeling with people. I only have one shot to do it, or maybe a couple."*

Early Life

Sandi Patty was born on July 12, 1957 in Oklahoma City, Oklahoma. (Some sources list July 14 as her birthdate.) Her mother, Carolyn Patty, was a church pianist; her father, Ron Patty, was a minister who used music to spread the Christian Gospel. After Sandi Patty made her musical debut, at the age of two, when she sang "Jesus Loves Me" at a Church of God service, she, her parents, and her two brothers began touring small churches around the country as the Ron Patty Family. "I really wasn't a rotten kid," Patty said to Susan Reed for *People* (December 2, 1985). "I had a messy room, but I got along with my parents and I enjoyed school. Saying you were 'born again' has taken on a negative idea for the general public, but I knew that one day I would have to make a personal commitment to Jesus Christ. It was my eighth birthday and I decided that was as good a time as any. It was very special, a personal and public commitment."

When she was growing up, Patty never intended to become a professional singer; she wanted instead to be a music teacher. She spent two years studying music at San Diego State University, in California, before transferring to Anderson University, a Church of God college in Anderson, Indiana. To help pay her tuition, Patty sang on commercials for Juicy Fruit chewing gum, a fast-food chain, and the Ohio State Fair. At Anderson she met John Helvering, whom she married shortly before she graduated.

Life's Work

Meanwhile, impressed by her talent, Helvering persuaded Patty to record an album, which she produced herself; her last name was mistakenly spelled "Patti" on the album cover, and rather than go through the expense of changing it, she allowed it to remain. The couple planned to sell the disk after church concerts to earn extra income. Patty recalled to Charles W. Phillips for the *Saturday Evening Post* (May 1983), "John was a business major in college, and I was getting my teaching credentials. A week before our wedding, a record company executive called and said he had heard my custom album and wanted to talk with me. I told him I was getting married on Friday and didn't want to think about anything else for a couple of months. He understood and waited about eight weeks before he called back and set up a meeting. Everything started to mushroom from that point on. We hadn't planned on a music career, but it felt right." In 1979 Patty signed a contract with the independent Christian label Benson Records; that same year she released the album *Sandi's Song.* She then went on a series of musical ministry tours, including several with the acclaimed Christian music group the Bill Gaither Trio, winning a growing number of loyal fans in the process. Patty next recorded *Love Overflowing* (1981) and *Lift Up the Lord* (1982). In 1982, at the 13th Annual Dove Awards, she was named "artist of the year" and "female vocalist of the year" by the Gospel Music Association. She retained the title "female vocalist of the year" for an unprecedented 10 years in a row and also garnered the title "artist of the year" several more times during that decade. In addition, she was named *Billboard's* "inspirational artist of the year" each year from 1986 through 1989.

In 1983 Patty won her first Grammy, for best gospel performance by a duo or group, for the song "More Than Wonderful," a duet she had recorded with Larnelle Harris. Over the next decade she won four more Grammys—one in 1985, for a duet with Harris titled "I've Just Seen Jesus"; two in 1986, for "They Say," a duet with Deniece Williams, and the solo effort "Morning Like This"; and one in 1990, for the album *Another Time, Another Place.*

During the 1980s and early 1990s, Patty released several albums, including five that went gold (meaning sales of at least half a million copies): *The Gift Goes On* (1983), *Songs from the Heart* (1984), *Make His Praise Glorious* (1988), *The Finest Moments* (1989), and *Another Time, Another Place* (1990). Three of her recordings from this period achieved platinum status (sales of at least a million copies): *More Than Wonderful* (1983), *Hymns Just for You* (1985), and *Morning Like This* (1986).

Throughout her career Patty had presented herself as wholesome, family-oriented, and devoted to her ministry. Thus, it shocked many of her fans when, in 1992, she filed for divorce from, John Helvering. Then, at a press conference held in 1993, Patty revealed that she had been sexually abused as a child by a family friend. In 1995, at another press conference, Patty admitted that she had been unfaithful while married to Helvering. Later that year she married Don Peslis, a backup singer with whom she had conducted an affair. With the news of the infidelity spreading through the Christian-music

Affiliation: Country Music and Patriotism

By the mid-1980s, thanks to her prolific touring and recording, most fans of Christian music were familiar with Patty's work, but she remained largely unknown to mainstream audiences. That changed on July 6, 1986, when her rendition of the "Star-Spangled Banner" was televised at the end of ABC's *Liberty Weekend* programming, aired in honor of the centennial and rededication of the Statue of Liberty. Patty had recorded the song as a track on *They Come to America* (1986), the official album of the Statue of Liberty-Ellis Island Foundation, and A&M Records, the company that distributed the album, had sent a copy to ABC Television executives. Because the decision to play the track over the closing montage of the broadcast was made at the last minute, ABC officials were unable to alert Patty that her song was airing. "It was the strangest feeling to be watching the celebration at home with my family and suddenly to hear myself singing on television," she told Miller. "I had no idea that was going to happen. I was shocked, but pleasantly shocked."

Following the broadcast, ABC was flooded with more than 1,000 calls asking the identity of the singer. George H. W. Bush, then vice president, subsequently asked Patty to the White House for tea, and Johnny Carson asked her to make the first of four visits to the *Tonight Show.* As her popularity with non-Christian audiences grew, she made numerous other public appearances, including performances at the Fiesta Bowl and Disneyland.

world, several radio stations refused to play her records. "I got a variety of letters," she told Wayne Bledsoe in an interview for the *Knoxville (Tennessee) News-Sentinel* (November 10, 2002). "I got people saying 'Hey, we love you. Whatever you're going through, take your time and do what you need to do, but come back.' And I got letters from people who were very hurt and angry and very confused, and I totally understand that. . . . I was able to write them back and say, 'You know what? I understand. I've let God down and some friends and fans down' and I had to do some healing and reconciliation." The controversy prompted Patty to stop touring for a while.

She continued to record, however; in 1996 Patty made three highly successful albums: *0 Holy Night, An American Songbook,* and *It's Christmas.* The following year she sang the "Star Spangled Banner" at President Bill Clinton's inaugural gala, the second of three such galas at which she has performed. In 1998 she recorded *Artist of My Soul* and *Libertad Me Das* (You Set Me Free), which won a Dove Award as best Spanish-language album of the year. That year, buoyed by support from Peslis and her fans, she began touring again.

Patty continues to record regularly. Her recent releases include *Together: Sandi Patty and Kathy Troccoli* (1999), *These Days* (2000), *For God and Country* (2001), *All the Best Live* (2001), *Take Hold of Christ* (2003), which was nominated for a 2004 Dove Award for "inspirational album of the year," and *Hymns of Faith . . . Songs of Inspiration* (2004). She has also begun to branch out from the world of Christian inspirational music by performing with regional and national symphony orchestras. During those performances she sings selections from Disney soundtracks and Broadway shows, as well as patriotic and big-band tunes.

Personal Life

Patty and Peslis have eight children—four from Patty's previous marriage, three from Peslis's, and one the couple adopted after their marriage. They live in Anderson, Indiana. Speaking about how she and her husband juggle parenthood and demanding careers, Patty told Alyssa Roggie for the Lancaster, Pennsylvania, *Intelligencer Journal* (April 21, 2000), "It keeps us insanely busy. But you know what, it's what we signed up for. We love the business, and we love the kids. We just have to take one day at a time and enjoy the chaos."

Further Reading

Chicago Tribune C p6 Sep. 25, 1986, with photo
Knoxville (Tennessee) News Sentinel G p1 Nov. 10, 2002, with photo
People p193 Dec. 2, 1985, with photo
Saturday Evening Post p16+ May 1983, with photo, p64+ Dec. 1986, with photo, p44+ Jan. 1989, with photo

Luciano Pavarotti

Opera singer

Born: October 12, 1935; Modena, Italy
Died: September 6, 2007; Modena, Italy
Primary Field: Opera
Group Affiliation: Metropolitan Opera

Introduction

As Martin Mayer wrote in Esquire *(November 1972), "the most plausible candidate in years for the title of The New Caruso" is big, outgoing tenor Luciano Pavarotti, who began singing opera professionally in his native Italy in 1961, made his debut at the Metropolitan Opera in 1968, and reached superstardom at the Met in 1972. Combining power with quality, Pavarotti is, in the consensus of critics, the best Italian bel canto singer in the opera world today. Even when in prolonged flight in the highest register, his perfectly pitched voice never loses its purity of tone and articulation as it soars out over the orchestra to the back of the largest of opera houses. Pavarotti, an amiable applause-lover who does not like operas in which the soprano or baritone can upstage him, such as* La Traviata, *naturally prefers roles such as the Duke of Mantua in* Rigoletto. *His other favorites include Tonio in* La Fille du Regiment, *with its spectacular sequence of high C's; Arturo in* 1 Puritani, *which is even more challenging; and Elvino in* La Sonnamhula. *He looks forward to the day—three or four years hence, by his reckoning—when his voice will be dark enough for tenore spinto roles like Cavaradossi in Puccini's* Tosca *and Manrico in Verdi's* Il Trovatore.

Early Life

Luciano Pavarotti was born on October 12, 1935 in Modena in the Po River valley of Italy. "That's where I learned to be happy," he told Hubert Saal of *Newsweek* (March 5, 1973). "I'm a country boy. Modena is a city with 10,000, all my friends and most of them my relatives." In the *Saturday Review* (February 3, 1973) Irving Kolodin quoted him on the subject of his birthplace: "Everybody sings. We have an old opera house seating 1,200 where visiting companies from Bologna or Parma put on a few performances a year, and the local forces mount an annual production." Pavarotti's father, Fernando, a baker by trade, sings in the chorus of local productions and, according to Pavarotti, still has a "beautiful" tenor voice. In the interview with Kolodin, Pavarotti said that he would like soon to create a Christmas record on which his father would render "Panis Angelicus." While the father often attends his son's performances, Pavarotti's mother, Adele (Venturi) Pavarotti, a former tobacco factory worker, is confined to her home by a severe heart ailment. She has seen him perform professionally only once, and on that occasion the excitement was so much for her that she required medical attention. The tenor has a sister, Gabriella.

The solid muscle that undergirds Pavarotti's copious flesh was developed when, as a slimmer youth, he was an all-around athlete, especially good at European-style football, called soccer in America. But he was above all "born to be a singer," as he has said. "Our house was full of records, and I went to the opera a lot." He also sang in the children's choir of the local church. Among his childhood friends was soprano Mirella Freni, a native of Modena, who often performs with him.

Before daring to gamble on a professional career, Pavarotti thought he had better prepare himself for a more secure livelihood. His mother, dreaming of an ultimate bank presidency, wanted him to become an accountant, but he rejected that possibility in favor of teaching. With good grades behind him, he qualified for the teacher-training program at the Instituto Magistrale in Modena, where he graduated in 1955. He taught elementary school for two years before deciding to try for a professional career as a singer. When he did so decide—with his father's encouragement—he switched to the selling of insurance, an occupation that would allow him greater freedom in studying voice where and when he wanted. Most of his vocal training was received in Mantua. His father constantly goaded him on by telling him that he was singing below his potential.

Life's Work

In 1961, as a reward for winning the Concorso Internationale, Pavarotti made his professional debut in the role of Rodolfo in *La Boheme* at the Teatro Municipale in the Po valley city of Reggio Emilia. In the two years that followed he sang in opera houses all over Italy, including the major houses in Venice and Palermo, and then he ventured abroad, to Holland, Austria, Switzerland, Spain, Poland, Hungary, Czechoslovakia, and Great Britain. He made his debut in Amsterdam as Edgardo in *Lucia di Lammermoor,* in Dublin as the Duke in *Rigoletto*, and at Covent Garden, London as a replacement for the ailing Giuseppe Di Stefano in the role of Rodolfo. In 1964 he returned to Britain as Idamante in Mozart's *Idomeneo*.

In 1965, after making his North American debut opposite Joan Sutherland in *Lucia di Lammermoor* in Miami, he toured Australia with the soprano in *L'Elisir d'Amore* and other productions. Pavarotti, who says that he has always found it easier to learn from actual experience than in the abstract, under formal teachers, had a pure voice but one lacking in consistent strength at the time he met Miss Sutherland. From her he learned to breathe from the diaphragm. "When she sing I touch her stomach," he has recalled in his fractured English, "and then I tried to do the same."

Donizetti wrote nine high C's into Tonio's first-act aria in *La Fille du Regiment,* but on the rare occasions when tenors have attempted the role they have usually had the notes transposed down to a lower key. In rehearsing to sing opposite Joan Sutherland in the opera at Covent Garden in 1966, Pavarotti was tricked into daring to ascend to the long plateau of high C's by conductor Richard Bonynge, Miss Sutherland's husband. Bonynge, at the piano, led Pavarotti to believe that he would play the most difficult section of the aria a tone lower, but after playing the B flats that precede it, he transposed back up, and Pavarotti sang the high notes without any trouble before he realized he was no longer singing B flats.

Ever since, he has fearlessly soared up the full octave whenever he has sung Tonio. After hearing him sing it recently, Irving Kolodin asked him whether the "beautifully frontal head tone," or *dans la masque*, as the mellow sound of French tenors used to be called, was "happenstance or subtly associated with the language itself." Pavarotti told him: "When I first started singing this part, critics liked my voice but referred to the 'Austriaco-Ungarico' pronunciation of the text, and they were right! But little by little I learned the right way to sing in French, and now it comes very easy."

In 1966 Pavarotti opened the Rome Opera season as the Duke of Mantua in *Rigoletto* and made his debut at La Scala, Milan as Tybaldo in *I Capuletti ed i Montecchi.* Later in the 1966-67 season at La Scala he sang the tenor part in Verdi's *Requiem* under the direction of Herbert von Karajan on the occasion of the centenary of Arturo Toscanini's birth. Early in 1967 he made his debut with the San Francisco Opera in his mascot *La Boheme* role, Rodolfo, and he sang Tybaldo with the La Scala company at Montreal's Expo '67 the following summer. By 1968 his repertoire also included Lieutenant B. F. Pinkerton in *Madama Butterfly*, Arturo Talbot in *I Puritani,* and the Chevalier des Grieux in *Manon*.

In 1972 Pavarotti took part in the Met's spring tour and the three-week Verdi Festival at the opera house in New York that followed. He made his American concert debut at the Garden State Arts Center in New Jersey in June 1972, and back at the Met at the end of the year he sang two different roles on successive nights: his scheduled Edgardo in *Lucia di Lammermoor* and, to help out the Met management in an emergency, a Rodolfo originally assigned to Nicolai Gedda.

Robert T. Jones reported in *Time* (January 31, 1972) that when Pavarotti sang opposite Beverly Sills in Bellini's *I Puritani* in Philadelphia "his blazing high notes had the audience alternately gasping and yelling." Pavarotti was "thrilled" by the bravos he received when he and Joan Sutherland took their *La Fille du Regiment* to the Met in February 1972, and he was "happy" that Harold C. Schonberg of the *New York Times* praised his lyrical second-act aria more than the first-act aria with the high C's. "I want to be known as a tenor of line, not a tenor of the top," he explained. "That is what I work for."

Pavarotti delved into song literature for a concert series he gave in major American cities in February 1973, presenting selections from such composers as Gluck, Monteverdi, and Corelli ("*the* composer," in his opinion), some nonstandard arias, and some Italian dialect songs. After witnessing the culminating concert, in Carnegie Hall in New York City, Hubert Saal wrote in *Newsweek* (March 5, 1973), "Just to hear that sweet, clear, pure sound, that astonishing light and flexible voice flow from that gargantuan physique is breathtaking. . . . Pavarotti is musical as well as gifted. He exercised the self-control of an ascetic, tracing beautiful

Affiliation: Metropolitan Opera

When Pavarotti made his debut at the Metropolitan Opera in New York singing Rodolfo, Peter G. Davis wrote in the *New York Times* (November 21, 1968): "Mr. Pavarotti triumphed principally through the natural beauty of his voice—a bright, open instrument with a nice metallic ping up top that warms into an even, burnished luster in mid-range. Any tenor who can toss off high C's with such abandon, successfully negotiate delicate diminuendo effects, and attack Puccinian phrases so fervently is going to win over any La Bohdme audience, and Pavarotti had them eating out of his hand." On the negative side, Davis voiced a common opinion of critics at the time when he wrote, "As far as acting tenors go, Mr. Pavarotti is not the worst, but his generally stiff and unconvincing stage presence did leave something to be desired."

Forced by an attack of influenza to withdraw from his Met engagement in December 1968, Pavarotti returned to Italy and did not come back to the United States for three years. During those years he sang in *La Traviata* and *I Lombardi,* among other productions, at the Rome Opera; sang in *Un Ballo in Maschera* over Italian radio; and made recordings of *Beatrice di Tenda* (in which he sang Orombello) and *La Fille du Regiment* with Joan Sutherland on the London label. Later he recorded Calaf (a role he may never sing on stage) to Sutherland's Turandot, Riccardo in *Un Ballo in Maschera* and his accustomed roles in *Lucia di Lammermoor, Rigoletto,* and *Der Rosenkavalier* as well as the *Verdi Requiem* and several recital discs.

When Pavarotti returned to the Met as Rodolfo, Harold C. Schonberg of the *New York Times* (March 12, 1971) observed, "With the lyric sound comes a good deal of vocal heft, a perfectly equalized scale up to B (the G at the end of Act I was not as well managed), poise, and security. And faultless intonation too. . . . This is a suave voice of championship calibre . . . a golden-age voice."

lines, phrasing elegantly, coloring his songs in soft shades, charging them with more feeling and urgency for being restrained."

"His voice is not a big one, as tenors go," Robert T. Jones observed in *Time* (January 31, 1972), but it is brilliant from top to bottom and as perfectly focused as a laser beam. He phrases elegantly, attacks tones cleanly." And in *Life* (April 7, 1972) Joan Downs wrote: "His voice is absolutely unclouded, he can sing with subtlety or fire, and that high C is securely followed by a full D, eliminating most competitors in a world where high notes are a man's stock in trade. Caruso fans compare him to Caruso, Gigli fans link him with Gigli, and he reminds some of Bjoerling." Others are reminded of big, ebullient Leo Slezak, and Pavarotti himself in one interview said that he felt closest to Giuseppe Di Stefano. In another interview he asserted, without mentioning Franco Corelli, that he considered Nicolai Gedda and Alfredo Kraus to be his only competitors in bel canto repertory. The roles he has staked out for himself in the future, as his voice darkens further, include, besides those in *Tosca* and *Il Trovatore,* the lead tenor parts in *Parisina d'Este* and William Tell and the title role in *Idomeneo* ("when I'm old").

Criticism of his acting notwithstanding, Pavarotti takes dramatic values seriously and handles dramatic roles more easily as he grows older. When he does stand rigid, it is usually because what he is singing—such as the string of high C's in *La Fille du Regiment*—would be impossible with motion. Some critics have also faulted Pavarotti for his "old-fashioned" style, especially his habit of stepping out of a role to acknowledge applause with boyish delight. Pavarotti's defense is, as he put it on one occasion, "When you're an Italian opera singer, you're an Italian opera singer."

Pavarotti told Milton Mayer in the *Esquire* interview that he never goes to opera because he then "suffers" more in empathy with the singers than he does when he is on stage himself, and also because he wants his own performances to be as spontaneous as possible, uninfluenced by the interpretations of others. For the latter reason he also does relatively little rehearsing, outside of his private memorizing and practising of roles, with the help of a tape recorder, which he takes to bed with him. Except when preparing for roles, he studies without a coach, for about six hours a day, with one half hour set aside for vocalizing. Normally a ten-and-a-half-hour sleeper, Pavarotti sleeps twelve hours on the night before a performance, and on the day of performance he controls his enormous appetite, taking a "light" meal (such as spaghetti with olive oil and steak and salad) at one o'clock in the afternoon. Following a performance he usually goes directly to his apartment or hotel room to take a hot bath and rest.

In the early 1980s, Pavarotti formed The Pavarotti International Voice Competition for young singers. He performed with the winners in 1982 in excerpts of *La bohème* and *L'elisir d'amore.* The second competition, in 1986, staged excerpts of *La bohème* and *Un ballo in maschera.* To celebrate the 25th anniversary of his career, he brought the winners of the competition to Italy for gala performances of La bohème in Modena and Genoa, and then to China where they staged performances of *La bohème* in Beijing (Peking). The third competition in 1989 again staged performances of *L'elisir d'amore* and *Un ballo in maschera.* The winners of the fifth competition accompanied Pavarotti in performances in Philadelphia in 1997.

In 1985, Pavarotti sang Radames at La Scala opposite Maria Chiara in a Luca Ronconi production conducted by Maazel, recorded on video. His performance of the aria "Celeste Aida" received a two-minute ovation on the opening night. He was reunited with Mirella Freni for the San Francisco Opera production of La bohème in 1988, also recorded on video. In 1992, La Scala saw Pavarotti in a new Zeffirelli production of *Don Carlos*, conducted by Riccardo Muti. Pavarotti's performance was heavily criticized by some observers and booed by parts of the audience.

Pavarotti became even better known throughout the world in 1990 when his rendition of the aria "Nessun Dorma" from Giacomo Puccini's Turandot was taken as the theme song of BBC's TV coverage of the 1990 FIFA World Cup in Italy. The aria achieved pop status and remained his trademark song. This was followed by the hugely successful Three Tenors concert, held on the eve of the World Cup final at the ancient Baths of Caracalla in Rome with fellow tenors Plácido Domingo and José Carreras and conductor Zubin Mehta, which became the biggest selling classical record of all time. Throughout the 1990s, Pavarotti appeared in many well-attended outdoor concerts, including his televised concert in London's Hyde Park, which drew a record attendance of 150,000. In June 1993, more than 500,000 listeners gathered for his free performance on the Great Lawn of New York's Central Park, while millions more around the world watched on television. The following September, in the shadow of the Eiffel Tower in Paris, he sang for an estimated crowd of 300,000. Following on from the original 1990 concert, the Three Tenors concerts were held during the Football World Cups: in Los Angeles in 1994, in Paris in 1998, and in Yokohama in 2002.

In 1995, Pavarotti's friends, the singer Lara Saint Paul (as Lara Cariaggi) and her husband showman Pier Quinto Cariaggi, who had produced and organized Pavarotti's 1990 FIFA World Cup Celebration Concert at the PalaTrussardi in Milan, produced and wrote the television documentary The Best is Yet to Come, an extensive biography about the life of Pavarotti.

On December 12, 1998, he became the first (and, to date, only) opera singer to perform on Saturday Night Live, singing alongside Vanessa L. Williams. He also sang with U2 in the band's 1995 song "Miss Sarajevo" and with Mercedes Sosa in a big concert at the Boca Juniors arena La Bombonera in Buenos Aires, Argentina, in 1999. In 1998, Pavarotti was presented with the Grammy Legend Award.

He received an enormous number of awards and honors, including Kennedy Center Honors in 2001. He also holds two Guinness World Records: one for receiving the most curtain calls (165) and another for the best-selling classical album (*In Concert* by the Three Tenors; the latter record is thus shared by fellow tenors Plácido Domingo and José Carreras).

In late 2003, he released his final compilation—and his first and only "crossover" album, *Ti Adoro*. Most of the 13 songs were written and produced by Michele Centonze, who had already helped produce the "Pavarotti & Friends" concerts between 1998 and 2000. The tenor described the album as a wedding gift to Nicoletta Mantovani. That same year he was made a Commander of Monaco's Order of Cultural Merit.

Pavarotti began his farewell tour in 2004, at the age of 69, performing one last time in old and new locations, after more than four decades on the stage. On March 13, 2004, Pavarotti gave his last performance in an opera at the New York Metropolitan Opera, for which he received a long standing ovation for his role as the painter Mario Cavaradossi in Giacomo Puccini's *Tosca*. On December 1, 2004, he announced a 40-city farewell tour. Pavarotti and his manager, Terri Robson, commissioned impresario Harvey Goldsmith to produce the Worldwide Farewell Tour. His last full-scale performance was at the end of a two-month Australasian tour in Taiwan in December 2005.

On February 10, 2006, Pavarotti sang "Nessun Dorma" at the Winter Olympics opening ceremony in Turin, Italy, at his final performance. In the last act of the opening ceremony, his performance received the longest and loudest ovation of the night from the international crowd. Leone Magiera, who directed the performance, revealed in his 2008 memoirs, Pavarotti Visto da Vicino, that the performance was prerecorded weeks earlier. "The orchestra pretended to play for the audience, I pretended to conduct and Luciano pretended to sing. The effect was wonderful," he wrote. Pavarotti's manager, Terri Robson, said that the tenor had turned the Winter Olympic Committee's invitation down several times because it would have been impossible to sing late at night in the subzero conditions of Turin in February. The committee eventually persuaded him to take part by prerecording the song.

He posthumously received the Italy-USA Foundation's America Award in 2013.

Personal Life

On December 13, 2003, Pavarotti married his former personal assistant, Nicoletta Mantovani (born 1969), with whom he already had a daughter, Alice. Alice's twin brother, Riccardo, was stillborn. Pavarotti had three other daughters by his first wife Adua, to whom he was married for 34 years: Lorenza, Cristina, and Giuliana.

Brown-eyed, black-haired Luciano Pavarotti is about six feet tall and weighs at least 300 pounds, according to most observers. The exuberant singer good-naturedly disputes the common estimate of his weight, without supplying any figure as the correct poundage. The food that he devours in large quantities—along with mineral water, Coca Cola, or, more rarely, wine—is usually cooked by himself. Outside of the culinary arts, his recreations are studying languages, watching old movies on television, playing the piano, visiting and entertaining friends, swimming, and playing tennis. He is extraordinarily agile for his size

Unspoiled by the success that brings him up to $5,000 a night, and not fitting the temperamental mold of his profession, Pavarotti has a warm manner and an easy smile, speaks without rancor of his rivals, dispenses kisses (to women) with his autograph, and likes to tell jokes of which tenors are the butt. "I must enjoy myself when I sing . . . ," he told Louis Snyder of the *Christian Science Monitor* (May 26, 1972), "If everything is lovingly done, everything will be all right." Verdi and Corelli are the composers with whom he feels the most affinity.

During his international "farewell tour", Pavarotti was diagnosed with pancreatic cancer in July 2006. The tenor fought back against the implications of this diagnosis, undergoing major abdominal surgery and making plans for the resumption and conclusion of his singing commitments. He died at his home in Modena on September 6, 2007.

FURTHER READING

Esquire 78:184+ N '72 por
Life 72:65+ Ap '72 pore
N Y *Post* p!5 Je 3 '72 pors
NY Times II p15+ F 13 '72 por
Opera N 33:30 D 21 '68 por
Sat R 1:46+ F 3 '73 pors
Wright, W., *Pavarotti: My World* (1995)

JEREMY PELT

Trumpeter

Born: Nov. 4, 1976; California
Primary Field: Jazz
Group Affiliation: Ensembles and big bands, including Frank Foster and Charles Mingus

INTRODUCTION

The veteran jazz critic Nat Hentoff has been quoted widely as writing for the Wall Street Journal, "It is the beat of Jeremy Pelt's heart that underscores the future of jazz." A sophisticated trumpet player from a young age, Pelt began performing in the famed Mingus Big Band in 1999, just a year after finishing college. He then made a name for himself in collaborations with such contemporary jazz stars as Roy Hargrove, Ravi Coltrane, Greg Osby, and Cassandra Wilson. In 2002 Pelt made his debut as a bandleader with his first solo album, Profile, *a collection of mostly original tunes that was hailed as a boundary-pushing entree into post-bop jazz. His third album,* Close to My Heart *(2003), featured Pelt's takes on jazz standards by masters including Duke Ellington and Charles Mingus, while his fourth,* Identity *(2005), showcased his continued experimentation, and his fifth,* Shock Value: Live at Smoke *(2007), showed his range, with an electric, rock-influenced sound. Pelt's most recent album,* November *(2008), has been hailed as representing another step in his progression as an artist. C. Michael Bailey wrote for the Web site* All About Jazz *(July 20, 2008) that the album is "a fully realized post-bop suite. . . . Pelt's compositions are all tightly angular and anxious, both probing and airy. His trumpet is tart and sweet, the tone very much his own." Pelt was named Rising Star on the Trumpet five years in a row by* Down Beat *magazine and was nominated as "best emerging jazz star" by the Jazz Journalists' Association in 2005.*

EARLY LIFE

Jeremy Pelt was born on November 4, 1976 in California. He began playing the trumpet in elementary school, focusing mainly on classical music. When he entered high school and found that his school lacked an orchestra, he joined the jazz band, whose director introduced him to the music he would grow to love. "That is kind of how the ball got rolling," Pelt told R. J. Deluke for the Albany, New York, *Times Union* (June 24, 2004). "I met my teacher, and he hipped me to jazz. Being the curious person that I was, I really wanted to investigate all the songs that we were playing, such as 'So What' and 'My Little Suede Shoes.'" At a time when most of his peers were listening to pop and hip-hop, Pelt immersed himself in the music of the trumpeters Miles Davis, Lee Morgan, and Freddie Hubbard.

Following his graduation from high school, Pelt attended the Berklee College of Music, in Boston, Massachusetts. In addition to loving jazz, he was an avid fan of film music. He and a trumpet playing friend "were big John Williams fans," he told Deluke, referring to the composer of music for *Star Wars, Raiders of the Lost Ark,* and many other movies. "Every film that came out, we would get the soundtrack and listen to it." Pelt studied jazz improvisation and film scoring while playing with various jazz groups around the Boston area. He graduated in 1998 with a B.A. in professional music.

LIFE'S WORK

Having made many valuable connections at Berklee, Pelt moved to New York City to take on the challenging task of becoming a full-time musician. "There weren't many places to play the kind of jazz that we wanted to play, which was loud and exciting," he told Deluke of his experiences in Boston. "A lot of gigs you would get as a student would be society gigs, or part of cover bands, stuff like that." Once in New York he served as a sideman in the bands of several older musicians he admired, including the drummers Lewis Nash and Louis Hayes and the bassist Lonnie Plaxico. He also earned a chair in the Ralph Peterson quintet, playing on the albums *The Art of War* (2001) and *Subliminal Seduction* (2002).

In addition to small ensembles, Pelt has played in several big bands, most notably those of Frank Foster and Charles Mingus (the latter of which performs and reinterprets the music of the bassist and composer Mingus under the direction of his widow, Sue). He first took an interest in the Mingus band when a friend who was a member, his fellow trumpeter Philip Harper, invited him to sit in on their sessions. "I'd be down there every week, like a little lap dog at the side of the stage, hungry to sit in and impress Sue Mingus, who would be in the back," he recalled to Deluke. "I met her a couple times; she'd add you to the list, but whether you'd get the call is another thing." Pelt did indeed receive a call from Mingus, joined the band in 1999, and was a featured soloist on their 2005 album, *I Am Three.* Pelt has also played at various times in bands led by Ravi Coltrane, Cassandra Wilson, and Greg Osby.

In search of more experience playing traditional jazz, Pelt performed in the band led by the Grammy Award–winning saxophonist Frank Foster, who had joined the Count Basie Orchestra in 1953 and, following Basie's death, led it from 1986 to 1995. "That's the foundation of my training right there," Pelt told David Adler for *Down Beat* (February 2003). "The Mingus band is fun, but it's raw, and you're not concentrating too much on reading. So when you play with a more traditional band ... it will kick your a**." Pelt has also played with the Village Vanguard Orchestra, the Duke Ellington Big Band, and the Roy Hargrove Big Band.

Pelt formed his own quintet and released his first album as a bandleader in 2002. Widely hailed as a promising debut, *Profile* featured mostly original songs composed and performed by Pelt on trumpet, with Robert Glasper on piano, Gerald Cannon on bass, Ralph Peterson on drums, and Jimmy Greene on tenor saxophone. "In addition to his formidable trumpet chops, Pelt displays a mature and engaging compositional voice," David Adler wrote for allmusic.com. "On 'Pieces of a Dream' and the bright bossa 'We Share a Moon,' he builds forms around unexpected rhythmic contours, pushing himself and the band well beyond the safe zone.... Cannon and Peterson, the session's veterans, provide a robust rhythmic engine without overshadowing Pelt's precocious musicianship."

Pelt's subsequent recordings exhibited a mastery that many critics found remarkable in such a young player. His sophomore album, *Insight* (2003), was heavily influenced by hard bop, a genre of jazz with a strong percussive element and blues influence. "I love that style so much …," Pelt wrote in the album's liner notes, as quoted by Chris Searle for the *Morning Star* (October 15, 2003), a British publication. "I'm always trying to figure out how to add to it and move forward." "There is nothing imitative or merely nostalgic about Pelt's playing," Searle wrote. "It draws on the achievements of the great Jazz Messenger horns like Lee Morgan or Freddie Hubbard, but creates a sound that is scintillatingly new.... A poignantly lyrical 'I Wish You Love' makes it seem that the mouthpiece is only brushing Pelt's lips, so soft and balladic is his sound. . . . A mesmerising version of Herbie Hancock's 'Madness' with curvaceous solos by [saxophonists Greene and Myron Walden] is another powerful track, building *Insight* as an hour of understanding that this genre still has many roads to travel."

Close to My Heart (2003) featured Pelt leading a somewhat expanded band that included cello, viola, violin, and guitar—in addition to the usual drums, bass, piano, and trumpet—in standards by masters including Mingus and Duke Ellington. Pelt's goal, as stated in the liner notes, was "to try and define a voice within my compositions, as well as establish a firm musical direction." "Pelt opens with a melody statement on Charles Mingus' 'Weird Nightmare' that does justice to the title and hews to the theme through a harmonically bold improvisation," Ted Panken wrote for *Down Beat* (January 2004). "Pelt sustains the mood of burnished daring through a session comprising less traveled compositions and romance-oriented standards that aren't in the fake books." Francis Davis, writing for the *Village Voice* (August 24, 2004), however, was more ambivalent. "Things go wrong right away with Charles Mingus's 'Weird Nightmare,' one of five tracks where a string quartet arranged by David O'Rourke enfolds Pelt and the first-call rhythm section of Mulgrew Miller, Peter Washington, and Lewis Nash in perfumed gauze," Davis complained. Still, he allowed that "Pelt bows to no one in speed or dexterity" and that he had "depth of emotion on ballads . . . to spare."

In 2004 Pelt took time off from recording to tour as part of the drummer Louis Hayes's band. He returned to the studio in 2005 to record *Identity,* which represented another major step in his musical evolution. With some of its tunes strongly influenced by Miles Davis and the 1970s jazz-rock fusion he pioneered, *Identity* was Pelt's first album to use electric instruments. "Featuring 10 original compositions by Pelt, the disc also showcases his growing confidence as an improviser and skill as a bandleader," Terry Perkins wrote for the *St. Louis Post-Dispatch* (March 8, 2007).

Identity continued themes that Pelt had begun exploring in 2004, around the time that the composer/trumpeter Dave Douglas invited Pelt to play a double bill with him at the jazz and avant-garde music venue Tonic, in New York. Pelt surprised Douglas by offering to play with a fusion influenced band he had put together, called Noise (later renamed Wired). "It was a shock when Jeremy told me what he wanted to do," Douglas recalled to Jennifer Odell for *Down Beat* (June 2007). "I see someone who's coming up playing traditional music of the 1940s, '50s and '60s and making a sharp turn." Despite his initial surprise, he welcomed Pelt's new band onto the bill. "Not only was I listening to Billie Holiday and Dinah Washington, but I also used to listen to Jimi Hendrix," Pelt explained to Odell. "I can listen to all of that and now it's like I have an opportunity to adapt all these influences to my own creation. So why not do it?"

That performance was the first of many for Noise. Pelt recorded a live album, *Shock Value: Live at Smoke,* featuring the band's set at the iconic Harlem jazz club of the title, in 2007. Audience reactions were mixed; though some embraced the new sound, others wanted Pelt to play more standards, such as those on *Close to My Heart.* "We were rocking out and they were just looking at me," he recalled to Odell. "You could tell they didn't appreciate it. They didn't like it one bit." Even so, critics and friends admired Pelt's spirit of adventure. "A lot of people have the perception that if you take a bold step, you're undoing everything you've done before," Douglas told Odell. "I don't see that happening to Jeremy. He wants to take a step forward." "For sure, a bit of it sounds like an exercise in style," Ben Ratliff wrote for the *New York Times* (October 28, 2007), "but there's art here too. The constant volume and droning resonance of the band drive the players to focus and intensify their work, to make it matter; everyone's playing, especially Mr. Pelt's, is wise and serious." *November* (2008) continued Pelt's negotiation between tradition and innovation. Nate Chinen wrote for the *New York Times* (July 20, 2008), *"November.* . . occasionally owes a surface debt to the music of Wayne Shorter, around 1965: the searching harmonies and streamlined pulse are there, as is Mr. Shorter's instrumental timbre, thanks to the tenor saxophonist J. D. Allen." Chinen also, though, emphasized the album's ability to evade "its own retro impulse." "Mr. Pelt plays brilliantly, with warmth and depth," Chinen wrote. "He makes each of his nine compositions feel like a personal discovery." Michael Bailey, in his assessment for allaboutjazz.com, drew an even more direct line between Pelt and his forebears: "In the same way that Roy Hargrove's *Earfood* (2008) updated Lee Morgan's *Cornbread* (1965), so Jeremy Pelt's *November* updates Miles Davis' *Miles Smiles* (1966). If creativity and art can be evaluated on both the vertical and horizontal, Morgan's and Davis' offerings represent horizontal progressions of the art of jazz into new areas, where Hargrove's and Pelt's are vertical elaborations of those previous collections."

In 2007 Pelt was asked to co-curate the Festival of New Trumpet Music, a not-for-profit event held yearly in New York City, showcasing the best up and-coming jazz trumpeters, and he was a curator and board member of the 2008 festival. He continues to play with a variety of groups, including Wired and several other, more traditional ensembles. "I look for anything that's a learning experience and a challenging experience," Pelt told Deluke. "I don't really like to deal with titles—'mainstream' and this and that." According to his Web site, his next album, *Men of Honor,* was to be released in January 2010.

Personal Life

Pelt lives in New York City.

Further Reading

(Albany, New York) *Times Union* P p24 June 24, 2004; *Down Beat* p26 Feb. 2003, p8 June 2007
peltjazz.com

Itzhak Perlman

Violinist

Born: August 31, 1945; Tel Aviv, Israel
Primary Field: Classical musician
Group Affiliation: American Tour

Introduction

Israel-born Itzhak Perlman has been widely acclaimed as the most gifted violinist of the younger generation. Although he has been crippled by polio since his early childhood, Perlman overcame his handicap and was a recognized performer in Israel before he entered his teens. Brought to the United States by Ed Sullivan at thirteen, he soon attained international success, and when he won the coveted Leventritt prize in 1964 his future was assured. Since then, Perlman has performed with all the major American symphony orchestras. His recital tours have taken him to every major city in the United States, and to Canada, South America, Europe, Israel, the Far East, and Australia. Among the many critics impressed by Perlman's technical facility, richness of tone, and individuality of style are Arthur Bloomfield o£ the San Francisco Examiner, *who finds "an inner warmth and wit about his music- making which rather reminds one of Kreisler," and Daniel Webster of the* Philadelphia Inquirer, *who believes that Perlman "breathes a new life into the violin recital."*

Early Life

Itzhak Perlman, the son of Chaim and Shoshana Perlman, was born on August 31, 1945 in Tel Aviv, where his father was a barber. His parents, both natives of Poland, met and married in Palestine, where they had immigrated in the mid-1930's. Perlman once said that he cannot remember a time when he did not want to play the violin. According to his mother, when Itzhak was three years old he heard a violin recital on the radio and immediately wanted to become a violinist. Soon he began to practice, first on a toy fiddle, and then on a standard-sized violin that his parents bought him second-hand for the equivalent of six dollars.

When Itzhak Perlman was four years and three months old, he was stricken with poliomyelitis, which left him permanently disabled. (He still walks with leg braces and crutches and plays the violin sitting down.) After a year's convalescence, during which he continued to practice the violin, Perlman enrolled in the Tel Aviv Academy of Music, where he studied under Madame Rivka Goldgart on a scholarship from the America-Israel Cultural Foundation. Within a few years he was appearing regularly with the Ramat-Gan Orchestra of Tel Aviv and the Broadcasting Orchestra in Jerusalem. He was only ten when he gave his first solo recital.

In 1958 Itzhak Perlman came to New York City for two highly successful guest appearances on the CBS-TV *Ed Sullivan Show*, during which he played Rimsky-Korsakov's *Flight of the Bumblebee* and abbreviated versions of the finale of the Mendelssohn violin concerto and Wieniawski's *Polonaise Brillante*. He decided to remain in New York, where he was soon joined by his parents. During his first year in the United States he toured twenty American and Canadian cities, under the sponsorship of the Zionist Organization of America, which also arranged for him to gain admission to the Juilliard School. While studying there, Perlman completed his secondary schooling under a special arrangement with the New York City board of education.

Aided by scholarships from Juilliard, from the Katherine Tuck Fund in Detroit, and from the America-Israel Cultural Foundation, Perlman spent five years in the preparatory division of the Juilliard School. He then entered its regular division, where he eventually earned a diploma. With the help of a Lado scholarship, he spent several summers at the Meadowmount School of Music in upstate New York. While studying at Juilliard, he concertized with the Youth Symphony of New York and the National Orchestral Association.

In an interview with Shirley Fleming for *High Fidelity* (November 1970) Perlman paid tribute to his teachers at Juilliard, Dorothy DeLay and Ivan Galamian. Miss DeLay he characterized as "the kind of teacher who doesn't tell you what to do but inspires you to tell her what you want to do." Galamian, according to Perlman, "has an approach to technique that works for ninety people out of a hundred" and "knows exactly what he wants" from a pupil and "what each one is capable of."

Life's Work

Performing Wieniawski's Violin Concerto No. 1 in F Sharp Minor, Perlman made his Carnegie Hall debut on March 5, 1963 in a National Orchestral Association concert conducted by John Barnett. Although the

Affiliation: American Tour

In the 1965-66 season Sol Hurok sent Perlman on his first major concert tour, covering thirty American cities from coast to coast. Donal Henahan, who saw him in Chicago, wrote in the Chicago *Daily News* (November 29, 1965): "It was possible to imagine that Itzhak Perlman was born with a violin protruding from his left clavicle and never had to learn to play it, any more than he had to learn to breathe." In February 1966 he appeared at Philharmonic Hall with the National Symphony under Howard Mitchell, in a performance of Karl Goldmark's Violin Concerto in A Minor. A few days later he captivated audiences at Toronto's Massey Hall, when he played Paganini and Prokofiev with the Toronto Symphony under Seiji Ozawa.

The highlight of Perlman's fifty-concert tour in 1966-67 was his performance in Honolulu of Stravinsky's rarely heard Violin Concerto, with the composer himself conducting. A critic for the Honolulu *Star-Bulletin* reported that there "followed a fantastic tableau, Stravinsky holding the hand of the youthful violinist, both beaming." In March 1967 Perlman collaborated with the Soviet cellist Mstislav Rostropovich at Carnegie Hall in a performance of the Brahms Concerto in A for Violin and Cello, in which, according to Howard Klein of the *New York Times* (March 8, 1967), Rostropovich dominated musically and technically, but with Perlman holding his own. That summer the peripatetic violinist performed at the Hollywood Bowl, the Merriweather Post Pavilion in Washington, D.C., the Ravinia Festival in Chicago, and the Berkshire Music Festival in Tanglewood, Massachusetts.

During the heavily booked season of 1967-68, Perlman gave recitals in Philadelphia, Los Angeles, Portland, Denver, Dallas, Pittsburgh, and in Kalamazoo, Michigan—where he replaced an ailing Nathan Milstein. He joined another former child prodigy conductor Lorin Maazel and the Philadelphia Orchestra at Carnegie Hall in Edouard Lalo's *Symphonie Espagnole* and then embarked on a tour that included Lisbon, Trieste, Naples, Perugia, London, Paris, Edinburgh, Copenhagen, the Hague, and Tel Aviv. At the opening concert of the fiftieth season of the *Orchestre de la Suisse Romande* in Geneva in October 1968, Perlman received a ten-minute ovation for his rendition of the *Tchaikovsky Violin Concerto,* which, to Franz Walter of the *Journal de Geneve,* was richly deserved. "It was an unforgettable experience . . . to make the acquaintance with this extraordinary young artist. He has demonic power and an impressive technique," Walter informed his readers.

performance received no press coverage because of a newspaper strike, he came to the attention of such violinists as Isaac Stern, Yehudi Menuhin, and Zino Francescatti. It was Stern who brought him into contact with the impresario Sol Hurok.

Perlman was the youngest of nineteen contenders in the twenty-third annual contest of the Edgar M. Leventritt Foundation, one of the most prestigious and demanding of international musical competitions. On April 21, 1964, at Carnegie Hall, he emerged in first place among the four finalists who performed before a distinguished panel of judges that included Isaac Stem, George Szell, Lukas Foss, Joseph Fuchs, and William Steinberg. In reviewing the performance for the New York *Herald Tribune* (April 22, 1964), William Bender cited the "warmth and individuality," the "big, rich tone," and the "faultless" intonation that Perlman displayed in selections from Tchaikovsky, Mozart, Bach, and Wieniawski. In addition to receiving the $1,000 Leventritt Memorial Award, Perlman was guaranteed solo appearances in 1964 and 1965 with the New York Philharmonic and the symphony orchestras of Cleveland, Detroit, Pittsburgh, Denver, Buffalo, and New Haven. He suffered a temporary setback when the 200-year-old Guamieri violin that he had borrowed from Juilliard's rare instrument collection for the competition was stolen in the accompanying hullabaloo. Although it turned up the next day in an Eighth Avenue pawnshop, where it had been pawned for $15, the publicity given the incident by the press distracted public attention from Perlman's achievement.

Soon after winning the Leventritt award, Perlman, now under Hurok's management, returned to the Ed Sullivan show for two appearances and performed Tchaikovsky's Violin Concerto with the National Symphony Orchestra in Washington, D.C. When he repeated the Tchaikovsky work that October at Carnegie Hall with the Israel National Youth Symphony, he "stole the show," according to William Bender of the New York *Herald Tribune* (October 12, 1964), who wrote: "His flow of pure, sweet tone is unceasing. His bow arm is unfailingly strong and steady, and the fingering . . . is dazzlingly swift and accurate. There is a joy and bounce to his playing that had old-timers . . . reaching back in their memories to the days of the youthful Heifetz to find a parallel."

In January 1965 Perlman visited Israel for the first time since 1958. He gave a series of eight concerts, climaxed by a performance of the Sibelius and Tchaikovsky concertos at Tel Aviv's Mann Auditorium that brought him a fifteen-minute ovation. As quoted in *Time* (January 15, 1965), the Israeli critic Michal Smoira wrote in the Tel Aviv newspaper *Haaretz*: "His ability and general knowledge of music are so superb . . . that his technique and manual ability are taken as a matter of course. . . . Perlman creates a tonal feeling which sings in the ear and shakes the soul."

Making his debut with the New York Philharmonic under William Steinberg at Philharmonic Hall in May 1965, Perlman received five curtain calls for what Robert Sherman of the *New York Times* (May 10, 1965) described as "a warm, captivating performance" of Max Bruch's Concerto for Violin and Orchestra in G Minor. In October 1965, at Carnegie Hall, he played the Sibelius Violin Concerto in D Minor with the visiting Detroit Symphony under Sixten Ehrling in a memorial concert honoring the late Adlai E. Stevenson. Reviewing Perlman's performance in the *New Yorker* (November 6, 1965) Winthrop Sargeant wrote: "There is . . . nothing in the whole field of violin playing that he cannot do. . . . I cannot remember when a first encounter with a violinist has made such an impression on me."

In April 1969 Perlman gave an interpretation of Paganini's Violin Concerto No. 1 in D at Philharmonic Hall. Two weeks later he gave a critically acclaimed concert in the Hunter College series, playing Beethoven's "Kreutzer" sonata along with works by Stravinsky, Paganini, Chopin, Ravel, and Jean Marie Leclair. In December he and the great young Russian pianist Vladimir Ashkenazy collaborated with impressive musical rapport when they appeared in a concert at the Grace Rainey Rogers Auditorium of the Metropolitan Museum of Art, featuring Bach and Shostakovich. Among Perlman's credits for 1970 were recitals at Toronto and Stratford, Ontario; a performance with conductor George Szell at Philharmonic Hall; and another Hunter College concert that included works by Faure, Bach, Bartbk, Paganini, and Sarasate.

Perlman's performances in 1971 included his playing of Dvorak's rarely performed Violin Concerto in concerts at Philharmonic Hall and Washington's Constitution Hall; a Philharmonic Hall presentation of Mozart, Beethoven, and Prokofiev sonatas with Ashkenazy; recitals at the Tanglewood and Wolf Trap summer festivals; and an interpretation of Alban Berg's Violin Concerto in a Philharmonic Hall concert conducted by Leonard Bernstein. In 1972 he returned to Hunter College for a program of Brahms, Ives, Paganini, Wieniawksi, and Tartini; concertized in England and Canada; and received a standing ovation after performing Mendelssohn's Violin Concerto with the Israel Philharmonic, conducted by Zubin Mehta, at the Kennedy Center Concert Hall in Washington, D.C.

With William Steinberg conducting the Pittsburgh Symphony Orchestra and David Bar-Illan at the piano, Perlman appeared at Carnegie Hall as soloist in an all-Mendelssohn concert in January 1973. Undisturbed by a telephoned threat against his life, in March of that year Perlman gave a memorable recital at New York's Museum of Modern Art. During the 1973-74 season he gave another Hunter College recital; appeared in New York with the Philadelphia and Baltimore orchestras; performed in two Carnegie Hall chamber music concerts with Isaac Stern; and went on a tour of the United States and Canada. The highlight of Perlman's 1974-75 season was his Carnegie Hall concert in on January 30, 1975, during which he played a new work, *Chiaroscuro*, which the composer, Robert Mann, wrote especially for him. Of that concert Donal Henahan wrote in the *New York Times* (February 1, 1975): "Perlman . . . now has taken the quantum leap into a tiny group of artists—the names of Rubinstein and Segovia come most quickly to mind—who make audiences fall deeply in love with them."

Performing on a $60,000 Stradivarius violin that he bought after a three-year search, Perlman now makes more than 100 concert appearances annually. To iron out the trouble spots that occasionally arise in his playing, he spends many hours practicing. He also devotes some of his time to private teaching. In recent years he has taken part in the Aspen Music Festival in Colorado. For the Angel, London, and RCA Victor labels he has recorded most of the standard works in the violin repertory, including the concertos of Bach, Paganini, Mendelssohn, Bartók, Wieniawski, and Sibelius. Perlman also appears on recordings with pianist Vladimir Ashkenazy, with Israeli violinist Pinchas Zukerman, and with the conductors Daniel Barenboim, Seiji Ozawa, Lawrence Foster, and André Previn. An Angel album of Scott Joplin rags, performed by Perlman and Previn, was released in 1975.

Although he has never been billed or marketed as a singer, he sang the role of' "Un carceriere" ("a jailer") on a 1981 EMI recording of Puccini's "Tosca." He had earlier sung the role in a 1980 Concert telecast as part of the Live from Lincoln Center series with Luciano Pavarotti as Cavaradossi and Zubin Mehta conducting the New York Philharmonic.

On July 5, 1986, he performed on the New York Philharmonic's tribute to the 100th anniversary of the Statue of Liberty, which was televised live on ABC Television in the United States. The orchestra, conducted by Zubin Mehta, performed in Central Park.

In 1987, he joined the Israel Philharmonic Orchestra (IPO) for their concerts in Warsaw and Budapest as well as other cities in Eastern bloc countries. He toured with the IPO in the spring of 1990 for its first-ever performance in the Soviet Union, with concerts in Moscow and Leningrad, and toured with the IPO again in 1994, performing in China and India.

In 2015 on a classical music program entitled The Chamber Music Society of Lincoln Center produced by WQXR in New York City, it was revealed that Perlman performed the violin solo on the 1989 Billy Joel song The Downeaster Alexa.

While primarily a solo artist, Perlman has performed with a number of other notable musicians, including Yo-Yo Ma, Jessye Norman, Isaac Stern, and Yuri Temirkanov at the 150th anniversary celebration of Tchaikovsky in Leningrad in December 1990. He has also performed (and recorded) with good friend and fellow Israeli violinist Pinchas Zukerman on numerous occasions over the years.

Personal Life

On January 5, 1967, in a ceremony at the America-Israel Culture House in New York City, Itzhak Perlman married Toby Lynn Friedlander, a native New Yorker, who is also a violinist and a Juilliard School graduate. They met in 1964 at a summer camp concert at which Perlman was performing. They live in New York City with their five children: Noah, Navah, Leora, Rami and Ariella. Perlman is a distant cousin of Canadian comic/TV personality Howie Mandel.

A short, huskily built man with blue eyes and curly dark hair, Perlman has an informal manner, an acute sense of humor, and what Donal Henahan once described as "a great, booming, bass-baritone laugh." A write for *High Fidelity* (March 1966) reported that during his first recording session for RCA Victor, Perlman gave "a very plausible imitation of Napoleon" and "invented a collection of excruciatingly bad puns on composers' names." He and his wife are both fond of spectator sports, especially basketball, and attend the games of the New York Knickerbockers whenever possible. Completely adjusted to his physical handicap, Perlman told Donal Henahan in the *New York Times* interview: "Nothing bothers me.... I'm never afraid of an audience. You have to a little bit of a ham to enjoy the audience, and I do."

Perlman has begun to conduct, first taking the post of principal guest conductor at the Detroit Symphony Orchestra. He served as music advisor to the Saint Louis Symphony Orchestra from 2002 to 2004. In November 2007, the Westchester Philharmonic announced the appointment of Perlman as artistic director and principal conductor. His first concert in these roles was on October 11, 2008, in an all-Beethoven program featuring pianist Leon Fleisher performing the Emperor Concerto.

US President Barack Obama presented the Presidential Medal of Freedom to Perlman on November 24, 2015 at the White House in Washington, DC.

Further Reading

Esquire 69:12+ Je '68 por
Hi Fi 20:MA6+ N '70 por
N Y Times II p15+ Mr 8 '70 por
Parade p30 S 10 '67 pors
Time 85:49 Ja 15'65 por
Fiddler to the World: The Inspiring Life of Itzhak Perlman, Ap '92

Katy Perry

Singer and songwriter

Born: October 25, 1984; Santa Barbara, California
Primary Field: Pop
Group Affiliation:

Introduction

Until her mid-teens the phenomenally successful pop singer/songwriter Katy Perry heard pop, rock and roll, and other secular music only by chance or on the sly, because her parents allowed her to listen only to gospel and other Christian songs. Perry started singing in a church choir at age nine, and when she entered her teens, she began to write faith-based songs herself. Determined to make it big in the music world, she quit school at fifteen and then, in Nashville, Tennessee, polished her skills in singing, songwriting, and playing the guitar. She recorded ten of her religious songs for a Christian label, which released them on an album just before her sixteenth birthday. Called Katy Hudson *(Perry's original name), the album attracted no notice, and Perry turned away from Christian themes in her songwriting. During the next half-dozen years, she teamed up with accomplished professionals while under contract with Def Jam and then with Columbia, but both labels dropped her without marketing any of her work. In 2007 she signed with the newly formed Capitol Music Group, and the next year the label released her album* One of the Boys. *By that time she had become an international sensation, thanks to her hit song "I Kissed a Girl," which reached the number-one spot on charts in twenty countries and earned Perry a Grammy Award nomination.*

Early Life

The second of the three children of Keith and Mary (Perry) Hudson, Perry was born Katheryn Elizabeth Hudson on October 25, 1984, in Santa Barbara, California. She adopted "Perry" as her surname after recording her first album, to prevent being confused with the actress Kate Hudson. Perry's sister, Angela, who is two years her senior, has sometimes assisted her on concert tours. Her brother, David, is three years her junior. Her father and mother have said that they were hippies during the 1960s. Before they became parents they rediscovered their Christian faith; after years as itinerant or storefront preachers, they founded the nondenominational Keith and Mary Hudson Ministries, based in Irvine, California. Their website, after noting that they are Katy Perry's parents, identifies Keith Hudson as an evangelist and "end-time messenger" for God. According to their posted itinerary, they preach widely in the United States and overseas; at some of their stops, Mary Hudson holds conferences designed specifically for women. The Hudsons have published two faith-centered books; a third is scheduled to appear in 2012.

During Perry's earliest years her parents were mostly on the road, and the family moved frequently; they later returned to Santa Barbara, where Perry attended Christian elementary and middle schools and Christian summer camps, among them a "surf camp where the kids prayed for big waves," Melena Ryzik wrote. According to Perry, the Bible was the only book her mother ever read aloud to her when she was a child, and her parents banned from their home most TV shows, all music videos, and virtually all recorded music except religious songs. Perry sometimes heard popular music at friends' houses, however, and according to Sheryl Garratt, writing for the *New York Post* (7 Dec. 2008), she "us[ed] a down comforter to seal up the cracks in her bedroom door-and muffle devil's music by the likes of Queen."

Freddie Mercury, Queen's lead vocalist, "became her idol," Garratt added, "and rock 'n' roll her mission." While Perry has remained a Christian-she was "born again" at thirteen and had the name "Jesus" tattooed on the inside of her left wrist at eighteen-she has described her beliefs as different from those she held as a child. "Though she says she doesn't take the Lord's name in vain, she regularly flouts many of the other commandments she grew up with," Melena Ryzik noted.

Interviewers have often asked Perry about her parents' reactions to her work, given the disparity between the messages of Christianity and Christian songs, on one hand, and Perry's song lyrics and decidedly immodest apparel and behavior, on the other. In a representative response Perry told Tamara Palmer for the Phoenix, Arizona, *Metromix* (27 Jan. 2009), "My family definitely are very supportive. I have pushed their envelope from the day I was born. I was always the kid at the dinner table who, if there was a line you shouldn't cross, I took a big leap over it. That kind of has always been me; there's never really been an edit button on my keyboard of life. And I guess my parents weren't ever so shocked when I was singing very frank or honest songs." Noting that her father has four tattoos that say "Jesus," she likened him to a "modern rock 'n' roll pastor." Keith Hudson told Colette M. Jenkins for the Akron, Ohio, *Beacon journal* (3 Sep. 2010), "Sometimes when you bring children up in a good environment, they want to try something different. We might not always agree with what they're doing, but they're still our children." He also said that Perry "has a great deal of notoriety, but she's still our daughter. We have a great relationship with her, we love her and pray for her and want the best for her."

When she was nine Perry became a choir girl at her parents' church. Around that time her sister began to take singing lessons, and "Katy insisted on joining in too," Leah Greenblatt wrote for *Entertainment Weekly* (1 Aug. 2008). By age thirteen she had become determined to pursue a career in music, and she started learning to play the guitar. After her freshman year at Dos Pueblos High School, a public school in Goleta, California, near Santa Barbara, she earned a General Equivalency Diploma (GED) and ended her formal education. "I left school because I knew who I was and what I wanted," she told Edna Gundersen for *USA Today* (19 Aug. 2010). She told Sheryl Garratt, "As much as I am cheeky and full of opinions, essentially I know what I'm doing. . . . I feel I've got a good head on my shoulders."

Her parents approved her decision to quit school, albeit with misgivings, and when she was fifteen, determined to launch her career, she began to travel frequently to Nashville, where her parents "had some connections in the gospel industry," she told Greenblatt. In Nashville she devoted many hours to improving her guitar playing, and with the help of veteran gospel musicians, she honed her songwriting skills. She landed a deal with a Christian music label called Red Hill Records, which released her first album, *Katy Hudson,* just before she turned sixteen. Its ten tracks, all with religious messages, included "Faith Won't Fail," whose refrain is, "He'll prevail / In the midst of all my trials and tribulations / And He'll prevail / In the midst of all my sin and temptations / He'll prevail / When I fail and He will pick me up / For time and time again my faith won't fail." Perry performed at a series of churches and other places to promote the album, but it received little attention and attracted few buyers. Described by Stefanie Cohen for the *New York Post* (15 Aug. 201 O) as "a collision of gospel sentiment and Alanis Morissette angst" and by the *New York Times* (16 June 2008) critic Jon Caramanica as "a moody, eclectic collection of Christian contemporary music," it soon disappeared, as did Red Hill, which went bankrupt at the end of 2001. One of the album's coproducers, Tommy Collier, told Cohen, "Katy was kind of a diamond in the rough. You could tell she was gonna be an expensive race car, but she didn't know how to drive it yet." Earlier in 2001 Perry (as Katy Hudson) had performed as an opening act for Phil Joel, a New Zealander, who was touring to promote his album *Watching Over You* in the United States.

Life's Work

With the aid of industry contacts, Perry met the music producer and songwriter Glen Ballard, who had collaborated with artists and groups including Michael Jackson, Van Halen, and Aerosmith and, perhaps most famously, had cowritten and produced Alanis Morissette's Grammy Award-winning album, *jagged Little Pill* (1995). "I was first impressed by [Perry's] musicality and taste," Ballard told Lisa Robinson for *Vanity Fair* (June 20Il), as quoted by Jeff Dedekker in the Regina, Saskatchewan, *Leader-Post* (27 June 2011). "The unusual way she played the guitar demonstrated that she was a seeker. Katy communicates fun and passion; her music sounds like a celebration but it's clearer to me that there's great intelligence behind it. Katy's emotional range and stylistic range are enormous." With her parents' reluctant permission, at seventeen Perry moved to Los Angeles, California, where for the next three years or so, she worked with Ballard and reinvented herself as a pop singer. After a string of rejections from record labels, Perry signed with Island Def Jam Records, but in 2005, for reasons never made public, Def Jam shelved the album she and Ballard had recorded, and soon afterward the label dropped Perry. One of her collaborations with Ballard, a song called "Simple," was included on the soundtrack for the film *The Sisterhood of the Traveling Pants* (2005).

Perry next signed with Columbia Records, which teamed her up with the Grammy-nominated writing and production group the Matrix (Lauren Christy, Graham Edwards, and Scott Spock), who had collaborated with musicians including Christina Aguilera, Avril Lavigne, Shakira, and Korn. Along with Adam Longlands, Perry provided vocals for a Matrix-produced rock album, but Columbia ended its association with her before the project was completed. In an interview with Monica Herrera for *Billboard* (31 July 2010), Perry compared her experiences with Def Jam and Columbia to "taking a kid to Disneyland and then making them wait outside. The people just wouldn't let me through · the gates-what could I do?" During that period Perry supplemented money she borrowed from her parents by securing a few jobs. One involved critiquing demo tapes for Taxi Music, an independent artist-and-repertoire (A&R) company based in Calabasas, California.

Perry got her big break in 2007, when a record industry publicist, Angelica Cob-Baehler, and an A&R executive, Chris Anokute, recommended her to Jason Flom, the chairman of the newly formed Capitol Music Group. Perry, having reclaimed the songs she had recorded for Def Jam and Columbia, now re-recorded them for Capitol with various producers under Flom's direction. In November 2007 Capitol released her debut single, "Ur So Gay," with an accompanying music video. Cowritten by Greg Wells, the song is about a "metrosexual" man (or such men in general); it starts with the lines "I hope you hang yourself with your H&M scarf *I* While jacking off listening to Mozart." Writing for the *New York Times* (7 Nov. 2010), Alex Hawgood described it as "a jab at image-conscious straight men that many critics said was homophobic." "Ur So Gay" failed to reach the Billboard Hot 100 chart, but it created a buzz on the Internet, and the superstar Madonna praised the song on Ryan Seacrest's morning radio show.

Perry attracted a huge amount of attention worldwide with her next single, "I Kissed a Girl," which was produced by Dr. Luke. It contains the lyrics "It's not what I'm used to / Just wanna try you on / I'm curious, for you, / Caught my attention / I kissed a girl / And I liked it / The taste of her cherry chapstick / I kissed a girl / Just to try it / I hope my boyfriend don't mind it / . . . / You're my experimental game / Just human nature." "I Kissed a Girl" was extremely popular: it sold more than four million digital downloads, and it held the number-one spot on the *Billboard* Hot 1 00 chart for seven consecutive weeks and reached the top spot on charts in more than twenty countries. It was also widely condemned, both by those who interpreted it as promoting homosexuality or bisexuality and those in the lesbian and gay community who found it offensive or "felt used" by Perry, as Barry Walters, a music critic for *Spin* and *Rolling Stone,* told Alex Haywood. "I Kissed a Girl" was the lead song on Perry's album *One of the Boys* (2008), which spawned two additional Top I 0 singles ("Hot N Cold" and "Waking Up in Vegas"). The album peaked at number nine on the Billboard 200 chart and has since sold more than seven million copies worldwide. "I Kissed a Girl" earned Perry a Grammy Award nomination for best female pop-vocal performance.

Affiliation: Top-Selling Pop Artists

With her next album, *Teenage Dream* (2010), which she made with A-list producers who had worked with artists including Beyonce, Rihanna, and Britney Spears, Perry became the first woman—and only the second person, after Michael Jackson—to see five songs in succession from the same disk land at the top of the Billboard 200 chart. Although most professional reviewers have not greeted her work enthusiastically, to date sales of Perry's singles have surpassed 50 million digital downloads, and in total *One of the Boys* and *Teenage Dream* have sold upwards of 14 million copies. As of mid- November 2011, Perry had earned more than two hundred nominations for music awards worldwide and won more than sixty. Her honors include a total of six awards (in 2009, 2010, and 2011) from the American Society of Composers, Authors, and Publishers (ASCAP), three People's Choice Awards, three MTV Europe Music Awards, three MTV Music Video Awards, a BMI Award, and a Brit Award.

Writing for the *New York Times* (19 Aug. 2010) around the time of *Teenage Dream's* release, Melena Ryzik noted that in gaining fame, Perry has followed the "modern pop star playbook," which calls for "relentless promotion, corporate crossover, brand development and cheeky over-the-top persona." Perry, Ryzik continued, has "proved adept at working those angles, making an unlikely turnaround from gospel singer to provocative starlet ... and pop-culture personality." During performances Perry typically changes into an array of flamboyant, one-of-a-kind outfits, and she has posed topless or scantily clad for *Esquire, Rolling Stone,* and other national magazines. She is also !mown for using profane language and for her "cheeky sense of humour," "strong, throaty voice," and "ear for anthemic hooks," Sheryl Garratt wrote for the London *Observer* (10 Aug. 2008). In the *New York Times* (20 June 2011), the music critic Jon Pareles described Perry as "a bubblegum pop act for a raunchy era: not uncommercially wholesome, intermittently crude with a wink."

Its popular success notwithstanding, the reactions of most music critics to *One of the Boys* were lukewarm or negative. In an assessment for the *New York Times* (16 June 2008), Jon Caramanica wrote that Perry's "ideas about gender and sexuality seem as situational as her highly amalgamated style. Hers is a neatly commodified kind of rebellion: looks from Dita von Teese, production by way of Britney Spears and Alanis Morissette, vocals à la Ashlee Simpson and Avril Lavigne." He also wrote, "Ms. Perry . . . has an easy way with melody and is best served by producers who give her room to emote. Dave Stewart (of Eurythmics) takes the helm on 'I'm Still Breathing,' a calm and certain obituary for a dead relationship. And 'Thinking of You,' produced by the underappreciated Butch Walker, is gently and compellingly angry." Alex Miller, the reviewer for the British weekly *NME* (ll Sep. 2008), gave *One of the Boys* three stars out of ten and warned readers, "If you've got even a passing interest in actually enjoying a record, don't buy this one." In a scathing review for the *All Music Guide,* Stephen Thomas Erlewine wrote, "Given [Perry's] long line of botched starts, maybe it makes sense that the twenty-four-year old trollop is singing with the desperation of a fading burlesque star twice her age, yet Perry's shameless pandering on *One of the Boys* is startling, particularly as it comes in the form of some ungodly hybrid of Alanis Morissette's caterwauling and the cold calculation of Britney Spears in her prime. . . . [Perry] sinks to crass, craven depths that turn *One of the Boys* into a grotesque emblem of all the wretched excesses of this decade."

Perry's "California Gurls," an electropop song made for her third studio album, reached the number-one spot on the *Billboard* Hot 100 singles chart within four weeks of its release, in May 2010, making it the fastest-rising single by a Capitol Records artist since Bobbie Gentry's "Ode to Billie Joe" in 1967. The song, in which the rapper Snoop Dogg joined Perry, spent seven consecutive weeks atop the Billboard Hot 100 chart; it has since sold more than five million digital downloads. "California Gurls" is the first track on *Teenage Dream,* which arrived in stores on August 24, 2010. *Teenage Dream* debuted at number one on the Billboard 200 chart and sold 192,000 copies in its first week; it has since sold more than seven million copies worldwide. The disk produced four additional number-one singles ('Teenage Dream," "Firework," "E.T." [with Kanye West], and "Last Friday Night [T.C.I.F]"), making Perry the first woman and only the second artist to have five number-one singles from the same album; Perry also became the first artist in the half-century history of the *Billboard* Hot I 00 chart to have at least one song remain in the Top 10 for a complete calendar year. She launched a worldwide tour in support of the album in February 2011.

In a review of *Teenage Dream* for the Brisbane, Australia, *Courier Mail,* Cameron Adams wrote, "There is some fine pop here," citing in particular "Teenage Dream, " "Firework," and "Not Like the Movies," but also complained, "For a smart woman, Katy Perry makes some seriously dumb pop songs. Her unavoidable No. 1 'California Gurls' kills brain cells upon impact . . . . Perry is an adequate if unremarkable pop star, but she knows to surround herself with the right crew to dumb things down to bring sales up." "Give Katy Perry credit: She knows how to make a song that will totally rule on radio . . . ," Chuck Arnold and Jessica Herndon wrote for *People* (6 Sep. 2010). "Hitmakers like Dr. Luke, Max Martin, Christopher Tricky' Stewart and Stargate ... help give *Teenage Dream* a youthful bounce and sheen on giddy pleasures like 'Peacock,' a strutting standout. But when things slow down and turn serious in the second half on dreary tunes like 'Who Am I Living For?' and 'E.T,' it's a rude awakening from all the fun." Greg Kot, the *Chicago Tribune* (22 Aug. 2010) reviewer, found little to like in *Teenage Dream* and gave it one star out of four. "Katy Perry seems like a likable enough goofball, the kind of diva whose flashy trash fashions and offbeat humor promise something more interesting than formula pop. But formula pop is exactly what she dishes out, . . . split between girls-gone-wild clichés and melodramatic power ballads. The Frankenstein-like productions . . . sap the music of personality, presence, surprise. Too often she sounds robotic, like a wind-up toy incapable of singing with any elegance or nuance. She either stutters for effect . . . or lands on the beats so emphatically . . . that it's almost comical. . . . Singing ability is not a prerequisite for making great pop music, but original ideas and inventive presentation are—and both are lacking."

In November 2012, Perry began work on her fourth album, *Prism.* Perry revealed to MTV during the 2013 MTV Video Music Awards that after periods of self-reflection, she "felt very prismatic," which inspired the album's name. "Roar" was released as the lead single from *Prism* on August 10, 2013. It was promoted at the MTV Video Music Awards and reached number one on the *Billboard* Hot 100. "Unconditionally" was released as the second single from *Prism* on October 16, 2013, and peaked at number 14 in the United States.

Prism was released on October 18, 2013, and debuted at number one on the *Billboard* 200 chart. Four days later, Perry performed the songs from the album at the iHeartRadio Theater in Los Angeles. "Dark Horse" was released as the album's third single on December 17, 2013, and became her ninth number-one single on January 29, 2014. In 2014, "Birthday" and "This Is How We Do" followed as the album's fourth and fifth singles, and reached the top 25 on the Hot 100.

On November 23, 2014, the NFL announced that Perry would perform at the Super Bowl XLIX halftime show on February 1, 2015. Lenny Kravitz and Missy Elliott served as special guests for the show. Two days after the halftime show, the *Guinness World Records* announced that Perry's performance garnered 118.5 million viewers in the United States, and became the most watched and highest rated show in Super Bowl history. The viewership was higher than the game itself, which was viewed by an audience of 114.4 million.

The International Federation of the Phonographic Industry (IFPI) ranked her fifth on the list of Top Global Recording Artists of 2013. On June 26, 2014, she was declared the Top Certified Digital Artist Ever by the Recording Industry Association of America (RIAA) for certified sales of 72 million digital singles in the United States. On June 17, 2014, Perry announced that she had founded her own record label under Capitol Records, titled Metamorphosis Music. Ferras was the first artist to get signed to her label, and Perry served as an executive producer on his self-titled EP. She also recorded a duet with him on the EP, titled "Legends Never Die." She ranked seventh on the 2013 *Forbes* list for "Top-Earning Women in Music" with $39 million earned, and fifth on their 2014 list with $40 million. With earnings of $135 million, *Forbes* also ranked Perry number one on their 2015 "Top-Earning Women in Music" list as well as the "World's Highest-Paid Musicians" and declared her the highest earning female celebrity in 2015, placing her at number 3 on the *Forbes* Celebrity 100 list.

Throughout her career, Perry has won five American Music Awards, fourteen People's Choice Awards, and four Guinness World Records. Perry was declared the Top Global Female Recording Artist of 2013 by the International Federation of the Phonographic Industry (IFPI).

Personal Life

Perry's fashion often incorporates humor, bright colors, and food-related themes such as her trademark spinning peppermint swirl dress. *Vogue* described her as "never exactly one to shy away from the outrageous or the extreme in any realm," while *Glamour* named her the "queen of quirk."

Perry has supported various charitable organizations and causes during her career, especially organizations aimed at improving the lives and welfare of children. She has also supported organizations aimed at aiding people suffering with diseases including cancer and HIV/AIDS. The proceeds from Perry's single "Part of Me" were donated to the charity MusiCares, which helps musicians in times of need.

Further Reading

Cohen, Stefanie. "Katy-clysmic!" *New York Post*. NYP Holdings Inc., 15 Aug. 2010. Web. Jan. 2012.

Friedlander, Noam. *Katy Perry*. New York: Sterling, 2012.

"Katy Perry on Her Religious Childhood, Her Career, and Her Marriage to Russell Brand." *Vanity Fair*. Conde Nast Digital, 3 May 2011. Web. Jan. 2012.

"Katy Perry Talks Body Image, Fame and Politics in Rolling Stone Cover Story." *Rolling Stone*. Rolling Stone, 22 June 2011. Web. Jan. 2012.

Houston Person

Saxophonist; music producer

Born: Nov. 10, 1934; Florence, South Carolina
Primary Field: Jazz
Group Affiliation: Band leader and sideman

Introduction

In a career spanning more than 40 years, the tenor saxophonist Houston Person has played thousands of shows around the United States and been featured, ei-

ther as a leader or sideman, on more than 200 jazz albums. Person is often referred to as the heir to the soulful, big-toned sound championed by the saxophonist Gene Ammons, and while he is proficient in jazz styles ranging from acid to bop, he is best known for playing blues-tinged ballads. Person collaborated with the vocalist Etta Jones, who joined Person's band in the early 1970s, for more than 30 years, achieving what Samuel G. Freedman described in the New York Times *(May 5, 2002) as "perhaps the most productive such partnership in jazz history." His many albums include* My Romance *(1998),* Soft Lights *(1999), and* Sentimental Journey *(2003), each of which reached number one on the* Jazz Week *album chart. His album* Something in Common *(1990) won the Independent Jazz Record of the Year Award. In addition, Person has produced jazz albums for a number of leading performers, including two for Etta Jones,* Save Your Love for Me *(1980) and* My Buddy: Etta Jones Sings the Songs of Buddy Johnson *(1998), both of which were nominated for Grammy Awards. "[Jazz] is American and it's free," Person told* Current Biography *when asked about his love for the music. "You can listen to your own drummer in expressing yourself."*

Early Life

Houston Person was born in Florence, South Carolina, on November 10, 1934. Growing up in the racially segregated South taught him self-reliance. "In a backwards kind of way," he told Freedman, growing up in that difficult time "was beneficial, because it taught you that nothing was ever going to be handed to you." As a boy he studied piano; when he was 16 his father, who worked for the U.S. Department of Agriculture, bought him his first saxophone. "I loved jazz as a kid," he told Thomas Staudter for the *New York Times* (September 22, 2002), "especially the music of saxophonists like Lester Young and Illinois Jacquet. My brother Charles and I used to bring our records down to the local radio station for them to play." Person was also influenced in his youth by gospel and rhythm-and-blues music, both of which, according to Freedman, he learned how to play on his saxophone by "osmosis." In addition, Person's mother, an English teacher, required her son to listen to the New York Metropolitan Opera's Saturday-afternoon radio broadcasts.

In 1952 Person enrolled at South Carolina State College, in Orangeburg, where he was a member of the marching and jazz bands. He left the school three years later to join the United States Air Force and was stationed in Germany; there, along with fellow musicians Eddie Harris, Cedar Walton, Lanny Morgan, and Don Menza, all of whom went on to successful careers in jazz, he performed on weekends at a nightclub in Heidelberg. After being honorably discharged with the rank of corporal, in 1958, Person attended the classically oriented Hartt School of Music, in Hartford, Connecticut, where his classmates included the future recording star Dionne Warwick. He left the school in around 1961, without a degree.

Life's Work

From 1963 to 1966 Person was a member of the organist Johnny Hammond Smith's band and contributed to more than a half-dozen albums, including *Black Coffee* (1962), *Open House* (1963), and *Stinger(1965).* In the mid-1960s he formed his own band and signed with the Prestige record label. While recording with Smith and other performers, in particular the organist Don Patterson (a trend of the time found saxophonists frequently teaming with organists), Person began releasing his own albums, including *Chocomotive* (1967), *Blue Odyssey* (1968), and *Goodness!* (1969), which became Person's first hit record. As quoted on the Web site *artistdirect.com,* Michael Erlewine for *All Music Guide* called *Goodness!* "one of the best examples of Person's late-'60s/early-'70s style. Small organ combo with that funky sound. Perhaps too formulaic, but still nice."

According to Thomas Staudter, during the late 1960s Person developed into a "triple threat: a band leader; a musical director for Ms. Jones and a record producer for dozens of jazz notables." He has produced records by Freddy Cole, Charles Brown, Buck Hill, Dakota Staton, and Ernie Andrews, among others. "Houston has the kind of discipline and demeanor that helps him get the most out of the other musicians he works with," Joe Fields, . the head of HighNote Records, Person's label, told Staudter.

Among the albums Person released in the 1970s were *Person to Person* (1970), *Houston Express* (1971), *Sweet Buns and Barbeque* (1972), and *What It Is* (1974). In a review of *Person to Person* that appears on the Microsoft Network Web site, Richie Unterberger wrote for the *All Music Guide,* "The material gets a little close to pop at times . . . but Person's tone is always earthy (never more so than on Ray Charles' 'Drown in My Own Tears')." (*Person to Person* and *Houston Express* were combined on a single album and re-released

Affiliation: Etta Jones

In 1968, at a club in Washington, D.C., Person performed with Etta Jones for the first time. He did not enter their subsequent, longtime partnership by design. Speaking of how he and Jones came to play together so often, Person explained to Freedman, "If I'd get a gig, I'd ask [Jones], 'You want to go?' and she'd say, 'Yeah.' And it went along like that for a while. Then one day she heard from someone else that I had a gig and she said: 'You're not taking me along? Why don't you just take me on all the gigs?'" While Person produced their recordings, booked their engagements at clubs, worked on building their mailing list, and served as Jones's manager, the duo played as many as 200 dates a year for most of their 35 years together. Offering interpretations of others' music only, they often played at lesser-known clubs, such as the New Apartment Lounge, in Chicago, and Trumpets, in Montclair, New Jersey. Many of their fans were African-American. "We took our case to the people," Person told Freedman. "There's this idea that black people don't listen to jazz. Well, black people love jazz. It's a creation of black people. They love it when it has those elements of blues, swing, dancing. It's a music that's supposed to be a relief, that's supposed to be fun." Quoted by Freedman, Dan Morgenstern, director of the Institute of Jazz Studies at Rutgers University in Newark, New Jersey, said of Person and Jones, "What they did was classic. For a tenor sax and a lady singer, it was really one of a kind. Billie Holiday and Lester Young come to mind, but they worked together only episodically. Houston and Etta worked together so long and so consistently, they established a unique rapport. Every phrase, every gesture, they were attuned to each other." Daryl Sherman, a pianist and vocalist and sometime collaborator with Person, commented to Freedman, "When you have a horn player and singer, it's a conversation. And [Person and Jones] knew each other so well and knew their material so well that they could finish each other's sentences." Among the more than 20 albums they recorded together are *Etta Jones '75* (1975), *If You Could See Me Now* (1978), *The Heart and Soul of Etta Jones* (1985), *Sugar* (1990), and *At Last* (1993). In a review of *Sugar,* Mike Joyce wrote for the *Washington Post* (February 1, 1991), "It's another soulful, sensuous and sassy set of ballads and blues-old-fashioned, uncluttered and no doubt likely to win a mere fraction of the attention it deserves. As usual, Jones and Person make for a wonderfully expressive combination." Two albums produced by Person and featuring vocals by Jones, *Save Your Love for Me* (1980) and *My Buddy: Etta Jones Sings the Songs of Buddy Johnson* (1998), received Grammy Award nominations for best jazz vocal performance. (Person also played saxophone on those recordings.)

Regarding Jones's death from breast and lung cancer, in October 2001, Person told Freedman, "I've gotten my recognition. But I designed the group so that Etta and I shared half and half, and it hurts me that she didn't get what she deserved. She was out there for so many years. I would've liked to have seen her get a Grammy, get a write-up in the jazz periodicals." He said to Thomas Staudter, "We had a fun, wonderful run together. Etta really knew how to make an audience feel happy. She was full of swing, and we always liked the same qualities in music, which made it easy to work with her. She was down to earth, too, and had no ego. Etta simply loved good music and lived for it." (Contrary to some reports, Person and Jones were never married.)

as part of the *Legends of Acid Jazz* series, in 1976.) According to the jazz critic Gary Giddins, writing for the *Village Voice* (May 28, 2002), Person is "inspired throughout" his album *The Big Horn* (1976). "I have always admired Houston Person for his huge tone, bluff humor, and pointed obbligato," Giddins stated. ("Obbligato" refers to a melodic accompaniment to a solo or main melody.) Person's subsequent albums include *Heavy Juice* (1982), *Basics* (1987), *Why Not* (1990), which won an Indie Award from the Association for Independent Music, and *Horn to Horn* (1994). Released by HighNote Records, *My Romance* (1998), *Soft Lights* (1999), *In a Sentimental Mood* (2000), and *Blue Velvet* (2001) all x:eached number one on the Yellow Dog Jazz Chart (formerly known as the Gavin Jazz Chart), published by *JazzWeek,* an on-line magazine. *Dialogues,* which Person recorded with the eminent bassist Ron Carter, was released in April 2002. Freedman quoted Carter as having said of Person, "He knows the whole realm of jazz history." Speaking of Person's relatively low profile as a performer, Carter added, "If Houston Person is under the radar, then the radar is jammed."

Regarding Person's release *Sentimental Journey* (2003), in *All Music Guide,* as quoted on *artistdirect.com,* Scott Yanow called Person the "last in a tradition of tough-toned but warm tenors able to straddle the boundaries between soul-jazz, hard bop, and soulful R&B." Person, Yanow noted, is an "expert at caressing and uplifting melodies. . . . *Sentimental Journey* is a strong example of his talents." Another Person album, *Social Call,* also arrived in 2003.

In May 2002 Person and his quartet played a concert at St. Philip's Church, in the Harlem section of New York City. (In addition to Person, the group currently features Stan Hope on piano, Chip White on drums, and Nat Reeves on bass.) Describing the occasion, Freedman wrote, "For 25 songs over . . . three hours, Mr. Person and his quartet rendered the daytime nocturnal. He essayed standards from Ellington and Jobim, pushed the tempo into hard bop, brought calypso syncopation to 'I'll Remember April.' And when someone flipped off the fluorescent lights and Mr. Person played the opening bars of 'Since I Fell for You,' women clasped their hands, swayed their heads and softly sang along."

In addition to his recordings and performances as a band leader, Person has also been featured as a sideman on more than 100 albums, including Johnny Lytle's *Moonchild* (1962); Gene Ammons's *Boss Is Back* (1969); Tiny Grimes's *Profoundly Blue* (1973); Ran Blake's *Suffield Gothic* (1983); Cecil Brooks III's *Collective* (1989); Buck Hill's *Impulse* (1992); and Lena Horne's *We'll Be Together Again* (1994). In 1982 Person was honored with the prestigious Eubie Blake Jazz Award. Hartford County, Maryland, honored Person by declaring September 25, 1982 Houston Person/Etta Jones Day, and Washington, D.C., did the same on April 2, 1983.

Personal Life

Person was inducted into the South Carolina State College Hall of Fame in 1999. He lives with his wife, Rhona, in Croton Falls, New York. The couple have four daughters and one son.

Further Reading

artistdirect.com
jazzweek.com
New York Times II p1 May 5, 2002, with photos
XIV (Westchester) p10 Sep. 22, 2002, with photo
Village Voice p74 May 28, 200
Washington Post N p14 Feb. 1, 1991
yellowdogjazz
Kernfeld, Larry, ed. *New Grove Pictionary of Jazz,* 1988

Sam Phillips

Record producer; businessman

Born: Jan. 5, 1923; Florence, Alabama
Died: July 30, 2003; Memphis, Tennessee
Primary Field: Rock
Group Affiliation: Numerous recording artists, including Elvis Presley

Introduction

"Sam Phillips is not just one of the most important producers in rock history," Richie Unterberger wrote for the All-Music Guide *(on-line). "There's a good argument to be made that he is one of the most important figures in 20th-century American culture." In 1951 Phillips produced what has been called the first rock and roll song, Jackie Brenston's "Rocket 88." He also cut early records by such legends as B.B. King and Howlin' Wolf as well as other blues artists, retaining in those recordings a raw energy that no other producer at the time succeeded in capturing on vinyl.*

Early Life

Sam Phillips was born into a poor family on January 5, 1923 in Florence, Alabama. As a youngster he worked in the fields alongside African Americans and became familiar with spirituals and the blues. "Growing up, I loved black people," Phillips told Norm Shaw for *Blue-Speak* (June 1996, on-line). "I could listen to them sing forever. I heard a lot of words I could equate with. Sure I was young, but the bigger I got, the more I understood that I had been hearing this stuff all my life." He learned to play many instruments (most likely at school), ranging from the drums to the sousaphone, and with his unusual energy and determination, he dominated his high-school band. He also organized a smaller band, from members of the marching band, to play for the high school, and while serving as president of the 11th grade, he formed a choir. Outside school, by his own account, he learned a great deal about life from an elderly man known as Uncle Silas, who had been blinded by syphilis. The disdain that his close contact with African-Americans provoked in many of his white peers still angered him decades later. "Let me tell you, you cannot express to people how much the black man has meant to our culture," he told Shaw. "People just do not know the integrity of the people. I know what I have learned from black people. I have learned, man, that everyone is the same."

Sam Phillips.

LIFE'S WORK

Phillips quit school after the 11th grade and found work as a radio announcer and engineer. His first disc-jockey position was in Muscle Shoals, Alabama. In 1945, now married and a father, Phillips moved his family to Memphis, where he had landed a job as a disc jockey at radio station WREC. In addition to working there, in January 1950 Phillips opened his own studio, the Memphis Recording Studio—the first such facility in that city. He started to record blues artists and, to make ends meet, also recorded at private functions. "My conviction was the world was missing not having heard what I heard as a child," he told Bill Ellis for the Scripps Howard News Service, as reported in the *Naples* [Florida] *Daily News* (January 21, 2000, on-line). "And nobody was crazy enough to do what I did then with no money, just hard work. I was already working myself to death at the radio station and recording weddings and funerals and anything else. I don't feel I made any sacrifice. The only thing that frightened me was that I wanted to make sure that my children—Knox and Jerry, [wife] Becky and my momma didn't suffer from my malfeasance of thinking."

During the 1950s Phillips, who had been sleeping less than five hours a night while trying to work multiple jobs, endured two nervous breakdowns and underwent electric shock therapy. In addition, his failure to pay his income taxes on time led to difficulties with the Internal Revenue Service; reportedly, an agent who saw how ravaged he looked took pity on him and gave him more time to wipe out his debt to the IRS.

In 1951 Phillips quit his job as a disc jockey at WREC. At about the same time, frustrated by the repeated arguments over talent acquisition that he had had with executives at various record labels, he decided to try his hand again at launching a label of his own. In 1952 he started Sun Records, with the motto, "We record anything—anywhere, anytime." Unlike any other label then in business, Sun Records was staffed entirely by women. The label began working with local blues artists, mostly musicians who had never before had a chance to record. "Knowing how poor [the musicians] were and how poor I was, nobody did more in my opinion to help people in a certain way than I did, many ways psychologically, to make them feel they had achieved something in life," Phillips told Jackson Baker for the *Memphis Flyer* (June 8, 2000, online). "One thing I never did. I never slighted one person who came in there for an audition. Not one damn penny did they pay me before we signed a contract and had sessions." In 1953 Sun had its first national hit—"Bear Cat," by Rufus Thomas. (Sun would later lose a lawsuit that was filed to protest the record's similarity to another song.) Over the next couple of years, Sun produced high quality electric blues records, some of which became successful singles, by such bluesmen as James Cotton, Little Milton, and Junior Parker. The label also produced white country musicians, among them Douglas Poindexter.

In 1954 Phillips met Elvis Presley, then a shy teenager, who, according to various sources, was interested in either recording songs for his mother or making a vanity record for himself. Phillips arranged for Presley to cut a disk on July 5, 1954, with backing musicians who he thought would interact well with the young singer/guitarist. The session wasn't going particularly well until, during a break, Presley and the other musicians started jamming with Presley on the blues song "That's Alright, Mama." Excited by what he heard, Phillips told the musicians to keep working on that track. Presley ultimately recorded five singles for Sufi in the blues and country veins. "I was trying to find a white person ... who could sing with the same feeling [as a black person] but *not* try to copy these people," Phillips told Jackson Baker. "*That* would have been a joke. I honestly believe had we not done what we did with Elvis, or with somebody, and got that feel over and broke down a little bit of the wall or if somebody else hadn't done the same type of thing, I honestly feel that we would have still had segregation in music." In 1955 Presley recorded his first hit for Sun, "Baby Let's Play House," which reached number 10 on *Billboard's* country chart.

Toward the end of that year, in a well-known and—in retrospect—shortsighted business move, Phillips sold the contract of the still little-known Presley to RCA for $35,000 ($40,000, according to some sources), so as to keep his label afloat and sign new artists. "I sold Elvis for a reason and that was a legitimate deal," Phillips told Bill Ellis. "And that was done to help take [off] some of the burden put on my many years as an independent. [RCA] gave what then was an awful lot of money." Right after Phillips sold Presley's contract, Sun had its biggest hit up to that date, with Carl Perkins's "Blue Suede Shoes."

Throughout the rest of the 1950s, Phillips continued to record a roster of future rock greats. His decision to switch Sun's focus from blues to rock and roll drew some criticism, from, for example, the former Sun artist Rufus Thomas. Among others whom Sun recorded in the late 1950s were Jerry Lee Lewis, Roy Orbison, Johnny Cash, and Sonny Burgess. Toward the end of the decade, Phillips delegated more responsibility to other Sun producers so that he could spend more time on the business side of the label. Meanwhile, rock and roll was beginning to fade as a style, and Sun was unable to adapt to new forms of rock. Cash, Orbison, and Perkins left Sun for other labels (and future success); Jerry Lee Lewis stayed put, but his career ran into trouble due to scandal. Nevertheless, the label still had some life left in it. The country

Affiliation: Recording

During this period Phillips recorded pieces by B. B. King and Howlin' Wolf (Chester Burnett) and also produced Jackie Brenston's "Rocket 88," which several rock scholars have labeled the first rock and roll record ever cut. "If you had to do something too many times," Phillips said, "it could really get to where it didn't have the spontaneity. And anything that didn't sound spontaneous really was no good." Later in the 1950s, at his now legendary Sun Records studio, he recorded the first Elvis Presley singles and produced the work of such rock and roll luminaries as Jerry Lee Lewis and Roy Orbison. In addition, Sun produced several records by some of the best blues and country musicians of the day. After Phillips sold Sun, in the late 1960s, he built a successful career in real estate and as an investor in radio stations. The Sam Phillips Recording Service still operates in Memphis, Tennessee.

"A lot of artists had been kicked around. I hate to say this, but some of the independent labels, they just didn't do black folks right," he told Bill Ellis. "I'm not saying I'm an angel or anything. But there's nobody in this world that knew more about what they were feeling than me, because I had come through the Depression. I happen to have white skin and that made it better for me. And yet it was so damn bad. I couldn't believe that life could be this bad. And then I'd look around and see my black brothers and know they got what was left of the hog [while] we got the best part of the hog. And so I was equipped." Even on those early records, Phillips's production had a distinct style. He made the sounds of instruments more prominent on recordings than was common at the time and would even record fuzzy guitars. As a result, the blues songs he recorded were rawer, more energetic, and closer to the sound of live music than those produced elsewhere. After producing the disks, Phillips would license the masters to such labels as Chess and RPM. Toward the end of 1950, Phillips started his own record label with his friend Dewey Phillips (no relation), a disc jockey. Called Phillips, the label folded after only one release, "Gotta Let You Go," by the bluesman Joe Hill Louis.

singer Charlie Rich recorded some minor hits for Sun in the late 1950s and early 1960s; he left the label in 1964. In addition, Carl Mann made the singles charts with "Mona Lisa." Sun continued to release records in the 1960s, but more and more infrequently; by the middle of the decade, the label's operations were beginning to wind down. Phillips wasn't hurting, however, because he had begun investing in radio stations, real estate, and the Holiday Inn hotel chain. In 1969 he sold the entire Sun catalogue to Shelby Singleton. During its 16-year run, Sun had released 226 singles.

The red-bearded Phillips was said to look about 30 years younger than his real age. He was known as being down to earth, direct, and proud of his accomplishments but not arrogant. "God didn't make us perfect or He wouldn't have messed around with Adam and Eve and the apple," Phillips told Jackson Baker. "I am honest, and some things turn on the fact of what you believe honesty to be." His children now run the family studio—the Sam Phillips Recording Service—and a music-publishing company in Nashville.

Personal Life

A resident of Memphis, which he loved with a "religious fervor," in his words, Phillips late in his life spent most of his time working with the radio stations he owned in Alabama. "I'll never retire," he told an Associated Press reporter, as quoted in the *Jefferson City* [Missouri] *News Tribune* (July 13, 2000, on-line). "I'm just using up somebody else's oxygen if I retire." In 1986 he was inducted into the Rock 'n' Roll Hall of Fame. In 1997 the University of Mississippi gave him the title of honorary professor of southern studies. "I'm happy we were able to contribute, at least in my opinion, to what music has done, and is continuing to do, as one of the greatest ambassadors we have, both for nations around the world and racial desegregation," Phillips told Gary Graff for *Elvis World News* (June 17, 2000, on-line). "We now get to hear R&B and don't worry whether it's white or black. I feel like we made a hell of a contribution."

Sam Phillips died on July 30, 2003 in Memphis, Tennessee of respiratory failure. He was survived by his wife, his two sons, two granddaughters and a great-grandson. At the time of his death, the Sun Records studio was named a National Historic Landmark.

Further Reading

All Music Guide (on-line)
Bluespeak (on-line)
Naples [Florida) *Daily News* (on-line) Jan. 21, 2000
Newsweek p54+ Aug. 18, 1997
Rolling Stone p53+ Feb. 13, 1986, with photos

Phish

Musical group

Jon Fishman
Drummer
Born: Feb. 19, 1965; Syracuse, New York

Mike Gordon
Bassist
Born: June 3, 1965; Sudbury, Massachusetts

Page McConnell
Keyboardist
Born: May 17, 1963; Basking Ridge, New Jersey -

Trey Anastasio
Songwriter; guitarist
Born: Sep. 30, 1964; Princeton, New Jersey

Primary Field: Improvisational rock
Group Affiliation: Phish

Introduction

"Given their sense of community, their ambition and their challenging, generous performances, Phish have become the most important band of the Nineties," Matt Hendrickson wrote for Rolling Stone *(October 1, 1998). Three members of Phish—Trey Anastasio, Jon Fishman, and Mike Gordon—have played together since about 1983; the fourth current member, Page McConnell, joined them two years later. The band's upbeat and sometimes humorous works have earned it many comparisons to the Grateful Dead, who for decades toured the United States playing improvisational rock music. Like the Grateful Dead, Phish has attracted a large*

number of fans who have embraced hippie lifestyles and spend their free time following the band.

Early Lives

Trey Anastasio was born Ernest Giuseppe Anastasio III on September 30, 1964 in Princeton, New Jersey. He met his future songwriting partner, Tom Marshall, while both were attending Princeton Day School. During his adolescent years Anastasio helped his mother, Diane Anastasio, write songs for children's records. Among the ones that he still plays are "Golgi Apparatus" (recorded for the Phish album *Junta)* and "Makisupa Policeman," written when he was 12 years old. As a teenager Anastasio played guitar with the Princeton-based bands Space Antelope and Falling Rock. After graduating from high school, he enrolled at the University of Vermont, in Burlington. He and another student at the school, the drummer Jon Fishman (born on February 19, 1965 in Syracuse, New York), heard each other practicing through dormitory walls and began playing music together. They were soon joined by a third undergraduate, the guitarist Jeff Holdsworth, and then a fourth, the bassist Mike Gordon (born Michael Elliot Gordon on June 3, 1965 in Sudbury, Massachusetts), whom they recruited through an ad. (Gordon's father, Robert Gordon, founded the mini-mart chain Store 24.)

The four instrumentalists shared a love for improvised music, including Frank Zappa's and the Grateful Dead's songs as well as jazz. The band's first off-campus show took place in 1983, at a Reserve Officers Training Corps (ROTC) dance, at which disapproving audience members attempted to drown out the band by turning up the volume on a recording of Michael Jackson's hit record *Thriller.*

Lives' Work

Phish began securing frequent dates at the Burlington bar Nectar's, and the members put together their first demo recordings. "Had we not come from Burlington we wouldn't have made it as a band," Anastasio told Steve Rosenfeld for the *Burlington Times* (March 9, 1992), as quoted on the *Phish Archive;* "there would have been pressure to play other kinds of music, to do certain kinds of gigs. Also, in Burlington there *are* all these musical influences. There are so many good players." For brief periods around this time, the percussionist Marc Daubert and, occasionally, a flamboyant vocalist named Steve Pollak, who called himself the Dude of Life, performed with the band; the Dude of Life continued to collaborate with the group sporadically over the years. Meanwhile, Phish performed at nearby colleges, offering mostly obscure jazz and blues songs by other artists.

During the fall semester in 1984, the University of Vermont notified Anastasio that he would be suspended the following semester, as punishment for stealing human body parts from the school's anatomy lab as a practical joke. (Some sources reported that the suspension took effect at the beginning of the 1986 spring term.) After he left Vermont Anastasio returned to Princeton, where he resumed his friendship with Tom Marshall. The two worked on new music that later reappeared on the first official Phish cassette release, *The White Tape* (1986). In 1985 the band played at the Goddard College Springfest, in Plainfield, Vermont, an event organized by Page McConnell. (McConnell, born on May 17, 1963 in Basking Ridge, New Jersey, is the son of Mary Ellen McConnell and Jack B. McConnell, the latter of whom, a physician, helped to develop the medication Tylenol, among other major accomplishments.) Page McConnell persuaded the group to take him on as a keyboardist. Influenced by such jazz pianists as Fats Waller, Art Tatum, and Thelonious Monk, McConnell brought a jazzier edge to the band. Not long after his arrival, Holdsworth quit, for reasons connected with his becoming a born-again Christian, according to various sources.

In the fall of 1986, Anastasio and Fishman transferred to Goddard College. While there Anastasio studied in his free time with an off-campus composer named Ernie Stiles. "At his best, Trey was writing music beyond the level of what we could play, and we all became better players trying to learn it," Fishman recalled to Will Dana for *Rolling Stone* (July 19, 2001). For his senior thesis Anastasio wrote and recorded *The Man Who Stepped into Yesterday,* a concept album about the protagonist's attempts to free the imaginary land of Gamehenge from the rule of an evil king. Although *The Man Who Stepped into Yesterday* is not considered an official Phish album, the band has often included songs from it in its live shows and has occasionally played the entire work live.

In 1988, at a cost of about $5,000, Phish made *Junta,* an album recognized as its first; they sold the recording, which was available only as a cassette, at concerts. "We didn't want to be dependent on record companies or any outside force," Anastasio told Jon Pareles for the *New York Times* (December 8, 2002). Junta features

Affiliation: Improvisational Rock

Adopting a practice of many Grateful Dead aficionados, many Phish enthusiasts tape each Phish performance they attend and trade copies of their tapes; since every show is markedly different from all previous ones, the tapes are prized. Thanks to their many devotees, Phish has drawn as many as 135,000 ticket buyers to a single show, even though the band has never had a Top 40 single, and none of its dozen albums has been outstandingly successful commercially.

Despite that success, some music critics have complained that Phish's recorded music as too "safe"—that is, lacking in the spontaneity and risk-taking that characterize their live performances. During their concerts, the band draws from an array of musical genres including bluegrass, progressive rock, jazz, and country, switching from one style to another with ease. Phish is also renowned for its improvisational jams, in which a piece four or five minutes in length on one of their recordings may continue for as long as an hour on stage. Illustrating its members' creative and musical abilities, Phish has even played a lengthy improvisational jam based on the theme music for National Public Radio's news program *All Things Considered.* While jamming, members of the band often engage in such antics as jumping on trampolines, roller blading on stage, or "playing" vacuum cleaners or other household appliances. Phish is famous for its psychedelic light show as well; indeed, many consider the group's lighting director, Chris Kuroda, a member of the band. "We treat people who come to our shows exactly like we do each other," Anastasio told Tim Perlich for the *Philadelphia In*quirer (December 12, 1992), as printed on the *Phish Archive* (on-line). "We like to think they have the same musical standards that we do. We just love playing live and we focus so much of our energy into putting on a show and trying to make every show unique by playing different songs, improvising and allowing spontaneous things to happen. I think people respond to that."

several 10- to 12-minute jam pieces along with shorter works, such as "Dinner and a Movie," whose lyrics consist of one line: "Let's go out to dinner and see a movie." At about this time the members of the band quit their day jobs, to devote themselves to touring and other Phish-related activities. In 1989, after a successful stint the year before at the Paradise Theater in Boston, Massachusetts, the group embarked on its first tour outside New England. Playing throughout the southeastern U.S., Phish became known for clowning and wearing wild attire. Fishman, for example, would occasionally appear on stage naked or wearing bizarre outfits, while Anastasio and Gordon would sometimes play solos while jumping on trampolines. Occasionally each of the band members throws a colored beach ball into the audience and then lets the movements of the ball dictate the song's pitch and tempo. In the fall of 1990, Phish released its second album, *Lawn Boy,* on the Absolute A-Go-Go label, a subsidiary of the independent label Rough Trade. With fewer long jams than Junta, the record contains primarily studio versions of the band's best—Phish produces "mostly nonsense," Moon wrote that the band's music "revolves around changes in texture and color rarely found in arena-level rock." Consistently selling out 15,000- to 20,000-seat venues, Phish became the most successful jam band in the U.S; after the disbanding of the Grateful Dead, in the wake of the death of that group's singer and guitarist, Jerry Garcia, in August 1995.

In early 1996 Anastasio released his first non-Phish recording, *Surrender to the Air,* whose sound some critics compared to that of the free-jazz musician Sun Ra's work. In the fall of that year, Phish returned with *Billy Breathes,* produced by Steve Lillywhite and recorded in a studio constructed in a converted barn in Bearsville, New York. Featuring upbeat, concise pop songs, *Billy Breathes* received better reviews than any Phish album up to that date and charted at number seven on the *Billboard* album list; the single "Free" received heavy airplay on mainstream rock radio stations. In his review for *Entertainment Weekly* (October 18, 1996), David Browne noted that on *Billy Breathes,* "pianos and guitars glisten like sundrenched streams, and each song averages only one solo instead of the usual two or four." According to Bob Gully in *Spin* (October 15, 1996, on-line), "This album finally hits the perfect middle ground between the band's loopy explorations and their blooming pop craft." "I've always known that we could make a great album," Anastasio told Neil Strauss for the *New York Times* (October 17, 1996). "We just weren't focused on records over the years, because we were so focused on playing live, almost to an absurd degree. When I was writing songs, I was writing for the show. I would think, 'I wish we had a song that I could throw in two-thirds of the way through the second set that had a piano solo.' Then at the end of the tour, we'd go in and record an album with songs like that." Anastasio also noted that "by taking time off from touring and going into this barn up in the woods and telling everyone to leave us alone, we could reinvent ourselves and kind of rediscover a lot of interpersonal things." In the summer of 1996, Phish organized a two-day concert, called the Clifford Ball, at an abandoned air-force base in Plattsburgh, New York. About 135,000 people attended the show.

Phish's second live album, *Slip, Stitch & Pass* (1997), recorded in Germany, received mixed reviews, but the band's popularity continued unabated. Some 70,000 fans attended a concert in the small town of Limestone, Maine, that year. In 1998 Phish released *Story of the Ghost,* a studio album that features the radio hit "Birds of a Feather" and, like *Billy Breathes,* offers shorter pieces rather than epic jams. Described by Michael Gallucci in *All Music Guide* (on-line) as "their most commercially accessible offering," it reached number eight on the *Billboard* album chart. Gallucci also felt that "despite some good songs ... *The Story of the Ghost* is occasionally sloppy, a bit smug and often quite boring." Johnny Black, in the British magazine *Q* (October 2000, on-line), by contrast, praised the album; in it, he wrote, Phish "display not just a gorgeous blend of voices in tight arrangements punctuated by cartwheeling instrumental improvisations, but a surprising ability to knock off three-minute pop goodies with aplomb." Greg Kot agreed, writing for *Rolling Stone* (October 29, 1998, on-line), "Phish exploit their subtlety like never before, with airy, uncluttered grooves and relaxed vocals that sound as if they were delivered between catnaps." Phish next released *Hampton Comes Alive* (1999), a six-disc box set that contains four full live sets recorded over two nights. In the *All Music Guide* (on-line), Stephen Thomas Eriewine hailed the recording as "the fullest representation of the band yet available. . . . The group's eclecticism, stretched to a full-length running time, becomes stunning, since it all seems seamless." On New Year's Eve 1999, at the Big Cypress Indian Reservation, in the Florida Everglades, in front of approximately 80,000 people, Phish held what many believe to be the longest concert in recorded history. The show continued for nine hours and 32 minutes.

Phish's album *Farmhouse* (2000) was one of their most critically acclaimed. Recorded in Anastasio's converted barn near Burlington, Vermont, the album features the single "Heavy Things," which received a fair amount of radio exposure. In a review for *Q* (October 2000, on-line), David Henderson wrote that the material was "full of warmth, depth and simple beauty. Still with all [Phish's] trademark twists, this is understated, riddled with melody and gloriously uplifting." Dan Aquilante, in the *New York Post* (May 16, 2000), characterized *Farmhouse* as "the most lovable collection of goodtime tunes the band has ever gathered for a single disc. This is a great album of modern country rock that closes the artistic gap between the Vermont band and San Francisco's defunct Dead.... There isn't a bad song on *Farmhouse.* The disc is pleasing to the ear and soothing to the soul. This is an album that will spur interest in the band well outside of its giant cult community." In a dissenting opinion, Jon Pareles wrote for *Rolling Stone* (May 25, 2000, on-line), "There's a thin line between mellow and torpid, and Phish repose on that line all too calmly on *Farmhouse."* The band's tours during the summer of 2000 included two unannounced appearances with the rap-metal star Kid Rock.

There soon followed the surprising announcement that Phish would take a break from touring for an undetermined period starting after its October 8, 2000 show. Reasons for the planned sabbatical included members' exhaustion after years on the road and their desire to have more time with their families. For his part, Anastasio told Will Dana, "I was starting to feel in the last couple of years that I was spending more time dealing with the personnel crises of the enormous organization we had made than writing music. There are forty people working in the office, and people want to have lunch, because, you know, there's a problem known live songs up to that time, among them "Bouncing Around the Room" and "Split Open and Melt." *"Lawn Boy* stands as one of the '90s' most underrated albums," Ben French wrote for *Nude As the News* (July 14, 1997, on-line), adding that it was "loaded with bombastic ingenuity" and was unusually "ambitious" and "difficult."

During the summer of 1991, Phish toured the U.S. and also recorded its third album, *A Picture of Nectar* (named for Nectar Rorris, the owner of Nectar's). That August the Rough Trade label folded, and Phish signed with Elektra Records. The band's major-label debut, *A Picture of Nectar* was released in February 1992 and became a hit in New England, in terms of number of records sold. In the *All Music Guide* (on-line), Stephen Thomas Eriewine described it as Phish's "best and most accomplished album," noting that it "incorporates a remarkable mixture of styles, from country, jazz, and calypso to straight-up rock & roll. Lyrically, the band's trademark goofiness is intact, but the playing is more muscular and Trey Anastasio's arrangements have increased intensity and focus. In fact, it's a surprisingly tight record for a band that built their reputation on endless concert jams." Phish broadened its fan base with a busy national tour in the summer of 1992; in addition, the band played a handful of shows in the first HORDE Festival (the acronym stands for Horizons of Rock Developing Everywhere), opened for the legendary musical group Santana at several concerts, and played their first European tour.

Phish's fourth album, *Rift* (1993), was its first to be produced by someone outside the band-in this case Barry Beckett, who had produced for Aretha Franklin, Bob Dylan, and Dire Straits. Each song on *Rift* represents a different dream during one man's night of sleep. Moodier than previous Phish records, Rift also consists of more tightly constructed songs and less experimentation with different styles. For those reasons, it disappointed many fans and critics; on the other hand, it reached number 51on *Billboard's* Top 200 album chart, and the single "Fast Enough for You" received some radio airplay. Stephen Thomas Erlewine, in a review for the *All Music Guide* (on-line), complained that *Rift* "doesn't live up to the surprising, adventurous music on *Nectar.* Instead, most of the album sounds like an uninspired retread, as the band tries to fashion their songs into a loose concept album. The concentration on thematic unity tends to rob Phish of the loose spontaneity that makes them unique and makes *Rift* a bland, tedious listen." "I always look back at *Rift* with a lot of dismay because it was a really fertile time for us—the music was just pouring out—but I think we were so excited about this conceptual thing that we kind of beat it into the ground," Anastasio told Alan Paul for *Guitar World* (December 1996, on-line). "It could have been great, but we tried to cram every idea we had into it. As a result, it's largely unlistenable." During its subsequent tour the band began to perform in larger venues, before crowds of up to 15,000; to make sure that fans could still tape the shows, Phish reserved seats with especially good acoustics for ticket buyers who planned to make recordings.

In an interview with Liane Hansen for National Public Radio's *Weekend Edition* (October 23, 1994), as quoted on the *Phish Archive* (on-line), Anastasio referred to the taping of their shows by fans as "the key to [the band's] existence . . . because the live show has always been so much a part of what we do, so much a focus of our energy.... Before we ever even signed with a major label, we were touring the whole country . . . and there was no records available of Phish at all. It was purely through tapes being traded and word of mouth, so it's always been a real underground phenomena, and the taping has been such a big part of it . . . It keeps you on your toes. You can't do the same show twice. . . . You can't tell the same joke twice. You can't do anything twice, 'cause everybody knows."

In 1994 Phish released both *Crimes of the Mind* and *Hoist,* the latter of which features the single "Down with Disease," for which the band made its first and only video. Produced by Paul Fox, *Hoist* sold better than any previous Phish album, climbing to number 34 on the *Billboard* album chart. The disc was more upbeat and varied than *Rift.* In the *Hartford Courant* (March 31, 1994), John M. Moran wrote that the record "demonstrates that Phish is . . . finally bringing its musical vision into line with its considerable instrumental talents. Guitarist and lead singer Trey Anastasio, who co-wrote 10 of the 11 cuts on the album, is in particularly fine form. His songwriting skills are sharper than ever, his guitar work shines and his vocals reach new levels of expressiveness." "We were definitely out to make this one more accessible," McConnell told Steve Morse for the *Boston Globe* (March 27, 1994). "Our previous albums had their good and bad sides, but none of us spent much time listening to them. We wanted to make one we might really like to listen to." Also in 1994 Phish launched its Halloween-show tradition of performing every song on an album by another artist or group. The band closed the year with an appearance on the *David Letterman Show* and its first performance at the 20,000-seat arena Madison Square Garden, in New York City. Notwithstanding some Phish members' criticism of their first live album, *A Live One,* the double-disc recording rose to number 18 on the *Billboard* album chart and received positive reviews.

For many music critics and others, hearing *A Live One* provided the first clues to Phish's popularity. In *Rolling Stone* (August 24, 1995, on-line), Tom Moon called the record "the definitive statement of the jam-band aesthetic," and described the album's 12 selections as "precision minded and crisply executed, notable for their elaborate tension-building schemes and chamber-group division of labor, in which the roles of soloist and accompanist are fluid." While he warned that "until the solos start," with their salary, or someone asks, 'How come I'm not involved in this decision-making process like I was when you were a smaller band?' I always feel, because of my role in this thing, a kind of responsibility. I want everybody to be happy." Anastasio also told Ana that a lot of the material in *Farmhouse* had come from his own solo work or was not of recent vintage. "I didn't want to do another album like that," he told Ana, "because at that point it's not even Phish anymore." Anastasio recalled to Jon Pareles that after the band's last show, the members met backstage and talked about "this grand experiment. What if we now left and had as many musical experiences as we could? Musicians improve by playing with musicians who are better than them. So we would all leave our little cocoon. And the only way we could be sure that this experiment was to work was to have no definite plan for coming back. As soon as we had a plan, then no one would really fully embrace their other projects. That being said, I think we all pretty much knew we were going to come back."

The hiatus did not apply to the release of archival recordings. In November 2000 Elektra released *The Siket Disc* (named for the recording engineer John Siket), which contains improvisational material from the recording sessions that produced *Story of the Ghost.* The year 2000 also saw the release of the filmmaker Todd Phillips's documentary *Bittersweet Motel,* which shows scenes from Phish's 1997 tour. Also during this period, Anastasio released *Trampled by Lambs and Pecked by the Doves* (2000), a collection of demos recorded in 1997 that featured most of the material on *Story of the Ghost* and *Farmhouse* (albeit in a different form). In addition, he formed the band Oysterhead with the bassist Les Claypool of Primus and Stewart Copeland, the former drummer of the Police, with the intention of playing just one gig at the New Orleans Jazz and Heritage Festival in May 2000. Pleased by the experience of playing together, the three recorded an album, *The Grand Pecking Order* (2001). In the *All Music Guide,* Steve Bekkala wrote of that work, "Over the span of 13 tracks, the trio succeeds admirably at finding the common ground between their seemingly disparate styles.... The musicians seem to be carefully listening and playing off of one another at all times-and enjoying themselves doing so. This dedication injects electricity into the instrumental interplay and keeps the songs fresh and lively." Anastasio, Claypool, and Copeland toured together to promote the Oysterhead recording. In the spring of 2002, Anastasio released an eponymous solo album, which consists primarily of structured compositions. Like *The Grand Pecking Order,* it advanced to *Billboard's* Top 50 albums. Anastasio also spent several months transcribing the Phish song "Guyute" for orchestra; the Vermont Youth Orchestra performed the piece in February 2001.

During this period two other members of Phish—Jon Fishman and Page McConnell—contributed to 2002 debut albums, each named for the band that made it: Fishman with his side project Pork Tornado, a group that specializes in a mixture of jazz, blues, and funk, and McConnell with a newly formed ensemble, Vida Blue, which joins jam-band textures with electronica influences. Mike Gordon directed a film on bass playing and bassists, Rising *Low,* which won the Audience Award at the SXSW (South by Southwest) Festival. Gordon and McConnell performed for Gov't Mule's *The Deep End, Volume One* (2001), which, like Rising *Low,* was a tribute to Gov't Mule's bassist Allen Woody, who had died the year before.

In 2002 and 2003 Phish released a total of 20 live albums (each containing three or four CDs), sold separately but considered a set. In December 2002 Phish's jam-oriented studio album *Round Room,* a collection of five extended pieces, made its appearance. Speaking of *Round Room,* Anastasio told Jon Pareles, "It's just the four of us in the Barn, ripping it up. We hadn't played together in a long time. We weren't tight. But we decided that that was more exciting than having it be 'right.' If we stop perfecting it, then it sounds like Phish." The record struck Stephen Thomas Erlewine, writing for the *All Music Guide,* as "ramshackle, laid-back and haphazard.... What's weird is that there's very little shape to the songs. Often, only a bare sketch of a song is discernable, and even those are never played as if that sketch is final." Tom Moon, by contrast, wrote in his review for *Rolling Stone* (January 3, 2003, online), "Virtually everything on these seventy-eight minutes breathes with an anxious, edge-of-the-seat intensity that's missing from their previous studio efforts. Phish on record may never approach the energy of their live shows. But on *Round Room,* they're doing more than jabbering and jamming-they're sounding happy to be working together, and that allows them to reach truly new places."

Phish performed together for nearly 20 years before going on hiatus in August 2004. They reunited in March 2009 for a series of three concerts played in the Hampton Coliseum in Hampton, Virginia, and have since resumed performing regularly.

Phish's fourteenth album, *Joy*, produced by Steve Lillywhite, was released September 2009. The band announced a "save-the-date" for a three-day festival on October 30 & 31 and November 1. Phish.com contained an animated map of the United States, and individual states were slowly removed from the map, leaving California. Confirming several rumors, the band announced that Festival 8 would take place in Indio, California.

In June 2012, Phish headlined Bonnaroo 2012 with the Red Hot Chili Peppers and Radiohead. Phish also performed for the first time ever a show in Oklahoma at the Zoo Amphitheater in August. For the fourth consecutive year, Phish has performed a set of sold-out New Year's shows at New York City's Madison Square Garden, which culminated with a three-set show to ring in 2013. Phish went back on tour in the summer of 2013 to celebrate their 30th-year anniversary. The band released a new album, *Fuego,* in 2014.

Personal Lives

All the members of Phish live near Burlington, Vermont. Anastasio, Fishman, and McConnell are married; Anastasio has two daughters, Fishman one. In 1997 the members of Phish formed the Waterwheel Foundation, which gives grants to Vermont-based charitable organizations that focus on environmental concerns, social issues, or the arts. The Vermont-based company Ben & Jerry's Homemade honored Phish by naming an ice cream for them: Phish Food, which contains fish-shaped chunks of chocolate. "I know I will never ever be in a situation like Phish again," Fishman told Pareles. "Not in terms of success or making money, but the productivity, the discipline, the inter-band relationships, the considerateness, the way it fits into all our lives. Everything must end, but if it ends when my life does, so be it, and if it ends before that, it'll really be a sad day."

Further Reading

Boston Globe C p5 Mar. 27, 1994
Down Beat p49 Feb. 1999, with photo, p12 June 2000, with photos
Guitar World (on-line) Dec. 1996
New York Times C p5 Oct. 17, 1996, II p33 Dec. 8, 2002
Phish Archive (on-line)
Rolling Stone p20+ Oct. 1, 1998, p33+ July 19, 2001
Yankee p54+ July/Aug. 2001, with photos
The Phish Book, Phish, Villard Sept. 15, 1999
Phish: The Biography, Puterbaugh, P. Da Capo Press Oct. 26, 2010

John Popper

Harmonica player, singer, songwriter

Born: March 29, 1967; Cleveland, Ohio
Primary Field: Blues
Group Affiliation: Blues Traveler

Introduction

The singer, songwriter, and world-class harmonica player John Popper is the front man of the jam band Blues Traveler, which he formed in the late 1980s. The group had its mainstream breakthrough in 1995, with the Grammy Award-winning single "Run-Around," which spent nearly a full year on the charts. Although Blues Traveler's success was periodically slowed by Popper's health issues—which included injuries sustained in a serious auto accident, an angioplasty, and gastric-bypass surgery—as well as by the death in 1999 of its bass player, the group has enjoyed a consistently loyal following and has released critically acclaimed albums including Travelers & Thieves *(1991),* Save His Soul *(1993),* Four *(1994),* Live from the Fall *(1996),* Straight on Till Morning *(1997),* Bridge *(2001),* Truth Be Told *(2003), and* Bastardos! *(2005). Popper recently formed a side group, John Popper and the Duskray Troubadours, which he conceived, according to a band press release, as a "scrappy, roots-rock alter ego of Blues Traveler."*

Early Life

John Popper was born on March 29, 1967, in Cleveland, Ohio. His father, Robert, was a native of Hungary who immigrated to the United States in the 1950s to escape his birth country's Communist regime. Popper, who studied the piano, guitar, and cello before settling on the harmonica, is reportedly related to David Popper (1843–1913), a noteworthy cellist and composer. When

Popper was young his family moved to the East Coast, eventually settling in Princeton, New Jersey. While attending Princeton High School, Popper met the drummer Brendan Hill, and they began performing as a duo, mimicking the John Bel us hi/ Dan Aykroyd act known as the Blues Brothers. "I actually got into the blues because of the [1980 film] Blues Brothers, because what I really wanted to be was a comedian, just like John Belushi," Popper told Alan Niester for the Toronto, Ontario, *Globe and Mail* (9 July 1997). "That led me to Paul Butterfield, and that led to me to the old blues guys, and that led me to Jimi Hendrix. When I heard Hendrix, I knew I wanted to be a musician." (Years later Popper had a cameo in the 1998 Blues Brothers sequel.)

Life's Work

Shortly after Popper graduated from high school, in 1986, he and Hill—along with the guitarist Chan Kinchla and the bassist Bobby Sheehan—formed Blues Traveler. The four moved to New York City, and Popper enrolled at the New School for Social Research. There, he told Niester, "the school band was jazz-oriented, it was a very big bebop school. They used to let me do the solos. Sure, rock 'n' roll was my vocabulary, but there's definitely a big bebop influence [in my harmonica playing]." Attending classes by day, Popper played local clubs with his bandmates at night. They quickly earned a reputation for lengthy improvisational shows that put them "at the forefront of an emerging movement of rootsy jam bands, a vibrant community that also produced Phish and the Spin Doctors," according to the band's website. Popper told Steve Hochman for the *Los Angeles Times* (20 Sep. 1991), "Here's our shtick line to describe our music: It's our garage band attempt at our appreciation of jazz improvisation through the reality of rock 'n' roll. Rock has its own vocabulary, but you can approach it with freedom."

Fans began following Blues Traveler from venue to venue. "They're bored, and I think they're fans of real music," Popper told Hochman. "I keep getting surprised everywhere we go how many there are." The band was signed by A&M Records in 1989, and Popper left the New School without earning his degree. An eponymous debut album was released in 1990 and included eleven original songs, all written or cowritten by Popper. "Blues Traveler's *loose* jam structures on basic blues riffs mark them as a band in the tradition of such predecessors as the Grateful Dead," William Ruhlman wrote in a review of the recording for the *All Music Guide* website. "Unlike that communal effort, however, this group has a distinct focal point in virtuoso harmonica player and vocalist John Popper." In 1991 the band's sophomore effort, *Travelers & Thieves,* made an appearance on the Billboard 200 chart. Blues Traveler toured relentlessly, playing some 250 shows that year. "We've always been predominantly a live band," Popper told Scott Brodeur for *Billboard* (25 Jan. 1992). "Our studio albums are nice tries, but the live shows just totally blow them away." In the summer of 1992, when the band was three weeks into the recording of its third studio album, Popper crashed his motorcycle on the way to the studio, near New Orleans, Louisiana. Riding an estimated 70 miles per hour, he broke his arm and shattered his leg. After he recovered the band resumed recording and touring, with Popper playing some shows in a wheelchair for a while.

That year Blues Traveler helped found the Horizons of Rock Developing Everywhere (H.O.R.D.E.) music festival, which also featured such bands as the Spin Doctors, Phish, and Widespread Panic. The festival became a popular annual event and was mounted until 1998. "Forget Woodstock: The '90s version of a Generational Celebration has gone mobile," Gina Arnold wrote about the phenomenon for the *San Francisco Chronicle* (1 Sep. 1995). "Judging by the number of traveling multi-act bills crossing the nation this summer, musical fun in the summer sun is also clean, well-organized, streamlined and financially successful—in short, everything Woodstock wasn't." Arnold continued, "Now in its fourth season, the 23-date H.O.R.D.E. tour is outselling Lollapalooza. Unlike the latter, which aims at 15- to 25-year-old alterna-youth, H.O.R.D.E.—dubbed 'Hippiepalooza' by industry insiders—is meant to appeal to a cross-section of fans, particularly those with a penchant for '70s-sounding, Southern white, blues-rock jamming."

Blues Traveler released the album *Save His Soul* in 1993, followed by *Four* (1994), the recording that brought the band its first mainstream success. Thanks in large part to the infectious song "Run-Around," which spent forty-nine straight weeks on the singles chart, the album peaked at number eight on the Billboard 200, marking the first time a Blues Traveler album had made it into the-top ten. The album ultimately sold more than six million copies, and the single earned Popper and his cohorts a Grammy Award for best rock vocal performance by a group or duo. In 1995 Popper played a small role in an episode of the popular sitcom *Roseanne,* and the following year Blues Traveler recorded the theme song that was played during the show's final season (1996-97). Reportedly hoping to ensure their fan base that the hit single, Grammy Award, and TV exposure had not altered their core values, the band next released *Live from the Fall* (1996), a double-disk live recording filled with lengthy jams.

Straight on Till Morning (1997), the group's next studio effort, was generally well received and reached number 11 on the album chart. In a review for the Newark, New Jersey, *Star-Ledger* (6 July 1997), Jay Lustig called the recording "positively infectious" and wrote, "Blues Traveler has gone in a more accessible direction, with Popper singing from the heart." In his review for the *All Music Guide* website, Stephen Thomas Erlewine wrote, "The commercial success of Four was a mixed blessing for Blues Traveler. It did give them a wider audience, but it also put them in the delicate position of pleasing their new, hook-happy fans while retaining their hardcore, jam-oriented cult following. They skillfully manage to do just that on *Straight on Till Morning,* the bluesy, ambitious follow-up to *Four.*" He continued, "On the whole, *Straight on Till Morning* is a tougher album than any of its predecessors, boasting a gritty sound and several full-on jams. But the key to the album is its length and its sprawling collection of songs, which find Blues Traveler trying anything from country-rock to jangling pop/rock. They manage to be simultaneously succinct and eclectic, and they occasionally throw in a good pop hook or two. Blues Traveler are still too loose to be a true pop/ rock band . . . but *Straight on Till Morning* is the first studio record that captures the essence of the band." Popper told Alan Niester, "On *Four,* I was very much aware of the fact that nobody had really heard me play harmonica before, and that was a kind of gimmick factor in my mind. So I was playing in a sort of 'Hey, look at me, look what I can do' mode. On this album *[Straight on Till Morning],* I didn't have to worry about that. I could play more melodically. 1 didn't have to show my chops off."

While on vacation in Hawaii in May 1999, Popper, who then weighed more than 400 pounds, felt crushing chest pain. He subsequently underwent an angioplasty to clear an artery that had been almost completely blocked. He spent the next few months recuperating and completing a solo album, *Zygote* (I999). While the album received little attention from anyone _ other than Blues Traveler's core fans, in a review for the *All Music Guide* website, Stephen Thomas Erlewine praised the "supple singing, elongated phrasing, affection for blues-rock, and astounding harmonica playing" and opined that *Zygote* "make[s] the case that Popper is a worthwhile solo artist in his own right."

On August 20, 1999, Bobby Sheehan was found dead of a drug overdose. Chan Kinchla's younger brother Tad joined the group to play bass in his stead, and a fifth member, the keyboardist Ben Wilson, was subsequently added. While working on a new studio album, the reconfigured group made available for download on its website a four-song EP, *Decisions of the Sky—A Traveler's Tale of Sun and Storm.*

In 2000 Popper had gastric-bypass surgery. By the time Blues Traveler's next studio album, *Bridge* (2001), was released, he had lost more than 100 pounds. The new album divided critics. A reviewer for *Entertainment Weekly* (1 June 200 I), for example, wrote, "What's always lifted [the group] above their peers are Popper's percussive harmonica and those wonderfully melodic songs—both of which are abundant here," while a contributor to the music website *SonicNet* asserted, "On *Bridge,* they're still traveling down the long and winding improvisational road, with most of the tracks averaging around five minutes in length. . . . This time out, though, the songs feel like they're twice that."

After releasing another live album, *Live: What You and I Have Been Through,* in 2002, the group returned to the studio to record *Truth Be Told* (2003). In a review for the *Baltimore Sun* (24 July 2003), Rashod D. Ollison wrote, "The musicianship throughout is tighter than a pickle jar lid, more focused than on previous efforts." Eric Ward, reviewing *Truth Be Told* for *Glide Magazine* (25 Aug. 2003), wrote, "It's easy to claim that life on the road, long tours and some struggling years together give a band some legitimacy, but when you've endured well over a decade that included a severe motorcycle accident, major surgery, creating your own touring festival, a Grammy, a founding member's death and over 10 million in album sales, you've pretty much seen it all. Though with a skewed line-up that for now seems solidified, the Blues Traveler story is apparently far from over." Ward continued, "*Truth Be Told* is Blues Traveler finally back to business, pushing forward rather than merely looking back. . . . [It's] vintage Blues Traveler, complete with self-disclosing lyrics, fiery harmonica, powerful solos and those Popper ballads that never fail to evoke emotion. Still far from a throwback, and miles from the repetitive- beat-bandwagon most [music groups] have succumbed to, it's the album you hoped they'd make once everything they've been through eventually settled down."

Bastardos! (2005) met with similar praise. Stephen Thomas Erlewine wrote for the *All Music Guide* website, "What makes it one of their best [albums] is how the band stretches from psychedelia to soulful pop and back toward their signature blues-rock, writing sturdy songs all the while. It's strong on a song-by-song basis, particularly since each track is sonically distinct, but all the moods complement each other, resulting in an album that might not be the most representative Blues Traveler album (although it isn't all that far removed from their trademark sound, either), but is certainly the richest, most diverse album they've ever done, and quite arguably their best."

In 2006 Popper released *The John Popper Project,* a collaborative effort that featured DJ Logic (a Bronx-born turntable artist), Tad Kinchla, and several other guest artists. "Forget everything you ever knew about John Popper and Blues Traveler. This is no jam band but they can play some," Thom Jurek wrote for the *All Music Guide.* "This is one steamy, groove-laden set that offers a view of Popper as not just a harmonica master who can play dozens of them through more effects that you can shake a speaker at, but as a serious funk and futuristic R&B vocalist."

In 2007 Blues Traveler recorded *Cover Yourself,* on which they reinterpreted or rearranged several songs in their catalog, including "Run-Around." They followed that with *North Hollywood Shootout* (2008), which received generally lukewarm reviews. Writing for *Slant Magazine* (24 Aug. 2008), Jonathan Keefe called it a "slightly over-reaching attempt at reclaiming some of their former commercial relevance," and Andrew Leahey, in a review for *Paste Magazine* (29 Aug. 2008), wrote that the album "lacks the cohesion of Blues Traveler's previous work." Most reviewers were particularly perplexed by a track that featured the actor Bruce Willis performing a rambling monologue, "a move that is either unexpectedly awesome or sadly misguided," Leahey wrote.

Popper's latest recording, *John Popper & the Duskray Troubadours* (2011), is the result of a side project separate from Blues Traveler. The Troubadours include the bassist Steve Lindsay, the drummer Mark Clark, the guitarists Kevin Trainor and Aaron Beavers, and the multi-instrumentalist Jono Manson, who also engineered and produced the recording. Stewart Oksenhorn wrote for the *Aspen (Colorado) Times Weekly* (6 Mar. 2011) that the new band is providing a chance for Popper, whom he described as a "superhuman musician [who takes] the harmonica places nobody could have imagined," to take artistic chances. Still, he wrote, "the Duskray Troubadours are not a huge gamble. For one thing, the group has already recorded a self-titled album that was released this past week. *John Popper and the Duskray Troubadours* is 12 songs that are a step away from Blues Traveler material—mellower, more focused on the songs and less so on the harmonica and guitar solos. And Popper's principal partner in the band, Jono Manson, is hardly an unknown quantity [in the music world]."

Personal Life

An avid collector of firearms, Popper owns a reproduction of an 1858 cannon. Because the law prohibits him from firing actual cannon balls, he has been known to use it to launch cans of dog food up to one thousand yards. "If you ever see a guy with dog food in the trees, he probably owns a cannon," he quipped to Jeff Spevak for the *Rochester (New York) Democrat and Chronicle* (28Apr. 2011).

In 2007 Popper, who had been arrested four years earlier for marijuana possession, was stopped while speeding in his SUV in Washington State. Police found several handguns and rifles, a set of brass knuckles, and a Taser, as well as a small quantity of marijuana. Because he had permits for the firearms and agreed to surrender the brass knuckles and Taser, he was charged only with drug possession.

Popper, who is unmarried, generally identifies himself as a libertarian, although he rarely expresses political opinions in his music. "All you do, when you talk about politics, is alienate people," he told Spevak. "The stuff I write about is beyond that. It's beyond people's opinions. I try to look for a basic idea that we can all relate to. Love being good, hearts being broken. I'm a uniter."

Further Reading

Oksenhorn, Stewart. "John Popper Brings Duskray Troubadours to Aspen." *Aspen Times Weekly.* Aspen Times, 6 Mar. 2011. Web. Jan. 2012.

Ollison, Rashod D. "Blues Traveler Has Survived the Perils of Rock." *Baltimore Sun.* Baltimore Sun, 24 July 2003. Web. Jan. 2012.

Sessa, Sam. "Odd Pairing Clicks." *Baltimore Sun.* Baltimore Sun, 19 Oct. 2006. Web. Jan. 2012.

Ward, Eric. "Blues Traveler: *Truth Be Told.*" *Glide Magazine.* Glide Publishing LLC, 25 Aug. 2003. Web. Jan. 2012.

Elvis (Aron) Presley

Singer, actor

Born: January 8, 1935; Tupelo, Mississippi
Died: August 16, 1977; Memphis, Tennessee
Primary Field: Rock and roll; pop music
Group Affiliation: Solo Performer

Introduction

Out of the hillbilly tunes, Negro blues and gospel songs of the American South developed the unique singing style of Elvis Presley. His guitar strumming and bodily gyrations brought him the adulation of millions of teenage fans, who purchased his recordings of such tunes as "Blue Suede Shoes" and "Hound Dog" in astronomical quantities. Presley first came to fame in 1956 when the quaking rhythms of rock 'n' roll began to pour from the jukeboxes of the United States. After he had conquered the recording industry Presley performed on television, and became a box-office hit when he starred in several Hollywood motion pictures. From 1958 to 1960 he served in the United States Army, attaining the rank of sergeant, and was stationed in Germany.

Elvis Presley.

Early Life

Elvis Aron Presley, who was of Irish descent, was born in Tupelo Mississippi on January195 to Vernon Elvis and Gladys Presley. His twin brother, Jessie Aaron, the only other child in the family, died at birth. Vernon Presley, who worked as a cotton farmer, carpentry foreman, and factory worker, built his own home for his ardently religious family. Elvis had his first singing experiences in the choir of the local church of the Assembly of God and later at revivals and camp meetings. While still in elementary school he entered an amateur singing contest sponsored by WELO radio station and the Mississippi-Alabama Fair in which he won fifth prize.

The boy received his first guitar as a birthday present when he was about twelve. He taught himself to strum chords, although even once he became a professional he could not read music, and learned hillbilly tunes and Negro blues songs by listening to phonograph records. Moving with his family to Memphis Tennessee in 1949, he attended the L.C. Humes High School, from which he graduated in June 1953. He then became a truck driver for the Crown Electric Company, and at night studied to be an electrician.

That summer, Presley went to the Sun Record Company, which had a department that would cut personal records; there he paid $4 to make a recording of "My Happiness" and "That's When Your Heartaches Begin" as a present for his mother. Sam Phillips, the president of the Sun Record Company, which specialized in hillbilly music, heard the performance and later signed a contract with Presley.

Life's Work

A year later, Presley made his first commercial coupling, "That's All Right, Mama" and "Blue Moon of Kentucky" for Sun. The record was heard over the radio program of Memphis disc jockey Dewey Phillips in the summer of 1954. That night, Phillips played each side seven times in response to forty-seven telephone calls and seventeen telegrams. In the following week Memphis stores sold some 6,000 copies of the record.

As a result of this initial success, impresario Colonel Thomas A. Parker signed Presley for a personal-appearance tour as The Hillbilly Cat. He also performed weekly on Louisiana Hayride over station KWKH in Shreveport, Louisiana. In the autumn of 1955 Presley was booked for a disc-jockey's convention in Nashville, Tennessee. By this time he had developed his own style of "rock 'n' roll," a variety of popular music which combines highly emotional, primitive, revivalist, and hillbilly elements.

At the convention his singing impressed RCA Victor talent scout Steve Sholes, who induced his firm to buy Presley's contract and five master discs from the Sun company for $35,000. In addition, RCA Victor paid Presley $5,000. He used the money to buy the first of several Cadillacs.

RCA Victor pressed all five of Presley's records under its own label and released them simultaneously. Within three months Presley discs accounted for more than half of the firm's popular-music production, and he was engaged for his first national TV appearance on Jackie Gleason's Stage Show. He sang "Heartbreak Hotel," and the record of this tune became the number one recording in the United States in popularity, selling over 1,000,000 copies within several weeks. By May 1956 seven of RCA Victor's fifteen best-selling popular discs had been recorded by Presley.

Love Me Tender, Presley's first film, was released by Twentieth Century-Fox Film Corporation in November 1956 and was followed by Paramount's *Loving You,* in July 1957. For his third film, MGM's *Jailhouse Rock* (November 1957), Presley earned $250,000 plus 50 per cent of the net profits. If Presley's motion pictures were not artistic triumphs, they were profitable.

Presley's career was interrupted when he was inducted into the army on March 24, 1958. After receiving basic training and advanced instruction in tank corps activities at Fort Hood, Texas, he was assigned to the 3d Armored Division in Germany as a truck and jeep driver. He maintained a seven-room house in Germany, which he shared with his father and grandmother, but performed the normal duties of an enlisted soldier.

Military service did not diminish Presley's popularity with his teen-age following. His film *King Creole* was released in July 1958, and his recordings, which were made before his induction, were released throughout his time in the army and command a high place on lists of best-selling discs. In 1958, although he was serving in the army, Presley earned about $2,000,000, largely from his records and his movies.

Despite his worries that military service would ruin his career, Parker convinced Presley that to gain popular respect, he should serve his country as a regular soldier rather than in Special Services, where he would have been able to give some musical performances and remain in touch with the public. However, RCA producer Steve Sholes and Freddy Bienstock of Hill and Range had carefully prepared for his two-year hiatus. Armed with a substantial amount of unreleased material, they kept up a regular stream of successful releases. Between his induction and discharge, Presley had ten top 40 hits, including "Wear My Ring Around Your Neck," the best-selling "Hard Headed Woman," and "One Night" in 1958, and "(Now and Then There's) A Fool Such as I" and the number one "A Big Hunk o' Love" in 1959. RCA also generated four albums compiling old material during this period, most successfully Elvis' *Golden Records* (1958), which hit number three on the LP chart

Presley returned to the United States on March 2, 1960, and was honorably discharged with the rank of sergeant on March 5. The train that carried him from New Jersey to Tennessee was mobbed all the way, and Presley was called upon to appear at scheduled stops to please his fans. On the night of March 20, he entered RCA's Nashville studio to cut tracks for a new album along with a single, "Stuck on You," which was rushed into release and swiftly became a number one hit. Another Nashville session two weeks later yielded a pair of his best-selling singles, the ballads "It's Now or Never" and "Are You Lonesome Tonight?," along with the rest of Elvis Is Back! As a whole, the record "conjured up the vision of a performer who could be all things," in the words of music historian John Robertson: "a flirtatious teenage idol with a heart of gold; a tempestuous, dangerous lover; a gutbucket blues singer; a sophisticated nightclub entertainer; [a] raucous rocker."

Presley returned to television on May 12 as a guest on *The Frank Sinatra Timex Special*—ironic for both stars, given Sinatra's not-so-distant excoriation of rock and roll. Also known as *Welcome Home Elvis*, the show had been taped in late March, the only time all year Presley performed in front of an audience. Parker secured an unheard-of $125,000 fee for eight minutes of singing. The broadcast drew an enormous viewership.

G.I. Blues, the soundtrack to Presley's first film since his return, was a number one album in October. His first LP of sacred material, *His Hand in Mine*, followed two months later. It reached number 13 on the U.S. pop chart and number 3 in Great Britain, remarkable figures for a gospel album. In February 1961, Presley performed two shows for a benefit event in Memphis, on behalf of 24 local charities. During a luncheon preceding the event, RCA presented him with a plaque certifying worldwide sales of over 75 million records. A 12-hour Nashville session in mid-March yielded nearly all of Presley's next studio album, *Something for Everybody*. As described by John Robertson, it exemplified the Nashville sound, the restrained, cosmopolitan style that would define country music in the 1960s. Like much of what was to come from Presley himself over the next half-decade, the album is largely "a pleasant, unthreatening pastiche of the music that had once been Elvis's birthright." It would be his sixth number one LP. Another benefit concert, raising money for a Pearl Harbor memorial, was staged on March 25, in Hawaii. It was to be Presley's last public performance for seven years.

Parker had by now pushed Presley into a heavy film making schedule, focused on formulaic, modestly budgeted musical comedies. Presley at first insisted on pursuing more serious roles, but when two films in a more dramatic vein—*Flaming Star* (1960) and *Wild in the Country* (1961)—were less commercially successful, he reverted to the formula. Among the 27 films he made during the 1960s, there were few further exceptions. His films were almost universally panned. Nonetheless, they were virtually all profitable. Hal Wallis, who produced nine of them, declared, "A Presley picture is the only sure thing in Hollywood." In the first half of the decade, three of Presley's soundtrack albums hit number one on the pop charts, and a few of his most popular songs came from his films, such as "Can't Help Falling in Love" (1961) and "Return to Sender" (1962). ("Viva Las Vegas," the title track to the 1964 film, was a minor hit as a B-side, and became truly popular only later.) But, as with artistic merit, the commercial returns steadily diminished. During a five-year span—1964 through 1968—Presley had only one top-ten hit: "Crying in the Chapel" (1965), a gospel number recorded back in 1960. As for non-film albums, between the June 1962 release of *Pot Luck* and the November 1968 release of the soundtrack to the television special that signaled his comeback, only one LP of new material by Presley was issued: the gospel album *How Great Thou Art* (1967). It won him his first Grammy Award, for Best Sacred Performance. As Marsh described, Presley was "arguably the greatest white gospel singer of his time [and] really the last rock & roll artist to make gospel as vital a component of his musical personality as his secular songs.

However, by 1968, Presley was deeply unhappy with his career. Of the eight Presley singles released between January 1967 and May 1968, only two charted in the top 40, and none higher than number 28. His forthcoming soundtrack album, *Speedway*, would die at number 82 on the *Billboard* chart. Parker had already shifted his plans to television, where Presley had not appeared since the *Sinatra Timex* show in 1960. He maneuvered a deal with NBC that committed the network to both finance a theatrical feature and broadcast a Christmas special. Recorded in late June in Burbank, California, the special, called simply *Elvis*, aired on December 3, 1968. Later known as the *'68 Comeback Special*, the show featured lavishly staged studio productions as well as songs performed with a band in front of a small audience—Presley's first live performances since 1961. The live segments saw Presley clad in tight black leather, singing and playing guitar in an uninhibited style reminiscent of his early rock-and-roll days. Director and coproducer Steve Binder had worked hard to reassure the nervous singer and to produce a show that was far from the hour of Christmas songs Parker had originally planned. The show, NBC's highest rated that season, captured 42 percent of the total viewing audience.

By January 1969, the single "If I Can Dream," written for the special, reached number 12. The soundtrack album broke into the top ten. Buoyed by the experience of the *Comeback Special*, Presley engaged in a prolific series of recording sessions at American Sound Studio, which led to the acclaimed *From Elvis in Memphis*. Released in June 1969, it was his first secular, non-soundtrack album from a dedicated period in the studio in eight years. As described by Dave Marsh, it is "a masterpiece in which Presley immediately catches up with pop music trends that had seemed to pass him by during the movie years. He sings country songs, soul songs and rockers with real conviction, a stunning achievement."

Following the success of the *Comeback Special,* Presley wanted to resume regular live performing. In May, the brand new International Hotel in Las Vegas, boasting the largest showroom in the city, announced that it had booked Presley, scheduling him to perform 57 shows over four weeks beginning July 31.

Presley took to the stage without introduction. The audience of 2200, including many celebrities, gave him a standing ovation before he sang a note and another after his performance. A third followed his encore, "Can't Help Falling in Love" (a song that would be his closing number for much of the 1970s). At a press conference after the show, when a journalist referred to him as "The King," Presley gestured toward Fats Domino, who was taking in the scene. "No," Presley said, "that's the real king of rock and roll." The next day, Parker's negotiations with the hotel resulted in a five-year contract for Presley to play each February and August, at an annual salary of $1 million.

Presley returned to the International early in 1970 for the first of the year's two month-long engagements, performing two shows a night. Recordings from these shows were issued on the album *On Stage*. In late February, Presley performed six attendance-record–breaking shows at the Houston Astrodome. In April, the single "The Wonder of You" was issued—a number one hit in Great Britain, it topped the U.S. adult contemporary chart, as well. MGM filmed rehearsal and concert footage at the International during August for the documentary *Elvis: That's the Way It Is*. Presley was by now performing in a jumpsuit, which would become a trademark of his live act.

The album *That's the Way It Is*, produced to accompany the documentary and featuring both studio and live recordings, marked a stylistic shift. As music historian John Robertson notes, "The authority of Presley's singing helped disguise the fact that the album stepped decisively away from the American-roots inspiration of the Memphis sessions towards a more middle-of-the-road sound. With country put on the back burner, and soul and R&B left in Memphis, what was left was very classy, very clean white pop—perfect for the Las Vegas crowd, but a definite retrograde step for Elvis."

The U.S. Junior Chamber of Commerce named Presley one of its annual Ten Most Outstanding Young Men of the Nation on January 16, 1971. Not long after, the City of Memphis named the stretch of Highway 51 South on which Graceland is located "Elvis Presley Boulevard." The same year, Presley became the first rock and roll singer to be awarded the Lifetime Achievement Award (then known as the Bing Crosby Award) by the National Academy of Recording Arts and Sciences, the Grammy Award organization. Three new, non-film Presley studio albums were released in 1971, as many as had come out over the previous eight years. Best received by critics was *Elvis Country,* a concept record that focused on genre standards. The biggest seller was *Elvis Sings the Wonderful World of Christmas,* "the

Affiliation: Solo Peformer

Throughout 1956 Presley luxuriated in a popularity seldom equaled in American entertainment He earned $50,000 for three spots on the *Ed Sullivan* television program and signed a seven-year movie contract with Hal Wallis Productions. But Presley made his strongest impact in his personal appearances, mainly upon impressionable audiences of teen-age girls.

"They get set off by shock waves of hysteria," reported a *Life* writer (August 27, 1956), "going into frenzies of screeching and wailing, winding up in tears." Carlton Brown, writing in *Coronet* (September 1956), described Presley's stage presence in these words: "irregular stress on syllables gave the song an urgent jerkiness that the singer's actions gamed out visually. His legs spread in a straddling stance, he whacked his feet. . . like a cowboy riding a bronco with a rock-and-roll buck." It was these supplementary body movements which drew condemnation from the press.

"His movements and motions during his performance, described as a 'strip-tease with clothes on,' were not only suggestive, but downright obscene," according to an editorial in the Roman Catholic publication *America* (June 23, 1956), which concluded: "If the agencies would stop handling such nauseating stuff, all the Presleys of our land would soon be swallowed up in the oblivion they deserve."

Far from being "swallowed up," Presley earned an estimated $1,000,000 by the end of 1956. Exploiting the boom, his business managers were preparing to sell between $19,000,000 and $24,000,000 worth of merchandise under Presley's name. The merchandise included such items as a Hound-Dog-Orange lipstick, named after a Presley hit song.

truest statement of all," according to Greil Marcus. "In the midst of ten painfully genteel Christmas songs, every one sung with appalling sincerity and humility, one could find Elvis tom-catting his way through six blazing minutes of 'Merry Christmas, Baby,' a raunchy old Charles Brown blues. . . . If [Presley's] sin was his lifelessness, it was his sinfulness that brought him to life."

MGM again filmed Presley in April 1972, this time for Elvis on Tour, which went on to win the Golden Globe Award for Best Documentary Film that year. His gospel album *He Touched Me*, released that month, would earn him his second Grammy Award, for Best Inspirational Performance. A 14-date tour began with an unprecedented four consecutive sold-out shows at New York's Madison Square Garden. The evening concert on July 10 was recorded and issued in LP form a week later. *Elvis: As Recorded at Madison Square Garden* became one of Presley's biggest-selling albums. After the tour, the single "Burning Love" was released—Presley's last top ten hit on the U.S. pop chart.

In January 1973, Presley performed two benefit concerts for the Kui Lee Cancer Fund in connection with a groundbreaking TV special, *Aloha from Hawaii*. The first show served as a practice run and backup should technical problems affect the live broadcast two days later. Aired as scheduled on January 14, *Aloha from Hawaii* was the first global concert satellite broadcast, reaching millions of viewers live and on tape delay. Presley's costume became the most recognized example of the elaborate concert garb with which his latter-day persona became closely associated. As described by Bobbie Ann Mason, "At the end of the show, when he spreads out his American Eagle cape, with the full stretched wings of the eagle studded on the back, he becomes a god figure." The accompanying double album, released in February, went to number one and eventually sold over 5 million copies in the United States. It proved to be Presley's last U.S. number one pop album during his lifetime.

RCA, which had enjoyed a steady stream of product from Presley for over a decade, grew anxious as his interest in spending time in the studio waned. After a December 1973 session that produced 18 songs, enough for almost two albums, he did not enter the studio in 1974. Parker sold RCA on another concert record, *Elvis: As Recorded Live on Stage in Memphis*. Recorded on March 20, it included a version of "How Great Thou Art" that would win Presley his third and final competitive Grammy Award. (All three of his competitive Grammy wins—out of 14 total nominations—were for gospel recordings.) Presley returned to the studio in Hollywood in March 1975, but Parker's attempts to arrange another session toward the end of the year were unsuccessful. In 1976, RCA sent a mobile studio to Graceland that made possible two full-scale recording sessions at Presley's home. Even in that comfortable context, the recording process was now a struggle for him.

Despite the concerns of his label and manager, in studio sessions between July 1973 and October 1976, Presley recorded virtually the entire contents of six albums. Though he was no longer a major presence on the pop charts, five of those albums entered the top five of the country chart, and three went to number one: *Promised Land* (1975), *From Elvis Presley Boulevard, Memphis, Tennessee* (1976), and *Moody Blue* (1977). The story was similar with his singles—there were no major pop hits, but Presley was a significant force in not just the country market, but on adult contemporary radio as well. Eight studio singles from this period released during his lifetime were top ten hits on one or both charts, four in 1974 alone. "My Boy" was a number one adult contemporary hit in 1975, and "Moody Blue" topped the country chart and reached the second spot on the adult contemporary chart in 1976. Perhaps his most critically acclaimed recording of the era came that year, with what Greil Marcus described as his "apocalyptic attack" on the soul classic "Hurt." "If he felt the way he sounded," Dave Marsh wrote of Presley's performance, "the wonder isn't that he had only a year left to live but that he managed to survive that long." "Way Down," Presley's last single issued during his lifetime, came out on June 6. His final concert was held in Indianapolis, Indiana at Market Square Arena, on June 26.

Between 1977 and 1981, six posthumously released singles by Presley were top ten country hits. Graceland was opened to the public in 1982. Attracting over half a million visitors annually, it is the second most-visited home in the United States, after the White House. It was declared a National Historic Landmark in 2006. Presley has been inducted into five music halls of fame: the Rock and Roll Hall of Fame (1986), the Country Music Hall of Fame (1998), the Gospel Music Hall of Fame (2001), the Rockabilly Hall of Fame (2007), and the Memphis Music Hall of Fame (2012).

Personal Life

Elvis Presley weighed 185 pounds and stood six feet one inch in height when he was drafted into the United

States Army. At that time, he was a "lanky, loose-jointed, sullenly handsome youth with sideburns" in civilian life. He had a classic Barrymore profile, wavy brown hair, blue eyes, and long, thick eyelashes. He dressed flamboyantly for his stage appearances and tended to be ill at ease when not performing. He neither smoked s nor drank. In addition to strumming a guitar, he played the piano. Presley bought his family a seven-room ranchhouse in Memphis and persuaded his father to retire at the age of thirty-nine. His hobbies were sports cars, motorcycles, collecting teddy bears, swimming, water skiing, boxing, and football.

Having made twenty-one records which sold more than 1,000,000 copies each, and haying consistently topped popularity polls in 1956, 1957, and 1958 Elvis Presley was often the subject of speculation as to the source of his success. Perhaps the most penetrating analysis was written by James and Annette Baxter in *Harper's Magazine* (January 1958): "Admonished that there were those who found his hip-swiveling offensive, Elvis is said, to have replied, 'I never made no dirty body movements.' And this is believable; Elvis moves as the spirit moves him; it all comes naturally. . . But Presley's stunning rapport with his own generation is something more than the ageless call of the wild. . . In the back-woods heterodoxies of Elvis the [teen-ager] recognizes a counterpart to his own instinctive rebellion. . . in his voice the teen-ager hears intimations of a world heavily weighted with real emotion."

While in Germany, Presley met 14-year-old Priscilla Beaulieu. Shortly before Christmas 1966, more than seven years since they first met, Presley proposed to Priscilla Beaulieu. They were married on May 1, 1967, in a brief ceremony in their suite at the Aladdin Hotel in Las Vegas. Presley's only child, Lisa Marie, was born on February 1, 1968. By 1971, Presley and his wife had become increasingly distant, barely cohabiting. In 1971, an affair he had with Joyce Bova resulted—unbeknownst to him—in her pregnancy and an abortion. He often raised the possibility of her moving into Graceland, saying that he was likely to leave Priscilla. The Presleys separated on February 23, 1972, after Priscilla disclosed her relationship with Mike Stone, a karate instructor Presley had recommended to her.

Five months later, Presley's new girlfriend, Linda Thompson, a songwriter and one-time Memphis beauty queen, moved in with him. Presley and his wife filed for divorce on August 18. Presley's divorce took effect on October 9, 1973. Presley and Linda Thompson split in November 1976, and he took up with a new girlfriend, Ginger Alden. He proposed to Alden and gave her an engagement ring two months later, though several of his friends later claimed that he had no serious intention of marrying again.

By early 1977, journalist Tony Scherman wrote that "Presley had become a grotesque caricature of his sleek, energetic former self. Hugely overweight, his mind dulled by the pharmacopoeia he daily ingested, he was barely able to pull himself through his abbreviated concerts." In Alexandria, Louisiana, the singer was on stage for less than an hour and "was impossible to understand." Presley failed to appear in Baton Rouge; he was unable to get out of his hotel bed, and the rest of the tour was cancelled. Presley was scheduled to fly out of Memphis on the evening of August 16, 1977, to begin another tour. That afternoon, Ginger Alden discovered him unresponsive on his bathroom floor. Attempts to revive him failed, and death was officially pronounced at 3:30 pm at Baptist Memorial Hospital.

Further Reading

Colliers 138:109+ O 26 '56 pors
Coronet 40:153+ S '56 por
Harper 214:86 Ap '57
Life 41:101+ Ag 27 '56; 44:117+ Ap 7 por; 45:77+ 0 6 '58 pors
Look 20:82+ Ag 7; 9+ N 13 '56; 22: 113+ D 23 '58 pors
International Motion Picture Almanac, 1959
Who's Who in Rock 'n' Roll (1958)

Dafnis Prieto

Drummer and composer

Born: July 31, 1974; Santa Clara, Cuba
Primary Field: Jazz, Folkloric music
Affiliation: Bandleader of various ensembles

Introduction

Working with both modern kits and traditional percussion instrumentation, fusing the Afro-Cuban rhythms of his homeland with cutting-edge jazz and a host of other influences, the Cubanborn percussionist, bandleader, and composer Dafnis Prieto is one of the most technically accomplished and innovative drummers working today. His arrival in the United States in 1999 was compared to an asteroid strike by Ben Ratliff of the New York Times *(17 Jan. 2002), and in the years since, he has played with a veritable who's who of contemporary musicians, both in the jazz world and beyond.*

Early Life

Dafnis Prieto was born on July 31, 1974, in Santa Clara, the capital of the province of Villa Clara in central Cuba. His father earned his living as an elevator mechanic. Trained as an accountant, his mother kept the books at a factory that produced equipment for sugarcane processing facilities. Prieto grew up in a largely Afro-Cuban neighborhood, an environment that helped inspire his lifelong passion for music. "I was surrounded by music," he told Tomas Pena for *All about Jazz* (22 Dec. 2004). "Music was everywhere; on the radio and in the streets." The young Prieto was especially fascinated by the *comparsas,* bands of musicians who perform in Cuban conga parades as part of the festival of Carnival. During the lead up to the celebration, the *comparsas* would practice in Prieto's neighborhood, sometimes right in front of his family's home. Though only six or seven at the time, Prieto was enthralled by the sounds and rhythms. His mother recognized his growing obsession and, Prieto recalled to Pena, "Whenever the comparsas would rehearse in front of my house [she] would get very nervous. She knew I was about to get lost . . . . Invariably, I would always find a way to sneak out of the house and follow the comparsas." Prieto's musical education commenced soon afterward. He joined a local social club that provided musical instruction. There, he learned *son, guaracha, rumba,* and other standard rhythms of Cuban music. For his musical instrument, he initially took up the Spanish guitar. Then, one of his instructors decided to form the social club's music students into a band. There were already half a dozen guitar players, so the teacher asked some of them to select other instruments. "As fate would have it," Prieto told Pena, "I picked the bongos." His choice was hardly surprising, given that his childhood was saturated with the percussive rhythms of Cuban music. "[E]verywhere—in the streets, coming out of open windows—I heard the sound of drums that captured Cuban music's African influence," Prieto told Drozdowski. "It was in the air every day." During one of the band's shows, the clave player failed to appear-the clave is a percussion instrument consisting of two short and thick wooden sticks that are rhythmically banged together. Without any prompting, the bongo-playing Prieto started making the sounds of the clave with his mouth. Impressed by this display, his music instructor spoke to Prieto's mother and recommended that she send him to the local music conservatory.

At the age of eleven, Prieto graduated to a full drum kit and began a four-year stint at the music conservatory of the Santa Clara School of Fine Arts, where he was trained as a classical percussionist. Several years later, he was accepted at the National School of Music in Havana and moved from Santa Clara to the Cuban capital to take up his studies. At the National School of Music, he continued his education in classical percussion. Living in Havana, Prieto was introduced to new forms of music; he quickly developed a passion for jazz and started experimenting with it in his spare time. Early on, he was drawn to such American jazz composers as the pianist Armando "Chick" Corea and the saxophonist John Coltrane, listening every day to the latter's 1964 studio album *A Love Supreme.* Elvin Jones, who drummed for Coltrane, was another influence. As Prieto immersed himself in the medium, he studied the saxophonist Michael Brecker, the drummer Steve Gadd, and the pioneering multiinstrumentalist Ornette Coleman. One of jazz's great innovators, Coleman played a key role in the emergence of both free jazz and avant-garde jazz.

Despite being introduced to the work of such luminaries, Prieto was isolated from much of the jazz world in Cuba, and his education in the medium was far from complete. Nevertheless, his capabilities as a musician were undeniable even as a teenager, and while still studying at the National School of Music, he went on his first overseas tour, performing at jazz festivals in Europe. As the artist grew more seasoned, he became enamored with avant-garde jazz, an especially unconventional and groundbreaking form that embraces unusual structures, rhythms, and instrumentation. In 1 992, Prieto graduated from the National School of Music. For the commencement ceremonies, he put together a band and played an avant-garde jazz composition he had created. "The group," he recalled to Pena, "consisted of four horns, a bass, and myself on the traps, kettle drums, and whistle. It was a rather revolutionary concept."

Life's Work

After completing his studies at the National School of Music, Prieto became a full-time professional musician. He went on tour in support of the pianists Ramon Valle and Carlos Maza, as well as the multi-instrumentalist Bobby Carcassés, joining his band Columna B. "It was fun, I learned a lot sharing the music with them," Prieto told Pena, "but I was also interested in playing with other musicians." The Cuban jazz scene, while vibrant, was not especially large, and it was cut off from the major jazz currents in the United States. Prieto started to feel constricted. It was not easy to support himself, either. "The avant-garde scene in Cuba is really small and it is very hard to make a living as a jazz musician," he told Pena. "To survive you have to travel out of Cuba, make money (American dollars), and spend it in Cuba. Besides, I didn't have a place to live in Havana because my family lived in Santa Clara, so I had to rent places all the time."

The year 1996 was a seminal one for Prieto. The American jazz saxophonist Steve Coleman visited Cuba, and he and Prieto embarked on a serendipitous collaboration. "With Steve, more than playing in his band, I did research," Prieto told Ben Ratliff for the *New York Times* (17 Jan. 2002). "I looked at South Indian music; we did a trio project about the sun, moon, and the Earth; and we did a thing about yin and yang." Prieto also traveled to Spain with Columna B. His wife, Judith Sanchez Ruiz, a professional dancer, had a two-year performance contract in Barcelona, and Prieto opted to stay with her for a year. "I decided then and there that I would not return to Cuba," Prieto told Pena. He soon received an offer to play with the Canadian jazz saxophonist Jane Bunnett and her band, Spirit of Havana, and subsequently went on tour in Canada and the United States. Visa troubles kept him from going back to Spain; he was forced to head home to Cuba, but only after giving serious thought to staying in New York City.

Three years later, in 1999, visa difficulties left Prieto stranded in Toronto, Canada. He headed to New York City, where he applied for residency. "I left Cuba because I felt suffocated professionally," he told Siddhartha Mitter for the *Boston Globe* (23 Feb. 2012). "I didn't have many options to do what I wanted to do musically." Elaborating further on his motivations to Ratliff, Prieto stated, "The kind of music I was doing there in Cuba was sort of on the side of jazz-avant-garde Latin music-and I didn't see myself in Cuba doing that for long. The only guys I saw playing that kind of music were the ones who were already playing with me, so there was nowhere to go.

Prieto received a warm welcome in New York and immersed himself in the local jazz scene. He played with dozens of musicians and fifteen different bands in just his first several years in the United States, including the avant-garde jazz great Henry Threadgill and his band Zooid, Eddie Palmieri's Latin jazz orchestra, and Claudia Acuna's South American-inflected jazz group. He also collaborated with his wife on some performances and studied American drumming traditions, exploring the work and styles of Max Hoach, Billy Higgins, and Ed Blackwell. Discussing Prieto's talents as a drummer, Brian Lynch, a trumpeter who played with him, observed to Ratliff, "He brings the intelligence level up.... He knows form, and he remembers things. He'll be swinging, he'll be in the clave rhythm, but he'll make these little shifts with it—just a little spurt, where there's an impossibly complex rhythm, but it's all precise."

Still, the transition was not an easy one. Raised in provincial Cuba, Prieto had found Havana overwhelming. New York City was even more intimidating. "I remember saying to myself, 'New York is the last place I ever want to live,' he told Pena. "Three years later I was not only living in New York but enjoying it." Soon, he was working again with Steve Coleman and teaming up with other jazz greats, such as the Cuban bandleader and pianist Chucho Valdes; he played drums on various live and studio recordings.

As a bandleader, Prieto released his first album, *About the Monks,* on the Zoho label in 2005. The album, Prieto explained to Pena, "is dedicated to the many people and artists who have inspired my soul." Prieto put together a six-person band for *About the Monks,* which features trumpet, bass, saxophone, piano, violin, and percussion. Reviewing the work for *Latin Jazz Comer* (18 ct. 2011), Chip Boaz described the music as "[moving] between hard-bop fire, modern play with time signatures, nods to Cuban tradition, and an inherent rhythmic complexity and drive that explodes from the speakers."

For *Absolute Quintet* (2006), Prieto's Grammy Award–nominated follow up to *About the Monks,* he included many of his bandmates from the first album. The eclectic lineup covers keyboard, percussion, saxophone, violin, and cello, with Threadgill playing alto saxophone on one track. Reviewing the release for *All about Jazz* (9 May 2006), Mark F. Turner wrote, "Like 2005's *About the Monks,* the new music has quirky rhythms and snaking patterns, matched with Prieto's ever-lively playing. But now he brushes his compositions with wider and more thoughtful strokes." Boaz wrote that "Prieto shatters all expectations with this album, plunging his musicianship in a completely new direction that edges on funky fusion." Despite such praise, *Absolute Quintet* did not capture the Grammy Award for best Latin jazz album, which went to the Brian Lynch/Eddie Palmieri Project for their record *Simpatico.* Based on his output, Prieto was also recognized at the Latin Grammys with a 2007 nomination in the best new artist category, though he did not win that honor.

For his third album, *Taking the Soul for a Walk* (2008), Prieto employed a sextet lineup of bass, piano, trumpet, percussion, and two saxophones. Released on Prieto's own Dafnison label, the record earned a positive critical reception. "Never has the line between traditional Latin-jazz and twenty-first-century post-bop been so wonderfully blurred as on *Taking the Soul for a Walk,"* wrote Michael]. West for *JazzTimes* (June 2008). "Prieto and his gang are as tight as they come."

Collaborating with the New York Afro Latin Jazz Orchestra and its director, Arturo O'Farrill, Prieto composed the title track to their 2008 album, *A Song for Chico,* in tribute to Chico O'Farrill, Arturo's father. The following year, the record earned the Grammy Award for best Latin jazz album. Since his arrival in the United States, Prieto has performed with many different lineups and has been a member of a number of different bands. There is no overlap from one project to the next, however. Each is distinct. "None of my bands play any of the same material," he told Drozdowsld. "I write for the group, for individual players, and for the moment—not by formula. Music should always be about honest communication. If we're going to say something pure and honest, it can't be premeditated." One of his bands, the Si 0 Si Quartet, is featured on his fourth album as a bandleader, *Live at Jazz Standard NYC* (2009). In addition to Prieto on the drums, the lineup includes Peter Applelbaum on the saxophone, Manuel Valera on the piano, and Charles Flores on the bass. "The drummer's writing sounds fresh and innovative, pulling colorful harmonies out of the group and constantly playing with rhythmic evolution," Boaz wrote in his review of *Live at Jazz Standard NYC* (18 Oct. 2011). "The most mature statement from Prieto that we've heard, this album overflows with intelligent risk talking, skillfully crafted drama, and masterful interplay that demands repeated listens."

In September 2011, the MacArthur Foundation contacted Prieto and informed him that he had been named one of twenty-two 2011 MacArthur Fellows. MacArthur Fellowships are anonymously awarded to American residents "across all ages and fields who show exceptional merit and promise of continued creative work,"

Affiliation: Jazz

Summing up his career, Chip Boaz for the *Latin Jazz Corner* (18 Oct. 2011) stated, "Prieto has shown himself to be a technically astounding drummer, an inspired bandleader, an edgy avant-garde musician, a supportive sideman, and a genre-bending composer that has contributed to jazz, Latin music, modern classical settings, and more." Prieto has released four albums as a bandleader—About *the Monks* (2005), the Grammy-nominated *Absolute Quintet* (2006), *Taking the Soul for a Walk* (2008), and *Live at Jazz Standard NYC* (2009). In 2007, he was nominated for a Latin Grammy in the best new artist category. In recognition of Prieto's potential as an artist, he received in 2011 the so-called "genius grant," a MacArthur Fellowship from the John D. and Catherine T. MacArthur Foundation. "My style is based on the rich polyrhythmic foundation that developed in Cuba because of the immersion of African culture there," Prieto told Ted Drozdowski for Broadcast Music Inc.'s *MusicWorld* (6 Feb. 2012), reflecting on his influences and evolution as an artist. "As I gained experience I found the freedom within my playing to feel open enough to create much more within those rhythms."

according to the MacArthur Foundation's website. Each unrestricted fellowship is worth $500,000 paid out over five years. For Prieto, the honor was well-timed. ''I'd been kind of struggling to get my projects moving," Prieto told Mitter. "The MacArthur will really help me get through a lot of barriers." He has planned to use the fellowship to finish an album with one of his bands, the Proverb Trio, which consists of Prieto, Jason Lindner on the keyboard, and the rapper Kokayi. Among other projects, he also plans to use the fellowship to help him publish a book about the art of drumming.

Since 2005, Prieto has served as an adjunct instructor in music at New York University (NYU), and as an educator he has led drum workshops throughout the country. In addition to his MacArthur Foundation Fellowship, Prieto is the recipient of a 2005 grant from Chamber Music America's New Works: Creation and Presentation Program and was named the up-and-coming musician of the year by the Jazz Journalists Association in 2006, among other awards and honors. He counts the Spanish surrealist painter Salvador Dali as one of his favorite artists and as someone who has had a deep influence on his perspective as a musician.

In addition to the artists mentioned above, Prieto has played with such jazz icons as Branford Marsalis, Arturo Sandoval, and Herbie Hancock. Though he has made his name in the genres of jazz and Latin music, Prieto does not like to confine himself to labels. "I don't look at myself as a jazz musician," he told Eric Fine for *JazzTimes* (August 2008). "I studied classical music in the conservatory. I did research on folkloric music because I actually grew up listening to folkloric music in Cuba. I don't even like that much the [idea] of being a jazz musician. I try to do the music that represents my life now."

Personal Life

When not touring, Prieto makes his home in the New York City neighborhood of Washington Heights in upper Manhattan. He is separated from his wife Judith Sanchez Ruiz, with whom he has a son, Lucian.

Further Reading

Chinen, Nate. "Meditation, and Time with the Sticks." *New York Times*. New York Times Co., II May 20I2. Web. 2I Aug. 2012.

Drozdowski, Ted. "Catching Up with Dafnis Prieto, Winner of MacArthur Foundation Fellowship." *MusicWorld*. BMI, 6 Feb. 2012. Web. 21 Aug. 2012.

Fine, Eric. "Dafnis Prieto: Multilingual Rhythms." *JazzTimes*. JazzTimes Inc., Aug. 2008. Web. 21 Aug. 2012.

Mitter, Siddhartha. "Dafnis Prieto Plays More than Meets the Ear." *Boston Globe*. New York Times Co., 23 Feb. 2012. Web. 21 Aug. 2012.

Pena, Tomas. "Dafnis Prieto: About the Monks." *All about Jazz*. All about Jazz, 22 Dec. 2004. Web. 21 Aug. 2012.

"Prieto, Dafnis (Dafnis Prieto Rodriguez)." *Encyclopedia of Jazz Musicians*. Jazz.com, 2012. Web. 21 Aug. 2012.

Ratliff, Ben. "From Cuba, with Rhythm, Taking Jazz by Storm; Dafnis Prieto Makes His Mark in New York" *New York Times*. New York Times Co., 17 Jan. 2002. Web. 21 Aug. 2012.

PRODIGY

Music group

Liam Howlett
Lyricist; musician; producer
Born: Aug. 21, 1971; Cressing, England

Maxim Reality
MC; vocalist
Born: Mar. 21, 1967

Keith Flint
Dancer; vocalist
Born: Sep. 17, 1969; Chelmsford, Essex, England

Primary Field: Electronic dance music
Group Affiliation: Prodigy

INTRODUCTION

The British band the Prodigy "can fairly be described as the techno equivalent of [the rock bands] U2 or Oasis," David Pollock declared in the London Independent *(December 10, 2008, on-line); "the perfectly timed half-step they tread outside the pace of what's fashionable is just enough to ease them into the realm of the timeless rather than the overtly dated." The Prodigy was founded as a one-man act by the lyricist/musician/producer Liam Howlett in about 1989, when he was 18. Howlett, who got his start as a breakdancer and a deejay at raves in Essex, England, was soon joined by the dancer/vocalist Keith Flint and the MC/vocalist Maxim Reality; another dancer/keyboardist, Leeroy Thornhill, was a member from 1990 to 2000. Howlett leads the Prodigy, and his is the only name that has appeared on the group's record contracts. Arguably the most influential of the electronic dance bands that emerged in Great Britain in the 1990s, the Prodigy was largely responsible for awakening interest in that genre in U.S. audiences.*

EARLY LIVES

Liam Paul Howlett was born on August 21, 1971 in Cressing, in Essex, a county that borders Greater London in southeastern England. His father, who ran a grouting-implement factory, started him on piano lessons when he was very young. As a preadolescent Howlett became drawn to ska, hip-hop, and other music with a raw, dance-oriented edge; his favorite band was the Specials, whom he discovered on a British ska·compilation album that his father bought for him. By the time he reached high school, Howlett had become drawn to hip-hop and its culture. The seminal hip-hop film *Beat Street* (1984) introduced him to the music of artists including Grandmaster Flash and Afrika Bambaataa. At 14 Howlett began mixing songs he recorded from the radio by using the pause button on his cassette player. Soon afterward he bought a set of turntables. He also learned how to breakdance, then formed a breakdancing crew, the Pure City Breakers. His talent as a deejay earned him both first- and third-place honors at a deejay-tape competition that he had entered under two aliases. Commenting on hip-hop's influence on him, Howlett told Chris Heath for *Rolling Stone* (August 21, 1997, on-line), "It wasn't just the music. It felt real. It felt like it was from the street. I knew that it was a ghetto thing. I knew it was somewhere I could never go, so it was special. It was the fact that no one else liked it. It felt like it was my own thing. Once I got it loud up in my room, nothing else mattered."

While he was a high-school student, at Alex Hunter Humanities College, in Essex (in Great Britain, secondary-level schools are sometimes called colleges), Howlett deejayed with a hip-hop band called Cut 2 Kill. Because he was white, other hip-hop bands viewed Cut 2 Kill as outsiders; once, a rival group robbed them at knifepoint. Howlett left the band in about 1988, when his bandmates used his demos to get a record deal that excluded him. Convinced "that there was no room for white people" in hip-hop, as he told a writer for *Spin* (September 1997, on-line), he abandoned that genre. Howlett then got a job at a London-based graphic design magazine called *Metropolitan.* (Easily available sources do not reveal whether he earned a diploma from his school.) While listening to pirate radio stations at work, he heard about the burgeoning British rave scene. Shortly after he attended a rave for the first time, in 1989, at the age of 17, Howlett started deejaying at a popular rave haunt called the Barn, in the town of Braintree, Essex, and at other rave parties. He soon became a fixture on the scene and began to introduce original material that he created at his home studio under the moniker the Prodigy. Some sources have inaccurately

Affiliation: Electronic Dance Music

The Prodigy's first album, *Experience* (1992), is regarded as a classic by cognoscenti of electronic dance music. The next, *Music for the Jilted Generation* (1994), "broke free of *Experience's* rave conventions into a style that was entirely the Prodigy's own," Alex Petridis wrote for the London *Guardian* (August 1, 2008, on-line); with it, the band "reinvent[ed] themselves as parent-scaring antiestablishment figures." "None of their peers came up with anything like" the "gripping blend of distorted guitar, thumping warp-speed techno, drum 'n' bass breakbeats and rasping flute" that the Prodigy offered in their second disc, Petridis wrote. "Indeed, the sense of audacity that marks out the album's highlights quickly became the Prodigy's trademark." The group's third album, *Fat of the Land* (1997), became the first recording of electronic dance music to debut at number one on the *Billboard* 200 chart; it debuted at the top spot in 22 other countries as well and sold 8.5 million copies worldwide, and its singles "Firestarter," "Breathe," and the controversial "Smack My Bitch Up" were chart toppers, too. In 2002, after seven years of being on the road together, the Prodigy took a break from touring. Although the band remained intact, Flint and Maxim (as he is commonly known) were not included in the Prodigy's next album, *Always Outnumbered, Never Outgunned* (2004). In 2005 the group resumed giving performances, in support of their compilation album, *Their Law: The Singles 1990-2005*. Tickets to the dozens of concerts scheduled for the arena tour the Prodigy launched in late 2008 sold out in one hour. Reporting on one of those concerts, presented in Sheffield, England, a couple of months before their latest album, *Invaders Must Die* (2009), went on sale, Dave. Simpson wrote for the *Guardian* (December 16, 2008, on-line), "It's incredible that such preposterous anarchy on stage can produce such a thrilling, even dangerous racket. The Prodigy haven't changed-they've just turned everything up and added enough new cusses to run up a national debt at the swear box. The new material returns to their mid-90s trademark of making a simple and ostensibly meaningless slogan seem terribly important and threatening." *Invaders Must Die* was released on the Prodigy's own, new label, Cooking Vinyl. As of mid-2009 the Prodigy's five albums had sold a total of over 16 million copies worldwide, more than those of any other dance-music act. "For a band who started out being thought of as a novelty," John Robinson wrote for the *Guardian* (April 4, 2009, on-line), "the Prodigy have proved to endure remarkably well."

linked that name to the brand of Moog synthesizer that he used; rather, he chose it because he wanted a name that sounded "grand," as he recalled to a writer for *Q* (December 1997, on-line). "When I first thought of the name, obviously I didn't consider it could be four people," he said. "It was just me, faceless in my bedroom, writing music: the prodigy."

Howlett's skills won him a strong following at the Barn. Two of his most avid fans were Keith Flint (born on September 17, 1969 in Chelmsford, Essex, England) and Leeroy Thornhill (born on October 8, 1968). With the idea of building the Prodigy into a more prominent act, Flint and Thornhill offered to perform as stage dancers during Howlett's live sets. Howlett accepted their proposal and then decided to add an MC who would serve as the group's frontman. The band chose the reggae vocalist Maxim Reality (born Keith "Keeti" Palmer, the youngest of seven children, on March 21, 1967 in Peterborough, Cambridgeshire, England), who had been recommended to them by their soon-to-be manager, known only as Ziggy. Emulating an older brother, Maxim had begun working as an MC at 14. Commenting on his move from reggae to dance music, he recalled to the *Spin* writer, "In them days, to be a good MC, you had to write lyrics every day. I found the dance scene easy to MC to because there wasn't any lyrical foundation. Lyrics are just fillers. The last thing people want is to hear you talking about life and politics. In a way, it took a bit away from me; the lyrics I used to write were quite deep-politics, old age, everyday life. My lyric style was . . . reality. That's where the name 'Maxim Reality' came from."

Lives' Work

Now a quartet, the Prodigy performed on the United Kingdom club circuit for several months. (A female vocalist known as Sharky also appeared with them briefly.) At around that time Howlett secured a deal with XL Recordings; his was the only name on the contract (as it has been on all of Prodigy's succeeding contracts with record companies). The Prodigy's first single, "What Evil Lurks," was released in 1991; it sold around 7,000 copies. The group's second single, "Charly," which sampled the meow of a cat from a popular series of short TV films for children about public safety, reached number three on the British singles chart and helped increase recognition of the Prodigy on the rave circuit. The electronic-dance monthly *Mixmag* (August 1992) later criticized "Charly" for inspiring a slew of copycat singles that sampled children's-television themes; called "toy-town techno," such music was condemned as sacrilege by enthusiasts of breakbeat hardcore. (Hardcore was the musical genre most commonly associated with the British rave scene; it was characterized by the combination of four-to-the-floor rhythms, played in 4/4 time, with rapid-fire polyrhythmic breakbeats.) The magazine further blamed the group for ushering in rave's supposed downfall and for "turning dance music from an ultra-cool and wildly subversive folk devil into a national laughing stock"-"an opinion widely shared by the club cognoscenti," Alexis Petridis wrote for the London *Guardian* (August 24, 2004, on-line). Such criticism notwithstanding, the Prodigy's third single, "Everybody in the Place," reached the second spot on the U.K. charts.

In 1992 the Prodigy released their debut album, *Experience,* which entered the British charts at number 12 and sold more than 200,000 copies in Great Britain. In a review that appeared years later in the All Music Guide (on-line), John Bush wrote, "One of the few noncompilation rave albums of any worth, *Experience* balances a supply of top this siren whistles and chipmunk divas with Liam Howlett's surprising flair for constructing track after track of intense breakbeat techno. Almost every song sounds like a potential chart-topper (circa 1992, of course) while the true singles 'Your Love,' 'Charly,' 'Music Reach,' and 'Out of Space' add that extra bit of energy to the fray. More than just a relic of the rave experience, *Experience* shows the Prodigy near the peak of their game from the get-go." The Prodigy's 79-minute second album, *Music for the Jilted Generation* (1994), was inspired by the British Parliament's passage of the Criminal Justice and Public Order Act of 1994, a complex, wide-ranging piece of legislation that criminalized aspects of raves. Unlike *Experience,* which was largely made up of hyperfast breakbeats and helium-induced vocals, *Music for the Jilted Generation* experimented with various styles-ambient, industrial, funk, and rap; it relied more on slower tempos with harder-sounding beats and incorporated hallucinatory whooshing effects and the sounds of shattering glass. One of its singles, the multilayered, mid-tempo "Poison," featured Maxim growling a voodoo-like chant ("I got the poison / I got the remedy / I got the pulsating rhythmical remedy"); another, "Their Law," opened with a sample from the 1977 movie *Smokey and the Bandit* ("What we're dealing with here is a total lack of respect for the law"), which led to a grinding guitar riff that gave way to an anarchic chorus ("F* * * 'em and their law"), sung by the former Pop Will Eat Itself frontman Clint Mansell. *Music for the Jilted Generation* received widespread praise from critics and was nominated for a Mercury Music Prize (now known as the Barclaycard Mercury Prize), bestowed annually to the best album from the United Kingdom or Ireland. Paul Evans later wrote for *Rolling Stone* (February 2, 1998, on-line), "A soundtrack for those British rave hordes who dodge Tory truncheons, *Music* for *the Jilted Generation* thrills initiates with a political buzz Americans might miss. But the Prodigy's hard-core techno generates universal dance fever. Mastermind Liam Howlett mixes relentless jungle grooves that add guitars to the keyboard shudder 'Voodoo People' and then turn spacey on 'The Heat (The Energy).' 'No Good (Start the Dance),' with ecstatic vocal snippets, is as heady an anthem as any in a genre that exults in billboard statements; more ambitious is 'The Narcotic Suite.' The latter begins in woozy ganjaland and climaxes in an acid swirl, an echoing voice intoning, 'My mind is glowing.' Truly trippy." John Bush, in the All Music Guide, called the album "pure sonic terrorism," adding, *"Music for the Jilted Generation* employs the same rave energy that charged . . . *Experience* . . . up the charts in Britain, but yokes it to a cause other than massive drug intake. Compared to [the Prodigy's] previous work, the sound is grubbier and less reliant on samples; the effect moved the Prodigy away from the American-influenced rave and acid house of the past and toward a uniquely British vision of breakbeat techno that was increasingly allied to the limey invention of drum 'n' bass."

While electronic dance music was enjoying mainstream popularity in Europe, it appeared to have little appeal to Americans; although *Music for the Jilted Generation* reached number one on British album charts, in the U.S. it sold poorly, peaking at 198 on the *Billboard* 200 album chart. Determined to reach a much bigger audience, the Prodigy began to present themselves as a "hard dance band" and to perform at rock festivals in the U.S. and other sites overseas. "Making people dance when they're out of their heads on ecstasy wasn't really that much of a challenge," Howlett told Ben Thompson for the London *Independent* (June 29, 1997), referring to the rave scene. He added, "There was no one on the dance scene who could create the energy on stage that a rock band did."

The Prodigy's reputation as a live act was strengthened with their performance in June 1995 at the Glastonbury Festival, in Pilton, England—one of the world's largest outdoor music and performing-arts festivals. Over the next 12 months, the band toured other parts of Europe, Australia, and the U.S. March 1996 saw the release of "Firestarter," a paroxysmal dance track that sampled two grunge acts, the Breeders and the Art of Noise. "Firestarter," in which Flint provided punk-style vocals, became the Prodigy's first major international hit and immediately shot to number one on the U.K. singles chart. The accompanying video, in which Flint looked like a cross between the Sex Pistols' Johnny Rotten and the monstrous clown from Stephen King's *It,* went into heavy rotation in the U.S. on the music channel MTV. That, in turn, helped another single, "Breathe," to become a bestseller. A major bidding war among U.S. music labels ensued; it ended when the Prodigy signed a contract with Maverick Records, a subsidiary of Warner Bros.

In June 1997 the Prodigy released *Fat of the Land.* (The band's name appears on that album as simply Prodigy.) With sales of more than 200,000 copies in the U.S. in its first week in stores, the album debuted at number one on the *Billboard* 200 album chart-an extremely rare feat for an electronic-dance-music disk. *Fat of the Land,* which debuted at number one in 22 other countries as well, offered simplified melodies, sparser sampling, and Flint's snarling punk-like vocals. Many critics hailed the album as a masterpiece. In a representative assessment, Barney Hoskyns, writing for *Rolling Stone* (July 1997), began with a take on electronic dance music in general: "Rarely has a pop trend so shamelessly been spoon-fed to America as the catch-all genre dubbed 'electronica.' Rarely, indeed, has the music industry tried so hard to convince us that the Next Big Thing is in fact a done deal-that another wave of English boys holds the future in its hands and we'd better get used to it. ... Lately, dissenting voices have questioned the wisdom of the electronica hype. America, they argue, will never embrace the underground subculture of techno." Hoskyns continued, "Enter the Prodigy ... and their bullishly titled third album, *Fat of the Land.* To say that the Prodigy aren't self-effacing synth nerds would be a comical understatement. To suggest that they are the Sex Pistols of techno would not even be such an exaggeration. What the Prodigy have done, quite simply, is to drag techno out of the communal nirvana of the rave and turn it into outlandish punk theater-and they've done it brilliantly. . . . *Fat of the Land* is a thrilling, intoxicating nightmare of a record, an energy flash of supernova proportions." One of the tracks, "Smack My Bitch Up," whose lyrics consisted solely of the lines "Change my pitch up / Smack my bitch up," angered women's organizations; the accompanying video, shot from the point of view of a person (revealed at the end to be a woman) taking drugs and drinking at clubs before picking up a lap dancer and having sex with her, generated far more controversy.

Thornhill left the Prodigy in 2000, because of trouble with his legs and the desire to pursue a solo career. (He has since performed with the band occasionally but never rejoined it.) The group's single "Baby's Got a Temper" (2002) launched what the British critic Louis Pattison, writing for Amazon.com, described as a "disastrous" comeback campaign that "found the band stagnant and on the verge of self-parody." Although Flint and Maxim remained members of the band, neither contributed to the Prodigy's next album, *Always Outnumbered, Never Outgunned* (2004). (The title was inspired by that of Walter Mosley's 1997 novel, *Always Outnumbered, Always Outgunned.)* The decision to make the recording without Flint and Maxim was Howlett's, who felt that as a threesome the band was in a rut. "Success and happiness makes you lazy and slows you down," he commented to Angus Batey for the *Guardian* (February 6, 2009). Maxim concurred, telling Batey, "We toured for almost seven years straight, and we were in each other's space for so long we needed to get away from that and have some different thoughts." Being cut off from the Prodigy troubled Flint, however; he told Batey, "I had no creative outlet at all. It really screwed me up, and I screwed myself up. I'm quite self-destructive." (In an example of his self-destructiveness, he had what he termed "quite a bad accident" while racing with a motorcycle team.)

Performers who contributed to *Always Outnumbered, Never Outgunned* included Liam Gallagher (Oasis's frontman), Kool Keith, Juliette Lewis, Twista, and the Ping Pong Bitches. Critical reception to the album was decidedly mixed-it earned an eight out of

10 from the *Drowned in Sound* (August 25, 2004, on-line) reviewer, four out of five from a London *Observer* (July 18, 2004) critic, and two out of five stars from the *Guardian* (August 20, 2004) and *Rolling Stone* (September 20, 2004). Nevertheless, on the U.K. album charts, the album reached number one, where it remained for one week only.

Howlett, Flint, and Maxim joined to record the Prodigy's fifth studio album, *Invaders Must Die* (2009). The album's singles, including "Omen" and "Warrior's Dance," marked a return to the band's rave roots. *Invaders Must Die* debuted at the top spot on the U.K. album charts. Between the beginning of January and the end of August 2009, the Prodigy performed at more than 80 sold-out concerts, in Singapore and cities in Great Britain, Ireland, the European continent, the U.S., Puerto Rico, Australia, New Zealand, and Japan. The group planned to tour in support of the album through March 2010.

Personal Lives

In 2002 Howlett married the British singer Natalie Appleton, a member of the British-Canadian all-female pop group All Saints. Appleton's sister Nicole, a member of the same band, is married to Liam Gallagher. Howlett and his wife have a son, Ace Billy, born in 2004; Appleton also has a teenage daughter, Rachel, from her first marriage. In their house, outside Chelmsford, England—where their neighbors include Flint and his wife—Rowlett has a state-of-the-art recording studio. Maxim and his wife have two sons and a daughter.

Further Reading

Kerrang (on-line) June 1997

(London) *Guardian* (on-line) Aug. 20, 2004, Feb. 9, 2009

Mixmag (on-line) Aug. 1992

Rolling Stone (on-line) Aug. 21, 1997

Spin (on-line) Sep. 1997; XLR8R Web site

Reynolds, Simon. *Generation Ecstasy: Into the World of Techno and Rave Culture,* 1999

Bernard Purdie

Drummer

Born: June 11, 1939; Elkton, Maryland

Primary Field: Country music performer and recording artist

Group Affiliation: Solo artist

Introduction

Bernard "Pretty" Purdie is one of the few who arguably can claim to be, as his Web site calls him, "the world's most recorded drummer." Although the accuracy of his assertion has never been proved, the drummer's presence on dozens of iconic and genre-defining 20th-century songs and albums—works of jazz, soul, pop, rock, and acid jazz—and the myriad studio sessions he took part in during the 1960s, '70s, and '80s certainly place him in the running for that distinction; his Web site notes performances on more than 3,000 albums, among them works by James Brown, Aretha Franklin, Steely Dan, and Louis Armstrong.

Early Life

The 11th of 15 children, Bernard Purdie was born on June 11, 1939 in the town of Elkton, Maryland, near the Delaware border. At the age of six, he took up drumming, banging out rhythms on an improvised drum set comprised of his mother's kitchenware. "I knew right away that's what I wanted to do with the rest of my life," he told Segal. "No matter what happened, I wanted to play the drums." When he was 11 his mother died, and at 13 he lost his father as well; afterward Purdie's grandparents and "people all over town" raised him, as he told Bradley Bambarger for Newhouse News Service (June 8, 2006). Purdie was given music lessons early on by a drummer named Leonard Hayward (spelled "Heywood" in some sources), who played in a local orchestra. Hayward started Purdie out on trumpet and flute—not the drums—and while that teaching method initially confused the young musician, it paid off. As quoted in the transcript of a 2004 interview for the traveling Red Bull Music Academy, Purdie said that Hayward "wouldn't let me play the drums and I didn't understand this. Then one day [another musician] said: 'He wants you to learn music, dummy.' I'm like: 'Yeah, I knew that. [Of] course I knew that, this is the way you do it.' Boy, I was really dumb, but it worked. I learnt how to play the notes and when you hear notes you play the rhythms, patterns, all horn players play patterns. . . . Also what happened for me, instead of trying to give me a drum chart . . . I would take the horn chart and use that to follow where the music was going and it was the easiest thing in the world for me, 'cause I'm an ex-trumpet player." Purdie's early idols were such big-band jazz drummers as Sid Catlett, Louie Bellson, Gene Krupa, Cozy Cole, Papa Jo Jones, and Chris Columbus. He would eventually adopt the swinging high-hat technique used by those drummers. "Those swing drummers were timekeepers, and keeping time was what I was taught as my job," he told Bambarger. "To this day, that's what it's all about for me—keeping that beat happening and everybody's feet moving." When Purdie was 14 or 15, he used money he made by distributing advertising circulars to purchase his first drum set.

In addition to teaching Purdie music, Hayward let the young musician accompany his band to shows. One of Purdie's jobs was to keep alcohol away from Hayward, a heavy drinker. Purdie took advantage of that situation in order to sit in on the drums. He said in the Red Bull Music Academy interview, "Everyone was always watching [Hayward] to make sure that he never got hold of any alcohol when the gig was going. So he'd bring me along to make sure he didn't drink anything, stuff like that, and I'd have to walk around with this big tall glass of water—'I got your water Mr. Hayward, I got it!' Only the big tall glass of water was filled with either vodka or gin. So every time after one or two songs, he'd need a drink of water, and I'd be standing there. . . . So by the time of the first break. . . . Mr. Hayward would have to go out to the station wagon and fall right to sleep. And I'd go inside and sit at the drums and I'd have to finish the gig, big band with 14-piece orchestra." In his teens Purdie also played with a host of local country and bar bands, including one called Jackie Lee & the Angels. According to Purdie's Web site, he became his family's biggest breadwinner through his frequent gigs, which also allowed him to "feel my way into nearly every kind of music, 'cause I had to know all styles and was never afraid to try something new."

Purdie attended George Washington Carver High School until the 12th grade, when community efforts to integrate public schools led him to enroll voluntarily in a previously all-white school. After graduating he attended Morgan State University (then Morgan State College), in Baltimore, Maryland. In the early 1960s, after two years at Morgan State, Purdie moved to New York City with a band, which played its first show at a club where the uncle of one of the group's members worked. Mickey Baker and Sylvia Robinson, who performed as the R&B duo Mickey and Sylvia, were in attendance—and were impressed by Purdie's drumming. After the show they asked him to play on a re-recording of their 1957 hit song "Love Is Strange." He was paid $80 for four hours of work. (He told Bambarger that the song "ended up making millions, but I felt rich with that 80 bucks, even though it was all gone by Tuesday, what with me buying drinks for everybody.") Purdie then found work at a laundry and spent the hours after work outside the nearby Turf Club, asking the musicians for a chance to play. That led to further session work, and soon Purdie was working up to four sessions a day, six days a week. He became known in the New York recording industry as a "fixer," a drummer on call to play session drums and add needed over-dubs. He established himself as an eager and available musician, and the professionally made signs he set up while working, which read "You done hired the hit maker" and "If you need me, call me, the little old hit maker," added to his reputation as something of an eccentric. (He stopped displaying the signs toward the end of the 1960s, after a friend lectured him about his ego. "When she was done with me, I felt about an inch high and my behavior changed 180 degrees," the drummer told Bambarger.)

Life's Work

In the late 1960s Purdie became the house drummer for the jazz record label CTI (Creed Taylor International), owned by the producer Creed Taylor. He also played drums on numerous recordings for artists on Atlantic Records during that period. The first hit among the songs on which Purdie played during those years was the 1967 instrumental song "Memphis Soul Stew," by the saxophonist King Curtis (born Curtis Ousley). Purdie has credited Curtis with helping him find much of his recording work in the 1960s and early 1970s and with introducing him to Aretha Franklin. He told the Red Bull Music Academy interviewer that meeting Curtis in 1962 was "a highlight" in his life. "I didn't realize how big King Curtis was," he said. "All I knew was that he had the best band in the land. He had a 10-piece orchestra that was a funk band, a pop band, a classical band—whatever it took, the band smoked. . . . Meeting him elevated me automatically, 'cause he was the one who called me for 90% of the records that were done for Atlantic Records. He brought me in, he liked what I was doing."

The late 1960s were some of Purdie's most prolific years: he played drums on one or more tracks on James Brown's *Ain't That a Groove* (1965), Gabor Szabo's *Jazz Raga* (1966), Nina Simone's *Nina Simone Sings the Blues* (1967), Jimmy Smith's *Respect* (1967), David Newman's *Bigger and Better* (1968), and Gary McFarland's *America the Beautiful* (1969). He also played on two songs on the iconic soul singer Brown's groundbreaking album *Say It Loud—I'm Black and I'm Proud* (1969), "I Guess I'll Have to Cry, Cry, Cry," and "Let Them Talk." That year Purdie also released his own album, *Soul Drums*, as "Pretty Purdie." Reviewing a reissue of that record, Chris Ziegler wrote for the *OC Weekly* (June 10, 2005), "*Soul Drums*' monstrous production and Purdie's ferocious style make for a widely recognized but rarely available classic."

Affiliation: Jazz, Pop, Soul Music

Purdie told George Kanzler for the Newark, New Jersey, *StarLedger* (September 11, 1998) that he has recorded and performed so frequently because "I do it all." "I have never wanted to be categorized, yet I have been all my life," he said. "I've been called a funk drummer, a rock drummer, a soul drummer, an R&B drummer, a Latin drummer, a jazz drummer—but all I've ever wanted to be known as was a drummer, a good, soulful drummer." In addition to his work with others, Purdie has released original studio and live albums over the past few decades, among them *Soul Drums* (1969), *Soul Is . . . Pretty Purdie* (1972), *Soul to Jazz* (1997), and *Purdie Good Cookin'* (2007).

Purdie has a long-established reputation for his near-perfect musical timing and his innovative signature beat, the "Purdie Shuffle," a half-time groove created with six high-hat, bass-drum, and snare-drum tones and augmented with "ghost notes"—accents added by lightly brushing or tapping the snare drum. Purdie has performed his beat, or variations of it, on recordings of many popular songs, including "Home at Last," from the 1977 Steely Dan album, *Aja*. The beat has become a musical standard, one many drummers aspire to duplicate. David Segal wrote for the *New York Times* (March 30, 2009, on-line), "For bowlers the ultimate test is the 7–10 split. For card sharks it's the hot shot cut. For drummers it's the funky little miracle of syncopation known as the Purdie Shuffle." The Purdie Shuffle is challenging to play, and many drummers concede that only the beat's creator can pull it off perfectly. Jason McGerr, the drummer for the indie-pop band Death Cab for Cutie, told Segal, "It doesn't matter how much I practice, I will never play that shuffle like Purdie. It's because he has an attitude that seems to come through every time. He always sounds like he's completely in charge."

In 1970 Purdie played drums on the song "Soul Kiss" on the Dizzy Gillespie album *The Real Thing*. The next year he played on Gil Scott-Heron's *Pieces of a Man* and Galt MacDermot's *The Nucleus*. He also released the album *Stand by Me (Whatcha See Is Whatcha Get)* on the Flying Dutchman label. That album, recorded with his band, Pretty Purdie and the Playboys, featured guest performances by a host of well-known musicians, among whom were Gil Scott-Heron, Harold Wheeler, and Chuck Rainey. Several of the tracks were instrumental versions of soul songs; some had vocals provided by Purdie, Norman Matlock, and Scott-Heron. Purdie also released *Purdie Good! & Shaft*, an album of covers he recorded with other musicians that featured a version of "Theme from Shaft," the popular Isaac Hayes song from the cult "blaxploitation" film *Shaft*. According to a review on the Web site Must-Hear.com, "Far from groundbreaking, *Purdie Good! & Shaft* simply crackle with a raw uncluttered funk that is seldom heard in the age of technocratic music producers and $10,000 a day studios."

Purdie's profile was also given a major boost in the early 1970s when he was asked by Curtis to join his band, King Curtis and the Kingpins, who were to perform as Aretha Franklin's backing band for a series of shows. Purdie accepted the offer and later took over Curtis's spot as Franklin's music director, a position he held until 1975. (Curtis was murdered by a drug addict in the summer of 1971.) Among the band's members were Cornell Dupree on guitar and Billy Preston on organ. The concerts were recorded and preserved on the album *Live at Fillmore West* (1971). Purdie also played Curtis's original material as part of the Kingpins; a recording of the performance was released in 1971, also as *Live at Fillmore West*.

In 1972 Franklin's album *Young, Gifted, and Black* was released to popular and critical acclaim. It contained the song "Rock Steady," which includes one of Purdie's best-known drum performances, complete with his signature 16th-note high-hat beat. In 1972 another album of Purdie's work, *Soul Is . . . Pretty Purdie*, was released on the Flying Dutchman label. The album found Purdie and numerous studio musicians playing covers as well as originals, such as Purdie's "Song for Aretha." A description of the album on the Dusty Groove America Web site reads, "Purdie breaks out here in a compelling album of soul jazz tracks done in a number of styles. The approach is sort of big studio funk—with some cuts that have a harder sound, and others that open up in a groove that's gotten a lot more complicated than the early days."

In 1970 Purdie had played on Louis Armstrong's *Louis Armstrong and His Friends* (1970), which featured the popular song "What a Wonderful World" and was re-released in 1988 with that title. Later in the decade Purdie played on the soundtrack of the animated film *Fritz the Cat* (1972) and the albums *Abandoned Luncheonette* (1973), by Hall & Oates; *Bolivia* (1973), by Gato Barbieri; and *Foreigner* (1973), by Cat Stevens. Among the noteworthy songs from that period featuring Purdie's work are B.B. King's "The Thrill Is Gone" and Percy Sledge's "When a Man Loves a Woman." Purdie is also known as one of the session drummers for the 1977 album *Aja*, by the jazz-rock band Steely Dan. The album was a critical success and reached number three on the U.S. album charts. Purdie played on the songs "Deacon Blues" and "Home at Last," the latter famously showcasing the Purdie Shuffle. Other Steely Dan albums with Purdie's work include *The Royal Scam* (1976) and *Gaucho* (1980).

In 1980 Purdie recorded with Dizzy Gillespie at the Montreux Jazz Festival in Switzerland, which resulted in the album *Digital at Montreux* (1980). In 1983 Purdie toured with Gillespie. He played on B.B. King's *There Must Be a Better World Somewhere* (1981) and recorded frequently during the 1980s with the jazz and funk saxophonist Hank Crawford, performing on *Indigo Blue* (1983) and *Mr. Chips* (1987). He played on two songs on Dizzy Gillespie's *Rhythmstick* (1990) and teamed up with Chuck Rainey and the percussionist Pancho Morales, among others, for the 1993 release *Coolin' Groovin' (A Night at On-Air)*, which was recorded live in Japan. Also in 1993 he also played on three songs each for Al Green's *Don't Look Back* and *The Fugs Second Album*, by the garage-rock band the Fugs. In 1995 he contributed drums to the critically acclaimed *Pushing Against the Flow*, by the acid jazz group *Raw Stylus*; that album, the only one by the group, brought together a large number of contributing musicians and merged soul, jazz, and hip-hop. Purdie also recorded drums for the electronic group Coldcult's 1997 album, *Let Us Play.*

The year 1996 saw the release of *Soul to Jazz*, the first recording in the U.S. in more than 20 years to be released under Purdie's name. The album, which included several soul and jazz covers, was followed by *Soul to Jazz II* (1998). For the followup recording Purdie enlisted guests from his past, Hank Crawford and Cornell Dupree. Douglas Payne wrote for the All About Jazz Web site (July 1, 1998), "*Soul to Jazz II* isn't as earth-shattering or hip-shaking as the premise promises. But the ultimate joy is hearing three soul sax giants (Hank Crawford especially) waxing eloquently in their own mighty soulful way."

Purdie has generated criticism and controversy for his claim, made at least as long ago as the late 1970s, that he was paid to provide, dub over, or "fix"—without credit—the percussion work on roughly 20 tracks by the Beatles. (He has said that he will make the case for that claim in a forthcoming autobiography.) His claim is still brought up in interviews, and he has stood by it. He told the Red Bull Music Academy interviewer, "People don't understand that fixing records was a way of life in the '60s and the '70s. 98% of self-contained groups are not on their own albums and I was one of the few drummers that could go in, join the group and make the records. . . . It was just a job to me, and the Beatles' music was just another job for me. . . . Half of the songs that I played on, I played on 21 of the Beatles tracks—half of them had no drums." He added that the Beatles' manager, Brian Epstein, "spent an amount of money to promote the Beatles that was unheard of in the '60s. [The Beatles' drummer, Ringo Starr,] had his place in the Beatles 'cause that's who they wanted and that's who they could control. . . . He looked the part and he's the one they chose, but when it came to those records and the fixing of those records, 98% of them were first recorded early in England and brought to the USA to be fixed. . . . There are four drummers on the Beatles music, and Ringo's not one of them." Purdie's assertion has brought him death threats.

While most of the recordings for which Purdie played in the late 1990s and 2000s were reissues and compilations, he has performed recently on a few original releases. He played on the song "Modern Jive" on Sugarman & Co's *Pure Cane Sugar* (2002), released by Daptone Records, and on *Steel Reelin'*, a 2006 record by the Steely Dan collaborator Elliot Randall. In 2007 Purdie released *Purdie Good Cookin'*, a live album that featured several musicians from Portland, Oregon. Since the early 1990s Purdie has also played occasional shows with the New Jersey-based R&B band the Hudson River Rats, fronted by Rob Paparazzi, who has since become a friend and business partner of Purdie's. Paparazzi played harmonica and provided vocals for *Purdie Good Cookin'* and has also served as Purdie's music director on tours of Europe and Japan. Purdie contributed to the Hudson River Rats' albums *Get It While You Can* (2003) and *First Take* (2007). In March 2009 Purdie began playing drums in the Broadway revival of *Hair* and is credited on the musical's cast recording. Purdie also appeared as Uncle Bill in the independent 2008 crime film *Priceless*.

The Purdie Shuffle, according to Purdie, was influenced by the rhythmic sounds of the train that regularly passed his childhood home. He told Segal, "When I first started working this out, I was 8 years old, and I called it the locomotion because that's what I was trying to capture: whoosh, whoosh, whoosh." The beat began as a standard drum shuffle, but as Purdie developed it he added lightly brushed "ghost notes," and instead of tapping the high-hat, he used a pattern in which he moved his right hand up and down to strike the side of the high-hat and then the top in repetition, creating what Segal described as a "tock-tick tocktick sound." Purdie described his shuffle to the Red Bull Music Academy interviewer as "quarter notes, eighth notes, 16th notes, 32nd notes, dotted notes, triplets, half notes, whole notes, everything except 64th notes. A combination of high-hats and kick drums, putting it all together with the dotted feel, the loping feel, and allowing it to breathe in a two bar phrase. Not one bar, 'cause the worst thing you can do is trying to put all this into one bar, it's a two bar phrase, and if you put it into half time, you automatically fall into what is necessary for the shuffle." He noted that the reason the shuffle challenges drummers is that most, instinctively, want to play it faster than it should be played. "The best part of it is, the slower you do it, the better it is. Which is why it's so hard for people to do, 'cause a lot of people don't want to play slow," he said. Segal wrote about the Purdie Shuffle, "If you can listen without shaking your hips, you should probably see a doctor." The shuffle is a versatile beat; the Steely Dan member Donald Fagen told Segal that the beat unexpectedly fit the song "Babylon Sisters," from *Gaucho*. "I guess we expected more of a regular shuffle, and he started playing something very complex," Fagen said. "We were amazed, because it was perfect for the tune. 'Babylon Sisters' has this dark mood to it, and the beat seemed to accentuate the floating dark mood that the song required."

Personal Life

Purdie has seven children, including three with his second and current wife, Barbara. He also has 12 grandchildren and 10 great-grandchildren. He has shown no sign of retiring soon from live performances. Paparazzi told Bambarger, "Bernard just loves playing music for people; it doesn't matter what it is—a giant concert, a serious recording session, a drum clinic or someone's wedding. He's played with some heavy cats, and he's got great stories to tell. But he's never intimidating; he's good at just being one of the guys."

Further Reading

allmusic.com
bernardpurdie.com
New York Times C pl Mar. 31, 2009
Newhouse News Service June 8, 2006

Patricia Racette (rah-SET)

Singer

Born: 1966 (?); Bedford, New Hampshire
Primary Field: Opera singer
Group Affiliation: Solo performer with multiple opera companies

Introduction

Patricia Racette has been hailed as one of the greatest sopranos the U.S. has produced in recent years. In such prestigious halls as the Metropolitan Opera House, in New York City, the Opera Bastille, in Paris, the Royal Opera House, in London, and La Scala, in Italy, she has sung some of the most famous roles in the operatic canon, among them those of Violetta in La Traviata, Donna Elvira in Don Giovanni, Micaela in Carmen, Mimi and Musetta in La Boheme, and the title characters Jenenufa and Iphigenia in Tauris.

Early Life

Her voice "was more or less there from the first," the singer recalled to J. A. Van Sant for *American Record Guide* (January/February 1998). Born in around 1966, Patricia Lynn Racette grew up in the small, blue-collar town of Bedford in southern New Hampshire. A descendant of French Canadians, she was raised in the Catholic faith. Her father, Paul Racette, delivered Pepsi products; her mother, Jackie Racette, worked in a grocery store. Although no one in her family was particularly musical, Patricia became fascinated with music at an early age. As she recalled to Cori Ellison, "When I was about 6, I saw a guitar in a store window. I got that sort of 'elevator stomach' you get when you're infatuated. I thought, 'I have to have that instrument.' [Every day] I spent five hours in my room after school writing songs, tape-recording myself and then harmonizing with myself. That was my oasis, my refuge." In about 1984 Racette enrolled at the College of Music of the University of North Texas (UNT) at Denton. "In order to be in [the UNT] music school you had to have an instrument," she told Davin Steinberg for the *Albuquerque Journal* (June 22, 1997). "My instrument is my voice, so I took voice lessons, and the [classical] literature was slowly introduced to me. I loved the way it made me feel, intellectually. And my voice was suited for it." As an undergraduate, she told Eric Myers, "I got seduced into this whole world of opera and theater and all that it meant. I'd never really been exposed to it. If I had to choose one moment that really hooked me into opera, it was hearing [Renata] Scotto's recording of [Puccini's] *Suor Angelica.* I remember sitting on the floor of my cheap little college apartment and just getting chills up my spine." Racette earned a bachelor of music degree in 1988.

Life's Work

After her graduation Racette won first prize in a national the San Francisco on the of which she was accepted into the SFO's Merola Opera Program, an intensive 11-week summer course. The program offers individual coaching by professional singers and classes in such subjects as musical style and interpretation, acting, movement, and diction; at the end of the summer, students perform in two fully staged operas. While at Merola Racette began to build her reputation as a singer who thoroughly immersed herself in the characters she portrayed; as she told Bryce Hallett for the *Sydney Morning Herald* (January 9, 2002), "I believe it's incumbent on the artist to not only do the research and explore the character and the world they are in, but to make a soul search within oneself. When I am playing a scene, I need to find the truth and have it relate to my own experience in some way. It has to be believable. The drama and the character are as important as the music, and affect the way I sing." After the summer the SFO named Racette an Adler Fellow for the 1989-90 season; as such, she participated in a performance-oriented residency in which she received intensive training and sang in SFO productions. Racette made her SFO—and professional—debut as Mistress Ford in matinee performances of Giuseppe Verdi's comic opera *Falstaff;* she also appeared as the high priestess in Verdi's *Aida.* The latter production was moved from the War Memorial Opera House, the SFO's home, to San Francisco's Masonic Temple, because of damage caused by the 1989 Lorna Prieta earthquake. While performing at the new site, Racette told Bruce Duffie for *Opera Journal* (March 2001), she felt the power of her art. "There was an energy in that place," she recalled. "[The earthquake] was a terrible event, but it was not something that devastated the entire city. It devastated a lot of things, but the response, the need to be moved, to experience something beautiful and something pure just by its very essence, was so overwhelming."

On October 12, 1991 Racette appeared for the first time as an SFO principal artist, in a company production of Bizet's *Carmen,* in which she played Micaela, Carmen's rival for the love of Don Jose. The audience rewarded her with a warm ovation; in a review for *Opera News* (February 3, 1996), David McKee praised her for "[rendering] the evening's single finest vocal vignette." Racette then traveled to the Grand Theatre de Geneve, in Switzerland, and the Lisbon Festival, in Portugal, where she reprised her role as Micaela. In 1993 she appeared for the first time in a leading role in a Mozart opera-that of Donna Elvira in *Don Giovanni-at* the Opera Theater of St. Louis, in Missouri. A year later, with the same company, she sang the part of the title character in Gluck's *Iphigenia in Tauris.* Charles MacKay, the general director of the theater, told J. A. Van Sant, "Pat Racette is one of the finest lyric sopranos before the public today. Her Elvira was ravishingly sung, with great clarity and rich, distinctive tone. She makes every role a part of her voice. I could not admire her more." Also in 1993 Racette appeared in Puccini's *Turandot* at the Welsh National Opera; she sang the part of the slave girl Liu, who kills herself out of love for Turandot's would-be suitor. Next, for the first time, she sang the part of the fatally ill seamstress Mimi, the heroine of Puccini's *La Boheme,* in an SFO mounting of the opera; she opened the San Diego Opera's 1994-95 season in the same role. At her New York Metropolitan Opera debut, on March 4, 1994, the versatile Racette assumed a different major role in *La Boheme*—that of Musetta. She told Denis Paiste for the *New Hampshire Sunday News* (October 30, 1994). "What's difficult is to be a truly world-class success in both [roles]. That's what I would like to try to do. When I'm doing one, I want to be doing the other. I truly love both parts." Later, as Mimi or Musetta, Racette debuted at major European opera houses in England, France, and Austria. Meanwhile, in 1994-95, she had sung the role of the compassionate schoolteacher Ellen Orford in Benjamin Britten's *Peter Grimes* with the Vancouver Opera of British Columbia. (Five years later she performed that part at Milan's Teatro alla Scala, known familiarly as La Scala.) Also in 1994-95 Racette appeared as Fiordiligi in Mozart's *Cosi fan Tutte* with the Philadelphia Opera.

In 1996 Racette gave what Peter G. Davis, in a review for *New York* (September 2, 1996). described as a "compelling" performance in the title role of *Emmeline* (music by Tobias Picker, libretto by J.D. McClatchy). in its world premiere at the Santa Fe Opera, in a production staged by Francesca Zambello. An Oedipal tragedy set in 1840s Maine, *Emmeline* follows a young woman who is forced to work in a textile mill to help support her desperately poor family. Impregnated by the mill's foreman (who is also the owner's son-in-law), she gives up her baby, who she thinks is a girl. Years later, she marries a far younger man who turns out to be her own son. Speaking of the opera, Racette told Cori Ellison, "It's this incredible Yankee sensibility, that Puritan residue. And the Merrimack River that figures so prominently in the book—my dad grew up swimming in it. I know what it smells like in the summer. I know what Maine winters are like. You'd think these things are far removed from creating a character. But knowing them adds such an important layer." Racette told David Steinberg, "*Emmeline* was something I was very proud of, and it was something that involved me artistically in a way nothing else had. You're creating a role among the composer and librettist and director. I really created the character. That was a rich feeling. to be able to participate at a fundamental level in the creation of a piece." In the *Wall Street Journal,* as quoted on Racette's Website,

Heidi Waleson wrote that as collaborators, Picker and McClatchy had "arrived at an emotional truth about the nature of love, particularly the love between mother and child, and created a tour-de-force role for the soprano along the way." After seeing Racette in *Emmeline* when it was mounted for the first time at the New York City Opera, in April 1998, Bernard Holland wrote for the *New York Times* (April 2, 1998), "Patricia Racette in the title role is a happy bit of casting. The part is not a virtuoso one, nor does it particularly try the parameters of a normal soprano voice. It does require, however, an unforced naturalness and an unconscious purity. of spirit. Ms. Racette projects both very well."

In 1997, at the celebrated Santa Fe Opera Festival, Racette appeared for the first time as Violetta in Verdi's *La Traviata* and received what J. A. Van Sant described as "a rare standing ovation" on opening night. Van Sant wrote that he "had not heard the first act coloratura scene so well sung in decades." He added, "Racette ably met the wide-ranging demands of the other three scenes of Verdi's marathon part, [which] embodies not only stringent coloratura singing but lyric and dramatic in full measure." On November 23, 1998 Racette again sang the part of Violetta, in Franco Zeffirelli's staging of *La Traviata* at the Metropolitan Opera (often referred to as the Met). Met officials had chosen Racette to replace the soprano Renee Fleming, who had left the production only a month before its scheduled opening (and who had accepted the role after Angela Georgiu had bowed out); the officials had turned down Zeffirelli's next choice for the role-the young Albanian soprano Inva Mulain favor of Racette. Mike Silverman of the Associated Press, as quoted on the Web site of the *Turkish Daily News* (December 6, 1998), praised the Met's decision to cast Racette: "In Patricia Racette, the Met has a singing actress of the first rank-and that's what it takes to do justice to the role of Violetta. . . . Racette captures the quicksilver emotion of the part—Violetta's surprise and alarm at her own response to Alfredo's declaration of love, for instance. In her aria about the joys of freedom, 'Sempre libera,' she sings the second verse as someone who is protesting too much and about to get deeply involved.... Her wraith-like appearance in Act 4 as she nears death provides a startling contrast to the glamour she exudes in the earlier scenes. Her singing is especially impressive here—a gorgeous 'Addio, del passato,' complete with high pianissimo that provoked the biggest ovation of the night. Vocally, she is equal to every challenge of this most demanding role." In a review for *Opera News* (March 1999), John W. Freeman wrote, "Racette's Violetta, if neither brilliant nor deeply impassioned, came across as a thinking, feeling characterization, neatly and expressively sung." The critic Justin Davidson, by contrast, found fault with the singer's interpretation; he wrote for *Newsday* (November 25, 1998), "Racette ... sang the title role with an agile, alabaster voice and a feathery pianissimo, but her notes clicked into place like so many tiles. She supplied none of the giddiness and desperation that is written into the first act's wrenching tug-of-war between her fierce desire for independence and the temptations of falling in love." Racette has since performed the role of Violetta at the Opera Bastille, the Houston Grand Opera, and the Dallas Opera, among other places.

Affiliation: Operetic Performances

Her acclaimed performance as the titular heroine in the world premiere of Tobias Picker's *Emmeline*, with the Santa Fe Opera in 1996, was seen by thousands of television viewers when a videotape of the production aired the following year on PBS's *Great Performances* series. In a review of that broadcast for the *San Francisco Examiner* (March 31, 1997), Allen Ulrich de- scribed Racette as "a radiant Emmeline, as credible at 13 as at 35, with a soprano that has acquired a remarkable range of color and an individuality that spell imminent stardom." "What makes Racette's voice distinctive is its timbre, which combines a heartbreakingly poignant quality with a strong, focused 'ping,' particularly in the upper range," Eric Myers wrote for *Opera News* (June 2002). "For all its vulnerability, it is still a powerful sound, made-to-order for those opera heroines who combine victimhood with flashes of defiance." Racette has also earned plaudits for her skills as an actress; as Cori Ellison wrote for the *New York Times* (March 29, 1998), "Racette's unique blend of strength and pathos, combined with a robust, plangent, bronze and-honey voice and an ineffable, unteachable gift that the Italian operagoers call anima, or soul, keeps her very much in demand in French and contemporary opera." Racette's honors include the 1994 Marian Anderson Award and the 1998 Richard Tucker Award; the Dallas Opera named her the Maria Callas Debut Artist of the Year for the 1999–2000 season. ''I'm still not certain where my voice is ultimately going," Racette told Ellison. "But my voice will tell me."

In April 1999, along with the Canadian baritone Russell Braun, Racette made her New York City recital debut, with a concert at the Walter Reade Theater, at Lincoln Center. In the next month she filled the role of the soprano soloist in a performance of Beethoven's Symphony No. 9 (known as the *Choral* Symphony), conducted by Christoph von Eschenbach at his final concert as music director of the Houston Symphony. Also that year, with both the Houston Grand Opera and Opera Australia, in Sydney, she performed the part of Margherita in Arrigo Boito's *Mefistofele.* In April 2000, at the Houston Grand Opera Racette appeared in the world premiere of Carlisle Floyd's *Cold Sassy Tree,* based on a novel by Olive Ann Burns. She sang the role of Love Simpson, a young woman who marries her much older em- player three weeks after the death of his first wife, thus scandalizing the residents of a Georgia town at the turn of the last century. In October of that year, she sang the title role in Leo Janacek's *Jenufa* with the Washington Concert Opera, which offers unstaged versions of rarely heard operatic works. Jenufa, a young resident of a Moravian village, is abandoned by the lover who impregnated her; her stepmother, eager to marry her off, drowns the newborn baby. Although the illegitimate birth and murder become public knowledge, the stepbrother of Jenufa's lover asks for her hand in marriage. In a review for the *Washington Post* (October 16, 2000) of the concert opera's presentation, Phillip Kennicott wrote, "[Patricia Racette), a soprano currently on the most precipitous upward arc of her career, focused on the frailties, vulnerability and youth of her character The sound is lovely, sweet and evenly produced, powerful when necessary, and rarely if ever unbeautiful or pinched. In any case, Racette has a major Jenufa in her." Racette then performed Jenufa at Chicago's Lyric Opera, in a production staged by Richard Jones, and later reprised the role with the SFO.

With the Pittsburgh Opera in 2002, Racette sang the title role, that of a Japanese geisha, in Puccini's *Madama Butterfly.* In the same year, with theSanta Fe Opera, in Tchaikovsky's *Eugene Onegin,* she sang the part of Tatiana, a simple country girl who is spurned by the sophisticated Onegin—who years later, when she is married and unavailable to him, falls in love with her. Also in 2002 Racette performed at the SFO as Desdemona in Verdi's *Otello,* an opera based on Shakespeare's *Othello.* "Racette is a radiant bright spot in director Emilio Sagi's otherwise lackluster production . . . ," Georgia Row wrote for the *Contra Costa Times* (October 12, 2002). "The soprano's soaring vocalism and poised stage presence were tremendous assets throughout."

Racette has contributed to two recordings: on the Polygram label, with James Levine conducting, Verdi's *I Lombardi* (1997), featuring performances by Luciano Pavarotti, Samuel Ramey, and June Anderson; and on the Angel Classics Label, with James Conlon conducting, Alexander von Zemlinsky's *Der Traumgorge* (2001). In May 2003 Racette appeared as Violetta in *La Traviata* at the Opera Bastille. Other performances by her in 2003 include that of the title role in Janacek's *Katya Kabanova* with the San Diego Opera, in July, and that of Leonora in *Il Travatore* with the Opera Company of Philadelphia, in October.

Personal Life

According to J. A. Van Sant, "Racette's spirit, her jokes and wit, endear her to colleagues, but her sense of purpose is respected by opera management." Racette maintains homes in New York City and the outskirts of Santa Fe with her life partner, the mezzo-soprano Beth Clayton, whose highly praised performances include her portrayal of the title character in the world premiere of Deborah Dratell's opera *Lilith.* The couple have a poodle named Sappho. In her leisure time Racette enjoys the kick-boxing exercise tae-bo.

Further Reading

American Record Guide p30+ Jan./Feb. 1998
Dallas Morning *News* p11 Jan. 28, 2000
Opera News p27+ Feb. 3, 1996, p8+ Dec. 1, 2000
San Francisco Chronicle V p1 June 4, 2001

Radiohead

Musical group

Colin Greenwood
Born: Jan. 26, 1969; England

Jonny Greenwood
Born: Nov. 5, 1971; England

Ed O'Brien
Born: Apr. 15, 1969; England

Phil Selway
Born: May 23, 1967; England

Thom Yorke
Born: Oct. 7, 1968; Scotland

Primary Field: Alternative rock
Group Affiliation: Radiohead

Introduction

Pigeonholed at first with the "alternative" rock bands that debuted in the wake of Nirvana's success in the early 1990s, the British group Radiohead has continued to explore new musical idioms and to bring experimental ideas and structures into the mainstream, thereby inviting comparisons to performers ranging from Pink Floyd to the Beatles. Radiohead's music—described as ethereal, dense, mournful, and majestic—features the tenor voice of its lead singer and lyricist, Thorn Yorke, whose sound is among the most distinctive in rock music today. Yorke founded Radiohead in collaboration with the bassist Colin Greenwood in about 1988; shortly afterward, the group expanded to include the guitarist Ed O'Brien, the drummer Phil Selway, and the guitarist Jonny Greenwood.

Early Lives

The members of Radiohead were all born within four and a half years of one another in England (with the exception of Yorke, who was born in Scotland and spent his early years there). The oldest of the five is Phil Selway, whose date of birth is May 23, 1967; the youngest is Jonny Greenwood (November 5, 1971). In between are Thorn Yorke (October 7, 1968), Colin Greenwood (January 26, 1969), and Ed O'Brien (April15, 1969). All of them attended the Abingdon School, a private boys' boarding and day school near Oxford. Colin Greenwood and Yorke became friends there when they discovered that they shared a liking for both crossdressing and the post-punk bands Joy Division and Magazine. They decided to form a band themselves. Their first recruit was Ed O'Brien, whom they approached because he seemed "cool," as one of them put it, and reminded them of the British rock icon Morrissey, the vocalist of the band the Smiths. Christening themselves On a Friday, the trio played a few gigs in 1988, accompanied by a drum machine. After the machine broke down, they sought out Phil Selway, who was playing with another band but agreed to join them. Before long Greenwood's younger brother, Jonny, asked to become a member of their group. Although they considered him too young and inexperienced, they occasionally allowed him to perform with them, on harmonica.

Lives' Work

Each member of the band attended a different college. Yorke studied fine art and literature at the University of Exeter; O'Brien majored in politics at the University of Manchester; Colin Greenwood and Selway both studied English, the former at Cambridge University and the latter at the University of Liverpool; and Jonny Greenwood dropped out of college after three months. When the young men returned home on school holidays, they practiced and performed together. After the last of the four older musicians graduated from college, they reformed the group, in Oxford, with Jonny Greenwood as a full member on guitar. Inspired by the title of a song on the 1986 Talking Heads album *True Stories,* they changed their name to Radiohead. After their first official gig, in 1991, they received more than 20 contract offers from record companies. They still had not made a deal when, in early May 1992, they released the EP *Drill* and opened shows for such established rock acts as PJ Harvey, Tears for Fears, and James. Soon afterward they signed to the *EMI*/Capitol record label and, in September 1992, released their first single, "Creep." The alienation and romantic frustration expressed in the song-its lyrics proclaim, "I'm a creep / I'm a weirdo / What the hell am I doing here? / I don't belong here"-were to take their place among the group's major themes. "Self-loathing is something we can all relate to," Ed O'Brien explained, as quoted by David Sprague in *Billboard* (May 15, 1993). The single became a minor hit in England. It was followed by the singles "Anyone Can Play Guitar" and "Pop Is Dead."

In February 1993 Radiohead released their first album, *Pablo Honey,* which consisted primarily of mid-tempo, plaintive songs with a heavy focus on guitars. For the most part both the British and American music press ignored the recording. Although noting that it offered "clever lyrics and good hooks," Mario Mundoz wrote for the *Los Angeles Times* (June 27, 1993) that the album did not "really deliver anything you haven't heard before, steering too close to Smiths-like melodies and trying ever so hard to be depressed in the way the Cure popularized." Despite the lack of attention, Radiohead continued to work hard, embarking that summer on a tour of Europe, during which they opened for other acts. The band's fortunes suddenly changed when American MTV and alternative radio stations started playing "Creep" heavily, apparently having recognized that the song's self-deprecatory lyrics and sharp guitar bursts fit comfortably with the grunge-rock scene that was so prominent at that time. The band soon supported Belly and Tears for Fears on a U.S. tour, during which they found that most concertgoers were interested only in "Creep." Thanks to its success in the U.S., "Creep" was re-released in England at the end of 1993, and this time it made the Top 10, while *Pablo Honey* sold enough copies to earn a gold certification. Radiohead spent the summer of 1994 performing dates around the world. During the year that followed their return to England, the group released *Iron Lung,* a series of EPs, which featured a continuation of the *Pablo Honey* sound with an increased emphasis on low-key acoustic numbers.

Eager to change the media perception that they were a one-hit wonder, Radiohead entered the studio with the producer John Leckie to record their sophomore album. The first results were heard in February 1995, when the single "High and Dry," a soaring acoustic ballad and their most sophisticated record until then, was released. In *The Bends,* which was released the following month, the group added a stronger dose of synthesizers and offered more dynamics than on their debut album. The lyrics, again mostly self-deprecatory, this time tackled the themes of isolation and loneliness as they applied to society in general, rather than just the singer; most critics found them to be of a higher quality than the group's earlier efforts. "Fake Plastic Trees," a mostly acoustic song about lonely people in an age defined by marketing, was released as a single in May 1995 and quickly became a fan favorite.

The Bends received strong reviews from some members of the press, who compared Radiohead favorably to such rock legends as U2 and complimented the band for writing songs that were more mature than their earlier work. "What makes *The Bends* so remarkable is that it marries such ambitious, and often challenging, instrumental soundscapes to songs that are at their cores hauntingly melodic and accessible," Stephen Thomas Eriewine wrote for the *All Music* Guide (on-line). Other critics were less friendly. "The sonics are frequently more compelling than the songs they embellish," Mark Jenkins complained in the *Washington Post* (April 7, 1995). American radio and MTV ignored the singles from *The Bends,* which were very different from "Creep," and record sales were low. Similarly, in Britain, during a summer in which the airwaves were dominated by anthemic Britpop by the likes of Blur, Oasis, and Pulp, Radiohead's somber musings were not popular.

Meanwhile, the band continued to perform live, supporting R.E.M. on their *Monster* tour. The third single of *The Bends,* "Just," was released in August 1995, and thanks to its louder guitars and stark, haunting video, Radiohead began to be noticed again. In 1996 rock radio and MTV began to play "Fake Plastic Trees" in heavy rotation, and *The Bends* returned to the British Top 10 and went gold in America. During the first half of 1996, the band toured to promote *The Bends.* Then they began work on their third album. Released in July 1997 and titled *OK Computer,* the album found Radiohead moving in distinctly new directions, combining progressive-rock experimentation with punk fury. For some tracks the band abandoned conventional song structures and used various synthesizers and production effects, taking their cue from such diverse sources as the film music of Ennio Morricone, *Bitches Brew*-era Miles Davis, and 1970s German psychedelia. Yorke's lyrics, which in some songs were much more abstract than before, did not dwell on his personal life. "I came to the realization I was being selfish in the past," he was quoted as saying on *MTV* (on-line), "and that was a good thing. It happened after *The Bends.* A drunk bloke comes up in the bar or a girl comes up in the street and says, 'Thank you, that record helped me through a difficult time.' And you stop being the selfish wanker you've always been. . . . I think there was a genuine point where it really was important for me to say things on a personal level to get these things sorted out for myself. But once it was out, it was done. With this album, I am moving on."

Containing multiple sections and ambitious lyrics, "Paranoid Android," the first single from *OK Computer,* was compared to Queen's multi-part operatic single "Bohemian Rhapsody." "Please could you stop the noise," Yorke sang, "I'm trying to get some rest from all the unborn chicken voices in my head." The surreal animated video of "Paranoid Android" attracted a lot of attention as well. The singles "Karma Police" and "No Surprises" received heavy airplay in both England and the United States. *OK Computer* was acclaimed in the press, with several magazines naming it "album of the year." Noting for *All* Music Guide (online) that it had "establishe[d] Radiohead as one of the most inventive and rewarding guitar-rock bands of the '90s," Stephen Thomas Erlewine declared that *OK Computer* was "a thoroughly astonishing demonstration of musical virtuosity, and becomes even [more] impressive with repeated listens, which reveal subtleties like electronica rhythms, eerie keyboards, odd time signatures, and complex syncopations." Apparently surprised by all the praise, Radiohead's members insisted that they didn't think the record worthy of the hype. Yorke told Aidin Vaziri for *Guitar Player* (October 1997), for example, "We got bored with being just a rock band, and we started considering what else was going on around us. Rock wasn't speaking to us. There was no intention to be difficult. Every record we make is, to some extent, the band absorbing stuff we've fallen in love with and then attempting to pay homage to it-and failing." The EP *Airbag/How Am I Driving* (1998), released while the band was touring, featured all the bonus tracks on the singles from *OK Computer.*

Radiohead returned to the studio in 1999 to record their highly anticipated fourth album. Difficulties soon arose, however, because Yorke suffered a bout of writer's block and then, having become fascinated by such experimental electronica acts as Aphex Twin and Autechre (Sean Booth and Rob Brown), would often bring only programmed drum machines or other electronic sound equipment to the studio. "It was about generating bits of work that may be incomplete and may not be going anywhere," Yorke told Danny Eccleston for *Q* (October 1999). "And by the time you finish it, it may be unrecognizable. But it might be far better than what you started with. That's what I hoped we were trying to do-regardless of where the music was coming from, and regardless of which members of the band were involved." His colleagues struggled with Yorke's new vision. "If you're going to make a different-sounding record," O'Brien told Eccleston, "you have to change the methodology. And it's scary—everyone feels insecure. I'm a guitarist and suddenly it's like, well, there are no guitars on this track, or no drums. [We] had to get our heads round that. It was a test of the band, I think." Despite such stumbling blocks, Radiohead continued recording, and in 2000 its new tracks began to be heavily circulated over the Internet, on Napster and other servers. Although arguments about choices of songs for the new album almost caused the musicians to split up, they launched a tour of Europe and Great Britain over the summer, during which they introduced many of their new songs. *Kid A,* released in October 2000, surprised many listeners by its reliance on a minimalist electronic sound and the near absence of conventional songs. In one song, "The National Anthem," the group incorporated avant-garde, Mingus-style horns. In others, Jonny Greenwood experimented with little-known instruments, using the Ondes Martenot, an electronic instrument that consists of a keyboard, a ribbon, and a ring and is best known for its use in the work of the 20th-century French composer Olivier Messiaen and in the theme of the television series Star *Trek.* Its unusualness notwithstanding, *Kid A* debuted on the American and British album charts at number one, thus becoming the first British album to hit the number-one spot in the U.S. since 1997.

Although critical reaction to *Kid A* was more reserved than it had been for *OK Computer,* most reviewers seemed to like it. In *Entertainment Weekly* (October 6, 2000), David Browne wrote, "Songs float by on the faintest of heartbeat pulses, intergalactic noises streaking like comets across the melodies. Ecclesiastical keyboards gently nudge the songs along." Browne concluded that despite its weaknesses, "it is a genuinely challenging work in a generally unchallenging time." In *All Music Guide* (on-line), Stephen Thomas Erlewine judged *Kid A* to be "a record that's intentionally difficult to grasp, which makes it seem deeper on first listen than it actually is. . . . The music is never seductive-it's self-consciously alienating, and while that can be intriguing at first, there's not enough underneath the surface to make Radiohead's relentless experimentation satisfying. Still, an experiment that yields mixed results still yields results, and there are some moments here that positively shimmer with genius." "With us, it's never going to be a case of 'let's tear up the blueprint

Affiliation: Electronic Music and Rock

While the guitars that dominated their early work are still occasionally prominent, their increasing use of synthesizers and sophisticated production technology has pushed the boundaries between electronic music and rock. Radiohead's first hit single, the so-called loser anthem "Creep," was released in 1992. *OK Computer* (1997), the band's third album, is widely considered Radiohead's masterpiece; several magazines have hailed it as one of the greatest, if not *the* greatest, rock album ever recorded. The group's members—five natives of Great Britain—have downplayed their experimental edge; as Thom Yorke told a writer for *Entertainment Weekly* (October 24, 1997), "We write pop songs. As time has gone on, we've gotten more into pushing our material as far as it can go. But there was no intention of it being 'art.' It's a reflection of all the disparate things we were listening to when we recorded it." Radiohead's influences range from the jazz bassist and composer Charles Mingus to the jazz harpist and pianist Alice Coltrane to the electronic artist Richard D. James, known as Aphex Twin, to the rock icon David Bowie. Radiohead's lyrics, many of which criticize aspects of contemporary life, contain much ingenious wordplay. Speaking about *OK Computer,* Yorke told the writer for *Entertainment Weekly,* "If it's about anything, it's just dealing with noise and fear, and trying to find something beautiful in it"-a statement that might serve as a summing-up of the band's philosophy.

and start from scratch,"' Jonny Greenwood told Simon Reynolds for the *Wire* (July 2001). "When the *Kid A* reviews came out accusing us of being willfully difficult, I was like, 'If that was true, we'd have done a much better job of it.' It's not that challenging-everything's still four minutes long, it's melodic." The band's decision not to release any singles from *Kid A* or to make videos related to it prompted some in the press to accuse Radiohead's members of pomposity. In response, O'Brien explained to Oldham, "There weren't any singles of *Kid A* because there weren't any singles on the record as far as we're concerned. We didn't do videos because there weren't any singles. There's no great mystique to it."

In June 2001 Radiohead released their fifth album, *Amnesiac,* culled from the same recording sessions that generated *Kid A.* Although expected to be a return to the more conventional sound of *The Bends,* the record turned out to be even more dense and experimental than *Kid A.* Nevertheless, it topped the charts in the United Kingdom, while hitting the number-two position in the United States. As with *Kid A,* the album drew heavily from minimalist electronica, with lyrics heavy with paranoid phrases that were reminiscent of nursery rhymes. "You can see the shared genes: the jazz spasms and electronic pulsings, the chill blood, and most of all, the chronic hypersensitivity to the world outside," Victoria Segal noted in her favorable review for *NME* (on-line). "It feels like a record that would blister if you touched it, allergic to modern life, shut away in a protective tent. It reports on half-remembered contact and conflict, blurred images seen through milky plastic." "The human touch and its visceral impact are no longer central to the music," Jon Pareles wrote in his critique of the album for *Rolling Stone* (June 21, 2001, on-line). "The songs on *Amnesiac* are barely populated vistas, subdued and ambient but not at all soothing. Electric guitars are scarce, and never heroic. Instead, there are semiautomatic rhythm loops, indecipherable background voices, pockets of static, and writhing string arrangements with electronic penumbrae. And when the band does write a melody with a grand arc, the arrangements leave Yorke sounding not triumphant but stranded." Stephen Thomas Earlewine, in the *All Music Guide* (on-line), wrote, "*Amnesiac* plays like a streamlined version of *Kid A,* complete with blatant electronica moves and production that sacrifices songs for atmosphere."

Hail to the Thief, a mix of piano and guitar rock, electronics, and lyrics inspired by war, was the band's final album for their record label, EMI and was released in 2003. Radiohead self-released their seventh album, *In Rainbows,* in 2007 as digital download. Customers could set their own price for the music. The album saw chart success. Their eighth album, *The King of Limbs* was self-released in 2011 and was an exploration of rhythm and quieter textures.

After the King of Limbs tour, Radiohead entered hiatus with band members working on solo projects. On Christmas Day 2015, Radiohead released a new song, "Spectre", on the audio streaming site SoundCloud. On January 21, 2016, it was announced that Radiohead would begin a new world tour in July with several festival dates.

Current band members:

Colin Greenwood – bass guitar, keyboards, percussion (1985–present)

Jonny Greenwood – guitar, keyboards, ondes Martenot, analogue synthesisers, drums (1985–present)

Ed O'Brien – guitar, percussion, backing vocals, drums (1985–present)

Philip Selway – drums, percussion, backing vocals (1985–present)

Thom Yorke – lead vocals, guitar, keyboards, piano, bass guitar (1985–present)

Personal Lives

Because of the somber take on modern life in their music, many listeners have assumed that the members of Radiohead are cynical and depressed, but the men have insisted that that is not the case. Many of their lyrics, they have maintained, are based on one incident and do not reflect an overarching view of life. The performers are often described as low-key and polite; Yorke, however, who told Jon Wiederhorn for *Rolling Stone* (September 7, 1995) that he has "always been melodramatic about everything," is known for his emotional outbursts. "The only time I feel comfortable is when I'm in front of a mike," Yorke confessed to Wiederhorn. "I'm obsessed with the idea that I'm completely losing touch with who I am, and I've come to the conclusion that there isn't anything to Thorn Yorke other than the guy that makes those painful songs."

Further Reading

Addicted to Noise (on-line)
All Music Guide (on-line)
Entertainment Weekly p32+ Oct. 24, 1997
Guitar Player p27+ Oct. 1997, with photo
New Music Express (on-line) Dec. 23, 2000
Q (on-line) Oct. 2000
Rolling Stone pl 9+ Sep.7, 1995, with photos
BBC News, Dec. 15, 2015

Rakim

Rapper

Born: Jan. 28, 1968; Long Island, New York
Primary Field: Hip-hop
Group Affiliation: Eric B.

Introduction

Rakim is one of the most important figures in the history of rap music. In 1985 he formed a partnership with DJ Eric B. to record the songs that would make up the groundbreaking album Paid in Full *(1987). The album's first single, "Eric B. Is President," was wildly popular among hip-hop aficionados. "Its signature chunky beats, heavy-duty synth bass and flurry of scratches mesmerized listeners," Brolin Winning wrote for* Remix *(May 1, 2004). Though it never received major radio play, the album has sold millions of copies and influenced countless hip-hop artists from the late 1980s to the present day. The duo released three more well-received albums before parting ways in 1992. After the resolution of legal issues that delayed the start of his solo career, Rakim reappeared with* The 18th Letter *in 1997 and, two years later,* The Master. *Following an abortive attempt to record an album on the rapper Dr. Dre's Aftermath label in 2000, Rakim started his own label, G&E Trust, which is slated to release his album* The Seventh Seal *in late 2008.*

Early Life

Rakim Allah was born William Michael Griffin Jr. in the predominantly black town of Wyandanch, Long Island, New York, on January 28, 1968. He grew up with a deep appreciation for jazz, soul music, and rhythm and blues. The famous R&B star Ruth Brown was one of his aunts; his mother, a fan of jazz and opera, enjoyed singing along with records; and his brothers played a variety of musical instruments. Rakim played tenor and baritone saxophone in high school, where he also excelled at football and received good grades. For a time in his teens, he also experimented with drugs and became involved in petty crime and other kinds of trouble. Then, at 16, he joined the sect of Islam called the Nation of Gods and Earths, known popularly as the Five-Percent Nation; at that time he took the name Rakim Allah. Rakim began writing raps while still in high school and caught the attention of Eric Barrier, better known as DJ Eric B., who was then working at the WBLS radio station and seeking an MC with whom he could make music. The two began working together in 1985. ("MC" generally stands for "master of ceremonies"; in the world of hip-hop, it is an acronym for "mic controller".)

Life's Work

In 1986 Rakim and Eric B. released their first single, "Eric B. Is President," a song about Barrier's DJ skills, on Zakia, a small record label based in the New York City neighborhood of Harlem. As DJ, Eric B. composed most of the music and put together the samples and beats while Rakim rapped over them. The single, whose B-side was "My Melody," became an instant underground hit. Various DJs have since remixed the song more than 30 times. Sparsely produced and more heavily reliant on sampling than any other hip-hop song up to that time, the single was like nothing that had come before it. With a rhythmic complexity akin to that of jazz, Rakim delivered a self-reflexive ode to the addictive power of the microphone: "I came in the door / I said it before / I never let the mic magnetize me no more." According to Jess Harvell, writing for *PitchforkMedia.com* (June 2, 2005), "Rakim's innovation was applying a patina of intellectual detachment to rap's most sacred cause: talking . . . about how you're a better rapper than everyone else."

Rakim.

The single attracted the notice of a larger music label, 4th and Broadway Records, which brought out Rakim and Eric B.'s first full-length album, *Paid in Full,* in 1987. Though it did not achieve mainstream success on its initial release, the album later reached platinum status—sales of one million or more units—and is widely regarded as one of the best rap records of all time. "Rakim basically invents modern lyrical technique over the course of *Paid in Full,"* Steve Huey wrote for the All Music Guide Web site, "with his complex internal rhymes, literate imagery, velvet-smooth flow, and unpredictable, off-the-beat rhythms."

In the mid-1980s hip-hop music tended to be simple, using rhymes only at the ends of lines to tell easy-to-follow stories. Rakim's lyrics, by contrast, contained metaphors with multiple meanings, assonance, alliteration, internal rhyme schemes, and other devices that had theretofore been used only in literature. Also unprecedented in hip-hop were complex rhythms and seemingly effortless word flow. Rakim has credited his skill in that area to his early exposure to jazz. "I listened to John Coltrane and Thelonious Monk when I was coming up," he told Jim Farber for the New York *Daily News* (November 18, 1997), "They gave me different timings and rhythms." A decade later he described his songwriting process to *PitchforkMedia.com* (October 24, 2007). "When I get a beat," he said, "I can see a million rhythms in the beat. I can see the slowest rhythm in the beat, and I can settle with that and write a song. Or I can look for the most intricate rhythms in the beat, and I can build my style and build my concept on that. That's how I challenge myself, by making sure that when the music comes to me, I'm giving the best of Rakim that I can for that track." Rakim's lyrics are also dense with rhyme and meaning. For example, this short passage from "Eric B. Is President" contains 18 rhyming or otherwise similar-sounding syllables: "I keep the mic at Fahrenheit, freeze MCs, make 'em colder / The listeners system is kicking like solar / As I memorize, advertise like a poet / Keep it gain', when I'm flowin' smooth enough, you know it's rough."

Rakim was also one of the first rappers to express his Islamic beliefs openly in his music. Unlike such soon-to-be-popular rap groups as N.W.A. and Public Enemy, however, he put his love of language before his message, occasionally creating outlandish images in service of a rhyme, as in the track "My Melody": "You scream I'm lazy, you must be crazy / Thought I was a donut, you tried to glaze me." "You don't go to Rakim for political insight, inner turmoil, or sex chat," Jess Harvell wrote. "You go to Rakim for an endless display of pure skill."

Rakim and Eric B. signed with Universal Records for their next release, *Follow the Leader* (1988). The album represented a more refined continuation of the duo's simple beats and sophisticated lyrics. Harvell wrote: "The title track fleshes out Rakim's metaphorical conceit via hellish high-speed-chase music. The beats rattle, the bass seethes, the flutes and strings screech like Blaxploitation crossed with the cheap urgency of an Italian zombie movie. But what's scariest and most exhilarating is how, for all the track's runaway train momentum, it feels inexorable, implacable, utterly in control of itself. Rakim's delivery of the final verse may be the most exciting-at least in terms of breath control-slice of rap the genre has yet delivered." Rakim and Eric B. were guest artists on the song "Friends" by the R&B musician Jody Watley in 1989, which was the first-and, to date, last-time they made it into the Top 10 on the pop charts. It was also one of the first appearances of a rap artist on a song of another genre. The duo signed a deal with MCA for their next release, *Let the Rhythm Hit 'Em* (1990), an album that showcased their technical expertise. "As the bass-drum backgrounds wash over him, Rakim sprays out rhymes like a Gatling gun or-in the preferred parlance of rap-like an Uzi," David Hiltbrand wrote for *People* (August 6, 1990). At the time of the album's release, there was a growing trend toward politics in hip-hop, and though Rakim was far from apolitical, language remained his primary focus. Some critics saw that as a shortcoming. "At a time when West Coast MCs like Ice-T and Ice Cube were mainly interested in getting a political message across," Alex Henderson wrote for the All Music site, "Rakim's goal was showing how much technique he had. . . . There are a few message raps (including 'In the Ghetto'), although Rakim spends most of his time finding tongue-twisting ways to boast and brag about his microphone skills. The overall result is a CD that is enjoyable, yet limited." The duo's fourth and final release was *Don't Sweat the Technique* (1992). The record earned good reviews for its flawless production and jazz influences and for the political themes on tracks such as "Casualties of War." Legal and financial disputes caused Rakim and Eric B. to part ways once the album was finished. Rakim told Jim Farber that the trouble had begun when Barrier wanted to record a solo album. "I had to sign [a paper] for him when he wanted to record but when it came time for him to sign for me, he was scared," he said. "We had two albums left on our contract [with MCA]. He thought those albums would be the last and then MCA would just pick me up. I cannot understand that to this day. He's my partner. I would make sure they took care of him. But once he started showing his colors, I just l'et him get into his own thing."

Rakim began working on a solo album for MCA in 1992. Soon, however, the MCA staff members with whom he worked fell victim to a company purge, then absconded with the unfinished tapes of nine of Rakim's songs and sold them to radio and mix-tape deejays. Almost five years passed before Rakim recorded another album, partly because he was discouraged and partly because of his dislike of the by-then-dominant "gangsta rap" genre. "I didn't want to be labeled as a gangsta because it's majority rules [in music]," he told Farber. "I wanted to go against the grain." He added that at the time of his interview with Farber, late 1997, rap artists seemed "more free to express themselves." That year, with Universal, Rakim recorded a much-anticipated

Affiliation: The Hip-Hop Sound

Discussing the minimalist production values of *Paid in Full*, Harvell referred to the record's sound as "hip-hop's garage-rock—a street reaction against the first wave of crossover pop-rap," and Winning described it as "unrelentingly dope: all snappy drum breaks, funky guitar licks, thick bass and rugged cuts." Sampling other songs more heavily than his predecessors had, Barrier in turn created what would become some of the most frequently sampled beats in hip-hop. The second and third singles from the album, "I Ain't No Joke" and "I Know You Got Soul," drew on songs by James Brown and Bobby Byrd. His use of that music set in motion the practice of pillaging old funk records for sounds used in new songs, which continues to this day. It also brought 4th and Broadway label copyright infringement lawsuits from Brown and Byrd, which were settled out of court but sparked an ongoing debate over the legality and ethics of using sampled sound in hip-hop music.

comeback album, *The 18th Letter.* Debuting at number four on the *Billboard* charts, it was beloved by critics and fans alike. On *The 18th Letter,* Rakim mixed his smooth, laidback style of rapping with a contemporary technique. "The beats are fresh, the rhymes are solid, the samples are perfect," Ryan Schreiber wrote for *PitchforkMedia.com* (1998). "Rakim is still a master lyricist and he proves it with lines like 'I used to roll up / This is a hold up / Ain't nuthin funny / Stop smiling, be still / Don't nothin move but the money.'" His heavily spiritual follow-up album, *The Master* (1999), was similarly acclaimed, with Angus Batey, writing for the London *Times* (November 27, 1997), hailing Rakim as "his genre's Bob Dylan—a gifted, if often abstract visionary whose followers hang on his every syllable." Rakim signed to the rapper Dr. Dre's Aftermath Entertainment label in 2000 and began working on an album tentatively titled "Oh, My God." Though he contributed work to songs released by several of his label mates, he shelved his own album in 2003 due to creative differences with Dr. Dre. Later that year Rakim released *Paid in Full: The Platinum Edition.* According to an accompanying press release, the two-disc set included a remastered version of the original album along with "the original mix of 'My Melody' (heretofore unavailable on CD), the enhanced video for 'Paid in Full,'" and "deluxe packaging" featuring "all of the elements of the original album, updated liner notes from essayist Tom Terrell, rare photos and ephemera, plus a special foreword." (In 2004 Rakim and Eric B. sued the Def Jam, Island, and Universal record labels for money owed to them for *Paid in Full,* which was estimated to have sold more than 10 million copies by then.) Rakim signed with Dreamworks to record his next album, but the label dissolved before he could begin work on it.

In 2004, upon his arrival at the Roseland Ballroom, in New York, to play a date with Ghostface (also known as Ghostface Killah) of the Wu-Tang Klan, Rakim was arrested on a 2001 warrant associated with a paternity suit. Rakim claimed to have had no prior knowledge of the warrant, arguing that he would not have signed on to play the highly publicized date if he had been a fugitive from justice. The suit—filed by the mother of his then 14- year-old son, a woman with whom he had had a tumultuous relationship and frequent financial disputes—was not the first of its kind. According to Rakim's attorney, Robert Kaline, the rapper agreed to pay $2,000 in child support "out of an abundance of caution" and was released the next day. Rakim's live album *The Archive: Live, Lost and Found* (2008) offers, in addition to live recordings, four previously unreleased tracks. Rakim played several dates on the Rock the Bells Tour and the Paid Dues Independent Hip Hop Festival in the summer of 2008, sharing the stage with artists including Mos Def, Ghostface, A Tribe Called Quest, Brother Ali, and the band Rhythm Roots Allstars. The release date of Rakim's newest album, *The Seventh Seal,* was pushed back several times and was most recently set for late 2008.

In his October 24, 2007 interview with *PitchforkMedia.com,* Rakim explained his decision to incorporate a live band in his performances: "The essence of hip-hop is that live band. That's why we had the turntables. When it started, we were scratching live bands. These 60s, 70s funk bands, rock'n'roll—we were taking the records and scratching them. If we would have been in the environment where we had drummers and horn players and guitar players—that's not that common in the ghetto. If we would have had guitar players, bass players, drummers, saxophonists, then you might have seen something different with hip-hop, as far as bands being more incorporated, because that's what it is. I don't want to take the DJ element out of it, but at the same time, I just want to let the crowd know that this is why we sample: that live band. I want them to respect that live band."

As one of hip-hop's pioneers, Rakim sees himself as a custodian of the music's legacy. "At this point in hip-hop, [the history] definitely needs to be expressed a little more and put in front of [fans'] faces so that they won't forget where the essence of hip-hop came from," he told *PitchforkMedia.com* in 2007. "If I'm one of the artists that knows about it then yeah, I'm responsible to keep that alive and keep it in the listeners' faces and give them access to it." In addition to stressing the importance of hip-hop's history, Rakim called upon fans and artists to keep the genre alive. "When they created jazz years ago it was the best thing to happen since fried ice cream," he said in the same interview. "But then you look at it now-it's not so popular as far as [being] universal. . . . The same thing can happen in hip-hop if we take it for granted and don't cherish it."

Personal Life

Rakim currently lives in New York City with his girlfriend and their three children.

Further Reading
All Music Guide Web site;
Miami (Florida) Times D p1 Nov. 20, 1997;
(New York) *Daily News* p46 Nov. 18, 1997;
PitchforkMedia.com Oct. 24, 2007;
popmatters.com Nov. 19, 2003; *Remix* p5 May 1, 2004

Dianne Reeves

Singer

Born: Oct. 23, 1956; Detroit, Michigan
Primary Field: Jazz
Group Affiliation: Solo performer

Introduction

The late, celebrated jazz vocalist Joe Williams told a writer for Down Beat *in 1997 about the singer Dianne Reeves, "I think Dianne's the legitimate extension of all the good things that have gone on before, from Ethel Waters to Ella Fitzgerald and Sarah [Vaughan] and Carmen [McCrae]. . . . She is earth mother, lover, she is the hurt child; she manages to get inside each one of those things." Though known primarily as a jazz vocalist, Reeves draws on a variety of influences, among them African, Brazilian, and Caribbean music and gospel, rhythm and blues, and pop. The albums of the four-time Grammy Award-winner include* In the Moment: Live in Concert *(2000),* The Calling: Celebrating Sarah Vaughan *(2001),* A Little Moonlight *(2003), and the soundtrack to the film* Good Night, and Good Luck *(2005).*

Early Life

Dianne Reeves was born on October 23, 1956 in Detroit, Michigan, into a musical family. Her mother, Vada Swanson, a nurse, played the trumpet; her father sang tenor; her uncle Charles Burrell played the bass in the San Francisco and Colorado Symphony Orchestras; and one of her cousins is the keyboardist George Duke. Reeves was only two years old when her father died. Her mother then moved with Reeves and her sister, Sharon, to Denver, Colorado, to be close to the girls' grandmother, Denverada, and their aunt, Mary Beth Mitchell. Reeves found her female relatives to be a source of strength and inspiration. "They were all fighters, and I picked that up from them," she told John Pitcher for the *Rochester (New York) Democrat and Chronicle* (June 3, 2002). "But they were also rich in their collective spirituality and always found a way to celebrate and support the aspirations of their children."

As a youngster in the 1960s, Reeves was one of the first African-American students to participate in Denver's busing program, in which black children were required to commute to predominantly white schools in order to integrate the school system. "They were sending us off to neighborhoods that we didn't even know existed, and the authorities didn't do anything to prepare us for what we were in for," Reeves told Pitcher. At the school where she was sent, Hamilton Junior High, many parents of white students were hostile toward the young African-Americans. "It dawned on me that this was truly ignorance—ignorance in not wanting to understand one another," Reeves told an interviewer for the Europe Jazz Network Web site. Reeves participated in events, such as assemblies and sit-ins, designed to enlighten the adults in the community. A choir teacher who was sympathetic to the black children's predicament sought to diffuse the tension by helping to put on a show of songs and skits featuring all the eighth-grade students; the songs included "You've Got a Friend" and "He Ain't Heavy, He's My Brother"—"the kind of music that had a positive message," Reeves told Pitcher. She recalled to the interviewer for the Europe Jazz Network Web site, "Fortunately it all ended in a positive way. People started to look at themselves and be kind of ashamed of the way they acted." That experience led Reeves to realize, as she told Norman Provizer for the Denver *Rocky Mountain News* (April 7, 2001), "that music—art—can have a soothing impact, especially on young people. After that, I decided that I loved what the music made me feel, and I knew I wanted to sing."

When Reeves's uncle Charles Burrell learned that his niece had a strong singing voice, he promptly took an interest in cultivating her talents and broadening her musical horizons. As Reeves told John Pitcher, her uncle "started giving me every jazz record he could find. . . . I heard Ella Fitzgerald, Billie Holiday, Sarah

Vaughan, and I became hooked on that kind of singing." At 17 Reeves got the opportunity to meet one of her idols when her cousin George Duke secured backstage access for her at a Cannonball Adderley tribute concert. While standing in the wings, Reeves struck up a conversation with a friendly woman who expressed an interest in the teen's career ambitions. "I told her I listened to Sarah Vaughan. I just talked and told her all about Sarah Vaughan," Reeves recalled in an interview with Adrian Chamberlain for the Victoria, British Columbia, *Times Colonist* (June 28, 2005). Several minutes later the woman was called onstage to perform and was introduced to the audience—as Sarah Vaughan. "I stood in the wings and listened to her. I just disappeared afterwards," Reeves admitted to Chamberlain. "I didn't know what to say."

Life's Work

While attending George Washington High School, Reeves was a member of a jazz band and sang at her own prom. When she performed with the school band at a convention of the National Association of Jazz Educators, in Chicago, Illinois, the famous trumpeter Clark Terry, impressed by the 16-year-old girl's voice, asked her to join his group. Soon Reeves found herself performing with Terry's bands, which featured the jazz luminaries Tommy Flanagan and Eddie "Lockjaw" Davis, among others. Meanwhile, after graduating from high school, she enrolled at the University of Colorado at Denver, leaving after a year. At the invitation of Philip Bailey, a member of the group Earth, Wind & Fire, who had heard about Reeves's talent through mutual friends, Reeves moved in 1976 to Los Angeles, California, to become the vocalist for another band that Bailey had formed. She quit the group a year later. "I really wanted to sing jazz," she explained to Norman Provizer, "and what they were doing wasn't really jazz-oriented. It was great music, but there was a really great jazz scene in Los Angeles at the time, and I wanted to be part of it." She performed with Caldera, a Latin-jazz group, in which she met the keyboardist Eduardo del Barrio, who was to become her frequent songwriting collaborator. From 1978 to 1980 she held a full-time gig with the pianist Billy Childs. "Billy gave me license to go anywhere musically," she said, as quoted by the Europe Jazz Network Web site. In 1981, when she heard that the pianist Sergio Mendes needed a singer, she gave an audition and before long was touring the world with Mendes and his band. Having acquired from Mendes an appreciation for Brazilian music, Reeves recorded her first album, *Welcome to My Love,* for the Palo Alto Jazz label, in 1982. Shortly thereafter she relocated to New York City in order to collaborate with the singer Harry Belafonte, whom she has credited with teaching her the importance of lyrics. While on the East Coast, Reeves continued performing live. In a review of one of her shows for *Newsday* (May 2, 1985), Wayne Robins praised Reeves's "awesome technical gifts: Pitch that you could set a tuning fork by is matched by enough lung power to raise the roof at a Pentecostal church service." She also released a second album with Palo Alto, *For Every Heart* (1985), before returning to Los Angeles in the following year.

Reeve's 1987 album, the rhythm-and-blues-inflected *Dianne Reeves,* released on Capitol's Blue Note label, earned the singer widespread attention. The album included the R&B ballad "Better Days," a poignant

Affiliation: Grammy Award

Given her history with the Grammy Awards, Reeves was pleased but not particularly hopeful when her album *In the Moment: Live in Concert* (2000) was nominated for the honor. She had planned to attend the awards ceremony, but a family emergency necessitated her presence in Denver, where she and her relatives watched the ceremony on television. While Reeves was watching the show, a friend from the East Coast (whose telecast was an hour ahead of Denver's) called with the news that Reeves had won the award for best jazz vocalist. Reeves was elated. "Everyone just started coming over. It was family, kids, cousins. Old friends were coming by, calling. Everybody was jumping around. It was really wonderful," she told Norman Provizer. Because Reeves could not be present at the live ceremony, her family and friends reenacted the event for her, even presenting Reeves with a photo of the Grammy Award and having her deliver an acceptance speech. Winning the Grammy was important to Reeves partly because, she told Provizer, it brought about "a healing experience. . . . There were people with whom I'd had misunderstandings and people with whom I'd fallen out of touch. They called. We talked and things were forgiven. You can say you're a Grammy winner, and maybe some things change. But most important, it brought people I really love together."

melody about Reeves's grandmother, which became a hit; Reeves praised her grandmother to Norman Provizer as "a very strong and wise person who really kept the family close." She also told *Jet* magazine (December 26, 2005- January 2, 2006) that the song was "dedicated to grandmothers everywhere." *Dianne Reeves* was nominated for a Grammy Award. In 1989 she released *Never Too Far,* followed two years later by *I Remember.* In 1992 Reeves moved back to Denver to be closer to her family. Her return to her childhood home apparently had a positive influence on Reeves's music: in 1994 she released *Art and Survival,* which, she told Provizer in 2001, was "the most important record I've ever made." Reeves then proceeded to record albums at the rate of one a year, including the Grammy-nominated *Quiet After the Storm* (1995), *The Grand Encounter* (1996), and another Grammy nominee, *That Day* (1997). Two years later came still another Grammy nominee, *bridges* (1999).

As a tribute to her longtime idol, Sarah Vaughan, Reeves recorded an album of classic Vaughan songs entitled *The Calling: Celebrating Sarah Vaughan* (2001). "When I was in high school, in the beginning of trying to find my own voice, dealing with my own raging hormones and angst—in the midst of all that, I heard her voice," Reeves recalled to Norman Provizer. "I heard her voice and a light came on. It opened a door to my understanding of my own voice and how I would use it." For her work on *The Calling,* Reeves won a second Grammy Award. She secured a third for *A Little Moonlight* (2003), which Nate Chinen described for the *New York Times* (February 7, 2006) as "an exquisitely focused standards album and her finest recorded work." Reeves became the first singer in any genre to win Grammy Awards for three consecutive releases. She next appeared as a 1950s TV-studio singer in *Good Night, and Good Luck,* a 2005 film about the broadcast journalist Edward R. Murrow, directed by George Clooney. Reeves also recorded the film's soundtrack. Both the movie and the album earned honors, which included a fourth Grammy Award for Reeves. "The powerful but mellow alto of Ms. Reeves wafts through the film, as ubiquitous and atmospheric as the smoke from Murrow's cigarettes," Nate Chinen wrote. Chinen described the soundtrack album, also called *Good Night, and Good Luck,* as "the leanest, most instantly gratifying album of [Reeves's] career." Also in 2005 she released *Christmas Time Is Here,* an album of what the *Sacramento (California) Observer* (November 9, 2005) called "stylish and sophisticated renditions of classics" delivered with a "strong, agile voice, rhythmic virtuosity and improvisational ease." Reeves's 2006 tour schedule included venues in the United Kingdom, the Netherlands, Norway, Spain, and Australia as well as the U.S.

Throughout her career Reeves has performed live as well as on recordings. In 2001 she appeared as part of the Jazz at Lincoln Center program in New York City. Writing about her performance, Ben Ratliff declared in the *New York Times* (February 20, 2001) that Reeves "sings the truest note in jazz. Ms. Reeves stays perfectly on pitch, and her notes, individually packaged like Valentine chocolates, have a perfect roundness." The following year she performed at the closing ceremony of the 2002 Winter Olympic Games, in Salt Lake City, Utah, She has since been awarded the Ella Fitzgerald Award at the Montreal International Jazz Festival, and in 2003 she received an honorary doctorate from the Berklee College of Music. Since 2002 she has held the position of creative chair for jazz with the Los Angeles Philharmonic Association.

Personal Life

Reeves continues to make her home in Denver.

Further Reading

(Denver, Colorado) *Rocky Mountain News* E pi Apr. 7, 2001

New York Times E p5 Feb. 20, 2001, E pi Feb. 7, 2006

Newsday p35 May 2, 1985

Rochester (New York) Democrat and Chronicle C pi June 3, 2002

(Victoria, British Columbia) *Times Colonist* D p5 June 28, 2005

L.A. Reid

President of Arista Records; songwriter; record producer

Born: 1956; Cincinnati, Ohio
Primary Field: R&B
Group Affiliation: Deele

Introduction

Although Antonio "L. A." Reid was for several years a drummer with the successful R&B group the Deele, it is in his behind-the-scenes work in the world of music that he has been most influential. In the mid-to-late 1980s, working with Deele bandmate Kenny "Babyface" Edmonds, Reid wrote and produced songs for some of the most important R&B artists of the time. In the process, he won three Grammy Awards for writing and production, and had 33 of the songs that he co-wrote and/or coproduced hit number one on the American singles charts.

Early Life

One of the four children of Emma Reid, the songwriter, musician, producer, and executive was born Antonio Reid in 1956 in Cincinnati, Ohio. He was raised in the Cincinnati suburbs of Mount Auburn and Madisonville. "We moved around a lot," he told Nager. "I want to say we come from the ghetto, but the truth is that I don't recall being that poor. I don't have a rags-to-riches story. My mother always worked, so I always had clothes and shoes. When I started getting into music, my mother supported me and was helping me buy instruments." Reid became entranced by such artists as Led Zeppelin, Jimi Hendrix, Sly Stone, Stevie Wonder, and Miles Davis, and saved whatever money he could to buy 45s. He especially loved James Brown. "I used to have a karate class in Evanston," he told Nager. "And when I would wait for the bus, I would go stand in front of the [old King Records building] and just stare at it. James Brown was there, and I was drawn to him and the music he created." Reid attended Hughes High School; by the time he graduated, in 1974, he was playing drums in several musical groups. Dave Parker, a baseball player who was then with the Pittsburgh Pirates, paid the expenses for one of the groups to record some of their material. One of the songs was played on the Pittsburgh radio station WCIN, while another was later used on a compilation record issued by another Pittsburgh station, WEBN.

Life's Work

Reid later formed a group called Essence, which played mostly original material. After several personnel changes, they renamed themselves the Deele but continued to play slick R&B and funk. "We called the group the Deele, because it implied that we were gonna get a record deal," he told Nager. One of the new members of the Deele was Kenny "Babyface" Edmonds. Reid and Edmonds soon became fast friends and successful musical collaborators. "We just really liked each other," Reid recalled to Nager. "Our musical ideas kind of worked together real well. [Babyface] was a very melodic guy, and I was a very rhythmic guy. We liked each other's company, we admired each other's taste, whether it be in music or in things other than music. We forged an amazing relationship that lasted many years." In 1983 the group was signed by Solar, the label of the famed R&B group Midnight Star. The Deele's first single, "Body Talk," released that year, was featured on an episode of the hit television show *Miami Vice.* Although it hit only number 77 on the pop chart, it reached number three on the R&B chart. The group followed that song up with two more charting singles, "Just My Luck" and "Surrender." In 1984 the Deele released their debut album, *Street Beat,* which managed to crack the Top 100 on the national album chart. "Though the record . . . is pleasant, synthesized soul and lite funk, it doesn't show many signs of innovation, and only the hit singles demonstrate much songcraft," Leo Stanley noted for the *All Music Guide* (on-line). During the recording of the album, Reid learned a great deal from Reggie Calloway, the Midnight Star trumpeter and producer, who produced *Street Beat.* "This guy probably doesn't even know how much impact he's had on my life," Reid told Nager. "Reggie kind of taught me the importance of making sure that every song you record is the absolute best song that you can find and has the absolute best performance by the artist. It was that basic training. I like to think of it as boot camp that really sort of paved the way for what we do now at LaFace, and so many of the other artists and labels that I associate with. But it all came from there."

Material Thangz (1985), the Deele's second album, was not as successful as their debut, with only the title cut making its way to the singles chart. Meanwhile,

Affiliation: Recording

In 1989 he and Babyface established their own record label, LaFace, which would go on to record some of the most successful and important R&B acts of the 1990s, including TLC, Usher, and Toni Braxton. Recently named the president of Arista Records, Reid is now the head of one of the largest pop labels in the United States, one that boasts contracts with Santana, Aretha Franklin, Carly Simon, and Whitney Houston, among other musicians and groups. "In my career I've always kind of been the guy behind the guy," Reid remarked to Larry Nager for the *Cincinnati Enquirer* (October 17, 1999, on-line). "Even when it was the Deele and it was in Cincinnati, Ohio, I was the guy behind those other guys. I wasn't the lead guy. I was at times maybe the spokesperson, because I was the leader of the band. But I wasn't the visual guy, I wasn't the lead singer, I wasn't out front. But I was kind of married to the business and the creative aspect together. It was never purely creative, it was always kind of both. And so as I've grown, I've found that my love, my passion and my talent is really to make others happen and not necessarily promoting me."

however, Reid and Babyface were becoming known as one of the hottest songwriting/production teams in the R&B world. Reid moved to Los Angeles, where, with Babyface, he produced and wrote for other artists on the Solar label; those performers included Shalimar, the Whispers, and Pebbles. The last-named artist, whose real name is Perri McKissack; married Reid. During the second half of the 1980s, Reid and Babyface produced and/or wrote songs for some of the most popular artists of the time, among them Bobby Brown, Sheena Easton, Karyn White, Paula Abdul, the Jacksons, Whitney Houston, Boyz II Men, and Bell Biv Devoe. The final Deele album featuring Reid and Babyface, *Eyes of a Stranger* (1987), contained two hit singles, "Two Occasions" and "Shoot 'em Up Movies," and became a certified gold release.

Despite their success, Reid and Babyface felt that they were missing out on financial rewards. "At that point I decided I wanted some ownership in the game," Reid told Nager. "We were having a lot of success, making a lot of records, selling a lot of records, not making a lot of money. We wanted equity participation and you can't have equity participation if you're work-for-hire. And as producers we were work-for-hire. So I figured it out. I want a label." In 1989 Reid and Babyface formed LaFace Records, a five-year, $20 million joint venture with Arista Records, which agreed to distribute their products. (The name "LaFace" combined parts of Reid's and Edmonds's stage names.) While Babyface continued writing, producing, and performing, Reid mostly stayed behind the scenes. "I've kind of retired from the studio," Reid told Nager. "[Babyface has] obviously kept it up and done an amazing job at it. We still talk every day and have co-ownership of our label. But for the most part, he pursues his career, and I retired to the boring job of being a record company executive."

Reid immediately began looking for artists to sign to the label. In 1991, in one of his first major successes, he signed the all-female R&B group TLC, which was managed by Pebbles. The group had three consecutive Top 10 hits the following year, and their debut album was also quite successful. Reid also brought the R&B singer Toni Braxton to the label. Her first album, released in 1993, sold more than seven million copies and earned her Grammy Awards in the categories of best new artist and best female R&B artist. "I look for stars, y'know? More than I look for people who sing or for people who play, I look for people who I think are stars," Reid told Nager. "People who have the ability to make you love them, and to make people around the world love them. And that becomes the most important thing to me. There are great singers all over the world. In any Baptist church in America you can find the greatest singers in the world. But it doesn't always translate to superstardom. I don't know what it is. It's something that I feel when I meet an artist, when I watch an artist. Whatever it is, let's put it this way, TLC has it, Madonna has it, Toni Braxton has it, Usher has it, Puff Daddy has it."

In September 1993 Reid and Edmonds split as a production team. "There were a lot reasons," Reid told Sonia Murray for the *Atlanta Journal-Constitution* (July 2, 2000, on-line). "No. 1 was, I think I used to [upset him) because I would sit in the studio and be on the telephone.... No. 2: I started to have a true love of the business ·and working with other artists. No. 3: In some respects, Kenny might have felt like Kenny needed to grow as a writer and producer and he needed to do it by himself. . . . And I supported that." Reid faced tension in other areas, personal as well as professional, over the next couple of years. In 1995 he and Perri McKissack divorced, and in 1997 Toni Braxton sued LaFace, holding the company responsible for the conditions that led her to file for bankruptcy. Reid responded to the latter development philosophically, telling Sonia Murray, "It's just a fact. of life, at a certain point all labels have legal issues. I think the fact that LaFace was such a proud company, and is such a proud company, that there simply were people around that really wanted to [hurt) this company. And as artists become successful, they become prone to listening to people."

In spite of such troubles, LaFace continued to be successful, grossing around $100 million annually. Among the other popular acts signed by Reid were the southern rap groups Outkast and the Goodie Mob and the soul crooner Usher. TLC's *CrazySexyCool* (1994) sold more than 13 million copies, making those artists the best-selling female group in the country. The record was later named the bestselling hip-hop album of the 20th century by the Recording Industry Association of America. In 1995 LaFace announced that it had renewed its agreement with Arista and its parent company, BMG, which invested an estimated $100 million in the label over five years. "We are doing exactly what the major labels do, just on a smaller scale," Reid told Rhonda Reynolds and Ann Brown for *Black Enterprise* (December 1994). "The difference is we understand black artists. We understand how to market them better than anybody." In 1997 LaFace released the soundtrack to the film *Soul Food;* Edmonds produced both the soundtrack and the film, which earned $11.4 million in its first weekend in theaters.

In 2000 Reid married Erica Holton, an Atlanta schoolteacher, in a ceremony on the Isle of Capri, off the coast of Italy. Soon afterward he was named president of Arista. Although the choice of Reid was not controversial, the move itself caused a stir, since it meant that Arista's founder, Clive Davis, was being forced to step down after 25 years at the helm of the label. As a result of the decision, some executives and performers left Arista, explaining that they wanted to work only with Davis; many others, inside and outside the recording industry, were excited to see an African-American chosen to head a major label. Despite the popularity of many African-American recording artists, few blacks held positions of power within the field. Reid was invigorated by the leap from running a small label to being the head of a major record company that was home to superstars. "I really need the challenge," he told Sonia Murray. "I love music first and foremost. And I haven't been able to work in all genres of music.... I've been sort of pigeonholed into the box of doing R&B and obviously some rap music. Although it's music that's crossed over . . . I have to tell you, I'm a little bored. I love working with the artists that I've worked with. I don't like the idea of having a small company, though. Because in a small company, I'm far too dependent on a couple of people, a couple of artists." Regarding his plans for Arista, Reid told the same interviewer that while he wanted to maintain the company's strengths—R&B and pop—he was also interested in opening up new markets. "In recent years, Arista has had marginal success in rock music. That's an area that's really going to require a lot of time and attention.... Also, I think when you look at the Latin population in the country and the fact that Arista basically has one artist—which would be Carlos Santana—who makes music that is appealing to that population of people, I think that there's obviously some room for growth there." After Reid was named president of Arista, the company acquired LaFace. In 2001 Reid amazed observers when he signed Whitney Houston to a $100 million multi-album deal. During that year rumors abounded that Reid was under heavy pressure to increase sales.

Personal Life

Reid has three children: Aaron, Ashley, and Antonio Jr. He lives and works in Atlanta and also has an office in New York City. He is a partner in Justin's, an Atlanta restaurant, along with the rapper and producer Sean "Puffy" Combs. Reid helped Combs's Bad Boy Records in its distribution deal with Arista. "All the success and all, I certainly don't take it lightly and I count my blessings," Reid told Nager. "But now, I'm more concerned with having peace and just happiness in life. I'm not trying to say that I haven't been happy and I haven't been peaceful but it just hasn't been at the forefront of my desire, and now it is. Simple as it may sound, I just want peace and love."

Further Reading

All Music Guide (on-line)
Atlanta-Journal Constitution (on-line) July 2, 2000
Black Enterprise p94+ Dec. 2000
Cincinnati Enquirer (on-line) Oct. 17, 1999
Fortune p40 Apr. 2, 2001, with photo
Jet p46+ May 22, 2000, with photo
New York p34+ Jan. 29, 2001

Keith Richards

Musician; songwriter

Born: Dec. 18, 1948; Dartford, England
Primary Field: Rock and roll
Group Affiliation: Rolling Stones

Introduction

It has been said that if Mick Jagger is the heart of the Rolling Stones, Keith Richards, its lead guitarist, is the group's musical soul. It is Richards who is responsible for the Stones' signature aggressive, gritty sound, so prominently featured in such classics as "(I Can't Get No) Satisfaction," "Brown Sugar," and "Honky Tonk Women," which Richards also wrote, and one music critic has called him "perhaps the most rhythmically assured guitarist in rock." A decade-long addiction to heroin, which led many to speculate he would become rock's next drug fatality, culminated in a highly publicized drug bust and rehabilitation in 1977 and contributed to Richards's reputation as the rude boy of the Rolling Stones—an image that has been enhanced by his guitar-playing style.

Early Life

Keith Richards was born in Dartford, a suburb of London, England on December 18, 1943, the only child of Bert and Doris (Dupree) Richards. His parents, he told Robert Greenfield for a 1971 Rolling Stone magazine interview, were "English working class . . . struggling, thinking they were middle class." Bert Richards worked as a foreman in a General Electric factory. "My dad worked his butt off in order to just keep the rent paid and food for the family," Richards has recalled. Richards's maternal grandfather, Theodore Augustus Dupree, played the saxophone, fiddle, and guitar and had a dance band in the 1930s.

When he was fifteen, Richards was expelled for habitual truancy from the Dartford Technical School. A sympathetic counselor sent him to art college in nearby Sidcup, where he was introduced to blues music and where he jammed on the guitar with students in a room next to the principal's office, playing songs by Little Walter and Big Bill Broonzy. At that time, rock-'n'-roll in Britain was "a brand new thing," Richards later explained to Kurt Loder for *Rolling* Stone (December 10, 1987). "The world was black-and-white, and then suddenly it went into living color."

In about 1960 Richards bumped into Mick Jagger, a childhood friend who also lived in Dartford, on a commuter train. Richards was en route to art school, and Jagger was on his way to the London School of Economics. They found they had a common interest in rhythm-and-blues and a mutual friend in Dick Taylor, who was also a Sidcup art student. Richards began jamming at Taylor's home with Taylor, Jagger, and other members of a group that called itself Little Boy Blue and the Blue Boys. From that point on, Taylor has recalled, "Mick and Keith were together. Whoever else came into the band or left, there'd always be Mick and Keith."

Life's Work

In March 1962 the group found "the only club in England where they were playing anything funky as far as anybody knew," Richards recalled to Stanley Booth in an interview for Booth's book Dance with the *Devil:* The Rolling *Stones* and *Their Times* (1984). That club was a small room under a tea shop in the London borough of Ealing, where they met Brian Jones, a guitarist with whom Richards felt an immediate rapport. Jones and Richards played together not as "lead" and subordinate "rhythm," but in full interaction, along with Taylor on bass guitar, Ian Stewart on piano, and Jagger as the vocalist. Taking the name the Rolling Stones from the song "The Rolling Stone Blues," by bluesman Muddy Waters, the group, with Mick Avory on drums, made its debut on July 12, 1962 at the Marquee, a club in Soho. "Brian was the one who kept us all together then," Richards later recalled. "Mick was still going to school. I'd dropped out. So we decided we got to live in London to get it together. Time to break loose. So everybody left home, upped and got this pad in London. Chelsea." When the Rolling Stones started, only a few groups were playing rock-'n'-roll in England, and the early dates were few and far between. During the winter of 1962, they dropped Taylor for Bill Wyman, a bass guitarist with better amplifiers, and replaced their drummer with Charlie Watts. "When we got Charlie, that really made it for us," Richards later said. "We started getting a lot of gigs." The Stones' big break came that winter with a gig at the Crawdaddy Club in suburban Richmond. It turned into a regular Sunday-night engagement, drawing what would become known as "swinging London," as well as Andrew Loog Oldham, who became their manager. At the age of nineteen, Oldham got the Stones out of the London clubs and into ballrooms all over Britain ("where the kids were," Richards once explained). Oldham also procured a record contract for the group, on extremely favorable terms, with Decca and dropped Stewart from the group because his looks were "too normal." (Stewart continued to record with the Stones and later acted as band manager.) He also persuaded Richards to drop the "s" from his name (which he later resumed) to capitalize on the popularity of the British pop star Cliff Richard.

The first Rolling Stones single, Chuck Berry's "Come On," was released on June 7, 1963, the date of their first television appearance. Although Oldham at first wanted the band to promote a somewhat tidy image (they wore neat, hound's-tooth jackets and their haircuts were only marginally longer than those of the Beatles), the Stones provoked calls from viewers criticizing them as "scruffy." Soon Oldham realized that the more the band annoyed parents, the more it would delight teenagers, and the image of the Stones as surly, rebellious, and menacing—the antithesis of the clean-cut, lovable Beatles-was established.

During the fall of 1963 the Stones toured Britain with Bo Diddley, the Everly Brothers, and Little Richard. Excitement was starting to build, and sustained frenzy erupted during their second domestic concert tour, in early 1964. "There was a period of six months in England we couldn't play ballrooms anymore because we never got through more than three or four songs every night, man," Richards recalled to Greenfield. "Chaos. Police and too many people in the places, fainting. You know that weird sound that thousands of chicks make when they're really lettin' it go. They couldn't hear the music. We couldn't hear ourselves, for years." The band's first album, *The Rolling Stones*, released in May 1964, went straight to the top of the pop charts, breaking the domination held by the Beatles through most of 1963. The Stones also managed to outstrip their rivals in two 1964 popularity polls. Their early music, however, unlike the Beatles', was not their own: instead, they borrowed from other artists, most prominently from Chuck Berry, whose guitar style and voice were imitated by Richards and Jagger, respectively.

The Rolling Stones started creating their own sound when, in 1964, Oldham locked Richards and Jagger into the kitchen of the northern London basement apartment they were sharing and threatened not to let them out until they wrote a song. The first efforts of the "Glimmer Twins," as they came to be called, included "Time Is on My Side," "Get Off of My Cloud," and "Heart of Stone." As Richards told Robert Greenfield, "The first things, usually I wrote the melody and Mick wrote the words. . . . Every song we've got has pieces of each other in it." In 1964 the Stones released a series of singles that rose high on the pop charts, including "Time Is on My Side," "The Last Time," and "Little Red Rooster," which was banned in the United States because of its blatantly sexual lyrics. The song "(I Can't Get No) Satisfaction," released in the summer of 1965, featured the famous introductory guitar riff that Richards invented. That song became the Stones' first number-one song on the charts, and it propelled the group to international superstardom. "I learned how to write songs just by sitting down and doing it," Richards told Greenfield. "For me it seems inconceivable that any guitar player can't sit down and write songs." A follow-up single, "Get Off of My Cloud," was released and reached the number-one position on the charts by the end of 1965. Following the release of the albums *12* x *5* (1964) and the *Rolling* Stones *Now* (1965), their fourth album, *Out of Our Heads* (1965), containing the song "Satisfaction," reached the number-one position in England and the number-two spot on the charts in the United States. By the time of that release, the Stones had developed a distinct musical identity, heavily influenced by the blues, which further evolved with December's Children in 1965 and *Big Hits* (*High Tide and Green Grass)* in 1966.

In contrast to the usually upbeat and positive sound of the Beatles, Richards and Jagger created music that was raunchy and aggressive and which often dealt with taboo themes, such as rape, in "The Midnight Rambler," and sexual domination, in "Under My Thumb." The sexually suggestive gyrations of Mick Jagger in the Stones' performances enhanced their raunchy reputation and their appeal to teenagers, who came to the Stones' concerts to "work it out." The Stones first toured the United States in 1964, and they made two North American visits in 1965. They also toured Europe in that period, and by 1966 the group was traveling to Australia and New Zealand as well.

During those years, the group's wild lifestyles were well documented by the press. "It wasn't a created image, or a phony thing," Richards told an interviewer for New York Newsday (January 25, 1983). "Things did happen to us. We'd go to a restaurant because we wanted some food, and get thrown out because we didn't have a tie." To many, Richards appeared to epitomize the self-destructive behavior for which the Stones were famous. "Keith represents an image of what the public thinks the Stones are like," Bill Wyman, the Stones' bass player, once told an interviewer. "Gypsy, pirate, drinking, smoking, finally heavy drug taking, swearing. People see· Keith and they see the Stones."

Both the Beatles and the Rolling Stones were helping Britain make inroads into its chronic payments deficit, but while the former had been honored by Queen Elizabeth II, the Stones were frequently harassed by the authorities. In February 1967 police raided a party at Redlands, the fifteenth-century moated Sussex cottage that Richards had bought the previous year, and confiscated illegal drugs. It was after that raid, while the Stones were vacationing in Morocco, that Richards became involved with the actress Anita Pallenberg, who was Brian Jones's girlfriend at the time. When Jones and Anita Pallenberg quarreled en route to Morocco, Richards and the actress went off together, beginning a long-term liaison. After another European tour, extending as far east as Warsaw and Athens, Richards returned to England to stand trial for permitting hashish to be smoked on his property. Found guilty, he was sentenced to a year in jail on June 29 and spent a night at the notorious Wormwood Scrubs prison before being released on bail; Jagger and another defendant were convicted on lesser charges. Richards's sentence was overturned on appeal on July 31.

A projected United States tour was endangered by the drug arrests, and the Stones lay low for the rest of 1967 and in 1968, playing no concerts. They released the albums *Got Live If You Want It*, *Between the* Buttons, and *Flowers* in 1967. In May 1968 the band released the single "Jumpin' Jack Flash," which was to become a perennial stage vehicle for Jagger. Towards the end of the year, they issued one of their finest albums, Beggar's Banquet, which included the song "Sympathy for the Devil." The political upheavals of 1968 were reflected in another song on the LP, "Street Fighting Man."

In May 1969 Brian Jones was dropped from the group and replaced by Mick Taylor. Jones had lost creative control to Richards and Jagger and had be- gun to miss dates and recording sessions because of his increasing addiction to drugs. When Jones was found drowned in the swimming pool of his Sussex estate on July 3, 1969, the Stones' reputation reached a new level of notoriety. Two days later, they performed a free memorial concert-their first public appearance in over two years-in London's Hyde Park. Also in July, the Stones released one of their most popular singles, "Hanky Tonk Women," with "You Can't Always Get What You Want" on the flip side of the American release. Late in the year, while on a new American tour, the Stones released the album Let *It Bleed,* which included the numbers "Gimme Shelter" and "Midnight Rambler." Their American tour ended on December 6, 1969 with a free concert at the Altamont Speedway in Livermore, California, where one member of a contingent of Hell's Angels who had been retained to keep order stabbed a spectator to death during the performance. That scene was recorded on film by Albert and David Maysles and appeared in their 1970 documentary *Gimme Shelter*.

Heavily in debt for back taxes, the Stones found relief by moving to France in 1971. In the same year, the group also left Decca (London had handled the American releases) to record on its own label, Rolling Stones Records. Atlantic Records was retained to manufacture and distribute the group's discs in North America. The Stones' first album for their own label was *Sticky Fingers*, which contained a glossary of drug jargon and included the songs "Brown Sugar," "Sister Morphine," and "Can't You Hear Me Knocking," another showcase for Richards's guitar work. At about this time, Richards and Anita Pallenberg, who had previously been sniffing or skin-popping heroin, began mainlining the drug at the villa they had rented on the Riviera.

In April 1972 the Stones released *Exile* on *Main* Street, which was recorded at Richards's villa and included the number "Tumbling Dice." In December a warrant was issued for the arrest of Richards and Anita Pallenberg, but they had moved to the West Indies before returning to their home in Chelsea for Christmas. Richards has admitted that both *Sticky* Fingers and *Exile* on *Main* Street were recorded by the Stones when they were high on drugs.

The Stones played North America in 1972 and Australia, New Zealand, Britain, and the European Continent in 1973. The following year there was no tour, but a film, *Ladies* and *Gentlemen, The Rolling Stones*, of the Stones in concert, made during their 1972 tour, was released. Mick Taylor, who had become a heroin addict, quit the group near the end of 1974. He was succeeded by Ron Wood the following year, when the band played a forty-two-stop tour of North America.

While Richards was in Toronto in February 1977 for club dates that were to form the basis of a new Stones album, police searched his hotel room and found enough heroin-twenty-two grams-to arrest him not only for possession but also for intent to traffic—a crime with a possible penalty of life imprisonment. With his freedom and the future of the Rolling Stones at stake, Richards, with Anita Pallenberg, underwent drug rehabilitation. As Richards told Jim Jerome for a *People* (November 21, 1977) magazine article, "I had reached the point of no return. I had this realization that I was endangering everything I wanted to do and what people around me wanted to do." The Stones did not play in public in 1977 but performed in the United States in June and July 1978. In October of that year, Richards pleaded guilty to a reduced charge of heroin possession and was put on probation for one year and ordered to stage a charity performance for the Canadian National Institute for the Blind. 'That concert took place in April 1979 in Oshawa, Ontario.

Affiliation: Rolling Stones

As Jon Pareles commented in the *New York Times* (October 9, 1988), "Fans always assumed that . . . Mr. Richards was the raunch specialist, with his rhythm guitar chords cross-cutting the beat, his leads and fills slicing nasty curlicues into a song, [and] his tone distorted a dozen ornery ways." Although he and his fellow Rolling Stones are now middle-aged, Richards remains as committed as ever to playing rock-'n'-roll. "It's a fallacy that rock-'n'-roll is a juvenile, teenage music," he has said. "It ain't like tennis—there's not a certain amount of years." After Mick Jagger refused to tour with the Stones to promote their 1986 album, *Dirty Work,* Richards produced his own album, *Talk Is Cheap,* released in 1988, and went on tour with the core musicians from that LP, calling themselves the X-Pensive Winos. "I've learned that if you give me the right bunch of guys, in a week I'll have 'em sounding like they've been together for years," Richards commented recently. "It's probably because *I* need it so much myself." The Stones regrouped in 1989, and in August of that year they began a thirty-six-city tour of the United States and Canada to promote their album *Steel Wheels.*

Jim Jerome reported that Richards, after he was off heroin, looked healthier and more alert and confident than he had in years. Richards spent most of 1977 at a rented house in Salem, New York. At the time, he owned a house in the Chelsea section of London, which he rarely lived in because of his tax status, a flat in Paris, a house in Jamaica, and a seventeenth-century castle overlooking the English Channel in Chichester. By the end of the year, Richards had reached the point where he could analyze how he became addicted to heroin. As he explained to Jim Jerome, he had used drugs to "take the edge off" the disorientation he felt when not on tour or recording. ''I'm somebody who's always got to have something to do, who needs continuity rather than these constantly shifting extremes," he told Jerome. Since he gave up drugs, Richards's therapy consisted of playing more music. "The whole idea is just to keep going, keep playing, never stop," he told an interviewer for the *Chicago Tribune* (April 17, 1986). "It doesn't matter if you're doing it for an audience. That's been a great help to me."

Asked by one interviewer late in 1981 how heroin had affected his playing, Richards said, "I don't think it hurt my music. . . . I may have played a little cooler, but not much." But, at about the same time, he told Kurt Loder in a *Rolling Stone* (November 12, 1981) interview, "Thinking about it, I would probably say yeah, I'd probably have been better, played better, off of it."

After performing in public only twice in three years, the Stones made a fifty-concert tour of the United States in the fall of 1981, playing to more than two million people and grossing more than $50 million. Also in that year, the Stones' new album, *Tattoo* You, topped sales in the United States for nine weeks. Robert Palmer of the *New York Times* (February 6, 1983), reviewing a Hal Ashby film made from three of their performances during the 1981 tour, Let's Spend the *Night Together* (1983), described Richards as being in peak form, healthy and "breathing fire onstage."

The Stones wrapped up a tour of England, Ireland, and continental Europe with a concert at Leeds, England on July 25, 1982. In 1983 the Stones signed a contract with CBS Records to supply, starting in 1985, four Rolling Stones Records albums for distribution, for a reported figure of between $20 million and $25 million. By 1985, when the band began ten months of work on the album *Dirty Work* (1986), the Stones had not played together, except sporadically, for a couple of years.

That album marked the demise—at least temporarily—of the Stones as a group, since Mick Jagger, who had released his first solo album in 1985, refused to go on tour in 1986 to promote *Dirty Work.* With the benefit of hindsight, Richards has said that his relationship with Jagger deteriorated after he gave up heroin and made it known that he wanted to become more actively involved in the business end as well as the musical end of the Stones—a move that he believes Jagger interpreted as some kind of power play. With Jagger involved in making another album and the Stones scattered, Richards signed a long-term record deal with Virgin Records in 1987 and began work on his first solo album, *Talk Is* Cheap. "The whole idea is, I gotta work," Richards told Rolling Stone (September 10, 1987). "I can't sit on my ass—I go crazy, you know?" He also acted as musical director for the 1987 film *Chuck Berry Hail! Hail! Rock 'n' Roll* and produced the soundtrack album. Reviewing that album in the *New* York *Times* (October 21, 1987), Robert Palmer said that it had the "raw guitar textures and an explosive live sound reminiscent of some Rolling Stones concert recordings." Richards also produced and played the guitar on Aretha Franklin's single "Jumpin' Jack Flash."

Talk Is Cheap, released in October 1988, was written and produced by Richards and the drummer Steve Jordan. Other members of the band that Richards put together for the album were the guitarist Waddy Wachtel, the keyboardist Ivan Neville, the saxophonist Bobby Keyes, and the bassist Charley Drayton. The album includes the song "You Don't Move Me," with its clearly implied anger at Jagger over his decision to make two albums, both of which were indifferently received by the public, as evidenced in the lines: "Now you want to throw the dice/you already crapped out twice." Reviewing the album in the *New York Times* (October 9, 1988), Jon Pareles wrote that it "sounds loose, sloppy, thrown-together, unfinished. That's why I like it-it's a relief to hear a musician open the lid on canned music.... Songs sprawl as the musicians try out riffs and grooves, and the singer—Mr. Richards, with his bomb-crater of a voice-shouts and growls his lines in any spaces left by the band." Pareles also noted that "albums like *Talk Is* Cheap . . . reclaim music as work in progress, bringing rock listeners as close to the moment of creation as the musicians dare."

In the fall of 1988 the core musicians from the album, calling themselves the X-Pensive Winos, went on a three-week, ten-city tour of the United States. Writing in the *New York Times* (December 1, 1988) about their concert at New York City's Beacon Theater, Jon Pareles described them as "a rowdy bunch, wandering the stage, grinning and cackling at one another's stomps and twangs. Mr. Richards laughs the hardest, bending to fling a power chord or kicking waist-high at the end of a verse." Commenting on Richards's guitar playing, Pareles added: "Mr. Richards casually displayed guitar techniques from gnarled blues phrases to the terse plunks of dub reggae, from the fast scratching of funk rhythm guitar to linear, melodic lead guitar. Like the great blues guitarists, he doesn't bother with hyperspeed or fancy harmonies; he just makes the instrument sing and snarl and snicker."

Richards and Jagger resolved their differences in late 1988, and in January 1989 they traveled to Barbados to begin writing songs for a new Rolling Stones album. In just two weeks, the pair churned out forty songs, nine of which were selected for their thirty-fourth album, Steel Wheels, which was released in August 1989. *Steel Wheels*, in the opinion of Nicholas Jennings of Maclean's (September 11, 1989), "bristles with more bravado than the Stones have demonstrated since they released the supercharged, disco-flavored *Some Girls* in 1978. Although the new record lacks the unpredictable, menacing tone of the Stones' best work, it may well become known as a minor classic itself, largely because it captures the creative sparks that fly when the willful Jagger and the more visceral Richards work together." The Stones played before huge crowds in every city they visited, and when it was announced that the band would perform four shows at New York's Shea Stadium in October, some 300,000 tickets were sold in just six hours. On August 31, 1989 the Stones kicked off the tour with a sold-out concert at Veterans Stadium in Philadelphia.

In the 1990s and 2000s Richards contributed to a wide range of musical projects as a guest artist. A few of the notable sessions include guitar and vocals on Johnnie Johnson's 1991 release *Johnnie B. Bad* and lead vocals and guitar on "Oh Lord, Don't Let Them Drop That Atomic Bomb on Me" on the 1992 Charles Mingus tribute album *Weird Nightmare*. He duetted with country legend George Jones on "Say It's Not You" on the Bradley Barn Sessions (1994). He partnered with Levon Helm on "Deuce and a Quarter" for Scotty Moore's album *All the King's Men* in 1997. His guitar and lead vocals are featured on the Hank Williams tribute album *Timeless* (2001) and on veteran blues guitarist Hubert Sumlin's 2005 album *About Them Shoes*. Richards also added guitar and vocals to Toots & the Maytals' recording of "Careless Ethiopians" for their 2004 album *True Love* and to their re-recording of "Pressure Drop", which came out in 2007 as the B-side to Richards' iTunes re-release of "Run Rudolph Run."

During his years as a heroin addict, Richards was sometimes described as a glassy-eyed walking corpse, and it was widely speculated that he would become the rock world's next drug fatality. His emaciated junkie look has disappeared, although his craggy features are deeply lined. Once described by a journalist as resembling a "rakish highwayman," Richards is a slender, yet muscular, five feet, ten inches tall, with black hair and brown eyes. Interviewers often comment on his intelligence, charm, and maturity. He wears a death's-head ring on his right hand as a *memento mori*, smokes Marlboro cigarettes, and drinks generous quantities of Rebel Yell bourbon. "Drink has never been a problem," he told Jim Jerome. "I've written some of my best things pissed out of my mind." In January 1989 the Rolling Stones were inducted into the Rock-'n'-Roll Hall of Fame.

Personal Life

Richards maintains cordial relations with Italian-born actress Anita Pallenberg, the mother of his first three children. Richards and Pallenberg, who never married, were a couple from 1967 to 1979. Together they have a son, Marlon Leon Sundeep (1969) and a daughter, Angela (1972) Their third child, a son named Tara Jo Gunne died in June 1976 at just over two months old of sudden infant death syndrome (SIDS)

Keith Richards and Patti Hansen, the actress and model, were married on his fortieth birthday, December 18, 1983, in Cabo San Lucas, Mexico in a civil ceremony, with Mick Jagger standing in as best man. Richards and his wife have two daughters, Theodora (1985) and Alexandra (1986). Keith Richards has five grandchildren.

Richards still owns Redlands, the Sussex estate he purchased in 1966, as well as a home in Weston, Connecticut and another in the private resort island of Parrot Cay, Turks & Caicos. His primary home is in Weston. In June 2013, Richards said that he would retire with his family to Parrot Cay or Jamaica if he knew his death was coming.

Gus and Me: The Story of My Granddad and My First Guitar was published in 2014. It is a children's book that Richards created with his daughter, Theodora. She reportedly did pen and ink illustrations for the book, which was inspired by the man she's named after, Richards' grandfather Theodore Augustus Dupree.

Richards has a collection of approximately 3,000 guitars. Even though he has used many different guitar models, in a 1986 *Guitar World* interview Richards joked that no matter what model he plays, "give me five minutes and I'll make 'em all sound the same." Richards has often thanked Leo Fender, and other guitar manufacturers for making the instruments, as he did during the induction ceremony of the Rolling Stones into the Rock and Roll Hall of Fame.

Further Reading

NY *Newsday* p4+ Ja 25 '83 par, II p3 Ap 13 '86 por, II p4 0 9 '88 pors

Rolling Stone p25+ N 12 '81 pors, p65+ D 10 '87 pors, p53+ 0 6 '88 pors

Norman, Philip. *Symphony for the Devil: The Rolling Stones Story* (1984)

The Rolling Stone Interviews: Talking with the Legends of Rock & Roll 1967-1980 (1981)

Weiner, Sue and Howard, Lisa. *The Rolling Stones A to Z* (1983)

Who's Who in America, 1988-89

Life, Richards, K, Fox, J, Back Bay Books, May 3, 2011

Gus & Me: The Story of My Granddad and My First Guitar, Richards, K, Richards, T, Little Brown Books for Young Readers, 2014

Rihanna (REE-anna)

Singer

Born: Feb. 20, 1988; Saint Michael, Barbados
Primary Field: Teen pop and American R&B
Group Affiliation: Solo performer

Introduction

Def Jam Recordings head Shawn Carter, better known as the rapper Jay-Z, reportedly gave Rihanna two choices after hearing her audition for the label in early 2005. Def Jam executives "locked me into the office—till 3am," the Barbados-born singer told Sylvia Patterson for the London Observer *(August 26, 2007). "And Jay-Z said, 'There's only two ways out. Out the door after you sign this deal. Or through this window.' And we were on the 29th floor." Rihanna, just 16 at the time, chose the former, launching a career that as of 2007 has yielded three hit albums, two number-one singles on* Billboard's *Hot 100 chart, and a host of awards, including Monster Single of the Year and Video of the Year honors, both for the smash "Umbrella," at the 2007 MTV Video Music Awards. The singer has built a reputation for recording summer hits, including "Pon de Replay" and "SOS." "The 19-year-old ingénue, who butterflied her way from Bajan dancehall queen to American pop princess in a few short years, has executed a genre-swapping crossover move as smooth as her elastic-limbed choreography," Shanel Odum wrote for* Vibe *(July 2007), adding that the singer "seductively straddles the line between doe-eyed sweetheart and sassy sex kitten."*

Early Life

The oldest of three children, Robyn Rihanna Fenty was born on February 20, 1988 in Saint Michael, Barbados. Her father, Ronald, is a native of that Caribbean island; her mother, Monica, is Guyanese. Throughout Rihanna's childhood her father struggled with addictions to alcohol and crack cocaine, leaving her mother to care for her and her two brothers, Rorrey and Rajad, while working accounting jobs. Ronald's substance-abuse problems led to frequent arguments with Monica. As she watched her parents fight, Rihanna internalized her feelings and kept mostly to herself. Around the time that she turned eight, she began having bad headaches, and for years doctors were unable to figure out their cause. "They even thought it was a tumor, because it was that intense," Rihanna told Margeaux Watson for *Entertainment Weekly* (June 29, 2007). The headaches stopped when she was 14, after her parents divorced. Rihanna stayed with her mother and has remained in touch her father, who eventually overcame his addictions. "Everybody has something that makes them stronger in their life," she told Georgina Dickinson for the English publication *News of the World* (September 2, 2007). "My childhood experiences helped to make me a stronger person and a stronger woman. That is very necessary in this industry and in this career. I need to be strong and I need to be very responsible."

Rihanna told Derek Paiva for the *Honolulu Advertiser* (September 15, 2006) that she "always sang" while growing up, "but no one ever was really pushing me to do it." As a child she listened to a mix of Caribbean music-her mother would often play reggae records around the house-and American hip-hop and R&B. In interviews she has cited Whitney Houston and Mariah Carey as major influences on her style. Despite her interest in singing, she was an introvert and a tomboy. Adding further to her feelings of isolation, her schoolmates teased her for her light skin color. "I had to develop a thick skin because they would call me white," she told Watson. By her early teens she had overcome her shyness enough to start a singing group with two female classmates. In 2004, the same year Rihanna won her school's beauty pageant, the trio landed an audition with Evan Rogers, one-half of Syndicated Rhythm Productions, the producing/songwriting team behind hits for musical acts including 'N Sync and Christina Aguilera. The audition came about after Rogers's wife, a native of Barbados, heard about Rihanna while she and her husband were vacationing there. "The minute Rihanna walked into the room, it was like the other two girls didn't exist," Rogers told Watson, recalling the audition he conducted in his hotel room. "She carried herself like a star even when she was 15." Rihanna sang "Emotion," a song by the popular American group Destiny's Child, and though Rogers thought that her voice was rough, he decided to fly the singer to New York to record a demo. Rihanna and her mother spent the next year flying back and forth between Barbados and Rogers's home in Stamford, Connecticut. After Rihanna turned 16, she moved in with Rogers and his wife, finishing her high-school coursework with the help of tutors.

Life's Work

As the teenage Rihanna adjusted to life in the public eye, she thanked her mother for helping her to develop a mature outlook. "I know a lot for my age," she told Amina Taylor for the London *Guardian* (November 25, 2005). "My mom raised me to be a child and know my place but also to think like a woman. She never held back from me in terms of being too young to know certain things, so fortunately I am very mature for my age. In this business you have to work with the things that get thrown your way, the good, the bad and the ugly." The "ugly" included losing friends. "When I signed my recording deal, a few fake friends and I parted ways," she told Taylor. "I gained some who wanted to get close to me because of the deal, so they had to go as well."

In April 2006, eight months after releasing her debut, Rihanna returned with *A Girl Like Me.* Among the new musical styles the singer explored on that album was 1980s pop, echoed in her song "SOS," which was built around a sample from Soft Cell's 1981 hit "Tainted Love" and reached number one on the *Billboard* Hot 100 chart. Critics again praised Rihanna for recording the "song of the summer," and the sportswear company Nike decided to use "SOS" in one of its promotions, making Rihanna the first non-athlete to endorse the brand. "SOS" also reached number one on *Billboard's* Pop and Hot Dance Airplay charts and made top 10 lists in Europe. "Unfaithful," the album's second single, reached number six on the *Billboard* Hot 100. "We Ride" failed to make the Hot 100 but climbed to number one on the Hot Dance Club Play chart.

As with Rihanna's first album, many critics found *A Girl Like Me* to be a spotty collection. Writing for the *New York Times* (April 24, 2006), Sanneh found that despite the standout "SOS," "this scattershot album is full of duds." Barry Walters, reviewing the album for *Rolling Stone* (May 26, 2006), agreed, though he saw the singer's second album as an improvement over her first. The album reached number five on the *Billboard* 200. Rihanna was nominated for two awards—Best New Artist in a Video and Viewers' Choice—at the 2006 MTV Video Music Awards, held on August 31.

Rihanna soon had to contend with rumors that she and Jay-Z were romantically involved and that she was in the midst of a feud with Jay-Z's girlfriend, the former Destiny's Child lead singer and top-selling solo artist Beyoncé Knowles. Rihanna denied the rumors. Even as they persisted, critics continued to compare the two female artists, with some calling Rihanna the "Bajan Beyoncé." ("Bajan" is another term for "Barbadian.")

As Rihanna prepared to record her next album, *Good Girl Gone Bad,* she decided to distance herself from the image of her that DefJam had attempted to project. "I got really rebellious," she told Watson. "I was being forced into a particular innocent image and I had to break away from it." On a superficial level, that meant cutting and dyeing her hair and trading her long brown locks for a jet-black "shiny new power-bob haircut," as Craig McLean wrote for the London *Daily Telegraph* (May 31, 2007). Rihanna told McLean, "Now I'm on a mission and I have a vision. The haircut is very liberating. The title [of her second album] *Good Girl Gone Bad* symbolizes that. It symbolizes freedom."

For the third summer in a row, Rihanna released what many called the song of the season, as "Umbrella," the first single from *Good Girl Gone Bad,* topped the *Billboard* Hot 100 chart for seven weeks in June and July. It also reached number one on *Billboard's* Hot Dance Club Play, Hot Digital, and Pop 100 charts. In the United Kingdom the song held the top spot for 10 weeks, besting Whitney Houston's record for most weeks at number one for a female artist. Rihanna said that she knew "Umbrella" would be a hit as soon as she heard it, and she urged the song's producers, who initially were not sure who they wanted to record it, to choose her. "I said: 'Listen, Umbrella is my song!'" she told Matt Glass for the British newspaper *Daily Star* (July 18, 2007), recalling the night she met one of the producers. "He must've thought I was really pushy and laughed it off. But I turned his face back to my own: 'No, I'm seriously need Umbrella.' Two days later, we found out the song was mine." On "Umbrella" Rihanna had help from Jay-Z, who agreed to rap in the song's introduction. Other high-profile guest artists who collaborated on *Good Girl Gone Bad* included the solo star and former 'N Sync singer Justin Timberlake, who wrote and sang background vocals for the song "Rehab." Further ensuring the song's success, Rihanna—long known for her beauty—filmed a portion of the video naked but for the silver paint covering her body.

The much-in-demand producer Timbaland oversaw the recording of three songs, and the singer and songwriter Ne-Yo penned "Hate That I Love You" and "Question Existing," a song about the downside of pop stardom. "Ne-Yo just knew how to say exactly what I feel . . . ," Rihanna told Patterson. "With success has come a latta great stuff, but there's cons, too. Who to trust is a huge one." Rihanna told Sanchez her star status made it hard for her to date: "Every time I meet someone now, I always keep my guard up," she said. "I guess that can get in the way sometimes. It's like a reflex action."

Good Girl Gone Bad met with mostly favorable reviews. "All other contenders may want to consider finding a beach towel to throw in: Rihanna has got the summer locked up," Sarah Rodman wrote for the *Boston Globe* (June 12, 2007). In his review for the *New York Times* (June 4, 2007), Sanneh wrote that the album "should secure [Rihanna's] place on pop music's A-list. She has an instantly recognizable voice (giddy enough for teen-pop, plaintive enough for R&B), great taste in beats.... This CD sounds as if it were scientifically engineered to deliver hits." Tom Breihan, writing for the popular on-line music Web site Pitchfork.com (June 15, 2007), criticized Rihanna for failing to reflect enough of her personality in her songs—a criticism echoed by other writers. "The chief characteristic of Rihanna's voice, after all, is a sort of knife-edged emptiness, a mechanistic precision that rarely makes room for actual feelings to bulldoze their way through," Breihan wrote. Still, he praised the album for its diverse mixture of sounds, writing, "*Good Girl Gone Bad* makes for an unexpectedly varied and satisfying listen." The album reached number two on the *Billboard* 200. Its second single, "Shut Up and Drive," which samples another 1980s song, New Order's "Blue Monday," peaked at number 15 on the Hot 100 chart.

Rihanna rose to widespread prominence and became a household name with the release of *Good Girl Gone Bad* and its chart-topping lead single "Umbrella" in 2007. The album and its 2008 *Reloaded* re-release were nominated for nine Grammy Awards, winning Best Rap/Sung Collaboration for "Umbrella." From 2009 to 2012 she annually released four Recording Industry Association of America (RIAA) platinum certified albums: *Rated R* in 2009, *Loud* (2010), *Talk That Talk* (2011), her first Billboard 200 number one album *Unapologetic* (2012) and *Anti* (2016). Rihanna has sold over 200 million records worldwide, making her one of the best-selling artists of all time. On July 1, 2015 the Recording Industry Association of America (RIAA) announced that Rihanna had surpassed more than 100 million Gold & Platinum song certifications. In doing so Rihanna has the most Digital Single Awards and is the first and only artist to surpass RIAA's 100 million cumulative singles award threshold.

On June 8, 2007 Gillette, manufacturer of a women's razor, gave Rihanna its 2007 Celebrity Legs of a Goddess award. The company also insured the star's famously shapely legs for $1 million. The next month Rihanna performed in Tokyo, Japan, as part of Live Earth, a worldwide series of concerts meant to raise awareness of climate change. At the 2007 MTV Video Music Awards, held in Las Vegas, Nevada, on September 9, Rihanna-in addition to

Affiliation: Breaking Into the Industry

By January 2005 Rogers had produced a four-song demo recording, which he began sending to record labels. The first to respond was Def Jam Recordings, and Rihanna was invited to audition for the company's newly named CEO and president, Shawn ("Jay-Z") Carter. "I had butterflies," she told Patterson. "I'm sitting across from Jay-Z. Like, Jay-Zee. I was star-struck." She sang three songs, including "Pon de Replay," which Rogers co-wrote. Jay-Z was impressed with what he heard. "After my audition, he clapped and said: 'OK, at Def Jam we don't sign songs, we sign artists and we want you,'" she told Nui Te Koha for the Australian *Sunday Sun Herald* (July 8, 2007). Rihanna has claimed that Jay-Z kept her locked in an office for some 12 hours, until she signed with Def Jam.

On August 30, 2005 the label released Rihanna's debut album, *Music of the Sun*. The album's first single, "Pon de Replay," reached number two on the *Billboard* Hot 100 chart, and many critics called it the song of the summer. "An inspired mix of Jamaican reggae and American R&B, 'Pon de Replay' is the ideal single for a late summer heatwave," Adrian Thrills wrote for the London *Daily Mail* (September 2, 2005). "One of the catchiest songs to come out of the Caribbean in years, it also acts as the perfect primer for Rihanna's first album." Though the single was well received, critics were not as enthusiastic about the album as a whole. "A hard beat and a soft voice: it's a reliable formula, and on her debut album, *Music of the Sun*, Rihanna spends 25 minutes sticking to it . . . ," Kelefa Sanneh wrote for the *New York Times* (September 5, 2005). "Just one problem: this CD is twice that long, and Rihanna sounds a bit stranded when she doesn't have a beat to ride." Despite such criticism, the album reached number 10 on the *Billboard* 200 chart. The second single, "If It's Lovin' that You Want," was less successful, peaking at number 36 on the Hot 100.

performing-took home Monster Single of the Year and Video of the Year honors, both for "Umbrella." Later that month she received three nominations for the MTV Europe Video Music Awards, among them solo artist of the year.

Personal Life

Rihanna lives in Los Angeles, California. She has named Madonna as her idol and biggest influence. She said she wants to be the "black Madonna". "I think that Madonna was a great inspiration for me, especially on my earlier work. If I had to examine her evolution through time, I think she reinvented her clothing style and music with success every single time. And at the same time remained a real force in entertainment in the whole world." She also cites Whitney Houston as a major influence and idol, and Mariah Carey and Beyoncé Knowles as major influences.

On February 8, 2009, Rihanna's scheduled performance at the 51st Grammy Awards was cancelled. Reports surfaced that then-boyfriend, singer Chris Brown, had beaten her. He was arrested and later charged with assault and making criminal threats. Due to a leaked photograph from the Los Angeles Police Department obtained by TMZ.com—which revealed that Rihanna had sustained visible injuries—an organization known as STOParazzi proposed "Rihanna's Law," which, if enacted, would "deter employees of law enforcement agencies from releasing photos or information that exploits crime victims." On June 22, 2009, Brown pled guilty to felony assault. Brown received five years probation and was ordered to stay away from Rihanna.

Further Reading

(Australia) *Sunday Sun Herald* E p5 July 8, 2007
Entertainment Weekly p 80 June 29, 2007
Honolulu Advertiser T p14 Sept. 15, 2006
(London) *Daily Mail* p53 Sept. 2, 2005
(London) *Daily Telegraph* p34 May 31, 2007
(London) *Guardian* p9 Nov. 25, 2005
(London) *Observer* p14 Aug. 26, 2007
(London) *Times* p16 Sept. 2, 2005
People p49 Aug. 29, 2005
Rihanna: The Unauthorized Biography, White D., Michael O'Mara Sept. 1, 2013

Nile Rodgers

Guitarist, songwriter, music producer

Born: September 19, 1952; New York City
Primary Field: Hip-hop, disco-soul-funk, R&B
Group Affiliation: Chic

Introduction

*Nile Rodgers may not be a household name, but for the past thirty-five years, his work has been familiar to nearly everyone who follows pop music. In the late 1970s and early 1980s, as the guitarist and coproducer for the disco soul-funk band Chic—which he cofounded with his longtime collaborator, the late Bernard Edwards—he wrote such hits as "Le Freak," "Dance, Dance, Dance," and "Good Times." The last-named song is not only one of Chic's best-known works but also one of their most influential: as an example, for the groundbreaking song "Rapper's Delight/' the hip-hop group Sugar Hill Gang sampled the bass line of "Good Times," which also inspired the art-rock group Queen's hit "Another One Bites the Dust." Beginning in the 1990s Rodgers's songs were also sampled by such hip-hop artists as the Notorious B.I.G. The songs Rodgers wrote for others in the 1970s and '80s include some of the most anthemic hits of modern times, among them Sister Sledge's "We Are Family" and Diana Ross's "I'm Coming Out"; he has also produced albums by such megastars as Ross, David Bowie, Madonna, Duran Duran, Mick Jagger, and Jeff Beck. For much of the 1990s and the first decade of the 2000s, Rodgers composed and produced music for high-profile films—*Beverly Hills Cop III, Rush Hour 2*, and others. In 2011 he published a memoir,* Le Freak: An Upside Down Story of Family, Disco, and Destiny.

Early Life

Nile Gregory Rodgers was born on September 19, 1952, in New York City. He provided a detailed account of his childhood in an essay for the *New York Times* (11 Sep. 2011), which was adapted from his memoir. His mother,

Beverly, conceived him when she was only thirteen years old; his father, Nile Rodgers Sr., was sixteen. A wedding was planned, but Beverly changed her mind at the last minute. Beverly, whom Rodgers described as smart and beautiful, later met Bobby Clanzrock, a white, Jewish man who became Rodgers's stepfather. With his mother and stepfather, Rodgers moved frequently around New York, settling in 1959 in an apartment in Greenwich Village, the bohemian center of Manhattan. That was when it occurred to Rodgers that his parents were "different," as he wrote. In that era, even on the progressive streets of Greenwich Village, the sight of a white man and a black woman walking together caused some people to stare. Beverly and Bobby, who listened to a lot of jazz, used the Beat slang of the time and took many drugs-most devastatingly, heroin. "Beverly and Bobby may not have been model parents," Rodgers wrote, "but they were a really good fit for each other; art, literature and especially their love of music bonded them together. But as they spiraled deeper and deeper into addiction, they were also increasingly self-centered, not infrequently criminal and less and less interested in the responsibilities of raising a kid. On some level, it was great to be treated like a peer, to be on a first-name basis with my parents, but it wasn't exactly a substitute for the usual parental cocktail of nurturing and discipline. Respect? Yes, there was plenty of that. If I had a problem, we'd 'rap on it.' Then they'd ask me something like: 'Are we copacetic?' If I said, 'Yeah, I guess so,' the matter would be settled with a five slap or some other affirming gesture." Rodgers sometimes saw his biological father, a gifted percussionist drawn to Afro-Cuban rhythms. Nile Sr., who in his son's recollection was warm and kind—if mentally unstable and addicted to drugs—taught his young son to listen to rhythm patterns. Rodgers also studied music in public school, and by the time he was 14 years old, he was already fairly proficient on a number of musical instruments.

Life's Work

While still in his teens, Rodgers began his music career in New York City as a session guitarist. He went on tour with the Sesame Street band and then played in the house band of the well-known Apollo Theater, in Harlem, backing such big-name acts as Aretha Franklin, Ben E. King, Parliament Funkadelic, and Screaming Jay Hawkins. In 1970 Rodgers met the bassist Bernard Edwards, and the two began a musical partnership that would last a quarter century. They formed the Big Apple Band, serving as backup musicians for an E&B group called New York City—which had a minor hit with ''I'm Doing Fine Now," toured extensively, and in 1973 opened for the Jackson 5 on the US leg of that supergroup's first international tour. After New York City broke up, Rodgers and Edwards met the drummer Tony Thompson, with whom they formed a funk-rock band called the Boys. They had a hard time getting signed, because, they were told, a black rock band would be hard to promote. As a result Rodgers, Edwards, and Thompson toured often as the Big Apple Band, working alongside such renowned vocalists as Ashford & Simpson and Luther Vandross. Because there was another act called Big Apple Band, Rodgers and Edwards changed their band's name to Chic— which, in addition to Rodgers, Edwards, and Thompson, included the singers Alfa Anderson and Norma Jean Wright (who was later replaced by Luci Martin). Chic's first single was the demo "Dance, Dance, Dance (Yowsah, Yowsah, Yowsah)," which they pitched unsuccessfully to several big record labels. After a small record label, Buddha, released it in 1977, the song became a huge hit in dance clubs, which led to a major record deal with Atlantic. After Atlantic re-released "Dance, Dance, Dance," the song became a Top 1 0 hit. Chic's self-titled debut album, which came out in 1977, showcased the group's mix of the Euro-discu, E&B, funk, and soul genres. Despite being panned by most rock critics-who heard too much disco in Chic's music—the record was very popular, thanks in part to the group's second single, "Everybody Dance." Rodgers and Edwards cowrote all of the group's songs and served as Chic's leaders and producers, an arrangement that would continue with future Chic albums.

Chic truly hit the big time with their second album, *C'est Chic* (1978), which featured the popular songs "I Want Your Love," "Chic Cheer," and "Le Freak." Robert A. Hull, writing for the *Washington Post* (23 Sep. 1979), called "Le Freak" one of the "goofiest and funniest singles of this dull decade—one can hear the song 50 times and not be able to pinpoint its hypnotic appeal." *C'est Chic* came out at the height of disco fever and climbed to number one on the Billboard R&B chart and number four on the Billboard 200 chart. In a review for *AllMusic,* Jason Birchmeier wrote about the significance of the album: "Producers Bernard Edwards and Nile Rodgers were quite a savvy pair and knew that disco was as much a formula as anything. As evidenced here, they definitely had their fingers on the pulse of the moment, and used their perceptive touch to craft one of the few truly great disco albums. In fact, you could even argue that *C'est Chic* very well may be the definitive disco album. After all, countless artists scored dance-floor hits, but few could deliver an album this solid, and nearly as few could deliver one this epochal as well. *C'est Chic* embodies everything wonderful and excessive about disco at its pixilated peak." Chic followed their sophomore album with another hit record, titled *Risque* (1979). Considered to be one of the group's quintessential albums, *Risque* featured such hits as "My Feet Keep Dancing," "My Forbidden Lover," and "Good Times." In his review Hull observed that has "an abundance of inspiring music guaranteed to motivate a veritable symphony of pelvic distortion on any dance floor. [One] quick listen, and it's easy to hear why all cuts from the album are currently climbing the disco charts. The key to Chic's entrancing sound is Nile Rodgers' guitar work and Rodgers/Bernard Edwards' sweeping production. This team's devotion to detail was not apparent on Chic's cliché-hit, 'Dance, Dance, Dance (Yowsah, Yowsah, Yowsah),' but with 'I Want Your Love,' possibly Chic's greatest tune, Edwards & Rodgers' craftsmanship hit its stride." The album peaked at number 5 on the *Billboard* 200 chart.

As the 1980s commenced, disco began to lose its grip on the public. Chic's *Real People* (1980) sold fairly well, peaking at number 30 on the Billboard 200 chart, but it was clear that the group's popularity was falling. The following year the group released *Take It Off* (1981), which clearly represented an attempt to reduce its Euro-disco feel; Chic's music had always contained elements of funk and soul, but those were more pronounced now, as were pop and rock sounds. The album, which peaked at number 124 on the Billboard 200 chart and number 36 on the R&B chart, impressed some notable critics, such as the music journalist and blues historian Robert Palmer. In his review of the album for the *New York Times* (23 Dec. 1981), Palmer wrote: 'The key to Chic's new direction turned out to be the same Chic rhythm section that powered the group's disco hits. The new album, *Take It Off,* succeeds brilliantly because it throws the spotlight squarely on Mr. Rodgers's guitar, Mr. Edwards's bass and Tony Thompson's drums. The sweet, elegant string arrangements that figured so prominently in the earlier Chic hits have been scrapped, and the new album's group vocals are lean, almost percussive. The first single to be released from the album, 'So Fine,' uses Mr. Rodgers's guitar as its lead instrument. He picks tricky, clipped rhythm figures, sounding at times a little like the late jazz guitarist Wes Montgomery, while the band punctuates with stop-time rhythms. The vocalists fill in like a horn section. On other numbers, Mr. Edwards's bass takes the lead, and the voices and other instruments fall into place around it, like iron filings around a magnet. The deliberately sparse production emphasizes that this is the sound of a few gifted musicians working closely together." Chic's last two

Affiliation: Producer

More significantly during that decade, Rodgers was considered the "hottest record producer in the business," in the words of Dennis Hunt, writing for the *Los Angeles Times* (9 Nov. 1985). Initially, in working on songs for other acts, he shared songwriting responsibilities with Edwards. In 1979 Rodgers, while still with Chic, had produced and cowritten most of the tracks for the Sister Sledge album *We Are Family,* including the title song, which became a huge hit and one of the most recognizable songs of the 1970s. He also wrote and coproduced all the songs for the next Sister Sledge album, *Love Somebody Today* (1980). Rodgers performed the same services for *Diana* (1980), the Diana Ross album that included such hit singles as "Upside Down" and "I'm Coming Out." Then, in the same year that Chic's members went their separate ways, Rodgers coproduced David Bowie's *Let's Dance* (1983), Bowie's best-selling album to date, containing the hits "Let's Dance," "China Girl," and "Modern Love." Rodgers also contributed his guitar playing to that art-rock dance record. The following year he produced Madonna's album *Like a Virgin* (1984), among whose hits were the title song and "Material Girl." Also that year Rodgers mixed the Duran Duran single 'The Reflex," which later hit number one on the Hot 100 chart, and "The Wild Boys," which reached number two on the chart. In a 1985 interview with Hunt, Rodgers conceded, "I work too much. I should learn to say no. I always bite off more than I can chew." Rodgers also produced Mick Jagger's *She's the Boss* (1985), Jeff Beck's *Flash* (1985), Duran Duran's *Notorious* (1986), Debbie Harry's *One More into the Bleach* (1988), and *Family Style* (1990), by the blues guitar-playing brothers Jimmie Vaughan and Stevie Ray Vaughan. In the 1990s Rodgers's work was frequently sampled by rappers such as MC Lyte, Puff Daddy, Notorious B.I.G., Faith Evans, and Will Smith.

albums of that era—*Tongue in Chic* (1982) and *Believer* (1983)—yielded no hit songs and were largely ignored, except by the band's die-hard fans.

Chic disbanded in 1983. That same year—before Chic officially broke up—Rodgers's debut solo album, *Adventures in the Land of the Good Groove,* came out. The album, which featured Edwards on bass, for the most part eschewed disco in favor of funk ("Yum-Yum") and R&B ("My Love Song for You"). Two years later Rodgers released *B-Movie Matinee,* which, full of synthesizer-driven pop and dance songs, was a departure from both his first solo album and his work with Chic. With the exception of the song "Let's Go Out Tonight," which reached number 88 on the Billboard Hot 100 chart, the album did not generate any hits.

In 1992 Chic reunited and released *Chic-Ism,* an album of new songs that recalled the band's glory days. The record, which made it to number 39 on the R&B chart, had no hit singles but included the critically successful tracks "Chic Mystique" and "Your Love." In an interview with Larry Flick for the *New York Times* (15 Feb. 1992), Edwards explained why he had gotten back together with Rodgers to re-form Chic: "I think we realized that we share a creative bond that we have not been able to match with other people. More than anything, we genuinely missed making music together." In 1996, in a series of commemorative concerts in Japan, Rodgers performed alongside Edwards, Sister Sledge, Steve Winwood, Simon Le Bon, and the Guns N' Roses guitarist Slash. During that trip, soon after one of the performances, Edwards died of pneumonia. Recalling the incident two years later in an interview with Neil Strauss for the *New York Times* (2 Apr. 1998), Rodgers said: "He died on the last night of the show, and being the kind of musician he is, there's no way he's just going to leave the stage or cancel the show. Midway through the concert, we were doing 'Let's Dance,' and all of a sudden, the bass dropped out at the beginning of the verse. I thought: 'Wow, that's clever... .' And I turned around and didn't see him. He had passed out, and the roadies had picked him up and placed him behind the stage, and he was sitting there playing. When we took a break in the middle of the show to change clothes, I realized how incredibly sick he was. This is a person I love closer than any family member, a person I know better than anyone who has ever walked this earth, and I knew there was no way he was leaving that stage. That's how we were brought up." Rodgers added: ''I'll never forget his last speech to the people from Japan. He told them he was a little sick with the Tokyo flu, but he was still here. He told me how much he loved me and how we've been together a long time, and he would do anything for me. Then we went into 'Good Times' and everybody in the house started singing it with us: 10,000 people who didn't even speak English singing 'Good Times' at the top of their lungs. At the end of the show, Bernard was crying in my arms, and he just said: 'You know, man, we did it. This music is bigger than us.'"

In addition to composing and producing songs for his own groups and other artists, Rodgers has created soundtracks for several films, including *Coming to America* (1988), *Blue Chips* (1994), *Beverly Hills Cop III* (1994), and *Rush Hour* 2 (2001). His songs-particularly those he wrote for Chic, Diana Ross, and Sister Sledge-have been used in more than one hundred films and TV shows. Rodgers's memoir, *Le Freak: An Upside Down Story of Family, Disco, and Destiny,* was well-received by critics. A reviewer for *Publishers Weekly* (3 Oct. 2011) wrote, "Rodgers's page-turning memoir is packed with emotionally charged vignettes of a tumultuous childhood and equally dramatic adulthood that found him awash in cash, cars, and celebrities.... While the story of velvet ropes and addiction is a common one, Rodgers's version emphasizes the arc of his life, rather than relying on salacious details or name-dropping to provide a narrative. His storytelling skills propel the reader through the book.... Remarkable for its candor, this rags-to-riches story is on the year's shortlist of celebrity memoirs." Luke Bainbridge wrote for the *London Observer* (5 Nov. 2011), "This is a rich, warm tale of a fascinating life in the golden age of New York-and pop."

Personal Life

Rodgers has received many honors, including the National Academy of Recording Arts and Sciences New York Chapter's Governor's Lifetime Achievement Award. In 2005 he was inducted (along with Edwards) into the Dance Music Hall of Fame, in New York. Chic has been nominated to the Rock and Roll Hall of Fame six times—in 2003, '06, '07, '08, '10, and '11. Rodgers served as co-musical director for the tribute concert to Ahmet Ertegun (the founder and president of Atlantic Records) at the Montreux Jazz Festival in the summer of 2006.

Rodgers is the founder of the We Are Family Foundation, a not-for-profit organization dedicated to the vision of a "global family,'' according to its website. The foundation's goal is to inspire and educate children and promote cultural understanding.

In 1998 Rodgers founded Sumthing Distribution, a nationwide record distributor and creative outlet for independent artists and record labels. Most notably, it has created soundtracks for such popular video-game franchises as Resident Evil and Halo.

In 2010 Rodgers had surgery to combat an aggressive form of cancer. In March 2011 he announced that, according to test results, he is "cancer-free."

Further Reading

Hunt, Dennis. "Producer Is Cuts Above the Field." *Los Angeles Times* 9 Nov. 1985: VI.

Palmer, Robert. "The Pop Life." *New York Times* 23 Dec. 1981: C12.

Rodgers, Nile. "Mr. Rodgers's Neighborhood." *New York Times T: Men's Fashion Magazine.* New York Times Co., 7 Sep. 2011. Web. Jan. 2012.

Richard Rodgers

Composer

Born: June 28, 1902; New York, New York
Died: December 30, 1979; New York, New York
Primary Field: Theater
Group Affiliation: Partner with Oscar Hammerstein

Introduction

Two of the outstanding musical successes of the 1940s, Oklahoma! *and* South Pacific, *were the work of composer Richard Rodgers. In these productions, as well as in* Carousel, Allegro, The King and I *and* The Sound of Music, *Rodgers and his collaborator, Oscar Hammerstein II, brought to the American stage an integration of music and drama which was considered by critics an indigenous art form, a combination of drama, music, and ballet drawn from native sources. Rodgers' earlier work for the Broadway theater was done in partnership with the late Lorenz Hart, with whom he created such hits as* I'd Rather Be Right, Babes in Arms, *and* The Boys from Syracuse. *In the course of several decades in show business, with a twenty-fifth anniversary marked by special events in 1950–51, he also wrote music for motion pictures and television series, produced legitimate drama, and coauthored several plays.*

Richard Rodgers.

Early Life

Born to William Abraham and Mamie (Levy) Rodgers in New York City on June 28, 1902, Richard Rodgers manifested his interest in music at an early age. Unlike his brother, Mortimer, who followed their father into the medical profession, Richard Rodgers more closely resembled his mother, "a merry, musical woman who liked to sing and play the piano." At the age of four he began to pick out the melodies from *The Merry Widow* and *Mademoiselle Modiste* on the piano, and by the age of fourteen had composed his first song, "My Auto Show Girl." About that time he also became active in amateur productions, particularly for the Akron Club, of which his brother was a member. Mimeographed copies of the songs he composed at that period were submitted to the music publishers, without success. As a sixteen-year-old freshman at Columbia College, he submitted the winning score for the annual varsity show, *Fly With Me,* thus becoming the first freshman ever to be so honored.

Through the interest of Columbia alumni (one of them Oscar Hammerstein, Jr., later to be Rodgers' collaborator) in the varsity show, Rodgers was brought into contact with a recent Columbia graduate, Lorenz Hart. Hart "knew something about lyric writing," said the composer, "but had no composer. I knew something about composing but had no lyricist." Of their decision to collaborate on words and music he said, "I left Hart's house having acquired, in one afternoon, a career, a partner, a best friend, and a source of lasting irritation." For the Lew Fields June 1919 production of *A Lonely Romeo,* Rodgers and Hart wrote "Any Old Place With You." Leaving Columbia at the end of his sophomore year, Rodgers worked with Hart and Herbert Fields on *Melody Man,* presented on Broadway under the joint pseudonym of Herbert Richard Lorenz. In 1920 he also assisted Sigmund Romberg in composing *The Poor Little Ritz Girl.*

Life's Work

Since work in the theater was difficult to find that year, Rodgers began a two-year study of music at the Institute of Musical Art under Walter Damrosch. There he was assigned to write the annual show. With the employment situation unimproved after two years, he and Hart began to put on a number of amateur productions for schools, churches, and synagogues. Discouragement with this field had almost brought Rodgers to the point of accepting a job as a salesman of children's wear when he was approached by Benjamin Kaye, a theatrical lawyer, about writing an amateur musical for the Theatre Guild, which needed new tapestries and wanted to stage a Sunday night show to pay for them. With the proviso that Hart was to be his lyricist, Rodgers eventually consented to do the unpaid work, and from this emerged the Guild's *Garrick Gaieties* of 1925, which opened "to the hosannas of public and critics and soon became a riot with nightly performances and two matinees a week." It had a successful run of 214 performances on Broadway.

Affiliation: Oscar Hammerstein

A revival of the *Connecticut Yankee* later in 1943 had a moderate success. The notices of the critics, in general, expressed enthusiasm chiefly for the retention of the four Rodgers hit tunes from the original. For the winter 1944 season Rodgers joined Hammerstein (who had become his permanent collaborator following Hart's death) in producing *I Remember Mama,* a comedy-drama considered "engrossing" and "delightful" by the reviewers. "The Rodgers-Hammerstein duo have added a new category," said *Variety,* "to their list of accomplishments."

The success of the *Garrick Gaieties* was repeated in 1925 with Rodgers and Hart's *Dearest Enemy,* which presented their song, "Here in My Arms." In 1926 they had four productions on Broadway, *The Second Garrick Gaieties, The Girl Friend, Peggy Ann,* and *Betsey,* and one in London, *Lido Lady.* Of these only *Betsey* was a failure. The year 1927 saw their *Connecticut Yankee* and *She's My Baby* on the New York stage, and *One Dam' Thing After Another* on the London stage. They rounded off the decade of the 1920s with *Present Arms* and *Chee Chee* (another unsuccessful musical) of 1928 and *Spring is Here* and *Heads Up* of 1929. Lincoln Barnett, in the *Ladies' Home Journal,* recalled "Blue Room", "Mount Greenery", "Thou Swell", "My Heart Stood Still", "You Took Advantage of Me", and "With a Song in My Heart" as the outstanding Rodgers and Hart song successes of those years. His choice from the next decade included "Small Hotel", "Where or When", "Johnny One Note" "This Can't Be Love," and "Bewitched, Bothered and Bewildered." These were culled from 1930's *Simple Simon* and *Evergreen,* (London) 1931's *America's Sweetheart,* 1935's *Jumbo,* 1936's *On Your Toes,* 1937's *Babes in Arms* and *I'd Rather Be Right,* 1938's *I Married an Angel* and *The Boys from Syracuse,* and 1939's *Too Many Girls.* Rodgers was also part author of *On Your Toes* and *I Married an Angel.* Particularly significant in the development of his work, George Beiswanger pointed out in *Theatre Arts,* were *Babes in Arms,* the first Rodgers musical in which each song was a "plot" song; and *I'd Rather Be Right,* the first in which "the critics recognized purposes and effects akin to those of the Gilbert and Sullivan operettas." Of work done by Rodgers in Hollywood during this period, the composer "would like to forget," said *Time,* all except his scores for the motions pictures *Love Me Tonight* and *State Fair.*

That Rodgers was interested in aspects of the theater other than composing was indicated by the multiple commitments he took in the next decade. As well as composer, he was coauthor and co-producer of *By Jupiter* (1942), which the New York *Times* considered presented some of his "better tunes." When he and Lorenz Hart were commissioned shortly afterward by the Theatre Guild to do a musical version of Lynn Riggs's *Green Grow the Lilacs,* Rodgers was suddenly left alone to complete the work because of Hart's refusal to continue. In need of a collaborator, Rodgers turned to lyricist Oscar Hammerstein, and from their joint effort came the highly successful folk operetta, *Oklahoma!*

Of its opening in April 1943, the New York *World-Telegram* critic Burton Rascoe said. "Richard Rodgers has written for the show one of the finest musical scores any musical play ever had." Citing particularly "Oh, What a Beautiful Mornin' ", "People Will Say;" and "The Surrey With the Fringe on the Top," Lewis Nichols of the New York *Times* observed that Rodgers' "scores never lack grace, but seldom have they been so well integrated as this for *Oklahoma!"* "While the songs fit the period of 1900 perfectly in mood and character," remarked Howard Barnes of the New York *Herald Tribune,* "they are in no sense derivative. It is strictly a Rodgers score and an extraordinarily varied and beautiful one." In a retrospective consideration of the show written that June, Olin Downes brought out that "the music is not folk music, but that of a Broadway composer writing in popular vein, free, skillfully, and with taste, and a fortunate relinquishment of the jazzeries of previous fashion." *Time,* recapitulating the financial gains of the musical at the end of its five-year run—2246 performances—in 1948, reckoned that more than 500,000 albums of its music in records had been sold, two million copies of its sheet music, and profits of 25 to 1 paid to its backers.

An adaptation by Rodgers and Hammerstein of Ferenc Molnar's *Liliom* to the nineteenth century New England scene was the genesis of their March 1945 production, *Carousel.* The score, which included "June is Bustin' Out All Over," was considered by *Variety* to be "comparable to other Richard Rodgers standouts." Otis L. Guernsey, Jr., of the New York *Herald Tribune* found the score "a series of variations on the theme of love or sorrows; its avoids monotony only by its excellence." Other critics considered the music "delightful" (Louis Kronenberger, *PM),* "pleasantly melodious" (E. C. Sherburne, *Christian Science Monitor),*"one of the most beautiful Rodgers scores" (Lewis Nichols, New York *Times).* L. A. Sloper of the *Christian Science Monitor* dissented: "The songs are not so commendable. They are far too protracted, the melodies are not up to the usual Rodgers standard."

Rodgers, who was associated with the production of the Helen Hayes vehicle *Happy Birthday* in 1946, also assisted that year with Hammerstein in the presentation of Ethel Merman in *Annie, Get Your Gun,* an Irving Berlin musical. The following year he was co-producer of *John Loves Mary.* Toward the end of 1947, he and Oscar Hammerstein wrote the musical drama *Allegro* for fall presentation. "The first hearing of the score comes as something of a shock," Kyle Crichton wrote in a *Collier's* article, in which he also mentioned that the psychoanalytic qualities of *Allegro* had resulted from its authors' conviction that Broadway musicals were "in a rut": "It may not be operatic and it may not be contrapuntal, but it certainly is not Broadway." He further described it as a "morality play with music." William Beyer, in a critical study of musicals for *School and Society,* was of the opinion that *Allegro* was "less distinguished" than the other Rodgers' musical plays, "but achieves nevertheless rousing theatrical effectiveness because of the originality of form which it used."

Advance reports had prepared New York audiences for the extraordinary success of the Rodgers and Hammerstein interpretation of two stories drawn from James A. Michener's *Tales of the South Pacific.* Upon the opening of the musical drama *South Pacific* in April 1949, Richard Watts spoke of Rodgers' music as "haunting and beautiful, with half a dozen songs that are unforgettable." Among these were numbered "Some Enchanted Evening" "I'm in Love with a Wonderful Guy" "I'm Gonna Wash That Man Right Out of My Hair," and "Younger than Springtime." Brooks Atkinson characterized Rodgers' music as a "romantic incantation" and ended his "rave" review of the play with the remark, "Fortunately Mr. Rodgers and Mr. Hammerstein are the most gifted men in the business." Besides tributes to Hammerstein and Joshua Logan, director of the musical, *Variety* unequivocally decided that its "score is one of Richard Rodgers' finest—possibly the finest." "The canny team of Richard Rodgers and Oscar Hammerstein 2d," said Howard Barnes, "has written melodies and lyrics that clarify and advance the action rather than impede it." Rodgers and Hammerstein in 1950 produced the short-lived John Steinbeck play, *Burning Bright,* and started work on a dramatization of

Graham Greene's *The Heart of the Matter* for London production and on *The King and I.* They also completed arrangements for the London opening of *South Pacific.*

The King and I, a $340,000 musical version of Margaret Landon's novel *Anna and the King of Siam,* opened in New York on March 29, 1951. Adapted from the story of a British widow who in the 1860s became the tutor to the children of the King of Siam, the play was described by Brooks Atkinson as "an original and beautiful excursion into the rich splendors of the Far East, done with impeccable taste by two artists and brought to life with a warm, romantic score, idiomatic lyrics, and some exquisite dancing" (New York *Times,* March 30, 1951). Other critics, while cautioning the audience not to expect another *South Pacific,* commented upon the novelty, charm, and colorfulness of the production, naming "Getting to Know You", "Something Wonderful," and "I Have Dreamed" as among the show's "memorable" songs.

South Pacific received the New York Drama Critics Circle award as the best musical of the year, the Antoinette Perry award for the best score, a Pulitzer Prize as the best original American play, while the annual medal of the Hundred Year Association was bestowed upon Richard Rodgers and Oscar Hammerstein for their collaboration on it. *Oklahoma!* had already received a special Pulitzer Prize (1944), *I Remember Mama* the Theatre Club Award (1945), and *Carousel* a special citation from the Drama Critics Circle (1946). The composer was the recipient, as well, of two Donaldson awards, for the *Carousel* score (1945) and for that of *Allegro* (1948). His work on the 1945 motion picture, *State Fair,* for which he had written the song "It Might as Well Be Spring," brought him the Academy of Motion Picture Arts and Sciences award for music the following year. Richard Rodgers was president of the Dramatists Guild, and was a member of the board of directors of American Society of Composers, Authors, and Publishers. He held memberships in the Authors League of America and the National Association for American Composers and Conductors; and formerly was a member of the Independent Voters Committee of the Arts and Sciences. Articles by him appeared in the *American Mercury,* the New York *Times,* and the New York *Herald Tribune.* With Hammerstein he was a partner in the music publishing firm of Williamson Music, Inc. Rodgers and Hammerstein musicals earned a total of 35 Tony Awards, 15 Academy Awards, two Pulitzer Prizes, two Grammy Awards, and two Emmy Awards.

After Hammerstein's death in 1960, Rodgers wrote both words and music for his first new Broadway project *No Strings* (1962, which earned two Tony Awards). The show was a minor hit and featured the song, "The Sweetest Sounds". Rodgers also wrote both the words and music for two new songs used in the film version of *The Sound of Music.* (Other songs in that film were from Rodgers and Hammerstein.) At its 1978 commencement ceremonies, Barnard College awarded Rodgers its highest honor, the Barnard Medal of Distinction.

Personal Life

Noted for his calm approach to the task of writing music, Rodgers was heard to say that even the presence of his two daughters, Mary and Linda, in no way disturbed his sources of inspiration. These were the children of his March 5, 1930, marriage to Dorothy Feiner—"I am still married to her." They remained married until his death in 1979. During World War II the Rodgers Connecticut home was shared by the child of an English friend of theirs. The composer's only form of exercise was an occasional game of croquet. He was five feet seven inches tall, dark-haired and dark-eyed, and preferred to wear gray suits. His original manuscripts were gifts to his wife, and during his life it was planned that they would be given to the Juilliard School of Music. Of his unruffled relationship to his collaborator—Hammerstein, too, was a devoted family man, punctual, and painstaking—Amy Porter said in *Collier's:* "No two more untemperamental artists ever graced the theater."

Richard Rodgers died at his home in Manhattan, New York on December 30, 1979 after a long illness. He had earlier survived cancer of the jaw (1955), a heart attack, and laryngectomy (1974), which left his voice somewhat hoarse. He was survived by his wife and his two daughters. In 1990, Rodgers was posthumously awarded Broadway's highest honor: a theater named after him on 46th Street in Manhattan, New York. A devoted art collector, Rodgers is remembered in his old neighborhood of Mount Morris Park in Harlem, New York, for building a million-dollar recreation center and theater.

Further Reading

Collier's 115:18 My 26 '45
Good H 118:38 Je '44
Ladies' Home J 67:200 N '50
ASCAP Biographical Dictionary of Composers, Authors, and Publishers (1948)

International Motion Picture Almanac, 1950-51
Who's Who in America, 1950-51
Who's Who in the East (1948)
Who's Who in the Theatre (1947)
World Biography (1948)
Richard Rodgers, Hyland, WG, Yale University Press, 1998

Kenny Rogers

Singer

Born: 1939 (?);Houston, Texas
Primary Field: Country
Group Affiliation: The First Edition; solo performer

Introduction

Kenny Rogers, who in 1979 reached his apogee of popularity on the country-western scene, is a product of the so-called "crossover" phenomenon—an entertainer who has changed from one musical genre to another. But while most singers cross over from country to pop, Rogers has done the opposite. As lead singer for a rock group in the late 1960's and early 1970's he enjoyed some success with such hits as "Just Dropped In" and "Ruby." It was not until he went on his own as a country solo artist, however, that Rogers really hit his stride.

Early Life

Kenneth Ray Rogers was born in a federal housing project in Houston, Texas about 1939, one of the eight children of Edward Floyd Rogers, a shipyard worker who died in 1976, and Lucille (Hester) Rogers. "We were very poor," Rogers told Norma McLain Stoop of *After Dark* (November 1972), "but I was just a kid with nothing to compare it to, so I thought everybody lived like that, and those were really some of the happiest times of my life." Despite his problem with alcoholism, Rogers' father, an amateur fiddle player, had an affectionate relationship with his children and taught them to love music. As a boy, Rogers accompanied his family on trips to his grandfather's farm in Apple Springs, Texas, where relatives gathered from miles around for music-centered family reunions. At thirteen, while sick in bed with the measles, he taught himself to play the guitar.

An A student at Houston's Jefferson Davis High School, Rogers sang in the glee club and in his church choir and played guitar in a band that he had organized, called the Scholars. His most important musical influences at that time were Ray Charles and Sam Cooke. About 1957 Rogers and his band produced the hit single "Crazy Feeling," which sold a million copies. The Scholars appeared on *American Bandstand* (ABC-TV, 1957) and cut several additional singles that failed, however, to measure up to "Crazy Feeling." In an effort to sustain their sudden popularity the group even recorded "Kangewah," a song written by Hollywood gossip columnist Louella Parsons. "We figured she'd plug our record in her column," Rogers told *People* interviewer Sue Reilly (December 10, 1979). "It was a great idea but had no relationship to reality. We came home broke." According to Kenny Rogers' brother Leland, quoted by Peter H. Brown in *Parade* (February 17, 1980), "Kenny really thought he was 'it' then. He got all duded up like Elvis Presley and took his 'star role' to heart. He came back to Houston and told me: 'One thing I'm not gonna do is sign all those autographs. I haven't got the time for that stuff.' Well, brother, it was ten years before Kenny got another taste of success, and he's been signing autographs ever since."

The first member of his family ever to complete high school, Rogers wanted to become a professional musician but, in compliance with his parents' wishes, enrolled at the University of Houston after graduation from Jefferson Davis to major in commercial art. In 1960, however, after less than a year in college, he dropped out and joined the Bobby Doyle Trio, an avant-garde jazz band. He remained with the group for about six years, playing bass fiddle, and was for a time also a member of an outfit known as the Kirby Stone Four.

Life's Work

Aware of the continuing popularity of folk music, Rogers joined the New Christy Minstrels in 1966. He told Norma McLain Stoop: "I ... went with the New Christy Minstrels because, though it was a monetary step down, I felt it was a professional step up and would do something towards my future career." Again, sensing the shift away from folk music to folk-rock, Rogers and several other members of the Christy Minstrels tried to change the group's approach. "A few of us in the group worked in nine songs Mike Settle had written, in hopes the Christy Minstrels would record them," Rogers explained in the *After Dark* interview, "but their opinion was that they had a successful image and they didn't want to gamble with it."

In 1967 Rogers and three other members of the New Christy Minstrels—Mike Settle, Terry Williams, and Thelma Camacho—left the group to form the folk-rock band the First Edition. From the beginning, Rogers—who at that time sported skin-tight suits, a beard, and a gold earring—tried to make the group's music and image appeal to the widest possible audience. The band made its debut at Ledbetters, a nightclub in Los Angeles owned by Randy Sparks, the founder of the New Christy Minstrels. Its first hit, "Just Dropped In (To See What Condition My Condition Was In)," written by Rogers' high school friend Mickey Newbury to cash in on the psychedelic or acid-rock craze, hit the *Billboard* "Top 100" in February 1968 and remained on the chart for ten weeks.

During the nine years of its existence, the group, formally called Kenny Rogers and the First Edition, recorded four gold albums and nine gold singles. Among its LP's were *The First Edition* and *The Ballad of Calico*—a concept album about a ghost-town near Barstow, California. Its hit singles included "But You Know I Love You," Mel Tillis' "Ruby (Don't Take Your Love To Town)," "Tell It All, Brother," "Heed the Call," Mac Davis' "Something's Burning," and Alex Harvey's "Reuben James" (not to be confused with Woody Guthrie's World War II song of the same title). After recording for five years under the Warner/Reprise label the band switched to MGM Records in the summer of 1972, primarily because Rogers managed to persuade the president of the latter company, Mike Curb (who later became Lieutenant Governor of California), to offer the band a million-dollar advance guarantee-the largest in recording history. In the After Dark interview Rogers candidly acknowledged: "I've tried to approach the [music] business as a business-just that."

The First Edition also toured the United States, Canada, England, Scotland, and New Zealand and was featured on seventeen television network variety shows. In the fall of 1972 it became the first pop group to headline at the Persian Room of New York's Plaza Hotel and broke house attendance records. The band also sang the songs for the soundtrack of the movie *Fools* (Cinerama, 1970) and in 1971-72 starred in its own syndicated musical television series *Rollin'* On *the River* (known from the fall of 1972 on as *Rollin' With Kenny Rogers and the* First *Edition),* which was set on board a Mississippi riverboat. The show was telecast over 192 stations in the United States and Canada in the course of its two-year run. The personnel of the First Edition changed several times, and only Rogers and guitarist Terry Williams remained with the group for the full nine years. Other members have included Mary Arnold, Gene Lorenzo, Mickey Jones, Kin Vassy, and Jimmy Hassell.

Not completely comfortable in the folk-rock idiom, Rogers maintains that he had always been a country singer and that much of the music performed by the First Edition had its roots in the country-western tradition. "When you look at most of our big hits, they were really country records," he told Alanna Nash of Stereo Review (April 1980). "But Warner Brothers . . . did not *have* a country-music department, so they merchandised us as a pop act, or a rock act." Miss Nash backed up that assessment, noting that "the songs of the First Edition did not fit neatly into any one category. Ostensibly a Top-40 rock group, the band built most of its fame with several country-flavored numbers.... In retrospect, it appears that the First Edition played a not-too-small but largely unheralded role in helping bridge the gap between country and rock."

Eventually, the band's records failed to sell. "We reached a point of what I call creative stagnancy," Rogers explained to Alanna Nash. "We had done about everything there was, and there was just no fresh input." But he has also said: "I loved the First Edition. There never was one minute I didn't feel proud of its success." Perceiving an upsurge of interest in country music, Rogers switched his label to United Artists in 1976 and moved to Nashville to try his luck as a solo artist. With the help of producer Larry Butler and manager Ken Kragen, he worked out a unique new musical style analyzed by Alanna Nash as "a little contemporary folk, a little pasteurized country, a little half-baked rock-and-roll, a few string-swathed love songs and ballads, and lots of good-natured congeniality."

Four of Rogers' singles in his new musical vein made the country-music charts almost immediately: "Love Lifted Me," "Homemade Love," "Laura," and "While the Feeling's Good." His popularity with audiences received a further boost from an appearance on the Tonight *Show* and a headline engagement at the

Golden Nugget casino in i.as Vegas. But Rogers' reputation as a country singer was not firmly established until 1977, with the release of "Lucille," a ballad by Roger Bowling and Hal Bynum about the woes of a man deserted by his wife. "Lucille" went "gold," became the nation's number one country hit, and brought Rogers a Grammy from the National Academy of Recording Arts and Sciences for the year's best male country vocal performance at the twentieth annual awards ceremony. It won the Academy of Country Music's best single and best song awards and earned Rogers its best male vocalist award for 1977. In addition, the Country Music Association designated "Lucille" its song of the year.

After "Lucille," Rogers and the popular female country vocalist Dottie West collaborated on the album *Every Time Two Fools Collide*, which included the hit song "All I Ever Need Is You." The pair became a popular singing team and made frequent concert appearances together. "Dottie is a very good friend of mine," Rogers has said, "and the thing I enjoyed most about doing the album is that it was all so genuine. It was done for the right reason; we really enjoy singing together."

Rogers' recent country-western recordings include the albums *Daytime Friends*, *Kenny Rogers*, *Love or Something Like It*, and *Ten Years of Gold*. Among his hit singles are "I Wish That I Could Hurt That Way Again," "Heart to Heart," "Morgana," "You Decorated My Life," "She Believes in Me," "Coward of the County," and Alex Harvey's "Making Music for Money"—a lampoon of commercialism in the music business. But his most successful recording by far is the 1979 album *The Gambler*, which elevated Rogers to the status of the leading male country vocalist in the United States. The title song, written by Don Schlitz, had previously been recorded by a dozen different artists, including Johnny Cash and Bobby Bare, but it took Rogers' distinctive voice and style to make the song a hit. By the end of 1979 the album had sold more than 3,000,000 copies. In February 1980 it earned Rogers a second Grammy for best male country vocal performance. *The Gambler* was dislodged from the top of the charts only when it was superseded by Rogers' next album, *Kenny*, which eventually went platinum. In January 1980 Variety listed *Kenny* fifth among the bestselling albums in the United States. Rogers' *Gideon*, a concept album relating the life story of a cowboy, written by the former New Christy Minstrels singers Kim Carnes and Dave Ellingson, was released in the fall of 1980.

Taking a hardheaded view of his future prospects, Rogers often tells interviewers that he does not expect his popularity to last. As he explained to Alanna Nash: "I'm on a hot spell right now, and I figure I've got two and a half years left on it. The rule of thumb is about three years, because the record-buying public changes on that three-year cycle." He has therefore expanded the range of his activities. In December 1979 he hosted the CBS-TV special Kenny Rogers and *the'* American Cowboy, which included a Rogers outdoor concert in Los Angeles as well as footage of the life of modern-day cowboys in Nevada and Oregon. A reviewer for Variety (December 5, 1979) called it "a very professional and appealing product." Rogers made his acting debut in the made-for-television movie Kenny Rogers as *The* Gambler, a western adventure drama, based on his hit song, that was presented on CBS-TV in April 1980.

In *Kenny Rogers' America*, a special shown on CBS-TV in November 1980, Rogers performed his songs against a background of both rural and urban American scenes. During 1981 his single "Lady" and his album *Greatest Hits* made the lists of best-selling records, and his newest album, *Share Your Love*, on which he collaborated with Lionel B. Ritchie Jr. of the pop-soul group the Commodores, made its first appearance in the record shops.

Rogers views the so-called "bastardization" of country music—its fusion with rock, folk, and other elements—as a salutary thing. "It's brought a lot of

Affiliation: Solo Performer

"Lucille," the first of his country hits, went "gold" (earned $1,000,000) in 1977. His greatest success to date came with the 1979 album The Gambler, which went "triple-platinum" (sold more than 3,000,000 copies) and racked up higher first-day sales figures than any other album of the 1970's. As of late 1979 Rogers' recordings have grossed more than $100,000,000. His honors include a half-dozen Academy of Country Music and Country Music Association awards and two Grammies. Rogers has set attendance records at personal concert appearances across the United States, and he has also begun to make his mark as a nonsinging star of television specials. "I've never felt I'm a particularly good singer," Rogers told Alanna Nash in an interview for *Stereo Review* (April 1980), "but I've always felt that I have a very commercial voice.

people into the fold that wouldn't have listened to country music otherwise," he told Lynn Van Matre of the *Chicago Tribune* (August 12, 1979). "It used to be you either liked country music or you didn't, because it all sounded alike. Now it's no longer one-dimensional, and I think that's great." *To* aid aspiring musicians, Rogers collaborated on the book *Making It With Music* (Harper, 1978) with Len Epand. "The book heavily stresses what one should do to get started in the business," Rogers was quoted in *Contemporary Authors* as saying. "It's not designed to make a star out of someone who is not capable of or interested in becoming a star. It's designed to help a person with an average amount of talent who just wants to make a decent living in a very lucrative business."

Rogers' income was estimated in 1979 to be about $7,000,000 a year, and he is prudent in his handling of it. He owns a $4,000,000 mansion in the Bel Air section of Los Angeles, a 2 percent share in the Golden Nugget casino in Las Vegas, a $600,000 yacht, two private jets, two office buildings in Nashville and one in Los Angeles, and a fleet of cars, including a yellow Rolls-Royce. His honors for 1979 include the Academy of Country Music's best male vocalist and entertainer of the year awards and the Country ·Music Association's awards for duo of the year (with Dottie West), album of the year (for *The Gambler*), and male vocalist of the year. Rogers also holds *Billboard* magazine's 1977 ''crossover artist of the year" award, as well as three awards from the trade association for juke box operators and a British Country Music Association award. President Jimmy Carter invited Rogers to entertain at the White House in 1979 on the occasion of the signing of the Israeli-Egyptian peace treaty by Prime Minister Manahem Begin and President Anwar Sadat.

Although Rogers occasionally writes his own songs, such as "Sweet Music Man," most of the songs he performs are written by others. "I think I have an excellent ear for hit songs," he said in the *Stereo Review* interview. "I try to find songs that have a hook, that have something to say, that touch people, and then I do that song the way I think it should be done." Rogers' producer, Larry Butler, regularly sifts through an enormous number of songs for suitability. After Butler narrows the number to about thirty, Rogers listens to them, makes the final selections, and usually records the songs that same night. "I've found that by doing that, there's a certain spontaneity that happens," he has explained. "I probably sing it better later, but I don't think it does the song as much good." William Carlton of the *New York Daily News* (March 26, 1979) Wrote that Rogers "sings in a warm, supple, romantic, tender voice with a surprisingly wide range. His story songs are always fresh, tasteful, honest and intelligent, well-crafted and interesting. The man and his music are as welcome as old friends and family."

Personal Life

Kenny Rogers and Marianne Gordon, a former model and star of the country-western television comedy show *Hee Haw,* were married on October 2, 1977. Two of his previous marriages lasted a total of four and a half years and a third endured twelve years—until 1976. He admitted to Sue Reilly of *People* magazine (December 10, 1979) that his preoccupation with his musical career plays a large part in his "inability to sustain relationships." Rogers has a grown daughter, Carole Lynne, by his first wife, and a teenage son, Kenneth Ray Jr., by his third. The bearded, grizzled singer stands six-feet one inch tall and weighs 203 pounds. He enjoys golf, tennis, softball, and poker, and does not smoke or drink. With his tour band, Bloodline, Rogers maintains a rigorous concert schedule. In 1979 he sang before a total of some 2,000,000 people, and his engagements included a concert at Carnegie Hall. But despite the many demands of his profession, Rogers assured Alanna Nash: "I love what I'm doing. I would do it for a lot less money."

Further Reading

After Dark 5:30+ N '72 por
People 9:64+]a 9 '78 pors, 94::122+ D 1.0 '79 pors
Stereo R 44:68+ Ap '80 por
TV Guide 28:1.8+ Ap 5 '80 por
Contemporary Authors vols 85·88 (1.980)\
Encyclopedia of Pop, Rock and Soul (1974)
Who's Who in America, 1980-81

Roy Rogers

Singer

Born: November 5, 1912; Cincinnati, Ohio
Died: July 6, 1998; Apple Valley, California
Primary Field: Western "cowboy" music
Group Affiliation: Sons of the Pioneers, Cowboy Band

Introduction

Roy Rogers, who in 1948 completed his eleventh year as star of Western films for Republic Pictures Corporation, was described as the "world's top boots-and-saddle star." This was written of him in PM in1947, when Rogers was for the second year chosen one of the ten uppermost money-making American screen stars by the Annual Motion Picture Herald's poll of theater owners. The award also marked the fifth consecutive year in which he had won the first position as Western star, outranking all other screen cowboys in box office receipts. Rogers' rodeo appearances, his radio programs, later his television programs, and his recordings of old and new Western songs brought him a wider public.

Early Life

When Roy Rogers first came to the attention of motion picture audiences, his birthplace was given in publicity releases as Cody, Wyoming—a Western town seemed a fitting place of birth for a rising film cowboy. Sometime later at Rogers' request, his actual birthplace, Cincinnati, Ohio, was admitted to the press. There, on November 5, 1912, he was born, as Leonard Slye. (His name was later changed legally to Roy Rogers.)When he was seven years old, his father, Andrew E. Slye, moved the family of three girls and one boy to a farm in Duck Run, a small country town in Ohio. The Slye family's income was small, and the father worked in a shoe factory in the neighboring town of Portsmouth. During his youth Rogers helped his two sisters do farm chores. Of this period he was quoted as saying "I hardly wore shoes until I was almost grown." His earliest dramatic appearance was as Santa Claus in the play given by the grammar school he attended.

The youth's first ambition was to be a dentist. This was never realized because he left high school after two years to work with his father in the United States Shoe Company in Cincinnati. His spare time was spent in learning to play the guitar and other stringed instruments, a skill taught to him by his mother and father, both of whom played for the local Saturday night dances. About that time the young man learned to sing hillbilly and Western songs and to call square dances.

Life's Work

In 1929 the family was invited to California to visit one of Rogers' sisters. This first view of the West so impressed Rogers that, on returning to Ohio four months later, he was no longer content to live in Duck Run. In the fall of 1929 he set out again for California, taking time to travel throughout the West. He found a job as driver of a sand and gravel truck. Later he joined the migratory workers called "Okies" in their trek through the farms and ranches of the West Coast. For a while Rogers worked in a peach orchard in Tulare, California. His other jobs at this time included house painting and road building, and for a short period he was a cow hand on a New Mexico ranch. Here he was to ride the range, round up cattle, and acquire the many riding and shooting tricks to be required of him as a film cowboy.

While earning his living at this work, Rogers formed several cowboy bands. The first of these was organized when Rogers entered a radio station's amateur contest in Los Angeles. He did not win the contest, but someone who heard him suggested that he join a band for radio appearances. His first professional radio debut was in 1931 as a member of the *Uncle Tom Murray's Hollywood Hillbillies.* Shortly afterward he was able to join a small group of itinerant musicians, variously known as the International Cowboys, the Rocky Mountaineers, the 0-Bar-0 Cowboys, and the Texas Outlaws.

By this time the Sons of the Pioneers had become more stabilized, receiving engagements of three or four hours a day on a Los Angeles radio station and making recordings of hillbilly songs. One of these recordings, "The Last Roundup," was so successful that on the strength of it Rogers and his band were given bit parts in Western films by the Republic Pictures Corporation. This organization, which had been formed in 1935, was just beginning its production of improved Western films. (The studio's major star was then Gene Autry, the first motion picture cowboy to substitute a guitar for a gun and to appear in Westerns produced on a budget of much more than the customary $25,000.)

In 1937 Rogers was given his first opportunity as a star. According to several sources, Rogers was in a Glendale hat shop when a man dressed in the typical film cowboy outfit, rushed into the store, demanding a ten-gallon Western hat for a screen test. He let it be known that Republic was giving the test as part of its search for a new Western personality. Rogers raced to the studio and was given an audition. It resulted in a contract with Republic for the leading role in *Under Western Stars.*

Produced in 1937, *Under Western Stars* was the first Republic picture to be shown on Broadway and was described by Louella Parsons in the New York *Journal-American's Pictorial Review* as a "rootin' tootin' Western." It created the pattern for the approximately eighty pictures in which Rogers later appeared. The "singing Westerns," in which he starred, were, according to a film critic writing in the *Christian Science Monitor* for April 9 1944, formulated on the basis of a "little song, a little riding, a little shooting, and a girl to be saved from hazard." All of Roy Rogers' pictures adhered to this formula—costar of each film was his horse Trigger, which was a colt when Rogers bought him in 1936. Rogers raised and trained Trigger himself. The horse, which was said to perform fifty tricks, became so well known that in 1946 a picture, *My Pal Trigger,* was named after it. Rogers told *Saturday Evening Post* readers that his part in this film, a part which he termed "practically a supporting role to a horse," was his favorite.

Films in which Rogers appeared usually drew praise from the critics. The New York *Post* in 1944, described one film as "bang-up action, many dance *divertissements,* and a host of hummable tunes." A 1943 review in the *Christian Science Monitor* described another Rogers film as a "straight-shooting, hard-riding melodrama, carrying off story elements that are never novel, yet never seem to be hackneyed. . . [which] gives Rogers opportunity for singing interludes, a romantic moment or two, and chases (with gunfire) galore." A New York *World-Telegram* critic, writing for an August 1946 issue, found one film "just too simple-mindedly good and pure," but another described the same film as "just good, wholesome melodrama with the ever-charming Roy Rogers going through his homespun paces with customary naturalness." The general agreement voiced by the critics was that Rogers' good voice, "classically handsome features", "properly lean and lithe" figure, and "good rolling gait" adequately qualifyed him for the Western film tradition.

In addition to making four high-budget films a year, each at an estimated cost of $250,000, Rogers had, ever since his rise to prominence, appeared in rodeos in New York, Chicago, and other principal cities of the United States. He was also star of several radio shows on nation-wide hookups, including a long engagement on the *Saturday Nite Round Up* on NBC, sponsored by Miles Laboratories and the *Roy Rogers' Show,* sponsored by the Goodyear Rubber Company, over the MBS network. One recent venture was the Roy Rogers' Thrill Circus, which played an eight-day engagement in June 1947 at the New York Polo Grounds and was described as "a wild and fantastic dream of a circus in which the utterly impossible quite casually takes place," and in which Rogers' sharp-shooting performance "exemplified a three-gunman to the kids." In March1948 Rogers signed a new contract with Republic under which, reportedly, he received a 100 per cent increase in salary. Roy Rogers and the Sons of the Pioneers were featured in the Walt Disney *Melody Time,* which combined animation with "live" action. Subsequently, in August, announcement was made of his projected radio program for the 1948–49 season, the *Roy Rogers Show,* sponsored by Quaker Oats, to be broadcast over the Mutual network.

Affiliation: Sons of the Pioneers Cowboy Band

Rogers later organized a group known as the Sons of the Pioneers. This last one remained the permanent group and until the fall of 1948 appeared with Rogers in motion pictures, radio shows, and on recordings. After the expiration of their contract, Rogers was featured with Foy Willing and the latter's Riders of the Purple Sage.

The "barnstorming" troubadours had many failures before reaching popularity. At one town in New Mexico the band, its finances being low, was able to convince the manager of the local radio station to pay its lodging at a tourist camp in exchange for broadcasting some songs on the air. The band, however, did not have enough money to buy food, and during the performance Rogers appealed for contributions of home-cooked food from the listeners. One contribution of two lemon pies came from a local girl, Arlene Wilkins, with whom Rogers exchanged letters for three years until she came to Hollywood in 1936 to be married to him.

A seventeen-day show presented by Rogers in Chicago in October 1948 netted about $300,000. A survey by the trade journal, *Boxoffice,* showed in November 1948 that Rogers had once again placed first among Western stars.

Personal Life

Roy Rogers was the father of three children: Cheryl (adopted), Linda Lou, and Roy, Jr. After his first wife's death in November 1946 he was married on December 31, 1947, to Dale Evans, his leading lady in more than twenty films. (Thereupon Republic announced Mrs. Rogers would no longer be cast opposite her husband; an executive said, "Roy plays a strong, silent man of the West who never kisses his leading lady. No one would believe it, if Dale played opposite him now." The fans, however, thought differently and, in deference to their demands, the studio put Dale Evans back into the Rogers' films.) Roy Rogers had blue eyes, chestnut hair, weighed 170 pounds, and was almost five feet eleven inches tall. He was described as possessing an "accent still pleasantly rural," a shy smile, and homespun humor. He met his enthusiastic children admirers on a "man-to-man basis," and made a point of refusing cigarettes and drinks.

Later in life Roy Rogers developed heart disease and had heart surgery in 1977 and 1990. He died on July 6, 1998 in Apple Valley, California of congestive heart failure.

Further Reading

Collier's 12:27 TI 24 '48
Cue pl9 0 17 '42
N Y *Herald Tribune* IX p24 F 21 '43
N Y *Post* Mag p3 S 19 '48
NY *Sunday News* p95 *N* 17 '46
PM p22 My 20 '41
Tune-In p27 Je '45
International Motion Picture Almanac, 1947-48

Kurt Rosenwinkel

Guitarist; composer

Born: Oct. 28, 1970; Philadelphia, Pennsylvania
Primary Field: Jazz
Group Affiliation: Ensemble performer

Introduction

Since the mid-1990s Kurt Rosenwinkel has been hailed as one of the world's top jazz guitarists, acclaimed for the complexity and melodicism of his playing as well as his fondness for experimentation. His unique sound-which he augments with effects-laden vocals that follow his guitar lines has set him apart from others, and he has pushed the boundaries of contemporary jazz by incorporating elements of electronica into his material. A writer for allaboutjazz.com described Rosenwinkel as an "adventurous, searching artist whose playing is marked by a kind of kinetic melodicism, darkly delicate lyricism and cascading, horn-like lines" and one who has "established an instantly recognizable voice on the guitar—warm and fluid with a tinge of overdrive, a touch of sustain and echo with a penchant for dissonance. His singing quality on the instrument is all the more enhanced by the fact that he is often literally singing in unison."

Early Life

Kurt Rosenwinkel was born on October 28, 1970 in Philadelphia, Pennsylvania. He was raised in a musical family; his mother, who had trained as a concert pianist, and his father, an architect who enjoyed musical improvisation, played twin grand pianos. "Since I was a young kid, I felt like I had an internal impulse to make music," he recalled to Ted Panken for jazz.com (October 17, 2008). At nine Rosenwinkel began playing piano; at 12 he picked up the guitar, after hearing the Beatles' album *Sgt. Pepper's Lonely Hearts Club Band.*

Rosenwinkel was not exposed to jazz until he began to listen to it on the radio, during high school. From there, "I started getting into more advanced forms and more mature and deeper musics," he told Panken. "I developed a thirst for the more complicated music. I liked [the Canadian pop/rock group] Rush. I went from listening to hard rock, to progressive rock, to electric jazz and fusion, and then into acoustic jazz." As a sophomore he started playing with the regular jazz performers at the Blue Note club in Philadelphia; meanwhile, he studied the jazz standards in a volume of sheet music called *The Real Book.* At the club, he told Panken, "they'd welcome me up on the stage, and I'd call [the Victor Young jazz standard] 'Stella By Starlight' and they would launch into some intra that was all so new to me. I had no idea how they knew it. It wasn't in *The Real Book.* It was a great education for me about what jazz really is. It's not what you learn on the page; it's this whole tradition. So I really got a good dose of that-the spirit, improvisation, connecting with people, lifting things off the ground. That's how I fell in love with jazz." In an interview with Franz A. Matzner for allaboutjazz.com (December 9, 2009), Rosenwinkel said, "I committed to playing music for my life when I was nine! Since then, it's never been a question. So, I never committed to a career in jazz. It's all just music to me. Whether it's this or that, I like it all-mostly. I became a jazz musician because so much of the music I love is called that, and it inspired me to learn and grow in that direction."

During his high-school years, Rosenwinkel took jazz-piano lessons with Jimmy Amadie; his aim, at least in part, was to decide which instrument he wanted to focus on. After graduating, and settling on guitar, he enrolled at the Berklee College of Music, in Boston, Massachusetts. There, he met the faculty member and jazz vibraphonist Gary Burton, who in the 1960s had pioneered a four-mallet playing style (vibraphones are traditionally played with two mallets). After three years Rosenwinkel dropped out of Berklee to tour with Burton's band as a sideman, from 1991 to 1992. He told John Kelman for allaboutjazz.com (June 20, 2005), "Gary's band was the first really professional sideman gig that I had-it was the first international touring experience, it was the first kind of high profile scenario, so I really felt that it was a big break. It was a great experience from a professional point of view in terms of gaining experience and an entry into the world of what it means to be a jazz musician, what life is like as a jazz musician. Gary's a master musician, so listening to him play his solo pieces every night was the most musically inspiring experience for me in that band. He's a true master of the vibraphone."

Life's Work

Rosenwinkel next moved to New York City and joined Paul Motian's Electric Bebop Band, in which he was able to hone his improvisational skills. "In Gary's band the parameters of the music were very specific, very specified, very controlled," he told Kelman. "In Paul's band *some* of them were set; there were some basic premises, like we're going to play bebop tunes, and this is going to be the arrangement. . . . But beyond that there wasn't any musical guidance. . . . The entire experience for me was about absorbing [Motian's] time feel and his feel for music." Around that time Rosenwinkel also performed with the saxophonist Joe Henderson's group and had regular gigs at Smalls Jazz Club, in the Greenwich Village section of Manhattan, in New York City.

In 1995 Rosenwinkel won a Composers Fellowship from the National Endowment for the Arts. He used the money to record his first solo album, *East Coast Love Affair* (1996), released on the Fresh Sound New Talent label. Recorded live at Smalls, the album featured the trio he had formed with the drummer Jorge Rossy and the bassist Avishai Cohen. "I wasn't even thinking about any kind of long term strategy, in terms of kinds of albums I wanted to make," Rosenwinkel recalled to Kelman. "At the time I was in New York, living hand to mouth and developing music with my friends. I happened to be doing a lot of sessions with Jorge Rossy—I've known him for years. We were doing a lot of jam sessions at each others' houses and in the New York scene." The record consists of jazz standards along with two original tunes—the title track and "B Blues." Rosenwinkel's next album, *Intuit* (1998), released on the Criss Cross label, also comprised standards, composed by Irving Berlin, Charlie Parker, and George Gershwin, among others. For that album Rosenwinkel played alongside Michael Kanan on piano, Joe Martin on bass, and Tim Pleasant on drums. In a review for allaboutjazz.com, C. Andrew Hovan wrote, "The tunes are familiar, but how they're transformed is something else all together! Rosenwinkel gets a clean, yet warm sound from his guitar and his improvisations are imbued with the kind of advanced melodic development that marks his writing. . . . One gets the sense that Rosenwinkel is at one with the music at hand and even his shorter statements speak volumes to anyone with an ear for standards or jazz guitar. His sidemen certainly do justice to the material and provide great support, but it's really Rosenwinkel who steals the show here. Taken on its own terms, this one comes highly endorsed. It's even further proof, as well, that Rosenwinkel knows his history and is likely to become a force to be reckoned with over the next several years." David R. Adler wrote for the All Music Guide Web site, "Rosenwinkel's sound throughout this straight-ahead excursion is fairly dry—a touch of reverb, no shimmering delay, no ethereal vocalizing, a bit less distinctive than usual. His highly modern approach to harmony often comes through, however, even on vehicles as traditional as 'Darn That Dream.' And, as always, he uses the physical properties of the guitar to alter the sonic dimensions of his lines, as when he plays a long string of 16th notes near the bridge during his solo on 'When Sunny Gets Blue.'" Adler also noted that the "way he interacts with these [other] straight-ahead players says a great deal about his breadth as a jazz musician. It also foreshadows his later attempts to blur the boundary between standard and original repertoire." Of his penchant for playing standards, Rosenwinkel explained to Kelman, "I think, in terms of the feeling I want to get to, it's the same thing [as playing original material], but in terms of the actual music it's very different. I have an awareness of my own relationship to standards that has evolved over the years, and it's an important part of being a jazz musician. It's a good backdrop to really see how your playing is, it's almost this sort of neutral stylistic context where you can discover what kind of player you are, what the qualities of your playing are."

Affiliation: Creating a Sound

Commenting on Rosenwinkel's idiosyncratic guitar sound, the celebrated jazz tenor-sax player Joshua Redman told Andrew Gilbert for the *Boston Globe* (March 20, 2005), "He somehow manages to write music that is incredibly sophisticated and complex, but so excruciatingly beautiful. He's created his own harmonic world, which in and of itself is a huge accomplishment in jazz. He has this incredible sense of melodic clarity and lyricism. His sound is so personal."

Initially a sideman in the bands of the vibraphonist Gary Burton and the drummer Paul Motian, among others, Rosenwinkel first caught the attention of jazz critics with albums of standards. He then met with praise for his recordings of original music, including *The Enemies of Energy* (2000), *The Next Step* (2001), and *Heartcore* (2003), the last of which incorporated elements of hip-hop and electronica. Although not as progressive as his previous albums, Rosenwinkel's more recent releases-*Deep Song* (2005) and *Reflections* (2009), among others-have won the guitarist praise and expanded his audience. In a review of *Deep Song* for the *New York Times* (March 7, 2005), Ben Ratliff observed, "Kurt Rosenwinkel has become one of the better guitarists in jazz, patient and serious, with a misty tone and a desire to pilot his lyricism through greater areas of harmony."

Rosenwinkel's first album of original material, *The Enemies of Energy,* released on the Verve label in 2000, included the work of the tenor saxophonist Mark Turner (a Berklee classmate of Rosenwinkel's and one of his frequent collaborators, both on recordings and in live performance), the keyboardist Scott Kinsey, the bassist Ben Street, and the drummer Jeff Ballard. In a review for the *Toronto Star* (January 15, 2000), Geoff Chapman wrote, "Achieving a singular sound on guitar these days is tough but Kurt Rosenwinkel, though a newcomer to band leadership, may have done it. His mix of jazz and its musical cousins produces tightly woven fusion for thinking people that goes far beyond tinkling and tinkering with technique. With four sympathetic colleagues, notably tenor Mark Turner, Rosenwinkel colours a 10-tune session with clever writing, interesting execution and the ability to vary instrumental sonics. 'Grant' is just one excellent example of bringing disparate effects together in dense, sophisticated textures. Uptempo tunes like 'Point Of View,' 'Number Ten,' and 'Synthetics' feature fascinating interplay." Other critics, too, were pleased with the record—though not all. Jules Epstein wrote for the *Philadelphia Tribune* (February 11, 2000) that *The Enemies of Energy* "confines itself to stereotypic settings, atop which the few interesting saxophone lines are inadequate to generate real interest. It is appropriate to note that one song is titled 'synthetics,' an apt description of this approach to jazz."

Rosenwinkel next signed with the Impulse! label, for which he recorded an album entitled "Under It All"; when Universal later took over Impulse!, the record was shelved, and it has yet to be released. Rosenwinkel followed the release of *The Enemies of Energy* with that of *The Next Step* (2001), a live album recorded with Ballard, Street, and Turner for the Verve label. The guitarist told Kelman that he had had to fight Verve for full creative control over the album: "While with *Enemies* and *Under It All,* the core of those records was my quartet, which was a working band, they were very compositionally-motivated records. *The Next Step* was a record where I really wanted to capture the sound of the band live, and so we're playing original tunes, and that's an important part of it; but the real thing of it is the live interaction of the band. In the beginning I had to fight a little bit more to get the go-ahead from Verve for *The Next Step;* they wanted me to do a different record. But . . . after the record came out and it got a lot of critical acclaim, I think that from that point on they kind of trusted my instincts." A review by Mike Zwerin for the *New York Times* (September 26, 2001, online) read, "Rosenwinkel teams up here with ... Mark Turner; they are flavors of the day in New York. They are also fine, introspective players. They do represent a-if not the-next step.... Young and talented, they will certainly grow; they already deserve more than one good listen."

Rosenwinkel's next effort was *Heartcore* (2003), for which the guitarist composed all of the songs and recorded on studio equipment at his home in Brooklyn, New York. The record was a departure from Rosenwinkel's previous material; while it showcased more playing by Turner, Street, and Ballard, it also made use of electronic drums and synthesizers as well as digital sampling, and it included production work by the hip-hop artist Q-Tip of the group A Tribe Called Quest. Indeed, Rosenwinkel's inspiration for the album came from hip-hop; he explained for his Web site, "From record to record, I've always tried to make things more simple, more direct. . . . I wanted to have the same kind of immediacy that Q Tip's music has, He was always the voice over my shoulder: 'Keep it simple. Keep it direct.'" Rosenwinkel also noted, "A lot of the harmonic moments in hip-hop remind me of what I hear in, say, [the Austrian-born composer Arnold] Schoenberg's music. He'll create a chord that is very much dependent on the dynamics of the performance-the strings are mezzo piano, the oboe is mezzo forte, and the piccolos are piano piano. Together they produce a harmony that might not work in jazz theory, but works perfectly in reality. You hear the same things in a hip-hop mix. It's all in the ear-something works because it sounds like it works." He added, "Those kind[s] of lessons are very important for the jazz musician. It's a great antidote for the pedagogical, theoretical school of jazz."

In a review of *Heartcore,* Richard S. Ginell wrote for the All Music Guide Web site, "With this recording, guitarist Kurt Rosenwinkel creates a unique sound world, blending elements of jazz and rock with electronica, occasional Third World strains, and other grooves in an absorbing, inward journey that defies classification.... In a way, this is 21st century expressionism of a sort, creating levels of ambiguity and uncertainty, leaving the listener out on a limb yet always intrigued. Give it a shot; you may not want to leave this twilight zone." Matt Merewitz opined for allaboutjazz.com (October 28, 2003), "If this isn't the future sound of jazz, then I can't imagine what is."

Rosenwinkel's next release was *Deep Song* (2005), a return to form for the guitarist. Lloyd Sachs wrote in a review of the album for Amazon.com, "Having made a compelling departure into trippy fusion on his last CD, *Heartcore,* ... Rosenwinkel returns here to a more familiar post-bop sound, but with no loss of nerve or verve. Joined by a pair of frequent cohorts . . . he effortlessly moves in and out of the mainstream pocket, thriving on bright unison lines and sighing lyrical constructions. Rosenwinkel is a cerebral player, but with his naturally warm, tangy tone, he readily converts ideas to emotion, adding celestial seasoning to songs including the standard, 'If I Should Lose You,' with his subtle wordless vocals." Kelman observed, "Following the more mainstream *The Next Step* and an '03 take on electronica, *Heartcore, Deep Song* feels like a consolidation and acknowledgement of everything Rosenwinkel has done to date. While the instrumentation is more straightforward . . . this is far from a mainstream record, with an energy and modernity that is equally strong testament to Rosenwinkel the writer as it is Rosenwinkel the guitarist." The record revisited some songs Rosenwinkel had recorded earlier; Kelman wrote for allaboutjazz.com (February 28, 2005), "What is immediately striking is a sense of *authority* and even stronger sense of adventure in Rosenwinkel's playing." In 2008 Rosenwinkel released the double album *The Remedy* on the ArtistShare label. He recorded the work live at the Village Vanguard, in Manhattan, with the Kurt Rosenwinkel Group, consisting of Turner, the pianist Aaron Goldberg, the bassist Joe Martin, and the drummer Eric Harland. The album comprises more than 120 minutes of material, with some tunes upwards of 20 minutes long. *The Remedy* was well-received, landing at number 38 on the *Village Voice* 2008 *Voice* Jazz Poll Winners list.

Rosenwinkel's most recent disk, *Reflections* (2009), recorded under the name Kurt Rosenwinkel Standard Trio, marks the guitarist's eighth album as a bandleader and features Harland and the bassist Eric Revis. The album represented a return to standards, with songs by Thelonious Monk and Wayne Shorter. Tom Moon, in a review posted on the National Public Radio Web site (December 15, 2009), observed, "Rosenwinkel has cultivated his following by bucking tradition, so I was a bit dismayed to learn about his latest project. It's a set of mostly familiar ballads and jazz standards-the kind of program expected of a tradition-minded jazz musician. It seemed Rosenwinkel was following the conventional path. Then I heard his version of 'Reflections.'

Thelonious Monk's piece is usually treated as a kind of sacred text, but Rosenwinkel doesn't play it that way. There's a hint of restlessness in his approach, as if he's determined to find an entirely new language for it. . . . What I hear in this is someone thinking like a composer, shaping a musical narrative one carefully considered phrase at a time. It's a fundamentally different enterprise from the daredevil high-speed babble that usually happens when jazz musicians play standards. They're out to stun with genius technique. Rosenwinkel, a composer first and foremost, wants to illuminate the architectural 'soul' of the tunes instead."

Rosenwinkel's distinctive practice of singing wordlessly to accompany his guitar melodies has often been praised by jazz critics. Kelman noted, "Singing what he plays is, in fact, another key aspect of Rosenwinkel's sound. While other guitarists have used this as more of [a] novel effect, with Rosenwinkel it's a natural and integrated concept." "It's something that's always come naturally to me," Rosenwinkel explained to Kelman. "I've never worked on it ... it just always came naturally to me; I was always able to sing anything I played. It's like I'll have an impulse to sing something, and then my fingers will just be coordinated with that impulse. And then sometimes, vice versa; if I have a visual idea, I'll know how that will feel to sing it as well, so whether the melody comes from the voice or whether the melody comes from some visual idea, I can always play what I want to sing, and sing what I want to play." To amplify his singing, Rosenwinkel performs with a Levalier microphone clipped to his shirt and plugged into an amp and effects-loop pedal. He began to recognize the importance of his singing when he started gigging at Smalls. "I sing quite loudly, so even before I discovered that microphone [the Levalier] it had become part of my sound," he told Kelman. "That's the way I discovered that the voice was part of my guitar sound, in fact. People would come up after shows and say, 'What kind of effect are you using?' I'd say I was using a delay and a reverb, and they'd say, 'No, there's some kind of chorus effect or harmonizer,' and I didn't realize what they were talking about. Then I realized that what they were talking about was the voice and that's how I discovered that it was a part of my sound." From January 4 to January 9, 2011, Rosenwinkel held a residency at the Village Vanguard in New York City, performing standards and original compositions with the pianist Aaron Parks, the bassist Ben Street, and the drummer Ted Poor.

Rosenwinkel has contributed guitar to the Q-Tip albums *The Renaissance* (2008) and *Kamaal/The Abstract* (2009). Despite the complexity of his playing style and his innovative compositions, Rosenwinkel believes his music is generally accessible. He told Kelman, "I've never been trying to write something that's complicated, that's not my purpose at all in discovering sounds and organizing them into compositions. For me what that's all about is containing some kind of fascination, or mood, or some kind of aesthetic quality that's pleasing to the ear. I'm only a conceptualist insofar as it translates to actual sound. So for me, the stuff under the hood is really meant to be under the hood; it has to be there in order for the melodies to come out, for the mood to be accessible. But at the end of the day I *want* my music to be accessible because I want to communicate."

Personal Life

In 2003 he moved to Zurich, Switzerland, for a teaching job. He now lives in Berlin, Germany, where he is a professor of jazz guitar at the Jazz Institute of Berlin. He and his wife, Rebecca, a native of Switzerland, have two sons, Silas and Ezra.

Further Reading

allaboutjazz.com June 20, 2005, Dec. 9, 2009
Boston Globe Arts/Entertainment p9 Mar. 20, 2005
jazz.com Oct. 17, 2008
Ottawa Citizen Arts E p5 June 30, 2004

Diana Ross

Singer; actress; entertainer

Born: March 26, 1944; Detroit, Michigan
Primary Field: Pop
Group Affiliation: Supremes; solo performer

Introduction

In the 1960's glamorous Diana Ross led the sweet-harmonizing Supremes, the most popular exponents of the black pop music known as the "Motown sound," to primacy among all female singing trios internationally, with record sales (well over 12,000,000) second only to those of the Beatles. Miss Ross has since gone on to solo success, as a nightclub, concert, and television entertainer and, most recently, motion picture actress. When she was cast as Billie Holiday in Lady Sings the Blues (1972), some critics doubted that the "slinky," "bouncy," "brassy" graduate of the glossily packaged Supremes could interpret with credibility the tragic life of the legendary blues singer, who grew up in prostitution and died a hopeless drug addict in 1959. But those who accused Miss Ross of "plastic soul" were confounded. The film itself was widely panned, but as "Lady Day" she not only, in the words of Judith Crist (New York, October 30, 1972), "captured the high pitch and girlishness of the early Holiday songs and the pure soul sound she developed," but also portrayed Miss Holiday herself "with a grace and grit." The performance brought her Cue magazine's Entertainer of the Year award and a Golden Globe award and stirred rumors of a possible Academy of Motion Pictures Arts and Sciences Award nomination.

Diana Ross.

Early Life

Diana Ross, the second eldest of six children (three girls and three boys), was born in Detroit, Michigan on March 26, 1944 to Fred Ross, a factory worker, and Ernestine (Earle) Ross. The name Diana was a mistake on her birth certificate. Her mother named her Diane and that is the name by which she is known to family and intimate friends, although she uses Diana professionally. Miss Ross's parents, now separated, still live in Detroit.

When Diana was growing up, the Rosses lived in a third-floor walk-up apartment in the Brewster-Douglass Homes, a low-income housing project in a poor section of Detroit. "We . . . six kids . . . slept in the same room, three in a bed, with a kerosene lamp lighted to keep the chintzes [bedbugs] away," she has recalled, and she told William Wolf of *Cue* (January 13, 1973), "I suppose life was difficult, but as a child I didn't notice those things. . . . I never thought of it being a ghetto when I was there." In another interview, with Sandy Burton of *Time* (August 17, 1970), she spoke again about the apartment: "I remember when I was growing up that it was decorated nicely," with "a red velvet couch that I thought was beautiful."

Singing in the choir at the Olivet Baptist Church in Detroit was a Ross family tradition. "My grandfather was a minister," Miss Ross explained to Digby Diehl of *TV Guide* (December 7, 1968), "and his twelve children were brought up in the church singing, so it just seemed sort of natural." The closest she came to formal voice training was the instruction of the choir director and coaching in pop singing from a cousin.

At highly rated Cass Technical High School, where a B-plus average was a necessary qualification for matriculation, Miss Ross studied dress design, costume illustration, and cosmetology; was a member of the swimming team; and was voted the best-dressed girl in her class, a distinction that was doubly gratifying, since she made many of her own clothes. After school she worked as a bus girl in the basement cafeteria of Hudson's, a Detroit department store and harmonized on street comers and at social gatherings with two girl friends, Mary Wilson and Florence Ballard. As semi-professionals, calling themselves the Primettes, they made about fifteen dollars a week. Ironically, *Miss* Ross was rejected when she tried for a part in a high school musical. "You have a nice voice," the teacher in charge told her, "but it's nothing special." Diana, who believes in working hard to achieve her goals, was undaunted by the rebuff.

Meanwhile, in 1959, Berry Gordy Jr., a former automobile assembly-line worker, was launching the Motown—a contraction of "motor town"—Record Corporation, which injected new lifeblood into American pop music during the following decade, especially through Diana Ross and the Supremes. Discussing the place of Motown in the recent history of pop music, Geoffrey Cannon of the *Guardian* (May 1, 1972) wrote: "Black harmony music was first sung in church; but most of the black groups who were successful up to the 1960's in America were owned by white businessmen who turned their singing towards comedy or novelty, on the prima facie sensible notion that any sound that smacked of Gospel music would be unfamiliar and unattractive to the predominantly white national audience. It took Berry Gordy, a black man who has always put business first, to break a Gospel sound out from this ethnic barrier."

Life's Work

Even before she graduated from high school, Diana Ross was importuning Gordy to hire the Primettes, and to that end she even took a job in his office. As a secretarial assistant she lasted only two weeks, but in the early 1960's Gordy began using die Primettes for background singing in recordings by Mary Wells, Marvin Gaye, the Shirelles, and other early Motown stars, and soon he began grooming them for a career of their own. He renamed them the Supremes and processed them in Motown's Artists Development Department—where all of the company's potential stars are trained in grooming, charm, deportment, and so on—until they emerged as sleek, poised, and sophisticated pros.

In his *Guardian* article, Geoffrey Cannon wrote: "Gordy poured all his energy and money into what has been his most dramatic social achievement: getting universal acceptance, by means of Diana Ross, of the idea that black is beautiful. Dressed and made up extravagantly to look like a cat-goddess, Diana Ross exploited her wide-mouthed, small-nosed beauty to its limit. And she seemed on records to be none the less accessible by means of her untrained, breathy, little-girl voice, and by her singing of losing love."

The Supremes' first single, "I Want a Guy," backed by "Buttered Popcorn" (included in the Motown album *Meet the Supremes*) made no great stir in the recording industry, nor did their next eight. Not until Gordy assigned the writing team of Eddie Holland, Lament Dozier, and Brian Holland to tailor songs for them, in 1964, did they finally cut a hit, "Where Did Our Love Go?" A writer for *Time* (August 17, 1970) recalled: "Florence and Mary sang the background, while Diana did the lead in a voice that was equal parts coyness, sexiness, nicotine, and velvet. 'Baby, baby, where did our love go?' they purred together, and that little question sent them right to the top."

"Where Did Our Love Go?" the third single in Motown history to reach the number one position in national pop records sales, sold 2,000,000 copies. In the next twelve months, the group released five more chart-topping singles: "Baby Love," "Come See About Me," "Stop in the Name of Love," "Back In My Aims Again," and "I Hear a Symphony," thus becoming the only singing group ever to have six consecutive Gold Records (million-or-more sellers) in one year. By 1965 their personal appearances in North America and Europe were worth $5,000 apiece, and their total income for the year was $250,000 for each member of the trio.

In early 1966 the Supreme's big hit was "My World Is Empty Without You." In an interview with Gerald Nachman published in the New York Post of March 6, 1966, Miss Ross explained that the group's sound was not "deep rock 'n roll." She said, "It's more pleasant, more rounded and mellow. It's not shrill," and Mary Wilson added, "It has the beat but not the grinding noise." Echoing that description, Richard Goldstein wrote more than a year later in the *New York Times* (July 23, 1967): "In an era of cellophane screamers, the men at Motown were looking for the antithesis, a soft, silky pop queen. So Diana Ross learned to put vocal swerves into the most un-supple lyrics. Her notes grew slim and elegant. Finally, her body slung like six feet of limp wrist, she

Affiliation: Solo Career

On the eve of Diana Ross's departure from the Supremes, the group issued the successful recording "Someday We'll Be Together." At the close of a farewell performance at the Frontier Hotel in Las Vegas in January 1970 Diana Ross and the Supremes were presented with a plaque naming them the first entertainers ever elected to the Frontier Hotel Wall of Fame. When Miss Ross left, Jean Terrell replaced her as lead singer of the Supremes. Ten of the twelve number-one songs recorded by the Supremes during Miss Ross's tenure with them were included in the retrospective album *The Motown Sound.*

Embarking on her solo career, Miss Ross took her act into the best night and supper clubs, from the Empire Room in New York to the Eden Roc in Miami Beach, at a salary ranging upward from $25,000 a week. After seeing her perform at the Now Grove in Los Angeles, a critic for *Variety* (August 5, 1970) wrote: "She does both [Motown and non-Motown songs] equally well, but it is the Motown roots that give her a soaring lyrical sound and lowdown funk. But it is not just the music that makes her a star." The reviewer described her as a "total entertainer," a "wide-eyed, funny, hip and endearing street gamin with great vitality, confidence, and presence." A correspondent for Time (August 17, 1970) reported during the Now Grove engagement: "Diana . . . is still all static electricity."

Accompanied by Bill Cosby and her protégés, the juvenile Motown singing group the Jackson Five, among others, Miss Ross starred in her own television special, *Diana,* in April 1971. On that occasion she displayed another facet of her talent: pantomime. Her impressions of Harpo Marx, W. C. Fields, and Charlie Chaplin were highlights of the well-received program. She impressed the reviewer for *Variety* (April 21, 1971) as "something special . . . not so much as a singer—she's still warbling the same kind of rather bland soft rock ballads as ever—but as a fresh, pretty, and lively personality who can work with other performers in an easy kind of go-along way which gives a lift to both acts." By the end of 1972 Miss Ross was able to demand up to $105,000 in concerts.

stood under the velvet spotlight, a perfect summa-cum-laude Supreme."

In 1967 alone the Supremes earned seven Gold Records, including one for "The Happening." In that same year they indicated a new trend, in the direction of pop standards, in an album in which they reworked standards by Rodgers and Hart. Behind them now were a dozen best-selling albums, including *Meet the Supremes* (Motown 606), *At the Copa* (Motown 636), *Bit of Liverpool* (Motown 623), *Country Western and Pop* (Motown 625), and *More Hits* (Motown 627). In a retrospective review of the albums in the *Washington Post* (November 3, 1968), Hollie I. West wrote: "The melodies [of the Holland-Dozier-Holland songs] were simple, containing almost no linear development. But the rhythm songs like "I Hear a Symphony" . . . surged in a heavy two-beat style, attuned perfectly to the herky-jerky dances of the 1960's. . . . The team tailored the harmony comfortably to the Supremes' need—close, lush, and bright. But Holland-Dozier-Holland songs all seemed to fit into the same mold. No wonder that the Supremes felt pressed to revise their repertoire."

In line with revising their repertory, the Supremes got a new writing team, which created for them such songs as "Love Child," a hit in late 1968. They also regrouped, with Cindy Birdsong coming in to replace Florence Ballard, and changed their formal billing to "Diana Ross and the Supremes." In an article in the *Observer* (June 15, 1969), Tony Palmer described the revised group in performance: "With their neat little trouser suits, the Supremes look like three tiger-limbed ritual priestesses ooing and aahing with such immaculate togetherness that one is convinced one is seeing . . . treble." Among the other items Palmer noted in the Supreme "package" were "lacquered wigs and blasted smiles," "flaxen-waven inch-long fingernails," and "pouting super-lifted breasts." If their image was sexy, it was also clean, for the Supremes were tightly supervised in all their tours. Chaperones were part of a vast entourage attending to everything from makeup to choreography. In the entourage was a Motown orchestra, led by conductor-arranger Gil Askey.

When Miss Ross made her movie debut in the title role of *Lady Sings the Blues* (produced by Berry Gordy and released by Paramount in October 1972), many critics agreed with Richard Schickel of *Life* (December 1, 1971) that the film did an injustice to Billie Holiday by trying to "shoehorn one of the legendary tragedies of popular music into one of the most trivial and conventionalized of screen forms, the show-biz biography."

But it was difficult to find a reviewer who did not in one way or another agree with Schickel's assessment of Miss Ross's performance: "Singing, she does a fair imitation of the Holiday style. Acting, she does even more. Billie Holiday personified the vulnerability, terror, and confusion of the performer who can't hide in a crowd or in a role. Miss Ross, in an unself-conscious, bravura performance, makes us feel all of that." William Wolf of *Cue* (October 21, 1972), after observing that "the star hauntingly evokes the musical style of the late blues singer but at the same time creates her own singing magic," asserted: "If there's any justice, Diana Ross should be the biggest movie superstar to come along since Barbra Streisand, and she possesses deeper acting ability."

Miss Ross was named Female Entertainer of the Year by the National Association for the Advancement of Colored People in 1970. In the same year she received a Grammy award as leading female vocalist and a *Billboard* award for the same distinction, and she has been similarly honored with *Cash Box* and *Record World* citations. Her efforts in behalf of President Lyndon Johnsons Youth Opportunity Program won her a citation from Vice-President Hubert H. Humphrey. Although she hesitates to become politically active, she was sympathetic to the Poor People's Campaign in 1968 and gave benefit performances with other artists to aid the movement. Coretta Scott King and the Rev. Ralph Abernathy commended her publicly for her contribution to the cause of the Southern Christian Leadership Conference.

After the release of a modestly successful LP, *Last Time I Saw Him,* Ross had a third number-one hit with "Theme from Mahogany (Do You Know Where You're Going To)," from her second feature film, *Mahogany*. A year later, in 1976, she began recording disco music, scoring with the international hit, "Love Hangover," which gave the singer a fourth chart-topper in the US. A two-week stint at Broadway's Palace Theatre in 1977 led to the Emmy-nominated television special, An Evening with Diana Ross, and a Special Tony Award. She released *The Boss,* in 1979. That album continued her popularity with dance audiences as the title song became a number-one dance single. That year, Ross hosted her own HBO special, *Standing Room Only,* taken place in Las Vegas during Ross' "Tour '79" concert tour, with most of the performances coming from *The Boss* album.

In 1980, Ross released her most successful album to date, *diana*. Composed by Chic's Nile Rodgers and Bernard Edwards, the album included the hits "I'm Coming Out" and "Upside Down," the latter becoming her fifth chart-topping single. Prior to leaving Motown, Ross recorded the duet ballad "Endless Love," with Lionel Richie. The song would become her sixth and final single to reach number one on the *Billboard* Hot 100.

Ross had success with movie-themed songs. While her version of Holiday's "Good Morning Heartache" only performed modestly well in early 1973, her recording of "Theme from Mahogany (Do You Know Where You're Going To)" gave Ross her third number-one hit, in late 1975. Three years later, Ross and Michael Jackson had a modest dance hit with their recording of "Ease on Down the Road." Their second duet, actually as part of the ensemble of *The Wiz,* "Brand New Day," found some success overseas. Ross scored a Top 10 hit in late 1980 with the theme song to the 1980 film It's My Turn. The following year, she collaborated with former Commodores singer-songwriter Lionel Richie on the theme song for the film *Endless Love*. The Academy Award-nominated title single became her final hit on Motown Records, and the number-one record of the year. Several years later, in 1988, Ross recorded the theme song to *The Land Before Time*. "If We Hold on Together" became an international hit, reaching number one in Japan.

In October 1981, Ross released her first RCA album, *Why Do Fools Fall in Love.* The album sold over a million copies and featured hit singles such as her remake of the classic hit of the same name and "Mirror Mirror." Before the release of *Why Do Fools Fall in Love,* Ross hosted her first TV special in four years, featuring Michael Jackson in the special. In early 1982, Ross sang the "Star-Spangled Banner" at Super Bowl XVI and appeared on the dance show *Soul Train*. The program devoted a full episode to her and Ross performed several songs from the *Why Do Fools Fall in Love* album.

In 1982, she followed up the success of *Why Do Fools Fall in Love* with *Silk Electric,* which featured the Michael Jackson-written and -produced, "Muscles," resulting in another top-ten success for Ross. The album eventually went gold on the strength of that song. In 1983, Ross ventured further out of her earlier soul-based sound for a more pop rock-oriented sound following the release of the Ross album. The album featured the hit single, "Pieces of Ice," whose music video garnered heavy rotation on video channel stations.

In 1984, Ross released *Swept Away*. This featured a duet with Julio Iglesias, "All of You," which was featured on both the albums they had then released—his *1100 Bel Air Place* as well as her *Swept Away*. It became international hit, as did the ballad "Missing You," which was a tribute to Marvin Gaye, who had died earlier that year after the moving poignant music video made a rare premiere on that year's American Music Awards show. *Swept Away* proved to be a success garnering gold level sales.

Her 1985 album, *Eaten Alive,* found major success overseas with the title track and "Chain Reaction," although neither of the songs became the best-sellers she was once accustomed to in America. Both songs had strong music videos that propelled the tracks to success. The Eaten Alive video was patterned after the 1960s horror film, *The Island of Dr. Moreau,* while the "Chain Reaction" music video saluted the 1960s American Bandstand. "Experience," the third international single's video reignited the "Eaten Alive" romantic storyline with Diana and American actor, Joseph Gian. The track, Eaten Alive, a collaboration with Barry Gibb and Michael Jackson, became a top 20 hit internationally. The Barry Gibb-produced album garnered an international number one in "Chain Reaction" and a Top 20 selling album.

"The Force Behind the Power" sparked an international comeback of sorts, when the album went double platinum in the UK led by the No. 2 UK hit single "When You Tell Me That You Love Me." Ross would see the album perform successfully across Europe to Japan as "The Force Behind the Power" went gold there. That single would be a lucky charm when a duet version with Irish group, Westlife also hit No. 2 in the UK in 2005. The album produced an astounding 9 singles across international territories, including another Top 10, "One Shining Moment."

Ross had success in the UK through 1994, when "One Woman: The Ultimate Collection," a career retrospective compilation, would become number one in the UK, selling quadruple platinum in the UK. That album did well across Europe and in the anglosphere. The retrospective was EMI's alternative to Motown's box set *Forever Diana: Musical Memoirs.* Ross's music sold well in international markets from 1991 to 1994. Ross performed during the Opening Ceremony of the 1994 FIFA World Cup held in Chicago and during the pre-match entertainment of the 1995 Rugby League World Cup final at Wembley Stadium. On January 28, 1996, she performed the Halftime Show at Super Bowl XXX.

In 1999, she was named the most successful female singer in the history of the United Kingdom charts, based upon a tally of her career hits. Madonna would eventually succeed Ross as the most successful female artist in the UK. Later that year, Ross presented at the 1999 MTV Video Music Awards in September of the year and shocked the audience by touching rapper Lil' Kim's exposed breast, pasty-covered nipple, amazed at the young rapper's brashness.

In 2002, after spending two years away from the spotlight and after a stint in jail for committing a DUI, Ross returned to live touring, first in Europe and then in the United States all within the same year. In 2005, she participated in Rod Stewart's *Thanks for the Memory: The Great American Songbook, Volume IV* recording a duet version of the Gershwin standard, "I've Got a Crush on You." The song was released as promotion for the album and later reached number 19 on the *Billboard* Hot Adult Contemporary chart, marking her first *Billboard* chart entry since 2000. Ross was featured in another hit duet, this time with Westlife, on a cover of Ross's 1991 hit "When You Tell Me You Love Me," repeating the original recording's chart success, garnering a number 2 UK *Billboard* hit (number 1 in Ireland).

In June 2006, Universal released Ross's shelved 1972 *Blue* album. It peaked at number 2 on *Billboard's* jazz albums chart. Later in 2006, Ross released her first studio album in seven years with *I Love You.* It would be released on EMI/Manhattan Records in the United States in January 2007. EMI Inside later reported the album had sold more than 622,000 copies worldwide. Ross later ventured on a world tour to promote *I Love You,* which garnered rave reviews. In 2007, she was honored twice, first with the Lifetime Achievement Award at the BET Awards, and later as one of the honorees at the Kennedy Center Honors.

In February 2012, Ross received her first ever Grammy Award, for Lifetime Achievement, and announced the nominees for the Album of the Year. In May, a DVD of her Central Park concert performances, *For One & For All,* was released and featured commentary from Steve Binder, who directed the special. On November 6, 2012, Ross performed for a crowd in India for Naomi Campbell's then billionaire boyfriend, Vladimir Doronin, at his 50th birthday, earning $500,000 for the performance. Following her final stage exit, Ross tripped and broke her ankle. A month later, on December 9, she performed as the marquee and headlining performer at the White House-hosted *Christmas in Washington* concert, where she performed (in a leg cast) before President Barack Obama, America's first African-American president. The event was later broadcast as an annual special on TNT.

Ross continues to tour, completing a 2013 South American tour, a multi-city US late summer tour (Launched: August 2, in Los Angeles - September 13, in Dallas). On July 3, 2014, Ross was awarded the Ella Fitzgerald Award for "her extraordinary contribution to contemporary jazz vocals," at the Festival International de Jazz de Montréal.

Personal Life

Diana Ross is a willowy person, about five feet four inches tall and weighing in the nineties. Although she claims she hardly ever relaxes because her "mind is like a tape-recorder," she enjoys reading, chess, swimming, dancing, and tennis, in which she is sometimes coached by her friend, tennis pro Arthur Ashe. She has an extensive wardrobe, ranging from blue jeans to elegant suits, much of it designed by herself, and she drives a Rolls-Royce, a gift from Berry Gordy, who remains her manager.

Miss Ross and Robert Ellis Silberstein, a white public relations executive, were married in January 1971. Ross and Silberstein divorced in 1977, and Ross moved to New York City in the early 1980s, after living in Los Angeles since Motown relocated to the area in the early 1970s. Ross met her second husband, Norwegian shipping magnate Arne Næss, Jr. in 1985 and married him the following year. They have two sons together: Ross Arne (born in 1987) and Evan Olav (born in 1988). Ross and Næss divorced in 2000. Ross considers Næss the love of her life. Næss was later killed in a South African mountain climbing accident in 2004.

Further Reading

Cue 42:11+ Ja 13 73 pors
Ebony 25:120+ F 70 pors
Life 73:42+ D 8 72
N Y Sunday News Mag p4 My 10 70 por
Newsday II p3 Ja 7 73 por
Time 87:83+ Mr 4 '66 por; 96:50+ Ag 17 70 pors
Taraborrelli, J. Randy. *Diana Ross: A Biography* (2007)

Rick Ross

Rapper

Born: January 28, 1976; Cahoma County, Mississippi
Primary Field: Rapper
Group Affiliation: Solo performer

Introduction

Rick Ross first burst onto the hip-hop scene in 2005, with the rap single "Hustlin'," an anthem that glorified Miami, Florida, as a haven for drug trafficking. He achieved commercial success following the release of his first two studio albums, which contain songs in which he rhapsodizes about dealing drugs. However, the self-proclaimed hustler-turned-rapper found his credibility in question after it was revealed that he was once a Florida corrections officer. Despite the revelation, Ross's third album reached the top of album charts while his next one achieved platinum status.

Early Life

The rapper Rick Ross was born William Leonard Roberts II on January 28, 1976, in Coahoma County, Mississippi. He and his sister were raised by their single mother, Tommie Roberts, in Carol City, a poverty-stricken suburb located north of Miami with a predominantly African American population. His father left the family when Ross was young and has since passed away. During his early teens, Ross began to take an interest in rap music, writing and recording rap lyrics with his childhood friend Elric "E-Class" Prince and then selling the mixtapes to his junior high school classmates. (A mixtape is a collection of original and exclusive tracks recorded by aspiring hip-hop artists and DJs to showcase their talents and generate interest in their music.) He continued to hone his writing skills when he was a student at Carol City Senior High School. "At fifteen, I was writing rhymes, songs with structure, choruses, bridges, and intros," Ross told the Associated Press in an interview for the *Victoria* (Texas) *Advocate* (Aug. 11, 2006). In addition to music, Ross turned his attention to sports, becoming a member of his high school football team. Following his 1994 graduation from Carol City Senior High, Ross was awarded an athletic scholarship to Albany State University (ASU), a historically black institution in Albany, Georgia. He briefly attended ASU, where he majored in criminal justice before dropping out after only one semester.

Upon returning to Florida in 1995, Ross decided to pursue a career in rap music. He renewed acquaintances with his childhood friend "E-Class" Prince and signed with Poe Buy Entertainment (now known as Poe Boy Music Group), a management company founded by Prince and Alex "Cucci Pucci" Bethune, another childhood friend. Over the next few years, Ross performed at events in the local hip-hop scene with the Carol City Cartel, a group Ross founded, and also spent a significant amount of time writing lyrics and recording demos. In 2000 Ross, performing under the moniker Teflon Da Don (a reference to the nickname of the late mafia boss John Gotti, known as the "Teflon Don"), was featured on the single "Ain't SHf-IJ-I to Discuss," a track on fellow hip-hop artist Erick Sermon's third studio album, *Erick Onasis.* That same year Ross accepted an offer from Tony Draper to join the Houston, Texasbased Suave House Records, an independent Southern hip-hop label. Ross spent the next two years continuing to work on his solo material before moving to another record label, following a failed distribution deal. "Unfortunately, I was in a bad situation with Jcor Entertainment," Draper told the Ballerstatus.com website (6 Sep. 2007). "I had a joint venture deal with Jcor, who had their distribution deal with Interscope Records. Jcor was supposed to supply marketing dollars, but they didn't. They only paid $500,000 on a $5 million tab. So to not tie up my artist, I allowed Ross to go to Slip-N-Slide Records in 2002."

Under the new label Ross continued to independently produce a series of mixtapes while also serving as a ghostwriter for fellow Miami rappers and new labelmates Trick Daddy and Trina. Hoss, who also toured with Trick Daddy, earned co-writing credit for the single "Told Ya'll," a track from Trina's 2002 platinum-selling album *Diamond Princess,* which peaked at number 64 on the *Billboard* Hot R&B/Hip-Hop Songs chart. In return, Trina championed Ross's music. "I was on tour and I was taking his mixtapes on tour, promoting, pushing him before people knew who he was," she told HiphopDX.com (26 July 2011). Three years later the duo renewed their collaboration on the track "I Cotta," featured on Trina's 2005 disc *Glamorest Life,* which reached the top five of *Billboard's* Top R&B/Hip-Hop Albums and Top Hap Albums.

Life's Work

Ross jump-started his solo career in November 2005, with the recording of the song "Hustlin'," a Miami anthem about drug trafficking. "When I finished 'Hustlin',' I knew it was gonna be a hit," Ross told *Billboard* magazine (3 June 2006). He handed his single to several local urban radio announcers, including DJ Khaled, a producer and host at WEDR. The single became a regional hit after receiving frequent airplay from several local stations. At about this time Ted Lucas, the chief executive officer of Slip-N-Slide Records, was seeking to renegotiate his distribution deal with Atlantic Records and was being heavily courted by representatives from other record companies. One of these executives was Shakir Stewart, the senior vice president of A&E at Def Jam Records (headed by rapper and label president Jay-Z). "What made Rick Ross stand out was that he's a real lyrical guy," Stewart told *Billboard* (3 June 2006), adding, "It's not just about the beat and a one-liner." In January 2006 Def Jam Records reached a distribution agreement with Slip-N Slide Records and offered Ross a four-album deal reportedly worth $10 million. *Port of Miami,* Boss's major-label debut, was released in August 2006. The record sold 187,000 units in its first week, reaching the pinnacle of the *Billboard* 200 chart, as well as the number-one spot on *Billboard's* Top R&B/Hip-Hop Album chart. *Port of Miami* eventually attained gold status, with sales of at least 500,000 units. A review of the album for *Entertainment Weekly* (7 Aug. 2006) noted, "On *Port of Miami,* Ross turns the minute details of drug distribution and dealing into ominous, slow-rolling songs, like the hypnotic, organ-driven hit single 'Hustlin" and the Scarface-goes-South Beach stomp of 'Cross That Line.' In general, the whole 'crack-rap' trend ... is a disheartening one, but Ross's pulpy debut manages to enthrall despite the drug-centric lyrics." Brendan Frederick, who reviewed the album for *XXL* magazine (18 Aug. 2006), was equally complimentary, adding that "while the runaway success of 'Hustlin" could have positioned Ross for one-hit–wonder status, he confidently sidesteps this fate by delivering the goods on *Port of Miami.* With a cohesive sound the city can call its own, the bearded rapper gets the release he needs by exposing the dark side of the Sunshine State."

The album's success was spurred by the lead single, "Hustlin'," which was certified platinum by the Recording Industry Association of American (RIAA), with sales of at least a million units. "Hustlin'" had an accompanying music video that received heavy rotation on MTV, MTV2, and its hip-hop sister channel, MTV Jams, and peaked at number 11 on the *Billboard* Hot R&B/ Hip-Hop Songs chart and reached the top 10 of *Billboard's* Hot Rap Tracks. Ross was featured on the remix of singer Nelly Furtado's 2006 hit single "Promiscuous" and appeared on three tracks from DJ Khaled's 2006 release, *Listennn . . . the Album:* "Born-N-Raised," "Holla at Me," and "Watch Out." Ross also made several appearances on *We the Best Forever* (2007), DJ Khaled's follow-up. In September 2007, after reaching a compromise with Def Jam Records, the rapper's former label Suave House Records released *Rise to Power,* a collection of songs that were written

Affiliation: Rap Reputation

In July 2008, Ross found himself embroiled in controversy when a photograph of someone identified as Ross wearing a corrections uniform surfaced on the Internet after reportedly being leaked by fellow rapper Trick Daddy. Ross, who claimed to have been a drug trafficker and a member of the Carol City Cartel, a violent street gang, vehemently denied the allegations and claimed that the image in question had been doctored. However, the Smoking Gun website subsequently posted documentation (including employment application containing Ross's Social Security number and a certificate for perfect attendance) obtained from the Department of Corrections that revealed that he was employed as a corrections officer (at Dade County's South Florida Reception Center) from December 1995 to June 1997.

In January 2009, "Mafia Music," the lead track from Ross's third studio album, *Deeper than Rap,* was released. It featured lyrics that disparaged fellow rapper 50 Cent, whose real name is Curtis Jackson: "I love to pay her bills *I* Can't wait to pay her rent *I* Curtis Jackson baby mama *I* I ain't asking for a cent." The song sparked a feud with 50 Cent, who answered with the song "Officer Ricky (Go Head, Try Me)" and posted a series of Officer Ricky cartoons on the YouTube video-sharing website. In February 2009, 50 Cent also taped an interview with the mother of one of Ross's children and made it available on YouTube. That same month Ross's reported criminal past and gang member affiliations were again under dispute after the Smoking Gun posted the copy of a deposition by Rey Hernandez, a Miami Beach police officer who had arrested Ross in January 2008 on gun and drug charges. In the transcript Hernandez revealed that Ross had no arrests in the Miami-Dade County area prior to 2008; he also indicated that he could not find evidence that Ross had been affiliated with any local gangs. In March 2009, after months of denial, Ross made a complete reversal regarding the photo, confessing that the image was indeed authentic and admitting that he had previously worked as a corrections officer.

This revelation did not, however, affect the sales of Ross's recordings. In April 2009 *Deeper than Rap* became Ross's third consecutive album to debut at number one on the *Billboard* 200, with sales of 158,000 copies during its first week of release. It featured the single "Magnificent," a collaboration with the R&B singer John Legend that reached the top I 0 of *Billboard's* Hot R&B/ Hip-Hop Songs and Hot Rap Tracks. The disc, which also topped the charts in two other *Billboard* categories (Top R&B/Hip-Hop Albums and Top Rap Albums), was well received by the critics. *"Deeper than Rap* is just as certain as his first two studio albums, *Port of Miami* and *Trilla,* but reflects the view from the top, not the bot tom. Now, instead of climbing up to success, he's achieved it," Jon Caramanica wrote for the *New York Times* (22 Apr. 2009). Adding that the album is "a throwback to a time of sonic and attitudinal ambition in hip-hop-the Bad Boy era of the mid- to late '90s, with its warm soul samples connoting the new hip-hop luxury comes to mind. Few rap albums have sounded this assured, this sumptuous, in years." In a review for *Billboard* (9 May 2009), Monica Herrera added: 'The Miami-bred MC Rick Hoss has faced a number of career obstacles in recent months—from damaged street credibility to a multi-episodic beef—so it's all the more impressive that on his third album, *Deeper than Rap,* he presents his most cohesive work yet."

and recorded by Ross when he was a member of the label's roster.

In March 2008 Ross released his second studio album, *Trilla,* whose title drew inspiration from Michael Jackson's best-selling record. "I just remember bein' a kid when Michael Jackson's album *Thriller* came out. It was one of the first vinyl albums I bought, along with Run DMC's *Walk* This *Way,"* Ross said in an interview on DJBooth.net. "I just played it over and over for a year long. I just wanted to make my sophomore album that intense; just wanted to electrify everyone." Like its predecessor, the disc debuted at the top spot of *Billboard's* 200 and Top R&B Hip-Hop Album charts and went on to achieve gold certification; *Trilla* also reached number one on the *Billboard* Top Rap Albums chart. Notable tracks included the singles "Speedin'," a collaboration with R. Kelly that was a top-30 hit on *Billboard's* Bubbling Under Hot 100 Singles chart; and "The Boss," the platinum-selling second single that featured T-Pain and reached the top five of two *Billboard* categories: Hot R&B Hip-Hop Songs and Hot Rap Tracks.

In June 201 0 "Freeway" Rick Ross, a convicted Los Angeles drug lord, filed a $10 million copyright infringement suit against the rapper and his record labels, Def Jam and Universal Music Group, accusing them of unlawfully capitalizing on his name and image. The federal lawsuit was dismissed in November 2010 and he filed an appeal in state court the following April. Another measure by "Freeway" Rick Ross to block the release of the rapper's upcoming album also proved unsuccessful. *Teflon Don,* the rapper's fourth studio album, was released in July 201 0 and narrowly missed the top spot of the *Billboard* 200. It debuted in second place, selling more than 176,000 copies during its first week; the disc went on to achieve platinum status.

In February 2011 Ross secured a distribution deal for his label, Maybach Music Group (MMC), with Warner Bros., who beat out several record companies, including Bad Boy Records and Cash Money Records. As a solo artist Ross remained signed to Def Jam. In May 20 II MMG released its first compilation album, *Self Made Vol. 1,* featuring artists on the label's roster such as Wale, Meek Mill, and Pill. Ross made headlines again on October 14, 2011, when he was hospitalized twice in the same day following seizures during two separate flights to Memphis, Tennessee, where he was scheduled to perform. After a two-day hospital stay, Ross, who cited lack of sleep as the cause of his seizures, postponed several concert dates in order to rest and recover from his health scare. In November the rapper also announced plans to push back the release date for his next solo effort—*God Forgives, I Don't*—set for release in 2012. Ross was back in the news in February 2012, after a man was found murdered in front of a Miami home owned by the rapper, who has been ruled out as a suspect by local police.

Personal Life

In addition to his record label, MMG, Ross has also launched Rick Ross Charities, whose mission is to "strengthen the lives of today's at-risk youth from all backgrounds and create diversity by providing solid resources through education advocacy, mentoring programs, and financial resources to deserving students," according to the organization's website. The rapper also owns a Wingstop restaurant franchise in Memphis, Tennessee.

Further Reading

Caramanica, Jon. "Beyond Authenticity: A Rapper Hestages." *New York Times.* New York Times, 22 Apr. 2009. Web. 18 Mar. 2012.

Herrera, Monica. "Deeper than Hap." *Billboard.com.* Billboard, 9 May 2009. Web. 18 Mar. 2012.

Hoard, Christian. "Rick Hoss: Miami Hustler." *Rolling Stone* 15 June 2006: 30-32. Print.

Reid, Shaheem. "Rick Hoss Finally Admits Prison-Guard Past." *MTV.com.* MTV, 12 Mar. 2009. Web. 18 Mar. 2012.

"Rick Ross's Hood Dreams." *The Smoking Gun.* The Smoking Gun, 9 Feb. 2009. Web. 18 Mar. 2012.

Gabriel Roth

Founder of Daptone Records; songwriter; bass player

Born: In 1974; Riverside, California
Primary Field: Music producer
Group Affiliation: Multiple artists

Introduction

The songwriter, musician, arranger, and producer Gabriel Roth is the co-founder of the Brooklyn, New York-based Daptone Records, a label that specializes in music modeled on the funk and soul sounds of the 1960s and 1970s. Released on vinyl, recorded using vintage analog equipment, and packaged in retro cardboard sleeves, Daptone's albums emulate the look, spirit, and sound of those released by such genre-defining labels as Stax and Motown.

Early Life

Gabriel Roth was born in 1974. His parents, Diane and Andrew Roth, are lawyers, as is his sister, Samra. Roth grew up in Riverside, California, and attended Ponderosa High School. When he was a teenager, his parents, who frequently worked on civil rights and discrimination-related cases, began opening their home to children from varied racial and socioeconomic backgrounds who needed a place to stay; several became part of the extended family. While some journalists have assumed that the ethnic diversity of Roth's home predisposed him to enjoying soul music, he has denied a connection, pointing out that his African-American foster brother was a fan of the Caucasian pop musician Phil Collins.

Life's Work

Roth attended New York University (NYU), where he studied sound engineering, listened to records by the soul singer James Brown, and, by most accounts, smoked large amounts of marijuana. He also formed a short-lived band, "Dine-O-Matic," and began collecting rare funk and soul recordings. One of the labels that interested him was Pure Records, which had been established in the late 1980s in Paris, France, by a wealthy record collector, Philippe Lehman. Roth arranged to meet Lehman when the latter visited New York City. "Philippe and I just had a vision for the same style and sound—hot and nasty, '70s funk in the James Brown tradition," Roth was quoted as saying on the Drumsuite Web site. The pair began recruiting musicians and recording tracks in a small studio on Manhattan's Lower East Side. By 1997—the year after Roth earned a bachelor's degree, cum laude, from NYU—they had moved to an office on West 41st Street, under a store called Desco Vacuum. Borrowing the name, they dubbed their enterprise Desco Records. A highly specialized independent soul and funk label, Desco released music only on vinyl. Their first single was "Let a Man Do What He Wanna Do," performed by the Soul Providers, a house band that included Roth on bass. They quickly realized that their own "classic-funk stuff" was "only commercially viable if you lied about how classic the funk was exactly," Ezra Gale wrote for the *Village Voice* (March 4, 2009). As a result, they began misrepresenting their releases as lost vintage recordings. "I was about 19, 20 years old, and we were really into these old records," Roth told Terry Gross. "And we would make kind of these fake old records, you know, reissues of a sound. The first record album we did was a reissue of a soundtrack to a Kung Fu movie that never existed. You know, we just kind of made this stuff up. . . . And people were buying them. And then we said, 'Oh, great, man, people really like this music.' So . . . we'd do a real name and say, 'OK, this is a new record we just recorded.' And nobody was interested. We couldn't give them away. So we got kind of more into this fake thing." (In keeping with that strategy, Roth himself uses several aliases, including Bosco "Bass" Mann.) The Kung Fu record was called *The Revenge of Mr. Mopoji*. "We put the 'soundtrack' out as a reissue and took it around to record stores," Roth explained to Dan Daley. "These stores would never have touched a funk or soul record by a new band, but when they saw a 'reissue' they scooped it up. We heard people saying, 'Oh, yeah, my cousin had that movie on VHS.'"

Roth used similarly deceptive tactics when he released *Soul Explosion* (1998) by the Daktaris, who were described by Steve Huey for the All Music Guide Web site as "an Afro-beat group . . . recording compact, Fela Kuti-style grooves that sounded as though they'd come straight out of 1970s Nigeria." Huey continued, "At first, Desco did nothing to discourage that perception, packaging . . . *Soul Explosion* to look like an authentically African collector's dream, and even giving some of the band members Nigerian aliases. But in reality, the Daktaris were Brooklyn-based studio musicians, many

Affiliation: Soul, Pop Music

In an age of assembly-line pop recordings, Roth has succeeded (somewhat paradoxically) in satisfying people's desire for authenticity by manufacturing it: Daptone's strategy, informed by the discriminating tastes of Roth and his collaborators, shrewdly addressed the biases of consumers to carve out a niche market. "I think we've had a lot of luck as far as people not being able to judge us on who we are but on how they like the music," Neal Sugarman, Roth's partner, told Michaelangelo Matos for *Seattle Weekly* (May 18, 2005, on-line). "At the beginning, we'd get people thinking they were old records. . . . And they made unbiased decisions on it, not saying, 'Oh, this is a new record by a bunch of young white kids.' It was a record they already liked; when they found out, I think it impressed them more." When one of the label's most popular acts, Sharon Jones and the Dap-Kings, covered Janet Jackson's 1986 hit "What Have You Done for Me Lately" in 2001, performing the tune in their distinctive soulful style, the track was done so well that listeners erroneously assumed that Jackson had been covering a (nonexistent) 1970s-era Sharon Jones tune.

Some critics have accused Roth of fetishism, exploitation, and "wholesale appropriation of black tradition," as Saki Knafo, writing for the *New York Times Magazine* (December 7, 2008), reported. Others, however, have credited Roth and his artists for reviving interest in beloved but neglected music that was being forgotten in the current cultural landscape. "I've always just tried to make records that sound like . . . the records I like," Roth told Terry Gross for the National Public Radio program *Fresh Air* (November 28, 2007). "I never had too much of a very specific agenda that we were going to try to . . . something or try to pass something off. We just wanted to make records that felt good to us and sounded good to us." Dan Daley wrote for *Sound On Sound* magazine (June 2008): "I believe [Roth] when he says that [he is] not willfully making retro records for the sake of it. Daptone [is] not some super-cool karaoke cover factory . . . but a place where people who really love a certain kind of music use the tools of the time to continue to make new editions of that music." Knafo pointed out: "In an age of MP3s and computer-generated sounds, [Roth] has distinguished himself by making vinyl records featuring actual musicians manipulating real-life instruments. He has rejected the music industry, and in doing so, he has aroused its interest."

of them white." Roth admitted to Daley, "[People] just created their own assumptions. We had an ethnomusicologist in LA tell us that he had other Daktari records! It's kind of disconcerting, seeing how much bias people look at things through." Members of the Daktaris went on to form the Antibalas Afrobeat Orchestra, which also recorded on Desco.

During the late 1990s Roth and Lehman hosted a weekly radio show, *Across 110th Street*, on WKCR, a station based at Columbia University, in Upper Manhattan. They continued to build the Desco roster as well. In addition to their young house musicians, the two recruited a handful of soul and funk veterans, including Lee Fields, who had made a name for himself in the 1970s. During that period Roth also forged a working relationship with the artist who would become the most successful in his future roster, Sharon Jones. Jones had sung in talent shows and funk groups during the early 1970s and later participated in church choirs and wedding bands. She made her living, however, as a prison guard, among other such jobs. Jones's boyfriend (some sources say husband) was playing saxophone on a session with Fields and suggested they bring her in for backup vocals. Roth was impressed and began recording additional tracks with her, including a fiery prison rant called *Switchblade*. "Gabe had faith in me," Jones told Mike Greenhaus for Jambands.com (January 23, 2008). "Everyone else told me I was too old and didn't have the look. I was too fat and too black. But he really believed."

Although Desco was slowly building a following of record fans, by 2000 Lehman and Roth were arguing about money, and they decided to dissolve the company. Lehman went on to form Soul Fire Records, but Roth's debts, which included student loans, were so large that he was forced to take a job in the distribution division of Sony Records. "It was the last place in the world I wanted to be," Roth told Knafo. "They would joke about how awful the songs were, and how the [artists] were singing out of tune and how formulaic it was and blah, blah, blah, and when they were finished joking they'd put together a two- [or] three-million-dollar budget to promote the next video." Roth spent much of his time at Sony planning the resurrection of his own company, sketching possible logos and making long-distance calls at his desk. Despite his lack of loyalty to Sony, he was offered a promotion, which he declined.

In 2002 Roth partnered with the saxophonist Neal Sugarman, who had been one of the cornerstone artists in the Desco stable, to found Daptone. Many of the other musicians who had comprised the Desco collective re-joined them to form a new house band, the Dap-Kings, which was often fronted by Jones. *Dap Dippin' with Sharon Jones and the Dap-Kings* was the first album to be released on the fledgling label. Daptone initially recorded in a sublet basement studio in the Williamsburg section of Brooklyn, but after learning that a royalty check was due from distributors, Roth and Sugarman signed a long-term lease on a house in Bushwick, another section of Brooklyn, intending to convert it into an office and studio. When the royalties never arrived, the pair renovated the space themselves, with the help of other Daptone artists and Roth's parents. The studio, equipped with a 16-track tape machine rather than a digital setup, as well as other vintage equipment, was ready by 2003.

One night, after a session spent recording Sharon Jones and the Dap-Kings' second album, *Naturally*, Roth was involved in a car accident on the way home from the studio. His eyes were badly damaged when an airbag exploded in his face, temporarily blinding him; he has worn dark protective sunglasses ever since. Roth's recuperation took several months, and *Naturally* was not completed until early 2005. The band then embarked on a grueling 267-show tour, slowing down only briefly in the winter of 2006 to record a third studio album, *100 Days, 100 Nights*, which they released in October 2007. The album, whose cover features a glamorous shot of Jones in a vintage cocktail dress, has since sold more than 100,000 copies and remains among Daptone's most successful releases to date.

Some of the other main groups on the Daptone roster are the Menahan Band, the Budos Band, the Sugarman Three, the Mighty Imperials, the Daktaris, and Binky Griptite. Their work includes funk, soul, Afrobeat, boogaloo, and sometimes a fusion of all those musical styles and more, usually produced by Roth and backed by permutations of the same loose pool of musicians who still form the bulk of the label's session artists. During the late 1990s Roth had become interested in gospel music after meeting Cliff Driver, the organist and bandleader of Naomi Shelton and the Gospel Queens, a Brooklyn-based group. Roth eventually began playing bass and writing songs for the Gospel Queens, who later joined the Daptone roster. Some journalists have commented on the irony that Roth, who is Jewish by birth and now an atheist, writes gospel music. "Such is Roth's skill at creating a sense—or, some would say, an illusion—of authenticity," Knafo wrote, "that Driver, a consummate perfectionist, has incorporated the songs into his church repertory, regularly trotting them out before some of the more discriminating and faithful gospel audiences in the world." *What Have You Done, My Brother?*, Naomi Shelton and the Gospel Queens' first Daptone album, was released in 2009. (It does not mark the label's first foray into gospel. The previous year Daptone had released *Como Now*, a stirring album recorded at the Mount Mariah Church in Como, Mississippi.)

Daptone's rising profile and sales are due in large part not only to Sharon Jones and the Dap Kings but also to the label's contributions to mainstream pop and hip-hop hits. When the producer Mark Ronson was trying to manufacture a classic retro sound for the British singer Amy Winehouse using computers and sampling, he found that Daptone studios and the Dap-Kings provided a better solution. "We were using every computer trick in the book to make it sound old," Ronson told Ben Sisario for the *New York Times* (September 29, 2007). "But it was just so ridiculous. [As soon as we used the Dap-Kings] it just sounded a million times better." The resulting album, Winehouse's platinum, Grammy Award—winning *Back to Black* (2006), featured the Dap-Kings on six of its 11 tracks, including the hit single "Rehab." (Roth also served as sound engineer on the project.) The Dap-Kings then backed Winehouse on tour, and other popular British singers, including Lily Allen and Robbie Williams, began hiring the band. "The pop stuff is cool and it opens a lot of doors for us," Roth told Oliver Wang for *LA Weekly* (July 17, 2008), "[but] that's not really our meat and potatoes." In the U.S. several hip-hop artists—including Kanye West, Ghostface Killah, and Jurassic 5—also drew upon the Daptone roster, and the Dap-Kings have backed such performers as Al Green and Rod Stewart as well.

In February 2009 Daptone's Bushwick premises were burglarized, with thousands of dollars' worth of equipment stolen, including most of Roth's collection of rare, vintage microphones. His Trident series 65 mixing board and eight-track reel-to-reel tape machine remained, however.

Sharon Jones and the Dap-Kings' latest album, *I Learned the Hard Way* (2010), earned positive reviews. "The Dap-Kings succeed through attention to detail," Joe Tangari wrote for *Pitchfork.com* (April 5, 2010). "While a lot of music makes aesthetic or stylistic nods to the 60s, almost none of it actually captures the sonic character of the era. But on each of their albums, Jones and her collaborators, led by Gabriel Roth, have done just that." Daptone also distributes music under the imprints Ever-Soul Records and Dunham Records.

Personal Life

Roth and his wife, Veronica, have a daughter, Penelope.

Further Reading

Big Daddy p72+ Summer 2000
LA Weekly (on-line) July 17, 2008
New York Times Magazine p38 Dec. 7, 2008
Pop Matters (on-line) Mar. 7, 2008
Seattle Weekly (on-line) May 18, 2005
Sound on Sound (online) June 2008

Rick Rubin

Music producer

Born: Mar. 10, 1963; Long Island, New York
Primary Field: Rap
Group Affiliation: Various

Introduction

"Rubin is the musical equivalent of a great, modern chef—not only able to make magic with any given set of ingredients, but bold enough to mix styles and cultural origins in ways that enhance each element without betraying its authenticity," Andrew Gumbel wrote for the London Independent *(February 13, 2007), in describing the music producer Rick Rubin. From producing now-classic rap albums in the 1980s, including LL Cool J's Radio and the Beastie Boys' Licensed to III, to overseeing the making of such landmark rock albums as Slayer's* Reign in Blood *and the Red Hot Chili Peppers'* Blood Sugar Sex Magik, *to reviving the careers of the musical icons Johnny Cash, Donovan, and Neil Diamond, Rubin has redefined musical production over the last quarter-century, amassing a discography of more than 90 albums whose combined sales exceed 100 million.*

Early Life

The only son of Mickey and Linda Rubin, Frederick Jay Rubin was born on March 10, 1963 in the upper-middle-class area of Lido Beach, in Hempstead, on Long Island, New York. His father worked in the wholesale shoe business; both of his parents hoped that he would pursue a career in medicine or law. Rubin wanted early on to become a magician, spending hours at a time perfecting tricks in front of a mirror. During his teenage years his interests shifted to music, and he began teaching himself to play guitar. Soon afterward he formed a punk band called the Pricks. Meanwhile, he listened to music by artists ranging from James Brown, the Beatles, and Led Zeppelin to punk acts including Black Flag and the Germs. "Typically, people learn about music from older brothers and sisters, and I didn't have that, which forced me to create my own taste and really know what I like," Rubin recalled to Maureen Droney in an interview for *Mix* (October 2000).

In 1980, during his senior year at the racially mixed Long Beach High School, Rick developed an affinity for a newly emerging musical style called rap. He began frequenting record stores in New York City's East Village, purchasing the latest rap singles and mingling with young people in the city, who exposed him to still more cutting-edge music. In his senior year Rubin started Def Jam Records, using the school's four-track recorder to create his own hip-hop samples and beats. (The slang phrase *defjam* was used in the hip-hop community to describe the ideal musical sound.)

In 1981 Rubin enrolled at New York University (NYU), intending to major in philosophy before going on to law school. He later changed his focus to film and video. During his freshman year he formed another punk band, Hose, with his friends Joel Horne (on bass) and Rick Rosen (on vocals); Mike Espindle later replaced Rosen. In 1982, in Rubin's dorm room, Hose recorded an EP, which would become the first official release under the Def Jam label. Rubin managed to secure a gig for Hose at the New York club CBGB's. It was there that he struck up a friendship with three Jewish punk rockers then in their mid-teens: Adam Yauch, Mike Diamond, and Adam Horovitz, who went on to form the rap trio Beastie Boys. For a while, Rubin was the fourth member of the group, acting as the band's official deejay, under the name DJ Double R. During one of his weekly stops at another club, Negril, Rubin met DJ Jazzy Jay, a member of Afrika Bambaataa's group Universal Zulu Nation. After listening to a number of beats that Rubin had programmed on his drum machine, Jazzy Jay offered to help Rubin, introducing him to one of Rubin's favorite hip-hop groups at the time, the Treacherous Three-Kool Moe Dee, Special K, and DJ Easy Lee.

The Treacherous Three were known as the first hip-hop group to integrate rap and rock, using guitars to accent rap vocals on the song "Body Rock." Rubin, too, was interested in blending those genres, along with scratches from turntables. Due to contract obligations with another independent label, Special K offered to have his brother, T. La Rock, work in his place with Rubin and Jazzy Jay in using a deejay and drum machine as the central elements of a track. In December 1983 Rubin, T. La Rock, Horovitz, and Horovitz's best friend, Dave Skilken, recorded in Jazzy Jay's apartment a single entitled "It's Yours"—mixed and mastered at a cost of $5,000, supplied by Rubin's parents. The release of the 1984 musical film *Beat Street,* whose cast included Jazzy Jay, drew much attention to the rapper, which in turn led "It's Yours" to be played on radio stations across the country. In August 1984 Jazzy Jay introduced Rubin to a fast-talking rap promoter and producer named Russell Simmons. Simmons had risen to prominence as the head of his own hip-hop-based management company, Rush Productions, which represented popular acts such as Run D.M.C. As noted by Stacy Gueraseva in the book *Def Jam, Inc.* (2005), when Jazzy Jay told Simmons that Rubin had produced "It's Yours," he responded, "I can't believe you made that record and you're white! 'Cause that's the blackest hip-hop record that's ever been!" With Simmons's help, and more financial assistance from his parents, Rubin was able to get Def Jam Records-still headquartered in his dorm room-off the ground. After discovering a 16-year-old rapper named James Todd Smith III, who was going by the name LL Cool J, Rubin invited him to his dorm to rap over several beats that he had produced. The resulting single, "I Need a Beat," cost around $400 to produce and sold 120,000 copies, eventually attracting the attention of major record labels.

Life's Work

Rubin graduated from NYU with a degree in film and video in 1985. In November of that year, LL Cool J's album *Radio* was released. The first popular rap album to use traditional song structures, *Radio* received much critical acclaim. At his own request, Rubin was given a "reduced by" credit on the record rather than the usual "produced by" designation. In 1986 Rubin's vision of fusing rap and rock became a reality when he persuaded Run D.M.C. to collaborate with Aerosmith for a cover of the rock group's 1975 classic "Walk This Way." The video for the song became the first rap video ever played in heavy rotation on MTV. The song was featured on Run D.M.C.'s 1986 triple-platinum breakthrough album, *Raising Hell,* which was coproduced by Rubin.

With Rubin at the helm, Def Jam inked a lucrative distribution deal with Columbia Records and produced the Beastie Boys' debut album, *Licensed to Ill,* the first hip-hop album to win mainstream popularity and the first to reach the top spot on the *Billboard* Hot 100 chart. Part of the group's appeal was attributed to Rubin's use of hard-rock samples with the rappers' freestyle rhymes. Rubin also designed the album's controversial cover, which showed an airplane crashing into a mountain. He next produced Slayer's equally controversial third album, *Reign in Blood.* Rubin eliminated the thrash-metal group's complex song structures in favor of shorter, faster-paced songs with clearer production elements; that approach became known as the "Rubin touch." Slayer's vocalist and bassist, Tom Araya, recalled to Gueraseva, "He took our sound and kind of fine-tuned it: that Slayer sound that we could never capture in the studio. We kinda realized, 'Oh my God, this guy, he's got the touch of gold.'" Whereas the *Village Voice* had called Rubin "the king of rap" several years earlier, his association with Slayer-whom rumors had linked with devil worship-led the publication to label him "Satan's record producer." With subject matter including concentration-camp torture, *Reign in Blood* caused an uproar. Defending the record in an interview for the *Los Angeles Times* (April 16, 1989), Rubin said to Robert Hilburn, "Who said rock n' roll was supposed to be nice? Rock n' roll is about going against the rules." In 1987 Rubin produced the rap group Public Enemy's classic first album, *Yo! Bum Rush the Show,* and helped produce and assemble the first-ever rap-rock soundtrack, for the film *Less Than Zero.* Then, in the midst of the controversy surrounding Slayer and power struggles within Def Jam, Rubin decided to part ways with the company he helped found. He ended his partnership with Simmons amicably, deeming their friendship more important than their business arrangement.

In 1988 Rubin launched his own label, Def American Records, moved to Los Angeles, California, and concentrated for a time on his first love: hard rock. Over the next three years, he produced more Slayer albums, including *South of Heaven* and *Decade of Aggression,* and records by other against-the-grain acts, among them Danzig, Masters of Reality, and Wolfsbane. He even added comedy to his repertoire, producing an album for the profane comic Andrew Dice Clay. In 1990, while doubling as a freelance producer for major record companies, Rubin got the opportunity to produce the Red Hot Chili Peppers' next album under the Warner Bros. label. Over a six-month period, Rubin worked with the band through an extensive brainstorming, songwriting, and rehearsal process that would result in some of the group's best work. During that period he came across a poem by the group's singer, Anthony Kiedis, entitled "Under the Bridge." Although Kiedis was reluctant at first to make the poem into a song, Rubin persuaded him to present it to the band. Then, after feeling dissatisfied with the atmosphere in the recording studio, Rubin came across an empty mansion in Los Angeles's Laurel Canyon, once owned by the escape artist Harry Houdini and later inhabited by such luminaries as Rudolph Valentino, the Beatles, and Jimi Hendrix, and moved the band into the house to live in seclusion for a month. (Only the drummer, Chad Smith, refused to stay there, believing that the house was haunted.) On September 24, 1991 *Blood Sugar Sex Magik* was released to unanimous critical acclaim. Its first single, the ultra-funky "Give It Away," won a Grammy Award in 1992 for best hard-rock song, and "Under the Bridge" went on to reach number two on the *Billboard* charts. *Blood Sugar Sex Magik* is widely considered to be one of the seminal rock albums of the 1990s.

In the early 1990s Rubin was one of rock's busiest producers-for-hire, working with Tom Petty and the Heartbreakers to produce the album *Wildflowers* and producing a solo effort by Mick Jagger, *Wandering Spirit,* among other projects. Meanwhile, in 1993, after Rubin came across the word "def" in a dictionary, he not only dropped it from the name of his label, feeling that it had become overused-he conducted a funeral ceremony for it, complete with coffin and grave. The label became known simply as American Recordings. With the name change came a desire to work with different kinds of artists, which resulted in his "American Series" albums with the country-music legend Johnny Cash. For several weeks in the autumn of 1993, under minimal instruction from Rubin, Cash recorded the solo tracks for the *American Recordings* album in his living room, accompanying himself on guitar. Describing their first sessions together, David Kamp wrote for *Vanity Fair* (October 2004), "Rubin sat in his living room like the musicologist Alan Lomax on a Mississippi porch, listening and recording intently while a gnarled, authentic article of Americana banged away at his repertoire." The album immediately brought Cash renewed mainstream popularity. *Rolling Stone* gave a five-star rating to *American Recordings,* which went on to win a Grammy Award for best contemporary folk-song album.

During the same period, and through much of the decade, Rubin continued producing albums for Slayer *(Divine Intervention),* Danzig *(Danzig IV),* and the Red Hot Chili Peppers *(Californication),* in addition to recordings of the heavy-metal icons *ACIDC (Ballbreaker)* and the pop veteran Donovan *(Sutras).* Each of his successful albums with those groups resulted from a long, often tedious production process. Rubin had Donovan, for example, write an abundance of new material; the singer arrived at the studio with more than 100 songs. Referring to *Sutras,* which was several years in the making, Rubin explained to Craig Rosen *for Billboard* (August 31, 1996), "Artists that have made lots of records get into a very specific habit. They make a record, go on the road, and record again whether they are prepared to make a record or not, because that's the cycle. In the case of grown-up artists, which I like to call them, it's not easy to try to break that cycle. They should spend as much time as it takes to write, like they did on their first album, and not rush into making an album." Through hard work, Rubin was able to help veteran artists break out of their comfort zones. *Sutras* proved to be a hit and had drawn more media attention to the American Recordings label by the time Rubin's second album with Cash, *Unchained,* appeared in 1996. Backed on the record by Tom Petty and the Heartbreakers, Cash, at Rubin's urging, focused less on original material than on covers of songs whose styles were not normally associated with the country icon, among them Soundgarden's "Rusty Cage." Cash "thought I was insane," Rubin recalled to Kamp, when he first had the singer listen to the Soundgarden version of the song. Rubin's radical vision paid off, and the album took home a Grammy Award for best country album that year-despite being all but ignored by the country music community.

Rubin collaborated with the art-metal group System of a Down on their eponymous debut album, in 1998, and on their 2001 follow-up, *Toxicity.* The latter debuted at number one on the *Billboard* chart, and the magazine *Spin* named it the number-one record of the year. Keith Harris, in an album review *for Rolling Stone* (September 27, 2001), praised Rubin's production, remarking that it allowed the music to insist "on forward motion without trapping itself in a thrashy lock-step rut." In 2000 Cash released his third American Series record with Rubin, *American III: Solitary Man,* which featured covers such as Tom Petty's "I Won't Back Down," U2's "One," and Neil Diamond's "Solitary Man." Cash won another Grammy for the Neil Diamond cover, taking home the award for best song by a male country singer. In 2002 came Cash and Rubin's fourth collaboration, *American IV: The Man Comes Around,* which became Cash's first gold record in more than 30 years and represented even more radical departures for the singer, including covers of Depeche Mode's "Personal Jesus" and Nine Inch Nails' "Hurt." *American W* was the last collaboration between Rubin and Cash, who remained close friends until Cash's death, on September 12, 2003. Two more Rubin/Cash albums were released posthumously: *Unearthed* (2003), a boxed set featuring outtakes and alternative versions of songs, and *A Hundred Miles* (2006).

In the new millennium Rubin has continued to collaborate with recording artists in a wide range of genres, working on the rapper Jay Z's song "99 Problems" *for The Black Album* (2003), the metal group Slipknot's 2004 record *Vol. 3 (The Subliminal Verses)* (2004), and the Colombian pop artist Shakira's *Fijacion Oral Vol. 1* and its English language follow-up, *Oral Fixation Vol. 2,* both of which won numerous awards. Rubin's second

Affiliation: Uncommon Career Path

Since he began running the legendary Def Jam label out of his college dorm room in the 1980s, with his then-partner Russell Simmons, Rubin has won a reputation as a visionary among producers, offering advice on every aspect of an album, from its music to its cover art. "I'm just trying to make my favorite music. That's how I work; I just do things based on the way they feel to me. I want to be touched by the music I'm making. Luckily, other people have shared that response to my work over the years," Rubin explained to J. Freedom du Lac for the *Washington Post* (January 15, 2006). He added, "I don't even know what a traditional producer is or does. I feel like the job is like being a coach, building good work habits and building trust. . . . My goal is to just get out of the way and let the people I'm working with be their best."

While most producers begin their careers as studio technicians, Rubin "came up as a fan," as he told Josh Tyrangiel for *Time* (February 19, 2007). Much of Rubin's success lies in his practice of stripping songs of such common production elements as backup vocals and string sections, in order to focus on the essence of the material. David Hajdu noted for the *New Republic* (May 29, 2006), "His primary concerns as a producer are composition and performance, and his main objective is to capture the sound of people in the act of music making. He thinks of recording as [Thomas] Edison did, as the documentation of an art made by others rather than as a creative act in itself." His expertise brought him "best producer of the year" honors at the 2007 Grammy Awards, in recognition of his work on the Red Hot Chili Peppers' *Stadium Arcadium,* the Dixie Chicks' *Taking the Long Way,* and Justin Timberlake's *FutureSex/LoveSounds,* among a host of other records. Daron Malakian, the principal songwriter for System of a Down, told du Lac that Rubin might be described best as a "song doctor," adding, "If you play something for him, it's like going in for a checkup. He's like, 'Here, take a couple of these vitamins and see how you feel.' And the songs always feel better after his suggestions. And so do you." The comedian Chris Rock, a friend of Rubin's, said to Josh Tyrangiel, "Most producers have their own sound, and they lease it out to different people, but we know it's still their record. The records you make with Rick are your records. He makes it his job to squeeze the best out of you-and not leave any fingerprints." In 2007 Rubin's musical expertise was tapped by Columbia Records: since May he has been Columbia's co-head, with Steve Barnett, working to help the label adjust to changing times. As part of an agreement with Columbia, Rubin will continue to produce music with artists who have not signed with that record label.

most unlikely collaboration—after his partnership with Cash—came when he worked with the pop star Neil Diamond. Rubin helped Diamond to think of himself once more as a singer/songwriter, having him use his own early albums as a springboard to new material and even persuading him to play guitar again—which the artist had not done since the 1960s. Diamond's *12 Songs* (2005) became his most successful and critically acclaimed studio album in years, debuting at number four on the *Billboard* album chart. Rubin's influence was also in evidence during the subsequent tour for the album, as Diamond used tougher-sounding background arrangements for some of his classic songs. Diamond told Edna Gundersen *for USA Today* (July 7, 2006), "With Rick, I found the right path. He picked up on the vibe of acoustic guitar and understatement, something I haven't done in years and wasn't able to replicate until this album."

Rubin's success has not been founded on technical mastery; he does not read music, write lyrics, or know how to use a standard mixing board. As reflected in his accomplishments with Cash, Diamond, and other artists, Rubin's gift has been in his ability to put the musicians he works with—veterans and newcomers alike—at ease while guiding them toward their full creative potential, through hard work and patience. "I try to get them in the mind-set that they're not writing music for an album," he explained to Josh Tyrangiel. "They're writing music because they're writers and that's what they do." As a result, many of Rubin's projects take years to complete, which is why he often finds himself working on several projects at once. Because he grants almost full autonomy to the artists, frequent collaborators have described his studio atmosphere as a "real democracy." Rubin said to Tyrangiel, "In the old days, when I'd hear something that's not working, I'd say, 'O.K., this is how we're going to fix it.' Now I ask, 'How do we fix it?' And nine times out of 10, what they come up with is as good as or better than how I would've done it."

In 2006 Rubin was greatly in demand as a producer, overseeing the recording of albums for Slayer *(Christ Illusion),* the Red Hot Chili Peppers *(Stadium Arcadium),* and the Dixie Chicks *(Taking the Long Way).* He did additional work on Justin Timberlake's multiplatinum *FutureSex/LoveSounds,* working on the track "(Another Song) All Over Again," and produced U2/Green Day's cover of the Skids' song "The Saints Are Coming." Tyrangiel noted, "It's clear [Rubin's] aesthetic range is essentially limitless." Rubin was connected with 15 artists and recordings nominated for 2007 Grammy Awards; Rubin himself, who had been nominated for "producer of the year" on three previous occasions, took home his first Grammy in that category.

In May 2007 Rubin's career took a turn that surprised many observers, when he accepted an offer from Steve Barnett, the head of Columbia Records, to join him as co-head of the label. Barnett hoped that Rubin would provide fresh ideas for saving the record-label industry, in which the most successful CDs were selling 30 percent fewer copies than their counterparts in 2006. Rubin agreed with stipulations: that he not have to travel, wear suits, or maintain a desk or phone at any corporate office. He also strongly suggested that Columbia become the first major record company to "go green" and end the practice of packing its CDs in plastic cases. Columbia's willingness to accommodate Rubin led him to feel that he could be effective in his new post. "I felt like I could be a force for good," Rubin told Lauryn Hirschberg for the *New Y ark Times Magazine* (September 2, 2007). "In the past, I've tried to protect artists from the [Columbia] label, and now my job would also be to protect the label from itself. So many of the decisions at these companies are not about the music. They are shortsighted and desperate. For so long, the record industry had control. But now that monopoly has ended, they don't know what to do. I thought it would be an interesting challenge." In his new job Rubin must seek out fresh talent rather than concentrate on reinvigorating the careers of established artists. His major challenge, though, is one that faces not only Columbia but the entire industry: adjusting belatedly to an age when increasing numbers of people download music illegally, no longer listen to music on the radio, and learn about music primarily through word of mouth. Rubin has noted that for 50 years, record labels sold music through such channels as Tower Records and other major retail chains, MTV, and *Rolling Stone* and other large-circulation music magazines. Although Columbia has made some changes-creating a promotion division at Columbia that sells music directly to TV and a "word of mouth" department that spreads buzz through chat rooms—Rubin believes that such minor gestures may merely make Columbia the "best dinosaur" and that the time has come for more drastic action. Along with others in the industry, he has suggested the use of a subscription-based model, whereby subscribers would pay a monthly fee to gain access to music from a virtual library. That approach would require cooperation among record companies, and many, including Barnett, view it as risky. Rubin, however, sees no alternative. "Either all the record companies will get together or the industry will fall apart and someone like Microsoft will come in and buy one of the companies at wholesale and do what needs to be done," he told Hirschberg. He added, "The existing people will either get smart, which is a question mark. Or new people will understand what a resource the music business is and change it without us. I don't want to watch that happen."

Personal Life

An adherent of yoga and Zen Buddhism, Rubin shares his recently restored 1923 English Tudor style mansion, perched above Los Angeles's Sunset Strip, with his girlfriend. "Physically, he is little short of arresting—a big man, with a yawning pot belly and a beard so wide and long it could be its own ecosystem," Andrew Gumbel wrote. Rubin does not drink alcohol and, surprisingly for someone in his line of work, has never tried drugs. The film actor Owen Wilson, a longtime friend of Rubin's, said to Edna Gundersen about the producer, "We just have a good time laughing. He has a funny take on stuff. A lot of lines in my movies came directly from Rick." J. Freedom du Lac reported that Rubin often reads and meditates at home. "It's a big theme in my life, learning about myself and being a better person," Rubin told du Lac. ''I'm a work in progress; I have revelations every day."

Further Reading

Billboard Nov. 5, 2005, Aug. 31, 1996
(London) *Independent* World p26 Feb. 13, 2007
Los Angeles Times p65 Apr. 16, 1989
Mix (on-line) Oct. 2000
MTV Web site; *New Republic* p25+ May 29, 2006
New York Times E p1 Feb. 5, 2007
New York Times Magazine p28+ Sep. 2, 2007
Time p62+ Feb. 19, 2007
USA Today E p1+ July 7, 2006
Vanity Fair p200+ Oct. 2004
Washington Post N p1+ Jan. 15, 2006
Gueraseva, Stacy. *Def Jam, Inc.*, 2005

Rush

Rock band

Geddy Lee
Born: July 29, 1953; Willowdale, Ontario, Canada

Alex Lifeson
Born: Aug. 27, 1953; British Columbia, Canada

Neil Peart
Born: Sep. 12, 1952; Hamilton, Ontario

Primary Field: Rock
Group Affiliation: Rush

Introduction

In the history of rock, few bands have endured for as long as Rush, and fewer still have displayed such vigor and inventiveness after recording and performing for more than a quarter-century. Once dismissed as musical dinosaurs mired in 1970s progressive rock, the Toronto-based Rush is now spoken of in almost reverential terms by fans, and such groups as Primus, Metallica, and Dream Theater have cited Rush among their most important influences. Rush's three members—bassist and vocalist Geddy Lee, guitarist Alex Lifeson, and drummer Neil Peart—who have played together since 1975, have all been recognized as masters of their instruments.

Early Lives

Geddy Lee (born Gary Lee Weinrib on July 29, 1953 in Willowdale, Ontario, Canada) and Alex Lifeson (born on August 27, 1953 in British Columbia, Canada, with the surname Zivojinovich) met in Toronto as eighth-graders. Inspired by the then recent invasion of British acts who blended blues with guitar-crunching hard rock, the boys began playing music together in their basements. "When we were growing up," Lee told Dan Nooger for *Circus* (April 27, 1976, on-line), "the big bands were [Led] Zeppelin and [Jeff) Beck. We used to do a lot of Zeppelin material before we started writing our own stuff and I used to have to scream to hit the high notes." After a while Lee and Lifeson hooked up with John Rutsey, a drummer, and formed Rush, a name suggested by a friend of theirs. Lee and Lifeson also adopted stage names ("Geddy" is how Lee's Polish-born mother pronounced "Gary"; "Lifeson" is the English translation of "Zivojinovich").

Lives' Work

The band played their first gig at the Coffin, a makeshift club in the basement of a local Anglican church. There they met Ray Danniels, a high school dropout with a keen head for business. Danniels made deals with club owners in and around Toronto, and soon Rush was getting engagements in clubs, school gyms, youth centers, and any other place that would take them. The pay was minimal, and more often than not, patrons paid no attention while the group performed, usually presenting songs written by others. By continuing to accept such gigs despite such undesirable conditions, the band developed a strong work ethic. "It was just persistence," Lee told Debra Frost for *Circus* (February 14, 1977, online). "We only did tunes that we liked, and we'd sneak in an original here and there. Eventually we built up our own little following."

On the strength of that following, Rush recorded their first studio album—*Rush*, which Moon Records released in early 1974. The disc contained some songs that have become Rush chestnuts, among them "Finding My Way," "In the Mood," and "Working Man." Many critics dismissed *Rush* as a mediocre collection of Zeppelin-influenced blues-rock tunes, and it failed to generate much attention in either Canada or the U.S. The musicians were planning their first American tour, to support the album, when Rutsey announced that he was leaving the band. "It was obvious that his heart wasn't into it ...," Lee explained to Frost. "He just wasn't thinking the way Alex and I were and he decided it would be better for himself and for us if he left." After an extended search, Lee and Lifeson found a new drummer-Neil Peart (born on September 12, 1952 in Hamilton, Ontario). A self-educated high-school dropout who had spent a year in England playing with several bands, Peart impressed Lee and Lifeson with his powerful, intricate drumming, which favored syncopated beats over the straight-ahead rhythms used by most other percussionists at that time. Peart joined them on a tour of North America, during which they opened for such acts as Kiss, Uriah Heep, and ZZ Top, occasionally upstaging the headlining act. In the Midwest the trio discovered that Rush already had a fairly solid fan base, thanks in part to Donna Halper, a programmer at the Cleveland, Ohio, rock radio station WMMS, who had been inserting the Rush song "Working Man" into the station's daily rotation. During the tour, while the group's reputation as a top-shelf live act developed, sales of *Rush* began to rise, and Rush soon joined the roster of Mercury Records.

Meanwhile, Lee and Lifeson had discovered that Peart, an avid reader, could write lyrics. While still on the road, the band began writing songs for their next album, *Fly by Night.* Released in 1975, that record contains not only straightforward rockers, such as "Best I Can," but also epic-length pieces, with lyrics inspired by the writings of Tolkien, Ayn Rand, and Michael Moorcock. Fans' wildly enthusiastic responses to such songs as "Anthem," "Rivendell," and the seven-minute "By-Tor and the Snowdog," about a battle between an evil knight and a benevolent mythical beast, spurred the band to release another album, *Caress of Steel,* before the year was out. Two cuts from that disc, "Bastille Day" and "Lakeside Park," became staples of the band's live show, while "The Fountain of Lamneth," which took up one whole side of the album, demonstrated Rush's affinity for progressive rock. *Caress of Steel* struck critics as bloated and pretentious, and its sales lagged far behind those of its predecessor. Rush's subsequent live performances during the "Down the Tubes Tour," as they dubbed it, failed to generate much income; indeed, Lifeson, who had married and become a father by then, had to use the money remaining from his wedding gifts to support his family.

In the wake of the failure of *Caress of Steel,* Rush faced demands from their label to conform to a more mainstream sound. "There was a lot of pressure on us to be more accessible," Lee told *Current Biography.* "We responded with something that was even less accessible." Instead of a collection of three-minute pop songs, for *2112* (1976) Lee, Lifeson, and Peart produced a 20-minute title track, which told of how the discovery of a guitar by a young member of an oppressive futuristic society helped to free the minds of his compatriots. "We were kind of angry about how much pressure we were getting from everybody else to conform, and that whole album is about not conforming," Lee explained to *Current Biography.* "It's probably the most important record we ever did." With the liner notes from the album acknowledging "the genius of Ayn Rand," and with virtuoso playing by all three instrumentalists, *2112* catapulted Rush to official superstar status. Although, once again, they were an opening act, Rush's performances on their *2112* tour reinforced their standing as one of the premier rock acts of the late 1970s. Portions of the *2112* concerts were captured on the live collection *All the World's a Stage* (1976).

A Farewell to Kings (1977) features quieter songs, accompanied by classical guitar, synthesizers, and the temple blocks, chimes, and gong that Peart had acquired. In addition to such meditative reflections on the human condition as "Closer to the Heart," "Madrigal," and "Cinderella Man," the album includes the 11-minute "Cygnus X-1." Describing an astronaut's encounter with a black hole, the song was inspired by an article about black holes in *Time* magazine, and along with "Xanadu," a song based on Samuel Taylor Coleridge's poem "Kubla Khan," it established Rush as the thinking person's heavy-metal act. On their subsequent, seven-month "Drive Till You Die Tour," Rush was the headliner, and the band enhanced their show with rear-projected films (some of them made by Lee), laser effects, and an array of pyrotechnics. Taking advantage of the extra time allotted to them, they occasionally ended each show with a medley of songs, which they stitched together to form one long piece, and closed with a crowd-rousing explosion of fireworks and confetti. Lee explained to *Current Biography* that Rush's extravagant live show reflected concerts the musicians had seen while growing up, as well as experiences they had had as an opening act. "We opened for Kiss on our first couple of tours," he recalled. "And here we are, three Canadian musicians sitting on the side of the stage watching guys put makeup on and blow things up on stage. And, like their music or not, they worked really hard, and they tried to give an all-around performance and put on a show for their fans. So there was a work ethic that rubbed off on us, and we began to think, 'If we can play as well as we can, and add a show to that, that's gonna be kind of sensational.'"

A month after completing the tour, Rush released their sixth studio album, *Hemispheres* (1978), whose name refers to the left and right halves of the brain. Two concert tours and approximately 150 concerts later, the group made two albums that many casual admirers and die-hard fans consider to be their best—*Permanent Waves* (1980) and *Moving Pictures* (1981), for both of which the trio wrote shorter songs. Explaining Rush's reasons for this change, Lee told Howard Reich for the *Chicago Tribune* (November 14, 1982), "We got to a point where it was almost expected for us to do a 10- or 20-minute song on each album. It wasn't real challenging anymore, to be honest. It was like standing still. Sure, we could do another concept thing in a 20-minute piece, but that would really be like doing the same one again, except with different notes. It stopped becoming a challenge to write a tune that would be considered good simply because it lasted 10 minutes, and not good because it ran four minutes." "The Spirit of Radio" and "Free Will," from *Permanent Waves,* and "Tom Sawyer," from *Moving Pictures,* became radio hits. In addition, the instrumental "YYZ," from *Moving Pictures,* earned Rush their first Grammy nomination-for best instrumental-and the album itself went quadruple platinum. The live album *Exit . .. Stage Left* (1981) features highlights from the *Moving Pictures* tour.

In the next year Rush released *Signals,* a sleeker, more high-tech album that displayed Rush's continued interest in keyboard-driven rock. As he did for *Hemispheres,* whose songs examine the differences among people, Peart chose a theme for *Signals*—the idea of communication between people. The album generated the singles "Subdivisions," about suburban adolescents' isolation, and "New World Man," and also offered such songs as "The Analog Kid" and "Countdown," about the majesty of a shuttle launch.

Soon after the release of *Signals,* the band split from their longtime producer, Terry Brown. "For all intents and purposes, he was in the band; he was one of us, and that was great," Lee told Greg Armbruster for *Keyboard* (September 1984). "We made a lot of great albums together, but 10 records is a long time working with the same attitudes. Sometimes you have to have a radical change. Sometimes you have to shake yourself and make sure you're not falling asleep at the wheel, or falling into bad habits, or taking the easy way out every time." Working with the producer Peter Henderson, the group made the dark and introspective *Grace Under Pressure* (1984). That album includes "Afterimage," a tribute to the trio's friend Robbie Whelan, who had died in a car accident; "Between the Wheels," about what the group perceived as the decay of society; and "Red Sector A," which deals with the Holocaust. (Lee's parents survived incarceration in the Nazi concentration camp in Auschwitz, Poland.)

Rush left Henderson and linked up with the producer Peter Collins to make their next album, *Power Windows* (1985). An exploration of various forms of power, it includes such songs as "The Big Money," "Marathon," and "Manhattan Project," which deals

Affiliation: Rock

Some high-school and college instructors have made teaching tools of Rush's songs, which contain abundant references to literary material, ranging from the Greek legend of Sisyphus to J.R.R. Tolkien's fantasy series *The Lord of the Rings.* They have also fashioned a reputation for being one of the top live acts in rock music, touring the world extensively and putting on shows that blend music and spectacle. "I think we've remained true to our own style, but [we've] not been so close-minded as to ignore new things that are going on in music that we respond to," Lee told *Current Biography,* when asked about Rush's longevity. "We love writing music together," Lifeson explained to Chris Gill for *guitarworld.com* in 1997. "We laugh a lot together. When we work we like to be secluded. We go away to a studio in the country and take the weekends off to go home. We're around each other all the time-having dinner, sitting around in the evening when we've finished working-and all we do is goof around and laugh. We've always done that. It's made us want to be together. In fact, we look forward to it."

with the aftereffects of the bombing of Hiroshima, Japan, in 1945. "When I started that song, I only wanted to dramatize the event itself," Peart told Ernie Welch for the *Boston Globe* (December 5, 1985). "But after doing so much research, I realized just what had happened and began to empathize with the people involved. They weren't heartless, crazy monsters, just regular, patriotic people caught up in the momentum of events." Employing strings, keyboards, and, on "Marathon," a full choir, *Power Windows* offers a more polished sound that previous Rush discs. The radio-friendly single "Mystic Rhythms" helped propel sales of the record to more than one million copies by the end of the year.

The lushly orchestrated, keyboard-heavy *Hold Your Fire* (1987), which is widely regarded as the band's strongest effort from this period, boasts a string of Rush classics, including "Force Ten," "Mission," and "Time Stand Still," the first Rush song to include an outsider (Aimee Mann) on backup vocals. Written by Peart, "Time Stand Still" reveals the musicians' desire to focus less on their careers and more on their personal lives; the lyrics include the lines, "I want to look around me now / See more of the people / And places that surround me now." "All through the 70s our lives were flying by; we spent so much time on the road that it became like a dark tunnel," Peart told Brett Milano for the *Boston Globe* (November 19, 1987). "You start to think about the people you're neglecting, friends and family. So the song is about stopping to enjoy that, with a warning against too much looking back. Instead of getting nostalgic about the past, it's more a plea for the present." Such sentiments notwithstanding, Rush spent eight months on a concert tour in support of *Hold Your Fire.* Afterward, Lee, Lifeson, and Peart took a break from performing and recording that lasted about two years. "Call it maturity, but we discovered that we didn't have to be obsessed about Rush 24 hours a day," Lee told Nicholas Jennings for *Macleans* (September 30, 1991). "It was just one of the things that we do."

In late 1989 Rush released their 13th studio album, *Presto,* the first recording to bear the band's own label, Anthem. Produced by Rupert Hine, it relies on basic rhythms from each instrumentalist rather than synthesized sound. *"Presto* is kind of a renewal to me," Lee told Nick Krewen for *Canadian Musician* (April 1990). "It's a renewal of energy and a positive outlook, in musical terms and in personal terms, both in my place in the band and my feeling about recording." Highlights of the album are "Show Don't Tell," which was inspired in part by the 1925 trial of John Scopes, a high-school teacher who broke Tennessee law by teaching the theory of evolution; "The Pass," which addresses suicide; and "Superconductor," about the vagaries of fame. The video for "Show Don't Tell," which aired repeatedly on the cable music channel MTV, raised the band's profile. It also introduced the band to a new generation of listeners, many of whom responded enthusiastically to Rush's next recording, *Roll the Bones* (1991). That album debuted at number three on the *Billboard* charts, and within a week of its release, its single "Dreamline" had become the most requested song on rock-oriented radio stations; within a month, the album had sold a half-million copies. With *Counterparts* (1993), which is dominated by a hard-driving guitar, Rush reunited with Peter Collins. *Counterparts,* Lifeson told Andy Aledort for *Guitar World* (February, 1994), is "about the three of us playing together. There was something very satisfying about making this record. It took us back to what we've always been about as a three piece band." Another hiatus followed the release of *Counterparts.* "After 20 years, we needed to just explore ourselves as people," Lifeson told a reporter for *Billboard* (August 3, 1996). "Our lives had been centered around the band. When I think back over the last 20 years, I think in terms of tours, or where were we recording at any given time. My connection is always to the band, and we needed to break away from that." During this period Lee became a father for the second time and Lifeson released a solo album, *Victor* (1996). Peart engaged in various activities during his sabbatical: he produced and (along with several other drummers) performed on the two-volume *Burning for Buddy: A Tribute to the Music of Buddy Rich* (1994 and 1997, respectively); studied drum techniques with the renowned teacher Freddie Grubber; and wrote a book, *The Masked Rider* (1996), which describes his experiences while bicycling in West Africa.

Rush returned with *Test for Echo* (1996), their 16th studio effort. Centered on the concept of human interaction in a technological society, the album spawned two singles-the title track and the acoustic rocker "Half the World." "It was the most enjoyable [album] for us," Lifeson told Gerald Mizejewski for the *Washington Times* (November 7, 1996). "We were very unified in what the direction was. I think it shows on the album." *Test for Echo* debuted at number five on the *Billboard* charts, making Rush the only Canadian act with more than one *Billboard* Top 10 success. During the *Test for Echo* tour, the band performed for almost three hours without an opening act. "When you have 16 studio records out, we decided the only way we could do it is be so self-indulgent that we have the whole show to ourselves," Lee explained to Jancee Dunn for *Rolling Stone* (December 12, 1996). During their shows, Rush performed "2112" in its entirety, something they had never before done in concert.

At the beginning of 2001, the members of Rush reunited and began working on their first new record in five years. "At present, Alex, Neil and I are just about approaching the end of· our rather long and intensive writing sessions and have moved into the realm of album production," Lee wrote in a September 22, 2001 message on his Web site, *geddylee.net.* "Now I believe we are at the point where we are starting to feel pretty darn good about how we have spent the last 8 months, and what we have created."

Personal Lives

In August 1997 Peart's only daughter, Selena, was killed in a car accident at the age of 19. Less than a year later, his wife, Jackie Taylor, an art dealer, succumbed to cancer. In the wake of these tragedies, the group took another extended break. "We're brothers," Lifeson explained to Tom Harrison for the Vancouver *Province* (November 10, 1998, on-line). "We feel for each other, especially in a time like this. We have a great relationship that's been strong since day one." To satisfy fans eager for something new, Rush released the triple album *Different Stages* (1998), a collection of highlights from their last few tours, as well as a rare recording of a 1976 concert at the Hammersmith Odeon, in London. On other fronts, Lee and Lifeson contributed a recording of "0 Canada," the Canadian national anthem, to the soundtrack of the film *South Park: Bigger, Longer and Uncut* (1999). Peart, who married Carrie Nuttall, a photographer, in 2000, has been traveling extensively. Lifeson's activities include managing his music club cum cocktail lounge, the Orbit Room, in Toronto.

Lifeson and his wife, Charlene are the parents of two sons, Justin and Adrian. Lee, who with his wife, Nancy, has one son, Julian, and one daughter, Kyla, took the time off to record a solo album, *My Favorite Headache.* "I was not interested in stepping out as a solo artist," Lee told *Current Biography.* "I've had enough attention to last me two lifetimes. And I have no frustration working with Alex and Neil. But [with *My Favorite Headache],* there was something different at work. I was expressing myself in a different way." *My Favorite Headache* was made in collaboration with the Canadian musician and producer Ben Mink, a longtime friend of Lee's. Lee began writing songs with Mink as a way to remain artistically engaged when not working with Rush. "But even before that Ben and I would always say 'We should write something together.' So basically we made a pact [in 1997] that we would write one song before the end of the year." That one song led to 10 more, and the resulting album, released in November 2000, has generated positive reviews and strong sales.

The members of Rush have raised several million dollars for the United Way. In 1997 the group was awarded the Order of Canada, thus becoming the only rock act to be so honored. In 1999 they earned a star on the Canadian Walk of Fame, in Toronto. Also that year, in an on-line poll conducted by *JAM! Showbiz* (on-line), Rush was voted "Canada's most important musicians of all time."

Further Reading

Chicago Tribune VI p11 Nov. 14, 1982
Macleans p66+ Sep. 30, 1991, with photos
Rolling Stone p33 Dec. 12, 1996, with photos
Washington Post p24 May 4, 1990, with photo

S

David Sánchez (SAHN-chez, dah-VEED)

Saxophonist

Born: Sep. 1968; Guaynabo, Puerto Rico
Primary Field: Jazz
Group Affiliation: Solo and ensemble performer

Introduction

The saxophonist David Sánchez is regarded by many critics as one of the most exciting and important young artists to emerge on the jazz scene in recent years. A native of Puerto Rico, Sánchez made his mark in Latin jazz with his first solo recording, The Departure, *in 1994. Popularized by the trumpeter and bandleader Dizzy Gillespie, Latin jazz is known for its unique fusion of American jazz and the traditional, African-based music of South America and the Caribbean islands. Sánchez has transformed the music he heard as a child into a form that pushes the envelope of modern jazz interpretation.*

Early Life

David Sánchez was born in September 1968 in Guaynabo, a town of 100,000 on the outskirts of San Juan, Puerto Rico's capital. Inspired by his oldest brother, a percussionist in a band that included members. of the legendary Rafael Cortijo Combo, Sánchez took up percussion at the age of eight. His father was a professional baseball player who was disappointed that his son had decided to pursue musical careers rather than baseball. "I started playing on my brother's drum set and the conga," Sánchez told Isabelle Leymarie for the *Unesco Courier* (January 1997). "I had a particular liking for Cuban drummers such as Morigo Santamaria, Patato Valdes, Los Papines and El Nino, and jazzier groups such as Irakere." When Sánchez was 12 years old, his sister brought home a copy of the famed trumpeter Miles Davis's recording *Basic Miles,* an anthology that features John Coltrane on saxophone. "After I heard that record, I decided I would like to focus more on saxophone than on the [Latin] percussion I had been playing, and I decided I had to play this music, jazz," Sánchez told Howard Reich for the *Chicago Tribune* (March 26, 1995). When he was 14 Sánchez enrolled at La Escuela Libra de Musica (the Free School of Music) in San Juan. There, he began his formal classical training and concentrated on mastering the saxophone, while never completely abandoning percussion. Critics have noted the attention to rhythm that is evident in his music. "It is true, there is like a burst of rhythm, because when I grew up, that was my first instrument, percussion," Sánchez told Howard Reich for *Down Beat* (March 2001). "So when I play percussion in the band, I'm not doing it as just a show. Honestly, that's what I feel, that's what I hear." He also began playing with some of the local salsa bands, most notably Eddie Palmieri's group, which represented the vanguard of Latin jazz in Puerto Rico at the time. After he graduated from the Free School, he enrolled at the University of Puerto Rico, where he briefly considered abandoning music for a career in psychology. Following a year at the University of Puerto Rico, Sánchez won a scholarship to study jazz at Rutgers University in New Brunswick, New Jersey, a short distance from New York City, where members of his family lived.

Life's Work

Eddie Pahnieri and his band had meanwhile moved to New York, and Sánchez soon began playing with them again. He also collaborated with the pianist Danilo Perez, the percussionist Giovanni Hidalgo, and the trumpeter Charlie Sepulveda, who were all students at Rutgers. In an interview quoted on the official Web site of B. H. Hopper Management, which represents him, Sánchez recalled that playing with Pahnieri "was a great learning experience." Through Palmieri, Sánchez was introduced to many important musicians, among them Paquito D'Rivera, Claudio Roditi, and Dizzy Gillespie. Upon hearing the young saxophonist play, Gillespie invited Sánchez to join his Grammy Award-winning United Nations Orchestra. "There's a young tenor player from Puerto Rico," Gillespie announced, as quoted by *hoppermanagement.com.* "David Sánchez: good, very reserved mind, very old mind, knows his changes, knows where he's going and knows where he's coming from." Sánchez toured with Gillespie's ensemble from 1990 to 1992, when an illness forced Gillespie to retire from music. (He died in January 1993.) Sánchez then participated in the historic, month-long "Dizzy's Diamond Jubilee" at New York's Blue Note nightclub. He was also featured on the celebrated recording *To Bird with Love: Live at the Blue Note* (1992), a tribute to the jazz legend Charlie Parker. He spent the rest of 1992 performing in a series of concerts presented throughout Europe and the U.S. in honor of Gillespie's 75th birthday.

The following year Sánchez signed a deal with Columbia Records, and in 1994 he released his debut solo album, *The Departure.* Describing a live performance that Sánchez gave to promote the album, the *Chicago Tribune* (September 3, 1994) critic Howard Reich wrote, "Technically, tonally and creatively, [Sánchez] seems to have it all. His sound is never less than plush, his pitch is unerring, his rapid-fire playing is ravishing in its combination of speed, accuracy and utter evenness of tone. More important, Sánchez clearly commands the ability to create unconventional, unexpected melodic lines that consistently keep the listener on edge." *The Departure* featured an all-star cast of supporting musicians, among them Danilo Perez on piano, bassists Andy Gonzalez and Peter Washington, trumpeter Tom Harrell, drummer Leon Parker, and percussionist Milton Cardona. The album's blend of Caribbean and jazz sounds reflected Sánchez's musical upbringing. "The jazz tradition and the Afro-Cuban stuff . . . they're the same rhythms," he told Eugene Holley for *Down Beat* (August 1994). "That strong 6/8 thing with the triplet [feel]-that's a thing that we have in the Caribbean and Latin America, and the United States." That correlation was noted by several critics, and the album was widely praised. Don Heckman of the *Los Angeles Times* (October 7, 1994) wrote, "Several originals were based on Caribbean rhythms. One of the most impressive, the multimetric 'The Departure,' initially echoed the buoyant dance qualities of Rican bomba bands. But Sánchez's soloing . . . quickly moved into more exotic territory. His string of choruses-exploding with a collection of sounds that reached across the length and breadth of his instrument-provided the final evidence that Sánchez is quickly becoming a player to be reckoned with."

Sánchez next recorded *Sketches of Dreams* (1995), which inspired additional respect for his talents in both critics and peers. For that album he was joined by the musicians who had contributed to *The Departure* as well as by the percussionist Jerry Gonzalez and the pianist David Kikoksi. In a review of *Sketches of Dreams* for the *Washington Post* (May 19, 1995), Mike Joyce wrote, "What separates the young saxophonist David Sánchez from most of his peers is his musical conception, one in which cultural heritage outweighs the fashionable tenets of neo-traditionalism. . . . The tone of his tenor sax is full and robust, and he swings through the chord changes like someone . . . in love. His elliptical approach to Rodgers and Hart's 'It's Easy to Remember' is further proof of his unusual maturity." After the album's release Sánchez embarked on a nationwide tour, which also received rave reviews. After attending one of Sánchez's concerts, Howard Reich wrote for the *Chicago Tribune* (April 13, 1995), "Of all the splendid young tenor saxophonists emerging on the national stage, surely none has more smarts, more depth, more purpose or more savvy than David Sánchez. . . . As a performer, Sánchez seems to know precisely what he wants to achieve on stage and how to attain it, wasting no gestures in the process. . . . The intricacy of [his] melody lines and the exquisitely slow vibrato he produced reaffirmed that some of the most mature playing in jazz these days is coming from some of the youngest artists in the business."

In spite of a busy tour schedule, Sánchez found the time to record his third album, *Street Scenes* (1996). In *Billboard* (October 5, 1996), Paul Verna referred to it as a "compelling showcase for [Sánchez's] raw rich sax timbres and well-sculpted solos." Demonstrating his skill as a composer, Sánchez wrote all but one track (a

Affiliation: Latin Jazz

In the *New York Times* (June 26, 1996), Jon Pareles wrote, "Sánchez is carrying Latin jazz toward the millennium, testing new ways to integrate Caribbean rhythms and jazz swing." Sánchez has also demonstrated an appreciation for the historical precedents of his music. Commenting on his fifth album, *Melaza* (2000), Sánchez told Don Heckman for the *Los Angeles Times* (December 8, 2000), "What I was trying to do . . . was to basically take things that came from the folkloric traditions of Puerto Rico and combine them with jazz. Mix up loose rhythms and harmonies of jazz. . . . It was my way of paying a little tribute to the Puerto Rican people who developed the music that I inherited." Sánchez's saxophone playing has been featured on many albums, and he has appeared live, both as a headlip.er and an accompanying musician, at such prestigious events as the Montreal and San Francisco jazz festivals. Two of Sánchez's solo efforts; *Obsession* (1998) and *Melaza*, were nominated for Grammy Awards.

piece by Thelonious Monk) on *Street Scenes.* In an assessment of *Street Scenes* for the *Washington Post* (November 22, 1996), Geoffrey Himes wrote, "Sánchez has a brawny tone on the tenor sax and an unusual, biting edge on the soprano horn, and he bulls his way through the chord changes toward strong, surprising solos. Yet he invents variations not only on the harmonies but on the syncopated Latin rhythms as well. . . . His striking compositions range widely from straight-ahead be-bop to breezy Brazilian romance to danceable salsa." "This new music challenges the cultural legacy of Europe in the Americas," Peter Watrous wrote for the *New York Times* (December 22, 1996). "And with its polyglot way of thinking, [it] does everything it can to counter the magnetic pull of a Eurocentric way of hearing." Sánchez's Caribbean background has always been a primary source of inspiration. "I wanted to be in touch with my roots, which come from Latin America," he was quoted as saying by *hoppermanagement.com.* "I believe that Latin jazz was born in the U.S., but I also believe that we are really one: North America, South America, the Caribbean. There are native people in these places who are related to each other. I'm trying to put that together in my music, trying to get in touch with the unity of it all while I integrate the stylistic elements from the different regions." In his conversation with Isabelle Leymarie, he said, "In Puerto Rico, 90 per cent of the music has black roots. I'm thinking of bomba, of course, but also the more hybrid plena, which is played with tambourines and appeared after the First World War, and danza, which is orchestrated for European instruments. Danza comes from the old courtly dances like the minuet, and when it arrived in the Caribbean in the eighteenth century, it picked up African syncopation."

In his next offering, *Obsesión* (1998), Sánchez Continued to provide listeners with his unique blend of Puerto Rican musical traditions and modern mainstream jazz. Co-produced with the saxophonist Branford Marsalis, the album ventured even deeper into Sánchez's past, evoking sounds enjoyed by his father and his grandfather. *"Obsesión* is a watershed album for Sánchez-a tribute to what he describes as the Cuban, Brazilian and Puerto Rican influences in his music," Don Heckman wrote for the *Los Angeles Times* (June 28, 1998). In *Hispanic* (October 1998), Mark Holston wrote, "On *Obsesión,* [Sánchez] reaches for an audience beyond the jazz crowd that he's successfully courted in recent years by recording a program of well-known romantic standards of decades past." As Bruce Handy pointed out for *Time* (May 18, 1998), Sánchez had tried to update and personalize the traditional Latin pieces that he chose to include on the album. "The tunes are Latin standards from Puerto Rico, Cuba and Brazil, and Sánchez delights in reversing fields on them, turning a gentle Antonio Carlos Jabim song, for instance, into a rowdy Caribbean parade," Handy wrote. *Obsesión* was nominated for a Grammy Award for best Latin jazz performance in 1999.

Sánchez's fifth album, released in 2000, is *Melaza.* The title, which is Spanish for "molasses," alludes to the connection between the labors of black sugarcane workers in the Caribbean and the process of making music. In the album's liner notes, Sánchez described the trials and tribulations of these workers, many of whom were slaves. (Slavery persisted on some Caribbean islands until the late 1880s.) "The end result of their backbreaking work, after the refining process, was sugar—sweet, with a rich taste," Sánchez wrote. "Despite suffering and deprivation, we celebrate the sweet and rich culture that is a vital part of our world." Many critics singled out *Melaza* as the highlight of Sánchez's career up to that point. In a review for *Down Beat* (March 2001), Howard Reich wrote that the album was Sánchez's "most accomplished recording to date," and one that "fearlessly merges various forms of jazz improvisation with the intricate Puerto Rican bomba and plena rhythms he grew up hearing. The result is a surprisingly fresh, dramatically charged music that's rhythmically more volatile, melodically more angular and harmonically more complex than most listeners are accustomed to hearing from less adventurous Latin jazz ensembles." "It's definitely a lot of stuff I put in that music," Sánchez told Reich, "and I don't blame some people if it takes them a minute to understand what we're doing.... For people who listen to the regular, straight-ahead Latin jazz, it's not going to be easy for them ... but this is what I have to do now." *Melaza* garnered Sánchez another Grammy nomination for best Latin jazz performance, in 2001. *"Melaza* is a beginning," he was quoted as saying on the Web site for Sony Music, his current record label. "I'm excited because little by little I'm starting to find a voice, starting to hear something I didn't hear before. If I didn't hear it before, that means I'm starting to get close to finding something, some voice that hasn't been there before. That's the beauty of music for me."

October 2, 2001 marked the release of Sánchez's latest musical offering, *Travesfa.* The musician's explanation for the title of the album appeared on Sony Music's Web site: *"Traversfa* is a crossing—not really the journey itself, but the motion and the movement of it. It's part of life, it's living, moving forward." As of the end of October, little had been published about the album. In an unsigned, highly laudatory assessment for the *Washington Post* (October 12, 2001), the reviewer wrote, "Sánchez is able to communicate where he's coming from and where he's going with just a handful of notes. Yet it's not necessary to be familiar with his background to fall under the spell of his sensuous tone." Sánchez, who was the album's sole producer, enlisted the services of the alto saxophonist Miguel Zenon to accompany him on many of the album's tracks. The results, as reported by the *Washington Post* critic, "reveal by turns the impressive strides Sánchez has made as an interpreter and a composer."

Personal Life

Sánchez lives in the New York City borough of Brooklyn.

Further Reading

Billboard p91 Oct. 5, 1996
Calgary Sun (on-line) June 23, 1998
Chicago Tribune I p29 Sep. 3, 1994, with photo
Down Beat p84 Oct. 2000, p46+ Mar. 2001, with photo
Hispanic p102 Oct. 1998
Los Angeles Times p10 Oct. 7, 1994, p66 June 28, 1998, F p23 Dec. 8, 2000, with photo
New York Times II p44 Dec. 22, 1996, with photo
San Francisco Chronicle E p3 Dec. 7, 2000, with photo
Time p97 May 18, 1998, with photo
Unesco Courier p48+ Jan. 1997
Washington Post N p14 Nov. 22, 1996

Christian Scott

Trumpeter

Born: 1983; New Orleans
Primary Field: Jazz and bebop
Group Affiliation: Various

Introduction

"Pretty consistently I have had people ask me why I'm not playing bebop, or tell me I should be playing bebop," Christian Scott, a 25-year-old, Grammy Award-nominated jazz trumpeter, told R. J. DeLuke for the Albany, New York, Times Union *(June 22, 2006). He was referring to the style of jazz that was established in the 1940s and is characterized by breakneck melodies and rapid chord changes played by small combos. "But I was born in 1983," he added. "[Bebop] pre-dates my existence by 20, 30, 40 years. . . . It was something that I was practicing and listening to, and in my musical infancy could try to get my foundation together. But it wasn't what was affecting me in my life." Scott, a New Orleans, Louisiana, native, has released two critically acclaimed albums and collaborated with a host of artists of varied genres, including Prince, Randy Jackson, and Jill Scott; he has been compared to prominent jazz trumpet players of the past and present, from Miles Davis to Wynton Marsalis.*

Early Life

Christian Scott was born in 1983 into a New Orleans family chock-full of artists and musicians. His mother, Cara Harrison, had played classical music in high school and college; his father is a visual artist whose work incorporates photography, sculpting, and drawing; and his grandfather Donald Harrison Sr. was both a well-known folk singer and the "big chief" of three Mardi Gras Indian tribes, groups of African-American revelers who for generations have dressed in Native American garb and danced in the Mardi Gras parade in a display of solidarity with the plight of Native Americans. As a young boy Scott's twin brother, Kiel, demonstrated talent as a guitarist, while Scott was more interested in football, baseball, and basketball than in music. (Kiellater became a visual artist and a filmmaker.) But at age 12—a late bloomer by New Orleans standards-Scott decided that he wanted to play trumpet. "I used to get teased all the time because most guys start[ed] playing trumpet or trombone when they were 4 or 5, as soon as they could hold the instrument," Scott told R. J. DeLuke. Although his mother encouraged him to play music, she would have preferred that he play an instrument offering a stronger foundation in chords and harmonics, such as piano, violin, or cello. Soon, though, she became reconciled to his choice of the trumpet and even spent evenings clapping out rhythms for him as he learned. Though not a trained musician, Donald Harrison Sr. also helped Scott by humming classic jazz tunes and asking Scott to play them back to him.

The person who probably influenced Scott's musical development most was Donald Harrison Jr. As Scott began to learn trumpet, Harrison "was stopping by the house between gigs dressed in the most beautiful cream-colored suits the boy had ever seen," as Keith O'Brien wrote for the New Orleans *Times-Picayune* (April 27, 2003). Admiring his uncle's talent and style, Scott asked him for guidance. So Harrison gave his nephew a recording of the jazz trumpeter Clifford Brown playing the song "Donna Lee," by the saxophonist Charlie Parker, who had helped to start bebop and was known for his high-speed, difficult-to-imitate improvisations. Harrison knew that the challenge of learning to play such music would either deter Scott from pursuing jazz or help him develop his own style. "Two weeks later he had learned it," Harrison told Dan Ouellette for *Down Beat* (May 2006). "At that time, I decided to do whatever I could to help him develop." Soon the teacher and student became inseparable, spending whole weekends together; according to Scott's mother, even their mannerisms became almost indistinguishable. "One of the first things that my uncle taught me is how to have musical tact," Scott recalled to Krolick. "All too often young musicians are plagued with the reality of having the skills to play, whereas I was more or less conditioned from the beginning not to worry about whether people thought I could play. It was all about me emoting and being able to come across on an emotional level that made the listener feel what we played."

Scott was a quick learner, impressing his instructors at all levels of his education. During high school he attended the New Orleans Center for Creative Arts (NOCCA), a pre-professional arts training center that provides, among other educational services, half-day intensive instruction for high-school students in music and other arts. The center's music program boasts such successful alumni as Branford, Wynton, Delfeayo, and Jason Marsalis and Harry Connick Jr. "You're supposed to start there your sophomore or junior year," Scott told Yoshi Kato for the *San Jose (California) Mercury News* (September 13, 2007). "I started in my freshman year, and the curriculum was really easy for me, since I had been hanging out with, and learning from, my uncle." After Scott finished high school, Wynton Marsalis encouraged him to attend the prestigious Juilliard School of Music, in New York City. Instead, not wanting to commit himself to a narrowly focused sound or scene, Scott enrolled at the Berklee School of Music, in Boston, Massachusetts, where he received a full scholarship. "I needed to find out who I was," Scott told Ouellette. "I didn't want to be so defined at my age. I wanted to go into a classroom and see some dude with a mohawk and meet people who were into rock and hip-hop as well as jazz." At Berklee, Scott, along with other first-year students, was required to take a series of placement tests in harmony and ear training. It was common for a student to fail or not finish many of the tests, as most students stopped when they came across parts of the tests they did not understand. Scott was the only student in his class to complete and pass all of the tests, prompting administrators to insist that he be retested; when he passed the second round, some professors gave him tests in individual subjects. "And after I tested out [of] all of those, they figured I wasn't [messing] around," Scott told Kato.

Life's Work

Meanwhile, in 2000, Scott joined his uncle and the other members of the Donald Harrison Quintet on tour, performing at festivals and concerts across the country, including the New Orleans Jazz and Heritage Festival and the M&T Jazz Fest-Syracuse. Mark Bialczak wrote for the Syracuse, New York, *Post-Standard* (June 24, 2000) that as Scott began playing the tune "Christopher, Jr.," "eyes opened. Jaws dropped. The crowd shrieked. Uncle Don smiled as wide as the stage." Howard Reich, writing for the *Chicago Tribune* (December 14, 2000), described Scott's still-developing style during his show at Chicago's Metropolis Performing Arts Centre: "In the ballad, 'Misty,' he played the first refrain with a gauzy, breathy tone that provided some of his most individualistic music-making of the evening. And the way he dispatched his final 'Misty' solo, taking his time between gestures and ending with a disarmingly simple phrase, pointed to a young musician with poise." Reich also identified some flaws in Scott's performance—"his tendency to rely on familiar scale patterns, relatively simple chord structures and oft-repeated technical stunts"—which, Reich thought, suggested that it may have been too early for Scott to "step into the . . . spotlight." Rick Nowlin, a reporter for the *Pittsburgh Post-Gazette* (June 13, 2001), reviewed a concert at which Scott, who "quite literally just graduated from high school, pretty much stole the show." Those early listeners and reviewers were impressed not only with Scott's technical skills and range but also with the mature style he had developed at such a young age. Some drew parallels between Scott's trumpet playing and the early work of such jazz legends as Miles Davis and Louis Armstrong. They also took note of his ability to produce remarkably soft, "round, fuzzy notes" that did not sound as if they were made by a trumpet. Writing for the Newcastle upon Tyne, England, *Morning Star* (December 27, 2002) about Harrison's album *Kind of New,* on which Scott performed, Chris Searle called the trumpeter's playing "wistfully quiet, note-perfect, almost becalmed . . . [as] if he was mollifying brass, transforming metal into a muted woodwind." Scott produces those sounds, which have also been called "haunting," by means of his circular breathing of warm air through his instrument. To perfect the sound, he took advice from the veteran swing and bop trumpeter Clark Terry and ignored the instructions of textbooks and music teachers. "It took me two years of concentration to come up with that tone . . . ," Scott told Fred Shuster for the *Daily News of Los Angeles* (June 14, 2006). "I like it because it makes the trumpet sound like the human voice." Scott said that his breakthrough came when he decided to focus on capturing a specific sound. "The thing that I tried to emulate was my mother's singing voice," he said.

In 2002 Scott graduated from Berklee with degrees in professional music and film scoring, having completed the five-year program in just two years. The same year Scott released a self-titled, self-produced album and began shopping it to local music stores. After graduating Scott toured regularly with the guitarist Matt Stevens, the tenor saxophonist Walter Smith III, the

Affiliation: Bebop Influences

Scott was mentored by his uncle, the accomplished saxophonist Donald Harrison Jr., who advised him to develop his own style and to limit the influence of other contemporary trumpeters on his playing. Perhaps as a result, Scott learned to play soft, breathy, "round" notes that sometimes sound as close to a human voice as to a brass instrument, and when he was just 16, he made a name for himself when he accompanied his uncle's band on a nationwide tour. The pieces on his two albums to date, *Rewind That* (2006) and *Anthem* (2007), were deeply influenced by his personal experiences and his views on sociopolitical issues. Suggesting Davis's influence, both of Scott's records—especially *Anthem*—also demonstrate an enthusiasm for infusing jazz with elements from other musical genres, including funk, hip-hop, and indie rock, using heavy guitar riffs, for example, or overlaid rap vocals. Those choices, while eliciting some flak from jazz traditionalists, have also won him popularity and critical praise from those who support such innovation and boundary-pushing. "[Scott] embodies all we have grown to love from past jazz heavyweights while pushing boundaries with today's beboppers," Jake Krolick wrote for the music Web site Jambase.com in the fall of 2007. "When Scott plays his trumpet he blows down jazz barriers but also cultural, economic and emotional obstacles. Scott is one of the most progressive jazz musicians of our time, playing with a unique tone and candor. He is an artist for all the right reasons, who loves his chosen craft as well as embracing indie rock, neo-soul and hip-hop." Scott's first live album, *Live at Newport* (2008), was expected to arrive in stores on November 4, 2008.

keyboardist Zaccai Curtis, the bassist Luques Curtis, and the drummer Jamire Williams. In 2003 Scott and his sextet were invited to perform on their own stage at the New Orleans Jazz and Heritage Festival, as the trumpeter had long dreamed of doing. Scott also played more shows with his uncle. Reviewers continued to predict great things for the young man. In 2004, while promoting his self-titled record at a performance at a Virgin music store, Scott was approached by a former distributor for the record label Concord Music Group. Impressed by both the music and the packed crowd, the distributor asked to hear the whole album and urged him to send it to Concord; soon the label offered Scott a record deal. Scott accepted on the condition that he would not be required to play traditional jazz and would be able to incorporate elements from a variety of genres.

Scott was still in Boston when Hurricane Katrina caused flooding that ravaged his hometown in August 2005, an event that affected him deeply as a person and a musician. After the catastrophe Scott's family moved to Houston, Texas, and Scott relocated to New York City, a move he had been contemplating for some time. In March 2006 Concord Records released Scott's major-label debut album, *Rewind That,* which featured Scott's minimalist trumpet lines over Matt Stevens's heavy guitar work. The album consists of 11 tracks, including two covers—Miles Davis's "So What" and "Paradise Found," by Donald Harrison Jr. and nine original tunes that vary greatly in mood and tempo. Each one was inspired by a personal experience or, according to Scott, a specific conversation. "Rejection" is a somber ballad mourning a painful breakup, while "Suicide" is intended to call attention to trigeminal neuralgia, a rare nerve disease afflicting Scott's mother, which causes pain so intense that it has been dubbed "the suicide disease." The final song on the album, the funk-inflected "Kiel," is dedicated to Scott's twin brother, a visual artist who Scott said is "10 times more talented than I'll ever be," according to Jack W. Hill, writing for the *Arkansas Democrat Gazette* (September 8, 2006). Scott's uncle is featured on four of the tunes. *Rewind That* was met with many rave reviews, with critics praising Scott's ability to draw from Miles Davis's work of the 1970s and 1980s while incorporating elements from a variety of contemporary genres. Scott McLennan wrote for the Massachusetts *Telegram and Gazette* (August 10, 2006) that the album is "full of poise, passion and precision, linking traditional jazz to contemporary grooves." In the Victoria, British Columbia, *Times Colonist* (May 14, 2006), Joseph Blake identified Scott as "the future of jazz" and as being "wise beyond his years, a thoughtful, less-is-more master of his instrument and a very fine composer of urbane, modern music that is steeped in the blues and jazz tradition of his hometown, but, taking his cues from Miles Davis's electric bands, liberated and fearless enough to establish a new sound with his burnished, muscular playing." Although the vast majority of critics complimented what Ouellette called the trumpeter's "deep, smoky, reson[ant] tone," there were some critics who did not warm to Scott's style. Writing for the Raleigh, North Carolina, *News & Observer* (July 2, 2006), Owen Cordle complained, "Scott's [playing] often seems calculatedly world-weary and bloodless.... He's obviously a stronger jazzman than this album indicates. But as it is, there are breathy long tones and a fluffy delivery-the stuff of smooth jazz." By his own account Scott, who greatly values musical freedom, does not mind if some listeners are displeased. He told Fred Shuster, "Everyone wanted me to do a straight-ahead [jazz] album, but that's like meeting a woman and trying to be like her last boyfriend. You've got to be special." In 2006 *Rewind That* received a Grammy nomination for best new jazz album, and Scott was named by *Billboard* magazine as one of its "names to watch." As a result of the exposure from *Rewind That,* such non-jazz artists as Prince and the *American Idol* judge Randy Jackson invited him to collaborate with them; Scott wrote and recorded two songs for Prince's album *Planet Earth* and recorded a track for Jackson's upcoming album, *American Music, Volume 1. Ebony* magazine chose Scott as one of its "30 Young Leaders Under 30" in 2007.

Scott and his bandmates toured internationally in 2006 and 2007, performing in jazz clubs and other venues. While on the road, Scott woke up at 6:00 a.m. each day to compose the pieces that would make up his second album, *Anthem.* He told an interviewer for *Down Beat* (June 2007) to expect from that album an even broader array of musical elements than were heard on his first record, including indie rock, classical music, hip-hop, and R&B. Indeed, upon its release, in August 2007, *Anthem* was hailed as an innovative collection that stretched the limits of traditional jazz. Scott told Farai Chideya, host of the National Public Radio program *News and Notes* (September 5, 2007), that he sometimes referred to his music as "razz," a mixture of rock and jazz. Bob Karlovits noted for the *Pittsburgh Tribune-Review* (September 2, 2007), "Christian Scott is heading in the direction

Miles Davis would have been, were he still alive. This is not to elevate Scott to the Davis level, but it is to say *Anthem* is an album that looks for a legitimate new direction in music. . . . Scott is a fine trumpet player, but is showing here even more strength as a conceptualist." Scott played cornet and flugelhorn as well as trumpet on the 12 tunes, to add variety to the moods of the album. Most reviewers, however, considered the album as a whole to be significantly darker than his first collection; Charles J. Gans, writing for the Associated Press (August 30, 2007), called the album "edgier and more brooding." As with his first album, Scott drew from both personal experiences and his reactions to sociopolitical issues for each composition's emotional energy. "The thing about *Anthem,"* Scott told Kato, "is that it's so tied in to my life and the experiences of the last. year and my feelings about what has happened in New Orleans, what hasn't happened in Darfur, what is happening in Iraq. . . , So this music wasn't just about music; it became a musical interpretation of what I was going through." His feelings about the aftermath of Hurricane Katrina inspired several pieces, including "Void" and "Anthem (Antediluvian Adaptation)," the latter of which also features an angry rap from Brother J of the group X-Clan. The title of the ballad "Katrina's Eyes," however, refers not to the hurricane but to Scott's baby daughter. Scott's talent has earned him guest spots as a performer with the singer Jill Scott and the rapper Mos Def. He has said that he would most like to perform with the rock group Radiohead.

Scott has often felt pressure from the critical establishment to conform to the conventional path for jazz musicians. While he seems to have thrived on resisting that pressure, he recognizes a danger for other young musicians in a similar position. Though he agrees that music schools should expose students to the work of past jazz greats, he believes that forcing students to imitate them makes it difficult for them to find their own styles. "The main idea should not be to sound like guys that have already done what they needed to do," Scott told Krolick. "There's another strength, not taught, that makes musicians become individuals."

Scott planned to release his third record, *Live at Newport,* on November 4, 2008. The album features Scott's live performance at the JVC Newport Jazz Festival in Newport, Rhode Island, three songs from his previous two albums, and five new tracks, including "Died In Love," "Isadora," and "The Crawler." The album will be sold with a DVD of Scott's live performances and a behind-the-scenes look at his rehearsals prior to the Newport festival. Scott had small parts in the 2008 films *Leatherheads* and *Rachel Getting Married.*

Personal Life

Scott volunteers regularly for the nonprofit NO/AIDS Task Force in New Orleans. As of the spring of 2006, he shared an apartment in downtown Manhattan with his twin brother, Kiel, a student of filmmaking at New York University.

Further Reading

Daily News of Los Angeles U p6 June 14, 2006;
Down Beat p29 May 2006; Jambase.com;
(New Orleans, Louisiana) *Times Picayune* Living p1 Apr. 27, 2003;
San Jose Mercury News Music Sep. 13, 2007

Sean Paul

Singer-songwriter

Born: Jan. 8, 1973; Kingston, Jamaica
Primary Field: Jamaican dancehall reggae artist
Group Affiliation: Solo performer

Introduction

"Music is the voice of the Jamaican people,"' the dancehall-reggae singer/songwriter Sean Paul told Steve Garbarino for the New York Times *(May 30, 2004). "We think about it hour to hour, year to year. The speed of it changes, the voice changes. But it always depends on what is happening in our society." In the United States, the 34-year-old Sean Paul is the best-known performer of dancehall, a genre that originated in Jamaica, his native land, around the time of his birth. Dancehall mixes elements of rap and reggae; the singers, known as deejays or sing-jays, vocalize over a digitized bass-and-drum background, sometimes incorporating the melodies of others' earlier songs.*

Early Life

The singer was born Sean Paul Henriques to Garth and Frances ("Fran") Henriques on January 8, 1973 in Kingston, the capital of Jamaica, a small island nation less than 100 miles south of Cuba in the Caribbean Sea. (Some sources, among them the Library of Congress, have erroneously listed "Paul" as the singer's surname.) He and his younger brother, Jason "Jigzag" Henriques, were raised in Norbrook, a relatively well-to-do, uptown section of Kingston. In Jamaica Sean Paul is known as an "uptown" deejay, thus distinguishing him from most other dancehall artists, who grew up in impoverished neighborhoods. In recent years the incomes of at least one-sixth of Jamaica's population of 2.75 million have remained below the poverty level, with economic deprivation particularly severe in rural areas. In parts of Kingston and other cities, gang violence connected with the drug trade is common; the high level of violent crime has also been linked to the activities of the island's major political parties and their deeply entrenched patronage systems. Sean Paul explained to Joseph Patel for the *Boston Globe* (November 22, 2002) that neighborhoods like Norbrook are for "people who could afford luxuries like running water, people who could afford a car. It's not ghetto, but not American luxury by any means." With his very mixed genetic heritage, Sean Paul is typical of many Jamaicans, whose country's motto is "Out of many, one people." Both of his parents are native-born Jamaicans. Some of his father's forebears came to Jamaica from Africa; others were Sephardic Jews from Portugal who settled on the island in the 17th century. Sean Paul's mother is descended from immigrants from China and England. Sean Paul's skin tone is unusual among Jamaicans, and it led his childhood friends to refer to him as "copper-color Chiney bwoy," according to the Web site dancehallminded.com.

Sean Paul's father, a businessman, and his mother, a professional artist, were champion swimmers, his father in long-distance swimming and his mother in the butterfly stroke. His father also excelled at water polo; in recent years he has coached the national Jamaican water-polo team, and currently he is the vice president of the Amateur Swimming Association of Jamaica. In a conversation with Ian Burrell for the London *Independent* (September 2, 2005, on-line), Sean Paul described his father as a "hustler." He came from a good family but didn't do a lot of schooling," he said. "We had to go and get him and pick him up from the ghettos where he would be burning a chalice [marijuana pipe] with his friends. That kind of stuff happened regularly when I was a kid." When Sean Paul was 13 years old, his father was convicted of illegal narcotics trafficking and sentenced to prison; he spent the next six years behind bars. In his father's absence, Sean Paul has told interviewers, his mother provided comforting nurturance and firm discipline. His relationship with his father since the latter's release from prison, he told an interviewer for the "dot rap magazine" *Murder Dog* (June 2003, on-line), is "all good"; according to other reports, the two have only occasional contact.

During his early years Sean Paul attended the Hillel Academy, a nonsectarian, multicultural private school founded by Kingston's Jewish community. As a teenager he transferred to Walmer's Boys' School, a sports-oriented high school near downtown Kingston, where many of his classmates were economically disadvantaged and teased him about his middle-class lifestyle; some bullied him. He had little interest in academics and "wasn't a great student," as he told the *Murder Dog* interviewer. Starting at about 14 he became active in competitive swimming. Honing his skills in freestyle swimming and the backstroke, he joined the Jamaican national swim team, which participated in contests internationally as well as in Jamaica. He also joined the Jamaican national waterpolo team. Swimming, he told Ian Burrell, "taught me a lot of discipline. Exercise does a lot for the mind. Knowing that my father and mother were champions meant that I had a lot to look up to, to try and be a champion for Jamaica for myself. I'm still a swimmer and the swim team are my closest friends."

After he completed high school, Sean Paul attended the College of Arts, Science, and Technology (also called the University of Technology, Jamaica), where he studied hotel management and took classes in cooking. After two years he dropped out. He then worked briefly as a bank teller. He has recalled how impressed he was by a customer who deposited several million dollars during a single week. "It made me realize how much money was out there in the world," he said to Alana Wartofsky, who interviewed him for the *Washington Post* (September 13, 2000), "and [that] I should go out and get some of it." With the idea that he might accomplish that goal as a professional musician, in about 1994 Sean Paul began to spend much of his time writing songs.

Music, Sean Paul has said, has always been a big part of his life. His mother often played recorded music at home—he remembers in particular hearing songs by the Beatles-and as a Jamaican, as he told the *Murder Dog* interviewer, he would hear reggae music "all over the place, everywhere." Reggae originated in the 1960s in Jamaican shantytowns, providing an outlet for some of the many poverty-stricken residents who despaired of improving their lot in life. Associated with such performers as Bob Marley and the Wailers, Peter Tosh (one of the Wailers), Jimmy Cliff, and Desmond Dekker, reggae often focused on calls for social and political justice and other public issues. Dancehall reggae, or simply dancehall, came into being in the 1970s and took hold in Jamaica in the 1980s, when the digital revolution blossomed; it is distinguished from reggae by the bawdiness ("slackness," in Jamaican slang) of the lyrics and the presence in every song of an aggressive riddim (a Jamaican slang term for "rhythm"), a digitized bass and drum background whose beats are significantly faster than those of reggae. "The rhythm isn't merely a pattern of beats, it's an electronic composition—add some singing or shouting and your song is done," Kelefa Sanneh wrote for the *New York Times* (March 9, 2003, online). (There are dozens of riddims, with new ones being created each year. Each riddim has a name, such as Sleng Teng, Playground, Space Invaders, Ching Chong, Bookshelf, Bada Bada, Diwali, and Jonkanoo; often, the name is derived from the first song that used it.) Other characteristics of dancehall are singsong intonations and the use of a patois that is often unintelligible to non-Jamaicans. Dancehall rapping is called "toasting."

During Sean Paul's childhood his mother arranged for him to take piano lessons, but he disliked them and soon discontinued them. When he entered his teens, his mother, at his request, bought him an inexpensive electronic keyboard, which he used to create simple riddims. By that time he had become an ardent fan of dancehall and of such dancehall stars as Super Cat, Shabba Ranks, Major Worries, Papa San, and Lt. Stitchie; he also found hip-hop music from the U.S. to his liking. He enjoyed helping one of his aunts in her "sound system" business, called Sparkles Disco. The proprietors of such enterprises, which sprang up in Jamaica during the 1950s, travel with generators, records or CD players, and large speakers and provide music for street parties that they have organized. Attendees, sometimes numbering in the thousands, pay for admission and food and drinks. A sound system's major draw is brand-new music. Sean Paul sometimes performed his own songs at his aunt's street parties.

Life's Work

In the early 1990s Sean Paul tried without success. to form a business relationship with one or another experienced record producer. "No producer at the time would look at me as that kind of DJ," he recalled to Alana Wartofsky. "They said, 'No one's gonna hear that from you because you don't come from the ghetto, you don't really know these experiences, and because of your class and complexion. Your image is just different.... It's not marketable from you at this time.'" A turning point came in about 1993, when his father introduced him to a longtime acquaintance of his, Stephen "Cat" Coore, a founding member of the popular Jamaican reggae group Third World. Impressed by Sean Paul's musical talents, Coore arranged for him to record demos in the producer Rupert Bent's small music studio, which Third World used. Sean Paul soon gained access to other studios as well, and he started to become a familiar figure among Jamaican musicians. To make himself known among the public, he began making dub plates-one-off vinyl records-for sound systems in addition to his aunt's, among them Stone Love, Renaissance, and Coppershot, the last-named being that of his brother. (Jigzag Henriques has been involved in the making of all of Sean Paul's recordings.) By 1996, Sean Paul told the *Murder Dog* interviewer, "everybody was trying to get dubs from me." That year, with the producer Jeremy Harding, whom he had met in 1995, he recorded "Baby Girl (Don't Cry)," using Harding's Fearless riddim; it received wide radio play in Jamaica and became his first hit there (but is not included on any of Sean Paul's albums). During that period he became associated with the Dutty Cup Crew ("dutty" being slang for "dirty"), a group of aspiring deejays including Don Yute, Mossy Kid, Looga Man, Kid Kurupt, Chicken, Daddigon, and Froggy. (The names of some of them appear with alternate spellings on various Web sites.) During the next few years, in addition to performing occasionally with the Dutty Cup Crew, Sean Paul recorded several singles that enjoyed great popularity in Jamaica: "Infiltrate," made with Jeremy Harding's Playground/Zim Zimma riddim, and "Hackle Mi," also produced by Harding; "Nah Get No Bly (One More Try)," with Donovan Germain as producer; and "Excite Me" and "Deport Them," with Tony Kelly as producer. "Deport Them," made with Kelly's Bookshelf riddim, was aired by radio stations in Miami, Florida, and New York City as well as Jamaica. The reggae specialist Derek A. Bardowell wrote for the *Voice* (September 9, 2002) that at that time in his career, Sean Paul sounded like one of the originators of dancehall Super Cat, with "words crawling out of his mouth as if they'd endured piercing heat for some hours but delivered with the intensity of someone slightly irritated"-and like "a vexed weed head," or a person who smokes a lot of marijuana (as does Sean Paul). With the dancehall artist Mr. Vegas and the rapper DMX, Sean Paul recorded the song "Here Comes the Boom" (also called "Top Shotta" or "Top Shatter") for the soundtrack of the director Hype Williams's debut feature film, *Belly* (1998), starring DMX. Also with Mr. Vegas, he recorded the crossover hit "Hot Gal Today," made with the producers Steely and Clevie's Street Sweeper riddim, which in 1999 reached the top of the reggae charts in Jamaica and hit the number-six spot on *Billboard's* Top Rap Singles chart. Both "Hot Gal Today" and "Deport Them" appeared in the Top 100 on *Billboard's* R&B Singles chart, the former at number 66 and the latter at 85.

In June 2000 Sean Paul performed at Summer Jam, an annual outdoor concert sponsored by the New York City radio station WQHT (known as Hot 97 FM); other entertainers at the event included Jay-Z, Dr. Dre, Snoop Dogg, Eminem, and Aaliyah. His appearance at the concert followed by a few months the release of his debut album, *Stage One,* which became a big seller in Jamaica. Although *Stage One* sold poorly in the U.S., *Billboard* named it the number-four reggae album of the year, while ranking Sean Paul third among reggae artists of 2000. In a review of *Stage One* for the All Music Guide Web site, Rosalind Cummings-Yeates wrote, "Since [Sean Paul] possesses neither an unusual voice nor outstanding skill, this CD can become rather tiresome after awhile.... Still, there are some enjoyable tunes here." Alona Wartofsky credited part of Sean Paul's appeal to "the way he rides the beats." "Dancehall artists chant their lyrics over spare, percussive rhythm tracks," she explained, "and their gift for filling the space is as important as a rapper's talent for lyrical flow. Sean Paul's vocal style is reminiscent of vintage dancehall star Supercat, the words coming flat and fast." Wartofsky also wrote, "The 17 songs and eight skits and interludes ... suggest that Sean Paul is preoccupied with women: getting them to look right, getting them to act right, getting them into bed right, then getting rid of them." Noting that two of the tracks, "Next Generation" and "You Must Lose," deal with the issues of poverty and violence, she wrote, "These tracks suggest that perhaps Sean Paul, like so many dancehall stars before him, may find that his passions shift as his career develops." Sean Paul told Cary Darling for the *Miami Herald* (June 9, 2000), "That's my image, to be the player. But I'm trying to bring it forward with more conscious vibes."

With *Dutty Rock* (2002), made in collaboration with the producers Tony Touch, Rahzel, the Neptunes, and others, Sean Paul achieved great commercial success in the U.S. and Europe as well as in Jamaica. One of the disc's tracks, "Get Busy," was certified gold by the Australian Recording Industry Association and rose to the top spot on the *Billboard* Hot 100 chart. A second single, "Gimme the Light," which features catchy instrumentals created by the Miami-based producer Troyton Rami, reached number seven on the same chart. The popularity of "Gimme the Light" was attributed in part to its video, which celebrated popular Jamaican dance moves and enjoyed regular play on MTV. "Gimme the Light" refers to a potent form of hydroponic marijuana known as "dro" in American slang and contains the phrase "pass the dro." Speaking to Rashaun Hall for *Billboard* (November 23, 2002), Sean Paul explained

Affiliation: Reggae

After describing Sean Paul as "reggae's biggest success" since Bob Marley, Kelefa Sanneh, a pop-music critic for the *New York Times* (March 25, 2006), wrote that he "makes hits by making only minimal changes to the genre's standard operating procedure. He slides cool, tuneful rhymes over sharp dancehall beats.... What's most exciting about Sean Paul is his example: he has helped prove that the old model of crossing over is outdated. You don't need to overhaul your sound or hire an American star; all you need is a great beat and an infectious hook." *Dutty Rock* (2002), the second of the three albums that Sean Paul has released since 2000, has sold some six million copies worldwide; it won a Grammy Award as best reggae album in 2003 and earned Sean Paul a bevy of other honors, including the MTV Europe Award for best new act of the year. His single "Temperature," from *The Trinity (2005),* his third album, claimed the top spot on the *Billboard* Hot 100 singles chart in early 2006. "I try to write familiar songs, songs people can listen to in clubs," Sean Paul said to reporters for *Teen People* (March 1, 2003). "I try to keep it on an international vibe so all people can feel my music."

that, with words as well as music, he consciously tried to lure Americans into singing along with "Gimme the Light": "I've had a few other hits . . . and I noticed that people liked the songs but they couldn't understand certain things I was saying. Since I wanted to cross over into the hip-hop world, I figured I should start writing songs that hip-hop heads would be able to pick up easier. That's why 'Gimme the Light' is so successful. It has a good melody, it's on a straight dancehall riddim, and people can identify with the words." Another single from *Dutty Rock,* "Baby Boy," for which Sean Paul collaborated with the American R&B singer and megastar Beyoncé Knowles, spent nine weeks at number one on the *Billboard* Hot 100 chart in the summer of 2003. *"Dutty Rock* is almost revolutionary," Tim Sendra wrote for the All Music Guide Web site, in one of many favorable reviews of the album, in which he also described it as "infectious," "bursting with hooks and filled with energy," and "easy to dance to." Sean Paul "has a good ear for melody and his flat, distinctive voice is perfect for his singjay style." In 2003 *Dutty Rock* earned the Grammy and the *Source* magazine awards for best reggae album, and Sean Paul was named MTV Europe's best new artist.

Sean Paul's third and most recent album, *The Trinity* (2005), was three years in the making and was recorded entirely in Jamaica, using Jamaican artists. "I felt a sense of responsibility to give people a great record and also give a chance to younger people back home," Sean Paul said to Mark Edward Nero for the *San Diego (California) UnionTribune* (December 2, 2005). "So I went back there to do the album." *The Trinity* earned mixed reviews. Tim Sendra, for example, wrote that the preponderance of the album's tracks are "hypersexualized, tough, and semi-raw" and that "each song relies on standard synth sounds and straightforward beats and there are precious few surprises on the record, sound-wise." He continued, "[Sean Paul's] vocals are strong enough but, overall, lack the freshness and vigor of those on *Dutty Rock."* Such lukewarm assessments notwithstanding, "Temperature," a dance anthem and the second single to be released from the record (the first single was "We Be Burnin'"), became very popular, reaching number one on the *Billboard* Hot 100 chart.

Sean Paul's solo performances or collaborations with other artists are included on dozens of albums in addition to his own. Among them are *Platinum Jam '98, Df's Choice* (2000), *Reggae Gold 2000, Ultimate Dancehall* Mix, Vol. 1 (2000), Michael Knott's *Things I've Done, Things to Come* (2000), Riddim *Ryders,* Vol. 1 (2001), Kardinal Offishall's *Quest for Fire: Firestarter,* Vol. 1 (2001), and Choobakka's My *Time* (2002). Feature-film soundtracks to which he has contributed include *Shark's Tale* and *Chasing Liberty* (both 2004) and *Step Up* (2006). Sean Paul has also made many appearances on TV, on such programs as *The Tonight Show with Jay Lena, Late Night with Conan O'Brien, Live with Regis and Kathie Lee, It's Showtime at the Apollo,* and at the opening ceremonies of the 2007 Cricket World Cup.

In September 2006 Sean Paul began recording a new album. In light of the deaths of two of his friends from violence in Jamaica, many of its songs will address more serious issues than his earlier songs. "The content is just a little different than what people expect from me," he told MTV News (January 23, 2007, online). "[On] one or two of the songs ... it's not about partying, it's not about ladies; it's about the kids with the guns in the streets. It's more reality."

Personal Life

Sean Paul lives in a suburb of Kingston with his mother, grandmother, and brother. He donated $1 million to help victims of Hurricane Ivan, which caused widespread devastation in Jamaica in 2004.

Further Reading

All Music Guide Web site
Boston Globe C p14 Nov. 22, 2002
dancehallminded.com
DancehallReggae.com
(London) *Independent* (on-line) Sep. 2, 2005
Jamaica Gleaner (on-line) Dec. 18, 2003
Sean Paul's Web site
Washington Post G p1+ Nov. 24, 2002

Peter Seeger

Singer, songwriter

Born: May 3, 1919; New York, New York
Died: January 27, 2014; New York, New York
Primary Field: Folk music
Group Affiliation: People's Songs Union

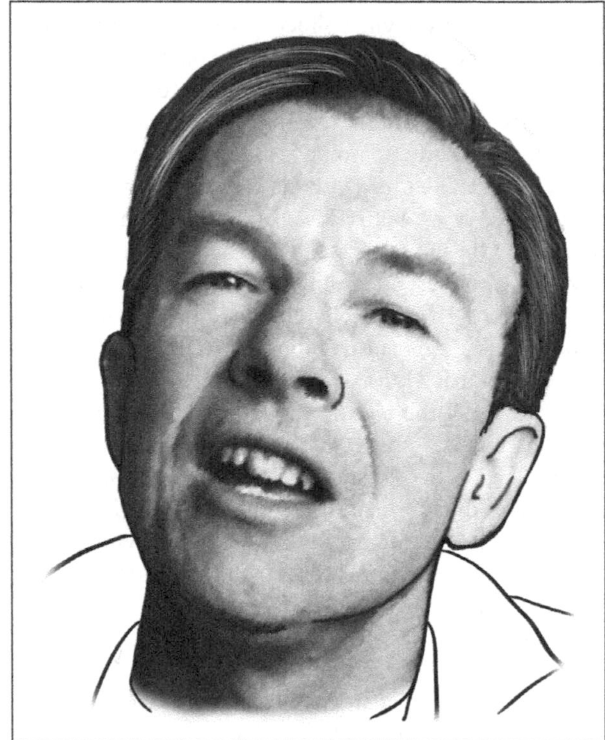

Pete Seeger.

Introduction

A "reincarnated troubadour," "America's tuning fork," and the "Thomas Jefferson" of folk music, Pete Seeger was perhaps more responsible than anyone else for the vogue of folk music in the United States. After taking to the road in the late 1930s, he presented a cross-section of American life in song to audiences throughout the world, and he was considered one of the best- informed scholars in folk music. A master of the five-string banjo, Seeger was also an authority on the guitar, the recorder, and the Trinidad steel drums. Over the years he recorded some fifty-two studio albums, twenty-three compilation albums, twenty-two live albums, and thirty-one singles for Folkways, Columbia, and other companies, and his activities also included song writing, film production, and research, editing, and writing in the folk music field. Although Seeger's acute sense of social justice and his insistence on freedom of speech and association brought him into conflict with the House Un-American Activities Committee and caused him to be blacklisted by television networks, he acquired a huge following, especially among young people, and his audiences included some Rockefellers as well as hoboes and migratory workers.

Early Life

Descended from Colonial settlers who came to New England some 300 years ago, Pete Seeger counted among his ancestors religious dissenters, Revolutionary War soldiers, and abolitionists. His family, mostly New Englanders and Pennsylvanians, was "shot through with pedagogues, doctors, occasional businessmen, and occasional artists." (The World War I poet Alan Seeger, author of the famous poem "I Have a Rendezvous with Death," was an uncle of his.) A native of New York City, Peter Seeger was born on May 3, 1919 to Dr. Charles Louis Seeger, a musicologist, conductor, author, and educator who was on the faculty of the University of California at Los Angeles, and to Constance de Clyver (Edson) Seeger, a violinist and teacher. He had two older brothers, Charles L. and John P.; through his father's second marriage, to the late Ruth Crawford Seeger (also a noted musicologist), he had a half-brother, Michael, and three half-sisters, Margaret (Peggy), Barbara Mona, and Penelope.

After completing his primary education at public schools in Nyack, New York and at the Spring Hill School in Litchfield, Connecticut, Seeger attended secondary school at Avon Old Farms, a private boarding school in Avon, Connecticut, where he took part in dramatics, edited the school paper, and had ambitions of becoming an artist or a journalist. Having been exposed mainly to classical music during his childhood, Pete Seeger had little contact with any music at the grass roots. His interest in folk music, and particularly in the five-string banjo, was first aroused when in 1935 he accompanied his father to a folk festival in Asheville, North Carolina. The experience was a revelation and opened a new world to him.

Life's Work

In 1936 Seeger entered Harvard University, where he majored in sociology and served as secretary of the Harvard Student Union. He decided to cut short his formal education, however, and left Harvard in 1938 during his sophomore year, to seek his fortune on the open road. Roaming through the New England countryside, he painted rural landscapes in watercolors and bartered them for his basic needs. In the next few years he covered thousands of miles, often by riding the rods or hitchhiking, traveling through the Depression-ridden United States as a folk singer. He performed on street corners and in hobo jungles, migrant camps, saloons, and churches. Along the way he learned "a little something from everybody," picking up songs and banjo techniques from farmers, workers, and mountaineers, and building a vast repertoire of ballads and blues, spirituals, lullabies, work songs, and country dance tunes.

Among the major influences upon Seeger's life and career during this period were the Oklahoma balladeer and folk composer, Woody Guthrie; the "king of the twelve-string guitar," Huddie Ledbetter (Leadbelly); and the curator of the Archive of American Folk Song at the Library of Congress, Dr. John A. Lomax, and his son, Alan. As part of his self-education as a folk musician, Seeger spent considerable time in Washington, listening to the recordings in the Archive of American Folk Song and working as an assistant in the archive, classifying records. He also accompanied the Lomaxes on field trips, recording songs in remote areas of the country, and he appeared on Lomax's CBS radio program, along with Woody Guthrie and Leadbelly.

In 1940 Seeger joined with Lee Hays, Woody Guthrie, Millard Lampell, and others in the Almanac Singers, a group that toured the United States and recorded albums of sea shanties, "sod- buster ballads," work songs, and union and topical songs. Later, Seeger teamed up with Guthrie, singing at migrant camps and union halls in the South and Southwest, touring Mexico, collaborating on the writing of labor and anti-Fascist songs, and singing on overseas broadcasts for the Office of War Information. Inducted into the Army in 1942, Seeger spent three and a half years with Special Services, entertaining troops in the United States and the South Pacific and adding soldier songs to his repertoire.

The folk music revival was given momentum by the appearance of the Weavers, a four-member singing group established in 1948 by Seeger, Lee Hays, Ronnie Gilbert, and Fred Hellerman. After making their professional debut at the Village Vanguard in New York City in late 1949 the Weavers appeared on national radio and television programs, sang in leading night clubs and in theaters throughout the United States, and turned such folk songs as "On Top of Old Smoky," "Goodnight, Irene," and "So Long, It's Been Good to Know You" into national hits. By 1952 sales of their recordings for Folkways and Decca exceeded 4,000,000 copies. The Weavers disbanded temporarily in 1952 and were reconstituted in 1955. Seeger left the group in 1957 because of other commitments. The group disbanded in 1964, but occasionally reunited, making their last appearance in 1980, shortly before the death of Lee Hays.

On his own, Seeger continued his folk singing tours in the 1950s, performing before capacity crowds in New York's Carnegie Hall and Town Hall and throughout the United States, Canada, and the British Isles. In the winter of 1954–55 he gave a series of six concerts entitled "American Folk Music and its Origins" at Columbia University's Institute of Arts and Sciences. He also was featured at the National Folk Festival in St. Louis, and in the late 1950s and early 1960s he helped to organize the Newport (Rhode Island) Folk Festivals, in which he was a participant.

In 1955 Seeger was called before a subcommittee of the House Committee on Un-American Activities investigating alleged subversive influences in the entertainment field. Refusing to answer questions put to him by the committee regarding his political beliefs and associations, Seeger chose to cite the First Amendment to the Constitution, guaranteeing freedom of speech and association, rather than the Fifth, allowing the individual to avoid self-incrimination, which would have safeguarded him from prosecution. "In my whole life I have never done anything of any conspiratorial nature," he declared at the time of the hearing. "I resent very much and very deeply the implication of being called before this committee."

Indicted on ten counts of contempt of Congress, Seeger went on trial before the United States District Court in New York City in March 1961, and was found guilty on all counts by a jury that had deliberated for one hour and twenty minutes. Upon being sentenced to one year in prison by Judge Thomas F. Murphy on April 4, 1961, Seeger declared: "I have never in my life supported or done anything subversive to my country. I am proud that I have never refused to sing for any organization because I disagreed with its beliefs." To illustrate his position he then offered to sing a song, but he was refused permission by the court to do so. Later he told an interviewer for *Variety* (March 21, 1962): "I'd sing for the John Birch Society or the American Legion, if asked. So far they haven't."

On May 18, 1962 the United States Court of Appeal by unanimous decision, reversed Seeger's conviction on the ground that the indictment had failed to define with sufficient clarity the authority of the subcommittee to hold the hearings. Although the indictment against Seeger had been dismissed, during that time he was still banned by some television networks and his concerts continued to be picketed by the American Legion and other organizations. When the American Broadcasting Company banned Seeger and the Weavers from its weekly folk music program *Hootenanny,* which made its television debut on April 6, 1963, several folk singers, including Joan Baez, declined invitations to appear on the program. The ABC network later issued a statement that it would consider using Seeger if he signed an affidavit regarding his political affiliations, but he refused to do so on constitutional grounds.

Pete Seeger's popularity stemmed largely from his informal style and his mesmeric ability to get his audiences to take an active part in his concerts. He sang in a light, pleasing tenor, trying to recreate the atmosphere in which the songs were originally sung. His long-necked five-string banjo, which became his trademark, was made to his own design, and he played it in several styles. His instruction manual, *How to Play the Five-String Banjo,* was published privately in 1948 and revised in 1954. His other publications included The *Twelve-String Guitar as Played by Leadbelly, The Steel Drums of Kim Loy Wong,* and several songbooks. Seeger served on the editorial staff of the folk music magazine *Sing Out!* and as an adviser to the new topical song periodical Broadside, and he wrote for these and other publications.

During his thirteen years with Folkways Records and Service Corporation, Seeger made forty albums, including four volumes of *American Favorite Ballads* and three volumes of *Frontier Ballads,* and children's songs, Civil War songs, industrial ballads, African freedom songs, and instructional records for banjo and guitar. In 1961 he signed a contract with Columbia Records, but he continued to record occasionally for Folkways. As a writer of songs Seeger also met with success. His "Where Have All the Flowers Gone?" became a hit in 1961. Another hit, which he wrote with Lee Hays, was "If I Had a Hammer," and he collaborated with the Weavers in writing "Kisses Sweeter Than Wine." In another, related activity Seeger produced educational short subjects through Folklore Research Films, which he and his wife founded. In the summer of 1963 Seeger embarked with his family on a global singing tour covering some twenty-one countries, including Australia.

The long television blacklist of Seeger began to end in the mid-1960s, when he hosted a regionally broadcast, educational, folk-music television show, *Rainbow Quest.* Thirty-nine hour-long programs were recorded at WNJU's Newark studios in 1965 and 1966, produced by Seeger and his wife Toshi, with Sholom Rubinstein. The Smothers Brothers ended Seeger's national blacklisting by broadcasting him singing "Waist Deep in the Big Muddy" on their CBS variety show on February 25, 1968, after his similar performance in September 1967 was censored by CBS.

Pete Seeger was one of the earliest backers of Bob Dylan and was responsible for urging A&R man John Hammond to produce Dylan's first LP on Columbia, and for inviting him to perform at the Newport Folk Festival, of which Seeger was a board member. There was a widely repeated story that Seeger was so upset over the extremely loud amplified sound that Dylan, backed by members of the Butterfield Blues Band, brought into the 1965 Newport Folk Festival that he threatened to disconnect the equipment. In fact, Seeger said, "I was at fault. I was the MC, and I could have said to the part of the crowd that booed Bob, 'You didn't boo Howlin' Wolf yesterday. He was electric!' Though I still prefer to hear Dylan acoustic, some of his electric songs are absolutely great. Electric music is the vernacular of the second half of the twentieth century, to use my father's old term."

A longstanding opponent of the arms race and of the Vietnam War, Seeger satirically attacked then-President Lyndon Johnson with his 1966 recording, on the album *Dangerous Songs!?,* of Len Chandler's children's song, "Beans in My Ears." Beyond Chandler's lyrics, Seeger said that "Mrs. Jay's little son Alby" had "beans in his ears," which, as the lyrics imply, ensure that a person does not hear what is said to them. To those opposed to continuing the Vietnam War, the phrase implied that "Alby Jay," a loose pronunciation of Johnson's nickname "LBJ," did not listen to anti-war protests as he too had "beans in his ears."

Seeger attracted wider attention starting in 1967 with his song "Waist Deep in the Big Muddy," about a captain—referred to in the lyrics as "the big fool"—who

Affiliation: People's Songs

After his discharge, with the rank of corporal, in December 1945, Seeger, along with others, founded People's Songs, Inc., and he became its national director. People's Songs, a union of songwriters, as well as a research center and clearing house for folk songs, grew out of Seeger's conviction that the United States was ripe for a folk music revival, which, he felt, would be given its main impetus by organized labor. The organization, which began rather modestly, had a membership of about 3,000 at its peak and counted among its leading members such singers, musicians, and scholars as Alan Lomax, Lee Hays, Woody Guthrie, Sonny Terry, Betty Sanders, Tom Glazer, and Waldemar Hille. It published a monthly bulletin and a *People's Song Book,* popularized current topical songs and traditional folk songs from all over the world, furnished songs to unions and other organizations on request, and conducted weekly "hootenannies," or informal folk song sessions. During the early postwar years Seeger also made a short folk music film, *And Hear My Banjo Play,* produced in 1946, and he appeared in a revival of the folk play *Dark of the Moon* when it was performed by the Los Angeles Repertory Theatre. In 1948 he toured the United States in behalf of the Progressive party's Presidential candidate, Henry A. Wallace.

drowned while leading a platoon on maneuvers in Louisiana during World War II. With its lyrics about a platoon being led into danger by an ignorant captain, the song's anti-war message was obvious— the line "the big fool said to push on" was repeated several times. In the face of arguments with the management of CBS about whether the song's political weight was in keeping with the usually light-hearted entertainment of the *Smothers Brothers Comedy Hour,* the final lines were "Every time I read the paper/those old feelings come on/We are waist deep in the Big Muddy and the big fool says to push on." The lyrics could be interpreted as an allegory of Johnson as the "big fool" and the Vietnam War as the foreseeable danger. Although the performance was cut from the September 1967 show, after wide publicity it was broadcast when Seeger appeared again on the *Smothers' Brothers* show in the following January.

At the November 15, 1969, Vietnam Moratorium March on Washington, DC, Seeger led 500,000 protesters in singing John Lennon's song "Give Peace a Chance" as they rallied across from the White House. Seeger's voice carried over the crowd, interspersing phrases like, "Are you listening, Nixon?" between the choruses of protesters singing, "All we are saying . . . is give peace a chance."

In 1982, Seeger performed at a benefit concert for Poland's Solidarity resistance movement. His biographer David Dunaway considers this the first public manifestation of Seeger's decades-long personal dislike of communism in its Soviet form, which developed after the 1956 repressions in Hungary. In the late 1980s Seeger also expressed disapproval of violent revolutions, remarking to an interviewer that he was really in favor of incremental change and that "the most lasting revolutions are those that take place over a period of time." In a 1995 interview he insisted that "I still call myself a communist, because communism is no more what Russia made of it than Christianity is what the churches make of it." In 2007, in response to criticism from a historian Ron Radosh, a former Trotskyite who now writes for the conservative National Review, Seeger wrote a song condemning Stalin, "Big Joe Blues": "I'm singing about old Joe, cruel Joe. / He ruled with an iron hand. /He put an end to the dreams / Of so many in every land. / He had a chance to make / A brand new start for the human race. / Instead he set it back / Right in the same nasty place. / I got the Big Joe Blues. / Keep your mouth shut or you will die fast. / I got the Big Joe Blues. / Do this job, no questions asked. / I got the Big Joe Blues." The song was accompanied by a letter to Radosh, in which Seeger stated, "I think you're right, I should have asked to see the gulags when I was in U.S.S.R [in 1965]."

Seeger continued to be active late in his life. On March 16, 2007, Pete Seeger, his sister Peggy, his brothers Mike and John, his wife Toshi, and other family members spoke and performed at a symposium and concert sponsored by the American Folklife Center in honor of the Seeger family, held at the Library of Congress in Washington, D.C., where Pete Seeger had been employed by the Archive of American Folk Song 67 years earlier. In September 2008, Appleseed Recordings released At 89, Seeger's first studio album in 12 years. On September 29, 2008, the 89-year-old singer-activist, once banned from commercial TV, made a rare national TV appearance on the *Late Show with David Letterman,* singing "Take It from Dr. King." On January 18, 2009,

Seeger and his grandson Tao Rodríguez-Seeger joined Bruce Springsteen, and the crowd in singing the Woody Guthrie song "This Land Is Your Land" in the finale of Barack Obama's Inaugural concert in Washington, D.C. The performance was noteworthy for the inclusion of two verses not often included in the song, one about a "private property" sign the narrator cheerfully ignores, and the other making a passing reference to a Depression-era relief office. On September 19, 2009, Seeger made his first appearance at the 52nd Monterey Jazz Festival, which was particularly notable because the festival does not normally feature folk artists. On December 14, 2012, Seeger performed, along with Harry Belafonte, Jackson Browne, Common and others, at a concert to bring awareness to the 37-year-long ordeal of Native American Activist Leonard Peltier. The concert was held at the Beacon Theater in New York City.

Over the years he lent his fame to support numerous environmental organizations, including South Jersey's Bayshore Center, the home of New Jersey's tall ship, the oyster schooner A.J. Meerwald. Seeger's benefit concerts helped raise funds for groups so they could continue to educate and spread environmental awareness. On May 3, 2009, at the Clearwater Concert, dozens of musicians gathered in New York at Madison Square Garden to celebrate Seeger's 90th birthday (which was later televised on PBS during the summer), ranging from Dave Matthews, John Mellencamp, Billy Bragg, Bruce Springsteen, Tom Morello, Eric Weissberg, Ani DiFranco and Roger McGuinn to Joan Baez, Richie Havens, Joanne Shenandoah, R. Carlos Nakai, Bill Miller, Joseph Fire Crow, Margo Thunderbird, Tom Paxton, Ramblin' Jack Elliott and Arlo Guthrie. Cuban singer-songwriter Silvio Rodríguez was also invited to appear but his visa was not approved in time by the United States government. Consistent with Seeger's long-time advocacy for environmental concerns, the proceeds from the event benefited the Hudson River Sloop Clearwater, a non-profit organization founded by Seeger in 1966, to defend and restore the Hudson River. Seeger's 90th birthday was also celebrated at The College of Staten Island on May 4. In 2010, still active at the age of 91, Seeger co-wrote and performed the song "God's Counting on Me, God's Counting on You" with Lorre Wyatt, commenting on the Deepwater Horizon oil spill. A performance of the song by Seeger, Wyatt, and friends was recorded and filmed on the Sloop Clearwater in August and released as a single and video produced by Richard Barone and Matthew Billy on election day November 6, 2012.

On October 21, 2011, in his last act as a social activist, at age 92 Pete Seeger was part of a solidarity march with Occupy Wall Street to Columbus Circle in New York City. The march began with Seeger and fellow musicians exiting Symphony Space (95th and Broadway), where they had performed as part of a benefit for Seeger's Clearwater organization. Thousands of people crowded Pete Seeger by the time they reached Columbus Circle where he performed with his grandson, Tao Rodríguez-Seeger, Arlo Guthrie, David Amram, and other celebrated musicians. The event, promoted under the name OccupyTheCircle, was live streamed and dubbed by some as "The Pete Seeger March."

Personal Life

On July 20, 1943 Peter Seeger married Toshi-Aline Ohta, who was of Japanese and Virginian parentage. The couple remained married until Toshi's death in 2013. They had a son, Daniel Adams, and two daughters, Mika Salter and Virginia S. (Tinya). The Seegers lived near Beacon, New York, some sixty miles north of New York City in a two-room log cabin overlooking the Hudson River, which they built with the help of friends. Tall and lanky, Pete Seeger stood at six feet one and a half inches, weighed 165 pounds, and had thinning brown hair and blue eyes. On his concert tours he drove around the country in an old station wagon and wore work shoes and vivid shirts, socks, and ties. His favorite recreations were skiing, sailing along the Hudson in a small boat, and rambling through the woods near his home.

Indifferent to material gain, Seeger often turned down bids for concert engagements to tour black colleges in the South or to give benefit performances for the Freedom Riders and for other causes. He was not particularly disturbed by the commercialism that generally accompanied the folk music boom of the 1960s. "Folk music is a living, vibrant thing again," he told an interviewer for *Look* (August 27, 1963). "To me, this is the musical reflection of a new national maturity; we are trying to identify with our country again." Of his own role as a folk singer Seeger said in an interview with J. C. Barden for *High Fidelity* (January 1963): "I feel I'm building a healthy musical life for people who seem to have lost it somewhere in the machine age."

Seeger died at New York-Presbyterian Hospital on January 27, 2014, at the age of 94. He was survived by two half-sisters, Peggy and Barbara, his three children, and eight grandchildren. Response and reaction to Seeger's death quickly poured in. President Barack Obama noted that Seeger had been called "America's tuning fork" and that he believed in "the power of song" to bring social change, "Over the years, Pete used his voice and his hammer to strike blows for workers' rights and civil rights; world peace and environmental conservation, and he always invited us to sing along. For reminding us where we come from and showing us where we need to go, we will always be grateful to Pete Seeger."

Further Reading

Hi Fi 13:51+ Ja '63 pors
Sing Out! 4:4+ My '54 por
Lawless, Ray M. *Folksingers and Folksongs in America* (1960)

Andrés Segovia

Spanish guitarist

Born: February 18, 1894; Linares, Spain
Died: June 2, 1987; Madrid Spain
Primary Field: Classical
Group Affiliation: Solo performer

Introduction

Andrés Segovia, the unchallenged master of the Spanish classical guitar during his lifetime, enjoyed one of the most successful and rewarding careers in the history of music. His artistry and the pervasive humanity revealed through his playing enriched the lives of music lovers for close to seven decades. Through his impeccable musicianship and technique he restored the guitar to a place on the concert stage and at the same time established it as perhaps the most popular instrument for amateurs. Indefatigable, even in his old age he committed himself to a strenuous concert schedule that took him to almost all parts of the globe. If his musical frame of reference in in the later part of his career seemed narrower and more subdued, turning away from the passion of former years, the reward was still great. For there remained the serene distillation of his art— the essence of a lifetime devoted to the creation of beauty.

Early Life

Andrés Segovia was born on February 18, 1894 in the Andalusian city of Linares, Spain and was reared in Granada. His father was a prosperous lawyer and hoped his son would ultimately join him in this profession. However, wishing to offer the boy as wide a cultural background as possible, he provided him with musical instruction at an early age. He was tutored in piano and violin but was unable to become enthusiastic about either. It was not until he heard the guitar in the home of a friend that his musical imagination was stirred. The color and richness of the instrument's sonority especially appealed to him. Disregarding the objections of his family and his teachers at the Granada Musical Institute, Segovia persisted in learning to play the guitar. When he could not find a competent teacher, he became his own teacher.

Life's Work

Applying his previously acquired musical knowledge to his study or the guitar, he developed his own technique. He had discovered quite early that certain piano exercises were especially beneficial in strengthening the fingers for the guitar. Although he admitted the influence of such earlier masters as Francisco Tárrega on his development, his style and technique remained generally his own. Not content with mastering the instrument, Segovia insisted that the guitar's rightful place was on the concert stage. The difficulties implicit in this decision would have seemed insurmountable to a less tenacious student. The guitar was considered unsuitable in the select music circles of the day. Its place was the tavern, its function, the accompaniment of lascivious songs and dances. More important was the fact that there existed no true repertoire for the guitar beyond this questionable if vital literature.

Despite these obstacles, Segovia continued to study and perfect his technique. As his artistry matured, his reputation began to spread and at the age of fifteen, in 1909, he made his public debut in Granada under the auspices of the Círculo Arífstico, a local cultural organization. Numerous concerts followed, including those in Madrid in 1912 and in Barcelona in 1916. In Madrid he had acquired from the craftsman Manuel Ramírez a guitar that he played for many years. In the mid-1930's he began using an instrument made by Hermann Hauser of Munich.

A limited repertoire remained a major difficulty during the early years of Segovia's career. His task of transcribing works for other instruments required much time and care. He relied primarily on Renaissance and baroque pieces composed for lute or Spanish vihuela. In Germany he began searching for music applicable to the guitar and discovered the lute works of Sylvius Leopold Weiss. They were relatively adaptable and generally quite effective. His most significant find was a group of Bach's works that were well suited to the guitar. It was Segovia's belief that many of Bach's solo pieces were originally written for lute and later transcribed by him for other instruments. Though authorities at the time were less than sanguine over the validity of this theory, they find no quarrel with Segovia's transcriptions of the master. The suitability of Bach's music for the classical guitar as demonstrated by Segovia proved to be one of the most delightful aspects of the guitarist's art.

Segovia's growing fame brought with it a rising interest in the instrument itself. The rich and vibrant sonority that Segovia produced, the sensuous and subtle nuances, and above all, the intimacy of its idiom excited in listeners the desire to learn to play the guitar themselves. During the span of Segovia's career he saw the guitar, which was "on the outskirts of music" when he was a boy, become one of the most popular and studied instruments in the world.

Leading composers too were finally realizing its possibilities and were beginning to compose for it. But there was a problem in that few of them understood the instrument sufficiently so that the success of their compositions often depended on the availability of Segovia's tutelage. As he has said, much of the modem repertoire was composed through him. Among early converts were Mario Castelnuovo-Tedesco and Alfred Casella, who wrote concertos for guitar. Through the years since then the instrument has achieved an estimable modern repertoire because of the efforts of such other composers as Turina, Torroba, De Falla, Tansman, Ponce, and Villa-Lobos. In his concert in Paris, in April 1924, Segovia played a solo piece written for the guitar by Albert Roussel and entitled simply *Segovia*.

On the advice of the noted violinist Fritz Kreisler, the manager Coppicus engaged Andrés Segovia for his first American tour. To the surprise and delight of Segovia, who enjoyed giving private performances, he made his first scheduled musical appearance in the home of three devotees in Proctor, Massachusetts. In January 1928 he appeared at Town Hall in New York City. On that occasion Olin Downes commented in the *New York Times:* "He belongs to the very small group of musicians who by transcendent powers of execution and imagination create an art of their own that sometimes seems to transform the very nature of their medium. He draws the tone colors of a half a dozen instruments from the one he plays. He has extraordinary command of nuances and seems to discover whole planes of sonority." Segovia's first concert in New York City was followed by five others there, all of which were sold out, and twenty-five in other cities. Before the tour was over critics were beginning to compare him favorably with Kreisler, Casals, and Paderewski. For the next ten years Segovia toured the United States annually and acquired a devoted following.

The outbreak of the Spanish Civil War forced Segovia to give up his home in Spain in 1936. After living for a time in Genoa, Italy, he moved to Montevideo,

Affiliation: Solo Performer

Having gradually won recognition outside his own country, by 1919 Segovia was ready for a full-fledged tour. He performed in that year in South America, where he gained an enthusiastic reception. Subsequent engagements kept him away from Europe until 1923. During this period Segovia was still considered something of a curiosity by the uninitiated. At his London debut the *Times* critic who had approached the idea of a classical guitar recital with more than a little skepticism came away a devoted follower. "We remained to hear the last possible note," he wrote, "for it was the most delightful surprise of the season." Perhaps his most important early success occurred at his Paris debut in April 1924. This had been arranged at the insistence of his countryman Pablo Casals, the cellist. The audience at the Conservatoire included a charmed circle of such musical celebrities as Paul Dukas, Manuel De Falla and Madame Debussy. He was an immediate sensation, winning from most critics warm praise for disclosing the glories of the Spanish guitar. With his successful Berlin debut later that year, his reputation became international.

Uruguay. From there he toured extensively in Central and South America. After an absence of five years Segovia returned to the United States, in 1943, under the management of S. Hurok. But the impresario found it less than easy to secure bookings for an artist whom audiences had almost forgotten. Hurok had to start all over again to build the guitarist's popularity, often guaranteeing local managers against loss, and before long he was again at the top. The burgeoning medium of television also helped secure his popularity by introducing him to a wider audience than he could have reached via the concert circuit. His concert circuit by the 1960s, however, covered almost every country outside the Communist bloc, and he gave about 100 concerts a year. In the spring of 1964 it was announced that during the following summer Segovia would conduct a master class at the University of California, Berkeley, to be televised over the National Educational Network.

Starting after World War II Segovia recorded more frequently, and the work of Andrés Segovia became available through his numerous phonograph recordings. The Segovia discography encompassed a large number of carefully programmed recitals that offer a wide variation in periods and composers, from the classical through the romantic to the modern. His records for Musicraft, Victor's British affiliate, and Decca enjoyed remarkable popularity. He won the 1958 Grammy award for Best Classical Performance by an instrumentalist.

Concerts and recordings never kept Segovia from sharing his knowledge and technique with others. He had many pupils and has taught at Santiago de Compostela in Spain and the Academy Chigi in Siena, among other schools. Perhaps the most famous of his pupils is he guitarist John Williams, but his recordings influenced many others, including Julian Bream and Christopher Parkening. Segovia's interest and influence aided in establishing the guitar as a serious part of the curriculum at music schools in Madrid, Barcelona, Florence, and London.

Personal Life

Tall and courtly, Andrés Segovia, who usually wore a string tie or flowing ribbon tie, had a charm and graciousness suggestive of a former era. "His manners have the elaborate simplicity of Don Quixote," Samuel Chotzinoff has observed, "though physically he more resembles Sancho Panza." When not on tour, he lived surrounded by fine Spanish antiques in his upper East Side apartment in Manhattan, which he shares with his wife, Emelia Segovia, a former student of his, whom he married in 1962. In 1981 Segovia was ennobled by King Juan Carlos I of Spain, who gave him the hereditary title of Marqués de Salobreña. His son from this marriage to Emelia, Carlos Andrés Segovia, currently holds that title. Segovia's earlier marriages ended in divorce. A son from an earlier marriage was a painter who lived in France. He also had a daughter, Beatrice.

A disciplined artist, Segovia practiced from five to six hours each day. But his world contained much more than his professional interests. He delighted in art and in reading poetry, history, and philosophy. He also enjoyed good food and drink and stimulating conversation. Among his friends in many parts of the world were Queen Elisabeth of Belgium and Prince Chigi of Siena, both of whom he visited annually. For some years he worked on an autobiography, part of which was published in 1976. He also published many of his arrangements and wrote a introductory book on guitar playing entitled *Segovia: My Book of the Guitar.*

Andrés Segovia died on June 2, 1987 in Madrid, Spain of a heart attack.

Further Reading

Hi Fi 11:10+ Jl '61 por

N Y Times Mag p36+ F 16 '64 pors

Chotzinoff, Samuel. *A Little Night Music* (1964)

Ewen, David. *Encyclopedia of Concert Music* (1959); *Living Musicians* (1940; First Supplement, 1957)

Who's Who in America, 1964-65

Rudolf Serkin

Pianist and composer

Born: March 28, 1903; Eger, Hungary
Died: May 8, 1991; Guilford, Vermont
Primary Field: Classical
Group Affiliation: Solo Artist

Introduction

Rudolf Serkin took American music-lovers by storm when he made his first United States appearance in 1935. Since that first concert Serkin was rated one of the finest pianists of his era. On June 20 he inaugurated the 1940 Lewisohn Stadium Concerts under the baton of Arturo Rodzinski, and continued to play concerts in America unit 1989.

Early Life

Rudolf Serkin was born in Eger, Bohemia, of Russian-Jewish parents. At four he could play the piano creditably and was able to read music with facility. On the advice of the celebrated Viennese pianist, Alfred Gruenfeld, his parents placed him under the tutelage of Professor Richard Robert in Vienna. At that time his parents were so poor that they had only one room for themselves and eight children. There, in the din and clatter, Rudolf learned to play, and at 12 made his debut as guest artist with the Vienna Symphony Orchestra.

Though he achieved great success and was offered a long tour by enthusiastic managers, his teacher and parents decided that he was still too young to undertake anything so strenuous. For several years he continued his studies, rounding out his technical knowledge of music by studying composition under Arnold Schonberg. When he finally inaugurated his career he established himself quickly as an important artist, giving concerts in France, Switzerland, Italy, Spain and Austria.

Life's Work

Herbert F. Peyser, writing in Berlin for the New York *Times* in 1931 made the comment that "Mr. Serkin is not a sensational pianist, though he can storm the clouds and summon the mellowest of thunders and dazzle like the best of them in the sheer resplendence of mechanics." He added: "a tall, gangling, bespectacled young man of 25 to 30, suggesting in his general appearance a somewhat overgrown high school student, his demeanor at the keyboard is, on the whole, tranquil and unmannered." His playing, in its limpid and subtle loveliness, called to mind the famous Walter Gieseking.

In 1935 Serkin appeared in the United States for the first time with Adolf Busch, the violinist, at the Coolidge Festival in Washington. When he made his American debut the following winter as soloist under the baton of Arturo Toscanini, conductor of the New York Philharmonic Symphony Orchestra, Leonard Liebling called him "an artist of unusual and impressive talents in possession of a crystalline technique, plenty of power delicacy and tone pure and full." Not to be outdone, Olin Downes claimed that he was "a masterly musician . . . a scholar and a profound one, without pedantry with the loftiest conception of beauty, whose every thought and emotion is for the glory of his art."

In 1937 he gave his first New York recital in Carnegie Hall, and Downes described him as: "a curious figure on the platform, because of his slightness and the fact that he is not tall and the nervous intensity of his walk to the piano, and his fantastical intentness on the work in hand . . . He played significantly always with a magnificent control and with a sovereign sense of form. Richness and complexity of detail never distracted him from issues, but only added to the richness of the effect, and in lyrical passages his tone was lovely in color, in nuance in capacity to carry, even when the key is barely pressed down by the finger."

After settling in the United States, Serkin added teaching to his list of activities. He was on the faculty at the Curtis Institute of Music in Philadelphia, serving as the director of the Institute from 1968 to 1976. During that time he continued giving concerts; in March 1972 he celebrated his 100th appearance with the New York Philharmonic with a performance of Brahms' First Piano Concerto. In 1951 he and Adolph Busch founded the Marlboro Music School and Festival in Marlboro, Vermont to promote chamber music in the United States. Many performances given at the Marlboro Festival were recorded and issued on Columbia Masterworks; these included many performance by Serkin but also other by guest musicians such as Pablo Casals.

Serkin also recorded extensively for Columbia Masterworks, and later Deutsche Grammophon and Telarc. His Columbia recordings of the piano concertos of Johannes Brahms with George Szell and the Cleveland

Affiliation: Solo Pianist

In 1937 Serkin, appearing with the National Orchestral Association under the direction of Leon Barzin, received the following comment from the well-known critic, Jerome D. Bohm: "His treatment of the music was perfectly proportioned, teeming with sensitively applied nuances, and invested with unceasing tonal loveliness and astonishing technical finish."

Orchestra were considered among the very best available, and many of his recording are still available.

Serkin was awarded the Presidential Medal of Freedom in 1963 and in March 1972 celebrated his 100th appearance with the New York Philharmonic by playing Johannes Brahms' Piano Concerto No. 1. The orchestra and board of directors named Serkin an honorary member of the New York Philharmonic-Symphony Society, a distinction also conferred on Aaron Copland, Igor Stravinsky, and Paul Hindemith. In 1986, he celebrated his 50th anniversary as a guest artist with the orchestra. He is also regarded as one of the primary interpreters of the music of Beethoven in the 20th century.

Personal Life

Since his first appearance in the United States with Adolf Busch, Serkin played several series in concert with the German violinist. As a matter of fact, so closely attached did they become musically, that Serkin stepped forward to tighten the bond by marrying Busch's daughter, Irene, in 1936. He and Irene had seven children, one of whom died in infancy. His son Peter Serkin is a famous pianist in his own right, and his daughter Judith Serkin is cellist and founder of the Brattleboro Music School. (Irene Busch Serkin died in 1998.)

Rudolf Serkin suffered from cancer late in life, and the disease forced him to quit his solo career and recording activities in 1989. He died of the disease on May 8, 1991 at his home in Guilford, Vermont.

Further Reading

Musician 41:57 Mr '36 por

Springf'd Repub E p6 Mr 3 '40

Time 28:22 D 28 '36 por

Thompson, 0. ed. *International Cyclopedia of Music and Musicians* 1939

Wier, A. E. ed. *Macmillan Encyclopedia of Music and Musicians* 1938

Rudolf Serkin: A Life, Lehmann, S, Oxford University Press, 2003

Shins

Music group

James Mercer
Songwriter; guitarist
Born: Dec. 26, 1970; Honolulu, Hawaii

Martin Crandall
Keyboardist; guitarist
Born: Apr. 20, 1975

Dave Hernandez
Bass guitarist
Born: Sep. 22, 1970

Jesse Sandoval
Drummer
Born: Nov. 15, 1974

Eric Johnson
Keyboardist; guitarist
Born: June 7, 1976

Primary Field: Indie rock
Group Affiliation: Shins

Introduction

In the 2004 film Garden State, *directed by and starring Zach Braff, the character played by Natalie Portman says to the Braff character, "You gotta hear this one song—it'll change your life." She was referring to "New Slang," by a then-underground indie-rock band known as the Shins. The film, produced for a modest $2.5 million, went on to gross more than $26 million, and the* *songs in it, handpicked by Braff, won a Grammy Award for best compilation soundtrack for a motion picture. Those developments propelled the relatively unknown group of Portland, Oregon-based musicians to mainstream stardom and helped their 2001 debut album,* Oh, Inverted World, *to achieve gold-record status, with sales increasing by approximately 400 percent. Since then the band has sold upwards of a million copies of its first two albums combined and debuted at number two (eventually reaching number one) on the* Billboard *200 album chart with its third record,* Wincing the Night Away, *which sold 118,000 copies in its first week.*

Early Lives

A son of Jim Mercer, a lieutenant colonel in the U.S. Air Force, and Alice Mercer, James Russell Mercer was born on December 26, 1970 in Honolulu, Hawaii. Due to their father's occupation, Mercer and his younger sister, Bonnie, had a peripatetic lifestyle, moving from city to city and country to country, which later contributed to the sophisticated and anecdotal nature of Mercer's lyrics. Early on in his childhood, Mercer's family traveled around the U.S. in a motor home, making stops in Utah, Kansas, and Alabama, before heading to Europe. They lived in Germany for a year before Mercer's father was transferred to Greece. At that point his mother decided to take him and his sister back to the United States, where they settled in Albuquerque, New Mexico, for several years. Back in the States, as Mercer recalled to Eliscu, "I didn't fit in. Kids were drinking and smoking pot and having sex. The social dynamic was much more mature than I was ready for at eleven. I became depressed for months. My dad and mom are both farm people and were not versed in child psychology. I remember that as being the end of my childhood." He went on to attend high school in England, spending a good deal of time on a Suffolk air-force base, where he began to develop an affinity for music. He listened to the likes of the Smiths, the Cure, the Beach Boys, and the Jesus and Mary Chain, and was greatly influenced by the group Pink Floyd's masterpiece, *Dark Side of the Moon.*

After returning to Albuquerque to attend college, Mercer picked up his first guitar (he had no formal training in music) and joined the local music scene—defined by hard punk acts such as Cracks in the Sidewalk, Big Damn Crazy Weight, and Elephant. His future band mates Martin Crandall, born on April 20, 1975, and Jesse Sandoval, born on November 15, 1974, were still in high school when they first met Mercer and his friend Neil Langford, a bassist, through other musicians. Mercer, who had played in such local groups as Orange Little Cousins, Subculture, and Blue Roof Diner, soon joined Langford, Crandall, and Sandoval in forming a lo-fi rock group called Flake. ("Lofi" is a subgenre of indie rock; the term refers to the use of low-fidelity recording methods, which produces more "authentic" sound. Many lo-fi artists use inexpensive cassette tape recorders in producing their music.) The "power punk pop" ensemble, as Mercer described them in an interview with *Ear Shot Magazine* (November 10, 2004, on-line), renamed themselves Flake Music after another Seat- tie-based group, also called Flake, threatened to sue them. Flake Music soon made a name for themselves with their frenetic, counterpoint guitars, mathematically calculated keyboard passages, and sometimes rambling fuzz-pop style. Over the next eight years, they released a number of records, including their 1993 debut, a seven-inch single on Resin Records called "Mieke"; a 10-inch EP under Spark Science Project, in 1995, that included the songs "Pull Out of Your Head Size," "Dying Lack of Spit," "Tott," "Nuevo," and "Dilly Dally"; another seven-inch single in 1996, under Headhunter/Cargo; and, with the band Scared of Chaka, a split seven-inch single on 702/Science Project that contained the songs "Submarines" and "The Shins." In 1997 Flake Music released their only full-length album, *When You Land Here, It's Time to Return,* on Omnibus Records, which was well received despite minimal exposure outside college radio stations.

Lives' Work

As early as 1996, Mercer—a self-described "control freak"—began to stray from Flake Music to begin work on a side project, which would result in the formation of the Shins. The band's name was based on both the Flake Music song of the same name and a fictional family in the Broadway show *The Music Man,* which was a favorite of Mercer's father. Because Neil Langford had gotten a job at about that time that involved piloting a corporate-owned hot-air balloon around the country, which forced him to be away from the band for long periods, the Shins started off as a duo, with Mercer on vocals and guitar and Sandoval on drums. Developing an affection for the "feel-good" retro-pop sound that harked back to the 1960s, as exemplified by such Beatles-inspired bands as Apples in Stereo and the Olivia Tremor Control, Mercer and Sandoval started playing together live, opening for acts including the American Analog Set and Cibo Matta. Speaking with Lindsey Byrnes for *Thrasher Magazine* (April 2004), Sandoval recalled, "We realized that we wanted to expand to a fuller sound on stage so we asked Dave [Hernandez, from the band Scared of Shaka] to play bass. Then we realized that we wanted keys, so we asked Marty [Crandall] to play keyboards." Later they added the drummer Ron Skrasek, with whom they had previously collaborated. Shortly thereafter, due to Scared of Chaka's heavy touring schedule, both Hernandez and Skrasek were forced to leave the band, reopening the bassist slot for Langford. Thus, for the most part, the members of Flake Music became the Shins.

In 1998 the Shins released a seven-inch single under Omnibus entitled "Nature Bears a Vacuum." (By 1999 Flake Music had run its course; as Mercer explained to Eliscu, "I was so sick of trying to pretend to be punk rock.") In 2000 the group released another seven-inch single, "When I Goose-Step." With those two records the band received some critical acclaim and found themselves touring with the indie favorites Califone and Modest Mouse as a supporting act. At a show in San Francisco, California, during the tour with Modest Mouse, the Sub Pop Records founder, Jonathan Poneman, was so impressed by the group that he signed them to a contract. The contract came as a relief for Mercer, who had had minimal financial success with Flake Music and had been living on credit cards for some time. "I had a conversation with my parents where I said, 'Look I'm going to make this one last push at music,'" he recalled to Eliscu. "I told them, 'If this doesn't work, I'll go back to school.'"

In 2001 the Shins debuted their single "New Slang" under Sub Pop, followed by the release of their first album, *Oh, Inverted World.* Drawing comparisons to other groups of the genre, such as Apples in Stereo and Modest Mouse, critics almost unanimously hailed the album as a triumphant return to a style of rock from an earlier era, when the Beatles and the Beach Boys reigned supreme. In a review for *Pop Matters* (November 10, 2001, online), Paul Bruno wrote that the album "is filled with musical allusions that will probably go over the heads of many backpack-and-thick-rimmed glasses wearing listeners: lots of Brian Wilson-like vocal lines, [Roger] McGuinnesque jangley guitar, some [Syd] Barrett-aid psych here and there," adding that "musically and lyrically, all the emotions are bubbling just beneath the surface but obvious to anyone who is paying attention." Critics noted the melancholic feel of such songs as "Caring Is Creepy," "The Past and Pending," and "Girl on the Wing," with their dreamy vocals and strummed guitar licks interspersed with space-like synthesizer sounds. "Weird Days" drew fond comparisons to the sun-induced rhythms of the Beach Boys, and other songs won praise for their complexity, evident in Kinks-like songs such as "Know Your Onion!" The album's centerpiece, "New Slang," was praised across the board; Eliscu noted for *Rolling Stone* (August 16, 2001) that "the most affecting song is 'New Slang,' a shuffling folk ballad with a spaghetti-western feel and a somber melody," while Bruno declared that it had "instant classic status written all over it."

Around that time Langford decided to pursue his air-balloon work exclusively, paving the way for Dave Hernandez (born on September 22, 1970) to rejoin the band. Soon after that, Mercer persuaded his Albuquerque-born bandmates to relocate to Portland, Oregon, which was home to such notable indie acts as the Decemberists and Sleater-Kinney. Martin Crandall noted to Douglas Walk, writing for *Billboard* (February 3, 2007), "Albuquerque's nice, but there's not much going on musically, unless you want to watch some ska bands."

The Shins had established a fan base in indie circles by the time their second album, *Chutes Too Narrow,* was released, on October 21, 2003. Produced by Phil Ek, the album featured cleaner production work than did *Oh, Inverted World,* and garnered even more praise as a result. Robert Christgau, writing for *Rolling Stone* (January 25, 2007), recalled *Chutes* as being "one of the deftest, subtlest and just plain loveliest guitar-rock albums of the decade." While many had seen the Shins' first album as a flash-in-the-pan fluke, *Chutes Too Narrow* converted skeptics. Mike Baker, in a review for *Splendid Magazine* (October 27, 2003, on-line), commented, "The Shins' second effort sparkles with a clarity that was not always evident on their debut and energizes with a spark and an enthusiasm that previously seemed forced." The poetic nature of Mercer's songwriting was most apparent on tracks such as "Mine's Not a High Horse," whose words include, "After that confrontation you left me wringing my cold hands," and "Kissing the Lipless," among whose lyrics is the line, "I want to bury in the yard / the grey remains of a friendship scarred." Marked by an anxious New Wave spirit and a stronger emphasis on guitars, the songs "Saint Simon" (featuring violin work by Annemarie Ruljancich), "So Says I," and "Those to Come" were considered standouts, as Baker remarked: "There is an album's worth of well written and ably conceived pop tunes, each of which capture the spirit of *Oh, Inverted World's* few truly inspiring songs." The album went on to win a Grammy nomination for best recording package and has sold nearly 400,000 copies to date.

Despite having firmly established themselves in the indie-rock world with their first two albums, the Shins were still relative unknowns on the mainstream music scene, Then, in 2004, Zach Braff's independent film *Garden State* featured two songs from the band's debut album, "Caring Is Creepy" and "New Slang." The film's endorsement helped quadruple sales of *Oh, Inverted World* and made the Shins known to millions of filmgoers. Three years later, on January 23, 2007, the band released its much-anticipated follow-up album, *Wincing the Night Away,* to equally favorable reviews and a number-two spot on the *Billboard* charts. A play on the name of a Sam Cooke song, "Twistin' the Night Away," the album's title referred to Mercer's woes as an insomniac. Mercer had brought other personal issues to his songwriting process for the new album, after finding himself alienated from old friends due to his success, trying to overcome a painful breakup with his girlfriend, and receiving death threats from crack-dealing former neighbors. "It started feeling like a David Lynch movie, where it's a normal scene and there's this latent dread and you don't know why," Mercer recalled to Brian Hiatt for *Rolling Stone* (November 30, 2006). "When we were mixing the record, I would say, 'More ghosts on the chorus.'" Considered the Shins' most experimental work to date, using elements ranging from hip-hop loops to psychedelic, ukulele-based Hawaiian folk meanderings, *Wincing the Night Away* included "Phantom Limb," the album's first single, which was followed by "Australia," "Sleeping Lessons," and "Spilt Needles." Jonathan Cohen wrote for *Billboard* (January 2 7, 2007), *"Wincing the Night Away* might actually be their best yet, a quietly ambitious effort that nudges the Shins' trademark indie pop into unexpected new directions. There's a drum machine beat, loping bass groove, strings and even flute on 'Red Rabbits,' ghostly reverb and noises on 'Black Wave,' and 'Spilt Needles' drops the jangle in favor of a dark melody and surreal lyrics."

While their music falls into a category—indie rock—whose name derives from the fact that many of its artists fail to be signed to major record labels, the Shins have almost singlehandedly catapulted indie rock into the mainstream. In addition to *Garden State,* "New Slang" has been used in commercials for McDonald's, Guinness, and other brands as well as on television shows, among them *Scrubs, Buffy the Vampire Slayer,* and *The Sopranos.* A handful of the group's other singles, including "Gone for Good," "Caring Is Creepy," "Pink Bullets," and "Phantom Limb," have been used in films including *In Good Company* and *Wicker Park* and in a variety of television shows, such as Ed, *One Tree Hill,* and *The O.C.* Although fans may interpret that widespread media exposure as evidence of "selling out," Mercer has defended the Shins' decision to license their material. "All this licensing and these different ways of exposing people to your music, it's just a way to compete with these big labels. The infrastructure that something like Warner Brothers or Sony has, they really can literally shove stuff down people's throats," Mercer

Affiliation: Group Leadership

The group, which performed for nearly a decade under a succession of names before becoming known as the Shins, is led by James Mercer. A songwriter and guitarist, Mercer "acquits himself quite well with a pen, and never allows his words to detract from (or often even draw attention from) the music," according to Josh Love, writing for *Stylus Magazine* (October 12, 2003, on-line); he was described as "one of indie-rock's most wordy and elliptical lyricists," by Kitty Empire, writing for the London *Observer* (April 1, 2007). The innovative quintet includes the keyboardist and sometime guitarist/bassist Martin Crandall, the bassist/guitarist Dave Hernandez, the drummer Jesse Sandoval, and the recently added multi-instrumentalist Eric Johnson, formerly of the Seattle, Washington-based group the Fruit Bats. The Shins have managed to transcend indie-pop clichés (such as cheesy keyboard passages and asinine lyrics) with innovative musical arrangements, complemented by Mercer's lyrical poetry. "Songwriting is really a weird process for me," Mercer explained to Jenny Eliscu for *Rolling Stone* (February 8, 2007). "It's almost as though you start fishing out into nothingness and there's these beautiful things out there that have yet to be realized. And it has to do with the math of the relationship between the actual notes and the harmonies and the chords. It's like you're putting your hand in a blind hole and feeling around, and once in a while you can grab onto something and keep it."

said to Wince Charming, in an interview for *Time Off* (January 2007, on-line). When they prepared to launch *Wincing the Night Away,* the Sub Pop label had to use unorthodox marketing methods, reaching younger fans through Web-based vehicles such as MySpace (the band currently has more than 154,000 "friends" listed on its MySpace page) and prospective older fans through sales at the java behemoth Starbucks. *Wincing* sold 118, 000 copies in the first week after its release.

On January 2, 2007, in an interview with Matt LeMay for the indie music Web site pitchforkmedia.com, Mercer announced that the multi-instrumentalist Eric Johnson (born on June 7, 1976), from the group Fruit Bats, had officially joined the Shins. Johnson had played with the group on its most recent tour, performing on guitar, keyboards, slide guitar, and even maracas. Mercer has insisted in interviews on his desire to collaborate with new musicians continually. On January 13, 2007 the Shins' celebrity status was highlighted by their appearance on *Saturday Night Live* with the actor Jake Gyllenhaal; they performed "Phantom Limb" and "New Slang." Discussing honors and distinctions he would like to see his band attain, Mercer told Douglas Walk, "There's always the cover of *Rolling Stone.* Or having a video on MTV that they're actually playing and not just at 3:30 in the morning."

The Shins began touring for *Wincing the Night Away* in February 2007, taking a break of several months the following spring and summer when Mercer's wife, the journalist Marisa Kula, gave birth to the couple's first child. (Mercer met Kula in April 2006, when she interviewed the Shins for an article she was writing. The band resumed their tour in the fall.

Personal Lives

The members of the Shins reside in Portland's more bohemian-friendly regions. Mercer lives in a former 1920s-era speakeasy, once occupied by one of Portland's indie legends, the late singer-songwriter Elliott Smith. Crandall lives in another storied Portland dwelling, the Alfred J. Armstrong House, which is listed in the National Register of Historic Places. In their spare time, the band members enjoy surfing, riding motocross, and playing video games.

Further Reading

Albuquerque (New Mexico) Journal Venue p18 Apr. 6, 2007

Billboard p28+ Feb. 3, 2007

(London) *Observer* p21 Apr. 1, 2007

Rolling Stone p22 Nov. 30, 2006, p71+ Jan. 25, 2007, p53+ Feb. 8, 2007

Thrasher (on-line) Apr. 2004

Time Off (on-line) Jan. 2007

Beverly Sills

Singer

Born: May 25, 1929; Brooklyn, New York City, New York

Died: July 2, 2007; New York, New York

Primary Field: Opera

Group Affiliation: New York City Opera

Introduction

One of the more gratifying experiences of the decade for American opera fans of the 1960s anxious to acclaim a locally bred and trained prima donna was the evolution of Brooklyn-born Beverly Sills from a predictably dependable performer with the New York City Opera Company into an international coloratura soprano of the first magnitude. Hers was by no means an overnight success story. Once known as Bubbles Silverman, Miss Sills began her career as a three-year-old child star of the Shirley Temple persuasion on a weekly radio program. She went into premature retirement at the age of twelve, emerging three years later to stage a comeback in touring musical companies. A ten-year apprenticeship on the road in everything from Gilbert and Sullivan to Bizet provided her with the experience that eventually brought her star billing at the New York City Opera. Her electrifying performance as Cleopatra in Handel's Julius Caesar in 1966 finally brought her the recognition her uncommon gifts had always deserved. With her interpretive skill only deepened by tragedies in her private life, Miss Sills came into a late-blooming dra-

matic and musical maturity that astonished even her colleagues in the New York City Opera Company.

Early Life

Of Russian-Jewish descent, Beverly Sills was born Belle Silverman in Brooklyn, New York on May 25, 1929 to Morris Silverman, an insurance broker, and Shirley (Bahn) Silverman. She had two older brothers, Dr. Sidney N. Silverman and Stanley S. Sills, an International Telephone and Telegraph Company executive. Mrs. Silverman interpreted her daughter's precocious musical talent and her blonde curls as signs that the family had been blessed with a second Shirley Temple. Adopting the stage name of Bubbles, the child made her radio debut when she was three on a Saturday morning children's program called *Uncle Bob's Rainbow House.* For four years she was its permanent fixture, come rain or come shine. At six Bubbles Silverman won a Major Bowes Amateur Hour prize, and by the time she was seven she had appeared in a couple of Twentieth Century-Fox films with Willie Howard. Shortly afterwards she was delighting the Major Bowes Capitol Family Hour audience weekly with her tap dancing and her memorized renditions of some twenty-two coloratura arias she had learned phonetically from her mother's Galli-Curci recordings. It was about this time that she made her concert debut. Even at that age Miss Sills was attuned to audience response. One winter evening Major Bowes asked Bubbles over the air if she had arrived by sled. She replied that she had none, and within a matter of weeks she had received dozens of sleds from compassionate listeners. From then on, Bubbles Silverman obtained the things she wanted by mentioning them on the air. A thirty-six week engagement on the marathon soap opera *Our Gal Sunday* gave her the opportunity to gain her first experience as a singing actress when she played a "nightingirl of the mountains." She also sang the original "Rinso White" jingle, one of the pioneer singing commercials, which had for its lyrics "Rinso White, Rinso White, Happy Little Washday Song." For a time she appeared on radio's *Cresta Blanca Hour*.

By that time Beverly Sills was twelve and becoming somewhat self-conscious. Because her days as a child prodigy were behind her, the Silvermans had decided their daughter should retire and devote some attention to her studies at Erasmus Hall High School in Brooklyn and the Professional Children's School in New York City. Meanwhile, she had also found time for daily French and Italian lessons, in addition to her

Beverly Sills.

daily voice lessons with the famous singer and teacher Estelle Liebling that she had taken since the age of seven and for weekly piano lessons in the Bronx with Paolo Gallico, the father of novelist Paul Gallico. Miss Liebling had been Amelita Galli-Curci's coach and until her death in 1970 remained the only voice teacher with whom Beverly Sills ever studied. Miss Liebling reminisced to Quaintance Eaton in an interview for the March 1, 1969 issue of *Opera News* that her small but enthusiastic student loved singing so much that she cried when told to be quiet for awhile. Although she brought Beverly up on taxing vocal exercises, Miss Liebling maintained that her pupil no longer needed them and at that time warmed up exclusively with arias. "She can do anything," declared Estelle Liebling flatly.

Life's Work

On her graduation from the Professional Children's School in 1945, Beverly Sills entered the American musical world in its most rigorous form: the national tour, with its succession of brief engagements and one-night shows, exhaustive repertory, and severe demands on versatility and stamina. During her first season with the Gilbert and Sullivan Opera Company, for instance, she sang six different leading roles. That was followed by tours in musicals under the auspices of J. J. Shubert, singing Rosemarie, Countess Maritza, and the Merry Widow, and her first concert tour. The teen-aged diva's debut in opera took place as Micaela in *Carmen* with the Philadelphia Civic Opera when she was seventeen. After that she toured coast-to-coast for two seasons with the Charles Wagner Opera Company, singing dozens of Micaelas and Violettas in *La Traviata,* on as many nights. "My voice was all right, but my feet were killing me," she said.

After eight unsuccessful auditions over a three-year period, Beverly Sills joined the New York City Opera, then housed in the City Center of Music and Drama, during the 1955–56 season, after her ninth attempt. Thus began the mutually beneficial relationship that gave the young company a soprano with a reputation for being a good trouper, while she in turn was guaranteed a secure home base and a springboard to fame. The brief reports on Beverly Sills's debut, as Rosalinda in *Die Fledermaus,* with the New York City Opera in late October 1955 that appeared in the *New York Times* and New York *Herald Tribune* anticipate her later triumphs. The reviewers not only were beguiled by the quality and technique of her voice but also by the assurance, vivacity, and personality of her characterization. The *Times* critic, Francis D. Perkins, remarked prophetically that the opera company had added an accomplished singing actress to its roster. "I'll sacrifice the beautiful note for the meaningful word or movement any time," Miss Sills often assured interviewers. "Anybody can drop pearls."

Beverly Sills created the title role in Douglas Moore's opera in the American folk idiom, *The Ballad of Baby Doe,* when it had its premiere at Central City, Colorado on July 7, 1956, and she repeated her initial success on its many revivals. (She also made an acclaimed recording of the opera.) When Moore's *The Wings of the Dove* had its premiere in October 1961, she sang the role of the Henry James heroine, Milly Theale. In addition to her contributions to contemporary American opera, Miss Sills sang many roles in the standard repertory with the New York City Opera. She was able to perform some eighty-five or ninety roles, ranging from Violetta in Verdi's *La Traviata* to Pamira in Rossini's *The Siege of Corinth.*

While appearing with the New York City Opera in Cleveland, in 1955, Miss Sills met Peter Bulkeley Greenough, a Boston Brahmin descended from John Alden, whose family holdings included the Cleveland *Plain Dealer*. They were married on November 17, 1956, and Beverly Sills found herself in charge of a twenty-five-room house and three small daughters—Lindley, Nancy, and Diana—from her husband's previous marriage. Although Miss Sills commuted to New York City from Cleveland and later from Boston, her career advanced little during that period. She was, however, happy with her family; a daughter of her own, Meredith (Muffy) was born in 1959 and a son, Peter Jr. (Bucky) arrived two years later. The day that tests proved that Muffy, then almost two and very bright, suffered from a profound loss of hearing was the worst day of her life, Beverly Sills told her husband, but only a few months afterwards the couple discovered that their baby boy was retarded. When they put Peter into a special school, they felt relieved by the knowledge that little worse could happen.

Determined to help Muffy in her fight to hear, Beverly Sills stopped singing and devoted herself to helping

Affiliation: Return to the New York City Opera

One of Beverly Sills's first feats after her return to the New York City Opera stage was her daring performance of all the female leading roles in Offenbach's *The Tales of Hoffmann* which she topped off with a startling high C sharp triple fortissimo that all but overpowered the orchestra. The New York Times critic Harold C. Schonberg recorded in his October 15, 1965 review that her interpretations were convincing, considering the contrasts between the characters of Olympia, Antonia, and Giulietta. The fact that she had attempted and brought off all three of the roles indicated a courage shared by few sopranos.

The 1966–67 season of the New York City Opera gave Miss Sills the chance to expand her repertory with a brief Mozart cycle that gave her the opportunity to appear as Donna Anna in *Don Giovanni,* Constanza in *The Abduction from the Seraglio,* and the Queen of the Night in The *Magic Flute,* in all of which she won critical acclaim. Commenting on her Donna Anna in the October 1, 1966 issue of the New York *World Journal Tribune,* critic Miles Kastendieck noted that Miss Sills had set a new standard for herself that season; what she achieved as Mozart's heroine enhanced her reputation as a singing actress.

the child master such simple skills as blowing out a candle, which took her weeks to learn. All that autumn and winter, New York City Opera Director Julius Rudel sent her a series of nonsensical, chatty notes filled with small talk about opera and with half-joking, half-serious references to roles in which she might conceivably—or inconceivably—appear, including that of Boris Godunov (written for a bass voice). But by the following spring, Rudel decided it was time for Beverly Sills to return to the lyric stage, and he had his secretary notify her of performances to be sung that season and of rehearsal dates, with a reminder for her to turn up on time.

Turn up on time she did, but it seemed as though a different singer had returned. Looking back on her return to opera after an absence of about a year and a half, Beverly Sills noted that she always looked upon herself as a good singer, although for a long time she considered herself as a product of other people's ideas. "After I came back, I talked back," she said. Above all, she stopped worrying about what anyone else might think. Miss Sills recalled that she used to speculate while walking along the street whether anyone else in the passing crowd had suffered as much as she. Once she had surmounted that negative approach and her bitterness and self-pity, she felt really free to release herself onstage. "I felt if I could survive my grief, I could survive anything," she explained to interviewers.

In the spring of 1966 Beverly Sills showed what she could accomplish with the meticulous demands of baroque opera when she sang Aricie in the first American staging of Rameau's little-known *Hippolyte et Aricie* by Sarah Caldwell's Opera Company of Boston. Her security, precision, and ease in negotiating the role's exacting scales, roulades, trills, and grace notes captivated the critics. Then, in October 1966, in the still-new house of the New York State Theatre in Lincoln Center, she helped to open the New York City Opera's autumn season in a sumptuous production of Handel's *Julius Caesar*. The fact that it was the first Handel opera to be staged by a major company in New York within living memory had quickened anticipation, but it turned out that the evening's special excitement was generated by Beverly Sills as Cleopatra. She not only managed the florid fioritura of the score with incredible ease but succeeded at the same time in creating the character of a superficial girl evolving into a queenly woman. And in spite of all the acrobatics, she never sacrificed the clarity of her diction, the floating gossamer of her pianissimi, and the warmth, body, purity, and color of her voice.

Opening the company's spring season, which also marked its twenty-fifth anniversary, a new production of Massenet's *Manon*, the New York City Opera's biggest success of 1968, returned on February 20, 1969. Again Beverly Sills appeared in the title role of a production that Harold C. Schonberg called "very likely the most beautiful ever staged in New York." According to Schonberg, Miss Sills's acting had improved over even its high standard of the previous season, in communicating the character of Manon in her downward path from innocence to worldly wisdom and eventual disaster. George Movshon of *Musical America* (May 1969) also found her Manon authentic and human and her singing delectable in the most unanimously acclaimed operatic production New York City had seen since the end of World War II. The usually captious Winthrop Sergeant of the *New Yorker* (March 1, 1969) wrote: "If I were recommending the wonders of New York City to a tourist, I should place Beverly Sills as Manon at the top of the list—way ahead of such things as the Statue of Liberty and the Empire State Building." The critical response was scarcely less adulatory the following autumn when, on the same stage, Miss Sills sang the emotionally and technically demanding title role in Donizetti's *Lucia di Lammermoor,* perhaps the supreme test for coloratura sopranos.

Meanwhile, Beverly Sills had obtained the cachet of foreign critics. That came in April of 1969 when she made her debut at Milan's La Scala as Pamira in Rossini's long-neglected opera *The Siege of Corinth,* in a revival that featured her fellow American singers Marilyn Hornee and Justino Diaz under the baton of Thomas Schippers. At a rehearsal the Italian members of the orchestra had given her a standing ovation, and by the end of the public performance Beverly Sills had not only been transformed into "La Sills" but had also picked up the Italian nicknames of "Il Mostro" and "La Fenomena." The influential Italian daily *La Stampa* headlined its story about the performance: "American interpreters of Rossini brought bel canto again to La Scala."

Other foreign engagements took Beverly Sills to the Teatro Colon in Buenos Aires, to Mexico City and Lausanne, to Santiago de Chile, Cologne, and to Vienna, where she sang at the State Opera in Mozart during the annual festival, a distinction of which she was especially proud. Her recordings included Handel's *Julius Caesar,* released by RCA Victor in 1967, *The Ballad of Baby Doe,* re-released on CD by Deutsche Grammaphon, and Bellini and Donizetti *Heroines* and *Scenes and Arias from French Opera,* both 1969 Westminster releases. Later recordings included, among others, versions of Donizetti's *Roberto Devereux, Lucia di Lammermoor, Anna Bolena, Maria Stuarda,* and *Don Pasquale; Offenbach's Tales of Hoffman; Bellini's I puritani, I capuleti e i Montecchi,* and *Norma;* Massenet's *Manon and Thaïs;* and Verdi's *La traviata* and *Rigoletto*.

Thanks to her wit, warmth, and utter lack of prima donna temperament. Beverly Sills took her sudden fame in stride. She assured *Newsweek's* music critic Hubert Saal in an interview published on April 21, 1969 that she would instantly trade her success without a regret if someone could guarantee her a healthy child. The best feature of her new success, she felt, was the chance it gave her to sing what she likes. "I love being able to sing well," she told Saal, "to have it just pour out of me. I'm happy onstage/." Miss Sills gave the impression of serenity onstage and at her vocal best traversed what seemed to be a three-octave range. An admirer of Maria Callas, she noted that she would not mind having a similar career—brief but brilliant and full of deep emotional involvement in her roles. "Opera is drama and music," she said. "They are inseparable and I won't take one without the other."

In 1969, Sills sang Zerbinetta in the American premiere (in a concert version) of the 1912 version of Richard Strauss's *Ariadne auf Naxos* with the Boston Symphony. Her performance of the role, especially Zerbinetta's aria, "Grossmächtige Prinzessin," which she sang in the original higher key, won her acclaim. Home video-taped copies circulated among collectors for years afterwards, often commanding large sums on Internet auction sites; the performance was finally released commercially in 2006, garnering high praise. The second major event of the year was her debut as Pamira in Rossini's *The Siege of Corinth at La Scala,* a success that put her on the cover of *Newsweek.*

Sills's high-profile career landed her on the cover of *Time* in 1971, where she was described as "America's Queen of Opera." The title was appropriate because Sills had purposely limited her overseas engagements because of her family. Her major overseas appearances were at London's *Covent Garden, Milan's La Scala, La Fenice in Venice, the Vienna State Opera, the Théâtre de Beaulieu in Lausanne, Switzerland,* and concerts in Paris. In South America, she sang in the opera houses of Buenos Aires and Santiago, a concert in Lima, Peru, and appeared in several productions in Mexico City, including *Lucia di Lammermoor* with Luciano Pavarotti. On November 9, 1971, her performance in the New York City Opera's production of *The Golden Cockerel* was telecast live to cable TV subscribers.

During this period, she made her first television appearance as a talk-show personality on *Virginia Graham's Girl Talk,* a weekday series syndicated by ABC Films. An opera fan who was talent coordinator for the series persuaded the producer to put her on the air, and she was a huge hit. Throughout the rest of her career she shone as a talk show guest, sometimes also functioning as a guest host. Sills underwent successful surgery for ovarian cancer in late October 1974 (sometimes misreported as breast cancer). Her recovery was so rapid and complete that she opened in *Daughter of the Regiment* at the San Francisco Opera a month later.

Following Sir Rudolf Bing's departure as director, Sills finally made her debut at the Metropolitan Opera on April 7, 1975 in *The Siege of Corinth,* receiving an eighteen-minute ovation. Other operas she sang at the Met include *La traviata, Lucia di Lammermoor, Thaïs,* and *Don Pasquale* (directed by John Dexter). In an interview after his retirement, Bing stated that his refusal to use Sills, as well as his preference for engaging, almost exclusively, Italian stars such as Renata Tebaldi—due to his notion that American audiences expected to see Italian stars—was the single biggest mistake of his career. Sills attempted to downplay her animosity towards Bing while she was still singing, and even in her two autobiographies. But in a 1997 interview, Sills spoke her mind plainly: "Oh, Mr. Bing is an ass. [W]hile everybody said what a great administrator he was and a great this, Mr. Bing was just an improbable, impossible General Manager of the Metropolitan Opera. . . . The arrogance of that man."

Sills was a recitalist, especially in the final decade of her career. She sang in mid-size cities and on college concert series, bringing her art to many who might never see her on stage in a fully staged opera. She also sang concerts with a number of symphony orchestras. Sills continued to perform for New York City Opera, her home opera house, essaying new roles right up to her retirement, including the leading roles in Rossini's *Il Turco in Italia,* Franz Lehár's *The Merry Widow* and Gian Carlo Menotti's *La Loca,* an opera commissioned in honor of her 50th birthday. *La Loca* was the first work written expressly as a vehicle for Sills and was her last new role, as she retired the following year. Her farewell performance was at San Diego Opera in 1980, where she shared the stage with Joan Sutherland in a production of *Die Fledermaus.*

Although Sills' voice type was characterized as a "lyric coloratura," she took a number of heavier spinto and dramatic coloratura roles more associated with heavier voices as she grew older, including Donizetti's *Lucrezia Borgia* (with Susanne Marsee as Orsini) and the same composer's *Tudor Queens,* Anna Bolena, Maria Stuarda and Queen Elizabeth in *Roberto Devereux* (opposite Plácido Domingo in the title part). She was admired in those roles for transcending the lightness of her voice with dramatic interpretation, although it may have come at a cost: Sills later commented that *Roberto Devereux* shortened her career by at least four years.

Sills popularized opera through her appearances on talk shows, including Johnny Carson, Dick Cavett, David Frost, Mike Douglas, Merv Griffin, and Dinah Shore. Sills hosted her own talk show, *Lifestyles with Beverly Sills,* which ran on Sunday mornings on NBC for two years in the late 1970s; it won an Emmy Award. In 1979 she even appeared on *The Muppet Show*. Down-to-earth and approachable, Sills helped dispel the traditional image of the temperamental opera diva.

In 1978, Sills announced she would retire on October 27, 1980, in a farewell gala at the New York City Opera. In the spring of 1979, she began acting as co-director of NYCO, and became its sole general director as of the fall season of that year, a post she held until 1989, although she remained on the NYCO board until 1991. During her time as general director, Sills helped turn what was then a financially struggling opera company into a viable enterprise. She also devoted herself to various arts causes and such charities as the March of Dimes and was sought after for speaking engagements on college campuses and for fund raisers.

From 1994 to 2002, Sills was chairman of Lincoln Center. In October 2002, she agreed to serve as chairman of the Metropolitan Opera, for which she had been a board member since 1991. She resigned as Met chairman in January 2005, citing family as the main reason (she had to place her husband, whom she had cared for over eight years, in a nursing home). She stayed long enough to supervise the appointment of Peter Gelb, formerly head of Sony Classical Records, as the Met's General Manager, to succeed Joseph Volpe in August 2006.

She co-hosted *The View* for Best Friends Week on November 9, 2006, as Barbara Walters' best friend. She said that she didn't sing anymore, even in the shower, to preserve the memory of her voice. Sills's voice was described at the same time "rich, supple," "silvery," "precise, a little light," "multicolored," "robust and enveloping," with "a cutting edge that can slice through the largest orchestra and chorus," soaring easily above high C. Her technique and musicianship were much praised. Conductor Thomas Schippers said in a 1971 interview with Time that she had "the fastest voice alive." The *New York Times* wrote that "she could dispatch coloratura roulades and embellishments, capped with radiant high Ds and E-flats, with seemingly effortless agility. She sang with scrupulous musicianship, rhythmic incisiveness and a vivid sense of text." Soprano Leontyne Price was "flabbergasted at how many millions of things she can do with a written scale." Her vocal range, in performance, extended from F3 to F6, and she said she could sometimes hit a G6 in warm up.

Personal Life

Because of her generously upholstered proportions (39-26-42), titian hair, five feet eight inches of stature, and 150-pound weight, Beverly Sills lent conviction to such voluptuous roles as Cleopatra, Manon, and the seductive Queen of Shemakha in *The Golden Cockerel.* Her hobbies included fishing and bridge. Gourmet cooking was a pastime she shared with her husband, who was financial editor of the *Boston Globe*. With their five children, the couple used to share a nineteen-room home in Milton, Massachusetts, but in the late 1960s the family moved to New York City.

Peter Greenough, Sills's husband, died on September 6, 2006, at the age of 89. They would have had their 50th wedding anniversary on November 17, 2006. On June 28, 2007, the Associated Press and CNN reported that Sills was hospitalized as "gravely ill," from lung cancer. With her daughter at her bedside, Beverly Sills succumbed to cancer on July 2, 2007, at the age of 78. She is interred in the Sharon Gardens Division of Kensico Cemetery in Valhalla, New York.

Further Reading

Hi Fi 19:24 F '69 por
Life 66:37+ Ja 17 '69 pors
N Y Sunday News mag p4+ Ap 14 '68 pors
N Y Times Mag p34+ S 17 '67 pors
Newsweek 73:69+ Ap 21 '69 pors
Who's Who of American Women, 1970-71

Russell Simmons

Founder and CEO of Rush Communications

Born: October 4, 1957; Queens, New York
Primary Field: CEO
Group Affiliation: Rush Communications

Introduction

Russell Simmons, the founder and CEO of Rush Communications, has been widely credited with breaking down the barriers between rap and mainstream pop music. Ever since 1986, when Run-D.M.C., a star rap act from Simmons's Def Jam record label, collaborated with the rock-'n'-roll band Aerosmith on their groundbreaking remake of "Walk This Way"—the first and most famous of several rap singles to become pop hits around this time—rap has steadily made its way not only onto pop radio and the national and international music charts, but also into movie soundtracks and advertising jingles. According to some observers, Simmons may even be responsible for the pervasiveness of rap in many aspects of mainstream culture. Over the past decade, his company has expanded to include publishing (with the magazine Oneworld*), fashion (with the Phat Farm line), television (with the show* Def Comedy Jam*), and film-making (with such Def Pictures releases as* The Nutty Professor*). Dean F. Landsman, the president of a radio-and record-industry consulting firm, told Jonathan Hicks for the* New York Times *(June 14, 1992) that he considered Simmons to be "the king of rap," and that Simmons's understanding of rap as "more than just music" was a major factor in his success. "It's an entire consumer and marketing field, of which he has a tremendous intuition as well as business and marketing sense."*

In all these endeavors, Simmons's goal has been "to present urban culture in its most true form to the people who love it, and to those who live it," as he explained in an undated editorial in Oneworld *(on-line). In 1988, a few years before Def Jam rappers such as L.L. Cool J and the Beastie Boys made an indelible impression on the sound of pop radio, Simmons told an interviewer, "There's a void, a lack of reality in black America. All the artists on black radio are so polished they are almost whitewashed. It has gotten to the point that images that are exclusively black . . . offend many blacks." Simmons has been quite successful in pursuing his goal: Rush Communications has grown to be the second-largest black-owned entertainment company in the U.S., with annual revenues of almost $50 million.*

Early Life

Russell Simmons was born in 1957, and he was raised in a relatively comfortable, middle-class home in the Hollis section of Queens, New York City. According to one account, his father, Daniel, was a professor of black history at Pace University; another reports that he was the supervisor of attendance in one or more New York City school districts. His mother, Evelyn, was a preschool teacher and artist. Russell is the second of his parents' three sons; the eldest, Daniel, is an artist, and the youngest, Joseph, is "Run" of Run-D.M.C., the first and, perhaps, the most famous of the rap groups that Simmons has managed.

As a teenager, Simmons spent several years as a warlord in a gang called the Seven Immortals (a relatively benign group, according to some accounts), and he made money by selling marijuana. "We used to stand on the corner and sell 40, 50 bags in six hours," he told Lucy Kaylin for *Gentlemen's Quarterly* (April 1993). (Although Simmons has made no apologies for his past dealings in marijuana and has credited his later success in business in part to this early exposure to cash flow, client relations, and networking, he has said that he regrets that information about his drug-dealing days has been published, perhaps because it sends the wrong message to wrong people.) When he was in the 11th grade, Simmons worked at an Orange Julius fast-food restaurant, but was fired after one month for throwing oranges into the street outside the shop. That was the first and last time that Simmons was an employee of a business other than his own. His mother told Kaylin that although Russell occasionally got into serious trouble, she never really worried about him. "There was some kind of cover over Russell," she said. "It would be raining on everybody else, and he'd just walk right through." During his teens, his friends nicknamed him Rush.

After graduating from high school, Simmons studied sociology at City College, a branch of the City University of New York, in the Harlem section of New York City. In Harlem, in about 1978, Simmons heard some of the earliest strains of rap, a style of music that combines strong, percussive rhythms with spoken words and that

Affiliation: Rush Communications

In 1990, two years after Rubin left Def Jam to found his own company, Simmons established Rush Communications, which continued to oversee the thriving Def Jam label, Def Pictures, and a fledgling television-production outfit. Having become interested in comedy, he also decided to research whether there was an audience for an African-American television comedy show. "Across the country, there [are] lots of discos and rap music clubs that become comedy clubs for one night out of the week. And those nights are always sold out," he told Christopher Vaughn for *Black Enterprise* (December 1992). "That told me there was an interest in African-American comedians, and I jumped to service that market." *Def Comedy Jam,* which was co-produced by Simmons and his TV-production outfit, Bernie Brillstein (who also worked on the films *Ghostbusters* and *Wayne's World),* and Brad Grey, was hosted by the comedian Martin Lawrence and featured other African-American comics as guests each week. Shortly after its debut, in 1992, it became, according to Jonathan Hicks, the "most-watched television show at midnight on Fridays." Hicks also noted that "virtually every joke was unprintable." Bill Cosby once likened the program to a "minstrel show," and said he felt that the show was telling African-Americans, "You can't come on the show unless you undignify your African-ness." *Def Comedy Jam* retained its popularity and its high ratings, however; it recently entered its seventh season, with the comedian Adele Givens as its first female guest host.

In 1993, Simmons expanded his communications empire to include the magazine *Oneworld,* which offers articles on music, fashion, and hip-hop personalities. Simmons's goal for the publication, according to an editorial he wrote on his Rush Communications Web site, is to "build bridges, and to give readers a unique view of the increasingly multiracial youth culture that we see all around us in music, fashion, and art." In the same year, Simmons launched a line of clothing called Phat Farm (in hip-hop slang, "phat," like "def," refers to something that is "cool" or "hip"). His first collection was described by Amy Spindler, a fashion correspondent for the *New York Times* (March 4, 1994), as "urban work wear"; the line was sold in a boutique in the fashionable SoHo district of Manhattan. Although, at the time of the first Phat Farm fashion show, Simmons told Spindler that he was less concerned with people buying the clothes than with their knowing that the product existed, Phat Farm's profits have been surprisingly high; in 1997, the enterprise grossed almost $10 million.

Recent offshoots of Rush Communications are the Rush Media Co., a marketing and advertising agency that produced award-winning advertisements for Coca-Cola in 1996, and SLBG Entertainment (the initials stand for Simmons, Lathan [that is, the director Stan Lathan], Brillstein, and Grey), which serves as an agency for actors and other entertainers.

Def Picture's most recent films include *The Addiction* (1995) and *The Funeral* (1996), both of which were directed by Abel Ferrara and starred Christopher Walken; *The Nutty Professor* (1996), which starred Eddie Murphy; *How to Be a Player* (1997); and *Gridlock'd* (1997), which featured the late rapper Tupac Shakur. In 1995, Simmons participated and appeared in *The Show,* a documentary about the rise of hip-hop in American culture. Simmons recently hired two African-American filmmakers, Stan Lathan and the producer Preston Holmes, to serve as president and co-chair, respectively, of Def Pictures.

---

was developed mainly by African-Americans in urban centers across the United States. Although it was quickly gaining popularity in New York City, rap had yet to gain the attention of major record companies. While at City College, Simmons and a close friend, Curtis Walker, began to promote rap parties and concerts both in Harlem and in Queens. Reportedly, it was out of these late-1970s parties that hip-hop, the popular subculture that is associated with rap music, was born. Meanwhile, in 1979, Simmons helped Walker (who at some point adopted the name Kurtis Blow) launch his career as a rap artist. The two friends co-wrote the single "Christmas Rappin," which became a hit that holiday season. With Kurtis Blow's success, Simmons took on the management of other local rap acts, some of which were completely unknown outside of their communities. "Russell could take a book of matches and make people think it would light the world," an old friend of Simmons's told Kaylin.

Life's Work

Although rap and disco are drastically different musical genres, in those days record companies lumped them together. Because of this, Simmons would frequent some of New York's trend-setting discotheques and would appeal to the management to have his artists' most recent recordings played. "I was so frustrated with that environment," Simmons told Kaylin. "But that was the only way into the record business." Among the bands he promoted during the early and mid-1980s was Run-D.M.C., which, in addition to his brother Joseph, featured Darryl "D.M.C." McDaniels and Jason "Jam Master Jay" Mizell.

In 1983, Simmons met Rick Rubin, a white student at New York University who also wanted to promote rap music. The two scrounged up $8,000 and founded Def Jam Records ("def" means "excellent" and "jam" connotes music in hip-hop parlance), and set up operations in Rubin's dorm room. Simmons told Alan Light for *Rolling Stone* (November 15, 1990) that his main reason for starting the company was that none of the existing record companies in New York would allow him to develop his artists the way he wanted. McDaniels explained to Nelson George for *Essence* (March 1988) that Simmons's sensibility played a role in Run-D.M.C.'s success: "Russell fixed up our whole image. He put the black hats and leather suits on us. In the studio, we rely on Russell's judgment, because he always knows what people want to hear. If it wasn't for Russell Simmons, rap wouldn't be where it is today."

Two years into their bare-bones operation in Rubin's dorm, Simmons's and Rubin's adept management skills and the growing popularity of rap led Al Teller, then the head of Columbia Records, to approach Def Jam with an offer to promote, market, and distribute Def Jam's new rap recordings for a share in their profits. In addition to the already- popular Run-D.M.C., Def Jam had discovered and contracted the 15-year-old rap sensation L.L. Cool J (James Todd Smith) and the first-ever white rap group, the Beastie Boys. With financial backing from Columbia, 1986 became a landmark year for Def Jam, with Cool J's first full-length album, *Bigger and Deffer*, selling 3.5 million copies and the Beastie Boys' *License to 111* approaching sales of 4.8 million. Run-D.M.C.'s *Raising Hell* sold 2.5 million copies and spawned rap's first top-five pop hit with their version of Aerosmith's "Walk This Way." According to Light, the memorable single "silenced all doubt about [rap's] staying power [and] dominated the radio for that whole summer."

According to Simmons, although Run-D.M.C., L.L. Cool J, and the Beastie Boys are all quite different from one another, each of the acts was extremely important to the evolution of rap as a popular musical genre. Cool J's single "I Need Love" was an early rap love ballad and thus attracted a far broader audience than traditional rap songs, with their abrasive lyrics, had in the past. The caustic music of the Beastie Boys, in contrast, was instrumental in bringing rap to white audiences, because, as Simmons explained to Light, they were able to draw on the work of such white rock-'n'-rollers as Led Zeppelin in the same way that black rappers were inspired by the rhythm-and-blues of James Brown. Another defining moment for rap came when Run-D.M.C.'s "Walk This Way" music video became one of the first rap videos to get significant airplay on MTV, which, in the early 1980s, had played rap music only reluctantly. "Run-D.M.C. didn't have to present a watered-down version of how they were or write a sell-out hit to get MTV to change their programming. They simply had to be themselves, and fans responded," Simmons wrote in an editorial in *Oneworld* (on-line). A second single from the *Raising Hell* album, "My Adidas," earned Run-D.M.C. a $1 million sponsorship contract with the athletic-shoe manufacturer Adidas; it was the first deal of its kind between an athletic-wear company and a nonathlete. *Raising Hell* concerts sold out across the country, even in cities where it was thought that rap was not popular and would not be well received.

The success of these albums prompted Def Jam to sign additional acts, such as Public Enemy, Oran "Juice" Jones, and the rap duo D.J. Jazzy Jeff and the Fresh Prince. Although some of Def Jam's artists have been criticized for their thug-like images and lyrics that seem to glorify violence and misogyny, Simmons has said that he has purposely tried to create images that are true to the urban African-American experience. As he explained to Stephen Holden for the *New York Times* (August 11, 1987), "In black America, your neighbor is much more likely to be someone like L.L. Cool J or Oran 'Juice' Jones than [the entertainer] Bill Cosby. A lot of the black stars being developed by record companies have images that are so untouchable that kids just don't relate to them. Our acts are people with strong, colorful images that urban kids already know. . . . If some of those images glorify an outlaw pose, it's just kids having fun." Simmons has also defended some of his artists' blatantly misogynist songs. "Those songs are about guys giving advice to women who are not together, who are playing themselves so cheap!" he told George. He added, "Rap is an expression of the attitudes of the performers and their audience. I don't censor my artists. I let them speak."

At the same time that Simmons and Rubin were developing the Def Jam record label, Simmons was also becoming involved in other media. In 1985, in cooperation with Warner Bros., his new company, Def Pictures, produced its first film, *Krush Groove,* a rap musical based loosely on his own life and the rise of hip-hop. The film, which cost only about $3 million to produce, grossed almost $20 million at the box office. Simmons's second film, *Tougher Than Leather* (1988), was a Dirty Harry-style film starring the members of Run-D.M.C. as themselves. Simmons admitted to David Hinckley for the *New York Daily News* (July 24, 1988) that because the film contained so many derogatory references to women, finding a distributor proved to be difficult. "We showed it to major companies and they went, 'Oh, you gotta fix that,'" he recalled. "What [they] don't get is that this movie insults *everyone.* It's not vicious, it's funny. . . . It has a song called 'Treat Her Like a Prostitute,' by Slick Rick. It could be very big. It's not against women. It's funny." Like *Krush Groove, Tougher Than Leather* was not a critical success, but it did well at the box office.

In 1994, Simmons sold the distribution rights to recordings produced by Def Jam to Polygram, a Dutch-owned record company, for $33 million. (He retains complete control over the musical products that emanate from Def Jam.) In *Fortune* (December 1997), Roy S. Johnson wrote that Simmons had recently become "frustrated by Polygram's unwillingness to invest in his other ventures, which target the growing hip-hop-influenced urban market." One of Simmons's lawyers told Johnson, "We're still trying to ascertain whether Polygram wants to be fair and whether it wants to be in the urban entertainment business. If people are less interested in urban culture, it makes it difficult for people who are interested in that culture to exist in that environment."

Personal Life

Although he has three offices in New York City and another three in Los Angeles, California, Simmons does most of his work at home—a triplex penthouse apartment in the Greenwich Village section of New York City that was once owned by the pop star and actress Cher. His cellular telephone—which, it is said, never leaves his side—rings constantly, and Simmons reportedly never misses a call. Speaking of Simmons's management style, his brother Joseph told Stephen J. Dubner for *New York* (December 21, 1992), "He's not scared to hire some of the strangest people. You go to his office and it looks like a costume party, the way those people are dressed. But they are the most professional." Simmons typically dresses in loose-fitting jeans, a hooded sweatshirt, and untied sneakers, even when attending important business meetings. Kaylin noted that he speaks with a slight lisp and has a roundish face that "slides easily between worried and silly at least a few times a minute." According to David Hinckley, Simmons usually begins his day at a late hour. He likes to work through the afternoon, break at about 8 p.m. for dinner, and then work far into the night, sometimes until 2:30 a.m. "Then we'll go somewhere till about 4:30," Simmons said. "Drink, tell jokes. It's cool."

Simmons recently founded the Rush Philanthropic Arts Foundation, which conducts a celebrity auction and other events to raise money for projects that help inner-city youth.

Further Reading

Essence p60+ Mar. 1988, with photos
Gentlemen's Quarterly pi68+ Apr. 1993, with photos
New York p69+ Dec. 21, 1992, with photo
New York Daily News C p24 July 24, 1988, with photos
New York Times III pi June 14, 1992, with photos
Rolling Stone pl06+ Nov. 15, 1990, with photos

Paul Simon

Singer-songwriter

Born: October 13, 1941; Newark, New Jersey
Primary Field: progressive folk
Group Affiliation: Solo artist; Simon and Garfunkel

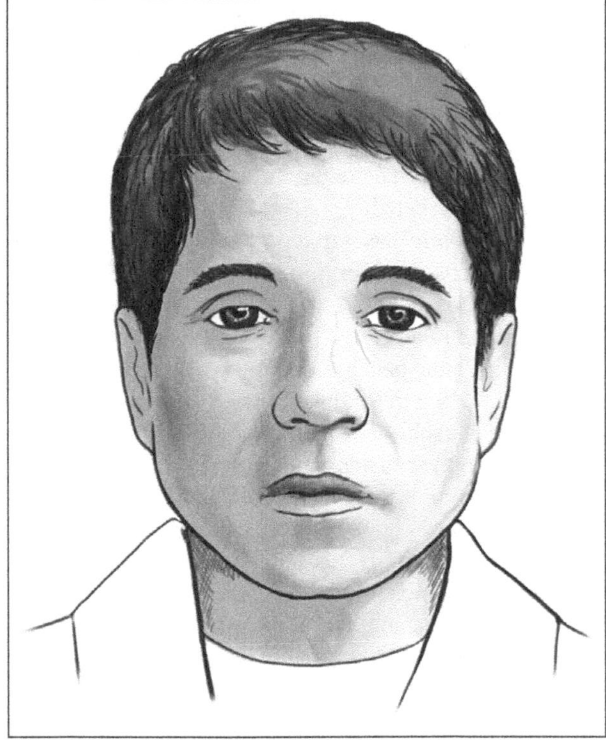

Paul Simon.

Introduction

Paul Simon ranks "among the most erudite and daring songsmiths in popular music," according to his inductee biography at the Rock and Roll Hall of Fame. In a career spanning more than fifty years, Simon has been praised as an innovator and a consummate craftsman for his performances, his lyrics, and his music. In collaboration with Art Garfunkel, Simon produced some of the best-loved songs of the sixties, and later, as a solo artist, he forged a genre of his own, fusing progressive folk and world beats in a fluid and ever-evolving style that has garnered Grammys, tributes, honors, and new generations of fans. "Paul Simon," writes Paul Zollo in a cover article for American Songwriter, *"is an ongoing creative phenomenon, an American treasure as significant to the art of songwriting as Cole Porter or Irving Berlin was in their day, a songwriter who continues to break new ground in an art form that has been profoundly impacted by his work. Unlike many of his peers who seem creatively disengaged, Simon has entered his 70th year as exultant about songwriting and record-making as ever."*

Early Life

Paul Frederic Simon was born on October 13, 1941, in Newark, New Jersey. In 1945 his family moved to Flushing, New York, where he spent the remainder of his childhood. Simon's parents, Louis and Belle Simon, were of Hungarian Jewish extraction. Both of his parents were teachers: Louis Simon held a doctorate in linguistics and was a professor of education at City College of New York, and Belle Simon taught elementary school, although she took time off to raise Paul and his younger brother Eddie. Simon's father was also a professional musician who played upright bass in clubs and on television programs such as the Jackie Gleason Show. In addition to their love of music, Paul and his father shared a love of the New York Yankees and the sport of baseball. In an article in the *New York Times*, Simon writes, "I was sitting on my father's lap listening to a Yankee game on our old Philco radio. It was 1948 and I suddenly realized I was a Yankee fan." He played baseball in high school for the "all-Queens second team," and has remained a fan throughout his life.

Growing up in Queens, Simon attended the same elementary school as his future musical collaborator, Art Garfunkel. He first heard Art sing in the fourth grade, and in high school the two boys briefly formed a duo called Tom and Jerry. The band performed at dances and produced one minor hit, but broke up after graduation, when Simon attended Queens College in New York and Garfunkel went to Columbia. It was only after college that they reunited and began their professional collaboration in earnest.

Life's Work

"I think you could look at my work as divided into three distinct periods," Simon explains in an interview with *American Songwriter*: "Simon and Garfunkel, pre-*Graceland* solo albums and *Graceland* to the present."

From the beginning of their partnership, Simon and Garfunkel showed a deep connection with the music of the Everly Brothers. "As teenagers," writes Andy Greene of *Rolling Stone*, "Paul Simon and Art Garfunkel used to sing Everly Brothers songs on the grounds of Forest Hills High School. They were their single biggest influence, with no close second." This is reflected in the use of close harmonies and in the "pristine and soulful" singing, which Simon attributed to the Everlys but which just as aptly characterizes the vocal style that he and Garfunkel created.

Rolling Stone has ranked Simon among the 100 greatest guitarists, observing that he speaks "as vividly through his guitar as through his lyrics." Initially, Simon was influenced by "early doo-wop and rock & roll," but he later became deeply involved in the folk revival, "traveling to England to study the acoustic mastery of Bert Jansch." This combination of rock and folk guitar created the musical underpinnings of Simon and Garfunkel's sound and was at least as important as the vocal harmonies.

A third element in this legendary musical partnership, and one which contributed greatly to its success, was Paul Simon's singular talent as a lyricist. In a 2011 interview, *American Songwriter* describes him as "surgically precise with words," and Simon then elaborates:

I guess clarity is the most important thing, although mystery is pleasurable too. The first line of a song is crucial. Listener attention is probably highest at the first line. I try to make those words interesting enough to keep the listener interested, . . . a quick image that tells a story or asks a question.

Many of Simon's lyrics stand on their own as poetry, although as he has pointed out, he develops his lyrics to fit the music rather than the other way around.

In 1963, the duo began performing in small clubs and were eventually noticed and signed by Columbia Records. Their first album, *Wednesday Morning 3 AM*, sold poorly when it was originally released in 1964, likely eclipsed by the simultaneous outbreak of Beatlemania. At this point, Garfunkel decided to return to Columbia, and Simon moved to England, hoping to launch a solo career. He had limited success in the UK, but he did sign with a British record company, Oriole, and produced a single hit called "He Was My Brother." Simon also made friends with such folk rock luminaries as Bert Jansch and Sandy Denny, and fell in love with Kathy Chitty, who would inspire two of his subsequent songs, "Kathy's Song" and "America."

The second stage in Simon's career, by his own reckoning, is his solo work prior to *Graceland*, which was released in 1986. This was Simon's time to define himself as a solo artist and, as he explains in an interview with *American Songwriter*, it was "liberating" not to be "writing for a duo anymore. . . . It freed me to write more rhythm songs. . . . My first songs after Art and I broke up were "Mother and Child Reunion" and "Me and Julio down by the Schoolyard."

These first solo efforts combined world rhythms; playful yet reflective and revealing lyrics; and creative, eclectic instrumentation. Simon's interest in world music is evident in the Jamaican-influenced "Mother and Child Reunion" and the Latin style of "Me and Julio," both hits from his first album of the solo period, *Paul Simon* (1972). He continued his experimentation with world music and with more introspective lyrics throughout the period, with *There Goes Rhymin' Simon* (1973); *Still Crazy after All These Years* (1975), for which he won two Grammys; and *Hearts and Bones* (1983).

The first half of this phase in Simon's career was undoubtedly the most productive and critically well-received. Stephen Holden of *Rolling Stone* considers the first two albums "fully realized work[s] of art, of genius in fact," and reserves special praise for *Rhymin' Simon*, which he calls "a sweeping outward gesture from the introspection of the first album [in which] Simon has triumphantly relocated his sensibility in the general scheme of things: as a musician, as a poet of the American tragedy, and most importantly as a family man." In a review of *Still Crazy*, however, *Rolling Stone*'s Paul Nelson refers to Simon not as a "genius" but as a "good middleweight" and to the album itself as a "grim and ambitious" effort in which Simon "paints himself into the usual corner under the familiar shadow of Bob Dylan." And as for *Hearts and Bones*, which sold poorly, critic Robert Christgau refers to it as "a finely wrought dead end." Discouraged, and fearful that his songwriting gift had begun to fail him, Simon was ready for something new.

The third phase of Paul Simon's career began with *Graceland*, which took his love affair with world music to new heights and generated a great deal of controversy in the process. As Christgau observes, "This isn't the mere exoticism that flavored past Simon hits with reggae and gospel and Andean pipes. It's a full immersion." The "groove" of the album "doesn't come from nowhere—it's indigenous to black South Africa. . . . On its own idiosyncratic terms, this is a real umbaqanga

Affiliation: Simon and Garfunkel

Simon returned to America in 1965, intending to attend law school, but fate intervened. One song from *Wednesday Morning* had begun to receive attention as a single: "The Sound of Silence." The producer of the original album, Tom Wilson, was encouraged and decided to try an electric-acoustic remix of the song, replacing the original purely acoustic accompaniment. Despite some artistic criticism of the overdubbing, the new "Sound of Silence" was a resounding success.

In 1966, riding on the wave of popularity from "The Sound of Silence," *Wednesday Morning 3 AM* was re-released as *Sounds of Silence* and quickly began to climb the charts. Over the remaining half-decade, Simon and Garfunkel created *Parsley, Sage, Rosemary, and Thyme* (1966), *Bookends* (1968), and *Bridge over Troubled Water* (1970), albums which represent, as *Rolling Stone*'s Nicholas Dawidoff writes, "among the most melodic, beautifully interwoven harmonies in American musical history." Simon and Garfunkel's work was also featured in the soundtrack of Mike Nichols' iconic film, *The Graduate.* In 1968, the duo received Grammys both for record of the year and best contemporary pop performance of a vocal duo or group for "Mrs. Robinson," and *The Graduate* won best original score. In 1971, *Bridge over Troubled Water* took the Grammy for album of the year, and the lead single, "Bridge over Troubled Water," garnered five Grammys—record of the year, song of the year, best contemporary song, best instrumental arrangement, and best engineered recording.

At the height of their popularity, however, Simon and Garfunkel's relationship had begun to unravel, and Simon announced the split in 1971. "There was no real pressure to stay together . . ." he recalls:

We didn't need the money. And musically, it was not a creative team, too much, because Artie is a singer, and I'm a writer and player and a singer. We didn't work together on a creative level and prepare the songs. I did that. When we came into the studio I became more and more me, making the tracks and choosing the musicians. (from *Paul Simon: A Life* by Mark Eliot)

Simon, in his own words, "just wanted out." There have been Simon and Garfunkel reunions over the years, but from that point onward, Simon's main focus was his career as a solo artist.

album: the rhythms and licks and colors that define the style can't go unchanged in this alien context, but I swear they remain undiluted. Yet at the same time it's a real Paul Simon album."

Simon's decision to use black South African artists, principally the vocal group Ladysmith Black Mambazo, reinforced the authenticity of the music, but it also created a firestorm of controversy because at the time there was a boycott on performing in South Africa due to its policy of apartheid. Students at Howard University were particularly incensed, claiming that Simon was violating the boycott. Simon responded: "When I went to South Africa [to work on the album], I in no way thought I was in defiance of the cultural boycott. The boycott is aimed at performing, and in fact, that is the definition of it" (from James McBride, *Washington Post*). Simon did not in fact perform in South Africa, he paid his musicians three times American scale and treated them and their music with great respect, even reverence. When he accepted his Grammy for *Graceland*, he spoke of "my deep admiration and love for the singers and musicians from South Africa who worked with me on *Graceland*... They live — along with other South African artists and their countryman — under one of the most repressive regimes on the planet today and still they are able to produce music of great power and nuance and joy. And I find that just extraordinary, and they have my great respect and love."

After *Graceland*, Simon has continued to grow and develop as an artist. In *The Rhythm of the Saints* (1990), Simon explores West African and Brazilian musical idioms, and, as John McAlley of *Rolling Stone* writes, "extends his reach not only further into the riches of world-beat music but further into the realm of the spiritual." *So Beautiful or So What,* released in 2007, effortlessly employs what Will Hermes of *Rolling Stone* calls "the common tongues of a polyglot modern world" in what amounts to a "spiritual meditation" that "sums up much of what makes Simon great." In 2015, *The Ultimate Collection: Paul Simon,* was released and charted number one in the UK, coinciding with Simon's "On Stage Together" tour with Sting.

Personal Life

Paul Simon was married to Peggy Harper from 1969 to 1975. They had one son, Harper. Simon married Carrie Fisher in 1983, but they divorced in 1984. He is presently married to folk singer Edie Brickell. They have three children, Adrian, Lulu, and Gabriel, and reside in New Canaan, Connecticut.

Further Reading

"100 Greatest Guitarists." *Rolling Stone*. Nov. 23, 2011.

Christgau, Robert. "South Africa Romance." *Robert Christgau.com*.

Eliot, Marc. *Paul Simon: A Life*. Wiley, 2010.

Greene, Andy. "Flashback: Everly Brothers Reunite for Simon and Garfunkel," *Rolling Stone*. September 30, 2013.

Holden, Stephen. "There Goes Rhymin' Simon." Rolling Stone. June 21, 1973.

"Interview: Paul Simon Discusses *Songwriter* and Songwriting." *American Songwriter.* Oct. 7, 2011.

Mastropolo, Frank. "51 Years Ago: Simon & Garfunkel Record Their First Classic, 'The Sounds of Silence.'" *Ultimate Classic Rock*. March 10, 2015.

McAlley, John. *Rolling Stone*. Nov. 15, 1990.

"Paul Simon," *Rock and Roll Hall of Fame*.

"Paul Simon Biography." *Biography.com*.

Zollo, Paul. "Paul Simon on Songwriting: I Know What I Know." *American Songwriter* September 1, 2011.

Frank Sinatra

Singer; actor

Born: December 12, 1917; Hoboken, New Jersey
Died: May 14, 1998; Los Angeles, California
Primary Field: American songbook
Group Affiliation: Solo performer

Introduction

Frank Sinatra, who first became popular in the early 1940's when his unusual style of singing love ballads made teen-aged girls squeal and swoon, was regarded as one of the biggest show business attractions of the twentieth century. During his resplendent career—marked by a professional comeback after a popularity slump—Sinatra developed into a baritone who charmed lovers of popular music of all ages. He also became a sensitive and versatile motion-picture actor, who won a 1953 Academy of Motion Picture Arts and Sciences Award as best supporting actor for his performance in From Here to Eternity. *His annual income by 1960 was estimated at $4,000,000; he could write his own contract at almost any night club; his Capitol albums were among the most popular records ever pressed; he appeared frequently on television; and he starred in a number of motion pictures each year. In the world of entertainment, "The Voice" came through more loudly and clearly than ever before.*

Early Life

Francis Albert Sinatra was born in Hoboken, New Jersey on December 12, 1917 (some sources indicate 1915), the only child of Anthony Martin and Natalie (Garaventi) Sinatra. His father, who was for many years a member of the Hoboken Fire Department, and his mother, who often sang at social affairs, were both born in Italy.

Frank first became interested in music when his uncle gave him a ukulele, and on summer nights he would sit on a curbstone under a street light singing while he strummed on the ukulele. At Hoboken's Demarest High School he joined the school band and helped to organize the glee club. Later, he took courses at Drake Institute. In these years Sinatra developed another lasting interest, boxing; he grew up in a tough neighborhood and became a good boxer in order to protect himself. When he left school he went to work for the now-defunct *Jersey Observer* in his home town, first as a helper on a delivery truck and later as a copy boy.

Life's Work

Apparently, Sinatra's decision to become a singer was a spur-of-the-moment affair. One day in 1936 he and his fiancée, Nancy Barbato, went to a Jersey City vaudeville house to see Bing Crosby, who was making a personal appearance there. Afterwards, Sinatra, who could not read music and who had never sung professionally before, suddenly announced that he, too, was "going to be a singer." He promptly quit his newspaper job and began singing with various local bands.

In 1937 Sinatra and three young instrumentalists from Hoboken performed on the *Major Bowes' Original Amateur Hour* as the Hoboken Four. They were awarded first prize and engaged for a tour with one of Bowes's traveling companies. After three months, a homesick Sinatra left the group and returned to Hoboken.

For the next year and a half, Sinatra sang at the Rustic Cabin, a North Jersey roadhouse, for $15 a week. When, in 1939, he got a $10 raise, he celebrated the occasion by marrying Nancy Barbato. At this time Sinatra performed without compensation on many local radio shows hoping to attract the attention of someone who could give him a good singing job.

Sinatra's efforts brought results: a trumpeter with Benny Goodman's band, Harry James, heard Sinatra sing on a broadcast from the Rustic Cabin. James, who was organizing his own orchestra, offered Sinatra a one-year, $75-a-week contract in 1939. After several months with Harry James, Sinatra broke the contract to join Tommy Dorsey and his band.

For three and a half years Sinatra sang with Dorsey, eventually becoming as much a celebrity as the band leader. His discs of "I'll Never Smile Again," "Night and Day," and "This Love of Mine," made with the Dorsey group, smashed sales records. At this time Sinatra developed his distinctive singing style, characterized by pausing, phrasing, and glissandi. Sinatra had noticed that Dorsey's success had come from his unusual method of phrasing with his trombone. "I figured if he could do that phrasing with his horn, I could do it with my voice," Sinatra once explained. Tying phrases together with moans to heighten the song's emotional content and inhaling in the middle of a note so that his voice seemed to glide effortlessly from note to note without breathing became Sinatra trademarks.

The crooner's success outlasted the war years. In 1943 he made his debut as a film star in *Higher and Higher* (RKO) and went on to make other musical confections like *Anchors Aweigh* (MGM, 1945), *Till the Clouds Roll By* (MGM, 1947), *It Happened in Brooklyn* (MGM, 1947), *The Kissing Bandit* (MGM, 1949), and *On the Town* (MGM, 1949).

In addition to his professional activities, Sinatra at this time was working with youth groups to promote religious and racial harmony. He donated his services to the RKO short subject *The House I Live In* (1945), which had for its message the essential importance of tolerance in a democracy. This musical film won a special Academy Award.

In the late 1940's Sinatra's career suffered a setback. His record sales slumped, his throat began hemorrhaging, the adulation of his public declined, and his film studio, MGM, dropped him from its roster. During this period he became involved with Ava Gardner in a romance that the pair pursued in various parts of the world, usually followed by a contingent of unwelcome reporters. In 1951 Sinatra and his first wife were divorced and he was married to Miss Gardner. When Sinatra sought the dramatic role of Angelo Maggio in the screen version of James Jones's *From Here to Eternity,* he had to "undergo the humiliation of a screen test" and he had to accept a salary of only $8,000 instead of his customary $150,000.

His performance in *From Here to Eternity* (Columbia, 1953) was to prove a turning point. In this expose of tarnished prewar Army brass and the injustices of barracks life Sinatra played a temperamental Italian-American GI who is confined to an Army stockade and killed by a sadistic sergeant. Many reviewers felt that Sinatra's acting was the biggest surprise of the film and six years after the picture was made Alfred G. Aronowitz of the New York *Post* (October 27, 1959) wrote that as Maggio, "Sinatra once strictly a song-and-dance man, had become an actor with a sensitivity that continues to overwhelm producers, directors, and critics." The film won seven Academy Awards, including one for Frank Sinatra as the best supporting actor of 1953.

In *The Man with the Golden Arm* (United Artists 1956), an unrelenting examination of drug addiction, Sinatra portrayed a "junkie," Frankie Machine, struggling to "kick" the habit. As an ex-soldier returning from World War II and floundering in his attempt to find a place in the civilian world, Sinatra played Dave Hirsh in *Some Came Running* (MGM, 1959). He appeared as a widowed hotel-owner in the comedy *A Hole in the Head* (United Artists, 1959).

Other motion pictures in which Sinatra starred include *Suddenly* (1954), *Young at Heart* (1955), *Not as a Stranger* (1955), *Guys and Dolls* (1955), *The Tender Trap* (1955), *Johnny Concho* (1956), *High Society* (1957), *The Joker Is Wild* (1957), *Pal Joey* (1957), *The Pride and the Passion* (1957), *Kings Go Forth* (1958), *Never So Few* (1960), *Can-Can* (1960), *Ocean's Eleven* (1960), *The Manchurian Candidate* (1962), *Von Ryan's Express* (1965), *None but the Brave* (1965), *Assault on a Queen* (1966), *The Naked Runner* (1966), and *The Detective* (1968).

On television Sinatra captivated audiences of CBS's *The Frank Sinatra Show* from October 1950 to April 1952 and of ABC's *Frank Sinatra Show* from October 1957 to June 1958. He also appeared as a guest star on various programs and on TV specials. He had interests in a Beverly Hills restaurant, the Sands Hotel in Las Vegas, Nevada, several music publishing companies, a talent agency, and Dorchester Company, a motion-picture producing concern. He tried his hand at writing such songs as "This Love of Mine," "Peachtree Street," "Take My Love," and "Manhattan Skyline." With John Quinlan, from whom he had taken voice lessons, Sinatra wrote *Tips on Popular Singing* (Embassy Music Corporation, 1941).

Few people argued about Sinatra's prestige as a performer, but many disagreed about Sinatra's personality. He appeared to be a man riddled with contradictions. Outside his California home, which he protected with a ten-foot brick wall, there was a sign reading: "If you haven't been invited, you better have a damn good reason for ringing this bell!" He carried on a feud with certain sections of the press, primarily over his desire for personal privacy. On the other hand, Sinatra's generosity with friends was legendary and he aided the careers of many show business performers. He often surrounded himself with a retinue of business associates and stars known as "The Rat Pack," who looked to him as their leader. Sinatra was "not simply the leader of the Rat Pack" but had "assumed the position of *il padrone* in Hollywood." He was asked by 20th Century Fox to be the master of ceremonies at a luncheon attended by President Nikita Khrushchev on September 19, 1959. *Nice 'n' Easy*, a collection of ballads, topped the *Billboard* chart in October 1960 and remained in the charts for 86 weeks, winning critical plaudits. Granata noted the "lifelike ambient sound" quality of *Nice and Easy*, the perfection in the stereo balance, and the "bold, bright and snappy" sound of the band. He highlighted the "close, warm and sharp" feel of Sinatra's voice, particularly on the songs "September in the Rain," "I Concentrate on You," and "My Blue Heaven."

Sinatra grew discontented at Capitol, and decided to part with Riddle, May, and Jenkins, to form his own label, Reprise Records. Under Sinatra the company developed into a music industry "powerhouse," which he later sold for an estimated $80 million. His first album on the label, *Ring-a-Ding-Ding!* (1961), was a major success, peaking at No.4 on *Billboard*. The album was released in February 1961, the same month that Reprise Records released Ben Webster's *The Warm Moods*, Sammy Davis, Jr.'s *The Wham of Sam*, Mavis River's *Mavis* and Joe E. Lewis's *It is Now Post Time*. On September 11 and 12, 1961, Sinatra recorded his final songs for Capitol. In an effort to maintain his commercial viability in the 1960s, Sinatra recorded Elvis Presley's hit "Love Me Tender," and later recorded works

Affiliation: Solo Performer

By 1942 Sinatra had decided that he was ready to strike out on his own. He left Dorsey to become the first of many soloists who broke away from bands and made successful careers as individual singers. Obtaining a booking for a personal appearance at New York's Paramount Theatre, Sinatra crooned from the last day of 1942 until eight weeks later, a period longer than any other solo engagement at the Paramount up to that time. His growing popularity landed him a spot as soloist on the radio program *Your Hit Parade,* which he held from February 1943 to January 1945, and brought him to the attention of Hollywood producers.

It was during this period, 1942–43, that Sinatra became the idol of the bobbysoxers. This was in part a result of some high-powered press-agentry. E. J. Kahn in the *New Yorker* (November 9, 1946) magazine reported that Sinatra's publicists launched a drive to link the words "Sinatra" and "swoon." Such nicknames as "Swoonlight Sinatra" and "Mr. Swoon" were created. Ironically, the nickname that eventually caught on did not mention swoon in any way. Throughout his career, Sinatra was "The Voice."

Throughout the United States girls and women formed Frank Swoonatra Fan Clubs. His performances, during which he stared intensely into the various eyes that were glued to him, were punctuated by shrieking and squealing and swooning and fainting. In the *New Yorker* (November 2, 1946) E. J. Kahn noted that it was during World War II that Sinatra became a teen-agers' hero, and that girls "turned to him as compensation for the absence of their young men."

by Paul Simon such as "Mrs. Robinson," the Beatles ("Something," "Yesterday"), and Joni Mitchell ("Both Sides, Now").

In 1962, Sinatra released *Sinatra and Strings*, a set of standard ballads which became one of the most critically acclaimed works of Sinatra's entire Reprise period. Frank Sinatra, Jr., who was present during the recording, noted the "huge orchestra," which Nancy Sinatra stated "opened a whole new era" in pop music, with orchestras getting bigger, embracing a "lush string sound." Sinatra and Count Basie collaborated for the album *Sinatra-Basie* the same year, a popular and successful release which prompted them to rejoin two years later for the follow-up *It Might as Well Be Swing*, arranged by Quincy Jones. The two became frequent performers together, and appeared at the Newport Jazz Festival in 1965. Also in 1962, as the owner of his own record label, Sinatra was able to step on the podium as conductor again, releasing his third instrumental album *Frank Sinatra Conducts Music from Pictures and Plays*.

In 1963, Sinatra released *The Concert Sinatra*, an ambitious album with a 73-piece symphony orchestra led by Nelson Riddle. The concert was recorded on a motion picture scoring stage with the use of multiple synchronized recording machines that employed 35 mm magnetic film. Granata considers the album to have been "impeachable" [sic], "one of the very best of the Sinatra-Riddle ballad albums," in which Sinatra displayed an impressive vocal range, particularly in "Ol' Man River," in which he darkened the hue. In 1964 the song "My Kind of Town" was nominated for the Academy Award for Best Original Song. Sinatra released *Softly, as I Leave You*, and collaborated with Bing Crosby and Fred Waring on *America, I Hear You Singing*, a collection of patriotic songs recorded as a tribute to the assassinated President John F. Kennedy.

Sinatra's phenomenal success in 1965, coinciding with his 50th birthday, prompted *Billboard* to proclaim that he may have reached the "peak of his eminence." In June 1965, Sinatra, Sammy Davis, Jr., and Dean Martin played live in St. Louis to benefit Dismas House, a prisoner rehabilitation and training center with nationwide programs that in particular helped serve African Americans. The Rat Pack concert was broadcast live via satellite to numerous movie theaters across America. The album *September of My Years* was released September 1965, and went on to win the Grammy Award for best album of the year. Granata considers the album to have been one of the finest of his Reprise years, "a reflective throwback to the concept records of the 1950s, and more than any of those collections, distills everything that Frank Sinatra had ever learned or experienced as a vocalist." One of the album's singles, "It Was a Very Good Year," won the Grammy Award for Best Vocal Performance, Male. A career anthology, *A Man and His Music*, followed in November, winning Album of the Year at the Grammys the following year.

In 1966 Sinatra released *That's Life*, with both the single of "That's Life" and album becoming Top Ten hits in the US on *Billboard*'s pop charts. *Strangers in the Night* went on to top the *Billboard* and UK pop singles charts, winning the award for Record of the Year at the Grammys. Sinatra's first live album, *Sinatra at the Sands*, was recorded during January and February 1966 at the Sands Hotel and Casino in Las Vegas. Sinatra was backed by the Count Basie Orchestra, with Quincy Jones conducting.

Sinatra started 1967 with a series of recording sessions with Antônio Carlos Jobim. He recorded one of his most famous collaborations with Jobim, the Grammy-nominated album *Francis Albert Sinatra & Antonio Carlos Jobim*, which was one of the best-selling albums of the year, behind the Beatles's *Sgt. Pepper's Lonely Hearts Club Band*. According to Santopietro the album "consists of an extraordinarily effective blend of bossa nova and slightly swinging jazz vocals, and succeeds in creating an unbroken mood of romance and regret." Writer Stan Cornyn noted that Sinatra sang so softly on the album that it was comparable to the time that he suffered from a vocal hemorrhage in 1950. Sinatra also released the album *The World We Knew*, which features a chart-topping duet of "Somethin' Stupid" with daughter Nancy. In December, Sinatra collaborated with Duke Ellington on the album *Francis A. & Edward K.* According to Granata, the recording of "Indian Summer" on the album was a favorite of Riddle's, noting the "contemplative mood [which] is heightened by a Johnny Hodges alto sax solo that will bring a tear to your eye." With Sinatra in mind, singer-songwriter Paul Anka wrote the song "My Way," using the melody of the French "Comme d'habitude" ("As Usual"), composed by Claude François and Jacques Revaux. Sinatra recorded it just after Christmas 1968. "My Way," Sinatra's best-known song on the Reprise label, was not an instant success, charting at #27 in the US and #5 in the UK, but it remained in the UK charts for 122 weeks, including 75 non-consecutive weeks in the Top 40, between April 1969 and September 1971, which was still a record in 2015. Sinatra told songwriter Ervin Drake in the 1970s that he "detested" singing the song, because he believed audiences would think it was a "self-aggrandizing tribute," professing that he "hated boastfulness in others."

On November 2, 1970, Sinatra recorded the last songs for Reprise Records before his self-imposed retirement, announced the following June at a concert in Hollywood to raise money for the Motion Picture and TV Relief Fund. He finished the concert with a "rousing" performance of "That's Life," and stated "Excuse me while I disappear" as he left the stage. He told *Life* journalist Thomas Thompson that "I've got things to do, like the first thing is not to do *anything* at all for eight months . . . maybe a year," while Barbara Sinatra later claimed that Sinatra had grown "tired of entertaining people, especially when all they really wanted were the same old tunes he had long ago become bored by." While he was in retirement, President Richard Nixon asked him to perform at a Young Voters Rally in anticipation of the upcoming campaign. Sinatra obliged and chose to sing "My Kind of Town" for the rally held in Chicago on October 20, 1972.

In 1973, Sinatra came out of his short-lived retirement with a television special and album, both entitled *Ol' Blue Eyes Is Back*. The album, arranged by Gordon Jenkins and Don Costa, was a success, reaching number 13 on *Billboard* and number 12 in the UK. He initially developed problems with his vocal cords during the comeback due to a prolonged period without singing. He began what Barbara Sinatra describes as a "massive comeback tour of the United States, Europe, the Far East and Australia." In October 1974 he appeared at New York City's Madison Square Garden in a televised concert that was later released as an album under the title *The Main Event—Live*. Backing him was bandleader Woody Herman and the Young Thundering Herd, who accompanied Sinatra on a European tour later that month.

In 1975, Sinatra performed in concerts in New York with Count Basie and Ella Fitzgerald, and at the London Palladium with Basie and Sarah Vaughan, giving 140 performances in 105 days. In August he held several consecutive concerts at Lake Tahoe together with the newly-risen singer John Denver, who became a frequent collaborator. Sinatra had recorded Denver's "Leaving on a Jet Plane" and "My Sweet Lady" for *Sinatra & Company* (1971), and according to Denver, his song "A Baby Just Like You" was written at Sinatra's request for his new grandchild, Angela. During the Labor Day weekend held in 1976, Sinatra was responsible for reuniting old friends and comedy partners Dean Martin and Jerry Lewis for the first time in nearly twenty years, when they performed at the "Jerry Lewis MDA Telethon." That year, the Friars Club selected him as the "Top Box Office Name of the Century," and he was given the Scopus Award by the American Friends of Hebrew University in Israel and an honorary Doctor of Humane Letters from the University of Nevada.

On March 14, 1977, he recorded with Nelson Riddle for the last time, recording the songs "Linda," "Sweet Loraine," and "Barbara." The two men had a major falling out, and later patched up their differences in January 1985 at a dinner organized for Ronald Reagan, when Sinatra asked Riddle to make another album with him. Riddle was ill at the time, and died that October, before they had a chance to record.

In 1980, Sinatra's first album in six years was released, *Trilogy: Past Present Future*, a highly ambitious triple album that features an array of songs from both the pre-rock era and rock era. It was the first studio album of Sinatra's to feature his touring pianist at the time, Vinnie Falcone, and was based on an idea by Sonny Burke. The album garnered six Grammy nominations—winning for best liner notes—and peaked at number 17 on *Billboard*'s album chart, and spawned yet another song that would become a signature tune, "Theme from New York, New York." That year, as part of the Concert of the Americas, he performed in the Maracana Stadium in Rio de Janeiro, Brazil, which broke records for the "largest live paid audience ever recorded for a solo performer." The following year, Sinatra built on the success of *Trilogy* with *She Shot Me Down*, an album that was praised for embodying the dark tone of his Capitol years. Also in 1981, Sinatra was embroiled in controversy when he worked a ten-day engagement for $2 million in Sun City, in the internationally unrecognized Bophuthatswana, breaking a cultural boycott against apartheid-era South Africa. President Lucas Mangope awarded Sinatra with the highest honor, the Order of the Leopard, and made him an honorary tribal chief.

Santopietro stated that by the early 1980s, Sinatra's voice had "coarsened, losing much of its power and flexibility, but audiences didn't care." In 1982, he signed a $16 million three-year deal with the Golden Nugget of Las Vegas. Kelley notes that by this period Sinatra's voice had grown "darker, tougher and loamier," but he "continued to captivate audiences with his immutable magic." She added that his baritone voice "sometimes cracked, but the gliding intonations still aroused the same raptures of delight as they had at the Paramount Theater." That year he made a reported further $1.3 million from the Showtime television rights to his "Concert of the Americas" in the Dominican Republic, $1.6 million for a concert series at Carnegie Hall, and $250,000 in just one evening at the Chicago Fest. He donated a lot of his earnings to charity.

Sinatra was selected as one of the five recipients of the 1983 Kennedy Center Honors, alongside Katherine Dunham, James Stewart, Elia Kazan, and Virgil Thomson. Quoting Henry James, President Reagan said in honoring his old friend that "art was the shadow of humanity" and that Sinatra had "spent his life casting a magnificent and powerful shadow."

In 1984, Sinatra worked with Quincy Jones for the first time in nearly two decades on the album, *L.A. Is My Lady*, which was well received critically. The album was a substitute for another Jones project, an album of duets with Lena Horne, which had to be abandoned. In 1986, Sinatra collapsed on stage while performing in Atlantic City and was hospitalized for diverticulitis, which left him looking frail. Two years later, Sinatra reunited with Martin and Davis, Jr. and went on the Rat Pack Reunion Tour, during which they played a number of large arenas. When Martin dropped out of the tour early on, a rift developed between them and the two never spoke again.

In 1990, Sinatra was awarded the second "Ella Award" by the Los Angeles-based Society of Singers, and performed for a final time with Ella Fitzgerald at the award ceremony. Sinatra maintained an active touring schedule in the early 1990s, performing 65 concerts in 1990, 73 in 1991 and 84 in 1992 in seventeen different countries. In 1993, Sinatra returned to Capitol Records and the recording studio for *Duets*, which became his best-selling album. The album and its sequel, *Duets II*, released the following year, would see Sinatra remake his classic recordings with popular contemporary performers, who added their vocals to a pre-recorded tape. During his tours in the early 1990s, his memory failed him at times during concerts, and he happened to faint onstage in Richmond, Virginia, in March 1994. His final public concerts were held in Fukuoka Dome in Japan on December 19–20, 1994. The following year, Sinatra sang for the very last time on February 25, 1995, before a live audience of 1200 select guests at the Palm Desert Marriott Ballroom, on the closing night of the Frank Sinatra Desert Classic golf tournament. *Esquire* reported of the show that Sinatra was "clear, tough, on the money" and "in absolute control." Sinatra was awarded the Legend Award at the 1994 Grammy Awards, where he was introduced by Bono, who said of him, "Frank's the chairman of the bad attitude . . . Rock 'n roll plays at being tough, but this guy is the boss – the chairman of boss . . . I'm not going to mess with him, are you?"

In 1995, to mark Sinatra's 80th birthday, the Empire State Building glowed blue. A star-studded birthday tribute, *Sinatra: 80 Years My Way*, was held at the Shrine Auditorium in Los Angeles, featuring performers such as Ray Charles, Little Richard, Natalie Cole and Salt-N-Pepa singing his songs. At the end of the program Sinatra graced the stage for the last time to sing the final notes of the "Theme from New York, New York" with an ensemble.

Personal Life

Frank Sinatra and Nancy Barbato were married on February 4, 1939 and had three children, Nancy Sandra (who became the wife of the singer Tommy Sands), Franklin Wayne, and Christina. Although the couple was divorced in 1951, Sinatra remained devoted to his first wife and his children. On November 7, 1951 he was married to Ava Gardner; this marriage ended in divorce on July 5, 1957. Sinatra continued to feel very strongly for her, and they remained friends for life. He was still dealing with her finances in 1976.

Sinatra reportedly broke off engagements to Lauren Bacall in 1958, and Juliet Prowse in 1962. He married Mia Farrow on July 19, 1966, a short marriage which ended with divorce in Mexico in August 1968. They remained close friends for life, and in a 2013 interview Farrow admitted that Sinatra might be the father of her son, Ronan Farrow (born 1986).

Sinatra was lastly married to Barbara Marx from 1976 until his death. The couple married at Sunnylands, in Rancho Mirage, California, the estate of media magnate Walter Annenberg, on July 11, 1976.

Frank Sinatra died with his wife at his side at Cedars-Sinai Medical Center in Los Angeles on May 14, 1998 of a heart attack. He was survived by his wife Barbara, his three children, and two grandchildren.

Further Reading

Kahn, E. J. *The Voice; The Story of an American Phenomenon* (1947)

Who's Who in America, 1960-61

Consiglio, Tony; Douskey, Franz. *Sinatra and Me: The Very Good Years (2011)*

Fuchs, Jeanne; Prigozy, Ruth. *Frank Sinatra: The Man, the Music, the Legend (2007)*

Slash

Guitarist

Born: July 23, 1965; Stoke-on-Trent, England
Primary Field: Rock
Group Affiliation: Guns N' Roses

Introduction

With his long ringlets of dark hair and signature top hat, the guitarist Slash, formerly of the popular band Guns N' Roses, is one of the most recognizable figures in the world of rock music. He is also one of rock's archetypes: his rise to the top of the charts during the late 1980s and 1990s was marked by drug addiction, alcoholism, sexual exploits, and infighting among his fellow band members—all of which he has chronicled in his eponymous memoir, published in 2007. (The book's cover declares, "It seems excessive, but that doesn't mean it didn't happen.") While much media attention has been paid to his lifestyle, Slash's talents and musicality are also widely recognized. Jed Gottlieb wrote for the Boston Herald *(May 18, 2007), "Slash is the sleaziest sleaze-rock guitarist of all time: a Gibson master second only to [Jimmy] Page and [Joe] Perry; a guy who legitimized metal guitar by infusing blues riffs with a genuine punk aesthetic," and Christina Taylor wrote for the Stoke-on-Trent, England,* Sentinel *(June 1, 2007), "Slash has long been established as one of the best guitarists of his generation and continues to set the benchmark for aspiring musicians everywhere." Now a happily married father of two—and reportedly free of his chemical dependencies—Slash is the lead guitarist of the group Velvet Revolver, and he recently appeared as a character in an edition of the blockbuster video game Guitar Hero.*

Early Life

The musician was born Saul Hudson on July 23, 1965 in Stoke-on-Trent. (He was given the nick name Slash as a teen, reportedly because he was always dashing around.) His mother, Ola, an African-American costume designer, had met his father, Anthony, a white British painter, during a period in which they were both living in Paris, France. Not long after Slash was born, his mother moved to California to further her career. Her clients included the Pointer Sisters, Ringo Starr, Diana Ross, and John Lennon, among other music luminaries. Slash and his father joined her four years later, and the family settled in the Laurel Canyon section of Los Angeles. In *Slash,* co-written with Anthony Bozza, the musician recalled, "My first memory of Los Angeles is the Doors' 'Light My Fire' blasting from my parents' turntable, every day, all day long." His parents also exposed him, he wrote, "to everything from Beethoven to Led Zeppelin." As demand for his mother's costumes grew, his father found ample work designing album covers for such recording artists as Neil Young and Joni Mitchell. Many musicians lived in Laurel Canyon, known for its artistic, bohemian atmosphere. Slash wrote in his memoir, "The essence of pot and incense usually hung in the air." His parents often took him to concerts, recording studios, and rehearsal spaces, and he developed a love of music at an early age, listening to the radio almost constantly. He was also passionate about drawing. (Mitchell included a series of his animal drawings in an unpublished book of her verse called "The Bestiary.") "He was drawing from the time he could pick up a pencil," his mother told Jeffrey Ressner and Lonn M. Friend for *Rolling Stone* (January 24, 1991, on-line).

Slash's parents separated when he was eight years old, a year after his brother, Albion, was born. Not long after that, his mother began an affair with the famed rocker David Bowie, for whom she had designed costumes. "Bowie came by often, with his wife, Angie, and their son, Zowie, in tow," Slash recalled in his book. "The seventies were unique: it seemed entirely natural for Bowie to bring his wife and son to the home of his lover so that we might all hang out. At the time my mother practiced the same form of transcendental meditation that David did. They chanted before the shrine she maintained in the bedroom." While Slash had some difficulty adjusting to having a new father figure around, he has credited the older musician with teaching him that "being a rock star is the intersection of who you are and who you want to be." Slash and his brother were shuttled to their maternal grandmother's home, in Hollywood, when Ola was working, and they eventually moved in with her. "I've been shocked at a lot of things I've read where it sounds like I left him on somebody's doorstep in a basket," Ola told Ressner and Friend. "They make it seem as if he never had a family and grew up on the streets like an urchin, but that's not true. It's just part of his image. He's not all leather and tattoos."

During his early teens Slash developed a love for BMX riding and won several competitions in his age division. At around the same time, he began experimenting with drugs and committing petty crimes. If he liked a band, for example, he shop lifted all of their albums from local record stores. He was kicked out of one of the junior high schools he attended for stealing several BMX bikes. "I did wander off at a young age, but it wasn't because of my parents. It was just 'cause I was tripped out and getting into all kinds of stuff," he told Giles Smith for the London *Independent* (July 17, 1995).

Slash and his best friend, Steven Adler—who would later become the drummer of Guns N' Roses—had dreams of starting a rock band, so during the summer before high school, Slash started taking guitar lessons, using an old flamenco guitar that his grandmother had given him. While his instructor, Robert Wolin, taught him the fundamentals, he learned how to improvise and play numbers by his favorite artists and groups-Cheap Trick, AC/DC, Van Halen, Ted Nugent, and Aerosmith-from a bargain-bin book he had picked up called *How to Play Rock* Guitar. He recalled in his memoir, "Finding guitar was like finding myself; it defined me, it gave me purpose. It was a creative outlet that allowed me to understand myself. The turmoil of my adolescence was suddenly secondary; playing guitar gave me focus. I didn't keep a journal; I couldn't seem to vocalize my feelings in a constructive fashion, but the guitar gave me emotional clarity." When Slash entered Fairfax High School, in 1979, he felt alienated. "I had long hair, and the schools I went to were filled with kids of bankers and real-estate agents," he told Ressner and Friend. "It wasn't like any of them came from the same background I had." He managed, however, to find his own circle of friends, thanks to his guitar playing. He became particularly close to Marc Canter, whose family owned the famous Canter's Deli in Los Angeles, and Matt Cassel, whose father was the veteran character actor Seymour Cassel. (The elder Cassel was responsible for giving Slash his nickname.)

During high school Slash formed his first rock band, Tidus Sloan, which played birthday parties, an occasional Bar Mitzvah, and concerts in the school's auditorium. Slash's time at Fairfax High was cut short when he was expelled for flipping over a teacher's desk. He attended other schools, including Beverly Hills High, before dropping out permanently during his junior year. Throughout the early 1980s, Slash held a number of odd jobs, including stints at a movie theater, a music store, and Canter's Deli. At the same time he tried to put together a band that could compete with the so-called hair-metal groups, such as Great White and Poison, that were popular at the time. (Hair-metal bands were known as such because of the long, teased, and gelled hairstyles favored by their members; Slash found their music and their posturing vapid.) For the next several years, he played in a variety of bands, including a hard-rock act called Road Crew he founded with Adler and a funk collective known as Black Sheep.

Life's Work

The early history of Guns N' Roses is muddled. Early incarnations of the group were called Rose and Hollywood Rose. In mid-1985 the band-with a new, soon-to-be-iconic name-went on its first club tour, along the West Coast: its members, now considered the classic lineup, included Slash, Adler, Axl Rose, Izzy Stradlin, and Duff McKagen. The band's raw musical style—a hybrid of punk, heavy metal, and classic rock—changed Los Angeles's hair-metal scene seemingly overnight. Slash wrote in his memoir, "There was not a bit of the typical L.A. vibe going on where the goal is to court a record deal. There was no concern for the proper poses or goofy choruses that might spell popular success; which ultimately guaranteed endless hot chicks. That type of calculated rebellion wasn't an option for us; we were too rabid a pack of musically like-minded gutter rats. We were passionate, with a common goal and a very distinct sense of integrity. That was the difference between us and [other bands.]"

In 1986 the group released an independent EP called *Live ?!*@ Like a Suicide,* which featured cover art by Slash. (The recording is often referred to simply as *Live Like a Suicide.)* With a limited release of 10,000 copies, it failed to generate much industry attention. That lack of attention did not last long, however. The band's next effort, for Geffen Records, the full-length *Appetite* *for Destruction,* released on July 21, 1987, went on to become the biggest-selling debut album of the 1980s and was listed among the top 100 albums of all time by the editors of *Rolling Stone.* Because the band's original album cover, featuring a woman who looked as if she had been sexually violated, was banned from stores, and MTV initially refused to play the graphic video for the debut single, "Welcome to the Jungle," 13 months passed before *Appetite for Destruction* reached the number-one spot on the *Billboard* album charts. To date the album has sold more than 28 million copies worldwide and-with its second cover, which features a stylized cross and skulls representing the band members-reportedly still sells 9,000 copies a week. Besides "Welcome to the Jungle," the album contains the hits "It's So Easy," "Mr. Brownstone," "Paradise City," and "Sweet Child O' Mine." In a review for the All Music Guide Web site, Stephen Thomas Erlewine wrote, "Guns N' Roses' debut, *Appetite for Destruction,* was a turning point for hard rock in the late '80s-it was a dirty, dangerous, and mean record in a time when heavy metal meant nothing but a good time. On the surface, Guns N' Roses may appear to celebrate the same things as their peers-namely, sex, liquor, drugs, and rock & roll-but there is a nasty edge to their songs. . . . [They have] a primal, sleazy sound that adds grit to already grim tales." He concluded, "As good as Rose's lyrics and screeching vocals are, they wouldn't be nearly as effective without the twin-guitar interplay of Slash and Izzy Stradlin who spit out riffs and solos better than any band since the Rolling Stones and that's what makes *Appetite for Destruction* the best metal record of the late '80s." Commenting on the album's 20th anniversary, Slash told a writer for *GQ* (October 2007), "It was blatantly in-your-face about stuff that kids deal with on a daily basis. It was just, like, screaming reality. And it became a badge of honor, like 'This is who I am.' We were like a combustible M-80; we took it all over the edge."

The group's next albums, *Use Your Illusion I* and *Use* Your *Illusion II,* were released simultaneously on September .17, 1991. The albums, which went on to sell some seven million copies each worldwide, marked a major departure from the band's gritty, unpolished hard-rock roots. Incorporating a variety of genres (including blues, country, progressive, and electronica), the *Illusions* albums were deemed both artistically ambitious and brazenly self-indulgent by critics. Slash's guitar playing, however, was universally lauded, with critics impressed by his work on acoustic and flamenco guitars, in addition to his customary Les Paul. After the 28-month *Illusions* promotion tour, during which the band played 192 shows in 27 countries to more than seven million people, Slash officially became an American citizen.

Following the release of Guns N' Roses' next studio album, *The Spaghetti Incident?* (1993), an ill-received covers record, Slash found himself drifting away from the group, disgruntled because Rose had been consistently rejecting material he had written or arranged. When Rose overdubbed Slash's guitar parts for a Guns N' Roses cover of the Rolling Stones song "Sympathy for the Devil," which was featured in the film *Interview with the Vampire* (1994), Slash decided to form a group of his own. Slash's Snakepit, which included Gilby Clarke and Matt Sorum, released its first album, *It's Five O'clock Somewhere,* in February 1995. Though the album went platinum, it received tepid reviews. J. D. Considine, wrote for *Rolling Stone* (February 23, 1995, on-line), for example, "When he's onstage with Guns N' Roses, it's easy to see Slash as the strong, silent type, happily inscrutable behind his thick mop of curls. Unlike Axl Rose, who seems obsessed with verbalizing his deepest fears, Slash would rather let his fingers do the talking, an approach that has led to some remarkably expressive solos but hasn't told us much about the guitarist's inner life. *It's Five O'clock Somewhere* doesn't alter that image much, either. Even though this is a Slash solo project, the role he plays seems largely the same: He doesn't sing, he doesn't talk, and he generally leaves the lyric writing to others." Slash also worked on other outside projects, including music for Quentin Tarantino's film *Jackie Brown* (1997), while waiting for Rose to complete the material for the next Guns N' Roses album. He explained to Giles Smith, "Axl all of a sudden had this masterplan of how he wanted to approach the next Guns' release. I wanted to go back to doing old style, just heavy Guns N' Roses. But he's still on that long, mountainous trek." In October 1996, in a rambling fax sent to MTV News, Rose officially announced that Slash had left Guns N' Roses and that others in the group were being put on notice; those members departed shortly thereafter, and Slash is said not to have spoken with Rose since the split.

Slash spent the rest of the 1990s and early 2000s as one of the busiest session guitarists in the music business, playing for a wide variety of artists that included Insane Clown Posse, Blackstreet, Chic, Ronnie Wood, and Ray Charles, while contributing to the soundtracks of several films, including *The Kid Stays in the Picture* (2002), about the legendary film producer Robert Evans. In October 2000 Slash released his second Snakepit album, *Ain't Life Grand,* which went platinum. Most critics again made mention of Slash's superb guitar playing but failed to find any promise in the band as a whole. Rob Sheffield wrote for *Rolling Stone* (October 12, 2000), "As the poet [alluding to Axl Rose] once sang, it's hard to hold a candle in the cold November rain-but Slash is still hanging in there, shining the light within his soul as a lucid path back to the days when guitars were guitars, hair was hair. . . . The real problem is that great guitarists need great bands, and the Snakepit dudes are barely functional backup peons who don't even have cool names."

While touring with the hard-rock group AC/DC in 2000, Slash was rushed to the hospital for what he believed was exhaustion. He was instead diagnosed with a heart ailment known as cardiomyopathy and told that he had six weeks to live. He wrote in his memoir, "Fifteen years of overdrinking and drug abuse had swelled [my heart] to one beat short of exploding." Doctors implanted a defibrillator in his chest and advised him to stop drinking and using drugs—advice that he has reportedly

Affiliation: Drugs and Lifestyle

The journey from unknown to star was not easy for Slash. "We started out on the lowest rung of the ladder, as far as club bands are concerned," he told Caroline Ryder for *Swindle* (October 2006). "When we got signed [to Geffen] we were totally [messed] up. We got $7,500 bucks apiece and spent it all on drugs. We had nowhere to live. We were staying in cheap motels. We couldn't find anyone that wanted to produce us and manage us. Then we went on tour opening up for Aerosmith, and everything just sort of worked its way up." While touring—the band worked with such acts as Alice Cooper and Iron Maiden, in addition to Aerosmith—Slash found it easier to cope, but off the road he turned to increasingly dangerous drugs, including heroin. "We'd be on the road and we'd hear we sold a certain number of records," he explained to Ryder. "Then we went back to Hollywood and it's the same [stuff]: living in a cheap apartment and doing drugs all the time, except this time I didn't want to go out because people would recognize me." By his own admission, Slash spent most of the period from 1988 to 1990 abusing heroin and cocaine, and he also developed a problem with alcohol, drinking up to half a gallon of vodka a day, according to some reports. Still, he was able to work; Guns N' Roses released *GN'R Lies* (1988), which consisted of the *Live* EP plus four new tracks, and Slash also did session work for a number of artists, including Iggy Pop, Michael Jackson, Alice Cooper, and Lenny Kravitz (a fellow Fairfax High alumnus).

Guns N' Roses found themselves embroiled in controversies as their popularity increased. *GN'R Lies,* which featured the hit single "Patience" and went on to sell more than 12 million copies worldwide, also contained a song written by Rose called "One in a Million," which attacked-in exceedingly derogatory terms-immigrants, blacks, and homosexuals. As a result, members of the group were collectively referred to as racists; they were barred from participating in a benefit concert for the Gay Men's Health Crisis, in New York City, and were openly criticized onstage by the all-black hardrock group Living Colour when both bands opened for the Rolling Stones in 1989. Slash, who was never fond of the lyrics in the song, given his ethnic background, explained to Jon Bream for the Minneapolis *Star Tribune* (January 21, 1992), "When I first heard the lyric, I was, like, 'Axl, I know what you're saying, but I don't think people are going to take it right. I know my family isn't going to take it right.'" The Rolling Stones tour was also notable for an incident in which Rose threatened to kick Slash out of the group because of his heroin use. As a peacemaking effort, Slash agreed to address the crowd about the perils of heroin addiction during one of the shows, although he admitted in his memoir that he did so half-heartedly. On January 22, 1990, at the annual American Music Awards, Slash used several expletives during the 20-second, drunken acceptance speech he gave when *Appetite for Destruction* was honored as best rock album of the year. He recalled in his autobiography, "I was overwhelmed by the controversy [that resulted] because to this day the incident still doesn't mean that much to me. I was, however, responsible for the seven-second delay being instituted at all future live award ceremonies; plus Dick Clark wouldn't speak to me for eight years."

since tried to follow. In April 2002 Slash reunited with former Guns N' Roses bandmates Duff McKagen and Matt Sorum to play a benefit concert for their longtime friend, the drummer Randy Castillo, who had recently died of cancer. Realizing that their chemistry was still good, the three decided to start a new band that initially included Keith Nelson and Josh Todd, from the band Buckcherry. The latter two left after only a few months, and Slash, McKagen, and Sorum embarked on a year-long search for a singer. (They also added a mutual friend, Dave Kushner, on rhythm guitar.) After listening to hundreds of tapes and unsuccessfully auditioning dozens of singers (a project documented by VH1 on a short-lived reality series), they agreed on the former Stone Temple Pilots singer, Scott Weiland. The group settled on the name Velvet Revolver and contributed songs to two film soundtracks, a cover of Pink Floyd's "Money" for *The Italian Job* (2003) and an original song called "Set Me Free" for *The Hulk* (2003). Their first album, *Contraband,* was released in June 2004 and debuted at number one on the *Billboard* album charts. It has sold some four million copies worldwide, and the group won a Grammy Award for best hard-rock performance for the single "Slither."

In March 2006 Rose released a statement to the press claiming that he had once heard Slash make disparaging comments about Weiland, McKagen, and Sorum. While the incident briefly shook the relationship between Slash and his bandmates and put the future of Velvet Revolver in jeopardy, the dispute was eventually resolved, and in July 2007 the group released their sophomore album, *Libertad.* Despite being a commercial disappointment, the album garnered mostly positive reviews. Slash told Jacqui Swift for the London *Sun* (August 3, 2007), "On *Contraband* we barely scratched the surface of what we are capable of. Making *Libertad* we dipped in to see the band's individual and collective talents and we had also blossomed as a band. The relationships between the guys got more personal and we have a real camaraderie going. The sound is more musical and not as aggressive. We played more raw with little over-production. What you're hearing is how we played. It's better and more exciting and so . . . now I have a sense of accomplishment." In March 2008, after spending the previous month in rehab for undisclosed addictions, Weiland told the audience during a Velvet Revolver show in Glasgow, Scotland, that they were witnessing the band's final tour. Early the next month Slash confirmed reports that Weiland had left the group to rejoin Stone Temple Pilots. Since Weiland's departure, Velvet Revolver has auditioned hundreds of singers, both known and unknown, but has not chosen one. Slash is currently working on a solo album with guest singers and musicians including Izzy Stradlin, Duff McKagen, Lenny Kravitz, Sebastian Bach, Alice Cooper, and Vince Neil.

Personal Life

Slash currently lives in Los Angeles. He and his wife, Perla, have been married since 2000. They have two sons, London (born in 2002) and Cash (born in 2004). His self-titled memoir, written with Anthony Bozza, reached the *New York Times* nonfiction best-seller list soon after its publication. The book focuses largely on his time with Guns N' Roses, attempting to explain the band's breakup and to dispel rumors that the group will one day reunite. It also provides an unflinching look at Slash's addictions and excesses. Ian McCullough wrote for the Sydney, Australia, *Sunday Telegraph* (November 25, 2007), "Considering that at the height of the band's success he was drinking a gallon of vodka a day-and that was before he went out at night-it's remarkable he can remember anything." Alan Light wrote for the *New York Times Book Review* (January 27, 2008, on-line): "Most rock biographies are about getting to the Good Part. There's typically a bit of slogging through the star's unhappy childhood, the revelation of music's true power and a hard-fought rise to the top before the litany of debauchery and depravity begins-the part that fans actually want to read. . . . *[Slash* is] pretty much all Good Part."

In January 2007 Slash was honored with a star on the Rock Walk of Fame, in Los Angeles.

Further Reading

Boston Herald E p6 May 18, 2007; *Entertainment Weekly* p79 June 4, 2004
(London) *Independent* p4 July 17, 1995
(London) *Sun* Aug. 3, 2007
(Minneapolis) *Star Tribune* E p1 Jan. 21, 1992
New York Times Book Review (on-line) Jan. 27, 2008
Rolling Stone (on-line) Jan. 24, 1991, June 16, 2004
(Stoke-on-Trent, England) *Sentinel* p6 June 1, 2007
Swindle Oct. 2006
(Sydney, Australia) *Sunday Telegraph* p90 Nov. 25, 2007
Slash (with Anthony Bozza). *Slash,* 2007

Stephen (Joshua) Sondheim

Composer; lyricist

Born: March 22, 1930; New York City
Primary Field: Musical theater
Group Affiliation: Broadway

Introduction

Musical comedy, the United States's most significant contribution to the theatre arts of the world, has in the past few years been revitalized by the team of composer-lyricist Stephen Sondheim and producer-director Harold Prince. Repudiating the superannuated star vehicles and witless extravaganzas that have so long dominated Broadway, Prince and Sondheim have introduced a high intelligence quotient into their productions, which capture the angst-ridden spirit of the times without sacrificing the brio that characterizes American musical theatre at its best. Their first collaboration, in 1970, was Company, an astringent satire of contemporary urban life and marriage. A year later they produced Follies, an expressionistic treatment of show business nostalgia that one critic called "the first Proustian musical." Their latest contribution, A Little Night Music, *which opened in February 1973, is a bittersweet celebration of heterosexual love in all of its guises.*

Stephen Sondheim.

Early Life

Stephen Joshua Sondheim was born in New York City on March 22, 1930, the son of Herbert and Janet (Fox) Sondheim. His father was a prominent New York dress manufacturer. His mother, who is known to friends and associates as "Foxy," was first a fashion designer and then an interior decorator. Her married name is now Leshin. Sondheim has described his upbringing as "the best thing to be—typical upper-middle-class." A precocious child, he picked out tunes on the piano at the age of four and in the first grade read his way through the *New York Times.* When he was ten years old his parents divorced, and his mother sent him off to a military school. "I loved it because of all the rules and order, and because the school had a huge organ with lots of buttons," the composer told Charles Michener of *Newsweek* (April 23, 1973).

Shortly after the divorce, Sondheim's mother moved to Doylestown, Pennsylvania, where Oscar Hammerstein II, an old friend of the family, had a farm. The boy soon spent all his spare time at the celebrated lyricist's home. "Oscar was everything to me," recalled Sondheim to Michener. "He was a surrogate father and I wanted to be exactly like him. In a way I still do."

It was Oscar Hammerstein II who introduced the boy to the musical theatre. At the age of fifteen Steve Sondheim wrote his first musical, "By George," for the George School, a Quaker institution in Newton, Pennsylvania. Proudly showing it to his mentor, he asked him to criticize it objectively. Hammerstein not only told him it was the worst thing he had ever read but showed him why. "At the risk of hyperbole, I'd say that in that afternoon I learned more about song writing and the musical theater than most people learn in a lifetime," Sondheim recalled to Craig Zadan of *After Dark* (June 1971). ". . . He taught me how to build songs, how to introduce characters, how to make songs relate to characters, how to tell a story, how not to tell a story, the interrelationships between lyric and music—all, of course, from his own point of view."

As an apprenticeship to the practical side of musical theatre, Hammerstein let Stephen fetch coffee and type out scripts during rehearsals for his play *Allegro*, and later for *South Pacific* and *The King and I.* After graduating from the George School in 1946, Sondheim attended Williams College, where he majored in music. There he embarked on a course of study suggested to him by Hammerstein, in which he was first to turn a good play into a musical, then a mediocre play, then a non-theatrical work, and finally write his own original. When he graduated *magna cum laude* from Williams College in 1950 he was awarded the Hutchinson prize, a two-year fellowship to study music and compose. With it he finished his original musical and studied under the American composer Milton Babbitt in New York City.

Life's Work

Around 1953 Sondheim wrote the music and lyrics for a musical called "Saturday Night," which was to be produced on Broadway by Lemuel Ayers, the producer and set designer, but Ayers died suddenly, and the project was abandoned. While waiting for another chance to break into Broadway, Sondheim went to Hollywood and became coscriptwriter for the NBC Television comedy series *Topper*.

Two years later, playwright Arthur Laurents introduced Sondheim to Leonard Bernstein, who was then composing the score for a musical by Laurents about Manhattan street gangs. The play was to be an updated version of *Romeo and Juliet.* Impressed with his songs for "Saturday Night," Bernstein offered Sondheim the chance to write the lyrics for the new project. When *West Side Story* opened on September 26, 1957, with choreography by Jerome Robbins, it was acclaimed as a moving and innovative musical. After a triumphant Broadway ran of about two years it was made into a bit film (*West Side Story,* United Artists, 1961).

The spectacular success of *West Side Story* assured Sondheim of further Broadway assignments, and in 1958 he was hired to write both the music and lyrics for *Gypsy,* a Laurents play based on the memoirs of the stripper Gypsy Rose Lee. At the last moment, however, the star, Ethel Merman, refused to take a chance on an unknown composer, and Jule Styne was brought in to write the music. *Gypsy* opened to rave reviews on May 21, 1959 and achieved a two-year Broadway run.

For several years Sondheim worked with playwright Burt Shevelove on an idea for a play derived from the comedies of the classical Roman playwright Plautus. He finally persuaded Harold Prince, who had coproduced *West Side Story,* to back the project, and *A Funny Thing Happened On the Way to the Forum* opened on May 8, 1962, starring Zero Mostel. A low-comedy mélange of ancient Roman and American vaudeville comedy techniques accompanied by some rousing songs by Sondheim, the play proved enormously popular with audiences and ran for 964 performances. Ten years later its buffoonery still aroused immoderate laughter when it was revived on Broadway, with Jack Gilford in the starring role.

After *A Funny Thing Happened On the Way to the Forum*—from which he reportedly still derives more income than from any of his other shows—Sondheim entered a slump period. In 1964 he wrote the music and lyrics for *Anyone Can Whistle,* an offbeat satire by Arthur Laurents that folded after only nine performances. A year later he fared little better with *Do I Hear a Waltz?,* a humdrum musical adaptation of Arthur Laurents' play *The Time of the Cuckoo* for which Sondheim set lyrics to Richard Rodgers' tunes.

For several years no Sondheim songs were heard on Broadway. Then, in 1969, Harold Prince agreed to direct and produce a musical play based on several short one-act plays about marriage. The result was *Company,* which by the time it opened on Broadway on April 26, 1970 had evolved into an episodic play about a thirty-five-year-old New York bachelor who observes the interactions of in the words of the title song, "those good and crazy people, my married friends." *Company* jolted audiences with its abrasive approach to married life and urban society. "[It's the] concerts you enjoy together, Neighbors you annoy together, Children you destroy together, that keep marriage intact," one Sondheim song goes, but the play takes no less acerbic a view of single life. "The show is about the increasing difficulty of making one to one relationships in an increasingly dehumanized society," Sondheim has explained to interviewers.

Finding the play itself dehumanized, some critics objected to its hard, brittle quality. But practically all of them agreed that *Company* was a stylish, brilliantly executed departure from conventional American musical theatre. Plotless, resolutely unromantic, and tinged with misanthropy, the show bore little resemblance to the Rodgers and Hammerstein type of musical that had dominated the American stage for twenty years. Different too were Sondheim's songs, which provided a sardonic commentary on the action instead of developing character or furthering the plot as those in traditional musicals did. *Company* ran for eighteen months on Broadway and won many awards, including, for Sondheim, the Tony awards for best lyrics and score and the *Variety*-New York Drama Critics poll awards for best composer and lyricist.

While *Company* was still playing to standing-room-only audiences, Sondheim and Prince introduced another hit musical *Follies*, which opened on April 4, 1971. Inspired by Eliot Elisofon's photograph of Gloria Swanson standing in the rubble of the old Roxy Theatre, Follies concerns a reunion of former Ziegfeld girls at the theatre, now rundown and about to be demolished, where they used to perform. Now middle-aged and disillusioned, the former showgirls perform their old numbers on stage while a ghostly set of performers, representing their former selves, promenade in the background. The effect was a kind of baroque melancholy of lost hopes and broken dreams quite different from the geriatric optimism of Broadway's other nostalgia hit of the season, *No, No Nanette.*

Critics were sharply divided on their assessment of *Follies* and of Sondheim's score, most of which was a pastiche of the music of other days. Some found the music merely derivative, but T. E. Kalem of *Time* (April 12, 1971) wrote, "Sondheim's entire score is an incredible display of musical virtuosity. It is a one-man course in the theatrical modes of the '20s, '30s, and '40s musicals, done not as parody or mimicry, but as a passionately informed tribute." Sondheim again won the Tony and Variety-Critics Poll awards for his music and lyrics.

In a change of pace from the ironic statements of *Company Bud Follies,* Prince and Sondheim created a romantic, operetta-like musical in *A Little Night Music,* which is based on Ingmar Bergman's farcical but elegant film, *Smiles of a Summer Night,* which won a comedy prize at the 1956 Cannes festival. When the play opened on February 25, 1973, it was accorded the best reception of Sondheim's career. Even Clive Barnes of the *New York Times,* no fan of either *Company* or *Follies*, declared it a triumph. "Perhaps the real triumph belongs to Stephen Sondheim . . . he wrote the day after the opening. "The music is a celebration of 3/4 time, an orgy of plaintively memorable waltzes, all talking of past loves and lost worlds. . . . Then, of course, there are Mr. Sondheim's lyrics. They have the kind of sassy, effortless poetry that Cole Porter mastered. The mother announces grandly, 'I acquired some position—plus a tiny Titian,' and this is coming from a lyricist who only seconds before has dazzlingly made 'raisins' rhyme with liaisons.'" *A Little Night Music* won Sondheim his third straight Tony as the year's best composer and lyricist, and was voted the year's best musical by the New York Drama Critics Circle.

By Bernstein premiered at the off-Broadway Westside Theatre on November 23, 1975 and closed on December 7, running for 40 previews and 17 performances. Its lyrics and music were by Leonard Bernstein, with additional lyrics by others (including Sondheim). Conceived and written by Betty Comden, Adolph Green and Norman L. Berman and directed by Michael Bawtree, By Bernstein featured Jack Bittner, Margery Cohen, Jim Corti, Ed Dixon, Patricia Elliott, Kurt Peterson and Janie Sell. The two Sondheim contributions were "In There" (from the adaptation of The Exception and the Rule) and a song cut from *West Side Story,* "Kids Ain't (Like Everybody Else)." *Pacific Overtures* (1976), the most non-traditional of the Sondheim—Prince collaborations, explored the westernization of Japan.

Sweeney Todd: The Demon Barber of Fleet Street (1979), Sondheim's most operatic score and libretto (which, with *Pacific Overtures* and *A Little Night Music,* has been produced in opera houses), explores an unlikely topic: murderous revenge and cannibalism. The book, by Hugh Wheeler, is based on Christopher Bond's 1973 stage version of the Victorian original.

Merrily We Roll Along (1981), with a book by George Furth, is one of Sondheim's more traditional scores; Frank Sinatra and Carly Simon have recorded songs from the musical. According to Sondheim's music director, Paul Gemignani, "Part of Steve's ability is this extraordinary versatility." Although Merrily closed after 16 performances, its score has been subsequently recorded. Martin Gottfried wrote, "Sondheim had set out to write traditional songs ... But [despite] that there is nothing ordinary about the music." Sondheim and Furth have revised the show since its original production, and Sondheim later said: "Did I feel betrayed? I'm not sure I would put it like that. What did surprise me was the feeling around the Broadway community—if you can call it that, though I guess I will for lack of a better word—that they wanted Hal and me to fail." Merrily's failure greatly affected Sondheim; he was ready to quit theatre and do movies, create video games or write mysteries: "I wanted to find something to satisfy myself that does not involve Broadway and dealing with all those people who hate me and hate Hal." Sondheim and Prince's collaboration was suspended from *Merrily* to the 2003 production of *Bounce*, another failure.

Affiliation: Broadway

Probably no Broadway songwriter has composed musical scores more perfectly wedded to the plays for which they are written than Sondheim, whose songs purvey exactly the right moods of emotional ambivalence and complexity. His lyrics are universally acknowledged as the musical theatre's best: clever, razor-edged light verse laced with puns, literary allusions, and playful rhymes. For his work on *Company, Follies,* and *A Little Night Music,* Sondheim received the Tony awards for best composer and lyricist in 1971, 1972, and 1973, making him the only songwriter to be so honored three years in a row. Sondheim began his Broadway career in the 1950's as the lyricist for the landmark musical West Side Story. His other theatre credits include the lyrics for *Gypsy* and *Do I Hear a Waltz?* and the music and lyrics for *A Funny Thing Happened On the Way to the Forum* and *Anyone Can Whistle.*

However, Sondheim decided "that there are better places to start a show" and found a new collaborator in James Lapine after he saw Lapine's *Twelve Dreams* off-Broadway in 1981: "I was discouraged, and I don't know what would have happened if I hadn't discovered *Twelve Dreams* at the Public Theatre"; Lapine has a taste "for the avant-garde and for visually-oriented theatre in particular." Their first collaboration was *Sunday in the Park with George* (1984), with Sondheim's music evoking Georges Seurat's pointillism. Sondheim and Lapine won the 1985 Pulitzer Prize for Drama for the play, and it was revived on Broadway in 2008.

They collaborated on *Into the Woods* (1987), a musical based on several Brothers Grimm fairy tales. Although Sondheim has been called the first composer to bring rap music to Broadway (with the Witch in the opening number of "Into the Woods"), he attributes the first rap in theatre to Meredith Willson's "Rock Island" from *The Music Man.* Sondheim and Lapine's last work together was the rhapsodic *Passion* (1994), adapted from Ettore Scola's Italian film *Passione D'Amore.* With a run of 280 performances, *Passion* was the shortest-running show to win a Tony Award for Best Musical.

Assassins opened off-Broadway at Playwrights Horizons on December 18, 1990, with music and lyrics by Sondheim and its book by John Weidman. The musical closed on February 16, 1991, after 73 performances. Its idea derived from Sondheim's days as a panelist at producer Stuart Ostrow's Musical Theater Lab, when he read a script by playwright Charles Gilbert. He asked Gilbert for permission to use his idea; although Gilbert offered to write the book, Sondheim had Weidman in mind.

During the late 1990s, Sondheim and Weidman reunited with Hal Prince for *Wise Guys,* a musical comedy following brothers Addison and Wilson Mizner. A Broadway production, starring Nathan Lane and Victor Garber, directed by Sam Mendes and planned for the spring of 2000, was delayed. Renamed *Bounce* in 2003, it was produced at the Goodman Theatre in Chicago and the Kennedy Center in Washington, D.C. Although after poor reviews *Bounce* never reached Broadway, a revised version opened off-Broadway as *Road Show* at the Public Theater on October 28, 2008. Directed by John Doyle, it closed on December 28, 2008.

Asked about writing new work, Sondheim replied in 2006: "No . . . It's age. It's a diminution of energy and the worry that there are no new ideas. It's also an increasing lack of confidence. I'm not the only one. I've checked with other people. People expect more of you and you're aware of it and you shouldn't be." In December 2007 he said that in addition to continuing work on *Bounce*, he was "nibbling at a couple of things with John Weidman and James Lapine."

Lapine created a multimedia production, originally entitled *Sondheim: a Musical Revue,* which was scheduled to open in April 2009 at the Alliance Theatre in Atlanta; however, it was canceled due to "difficulties encountered by the commercial producers attached to the project ... in raising the necessary funds." A revised version, *Sondheim on Sondheim,* was produced at Studio 54 by the Roundabout Theatre Company; previews began on March 19, 2010, and it ran from April 22 to June 13. The revue's cast included Barbara Cook, Vanessa L. Williams, Tom Wopat, Norm Lewis and Leslie Kritzer.

Sondheim collaborated with Wynton Marsalis on *A Bed and a Chair: A New York Love Affair,* an Encores! concert on November 13–17, 2013 at New York City Center. Directed by John Doyle with choreography by Parker Esse, it consisted of "more than two dozen Sondheim compositions, each piece newly re-imagined by Marsalis." The concert featured Bernadette Peters, Jeremy Jordan, Norm Lewis, Cyrille Aimee, four dancers and the Jazz at Lincoln Center Orchestra conducted by David Loud. In *Playbill*, Steven Suskin described the concert as "neither a new musical, a revival, nor a standard songbook revue; it is, rather, a staged-and-sung chamber jazz rendition of a string of songs ... Half of the songs come from *Company* and *Follies*; most of the other Sondheim musicals are represented, including the lesser-known *Passion* and *Road Show*." Sondheim wrote additional songs for the film adaptation of *Into the Woods,* including "Rainbows."

Several benefits and concerts were performed to celebrate Sondheim's 80th birthday in 2010. Among them were the New York Philharmonic's March 15 and 16 *Sondheim: The Birthday Concert* at Lincoln Center's Avery Fisher Hall, hosted by David Hyde Pierce. The concert included Sondheim's music, performed by some of the original performers. In November 2015, Sondheim was awarded the Presidential Medal of Freedom by President Barack Obama in a ceremony at the White House.

Personal Life

Sondheim has been described as introverted and solitary. In an interview with Frank Rich he said, "The outsider feeling—somebody who people want to both kiss and kill—occurred quite early in my life." Interviewers find him outwardly gruff, candid, and assured in his opinions. He openly shows his disdain for critics who find fault with his music, but he does not hesitate to criticize his own work (he now finds most of his *West Side Story* lyrics "embarrassing"). He also admits to being "hyper-self-critical" of his work, with the result that he is "a terrible procrastinator."

Sondheim is an inveterate game player and puzzle solver who has decorated his town house in Manhattan's Turtle Bay with nineteenth-century board games, antique ninepins, and penny- arcade jackpot machines. The decor reportedly inspired British playwright Anthony Shaffer's *Sleuth*. With such friends as Leonard Bernstein, Phyllis Newman, or Anthony Perkins, Sondheim likes to spend evenings playing "cutthroat anagrams," and he has often invented elaborate variations of Monopoly based on a friend's personality or work. Until he became too busy, Sondheim used to make up the brain-teasing crossword puzzles in *New York* magazine. Murder mysteries are another kind of puzzle that Sondheim likes to solve; with Tony Perkins he wrote the screenplay for a mystery thriller entitled *The Last of Sheila* (Warner Brothers, 1973), which was chosen to represent the United States at the 1973 Cannes Film Festival.

Although he has been linked romantically with a number of women, including Lee Remick who starred in *Anyone Can Whistle,* Sondheim has never married. His bachelorhood has been compared, perhaps inevitably, with that of Robert in *Company*. Like Robert, he is hardly satisfied with his way of life. "One of the reasons I've been in analysis for years," he told Charles Michener of *Newsweek*, "is that there are things I miss—like having a permanent relationship, and I don't know how else to work for it." The composer is in a relationship with Jeff Romley, and lived with dramatist Peter Jones for eight years (until 1999).

Further Reading

After Dark 4:21+ Je '71 pors N Y Post pl3 Jl 31 '71 por
N Y Times II pl+ Mv 10 '70 por
Newsday A p9 Je 1 '70 por
Newsweek 81:54+ Ap 23 '73 pors *Time* 97:70+ My 3 '71 por; 101:58 + Mr 19 '73 por
Biographical Encyclopedia & Who's Who of the American Theatre (1966)
Ewen, David, ed. *Popular American Composers, First Supplement* (1972)
Who's Who in America, 1972-73
Sondheim, Stephen. *Finishing the Hat* (2010)

Omar Souleyman

Musician

Born: 1966; Ras Al Ain, Syria
Primary Field: Dance-folk-pop
Group Affiliation: Solo performer with various friends; Bjork

Introduction

Singer Omar Souleyman started performing his own unique style of traditional Middle Eastern dance-folk-pop music in his native Syria in the mid-1990s. After a decade of performing at weddings and other celebrations and releasing hundreds of cassette tapes of these shows, Souleyman made his worldwide debut with the album Highway to Hassake, *in 2007. It was well received by critics and the public. In 2009, Souleyman and his band began touring the United States, the United Kingdom, and Australia, where he performed at concert halls and big music festivals. Like his first worldwide release, Souleyman's subsequent albums* Dabke 2020 *(2009) and* Jazeera Nights *(2010) are compiled from live recordings at weddings and parties in his native country. However, the next album,* Hafiat Gharbia: The Western Concerts *(2011), is a collection of his live performances while on tour. Souleyman also collaborated with the eclectic Icelandic singer Bjork on several remixes in 2011.*

Early Life

Omar Souleyman was born in 1966 and grew up in Ras Al Ain, a small town in Syria's northeastern region, close to the Turkey's southern border. Souleyman was not raised in a musical family. However, as a boy he heard instruments such as the *rehab,* a Middle Eastern instrument with similarities to a violin and a banjo, though it usually has just one string; and the *bouzouki,* a type of lute often used in Balkan music. Souleyman dropped out of school-because of an eye injury, he has explained-and went on to work a variety of jobs, including as a stonemason.

Souleyman got the idea to pursue singing full-time because of encouragement from friends who had heard him sing at a few weddings. In the mid-1990s, he started performing at weddings and family parties, where he would sing folk poetry over traditional dance beats. In 1996, he met Rizan Sa'id, a young multi-instrumentalist who was playing keyboards. Souleyman asked Sa'id to join him, and the two slowly built up a reputation as a great party band. They continued to perform at weddings and family parties, with Souleyman singing folk poetry and Sa'id playing keyboards and synthesizers and driving the rhythm. Sa'id played not only Syrian styles of dance music but also blended in other Middle Eastern styles, such as Kurdish, Iraqi, and Arabic. The kind of music they performed is known as *dabke,* a sty1e of dance and party music particular to the Levant region of the Middle East, which mainly includes Syria, Lebanon, Israel, Jordan, and the Palestinian territories. The duo would sometimes perform with other musicians, such as violin players and percussionists. They also performed with musicians who played the *saz,* a kind of lute with a pear-shaped body; the *ney,* a kind of flute; and the bouzo11ki. By then, Souleyman's trademark look was set: large, dark sunglasses and a keffiyeh scarf on his head.

Life's Work

Souleyman's journey to wider mass appeal began when Zuhir Maksi, a local producer who had his own label, recorded him live at those parties and weddings and released a good deal of the recordings as cassette tapes for the general public. The Syrian people of the region soon developed a high opinion of Souleyman as a musician, and demand increased for his band to perform at parties and weddings. The tapes themselves were of inferior sound and production quality, but people who bought those tapes could hear the spirit and energy of the singer, and so the dynamic singer continued to be in demand.

Aside from helping to spread the word about Souleyman, Maksi would occasionally perform with him, whispering lines of poetry into his ear during the live show. Mark Gergis wrote about this phenomenon, which is unfamiliar to most Westerners, for the official Omar Souleyman website (May 2011): "This age old poet and singer relationship is a tradition in the region and often employs the poetry form called the *ataba— a* form of folk poetry still employed today. During a concert, the poet often stands very near to Souleyman, following him into the circle of dabke linedancers, and whispering verses relevant to the event and the families that host it into Omar' s ears. Acting as a conduit,

Affiliation: International Appeal

Even though Souleyman sings in Arabic, reviewers have called attention not only to his song titles but also the lyrics, which are provided by a variety of poets. In a review of *Jazeera Nights* for the *New York Times* (30 May 2010), Ben Ratliff wrote, "The songs are grave, direct, and Mr. Souleyman cheerleads around the lyrics." Hatliff added that the lyrics are "worth pondering" and provided a sample translation for readers: "'I will cry, and make the stones cry on everybody who said I made them cry,' Mr. Souleyman sings. 'I spent my life being afraid to die before we embraced / I will embrace you.'" In addition to the lyrics of *Jazeera Nights,* Ratliff praised the album's music, particularly the "high-speed beats and microtonal synth wails." In a profile of Souleyman for the Abu Dhabi-based publication the *National* (28 May 20 I 0), Dan Hancox wrote that there is a "tendency to see any folk music as an established set of standards, preserved in amber. Blessedly, its reality is one of complexity and constant evolution. Indeed, Souleyrnan has witnessed the Syrian musical scene change a great deal, even in the last few years." Souleyman told Hancox that his brand of Syrian/Arabie folk music has "sped up." When asked whether this was due to foreign influences, Souleyman replied, "No, we developed the speed. We started out with slower rhythms, but each year it's got faster by about ten beats per minute. The change came from the electronic keyboards—you can just turn the speed up and make it faster with your hand."

Souleyman and his band went on their first tour of Europe and the United States in 2009, during which they received positive reviews and much enthusiasm from concert attendees. The following year, the band went on tour again, playing such venues as New York City's SummerStage concert series in Central Park and at the hip London venue Scala. Writing about Souleyman's performance in the United Kingdom, Hancox stated: "It is amusing to behold an English crowd attempting to dance to something it doesn't quite know how to relate to. Fortunately, with Souleyman's help, inhibitions are quickly cast aside. He paces the edge of the stage clapping his hands, beckoning to the crowd. His most successful maneuver is to sweep his arm along and then up, an injunction to raise one hand into the air as the leader in a dabke dance would. It may be a long way from a Syrian wedding, but the crowd soon realizes that a lack of knowledge of the right steps is not a problem, and begin to make up their own: a mixture of naive attempts at dabke, flamenco, Bollywood hand-flourishes, fist-pumping, foot-stomping, rock mushing, even the festive footwork of an Irish ceilidh. It's a mess, but a glorious one."

Souleyman strides into the audience, vocalizing the prose in song before returning for the next verse." Souleyman later continued that tradition with Hassan Hamadi and Mahmoud Harbi, both well-respected local poets. The latter, Harbi, would eventually go on to tour internationally with Souleyman. In 1996, *Jani,* a live recording of Souleyman's performance at a wedding, was released. The recording was so successful that within a few years, Souleyman released hundreds of such recordings of different wedding performances. As his popularity continued to rise, he began performing at weddings and parties all over Syria. He was soon performing in other Middle Eastern countries, such as the United Arab Emirates, Lebanon, and Saudi Arabia. A recording that helped Souleyman gain further acclaim across the Middle East was his studio album *Khataba* (2005), which had a solidly produced sound and did not have any of the technical glitches of live cassette recordings. Although Souleyman's popularity was growing in the Arab world, he was still unknown to Western audiences at this time.

Highway to Hassake: Folk and Pop Sounds of Syria (2007) was the first collection of Souleyman's music released outside the Middle East. In 1998, almost a decade before the album's release, American musician Mark Gergis heard Souleyman's music during a visit to Syria. He did not see Souleyman live but did hear his wedding recordings, which were by this point fairly ubiquitous in Syrian cassette kiosks. Over the years and several trips to Syria, Gergis collected many such tapes. In 2006, he finally met Souleyman, which ultimately led to the release of *Highway to Hassake* on the Sublime Frequencies label, where Gergis had connections.

Highway to Hassake is a compilation of Souleyman's cassette recordings spanning more than a decade, starting from around 1996. On the compact disc, Souleyman sings his unique version of the dabke style, but he also incorporates Turkish pop music, the distinctive beat of Iraqi *choubi,* and ataba. Many music critics in the West, particularly the United States and England, wrote enthusiastically of the album's raw energy, which they viewed as a combination of Middle Eastern music—particularly Syrian folk styles—and electronic dance music. The CD features thirteen songs, including "Leh Jani" ("When I Found Out"), "Jani" ("She Came to Me"), and "Jalsat Atabat" ("Atabat Session"). In a review for the *Washington Post* (8 Jan. 2008), Chris Richards wrote, "The sonic anarchy on *Highway to Hassake* always stays tethered to Souleyman's voice. His vocal cords strain with startling urgency as he pleads his way through narratives worthy of Shakespeare (even though he's not singing in English). According to the liner notes, these songs recount tales of unrequited passion, meddling parents, star-crossed lovers and double-crossed fools."

Souleyman was not the only one to receive praise for *Highway to Hassake.* Music critics took note of Sa'id's talent as well. Commenting on Sa'id, Richards stated, "Equally compelling: the keyboard fireworks of Rizan Sa'id—a synthesizer virtuoso so nimble he could probably ace your favorite Van Halen guitar solo on the keypad of a touch-tone phone. Sa'id's riotous blips and drum machine thwacks jostle for position in Souleyman's breakneck beatscape, giving these tracks a kinetic energy that shines through the cassette tape hiss and across the cultural divide." *Highway to Hassake* also received enthusiastic reviews in the *Village Voice, Seattle Weekly,* and the London *Observer,* as well as many other publications across the globe. In addition to the album, a video widely available on YouTube featured Souleyman singing the song "Leh Jani" and helped the singer draw in even more fans.

Souleyman's next two albums were released internationally in 2009 and 2010. Like *Highway to Hassake,* they are compilations of his performances from a career that by that point spanned nearly a decade and a half. *Dabke 2020: Folk and Pop Sounds of Syria* (2009) features eight songs. Some have elaborate titles, such as "La Sidounak Sayyada" ("Til Prevent the Hunters from Hurting You"), "Laqtuf Ward Min Khaddak" ("I Will Pick a Flower from Your Cheek"), and "Kaset Hanzal" ("Drinking from the Glass of Bitterness"). Souleyman's third album, *Jazeera Nights* (20 I 0), also features dramatic titles, including "Labji Wa Bajji II Hajar" ("My Tears Will Make the Stones Cry"), "Hafer Gabrak Bidi" ("Will Dig Your Grave with My Hands"), and "Hot II Khanjar Bi Gleibi" ("Stab My Heart"). The album, like the two that came before it, received a great deal of glowing, if short, reviews.

Souleyman returned to New York City in the fall of 2010 to yet another hip music venue, the Music Hall of Williamsburg, in Brooklyn. Unlike some of his other live performances in the West, Souleyman was accompanied only by Sa'id, his keyboardist and composer, which created a mellower atmosphere than the typically frenzied state aroused by the up-tempo dance numbers with percussion. In a review of the concert for the *New York Times* (3 Nov. 2010), Ratliff wrote, "Mr. Souleyman wore his typical clothes: brown leather jacket over a floor-length tunic, aviator sunglasses, a red-and-white-checked keffiyeh. He started singing a poem in slow rubato over a single synthesizer chord. Mr. Sa'id filled in the pauses with fast, fluttering, modal figures; there were no percussion sounds. It wasn't as guttural and rending as this kind of song has been on his records; it was orderly and calming, quite beautiful."

In 2011, Souleyman went on tour once again to perform at festivals worldwide, including the Perth International Arts Festival in Perth, Australia; the Chaos in Tejas Festival in Austin, Texas; the Bonnaroo Festival in Manchester, Tennessee; the Field Day Festival in London, England; and the Isle of Wight Festival on the British Isle of Wight. Souleyman also played shows in Germany, France, Belgium, and the Netherlands. Despite playing concerts and music festivals all over the United States, Australia, and Europe, Souleyman did not play general-admission concerts in his home country of Syria. As before, he continued to perform regularly at parties and weddings there.

Souleyman's fourth album, also released by Sublime Frequencies, is titled *Hafiat Gharhia: The Western Concerts* (2011). The album is another collection of live material, this time compiled from Souleyman's concerts in the United States, Europe, and Australia, between 2009 and 2011. *Hafiat Gharhia* was favorably received, peaking at number ten on the Billboard Top World Albums chart after its release. In a review for Allmusic (2011), Thorn Jurek commented on how lively and exciting the sound is, a general consensus among music critics: "Sa'id is able to make his wildly modified keyboards and samplers capture the sounds of the ney, violin, and numerous percussion instruments, while [Ali] Shaker's electric saz is as expertly played as any guitar virtuoso's axe. Its amplified sound resembles a dead cross between a Fender Stratocaster and a sitar. In addition to these two, poet Zuhir Maksi literally stands close to Souleyman on-stage and whispers poetry or prose (both traditional and modern) into his ear. The singer transforms this in real time into a wailing live vocalization that is pure lightning-bolt energy, wailing with abandon atop the numerous rhythms, harmonies, and melodies being played with nonstop kinetic musical fire behind him." Jurek concluded that *Hafiat Gharbia* is "among the finest live albums of the twenty-first century thus far."

Music critics and music fans have not been the only ones singing the praises of Souleyman's band. On the National Public Radio (NPH) program *All Things Considered* (29 June 2009), on the series called *You Must Hear This,* on which musicians discuss other musicians they greatly admire, the eclectic singer-songwriter Bjork, of Iceland, recalled that the first time she heard Souleyman was on YouTube. "Some people," said Bjork, "call what he plays Syrian techno [sound bite of laughter]. . . . But I think what's refreshing about Omar Souleyman is just the party and fun, and it's really alive and very urgent, and he's not shy of using synths and electronics and drum machines and YouTube. So he's, like, really eager to make something that's vibrant today." In 2011, Bjork and Souleyman collaborated on several remixes of Bjork's songs, including "Tesla" and "Crystalline," for her musical and interactive project titled *Biophilia* (2011).

Personal Life

Omar Souleyman lives in Syria.

Further Reading

Carroll, Jim. "If You See One Syrian Wedding Singer This Year ... *"Irish Times.* Irish Times, 9 Sep. 2010. Web. 11 June 2012.

Gehr, Hichard. "Omar Souleyman, Arabian Idol." *Village Voice.* Village Voice LLC, 22 June 2010. Web. 11 June 2012.

Gergis, Marie "Bio." *Omar Souleyrnan.* Sublime Frequencies and Omar Souleyman, May 2011. Web. 11 June 2012.

Hancox, Dan. "Highway to Hipsterville." *Abu Dhabi National.* Abu Dhabi Media Company, 28 May 2010. Web. 11 June 2012.

Hatliff, Ben. "Cool Alchemy: Merging East and West for a Universal Beat." *New York Times.* New York Times, 3 Nov. 2010. Web. 11 June 2012.

Esperanza Spalding

Jazz Bassist musician

Born: 1984; Portland, Oregon
Primary Field: Jazz
Group Affiliation: Solo artist

Introduction

In the world of jazz instrumentalists, where women make up a small minority, female bandleaders are rare, and female standup-bass players rarer still. At the age of 25, Esperanza Spalding has won high acclaim as both. Influenced as much by R&B artists, including Stevie Wonder and Erykah Badu, as by such jazz icons as Wayne Shorter and Ron Carter, Spalding has performed with many jazz greats and recorded three albums as a bandleader, showcasing her eclectic sensibilities along with her vocal and compositional talents. After graduating from the prestigious Berklee College of Music, in Boston, Massachusetts, at the age of 20, Spalding was offered a teaching position there, making her the second-youngest person in the school's 60-year history (after the jazz guitarist Pat Metheny) to be hired as an instructor; she taught at Berklee for three years.

Early Life

Esperanza Spalding was born in 1984 in Portand, Oregon. Her mother raised Spalding and her older brother in a lower-middle-class Portland neighborhood called King. Because Spalding's mother was the only provider for her children, working a number of jobs, the family struggled financially, sometimes coming close to homelessness; Spalding remembers little about that, recalling mainly that she grew up with a loving and caring mother. From an early age Spalding loved music. She enjoyed listening to an oldies radio station, which played songs by Stevie Wonder, Sam Cooke, the Monkees, and others. One day she heard her mother trying, with difficulty, to play a relatively simple classical piece on the family's piano; Spalding, then four years old, went to the piano bench and played the piece by ear. During those years Spalding saw the famed cellist Yo-Yo Ma perform on the children's TV show *Mister Rogers' Neighborhood*, and she was transfixed. "Oh, I want to do that," Spalding remembers thinking. "That's what I want to do."

Because the local, free music program had no cellos, Spalding settled for a violin. Though she did not like to practice, her ability to play by ear allowed her to develop her music skills. She eventually joined the Chamber Music Society of Oregon, a nonprofit program that included a children's chamber orchestra, in which Spalding played, and a summer camp, where she took group lessons. Around the age of 12, she started getting private instruction. By age 15 she was the orchestra's concertmaster, or lead violinist. During those years, from fifth to eighth grade, Spalding was home schooled, in part because she had a poor immune system and was often ill, and in part because her mother generally disliked the public-school environment. Since her mother worked full-time, Spalding mostly educated herself—borrowing books from the library, having her mother check her work, and taking tests administered by the state. One of the most important lessons Spalding learned during that time, one that she applies today, was the importance of time management: with no schedule in place, she realized that the only way to get work done was to structure her own time.

Spalding attended the Northwest Academy, a private arts high school in Portland, on a full scholarship. One day during her freshman year, while walking through the halls of her school, she spotted a new standup bass on the floor of an empty classroom. She instinctively went inside, picked it up, and started to play. "I remember distinctly," she said, "the first thing you notice [about a bass] is the vibration is so powerful, particularly compared to a violin—or any other instrument. I felt it resonating through my whole system. I said, 'Wow. This is pretty hip.' And I just kept noodling around." Brian Rose, a jazz-improvisation teacher, came into the room and explained the concept of a walking bass line (a steady rhythm of quarter notes) and then showed Spalding a simple blues progression. That was an illuminating moment for Spalding. "I was like, 'Oh, cool, so you can just make up some accompaniment that fits into the harmony, but it can be whatever you *hear*.' And I really am an ear player on a lot of different levels, so that was really encouraging, because I always felt so behind everyone else in the classical world. My brain just never worked in a mathematical way and it was really discouraging, because I loved music, and I felt I was good at it." After a few minutes of playing blues on the standup bass, Spalding felt she had found "something I can relate to."

Within a few months Spalding was playing live gigs with a variety of bands—jazz, blues, rock, funk, and hip-hop groups. One that contributed significantly to her development as a singer and songwriter was the indie-rock band Noise for Pretend. The members of that already established group, both men, needed a bass

Affiliation: Jazz

While her tendency to cross musical boundaries has led some to question whether her music is really jazz, Spalding told *Current Biography*—the source of quotes for this article, unless otherwise noted—that she is not concerned with how people label her music: "I know that I like what I'm doing, and people seem to have a great time at the shows. And people that I really respect have invited me to play in their bands, only because of the music, not because of any hype or titles."

At the request of President Barack Obama, Spalding performed for him three times in 2009: twice at the White House—once for a tribute to Stevie Wonder and again as part of an evening of music and poetry—and once in Oslo, Norway, where Obama accepted the Nobel Peace Prize. Spalding's latest album, *Chamber Music Society*, a modern chamber-music record with elements of classical, folk, and world music as well as early-20th century jazz, was released in 2010. In a review for the *Washington Post* (August 17, 2010), Bill Friskics-Warren wrote that the album's "fusion of jazz, contemporary classical and other sources, including some understated funk, is as lively as it is original." In early fall Spalding began an international tour in support of the album. Another album, as yet untitled, will be what she called a "rocking funky singer-songwriter" jazz record; it is due out in the spring of 2011. Spalding's bass playing can also be heard on Joe Lovano's *Folk Art* (2009), a critically acclaimed post-bop album of original tunes by Lovano's band Us Five. Spalding has said that she would like to collaborate with the singer/songwriter Paul Simon and the hip-hip artist Andre 3000 of the rap group OutKast. She would also like to act in films and write music for large ensembles.

player who could also sing backup; Spalding had not done much singing, let alone while playing bass, but she said she could do it. Soon after joining the band, she started contributing lyrics and compositions, and before long she was writing most of the group's songs. "Composition is a huge part of my musical identity," Spalding said. She added that most teenagers "don't get a platform like that, that you can write stuff and have it played by these awesome grown-up musicians who are not only going to play it and take it seriously but contribute to it and give constructive feedback, and help make the arrangements better, etcetera." At the suggestion of a record-label owner, Spalding, at age 16, also became the band's lead singer. While with Noise for Pretend, she improved her composition, singing, and playing as well as the coordination required to sing and play bass at the same time. She also got better at commanding the attention of a live crowd, usually people in their 20s, 30s, and 40s "getting drunk and wanting to party." During that period Spalding was officially in four bands—including a jazz group, Trio Esperanza—and played with many others, among them a 14-piece jazz ensemble. At the suggestion of a band member, she learned to sing and play several jazz standards. Spalding's transition to jazz was not deliberate. "It wasn't like, Oh, I want to be a jazz musician now," she said. "It was like, I want to do this some more, because I'm really good at it and it's fun." The pace of her evolution as a musician was rapid. She told Marty Hughley for the *Oregonian* (August 16, 2002), "I feel like I've tried to cram 10 years of development into two years."

At 15 Spalding dropped out of high school. Later, after getting a GED, she spent a year in a conservatory program at Portland State University. Because her studies there were very intense, and because she already had a wealth of musical experiences, she had an easy time when she arrived on a full scholarship at the Berklee College of Music, in 2002. "I didn't really dig most of the classes at Berklee," she confessed. "Of course there were some teachers that opened my mind and taught me so much, but most of the curriculum I found to be pretty dry—compared to what I wanted to do." Spalding nonetheless enjoyed the environment at Berklee, where she could meet and play with gifted musicians from more than 50 countries. Spalding was also performing four or five nights a week, appearing with famous and influential musicians who included Pat Metheny, the saxophonist Joe Lovano, the singer Patti Austin, and many others. One encounter with Metheny made a lasting impression on her. At the time he was producing a recording of a student ensemble led by the vibraphonist Gary Burton. "Everybody had left the studio," Spalding recalled, speaking to Thomas Peña for jazz.com (May 28, 2008), "and I was there, probably practicing and Mr. Metheny walked in and asked me what I was planning to do with my life. I told him that I was thinking of leaving school and pursuing a degree in political science. He told me that he meets a lot of musicians, some great, some not so great and that I had [what he called] the 'X Factor.' Meaning, that if I chose to pursue a career in music and I applied myself, my potential was unlimited." Spalding graduated in 2005 and then, at the age of 20, accepted a teaching position at the school, which she held until 2008.

Life's Work

As she was finishing her studies at Berklee, Spalding recorded her first album, *Junjo* (2006), an instrumental-jazz record with bebop and Latin elements. Spalding had not envisioned the album as her debut. In Boston she had been playing Latin and improvisational music with the pianist Aruan Ortiz and the drummer Francisco Mela and asked them to record with her, "purely as a project for our enjoyment, and the desire to capture the music we were making." The resulting record, released on a small Spanish label, won attention from jazz fans, critics, and other musicians that far exceeded her expectations. Writing for allmusic.com, Michael G. Nastos called the album "an exercise in joy and freedom. . . . For sure, [Spalding] is an accomplished bassist, musician, and original thinker. *Junjo* is an auspicious beginning that should catch the ears of any lover of great music." Spalding wrote or co-wrote four of the nine tracks; the rest were her versions of songs by such jazz greats as Chick Corea ("Humpty Dumpty") and Jimmy Rowles ("The Peacocks"). Along with her bass playing, Spalding provided wordless vocals for nearly all the songs. In a short review for the *New York Times* (July 9, 2006), Ben Ratliff called the record "charming."

Late in 2007 Spalding began recording her full-fledged, self-titled debut album. *Esperanza* (2008) was more diverse and ambitious than her first record, encompassing a wider variety of sounds and styles, a gumbo of jazz, samba, bossa nova, neo-soul, and R&B. Spalding wrote the music and words for nine of the 12 songs and sang in English, Portuguese, and Spanish. She put unique twists on other people's songs; one of the three covers on the album is "Cuerpo y Alma" her version of the jazz standard "Body and Soul." The opening bass line provides a hint of the original tune, which vanishes when all the elements—the nonstandard time signature (5/4), Latin rhythm, and Spanish lyrics— come together to form an entirely new song. Other tracks, especially "Precious" (composed by Spalding), are much closer to neo-soul and pop than to jazz or Latin music. Still others, such as "I Know You Know," another Spalding original, float in between: the song begins with a funky bass line accompanied by drums and spare piano; Spalding sings the verse in a cool, neo-soul style, showing the influence of Erykah Badu, and then delivers the partly scatted chorus over a Latin rhythm. "She Got to You," another Spalding original, is also sung in English, between and along with bursts of alto-sax melodies. A mellow and soulful samba is heard on the album's last track, "Samba em Preludio," a song by the celebrated Brazilian guitar player Baden Powell. *Esperanza* debuted at number three on *Billboard's* top contemporary jazz albums chart, quickly moved up to number two, and remained on the chart for over a year.

"The ambition on display on *Esperanza,"* Thom Jurek wrote for allmusic.com, "is not blind; it's deeply intuitive, and her focus brings out the adventure on the album in all the right ways. By a lesser musician, even attempting something like this would have been disastrous." The fact that Spalding was only 23 years old did not go unnoticed by Jurek or other critics. "In sum," Jurek concluded, *"Esperanza* sounds like the work of a much older, more experienced player, singer, and songwriter. Spalding not only has these gifts in natural abundance but is disciplined in her execution as well." Writing for the *Chicago Tribune* (July 10, 2008), Ed Morales described Spalding's album as "picking up where the jazz fusion of the 1970s left off." He added: "The songs pulsate with complex arrangements, Spalding's uniquely expressive vocals and fat-bottomed bass playing, and challenging melodies and harmonies." The positive reception, however, was not unanimous. Some critics, among them Ben Ratliff of the *New York Times* (May 26, 2008), argued that Spalding's attempt to blend the various genres and styles was ambitious but ultimately unsuccessful. Ratliff, who conceded that Spalding's talent is "beyond question," argued: "This is mostly acoustic music played by jazz musicians and owes as much to Stevie Wonder as Wayne Shorter. It's an attempt at bringing this crisscrossing to a new level of definition and power, but its vamps and grooves are a little obvious, and it pushes her first as a singer-songwriter, which isn't her primary strength."

Acknowledging how different the songs on *Esperanza* are from one another, Spalding called the album an "appetizer sampler of all the elements that made up my musical identity." She conceded that the record is "all over the place" but said that that is because "I only got however many songs to make a statement about who I was." The album, she said, was meant to be an introduction to her various styles. "I really think I have a lot to offer long-term," she said, "and I want people to pay attention and experience my music." Because jazz artists and other musicians now make most of their money through touring rather than record sales, *Esperanza* was also meant to be an advertisement for music fans to see her in live performance, which, she said, is "where the magic happens."

Personal Life

Spalding lives in Austin, Texas, and New York City.

Further Reading

allaboutjazz.com
allmusic.com
Boston Globe D p11 Apr. 22, 2005
esperanzaspalding.com
New Yorker p32 Mar. 15, 2010
Oregonian p38 Aug. 16, 2002

Britney Spears

Singer

Born: Dec. 2, 1981; Kentwood, Louisiana
Primary Field: Pop
Group Affiliation: Solo performer

Introduction

At the age of 18, the singer Britney Spears has won honors and accolades—and also become the target of media critics, for reasons having nothing to do with her talent.

Her singles ". . . Baby One More Time" and "Sometimes," from her debut album, . . . Baby One More Time *(1999), soared up the record charts while drawing accusations that their lyrics condoned domestic abuse and masochism, interpretations that miss the mark, according to the singer. The criticism has done little to deter Spears's fans: they have purchased almost 12 million copies of her album, and her stadium concerts typically sell out the day tickets are made available. In* Entertainment Weekly *(December 24/31, 1999), Ken Tucker wrote that Spears has "chosen her . . . influences well: a bit of Janet Jackson in her take-charge dance moves, a smidgen of Mariah [Carey]'s sultry sassiness, some Stevie Wonder in her croon, and, behind the scenes, Backstreet Boys mentor Max Martin co-writing and co-producing unshakable hits."*

Early Life

Britney Spears was born in the small town of Kentwood, Louisiana, on December 2, 1981 to Jamie Spears, a construction contractor, and Lynne Spears, a second-grade teacher. She has an older brother, Bryan, whom she has described as protective, and a younger sister, Jamie Lynn, who is considering a singing career. Britney Spears has always loved to sing, and she remembers standing in front of the bathroom mirror while holding a hairbrush she pretended was a microphone. "My mom would have company over when I was little, and she was so used to [me singing all the time], she didn't even realize I was doing it," Spears told an interviewer for *TV Guide* (May 8, 1999). "And the company was always like, 'Lynne, tell her to be quiet.'" Spears, who remains a devout Baptist, made her first public appearance when she was four, singing "What Child Is This" in her church. When she was eight years old, she traveled with her mother to Atlanta, Georgia, to audition for the Disney Channel's *Mickey Mouse Club,* based on the original series, which aired in the 1950s. Although the producers considered her too young for the show, they were sufficiently impressed by her singing ability to refer her to an agent in New York. There, for the next three summers, Spears studied at the Professional Performing Arts School at the Off-Broadway Dance Center. The lessons paid off: she began to win parts in commercials, and in 1991 she landed a role in the Off-Broadway production of *Ruthless,* based on the 1956 film thriller *The Bad Seed.* When she was 11, Spears auditioned again for *Mickey Mouse Club,* and this time she was invited to join the cast. She performed for two seasons alongside fellow mouseketeers Justin Timberlake, JC Chasez, Christina Aguilera, and Keri Russell, each of whom has also gone on to fame as a singer or actor.

When the show was canceled, in 1993, Spears returned to Kentwood, where she completed one year of high school. During that time she lived a normal high-school life, attending the prom and other functions, but she quickly became discontented. "I went home and it was like a year and I was just like 'Eh,'" she told John Norris during an interview for the MTV Web site. "I wanted to sing and I wanted to perform and performing for all these functions in my home town just wasn't enough. You know?" At 15 she returned to New York to try to find singing jobs.

Life's Work

An executive at Jive Records, eager to win a share of the burgeoning teen market, heard a demo tape she had made and signed her to a development deal. Eric Foster White, a producer who had previously collaborated with the singer Whitney Houston, was assigned to work with her-an arrangement that delighted Spears, since Houston had long been an idol of hers. She also traveled to Sweden to work with the producer Max Martin, who had already teamed up with several other young performers-including the Backstreet Boys and Ace of Base—and has been credited with helping to rejuvenate pop music in the latter part of the 1990s.

In October 1998 Spears's first single,"... Baby One More Time," was released. To promote the song, Jive Records sent Spears on a cross-country tour of the nation's shopping malls, a strategy that had been used in the 1980s to launch the careers of Tiffany and Debbie Gibson, pop singers to whom Spears is often compared. Backed by two dancers and armed with promotional copies of the record, Spears was seen by thousands of teens, and by December of that year her single had sold 500,000 copies. Spears later toured as the opening act for 'N Sync, a band made up of five boys who were quickly becoming teen idols. This gave her even more exposure to her intended audience, and as a result her debut album, also called . . . *Baby One More Time,* quickly landed on the *Billboard* charts at number one.

The music industry showered her with honors. Spears won four *Billboard* awards, including female artist of the year, new pop artist of the year, Hot 100 Singles artist of the year, and female Hot 100 Singles artist of the year; several MTV awards; a Teen Choice Award; a People's Choice nomination for favorite female performer; and a 2000 Grammy nomination for best new artist. Her second album, *Oops! . .. I Did It Again,* was released in May 2000 and sold 1.3 million copies during its first week. In June the television special *Britney in Hawaii* aired on the Fox network.

In February 2001, Spears signed a multi-million promotional deal with Pepsi. Her self-titled third studio album, *Britney*, was released in November 2001. While on tour, she felt inspired by hip hop artists such as Jay-Z and The Neptunes and wanted to create a record with a funkier sound. The album debuted at number one in the *Billboard* 200 and sold over 12 million copies worldwide. Stephen Thomas Erlewine of AllMusic called *Britney* "the record where she strives to deepen her persona, making it more adult while still recognizably Britney. [...] It does sound like the work of a star who has now found and refined her voice, resulting in her best record yet." The album was honored with two Grammy nominations—Best Pop Vocal Album and Best Female Pop Vocal Performance for "Overprotected"— and was listed in 2008 as one of *Entertainment Weekly's* "100 Best Albums from the Past 25 Years." The album's first single, "I'm a Slave 4 U," became a top-ten hit worldwide.

Spears's performance of the single at the 2001 MTV Video Music Awards featured a caged tiger and a large albino python draped over her shoulders. It was harshly received by animal rights organization PETA, who claimed the animals were mistreated and scrapped plans for an anti-fur billboard that was to feature Spears. To support the album, Spears embarked on the Dream Within a Dream Tour. The show was critically praised for its technical innovations, the *pièce de résistance* being a water screen that pumped two tons of water into the stage. The tour grossed $43.7 million, becoming the second highest grossing tour of 2002 by a female artist, behind Cher's Farewell Tour. Her career success was highlighted by *Forbes* in 2002, as Spears was ranked the world's most powerful celebrity.

Spears released her fourth studio album, *In the Zone*, in November 2003. She assumed more creative control by writing and co-producing most of the material. *Vibe* called it "A supremely confident dance record that also illustrates Spears's development as a songwriter." NPR listed the album as one of "The 50 Most Important Recording of the Decade," adding that "the decade's history of impeccably crafted pop is written on her body of work." *In the Zone* sold over 609,000 copies in the United States and debuted at the top of the charts, making Spears the first female artist in the SoundScan era to have her first four studio albums to debut at number one. It also debuted at the top of the charts in France and the top ten in Belgium, Denmark, Sweden and the Netherlands. *In the Zone* sold over 10 million copies worldwide. The album produced the hit singles: "Me Against the Music," a collaboration with Madonna; "Toxic"—which won Spears her only Grammy for Best Dance Recording; "Everytime" and "Outrageous."

In March 2004, she embarked on The Onyx Hotel Tour in support of *In the Zone*. In June 2004, Spears fell and injured her left knee during the music video shoot for "Outrageous." Spears underwent arthroscopic surgery. She was forced to remain six weeks with a thigh brace, followed by eight to twelve weeks of rehabilitation, which caused The Onyx Hotel Tour to be canceled. During 2004, Spears became involved in the Kabbalah Centre through her friendship with Madonna.

October 2004, Spears took a career break to start a family. *Greatest Hits: My Prerogative*, her first greatest hits compilation album, was released in November 2004. Spears's cover version of Bobby Brown's "My Prerogative" was released as the lead single from the album. The second single was "Do Somethin'." The greatest hits album sold over 5 million copies worldwide. In September 2005, Spears gave birth to her first child, a son. In November 2005, she released her first remix compilation, *B in the Mix: The Remixes*, which consists of eleven remixes. It has sold over 1 million copies worldwide. In September 2006, she gave birth to her second child, a son. In November 2006, Spears filed for divorce from Federline, citing irreconcilable differences. Their divorce was finalized in July 2007, when the couple reached a global settlement and agreed to share joint custody of their children.

In October 2007, Spears released her fifth studio album, *Blackout*.. In the United States, Spears became the only female artist to have her first five studio albums debut at the two top slots of the chart. The album received positive reviews from critics and has sold over 3 million copies worldwide. *Blackout* won Album of the Year at MTV Europe Music Awards 2008 and was listed as the fifth Best Pop Album of the Decade by *The Times*. Spears performed the lead single "Gimme More" at the 2007 MTV Video Music Awards. The performance was panned by many critics. Despite the backlash, the single acheived worldwide success, peaking at number one in Canada and the top ten in almost every country it charted. The second single "Piece of Me" reached the top of the charts in Ireland and reached the top five in Australia, Canada, Denmark, New Zealand and the United Kingdom.

In September 2008, Spears opened the MTV Video Music Awards with a pre-taped comedy sketch with Jonah Hill and an introduction speech. She won Best Female Video, Best Pop Video and Video of the Year for "Piece of Me." A 60-minute introspective documentary, *Britney: For the Record*, was produced to chronicle Spears's return to the recording industry. Directed by Phil Griffin, *For the Record* was shot in Beverly Hills, Hollywood, and New York City during the third quarter of 2008. The documentary was broadcast on MTV to 5.6 million viewers for the two airings on the premiere night. It was the highest rating in its Sunday night timeslot and in the network's history.

In December 2008, Spears's sixth studio album *Circus* was released. It received positive reviews from critics and debuted at number one in the United States, and inside the top ten in many European nations. In the United States, Spears became the youngest female artist to have five albums debut at number one, earning a place in *Guinness World Records*. She also became the only act in the Soundscan era to have four albums debut with 500,000 or more copies sold. The album was one of the fastest-selling albums of the year, and has sold 4 million copies worldwide. Its lead single, "Womanizer," became Spears's first number one in the *Billboard* Hot 100 since "...Baby One More Time." The single was nominated for a Grammy in the category of Best Dance Recording. Spears embarked on The Circus Starring Britney Spears in March 2009. With a gross of U.S. $131.8 million, it became the fifth highest grossing tour of the year.

In November 2009, Spears released her second greatest hits album, *The Singles Collection*. The album's lead and only single, "3" became her third number one single in the U.S. In September 2010, she made a cameo appearance on a Spears-themed tribute episode of American TV show *Glee*, titled "Britney/Brittany." The episode drew *Glee*'s highest ratings ever.

Affiliation: Controversy

The title song's lyrics were criticized by some, who interpreted them as a celebration of domestic violence. The song's refrain, "Baby, hit me one more time," was taken literally by these critics, despite Spears's protests that its meaning was metaphorical; in the *Rolling Stone* interview, she said, "It means just give me a sign, basically. I think it's kind of funny that people would actually think [it meant to hit me physically]." A second single from the album, "Sometimes," caused similar concerns, when the lyrics "Sometimes I run from you /Sometimes I hide /Sometimes I'm scared of you" were thought to have masochistic overtones. Neil Strauss, a music critic for the *New York Times* (July 6, 1999), found fault with the song for other reasons. "These meanings-the hitting, the fear, the implication that when Ms. Spears says no she means yes-are not so much intentional as they are evidence of careless songwriting, glitches in the pop machine." Spears stirred still more controversy when she appeared scantily clad on the cover and inside photos of *Rolling Stone's* April 1999 issue. Fans were apparently less offended than media critics, as ... *Baby One More Time* went on to sell more than 11 million albums worldwide.

In March 2011, Spears released her seventh studio album *Femme Fatale*. The album peaked at number one in the United States, which tied her with Mariah Carey and Janet Jackson for the third-most number ones among women. It has sold 1,000,000 copies in the United States and 2.2 million worldwide, and has been certified platinum by the RIAA. The album's lead single "Hold It Against Me" debuted at number-one on the *Billboard* Hot 100, becoming Spears's fourth number-one single on the chart and making her the second artist in history to have two consecutive singles debut at number one, after Mariah Carey. The second single "Till the World Ends" reached peaked at number three on the *Billboard* Hot 100 in May, while the third single "I Wanna Go" reached number seven in August. *Femme Fatale* became Spears's first album in which three of its songs reached the top ten of the chart. The fourth and final single "Criminal" was released in September 2011. In April 2011, Spears appeared in a remix of Rihanna's song "S&M." It reached number one in the US later in the month, giving Spears her fifth number one on the chart. On *Billboard*'s 2011 Year-End list, Spears was ranked number fourteen on the Artists of the Year, thirty-two on *Billboard* 200 artists and ten on *Billboard* Hot 100 artists.

In June 2011, Spears embarked on the Femme Fatale Tour. The first ten dates of the tour grossed $6.2 million, landing the fifty-fifth spot on Pollstar's Top

100 North American Tours list for the half-way point of the year. The tour ended on December 10, 2011 in Puerto Rico after 79 performances. In August 2011, Spears received the MTV Video Vanguard Award at the 2011 MTV Video Music Awards. The next month, she released her second remix album, *B in the Mix: The Remixes Vol. 2*.

In May 2012, Spears was hired to replace Nicole Scherzinger as a judge for the second season of the U.S. version of *The X Factor*, joining Simon Cowell, L.A. Reid and fellow new judge Demi Lovato, who replaced Paula Abdul. With a reported salary of $15 million, she became the highest-paid judge on a singing competition series in television history. She mentored the Teens category; her final act, Carly Rose Sonenclar, was named the runner-up of the season. Spears did not return for the show's third season. Spears was featured on will.i.am's "Scream & Shout," which was released as a single from his fourth studio album, *#willpower* (2013). The song later became Spears's sixth number one single on the UK Singles Chart and peaked at #3 on US *Billboard* Hot 100. Scream & Shout was among the best selling songs of 2012 and 2013 with denoting sales of over 8.1 million worldwide, the accompanying music video was the third-most viewed video in 2013 on VEVO despite the video being released in 2012. In December, *Forbes* magazine named her music's top-earning woman of 2012, with estimated earnings of $58 million.

Spears began work on her eighth studio album, *Britney Jean*, in December 2012, and enlisted will.i.am as its executive producer in May 2013. *Britney Jean* became Spears's final project under her original recording contract with RCA, which had guaranteed the release of eight studio albums. The record received a low amount of promotion and commercial impact, reportedly due to contractual obligations for Britney: Piece of Me. Upon its release, the record debuted at number four on the U.S. *Billboard* 200 with first-week sales of 107,000 copies, becoming her lowest-peaking and lowest-selling album in the United States.

"Work Bitch" was released as the lead single from *Britney Jean* on September 16, 2013, one day earlier than expected after being leaked online. It debuted and peaked at number 12 on the U.S. *Billboard* Hot 100 marking Spears's 31st song on the chart and the fifth highest debut of her career on the chart, and her seventh in the top 20. It also marked Spears's 19th top 20 hit and overall her 23rd top 40 hit. It also entered the top 10 on the U.S Billboard Hot Digital Songs chart at number 6 and debuted at number 2 on both the U.S. *Billboard* chart's Hot Dance Club Songs and Hot Dance/Electronic Songs. Also its debut on the U.S. *Billboard* Pop Songs chart at number 25, marked Spears's 31st chart entry, pushing her past Mariah Carey (30) for the second-most entries to the chart's October 3, 1992, launch. The song marked Spears's highest sales debut since her 2011 number one hit "Hold It Against Me." The second single "Perfume" was premiered on November 3, 2013, two days earlier than originally announced. It debuted and peaked at number 76 on the U.S. *Billboard* Hot 100. "Perfume" also charted on the U.S. *Billboard* Pop Songs chart, it debuted at number 37, reaching number 22 weeks later. During the production of *Britney Jean*, Spears recorded the song "Ooh La La" for the soundtrack of *The Smurfs 2* earlier in 2013.

On January 8, 2014, Spears won Favorite Pop Artist at the 40th People's Choice Awards at the Microsoft Theater in Los Angeles. For the week of July 26, 2014, "Alien" debuted and peaked at number 8 on the US Bubbling Under Hot 100 Singles despite not being released as a single from *Britney Jean*.

Spears released "Pretty Girls," with Iggy Azalea, on May 4, 2015. The song debuted and peaked at number 29 on the Billboard Hot 100 and charted moderately in international territories. Spears and Azalea performed the track live at the 2015 Billboard Music Awards from The AXIS, the home of Spears's residency, to positive critical response. At the 2015 Teen Choice Awards, Spears received the Candie's Style Icon Award, her ninth Teen Choice Award.

Guy Blackman of *The Age* wrote that "[t]he thing about Spears, though, is that her biggest songs, no matter how committee-created or impossibly polished, have always been convincing because of her delivery, her commitment and her presence. [...] Spears expresses perfectly the conflicting urges of adolescence, the tension between chastity and sexual experience, between hedonism and responsibility, between confidence and vulnerability."

Personal Life

Spears had been linked with Justin Timberlake of 'N Sync, Spears has claimed that her concert and recording obligations get in the way of dating. In January 2004, Spears married childhood friend Jason Allen Alexander at The Little White Wedding Chapel in Las Vegas, Nevada. The marriage was annulled 55 hours later, following a petition to the court that stated that Spears "lacked understanding of her actions." In July 2004, Spears became engaged to American dancer Kevin Federline, whom she had met three months before. The romance received intense attention from the media, since Federline had recently broken up with actress Shar Jackson, who was still pregnant with their second child at the time. The stages of their relationship were chronicled in Spears's first reality show *Britney & Kevin: Chaotic*. They held a wedding ceremony on September 18, 2004, but were not legally married until three weeks later on October 6 due to a delay finalizing the couple's prenuptial agreement.

In February 2007, Spears stayed in a drug rehabilitation facility in Antigua for less than a day. The following night, she shaved her head with electric clippers at a hair salon in Tarzana, Los Angeles. She admitted herself to other treatment facilities during the following weeks. In October 2007, Spears lost physical custody of her children to Federline. The reasons of the court ruling were not revealed to the public.

In January 2008, Spears refused to relinquish custody of her sons to Federline's representatives. She was hospitalized at Cedars-Sinai Medical Center after police that arrived at her house noted she appeared to be under the influence of an illicit substance. The following day, Spears's visitation rights were suspended at an emergency court hearing, and Federline was given sole physical and legal custody of the children. She was committed to the psychiatric ward of Ronald Reagan UCLA Medical Center and put on 5150 involuntary psychiatric hold. The court placed her under temporary, and later, permanent conservatorship of her father James Spears and attorney Andrew Wallet, giving them complete control of her assets. She was released five days later. In July 2008, Spears regained some visitation rights after coming to an agreement with Federline and his counsel.

In May 2010, Spears's representatives confirmed she was dating her agent Jason Trawick, and that they had decided to end their professional relationship to focus on their personal relationship. In December, Spears and Trawick became engaged. In January 2013, Spears and Trawick ended their engagement.

Further Reading

Entertainment Weekly p28 Dec. 24/31, 1999, with photo
Forbes p164+ Mar. 20, 2000, with photo
MTV Web site
New York Times E p1 July 6, 1999
Newsweek p64 Mar. 1, 1999, with photo
Rolling Stone p46+ May 25, 1000, with photo
Rolling Stone (on-line) Apr. 1, 1999, with photos
TV Guide p30+ May 8, 1999, with photos, p28+ Oct. 9-15, 1999
Dennis, Steve. *Britney: Inside the Dream* (2009)

(Harvey) Phil(lip) Spector

Recording industry executive

Born: Dec. 26, 1940; New York City
Primary Field: Producer
Group Affiliation: Philles; Ronettes; Righteous Brothers; Beatles

Introduction

In a field dominated by the fame of singers, guitarists, and rock groups, Phil Spector has achieved international stardom as a producer, composer, and arranger of pop songs during his thirty-year career. The hits he created in the 1950s and 1960s-among them "To Know Him Is to Love Him" by the Teddy Bears, "He's a Rebel" and "Uptown" by the Crystals, "Be My Baby" by the Ronettes, and "You've Lost That Lovin' Feelin"' by the Righteous Brothers-are known to the trade as Phil Spector records. Spector's "wall of sound" recording style is internationally recognized, virtually eclipsing the names of the singing groups he produced in the early years of rock-'n'-roll. Having produced eighteen gold (million selling) records by 1966, Spector temporarily retired from the music business. He returned in 1970 to produce the Beatles' Let It Be *album and then worked on individual projects with George Harrison and John Lennon. In the late 1970s Spector released several collections of his greatest hits. He is currently working on the digital transfer of sixty of his tracks for their long-awaited debut on compact disc from Rhino Records of Santa Monica, California, in a boxed set, to be entitled "Wall of Sound: The Essential Phil Spector." In Janu-*

ary 1989 Spector was inducted into the Rock-'n'-Roll Hall of Fame.

Early Life

Phil Spector was born Harvey Phillip Spector on December 26, 1940 in the New York City borough of the Bronx, the only son and second child of Benjamin and Bertha Spector. His father, an ironworker, committed suicide by carbon monoxide poisoning when the boy was nine. In 1953 Bertha Spector arrived with Phil and his older sister, Shirley, to southern California, where she at first supported her family as a seamstress and then worked as a bookkeeper for California Record Distributors.

Life's Work

At the age of thirteen, Spector was given a guitar for his bar mitzvah, and he began playing jazz in local coffeehouses only three years later. Fascinated by the rhythm-and-blues sounds that he heard on radio stations specializing in black music, or "race music," as it was then called, Spector was writing songs and organizing his classmates into singing groups even before he graduated from Fairfax High School in Los Angeles. One such group, made up of Phil Spector, Marshall Leib, and Annette Kleinbard, was the Teddy Bears, whose song "To Know Him Is to Love Him" was Spector's first big hit. The title was inspired by the epitaph on his father's tombstone.

Released on Dore Records in August 1958, "To Know Him Is to Love Him" languished for weeks until a disc jockey in Minneapolis began playing the song, generating 20,000 orders for it and catapulting it to the number-one position on the *Billboard* Hot 100 singles chart. "To Know Him is to Love Him" remained on the charts for twenty-three weeks and sold over one million copies in the United States alone, leading to a guest engagement for the Teddy Bears on Dick Clark's nationally broadcast American *Bandstand* television show.

"To Know Him Is to Love Him" was recorded thirty years later by Emmylou Harris, Dolly Parton, and Linda Ronstadt, and in 1988 it earned a BMI Award as the Most Performed Country Song of the year. The Teddy Bears' success as a group proved less enduring. The teenaged performers received only $3,000 of the $20,000 in royalties they were due under their contract with Dore, and, after a follow-up song flopped, the Teddy Bears moved to Imperial Records, where they cut three singles and an album, all of which were unsuccessful. The group folded in the wake of those failures and a serious auto accident suffered by Annette Kleinbard, the lead singer. Miss Kleinbard is better known today as Carol Connors, who collaborated on the theme song for the award-winning film *Rocky* (1977).

Spector's work with the Teddy Bears so impressed Lester Sill, the head of Trey Records, that he hired the precocious eighteen-year-old to produce Kell Osborne's "The Bells of St. Mary's" (1959] and two singles by a new group organized by Spector-the Spectors Three. The singles failed to reach the charts, and the group was relatively short-lived—unlike Spector's relationship with one of its members, Annette Merar (Mirar, according to some sources). The two were married shortly after that.

While under contract to Lester Sill, Spector worked as a court stenographer from 1959 to 1960 to help pay his tuition for one year at the University of California at Los Angeles following his high school graduation. Unable to continue to afford college, he left UCLA and Trey Records in 1960 for New York City, where he hoped to use the fluency in French that his mother had taught him to get a job as an interpreter with the United Nations. But he fell in with a group of musicians shortly after his arrival and never showed up for his scheduled interview.

Within weeks Spector was playing guitar as a session musician with two of his boyhood idols, Jerry Leiber and Mike Stoller, who composed songs for Elvis Presley. Leiber and Stoller also produced the Drifters and the Coasters for Atlantic Records, where Spector soon became head of artists and repertory. He not only collaborated with the ex-Drifter Ben E. King on "Spanish Harlem" in 1960, which reached number ten on the charts, but is also widely believed to have played a role in its production, though it is officially credited only to Leiber and Stoller. Spector was also involved in the making of Ben E. King's number-four hit "Stand by Me" and Nino Tempo and April Stevens's number-one hit "Deep Purple," both for the Atlantic label. Spector's other Atlantic productions of 1960–61 included songs for La Vern Baker, Billy Storm, and Ruth Brown.

Spector worked as a freelance producer for other labels after Leiber and Stoller had accepted as much work as they could handle. For the Dunes label, he produced Ray Peterson's number-nine hit "Corinna, Corinna" in 1960 and Curtis Lee's number-seven hit "Pretty Little Angel Eyes" the following year. For the Musicor label, he made Gene Pitney's "Every Breath I Take," in which the echo and percussion effects presaged Spector's later trademark sound. For Hill and Range Music, the publishing house known for handling most of the original songs written for Elvis Presley, Spector produced demo records with the legendary rhythm-and-blues composer Doc Pomus. Rumors that Spector worked on the demos for the first album Presley made after his discharge from the army have never been confirmed.

In 1961 Spector returned to Los Angeles to produce "Be My Boy" by the Paris Sisters on Lester Sill's Gregmark label. Although the song rose to only number fifty on the charts, his next vehicle for the Paris Sisters, "I Love How You Love Me," turned out to be his biggest hit since 1958. The number-five song sold more than one million copies and prompted Sill to offer him a partnership in a new label, Philles (for Phil and Les) Records, whose slogan was "Tomorrow's Sound Today." Around that time, Spector also established Mother Bertha, a publishing company to be run by its namesake, Bertha Spector.

Consisting of five New York City high school girls, Spector's first group for Philles, the Crystals, established the label with their debut single, "There's No Other (Like My Baby)," which rose to number twenty in 1962. The Crystals' next release, "Uptown," not only climbed to number thirteen on the charts, but also inspired a string of imitations, notably "Up on the Roof" and "Under the Boardwalk," both by the Drifters. Written by Barry Mann and Cynthia Weil, "Uptown" opens with a moody, trilled bass and delicately plucked mandolin and then soars skyward on a densely packed violin arrangement punctuated by woodblock and castanets, as the Crystals sing of the joys and frustrations of urban life.

In late 1962 Spector bought out his partner and assumed sole ownership of Philles Records. Aside from the Crystals' single "He Hit Me (and It Felt like a Kiss)," which was withdrawn during Spector's quest for control of the company, Philles scored a number of successes in 1962 and 1963. The Crystals' "He's a Rebel," written by Gene Pitney, became the label's first chart-topping hit. Although credited to the Crystals, the lyrics were actually sung by Darlene Love, a Los Angeles-based session vocalist with the Blossoms. As a member of Bob B. Soxx and the Blue Jeans, she recorded a version of "Zip-A-Dee-Doo-Dah" for Philles in 1962 and substituted for the Crystals on their 1963 hit "He's Sure the Boy I Love." That year the Crystals were signed to tour England after making "Da Doo Ron Ron" and "Then He Kissed Me," both top ten hits written by Jeff Barry and Ellie Greenwich, with whom Spector often collaborated as a composer.

Spector scored an even bigger hit in 1963 with "Be My Baby" by the Ronettes, three dancers turned singers who were led by Veronica ("Ronnie") Bennett, whom Spector married in 1967 or 1968 after their affair ended his first marriage. "Be My Baby," featuring an impassioned lead vocal backed by an overdubbed, layered chorus, rose to number two on the charts and led to a British tour for the Ronettes with the Rolling Stones in 1964. In England Spector played the organ on the Rolling Stones' song "Now I've Got a Witness" on their debut album and the guitar on the group's 1964 single "Play with Fire." He found his own music popular with many British artists, including the Beatles, the Searchers, Dusty Springfield, and Petula Clark.

Despite those testimonials to Spector's influence in England, he began to experience setbacks in the United States as British groups came to dominate the charts in 1964. The Ronettes' follow-ups to "Be My Baby" failed to make the top ten, and his other artists were becoming restive with the demands placed upon them by their perfectionist producer, who required them to spend long hours recqrding and re-recording songs that were sometimes withheld indefinitely. By 1965, the Crystals, Darlene Love, and the Blossoms had left Philles.

Nevertheless, in 1965 the Philles label achieved what many critics consider to be, in the words of Michael Aldred writing in *Goldmine* (June 17, 1988), "Spector's greatest artistic and commercial triumph": "You've Lost That Lovin' Feelin'" by the vocal duo the Righteous Brothers. "Spector's recording of it," to quote Aldred, "was brilliant, spectacular, and dynamic. It remains an unsurpassed masterpiece." Three more top ten hits of 1965 by the Righteous Brothers followed: "Just Once in My Life," "Unchained Melody," and "Ebb Tide."

The following year Spector's musical fortunes were mixed, despite his having amassed a fortune that made him a multimillionaire at the age of twenty-five. (He had just been dubbed "the first tycoon of teen" in a memorable profile by Tom Wolfe.) The Ronettes' "Walkin' in the Rain" earned Spector and his engineer, Larry Levine, a special citation for special effects (thunder)—the only Grammy ever awarded for a Phil Spector record. In the summer of 1966, the Ronettes—minus Ronnie Bennett, whose impending marriage to Spector was reportedly contingent upon her ceasing to perform

Affiliation: The Beatles

After releasing the *River Deep—Mountain High* album in 1969 (through a distribution arrangement with A&M Records that reactivated Philles) and recording a group called the Checkmates, Ltd., Spector returned to the music business. In 1969 he was entreated by the manager of the Beatles to produce their final album, *Let It Be,* from the tapes of their disjointed sessions of January 1969. Spector agreed and produced John Lennon's "Instant Karma" before completing *Let It Be* in 1970. The album rose to the top of the charts and generated three number-one singles: "Get Back," "Let It Be," and "The Long and Winding Road."

John Lennon and George Harrison enlisted the services of Spector for the solo albums that followed *Let It Be.* In 1970 he produced Lennon's Plastic Ono Band and Harrison's *All Things Must Pass,* which reached number six and number one on the charts, respectively. He then released Lennon's *Imagine* in 1971 and his *Sometime in New York City* in 1972. In the same year he worked on Harrison's *live* benefit album *The Concert for Bangla Desh* and, in 1973, on Harrison's *Living in the* Material *World* before parting company with both former Beatles.

or record—opened for the Beatles on their final tour of the United States. But Spector had a bewildering failure that year with Ike and Tina Turner's "River Deep—Mountain High," though it is now generally recognized as a minor classic. Written by Spector with Barry and Greenwich, the song represented one of Spector's inspired production jobs, with its multilayered orchestrations, percussion, choruses, and Tina Turner's lung-bursting vocals.

"River Deep—Mountain High" climbed no higher than number eighty-eight on the American charts and vanished from the charts after only three weeks, leading Spector to close down Philles Records. It received poor reviews and very little airplay: pop stations found it too rhythm-and-blues, and rhythm-and-blues stations considered it too pop. Meanwhile, it soared to number three in England, where it was admired by the likes of George Harrison of the Beatles. Four years later, after the belated release of the River Deep—Mountain High album, the song was successfully revived in a combined recording by the Motown trio the Supremes and the quartet the Four Tops. It became a European hit for the Australian rock group the Easybeats, and the song was later recorded by such diverse artists as Deep Purple, the blues band Brian Auger and the Trinity, and the punk group the Flamin' Groovies.

Those transatlantic discrepancies in the reception of "River Deep—Mountain High" perplexed Spector until at least 1969 and led to much searching for explanations. Some people highlighted the role played by strict categorization of the song into either pop or rhythm-and-blues; others simply held that Spector's time had come and gone; still others, disavowing an outright conspiracy theory, hinted that the industry may have turned against him for the mere pleasure of mowing down a giant. To many of the newer breed of disc jockeys, Spector's records seemed gimmicky and out-of-date; the more complex his "wall of sound" productions became, the less airplay they were given on the radio. Another reason for Spector's temporary eclipse in the late 1960s may have been his staunch refusal to imitate the styles characterizing the so-called British invasion at a time when his favored artistic vehicle—"girl groups" (as they were called) of black teenagers who were often discovered singing in the high schools—was increasingly unavailable.

Spector provided a rare explanation of his motives for temporarily withdrawing from the music business in an interview with Peter Bart for the *New York Times* (July 10, 1966). "Art is a game," said Spector. "If you win that game too regularly it tends to lessen your motivation. That's why I lost interest in the record business. If I stayed at it I would just be playing for public approval, not for what suits me." In an interview with Jann Wenner, the founding editor of *Rolling* Stone, three years later, Spector asserted that the quality of popular music had deteriorated in his absence, saying, "It bothers me enough to get back in [the recording industry]."

In the meantime, Spector ventured into the motion picture industry. In 1964–65 he financed and served as musical director of a concert film called *The Big TNT Show,* featuring the Ronettes, the Byrds, the Lovin' Spoonful, and Bo Diddley, among others. The movie became a staple at revival theatres and college screenings in the 1970s and 1980s and was reissued as part of the home-video compilation That Was Rock (1983). In 1965 he produced the television documentary *A Giant Stands 5 Ft. 7 In.* (Spector's height—his weight was 131 pounds at the time). He had one comic cameo appearance in a 1968 episode of the television series *I*

Dream *of* Jeannie and a bit part in Dennis Hopper's hit movie Easy Rider (1969). He also provided financing for Hopper's ill-fated *The Last Movie* (1970).

Spector's productions during the remainder of the decade included Cher's *A Woman's Story* [1974), Dion's *Born to Be with You* (1975), and Leonard Cohen's *Death of a Ladies' Man* (1977), all of which were recorded on his new label, Warner-Spector Records. In the mid-1970s he established yet another label, Phil Spector International (PSI), on which he reissued some of his early hits as well as new material that had just been released for Warner-Spector. Much better received than the aforementioned albums were four greatest-hits collections: *The* Best *of the* Spector Sound (1975 and 1976) by Polygram in England, *Phil* Spector's Greatest Hits [1977) by Warner-Spector, *Phil* Spector *74/79* by PSI, and *Wall of* Sound (1981) by PSI's British branch. Aside from those collections and his work on the forthcoming set from Rhino Records, Spector's most recent work was producing the Ramones' End *of the Century* album in 1980 and coproducing Yoko Ono's *Season of Glass* album in 1981.

Personal Life

Phil Spector is a slender, dark-haired man who looks younger than his forty-eight years. His marriage to Ronnie [Bennett) Spector ended in divorce in 1974. With her, he adopted three children: Gary Phillip and Louis Phillip, who are twins, and Donte Phillip, aged nineteen. *Who's Who in America* lists two other children, the twins Nicole and Phillip. From 1965 until recently Spector's home was a heavily guarded twenty-one-room mansion in Beverly Hills. He currently lives in a huge home in Pasadena, California. He is an enthusiastic gun collector and student of karate.

Further Reading

Goldmine p6+ Je 17 '88 pors, p26+ Jl 1 '88 pars
People 31:84+ F 6 '89 pars
Betrock, Alan. *Girl Groups* (1982)
Herbst, Peter, ed. *The Rolling Stone Interviews, 1967-1980* (1981)
Ribowsky, Mark. *He's a Rebel* (1989)
Stambler, Irwin. *Encyclopedia of Pop, Rock, and Soul* (1974)
Who's Who in America, 1988-89
Wolfe, Tom. *The Kandy-Kolored Tangerine-Flake Streamline Baby* (1965)

Regina Spektor

Singer; songwriter

Born: Feb. 18, 1980; Moscow, Russia
Primary Field: Anti-folk
Group Affiliation: Solo performer

Introduction

"If I wasn't gonna be a musician, I'd probably be an actor . . . ," Regina Spektor told Michael Dwyer for the Age *(December 8, 2006). "I love roles and I love portraying people." Indeed, it is through her idiosyncratic third-person character studies, set against a blend of classical piano, folk, jazz, and punk-rock rhythms, that Spektor-a 27-year-old, Soviet-born, Bronx-bred singer-songwriter-has established herself as the queen of the so-called anti-folk scene of the Lower East Side, the famed mecca for emerging talent in New York City.*

Early Life

One of the two children of Jewish parents, Regina Spektor was born on February 18, 1980 in Moscow, Russia, in what was then the Soviet Union. Her father, a photographer and violinist, and her mother, a teacher of music history, encouraged her early interest in music. At the age of six, Spektor began her training on piano. She has cited a range of famed classical composers, including Tchaikovsky, Mozart, and Chopin, as influences. "For me it was all classical music," she told Shane Roeschlein for Themusicedge.com (March 25, 2005). "We had records, went to concerts, ballets and operas. There were also these bards that were writing simple songs musically but deep and beautiful and poetic lyrics." Spektor's father also exposed her to an eclectic mix of European and British pop music, frequently playing tapes with songs by such British rock legends as the Beatles, Queen, and Moody Blues. The Beatles' songs were "the first . . . pop music I knew growing up in Russia . . . ," Spektor wrote in a piece for *Harp Magazine* (July/August 2006, on-line). "I learned all the songs phonetically even though I couldn't understand a word." In addition to their shared enthusiasm for music, the Spektor family—which included Regina's younger brother, Bear—felt a bond because of their Jewish identity, having withstood a wave of anti-Semitism that spread throughout the Soviet Union in the 1970s and 1980s. "The fact that I'm Jewish is definitely one of the most important, defining things in my life," Spektor told Mark Huntley for the *New York Sun* (April 21, 2005). "Not necessarily the religion, but the ethnicity. I was aware of it when I was very young-having certain customs in the family, always knowing in Russia that I was different."

In 1989, with the advent of *perestroika,* the political and economic reform movement initiated by then-Soviet premier Mikhail Gorbachev, Spektor's family fled Russia under new laws permitting mass emigration. After spending several months in refugee camps in Italy and Austria, they arrived in New York City, in August 1989, settling in the borough of the Bronx. Spektor, then nine, wished to resume her piano playing, but with no access to a piano (the family's Petrof piano was left behind in Russia) and little money for lessons, she resorted to "practicing on window sills and tables," as she told Anthony Mason for CBSnews.com (January 21, 2007). She was later able to practice on a piano discovered in the basement of a local synagogue. Matters improved again after Spektor's father met Samuel Marder, a concert violinist, on the subway. Marder's wife, Sonia Vargas, a professor at the Manhattan School of Music, later met Spektor and offered to give her free lessons; that arrangement lasted until Spektor turned 17. "In a lot of ways, [my family] had failed in the American sense of owning this or owning that, but we have been overly successful in terms of education," Spektor said to Jon Caramanica for *New York Magazine* (June 12, 2006). "We've always had educators come into our lives when we needed them."

In her teens Spektor attended the Frisch Yeshiva High School, in Paramus, New Jersey, then transferred to Fair Lawn High School, in Fair Lawn, New Jersey. Meanwhile, as her music lessons continued, she grew frustrated by what seemed to be the limits of her ability on piano. "Playing piano is almost like being an athlete," she explained to Caramanica. "The art happens amidst routine. For me, it was always a real struggle. I wasn't consistent enough to make that my art." Spektor instead found her creative freedom in songwriting and, later, singing, inspired in part by peers who heard her sing her own songs during a summer sojourn in Israel and encouraged her to continue doing so. "[Singing and songwriting] had never occurred to me," Spektor admitted, as quoted by a writer for the EMI Music Publishing Web site. "To me, the mentality was you sit at the piano and play Bach or Mozart or Chopin. You didn't ever improvise, so the idea of writing my own music was an intimidating one." Spektor soon ended her classical training and began to compose original a capella songs, slowly blending them into her piano performance. She found the transition from classical music to be difficult at first. As she told Caramanica, "It was very painful to be so crude. You go from being at a certain level to being an Oompa-Loompa person. You don't have the dexterity." Caramanica reported, "Having not been raised on pop music, she also didn't have the traditional songwriting reference points, or boundaries, all of which proved to be a boon. Her songs quickly grew florid and intricate, her lyrics teeming with oddball characters that she didn't discover and inhabit so much as cut from whole cloth."

At the renowned Conservatory of Music at Purchase College, a division of the State University of New York (SUNY-Purchase), Spektor majored in studio composition and completed her studies in three years. During that time she put on live shows for the Purchase community. With her quirky, folksy, piano-driven pop beginning to generate positive buzz, Spektor teamed with the jazz bassist Chris Kuffner in early 2001 to record her first, independently produced album, *11:11,* which had a modest printing of 1,000 copies but sparked local fanfare.

Life's Work

After her graduation, in 2001, Spektor returned to New York City and began to perform in such venues as the Knitting Factory, the Sidewalk Cafe, and the Living Room in the East Village and Lower East Side, home to a thriving musical subgenre known as anti-folk; that performance style combined the sparse acoustic sounds of 1960s American folk music with the raw energy of 1970s punk rock and ironic, stream-of-consciousness lyrics. "I don't think [anti-folk is] necessarily a sound of music, or a type of music," Spektor explained to Noel Murray for avclub.com (June 21, 2006). "It's

Affiliation: Anti-Folk

Though her broad vocal range and charismatic stage presence have called to mind the modern folk-rock chanteuses Tori Amos, Ani DiFranco, Fiona Apple, and Joni Mitchell, Spektor has departed from their confessional song styles to spin tales comparable in their detachment to the narrative conventions of film and short fiction. Spektor's musical style, which has been described variously as quirky, discordant, melodic, angry, and poetic, has wowed audiences and left critics scrambling for adjectives. Writing for *Blender* (December 2004), Pauline O'Connor called Spektor's music "a weirdly ancient-sounding mash-up of pre-rock and art-school piano delivered in a voice that swoops from whisper to moan and back again," while JR Griffin, in the *Alternative Press* (August 2006), likened her to "that crazy girlfriend you just know is a heap of trouble, but even still, she's so hard to resist." Mainstream record executives, who overlooked Spektor during her days as a fixture in the college and local indie-music scene, have also come to regard her as a "genius" and a "culture-changing artist," as Susan Visakowitz noted in *Billboard* (January 13, 2007).

Spektor has recorded five albums, three of them produced and released independently. While *11:11* (2001) and *Songs* (2002) established Spektor in the indie-music world, her third album, *Soviet Kitsch,* released in 2004, broadened her appeal to the mainstream audience. Described as "beautifully strange" by Jonathan Durbin, writing for *Paper Magazine* (April 2004), *Soviet Kitsch* drew the attention of Julian Casablancas, lead singer of the esteemed modern rock band the Strokes, who in 2003 invited Spektor to perform as the opening act for the group's North American tour. Their high-profile collaboration later spawned the popular duet "Post Modern Girls & Old Fashion Men" and landed Spektor a coveted recording deal with Sire Records, which reissued *Soviet Kitsch* in 2004 to critical acclaim. The noted singles "Ode to Divorce," "Chemo Limo," and "Your Honor" from *Soviet Kitsch* confirmed Spektor's talents as a genre-hopping musical wordsmith. In June 2006 Spektor released *Begin to Hope,* her first original recording for the Sire label. In her review of *Begin to Hope* for *Rolling Stone* (June 29, 2006), Jenny Eliscu praised Spektor's "gorgeous, fluttery voice, her burgeoning writer chops and her God-given quirks," while Amanda Petrusich, in *Paste* (June/July 2006), pronounced Spektor's latest offering to be "as elegant as it is addictive."

more like an attitude. People with acoustic instruments, playing songs and singing in their own voice. Not in a really stylized way, but kind of conversational." Spektor quickly emerged as a fixture in the anti-folk scene, drawing a devoted local audience with songs in which she strived for "really intelligent lyrics" and "a punk attitude," as she put it in an interview with Jeff Guinn for the *Fort Worth Star Telegram* (April 18, 2004). In early 2002 Spektor released her second album, entitled simply *Songs,* which veered from the jazzy sounds of *11:11* to reveal "a more intrepid spirit: revisionist stories about Samson and Delilah, Oedipus Rex, and more, delivered in an extraordinarily powerful voice with a slight pinch, giving it a naive edge," Jon Caramanica wrote. "It's fabulist cabaret as incisive emotional therapy." *Songs* showcased Spektor's powerful vocals and versatility, proving her to be an "Old World soul in a New World reality," in the view of George Varga, writing for the Copley News Service (November 17, 2006). Spektor told Varga, "You feel this [old] world, in which your parents, grandparents and childhood reside. You also have all the literature and art that comes with that, and the language. Then, you have the new world, which is very modern and is sort of your future, and you are always trying to keep the two connected. So, it's kind of like making these little sutures to keep the two worlds together."

Songs emerged as a bona fide hit among many of New York City's music fans and made converts of contemporaries including the acclaimed singer-songwriter David Poe and Allan Bezzozo, the drummer for the alternative rock group They Might Be Giants. "I never had enough money to do a big run so I'd do 200 at a time, sell them out, and then make more," Spektor told the writer for the EMI Publishing Web site. One of Spektor's spunky performances impressed Gordon Raphael, then the record producer for the popular garage-rock band the Strokes. Raphael wrote for a British music Web site, as quoted by Caramanica, "[Spektor is] a revelation . . . one of the purest musical offerings I've ever seen, certainly among the most brilliant." At Raphael's urging, Spektor recorded "Poor Little Rich Boy," a hit on the local club circuit; on that song she played piano with one hand while striking a drum with the other, creating an unusual, frenetic melody. That single was included on Spektor's third album, *Soviet Kitsch* (2004), which revealed the variety of influences on the songwriter, ranging from the jazz singer Billie Holiday to the Icelandic rock artist Björk. It also featured contributions from highly regarded New York City musicians, including the guitarist Oren Bloedow, the bassist Graham Maby, and the cellist Jane Scarpantoni. Commenting on the album, Spektor told the writer for the EMI Publishing Web site, "I don't have an overall sound. I tend to think of each song as its own little world, so one can be a complete punk song, while another could be a chamber ensemble with strings." *Soviet Kitsch* attracted a strong cult following, with songs that featured memorable characters, imaginative, wry narratives, and quirky wordplay, closer in form to short stories and films than to conventional pop songs. "I'm much more attracted to fiction and novels and movies-things that are less autobiographical and more mythological," Spektor told Kristyn Pomranz for the St. Louis, Missouri, *Riverfront Times* (November 8, 2006). "I guess they're not fantasies that are made up altogether but observations. Characters that I've seen or glimpsed." Spektor's interest in "character exploration," as she put it for Ernest Jasmin in the Tacoma, Washington, *News Tribune* (April 5, 2005), also rendered the songs "personal, because they're rooted in real emotions."

As *Soviet Kitsch* had confirmed Spektor's status in the anti-folk movement, her subsequent stint on the Strokes' North American "Room on Fire" tour, in 2003, made her known her to a mainstream audience. Invited by Julian Casablancas, the lead singer of the Strokes, to open for the band, Spektor-who was still not signed to a record label paid her own expenses to perform with musicians she admired. "[The Strokes] were the closest I had heard rock come to classical," she told Nick Catucci for the *Village Voice* (June 26, 2006). "Their music is extraordinarily orderly and composed. It's almost like Mozart." On the tour Spektor's ironic, reflective numbers proved to be an odd contrast to the gritty songs of the band-and drew mixed responses from fans. "I got tougher toward the end of the tour," she told Jeff Gunin for the *Fort Worth (Texas) Star Telegram* (April 18, 2004), "but a couple of nights, I ran offstage when I was done playing so nobody would see me cry." Still, Spektor's work impressed Casablancas, who asked her to record a song with the band, "Post Modern Girls & Old Fashion Men," featured on the Strokes' sophomore album, *Room on Fire* (2003). In the wake of Spektor's tour and collaboration with the Strokes, major record labels took notice of her. Sire Records, owned by the Warner Music Group, signed Spektor to her first professional recording contract. Sire reissued *Soviet Kitsch* in 2004, through the mass distribution network of Warner Bros. Records. On Spektor's initiative, Sire also mounted an "old-school, word-of-mouth" sales campaign sustained by "hard work and belief," as the label's president, Michael Goldstone, told Susan Visakowitz for *Billboard* (January 13, 2007). The rerelease of *Soviet Kitsch* received enthusiastic reviews from critics. Writing for the *Bangor (Maine) Daily News* (April 2, 2005), Dale McGarrigle praised Spektor for "straddl[ing] the line between confessional angst and funny, observational songwriting. Spektor's primary strength is her expressive, elastic voice." In the *Lancaster (Pennsylvania) New Era* (April 14, 2005), Judy Jarvis hailed one of Spektor's musical signatures-the ability to "meld her voice to fit the tone of her song" and create "separate and unique worlds with each track."

In 2006 Sire Records issued Spektor's second major-label release, *Mary Ann Meets the Gravediggers and Other Short Stories,* a compilation album of older tracks that served as an introductory offering for the European market. In June of that year, Spektor released her first new album under the Sire label, *Begin to Hope,* recorded the previous summer under the direction of David Kahne, the Grammy Award-winning producer of records by Paul McCartney and Tony Bennett. Though Spektor remained wary of the "big machine" aspect of a major record label, as quoted by Bob Gendron for the *Chicago Tribune* (April 21, 2006), she reveled in the luxury of bigger budgets and flexible studio time afforded a label signee. "My other records I had to speed-record," she said to Michael Dwyer.

"You know, you have a couple of days and no budget and no players and then you get three string players and you have four hours with them. This record, I had more of a chance to really learn about sounds and arranging." *Begin to Hope* marked a departure for Spektor, incorporating a wider mix of electronic instrumentation and natural percussion for more "radio-ready pop, if indeed radio were ready for Spektor's whimsy and warmth," Jon Caramanica wrote. At its core, though, *Begin to Hope* was quintessential Spektor, weaving the raw and the tender into sometimes fantastical narratives that some took as evidence of a range of colorful experiences on the singer's part. Spektor dismissed speculation that she had "lived" the tales in her songs, insisting on her role as a storyteller. Discussing the album's personal, introspective feel, Spektor chalked it up to "becoming less of a narrator and more of a character. . . . I was always used to observing and writing third-person narrative stories about things I was seeing. Then, as time went on, I started placing myself in these scenes, more like an actor," as she told Stirling. While songs including "Lady," an ode to Billie Holiday; "Samson," about the Old Testament figure with Herculean strength; and "Summer in the City," a tale of bizarre discovery on New York's Delancey Street, garnered critical praise for their eclecticism, innovation, and quirky insight, it was the single "Fidelity," a "sweet, reflective love song," as described by Andrzej Lukowski for the London *Evening Standard* (February 16, 2007), that propelled Spektor's album into mainstream popularity. The song's music video netted 200,000 hits over two days on the popular video-sharing Web site YouTube and went on to be included in the VHI cable channel's "You Oughtta Know: Artists on the Rise" video series. In December 2006 *Begin to Hope* reached the number-one spot on the Apple Computer iTunes alternative-album chart in the United States. Two months later Sire released an EP, called *Live in California 2006,* containing two songs from *Begin to Hope* and another two from *Soviet Kitsch.*

Personal Life

Spektor lives in New York City. "New York feeds me creatively," she told Imogen Tilden for the London *Guardian* June 23, 2006). "A lot of my inspiration comes from walking in the streets. It's a kind of country of its own. This is the place that makes me feel more at home than anywhere else on the planet."

Further Reading

Billboard Jan. 13, 2007
EMI Music Publishing Web site
(London) *Guardian* Film and Music p3 June 23, 2006
Musicedge.com Mar. 25, 2005
New York Sun p20 Apr. 21, 2005
(St. Louis, Missouri) *Riverfront Times* Music Nov. 8, 2006
(Tacoma, Washington) *News Tribune* F p7 Apr. 8, 2005
Womanrock.com

Bruce Springsteen

Musical Artist, Songwriter, Band Leader

Born: September 23, 1949; Long Branch, New Jersey
Primary Field: Rock and Roll
Group Affiliation: E Street Band

Introduction

Bruce Springsteen is an American musician, singer, songwriter and leader of The E Street Band. As "The Boss", Springsteen presents a musical catalog that details the struggles, concerns, and grace of working-class America, infused with New Jersey sensibilities. Using a combination of commercially successful rock albums, folk-roots projects, and lengthy, intense stage performances, Springsteen's distinctive voice provides a soundtrack for American life.

Early Life

Born on September 23, 1949, in Long Branch, New Jersey, Bruce Frederick Joseph Springsteen was the firstborn of Douglas and Adele Zerilli Springsteen, preceding the births of his sisters Virginia and Pamela.

Springsteen is a Dutch word for "jump stone." His Dutch-Irish-American father worked at several vocations between intervals of unemployment. His Italian-American mother worked as a legal secretary, providing steady income to the family.

In a 2012 interview with *The Mirror*, Springsteen remarked, 'Work creates an enormous sense of self . . . I saw that in my mother . . . I picked up a lot of things from her in the way that I work . . . I also picked up a lot of the failings of when your father doesn't have those things. . . ."

The independent spirit reflected in his music was first evidenced in his conflicts with nuns at St. Rose of Lima Catholic School, while values and influences learned there later informed his work. A 2012 interview revealed that his Catholic upbringing influenced his music more than his political ideology, providing him a "very active spiritual life."

Challenges with authority continued through his years at Freehold Borough High School, regarded as an outcast loner for which rock music was his lifeline: "Until I realized that rock music was my connection to the rest of the human race, I felt like I was dying." After graduation, he briefly attended Ocean County College, but soon dropped out. Speaking to *Entertainment Weekly* in 2003, Springsteen remembered: "I was . . . a smart young guy who didn't do very well in school . . . my intelligence was elsewhere . . . I had tried to go to college . . . I just looked and acted different, so I left school."

At age 18, he was classified as 4F with a failed physical and erratic behavior during the military service intake exam.

Life's Work

Adele Springsteen's affection for Elvis Presley and Frank Sinatra provided context and influence to her young musician son, in addition to the Beatles' 1964 appearance on television's *Ed Sullivan Show*. Performing at small local venues, he was a member of several bands playing in clubs along the Eastern Seaboard to good reviews and increasing critical recognition. The bands drew inspiration from heavy-metal, progressive rock, folk, rockabilly, church music, blues, jazz, and soul, molding a new genre called the "Jersey Shore" sound. During this time, he met the founding members of his E Street Band and acquired the grudgingly accepted nickname "The Boss" for his habit of collecting the band's nightly pay and ensuring distribution to his bandmates.

Springsteen was noticed by manager Mike Appel, who arranged Springsteen's audition & contract with Columbia Records in May 1972. Members of the future E Street Band joined Springsteen on his debut release, *Greetings from Asbury Park, N.J* (January 1973). His second album, *The Wild, the Innocent & the E Street Shuffle* (September, 1973) had rhythm and blues sensibilities that reflected young urban street life. Both albums garnered critical respect if not retail sales, though his dynamic live performances increased and inspired his devoted fan base.

For his third album, Springsteen and new producer/agent Jon Landau spent 14 months creating *Born to Run,* with the assistance of Steve Van Zandt required to create the sounds in studio that the frustrated Springsteen heard only in his head. A transitional album that solidified his connection to New York and the Jersey

Bruce Springsteen.

Shore and the dawning of adulthood for teenagers and young adults, Springsteen regarded *Born to Run* as "the album where I left behind my adolescent definitions of love and freedom—it was the dividing line." The album garnered widespread critical and popular acclaim, with nearly every song receiving perennial airplay thereafter.

Troubles with former management kept Springsteen out of the studio for over a year until a legal settlement permitted release of *Darkness on the Edge of Town*. Throughout the rest of the '70s, he toured extensively with the just-forming E Street Band, becoming legendary for the intensity and duration of his concerts. Commitment to his stage art convinced Springsteen to embrace free weights, running, and a mostly vegetarian diet, allowing him to maintain performance standards to this day.

Springsteen's working-class musical voice arrived with 1980s *The River*, yielding his first Top Ten single, "Hungry Heart." Influenced by early rock and folk, the album spanned '80s party rock anthems to emotionally intense ballads. The album's success sent Springsteen onto his 1980–81 world-wide tour.

The explosiveness of this tour was countered with the dark, contemplative nature of 1982's solo folk acoustic album, *Nebraska*, recorded alone at home on a simple tape deck. Springsteen's common musical themes of blue-collar people coping with life challenges and turning points took a darker turn here, with no salvation or grace found at the end of the stories told.

Disguised within a near-irresistible rock band soundtrack, the dark themes of *Nebraska* were carried forward into one of the highest selling albums of all time, 1984's *Born in the USA*. Its patriotic attachment to U.S. political and sociocultural issues presented contrast to the simultaneous patriotism promoted by Ronald Reagan, whose focus affirmed values of prosperity, expansion, and world domination. Springsteen remarked, "My work is often claimed by different political groups because there is a feeling of patriotism underneath. But it's a very critical, questioning, often angry, patriotism. That's not something I'm prepared to give up because somebody might simplify what I'm saying."

During the *Born in the USA* Tour, Springsteen met and married model/actress Julianne Phillips (May, 1985). Cultural and age differences, tour life, and infidelity compromised the marriage. 1987's *Tunnel of Love* is subsequently one of Springsteen's most autobiographical albums, documenting themes of relationship conflicts. Separated by early 1988, their divorce was finalized in March, 1989.

Springsteen met Patti Scialfa in the 1980s, and she joined the E Street Band on their 1984 *Born in the USA* and the 1988 *Tunnel of Love Express* tours. They began living together after his 1988 separation, and married in 1991 after the birth of their first child. Two other children soon followed, and 1994 ended with the rock star in the role of husband and father.

After the 1988 *Tunnel of Love* tour, Springsteen headlined Amnesty International's "*Human Rights Now!*" tour after a successful concert in Berlin that was considered influential in the ultimate dismantling of the Berlin Wall. Buying a Los Angeles mansion, he dissolved the E Street Band in late 1989, and started family life with Scialfa. Hiring studio musicians, he produced two introspective albums (*Human Touch* and *Lucky Town*) (March 1992) that revealed a new confidence and happiness not found in previous albums.

However, his work was poorly received by fans, who now viewed him as "going Hollywood" as a "limousine liberal," who instead valued his former insights pertinent to the genuine struggles of working class, blue-collar people. When his artistic sensibilities returned to more topical, socially conscious writings, audiences and accolades returned as well.

1994's brief reunion with the E Street Band produced Springsteen's *Greatest Hits* album. Though largely panned by critics as being too commercial and missing key works from his catalogue, the exercise refocused and reenergized Springsteen, renewing his intrinsic voice and social conscience.

He won an Oscar for his 1994 theme song "Streets of Philadelphia" for the movie *Philadelphia*, with both works bringing the topic of AIDS into the national conversation. 1995's sparse, acoustic album *The Ghost of Tom Joad,* inspired by Steinbeck's *The Grapes of Wrath,* provided a sobering viewpoint for immigrants and society's fringe elements, and was better received by fans and critics.

Following *The Ghost of Tom Joad* tour, Springsteen returned to his New Jersey roots in both his professional sensibilities and personal life. The Springsteens moved back to New Jersey, desiring a lower-key childhood than could be found in Los Angeles, and Springsteen subsequently regained his professional voice.

Springsteen ultimately acknowledged that the 1990s were a "lost period" for him. 2014's *Rolling Stone* interview revealed that his isolation from musical peers, producers, and band members negatively affected his artistic development:

Some people would say I didn't do my best work....We lost our recorded intensity. We went from being good producers in the 1980s to not very good in the 1990s. . . . We needed to interact with . . . people who were making [a lot of modern] records all the time and [understanding how] modern records were sounding. . . . You have different levels of sensitivities about these things at different times. . . . *Streets of Philadelphia* and *The Ghost of Tom Joad* led me back to topical writing, which really lead me back to the Band, which was a place where that writing expands and reaches the greatest audience.

Springsteen ended the decade by reuniting with the E Street Band for their 1999-2000 *Reunion* tour.

In 2014, Springsteen told *Rolling Stone:* "An outgrowth of having a long career is that I have a lot of interesting things around that I get to revisit, and someday get to the place where they become something that I want to do next."

Springsteen's work in the 2000s can be characterized by frequent tours, individual and collaborative projects, and philanthropic and political projects which further his multiple interests.

Quoted in the 2014 book *Springsteen on Springsteen*, he explains his near-continuous touring: "The long conversation with my fans has been one of the most valuable experiences of my life." Between and during his world tours (*The Rising* (2002–3003), *Vote for Change* (2004), *Devils and Dust* (solo) (2005), *The Seeger Sessions* (2006) *Magic* (2007), *Working on a Dream* (2009), and *Wrecking Ball* (2012–2013)), Springsteen has lent his voice to philanthropic and political causes.

In the early 2000s, he promoted revitalization efforts for Asbury Park, New Jersey, a town that has provided support throughout Springsteen's career. In 2012, he and the Band performed on a telethon and benefit concert for Hurricane Sandy Relief. At times, his work is increasingly political, as first evidenced in "The Rising" and continuing with political campaign support and appearances for candidates John Kerry and Barack Obama.

Recent albums have included an acoustic compendium of previously unreleased work (*Devils and Dust (*2005)), and an American roots project (*We Shall Overcome: The Seeger Sessions (2006)*). The E Street Band's talents were featured in 2007's *Magic*, an energetic album that offers commentary on global war and societal disillusionment. 2012's *Wrecking Ball*, an album with rock, hip-hop and Irish folk influences, offers indictments for Wall Street corruption, frustration with government accountability, but also hope for the American dream. 2014's *High Hopes* is a first: an album composed entirely of covers, outtakes and reimagined versions of previously released songs.

Springsteen's and The E Street Band's musical catalogue was recognized in 2005 by Sirius Satellite Radio, who created the *E Street Radio* channel, featuring his work, interviews, rare tracks, and concert recordings.

2009 provided the expansion of Springsteen's performance venues beyond his own tour stage. He and the Band performed at football's Super Bowl halftime show, and participated in several global music festivals in the Netherlands, France, England, and the United States.

Summarizing his musical ethos in a March 2012 speech to SXSW Festival, Springsteen states: "Authenticity is a house of mirrors ... it's the power and purpose of your music that matters."

Springsteen has sold more than 64 million albums in the United States and more than 120 million records worldwide. Awards include 20 Grammys, two Golden Globes and an Oscar, as well as induction into the Songwriters Hall of Fame and the Rock and Roll Hall of Fame in 1999. He is a 2009 Kennedy Center Honoree.

Affiliation: Rebirth and Redemption: The Rising

The September 11, 2001 attacks on New York City's World Trade Center provided inspiration to Springsteen and the Band for their first combined studio efforts in 18 years. Springsteen said he visited the beach in Asbury Park soon after Sept. 11, where a fan recognized Springsteen, and told him: "We need you now."

Springsteen responded with 2002's *The Rising*, a reflection on the 9/11 attacks that received critical and popular acceptance while becoming Springsteen's best-selling album of new material in 15 years. Though some songs had been written prior to the attacks (*My City of Ruins* was written for Asbury Park), their meaning and significance were reframed in light of the recent history. Many of the songs were influenced by phone conversations Springsteen had with family members of victims, whose obituaries had revealed Springsteen's influence on their lives. While fierce in tone, *The Rising* still offers more requiem than revenge, where the perished, the rescuers, and the mourning are recognized and honored.

Critics and fans of *The Rising* found a context of resilience and hope that expands beyond the 9/11 attacks. On the 10th anniversary of 9/11, Dan DeLuca of the *Philadelphia Inquirer* said: "The songs make contextual sense in the aftermath of 9/11, but the specific details that give them power are allusive...[the songs] are about the hollowing devastation of that day, but ... the sentiments are by no means frozen in time."

The Rising also constituted a revitalization of album production values compared to prior efforts. New producer Brendan O'Brian infused a new energetic viewpoint to Springsteen and the Band. Speaking in 2014 to *Rolling Stone*, Springsteen said: "Brendan O'Brien [was] the initiator of the modern sound of the E Street Band. . . . He immediately heard the Band in a very fresh and different way. He kick-started our recording career into another gear."

Personal Life

Springsteen is married to his bandmate, Patti Scialfa, with whom he shares three children: Evan (b. 1990), Jessica (b.1991) and Samuel (b. 1994). The family has homes in Colts Neck and Rumson, New Jersey, Wellington, Florida, and Los Angeles, California.

Further Reading

Bruce-Springsteen: How the Boss has evolved. http://www.telegraph.co.uk/culture/music/bruce-springsteen/10118386/Bruce-Springsteen-How-the-Boss-has-evolved.html

Burger, Jeff (Editor). *Springsteen on Springsteen.* Chicago Review Press, April 1, 2014.

Chilton, Martin. "Bruce Springsteen: How the Boss has Evolved." *The Telegraph,* December 18, 2014.

Greene, Andy. "A 54-Minute Conversation with Bruce Springsteen." *Rolling Stone*, January 9, 2014.

Marsh, Dave. *Glory Days: Bruce Springsteen in the 1980s.* Pantheon Publishing, April 12, 1987.

Martin, Gavin. "Why Bruce Springsteen is still attacking the 'fat bankers' and 'robber barons." *The Mirror (U.K.),* February 24, 2012.

Phillips, Christopher, Masur, Louis P. *Talk About a Dream: The Essential Interviews of Bruce Springsteen.* Bloomsbury Publishing USA, August 20, 2013.

Tucker, Ken. "Springsteen: The Interview." *Entertainment Weekly,* February 28, 2003.

Ringo Starr

Musician

Born: July 7, 1940; Liverpool, England
Primary Field: Rock music
Group Affiliation: The Beatles

Introduction

A prime factor in the popularity of the Beatles is their drummer, Ringo Starr, who joined England's shaggy-haired rock 'n roll quartet in August 1962. The favorite Beatle with American tans, Starr seems to have captured the imagination of teen-aged girls in the United States with his air of childlike innocence, and revenue from the sale of "I Love Ringo" buttons has contributed to the improvement of Great Britain's balance of trade. He has also endeared himself to American movie critics, who after watching him perform in the two Beatles films, A Hard Day's Night *and* Help!, *view him as the most promising comedian in the group and as a possible successor to Harpo Marx.*

Early Life

An only child, Ringo Starr was born Richard Starkey in Dingle, a working-class suburb of Liverpool, on July 7, 1940. His mother is Elsie (Graves) Starkey and his father (or stepfather, as one source has it) is Harry Starkey, a house painter. Mrs. Starkey sometimes helped the family finances by working in a fruit store and as a barmaid. The nickname Ringo was given to him by his mother, because of his passion for wearing rings. Between the ages of six and twelve, Ringo Starr spent most of his time in hospitals, suffering first from a burst appendix and later from peritonitis, a fractured pelvis, and pleurisy. During this period he underwent more than a dozen operations, and for a time it seemed doubtful that he would survive. Before he was fourteen, Ringo left school and took a job as an engineer's apprentice, working on swimming pool and playground projects for the firm of H. Hunt & Sons at a salary of about $15 a week. He later worked at odd jobs, including a stint as a waiter on a ship that ran between London and Wales. For a time he considered becoming a hairdresser.

Ringo Starr's interest in drums began early. "Ever since I can remember he's been tapping on things," his mother has recalled. He fashioned his first set of drums out of tin cans and made a bass drum from an old tea chest. After his parents bought him a set of drums one Christmas, he practiced for hours in his room, to the annoyance of his neighbors. About 1958 Ringo and a friend began to play together professionally. "We started playing on dances and things," he has recalled, as quoted by Alfred G. Aronowitz in the *Saturday Evening Post* (March 21, 1964). "We took an interest in it and we stopped . . . hanging around comers every night."

By playing in Liverpool clubs with such outfits as the Darktown Skiffles, Ringo earned as much as $1.50 an hour—more than his father made as a housepainter.

Life's Work

In 1960 Ringo Starr went to Hamburg, Germany, on an engagement with Rory Storme and the Hurricanes. There he made friends with the instrumental and vocal rock 'n' roll group known as the Beatles, who were performing at the Kaiserkeller on the Reeperbahn. Back in Liverpool, he filled in on several occasions for Pete Best, then the Beatles' drummer. After an executive at Electrical & Musical Industries Ltd. (EMI), with which the Beatles had just signed a recording contract, expressed some dissatisfaction with Pete Best's performance on the drums, the other three Beatles decided to replace him with Ringo. "I had a beard then," Starr told Paul Sann of the New York *Post* (September 14, 1964). "One day I'd be a scruffly article, . . . and then I'd shave and then I'd let it grow again. And then one day—it was in August 1962—John Lennon called me and he said 'You're in, shave your beard . . . but keep your sidies.' That's sideburns, you know."

Brian Epstein, the Beatles' manager, at first had some misgivings about Ringo. "To be completely honest, I was not at all keen to have him," Epstein wrote in his book *A Cellarful of Noise* (Doubleday, 1964). "I thought his drumming rather loud and his appearance unimpressive, and I would not see why he was important to the Beatles. But. . . . I trusted their instincts and I am grateful now. He has become an excellent Beatle and a devoted friend." Although it took some weeks until Beatle fans in the Liverpool clubs accepted the change, Ringo's status as a full-fledged Beatle was soon established. In the months that followed, the Beatles became more and more popular on the British scene, touring nightclubs, theaters, and concert halls, and recording such best-selling hits as their "Love Me, Do" and "She Loves You (Yeah, Yeah, Yeah)." Their concert at the London Palladium on October 13, 1963 brought them into the national limelight, and they had to be rescued by police from the thousands of teen-age fans who mobbed them. After their Royal Command Variety Performance at London's Prince of Wales Theatre in November 1963, they were visited backstage by Princess Margaret and the Queen Mother. "It was the first time I ever felt British," Ringo Starr has said, as quoted in the Saturday Evening *Post* (March 21, 1964). "You know, you never think about royalty. But the Queen Mother, she was a nice lady."

In February 1964, following an intensive publicity campaign launched by Brian Epstein, the Beatles embarked on their first tour of the United States. Even before their arrival, their recording of "I Want to Hold Your Hand" for Capitol Records reached the top of America's best sellers. Their appearances on the *Ed Sullivan Show* on CBS-TV brought that program the highest ratings in television history. They visited Washington, D.C. and Miami, Florida, where, according to Alfred G. Aronowitz, "they were greeted at the airport by a chimpanzee, four bathing beauties, a four-mile-long traffic jam and 7,000 teen-agers, who shattered 23 windows and a plate-glass door. The flight- engineer of the plane wore a Beatle wig." At an informal poll taken at one of their concerts at New York's Carnegie Hall, Ringo Starr was rated the most popular of the Beatles among American fans. When the Beatles returned to the United States in August 1964 and in August 1965 after visiting other parts of the world, Beatlemania had in no way diminished.

The Beatles' first film, *A Hard Day's Night* (United Artists, 1964), a good-natured spoof of Beatlemania in the vein of the old Mack Sennett or Marx Brothers comedies, gave Ringo Starr an opportunity to demonstrate his comic talents. An episode showing Ringo on a lonely stroll through London was described by Bill Rice in the *Washington Post* (August 14, 1964) as "a vignette that is Chaplinesque in its evocation of pathos and comedy." Penelope Gilliatt wrote in a review in the London *Observer* (July 12, 1964): "Ringo emerges as a born actor. He is like a silent comedian, speechless and chronically underprivileged, a boy who is already ageless." In their second film, *Help!* (United Artists, 1965), the Beatles are subjected to a mad chase through London, the Austrian Alps, and the Bahamas by an Oriental high priest and a mad scientist in pursuit of a sacred ring that Ringo had in his possession. Bosley Crowther commented in the *New York Times* (August 29, 1965): "The Beatles, for all their . . . good, clean boyish charm, have not yet . . . developed distinctive comic characters. Ringo is the most creative. He is the sad sack, the butt of the jokes, the one who inclines to be literal. The others . . . are just happy, glib young chaps."

Despite the enthusiasm of their fans, the Beatles have not been universally acclaimed. A writer for the *Washington Post* (February 12, 1964) noted when they first visited the United States: "Nothing we have exported in recent years quite justifies imported hillbillies who look like sheep dogs and sound like alley cats in agony," and evangelist Billy Graham has seen in the Beatles "symptoms of the uncertainty of the times and confusion about us." Their defenders range from members of the British Royal family to the folk singers Joan Baez and Bob Dylan and the veteran rock 'n' roll star Elvis Presley. The London symphony conductor John Pritchard has said of the Beatles: "I find them good entertainers . . . Their numbers are extremely good, absolutely technically all right— both harmonically and rhythmically." The wide acceptance of the Beatles is testified to by the fact that the United States government has beamed their songs to Communist countries over the Voice of America, and by the adoption of their tunes by the anti-Establishment Free Speech Movement at the University of California. Among their honors are an award from the British Songwriters Guild, a Grammy award from the National Academy of Recording Artists in the United States, and a number of Gold Record awards. Their heads have been sculptured in bronze, and their likenesses are represented in Madame Tussaud's famous wax museum in London. The A.N. Marquis Company has announced that the Beatles will be included in the 1966-67 edition of *Who's Who in America*, a distinction accorded only to a few select non-Americans. On his own, Ringo Starr has attained the honor of being teen-age America's nominee for President of the United States, and he has a "medal for bravery," sent to him by two female fans after he had his tonsils removed in December 1964.

For their economic services to England, Queen Elizabeth included the Beatles on her birthday honors list on June 11, 1965 and conferred on them membership in the Order of the British Empire (M.B.E.). The award drew criticism from those observers who thought it beneath the dignity of the Crown to confer such an honor upon a rock 'n' roll ensemble. Upon receiving the M.B.E., Ringo Starr said with characteristic modesty: "It's good to know we are some use."

The constant pressure of the Beatles' fame affected their live performances; Starr commented, "We were turning into such bad musicians ... there was no groove to it." He was also feeling increasingly isolated from the musical activities of his bandmates, who were moving past the traditional boundaries of rock music into territory that often did not require his accompaniment; during recording sessions he spent countless hours playing cards with their road manager Neil Aspinall and roadie Mal Evans while the other Beatles perfected tracks without him. In a letter published in *Melody Maker,* a fan asked the Beatles to let Starr sing more; he replied: "[I am] quite happy with my one little track on each album." In August 1966, the Beatles released *Revolver*, their seventh UK LP. The album included the song "Yellow Submarine," which was the only British number one single with Starr as the lead singer. Later that month and owing to the increasing pressures of touring, the Beatles gave their final concert, a 30-minute performance at San Francisco's Candlestick Park. Starr commented: "We gave up touring at the right time. Four years of Beatlemania were enough for anyone."

For the Beatles' seminal 1967 album, *Sgt. Pepper's Lonely Hearts Club* Band, Starr sang lead vocals on the Lennon–McCartney composition "With a Little Help from My Friends." Although the Beatles had enjoyed widespread commercial and critical success with *Sgt. Pepper,* the long hours they spent recording the LP contributed to Starr's increased feeling of alienation within the band. He commented, "[It] wasn't our best album. That was the peak for everyone else, but for me it was a bit like being a session musician. In February 1968, Starr became the first Beatle to sing during another artist's show without the other three present. He sang the Buck Owens hit "Act Naturally," and performed a duet with Cilla Black, "Do you Like Me Just a Little Bit?" on her BBC One television program, *Cilla.*

During the recording of the White Album, relations within the band became openly divisive. As the sessions progressed, their collective group dynamic began to decay; at times only one or two Beatles were involved in the recording for a track. Starr had grown weary of McCartney's increasingly overbearing approach and Lennon's passive-aggressive behavior, which was exacerbated by Starr's resentment of Yoko Ono's near-constant presence. After one particularly difficult session during which McCartney had harshly criticized his drumming, Starr quit the band for two weeks, taking a holiday with his family in Sardinia on a boat loaned by Peter Sellers. During a lunch break the chef served octopus, which Starr refused to eat. A subsequent conversation with the ship's captain regarding the behaviors of the animal served as the inspiration for his *Abbey Road* composition, "Octopus's Garden," which Starr wrote on guitar during the trip. He returned to the studio two weeks later, to find that Harrison had covered his drum kit in flowers as a welcome-back gesture.

On April 10, 1970, McCartney publicly announced that he had quit the Beatles. Starr released two albums before the end of that year: *Sentimental Journey,* a UK number seven hit composed of his renditions of many pre-rock standards that included musical arrangements by Quincy Jones, Maurice Gibb, George Martin and McCartney, and the country-inspired *Beaucoups of Blues,* engineered by Scotty Moore and featuring renowned Nashville session musician Pete Drake.

Starr was prolific in the early seventies. He played drums on Lennon's *John Lennon/Plastic Ono Band* (1970), *Ono's Yoko Ono/Plastic Ono Band* (1970), and on Harrison's albums *All Things Must Pass* (1970), *Living in the Material World* (1973) and *Dark Horse* (1974). In 1971, Starr participated in the Concert for Bangladesh, organized by Harrison, and with him co-wrote the hit single "It Don't Come Easy," which reached number four in both the US and the UK. The following year he released his most successful UK hit, "Back Off Boogaloo" (again produced and co-written by Harrison), which peaked at number two (US number nine).

In 1973, Starr earned two number one hits in the US: "Photograph," a UK number eight hit that was co-written with Harrison, and "You're Sixteen," written by the Sherman Brothers. Starr's third million-selling single and his second US chart-topper, "You're Sixteen" was released in the UK in February 1974 where it peaked at number four in the charts. Both songs appeared on Starr's debut rock album, *Ringo*, which was produced by Richard Perry and featured writing and musical contributions from Lennon and McCartney, as well as Harrison. A commercial and critical success, the LP also included "Oh My My," a US number five that was Starr's fifth consecutive top-ten hit. The album reached number seven in the UK and number two in the US. Author Peter Doggett describes *Ringo* as a template for Starr's solo career, saying that, as a musician first rather than a songwriter, "he would rely on his friends and his charm, and if both were on tap, then the results were usually appealing."

Goodnight Vienna followed in 1974 and was also successful, reaching number eight in the US and number 30 in the UK. Featuring musical contributions from Lennon, Elton John and Harry Nilsson, the album included a cover of the Platters' "Only You (And You Alone)," which peaked at number six in the US and number 28 in the UK, and Hoyt Axton's "No No Song," which was a US number three and Starr's seventh consecutive top-ten hit. The John-written "Snookeroo" failed to chart in the UK, however, when issued there as the second single from the album. Starr founded the record label Ring O'Records in 1975. The company signed eleven artists and released fifteen singles and five albums between 1975 and 1978, including works by David Hentschel, Graham Bonnet and Rab Noakes. The commercial impact of Starr's own career foundered over the rest of the seventies, however, although he continued to record and be a familiar celebrity presence.

Following Lennon's murder in 1980, Harrison modified the lyrics of a song he had originally written for Starr, "All Those Years Ago," as a tribute to their former bandmate. The track, which included vocal contributions from both Paul and Linda McCartney and Starr's original drum part, peaked at number two in the US charts, and number 13 in the UK. In 1981, Starr released *Stop and Smell the Roses.* The LP contained the Harrison composition "Wrack My Brain," which reached number 38 in the US charts, but failed to chart in the UK. Lennon had offered a pair of songs for use on the album: "Nobody Told Me" and "Life Begins at 40," but following his death, Starr did not feel comfortable recording them. Soon after the murder, Starr and his girlfriend Barbara Bach flew to New York City to be with Lennon's widow Yoko Ono.

From 1984 to 1986, Starr narrated the children's series *Thomas & Friends,* a Britt Allcroft production based on the books by the Reverend W. Awdry. Starr also portrayed the character Mr. Conductor in the program's American spin-off *Shining Time Station,* which debuted in 1989 on PBS. He left after the first season

During October and November 1988, Starr and Bach attended a detox clinic in Tucson, Arizona, each receiving a six-week treatment for alcoholism. On 23 July 1989, Ringo Starr & His All-Starr Band gave their first performance to an audience of ten thousand in Dallas, Texas. The band consisted of Starr and a varying assortment of musicians who had been successful in their own right with popular songs at different times. The concerts interchanged Starr's singing, including selections of his Beatles and solo songs, with performances of each of the other artists' well-known material, the latter incorporating either Starr or another musician as drummer.

In 1994, Starr began a collaboration with the surviving former Beatles for the *Beatles Anthology* project. They recorded two new Beatles songs built around solo vocal and piano tapes recorded by Lennon and gave

Affiliation: The Beatles

The Beatles' trademarks—their Edwardian style stovepipe trousers, four-button coats, and ankle-high polished boots, as well as their moplike, medieval style hairdos—are largely the creations of Brian Epstein. Their Liverpudlian speech has enlivened their press conferences, in which they good-naturedly make fun of virtually everything and everybody. Their songs—written mostly by John Lennon and Paul McCartney, with a few numbers contributed by George Harrison—deal with love in a casual way, without the agony of many American popular laments. Their musical style, sometimes referred to as the "Liverpool Sound" or "Mersey Beat" (named for the Mersey River that flows through Liverpool), is derived primarily from the American rock 'n' roll of the 1950's. Starr, who rarely takes part in the singing during the Beatles' performances, was pictured by Maureen Cleave in the New York *World-Telegram and Sun* (December 27, 1963): "Ringo sits marooned behind the drums. Like Harpo Marx, he never speaks on stage and rarely off it. As he says, a drummer knows his place. The others are teaching him to smile because he's got such nice teeth." Thus far, Ringo has not added to the musical repertoire of the Beatles, but he has reportedly been working on a song for three years and intends to present it to the group if and when he finishes it.

lengthy interviews about the Beatles' career. Released in December 1995, "Free as a Bird" was the first new Beatles single since 1970. In March 1996, they released a second single, "Real Love." Harrison refused to participate in the completion of a third song.

Starr guested on two songs from McCartney's 1997 album, *Flaming Pie*. McCartney had written a song about Starr's ex-wife Maureen, who died in 1994, called "Little Willow" and asked Starr if he would play on another song, "Beautiful Night." The day after the "Beautiful Night" session, the two recorded a jam session, which developed into another song, "Really Love You," notable for being the first official release ever credited to McCartney/Starkey. In 1998, he released two albums on the Mercury label. The studio album *Vertical Man* marked the beginning of a nine-year partnership with Mark Hudson, who produced the album and, with his band the Roundheads, formed the core of the backing group for the album. In addition, many famous guests joined on various tracks, including Martin, McCartney and, in his final appearance on a Starr album, Harrison.

Starr was inducted into the Percussive Arts Society Hall of Fame in 2002, joining an elite group including Buddy Rich, William F. Ludwig, Sr., and William F. Ludwig, Jr. On 29 November 2002 (the first anniversary of Harrison's death), Starr performed "Photograph" and a cover of Carl Perkins' "Honey Don't" at the *Concert for George* held in the Royal Albert Hall, London.

On April 4, 2009, Starr reunited with McCartney at the David Lynch "Change Begins Within" Benefit Concert at Radio City Music Hall. After separate performances from Starr and other artists, McCartney's set came last, and towards the end he announced "Billy Shears," whereupon Starr joined him to perform "With a Little Help from My Friends" and, with all performers, "I Saw Her Standing There" and "Cosmically Conscious."

Starr appeared on-stage during Microsoft's June 2009 E3 press conference with Yoko Ono, McCartney and Olivia Harrison to promote *The Beatles: Rock Band* video game. In November 2009, Starr once again performed the voice of Thomas the Tank Engine for "The Official BBC Children in Need Medley." This is the first number 1 UK hit Starr has been involved in since the Beatles disbanded in 1970 (not counting guest appearances on other singles by other artists).

In 2010 Starr self-produced and released his fifteenth studio album, *Y Not,* which included the track "Walk with You" and featured a vocal contribution from McCartney. Later that year, he appeared during *Hope for Haiti Now: A Global Benefit for Earthquake Relief* as a celebrity phone operator. On 7 July 2010, Starr celebrated his 70th birthday at Radio City Music Hall, New York with another All-Starr Band concert, topped with friends and family joining him on stage including Yoko Ono and his son Zak: McCartney made a surprise appearance. In 2011, readers of *Rolling Stone* magazine voted Starr as the fifth-greatest drummer of all time. Journalist Robyn Flans, a long-time contributor with *Modern Drummer* magazine, writing for the Percussive Arts Society stated: "I cannot count the number of drummers who have told me that Ringo inspired their passion for drums." Starr is considered to have influenced various modern drumming techniques, such as the matched grip, tuning the drums lower, and using muffling devices on tonal rings, as well as placing the drums on high risers for visibility as part of the band. According to Ken Micallef and Donnie Marshall, co-authors of Classic Rock Drummers: "Ringo's fat tom sounds and delicate cymbal work were imitated by thousands of drummers."

In January 2015 Starr tweeted the title of his new 11-track studio album, *Postcards from Paradise*. The album came just weeks in advance of Starr's induction into the Rock and Roll Hall of Fame, and was released on 31 March 2015 to mixed to positive reviews.

Personal Life

Ringo Starr was married in February 1965 to Mary Maureen Cox, a former hairdresser from Liverpool. Their son, Zak, was born on September 13, 1965. They have a home in Weybridge, a London suburb. Ringo's parents, long reluctant to leave their friends and relatives in Dingle, have finally been persuaded by their son to move into a new, $24,000 bungalow he purchased for them at Gate-acre Park, Liverpool. The shortest of the Beatles, Ringo Starr is five feet eight inches tall, weighs 134 pounds, and has blue eyes and brown hair streaked with gray.

Easygoing and happy-go-lucky, Ringo is by his own admission not the handsomest of the Beatles, but his wistfulness enchants his female followers. "He's like a little puppy dog," one teenage girl has explained. "I don't care when people talk about my big nose," Ringo once said. "Maybe if all the Beatles looked alike we wouldn't have made it." John Lennon has used Starr to chasten his own ego. "When I feel my head starting to swell I just look at Ringo and I know perfectly well we're not supermen" he once told an interviewer. Ringo owns thousands of rings—most of them sent to him by fans—and he wears as many as five at a time on his fingers, because, as he has said, "I can't fit them all through my nose." Like his fellow Beatles, he is a chain smoker. When he finds the time, he likes to do pottery or basketwork, read poetry and science fiction, listen to rhythm and blues or country and Western records, and answer his fan mail.

In 1980, while on the set of the film *Caveman*, Starr met actress Barbara Bach; they were married on 27 April 1981. In 1985, he was the first of the Beatles to become a grandfather upon the birth of Zak's daughter, Tatia Jayne Starkey. Starr and Bach split their time between homes in Cranleigh, Surrey; Los Angeles; and Monte Carlo. In the *Sunday Times* Rich List 2011, Starr was listed at number 56 in the UK with an estimated personal wealth of £150 million. In 2012, Starr was estimated to be the wealthiest drummer in the world.

Further Reading

Life 56:25+ Ja 31 '64 pors; 37:58B + Ag 28 '64 pors
N Y *Post* p25 F 13 '64 por; p21 S 16 '64 por
N Y Times Mag p124+ D 1 '63 pors
Newsweek 63:34+ F 24 '64 pors
Sat Eve *Post* 238:31+ Mr 21 '64 por
Epstein, Brian. *A Cellarful of Noise* (1964)
Barrow, Tony. John, Paul, George, *Ringo & Me: The Real Beatles Story* (2005)

Nina Stemme

Opera singer

Born: May 11, 1963; Stockholm, Sweden
Primary Field: Opera
Group Affiliation: Solo artist

Introduction

Many consider Swedish soprano Nina Stemme one of the finest contemporary operatic sopranos. Known for her interpretations of operas by German composers Richard Wagner and Richard Strauss, she diversifies with Italian opera as well. Fittingly enough, in both the Norwegian and Danish languages, her last name, stemme, means "voice." Director Francesca Zambello told Cori Ellison for the New York Times *(20 May 2012), "Who she is offstage is so different from who she is onstage. In life, she often seems so understated. Then she gets onstage, and some sort of primal creature takes over. She's an absolutely fearless singing actress for whom no challenge is too much."*

Early Life

Nina Stemme was born on May 11, 1963, and grew up in Stockholm, Sweden, in a family of amateur musicians. She began piano lessons at age six, after she auditioned for and was accepted into the Adolf Fredriks

Musikklasser (Music School). She studied both violin and viola before cultivating her voice. The first record she ever bought was a collection of Franz Schubert compositions performed by Dame Janet Baker, a mezzo-soprano. Choral music plays a large role in the Scandinavian countries. However, Stemme told Ellison, "Music was a big part of my life. But there was no thought of a career. In Sweden, nobody is supposed to stick out from the crowd."

Stemme, who was shy and more comfortable as a member of the chorus than in solo roles, carne to McLean, Virginia, for a year as an exchange student at Langley High School. Despite her initial shyness, Stemme's ability as a vocal soloist in the chorus won her awards. She received the second highest marks overall at her audition for the Virginia All-State Chorus, which gave her more confidence.

Upon her return to Sweden, Stemme pursued studies in economics and business administration at the University of Stockholm, planning to become an auditor. She was also singing and acting, and it soon became apparent where her true desires would lead. She attended a two-year program of study at Stockholm Opera Studio in her mid-twenties, beginning as a mezzosoprano and making her 1989 debut in Wolfgang Amadeus Mozart's *Nozze di Figaro* as Cherubino. She often sang in churches and hospitals to earn some money on the side.

After further vocal coaching, she switched to lyric soprano roles at the age of twenty-seven. Doing so meant starting over and facing her fear of failure. From 1990 to 1994, she studied at Stockholm's University College of Opera. Even before her graduation, Stemme was singing minor roles with the Royal Swedish Opera. She remains a member of the company, even though she now has an international career.

Life's Work

In 1993 Stemme was a finalist in the Cardiff Singer of the World competition. The same year she entered the operatic tenor Plácido Domingo's first Operalia contest, held in Paris. Despite a bout of food poisoning before the competition, she won. Domingo later asked her to sing with him in concerts in Paris and Munich. Domingo and Stemme later recorded Wagner's *Tristan und Isolde* with the two of them in the title roles. Stemme commented to Ellison, "Those competitions opened the door to the opera world. I got an audition for the Vienna State Opera and was offered a contract right away. But I felt I wasn't really ready yet. My technique was not settled enough."

Leery of burning out too quickly or ruining her voice by beginning a career at the Vienna level too soon, Stemme instead went to the smaller Cologne Opera for four years. There she learned the music of Giacomo Puccini and Giuseppe Verdi. As a resident member of the company—one not so demanding or prestigious as Vienna—she was able to start her family and develop her talent over time. At Cologne, she portrayed the title role in Puccini's *Madama Butterfly* for a matinee Red Cross benefit concert. Her portrayal led to an offer to do the role the following season, and eventually to Wagnerian opera.

Her decision to refuse the job at the Vienna State Opera proved beneficial to her growth as a vocalist, as Antonio Pappano, the music director of Covent Garden's Royal Opera House, told Jessica Duchen for *Opera News* (2012). "One thing that has enhanced her career is the fact that she's done so many different types of repertoire," he explained. "I think this also gives her a breadth and makes her a much more interesting artist than if she were singing only Wagner every day."

In 1996 Stemme received a personal scholarship from the famed Swedish soprano Birgit Nilsson. The two remained in contact, though Stemme did not fulfill her dream of singing the role of Wagner's Isolde for the older woman.

The word *opera*, meaning "works," is Italian, because the art form originated in Italy during the end of the sixteenth century. In 1637, the first opera house opened in Venice. Opera combines many aspects of the arts—music, dance, spoken text, costumes, and stage sets. Because words are sung rather than said, operas typically take longer to perform than plays. An early composer of operas described the dramatic singing style as being more than speech, but less than song.

Two types of opera soon developed as the form spread throughout Europe. *Opera buffa* was a comic, light opera. *Opera seria* was a dramatic opera, often concerned with stories of the gods. The former lends itself to lyrical voices and a light touch. The latter demands strong voices.

Working with the Cologne Opera, Stemme initially sang lyric opera roles, such as the Countess in Mozart's *Marriage of Figaro*, and light Italian works such as Verdi's *Suor Angelica*. She explained to Cori Ellison, "Italian opera requires a different approach, a different temperament, and I really want to find the color of it, which is a stretch for me. It helps the Wagnerian singing to do Italian repertoire."

Additional lighter roles included Verdi's *Tosca*. She also began singing Wagner's more lyric roles, such as Elisabeth in *Tannhäuser* and Elsa in *Lohengrin*. These were steps on her path to becoming a dramatic soprano. She explained the change in her voice to Duchen, noting, "I do know that it has grown and stabilized a bit, and since the size has increased I don't have a huge problem sounding through an orchestra. I've never heard my own voice! But this is what others tell me, and I think it must be true."

In 2000 Stemme took on the dramatic role of Senta in Wagner's *The Flying Dutchman*. Although she had expected the role to test the limits of her vocal ability, she found that her voice developed further during the experience. Other singers had warned Stemme that once she took on the roles of Isolde and Brünnhilde, she would be unable to go back to other roles, simply because singing Wagner strengthens the voice so much that it becomes overpowering in other, lighter roles. She found their warning to be accurate. As Stemme told Kate Molleson for Scotland *Herald* (7 Nov. 2012), "My heart is still with Puccini and Verdi but my voice is with Wagner and Strauss. Verdi was the music that opened my heart and soul to opera. Whereas Wagner has to come to you; you can't force yourself on to Wagner."

Stemme was initially hesitant to accept the offer to sing the female lead in Wagner's *Tristan und Isolde*. Commenting on its length—the three-act opera runs about five hours—she has likened filling the role of Isolde, which she first performed in 2003 at the Glyndebourne Festival and which brought her public acclaim, to running a marathon. Other noted sopranos, such as Linda Esther Gray and Helga Demesch, damaged their voices performing the role. She has since performed Isolde more than sixty times, finding something new in the role each time she sings it.

Affiliation: Opera Music

Booked for five years in advance, Stemme notes that she feels privileged to have a full calendar at a time when opera houses throughout Europe are closing because of financial difficulties. She has been a guest performer for many companies, including the New York Metropolitan Opera, Milan's La Scala, the Paris Opera, and the Royal Opera House in London. In addition, she has sung at many music festivals, such as the BBC (British Broadcasting Company) Proms in London, Germany's Bayreuth Festival, and the Salzburg Festival in Austria. Unlike some famous performers, Stemme does not knit or do other things backstage while waiting for long periods of time between entrances. Rather, she follows the show, attempting to remain in character, and claims never to be bored. In describing her process to Jessica Duchen for *Opera News* (2012), Stemme said, "Normally I use the first rehearsals to take in as much information as possible and to see what the director wants and sometimes they don't really know what I'm capable of doing until I get onstage. It all comes out in. the performance—more or less out of control!"

From the beginning of her operatic career, Stemme has impressed critics both in live performances and on recordings. As Marc Mandel wrote for *Fanfare* (1 Sept. 2007) of her recording of Richard Strauss's *Capriccio*, he "was particularly startled and impressed by Stemme's delivery of the harp-accompanied sonnet embedded in the scene. She's not just singing it through: she seems actually to be thinking hard about the sonnet, and weighing the difficulty of her position, at every step along the way." According to Anthony Tommasini, writing for *New York Times* (5 Feb. 2010), when Stemme performed the title role in Strauss's *Ariadne auf Naxos* with New York's Metropolitan Opera, she was "in excellent voice here, singing with earthy colorings, ample power, and vivid character."

In 2011 Stemme sang Wagner's complete *Der Ring des Nibelungen*, a sixteen-hour, four-opera cycle that is generally performed over the course of several days, for the first time. She took the challenging role of Brünnhilde, which she initially did not feel competent to undertake. That San Francisco Opera production, under Francesca Zambello, proved her wrong. It was the first of several performances leading to the celebration of Wagner's two-hundredth birthday on May 22, 2013. Describing Stemme's talent for *Opera News* (2012), Jessica Duchen referred to its 'irresistible magnetism" and noted that it is "a combination of purity, magnitude, and steely strength, built on a foundation of intelligence, focus, good sense, and absolute musicality."

Stemme fears that Wagnerian opera is becoming an endangered species in an age of declining patronage and tight budgets. The pieces are massive and expensive to produce. Indeed, the Washington (DC) National Opera delayed a production of the complete *Ring* cycle due to budget shortfalls. Stemme is contracted to perform the third of the four operas with the company, however, for a 2016 production, to be directed by Zambello.

Swedish singers have historically gravitated toward the notoriously difficult Wagner repertoire. Stemme explained this multigenerational tradition to Duchen, saying it is likely driven by that fact that Swedes are "well grounded in our relationship to nature and in our ability to relax and not take in the stress of city life. When you're grounded, you can tackle these extremely demanding parts without destroying yourself."

In 2012, the recording Stemme made of Ludwig von Beethoven's *Fidelio* with Jonas Kaufmann and the Lucerne Festival Orchestra, under the direction of Claudio Abbado, won a Gramophone Award. Stemme has done extensive recording, including three recordings of Wagner's *Tristan und Isolde*, first with Domingo as Tristan, then in 2008 with Robert Gambill on DVD, and again with Stephen Gould in 2012. Among her other recordings are Verdi's *Aida* and Strauss's *The Flying Dutchman*.

In 2006, Stemme was appointed Swedish Court Singer. Her performance of Isolde at London's Royal Opera House in 2010 earned her the Laurence Olivier Award for best role interpretation. Twice, in 2005 and 2012, the German magazine *Opernwelt* named her Singer of the Year. She also received *Opera News's* 2013 Opera News Award, which honors those who have made a significant contribution to that musical art form. SWEA International, a global network for women of Sweden, named Stemme Swedish Woman of the Year in 2014. She has three times been nominated for the Stockholm Prize.

Personal Life

Stemme is married to Bengt Gomer, a stage designer, with whom she has three teenage children According to Stemme, they provided her with an understanding of how the character of Salome in Strauss's opera was innocent, yet sending out sexual messages she did not understand. She also feels that Wagner's music—with its overwhelming emotion—speaks to teenagers. Stemme travels for performances and is attracted to new works. Speaking of her family, she explained to Richard Speer for *Opera News* (2007), "I can't complain, because they're incredibly supportive. But we do have to plan differently. We live in Stockholm, so I go do new productions and then try to be home between the productions." When apart, family members rely on the Internet phone service Skype to stay in touch.

Although she most enjoys performing Wagner, Stemme prefers to listen to Mozart. Her favorite soprano, to whose recordings she always returns, is the twentieth-century Norwegian Kirsten Flagstad. She refers to dark chocolate and malt whiskey as her guilty pleasures. Stemme takes seriously her responsibility to her talent. She told Molleson, "At the end of the day I'm the only one who's responsible for my voice. People will just try to use it. They tried to get me to sing dramatic repertoire too early, but I said no. And one no gives you more respect than one yes too many." Her personal creed is "hurry slowly."

Further Reading

Duchen, Jessica. "Woman of the Year." *Opera News* Nov. 2012:24–29. Print.

Ellison, Cori. "A Drama Queen with Her Head on Straight." *New York Times* 20 May 2012: 11(L). Print.

Molleson, Kate. "The Essential Isolde." *Scotland Herald*. Herald & Times Group, 7 Nov. 2012. Web. 4 June 2014.

Moss, Stephen. "Nina Stemme: I Am Always Questioning Myself: Could It Be Better?" *Guardian*. Guardian Media, 2 May 2013. Web. 4 June 2014.

Serinus, Jason Victor. "Frank Talk from Nina Stemme." *San Francisco Classical Voi*ce. San Francisco Classical Voice, 2011. Web. 4 June 2014.

Tommasini, Anthony. "The Opera in an Opera Overcomes Illnesses." *New York Times*. New York Times, 5 Feb. 2010. Web. 4 June 2014.

Wasserman, Adam. "Nina Stemme." *Opera News*. Apr. 2014: 24–25. Print.

Isaac Stern

Violinist

Born: July 21, 1920; Kreminiecz in the Soviet Ukraine
Died: September 22, 2001
Primary Field: Classical
Group Affiliation: Solo performer

Introduction

"We do not know how many hours Isaac lives in a day. We only know that it must be more than twenty-four," the conductor Zubin Mehta said of his friend Isaac Stern, as quoted in Time *(July 7, 1980). Stern, who emigrated from the Soviet Union as an infant but studied exclusively in the United States, was considered the first American violin virtuoso. His taste and facility were said to be unsurpassed, and his energy was legendary. He played as many as 200 concerts in a year, made some 100 recordings, and performed in virtually every major country in the world, although he refused to play in Germany. He visited that country once, in 1999, to give a series of master classes but never performed publicly there.*

Early Life

Isaac Stern was born in the town of Kreminiecz (or Kremenets), in the Soviet Ukraine, on July 21, 1920 to music-loving parents. His father, Solomon Stern, was a contractor by trade but an artist at heart. His mother, Clara Stern, studied voice with Aleksandr Glazunov at the Imperial Conservatory in St. Petersburg. When Isaac was ten months old, his parents, fleeing the adversities resulting from the Revolution, took him with them to the United States, settling in San Francisco.

When Isaac Stern was six, he began to take piano lessons because his parents considered music essential to a general education, even though he did not demonstrate a special affinity for it. "I didn't go to a concert at the age of two, and I never begged for a tiny violin;' he told Joseph Wechsberg, as quoted in the *New* Yorker (June 5, 1965). It was not until he was eight that he began to show an interest in the violin, prompted by the fact that a boy who lived across the street played the instrument. Even after he was provided with a violin, Isaac did not immediately reveal his gift. But when he was ten, after receiving instruction from a succession of mediocre teachers, his talent came to the surface. "Something suddenly seemed to happen under my fingers," he told Wechsberg.

While Stern was studying the violin at the San Francisco Conservatory of Music, his budding talent came to the attention of a wealthy woman who agreed to finance his musical training. Perhaps most significant, Naoum Blinder, a violinist of the Russian school, who was then the concertmaster of the San Francisco Symphony, took him under his wing. Except for a brief interlude with Yehudi Menuhin's teacher, Louis Persinger, Stern studied with Blinder until he was eighteen. His progress was slow but sure. Blinder's unorthodox teaching methods neglected such "necessities" as scales, exercises, and etudes and focused on cultivating Stern's independence, musical instinct, and natural technique. Blinder enabled Stern to be his own teacher. "He allowed me to learn: he didn't impose," Stern told Edward Greenfield in an interview for the *Guardian* (February 16, 1987). "If something was going the wrong direction, he'd stop me. Otherwise he'd let things develop.... He taught me to teach myself, which is the greatest thing that a teacher can do."

Stern's musical education took place in the audience as well as behind the music stand. He listened to Rachmaninoff playing Beethoven's piano sonatas and to the Budapest Quartet performing the complete cycle of Beethoven quartets. He heard Wagner's ring cycle performed by Kirsten Flagstad, Lauritz Melchior, and Lotte Lehmann, at the San Francisco Opera, and he attended recitals by Artur Schnabel, Fritz Kreisler, and Bronislaw Huberman.

Life's Work

Sources differ as to when Stern actually made his professional debut. According to some authorities, he made his first appearance, as a guest artist with the San Francisco Symphony Orchestra under Pierre Monteux, at the age of eleven. But the *New Grove Dictionary of Music and* Musicians (1980) indicates that he made his recital debut in 1935 and first appeared with the San Francisco Symphony under Monteux in 1936 and that in the same year he also played with the Los Angeles Philharmonic under Otto Klemperer. Edward Greenfield wrote in the *Guardian*, "By the time he was fourteen, Stern was being brought in to play quartets and quintets once a week with the front-desk players of the San Francisco Symphony." And Joseph Wechsberg noted in the *New Yorker* that Stern made his local debut at fifteen, performing the Bach D Minor Concerto for two violins with Blinder and the San Francisco Symphony under Monteux.

When, on October 11, 1937, the seventeen-year-old Stern made his New York City debut at Town Hall, he received thoughtful approval rather than raves. A critic for the *New York Herald Tribune* predicted, "An unusually promising young musician whose talent seems to be following a normal and judicious course of development, he should become an artist of exceptional consequence." Irving Kolodin remarked of Stern in the *New York Sun* (October 12, 1937): "He does already possesses one indispensable trait of a fine violinist. That is a solid and well-rounded tone." Stern was disappointed with the reactions of the critics. "They admired my tone and carped at my intonation," he recalled, as quoted in People (January 31, 1977). "The consensus was that I should go far. I did. I packed up my violin, convinced I didn't know my elbow from A flat, and went back to California."

Stern's manager, the legendary impresario Sol Hurok, whom he considered a father figure, could wangle only a handful of dates a year for him but retained his faith in the young violinist. Remembering the hardships of those early days, Stern told S. E. Rubin, as reported in the *New York Times Magazine* (October 14, 1979): "I played seven concerts the first year, fourteen the next. I traveled in upper berths in trains. I practiced day and night. What did I know from Carnegie Hall, from arts councils, from big interviews? I worked my head off.... I had a tough, hardening apprenticeship. It taught me the value of values."

His arduous apprenticeship paid off. Stern's Carnegie Hall debut, on January 8, 1943, was the turning point in his career, for no less an authority than Virgil Thomson, writing in the *New* York *Herald Tribune* (January 12, 1943), proclaimed him "one of the world's master fiddle players." After his wartime performances for Allied troops in Greenland, Iceland, and the South Pacific, Stern was deluged by tour and recording offers. He made his screen debut in the 1946 film *Humoresque*, in which his hands were shown as those of John Garfield, who portrayed an ambitious young violinist involved with a wealthy patroness, played by Joan Crawford. By 1947 Stern was playing ninety concerts a year. He made his European debut in 1948, at the Lucerne (Switzerland) Festival, under Charles Munch, and went on to perform in nine European countries that summer alone. His 1949 concert tour comprised 120 concerts in seven months throughout the United States, Europe, and South America. By the time Stern reached his mid-thirties, he was recognized as one of the great violinists of his generation, along with Jascha Heifetz, Nathan Milstein, and Yehudi Menuhin. In 1950, at Pablo Casals's Prades Festival, the renowned cellist pronounced Stern a worthy descendant of Eugene Ysaye, the Belgian violinist who, along with Paganini, is one of Stern's heroes. Fittingly, in 1953 Stern played the role of Ysaye in the film *Tonight We Sing*, a biography of Sol Hurok.

By the 1970s Stern was said to be the world's highest-paid violinist, earning as much as $10,000 a performance and playing as many as 200 concerts a year. He earned the admiration of his peers, including Yehudi Menuhin, who was moved to say of him: "His playing has warmth, musicality, good taste, discipline, and spontaneity. There is no self-consciousness. It's all of one piece." Such unqualified approval is notable in the light of Stern's eclecticism, for his repertoire spans a wide range of musical history, including premiere performances of contemporary works by Leonard Bernstein, Peter Maxwell Davies, Paul Hindemith, Krzysztof Penderecki; George Rochberg, William Schuman, and Henri Dutilleux.

In an article for the *New York Times* (April 8, 1979), Peter G. Davis

Affiliation: The "Kosher" Nostra

Stern's record as a talent scout reads like a Who's Who of music. Among his discoveries are Pinchas Zukerman, Itzhak Perlman, Miriam Fried, Shlomo Mintz, Sergiu Luca, the cellist Yo-Yo Ma, Joseph Swensen, and Cho Liang Lin—a coterie of protégés dubbed the "kosher nostra." One music manager, quoted in the *New York Times Magazine* (October 14, 1979), called him "the biggest powerbroker in the music business." In addition, Stern was largely responsible for launching the drive to save Carnegie Hall from the wrecker's ball. He founded cultural councils in the United States and Israel, and he campaigned for civil rights. "I've never been able to live in a cocoon," Stern has said, as quoted in *Time.* "I have a long buttinsky nose." The pianist Eugene Istomin believed that Stern's broad spectrum of activity resulted from "his *total* need to communicate with other people."

called attention to Stern's "catholicity of taste that has drawn him to violin music of all periods" and "his stylistic flexibility." He noted that Stern "invariably seems to perceive all music from the inside with an instinctual sense of what is right in terms of tone, gesture and expression—a treasurable gift." Although not a flawless technician, Stern was flexible and in full command of his instrument. He was known to devise new fingerings of a difficult passage spontaneously during a performance. In a review for the *New* York Times (January 25, 1964), Harold C. Schonberg described "a typical Stern evening," in which the violinist played program of· Brahms, Bach, Prokofiev, Ernest Chausson, and Joseph Wieniawski. Accompanied by Alexander Zakin, his piano accompanist since 1940, Stern played with "surety and precision . . . , cleanly turned phrasing, strong rhythm and impeccable technique." Another landmark was Stern's 1968 silver anniversary concert at Carnegie Hall, commemorating his first appearance there twenty-five years earlier. For that concert, he and Zakin revived the violin arrangement of Brahms's Op. 120, no. 2, for clarinet and piano and also presented Bach's Sonata in E, along with Bartok's Second Sonata, two Mozart movements, and Ravel's Tzigane. In the words of Donal Henahan of the *New York Times* (December 2, 1968), "As impressive as anything else in the recital ... was the ease with which he changed styles in the program's later works.... For the Bartok, which is uncongenial to the violin in many ways, Mr. Stern put aside any search for tonal sheen and made music Bartok's way. A moment later, the same violin was singing the sweetest and gentlest Mozart, putting each grace note and turn in place, as the gallant style demanded." ·

In describing his objective of attaining top musical quality to Flora Lewis, who interviewed him in Paris for the *New York Times* (July 1, 1980), Stern said: "It's when what comes out is as near as possible to an ideal realization of the way music is written, not just the notes, which are dead, but also the music between the notes, without any interference in the ear of a bad sound, a mistake or an ugly sound, one that doesn't belong. It's like a beautiful woman, perfectly dressed in elegant clothes with colors that go well together, moving with special grace through a garden on a lovely day. It's when everything is right."

Commenting on Stern's down-to-earth stage presence, Louise Sweeney wrote in the *Christian Science Monitor* (September 30, 1980): "Perhaps because Stern just lets the music shine through him, there is little of the star bravura or mystique about his appearances on stage. He walks briskly, matter-of-factly on and off stage, his violin held out slightly in front of him like a staff in his left hand, his right hand grasping the bow. When he performs, he plants his feet wide apart, stands sturdy as an oak tree, and goes about the business of making sublime music without any theatrics."

Stern enriched his already extensive performance repertoire by forming a trio with the pianist Eugene Istomin and the cellist Leonard Rose. Inaugurated at the Israel Festival in 1961, the trio remained in existence until 1983 but performed only occasionally, because of the full solo schedules of its members. "We do it for our own satisfaction and that feeling of freshness," Stern explained to Jane Perlez of the *New* York Post (December 12, 1974). "One of the special qualities we enjoy is the sense of spontaneous pleasure. . . . On stage we listen to each other and play to each other. . . . It is a very intimate language-like a glance between close friends who know each other very well." Although star soloists are reputed to have immense egos, incompatible with the cooperation required for chamber performing, Stern denied that he had such problems. "I've no need of being the great 'I am' constantly," he told Alan M. Kriegsman of the Washington *Post* (November 17, 1973). "Each kind of music has its own dynamics, its own form, its own joys. Being able to perform as a soloist, and knowing the power one has as a soloist, makes the chamber music experience that much larger." The trio concentrated on eighteenth- and nineteenth-century works and achieved particular acclaim for the Beethoven programs it performed around the world in 1970 and 1971 in honor of the 200th anniversary of the composer's birth. The trio made several recordings, including a complete set of Beethoven's piano trios. After Leonard Rose died in 1984, Stern formed a new trio with Emmanuel Ax and Yo-Yo Ma.

In the 1970s and 1980s, Stern became increasingly involved in television, particularly in such series as *Tonight at Carnegie Hall* and *Live from Lincoln Center*. In addition to his frequent appearances as a guest artist, he generated ideas for programming. "He's a TV natural," the producer Ruth Leon said. "He understands television, he's fascinated by its possibilities, and he's the sort of person who can come up with an idea and then keep wheedling people until that idea comes to fruition."

The motion picture *From Mao to Mozart: Isaac Stern in China* chronicles the violinist's 1979 tour of the People's Republic of China, during which he gave master classes to young Chinese musicians. The film won the Academy Award for the best full-length documentary of 1981and special mention at the Cannes Film Festival. Stern's screen presence was described in the *Nation* (April 25, 1981) as being "as inspiring as a flourish of trumpets." The reviewer went on to say that "the mere sight of a human being causes him to glow with pleasure, as though he were encountering this marvel of nature for the first time."

Ever eager for opportunities to deploy the power of music, Stern devoted May and June of 1980, the year in which he turned sixty, to serving as "doctor" to two ailing French orchestras, the Orchestre National de France and the Nouvel Orchestre Philharmonique. The cure involved an intensive regimen of rehearsals and eighteen concerts comprising twenty-five works, and it helped to persuade the temperamental members of the two orchestras to cooperate. His energy never fading, Stern went on to Washington, D.C., to perform in five concerts under five different conductors, and he was also booked for concert dates in San Francisco and Los Angeles. By December 1980 he had played sixty concerts in four countries.

Stern has also used his violin as an effective cultural and political tool. In 1956, before any official cultural exchanges had been established, he performed in the Soviet Union. Just as Sol Hurok had encouraged Stern during his lean years, Stern became a mentor to many young musicians, and in doing so he served as a talent scout for Hurok. Among Stern's protégés was the violinist Pinchas Zukerman, who was discovered as a child prodigy in Israel. Others include the violinists Itzhak Perlman, Miriam Fried, Shlomo Mintz, Sergiu Luca, Joseph Swensen, and Cho Liang Lin, the cellist Yo-Yo Ma, and the pianist Yefim Bronfman.

Determined to safeguard Carnegie Hall from threatened demolition in 1960, Stern organized the Citizens' Committee to Save Carnegie Hall. When he succeeded and became president of the Carnegie Hall corporation, detractors accused him of having a conflict of interest. There were complaints that Stern ran the hall like a "mom-and-pop" store and that he filled its schedule with concerts by himself and his protégés, including events like "Isaac Stern and His Friends," a chamber music series designed to invoke the informality of a living-room gathering. Defenders maintained that Stern, who was president until his death, played no part in programming decisions. Stewart Warkow, the corporation's executive director, said, as quoted in *New York* (March 12, 1979) magazine: "Isaac has never sat me down and said use so-and-so. He's too honest for that." In later years Stern reduced his personal involvement, although he spearheaded a multimillion-dollar project in the late 1980s to renovate the hall and protect it from the vibrations of the subways below.

Stern's political activism prompted him to campaign for a number of Democratic candidates, including Lyndon B. Johnson and Hubert Humphrey. He also put his causes on presidential agendas. Having introduced the idea of an arts council during John F. Kennedy's presidency, Stern founded and oversaw the creation of the National Council on the Arts, which was the precursor of the National Endowment for the Arts, during the Johnson administration. His support of the arts extended to testifying before Congress in February 1970 to urge the legislature to increase its allocation of federal funds to the arts, warning that the United States was in danger of becoming "an industrial complex without a soul."

Israel was the object of Stern's consuming passion, so much so that he was, in effect, a one-man diplomatic service to the Jewish state. In addition to performing there frequently, he was the chairman, since 1964, of the America-Israel Cultural Foundation, which raised funds for Israel's cultural organizations and subsidized Israeli musicians. In 1973 he founded the Jerusalem Music Center, where musicians from many nations give master classes.

Stern's unyielding commitment to his beliefs occasionally threatened to disrupt his schedule of musical engagements. In March 1965 he attempted to cancel an appearance with the National Symphony in Washington in order to go to Selma, Alabama to support civil rights demonstrators there, but he was dissuaded by the National Symphony conductor, Howard Mitchell. In 1967 he boycotted the Athens music festival in a protest against the repressive Greek military junta, and he became the first American artist to sever relations with the USSR in outrage over its restrictions on Soviet artists. In 1974, when the United Nations Educational Scientific and Cultural Organization suspended cultural aid to Israel, Stern organized a musicians' boycott of UNESCO events. On other occasions politics served as a context for Stern's music. After the Six-Day War in 1967, Stern performed the Mendelssohn ·Concerto with the Israel Philharmonic, conducted by Leonard Bernstein, on Mount Scopus. That concert formed the basis of the film *A* Journey to *Israel.* During the Gulf War in 1991 he put on a gas mask and played a sarabande by Bach when a missile attack interrupted a performance.

Stern received wide recognition for his prodigious talent and contribution to cultural life. In 1974 he was made a commandeur of the French Ordre de la Couronne and in 1979 he became an officier of the Ordre de Legion d'Honneur. In December 1984 President Ronald Reagan presented him with the Kennedy Center Honors Award. CBS Masterworks named him its first Artist Laureate in 1985, and in 1986 the editors of the *Musical America International Directory of the Performing Arts* selected him as Musician of the Year. In 1987 he received the Wolf Prize, one of the most prestigious and lucrative prizes in the arts and sciences, awarded by the Wolf Foundation, which had been established by the Israeli parliament in 1975 on the initiative of Dr. Ricardo Subirana Lobo Wolf and his wife, Francisca. The award, which he shared with the Polish composer Krzysztof Penderecki, was presented in recognition of Stern's "everlasting humanistic contribution as an artist and educator, which transcends the boundaries of musical performance." Other honors that Stern received include an Emmy Award for the CBS telecast of the post-renovation opening of Carnegie Hall and the Gold Baton Award from the American Symphony Orchestra League.

Personal Life

Wearing horn-rimmed bifocals over hazel eyes, the rotund, five-foot-six violinist was said to resemble a "cuddly teddy bear." His first marriage, in 1948, to the ballerina Nora Kaye, ended in divorce. He lived with his second wife, Vera Lindenblit Stern, whom he met in Israel on August 1, 1951and married on August 17, after only four meetings over a period of sixteen days. The Sterns had three children: Shira, Michael, and David. They divided their time between a duplex apartment on Central Park West in New York City and a forty-acre estate in western Connecticut. Stern's favorite activities were playing tennis, during which he wears a glove to protect his strong, dimpled hands from blisters and took care to follow through on his swing to avoid tennis elbow, and watching spectator sports. He was known to practice his violin playing while watching football on television with the sound turned off. His habits were erratic. He worked best under pressure, practicing anywhere from half an hour to fourteen hours a day, preferring to do so at night and in the small hours of the morning. His two most prized instruments were Alard Guarneri "del Gesù" violins.

Isaac Stern's second marriage ended in divorce in 1994. In 1996 he married Linda Reynolds, who survived him. In 1999 he published an autobiography, *My First 79 Years,* which was written with the novelist Chaim Potok.

Isaac Stern explained his artistic creed during his interview with S. E. Rubin for the *New* York *Times Magazine* [October 14, 1979). "I would do better if I lived more healthily, exercised more, ate less," he said. "I'm a hog. I love food and drink. I love tastes and textures. I think I could be called a sensualist. But that is the power source of my playing. When I'm caressing music, it is very sensual. I love feelings and I love gratifying the senses. I would find it difficult to be abstemious."

Isaac Stern died at a Manhattan hospital on September 22, 2001 from heart failure after an extend hospital stay.

Further Reading

Christian Sci Mon B p2+ S 30 '80 por
Newsweek 96;93+ N 17 '80 pors
New Yorker 41:49+ Te 5 '65 por
NY Times Mag p40+ 0 14 '79 pors
People 7:47+ fa 31'77 pors, 14:32 S 29 '80 por
Stereo Review 50:45+ F '85 pors
Time 116:64+ 117 '80 pors
Washington Post C p1+ N 17 '73 por, M p1+ 0 5 '80 por
International Who's Who, 1989-90
New Grove Dictionary of Music and Musicians (1980)
Who's Who, 1989
Who's Who in America, 1988-89

STEW

Musician; songwriter

Born: Aug. 16, 1961; Los Angeles, California
Primary Field: Rock; musical theater
Group Affiliation: Negro Problem and solo performer

INTRODUCTION

"We have these fans who think it's wrong that we're not more famous," the rock musician Stew explained to Deborah Sontag for the New York Times *(May 21, 2007), referring to himself and his partner, Heidi Rodewald. "But we know that fame just isn't the judge of quality, except in America. Only in America do they go; 'You've made six records? You're making a play? But I've never heard of you."' Stew's musical, Passing Strange, which debuted in October 2006 at the Berkeley Repertory Theater, in California, and had a successful limited engagement at the Public Theater in New York in the spring of 2007, has helped to grant his fans' wishes, winning acclaim and followers for its innovative and experimental approach to musical theater.*

EARLY LIFE

Stew was born Mark Stewart on August 16, 1961 in the middle-class Fairfax District of Los Angeles, California, a neighborhood he described to David Ng for the *Village Voice* (May 2, 2007) as "a black-Jewish-Mexican-Asian bubble of liberalism." Early on his family exposed him to a wide variety of music; his sisters and cousins eagerly awaited new albums by artists and groups ranging from the Beatles to James Brown. That eclecticism influenced Stew's own tastes and would inform his work as a musician. When he was eight years old, he started taking piano lessons; he took up the guitar at 12. He recalled to Gary Shipes for the *Stuart (Florida) News/ Port St. Lucie News* (December 19, 1997), "I remember being at my cousin's house when I was really little and being faced with this terrible dilemma. James Brown was on TV at the same time as The Beatles' cartoon. We didn't know what to do, so we had to jump between the two. That's still my musical philosophy in a nutshell." In addition to musicians, Stew's role models included comedians; he grew up idolizing such stand-up comics as Richard Pryor and Lenny Bruce- (influences that would later be exemplified in his lyrics).

Stew has recalled that while there was pressure from African-American students in the schools he attended to listen only to R&B and other black music, he enjoyed music that included punk, hard rock, progressive rock, and New Wave. "In my junior high school," he said to Jim DeRogatis for the *Chicago Sun-Times* (August 2, 2002), Stew and his friends "used to have to get protection from guys on the football team because the hardcore guys in school would beat us up if they heard us listening to, like, the Who." Stew has taken exception to what he sees as the different standards applied to black and white musicians and music fans, telling Gilbert Garcia for the *Phoenix (Arizona) New Times* (October 22, 1998), "It's okay for skinny English white guys to try to [appropriate the] blues, and it's okay for skinny New York white guys like David Byrne to try to pretend they're African, but I'm playing so-called 'white music'? ... Paul Simon can find some Brazilian or African music history, but if you're black, you're supposed to do what your neighborhood's doing. Well, my neighborhood wasn't that boring." In his teens, in the mid-1970s, Stew sang gospel music in a choir in a Baptist church in Los Angeles, played the guitar and piano in a number of garage bands, and made his first recording with a band called the Animated. Also during his teenage years, Stew began immersing himself in art history. He started reading about Dadaist performance art and Viennese Actionism (a brief movement in 20th-century art that surfaced in the 1960s). The concept of melding performance art and music soon became his passion.

LIFE'S WORK

After attending Fairfax High School for a year and a half, Stew went on to graduate from Hamilton High School in 1979. He enrolled at Los Angeles City College several times for the sole purpose of having access to film equipment; he never graduated. Feeling constricted by middle-class life in Los Angeles, the musician relocated to New York City before he was 20. There, he performed with what he has described as a "found-object all-percussion performance combo" as well as with a more conventional R&B/pop band. (The drum set Stew used in the "found-object all-percussion performance combo" consisted of discarded objects he found on the street on the way to his gigs.) At 21 he began traveling in Europe, settling in the early 1980s in Berlin, Germany, where he fell in with artists in an underground bohemian scene. For a number of years, he traveled extensively around the continent with a collective whose members performed a hybrid of musical theater and performance art. Stew's exposure during those years to German cabaret and to the works of the German playwright Bertolt Brecht and the Belgian singer-songwriter Jacques Brel had a significant impact on his life and art; the lyrics in his subsequent work, packed with cultural allusions and quotations, reflect those influences. In Europe Stew met his first wife, to whom he was married for 12 years and with whom he fathered a daughter.

Stew next returned to his work with more conventional bands—and to Los Angeles, where an indie-rock scene was thriving. In the early 1990s he performed with a series of bands, including ImPOPisation, Crazy Sound All Stars, and Popular Front, before teaming up with the drummer Charles Pagano in an experimental group affiliated with a local art gallery. Although the group's sound—characterized by heavy use of tape loops and improvisation—appealed to him, he found that the verse-chorus-verse format of his lyrics were at odds with the group's avant-garde style. He explained to Garcia, "I was pretty much closeted about being a pop songwriter. It's almost exactly as if you were a gay person wanting to come out in front of all these straight people, and you didn't want to freak them out too much. So you dropped little hints here and there. Every couple of songs I showed the band, it would get a little more melodic." After the departure of the group's original bassist/guitarist, Stew stayed on with the band, which came to be known as the Negro Problem. The group's other musicians—all of them white—included Pagano, the keyboardist/accordionist Jill Meschke Blair, the bassist Gwynne Kahn (who had formerly been in the band Pandoras), and an auxiliary member, the multi-instrumentalist Probyn Gregory, who also played with the Wondermints. In late 1995 they released a collection of singles (including an innovative cover of Richard Harris's "MacArthur Park" and a multi-part pop operetta entitled "Miss Jones") in a limited-edition boxed set. Then, after Blair filled in as keyboardist for the British band Elastica's lucrative U.S. tour, she returned to the Negro Problem with enough money to buy an eight-track recorder, which the group used to record their first album, *Post Minstrel Syndrome.*

Made for the modest sum of $900, *Post Minstrel Syndrome* was distributed nationally, due almost solely to the critical acclaim it received. (The band's name, a phrase first used by whites in the Reconstruction era who were wary of integration, was also an attention-grabber; as Gilbert Garcia wrote, "Not since the ... heyday of the Dead Kennedys has an American band managed to make people squirm so readily at the mere mention of its moniker.") "We just thought it was hilarious," Stew said to Gary Shipes about the band's name. "Though there is a serious side to it, because I'm a black person making this music, we're always going to run into the race issue. And as a band, we always thought of some record executive wringing his hands and saying, 'God, they could be so massive if it wasn't for the Negro problem.'" The group sought to challenge the idea of the divide between so-called "white" and "black" music, categories that had no place for an otherwise white band that was fronted by an African-American-and that counted among its influences artists as far-ranging as Sly Stone, George Clinton, Stephen Sondheim, and Burt Bacharach. Critics lauded *Post Minstrel Syndrome's* sophisticated blend of pop melodies, pun-happy lyrics, and psychedelic touches reminiscent of Jimi Hendrix and the Chambers Brothers. Shipes wrote that *Post Minstrel Syndrome* "delivers delectable melodies tinted with timely racial views that swing between satire and despondency," adding that it was "simply the best album of 1997." Stew told Shipes about the work, "I wanted to make an album that sounded like

Affiliation: Musical Theater

Passing Strange, performed by an all-black cast with Stew as the guitar-playing onstage narrator, uses rock to tell the story of a character called Youth-whose travels from California to Europe, search for identity, and adventures with sex and drugs draw on Stew's own past. Prior to *Passing Strange,* Stew served as the frontman for the band the Negro Problem, which released the critically acclaimed albums *Post Minstrel Syndrome* (1997), *Joys & Concerns* (1999), and *Welcome Black* (2002); his albums with Rodewald are *Guest Host* (2000), *The Naked Dutch Painter . .. and Other Songs* (2002), and *Something Deeper Than These Changes* (2003). Stew's category-resistant songs often contain social commentary, while their melodies have inspired comparisons to 1960s pop; his influences include a wide variety of acts, from R&B artists to the principal figures of the British Invasion.

some curio recorded in 1968, some dusty jewel box you'd find in an attic." The album included five hidden tracks, featuring three solo acoustic performances by Stew that hinted at the introspective sound of his future solo efforts.

Following the departures of Blair and Kahn, Stew quickly added the former Wednesday Week musician Heidi Rodewald, with whom he became romantically involved, as both bassist and keyboardist. Since 1997 Rodewald has served as cowriter, arranger, and producer of songs by Stew and the Negro Problem. In 1999 the Negro Problem released their follow-up album, *Joys & Concerns,* which included work by guest musicians Probyn Gregory and Lisa Jenio. A much darker, melancholic work than their debut, the album was inspired by Stew's personal troubles, among them the breakup of his 12-year marriage and his hand-to-mouth existence as a musician living on the earnings from relatively obscure albums. "I was very depressed back then," he recalled to Sara Scribner for the *Phoenix New Times* (September 28, 2000). "The hard part was not being with my kid." He added, however, "I wasn't depressed at all making this record. It was a very happy experience." Like their debut, the band's sophomore effort garnered unanimous praise from critics. Matthew Greenwald, in a review for the All Music Guide Web site, called the album "easily one of the finest power pop records of 1999," adding that it created a "post-psychedelic LA feel that is infectious." The glowing feedback was not enough, however, to bring the group financial stability or keep its members from seeking more lucrative projects. Pagano's departure from the group, in late 1999, marked the beginning of the Negro Problem's dissolution (though he continued to appear with them occasionally). Stew, for his part, was now free to experiment with songwriting for solo acoustic guitar.

Stew realized that desire in 2000, with the release of *Guest Host,* a record that received "album of the year" honors from *Entertainment Weekly.* He attributed much of the success of *Guest Host* to his relationship with Rodewald, who co-produced the album. Stew told Scribner, "She really helped me in knowing when to stop. With Negro Problem, I would say, 'One more triangle overdub!' Those guys wouldn't tell me to stop. If I said, 'Hey, dude, I'm hearing fuzz accordion and bagpipes,' they'd be like, 'Okay, dude, I think I know a bagpipe player!' She'd stop it right there." Sean Westergaard, writing for All Music Guide, called the album a "sunny pop masterpiece" and praised in particular Stew's lyrics and gift for storytelling. A song called "The Stepford Lives," whose title is a play on that of the film *The Stepford Wives,* was considered a highlight of the album, with lines such as, "A husband named 'honey' with too much money / He's sort of a jerk he told her not to work." The song "Rehab" includes the lines, "When she got out of rehab for the very first time / she was very very very very very very very very very optimistic very very very very very very very very very very very optimistic"; as the song's last verse begins, the character enters rehab for the 22nd time.

In 2002 *Entertainment Weekly* picked as "album of the year" Stew's next solo record, *The Naked Dutch Painter. . . and Other Songs*, which was recorded during live sessions at the Knitting Factory in Los Angeles and enhanced with overdubbing in a studio. Matthew Greenwald wrote about Stew and the album, "Filled with kaleidoscopic originality and an iconoclastic point of view, he remains one of the finest songwriters to come out of Los Angeles in decades, and this, his sophomore solo album, underlines the fact. One of Stew's greatest strengths is not just his melodic sensibility, but his ability to use lyrics as musical phrases." Songs such as "Single Woman Sitting" and "Giselle" were particularly noted for their formally elegant narrative structures; their subject matter ranges from sex and drugs to rock music to race. The latter song, about an intellectual young woman who carries a switchblade and takes acid, has lyrics that include: "Her cat has a personal chef / Her dog wears a dead-mink sweater / Her rabbit won't pose for Hef / She wears leather / whatever / the weather / Giselle is the cross and the nails and the crown and the thieves / She howls at the street lights and dances whenever she pleases." (A number of Stew's songs have centered on such unconventional, defiant women.) "The Negro Problem is like having a party, and the solo records are like writing a letter," Stew explained to Erin Aubry Kaplan for *LA Weekly* (April 12, 2002). "I wouldn't tell the *Naked Dutch Painter* story at a party, but I would tell it in a letter."

In late 2002 Stew returned to the studio to record *Welcome Black,* a Negro Problem album whose personnel consisted of only Stew and Rodewald, playing different instruments under the pseudonyms Vox Marshall, Sigfried Gretsch, Ennio Lessaconi, and Eddie Munch. The following year brought Stew's third solo effort, *Something Deeper Than These Changes.* Matt Cibula, in a review of that record for *Pop Matters* (November 13, 2003, on-line), wrote that Stew was "the best songwriter in the United States," adding, "It's the most melodic set of songs he's ever done, but it's also more overtly *folky* than any of his other records, too: hushed, soft, minimal."

In 2004 Stew put his two main projects—his solo work and work with the Negro Problem—on hold and began touring the country with Rodewald to appear in various versions of a cabaret called *Travelogue,* with many of the shows at Joe's Pub in New York City, a 180-seat performance space connected with the Public Theater. Like his previous live acts, Stew's cabaret was complete with storytelling and humor between songs. The move into the theater realm came about when the Public's proprietors sought to turn the music fans who patronized Joe's Pub into theatergoers; having observed the theatrical elements in Stew's rock shows, Bill Bragin, the director of Joe's Pub, suggested that the musician could help achieve the theater's goal. A meeting with the Public's then dramaturge, Rebecca Rugg, left Stew feeling reluctant, as he recalled to Mike Boehm for the *Los Angeles Times* (October 22, 2006): "I said, 'Becca, I don't want to do theater, because I don't know anything about doing theater.'" After Rugg introduced Stew to the theater director Annie Dorsen, who challenged him and Rodewald to create a story that would be told through rock music, the musician was persuaded. Over the next two years, Dorsen, Stew, and Rodewald transformed *Travelogue* into *Passing* Strange, a semi-autobiographical odyssey that follows a character named Youth from middleclass Los Angeles to Europe and back. *"Passing Strange* is more like a rock concert than a musical," Stew told David Ng. "When people hear the album for this, I don't want them to think, 'Wow, that's a great show-tunes album.' I want them to think that it's a great rock album, period."

When the rock musical opened at the Berkeley Repertory Theater, in Berkeley, California, in October 2006, many critics complained that the nearly three-hour production was episodic and unfocused. Stew and his collaborators largely rewrote the show in the months leading up to its New York debut. *Passing Strange* opened at the Public in May 2007 to mixed-to-good reviews. The actors in the show's all-black cast played multiple roles; Stew narrated the different stages of Youth's life, as the character tries to "find" himself and make connections with those around him. Charles Isherwood, in a review for the *New York Times* (May 15, 2007), wrote, "Bald and big-bellied, with a neat goatee and quirky eyeglasses, [Stew] has an air more professorial than swoon-inducing.... But Professor Stew can also play a mean guitar, and when necessary, he strides the stage like an evangelical preacher, or a preening rocker, to whip the audience into a froth. Part concert, with Stew leading an onstage band; part book musical with a full (and terrific) cast, *Passing Strange* defies generic categories. . . . Because Stew's aesthetic and moral awakening takes place against a shifting backdrop, no other characters stick around long enough to claim a full role in the proceedings, despite perfectly pitched comic performances from the whole cast. The spectacle of watching a young man try on various emotional and artistic attitudes will strike happy chords in the hearts of ex-dreamers of youthful dreams, but colder eyes may see it as an extended exercise in musical navel-gazing." Isherwood also, however, wrote that the show was "full of heart." Mark Blankenship, writing for *Variety* (May 14, 2007), called Stew "a cerebral writer" and noted that the arguments he makes in his lyrics reveal "a humanity that makes them just as accessible as drama as they are as social analysis." Stew considers the innovative play to be just an extension of his music, admitting to David Ng, "I'm not a playwright, and I'm comfortable with that. . . . We don't think theater is some sort of pinnacle. We've been invited to this big party, and the truth is that we're really here to take the sandwiches."

Personal Life

Stew is an insatiable reader who claims to make a beeline for the bookshelves of any house he enters. Despite critical acclaim, sales of his albums average around 3,350 copies; to date, he has drawn his largest audience with "Gary's Song," which he wrote for a 2005 episode of the TV cartoon *SpongeBob SquarePants.* Stew is the subject of a documentary entitled *What's the Problem?,* directed by Jeffrey Winograd and tentatively scheduled for release in 2007.

Further Reading

All Music Guide (on-line)

Los Angeles Times F p2 Sep. 22, 1997, E p34 Oct. 22, 2006

New York Times E p1 May 21, 2007

Phoenix (Arizona) New Times Music Sep. 28, 2000

Stew's Web Site; *Stuart (Florida) News/Port Lucie News* D p1 Dec. 19, 1997

Village Voice p65 Sep. 17, 2002, May 2, 2007

Rod Stewart

Musician; recording artist

Born: Jan. 10, 1945; London
Primary Field: Blues, heavy metal, pop
Group Affiliation: Jeff Beck Group; The Faces; solo performer

Introduction

Rock music's reigning male sex symbol, raucous, raspy-voiced Rod Stewart, began his career in the mid-1960's with various groups, notably two led by Long John Baldry, in his native England. In the late 1960s he was the lead singer with the Jeff Beck Group, from which he went into a seven-year association with The Faces. His ascent to superstardom might be dated from 1971, when his album Every Picture Tells a Story, *with its hit single "Maggie May," shot to the top of the charts in both England and the United States (where he now lives). Since then Stewart has had a succession of hits, including the gold (million dollar-earning) albums* Never a Dull Moment *and* Atlantic Crossing *and the platinum (million copy-selling) LP* Night on the Town. *His 1979 release* Blondes Have More Fun *also went platinum and spawned the hit single "Da Ya Think I'm Sexy?"*

Rod Stewart.

Early Life

Roderick David Stewart was born on Archway Road in the Highgate section of North London on January 10, 1945, the fifth child of Scottish-born Bob and Elsie Stewart, the proprietors of a small tobacco-newspaper-confectionery store. One of his earliest memories is of the pictures of Scottish soccer players that his brothers had on their walls, and another is of the family gathering around the piano for sing-a-longs, in which his brother Don would do Al Jolson impersonations. Jolson's brash performing style appealed to Rod; growing up, he saw the films *The Jazz Singer, The Jolson Story, starring Larry Parks,* and *Jolson Sings Again,* and in adolescence he began collecting a complete library of Jolson records, which he still owns.

At the William Grimshaw Secondary Modem School in Hornsey, Stewart captained the soccer team, and he later played on the Middlesex Schoolboys Team. In 1961 he signed a professional contract with the Brentford Football Club, but his love of music ultimately prevailed over his love of soccer. He had been playing guitar and banjo at school events from his early teens, and three of his schoolmates, Ray and Dave Davies and Pete Quaife, later became members of the rock group the Kinks.

Stewart took part in the Aldermaston "Ban the Bomb" marches of the early 1960's, often leading the protesters in song. At first the music to which he aspired was the topical folk variety exemplified by Ewan McColl, Alex Campbell, the Thames Side Four, Ramblin' Jack Elliott, Woody Guthrie, and especially Derroll Adams. Later he was attracted to rhythm and blues, and the single most enduring influence on him was the "soul"-based singing of the late Sam Cooke.

While working at grave-digging and other jobs, Stewart frequented the clubs in and around London where the Rolling Stones, the Who, the Yardbirds, and other young rock or rhythm and blues groups could be heard. In 1963 he began playing part-time harmonica with the rhythm and blues combo the Five Dimensions, and the following year he joined Long John Baldry's

Hootchie Coochie Men as a vocalist. During his tenure with Baldry's group he was given the nickname "Rod the Mod," because of his dandyish style of dress and grooming, and he began to attract attention with his detached performing style, which he originally adopted as a refuge from stage fright. The first single under his own name was the Decca release "Good Morning Little Schoolgirl," with "I'm Gonna Move to the Outskirts of Town" on the flip side.

After Baldry disbanded the Hootchie Coochie Men, Stewart did some gigs with the Soul Agents before rejoining Baldry in a new group, Steampacket. While with Steampacket, he recorded two singles for Columbia Records. One was "The Day Will Come," backed by "Why Does It Go On," and the other was a cover of Sam Cooke's "Shake," with "I Just Got Some" on the B side. Following the dissolution of Steampacket, he sang briefly with Shotgun Express and then entered the most important stage of his early career, his association with Jeff Beck.

Life's Work

It was as a member of the Jeff Beck Group that Stewart began to attract a following in America, which the group successfully toured in 1968. Equally successful was the album by the group released by Columbia at the end of the tour, *Truth*, for which Stewart and Ron Wood wrote several songs. The group returned to the United States for an engagement at the Fillmore East Theatre in New York City in January 1969, and later that year they recorded the LP *Beck Ola* (Columbia), which represented a shift from blues to "heavy metal."

When Beck broke up his band, Stewart and Wood joined The Faces (originally, The Small Faces), and they remained with that group for seven years, until it split up in 1976. As lead singer with The Faces, Stewart enhanced his reputation in the United States, which the group toured often. "A reputation for beer, football, cockney humor, and parties appeared very British and gained a strong cult following for The Faces," Tony Jasper observed in *Rod Stewart* (1977).

The seven albums Stewart made with The Faces, including *A Nod's as Good as a Wink to a Blind Horse* (Warner Brothers, 1972) and *Coast to Coast Overture* (Mercury, 1974), tended to be overshadowed by Stewart's solo discs. The first of his solo LP's was *An Old Raincoat Won't Ever Let You Down* (Vertigo, 1970), released in the United States as *The Rod Stewart Album,* a mixture of original compositions and covers of blues, folk rock, and traditional melodies demonstrating Stewart's broad musical range. Richard Cromelin wrote in his book *Rod Stewart* (1976): "The record is somewhat tentative in feel . . . but it immediately marked Stewart as an innovator in rock singing technique and an effective reviver of several neglected musical directions." Stewart's second solo album, *Gasoline Alley* (Vertigo, 1970), was reissued together with the first in a double package by Mercury Records in 1976.

Stewart's status as a rock star was clinched when his album *Every Picture Tells a Story* (Mercury, 1971) hit the top of the LP charts on both sides of the Atlantic and the track "Maggie May" did the same on the single charts. "Maggie May" was written by Stewart in collaboration with arranger Martin Quittenton. The other cuts on the album included the hymn "Amazing Grace," songs by Bob Dylan, and soul music. Richard Cromelin noted that the album had "an assurance and authority that lent a new dimension and power to his [Stewart's] basic ingredients" and that "Stewart exploits the raw, earthy qualities of his style as well as he ever has."

When Stewart and The Faces performed at Madison Square Garden in November 1971, Don Heckman of the *New York Times* (November 28, 1971) wrote: "The support it [The Faces] provides the lead singer is only minimally effective. But Stewart doesn't need much help. He has the almost hypnotically appealing stage presence of a Mick Jagger; one watches his strutting cock-of-the-walk antics even while he isn't singing. And his voice—slightly hoarse-sounding, but ringing with a crackling masculine authority—is an unmistakably original expression."

Stewart's Mercury solo singles "You Wear It Well"/"Lost Paraguayos" and "Angel"/ "What Made Milwaukee Famous (Has Made a Loser Out of Me)" were issued in 1972. Reviewing *Never a Dull Moment* (Mercury, 1972), Stewart's fourth album, in the *New York Times* (September 24, 1972), Lorraine Alterman described the recording artist as "a master of phrasing and control" who "projects all of the passion or irony or hurt that belongs to each set of lyrics." Like *Every Picture Tells a Story, Never a Dull Moment* went "gold," surpassing $1,000,000 in sales. Meanwhile The Faces continued to build their reputation for unpredictable performances, adding a circus trapeze and high wire act to their act in the latter half of 1972. In December 1972 Stewart appeared in a London revival of the rock opera *Tommy*, singing "Pinball Wizard."

The compilation *Sing It Again, Rod* (Mercury, 1973) included a "cover" of Tim Hardin's "Reason to Believe" that received much air play. The solo album *Smiler* (Mercury, 1974) contained compositions by Stewart in collaboration with Quittenton and Wood, selections from the works of Bob Dylan, Chuck Berry, Paul McCartney, Sam Cooke, and Elton John, and an instrumental version of Lerner and Loewe's "I've Grown Accustomed to Her Face." Of the album Tony Jasper wrote in his book on Stewart: "Rod performed this variety of songs with great skill and gave practical evidence of the remark that he could sing 'anything, virtually everything.'"

Affiliation: Style

Stewart's rough but expressive tenor voice is one of the most distinctive in current pop music. In concert Stewart is a colorful performer, known for his dyed-blond haystack head of hair, his makeup, his outrageously foppish costumes, including skin-tight pink pants, and his penchant for low comedy and broad melodrama; he is also energetic, leaping about as if he were playing soccer. In fact, he was once a professional footballer and is still an amateur one, along with his friend and fellow rock star Elton John, and earlier in his career the dominant image he projected was that of a tough street "jock." That "macho" image still comes through, but subtly, in a wink, a tongue in cheek, or the studied disarray of his elegant attire as he struts about the stage. The result is a paradoxical persona—the effeminate roustabout, the womanizing dandy. Reviewing *Blondes Have More Fun* in the Washington Post, Harry Sumrall credited Stewart the lyricist and performer with a "sense of sloppy sophistication." In his "finely crafted" compositions, Sumrall wrote, "melodies, rhythms, and harmonies all seem rough around the edges, yet they are tightly controlled."

But some critics and fans wondered if the "working-class kid" might not be losing his "earthy" quality in the *dolce vita* of show business in which he was becoming immersed, and there was a similar reaction in some quarters to his next solo album, *Atlantic Crossing* (Warner Brothers, 1975); Among the cuts on *Atlantic Crossing* was "Sailing," which was a massive hit in England. After leaving The Faces Stewart recorded *A Night on the Town* (Riva, 1976), which included four songs written by him, the best of which were "The Killing of Georgie," about the death of a New York homosexual friend of his, and "Tonight's the Night." The latter became a major hit despite the restricted radio play resulting from the explicit language used in describing a girl losing her virginity.

With a new back-up group he organized—a group consisting of pianist Kevin Ravinger, bassist Phil Chen, and guitarists Gary Grainger, Billy Peek, and Jim Cregan—Stewart cut *Footloose and Fancy Free* (1977). Also in 1977 Private Stock brought out *A Shot of Rhythm and Blues,* containing songs recorded between 1964 and 1966. That album became the subject of a legal battle, with Stewart claiming that the tracks had been intended for demonstration only.

On his most recent tracks Stewart, whose rapport with his musicians gives his recordings a festive air of easy give-and-take, is backed by a group that includes Carmine Appice on drums and Nicky Hopkins on piano. *Blondes Have More Fun* (Warner Brothers, 1979) sold better than any previous Stewart album, and its cut "Da Ya Think I'm Sexy?" became the fastest-selling single in Warner Brothers history. In his review in the *Washington Post* (January 17, 1979), Harry Suinrall wrote: "The record is imbued with the character and vocal style that are Stewart's alone. [It] bristles with a rough-edged excitement and energy that are the equals of his earlier work. Whether prancing away on the disco-like 'Da Ya Think I'm Sexy?' boogeying on 'Blondes Have More Fun,' or playing the part of the ragtag crooner on 'The Best Days of My Life' Stewart [draws] the listener into the spirit of enjoyment that he obviously brings to and takes from his music."

Stewart sold out Madison Square Garden in New York City when he performed there on four successive nights in June 1979. John Rockwell wrote in the *New York Times* (June 7, 1979): "He gave an old fashioned rock- and-roll show, and it was a humdinger. . . . He pranced and strutted about the stage with real enthusiasm, and the enthusiasm was contagious. [He] is a lithe and extremely sexy man [who] also happens to be about the best male singer in rock, with a fervent, husky, plaintive tenor that he phrases with real musicality. His band is a confident one, and his tunes are catchy and melodic. . . . [Stewart] doesn't approach the great work of the Beatles, the Rolling Stones, Bob Dylan, Neil Young, and so on. But as an entertainer he has few peers."

Stewart moved to a more new wave direction in 1980 by releasing the album *Foolish Behaviour*. The album produced one hit single, "Passion," which reached

No. 5 on the US *Billboard* Charts. In August 1981, MTV was launched in the US with several of Stewart's videos in heavy rotation. Later in 1981, Stewart added further elements of new wave and synthpop to his sound for the *Tonight I'm Yours* album. The title song reached No. 20 in the US, while "Young Turks" reached the Top 5 with the album going platinum. Stewart's albums between *Tonight I'm Yours* (1981) and *Out of Order* (1988) received harsh reviews from many critics. He was also criticized for breaking the widely observed cultural boycott of apartheid South Africa by performing at the Sun City resort complex in the bantustan of Bophuthatswana as part of his *Body Wishes* (1983) and *Camouflage* (1984) tours.

In 1988, he returned with *Out of Order,* produced by Duran Duran's Andy Taylor and by Bernard Edwards of Chic. "Lost in You," "Forever Young," "Crazy About Her," and "My Heart Can't Tell You No" from that album were all top 15 hits on the *Billboard* Hot 100 and mainstream rock charts, with the latter even reaching the Top Five. "Forever Young" was an unconscious revision of Bob Dylan's song of the same name; the artists reached an agreement about sharing royalties. The song reached No. 12 in the US. In September 1988, Stewart performed "Forever Young" at the 1988 MTV Video Music Awards at the Universal Amphitheatre in Los Angeles, and in 1989 he received a Grammy Award nomination for Best Male Rock Vocal Performance for the song.

Released in 1991, the *Vagabond Heart* album continued Stewart's renewal and inspiration. The lead single "It Takes Two" with Tina Turner, was released in 1990 in advance of the full album's release, and reached number five on the UK charts, but did not chart in the US. The follow-up songs from *Vagabond Heart* both reached the *Billboard* Hot 100 in 1991, with "Rhythm of My Heart" peaking at No. 5 and "The Motown Song" peaking at No. 10.

At the 1993 Brit Awards in London, Stewart picked up the prize for Outstanding Contribution to Music. Stewart brought back the Faces on stage for an impromptu reunion. In 1993, Stewart recorded "All For Love" with Sting and Bryan Adams for the soundtrack to the movie *The Three Musketeers;* the single reached number one in the US and number two in the UK. Also in 1993, Stewart reunited with Ronnie Wood to record an MTV Unplugged special that included "Handbags and Gladrags," "Cut Across Shorty," and four selections from Every Picture Tells a Story. The show also featured an acoustic version of Van Morrison's "Have I Told You Lately," which topped the *Billboard* adult contemporary chart and No. 5 on the *Billboard* Hot 100. A rendition of "Reason to Believe" also garnered considerable airplay. The resulting Unplugged...and Seated album reached number two on the *Billboard* 200 album charts.

Stewart was inducted into the Rock and Roll Hall of Fame in 1994 by Jeff Beck. On December 31, 1994, Stewart played in front on 4.2 million people on Copacabana beach in Rio, and made it into the *Guinness Book of World Records* for staging the largest free rock concert attendance in history.

The latter half of the 1990s was not as commercially successful, though the 1996 album *If We Fall in Love Tonight* managed to go gold and hit No. 19 on the *Billboard* album chart, thanks in large part to an appearance on *The Oprah Winfrey Show.* In June 2002, Stewart performed "Handbags and Gladrags" at the Party at the Palace held at Buckingham Palace Garden, a concert which celebrated the Golden Jubilee of Elizabeth II and featured stars from five decades of music.

By 2002, Stewart had sold over 100 million records during his career. Stewart then concentrated on singing 1930s and 1940s pop standards from the Great American Songbook, written by songwriters such as Irving Berlin, Cole Porter, and George and Ira Gershwin, with great popular success. These albums have been released on Clive Davis's J Records label and have seen Stewart enjoy album sales equal to the 1970s.

The first album from the songbook series, *It Had to Be You: the Great American Songbook,* reached number four on the US album chart, number eight in the UK and number ten in Canada when released in late 2002. The second series album, *As Time Goes By: the Great American Songbook 2,* reached number two in the US, number four in the UK and number one in Canada. A musical called *Tonight's The Night,* featuring many of Stewart's songs, opened 7 November 2003 at London's Victoria Palace Theatre. It is written and directed by Ben Elton, who previously created a similar production, *We Will Rock You,* with music by Queen.

In 2004, Stewart reunited with Ronnie Wood for concerts of Faces material. A Rod Stewart and the Faces best of album, *Changing Faces,* reached the Top 20 of the UK album charts. *Five Guys Walk into a Bar...,* a Faces box set compilation, went into the shops. Stewart has also mentioned working with Wood on an album to be entitled *You Strum, I'll Sing.* In late 2004, *Stardust: the Great American Songbook 3,* the third album in Stewart's songbook series, was released. It was his first US number one album in 25 years, selling over 200,000 albums in its first week. I His version of Louis Armstrong's "What a Wonderful World," featuring Stevie Wonder, made the Top 20 of the world adult charts. He also recorded a duet with Dolly Parton for the album *Baby, It's Cold Outside.* Stewart won his first ever Grammy Award for this album.

The fourth songbook album, *Thanks for the Memory: The Great American Songbook 4* was released in 2005 and included duets with Diana Ross and Elton John. Within weeks of its release, the CD made it to number two on the Top 200 list. In late 2006, Stewart made his return to rock music and his new approach to country music with the release of *Still the Same... Great Rock Classics of Our Time,* a new album featuring rock and southern rock milestones from the last four decades, including a cover of Creedence Clearwater Revival's "Have You Ever Seen the Rain?," which was released as the first single. The album debuted at number one on the *Billboard* charts with 184,000 copies in its first week. The number one début was helped by a concert in New York City that was on MSN Music and an appearance on Dancing with the Stars. On October 19, 2010, Stewart released another edition of his *Great American Songbook* series titled *Fly Me to the Moon...The Great American Songbook Volume V* on J Records.

Stewart headlined the Sunday show at the 2011 Hard Rock Calling Festival on June 26 in London's Hyde Park. Stewart signed on to a two-year residency at the Colosseum at Caesars Palace, Las Vegas, beginning on August 24. Performing his greatest hits, the residency also saw him perform selected tracks from his upcoming, untitled blues album. In October 2012, Stewart's autobiography titled *Rod: The Autobiography* was released.

On November 26, 2012, Stewart's recording of "Let It Snow! Let It Snow! Let It Snow!" reached the top of the *Billboard* Adult Contemporary Chart. Stewart has had the number one song on this chart three times previously, the last being in 1993 with "Have I Told You Lately," giving him the second-largest hiatus between number ones in the history of the chart. The song remained in the No. 1 spot for a total of five weeks, tying it for the longest-leading holiday title in the chart's 51-year history.

In May 2013, Stewart released *Time*, a rock album of his own original material. It marked a return to songwriting after what Stewart termed "a dark period for twenty years"; he said that writing his autobiography gave him the impetus to write music again. The album entered the UK Albums Chart at No. 1, setting a new British record for the longest gap between chart-topping albums by an artist. Stewart's last No. 1 on the chart had been *Greatest Hits Volume 1* in 1979 and his last studio album to top the chart was 1976's *A Night on the Town.*

Personal Life

Rod Stewart and Alana Collins Hamilton, the ex-wife of the actor George Hamilton, were married in April 1979. They have a daughter, Alana Kimberly. Before his marriage, Stewart had had a succession of affairs, including a two-and-a-half-year marriage with Britt Ekland, beginning in 1975. A $15,000,000 breach-of-trust suit filed by Miss Ekland was settled out of court, with a reported $500,000 property settlement. His marriage to Alana Hamilton ended in 1984. He was married to model Rachel Hunter from 1990 to 2006 and to Penny Lancaster since 2007. Stewart is known for his liaisons with women and has had eight children, by five different mothers.

"My passions are soccer, drinking, and women, in that order," Colin Dangaard and Daphne Davis quoted Stewart as saying in *Us* (May 20, 1979). His other interests include vintage automobiles.

Further Reading

Newsweek 80:75+ S 11 '72 por

People 11:80+ F 5 79

Rolling Stone p53 + N 6 75 pors, p46 Ap 6 78 pors

Time 102:99 +N 12 73Cromelin, Richard. *Rod Stewart* (1976)

Stambler, Irwin, *Encyclopedia of Pop, Rock, and Soul* (1977)

Stewart, Rod. *Rod: The Autobiography* (2012)

Leopold Stokowski

Orchestra conductor; composer

Born: April 18, 1882; London, England
Died: September 13, 1977; Nether Wallop, England
Primary Field: Classical
Group Affiliation: Solo performer

Introduction

In his book Music for All of Us *Leopold Stokowski wrote: "Formerly, music was chiefly confined to privileged classes in cultural centers, but today, through radio and records, music has come directly into our homes no matter how far we may live from cultural centers." In the decades since these words were written, Stokowski, acknowledged as one of the greatest conductors, helped through his study of acoustics and recordings to make it possible for music to be reproduced in the home with greater fidelity of tone and considerably less distortion. He foresaw and worked for binaural broadcasting with its greater tonal perspective. He was also concerned with the problem of giving contemporary composers an opportunity to be heard under the most favorable circumstances.*

In Carnegie Hall on October 17, 1953 he conducted the first major concert of contemporary Canadian music ever given in the United States, the first of a series under the auspices of the Contemporary Music Society. The programs were divided between American contemporary music and "seldom heard masterpieces."

Early Life

Leopold Anton Stanislaw Stokowski was born in London, April 18, 1882 of a Polish father, Josef Boleshaw Kopernicus Stokowski. His mother was Irish. Leopold was named for his grandfather, Leopold Stokowski of Krakow and Lublin.

From his earliest days he was interested in music and learned to play the piano and violin. Before he could reach the pedals he was playing parts of the organ works of Bach on a four-manual organ. At the Royal College of Music in London he studied harmony, counterpoint and composition under Sir Charles Parry and Sir Edward Elgar. He continued his education at the Paris Conservatoire and in Germany, concentrating upon the fugue and orchestration.

He subsequently studied different kinds of music during his travels in Arabia, China, India, Java and Bali. He was a Fellow of the Royal College of Music and a Bachelor of Music of Queen's College, Oxford. While a student in London he was organist of St. James' church in Piccadilly.

In 1905 he came to New York to be organist and choirmaster at St. Bartholomew's church. (The story that he was known there as Leo Stokes is wholly legendary.) In 1908 he left the sphere of church music to begin his career as an orchestra conductor in Cincinnati.

Life's Work

This transition from the choir loft to the podium was not as strange as it might seem. The modern pipe organ with its orchestral stops and great variety of color, somewhat approximates a symphony orchestra. Furthermore, familiarity with great organ literature, particularly the works of Bach, provided a sound musical background for the future conductor.

In 1912 Stokowski left Cincinnati to assume the leadership of the Philadelphia Orchestra. Here his innovations and successes made him one of the most controversial figures of the American musical scene.

Charles O'Connell, who was associated with Stokowski for eighteen years, writes in his book *The Other Side of the Record,* "I am told that Stokowski had periods of being a martinet, . . . of being an amiable friend or a remote and Olympian deity. I never have witnessed any of these manifestations during the last eighteen years."

O'Connell continues: "With his men he is pleasant, slightly aloof, impersonal and correct in his rehearsal deportment and quite insistent upon the incompatibility of mercy and justice. He will not for one moment tolerate inattention or stupidity. . . . The superb, the incredible legato of which the Philadelphia Orchestra alone seems capable is the result of Stokowski's insistence on free bowing; that is, the players were not obliged to follow the bowing of the section leader but handled their instruments in the way that was most natural and easy for them in producing the effect the conductor demanded."

Stokowski's years in Philadelphia were far from serene either for him or for his audiences. He was intolerant of late-comers and "traincatchers" and frequently chastised them publicly. His critics accused him of using these tactics to make the headlines. He had violent disagreements with his board of directors over modern music.

During the Depression financial support for the Orchestra fell off appreciably. In 1932 the directors announced that there would be no modern compositions or "debatable music" played that year. When Stokowski, who had been in. New Mexico, returned, he called in reporters and gave them a statement. He "would play a modern piece whenever he saw fit to do so and he would play it twice for whoever cared to listen." The press sided with him and another Stokowski victory was won.

It was inevitable that these clashes would one day not resolve themselves. He resigned in 1936 as musical director, continuing to conduct concerts each season until 1941. He had organized the All-American Youth Orchestra in 1940 with which he toured this country, South America, and the West Indies.

Again the skeptics were openly scornful of an attempt to play virtuoso symphonic pieces with an orchestra of young musicians who had never before played together. In a very short time Stokowski had welded into shape a remarkably fine organization.

Glenn Dillard Dunn of the Washington *Times-Herald* wrote: "I can assure Americans of either continent that this is just what Stokowski said it would be: one of the great orchestras of the world." However, since its members were of draft age, it had to be disbanded during World War II.

Stokowski was co-conductor with Toscanini of the NBC Symphony from 1941 to 1944. He led the New York City Symphony in 1944 and 1945, the Hollywood Bowl orchestra from 1945 to 1947, the United States Army Band at Fort MacArthur, California, and was co-conductor in 1948 and 1949 of the New York Philharmonic. He was a guest conductor all over the world, giving concerts with the Saint Cecilia Orchestra of Rome, the Royal Philharmonic Orchestra, the Philharmonia, the Berlin Philharmonic, the Suisse Romande Orchestra, the French National Radio Orchestra, the Czech Philharmonic and numerous other ensembles in Germany, Holland, Switzerland, Austria, and Portugal. In 1970 re returned to the Philadelphia Orchestra and made two LP recordings with them.

Stokowski's transcriptions of Bach's organ works brought the wrath of the purists upon his head. On the other hand, they also brought the music of Bach to thousands who might never have heard it. Of this the conductor himself said "The most free and sublime instrumental expressions of Bach are his greater organ works, and of these the greatest is the *Passacaglia in C minor*. Unfortunately one does not often enough have opportunity to hear it, and so, to bring it nearer to those who love Bach's music, I have made it for orchestra."

The late Lawrence Gilman, reviewing a concert for the New York *Herald Tribune* (April 4, 1937) wrote glowingly of an interpolated number *Mein Jesu, was für Seelenweh befällt dich in Gethsemane* (My Jesu, what befell thee in Gethsemane) "There is no more beautiful and poignant music than this in all of Bach's innumerable utterances of mystical and sacred grief; and Mr. Stokowski's setting for the strings, of magnificent felicity, made it well-nigh insupportable".

Stokowski worked with RCA Victor and with Dr. Harvey Fletcher of the Bell Laboratories to improve radio and recording techniques. Long opposed to broadcasting from "dead" studios, he struggled consistently to persuade radio technicians to broadcast from acoustically "live" studios. His persistence in this field was largely responsible for the greater realism in reproduced music that started in the 1950s, now accepted as a matter of course. He was among the first to make stereophonic recordings, starting with experimental recordings in the 1930s. In 1954 he made his first commercial stereo recordings for RCA Victor with the NBC Symphony.

Not only did he work closely with the engineers on every broadcast and recording session but he seated his orchestra differently for each composition to be played. Charles O'Connell says of this: "He decided that, given sympathetic cooperation in the recording room, he could accomplish more by manipulation of the orchestra than by revolving a rheostat."

He was first lured to Hollywood to make *The Great Broadcast of 1937*. This was followed by *One Hundred Men and a Girl,* and *Fantasia* (1941) which he made with Walt Disney, featuring Stravinsky's *Le Sacre du Printemps,* and *Carnegie Hall* (1947).

An enthusiast for modern music, Stokowski was the first to conduct in this country Gustav Mahler's *Symphony of a Thousand* (Symphony 8), Stravinsky's *Le Sacre du Printemps* and important works of Arnold Schoenberg, Serge Prokofieff, and Dmitri Shostakovich.

He also gave the first performance of a number of American compositions including Ernest Schelling's *A Victory Ball,* Aaron Copland's *Dance Symphony,* Walter Piston's *1929 Suite for Orchestra,* Abram Chasins' *Second Concerto in F-Sharp Minor for Piano and Orchestra,* Samuel Barlow's Babar and Elie Siegmeister's *Harvest Evening from the Prairie Legend.*

In April 1952 Stokowski conducted over CBS a concert from Columbia University as the climax of its Festival of American Music. He was subsequently given the Alice M. Ditson Memorial Fund award as a tribute to the conductor's "adventurousness".

During the season of 1952–1953, under the auspices of the American Composer's Alliance and of Broadcast Music, Incorporated, he presented two concerts at the Museum of Modern Art. Here, under nearly ideal circumstances, several new composers were introduced to the public. An unusual feature of these concerts was the tape-recording of the performances as they took place.

Of this innovation Stokowski said in an introductory speech, "The conventional composer usually has to wait for somebody else to play his music and it might be to his advantage to work, like the painter, directly on the materials of sound—the tape-recorder, for instance."

In September 1953 it was announced that Stokowski would conduct the six Sunday radio concerts sponsored jointly by the Columbia Broadcasting System and the American Composers' Alliance. The program, featuring the CBS radio orchestra, and offering both contemporary and classical music, is entitled *Twentieth Century Concert Hall.*

Stokowski conducted the NBS Symphony in 1954, making a series of recordings for RCA. When the orchestra was disbanded after the death of Arturo Toscanini, it was reestablished as the Symphony of the Air, with Stokowski as its music director. He led the orchestra until it disbanded in 1963. Stokowski was also the Music Director of the Houston Symphony Orchestra from 1955 to 1961, where he gave the U.S. premiere of Shostakovich's 11th Symphony on April 7, 1958. He founded the American Symphony Orchestra in 1962 and served as its Music Director until 1972, when he returned to England. His last public appearance took place on July 22, 1975, when he performed several of his Bach transcriptions with the Rouen Chamber Orchestra. He continued to make recordings until shortly before his death.

Personal Life

Stokowski became an American citizen in 1915. In 1911 he married the concert pianist Olga Samaroff; they were divorced in 1923. His marriage to Evangeline Brewster Johnson in 1926 ended in divorce in 1937. On April 21, 1945 he married Gloria Vanderbilt di Cicco; they divorced in 1955. He had a daughter, Sonia, by his first marriage; two daughters, Lyuba and Sadja by the second marriage, and two sons by his third marriage.

He had blue eyes and gray hair. Concerning his famous hands which were the subject of much comment and some derision, O'Connell wrote "the illusion of beauty that they give comes from the instinctive grace with which they are used". He was famous for conducting without a baton, using only his hands.

Stokowski was a member of the American Federation of Musicians in Philadelphia and Los Angeles. He received the Order of Polonia Restitute, Officer of the Crown of Rumania and Chevalier of the Legion of Honor. He held honorary degrees from the University of Pennsylvania and the University of California.

His book, *Music for All of Us* (1943), was translated into five languages. He composed *Dithyrambe* for flute, cello and harp, which was played in Philadelphia on November 15, 1917. Among his other compositions are *Negro Rhapsody, Prelude on Two Ancient Liturgical Melodies,* and *Benedicite Omina Opera* for organ.

On June 14, 1953 Leopold Stokowski conducted the Bergen, Norway Symphony Orchestra at the World Music Festival which was broadcast to the United States.

Affiliation: Solo Performer

Virgil Thomson wrote, "He has violated tradition and made tradition. His first violation of tradition was to arrive at the top of the conducting profession by an unorthodox and improbable route. The best conductors have mostly learned their job in the theatre . . . Mr. Stokowski came from the Royal College of Music to St. Bartholomew's Church as a perfectly good organist in the English style, no more. He went from there to conduct in Cincinnati . . . He stepped up to Philadelphia and made colossally good" (New York *Herald Tribune,* November 17, 1940).

Stokowski always had certain fundamental beliefs in his music and in himself. He was also able blithely to disregard his critics and to pursue his beliefs if need be in open defiance. He was able to transform a somewhat mediocre Philadelphia Orchestra into an instrument of such beauty and fame that he was given the Bok award as "the person who has done the most for Philadelphia." He accomplished this by engaging only the finest players for each section. Then he permitted these players some freedom of expression even as he kept a firm hand on the ensemble.

Leopold Stokowski died on September 13, 1977 in Nether Wallop, Hampshire, England of a heart attack and was buried at East Finchley Cemetery.

Further Reading

Mus Am 61:4 Mr 25 '51
N Y *Herald Tribune* Ap 14 '37
N Y Times Ja 13 '36; O 27 '52
Newsweek 17:60 Mr 24 '41
Times 47:69+ F 18 '46 por
Washington Times Herald Jl 13 '40
Brooks, D. *International Gallery of Conductors* (1951)
Columbia Encyclopedia (1950)
Ewen, D. *Dictators of the Baton* (1943)
International Motion Picture Almanac, 1950-51
O'Connell, C. *The Other Side of the Record* (1947)
Reis, C. *Composers in America* (1947)
Thompson, Oscar, ed, *The International Cyclopedia of Music and Musicians* (1949)
Who is Who in Music (1951)

Robert Stolz

Composer and conductor

Born: August 25, 1886; Graz, Austria
Died: June 27, 1965; West Berlin, West Germany
Primary Field: Opera
Affiliation: Solo conductor

Introduction

During World War II Robert Stolz, the composer of Two Hearts in Three-Quarter Time, *wanted to write the death dirge for Adolf Hitler's funeral. This self-exiled Viennese musician, who had left his home because of Hitler, began his career at the age of seven as a pianist; he was a full-fledged conductor by the time he was seventeen and remained busy directing orchestras and writing music ever since. Composition came very easily to Stolz, who wrote many sure-fire operettas, dozens of musical scores for motion pictures, and more than a thousand songs. After the Anschluss (the Nazi occupation of Austria), Stolz came to America, where he helped to revive an interest in melodious Viennese operettas.*

Early Life

The man who was considered by some critics to be the musical heir of Johann Strauss was born on August 25, 1886 in Graz, Austria, the son of Jakob and Ida (Bondy) Stolz. His family was an extremely musical one; his father had studied with Anton Bruckner and was a well-known opera conductor who had led the first performance in Vienna of Wagner's *Tannhäuser* (1845). His great aunt, Therese Stolz, the most famous Italian opera singer of her time, is prominently mentioned in the memoirs of Verdi.

As a child, Stolz received his early musical training from his father; later he became a pupil of Robert Fuchs, the noted professor of theory at the Vienna Conservatory. Stolz completed his musical studies under a protégé of Wagner, Engelbert Humperdinck, the composer of *Hänsel und Gretel* (1893).

When he was only seven years of age Stolz, accompanied by his father, made a concert tour of Europe, giving piano recitals of Mozart's music. Four years later his first composition was published by Adolf Fürstner, an important music publisher in Berlin. At seventeen Stolz was recognized as a composer and was commissioned to write the music and conduct the band for the Cirque Henri, Europe's largest circus.

Life's Work

Thereafter Stolz was engaged as opera and operetta conductor in Brünn (now Brno), Prague, Mannheim, and other cities; finally, he was made the conductor at one of the most famous musical institutions in the world, the *Theater-an-der-Wien.* It was at this same theatre that Mozart had conducted the first performance of his *Magic Flute* (1791) and that Beethoven had presented his *Fidelio* (1805) to the world. The conductorship of the *Theater,* which was rivaled in prestige only by the conductorship of the Vienna Grand State Opera, was a post for which most musicians would have given their eyeteeth. Stolz's immediate predecessor had been the late Artur Bodanzky, the celebrated conductor of Wagnerian operas. During the twelve years that Stolz was associated with the *Theater-an-der-Wien* he conducted the world premiere performances of many operetta favorites such as Franz Lehar's *The Merry Widow* (1905) and *Count of Luxembourg* (1909), and Oscar Straus' *The Chocolate Soldier* (1908). Every year Stolz also appeared as guest conductor with some of the major European orchestras, including the Vienna Philharmonic Orchestra and the BBC Symphony Orchestra. By 1943, Stolz had conducted over 17,000 performances and concerts throughout the world.

Although Stolz was of "pure Aryan" stock, he became a voluntary exile from Vienna as soon as Hitler and his henchmen arrived there in March 1938. "I left Vienna," explained Stolz, "because I believed in democracy and abominated the anti-Semitic excesses of the present regime. Throughout my career I have had Jewish lyric writers, publishers, and producers. Only the renegades to art have remained in Germany today."

Upon leaving Vienna, Stolz went to Paris where he remained for nearly two years before he sailed for the United States. He had no sooner arrived in Paris, however than Leo Ritter, Hitler's president of the German Association of Composers, Authors, and Agents, tried to tempt Stolz back to Germany with all sorts of offers. "Come back to Germany," said Herr Ritter. "You shall have carte blanche. You may name your price, your theatre, your conductor, your singers. The Führer will permit you to realize your wildest ambitions." But Stolz continued to refuse every one of these offers. "I would rather spend the rest of my days in a cubbyhole in America," he said, "than occupy a palace in Vienna under the present circumstances."

Stolz, whose New York apartment in the 1940s could scarcely be described as a "cubbyhole," was active as a conductor since his arrival in the United States in 1940. During seasons after his arrival, his conducting of the successful New York revivals of Viennese operettas has caused much favorable comment: The Viennese operettas presented by Robert Stolz with spectacular success were Johann Straus' *Die Fledermaus* (April 1942), *The Gypsy Baron* (June 1942), which received high praise and was repeated at the Lewisohn Stadium (August 1943), and *The Beggar Student* (September 1942) by Carl Milloecker. A New York *Herald Tribune* reviewer remarked of Stolz's ability as a conductor: "The precision, nuance, and overall fire that he obtained from his orchestra were remarkable, as was the coordination of the entire performance under his baton." Another critic, Noel Straus of the New York *Times,* stated: "Under Mr. Stolz's knowing baton every number, from the overture on, boasted the typical Viennese rhythmic nuances without which the polkas, waltzes, and other infectious melodies of the operetta lose their essential quality. His conducting was excellent in all respects." In August 1943 Stolz conducted with outstanding success the New Opera Company's production of his new musical version of Lebar's *The Merry Widow.*

The music of Stolz was played and sung in Germany during the war, although no royalties from the performing rights ever were sent to the composer. Besides his most famous work *Zwei Herzen im Dreiviertel Takt. (Two Hearts in Three-Quarter Time* [1931]) By 1943 Stolz had composed thirty-seven operettas, fifty-four scores for musical motion pictures (including *Spring Parade* [1940] with Deanna Durbin '41), 1,200 songs, a number of suites and orchestral pieces and one grand opera, *Roses of the Madonna.* One of his operettas, *Wild Violets* (1932), enjoyed a 400-performance run at the Drury Lane in London. Broadway audiences best remembered his *Sky High* (1925); *The Blue Train* (1927); and *Two Hearts.* The composer claimed that the melodic idea of *Two Hearts* came to him one evening while he was seated with friends at his favorite table in Vienna's famous Sacher Cafe. "Animated conversation was going back and. forth" he recalled. "I seized a pencil and scribbled on the menu the tune that was to become so popular." The proprietor of the Sacher begged for and received the original, which he placed in a gilt frame and hung in the main dining room.

Before Stolz would discuss his attitude toward contemporary music, he insisted that a distinction be made between "modern" music and "freak" music. Of the "moderns" his favorites were Stravinsky "at his best," Ravel, and Sibelius; in the latter category Stolz

Affiliation: Famous American Symphony Orchestras

Stolz won wide acclaim not only for his sensitive interpretation as conductor, but also for his musical streamlining of this presentation of the operetta. His comprehensive reshuffling of the original score and his own ballet arrangements were credited with placing the operetta on the hit class. In August 1943 too Stolz broke all-time attendance records with his concert of Viennese music with the Philadelphia Symphony Orchestra at the Robin Hood Dell. He drew a crowd of 24,000 people, against the previous record of 15,000.

included the atonal and "cerebral" composers, all of whom could be thrown out of a high window as far as he is concerned.

In late 1943 Stolz went to Hollywood to write and direct the musical score for the United Artists' film *It Happened Tomorrow,* starring Dick Powell, Linda Darnell, and Jack Oakie. This score was nominated for an Oscar. "Music is dead in Vienna, as in all occupied countries," Stolz said upon his arrival. "Austria will make a comeback, but not immediately, because the people are sick at heart and apathetic. But one country will be the same, immediately, overnight, when Hitler is gone. That is France, whose spirit will reawaken quicker than Austria's because it hasn't been under the Nazi yoke so long."

In 1946 Stolz returned to Vienna and lived there for the rest of his life. In 1952 he began to compose operettas for the Vienna Ice Revue, dedicating the first of 19 to the European Champion Eva Pawlik. In the 1960s and 1970s he made many recordings of famous operettas by Johann Strauss, Lehár, and other famous composers. He received many honors late in life, including becoming the first honorary member of the Vienna Volksoper in 1964 and receiving the Jerusalem Medal in 1971 for assisting the flight of Jewish citizens during the war years. He conducted using a baton inherited from Franz Lehár that was originally owned by Johann Strauss.

Personal Life

During the war years, the composer's strongest ambition is to write the funeral march for Hitler: "I trust," he said at that time, "I shall have the opportunity to begin work on it very soon." He believed that Germany would remain sterile artistically and musically as long as Hitler remained in power. "How is it possible to work in Hitlerland?" he asked. "All the spirit's gone. The men drink watered raspberry syrup. The girls dress and make up like mothball bags and nobody smokes—well, of course, not 'nobody.' But Hitler is the model for everything and he doesn't smoke. And when the girls look like that, how can you write Viennese operettas?"

Robert Stolz was married five times; his fifth wife, Yvonne Louise Ulrich, emigrated with him during the war and was his manager until his death. Stolz died on June 27, 1975 in West Berlin and was buried in Vienna's Zentralfriedhof cemetery near Johannes Brahms and Johann Strauss. After his death a memorial statue was erected in the Wiener Stadtpark (Vienna City Park).

Further Reading

Boston Sunday Post N 3 '40
Etude 59:225-6+ Ap '41 il por
N Y *Herald Tribune* VI p2 Ja 5 '41;Je 20 '42; S 26 '42
N Y Times Ap.12 '42; p21 My 19 '43
N Y World-Telegram p7 Je 25 '40
Philadelphia Inquirer Ag 30 '42
PM p13 010 '40
International Motion Picture Almanac 1941-42
Macmillan Encyclopedia of Music and Musicians 1938

George Strait

Singer

Born: May 18, 1952; Poteet, Texas
Group Affiliation: Solo artist

Introduction

Known to many of his fans as "the Pope of Texas," the singer George Strait has become such a country-music icon that the Texas state legislature once stopped sessions to investigate a rumor that he had died in a plane crash. Since bursting onto the country-music scene, in 1981, Strait has virtually redefined modern country music with a string of 24 hit albums, more than 35 chart-topping singles, and numerous Country Music Awards. His blend of honky-tonk, western swing, and romantic ballads has set him apart from other contemporary singers and opened the door for a new generation of country artists. He was the first in what is now a long line of country crooners clad in starched shirts, pressed jeans, and oversized hats, and his appeal has as much to do with what he represents as it does with his considerable talent. "George is the gentleman cowboy we all used to dream about," his fellow country star Patty Loveless told a reporter for People *(November 17, 1997).*

Early Life

The second of three children, George Harvey Strait was born on May 18, 1952 in Poteet, Texas. When he was a child, his mother left home with his sister, and George and his brother were raised by his father, a math teacher at the local high school. "It wasn't exactly a country music upbringing," he recalled to Bob Allen for the *Washington Post* (November 8, 1986). "My dad didn't even have a record player, and when he listened to the radio, it was usually the news or the cow market reports or something like that." A fourth-generation Texan, Strait spent his childhood roping, riding, and branding cattle on his family's 2,000-acre ranch in nearby Pearsall, while developing his interest in music. "Growing up, I pretty much listened to all kinds of music, even rock and roll.... I'd buy all the sheet music I could find," Strait told Marty Racine for the *Houston Chronicle* (August 7, 1983), as reprinted on the *No Place but Texas* Web site. "I just taught myself how to play the guitar and sing." As he improved musically Strait began playing in his spare time with what he described to Allen as "some of your basic high school garage bands. We'd play 'Gloria,' 'Louie Louie,' and stuff like that."

After graduating from high school, Strait attended Southwest Texas State University, in San Marcos, but before long he realized that college did not particularly interest him. He dropped out of school and eloped to Mexico with his longtime girlfriend, Norma Voss; they later repeated their vows in a church service, on December 4, 1971. Strait joined the army and was stationed in Hawaii, where his and Norma's first child, Jenifer, was born, on October 6, 1972. In 1973 he successfully auditioned to be lead singer for a country-and-western band at the Schofield Barracks. The newly formed band was soon performing at army functions, first under the name Rambling Country and later as Santee. "I always knew I wanted to be a country singer," Strait told Bob Allen. "But it wasn't until I got to Hawaii that I really got serious about it."

Life's Work

After his military discharge Strait reenrolled at Southwest Texas State University to study agricultural education. His announcement, placed on a campus bulletin board, that he was a singer in search of a band resulted in the formation of a group known as Ace in the Hole. Having rehearsed their rollicking country-and-western sound in a nearby run-down house, they began to take their act on the road, sometimes traveling as far as 200 miles for a gig. "We played everything back then," Strait recalled to Marty Racine. "We played weddings or any kind of function they would pay us money to do." Ace in the Hole soon gained a solid reputation.

Despite the band's success, by 1979 Strait "was just fixin' to go ahead and quit," he told Bob Allen. "I was 27 years old, I'd been playing for six or seven years, and I was beginning to think I just wasn't good enough and maybe ought to try something else." He gave his band notice and successfully applied for a job with a Uvalde, Texas, firm that designed cattle pens. At first his plan for a career change seemed sensible, but Strait's wife soon realized otherwise. "George was moping around the house so much I couldn't stand it," Norma Strait told Montgomery Brower for *People* (June 3, 1985). "I figured I didn't want to live in Uvalde with him like that, so we talked about his hopes in music. I wanted him to give it one more try."

Erv Woolsey, a Texas club owner who had formerly worked with MCA Records, arranged for Strait to perform for several of the label's higher-ups. Strait impressed them, and he signed a contract with MCA in 1980, just six months after his crucial talk with his wife. In the spring of 1981, Strait's first single, "Unwound," was released; his son, George Jr. (who is also known as "Bubba"), was born almost immediately afterward, on May 14. "Unwound" shot to number four on the charts, and the album containing the single, *Strait Country,* went certified gold. Since then the country music charts have rarely been without at least one George Strait single or album.

In June 1982 Strait released his second album, *Strait from the Heart,* which contains some of his best-known singles, among them "Amarillo by Morning," "Marina Del Rey," and the number-one hits "Fool Hearted Memory" and "A Fire I Can't Put Out." His next two albums, *Right or Wrong* (1983) and *Does Fort Worth Ever Cross Your Mind* (1984), would prove no less successful, yielding a total of four chart-toppers and going gold and platinum, respectively. In 1984 he won the *Billboard* award for top male country artist. To support record sales Strait toured aggressively across the country with Ace in the Hole, playing a jaw-dropping 250 dates per year. Most shows were marathons that lasted four or more hours and drew praise for their high energy. Although the daily grind of stardom was beginning to wear on Strait, he resisted easing his pace. "I'd be crazy to slow down right now; things are going too good," he explained to Brower. "I have to hit it full steam until I can't stand it anymore." In short order he released three more albums, the triple-platinum *Greatest Hits* (1985), *Something Special* (1985), and #7 (1986).

After 10 years in the limelight, the strain of his touring schedule finally caught up with him. "There were times earlier in my career when I was working like 200 or 250 dates a year the way a lot of young artists are doing today," Strait said to Jack Hurst for the *Chicago Tribune* (October 18, 1992), "and I remember getting to October and November when we started slowing down for Christmas and being burned out so bad I didn't think I could go another year. It got to the point where I would start feeling that way several times during the year. I figured out that I had to get some time away from the music business." Strait had appeared with Ace in the Hole in the James Glickenhaus film *The Soldier* (1982), and in the following years had hoped to star in a movie. Thinking that working on a film would be a good diversion from music, he read several scripts and settled on the drama *Pure Country* (1992), in which he played an overworked country star who undergoes a spiritual reawakening when he returns to Texas cattle country. In a review for the *Washington Post* (October 26, 1992), Richard Harrington called *Pure Country* "a pleasant, low-key country-and-western film." Roger Ebert of the *Chicago Sun-Times* (October 23, 1992) wrote, "Strait is not an actor in the class of [John] Mellencamp or [Willie] Nelson, but he is genuine and has a winning smile, and holds his own in a screenplay that makes few demands." While the film was a moderate hit, the soundtrack album stormed the charts-going quintuple platinum-and spawned three number-one hits. Strait's son joined him for a duet on the single "Heartland."

Strait returned to music in 1993. That year he released *Easy Come, Easy Go*, which featured a hit single of the same name. That album was followed by the platinum-selling *Lead On* (1994). His next effort, *Strait Out of the Box* (1995), went quintuple platinum and became the highest-selling boxed set in music history. The collection, spanning the first 15 years of Strait's career, featured 72 of his top-10 hits, duets with such music luminaries as Frank Sinatra and Hank Thompson, and three early songs that Strait had recorded for a small company before he signed with MCA. The set also offered a new chart-topping song, "Check Yes or No," which became his 35th number-one single and received numerous awards, including a Country Music Award for single of the year.

Strait had another excellent year in 1998. He released the studio album *One Step at a Time,* which loosened the *Titanic* soundtrack's seemingly unshakeable grip on the number-one position on the pop charts and which yielded four top-10 hits. In a review of *One Step at a Time* for the *Washington Post* (May 13, 1998), Bill Friskics-Warren wrote, "George Strait continues to outclass the spate of neo-traditionalist hat acts that he's inspired." The five Country Music Award nominations he

Affiliation: Return from Tragedy

A personal tragedy forced him to reevaluate his priorities. On the night of June 25, 1986, as Strait's daughter, Jenifer, was riding in a friend's car in San Marcos, Texas, the driver lost control; Jenifer was killed instantly. (She was the only fatality in the nonalcohol-related incident.) Strait was devastated. For more than a year, he refused to grant a single interview, ignoring warnings that retreating from the press might affect his record sales. "I just decided, 'If my career suffers, it suffers,'" he told Jack Hurst for the *Chicago Tribune* (November 23, 1995). "I couldn't suffer any worse than I was already suffering, and that was just the way it was going to be. And I've been that way ever since." In an attempt to lessen his pain, Strait recorded a Christmas album, *Merry Christmas Strait to You* (1986), and embarked on another grueling concert tour.

The following year Strait bounced back, with the release of *Ocean Front Property* (1987), his first album to debut at number one on the *Billboard* charts. The album produced three number-one hits: "All My Ex's Live in Texas," "Am I Blue," and "Ocean Front Property." He continued his domination of country music with two more platinum albums, *If You Ain't Lovin' You Ain't Livin'* (1988) and *Beyond the Blue Neon* (1989), and won a Country Music Award for entertainer of the year in November 1989. He accepted the award in his characteristically self-effacing manner, shaking his head while reaching for the envelope and saying, "Let me read that again." Strait kicked off the 1990s in his trademark furious style, releasing his 13th album, *Livin' It Up* (1990), which became his fastest seller ever. The single "Love Without End, Amen" reached number one on the country charts and stayed in the top spot for five consecutive weeks. Strait also strolled off with his second consecutive Country Music Award for entertainer of the year.

received in 1998 pushed him past Merle Haggard's record for total career nominations, and he won one prize. That summer Strait launched the George Strait Country Music Festival, which hosted a slew of country greats. Taking a cue from the acclaimed Lollapalooza rock festival, the traveling show cultivated a carnival atmosphere through such attractions as Straitland, a midway that offered games, food, and a dance floor surrounded by bales of hay. The festival was extremely popular, outselling Sarah McLachlan's much-hyped Lilith Fair, among other such events. Its success, the country singer Jo Dee Messina observed to Edna Gunderson for *USA Today* (March 9, 1999), "says a lot about the appeal of George Strait. He could do an arena tour and command any ticket price he wants, but he enjoys giving fans this festival."

In 1999, in addition to mounting the festival again, Strait released *Always Never the Same,* his 24th album. The first single, "We Really Shouldn't Be Doing This," a lilting ballad about a man who cannot forget a past lover, garnered praise from critics and topped the charts soon after its release. The tune inspired one *Billboard* critic to predict that "We Really Shouldn't Be Doing This" "will have couples swirling around a sawdust-covered dance floor and melting with delight." On March 7, 2000 Strait released *Latest Greatest Straitest Hits,* a collection of his more recent hit singles. In addition, the album featured two new recordings, one of which, "The Best Day," a ballad about a father and son, reached number one on the country charts.

Over the next fifteen years, Strait released: *George Strait* (2000), *The Road Less Traveled* (2001), *Honkytonkville* (2003), *Somewhere Down in Texas* (2005), *It Just Comes Natural* (2006), *Troubadour* (2008), *Twang* (2009), *Here for a Good Time* (2011), *Love is Everything* (2013), and *Cold Beer Conversation* (2015).

George Strait has more than 30 years in the recording business all spent with MCA Records. He has earned 60 No. 1 songs on all country charts and has more No. 1 hits than any other artist in any genre. His 44 *Billboard* magazine country No. 1's are a record, four more than Conway Twitty's total that includes several duets. Strait is also the first artist in the history of *Billboard* magazine to have at least one single enter the Top 10 of a *Billboard* chart for 30 consecutive years, starting in 1981 when his debut single "Unwound." Strait has sold more than 68 million albums in the United States and his certifications from the RIAA include 13 multi-platinum, 33 platinum, and 38 gold albums.

Personal Life

In 1971, George married his high school sweetheart, Norma. George Strait, Jr. was born ten years later. Their daughter Jenifer (born October 6, 1972) was killed in an automobile accident in San Marcos, TX, on June 25, 1986, at the age of 13. The family set up the Jenifer Lynn Strait Foundation, which donates money to children's charities in the San Antonio area. In February 2012, Strait became a grandfather, when his son George Strait, Jr., and his wife, Tamara, had their first child, George H. Strait, III.

Strait enjoys hunting, fishing, skiing, playing golf, and riding motorcycles. Along with his son, he is a member of the PRCA and partners in team roping competitions. George and his elder brother John Jr., hosted the annual George Strait Team Roping Classic, in which they competed against some of the best team ropers in the world. Strait has also said that he very seldom picks up a guitar when not in the studio or touring. He and his wife live in northwest San Antonio, as well as on a ranch near Cotulla in La Salle County between San Antonio and Laredo. Strait is a fan of the NBA's San Antonio Spurs and can be seen court-side at many of the Spurs' home basketball games.

Since 2010, Strait has served as spokesman for the Wrangler National Patriot program, a campaign designed to raise awareness and funds for America's wounded and fallen military veterans and their families. Strait states, "I've been a part of the Wrangler family for a long time, when they came to me with the idea for supporting fallen and wounded American veterans and their families, I knew I wanted to get involved."

He maintains his privacy fiercely, rarely granting interviews or doing publicity. "George is George," the Dixie Chicks singer Natalie Maines said to Gundersen. "He doesn't jump around a lot. He doesn't go for the glitz, the big lights, the stage scenery. He's a humble, nice Texan who stands there and sings songs that people really feel."

Further Reading

Chicago Tribune XIII p17 Jan. 13, 1985, with photo, XIII p22+ Oct. 18, 1992, with photo, V p2 Nov. 23, 1995, with photo

USA TodayD p1+ Mar. 9, 1999

Washington Post D p5+ Nov. 8, 1995, with photo

George Strait: The Story of Country's Living Legend

Bego, M. Kensington, Dec 1, 1996
King George the Triumphs and Tragedies in the Life of George Strait, Teutsch, A., JRAB Press, Dec 15, 2010

Igor Stravinsky

Composer; conductor

Born: June 17, 1882; Oranienbaum, Russia
Died: April 6, 1971; New York, New York
Primary Field: Classical
Group Affiliation: Solo composer

Introduction

It was said of Igor Stravinsky that "no other living composer has made a more notable contribution to the music of our Western world." Born in Russia, he achieved international fame as a musical innovator with L'Oiseau de Feu *(*The Firebird*),* Petrouchka, *and* Le Sacre du Printemps *(*The Rite of Spring*), which were written for Diaghilev's Ballets Russes before 1914. During World War I he lived in Switzerland and then in 1920 settled in France. From this time on his music developed increasingly in the direction of classicism. After 1939 he made his permanent home in the United States and he became an American citizen. His first full-length opera,* The Rake's Progress, *received its American premiere at the Metropolitan Opera in February 1953.*

Early Life

Igor Fëdorovich Stravinsky was born on the feast day of St. Igor, June 17, 1882, in Oranienbaum, near St. Petersburg, Russia. His father Fëdor Ignatevich Stravinsky, partly of Polish descent, came from an old and noble family bearing the name of Soulima-Stravinsky; his mother was from Little Russia. Since his father was the leading bass singer at the Imperial Opera in St. Petersburg, young Igor grew up in a musical atmosphere. He started taking piano lessons when he was nine years old and soon developed a taste for improvisation, but his parents had no thought of training him as a professional musician, and at the age of seventeen he was sent to study law at the University of St. Petersburg. It was agreed that he could have harmony lessons on the side, and he began to teach himself counterpoint at this time.

Life's Work

In the summer of 1902 Stravinsky showed some of his early efforts at composition to Nikolai Rimski-Korsakov, who encouraged him to continue his studies in harmony and counterpoint. Upon graduating from the university three years later, he decided to devote himself entirely to music, and he received private lessons in composition and orchestration from Rimski-Korsakov until the composer's death in 1908. The first of Stravinsky's compositions of which there is record was an unpublished Piano Sonata (1903–04), but his official Opus 1 was the *Symphony in E Flat* (1905–07), reportedly written in the academic style of Alexander Glazunov. His next two orchestral works, *Scherzo Fantastique* (1907–08) and *Feu d'Artifice* (1908), reflected the influence of the French impressionists. The first performances of these pieces in the winter of 1909 attracted the attention of the noted impresario, Sergei Diaghilev, who commissioned a new work from Stravinsky for a season of Russian ballet he was planning to present in Paris. This marked the beginning of an artistic collaboration that was to last for twenty years, during which time Diaghilev's Ballets Russes produced most of Stravinsky's new works for the stage. The first of these was *L'Oiseau de Feu* (The Firebird), a ballet based on a Russian fairy tale, which had its Paris premiere on June 25, 1910, and overnight established the unknown young composer as a musical celebrity. Although the score remained within the picturesque descriptive style of the Russian nationalist school, it proved, as one critic remarked, that Stravinsky "could rival, if not excel, his master in brilliance and glamour of orchestration."

The outbreak of World War I found Stravinsky living in Switzerland, where he remained for the next six years. During this period he began to experiment with various chamber orchestra combinations, but vocal music was his chief preoccupation and Russian folk material continued to be his main source of inspiration. Between 1914 and 1918 he worked intermittently on *Les Noces,* a ballet-cantata depicting a Russian village wedding, and another five years elapsed before he decided on the final scoring for voices, four pianos, and seventeen percussions instruments'. Rollo Myers has praised "the essential and profound originality of this masterpiece." Another ballet based on Russian folk lore was *Renard* (1916–17), a burlesque tale for dancers or acrobats, vocal soloist, and chamber orchestra. Neither of these works was produced until after the war, but in 1918 Stravinsky collaborated with the Swiss writer C. F. Ramuz on *L'Histoire du Soldat (The Story of a Soldier),* a theater work for dancers, actors, a narrator, and seven instrumentalists, which was presented in Lausanne that year. Described by Alexandre Tansman as "one of the most personal and engaging works of our time," *L'Histoire du Soldat* revealed the composer's interest in various popular dances, including ragtime.

At the conclusion of the war, Diaghilev suggested that Stravinsky write a ballet based on some manuscript fragments by the eighteenth century composer Pergolesi. The result was *Pulcinella* (1919–20), which marks the beginning of the so-called "neoclassical" phase of Stravinsky's musical development. After he settled in France in 1920, he became increasingly preoccupied with the composition of absolute music written in the various classical forms in which the style and spirit was akin to the masters of the baroque period. To this category belong the polyphonic *Octet* for wind instruments (1922–23), *Piano Concerto* (1923–24), *Piano Sonata* (1924), and *Sérénade in A* for piano (1925). The last of his works to use both a Russian subject and text was the one-act opera *buffa Mavra* (1921–22), based on a tale by Pushkin. During the early 1920's Stravinsky embarked upon a subsidiary career as a conductor and piano soloist playing his own works, and in 1925 he made his first concert tour of the United States. A significant landmark in the evolution of his neoclassical style was *Oedipus Rex* (1926–27), an opera-oratorio adapted from Sophocles by Jean Cocteau. The French text was then translated into Latin in order to attain "the least temporal and most universal means of expression." This was followed by the ballet *Apollon Musagètes,* which had been commissioned for a festival of chamber music held at the Library of Congress, in Washington, in April 1928. According to Abraham Skulsky *(Musical America),* Apollon was the first of Stravinsky's works in which melody was the most important element. That same year saw the premiere of *Le Baiser de la Fée (The Fairy's Kiss),* written for the Paris season of the dancer Ida Rubinstein. For this allegorical ballet, "inspired by the Muse of Tchaikovsky," Stravinsky borrowed most of his thematic material from that composer's works.

The 1930's were devoted to a further consolidation of the classical style. Prominent among Stravinsky's works of this decade was the *Symphonie de Psaumes,* composed "for the Glory of God" and dedicated to the Boston Symphony on the occasion of its fiftieth anniversary. Philip Hale judged this choral symphony to be "one of the sincerest expressions of Stravinsky's genius." The composer next wrote the *Violin Concerto* (1931) and *Duo Concertante* (1932) for the violinist

Affiliation: Composer

The innovations that won for Stravinsky "the incontestable leadership of modern Western music" were first revealed in his score for *Petrouchka.* According to Aaron Copland *(Our New Music),* they included the exploitation of ostinato and unusual rhythms, the bold use of unconventional harmonies (including the introduction of bitonality for the first time), and an orchestral timbre in which the tonal values of the various instruments and choirs were clearly distinguishable in the orchestral mass. The "dynamic verve" of this new style represented a revolt against the lush vagueness of late romanticism and impressionism. *Petrouchka,* a ballet about puppets at a Russian carnival, was first performed on June 13, 1911, with Vaslav Nijinsky dancing the title role, and immediately acclaimed as a masterpiece. It is generally agreed, however, that the composer's "most strikingly original" work is *Le Sacre du Printemps (The Rite of Sping),* a ballet representing pagan rites in ancient Russia, for which Nijinsky devised the choreography. At the historic Paris premiere on May 29, 1913, the music provoked a violent demonstration in the theater, and outraged listeners claimed that its pounding rhythms and harsh dissonances represented an attempt by Stravinsky "to destroy music as an art." Now considered "a landmark in the history of music," *Le Sacre* has been called "the most important symphonic creation of the twentieth century." Early in 1914, shortly before visiting Russia for the last time, Stravinsky completed *Le Rossignol (The Nightingale),* a three-act opera based on the Andersen fairy tale, which he had begun six years before. The score was later converted into a ballet, *Le Chant du Rossignol (The Song of the Nightingale),* which was staged in 1920.

Samuel Dushkin, with whom he gave a number of recitals. Then, at the request of Ida Rubinstein, he undertook the composition of Persephone, a "melodrama" for soloist, chorus, and orchestra, spoken recitation, miming, and dancing, set to a poem by André Gide. In his monograph on the composer, Eric White called the work "a pure and lucid example of the classical spirit working with full objective awareness and perfect control." In June 1934, two months after the Paris premiere of *Persephone*, Stravinsky became a French citizen. He made his second concert tour of the United States early in 1935, and during the remainder of that year completed an important *Concerto for Two Pianos,* without orchestral accompaniment. Two years later, he visited the United States again to conduct the world premiere at the Metropolitan Opera House of *Jeu de Cartes,* a satirical ballet based on a poker game, which had been commissioned by the American Ballet Company.

The composer returned to the United States to accept the Charles Eliot Norton Chair of Poetry at Harvard University for the academic year of 1939–40. After the fall of France, he settled in Hollywood, becoming an American citizen in December 1945. The critics have discerned in Stravinsky's recent work a tendency "to consolidate all his findings and to restate them in new terms," as well as "a new mellowness appropriate to his maturity." The *Symphony in C* (1939-40), composed for the fiftieth anniversary of the Chicago Symphony Orchestra, is said to present "a synthesis of his earlier classical usages," while the *Symphony in Three Movements* (1942-45) is "a summary of all the main characteristics exhibited in his total output up to that time." Of Stravinsky's score for *Orpheus,* which was given its premiere by the Ballet Society of New York in 1948, Robert Sabin observed in *Musical America:* "a supremely eloquent melos . . . treated with miraculous economy and purity of design." The *Mass in C* (1948) for male chorus and wind instruments reportedly shows the influence of his present enthusiasm for the Flemish contrapuntalists of the fifteenth century. Among the other works written during this decade are *Danses Concertantes* (1941-42), which the Ballet Russe de Monte Carlo staged in 1944; *Circus Polka* (1942), commissioned by Ringling Brothers for an elephant ballet; *Scènes de Ballet* (1944), written for Billy Rose's Broadway revue, The Seven Lively Arts; and *Ebony Concerto* (1945), for Woody Herman's swing band.

At an exhibition in 1947 Stravinsky came across *The Rake's Progress,* a set of engravings by the eighteenth-century English painter, William Hogarth, and the series at once appeared to him as the successive scenes of an opera. He asked the poet W. H. Auden to write an original English libretto using the Hogarth series as a point of departure. The text was completed in the spring of 1948 and the composition of the music occupied Stravinsky for the next three years. *The Rake's Progress* received its world premiere in Venice on September 11, 1951, and was introduced in the United States by the Metropolitan Opera in February 1953. A moral fable about a young rake's downfall and redemption, the opera returned to the traditional form of arias, duets, ensembles, choruses, concerted numbers, and other set pieces, linked by recitative. To Colin Mason *(Music & Letters),* it seemed "the greatest and most important neoclassic work that has yet been produced," and Nicolas Nabokov wrote in the New York *Herald Tribune* that it was "an unquestionable masterpiece whose Mozartian dimensions and transparent beauty have not been matched by any other work for the lyric theater in the first half of our century." In May 1952, shortly before celebrating his seventieth birthday, Stravinsky made his first public appearance in Paris in thirteen years, at the International Exposition of the Arts of the Twentieth Century, where his return was greeted with "a tremendous ovation." Six months later his second work set to an English text, the *Cantata on Anonymous Elizabethan Songs,* was presented for the first time.

Starting in the 1950s, Stravinsky began to experiment with the twelve-tone technique developed by Arnold Schoenberg. The first composition that was based completely on this technique was *In Memoriam Dylan Thomas* (1954). Other works in this style include *Agon* (1954–57), *Canticum Sacrum* (1955), *Threni* (1958), *A Sermon, a Narrative, and a Prayer* (1961, a work based on Biblical texts), and *The Flood* (1962), which used parts of the book of Genesis along with passages from the medieval York and Chester mystery plays.

In addition to the works already mentioned, Stravinsky wrote *Symphonies d'Instruments à Vent* (1920); *Capriccio* for piano and orchestra (1929); *Dumbarton Oaks Concerto, in E Flat,* for chamber orchestra (1937–38); *Norwegian Moods* (1942) and *Ode* (1943) for orchestra; *Sonata for Two Pianos* (1943–44); *Concerto in D* for strings (1946); works for string quartet, songs, and piano pieces. His unconventional arrangement of "The Star-Spangled Banner" led to an incident with the Boston police, who warned the composer (incorrectly) that he was violating the law. The incident developed into a well-established myth that Stravinsky was arrested for the piece. Most of his compositions have been recorded. Late in his life, he conducted recordings of virtually all his compositions for Columbia Masterworks. The musicologist and conductor Robert Craft assisted Stravinsky during this project. As a guest conductor, Stravinsky led nearly all the major orchestras of Europe and America. He was the author of an autobiographical *Chroniques de ma vie* (1935), and the text of his Harvard lectures was published in 1942 under the title *Poetique musicale.* Both of these books have been translated into English. Late in his life he coauthored with Robert Craft *Conversations with Stravinsky, Memories and Developments, Dialogues and a Diary, Themes and Episodes,* and *Retrospection and Conclusions.*

While critics are in agreement about the originality and importance of Stravinsky's Russian-inspired works, there is considerable difference of opinion over the value of his later output. His detractors maintain that he "retired into a self-made world of cerebral austerity from whence at certain intervals he offers a displeasing *pastiche*—a synthetic rehash of previously existing formulas" *(The Chesterian).* His champions find beneath the variety of his styles, forms, and techniques "a line of development that has been guided by a unified purpose." In the opinion of Arthur Berger *(Stravinsky in the Theatre),* it is "the restatement of organic principles, rather than the evocation of the past" that provides the real differentia of Stravinsky's classicism. The reason why Stravinsky's works seem "so fresh and new" and why he has become "one of the great reformers of music," according to Henry Boys *(The Score),* lies in "the intensity and persistence with which his genius seeks answers to its problems in the very bases of music."

Personal Life

A member of the National Institute of Arts and Letters, Stravinsky was awarded its Gold Medal for Music in 1951. On January 11, 1906, he married his cousin, Catherine Nosenkco, and they had four children: Theodore, a painter; Ludmilla; Sviatoslav (Soulima), a well-known pianist and teacher; and Milene. After the death of his first wife in 1939, he married Vera de Bossett Sudekine, a former dancer with the Diaghilev troupe, on March 9, 1940. The composer, who was called "a wiry, intense man," stood about five feet four inches tall and had light brown hair. Descriptions of his personality emphasize his energy and vitality, his sharp wit, and his "love for order and method." His faith was the Russian Orthodox. Robert Craft noted that Stravinsky prayed daily, before and after composing. He always composed at the piano, slowly, in what has been called "a day-to-day exploratory manner." "My only system," he remarked, "is my ear. I use no other guide."

In 1969 Stravinsky moved from Hollywood to New York, where he lived until his death on April 6, 1971 of a heart attack. He continued composing until shortly before his death. In 1982 the U.S. Postal Service honored him with a stamp in the Great Americans series, and in 1987 he was posthumously awarded a Grammy Award for Lifetime Achievement.

Further Reading

Atlan 184:21-7 N '49
Life 34:151 Mr 23 '53
N Y Times Mag p20 Je 15 '52 por
New Yorker 10:23-8 Ja 5 '35
Tempo No. 8 Summer '48
Time 52:46-51 Jl 26 '48 pors
Armitage, M. ed. *Igor Strawinsky* 0936)
Baker, T. ed. *Biographical Dictionary of Musicians* (1940)
Collaer, P. *Strawinsky* (1930)
Corle, E. ed. *Igor Stravinsky* (1949)
Dictionnaire Biographique Frangais Contemporain (1950)
Fleischer, H. *Strawinsky* (1931)
International Who's Who in Music (1951)
Lederman, M. ed. *Stravinsky in the Theatre* (1949)
Myers, R. H. *Introduction to the Music of Stravinsky* (1950)
Onnen, F. *Stravinsky* (1949)
Ramuz, C. F. *Souvenirs sur Igor Strawinsky* (1929)
Reis, C. *Composers in America* (1947)
Schaeffner, A. *Stravinsky* (1931)
Stravinsky, I. *An Autobiography* (1936); *Poetics of Music* (1947)
Tansman, A. *Igor Stravinsky* (1949)
Thompson, O. ed. *International Cyclopedia of Music and Musicians* (1946)
Who's Who (1952)
Who's Who in America, 1952-53
White, E. W. *Stravinsky's Sacrifice to Apollo* (1930); *Stravinsky* (1948)

Barbra Streisand

Singer, actress

Born: April 24, 1942
Primary Field: Broadway music
Group Affiliation: Solo performer

Introduction

"Everybody knew that Barbra Streisand would be a star, and so she is," wrote the New York Herald Tribune theater critic Walter Kerr in his opening-night report on the musical comedy Funny Girl. *He then devoted most of his review to the spectacular talents as singer, comedienne, and stage personality of the twenty-one-year old newcomer who, in her second Broadway appearance and first starring role, dazzled both critics and audiences.* Funny Girl *opened on March 26, 1964. In it, Barbra Streisand, in the part of Fanny Brice, fulfilled her promise as what Look called "the most-talked-about, sought-after performer in many, many years."*

When Barbra Streisand was asked for some biographical information to be included in the Playbill *for* I Can Get It For You Wholesale, *in which she played her first part on Broadway, she wrote: "Born in Madagascar, reared in Rangoon. . . and is not a member of the Actors' Studio." The theater program was printed accordingly, but no one was fooled by the romantic background that the young Broadway debutante gave herself.*

Early Life

Barbara Joan Streisand was born in Brooklyn, New York on April 24, 1942. Her father, a teacher of English and psychology, died at the age of thirty-four, when she was just fifteen months old. With a brother and sister, she was raised by her mother, who observed the Jewish dietary laws—thus making it difficult for her to indulge her passion for Chinese food—in the Williamsburg section of Brooklyn. "We weren't *poor* poor," she recalls, "but we didn't have anything."

By the time she was four, she had decided she would be an actress. When she was fourteen she announced to her family that she would spend the summer vacation working at the summer theater in Malden, New York. She spent hours going to the movies, watching TV, and devouring fan magazines during her years at Erasmus Hall High School. She graduated in 1959 with a 93 average and a medal in Spanish. By her own admission, she was an unhappy and unpopular student who never took part in school activities, and she wasted no time leaving home in Brooklyn, determined to become a star. At school she had refused her mother's pleas to study typing and stenography "just in case." As she explained to Arnold Abrams of *Newsday* (March 21, 1964), "I knew I had talent and I was afraid that if I learned to type I would become a secretary."

Life's Work

Never a conformist, Miss Streisand refused to make the rounds of Broadway producers. She also rejected the advice to change her name from Streisand to something that might look better on a theater marquee. Instead, she dropped an "a" from Barbara and began calling herself Barbra. She studied acting briefly with Allan Miller and Eli Rill, scrounged free lodging and meals from friends, and worked as a switchboard operator and as an usher in theaters. Her fortunes changed when she won a talent contest at a Greenwich Village bar as a singer, although she had never sung before. This led to an engagement at the bar and an audition at the Bon Soir, another Village club, which paid her $108 a week. (Three years later her fee for a one-night stand was $8,000.)

Barbra Streisand's engagement at the Bon Soir, where she introduced her version of "Who's Afraid of the Big Bad Wolf?" lasted eleven weeks. Then a number of television appearances in New York served to circulate more widely her reputation as "a character" and as a performer. On the Mike Wallace show *PM East,* a late-night TV program, she launched a tirade against milk that earned her near notoriety. Her first New York stage appearance was in the off-Broadway production *Another Evening With Harry Stoones,* in which she sang two songs to enthusiastic audience acclaim. The show lived up to its title, however, and ran only one evening, the night of October 21, 1961. That one performance was enough to win Barbra Streisand an engagement at the Blue Angel, a showcase for young talent on the verge of stardom. There Broadway producer David Merrick saw her and at once signed her for the role of Miss Marmelstein, the unnoticed and unloved secretary in the Broadway musical comedy version of Jerome Weidman's *I Can Get It For You Wholesale.* The show opened at the Shubert Theater on March 22,

1962 and was applauded by several critics especially as the occasion of the Broadway debut of a brilliant comedienne. Some theater commentators credited Barbra Streisand's performance with the fact that *Wholesale*, which itself received only mixed reviews, ran as long as nine months.

When the play closed in December 1962, Miss Streisand was besieged with offers from nightclubs, record companies, TV shows, and Broadway producers. She quickly became a national sensation. The late President John F. Kennedy saw her in a guest shot on the Dinah Shore television show and had her invited to entertain at the White House Correspondents' Dinner in May 1963. She appeared also on the Garry Moore, Jack Paar, Bob Hope, and Ed Sullivan TV shows, winning rave reviews from critics and acquiring a growing body of fans, particularly for her singing of a mournful "Happy Days Are Here Again," a gentle "Who Will Buy?," and a throbbing "Cry Me a River."

The Broadway premiere of *Funny Girl* was originally scheduled for February 13, 1964, but script and other trouble caused a number of delays. When the musical finally opened at the Winter Garden on March 26, 1964, after several postponed opening dates, there had been so many changes of director, producer, music, lyric, and book that little remained of the original production except Miss Streisand and the $900, 000 advance sale, for which she was largely responsible.

Barbra Streisand's concept of the role of Fanny Brice was typically original. She decided not to copy the style or mannerisms of the late great star of Broadway and radio but rather to approach the part as if she were portraying a fictional rather than a real person. "I've never heard her or seen her," she told John Keating of the *New York Times* (March 22, 1964). "When the show closes, that's when I'll listen to all her old records and radio tapes and see any movies she was in. But in the show, I approach the character as though she were not an actual person. I don't try to do an imitation of Fanny Brice; that would be like a nightclub act."

The New York critics generally approved of the way she handled the part. Norman Nadel wrote in the New York *World Telegram and Sun* (March 27, 1964), "For reasons of her own, Miss Streisand prefers to create a 1918 Barbra Streisand, and the justification is that she does it superbly. This young woman is a joy on any stage. A spontaneous comedienne, a big-voiced, belting singer and a brass gong of personality, she sets an audience tingling, time and time again," Capitol Records released the *Funny Girl* album in the spring of 1964.

Furious bidding by NBC and CBS for exclusive rights to Miss Streisand's television appearances ended on June 22, 1964, when she signed a ten-year CBS contract guaranteeing her artistic control over her programs and $100,000 to $300,000 a year. One special was planned for her during the 1964-65 season, and a series was projected for development in future seasons.

As fascinating to interviewers as Barbra Streisand's independence of mind and spirit is her appearance, which has evoked a wide range of comments, none of which included the words "pretty" or "attractive." In a *Coronet* article "as told to Dixie Dean Harris," Barbra Streisand described herself as an "ugly duckling." Norton Mockridge, after watching her in a nightclub engagement in New York's Basin Street East, wrote in his column for the New York *World-Telegram and Sun* (May 24, 1963): "Barbra Streisand is just about the darndest looking female I ever saw. Had she asked me, I surely would have told her to forget the theatre forever. She's ungainly, she has scrawny legs, angular arms, a flat facade, and a face that sometimes looks as though it came right out of *Mad Magazine*. Her eyes perpetually seem to be peering at each other, her nose proportionately shames Durante's, her gaping mouth slurs and twists and contorts when she sings and her hair is a squirrel's nest. . . I never dreamed she had the great, soaring, spectacular voice she reveals at Basin St. East. Listening to her is a glorious experience. Barbra Streisand is proof that beauty comes from within—and I'm mighty glad she proved me wrong."

Beginning with *My Name Is Barbra,* her early albums were often medley-filled keepsakes of her television specials. Starting in 1969, she began attempting more contemporary material, but like many talented singers of the day, she found herself out of her element with rock. Her vocal talents prevailed, and she gained newfound success with the pop and ballad-oriented Richard Perry-produced album Stoney End in 1971. The title track, written by Laura Nyro, was a major hit for Streisand.

During the 1970s, she was also highly prominent on the pop charts, with Top 10 recordings such as "The Way We Were" (US No. 1), "Evergreen (Love Theme from A Star Is Born)" (US No. 1), "No More Tears (Enough Is Enough)" (1979, with Donna Summer), which as of 2010 is reportedly still the most commercially successful duet, (US No. 1), "You Don't Bring Me Flowers" (with Neil Diamond) (US No. 1) and

"The Main Event" (US No. 3), some of which came from soundtrack recordings of her films. As the 1970s ended, Streisand was named the most successful female singer in the U.S.—only Elvis Presley and The Beatles had sold more albums. In 1980, she released her best-selling effort to date, the Barry Gibb-produced *Guilty*. The album contained the hits "Woman in Love" (which spent several weeks on top of the pop charts in the fall of 1980), "Guilty," and "What Kind of Fool."

After years of largely ignoring Broadway and traditional pop music in favor of more contemporary material, Streisand returned to her musical-theatre roots with 1985's *The Broadway Album,* which was unexpectedly successful, holding the No. 1 *Billboard* position for three straight weeks, and being certified quadruple platinum. The album featured tunes by Rodgers and Hammerstein, George Gershwin, Jerome Kern, and Stephen Sondheim, who was persuaded to rework some of his songs especially for this recording. *The Broadway Album* was met with acclaim, including a Grammy nomination for album of the year and, ultimately, handed Streisand her eighth Grammy as Best Female Vocalist.

At the beginning of the 1990s, Streisand started focusing on her film directorial efforts and became almost inactive in the recording studio. In 1991, a four-disc box set, *Just for the Record,* was released. A compilation spanning Streisand's entire career to date, it featured over 70 tracks of live performances, greatest hits, rarities and previously unreleased material.

Streisand finally returned to the recording studio and released *Back to Broadway* in June 1993. The album was not as universally lauded as its predecessor, but it did debut at No. 1 on the pop charts (a rare feat for an artist of Streisand's age, especially given that it relegated Janet Jackson's *Janet* to the No. 2 spot). One of the album's highlights was a medley of "I Have A Love" / "One Hand, One Heart," a duet with Johnny Mathis, who Streisand said is one of her favorite singers.

In 1993, *New York Times* music critic Stephen Holden wrote that Streisand "enjoys a cultural status that only one other American entertainer, Frank Sinatra, has achieved in the last half century." In September 1993, Streisand announced her first public concert appearances in 27 years (if one does not count her Las Vegas nightclub performances between 1969 and 1972). What began as a two-night New Year's event at the MGM Grand Las Vegas eventually led to a multi-city tour in the summer of 1994. Tickets for the tour were sold out in under one hour. Streisand also appeared on the covers of major magazines in anticipation of what *Time* magazine named "The Music Event of the Century." The tour was one of the biggest all-media merchandise parlays in history. Ticket prices ranged from US$50 to US$1,500, making Streisand the highest-paid concert performer in history. *Barbra Streisand: The Concert* went on to be the top-grossing concert of the year and earned five Emmy Awards and the Peabody Award, while the taped broadcast on HBO is, to date, the highest-rated concert special in HBO's 30-year history. Following the tour's conclusion, Streisand once again kept a low profile musically, instead focusing her efforts on acting and directing duties as well as a burgeoning romance with actor James Brolin.

Affiliation: Solo Performer

Miss Streisand won more laurels as a cabaret performer. When she opened at Hollywood's Coconut Grove in August 1963, columnist Sidney Skolsky wrote, "Barbra Streisand is the most uninhibited performer I've ever watched. . . She's the most fascinating young female singer to come along since Judy Garland first sang 'Over the Rainbow.'" Other critics, while emphasizing her uniqueness, have compared her with Edith Piaf, Helen Morgan, Lena Horne, and Ethel Merman in the impact she has on an audience and the star quality she radiates.

On records, Barbra has scored an equally extraordinary success. The *Barbra Streisand Album,* which she made for Columbia, immediately became the country's top-selling album by a female singer on its release in March 1963. To prove it was no fluke, she made another, entitled *The Second Barbra Streisand Album,* which John S. Wilson of the *New York Times* (October 20, 1963) called "a remarkable set of performances." He expressed awe at Miss Streisand's "fascinating imaginative way of developing a song" and went on to say: "She has considerable vocal range and such control that she can move quite readily from rough throatiness to a flawlessly pure tone in a single breath. An even more important element, however, is her complete involvement in each song, which enables her to give the song a positive interpretation that in most instances is decidedly original and brilliantly effective." Columbia released *The Third Barbra Streisand Album* early in 1964.

In 1996, Streisand released "I Finally Found Someone" as a duet with Canadian singer and songwriter Bryan Adams. The song was nominated for an Oscar as it was part of the soundtrack of Streisand's self-directed movie *The Mirror Has Two Faces.* It reached #8 on the *Billboard* Hot 100, and was her first significant hit in almost a decade and her first top 10 hit on the Hot 100 (and first gold single) since 1981.

In 1997, she finally returned to the recording studio, releasing *Higher Ground,* a collection of songs of a loosely inspirational nature which also featured a duet with Céline Dion. The album received generally favorable reviews and, remarkably, once again debuted at No. 1 on the pop charts. Following her marriage to Brolin in 1998, Streisand recorded an album of love songs entitled *A Love Like Ours* the following year. Reviews were mixed, with many critics complaining about the somewhat syrupy sentiments and overly-lush arrangements; however, it did produce a modest hit for Streisand in the country-tinged "If You Ever Leave Me," a duet with Vince Gill.

On New Year's Eve 1999, Streisand returned to the concert stage, selling out in the first few hours, eight months before her return. At the end of the millennium, she was the number one female singer in the U.S., with at least two No. 1 albums in each decade since she began performing. A two-disc live album of the concert entitled *Timeless: Live in Concert* was released in 2000. Streisand performed versions of the Timeless concert in Sydney and Melbourne, Australia, in early 2000. In advance of four concerts (two each in Los Angeles and New York) in September 2000, Streisand announced that she was retiring from playing public concerts. Her performance of the song "People" was broadcast on the Internet via America Online.

Streisand's most recent albums have been *Christmas Memories* (2001), a somewhat somber collection of holiday songs and *The Movie Album* (2003), featuring famous film themes and backed by a large symphony orchestra. *Guilty Pleasures* (called *Guilty Too* in the UK), a collaboration with Barry Gibb and a sequel to their *Guilty*, was released worldwide in 2005.

In February 2006, Streisand recorded the song "Smile" alongside Tony Bennett at Streisand's Malibu home. The song is included on Bennett's 80th birthday album, *Duets*. In September 2006, the pair filmed a live performance of the song for a special directed by Rob Marshall entitled *Tony Bennett: An American Classic.* The special aired on NBC November 21, 2006, and was released on DVD the same day. Streisand's duet with Bennett opened the special.

Streisand's 20-concert tour in 2006 set box-office records. At the age of 64, well past the prime of most performers, she grossed $92,457,062 and set house gross records in 14 of the 16 arenas played on the tour. She set the third-place record for her October 9, 2006 show at Madison Square Garden, the first- and second-place records of which are held by her two shows in September 2000. She set the second-place record at the MGM Grand Garden Arena, with her December 31, 1999 show being the house record and the highest-grossing concert of all time. This led many people to openly criticize Streisand for price gouging, as many tickets sold for upwards of $1,000. A collection of performances culled from different stops on this tour, *Live in Concert 2006,* debuted at No. 7 on the *Billboard* 200, making it Streisand's 29th Top 10 album.

In February 2008, *Forbes* listed Streisand as the No.-2-earning female musician, between June 2006 and June 2007, with earnings of about $60 million. On November 17, 2008, Streisand returned to the studio to begin recording what would be her sixty-third album and it was announced that Diana Krall was producing the album. Streisand is one of the recipients of the 2008 Kennedy Center Honors. On December 7, 2008, she visited the White House as part of the ceremonies.

On September 29, 2009, Streisand and Columbia Records released her newest studio album, *Love Is the Answer,* produced by Diana Krall. On October 2, 2009, Streisand made her British television performance debut with an interview on *Friday Night with Jonathan Ross* to promote the album. This album debuted at No. 1 on the *Billboard* 200 and registered her biggest weekly sales since 1997, making Streisand the only artist in history to achieve No. 1 albums in five different decades.

In September 2014, she released *Partners*, a new album of duets that features collaborations with Elvis Presley, Andrea Bocelli, Stevie Wonder, Lionel Richie, Billy Joel, Babyface, Michael Bublé, Josh Groban, John Mayer, John Legend, Blake Shelton and Jason Gould. This album topped the *Billboard* 200 with sales of 196,000 copies in the first week, making Streisand the only recording artist to have a number-one album in each of the last six decades. It was also certified gold in November 2014 and platinum in January 2015, thus becoming Streisand's 52nd gold and 31st Platinum album, more than any other female artist in history.

The RIAA and *Billboard* recognize Streisand as holding the record for the most top-ten albums of any female recording artist: a total of 33 since 1963. According to Billboard, Streisand holds the record for the female with the most number one albums. *Billboard* also recognizes Streisand as the greatest female of all time on its Billboard 200 chart and one of the greatest artists of all time on its Hot 100 chart. Streisand has 53 Gold albums, 31 Platinum albums, and 14 Multi-Platinum albums in the United States. In 2000, President Bill Clinton presented Streisand with the National Medal of Arts, the highest honor specifically given for achievement in the arts.

PERSONAL LIFE

Success and an income currently higher than $500,000 have not disconcerted Barbra Streisand. She lives in a luxurious duplex penthouse in Manhattan with her husband, Elliot Gould, whom she met in *I Can Get It For You Wholesale,* in which he was the leading man. They were married in March 1963. One of her few concessions to success is that her hair, which she wore in stringy beatnik style when she sang in Greenwich Village, is now done by a leading New York hairdresser. The color of her hair is reddish-brown, and her eyes are blue. She continues to be "clothes crazy," according to Eugenia Sheppard of the New York *Herald Tribune*, and has a vast collection of clothes acquired in second-hand thrift shops. She is especially attracted to the styles of the late 1920's and 1930's. She is a hearty eater, and her weight ranges from 110 to 125 pounds; she is five feet five inches tall. "If success changes me at all, I think maybe it will make me a little nicer—because I've been accepted," she told an interviewer for *Parade*.

Among Miss Streisand's admirers are composers Jule Styne, Johnny Mercer, and Harold Arlen. Styne, who has called her "one of the greatest singers of our time," described her talent this way: "Barbra is the first girl I have ever heard who is a great actress in each song. Barbra makes each song sound, like a well-written three- act play performed stunningly in three minutes. Although the same Barbra Streisand, she takes on an exciting new characterization for each song."

Perhaps the most penetrating evaluation of Barbra Streisand as a show-business phenomenon was made by Emory Lewis, editor of *Cue* magazine, in announcing on December 28, 1963 that she had won the magazine's "Entertainer of the Year" award. "Streisand is an original," he wrote, "and originals are rare in our industrial, homogenized society."

Streisand has been married twice. Her first husband was actor Elliott Gould, to whom she was married from 1963 until 1971. They had one child, Jason Gould, who appeared as her on-screen son in *The Prince of Tides.* Her second husband is actor James Brolin, whom she married on July 1, 1998.

FURTHER READING

Coronet 3:13+ Mr '64 por
N Y *Post* p37 S 13 '63 por
Newsday W p29 Mr 21 '64 por
Parade p14 S 8 '63 por
Sat Eve *Post* 236:22+ Jl 27 '63 pors
Time 83:62+ Ap 10 '64 pors
Andersen, Christopher. *Barbra: The Way She Is* (2006)

STROKES

Music group

Julian Casablancas
Singer; songwriter
Born: Aug. 23, 1978; New York City

Nikolai Fraiture
Bassist
Born: Nov. 13, 1978; Rio de Janeiro, Brazil

Albert Hammond, Jr.
Guitarist
Born: Apr. 9, 1979; Los Angeles, California

Fabrizio Moretti
Drummer
Born: June 2, 1980-

Nick Valensi
Guitarist
Born: Jan. 16, 1981; New York City

Primary Field: New Wave
Group Affiliation: Strokes

INTRODUCTION

Released in October 2001, the Strokes' debut album, Is This It, *went far toward changing the face of mainstream rock music, ushering in a new sound and a wave of garage bands heavily inspired by late-1970s underground rock. "On Jan. 1, 2001 rap-metal was in its death throes and angst-metal in its unfortunate life throes," Mark Lepage wrote for the* Toronto *(Canada)* Star *(October 12, 2003), describing the setting from which the Strokes emerged. "There was Eminem, Britney [Spears] and Jay-Z, Creed, Kid Rock and Matchbox 20. Into this came the dirty Converse sneakers and artfully trashed jackets of a crew of thrift-shop mods. The sound was a lean shot of contradictions: slacker-passionate, retro-neo, vocal lines descended from Italian crooners, a lean white-kid beat taken from the skinny-tie bands. The attack was indie, but the melodic sense classicist and irresistibly rock 'n' roll." "Fans and detractors alike heard and saw [the Strokes] as part of a movement; retro-rock was exploding, and this tidy, brilliant band seemed like the fuse," Kelefa Sanneh wrote for the* New York Times *(March 3, 2006).*

EARLY LIVES

The Strokes' vocalist, Julian Casablancas, was born on August 23, 1978 in New York City, to John Casablancas, the founder of the Elite modeling agency, and Jeanette Christjansen, the winner of the 1965 Miss Denmark title. After his parents divorced, when Casablancas was a child, he lived with his mother, who remarried. He has credited his stepfather, Sam Adoquei, a painter from Ghana, with beginning his education in music. "Every night he'd talk to me about artists and what made great artists great," Casablancas told lain Shedden. "He was the best teacher I ever had. Then I'd just go play guitar for hours and think I sucked and I had to get better." Casablancas, according to Ted Kessler in the London *Observer* (December 16, 2001), was "a disruptive, unruly presence" in school. When he was in his teens, his father enrolled him at the Institute Le Rasey, an international, bilingual boarding school in Switzerland. During his six months there, his stepfather sent him a tape of songs by the rock group the Doors. After listening to it repeatedly, he told Kessler, "it all fell into place. Sounds kind of corny, I realise, but I knew then how music was built." Also while at the school, Casablancas befriended Albert Hammond Jr., the school's only other American student, who was born on April 9, 1979 in Los Angeles, California. Hammond's father, Albert Hammond Sr., is a singer and songwriter; he is the co-writer of "It Never Rains in Southern California" and "To All the Girls I've Loved Before," the latter of which became a hit for Willie Nelson and Julio Iglesias, singing as a duo, and for several other performers. After Casablancas returned to New York, he and Hammond lost touch. Casablancas then entered the Dwight School, a private high school on New York's Upper West Side, where he met Nick Valensi (born on January 16, 1981 in New York City) and Fabrizio Moretti (born on June 2, 1980 in Rio de Janeiro, Brazil). The three of them, along with Nikolai Fraiture (born on November 13, 1978 in New York City), a friend of Casablancas's since kindergarten, formed a rock band. Shortly afterward, by chance, Casablancas was reunited with Hammond, who was studying filmmaking at New York University. Hammond soon joined the group, and the quintet christened themselves the Strokes. The band rented a small rehearsal studio, where they practiced for several years, often becoming frustrated with their slow progress. "We didn't know what we were doing," Casablancas told John Robinson for the London *Guardian* (June 28, 2001). "It sounded so bad, I remember us talking about what we wanted to do with it, and it was like, 'Throw it in the garbage.'" "We were searching for a sound for a long time and didn't know what it would end up being," Casablancas recalled to Richard Harrington for the *Washington Post* (October 26, 2001). "Anytime I would hear a song or a band, I would try to understand what their weak points were, as well as what their strong points were, and then absorb as much as I could and learn from their mistakes." Eager to learn more about music composition, Casablancas began taking classes at Five Towns College, in Dix Hills, on Long Island, New York, whose specialties include music and the performing arts. "I don't really believe that if you study the rules, it makes you uncreative," he told Harrington. "I think a lot of people study the rules too much and then don't know how to be creative. I just want us to learn the basic rules to help me figure out other songs and make me know more what I'm doing."

Lives' Work

When the Strokes gained confidence in the quality of their music, they started to perform at local clubs. At one of them, the Mercury Lounge, on Manhattan's Lower East Side, they caught the attention of Ryan Gentles, the club's booking agent. Gentles quit his job and became the band's manager, and, using his industry connections, he got the Strokes work as the opening act for such established bands as Guided by Voices and the Doves. Gentles played the group's three-song demo for Geoff Travis, the founder of Rough Trade Records, who quickly signed the group to his label. "After about 15 seconds, I agreed to release it," Travis told Ted Kessler. "What I heard in The Strokes were the song-writing skills of a first-class writer and music that is a distillation of primal rock 'n' roll mixed with the sophistication of today's society. The primitive in the sophisticated, to paraphrase [the filmmaker] Jean Renoir. It also has an unmacho quality that embodies grace and love, and it touches me."

Soon afterward, the members of the Strokes—who at the time were either students or workers in non-music-related jobs—embarked on a concert tour of England. "That's when our lives changed," as Casablancas told Neala Johnson for the Melbourne, Australia, *Herald Sun* (July 12, 2001). In addition to receiving rave reviews, the Strokes found themselves deluged by publicity and the focus of exaggerated claims made by writers for the British music press. "It never seemed like we had articles just saying we were a great band and people should check us out; from the get-go, it was 'This band is soooo hyped,'" as Casablancas told Sharon O'Connell for *Time* Out (August 29, 2001). "There was never any actual hype, there was just talk about the hype!" "We are not here to save rock 'n' roll! ... ," Casablancas also said to O'Connell. "We're not going to change your life, and the way everyone is idealising our arrival on the scene is ridiculous. Look, the bottom line is the music. That's it. Simple." The fever surrounding the Strokes in England soon spread to the United States, where the band's debut album, *Is This It,* was released in the fall of 2001 with great fanfare. "The Strokes are a body shot to popular music," Vaughn Watson wrote for the *Providence (Rhode Island) Journal-Bulletin* (September 27, 2001). "They make thoughtful and irreverent pop. Nearly every song on *Is This It* has a memorable hook, and the band unashamedly has a blast with all of it."

The hype surrounding the Strokes sparked a negative backlash from fans and critics who had wearied of hearing about the group. "That the Strokes are getting media attention should not, on its face, be the reason to love or hate the band," Jennifer Maerz wrote for *Salon.com* (November 28, 2001). "But even music purists have a tough time closing their eyes to hype, and the Strokes themselves are not blameless in creating an image for themselves. Singer Julian Casablancas is not only a noncommittal, take 'em or leave 'em slacker in his lyrics, he also plays at being combative during the band's live act." "Casablancas half-sang, half-sneered his way through *Is This It,* as if he could hardly be bothered to talk to you, wouldn't even deign to look at you," Laura Barton later wrote for the London Guardian (November 25, 2005). "They sounded so cool, they looked so cool, they were so very, very cool." The Strokes also inspired a wave of similarly minded groups. Craig McLean wrote for the London *Daily Telegraph* (January 12, 2006), "Without the Strokes' model of a groovy gang playing snappy guitar music, Franz Ferdinand, Kaiser Chiefs and Arctic Monkeys wouldn't exist."

The Strokes' sophomore effort, *Room on Fire* (2003), struck most reviewers as "a pretty straightforward re-run of their all-conquering, if strangely flimsy, debut *Is This It,*" as Ben Thompson wrote for the

Affiliation: Band Comparisons

Hailing from New York City, the Strokes have often been compared to groups associated with the Manhattan underground of earlier decades, among them the Velvet Underground (the band in which the rocker Lou Reed got his start), Television, and the Talking Heads. Writing for the London *Guardian* (February 6, 2001), Betty Clarke characterized the Strokes' music as "Chuck Berry to a Velvet Underground backing track, a simple and blistering formula that finishes abruptly after all of three minutes." The Strokes' guitarist Nick Valensi told Jay Mcinerney for *New York* (January 16, 2006), "The reason people liked the first record, maybe, was because it was kind of New Wave, kind of retro, and no one was doing that music then—the Ramones, Talking Heads, Blondie, the Cars. That music never went out of style, but no one was playing it. We were filling some kind of void in music."

The members of the Strokes—the lead singer, Julian Casablancas; the bassist, Nikolai Fraiture; Nick Valensi and his fellow guitarist Albert Hammond Jr.; and the drummer Fabrizio Moretti—became celebrities almost immediately after *Is This It* reached stores, with the media focusing as much on their personal styles and love lives as on their music. "The Strokes were so hip it hurt," Craig MacLean wrote for the London *Independent* (November 26, 2005), describing the band's arrival on the music scene as having been "a fashion moment rather than a proper rock event." In the *Weekend Australian* (August 25, 2001), Iain Shedden, writing shortly before the release of the group's debut album in the U.S., expressed the view that the Strokes were "arguably the most exciting band to come out of the US since Nirvana. They may not be as innovative or, in time, influential, but they have that special intangible something that makes you want to bounce off the walls when you hear them, just as the Velvets sometimes do." Wary of collapsing under the weight of the hype surrounding *Is This It,* the Strokes quickly produced a follow-up album, *Room on Fire* (2003), which was widely panned for resembling its predecessor too closely. By contrast, their next recording, *First Impressions of Earth* (2006), elicited favorable reviews.

London *Observer* (September 21, 2003). "There are the same number of songs (11), the same producer ... the same short, sharp songs of vaguely personalized alienation and breezy emotional underkill. In fact, clocking in at a terse 33 minutes, *Room on Fire* manages to be a full three minutes pithier than its famously compact predecessor." "The Strokes ... have been hailed as potential saviors (rather than imitators) of rock 'n' roll," Craig Semon wrote for the *Sunday Telegram* (November 2, 2003), a central Massachusetts newspaper. "Don't believe it. The so-called stroke of genius of a bunch of twentysomethings delving deep into the legacy of the NYC underground sounds somewhat generic and less exuberant on the second go-around. With lyrics and licks sounding virtually interchangeable from song to song, there is little that leaves a lasting impression here." "We felt we needed more material out there just to catch up with the attention we had been getting," Nick Valensi later told Neala Johnson for the *Herald* Sun (December 20, 2005). "But *[Room on Fire*] suffered from that. When I listen to that record now, I feel that if I'd had more time to really think about the songs and the guitar parts, and if the band had had more time to focus on the production, it would have been a lot more interesting. And that's a shame." The group's live performances at the time, however, were well-received. "Casablancas and his bandmates proceeded to destroy any lingering skepticism about their garage-rock credibility," Christopher Blagg wrote for the *Boston Herald* (May 17, 2004), after attending a Strokes concert. "Their balance of punk attitude and melodic hook-drenched songwriting was evident with the slamming guitar crunch of 'Trying My Luck' and the sneering barbs of 'The Way It Is.'"

After touring to promote *Room on Fire*, the Strokes disappeared briefly from the public spotlight, concentrating instead on their personal lives. In February 2005 Casablancas married Juliet Joslin, the Strokes' assistant manager; in that or the previous year (sources do not agree), Nikolai Fraiture had fathered a child with his wife, Ilona. In 2006 the band released a third album, First *Impressions of Earth,* a collection of songs that was seen as a departure from their previous material. "Musically, their characteristic leanness has filled out a little, the sound is less immediate, more labyrinthine, less recognizably Strokesian," Laura Barton wrote. "It is perhaps more of a cerebral album, after the vigorous physicality of *Is This It* and *Room on Fire*, and, as a result, it hits your brain before your belly." "There's some kind of distance from the past records," Casablancas told Steve Hochman for the *Los Angeles Times*

(January 1, 2006). "We don't want to do the same thing. The second record musically was different, but the production was the same and people swept the music under the rug." Jay McInerney wrote, "By almost any measure," First *Impressions of Earth* is "their best album. The propulsive rhythmic energy and the instant melodic appeal of the best songs provide a taut counter- point to the wounded sneer of Casablancas's lyrics, which are as disillusioned, doomy, and sarcastic as ever."

On their tour in support of *First Impressions of Earth,* the Strokes earned favorable reviews. Ryan White wrote for the *Oregonian* (April 4, 2006), "Casablancas has rediscovered his performer's mojo in a serious way.... Much like on their new record, the Strokes seemed focused on where they want to go, not where they've been." The Strokes' tour ended in October 2006. That month Albert Hammond released his first solo album, *Yours to Keep.* In September 2007 he reported on MySpace.com that he planned to release another solo disk. He and the other members of the Strokes also planned to record their fourth album in 2008.

Further Reading

Chicago Tribune C p3 Oct. 17, 2003
(London) *Guardian* p16 Feb. 6, 2001
(Melbourne, Australia) *Herald Sun* p40 July 12, 2001
New York p16+ Jan. 16, 2006
Time Out p19 Aug. 29, 2001

Taylor Swift

Singer

Born: December 13, 1989; Wyomissing, Pennsylvania
Primary Field: Country and pop music
Group Affiliation: Solo artist

Introduction

The singer Taylor Swift "is one of pop's finest songwriters, country's foremost pragmatist and more in touch with her inner life than most adults," Jon Caramanica wrote for the New York Times *(December 21, 2008). Since she made her recording debut, in 2006, the 21-year-old Swift—who writes or co-writes nearly all of her own material—has not only sold more than 13 million albums; she has also seen more than 25 million paid Internet downloads of her songs, more than any other country-music artist to date.*

Early Life

The daughter of Andrea and Scott Swift, Taylor Alison Swift was born on December 13, 1989 in Wyomissing, Pennsylvania. She has a brother, Austin, who is three years her junior. Swift's mother, who was a successful career woman before she began raising a family, chose the name "Taylor" to hide her daughter's gender—and avoid discrimination—from the girl's future prospective employers. Swift spent her early years on a Christmas-tree farm, which her father, who worked as a stockbroker, ran as a hobby. She was introduced to music by her grandmother Marjorie Finlay, who was an opera singer.

Taylor Swift.

After being exposed to a wide variety of musical genres, she felt particularly drawn to country music. "LeAnn

Rimes was my first impression of country music," Swift recalled to Amy Raphael. "I got her first album when I was six. I just really loved how she could be making music and having a career at such a young age." Early on Swift also developed a love of writing and started composing poetry. In the fourth grade she won a national poetry contest for a three-page poem titled "Monster in My Closet." Her mother noted to J. Freedom du Lac for the *Washington Post* (February 28, 2008), "She wrote all the time. If music hadn't worked out, I think she'd be going off to college to take journalism classes or trying to become a novelist. But her writing took an interesting twist when she picked up the guitar and applied her writing to music."

At the age of 10, Swift began performing at county fairs, festivals, and karaoke contests around her hometown. At 11 she gave her first major public performance, singing the national anthem at a Philadelphia 76ers basketball game. At 12 she learned to play the 12-string guitar; it has been noted that she would practice the guitar for hours at a time, until her calluses bled. (Swift now often plays a Swarovski-crystal-encrusted guitar.) She recalled to Bruce DeMara for the *Toronto Star* (January 12, 2008), "As soon as I picked up a guitar and learned three chords, I started writing songs. Songwriting just came as another form of expression." While attending Wyomissing Junior High School, Swift found it difficult to fit in with the other girls, which led her to channel her emotions through songwriting. One of her earliest songs, "The Outside," was later included on her debut album.

When Swift was 13 years old, her parents sold their Christmas-tree farm and moved the family to Hendersonville, Tennessee, near Nashville, the nation's unofficial country-music capital; there, Swift was able to focus on her music career. She recalled to Dan DeLuca for the *Philadelphia Inquirer* (November 7, 2007), "I literally walked up and down and knocked on doors and said: 'Hi, I'm Tay1or. I want a record deal.' When you've got nothing to lose, you have everything to gain." After rejecting a deal at RCA that would have prevented her from recording her own songs, she became, at 14, the youngest staff writer ever hired at the Sony Tree publishing house. Swift was home-schooled in the mornings before heading off to Nashville each afternoon for various writing assignments; it was during that time that she honed her songwriting skills.

Life's Work

Swift received her big break while performing at Nashville's famed Bluebird Café. There, she caught the attention of a music-business veteran, Scott Borchetta, who quickly signed her to his newly formed independent label, Big Machine Records. Swift "has a real inner vision, a real inner directedness," Borchetta explained to DeLuca. He added, "I thought: This girl has the potential to be a really big star. Her songs have these extraordinary takes on everyday life. There's a certain slant, a sense of humor and a sarcasm to them." Wanting to be embraced by the country-music audience, Swift appeared in a series of film shorts that aired on the Great American Country (GAC) cable network. She followed those in 2006 with her debut single, "Tim McGraw," named for her favorite male country music star; the song reached number six on the *Billboard* country-singles chart. In October of that year, she released her debut album, *Taylor Swift*, which arrived on the *Billboard* 200 chart at number 19 and sold 39,000 copies in its first week. Albums sales rose dramatically after the release of her second single, "Teardrops on My Guitar," about a secret high-school crush. After reaching the number two spot on the country-singles chart, the song achieved crossover status, peaking at number 13 on the *Billboard* Hot 100 chart. *Taylor Swift* went on to spawn three more Top 10 country singles ("Our Song," "Picture to Burn," and "Should've Said No"). The album reached number one on *Billboard's* top country-albums chart (after 39 weeks) and peaked at number five on the Billboard 200 chart; it has since sold more than 4.3 million copies in the U.S. and has been certified quadruple platinum by the Recording Industry Association of America (RIAA). It is also the longest-charting album by a female country artist in the era of Nielsen SoundScan (a sales-counting system established in 1991), with over 158 weeks logged on the *Billboard* 200 album chart.

Taylor Swift received widespread praise from critics. Nick Cristiano wrote in a review for the *Philadelphia Inquirer* (November 12, 2006), "[Swift] displays a maturity beyond her years while retaining the freshness of youth, just as her slightly husky voice balances between open-hearted innocence and life-scarred experience. There's feistiness to country-rockers 'Picture to Burn' and 'Should've Said No,' but no bubblegum angst or melodrama. Much of the music has a bracing acoustic country texture that reflects the taste and restraint of the singing and writing." Jon Caramanica declared for the *New York Times* (September 7, 2008) that the album is "a small masterpiece of pop-minded country."

Swift spent most of 2007 touring in support of her first album, performing mainly as an opening act for such country stars as George Strait, Brad Paisley, Kenny Chesney, Tim McGraw, and Faith Hill. In May of that year, Swift was nominated for the honor of top new female vocalist by the Academy of Country Music Awards. (She lost to Miranda Lambert.) Later that year she took home the Horizon Award, given by the Country Music Association (CMA), making her the second-youngest CMA winner ever. (The award is given annually to up-and-coming artists; previous winners include Carrie Underwood, the Dixie Chicks, and LeAnn Rimes, who at 15 became the youngest winner.) On October 14, 2007 Swift released a promotional EP, *Sounds of the Season: The Taylor Swift Holiday Collection*, exclusively through the discount-department-store chain Target. Also in 2007 Swift won the songwriter-of-the-year award from the Nashville Songwriters Association.

Swift continued to tour in 2008, with such country acts as Alan Jackson and Rascal Flatts, and made high-profile appearances at a wide variety of events. On February 10, 2008 she appeared at the 50th Annual Grammy Awards ceremony, held at the Staples Center in Los Angeles, California; she received a Grammy nomination in the best-new-artist category but lost to the British crooner Amy Winehouse. Swift next gave a memorable performance at the 43d Annual Academy of Country Music Awards ceremony, which was held at the MGM Grand Garden Arena on May 18, 2008 in Las Vegas, Nevada, where she was named top new vocalist. After beginning her performance of the song "Should've Said No" in an unassuming sweatshirt-and-jeans ensemble, she revealed a short black halter dress underneath, concluding the song under a waterfall. During the summer of 2008, Swift released a CD/DVD set, *Beautiful Eyes*, which featured alternate versions of previously released tracks and was sold exclusively at Wal-Mart. The DVD portion of the set included the music videos of some of her best-known singles (among them "Tim McGraw" and "Teardrops on My Guitar"), as well as various extras. The album debuted at number one on Billboard's top country-albums chart after selling 45,000 copies in its first week. During that same week Swift's debut album held the number-two spot, making her the first artist to hold the top two positions on the country-albums chart since LeAnn Rimes in 1997.

Swift released her much-awaited second album, *Fearless*, on November 11, 2008. The album debuted at number one on the *Billboard* 200 album charts and reportedly sold 592,304 copies in its first week of release. That figure marked the largest opening-week sales in the U.S. that year by a female artist in any musical genre and the fourth highest overall, behind Lil Wayne, AC/DC, and Coldplay. Fearless went on to hold the top spot on the *Billboard* 200 album chart for 11 nonconsecutive weeks, marking the first time in a decade that an album had spent that much time at the top of the charts; it also topped the *Billboard* top country-albums chart for 26 nonconsecutive weeks. The album produced five Top 10 hits ("Change," "Love Story," "Fearless," "You Belong with Me," and "Jump Then Fall") and eight Top 20 hits (including "You're Not Sorry," "White Horse," and "Untouchable"). It also became the first album in music history to produce 12 Top 40 hits. As with her debut, Swift wrote or co-wrote every song on *Fearless*. By the end of that year, she had become the top-selling musical artist of 2008 and the first artist in the history of Nielsen SoundScan to have two albums in the Top 10 on the year-end album chart, with *Fearless* and *Taylor Swift* finishing at number three and six, respectively. *Fearless* has since been certified sextuple-platinum by the RIAA. (On October 26, 2009 the album was re-released as *Fearless: Platinum Edition*, with six new songs.)

Fearless was also a major critical success. Jody Rosen, in a review for *Rolling Stone* (November 13, 2008, on-line), which gave the album four stars, called Swift "a songwriting savant with an intuitive gift for verse-chorus-bridge architecture" and wrote that her music "mixes an almost impersonal professionalism—it's so rigorously crafted it sounds like it has been scientifically engineered in a hit factory—with confessions that are squirmingly intimate and true."

In January 2009 Swift made her first musical guest appearance on *Saturday Night Live*, becoming the youngest country singer to appear on the show since its premiere, in 1975. Her massive popularity helped draw *SNL's* highest ratings since the vice-presidential candidate Sarah Palin's appearance on the show in November 2008. The following month Swift performed her song "Fifteen" with Miley Cyrus at the 51st Annual Grammy Awards ceremony. That April Swift launched her first North American headlining tour. Between the end of April and the beginning of October 2009, Swift performed in the U.S. and Canada at more than 50 concerts, all of which sold out, many in minutes; in November she performed several sold-out dates in England. The *Fearless* tour ran through June 2010 and included a series of concerts in Australia and three dozen additional shows in North America.

In 2009 Swift was showered with awards and accolades. In March she took home album-of-the-year honors for *Fearless*, the award for top female vocalist, and the video-of-the-year award (for "Love Story") at the 44th Annual Academy of Country Music Awards ceremony. She was also presented with the academy's Crystal Milestone Award, which is given for outstanding achievement in country music. (Swift is only the second artist to receive the prestigious award; Garth Brooks won it in 2007.) That summer Swift won two Country Music Television (CMT) Awards (video of the year and female video of the year for "Love Story") and two Teen Choice Awards (best album—*Fearless*—and best female artist). Then, on September 13, 2009, Swift became the first country singer in history to capture an MTV Video Music Award, when she won in the best-female-video category for her song "You Belong with Me." Her history-making win was largely overshadowed, however, by what happened immediately afterward. During Swift's acceptance speech the rapper and producer Kanye West came on stage and grabbed the microphone from her to declare that Beyoncé's video for the song "Single Ladies (Put a Ring on It)," nominated for the same award, should have won. He then handed the microphone back to Swift, who was visibly too shaken to finish her speech. When Beyoncé later won the award for best video of the year for "Single Ladies," she invited Swift back on stage to finish her acceptance speech. West, who was removed from the show for his actions, received thunderous criticism in the media the following day, even drawing a harsh comment from President Barack Obama. Following Swift's appearance on the daytime talk show *The View* two days later to address the matter, West contacted her to apologize personally; she has since forgiven him. On November 7, 2009 Swift returned to *Saturday Night Live*, as both host and musical guest. During her opening monologue, she made light of the Kanye West incident and poked fun at her personal life.

November 2009 brought Swift still more honors: she became the first solo female act in a decade to claim the entertainer-of-the-year award from the Country Music Association, and she picked up five prizes at the 37th Annual American Music Awards (AMA), including those for favorite female pop/rock artist, favorite female country artist, and AMA artist of the year. The following month Swift received eight Grammy nominations, including those for record of the year, song of the year, and album of the year.

On January 31, 2010 Swift performed with the singer Stevie Nicks and the singer-songwriter Butch Walker at the 52nd Annual Grammy Awards ceremony. Her album *Fearless* took home the Grammy for album of the year, making her, at 20 years of age, the youngest artist in history to win that prize. Swift also won Grammys for best country album, best country song ("White Horse," with co-composer Liz Rose), and best female country vocal performance ("White Horse"). The next month Swift made her feature-film acting debut, in Garry Marshall's romantic comedy *Valentine's Day* (2010), whose cast also included Julia Roberts, Ashton Kutcher, Anne Hathaway, Jessica Biel, Jamie Foxx, Kathy Bates, George Lopez, and Shirley MacLaine, among many others. Despite tepid critical reactions, the film was a box-office success, grossing more than $213 million worldwide.

Swift's third studio album, *Speak Now*, arrived in stores on October 25, 2010. Its lead single, "Mine," had been released the previous August; it has since sold over one million copies. Swift sang another, "Innocent," which is reportedly about Kanye West, at the 2010 MTV Music Video Awards ceremony on September 12. She wrote those and the 12 other tracks on *Speak Now*; like those on her first two albums, the songs are autobiographical, each representing a confession to a particular person. "Back to December," "Dear John," and "Better Than Revenge" are aimed at Taylor Lautner (who stars in the *Twilight* films), the singer-songwriter John Mayer, and Joe Jonas of the Jonas Brothers, respectively. Swift planned to tour internationally in support of the album in 2011. Swift carried out an extensive promotional campaign prior to *Speak Now*'s release. She appeared on various talk shows and morning shows, and gave free mini-concerts in unusual locations, including an open-decker bus on Hollywood Boulevard and a departure lounge at John F. Kennedy International Airport. She took part in a "guitar pull" alongside Kris Kristofferson, Emmylou Harris, Vince Gill, and Lionel Richie at LA's Club Nokia. The musicians shared the stage and took turns introducing and playing acoustic versions of their songs to raise money for the Country Music Hall of Fame and Museum. The album's lead single, "Mine," was released in August 2010, and five further singles were released throughout 2010 and 2011: "Back to

December," "Mean," "The Story of Us," "Sparks Fly" and "Ours." *Speak Now* was a commercial success, debuting at number one on the US *Billboard* 200 chart. Its opening sales of 1,047,000 copies made it the 16th album in U.S. history to sell one million copies in a single week. As of September 2011, *Speak Now* had sold over 5 million copies worldwide.

Swift toured throughout 2011 and early 2012 in support of *Speak Now*. As part of the 111-date world tour, Swift played shows in North America, Asia, Europe, Australia and New Zealand. Swift invited many musicians to join her for one-off duets during the North American tour. Appearances were made by Bieber, McGraw, James Taylor, Jason Mraz, Shawn Colvin, Johnny Rzeznik, Andy Grammer, Selena Gomez, Tal Bachman, Nicki Minaj, Nelly, B.o.B, Usher, Flo Rida, T.I., Jon Foreman, Jim Adkins, Hayley Williams, Hot Chelle Rae, Ronnie Dunn, Darius Rucker, and Kenny Chesney. Swift also performed numerous acoustic cover versions during her North American tour. In each city, she paid tribute to a homegrown artist. She said the cover versions allowed her to be "spontaneous" in an otherwise well-rehearsed show. The tour was attended by over 1.6 million fans and grossed over $123 million. Swift's first live album, *Speak Now World Tour: Live*, featuring all 17 performances from the North American leg of the tour, was released in November 2011.

At the 54th Annual Grammy Awards, Swift's song "Mean" won Best Country Song and Best Country Solo Performance. She also performed the song during the ceremony. Swift won various other awards for *Speak Now*. She was named Songwriter/Artist of the Year by the Nashville Songwriters Association in both 2010 and 2011. She was named Entertainer of the Year by the Academy of Country Music in both 2011 and 2012, and was named Entertainer of the Year by the Country Music Association in 2011. Swift was the American Music Awards's Artist of the Year in 2011, while *Speak Now* was named Favorite Country Album. *Billboard* named Swift 2011's Woman of the Year.

Swift's fourth studio album, *Red*, was released on October 22, 2012. She wrote nine of the album's 16 songs alone, while the remaining seven were co-written with various collaborators. Musically, while there

Affiliation: Country Music

Her two studio albums, *Taylor Swift* (2006) and *Fearless* (2008), both cracked the Top 10 of the Billboard 200 album chart, and *Fearless* was the first album in nearly a decade to hold down the number-one spot on that chart for more than two months, making Swift the biggest-selling artist of 2008 in any genre. Her third studio album, *Speak Now*, was released on October 25, 2010. While critics have praised her lyrics and voice—which one writer called "airy," another "light and breathy"—Swift's success has been attributed largely to her use of the Internet, particularly the social-networking site MySpace.com, to attract publicity and build a fan base. Amy Raphael wrote for the London *Observer* (February 1, 2009), "Swift is unlike any country star before her, her mainstream pop aesthetic attracting a devoted young audience in what is traditionally a middle-aged market. . . . The appeal is not just smart pop with country roots; here's a star who doesn't believe in the us-and-them divide between artist and audience. In this, she is following a country music tradition that dictates strong contact with fans. . . . So, despite her success, Swift is still the girl next door; the clean-living role model who is an antidote to Britney [Spears], a tonic in these days of destructive, dramatic pop stars." While remaining grounded in the country tradition, Swift has also incorporated elements of other genres in her music, which has contributed to her mass appeal. Sasha Frere-Jones, writing for the *New Yorker* (November 10, 2008), called Swift a "prodigy," adding, "What is surprising about Swift is her indifference to category or genre. She is considered part of Nashville's country-pop tradition only because she writes narrative songs with melodic clarity and dramatic shape—Nashville's stock-in-trade. But such songs also crop up in R&B and rap and rock. It is evidence of her ear that she not only identifies with songs in other genres but performs them, even though Nashville is a musically conservative place. . . . Swift is not an agent revolution; she, much like Beyoncé, is a preternaturally skilled student of established values. Her precociousness isn't about her chart success, but lies in the quality of her work, how fully she's absorbed the lessons of her elders and how little she seems to care which radio format will eventually claim her. Change the beat and the instruments around the voice, and her songs could work anywhere."

is experimentation with heartland rock, dubstep and dance-pop, it is typical Swiftian fare. As part of the *Red* promotional campaign, representatives from 72 worldwide radio stations were flown to Nashville during release week for individual interviews with She also appeared on many television talk shows and performed at award ceremonies in the U.S., the UK, Germany, France, Spain and Australia.

The album's lead single, "We Are Never Ever Getting Back Together," became Swift's first number one on the US *Billboard* Hot 100 chart. Six further singles were released: "Begin Again," "I Knew You Were Trouble," "22," "Everything Has Changed," "The Last Time" and "Red." "We Are Never Ever Getting Back Together" and "I Knew You Were Trouble" were both commercially successful worldwide. *Red* debuted at number one on the *Billboard* 200 with first-week sales of 1.21 million copies—this marked the highest opening sales in a decade and made Swift the first female to have two million-selling album openings. As of May 2013, *Red* had sold over 6 million copies worldwide. As part of The Red Tour, Swift played 86 dates in North America, New Zealand, Australia, Europe and Asia. She invited special guests such as Carly Simon, Tegan and Sara, Jennifer Lopez, Luke Bryan, Patrick Stump of Fall Out Boy, Ellie Goulding, Nelly, Sara Bareilles, Cher Lloyd, B.o.B, Lightbody, Train, Neon Trees, Flatts, Hunter Hayes, Emeli Sandé, and Sam Smith to duet with her on various nights of the tour. The tour was attended by over 1.7 million fans and grossed over $150 million.

Red did not win any Grammy Awards, but was nominated in a total of four categories. "We Are Never Ever Getting Back Together" was a Record of the Year nominee at the 2013 Grammy Awards, while *Red* was an Album of the Year nominee at the 2014 Grammy Awards. Swift was honored by the Association with a special Pinnacle Award for "unique" levels of success; Garth Brooks is the only other recipient. At the 2012 MTV Europe Music Awards, Swift won the honors for Best Female and Best Live Act. "I Knew You Were Trouble" won Best Female Video at the 2013 MTV Video Music Awards. She was named Best Female Country Artist at the 2012 American Music Awards and was named Artist of the Year at the 2013 ceremony. The Nashville Songwriters Association's Songwriter/Artist Award went to Swift for the fifth and sixth consecutive years in 2012 and 2013.

Swift's fifth studio album, *1989*, was released on October 27, 2014. Swift wrote one song alone, and co-wrote the remaining 12. Musically, it has been described as an album "driven by synths and drums in lieu of guitar." Swift herself described *1989* as her first "official" pop release. The critical response to *1989* was frequently positive. As part of the *1989* promotional campaign, Swift invited fans to secret album-listening sessions, called the "*1989* Secret Sessions," at her houses in New York, Nashville, Los Angeles and Rhode Island. Her "expert" use of various social media platforms was remarked upon by industry analysts. She also appeared on many talk shows, performed at award shows in the U.S. and England, and appeared as a contestant advisor for *The Voice*.

The album's lead single, "Shake It Off," was released in August 2014 and reached number one on the *Billboard* Hot 100. Four further singles have been released; "Blank Space" and "Bad Blood" (featuring Kendrick Lamar) both reached number one in the United States. "Style" and "Wildest Dreams" both peaked in the top ten of the *Billboard* Hot 100. *1989* sold 1,287,000 copies in the U.S. during the first week of release, selling more copies in its opening week than any album in the previous 12 years. This has made Swift the first and only act to have three albums sell more than one million copies in the opening release week. It later became the best-selling album of 2014, selling 3.66 million copies. As of February 2015, *1989* had sold over 8.6 million copies worldwide.

Prior to *1989*'s release, Swift wrote an op-ed for the *Wall Street Journal*, emphasizing the ongoing importance of albums, and, in November 2014, she removed her entire catalog from Spotify, arguing that the streaming company's ad-supported free service undermined the premium service, which provides higher royalties for songwriters. In June 2015, Swift criticized Apple Music in an open letter for not offering royalties to artists during the streaming service's free three-month trial period and stated that she would pull *1989* from the catalog. A day later, Apple announced that they would pay artists during the free trial period and Swift agreed to stream *1989* on the streaming service.

Swift was named *Billboard's* Woman of Year in 2014, becoming the first artist to be awarded this title twice. Also that year, she received the Dick Clark Award for Excellence at the American Music Awards. At the 2015 Grammy Awards, "Shake It Off" was nominated for three awards including Record of the Year and Song of the Year while, at the 2015 Brit Awards, Swift won the International Female Solo Artist category. Swift was named by *Time* magazine as one of the 2015 *Time* 100. Swift was one of eight artists to receive a 50th Anniversary Milestone Award at the 2015 Academy of Country Music Awards.

Personal Life

Swift, who has blond hair and blue eyes and is five feet 11 inches tall, lives in Nashville. Among her many philanthropic efforts, she has donated tens of thousands of dollars to the American Red Cross. She has landed several endorsement deals: she currently serves as the face of the l.e.i. clothing brand and has lent her name to its line of sundresses, which are sold exclusively at Wal-Mart. She has also released her own line of fashion dolls through the toymaker Jakks Pacific. In July 2008 Swift graduated from Aaron Academy, a private Christian school in Hendersonville, Tennessee, which serves as a base for home-schooled students. Swift's philanthropic efforts have been recognized by the Do Something Awards, The Giving Back Fund and the Tennessee Disaster Services. While promoting *1989*, Swift began to use social media to respond directly to her fans, and invited 100 fans to appear in the "Shake It Off" music video. Swift has sent holiday gifts to fans by post and in person, dubbed "Swiftmas," and has invited groups of fans to her home for album playback sessions. She has said that her fans are "the longest and best relationship I have ever had." Swift interacts with her fans heavily on social media, including Instagram and Tumblr. In 2015, she became the youngest woman ever to be included on *Forbes'* "100 Most Powerful Women" list, ranking number 64.

Further Reading

All Music Guide Web site
(London) *Sunday Telegraph* p12+ Apr. 26, 2009
Los Angeles Times F p13+ Oct. 26, 2008
New York Times AR p1+ Nov. 9, 2008, AR p1+ Aug. 2, 2009
New Yorker p88+ Nov. 10, 2008
(Ottawa, Canada) *Citizen* B p6 Sep. 4, 2007
Philadelphia Inquirer E p1+ Nov. 7, 2007
Taylor Swift Web site
Washington Post C p1+ Feb. 28, 2008
Jepson, Louisa. *Taylor Swift* (2013)

T

Tangerine Dream

German music group

Edgar Froese
Electronic musician
Born: June 6, 1944; Tilsit, East Prussia

Jerome Froese
Keyboardist
Born: Nov. 24, 1970

Primary Field: Rock and Roll, Electronic Music, Soundtrack Composers
Group Affiliation: Tangerine Dream

Introduction

Over the course of its 35-year existence, the German-based rock group Tangerine Dream has influenced the development of electronic music, perhaps more so than any other music act. In the band's early years, their members drew inspiration from psychedelic rock and classical minimalism to produce a series of records that are still hailed as visionary and avant-garde. Even as the band became more mainstream, in the late 1970s and early 1980s, their work anticipated much of 1980s pop music, in its heavy reliance on synthesizers with sequencer rhythms. During that time the band members also began composing film soundtracks; to date they have completed more than 60 original film scores, including those for Thief *(1981),* Risky Business *(1983), and* Legend *(1985). In doing so, Tangerine Dream helped push electronic music as an acceptable medium for film composition. "Some people think electronic music has to be cold and icy," the band's founder, Edgar Froese, told Robert Palmer for the* New York Times *(June 25, 1986), "but if you know how to use the instruments and put that particular human touch in it, it can sound beautiful." In the 1990s, as they became influenced by the very electronica artists they had inspired earlier, Tangerine Dream infused their increasingly produced sound with club rhythms. Remarking on this varied musical history, Froese, the only member of Tangerine Dream to have performed on all of the group's albums, told Ashley Franklin and Nick Willder for* SoundScapes *(online), "It's more like a long story which could be cut in different episodes. That was what Tangerine Dream was all about. Apart from the development in technology there is a kind of subjective personal diary. Whatever we went through as a band or as individuals can be seen in whatever we do on stage or record."*

Early Life

Edgar Froese was born on June 6, 1944 in Tilsit, East Prussia, which was then part of Poland. After Germany's defeat in World War II, Froese's family, like other German residents of East Prussia, were forced to relocate to Germany; Froese grew up in West Berlin. As a teenager he was taken with the Dadaist and surrealist movements in art, which stressed dreamlike and avant-garde images. He also enjoyed the writings of Gertrude Stein, Henry Miller, and Walt Whitman. In the mid-1960s Froese organized multimedia events at the home of the surrealist painter Salvador Dali in Spain. Inspired to work with music, Froese joined a rock band called the Ones, as a guitarist. The band released one single before breaking up in 1967. Froese then formed

Tangerine Dream, whose first lineup included the bassist Kurt Herkenberg, the drummer Lanse Hapshash, the vocalist Charlie Prince, and the flutist Voker Hombach. Over the next two years the group played at a variety of student events in West Berlin, in a psychedelic-rock style that centered on Eastern and jazz-inflected guitar lines and drug-influenced lyrics and was similar in that way to the music of their American contemporaries the Grateful Dead and the Jefferson Airplane. After a time the group's work began to Froese to seem futile. As he said to Andy Gill for the British magazine *Mojo* (April 1997, on-line), "What can you do if you're in a position where you can run round in circles and still never catch up what is already there? That period of time was when [Eric] Clapton was big with Cream, and [Jimi] Hendrix was big-what did it mean for a German to take a guitar and start playing like that? It was ridiculous."

Life's Work

In an effort to create original sounds, Froese formed a new version of Tangerine Dream in 1969, with the drummer Klaus Schulze and Conrad Schitzler, the latter of whom played wind instruments. The group began jamming in an improvised manner similar to that of the British psychedelic rockers Pink Floyd and the German avant-garde group Amon Diiiil. In 1969 Tangerine Dream recorded their debut single, "Ultima Thule," which featured both guitars and violins. After an unsuccessful trip to London, England, to recruit a lead singer for his new band, Froese returned to Berlin—"burned out and penniless," as he told Gill-to find a letter from the German record label Ohr. As Froese recalled to Gill, the letter said, '"We listened to your tape and it sounds great, we want to sign you!' I thought, "What tape?" The music in question was on a collection of improvised demos Tangerine Dream had recorded in an abandoned warehouse but had not expected to release. During the recording of the music, the band had filtered keyboard, guitar, and bass lines-as well as music produced with found objects-through various effects processors to create a sparse, almost trance inducing sound. Released as *Electronic Meditation* in June 1970, the band's first record has inspired a cult following with its raw sound. Klaus Schulze and Conrad Schitzler left for solo careers after the album was released. (Schulze would later become a founding member of the renowned German psychedelic group Ash Ra Tempel.) Following their departure, the organist Steve Schroyder and the keyboardist and drummer Christopher Franke joined the band. Not long after the lineup change, the band caused an outcry of protest when they appeared on television playing a piece written for guitar, cello, drums, and 12 pinball machines.

In 1971 Tangerine Dream released *Alpha Centauri,* on which the band increased their use of keyboards, relying less heavily on guitars. In particular they had drawn inspiration from the VCS3 synthesizer lent to them by a fellow music enthusiast. "We didn't know what it was about, we would just turn things right to left, left to right, get some sounds out of it, and put them straight on the record!," Froese told Gill. "It sounded as strange as we thought a sound could be at that time. That's all we could do on *Alpha Centauri!* So it's maybe a bit poor if you listen to it today, but back in '72 or '73 it sounded avant-garde!" Consisting of three slow-building pieces, *Alpha Centauri* helped pioneer the "space rock" sound, characterized by organ chords played slowly over gurgling synthesizers, improvised drumming, and flutes. Schroyder left the band after the album's release and was replaced by Peter Baumann. Baumann's first record with the group, *Zeit* (1972), pushed the boundaries of electronic music in a rock format, consisting as it does of one down-tempo composition in four movements, with no melody or drums and with such instruments as cellos and vibraphones thrown into the mix. That record has more in common with classical minimalist pieces by Steve Reich or Philip Glass than with the work of most rock acts. Remarking on the band's shift to mostly electronic instrumentation, Froese told Gill, "There was a gig somewhere in the South of Germany where we walked on-stage with the usual line-up and were playing some crazy free music with rock instruments, and all of a sudden we realised that if you do that for years you end up nowhere, with nowhere to go. Even though we were doing crazy things, the sound was pretty normal. We felt we had to make an absolute break, so after the gig we decided to sell everything we had in the way of normal instruments and do something completely new. At the same time, we were watching what was happening in the avant-garde community, where people were getting rid of harmonies and melody lines and so on. We knew we wouldn't make any money out of it, but we bought some little sine wave generators and microphones which we put on different things like calculators and stuff, and produced sounds which we then sent through echo and reverb units. It sounded so stupid that we thought we'd get some attention, at least!"

Affiliation: Soundtrack & Score Composers

In 1977 William Friedkin, the director of *The Exorcist,* asked the band to compose music for his upcoming film *Sorcerer* (1977). Without seeing any footage of the film, relying on a script alone, the band completed the score, which led to dozens of other film-scoring opportunities for the group. "Financially," Froese told Robert Palmer in 1986, "making sound tracks keeps us going independent of record companies. And artistically, seeing a vision and creating something in response to it is very much apart from sitting in front of a blank notebook not knowing what to do." After the live album *Encore* (1977), Baumann left Tangerine Dream for a solo career; he would later form Private Music, which became a major New Age label and featured such artists as Shadowfax, Yanni, and John Tesh. Replacing Baumann with Steve Jolliffe and adding the percussionist Klaus Kruger, Tangerine Dream put out *Cyclone* in 1978. The most controversial album of Tangerine Dream's career, Cyclone angered many of the band's fans with its addition of lyrics sung by Jolliffe and its general shift to a more mainstream sound. Jolliffe left the band after the record appeared, and the group returned to all-instrumental mode for *Force Majeure* (1979), albeit with more of a guitar-driven approach than on previous releases. After that record came out, Johannes Schmoelling joined the group on organ, while Klaus Kruger departed. Schmoelling's first concert with Tangerine Dream, at the Palast der Republik in East Berlin, was the first live performance by a Western rock group in a Communist nation in Eastern Europe. A recording of the performance was later released as the album *Pergamon* (1986). Schmoelling made his studio debut with Tangerine Dream on *Tangram* (1980), which found the band continuing to move in a more melodic and pop-friendly direction while still recording with mostly electronic instruments. "In the early '70s," Froese told Andy Gill, "we did 100 per cent improvised stuff, just sat down and started playing. . . . Then we moved on and started structuring things more, when technology became more reliable and flexible and you could store things and recall them better."

During the 1980s Tangerine Dream composed the music for more than 30 films, among them *Thief* (1981), the box-office smash *Risky Business* (1984), *The Keep* (1984), *Firestarter* (1984), *Vision Quest* (1985), Legend (1985), Three O'Clock High (1987), Shy People (1987), and *Deadly Care* (1987). Tangerine Dream's use of electronic instrumentation in their scores led many other film composers to experiment with synthesizers.

The year 1973 brought Tangerine Dream's album *Atem*, a somewhat more accessible work than *Zeit*. Through *Atem*, the band came to the attention of an influential British deejay, John Peel, who called it the record of the year. At this time the band refused to record any more music for the Ohr label, due in large part to the actions of its owner, Rolf-Ulrich Kaiser, who among other tactics allegedly spiked musicians' drinks with LSD in secret and recorded the musical results for another of his labels. With growing interest in their music, Tangerine Dream signed a five-year contract with the fledgling Virgin Records, which had recently become a major player in the record industry thanks to their release of Mike Oldfield's all-electronic album *Tubular Bells,* used to sinister effect in the 1973 film *The Exorcist.* Tangerine Dream's own all-electronic approach, however, brought them criticism from rock-music purists. During one of the group's performances, at about the time that *Phaedra* (1974) was released on the Virgin label, the audience pelted the band with apples and bananas, forcing the group to leave after 10 minutes of performing. At a concert in Paris an audience member in the balcony threw a plastic bag full of marmalade onto the band's equipment, ending the band's show. Froese told Gill, "In those days people were not very polite about what we did. In a *Melody Maker* interview in '73 or '74 . . . I said, 'In about 10 years' time, everybody will play synthesizers'-the guy stopped his tape recorder, said, 'You're an idiot,' and walked out. They thought we were aliens just fooling them." Years later John Bush, writing for the All Music Guide, nonetheless called Phaedra "one of the most important, artistic and exciting works in the history of electronic music." The record's slow-moving, occasionally melodic synthesizer lines play over complex, arpeggiated sequencer patterns and other eerie effects. Although the record received mostly negative reviews from the mainstream press at the time it appeared, it made the Top 20 on the British charts and was certified gold, meaning that it sold at least 500,000 copies.

As a result of their newfound popularity, Tangerine Dream was invited to play at the Roman Catholic Reims Cathedral, in France, on December 13, 1974. After the crowd, expected to be 1,500 people, swelled to almost 6,000, large numbers of audience members found themselves packed into the pews and unable to get out to use the bathrooms. As a result, some in the audience urinated against the pillars of the cathedral, causing a great public outcry-which led to, among other things, the group's being officially banned by Pope Paul VI from playing in Roman Catholic churches. Nonetheless, they were invited in 1975 to perform at several cathedrals affiliated with the Church of England, including Coventry Cathedral, York Minster Cathedral, and Liverpool Cathedral. That year Tangerine Dream released *Rubycon*, which features one 35-minute epic piece, on which the band added treated (as well as untreated) pianos and organs to their all-electronic sound. Tangerine Dream followed up the live album *Ricochet* (1975) with *Stratos/ear* (1976), for which they worked with more acoustic instruments, such as untreated piano, harpsichord, harmonica, and guitar. In addition the album's music showed a shift toward more conventional songwriting, with stronger melodies and rhythm.

Despite being seen as visionaries in some circles, the band was also derided for composing "by the numbers" when it came to their film scores. Writing about the band's score for the film *Legend*, for example, Fred Bayles of the Associated Press (July 30, 1986) noted, "Without a picture, the music is dull."

Longtime fans also complained that the band's music was becoming watered down. The group's 1981 album, *Exit*, contains shorter, more self-contained pieces with pop instrumentation and dance-floor influences. Although thematically concerned with the topical issue of nuclear war, the music was a far cry from the experimentation of the band's previous work. Tangerine Dream's next record, *White Eagle* (1982), focused on environmental concerns while retaining much of the sound of Exit. The group followed with *Logos: Live at the Dominion* (1982), which comprises a diverse cross-section of Tangerine Dream's music, moving from minimalist-influenced material to their more recent, conventionally structured pieces.

In 1983 the band released their last studio album for Virgin, *Hyperboea*, for which they added Eastern-influenced melodies to their sound. The band's next studio album, *Le Pare* (1985), released on the Jive Electro label, contains short compositions representing different parks from around the world. Le Pare marked the first time the group had used sampling technology on a studio record. The group utilized meditative Native American sounds on the track "Yellowstone Park," while "Central Park" is, in contrast, more modern in tone and had a danceable beat. Both critics and fans hailed the effort as among the band's best in years. After the album's release Johannes Schmoelling left the band and was replaced by Paul Haslinger, who came from a classical-music background and brought a more structured feel to Tangerine Dream's music. His first record with the group was *Underwater Sunlight* (1986), the theme of which is the underwater world. The band followed with *Tyger* (1987), which features more vocals than any previous Tangerine Dream album-specifically, Jocelyn Bernadette Smith singing verse of the English poet William Blake. That year the group also released *Canyon Dreams,* which was composed for a video of the same name, about the Grand Canyon. Fusing the band's earlier, progressive styles and their more modern leanings of the 1980s, the album brought the group their first of seven Grammy nominations. In 1987, after 16 years with the band, Christoper Franke left to focus on a solo career. His last concert-the band's 750th-was taped and released as the live album *Livemiles* (1988). "I felt I needed a creative break," Franke said of his reasons for leaving the group, as quoted on the Web site *Sound on Sound*. "Because I think we started to repeat ourselves. We ended up with so much equipment that we took on a lot of jobs to pay for it, became overworked and did too many things at the same time. We did not have time to explore our minds for fresh ideas or explore the great computer instruments we had at our disposal. Kids with much more time than us, but less experience, began producing better sounds, and I began to feel our quality was dropping. This was a very bad feeling for a group who always wanted to be on the cutting edge of music." Responding to such assessments, Edgar Froese told Ashley Franklin and Nick Willder, "I agree absolutely . . . it's not the same band any more. . . . Specifically the style of music is somehow related strongly to your consciousness. If consciousness changes, what you do will change, because your daily working, thinking, behaving process are absolutely linked 100% to your consciousness. That's why there is a development. We are not the same people anymore."

Optical Race (1988) was the group's first album to be released on their former bandmate Peter Baumann's label, Private Music Records. The album has been called one of Tangerine Dream's more accessible works. In 1990 Edgar Froese's son, Jerome Froese (born on November 24, 1970), joined Tangerine Dream as a keyboardist. The group's first album to feature his work is *Melrose* (1990), which consists of smooth yet technically complex music that, like a great deal of the band's more recent material, is often categorized as New Age-a designation with which Edgar Froese disagrees strongly. New Age music "is not the music we play," he told an interviewer for *Dream Collector* (June 1994), as quoted on the *Voices in The Net* Web site, "even if record dealers, music reviewers and listeners are always looking for a 'stylistic drawer' to put Tangerine Dream into. And, even more annoying than [New Age] music is the 'New Age' philosophy where everything is a caricature of a positive world. . . . 'New Age Music' is just the acoustical wallpaper for this world view, but this is exactly not the way we see the world around us. Tangerine Dream music is not the right choice for people who are still into baby food." Following the appearance of Melrose, Paul Haslinger left Tangerine Dream to compose film soundtracks; he would also form the Berlin Symphonic Film Orchestra and Sonic Images Records, one of the fastest-growing soundtrack labels in the world. Tangerine Dream's first album after his departure was *Rockoon* (1992), which features strong rhythms and was nominated for a Grammy Award. In 1993 the band collaborated with the actress Kathleen Turner on the album *Rumpelstiltskin*, on which Turner narrated the classic fairy tale of the title to musical accompaniment by Tangerine Dream. That year the band also released two live albums, *Dreaming on Danforth Avenue* and *220 Volt Live,* the latter of which was nominated for a Grammy Award. Those were followed by *Turn of the Tides (*1994), a concept album based on an excerpt from a story that Edgar Froese had written. In addition to the Froeses, the record features Linda Spa on saxophones and Zlatko Perica on guitar. Turn of the Tides opens with Tangerine Dream's interpretation of the Russian composer Modest Mussorgsky's *Pictures at an Exhibition.* The album as a whole was nominated for a Grammy Award. Less well-received was *The Dream Mixes* (1994), the first volume in a series of remixes of earlier work by Tangerine Dream. "It was a terrible thing," Froese told Franklin and Willder about the remixes. "I never ever had any desire to do it. It is something I'm really not interested in going through again. The reason is simply that if a band grows and becomes more and more popular, record companies have a commercial interest in releasing the back catalogue. So those companies said 'okay we want to release it.' I said 'great, but what and how?' And the answers I got were totally like scrambled eggs. They didn't know what to do, they didn't know how to do it. So I said, 'look, let's make an agreement: you have to support me in such and such a way, and I'll do it myself.' And that's the only reason I did it, otherwise the music would have been released in an almost crap direction."

In 1995 the band came out with the Grammy nominated *Tyranny of Beauty,* which found them fusing heavily produced, ambient music with dance-club beats, an approach they repeated on *Goblins Club* (1996). In 1997 the band released the live record *Tournado*, which was intended as a musical description of the landscape of the American Southwest. The record represented Tangerine Dream's departure from the more club-oriented releases for which they were becoming known, and a return to the more ethereal sounds of their earlier material. In 1998 came *Ambient Monkeys,* which features a variety of sound effects produced by animals and machines, from monkeys to ocean creatures to trains. While not a groundbreaking work, in many ways it was the band's most experimental album in almost two decades. The following year Tangerine Dream brought out soundtracks to two documentaries—*Transsiberia: The Russian Express Railway Experience*, whose soundtrack prominently features electronic rhythms, and *What a Blast: Architecture in Motion.* At this time the band formed their own record label. "If you want to do what you like to do: try to be honest with your fans, your audiences," Edgar Froese told Franklin and Willder for *SoundScapes*. "That's why we set up our own label; our own publishing company. Now we can be more creative in terms of releasing material, which we couldn't have before because everything had to be agreed by the companies." Also in 1999 the group released *Mars Polaris* and *Dream Encores*, the latter of which consists of the band's encores from live shows from past years. In 2000 the band released *Great Wall of China,* the soundtrack to the same-titled documentary, which accentuated the band's techno influences. More ethereal was *The Seven Letters from Tibet* (2000), based on the mystical properties ascribed by some to the number seven. In 2002 the group came out with *Inferno* (2002), a concept album based on the 13th- and 14thcentury poet Dante Alighieri's *Divine Comedy.* The album was recorded live in a European church with a small female choir and fuses progressive rock, electronica, classical music, and church music. A second Dante-inspired record is Tangerine Dream's *Purgatorio* (2004). The past couple of years have also seen releases of the group's live albums recorded in Germany, Canada, France, and Australia, respectively, as well as of the soundtrack album *Mota Atma* (2003). Reviewing that record for amazon.com, Jerry McCulley wrote, "This soundtrack (recorded in the fall of '02) . . . is a compelling summation of the band's various phases and enduring appeal. The brooding, sensuous textures of their expansive mid-'70s prime are often efficiently set here to the pulsing sequencer rhythms that propelled much of their film work from Sorcerer onwards, but deftly seasoned with samples and sparing uses of natural instruments that give it a deceptively transparent sense of the organic. Young Jerome Froese seems locked into his father's electro muse at the genetic level, producing one of T-Dream's most sonically elegant and rewarding modern albums."

The two current members of Tangerine Dream, Edgar Froese and Jerome Froese, both have solo careers. Jerome Froese has released several singles, while his father's solo efforts began with *Aqua* (1974), a collection of four free-form, tranquil pieces. Edgar followed in 1975 with *Epsilon in Malaysian Pale,* which mirrors Tangerine Dream's sound from that period. *Macula Transfer* (1976) consists of material written on airline flights, while *Stuntman* (1979) features a mix of short melodic pieces and all-electronic, ethereal sounds that pointed in the direction Tangerine Dream would take in the 1980s. *Kamikaze* (1982) and *Pinnacles* (1983) were followed two decades later by the five volumes in Froese's *Ambient Highway* series. Edgar Froese told Mark Naman for *STart Magazine* (October 1988) that when he formed Tangerine Dream he "had this crazy dream about using technology in the most advanced way possible. I'm still on that adventurous trip."

Personal Life

Both Edgar and Jerome Froese currently live in Berlin, Germany. Edgar's wife (who is Jerome's mother) has provided photographs for the Froeses' respective solo records.

Further Reading

Associated Press July 30, 1986
LiteraryMoose (on-line); Mojo Apr. 1997
New York Times C p25 June 25, 1986, with photo
Soundscapes (on-line)
STart Magazine p67+ Oct. 1988
Voices in The Net (on-line)

James Taylor

Singer; guitarist; songwriter

Born: March 12, 1948; Boston, Massachusetts
Primary Field: Pop
Group Affiliation: Solo performer

Introduction

Among the "new troubadours—" young singer-songwriters who are reshaping pop music into a gentler and more introspective mold after years of frenzied and deafening rock—the most successful and perhaps the best is James Taylor. An unknown barely out of his teens when his first record was released in 1969, Taylor has become one of the nation's best-selling recording artists and most sought after conceit performers. His songs, melodically uncomplicated but richly laden with evocative imagery, are often intensely personal narrations of his own struggles with drugs, alienation, and other afflictions of the affluent, middle-class youth culture to which he belongs, but they also convey feelings of joy, sorrow, and fear with a directness and dignity that span the generation gap.

Early Life

The second of the five children of Gertrude (Woodard) and Dr. Isaac M. Taylor, James Vernon Taylor was born on March 12, 1948 at Massachusetts General Hospital in Boston. His older brother Alexander and his younger brother Livingston and his sister Katherine have all followed him into the popular music business; only his youngest brother Hugh has never cut a record.

James Taylor was born while his father was interning at Massachusetts General. Dr. Taylor, who is descended from a well-to-do Southern Scottish family, has had a distinguished career at the University of North Carolina Medical School, where he retired as dean in

1971. The principal musical influence in the family was Mrs. Taylor, who had studied voice at the New England Conservatory of Music.

When James was a few years old, his family moved from Milton, Massachusetts, near Boston, to Chapel Hill, North Carolina, where they lived in a large, contemporary ranchhouse set on a spacious acreage of pasture and woods. Their summers were spent on Martha's Vineyard, an island retreat for the wealthy of Massachusetts. "We quite consciously set out to raise our children free of the hang-ups we see in ourselves and our generation," Dr. Taylor told a *Time* writer for a cover story on his son (March 1, 1971). "We weren't going to use that cop-out of 'because the Bible tells you so.'" Rather than formal religion, Gertrude Taylor recalls teaching her children to "believe in people" and to view the earth as a "beautiful, fragile place." Denied little, the Taylor children were, from all accounts, treated as rather special beings. "The basic orientation in my family," Livingston Taylor recalled for *Time*, "was that simply because you were a Taylor, you could and should be able to accomplish anything."

James Taylor attended public schools in Chapel Hill until he was sent as an eighth-grader to Milton Academy, an exclusive, highly-disciplined boys' school in Milton, Massachusetts. It was, apparently, the wrong school for him. "We just weren't ready for him," the school's dean, John Torney, was quoted as saying in *Time*. "James was more sensitive and less goal oriented than most students of his day. I'm sure James knew about drugs long before anyone else here."

James struggled through four years at the academy, his misery relieved by summers at Martha's Vineyard, by a trip to the Soviet Union in the summer of 1965, and by a drop-out episode when with his brother Alex he joined a North Carolina rock band called the Fabulous Corsayers. But by his senior year, James's adolescent unhappiness had taken a serious turn. It was time for him to plan for college, and he was considering Reed, Harvard, and Swarthmore. "But when I started applying," he told Susan Braudy for the *New York Times Magazine* (February 21, 1971), "I fell to pieces." He enrolled instead at McLean Hospital, a psychiatric institution for wealthy young people in Belmont, Massachusetts that was later to include Liwy and Kate Taylor among its patients.

"It's difficult for me to explain my state of mind at that time. . . . I felt really bad. It's an inseparable part of my personality that I have these feelings. I've never been able to put my finger on any specific explanation of what was or is the matter with me." Taylor's experience at McLean had its dark aspects, as he described in the song "Knocking 'Round the Zoo" ("Just knocking around the zoo on a Thursday afternoon/ There's bars on all the windows and they're counting up the spoons/ And if I'm feeling edgy, there's a chick who's paid to be my slave / But she'll hit me with a needle if she thinks I'm trying to misbehave"). Yet it was in McLean Taylor was able to reach the decision that he wanted to be a musician instead of a college student.

James Taylor.

Taylor spent some nine or ten months at McLean, during which time he graduated from the institution's high school. Not waiting for his formal discharge, he left the hospital for New York City in the summer of 1966. There he joined the Flying Machine, a rock band organized by his friend Danny (Kootch) Kortchmar with whom he had won a hootenanny contest when he was fifteen. In the group Taylor played guitar and sang many of the songs that were later to be released on his first album, including "Knocking 'Round the Zoo," "Night Owl," and "Rainy Day Man."

LIFE'S WORK

In the introduction to one of his songs Taylor recalls to audiences his "grim New York gig" with the Flying Machine: "We'd come to New York to form a rock-and-roll band like thousands of kids from the suburbs. Their idea of soul was to crank up the volume on the amplifiers their parents bought 'em." Despite his assessment of the group, the Flying Machine was better than most bands of its kind, and it managed to play regularly at the Village club, the Night Owl, for a few dollars a night. Taylor's personal problems grew worse in New York, however, as he became increasingly involved with drugs and eventually became addicted to heroin.

Fleeing New York, Taylor went to London in January 1968. Soon after his arrival he recorded a demonstration tape that he submitted to Peter Asher, a former rock performer who was then chief talent scout for the Beatles' Apple record company. Asher signed the young unknown American to a three-year contract, and Beatle Paul McCartney was so impressed with him that he played bass background for part of the album that Taylor made on the Apple label. That album, produced by Asher and entitled *James Taylor,* was released in the United States early in 1969. It received little promotion and sold poorly, but was highly praised by critics and soon became a rock cult item. A single from the album, "Carolina In My Mind," was released as a single and climbed up the Top Forty charts.

Meanwhile, James Taylor had returned to the United States in December 1968, more hooked on heroin than ever. He spent that winter in a hospital in New York and in Austin Riggs, another mental institution in Massachusetts, recovering his health and ridding himself of his drug habit. By July 1969, at the Newport Folk Festival, he was at the top of his form. The last scheduled performer at the festival, Taylor was cheered on by thousands of fans who stayed to hear him on a rainy Sunday afternoon.

Soon after Newport, Taylor had a motorcycle accident on Martha's Vineyard in which he broke both hands and a foot. He used the time of his convalescence to reassess his business life. As a result he broke his contract with the financially foundering Apple company and signed with Warner Brothers. At the same time Peter Asher, by then a close friend of Taylor's, left Apple to become the American singer's personal manager and producer. Late in 1969 he recorded his first album for Warners, *Sweet Baby James,* which was released in the spring of 1970.

Some critics, like Burt Korall of the *Saturday Review* (September 12, 1970), had found the production of James Taylor overly lavish. For *Sweet Baby James,* however, the accompaniments had been simplified, allowing Taylor's fine acoustical guitar playing to stand out, and for that reason Korall judged the second album to be superior. Of Taylor's songs on Sweet Baby James the *Saturday Review* critic wrote, "Again the songs are delightful and enriching. Taylor remains at his best unraveling personal situations that are universal in application. . . . One senses he is endeavoring to solve his own problems and, in the process, to help lift the weight of ours." The title song of the album is a tender lullaby written for Taylor's nephew and namesake, but the song that received the most attention was "Fire and Rain," whose lyrics express Taylor's pain in accepting the suicide of a girl he knew and in withdrawing from drugs. By early 1971 *Sweet Baby James* had sold some 1,600,000 copies, "Fire and Rain" had become a hit single, and the song and the album had been nominated for five Granny awards.

During 1970 Taylor's popularity grew at such an astonishing rate that it occasionally even caught his managers by surprise. When he was booked into the Gaslight Cafe in New York for a week in March, the proprietors found themselves turning away up

Affiliation: Connection with the Audience

Probably the major reason for Taylor's box-office draw is his personal magnetism, coupled with his ability to establish intimacy with audiences even within such cavernous halls as Madison Square Garden. But he is also considered a musician of considerable talents, who is especially admired as a guitarist. After hearing him at Washington's Cellar Door, William C. Woods (*Washington Post,* June 17, 1970), for example, wrote, "Almost all of his [guitar] work is permeated with the feel of the baroque the way the best of the Beatles is. . . . He also understands jazz. . . . And Lord knows he's familiar with country, rock, and blues . . . with the elusive essences of each music." Although his voice is less admired by music critics, they recognize the impact that its softness and pliancy can have upon his audiences. As one musically-trained coed told a *Time* writer, "I don't know why I love it. I know I shouldn't, because he doesn't really sing. He just sort of intones."

to 2,000 persons a night. That June, Taylor played to packed houses at two performances on a Friday night at Carnegie Hall. By the following winter when he toured twenty-seven cities across the country, his concerts sold out within hours of the time tickets went on sale. Early in 1971 Taylor performed in New York City to standing-room-only crowds at Fillmore East, Madison Square Garden, and Philharmonic Hall of Lincoln Center, where he was part of the Great Performers series, which usually features classical musicians. When Taylor returned to New York for four concerts at Carnegie Hall in late 1971, Don Heckman of the *New York Times* (December 1, 1971) found that the performer had "survived magnificently" the wave of publicity that had engulfed him. Calling the evening "a very nearly perfect pop music concert," Heckman wrote, "Mr. Taylor's . . . stage presence, as always, was that of a performer whose magic is so strong it virtually radiates out of his electric blue eyes. Every move he makes—gawky lopes to the piano, shy glances at the audience, awkward little bows of thanks—stamps him as an original."

Taylor's third album, *Mud Slide Slim and the Blue Horizon,* which was released by Warner Brothers in 1971, brought him acclaim from most critics and more Grammy award nominations. "Fire and Rain," "Something in the Way She Moves," "Carolina in My Mind," and many other Taylor songs have been recorded by such diverse vocalists as Melanie, Tom Rush, Harry Belafonte, and Andy Williams. Cashing in on Taylor's popularity, an outfit called Euphoria Records has released an album entitled *James Taylor and the Original Flying Machine,* which was compiled from demonstration tapes the musician made in 1967. In 1971 Taylor costarred with rock musician Dennis Wilson in Two-Lane Blacktop (Universal), one of the many youth culture "road" films that followed in the wake of Easy Rider. As a nameless, rootless young man who drives around the country in a souped-up 1955 Chevrolet looking for drag races, Taylor was scarcely called upon to act, but rather gave, as Bruce Cook of the *National Observer* (July 21, 1971) put it, a "tight-lipped, inarticulate portrayal of a tight-lipped, inarticulate character."

"Hey Mister, that's me up on the jukebox, / I'm the one that's singing this sad song, / And I cry every time you slip in one more dime,' James Taylor sang on *Mud Slide Slime* in a song that describes the disquieting, schizoid feeling of hearing oneself on the jukebox. He has much the same uncomfortable feeling about his newly-gained superstar status. "It's really odd," the singer told Bruce Cook of the *National Observer* (June 8, 1970). ". . . You get to be a big name, and all of these people are thinking about you . . . and they may share a conception of you that's really totally different from what you really are. So you can't be what you are. You've got to satisfy them by playing the role. So there's the point at which you don't run it any longer. It runs you." To insulate himself from the effects of fame, Taylor spends as much time as he can on Martha's Vineyard, where his mother (who is now separated from his father), two of his brothers, and his sister all live. He is building a house there on a twenty-seven-acre plot.

Taylor's artistic fortunes spiked again in 1975 when the Gold album *Gorilla* reached No. 6 and provided one of his biggest hit singles, a cover version of Marvin Gaye's "How Sweet It Is (To Be Loved by You)," which featured wife Carly in backing vocals and reached No. 5 in America and No. 1 in Canada. On the *Billboard's* Adult Contemporary chart, the track also reached the top, and the follow-up single, the feel-good "Mexico" also reached the Top 5 of that list. A critically well received album, *Gorilla* showcased Taylor's electric, lighter side that was evident on *Walking Man. Gorilla* was followed in 1976 by In the Pocket, Taylor's last studio album to be released under Warner Bros. Records. The album found him with many colleagues and friends, including Art Garfunkel, David Crosby, Bonnie Raitt and Stevie Wonder (who co-wrote a song with Taylor and contributed a harmonica solo). A melodic album, it was highlighted with the single "Shower the People," an enduring classic that hit No. 1 Adult Contemporary and almost hit the Top 20 of the Pop Charts. But the album was not well received, reaching No. 16 and being criticized, particularly by *Rolling Stone*. Still, *In The Pocket* was certified Gold.

With the close of Taylor's contract with Warner, in November the label released *Greatest Hits,* the album that comprised most of his best work between 1970 and 1976. It became with time his best-selling album, ever. It was certified eleven times Platinum in the US, earning a Diamond certification by the RIAA and eventually selling close to twenty million copies worldwide.

In 1977 Taylor signed with Columbia Records. Between March and April, he quickly recorded his first album for the label. *JT,* released that June, gave Taylor his best reviews since *Sweet Baby James,* earning a Grammy nomination for Album of the Year in 1978. *Rolling Stone* was particularly favorable to the album: "*JT* is the least stiff and by far the most various album Taylor has done. That's not meant to criticize Taylor's earlier efforts [...]. But it's nice to hear him sounding so healthy." *JT* reached 4 in the Billboard charts, selling more than 3 million copies in the United States alone. The album's Triple Platinum status ties it with *Sweet Baby James* as Taylor's all-time biggest selling studio album. It was propelled by the successful cover of Jimmy Jones and Otis Blackwell's "Handy Man," which hit No. 1 on *Billboard's* Adult Contemporary chart and reached No. 4 on the Hot 100, earning Taylor another Grammy Award for Best Male Pop Vocal Performance for his cover version. The success of the album propelled the release of two further singles—the up-tempo pop "Your Smiling Face" (an enduring live favorite) reached the American Top 20.

Back in the forefront of popular music, Taylor collaborated with Paul Simon and Art Garfunkel in the recording of a cover of Sam Cooke's "Wonderful World," which reached the Top 20 in the U.S. and topped the AC charts in early 1978. After briefly working on Broadway, he took a one-year break, reappearing in the summer of 1979 with the cover-studded Platinum album Flag, featuring a Top 30 version of Gerry Goffin and Carole King's "Up on the Roof." Taylor also appeared on the No Nukes concert in Madison Square Garden, where he made a memorable live performance of "Mockingbird" with his wife Carly. The concert appeared on both the No Nukes album and film.

In March 1981, James Taylor released the album *Dad Loves His Work,* whose themes concerned his relationship with his father, the course his ancestors had taken, and the effect he and Simon had had on each other. The album was another Platinum success, reaching No. 10 and providing Taylor's final real hit single in a duet with J. D. Souther, "Her Town Too," which reached No. 5 Adult Contemporary and No. 11 on the Hot 100 in *Billboard.*

During the late 1980s, he began touring regularly, especially on the summer amphitheater circuit. His later concerts feature songs from throughout his career and are marked by the musicianship of his band and backup singers. The 1993 two-disc *Live* album captures this, with a highlight being Arnold McCuller's descants in the codas of "Shower the People" and "I Will Follow." In 1995, Taylor performed the role of the Lord in Randy Newman's Faust.

After six years since his last studio album, in 1997 Taylor released *Hourglass*, an introspective album that gave him the best critical reviews in almost twenty years. The album had much of its focus on Taylor's troubled past and family. "Jump Up Behind Me" paid tribute to his father's rescue of him after *The Flying Machine* days, and the long drive from New York City back to his home in Chapel Hill. "Enough To Be on Your Way" was inspired by the alcoholism-related death of his brother Alex earlier in the decade. The themes were also inspired by Taylor and Walker's divorce, which took place in 1996. *Rolling Stone* found that "one of the themes of this record is disbelief," while Taylor told the magazine that it was "spirituals for agnostics." Critics embraced the dark themes on the album, and Hourglass was a commercial success, reaching No. 9 on the *Billboard* 200 (Taylor's first Top 10 album in sixteen years) and also provided a big adult contemporary hit on "Little More Time with You." The album also gave Taylor his first Grammy since *JT*, when he was honored with Best Pop Album in 1998.

Flanked by two greatest hit releases, Taylor's Platinum-certified *October Road* appeared in 2002 to a receptive audience. It featured a number of quiet instrumental accompaniments and passages. Overall, it found Taylor in a more peaceful frame of mind; rather than facing a crisis now, Taylor said in an interview that "I thought I'd passed the midpoint of my life when I was 17." Also in 2002, Taylor teamed with bluegrass musician Alison Krauss in singing "The Boxer" at the Kennedy Center Honors Tribute to Paul Simon. They later recorded the Louvin Brothers duet, "How's the World Treating You?" In 2004, after he chose not to renew his record contract with Columbia/Sony, he released *James Taylor: A Christmas Album* with distribution through Hallmark Cards. In the fall of 2006, Taylor released a repackaged and slightly different version of his Hallmark Christmas album, now entitled *James Taylor at Christmas,* and distributed by Columbia/Sony. In 2006, Taylor performed Randy Newman's song "Our Town" for the Disney animated film *Cars*. The song was nominated for the 2007 Academy Award for the Best Original Song. On January 1, 2007, Taylor headlined the inaugural concert at the Times Union Center in Albany, New York, honoring newly sworn in Governor of New York Eliot Spitzer.

Taylor's next album, *One Man Band* was released on CD and DVD in November 2007 on Starbucks' Hear Music Label, where he joined with Paul McCartney and Joni Mitchell. The introspective album grew out of a three-year tour of the United States and

Europe—featuring some of Taylor's most beloved songs and anecdotes about their creative origins—accompanied solely by the "one man band" of his long-time pianist/keyboardist, Larry Goldings. The digital discrete 5.1 surround sound mix of *One Man Band* won a TEC Award for best surround sound recording in 2008.

On November 28–30, 2007, Taylor, accompanied by his original band and Carole King, headlined a series of six shows at the Troubadour. The appearances marked the 50th anniversary of the venue, where Taylor, King and many others, such as Tom Waits, Neil Diamond, and Elton John, began their music careers. Proceeds from the concert went to benefit the Natural Resources Defense Council, MusiCares, Alliance for the Wild Rockies, and the Los Angeles Regional Foodbank, a member of America's Second Harvest—the Nation's Food Bank Network. Parts of the performance shown on *CBS Sunday Morning* in the December 23, 2007, broadcast showed Taylor alluding to his early drug problems by saying, "I played here a number of times in the 70s, allegedly." Taylor has used versions of this joke on other occasions, and it appears as part of his One Man Band DVD and tour performances.

In December 2007, *James Taylor at Christmas* was nominated for a Grammy Award. In January 2008, Taylor recorded approximately 20 songs by others for a new album with a band including Luis Conte, Michael Landau, Lou Marini, Arnold McCuller, Jimmy Johnson, David Lasley, Walt Fowler, Andrea Zonn, Kate Markowitz, Steve Gadd and Larry Goldings. The resulting live-in-studio album, named *Covers*, was released in September 2008. This album explores country and soul while being the latest proof that Taylor is a more versatile singer than his best known hits might suggest. The *Covers* sessions stretched to include "Oh What a Beautiful Morning," from the musical Oklahoma—a song that his grandmother had caught him singing over and over at the top of his lungs when he was seven years old. An additional album, called *Other Covers,* came out in April 2009, containing songs that were recorded during the same sessions as the original *Covers* but had not been previously issued.

During October 19–21, 2008, Taylor performed a series of free concerts in five North Carolina cities in support of Barack Obama's presidential bid. On Sunday, January 18, 2009, he performed at the *We Are One: The Obama Inaugural Celebration* at the Lincoln Memorial, singing "Shower the People" with John Legend and Jennifer Nettles of Sugarland. He was active in support of Barack Obama's 2012 reelection campaign, and opened the 2012 Democratic National Convention. He performed "America the Beautiful" at the President's second inauguration.

In March 2010, he commenced the Troubadour Reunion Tour with Carole King and members of his original band, including Russ Kunkel, Leland Sklar, and Danny Kortchmar. They played shows in Australia, New Zealand, Japan and North America, with the final night being at the Honda Center, in Anaheim, California. The tour was a major commercial success, and in some locations found Taylor playing arenas instead of his usual theaters or amphitheaters. Ticket sales amounted to over 700,000 and the tour grossed over $59 million. It was one of the most successful tours of the year.

After a 45-year wait, James earned his first No. 1 album on the *Billboard* 200 chart with *Before This World.* The album, which was released on June 16 through Concord Records, arrived atop the chart dated July 4, 2015 — more than 45 years after Taylor arrived on the list with *Sweet Baby James* (on the March 14, 1970 list). The album launched atop the *Billboard* 200 with 97,000 equivalent album units earned in the week ending June 21, 2015 according to Nielsen Music. Of its start, pure album sales equated to 96,000 copies sold—Taylor's best debut week for an album since 2002's *October Road.*

Personal Life

Taylor is six feet three inches tall and weighs 155 pounds. "Onstage and off," wrote Susan Brandy in her *New York Times Magazine* profile, "James looks like a handsome cowboy-Jesus with his long hair and his soared and scary blue eyes staring at yours, or lost gazing at the internal horizon." Taylor was married in November 1972 to singer-song writer Carly Simon. His marriage to Carly Simon ended in 1983. He was married to actress Kathryn Walker from 1985 to 1996. He married Caroline ("Kim") Smedvig in 2001. The couple reside in the town of Washington, Massachusetts, with their twin boys, Rufus and Henry, born in April 2001.

Although he received no formal religious training as a child, religion has played an important part in Taylor's life, and he told Miss Braudy, I think there's probably a God-shaped hole in everybody's being. Even if God only exists in people's minds, He's still a force. I believe in God, and I believe in Jesus, as a man, a metaphor, and a phenomenon."

Further Reading

Look 35 :M F 9 '71 pors
N Y Times Mag p28+ F 21 '71 pors
Nat Observer p20 Je 8 '70 por
Time 97:45+ Mr 1 '71 pors
White, Timothy (2002). *Long Ago and Far Away: James Taylor, His Life and Music.*

Koko Taylor

Singer; songwriter

Born: Sep. 28, 1935; Memphis, Tennessee
Died: June 3, 2009; Kildeer, Illinois
Primary Field: Blues
Group Affiliation: Willie Dixon

Introduction

"Blues is my life. It's a true feeling that comes from the heart, not something that just comes out of my mouth. Blues is what I love, and blues is what I always do." said Koko Taylor. According to the Web site of Alligator Records, her label since 1975, she was considered by many to be the "Queen of the Blues." "Possibly the last great tough, brassy blues woman alive," as the music critic Jeremy Hart wrote for Pop Matters *(2000, online), Taylor made her name "synonymous with Chicago blues," as her online* Rolling Stone *biography put it.*

Early Life

The youngest child of Annie Mae and William Walton, Taylor was born Cora Walton on September 28, 1935 just outside Memphis, Tennessee. According to most sources, she had two sisters and three brothers; in one interview, with Darlene Gavron Stevens for the *Chicago Tribune* (February 24, 1991), Taylor said she had three sisters and three brothers. Recalling to David S. Rotenstein for the *Charlotte Observer* (March 10, 1995) how she acquired the name Koko, she said, "When I was growing up I was a chocolate lover. I loved to eat chocolate candy, cake, cookies, whatever. And everybody started calling me a pet name, ... 'Little Cocoa'." Taylor's mother died when she was about four, and her father died before she reached her teens; for the next half-dozen years, her siblings took care of her. Beginning when she was old enough to do so—between six and eight years of age, as she has recalled—she picked cotton along with her brothers and sisters on the farm where the family lived as sharecroppers. "(My father] would make everybody in the household work," she told Darlene Gavron Stevens. "When we weren't in the fields working, we would cut wood for our cooking stove and we'd pick up kindling. I got used to working, and eventually I looked forward to it. This has stuck with me. It made a good, hardworking woman out of me. It made me strong, independent and honest." Taylor sang in the fields while picking cotton and in a local Baptist church choir. Her father encouraged his children to sing gospel music and warned them against listening to the blues, which he referred to as "devil's music." She and her brothers and sisters would sneak behind the house to sing and play music together. One brother made his own version of a guitar out of hay-bailing wire tied around nails; another brother made a kind of wind instrument by punching holes into a corncob. Making sure that their father did not know what they were up to, Taylor and her siblings would listen to the blues on a battery-operated radio (their home had no electricity), tuning in to B. B. King, who was then a disc jockey in West Memphis, Arkansas, and to the disc jockey Rufus Thomas, on WDIA in Memphis. One day when she was about 12, one of her brothers brought home a record by Memphis Minnie called "Me and My Chauffeur Blues." "Black Rat Blues," the song on the flip side, had a powerful effect on the young Taylor; as she told Michael Buffalo Smith in 2000 for *Gritz, the Online Southern Music Magazine,* "That was the first song that just stuck to my ribs, when it comes to the blues." Regarding that Memphis Minnie recording, Taylor told Ariel Swartley for the *New York Times Magazine* (June 29, 1980). "We had this—what we called graphonolia—that we wound up with our hands. That's how we played our music. I can remember the whole family listening to that record, playing it over and over. I learned it so well, I knew every word by [heart]."

Taylor attended school only sporadically; the highest grade she attended was the sixth. In 1953, at age 18, Taylor left Memphis with her boyfriend, Robert "Pops"

Taylor, a cotton-truck driver 12 years her senior. Owning little more than "35 cents and a box of Ritz crackers," as she recalled to John Floyd for the *Miami New Times* (October 21, 1999), they traveled to Chicago in search of work. The two were married later that year. Her husband found a job in a meat-packing plant, and Taylor earned $5 a day cleaning house and babysitting for families in the wealthy northern suburbs of Chicago. In their home, on the city's South Side, the hotbed of rough-edged Chicago electric blues, Pops would play guitar and Taylor would sing after work. Almost every weekend they would go to the so-called juke joints—the Queen Bee, Pepper's Lounge, and other gritty blues clubs in their part of town as well as on Chicago's West Side. "These were just little neighborhood tavern clubs where the black people went and drank and had a good time," Taylor recalled to Michael Buffalo Smith. "And they would have their band up there playing, and when I'd go in there, I'd just be going in there to have a good time too." With Pops's encouragement, Taylor began to join the musicians and sing on stage, performing with some of the leading Chicago musicians of the time—Muddy Waters, Howlin' Wolf, Elmore James, and Magic Sam. "They got to know me, and they started calling me Little Koko on their own," Taylor told Smith. '"We got Little Koko in the house, and we're going to get her up here to do a few tunes.' And that's what I did.... I'd just go up there and sing anything, just to be singing." Among the songs she performed in those venues were Brook Benton's "Make Me Feel Good, Kiddio" and Ike and Tina Turner's "I Idolize You."

Affiliation: Chicago and the World

Taylor began singing in public in the 1950s in Chicago clubs, just for the fun of it. Her career took off in 1965, when, thanks to her earlier, serendipitous encounter with the great traditional bluesman Willie Dixon, she recorded the single "Wang Dang Doodle," which sold a million copies and became her signature song. When Taylor was 61 and still singing at some 200 gigs a year, John Roos wrote in the Los Angeles Times (January 18, 1997), "This seemingly ageless wonder pours her heart out in one powerful song after another.... She's lost little of the fire and emotion she had [four decades ago].... Her raw voice growls and grunts, often building in intensity until it explodes with a killer line." Distinguished by her powerful, evocative voice and trademark growl, Taylor displayed "searing power and a steely emotional tautness . . . ," as David Whiteis wrote for the *Chicago Reader* (September 26, 1997) after attending one of her concerts, "and she radiates a warmth that borders on the spiritual: few performers in any genre are as capable as she is of generating genuine intimacy out of fervid house-rocking moments."

A sharecropper's daughter, Taylor sang in shows all over the world, appeared on television and in movies, and entertained at inaugural galas of two U.S. presidents. Among the most honored female blues singers of all time, she has won one Grammy Award and earned eight Grammy nominations for many of her albums. The mayor of Chicago, Richard Daley, presented Taylor with the city's Legend of the Year Award on March 3, 1993, which he proclaimed "Koko Taylor Day." In 1999 she received a Lifetime Achievement Award from the Memphis, Tennessee-based Blues Foundation, which has inducted her into its Blues Hall of Fame and recognized her achievements with 29 W. C. Handy Awards (considered equivalent to the Grammy Awards for the blues community). "A lot of people wonder what keeps me going," Taylor told an interviewer in 1992, as quoted on the African American Publications Web site. "It's for the love that I have for my music. This is my first priority: just to stay out here and sing the blues, make people happy with my music all over the world." In 2003 she received a Pioneer Award from the Rhythm and Blues Foundation and in 2004 an NEA National Heritage Fellowship.

Life's Work

Taylor's big break came when she met the bass player and composer Willie Dixon, a major contributor to the development of hard Chicago blues (and, later, an acknowledged influence on such groups as the Rolling Stones and the Grateful Dead). Dixon was also an arranger for Chess Records, which recorded many of the classic Chicago blues performers of the post-World War II generation, among them Sonny Boy Williamson, John Lee Hooker, Memphis Slim, and Buddy Guy as well as Muddy Waters and Howlin' Wolf. In a club one night in about 1962, Dixon approached Taylor as she came off the stage, and he exclaimed, as quoted on the Web site of the Richard De La Font Agency, which represented Taylor, "My God, I never heard a woman sing the blues like you sing the blues. There are lots of men singing the blues today, but not enough women. That's what the world needs today, a woman with a voice like yours to sing the blues." Dixon became Taylor's mentor and producer. In 1963 he produced Taylor's debut single, "Honky Tonky," for the USA label. Later he helped Taylor secure a contract with Chess Records, where he produced, among her earliest titles, the single "Wang Dang Doodle," which Dixon had written and recorded five years earlier with Howlin' Wolf. ("Wang dang doodle," Taylor told David S. Rotanstein, "means pitching a wang dang doodle on a Saturday night. What I would call a fish-fry, a romp-tromp good time, everybody partying, dancing, getting drunk, fighting, whatever comes first." In some interviews Taylor said that Dixon wrote "Wang Dang Doodle" for her.) The song urges the listener to tell various people—Razor Tootin' Jim, Fast Talking Fanny, Abyssinian Ned, Boxcar Joe—about plans for the evening: "We gonna romp and tromp till midnight / We gonna fuss and fight till daylight / We gonna pitch a wang dang doodle all night long." Taylor's rendition of Dixon's party song was a smash hit; it aired often on the radio, sold a million copies, and in 1966 climbed to number four on *Billboard's* rhythm-and-blues charts. "When I first heard 'Wang Dang Doodle' I thought it was the silliest song I had ever heard, but people just love that story," Taylor said, as quoted on the House of Blues Web site. "I can't do a show without that song, because the people won't let me off the stage without playing it." "Wang Dang Doodle" is included on many of the Taylor albums still available.

Dixon, with whom Taylor formed a close friendship, encouraged Taylor to write her own songs, advising her to find inspiration for them in her everyday life. She began doing so in about 1964, when she wrote "What Kind of Man Is This?," which she has described as a tribute to her husband, who became her manager. "It seems like I got the right man for a husband—one that's in my corner all the way when it comes to my career," she told Ariel Swartley. In the same vein, she told Michael Buffalo Smith, "There's plenty of women in their kitchen cooking apple pies that can sing as good as I can. Sing good as Aretha Franklin or Whitney Houston, but they can't get out there and do what they do, and why? Because, 'I got a husband,' first of all. And there ain't too many men that are gonna want their wife out there on the road. I traveled, and I had a husband, but my husband was right there with me. That makes a difference."

In the latter half of the 1960s, Taylor worked steadily in Chicago and toured widely in the South as well. She also made additional recordings with Chess Records and Dixon, including the albums *Koko Taylor* (1969) and *Basic Soul* (1972). Late in the 1960s, as a participant in the American Folk Blues Festival, she toured Europe and gained an enthusiastic following of blues fans there. In the largely male-dominated world of blues, Taylor had joined a number of outstanding women, among them Ma Rainey, Bessie Smith, Alberta Hunter, Dinah Washington, and Big Mama Thornton. "I'm showing the men that they're not the only ones,"Taylor told Swartley. "I can do just as good a job as they can at expressing the blues and singing the blues and holding an audience with the blues."

In the early 1970s Taylor became one of the first South Side blues artists to perform regularly at Kingston Mines and other clubs on Chicago's wealthier North Side. The steady change in the composition of her audiences from black to mostly white reflected the shrinking popularity of blues among African-Americans, who were gravitating toward jazz, soul, and rock and roll. In a conversation with Marty Racine for the *Houston Chronicle* (November 5, 1998), Taylor offered one explanation for the shift: "Blues is a reminder of hard times, slavery and just bein' black. Automatically, the black people don't need to be reminded of the way it was. We been there, we lived that."

In 1972 Taylor formed her own band, called the Blues Machine. (Its members have included, at various times, Vince Chappelle on drums, Cornelius Boyson on bass, Mervyn "Harmonica" Hinds on harmonica, Sammy Lawhorn and Mighty Joe Young on guitar, and Abb Locke on saxophone.) Taylor's fiery performance at the Ann Arbor Blues and Jazz Festival, in Michigan, recorded on the live album *Ann Arbor Blues and Jazz Festival 1972,* attracted the attention of Bruce Iglauer. Three years later, when Iglauer founded Alligator Records (now one of the biggest blues labels in the U.S.), Taylor was the first female artist he signed on. (The Chess Records label had come to an end that year, six years after its sale to GRT Records.) In 1999, for an article about Taylor's winning the Blues Foundation Lifetime Achievement Award, Iglauer told Niles Frantz, according to the foundation's Web site, "There is only one Queen of the Blues. [Taylor] is the blueswoman. I consider her music firmly in the tradition of the first generation of Chicago blues artists. She never wanted to sing anything but the blues, and she likes to leave the raw edges showing. In fact, she injects that rawness into all the music she sings. Koko is as tough as they come, and very proudly a country person in the best sense of what that means. She is the essence of what a blues musician should be."

In 1975 Alligator released Taylor's album *I Got What It Takes,* which features the standards "Big Boss Man," written by Luther Dixon and A. Smith, and "Voodoo Woman," which Taylor wrote. *I Got What It Takes* earned a Grammy Award nomination for best traditional blues album. Since then, the majority of Taylor's albums for Alligator have earned Grammy nominations. Earlier, on the Evidence label, Taylor made *South Side Lady* (1973), some cuts on which were recorded in a French studio and others live in the Netherlands during the 1973 American Folk Blues Festival tour of Europe. *The Earthshaker* (1978)—the title refers to Taylor herself—contains, among other songs, Taylor's "Please Don't Dog Me" and "I'm a Woman," Dorothy La Bostrie's "You Can Have My Husband (But Please Don't Mess with My Man)," and Willie Dixon's "Spoonful." Further cementing Taylor's reputation as a blues singer were her albums *From the Heart of a Woman* (1981), which includes swing, R&B, and soul as well as blues and is more tender than most of her other work; *Queen of the Blues* (1985), with contributions by the singer and guitarist Lonnie Brooks, the jazz guitarist Albert Collins, and the harmonica player James Cotton, among others; and *Live from Chicago—An Audience with The Queen* (1987), whose cuts include "Come to Mama," "Let the Good Times Roll," and Taylor's "The Devil's Gonna Have a Field Day." Taylor contributed to *Coast to Coast* (1989), an album by Paul Shaffer, the longtime bandleader for the CBS-TV program *Late Show with David Letterman.*

In February 1988 Taylor, her husband, and several members of her band were badly injured when their tour bus, with Pops at the wheel, tumbled off a cliff after a tire blew out. Neither Taylor nor the others, Dan Kening reported in the *Chicago Tribune* (May 4, 1990), had medical coverage; a benefit concert held by the Fabulous Thunderbirds, a blues, rock, and soul group, raised most of the money to pay the bills. Taylor, who had suffered a broken collarbone and several broken ribs, recovered after about six months and resumed her busy tour schedule. Then, in early 1990, her husband died, from maladies that she believes were related to the accident. "My work was the best thing happening for me—it gave me something to go on," she recalled to Don Snowden for the *Los Angeles Times* (September 6, 1990). "I just stay on the road—that's my life, and if I stay home too long, I get bored." She told Judy Hevrdejs for the *Chicago Tribune* (January 12, 1990), "Something magic happens when I get to a club or get on stage. [It's] the crowd, the musicians. Up on that stage, my personality changes. I put everything behind me when I perform. . . . I don't put a burden on my audience. I give them 100 percent of my energy." Taylor dedicated her next release, *Jump for Joy* (1990), to Pops. The disk includes four songs that Taylor wrote: the title track, "Can't Let Go," "Stop Watching Your Enemies," and "Tired of That." In a review of *Jump for Joy* for *People* (June 25, 1990), Roger Wolmuth wrote, "Taylor's energy and the mileage she has seen in 25 years of performing muscle her music beyond the merely raucous to believable reality. . . . For Taylor fans, this effort should serve as a reminder of just how good she still is."

Force of Nature (1993) earned Taylor another Grammy Award nomination, as did her next recording, *Royal Blue* (2000), both for best contemporary blues album. *Royal Blue* features several new songs written by Taylor, covers of songs by Ray Charles and Melissa Etheridge, and contributions by such guest artists as B. B. King, the blues and rock pianist Johnnie Johnson, the blues singer/songwriter Keb' Mo', and the blues-rocker Kenny Wayne Shepard. In a review of *Royal Blue* for *Amazon.com,* Matthew Cooke wrote, "Koko Taylor is the undisputed queen of Chicago blues vocals. . . . This record is . . . a characteristically well-informed tour of contemporary and electric blues, showcasing that gravelly, saucy growl that just gets more satisfying with age. . . . Investing each song with her time-tested, raspy wisdom, Taylor shows that her pipes are still, indisputably, in perfect working order." In 2002 Alligator Records released *Koko Taylor: Deluxe Edition,* a collection of some of her greatest hits.

Among the albums that feature Taylor are *Montreux Festival: Blues Avalanche,* recorded in Switzerland in 1972 and reissued in 1986; *Blues Deluxe,* recorded at the Chicago Blues Festival in 1980; *Willie Dixon: The Chess Box* (1990); *What It Takes: The Chess Years* (1991); *The Alligator Records 20th Anniversary Collection* (1992); and *B.B. King's Blues Summit* (1993). In 1990 Taylor made her movie debut, as a lounge singer in the director David Lynch's *Wild at Heart.* She also recorded two songs for the soundtrack, both composed by Lynch himself. She appeared as herself in the movie *Mercury Rising* (1998) and as a member of the so-called Louisiana Gator Boys in *The Blues Brothers 2000* (1998). Along with other world-famous artists, Taylor performed at galas celebrating the inaugurations of President George Herbert Walker Bush, in 1989, and President Bill Clinton in 1993. She appeared on the NBC television programs *Late Night with David Letterman* and *Late Night with Conan O'Brien;* FOX-TV's *New York Undercover;* CBS's *This Morning, Nightwatch,* and *Early Edition;* and the National Public Radio programs *All Things Considered* and *Crossroads.* The singer was also featured in such national publications as *People, Entertainment Weekly, Rolling Stone,* and *Life.* Taylor was named Chicagoan of the Year by *Chicago* magazine in 1998. Most of the 29 W. C. Handy Awards Taylor won between 1980 and 2002 were in the category contemporary female blues artist of the year. (Some have credited W. C. Handy, a Memphis composer and bandleader, with coining the term "the blues" in 1912, when he published his song "The Memphis Blues.")

Personal Life

Taylor had one daughter, called Cookie, and two grandchildren. In 1996 Taylor married Hays Harris, a tavern owner. The couple maintained a home on Chicago's South Side. Each of the two music clubs that Taylor herself opened in Chicago in the 1990s have closed. Speaking of her stature as a blueswoman, Taylor told Niles Frantz, "It makes me proud to be a role model for young people coming up that wants to sing and play the blues. I'm reaching for the sky, but if I fall somewhere in the clouds, I'll still be happy. I'm gonna keep on doin' what I'm doin', and hanging in there for the best."

Koko Taylor had an operation for gastrointestinal bleeding in 2003, but recovered from it to return to performing, scheduling close to 50 concerts per year. She died on June 3, 2009 in Chicago, Illinois of complications from a second operation surgery for gastrointestinal bleeding. She was survived by her second husband, her daughter, her two grandchildren, and three great-grandchildren.

Further Reading

African American Publications (on-line)

Alligator Records Web site; Blues Foundation Web site

Charlotte Observer (on-line) Mar. 10, 1995

Chicago Tribune XIII p4 June 5, 1988, with photos, VII p2 Jan. 12, 1990, with photos

Gritz: The Online Southern Music Magazine Nov. 27, 2001

New York Times Magazine p22+ June 29, 1980, with photos

Rolling Stone p56 Feb. 24, 1994, pSupp4 May 28, 1998

Rolling Stone (on-line)

Susan Tedeschi

Guitarist

Born: November 9, 1970; Boston, Massachusetts
Primary Field: Blues and soul
Group Affiliation: Derek Trucks

Introduction

The influential editor and musicologist Timothy White wrote for Billboard *(30 Jan. 1999) that Susan Tedeschi's voice can "seethe, whoop, and soar with enough sensual blunder to break the seal on whiskey bottles and tear the leaves from the trees." Music journalists writing today are fond of quoting the line, and most almost inevitably go on to compare Tedeschi to Bonnie Raitt or Janis Joplin. Tedeschi takes the comparisons in stride. "[R]eally, there aren't a lot of women you can be compared to when you do the blues, especially if you're white," she told Steve Morse for the* Boston Globe *(16 May 1993). "I'm not going to be compared to Koko Taylor, Etta James, or Big Mama Thornton, even though they're big influences on me."*

Early Life

Tedeschi (pronounced teh-DESK-ee) was born on November 9, 1970, in Boston, Massachusetts. The third and last of three children, she grew up in nearby Norwell. Her father, Richard, became interested in genealogy after he retired from his video business, and taught Tedeschi a great deal about her ancestry. Reportedly, the land on which she was raised had been given to the family centuries before by a British monarch, and Tedeschi is said to be a distant cousin of the late Diana, Princess of Wales. Several of her ancestors sailed to America on the *Mayflower,* and Abraham Lincoln appears on a distant branch of the family tree. Tedeschi's mother; Patricia, is of Irish ancestry.

The Tedeschi name may be familiar even to those who are not blues fans, because it is prominently displayed on some two hundred convenience stores throughout the Northeast. Tedeschi's paternal great-grandfather, Angelo, had opened his first location in 1923, selling imported Italian meats and cheeses from his home in Rockland, Massachusetts, and the chain is still run by members of the family.

Growing up, Tedeschi's home was always filled with music. Richard, who played the acoustic guitar and harmonica, had a large and eclectic record collection, and Tedeschi loved hearing him play music by the Beatles, Buddy Holly, and the Everly Brothers, as well as works by such blues artists as Lightnin' Hopkins and Mississippi John Hurt. Her family recalls that she was singing while still in her crib-even before she could talk-and by the time she was six years old, Pat, who was active in community theater, began arranging performances for her. Tedeschi made her theatrical debut in a production of *Oliver!,* playing a workhouse urchin.

At the age of ten, Tedeschi traveled to New York to audition for a role in the musical *Annie.* Although she did not win the part, during the trip she met country legend Johnny Cash, who was staying in the same hotel." I ran into [him]. Literally," she recalled to Kathaleen Roberts for the *Albuquerque Journal* (9 Feb. 2009). "He said, 'Slow down, little girl.' I didn't realize who he was at the time. I told him I was a singer and he said, 'I'm a singer too. Maybe we can sing together sometime."'

Tedeschi, who played the clarinet as a teenager, wrote her first song at age fourteen. She performed as a member of the Norwell High School concert band. By age sixteen, she was playing with a cover band called Third Rail, which performed songs by Heart, the Beatles, and the Eagles at private parties. She later joined a band called the Smoking Section, which had regular gigs at clubs around Massachusetts. "I really liked the biker bars," she recalled to Morse. "A lot of those Harley guys can be the best audience." Tedeschi admits that, early in her career, she sometimes used an ID card with a fake birth date in order to participate in open-mic nights or blues jams at certain venues. Despite those forays into rock, Tedeschi continued work in musical theater. When she was seventeen, she played the lead role in a production of *Evita* at the Hingham Civic Music Theater.

While deeply devoted to music, Tedeschi was unsure about pursuing it as a career and toyed instead with the idea of becoming a marine biologist. As a gift for her high school graduation, she was given tuition to attend a five-week summer program at the Berklee College of Music, in Boston. Already accepted at a college in Ithaca, New York, Tedeschi changed her mind midway through the summer and decided to stay at Berklee. Her parents were supportive of the decision, and in the fall of 1 988, she became a full-time music student.

Tedeschi remained interested in musical theater, and she initially based her singing style on that of popular female performers like Linda Rondstadt. She preferred, as she has told interviewers, to sing in a "pretty" manner. Her attitude changed when she joined Berklee's Reverence Gospel Ensemble, under the direction of Dennis Montgomery III, whom she still counts as a major influence. "I wanted to find something with a little more guts, a little more soul," she explained to Mark Small for *Berklee Today* (Fall 2000). "I loved the gospel choir. I had never been shy about singing in front of people, but singing in front of a whole bunch of people who could really sing was a little frightening."

As much as she loved singing gospel and performing in churches around Boston, Tedeschi saw little future in focusing solely on that genre. "I knew that as a young white girl, I couldn't make a living singing gospel," she told Small. Remembering her father's old Lightnin' Hopkins and Mississippi John Hurt albums—and influenced by a boyfriend who loved Magic Sam, Otis Rush, and Freddie King—she turned her attention to the blues. "The blues bring people together," she explained to Morse. "It doesn't matter what color or background you're from. Everyone can get inspired by the blues."

Life's Work

Tedeschi, who earned extra cash as a student by singing show tunes on the *Spirit of Boston,* a dinner-cruise ship, graduated from Berklee in 1991 with a degree in musical composition and performance. She began appearing regularly at area clubs, including Johnny D's in Somerville, the House of Blues in Cambridge, and the Yard Rock in Quincy. Wielding a new Fender guitar, she often worked with Adrienne Hayes, a fellow Boston-based guitarist and vocalist. In 1993, the pair joined forces with Annie Raines, a harmonica player, to form the first incarnation of the Susan Tedeschi Band. While the backup performers changed occasionally, the band ultimately featured a semiregular lineup that included the bassist Jim Lamond and the drummer Tom Hambridge. In 1994, the group won a Boston Battle of the Bands competition, and the following year they placed second in the National Blues Talent Competition held in Memphis, Tennessee.

In 1995, Tedeschi borrowed $10,000 and released her debut album, *Better Days,* which included several original tracks, as well as covers of such blues standards as Leiber and Stoller's "Hound Dog" and Elmore James's "It Hurts Me Too." The album coupled with multiple Boston Music Award nods, increased Tedeschi's visibility greatly. Soon she was being invited to open for such performers as Buddy Guy and B. B. King.

Tedeschi also found herself in great demand on the club and festival circuit, and for many days out of the year, she was on the road. She was backed on tour by her boyfriend at the time, guitarist Sean Costello, and his band, the Jive Bombers. Costello, who was widely considered among the most promising blues guitarists of his generation, suffered from bipolar disorder; he died in 2008, right before his thirtieth birthday, of an accidental drug overdose.

In 1998, Tedeschi released her next album, *Just Won't Burn,* on the Massachusetts indie label Tone-Cool Records. Richard Rosenblatt, Tone-Cool's president, was a musician himself—he had played the harmonica in a group called the Eleventh Hour Blues Band and Tedeschi knew that he loved and appreciated roots music. She also trusted his business integrity. "I don't want to be in debt, and [major] record labels are banks," she told Jim Beal Jr. for the *San Antonio Express-News* (12 May 2000). "Everything they give you, you owe them, and they're banks with very high interest rates. They'll try to sell you in a certain way. I don't want any part of that. I want to be known as a regular girl making good music." Most critics agreed that she was making good music. Jim McGuinness, for example, wrote for the Bergen County, New Jersey, *Record* (27 Feb. 1998), '*Just Won't Burn* brims with powerful vocals, blistering guitar licks, and a white-hot energy that suggest Tedeschi will be a major blues figure for years to come." Many music journalists were especially impressed at her brave inclusion of John Prine's "Angel from Montgomery," a song most people associated with Bonnie Raitt, whose cover version was widely considered definitive. Later that year, in the wake of *Just Won't Burn's* success, *Better Days* was reissued.

In 1999, while opening for the Southern blues/ rock legends the Allman Brothers Band, Tedeschi met Derek Trucks. His uncle, Butch Trucks, had been a founding member of the Allman Brothers, and Derek, a child prodigy who had learned the guitar at age nine, began touring with the group as a guest artist when he was thirteen. Considered a master slide guitarist, he had formed his own eponymous band in 1996, and in 1999, the year he met Tedeschi, he also became a formal member of the Allman Brothers. "The first time I heard Derek play, I got butterflies in my stomach and I actually cried," Tedeschi told Wayne Bledsoe for the *Knoxville*

Affiliation: Derek Trucks

During the early years of their marriage, Tedeschi and Trucks always toured and recorded separately. "He's got his thing and I've got my thing and they're both important," she told a reporter for the *Lancaster Intelligencer Journal* (31 Oct. 2003). "Both need to be [heard]." They backed an occasional track on each other's albums, and from time to time they performed gigs together as part of a casual band they called the Soul Stew Revival, which also included Trucks's younger brother, Duane, on drums.

That changed in 2010, when they decided to join forces as the Tedeschi Trucks Band. The eleven member group also featured Allman Brothers bassist Oteil Burbridge and his brother, Kofi Burbridge, a flutist/keyboard player from the Derek Trucks Band; drummers J. J. Johnson and Tyler Greenwell; vocalists Mike Mattison of the Derek Trucks Band and Mark Rivers; trombonist Saunders Sermons; saxophonist Kebbi Williams; and trumpet player Maurice Brown. The group's powerful sound and versatility have won over fans of both the Susan Tedeschi Band and the Derek Trucks Band.

The new group's first album, *Revelator,* recorded in their horne studio, was released in 2011 and won the Grammy Award for best contemporary blues album of the year. The following year, they released their sophomore effort, a live double album titled *Everybody's Talkin'.* In addition to their work in the studio, they tour widely, often accompanied by Charlie and Sophia. "I see Derek and I at seventy or eighty in rocking chairs, playing guitar together," Tedeschi told Mike Devlin for the Victoria, British Columbia, *Times Colonist* (22 June 2008). "We are doing this for life. It is our life."

News-Sentinel (26 Sep. 2003). Despite the difficulties of conflicting tour schedules, the two began dating, traveling to see each other whenever their performance schedules allowed.

Tedeschi's schedule became even more grueling in 2000, after she was nominated for a Grammy Award in the category of best new artist. She seemed an anomaly in a field that included Britney Spears, Christina Aguilera, Kid Rock, and Macy Gray. Many industry observers expressed shock. "Tedeschi has no music video. She doesn't do Tommy Hilfiger ads or bare her bellybutton on stage," Letta Tayler wrote for New York *Newsday* (20 Feb. 2000). "And she's up against some of the biggest names in pop, stars whose faces are plastered across billboards and whose songs are ubiquitous on radio and MTV."

Some cynically suggested that the National Academy of Recording Arts and Sciences, the organization that oversees the awards, was desperate to prove its credibility by nominating an artist with undeniable musical ability. (For one thing, none of the other nominees was an especially skilled instrumentalist.) Others maintained that the Academy's relatively new voting system was ensuring that skill and artistry, rather than merely sales figures, were being rewarded. Under the overhauled system, the nominees in the four top categories album of the year, record of the year, song of the year, and best new artist would be chosen by a blue-ribbon panel of twenty-five industry experts, rather than by the Academy's ten thousand rank-and-file members. Nevertheless, Christina Aguilera took home the 2000 Grammy for Best New Artist.

Tedeschi, who married Trucks on December 5, 2001, now faced the difficulties of juggling an increasingly high-profile career with a family life. Their son, Charles Khalil (named for saxophonist Charlie Parker, guitarist Charlie Christian, and writer Khalil Gibran), was born in 2002, and their daughter, Sophia Naima (whose middle name is derived from a John Coltrane ballad), followed in 2004. "The biggest problem that I have, career wise, is finding time to play music and write music when I'm not onstage," she told Jesse Fox Mayshark for the *New York Times* (5 Mar. 2006). "Because I'm Mom from six or seven in the morning up until a few minutes before I go onstage sometimes. So there's really no break."

With her mother-in-law providing childcare, Tedeschi continued touring, and although there were long gaps between albums, she continued to record. In 2002, she released *Wait for Me.* "With classy yet scorching performances and songs infused with roots rock, blues, funk, and even pop, it's a crossover album that oozes with integrity, terrific playing, and a loose yet distinctive direction," Hal Horowitz wrote in an undated review for the All Music Guide website.

Tedeschi next recorded the gospel-inspired cover album *Hope and Desire,* which was released on the Verve label in 2005, and she followed that in 2008 with *Back to the River,* which debuted at number one on the *Billboard* blues chart. The river referred to in the title is the St John's, in Jacksonville, Florida, where she and Trucks live when not on the road. ''I've always been near a river it seems, whether this one in Jacksonville, or the North River in Norwell, and both reflect very peaceful, calming places in my heart," she told Jay N. Miller for the *Patriot Ledger* (I0 Nov. 2008). Referring to the title track, which she cowrote with guitarist Tony Joe White, she said, "It is a song by someone who's been on the road a bit too long and reflects your desire to get back to your roots, your home, your family, all the more important things in life."

Although *Wait for Me, Hope and Desire,* and *Back to the River* were each nominated for a Grammy Award in the category of best contemporary blues album, it was not until Tedeschi and Trucks teamed up that she received one of the coveted statuettes.

Journalists frequently comment about the disparity between Tedeschi's blistering, bluesy voice and her outward "girl-next-door" appearance. She favors a fresh-scrubbed look, often wears flowery sundresses while performing, and plays a guitar decorated with stickers-some of them depicting storybook characters like Winnie the Pooh. Her background also strikes many as an unconventional one for a blues musician. Martin L. Johnson wrote for the *Mountain Xpress* (7 Oct. 2003), a North Carolina-based alternative paper, "While she'll never be able to boast the tortured biography of the musicians she most admires-[bluesman] Dr. John, for instance, took up piano after his 'strummin' finger' was shot off in a barroom fight—Tedeschi's talent and voice foretell a lengthy career."

Tedeschi believes that those disparities allow her to make music that transcends expectations. "If your intentions are good, and if the music's good, it doesn't matter if you're playing Indian classical music and you're from San Francisco, or if you're a girl from suburbia playing the blues," she told Joan Anderman for the *Boston Globe* (27 July 2001).

Personal Life

Like many recording artists, Tedeschi's personal life seemingly receives as much press attention as her music. She is married to guitarist Derek Trucks of the Allman Brothers Band, and the two frequently collaborate on projects.

Further Reading

Anderman, Joan. "Blues to Her Roots." *Boston Globe* 27 July 2001: D14.

Beal, Jim Jr. "Tedeschi Keeps Focus on Music, Not Image." *San Antonio Express-News* 12 May 2000: H14.

Bledsoe, Wayne. "Bliss amid the Blues." *Knoxville News-Sentinel26* Sep. 2003: 5.

Devlin, Mike. "Living a Blues Dream." (Victoria, British Columbia) *Times Colonist.* 22 June 2008: B1.

Johnson, Martin L. "Berklee Blues." *Mountain Xpress* 7 Oct. 2003:41.

Mayshark, Jesse Fox. "Ramblin' Man and Woman, Married With Kids." *New York Times.* New York Times, 5 Mar. 2006. Web. 10 June 2012. Mcguinness, Jim. "Pure as Her Driven Blues." (Bergen County, New Jersey) *Record* 27 Feb. 1998: 3.

Johnny Temple

Book publisher; bass guitarist

Born: Nov. 3, 1966; Washington, D.C.
Primary Field: Indie-rock
Group Affiliation: Girls Against Boys; Soulside; New Wet Kojak

Introduction

Describing the independent book publisher and musician Johnny Temple, Danny Goldberg, a music producer and record-label executive, told David Daley for the Hartford *(Connecticut)* Courant *(May 12, 2002), "He's really got a vision. . . . I've never known of anyone like Johnny, with that renaissance combination of interests and skills." As a bass guitarist, Temple is best known for his work with the indie-rock band Girls Against Boys, which has toured with such well-known groups as Foo Fighters, Rage Against the Machine, and Fugazi and released songs heard on the soundtracks of movies including* Clerks, Series 7: The Contenders, *and* Hedwig and the Angry Inch. *In 1997, after Girls Against Boys signed with a major record label, Temple used money from his advance to found a small, independent publishing company, the Brooklyn, New York-based Akashic Books, dedicated to what the company Web site calls "reverse-gentrification of the literary world"—that is, the distribution of literature ignored by major publishing houses to a readership that extends beyond the educated middle class. The company also aims to provide what it calls "a cure for the common novel." Akashic currently boasts dozens of titles in genres including literary fiction, mystery, crime, nonfiction, African-American interest, and gay and lesbian interest. In addition, Temple has written for several high-profile publications, including the* Nation.

Early Life

Johnny Temple was born on November 3, 1966 in Washington, D.C. His father, Ralph J. Temple, a lawyer, served for 13 years as the head of the local chapter of the American Civil Liberties Union (ACLU); his mother was a public defender. Temple grew up in a middle-class, mostly black neighborhood and attended private school until 10th grade, when he transferred of his own volition to a local public high school, Wilson, in the Northwest section of the city. The school "was ten percent white, but that was considered the white public school because it had so many more white kids than [other Washington public schools] . . . ," Temple told Williams Cole and Theodore Hamm for the *Brooklyn Rail-Express* (April 2003). "There was a chasm, you know, academically. In D.C. people will say, 'Oh, Wilson is just as good as any of the private schools.' Well, no it's not, and you really experience the difference in resources between a private school and a public school. It was just really interesting and so much of my life has grown out of that experience-everyone I played music with is from the public school system. I also became really interested in issues of race." While in high school Temple had an internship at an independent reggae record label, RAS Records. After graduating from Wilson, Temple attended Wesleyan University, in Middletown,

Connecticut, where he majored in African-American studies. He later earned a master's degree in social work from Columbia University, in New York City. Meanwhile, he had begun playing the bass guitar during his sophomore year of college, and during his junior year he joined a band called Lunchmeat, which included Temple's high-school friends Alexis Fleisig on drums and Scott McCloud on guitar. A few years later the band added the singer Bobby Sullivan, renamed itself Soulside, and was signed to the indie label Dischord. Those developments occurred at about the time Temple received his degree in social work. He told Mary Blume for the *International Herald Tribune* (January 12, 2007), "I loved social work, I loved working with juvenile delinquents, that was my area of focus. . . . I was sort of at a crossroads and I picked rock 'n' roll because I could return to social work, and I still could, but I knew I could never return to rock 'n' roll." Soulside recorded the albums *Trigger* (1988), *Hot Bodigram* (1990), and *Soon Come Happy* (1990), breaking up shortly after the last release.

Life's Work

Following the release of *House of GVSB,* Girls Against Boys left Touch and Go Records for a major label, Geffen Records. Temple resisted the move, explaining to Colatosti, "Now we've signed a contract with Geffen Records. This is not an independent company. It is a major recording corporation. This has helped us get some things that we couldn't get before, like more money so that we can all afford health insurance. But now we have to struggle to stay part of the independent music community. Geffen and other major corporations aren't really part of a music community. They are just trying to make money. Working with them means that we are associated with a business that focuses on the bottom line, and not with an independent label that is interested just in producing good music. The music industry is corrupt, market-driven and it is getting worse. It is disillusioning to work with a company that should be about promoting creativity but isn't." The band's first album with Geffen Records, *Freak*on*ica* (1998), received mixed reviews. The *Dallas Observer* (May 14, 1998) critic, Keven McAlester, found the album to be overly sanitized, writing, "Girls Against Boys used to be all about sex, and not just in its lyrics (though you'd find plenty there too.) The dueling basses of Eli Janney and Johnny Temple, the slurred come-ons of vocalist Scott

Affiliation: Girls Against Boys

McCloud, Fleisig, and Temple next joined the Fugazi drummer, Brendan Canty, in the studio for a project that culminated in the formation of Girls Against Boys. As McCloud recalled events to Jason Heller for the *Denver (Colorado) Westward* (September 5, 2002), "Girls Against Boys began as basically just an experiment. I think we wanted to give it a little more of a darker edge than Soulside, which was kind of more explosive, you know, more hardcore. We started out with a few studio freakout sessions where we just sort of laid down some weird tracks. It wasn't a real band then. We just kind of fantasized about playing shows. But those sessions did end up becoming that first EP we did, *Nineties Vs. Eighties.*" After Canty left the group, Girls Against Boys added another bassist, Eli Janney, who had acted as Soulside's sound technician, and who also added keyboards to the mix. The band—which called itself GVSB for short—released its first album, *Tropic of Scorpio,* in the early 1990s, before signing with the indie label Touch and Go Records. Three full-length albums followed: *Venus Luxure No. 1 Baby* (1994), *Cruise Yourself* (1995), and *House of GVSB* (1996). Girls Against Boys quickly became known for bass-heavy, sexually charged music, with Heidi Sherman remarking for *Rolling Stone* (May 28, 1999), "The band has churned out lo-fi, heavy grooves (they employ two basses) that can transform any club into a carnal pit, dense with sweat and pheromones." Temple told Camille Colatosti for *Witness* (on-line), "Girls Against Boys is both a creative and a social or political project. The music is discordant as far as loud rock music goes. Our musical roots are in the punk rock tradition, but we are not a punk rock band. Still, the passion and aggressiveness of punk informs the band. . . . When the band started in the early 1990s—our first album was in 1991—there was a boys' club mentality in rock music. There are so many more women in rock now than there were 10 years ago, and this is good. But back then we wanted to make a statement about the boys' club. We wanted to say that, even though the band is all men, we aren't part of the boys' club." In 1995, while still with Touch and Go Records, McCloud and Temple began a side project called New Wet Kojak, with Geoff Turner of Gray Matter and Nick Pelleciotto of Edsel. New Wet Kojak has released a self-titled record (1995) as well as *Nasty International* (1997), *Do Things* (2000), and *This Is the Glamorous* (2003).

McCloud, the preponderance of heavy grooves—all of it once added up to [a] kind of sultry-rock vibe.... Its title notwithstanding, *Freak*on*ica* offers precious little that could be mistaken for sensuality. The deficiency is confusing.... Girls Against Boys is capable of writing better songs than these. There's not much of the wit once evidenced in 'Kill the Sexplayer' or 'Cruise Your New Baby Fly Self,' not much of the catchy buzz that once propelled 'Crash 17 (X-Rated Car),' not much of the subdued grind that once carried 'Vera Cruz' and 'Zodiac Love Team.' What's left is ... well, not much." In stark contrast, Vicki Gilmer wrote for the Minneapolis, Minnesota, *Star Tribune* (August 7, 1998), "Subverting the conventions of lounge and disco music, the Washington, D.C. group's dance-cum-rock music is full of sexual innuendo, punkish vibrancy, and enough electronic manipulation to make it the dirtiest and darkest, but still danceable, soundtrack for the '90s, The band's latest album, *Freak*on*ica,* recorded at Minneapolis' Seedy Underbelly Studios, is roiled by the twin-bass slaughter of Eli Janney and Johnny Temple, while McCloud's guitar gives the songs enough of a Jurassic stomp to shake the rafters."

After Geffen Records signed Girls Against Boys, the band members received sizable record advances. At first Temple planned to use his share to launch his own record label; after realizing that the business side of music did not appeal to him, he decided to try his hand at publishing. Temple told Sarah Ferguson for the *Village Voice* (June 29, 1999), "Part of what motivated me to ... invest myself in independent publishing was because my band had made this jump from an independent label to a major one—a system I have absolutely no respect for. That gave me the motivation to create a counterbalance by investing myself in independent art." Akashic Books' first title was a reprint of an underground favorite, *The F**k-Up,* by Arthur Nersesian, in 1997; the book was later picked up by Simon & Schuster. Akashic has since published a wide variety of books, both fiction and nonfiction, many dealing with issues of race, class, or sexuality in urban settings. Temple has attempted not only to publish the work of writers from marginalized groups but to bring literature to a wider audience, telling Mary Blume, "I think that literature should be consumed by more than just the well-educated. Reverse gentrification is the notion that we don't need to just keep trying to sell books to the same people, these people for sure but also more of the population." Temple's venture outside the musical realm allowed him to delve into some of the issues that he had studied in college and graduate school. "I was always struggling with how to satisfy my passion for social justice and social issues," he told Janet Saidi for the *Los Angeles Times* (February 3, 2004), "and I never intended to go into book publishing—it was sort of a whim. I really feel that I've found something that satisfies my interest in politics and race and my various progressive passions." Other Akashic books have included *The Massage* (1999), by Henry Flesh, a novel about a masseuse in New York's gay underworld, and *R&B (Rhythm and Business): The Political Economy of Black Music* (2002), by Norman Kelley.

Mary Blume reported in early 2007 that Akashic "camps with a staff of four in a scruffy room in the former American Can Factory in Brooklyn." Akashic received a major boost in 2002, when Kaylie Jones, the daughter of the famed novelist James Jones, asked Temple to reissue a collection of her late father's short stories, *The Ice Cream Headache and Other Stories* (originally published in 1968) as well as his novel *The Merry Month of May* (1971). Temple was initially hesitant to take on those projects, since, as a small company, Akashic could not offer the same level of distribution as a major publishing house. Unlike bigger, long-established publishing companies, Akashic does not offer large advances but instead relies on a system similar to that of royalties paid by some independent music labels: writers receive half of the profits earned by their books. To save on expenditures, Akashic does not put writers up in expensive hotels or pay their plane fares during book tours; writers often transport themselves by car and stay in inexpensive motels. The appeal of Akashic for many writers is that they have greater agency in the publishing process, including input into their books' cover designs, layout, and marketing campaigns. Every piece of copy related to a book is a collaborative effort between the writer and Akashic. Ron Kovic, the author of the memoir *Born on the Fourth of July,* chose Akashic to reprint that 1976 Vietnam War classic because he was disgusted by the gory cover selected by his previous publisher; with Akashic he was given freer rein to present his book as he wished. Explaining why writers might choose Akashic over major publishing companies, Karin Taylor of the New York Small Press Center told the *Los Angeles Times* (February 3, 2004), "Authors will sometimes choose to go with Johnny Temple because that author knows that Johnny will put his heart, soul and whole effort into that book."

As for Temple's music career, Universal Music Group had purchased Geffen Records in 1999; GVSB subsequently came under pressure to deliver an album that would be accessible to a wider audience. Unwilling to compromise their aesthetic principles, GVSB asked to be released by the company and later signed with an indie label, Jade Tree, which released their first album in four years, *You Can't Fight What You Can't See* (2002). That album was produced by Ted Nicely, who had worked on two of the group's earlier indie albums, *Cruise Yourself* and *House of GVSB.* The new record was in many ways a return to the band's style prior to *Freak*on*ica,* with a less slick, more insistently powerful sound. "Once we got off Geffen," Temple told Brian Baker for the *Cleveland Scene* (March 7, 2002), "we were free to record the album that we've wanted to record for a couple years. We wanted it to be aggressive, upbeat, raw, with guitars, bass, drums, keyboards, and vocals upfront and urgent." Music aficionados were pleased with the shift away from the *Freak*on*ica* style; Heller wrote, "With GVSB already somewhat stigmatized by its new major-label association, *Freak*On*Ica* was, for many fans, the final straw. All of the familiar elements of the band's approach were still intact: the black humor, the brooding intensity, the pulverizing beats. And yet, its plastic production and near-pop sensibility steered *Freak*on*ica* dangerously close to the histrionic shlock dredged up by Nine Inch Nails and Prodigy.... *You Can't Fight What You Can't See* . . . . is a strong contender for the best yet. Allied with the flourishing independent label Jade Tree, the band is at a point where it has nothing to lose."

Although he now focuses most of his attention on his work for Akashic Books, Temple completed two European tours with Girls Against Boys in 2007. In 2008 he helped organize the third annual Brooklyn Book Festival, which introduced the public to writers and publishers from around the world. Currently, he serves as the chair of the Brooklyn Literary Council.

Personal Life

Temple lives in the Fort Greene section of Brooklyn with his wife and two children. Temple told Amy Freeborn for the *Advertiser* (July 4, 2002), "Being in a band is great but it can't be your only thing. I know for me personally, I'd be pretty miserable if all I did with my life was rock music."

Further Reading

Advertiser p58 July 4, 2002
Dallas Observer (on-line) May 14, 1998
Denver Westward (on-line) Sep. 5, 2002
Hartford (Connecticut) Courant p10 May 12, 2002
International Herald Tribune (on-line) Jan. 12, 2007
Los Angeles Times E p1 Feb. 3, 2004
(Minneapolis, Minnesota) *Star Tribune* E p3 Aug. 7, 1998
Rolling Stone (on-line) May 28, 1998
Village Voice (on-line) June 29, 1999
Witness (on-line) June 2001

Chris Thile

Bluegrass musician

Born: June 26, 1973; Pocahontas, Illinois
Primary Field: Bluegrass
Group Affiliation: Solo artist

Introduction

"Google the word 'mandolinist' and take a look at the suggestions that drop down in the search bar," David Weininger wrote for the Boston Globe *(19 Oct. 2013). "The name 'Chris Thile' is sure to be at, or near, the top." He explained, "It's a convenient shorthand for the fact that Thile has revolutionized his instrument—not only by furthering the evolution of bluegrass but by bringing the mandolin out of its niche and making it a viable contributor to a variety of styles."*

Early Life

Chris Thile was born on February 20, 1981, in Oceanside, California. He has an older brother, John, and a younger brother, Daniel. Commenting on the unlikelihood of a West Coast native taking an interest in bluegrass music and the mandolin, which are typically associated with Kentucky, Thile told Ralph Berrier Jr. for the *Roanoke Times* (20 Oct. 2006), "I'm from Southern California. My 'roots' are more likely the Beach Boys.

I've always been a bluegrass outsider. I don't identify with moonshining or coal mining."

Thile's father, Scott, was a professional piano tuner, and Thile remembers being surrounded by music from the time he was in diapers. When he was still a toddler, his parents regularly took him to That Pizza Place, a Carlsbad-area restaurant that hosted evenings of live bluegrass music. There he became fascinated by the sound of the mandolin, a stringed instrument belonging to the lute family. After his parents found a cassette tape of the Foggy Mountain Boys' *Flatt & Scruggs' Greatest Hits* in a drugstore bargain bin, he listened to it incessantly.

Almost immediately after being introduced to the instrument, Thile began pestering his parents for a mandolin of his own. Finally, when he was five years old, they agreed, allowing him to have a relatively inexpensive model handed down by a family friend. (One of the instruments he now plays, by contrast, is said to be worth $200,000.) They hired John Moore, a highly respected mandolin player who often performed at That Pizza Place, to teach him. "When he was a little kid, just learning, we'd sit down and I'd gauge how he was feeling," Thile's mother, Kathy, told Caroline Wright for *Bluegrass Now* magazine (Aug. 2002). "Some days he'd have more ability to stick to something than on other days. At only five, they're different from day to day! . . . We'd go for however long he could do it." She continued, "When he was a little older, he set himself up with a little star chart with his songs on it, and he'd do the song, then grade himself. I still have one where he wrote, *'Pritty Good!'*"

In 1989, when Thile was eight years old, he and two other youngsters—fiddler Sara Watkins, who was also eight, and her older brother, Sean, a twelve-year-old mandolinist and guitarist—formed the band Nickel Creek. The two families had met while attending shows at the pizza parlor, and the trio began playing their own gigs there, with Scott Thile on bass. Throughout the 1990s the band proved a popular feature at bluegrass festivals all over the country, and their busy touring schedule required the young members to be homeschooled.

Early on, Thile, who moved with his family to Kentucky in 1995 so his father could work as a musical instrument technician at Murray State University, recorded both with Nickel Creek and as a solo artist. Of his first solo effort, *Leading Off* . . . (1994), Stanton Swihart wrote for the AllMusic website, "According to the liner notes, in most ways Chris Thile was a typical thirteen-year-old when he put out this debut album . . . From the musical evidence, though, he was a typical teenager in the way that, say, Mozart was probably a typical teenager. The level of playing and compositional skill, not to mention the imagination, displayed on *Leading Off* . . . is no less than virtuosic."

Chris Thile.

Although Nickel Creek released *Little Cowpoke* in 1993 on the tiny label Choo Choo Records and followed it in 1997 with the self-released *Here to There*, most sources refer to their eponymous 2000 album as their debut. It was, more accurately, their major-label debut. Produced by the popular bluegrass and folk artist Alison Krauss, who had met the young musicians at a festival, and released by Sugar Hill Records, known for its seminal catalog of roots music, the album quickly went platinum. The recording also earned the group two Grammy Award nominations, in the categories of best bluegrass album and best country instrumental (for the song "Ode to a Butterfly"). Nickel Creek was nominated for a Country Music Association (CMA) Award for best vocal group and named one of the "Five Music Innovators of the Millennium" by the editors of *Time* magazine.

Despite the accolades, Thile, who at age twelve had become the youngest winner in the history of the National Mandolin Championships, is not especially proud of his earliest recordings. "Having come of age on record, it comes down to that classic cliché: the more you know, the more you don't know," he admitted to Matthews. "And I definitely thought I knew everything when Nickel Creek's first record came out. I was seventeen when we recorded it and eighteen when it was released. That music . . . just sounds unbearably smug to me. The know-it-all kid in class . . . it's hard for me to listen to it."

Life's Work

Nickel Creek released other well-regarded albums, including *This Side* (2002) and *Why Should the Fire Die?* (2005), before disbanding in 2006 to pursue other projects. Their farewell tour extended into 2007.

After leaving Nickel Creek, Thile, who had studied music at Murray State University for a few semesters before dropping out to focus on his professional career, joined fiddler and longtime friend Gabe Witcher, banjo player Noam Pikelny, guitarist Chris "Critter" Eldridge, and bassist Greg Garrison to form a new group, initially called Chris Thile and the How to Grow a Band. "The acoustic-music scene we all come from is really small," Eldridge told Dan Bolles for the Vermont alternative weekly newspaper *Seven Days* (5 Feb. 2008). "After a while you kind of get to know everyone else. It's a small community. So the band sort of formed through these mutual relationships. We're all guys around the same age who are on the same wavelength musically and as far as what our aspirations were." The group released their first album together, *How to Grow a Woman from the Ground*, in 2006 to positive reviews. In a review for Sing Out! (2007), Stephanie P. Ledgin called it "a colorful panorama of [Thile's] expansive creativity" and said of the band, "Each player is a perfectly matched complement to the others.

For a time, the group changed its name to the Tensions Mountain Boys (the pun becomes apparent when the name is said quickly). They ultimately settled on the Punch Brothers, a reference to a Mark Twain story, under which name they recorded such albums as *Punch* (2008), *Antifogmatic* (2010), *Who's Feeling Young Now?* (2012), and *Ahoy!* (2012). Signaling Thile's determination to push musical boundaries, *Punch* includes a genre-bending four-movement composition called "The Blind Leaving the Blind." "It's part modern chamber music and part song cycle—an impressionistic picture of a young marriage gone sour," Craig Havighurst wrote for National Public Radio (29 Feb. 2008). "It owes a debt to Bach, Bob Dylan, even the Beach Boys. And, of course, bluegrass."

Actor and comedian Ed Helms summed up the Punch Brothers' appeal in an article for *Paste* magazine (10 Aug. 2010), writing, "Their music is an impossibly perfect mixture of down-home charm and staggering sophistication"—a sentiment almost universally echoed by other music journalists. (Helms also concluded that the band members must be aliens, observing, "Frontman Chris Thile's mandolin playing defies the laws of physics. It is my belief that he has an additional six fingers on his left hand which are invisible.") In an interview with Hal Bienstock for *American Songwriter* (9 Jan. 2012), record producer T Bone Burnett called the Punch Brothers "one of the most incredible bands this country has ever produced" and described Thile as "probably a once-in-a-century musician, like Louis Armstrong was a once-in-a-century musician."

Thile has performed as a backup musician with a wide variety of other artists, including country music stars Dolly Parton and Dierks Bentley. He teamed up with fellow mandolinist Mike Marshall for *Into the Cauldron* (2003) and *Live*: *Duets* (2006) and paired with bassist Edgar Meyer for a category-defying album titled simply *Edgar Meyer & Chris Thile* (2008). Additionally, he was joined by guitarist Michael Daves on *Sleep with One Eye Open* (2011), a collection of traditional tunes from such bluegrass legends as Jimmy Martin and the Foggy Mountain Boys.

One of the most unusual collaborations Thile has ever undertaken came in 2011, when he, Meyer, fiddler Stuart Duncan, and acclaimed cellist Yo-Yo Ma recorded *The Goat Rodeo Sessions.* (In colloquial terms, a "goat rodeo" is a chaotic event that defies efforts to impose order on it—a reference to the seeming impossibility of four such disparate artists reaching any musical consensus.) "It's more of a little Frankenstein music monster. . . . I think what you have is a broad range on the spectrum of formal to informal music making," Thile told Gary Graff for *Billboard* (27 Oct. 2011). "Everyone" complements each other nicely. I think it's the kind of thing that maybe classical music listeners will think is bluegrass and bluegrass listeners will think it's classical. Hopefully it lands in the nebulous zone where it can't really be named." The quartet was featured on several late-night talk shows and also performed

Affiliation: Bluegrass Music

Yet some musical purists do not believe that the mandolin needed to be brought out of its niche. As a result, Thile—who was named a national mandolin champion at age twelve, earned the title of Mandolin Player of the Year from the International Bluegrass Music Association at age twenty, and won a 2012 MacArthur Foundation "genius grant" at age thirty-one—has not been fully embraced by certain segments of the music community. His detractors assert that he has veered too far away from the traditional bluegrass music that was pioneered by the legendary Bill Monroe in the late 1940s, with which the mandolin is most often associated. In response, Thile told Cameron Matthews for the country-music website *The Boot* (17 Feb. 2012), "We [the Punch Brothers] have a tremendous amount of respect for our predecessors on this group of instruments, which is commonly associated with bluegrass, but we're not interested in being museum curators of their work. Rather, we want them to influence our work." Addressing the same issue, he later told Cormac Larkin for the *Irish Times* (13 July 2012), "To me, it's always made sense to look forward when it comes to making music of any kind. . . . Bill Monroe and those guys weren't trying to sound like anyone. They were trying to create something new, and that's why their music is so important to so many people. I just think it's so funny when people decide that what we do isn't good because it doesn't sound like Bill Monroe. It's like saying that a zebra isn't a very good rhinoceros."

Thile has even recorded an album of Bach sonatas, written his own ambitious forty-minute, four-movement suite, and collaborated with celebrated cellist Yo-Yo Ma. Explaining why he feels comfortable transcending musical boundaries, he told Geoffrey Himes for the folk-music magazine *Sing Out!* (2008), "Genre distinctions are only good for record stores. It's all the same notes. In Western music there are twelve notes to choose from; [classical composer Gustav) Mahler used the same twelve as [bluegrass musician] Jimmy Martin."

live in concert. In 2013 the recording earned Grammy Awards for best folk album and best engineered nonclassical album.

Thile reunited with Sara and Sean Watkins in 2014 to record a new Nickel Creek album, *A Dotted Line* (2014), and to tour in celebration of the group's twenty-fifth anniversary. "Now we can look back and have a good laugh at ourselves—like looking at your baby pictures," Thile told Jim Farber for the *New York Daily News* (25 Apr. 2014).

Personal Life

Thile married fashion designer Jesse Meighan in 2003. The marriage was brief, ending in divorce the following year. Thile has said that his pain over the breakup was his inspiration for composing "The Blind Leaving the Blind." In December 2013 Thile married Claire Coffee, an actor best known for playing villain Adalind Schade on the hit television series *Grimm* (2011–). The wedding took place on a picturesque farm resort in the Great Smoky Mountains of Tennessee.

Thile lives in the New York borough of Manhattan. In 2012 he won a John D. and Catherine T. MacArthur Foundation Fellowship, commonly called the "genius grant," for "his adventurous, multifaceted artistry as both a composer and performer" and for "creating a distinctly American canon for the mandolin and a new musical aesthetic for performers and audiences alike."

Further Reading

Farber, Jim. "Nickel Creek, One of the Youngest Bands to Ever Celebrate a 25th Anniversary, Returns with Album and Tour." *New York Daily News*. NYDailyNews.com, 25 Apr. 2014. Web. 1 July 2014.

Graff, Gary. "Yo-Yo Ma Trades Bach for Bluegrass in *Goat Rodeo Sessions*." *Billboard*. Billboard, 27 Oct. 2011. Web. 1 July 2014.

Helms, Ed. 'The Slobbering Rave: Beware the Punch Brothers." *Paste*. Paste Media, 10 Aug. 2010. Web. 1 July 2014.

Himes, Geoffrey. "Punch Brothers: A Little of Everything Makes a Lot." *Sing Out!* Autumn 2008: 34–39. Print

Thile, Chris. "Chris Thile, Youngest MacArthur Genius of 2012, on His 'Dauntingly Lofty' New Status." Interview by Mallika Rao. *Huffington Post*. TheHuffingtonPost.com, 4 Oct. 2012. Web. 1 July 2014.

Thile, Chris. "Punch Brothers' Chris Thile Embraces 'Relative Incompetence.'" Interview by Cameron Matthews. *The Boot*. Townsquare

Media, 17 Feb. 2012. Web. 1 July 2014.
Weininger, David. "Not Enough Music in the Day for Mandolinist Chris Thile." *Boston Globe*. Boston Globe, 19 Oct. 2013. Web. 1 July 2014.

Hao Jiang Tian

Singer

Born: 1954; Beijing, China
Primary Field: Opera
Group Affiliation: New York City Metropolitan Opera

Introduction

Since Hao Jiang Tian made his debut with the New York City Metropolitan Opera, in 1991, the renowned basso cantante has given more than 1,300 performances in upwards of 40 roles with companies in Italy, France, Portugal, Germany, Argentina, Holland, Japan, and China, among other countries, and has performed with such opera greats as Placido Domingo, Luciano Pavarotti, and Kiri Te Kanawa. "If Tian's speaking voice is soft and buttery, his singing voice is molten chocolate," Chelsey Baker-Hauck wrote for the University of Denver Magazine *(Fall 2007). "Critics consistently praise his rich, full, flexible voice, which can command or caress a note with equal acuity."*

Early Life

Hao Jiang Tian was born in Beijing, China, in the late summer of 1954. His mother's birth name was Du Li, "Li" meaning "beauty"; she changed her name during Mao's rule, during which vanity and femininity were looked down upon, to Lu Yuan, which translates as "big land." At the age of 13, she left her home to join what Tian described in his autobiography as a military propaganda entertainment troupe. In it she met Tian Xiaohai, who was a year older. He later changed his name to Tian Yun, which means "cultivate." The couple performed in the People's Liberation Army Zhongzheng Song and Dance Ensemble, Tian Yun as conductor and Lu Yuan as composer, and had three children, including Hao Jiang Tian's older brother, Hao Qian ("big road"), and younger sister, Lin. Hao Jiang Tian was not formally named until he had to enroll in middle school, at the age of 14. Up until that time his family had called him Xiao Lu ("little deer"), a feminine name that his parents had begun calling him before his birth in hopes of having a girl. They decided on the name Hao Jiang, which means "roaring river."

As a child Tian spent much of his time drawing and dreamed of becoming an artist. He hated his piano lessons, often crying during practice sessions. "So one happiest day came when I heard an announcement from the loudspeakers: My piano teacher was arrested as a counterrevolutionary . . . ," Tian told a reporter for New York's WNYC radio program *Soundcheck* (May 30, 2008, online). "I ran to the courtyard, screaming and jumping with joy. Thirty years later, actually, I went back to Beijing - went to see him, and I told him I wanted to apologize to him because when he was arrested, I was so happy. And he laughed with tears in his eyes, and he said, 'Well, that was a crazy period, and it was so hard to figure out who was right and who was wrong.'"

Growing up under Mao's rule, Tian's parents were careful to maintain their allegiance to his Communist Party of China (CPC). Though they had both dedicated their lives to communism from a young age, their past came into question when it was discovered that they had once belonged to a propaganda performance troupe of the Kuomintang (KMT), also known as the Chinese Nationalist Party, a rival of the CPC. That discovery tarnished their names, and they were forced to leave Beijing. Tian-then 14-went with his sister to live for a period with his aunt on a farm; both later returned to the city to attend school. (Tian's brother, who was enrolled in the naval academy before authorities learned about his parents' past, was expelled afterward.) Tian's parents were banished to a "reeducation" camp in 1969. They would not return to Beijing until 1981.

Years earlier Tian's father had ordered him to demolish the father's record collection, in order to spare the family embarrassment or worse if the records were found by authorities. As Tian was packing for his trip to the country, he discovered a single surviving record behind the phonograph. It was of Beethoven's Sixth Symphony, which his father had once conducted. Tian has said that on that occasion, when his father played the record for him, he came to understand the power of music. "My first impression of Western music was in my father's eyes," he told Robert Lipsyte and Lois B. Morris for the *New York Times* (October 22, 2002). "He was a remote man who did not show emotion. But his face became so human, so tender, as he told me this was an interlude, here is the first theme. The change in my father's face was the music lesson that changed my life."

With his newfound love of music, Tian began learning the accordion and joined his school's Mao Zedong Thought Propaganda Team. He was 15 when he graduated from the school in 1970 and went to work at the Beijing Boiler Factory, which manufactured electricity generators. For seven years he cut steel sheets for a living while continuing to play the accordion, composing for and conducting the factory's Thought Propaganda Team. One day in the summer of 1975, Tian rode his bicycle to a friend's house for a visit; too tired to climb the stairs to the fifth floor, he yelled up to his friend's window. The friend was not at home, but a man who lived next door overheard Tian and asked him if he was a singer. Telling Tian he had a "big voice," the man suggested that he find a singing teacher. Tian recalled the event in *Along the Roaring River:* "[The man] turned out to be a professional singer, perhaps about forty, and although I don't remember his name or his face, the five minutes I spent with him changed my life." Tian took the man's advice to heart and soon began taking voice lessons with a family friend. He often feigned illness in order to leave work and practice.

In 1973 Mao's wife, Jiang Qing, had ordered the recruitment of young musicians to be trained at the Central Conservatory of Music in order to join the Central Philharmonic Society, China's foremost state-sponsored performing group. Tian auditioned for a spot in 1976. Later that year, after Mao had died, Jiang Qing and her "Gang of Four" were arrested, and the Cultural Revolution came to an end. Nonetheless, the Central Conservatory continued the program long enough to train a last class of 30 musicians; Tian was the only singer from Beijing who was selected. From that point on, Tian, who had secretly gone against cultural norms by drinking, smoking, and dating girls, dedicated himself wholly to singing.

At the conservatory Tian studied several forms of music, including revolutionary songs, folk tunes, classical music, and Italian opera, even taking a master class with the Italian opera star Gino Bechi, and honed his solo-singing skills. He soon received a full scholarship to attend the University of Denver's Lamont School of Music, in Denver, Colorado, and became determined to immigrate to the United States, where he could have a more fulfilling career. With the help of Martha Liao, a Denver-based geneticist and pianist whom he had met in China a year earlier, when she was a visiting scholar, Tian obtained a visa and immigrated to the U.S. in 1983. During a layover in New York City, he used some of the little money he had to buy a standing-room ticket to see Luciano Pavarotti perform at the Metropolitan Opera. (Ten years later to the day, Tian performed alongside Pavarotti in a production of *I Lombardi* at the Met.) The opera, Verdi's *Ernani,* was the first Western opera Tian had seen. "Before the end of the second act, I knew I had to become an opera singer," he wrote in *Along the Roaring River.*

Life's Work

After graduating with a master's degree in vocal performance in 1987, Tian spent the subsequent three years auditioning, participating in local voice competitions, and working as a singer in a Chinese restaurant. He made his first stage appearances with Opera Colorado, and during the same period he won six international singing competitions. Determined to have a career in opera, he traveled to New York City frequently to find an agent and audition for roles. After being rejected by the New York City Opera, he was signed to become a resident singer with the Metropolitan Opera, starting in the 1991-92 season. He moved to New Yark and married Liao. (Tian and Liao had each had a previous marriage that ended in divorce.)

Tian has won acclaim for many of his roles, including Philip II in Verdi's *Don Carlos,* Procida in Verdi's *I Vespri Siciliani,* and Mephistopheles in Gounod's *Faust.* He has performed with Germany's Berlin State Opera; Teatro Comunale, in Florence, Italy; Arena di Verona, in Italy; Teatro Colon, in Buenos Aires, Argentina; the Chicago Lyric Opera; and the Washington National Opera, in Washington, D.C., among others. He has also appeared on the concert stage with orchestras around the world, including the Philadelphia Orchestra, the Colorado Symphony, London's Orchestra of St. Martinin-the-Fields, and the Hong Kong Philharmonic. Discussing Tian's title role as the eighth-century Chinese poet in *Poet Li Bai,* performed with Colorado's Central City Opera, Bob Bows wrote for *Variety* (July 16-22, 2007), "Hao Jiang Tian . . . exudes jovial well-being as the

Affiliation: Culture

The Chinese-born singer entered his teens during Mao Zedong's Great Proletarian Cultural Revolution (1966-76), a political movement that sought to rid the nation of what was deemed to be educational and cultural elitism; only approved songs, plays, operas, and other items of entertainment could be performed, and everything representative of Western culture, from clothing to music, was forbidden. As a youth Tian bore the brunt of that and other forms of oppression: he was ordered to smash his father's collection of Western classical recordings to pieces and was present at the Tiananmen Incident in April1976, in which citizens publicly mourning the death of the popular Chinese premier Zhou Enlai were beaten, some fatally, by government security .forces in Tiananmen Square. "I'm glad I had that experience" of living through the Cultural Revolution, he told Marc Shulgold for the Denver, Colorado, *Rocky Mountain News* (December 13, 1998). "Most singers' lives are peaceful as they grow up. But not mine. Yet, whatever experiences I had from the past helped me to create a deeper feeling in my singing. You live, you have experiences-and that helps you express love, happiness, sadness."

As one of the first Chinese opera singers to have a lasting international career, Tian has experienced what he calls a prejudice against Asians in his chosen profession. "Especially when my career became global, I saw how great the disadvantages were for Chinese singers in the international opera world," he wrote in his autobiography, *Along the Roaring River: My Wild Ride from Mao to the Met* (written with Lois B. Morris, 2008). "There were so few of us singing· at the highest levels in those days. . . . The odds were stacked against us for many reasons-and not all of them related to skill. Too many people in the business thought that Asian singers could not master this form or that audiences would not wish to see or hear Chinese people in Western roles,"

Tian has nonetheless been celebrated and admired for his contributions to the opera world, in part for helping to create in the West "a new repertoire of Chinese opera-moving the field beyond stereotypes such as Timur [in Giacomo Puccini's *Turandot]* to authentic characters," as Andrew Druckenbrod noted for the *Pittsburgh Post-Gazette* (October 28, 2008). Tian has premiered the roles of Li Bai in Guo Wenjing's *Poet Li Bai,* Chang the Coffinmaker in Amy Tan and Stewart Wallace's *Bonesetter's Daughter,* and General Wang in Tan Dun's *The First Emperor.* After watching him perform in *Poet Li Bai,* the fine-arts critic Kyle McMillan wrote for the *Denver Post* (July 10, 2007, on-line), "[Tian] commands the stage from start to finish. Displaying amazing flexibility, he powerfully asserts his big, resonant voice and, a few moments later, caresses a phrase with supreme delicacy."

gifted wordsmith blessed with Mozart-like spontaneity and a Taoist disposition. Hao's expressive basso cantante captures Li Bai's sensitivity and visionary phrasing, while his imposing stature argues for immortality."

In reviewing the Baltimore Opera Company's 2008 production of Bellini's *Norma,* Tim Smith wrote for the *Baltimore Sun* (November 20, 2008), "As Oroveso, Norma's father and Druid elder, Hao Jiang Tian sang with admirable smoothness and solidity of tone and molded his phrases eloquently." Tian has been a U.S. citizen since 1995. He appeared as the Devil in Fresno (California) Grand Opera's production of *Faust* in April2009. The following September he taped a live performance of his autobiographical, one-man show *From Mao to the Met* at the Kaye Playhouse at New York City's Hunter College. (The performance was scheduled to air on PBS television stations in late 2009.) Tian expected to return to the Metropolitan Opera in January 2010 in the role of Timur in Franco Zeffirelli's production of *Turandot* and planned to present *From Mao to the Met* on April 11, 2010 at the Fresno Memorial Auditorium.

Personal Life

Tian's wife, Martha Liao, retired from her work as a genetic scientist to travel full-time with Tian. She serves as president of the Asian Performing Arts of Colorado, which she founded in 1987. She and Tian live in New York City with their English spaniel, Niu Niu, and their parrot, Luke. Though Tian intends to sing professionally for as long as he can, he has already planned on retiring to Colorado, where he hopes to spend his time exploring other art forms, such as writing poems and painting.

Further Reading

(Denver, Colorado) *Rocky Mountain News* D p25 Dec. 13, 1998

(Hong Kong) *South China Morning Post* p5 Sep. 24, 2003

New York Times E p1 Oct. 22, 2002

Pittsburgh Post-Gazette C p1 Oct. 28, 2008; TianHaoJiang.com

Timbaland

Hip-hop musician; record producer

Born: Mar. 10, 1971; Norfolk, Virginia
Primary Field: Hip-hop
Group Affiliation: Solo performer

Introduction

The success story of the acclaimed hip-hop musician and record producer Timbaland, according to Barry Walters in the Village Voice *(November 18, 1997), "starts with the drums-brittle, nervous, simultaneously small and loud, as if someone held a mike to a ticking clock prone to sudden spasms of syncopation." During the latter half of the 1990s, with such hit singles as "Pony" from Ginuwine's album* The Bachelor *(1996), Aaliyah's "One in a Million" from her 1996 album of the same name, and "The Rain" from Missy Elliott's* Supa Dupa Fly *(1997)—all of which achieved platinum status.*

Early Life

Timbaland was born Timothy Mosley on March 10, 1971 in Norfolk, Virginia. He and his younger brother, Sebastian (born Garland Mosley Jr.), were raised by their father, a truck driver, and his devoutly religious wife, a hospital worker. During his youth Timbaland had a passion for music; he "fiddled" with drums and guitar, as he recalled to Latta Taylor for *Newsday* (May 6, 2001), but he received no formal music training. After saving enough money from his various jobs as a grocery bagger, strawberry picker, and Red Lobster busboy, he bought himself a pair of Numark turntables. "It's hard to believe, but I didn't see Tim 'til late at night when we went to bed," Sebastian Mosley told Jeff "Chairman" Mao for *Vibe* magazine. ''I was always out with my friends doing he regular kid stuff, and he basically lived in our room by himself with his turntables, headphones on from sunup to sundown. . . . It seemed like he was born into music."

Life's Work

By his early teens Timbaland had begun calling himself DJ Timmy Tim and had become known locally for his skills as a deejay as well as his beatboxing (vocal percussion), He and his neighborhood friend Melvin "Magoo" Barcliff formed a group called S.B.I. (Surrouded by Idiots). Not long afterward he met the rapper and songwriter Missy Elliott, then a member of a local R&B group called Sista. After Elliott was discovered by DeVante Swing of the popular R&B band Jodeci, in about 1991, she called on Mosley to make the music for Sista's demo tape, Impressed, Swing showed Mosley how to use the studio equipment and helped him to develop his skills in production. Mosley took the apprenticeship seriously, often working in the studio for days on end with only an occasional break. "DeVante was hard on me and that made me really hard on myself," he recalled, according to a biography posted on the official Timbaland and Magoo Web site. At Swing's suggestion, Mosley adopted a new name—Timbaland. During this time the self-described "crew" Da Bassment came into being, with Timbaland, Missy Elliott, the three-man vocal group Playa, Ginuwine, and Magoo as members. Each eventually left to sign one or more record deals. Timbaland was picked up by Blackground Records, an Atlantic imprint, with whom he signed deals as solo artist and as a member of the rap duo Timbaland and Magoo. Wearing the hat of producer, Timbaland burst onto the music scene in 1996, with the Single "Pony" from Ginuwine's debut album, *Ginuwine . . . the Bachelor.* Described as playful and provocative, "Pony" spent many weeks on *Billboard's* R&B charts and went platinum. Timbaland followed that up with two singles, each of which reached number one on *Billboard's* R&B charts—Sisters with Voices; (SWV's) "Can We" and Aaliyah's "One in a Million," from her album of the same name (for which she worked with three producers in addition to Timbaland). Discussing the latter, Parry Gettelman wrote for the *Orlando Sentinel* (September 13, 1996), "Mosley favors a quiet storm approach that actually permits some ominous clouds on the horizon, in the form of tense, dub-derived beats.... Mosley and Elliott [who wrote and arranged for the album] provide settings distinctive enough to bring out a singular, smoldering sensuality."

In 1997 Timbaland teamed up with Missy Elliott on her album *Supa Dupa Fly,* for which he produced the hit song "The Rain." In the *Dallas Morning News* (July 13, 1997), Dave Michaels referred to "The Rain" as the "bright spot" on that disk, adding, "Timbaland weaves an ambient aural tapestry laced with the sounds of everything from wind chimes to the Millennium Falcon. Ms. Elliott's tender voice floats perfectly over the gusty track. It's a rare feat-beats and rhymes that fit together like two long-lost Platonic halves."

Later that year Timbaland and Magoo released their first album, *Welcome to Our World.* The record, which went platinum, included the gold debut single "Up Jumps Da' Boogie," a song that "slinks along at a snail's pace but feels much faster," as Barry Walters put it in his *Village Voice* article, "thanks to the fidgety drums, spooky P-Funk keyboards, an interpolation of Heatwave's 'Boogie Nights,' and the interchange of Timbaland's, Magoo's, Missy's, and Aaliyah's voices slicing up the funk like sushi—raw but tasty, shrewd, artful."

Although *Welcome to Our World* was the first album to showcase Timbaland as a lead rapper, his voice was already familiar to many people, thanks to his habit of interweaving an occasional rap of his own on tracks he produced for others. In their reviews of *Welcome to Our World,* some critics complained that Timbaland's vocal skills fell short of his production abilities-an assessment with which he agreed. "Even I say that I can't rap. I just do it 'cause my voice sounds good on my tracks," he explained, as quoted by Rob Brunner in *Entertainment Weekly* (November 20, 1998). Such judgments notwithstanding, his growing legions of fans deluged radio stations with requests for his songs. "I was looking down my playlist," one radio deejay told Janini Coveney for *Billboard* (September 13, 1997), "and any hour of the day between Puffy [Puff Daddy, the professional name of Sean Combs, now known as P. Diddy] and Timbaland and Missy, I'm playing something by them."

In late 1998 Timbaland released his first solo album, *Tim's Bio,* identified as the soundtrack to an imaginary movie titled "Life from Da Bassment." The album includes contributions by many of the artists Timbaland had previously worked with, including Magoo, Ginuwine, Nas, Missy Elliott, Aaliyah, Jay-Z, Kelly Price, and the newcomer Virginia Williams. "Without sacrificing his own indisputably individual production style," Carol Cooper noted for the *Village Voice* (December 15, 1998), *Tim's Bio* showed that Timbaland had become "strikingly looser about structure and tempo." In "Here We Come," a single that evoked the theme song from the animated TV series *Spider-Man,* "Magoo's staccato rhymes . . . hop and skip around the main pulse as if it were a maypole," Cooper wrote; in "Keep It Real," "Ginuwine and Timbaland have perfected a texture-based kind of call and response vaguely reminiscent of the way smooth Jamaican singers and gruff toasting deejays trade leads on a tune." Cooper and other critics also praised Timbaland for including many female vocalists on the album, something few other hip-hop artists had done. "When Timbaland works with women, his touch blossoms," David Browne wrote for *Entertainment Weekly* (December 18, 1998). "Timbaland won't want to hear this, but perhaps he should display his, well, *feminine* side more often?"

Timbaland scored another big hit with Aaliyah's "Are You That Somebody," recorded for the soundtrack to the film *Dr. Dolittle* (1998), starring Eddie Murphy. The rhythm of the song, Sasha Frere-Janes wrote in his *Village Voice* article, "is literally arresting: stopping, starting, and chunking along like a Metallica riff." The single was Timbaland's first to make it into the Top 10 pop-album charts.

The increasing numbers of hip-hop producers imitating Timbaland's eccentric beats received a rebuke on Missy Elliott's second album, *Da Real World* (1999): "Beat biter, dope style taker . . . stealing our beats like you're the one who made them," she rapped, as quoted by Simon Reynolds in the *New York Times* (August 1, 1999). Timbaland endeavored to create a fresh new sound for the album as well, one described by critics as a little harsher and more hip-hop than dance material (although the song "She's a Bitch" became a dance hit). Timbaland called it "real dark, real ghetto," as quoted by Reynolds. *Da Real World* reached number 10 on the pop charts, despite some reviewers' expressed disappointment with it. "Coming from a debut artist, *Da Real World* would be garlanded with acclaim," Reynolds remarked. "But given the widespread expectation that Ms. Elliott and Timbaland would rewrite the rhythmic rules

Affiliation: Producer

Timbaland built his reputation as one of the record industry's most innovative and trendsetting R&B and hip-hop producers. He followed up those successes with the platinum-selling *Welcome to Our World* (1997), which he made with one of his childhood friends, the rapper Magoo. Popular tracks including "Up Jumps Da' Boogie," from *Welcome to Our World,* and "The Rain" demonstrate Timbaland's distinctive sound, which the composer and musician Sasha Frere-Janes, in the *Village Voice* (April 18, 2000), described as incorporating "irregular hi-hat patterns, rhythmic hiccups, big Swiss cheese pauses, and noises drawn from video games, mouths, TV shows, anything and everything but the old-school funk records mined for hip-hop's first 15 years." While producing songs for such notable acts as Jay-Z, Lil' Kim, and Snoop Dogg, Timbaland also produced and rapped on his own solo album, *Tim's Bio: From the Motion Picture: Life from Da Bassment* (1998), and on a second collaboration with Magoo, *Indecent Proposal* (2001). Many other producers began to copy Timbaland's jittery beats, leading Frere-Janes to comment, "Timbaland sure is oil the radio a lot, even when. he's not. . . . No matter who the artist of record is, R&B in 2000 is Timbaland, just like funk in 1970 was James Brown."

of rhythm-and-blues and rap again, the response has been anticlimactic." "Enacting a scorched-earth policy," Sasha Frere-Janes wrote, "Tim got rid of the trademarks but forgot to replace them with anything, producing Da Real Nap." Such criticism failed to halt Timbaland's continuing success. With nine of his singles selling well enough to land them in the charts, *Billboard,* in its last issue of 2000, named him the year's Top Hot R&B/Hip Hop Producer.

Earlier, in the summer of 2000, at the invitation of the popular alternative singer Beck, Timbaland and Beck had recorded a cover of David Bowie's "Diamond Dogs" for the soundtrack to Baz Luhrman's film *Moulin Rouge* (2001). "He's the type of artist who inspires people," Beck, a longtime Timbaland fan, told Jeff "Chairman" Mao of his collaborator. "There are certain artists who give a sense of possibility. That's the kind of artist Tim is. He was definitely a major influence on my last album [*Midnight Vultures*]."

In 2001 Timbaland produced two of the year's best-selling singles—Missy Elliott's "Get Ur Freak On," from *Miss E . . . So Addictive,* and Aaliyah's "We Need a Resolution," from her eponymously titled album (the last one that she made before her death in a plane crash). He also served as the executive producer and scored the music for the film *30 Years to Life,* which was nominated for a Grand Jury Prize at the 2001 Sundance Film Festival. Directed by Vanessa Middleton, the film follows six friends living in New York City as they approach their 30th birthdays.

With the aim of helping other up-and-coming artists, Timbaland established his own record label, Beat Club, an imprint of Interscope. "I'm a great producer, so people need me more than I need them," Timbaland boasted to Steve Appleford for *Rolling Stone* (September 7, 2001). The first Beat Club release was Bubba Sparxxx's *Dark Days, Bright Nights* (2001), which Timbaland produced. In a review of the record for the *Los Angeles Times* (November 18, 2001), Marc Weingarten hailed it as one of "the best hip-hop albums of the year."

The year 2001 saw the release of *Indecent Proposal,* Timbaland and Magoo's second collaborative album. (Its appearance was delayed almost a year due to a disagreement with Virgin Records, the duo's label.) In comparing *Indecent Proposal* with *Welcome to Our World,* Marc Weingarten noted, "The will to party is still strong, but the mood is a bit darker. As usual, Timbaland's active imagination is hard at work, smearing sound effects like a finger-painting child across tracks already crowded with background vocals and syncopated beats." The album features cameos by Jay-Z, Ludacris, Playa, Tweet, Sin, and Petey Pablo. Beck and Aaliyah contributed the vocals for the closing track, "I Am Music." Alexis Petridis, a critic for the London Guardian (February 1, 2002), wrote that the album "manages to be simultaneously enthralling and underwhelming." While noting that, as before, Timbaland "is incapable of matching the aural splendour of his backgrounds with his vocals," Petridis declared, "Mosley may well be the most exciting record producer in the world." *Indecent Proposal* reached number three on *Billboard's* Top R&B/Hip Hop chart. That achievement notwithstanding, Timbaland told reporters that the record marked the last full-length release on which he would perform. "It's just too hectic; I don't want to do it no more," he told Letta Taylor for *Newsday.* He also said that he planned to focus his efforts on producing and adding groups to his label. According to Steve Appleford in *Rolling*

Stone, he hopes to sign the rap-metal group Linkin Park and dreams of working someday with the heavy-metal group Metallica.

The Beat Club is enjoying much success with Ms. Jade (born Chevon Young), whose album *Girl Interrupted* (2002) Timbaland produced. Meanwhile, Timbaland has continued to refine his sound, most notably on Missy Elliott's acclaimed album *Under Construction* (2002). Timbaland produced most of the tracks on that disk, including the single "Work It," a playful hip-hop bossa nova replete with sputtering beats and fuzzy synthesizers, which landed on many critics' "Best of 2002" lists.

Personal Life

In his leisure time Timbaland enjoys relaxing at home with friends; frequenting nightclubs, he told Letta Taylor, "ain't for me." He owns several high-priced automobiles, among them a $310,000 1998 Lamborghini Diablo Roadster, a $350,000 Bentley Azure VT, and an $85,0001998 Mercedes-Benz.

Further Reading

Billboard Sep. 13, 1997
Dallas Morning News C p8 July 13, 1997
Entertainment Weekly p125 Nov. 20, 1998, with photo
(London) *Guardian* p16 Feb. 1, 2002
Los Angeles Times VI p65 Nov. 18, 2001
New York Times 2 p27 Aug. 1, 1999
Newsday D p15 May 6, 2001, with photo
Orlando Sentinel p15 Sep. 13, 1996
Rolling Stone (on-line) Sep. 7, 2001
Village Voice p97 Nov. 18, 1997, with photo, p134 Dec. 15, 1998, p79 Apr. 18, 2000

Arturo Toscanini

Musical conductor

Born: March 25, 1867; Parma, Italy
Died: January 16, 1957; New York, New York
Primary Field: Classical
Group Affiliation: Solo conductor

Introduction

Arturo Toscanini, "the world's most famous conductor," became a legend within his own lifetime, celebrated for his profound knowledge of music, his brilliant rhythmic sense, his infallible ear, his "tenacious and communicative vitality," his fabulous musical memory, his ability to make great music one of the most exciting things in the world. There were other great conductors during his time, but to the critics, the musicians, and the people, Toscanini was "the maestro" of them all.

Early Life

It was in Parma, Italy that Arturo Toscanini was born, on March 25, 1867. His father, Claudio Toscanini, was a tailor and a fiery follower of the Italian patriot Garibaldi. Neither he nor Arturo's mother, the former Paola Montani, was a musician, but Parma was a musical town where a boy with talent could get ahead. At the age of nine Toscanini was attending the local conservatory of music, taking lessons on a half-sized cello. Within two years he had won a scholarship in Professor Carini's cello class, and his progress from then until his graduation, at the age of eighteen, with a *con lode distinta* (honors) certificate, was noteworthy.

Soon after his school days, at the end of a brief period with various small Italian orchestras, Toscanini became a cellist with Claudio Rossi's opera company and went on tour with this company. On June 15, 1886 there was to be a performance of Verdi's *Aida* in Rio de Janeiro. A few hours before the performance, however, the conductor withdrew, and there was no other to take his place. In the confusion someone reminded the distracted impresario of his young cellist, Toscanini, who, with his remarkable memory, "at least knew all the notes." Toscanini was bundled into a frock coat much too large for him, given a baton, and told to conduct. At the end of the first act there were wild demonstrations of approval, and the next morning a local critic wrote: "Brilliantly, expertly, enthusiastically, and vigorously, Mr. Toscanini saved us at the last minute." Years later, however, when an aged Brazilian was describing the perfection of that performance, Toscanini interrupted: "Ah, but he is wrong I made two mistakes, one in the first act, another in the third."

Life's Work

When Toscanini returned to Italy it was as a conductor rather than as a cellist, and as a conductor his reputation grew. Throughout the 1890's he conducted Verdi, Puccini, Alfredo Catalani, Wagner, and other composers in most of the cities of Italy—Turin, Verona, Novara, Palermo, Bologna, Brescia, Genoa, Rome, Milan. Then in 1898 he became chief conductor and artistic director of La Scala in Milan, the most famous, most wealthy, and best of Italy's opera houses. Immediately he instituted reforms in technique and interpretation as well as in repertory, insisting on rigorous rehearsals, on nearly unapproachably high standards of performance.

Even while he was still emerging from the rank and file of Italian conductors Toscanini had his own ideas on how things should be done. He believed that encores, for instance, were unnecessary. Audiences at La Scala believed differently, and when Toscanini sharply refused to permit one at the end of a magnificent burst of song, a near riot took place. Toscanini resigned his post. In the spring seasons of 1903 to 1904 and 1906 he conducted in Buenos Aires; in 1904 he was in Rome and Bologna; in 1905 and 1906 in Turin; and finally for the 1906 to 1907 season he returned to La Scala. He remained there until 1908, when La Scala's director, Gatti-Casazza, left to join the Metropolitan Opera Company in New York and took Toscanini with him.

Toscanini's first meeting with the members of the Metropolitan orchestra was inauspicious, for they made no attempt to conceal their contempt for the little, mustached Italian who was asking them to play the works of another Italian, Verdi. Toscanini saw their smiles, ordered them to put away those scores, and called for Wagner's *Götterdämmerung.* When he had finished putting them through the whole opera, without once consulting a "score, their smiles had vanished, and when it came time to perform Verdi their cooperation was wholehearted.

It was with *Aïda* that Toscanini made his Metropolitan debut on November 16, 1908, and the curtain had hardly dropped before he was being hailed as a "unique genius." Of the performance one critic wrote: "Toscanini brought to the understanding and emotions of the audience all of Verdi's score, body and soul, as it lives with him." A month later he was receiving the same sort of praise for his conducting of the *Götterdämmerung.* Until 1915 Toscanini remained at the Metropolitan, Manhattanites gaping at "his implacable, cyclonic tantrums, his insatiable interest in details of costuming and stage deportment, his lordly expenditure of extra rehearsal time, his intolerance of every sort of mediocrity, and his adamantine sense of discipline."

Toscanini's departure from the Metropolitan was accompanied by gossip. Some said he had suffered a nervous breakdown; others that there had been a dispute arising from his insistence on what he considered artistic performances and his requests for additional rehearsals. In any case Toscanini was back in Italy in 1915, offering his services to the Government and conducting charity performances at the Teatro del Verme. During the rest of World War I his conducting went to benefit war sufferers. Though a staunch Italian patriot, Toscanini never hesitated to play German music in Italy, even when war fever was at its highest.

With World War I over, and participation in the general elections of 1919—his only excursion into politics—behind him, Toscanini began the task of building up a new orchestra. Its personnel finally settled to his satisfaction, he arrived in America to give a series of concerts in the 1920 to 1921 season, and when these were over returned to Italy to rebuild the once proud La Scala Opera, closed since 1917. He remained with La Scala until the end of the 1928 to 1929 season, when, conscious of his age and of the added energy needed for operatic conducting, he decided to concentrate on symphonic work. It was always Toscanini's "way to tremble, to storm, to be emotional, in sympathy with each one of the singers; to experience with intense passion whatever happened to be well done or ill by the members of his troupe."

Meanwhile, in 1930 and 1931, he conducted Wagner at the festival at Bayreuth, the first foreign conductor invited there; in 1932 he conducted a Debussy memorial celebration in France; in 1933 he appeared in Sweden and in Denmark and conducted the Vienna Philharmonic; and in that year and again in 1935 he conducted concerts and operas at the Salzburg Festival. He was supposed to have conducted at Bayreuth again, in 1933, but he refused. The man who in 1931 had been handled roughly by his compatriots for refusing to play the *Giovanezza* (the Italian Fascist anthem) and who had headed a protest sent by famous musicians against the persecutions of their German colleagues for "political or religious reasons" sent a letter declining the invitation, stating in it: "I burn, I freeze, but I cannot be lukewarm."

Toscanini's last regular concert with the New York Philharmonic Symphony Orchestra took place in April

Affiliation: American Orchestras

Before 1929, however, Toscanini had achieved fame as a symphonic conductor, as a supreme interpreter of the works of Beethoven, Mozart, Haydn, and the other great masters of music. In the 1926 to 1927 season he appeared as a guest conductor of the New York Philharmonic Orchestra, and the following year became regular conductor, sharing the season with Willem Mengelberg. When, in 1928, the New York Philharmonic and the New York Symphony Orchestras were merged, becoming the New York Philharmonic-Symphony Orchestra, Toscanini was appointed principal conductor. Until 1936 he conducted this Orchestra during part of every season, leading it on a triumphal tour of Europe in 1930.

1936. From before dawn crowds lined the streets waiting to get in, and orchestra seats were bootlegged at $100. Cheer after cheer greeted the performance, and the shouting wouldn't be quieted until the Orchestra's manager stepped out to speak for Toscanini. "He asks me to say that he loves you all and begs to be excused," he said. The next day and for years after adulatory comment on Toscanini's performances with the New York Philharmonic poured forth. He had given the Orchestra, one said, "a discipline, a sound a style" all its own. Others recalled reverently his "many magical performances, his tireless quest for perfection, his abhorrence of all claptrap." Stokowski spoke of him as "the supreme master of all conductors."

But all had not been harmonious there, it was said. Players who had worked for Toscanini for half a season, according to *Fortune,* never seemed to play so well for other conductors during the rest of the season, for they were exhausted as well as inspired by his leading, a situation which made for jealousy and bitterness. The Philharmonic Society, too, had always to treat him with kid gloves, knowing, in the words of Olin Downes, that the handsome fee received for his services would not operate "for a second to detain him" if he were artistically displeased. In any case, according to *Fortune,* Toscanini left behind him not only an adoring public but a "complicated, gossip-ridden situation, and the same slackening of technique and of morale among the players that follows his departure in every orchestra he has ever conducted."

Any talk that he was growing older, his great days over, was soon stilled, for in August of that same year he set Salzburg agog with a heaven-storming performance. In December he conducted the Palestine Symphony Orchestra in its debut—"it is the duty of everyone to fight and help in this sort of cause according to one's means," he had told Bronislaw Huberman, organizer of the Orchestra. In 1937 he took this Orchestra around Palestine and again conducted at Salzburg. And on Christmas Eve of that year he was in the United States leading the National Broadcasting Company Symphony Orchestra in the first of a series of performances. Toscanini had been approached to conduct such an orchestra the winter before and had agreed to do so for $4,000 a broadcast (probably the highest price ever paid a conductor to that time), for his passage, and for payment of income taxes on his United States earnings. The Orchestra had been specially selected and specially trained, publicity had been feverish, passes to the broadcasts were treasures, and millions of people throughout the country heard the great Toscanini conduct for the first time. They continued to hear him through the season of 1940 to 1941, and there were few voices to decry their "almost slavish" admiration. Deems Taylor's voice was one of these, though. When he was threatened with the loss of his tickets to the broadcasts on the grounds that he "didn't like Toscanini anyway," he blasphemously cracked, according to *Time* Magazine: "I admit Toscanini was at the Last Supper, but I insist that he did not sit at the head of the table."

During the summer of 1940 Toscanini was on a tour of South America, each concert sold out weeks in advance. "Rarely," one commentator wrote, "has an artist received such an impetuous, almost frenzied reception" as he got. During the 1941 to 1942 season Toscanini limited his public appearances to a number of concerts with the Philadelphia Orchestra and five symphony concerts with the NBC Orchestra for the Treasury Department. But he was busy studying and reading, busy adding to the long list of the recordings he later made.

In the spring of 1942 Toscanini returned to the New York Philharmonic to conduct six post-season all-Beethoven concerts that were the finale to the Philharmonic's centennial year. At the first rehearsal, with no preliminaries, Toscanini "simply began to conduct the Orchestra for the first time after six years, and the Orchestra began to play as if the interval had been only one day." "They have remembered everything I taught them," Toscanini explained. "Nothing is missing." The concerts themselves were resplendent with the "profound truth, simplicity, nobility, and heroism which animate Toscanini's readings."

In the fall of 1942 Toscanini opened the Philharmonic's season, leading Berlioz' *Romeo and Juliet* symphony the first week and Shostakovich's famed Seventh Symphony the second. In November he conducted, as guest leader, the Philadelphia Orchestra, and presented the first of the twelve NBC concert broadcasts that he was to conduct during the 1942 to 1943 season, startling many of his adorers with a performance of Gershwin's *Rhapsody in Blue* that went "whooping down the groove." Benny Goodman was the soloist.

During the years of progress from conductor of small Italian orchestras to the most successful, most popular, and "greatest" leader of the world's most famous orchestras, the Toscanini legend grew. His memory was remarkable, the world learned. He was the man "credited with knowing by heart the whole standard operatic and symphonic repertory and in such detail that he remembers obscure misprints in various editions of each score." His memory, developed partly because his near-sightedness made it impossible to read a score during a performance, enabled him to learn a new symphony in three hours and then conduct it without consulting the score. It created a legion of stories like the following: A bassoon player once came to Toscanini in a panic, for his instrument was broken and couldn't produce an E-flat. Toscanini thought a moment and then said: "That's all right, you can play with us. The note of E-flat doesn't appear in your music tonight."

Musicians and laymen were aware of the infallible Toscanini ear, which heard "the merest imperfect stress by the fourteenth violinist." They came to know of his methods of rehearsal, his temper, to think of him as "a sort of tense and burning embodiment of impossible standards of perfection." At rehearsals Toscanini was painstaking and thorough. He began with the first note, "carve[d] each line of music like a sculptor, paying minute attention to every detail of the outline until, finally, he has moulded the entire composition into a work of art." At the men before him he mumbled, muttered, roared in four languages, mostly Italian. He would fall on his knees, clench his hands in prayer and beg: "Secondi violini, see I pray to you, give me the pianissimo I desire, I pray to you on my knees." But when the flautist failed to appear in time for his few notes, he would shriek, "Assassin!" and clutch his head in despair. "The tiniest technical error, a mistake in intonation or *solfeggio* or any raggedness" was a cause of acute suffering to him, and there were times when batons were broken like match sticks. "Many orchestral players," according to Oscar Levant, "consider Toscanini cruel, inflexible, and even petty." But, he said, "I know of no man who does not consider him the greatest conductor, *qua* conductor, with whom he has ever played."

Even at concerts Toscanini's emotions were sharp and violent. When performances went badly he suffered acutely, his temper was cyclonic, his harangues in rich Italian. When they went well he was happy. "His face beam[ed], his eyes glisten[ed], he [could] not control his lips from breaking into youthful smiles." But though his spirits rose and fell, in appearance he was usually calm. "He flicks his baton, establishes the pace. His left hand may rest easily on his hip at first. Soon it pleads for eloquence, stands out like a policeman's warning when he wants a pianissimo, quivers over his heart when he begs for special feeling." And all the while he sang along in a husky, croaking voice. (Once he was supposed to have interrupted a rehearsal to ask sharply: *"Who* is making that noise?") At concerts Toscanini was always modest, always sharing the applause with the orchestra, frequently refusing to return to the stage to acknowledge the audience's cheers. He never forgot that he was merely the conductor. As he once told his players who interrupted a magnificent rehearsal to applaud his reading: "It is not I gentlemen. It is Beethoven."

In a Toscanini recording of music one hears "razor-edge attacks, the radiant and beautifully shaped sonorities, the sharply contoured phrases, the transparent textures of balanced woodwinds or strings." There was an electric, dynamic exposition of the dramatic pages; the lyric pages drew a song from the orchestra incomparable for purity, serenity, and simplicity. And always there was a "fanatic adherence to the composer's wishes as expressed in the score," sometimes even more, for, as Puccini used to say: "Toscanini conducts a work not just as the written score directs, but as the composer had imagined it in his head even though he failed to write it down on paper."

He did this for the works of almost all the great composers, and he was considered by Ewen, for instance, to be greater in sheer versatility than any of his predecessors or contemporaries. His, said Ewen, was "a touch that can be so exquisite in Mozart, so heroic in Wagner, so poignantly lyrical in Verdi and Puccini, and so tremendously volcanic in the music of modern composers." That his conducting of Beethoven, Wagner, Brahms, Haydn, and the Italians, for instance, was magnificently vital and invigorating, phenomenally fresh even in a work he had led hundreds of times, every critic agreed. Yet there were some like Oscar Levant, who felt that he had built up "an amazing reputation" on the basis of a "really remarkable small range of interests," which excluded most Russian and most French music, except certain isolated works by Ravel and Debussy, and practically all English and American music. "He has," Levant continued, done very little contemporary music, has "sponsored no controversial music of merit. . . .invariably choosing contemporary works for which someone else has done the pioneering." Sigmund Spaeth agreed: "Much as I respect Toscanini as a musical genius," he said, "I am forced to regard him as a menace to American music. In preference to making some honest effort to discover first-rate American music, he plays the puerilities of tenth-rate Italian composers."

Though Toscanini frankly admitted that most modern music to him "lack[ed] something to say," he had, nevertheless, conducted early works by Debussy, Ravel, Elgar, Goossens, Pizzetti, Respighi, and Shostakovich; as he pointed out when this criticism was made: "I am the man who did Wagner when Wagner was new; who produced all the moderns from Strauss and Debussy to Malipiero and Sibelius. Now let the other men do what I did when I was young . . . I want, I crave the time in these, my last years, to come a little nearer to the secrets of Beethoven and a few other eternal masters."

Beginning in 1963, NBC Radio broadcast a weekly series of programs entitled *Toscanini: The Man Behind The Legend*, commemorating Toscanini's years with the NBC Symphony Orchestra. The show, hosted by NBC announcer Ben Grauer, who had also hosted many of the original Toscanini broadcasts, featured interviews with members of the conductor's family, as well as musicians of the NBC Symphony. It featured partial or complete rebroadcasts of many of Toscanini's recordings. The program ran for at least three years and was rebroadcast by PBS radio in the late 1970s.

In 1986, The New York Public Library for the Performing Arts purchased the bulk of Toscanini's papers, scores and sound recordings from his heirs. Entitled, "The Toscanini Legacy", the collection contains thousands of letters, programs, documents, over 1,800 scores and more than 400 hours of sound recordings. The Library also has other collections that have Toscanini materials in them.

Personal Life

He spent the last years in America in a sprawling twenty-room house in Riverdale New York, getting up at 6:30 each morning, spending his days and nights studying scores, reading, going over and over the works he had led, preparing himself for concerts, many of which, as always throughout his life, were for the benefit of worthy causes. He was a compact little man, with a crop of fine white hair and a mustache kept perky by an old-fashioned mustache iron. His eyes were nearsighted but flashing, his teeth were pure white, his stature was erect, and he gave "the impression of energy rather than of strength." He was quite uninterested in eating and frequently went through an elaborate banquet on just a bowl of soup. He drank wine occasionally but never smoked. "I kissed my first woman and smoked my first cigarette on the same day," he said. "I have never had time for tobacco since."

With him in Riverdale lived his wife, the former Carla dei Martini, whom he married in 1897. She was the one who took care of all his needs, who arranged for fresh clothing after rehearsals, who was in complete charge of all his financial affairs—a woman who always "was not nor wished to be anything but this man's wife." They remained married until her death on June 23, 1951. They had three children: Walter, an official of RCA; Wally, who was the Countess Castelbarco, wife of an Italian painter and poet; and Wanda, who was married to Vladimir Horowitz, the famous pianist. Toscanini's grandchildren were his great joy, and he loved to play with Wanda's daughter, Sonia. He was surprised one day in his studio playing *Heigh Ho, Heigh Ho, It's Off to Work We Go* from *Snow White* while she vigorously wielded a baton. "Her beat was correct," grandpa boasted.

Arturo Toscanini died in his sleep at his home in Riverdale, New York City on January 6, 1957. His body was returned to Italy and buried in the Cimitero Monumentale in Milan. In his will, he left his baton to his protégée Herva Nelli, who sang in the broadcasts of Otello, Aïda, Falstaff, the Verdi Requiem, and Un ballo in maschera. Toscanini was posthumously awarded the Grammy Lifetime Achievement Award in 1987.

Further Reading

Atlan 161:352-60 Mr '38
Collier's 100:17+ D 25 '37 pors
Etude 58:373+ Je '40 por·(Same abr. *Read Digest* 36:37-41 Je '40)
Fortune 17:62-8+ Ja '38 por
Harper 179:589-91 N '39
N Y Times VII p8 Ap 28 '40 il pors; VII p15 Mr 22 '42 por
New Yorker 5:23-6 F 23 '29
Sat Eve Post 205:14-15+ Ja 7 '33 por
Time 27:34+ F 3 '36 pors; 27:52-4 My11 '36 por; 34:65 D 11 '39; 35:45 J e10 '40 por; 39:39- 40 My 4 '42 por
Ewen, D. *Dictators of the Baton* 1942
Ewen, D. ed. *Living Musicians* 1940
Gilman, L. *Toscanini and Great Music* 1938
Mason, D. G. *Tune in, America* p36-48 1931
Men of Turmoil p249-57 1935
Nicotra, T. *Arturo Toscanini* 1938
Shore, B. *Orchestra Speaks* p159-82 1938
Stefan, P. *Arturo Toscanini* 1938
Thompson, 0. ed. *International Cyclopedia of Music and Musicians* 1939
Westrup, J. A. *Sharps and Flats* p190-9 1940
Who's Who in America 1942-43
Woolf, S. J. *Drawn from Life* p188-97 1932
Sachs, H., *The Letters of Arturo Toscanini,* Knopf, Ap 23 2002
Civetta, C., *The Real Toscanini: Musicians Reveal the Maestro,* Amadeus Press, S 1 2012

Travis Tritt

Country musician

Born: Feb. 9, 1963; Marietta, Georgia
Primary Field: Country
Group Affiliation: Solo performer

Travis Tritt.

Introduction

"I refuse to be muzzled," the country musician Travis Tritt told Kate Meyers for Entertainment Weekly *(June 10, 1994). "I was brought up in a family where above everything else, you tell the truth. If you don't want to know how things are, don't ask me." During the early years of his career, Tritt made waves in the country-music world because of his outspokenness and his refusal to conform to the stylistic and musical conventions of country music. Eschewing the traditional cowboy hat worn by most performers in the genre, Tritt kept his hair long and favored leather clothing over mainstream country garb.*

Early Life

Travis Tritt was born in Marietta, Georgia, outside Atlanta, on February 9, 1963 to James Tritt, a bus driver and former farmer, and Gwen Tritt, a bookkeeper. Along with his younger sister, Sheilah, he grew up on a 40-acre property. The Tritt family was prominent in Marietta, having once owned much of northeastern Cobb County; several roads, neighborhoods, and an elementary school bear the Tritt name. Travis's love of music began in childhood; he sang gospel in a youth choir at First Assembly Church of God and taught himself to play guitar at age eight. He began to write songs at 14 (around the time his parents divorced) and played in bluegrass, rock, and country bands as a teenager. Known in school for his Elvis Presley impersonation, he was similarly influenced by such bluegrass performers as Merle and Doc Watson, as well as by Johnny Cash, Willie Nelson, George Jones, Merle Haggard, and the southern rock band Lynyrd Skynyrd. He embarked on his musical career despite. his parents' reservations and struggled through the early 1980s while holding a variety of jobs. While he was working at an air-conditioning company, its president, a guitarist who had abandoned his goal of being a professional musician, urged Tritt to pursue his dream; in 1984 the young man quit to do just that. "I didn't want to wind up sitting on a porch when I'm old and wondering if I could have done it," he told Cynthia Sanz and Gail Wescott for *People* (June 1, 1992).

Life's Work

Tritt, who had recorded his first demo in 1982, cut several more songs over the next few years while also touring the honky-tonk circuit. After signing a major-label deal in 1989, he released his first Top 10 single, "Country Club"; an album of the same name followed, in 1990. His second album, *It's All About to Change* (1991), went multiplatinum. Among its hits was the number-one "Here's a Quarter (Call Someone Who Cares)," which he wrote while going through his second divorce, and the ballad "Anymore." *T-R-0-U-B-L-E,* his follow-up album, released in 1992, did not sell as well as his first two and did not receive as much critical acclaim. "Tritt's third album is so moany-whiny and self-pitying that he counteracts the affection and admiration he earlier won," Ralph Novak wrote for *People* (October 26, 1992). "Consider the titles: 'Looking Out for Number One,' 'I Wish I Could Go Back Home,' 'Leave My Girl Alone.' Not even the clever, jaunty title tune can relieve the oppressive tone." The album went gold nevertheless, on the strength of the number-one single "Can I Trust You with My Heart." Tritt's next album, *Ten Feet Tall and Bulletproof* (1994), went platinum, partly due to the hit "Foolish Pride." Another notable song on the album was "Old Outlaws Like Us," which featured performances by the country legends Waylon Jennings and Hank Williams Jr. Tritt has said that he composed the song late at night while thinking about his musical influences. "From the humorous macho self-ridicule of the title cut to the sensitivity of 'Foolish Pride,' from the Tritt-Waylon Jennings-Hank Williams Jr. teaming on 'Old Outlaws Like Us' to the sizzling rage of Marty Stuart's 'Hard Times and Misery,' this is a package that under- scores the wide diversity of Tritt's artistry," Jack Hurst wrote of the album for the *Chicago Tribune* (May 8, 1994).

A scant five years after his first major-label release, Tritt came out with *Greatest Hits: From the Beginning* (1995). Featuring the number-one single "The Whiskey Ain't Workin'"—which Tritt and his fellow country musician Marty Stuart had been singing together on their "No Hats" tour—the album went platinum. In 1996 Tritt released *The Restless Kind,* which was considered a departure for him because of its stripped-down sound and use of traditional instrumentation, including fiddle and Dobra. "The whole album talks about growing up," he said in an interview posted on the Country Stars Web Site. "Every young guy I've ever known in my life, practically, wanted to get away. And a lot of them end up going out and sowing their wild oats, and they end up coming back to the very thing they tried to get away from. I think that this album is probably a very good representation of that journey."

Tritt described his next album, *No More Looking Over My Shoulder* (1998), as "definitely a sample of what's been going on in my life, being married recently and having a brand new baby," as he told Ron Tank for the CNN Web site (October 16, 1998). "The music is still out on the edge, but it's a little bit different message than it had in the past. It's reflective of how happy I am as a husband and father." Tritt's penchant for mixing rock influences into his music was still on display—the album included two cover songs by rockers, one by Bruce Springsteen, the other by Jude Cole—but the slick production associated with Nashville's star artists was also evident. The disk did not enjoy as much commercial success as had most of his others.

In 1999, dissatisfied with what he viewed as a lack of publicity, Tritt left his label, Warner Brothers. "The last album that I did for Warner Brothers got no promotion, no backing," he told King. "It was almost like the label said, 'Tritt's records sell themselves; we have other fish to fry.'" After taking a two-year hiatus from touring and recording (during which he did not listen to country radio), Tritt signed a contract with Columbia Records in 2000 and released *Down the Road I Go.* The album scored four hit singles, including "It's a Great

Day to Be Alive" and the ballad "Best of Intentions." For the first time in Tritt's recording career, a bluegrass influence could be discerned in his work; Tritt played banjo (a traditional bluegrass instrument) on several of the album's tracks. In a review of one of his live performances, Jeffrey Lee Puckett, writing for the (Louisville) *Courier-Journal* (November 16, 2002, on-line), characterized the changes in Tritt's sound since his early days with Warner Brothers Records: "When Tritt was filling arenas his shows often seemed more like warmed-over Lynyrd Skynyrd than traditional country.... [Now] his approach is a bit more mellow and grounded more strongly in the past; fiddles and pedal steel are part of the sound, not tacked on for the sake of appearances." Though *Down the Road I Go* sold well, reviews were mixed. "After taking 18 months off ... Tritt emerges sounding strangely like Kenny Rogers, right down to the hokey catch in the voice and the melodramatic story song, in this case an ill-advised tribute to a couple of sadistic thugs, 'Modern Day Bonnie and Clyde,'" a *People* (November 13, 2000) critic wrote. "Tritt's slightly gravelly voice has always resembled Rogers's, of course. But that hardly obliges him to emulate the schmaltzier, least admirable aspects of the Gambler's style. Happily, Tritt sounds more like himself on the trenchant 'Southbound Train' . . . and 'Just Too Tired to Fight It.'"

In 2002 Tritt issued *Strong Enough.* Featuring his writing or co-writing on nine of the 12 tracks, the album had strong commercial appeal. *"Strong Enough* is Tritt doing what he does best, flexing his vocal muscles on up-tempo cuts ... and running on pure emotion on the ballads ... ,"Todd Sterling wrote for the Country Review Web site. "Travis Tritt may be on his eighth studio album, but he still sounds like he's having the time of his life.... There's enough fiddle and Dobra to please the older crowd, plenty of ballads to prick the hearts of the sensitive, and a handful of country rockers to keep the rowdies up until the wee hours playing air guitar and tabletop drums. Who said country music was dead? It isn't here." In *People* (October 21, 2002), Ralph Novak called Tritt "the George Jones of his generation, a throwback to elemental country music," and gave the album an "A" rating.

Also in 2002 Rhino Records released two compilations of Tritt's work, *The Rockin' Side* and *The Lovin' Side,* the first containing his rock-influenced numbers and the latter his romantic ballads. "Put simply, Tritt is a double threat and one hell of a Southern rock singer when he wants to be," Michael Paoletta wrote of *The Rockin' Side* for *Billboard* (February 16, 2002). Paoletta also gave high marks to the companion collection of ballads: "Tritt's dead-on delivery of such neoclassics as 'Between an Old Memory and Me' are whiskey-tinged, [Vern] Gosdin-esque perfection, delivering a mixture of regret, self-pity, and resignation that is the sole property of country music at its best." A reviewer for *Country Music* (June/July 2002) was not as pleased with the division of Tritt's songs along stylistic lines, pointing out, "Tritt's music always worked best when alternating his sensitivity with his swagger." Describing *The Lovin' Side,* the

Affiliation: Country Music and Individuality

He refused to live in Nashville (the accepted center of the country-music scene), employed a Hollywood agent, and vocally criticized his industry for embracing what he saw as a formulaic sound. ("I think the Nashville community is starting to realize that the cookie-cutter mentality is, in the end, not productive," he told an interviewer for the Country Stars Web site. "It may produce a tremendous amount of revenue for a certain period of time, but it has no longevity.") Musically, Tritt separated himself from the pack by incorporating rock into his sound. His first album, *Country Club* (1990), featured the song "Put Some Drive in Your Country," which acknowledged his love of the classic country sound embodied by such performers as Roy Acuff and George Jones but also recalled the excitement he felt upon discovering such "outlaw" country artists as Waylon Jennings and Hank Williams Jr., who were also influenced by rock music. Despite his image as a rebel and outsider, Tritt quickly rose to fame and eventually came to be accepted by the country-music establishment. He has sold some 20 million albums, recorded three number-one hits on the country music charts, and won two Grammy Awards. He has also collaborated with older, more traditional artists and appeared at the Grand Ole Opry. "For years, I've heard people talk about the outlaw image, [calling me] a rough-around-the-edges country rocker," he told Angela King for *Billboard* (September 14, 2002). "Then *[Down the Road I Go* (2000)] came out, and they are calling me a traditionalist. People like to try and put a label on things, put you in a box. I hate those boxes. It limits you if you're trying to do different things and experiment with music."

reviewer wrote, "The ballads collection features several memorable cuts . . . but even the best of Tritt's sensitive stuff pales in comparison to rockers like the hayseed-meets-hellion 'Ten Feet Tall and Bulletproof.'"

Rhino Records released another collection of Tritt's songs, *The Essentials,* in 2003. In March of that year, Tritt publicly criticized Natalie Maines, a singer in the country group the Dixie Chicks, after she told a London audience, "We're ashamed the president of the United States is from Texas," as quoted on the *CBS News* Web site (March 15, 2003). Tritt said that it was cowardly of Maines to attack President George W. Bush while she was overseas and dared her to make the same remark in the Houston Astrodome. In response to Maines's comment, many country radio stations stopped playing Dixie Chicks songs and some fans boycotted the group; Tritt urged them on, telling people to "hit 'em in the pocketbook," as quoted on the Boston Channel Web site (March 18, 2003). "I feel it is one of our God-given rights as Americans to speak our minds freely and honestly. The First Amendment is one of the things that makes our country great. However, in such a fragile time in the world, with that privilege comes the need to be responsible and mindful of the repercussions." Tritt, who often visits military bases to meet soldiers and has performed at a rally in support of American troops, said that the morale of servicemen and -women could be damaged if they heard negative comments about U.S. military policy.

Tritt assembled a large cast of guest musicians for his 2004 studio release, *My Honky Tonk Hist*ory. Again, the result is a rocking blend of country, blue. The fourth, especially noteworthy of the album's 12 tracks, "What You Say," features a duet between Tritt and the roots rocker John Mellencamp, set off by the twang of a banjo played by Bela Fleck. In *All Music Guide* (on-line), the reviewer Thom Jurek wrote of the album, "In all, *My Honky Tonk History* is a solid, sure-voiced outing from an enduring and committed artist."

Tritt has received many awards and honors. In 1991 he won the Horizon Award from the Country Music Association (CMA) and the TNN Music City News Song of the Year Award. In 1992 he was inducted into the Grand Ole Opry cast, was given the Vocal Event of the Year Award by the CMA, was named a star of tomorrow by TNN Music City News, and won a Grammy for best vocal collaboration for his duet with Marty Stuart, "The Whiskey Ain't Workin'." In 1993 he won the Vocal Event of the Year Award from the CMA once again and captured an award for vocal collaboration of the year from the TNN Music City News. In 1998 he received his second Grammy Award, for best country collaboration with vocals, with Earl Scruggs, Emmylou Harris, Joe Diffie, Marty Stuart, Merle Haggard, Pam Tillis, Patty Loveless, Randy Travis, and Ricky Skaggs for the song "Same Old Train." He was presented with a Public Service Award from the Department of Veteran Affairs in 2003 for his support of veterans. Tritt, who portrayed a disabled Vietnam veteran in three of his music videos and was a spokesman for Disabled American Veterans from 1994 to 1996, received the Veterans Administration's Secretary's Award in 1993 and the Hall of Fame Award from the Veterans of Foreign Wars in 2001.

Tritt has participated with other country stars in a series of radiothons to benefit St. Jude Children's Research Hospital, in Memphis, Tennessee. In August 2002 he donated $25,000 to the Sipesville, Pennsylvania, Volunteer Fire Company, which led the rescue of nine miners trapped underground for three days in late July of that year. The state of Georgia renamed a three-mile stretch of route 92 "Travis Tritt Highway" in 2001, and a Winchester gun, dubbed the Travis Tritt Tribute Rifle, has been created in his honor.

Tritt has appeared in several movies and television shows. His big-screen film cameos include *The Cowboy Way* (1994), *Sgt. Bilko* (1996), *Fire Down Below* (1997), and *Blues Brothers 2000* (1998); on TV he had parts in the films *Rio Diablo* (1993), which co-starred the singers Kenny Rogers and Naomi Judd; *Christmas in My Hometown* (1996), in which he played a sheriff; and *Outlaw Justice* (1999), in which he worked with Rogers again. Among the TV shows in which he has appeared are *Tales from the Crypt* (1995), *The Jeff Foxworthy Show* (1995), *Dr. Quinn, Medicine Woman* (1996), *Diagnosis Murder* (1999), *Touched by an* Angel (1999), and *Arli$$* (1999). He also hosted the weekly television program *Country Countdown with Travis Tritt* on VH1 in the 1990s. His autobiography, *Ten Feet Tall and Bulletproof,* co-written with Michael Bane, was published in 1994.

Personal Life

Tritt, who admits to being "the ultimate control freak," was divorced twice before finding success in his music career. His first marriage, to his college sweetheart, ended after two years; his second lasted four years. (He has admitted that his heavy drinking contributed to the failure of that marriage and has since curbed such excesses.)

On April 12, 1997 he married the model Theresa Nelson. The couple live on a 75-acre farm in Hiram, Georgia, outside Atlanta, with their three children-a daughter, Tyler Reese, born in 1998; a son, Tristan James, born in 1999; and a second son, Tarian Nathaniel, born in 2003. Tritt enjoys riding horses and Harley-Davidson motorcycles in his free time. "I like to do a little bit of a lot of different things," he told M.B. Roberts for *Country Music* (June/July 2002). "That's the way my music has always been. There's certain days when I feel like doing nothing but rock. Some days, it's straight-ahead country. Some days, bluegrass or the blues. I like being able to do all those different things."

Further Reading

Country Music p74 Oct./Nov. 2001, with photos
Country Stars Web site
People p25 Oct. 26, 1992
Travis Tritt Web site
Tritt, Travis and Michael Bane. *Ten Feet Tall and Bulletproof,* 1994

Richard Tucker

Singer

Born: August 28, 1913; Brooklyn, New York
Died: January 8, 1975, Kalamazoo, Michigan
Primary Field: Opera
Group Affiliation: Solo performer

Introduction

Leading tenor of the Metropolitan Opera Association, Richard Tucker celebrated the tenth anniversary of his debut with the Met on January 2, 1955 with his portrayal of Riccardo in Un Ballo in Maschera. *He was a renowned cantor and former businessman who sang at La Scala in Milan, Italy, on radio and television, in oratorio and concert, and was known for his recordings. Coming to the Metropolitan as an inexperienced opera singer, he learned his roles from season to season. The* San Francisco Examiner *(December 6, 1953) considered that he "is the best tenor in the world today, and he has been for some time."*

Early Life

One of the five children of Samuel and Fanny (Chippen) Ticker, Reuben Ticker, later to be known as Richard Tucker, was born in Brooklyn, New York, on August 28, 1913. Samuel Ticker, an emigrant from Bessarabia, was a furrier and occasionally officiated as a cantor. When Reuben was six, he began singing in the choir of the Allen Street synagogue on Manhattan's lower East Side.

After attending New Utrecht High School in Brooklyn, where he played baseball, football, and basketball, he decided to work during the day and study voice in the evening. First he worked as a runner for a Wall Street brokerage firm and then errand boy in New York's garment district. Raising $3,500, he opened a shop of his own where he dyed silk linings for fur coats. In the meantime, his singing was not neglected; at twenty, he had established himself as an outstanding cantor in Brooklyn. Among the famous voice teachers with whom he studied was Paul Althouse, who had been a Wagnerian tenor.

Life's Work

Professional operatic experience preceding the singer's recognition was extraordinarily brief. It included a concert at Town Hall in 1939 in which he sang tenor solos from Rossini's *Stabat Mater,* and an engagement with the *Chicago Theatre of the Air* over WGN radio station. A contestant in the *Metropolitan Auditions of the Air,* he won second place. It was about this time that the singer took the name of Richard Tucker. In 1944 Tucker obtained an audition with the Metropolitan's general manager, Edward Johnson; the result was his engagement as a leading tenor for the opera company.

At the time, Tucker was an established cantor of the Brooklyn Jewish Center and an independent businessman. According to Wambly Bald of the *New York Post Magazine* (April 18, 1949), Tucker told Johnson, "I refuse to join the opera company if I have to sing small roles. If I start, it must be as a leading man." Tucker made his debut at the Metropolitan on January 25, 1945 as Enzo Grimaldo in *La Gioconda.* Sharing honors with Stella Roman, Tucker headed the cast.

Affiliation: Solo Opera Singer

The part of Radames was sung by Tucker in Arturo Toscanini's presentation of *Aïda* over radio and television in 1949, winning fresh plaudits for the singer. In the same season he appeared for the first time at the Metropolitan in *La Bohème*. After only two performances in the role, Tucker recorded *La Bohème* for Columbia Records. Praising the singer's work in *Manon Lescaut,* presented later in the year, Howard Taubman of the New York *Times* wrote that "as with everything he has been doing this season, his performance had high distinction." He added that Tucker "is now among the finest tenors . . . and he is still developing."

While considering the "formidable role too heavy for his essentially lyric type of voice," the New York *Times* critic went on to say that Tucker "was enthusiastically received by the large audience . . . He sang with warmth and expressiveness and his acting was natural and easy." To hold the position he had achieved meant hard study, for in this and succeeding seasons, Tucker was singing his roles at the Metropolitan for the first time on any stage. Among his roles in 1946 was that of Dimitri in *Boris Godunoff,* performed on November 21, with Risë Stevens and Ezio Pinza in the cast.

The first operatic tenor to be invited to Italy following World War II, Tucker scored a success in Verona in the summer of 1947, appearing in *La Gioconda* for five performances. Another member of the cast was Maria Callas. Of a reappearance in the same opera at the Metropolitan in December of the same year, Jerome D. Bohm of the New York *Herald Tribune* wrote that "the most distinguished singing of the evening was that of Mr. Tucker . . . Not only has his fine tenor voice grown much more powerful but it is now produced with a concentrated freedom which permits him to project it throughout its range with unfailing tonal persuasiveness and telling expressivity."

In addition to singing at the Metropolitan, Tucker was in demand for concert work. The *New York Herald Tribune* (April 17, 1948) reported that he had consented to sing at a concert to be held at Carnegie Hall in celebration of the twentieth anniversary of Birobidzhan (the Jewish-Autonomous Region, U.S.S.R.), believing the program was a benefit for Jewish children in Israel. When he learned that it was not and that it was to feature an address by the Soviet Ambassador Alexander S. Panyushkin, Tucker withdrew.

In January 1949 Tucker sang with the Vinaver Chorus at Town Hall in a concert of Biblical and Hebraic music. The New York *Herald Tribune* critic commented that Tucker's "executions of the florid cantilations was deeply moving and his powerful and uncommonly sympathetic voice, his excellent vocal production, lent themselves to many and subtle nuances."

Noel Straus of the New York *Times* (December 17, 1951) in reviewing a performance of *La Bohème* commented: "The outstanding vocalism of the evening was that of Mr. Tucker. Not since [Enrico] Caruso has this reviewer heard any tenor who delivered Rodolfo's music with more fervor or greater accuracy." The tenor appeared in the same season in the new staging of *Rigoletto* and *Così fan tutte,* the latter under the direction of Alfred Lunt. In 1951 and 1952 Tucker was heard in Felix Mendelssohn's *Elijah* under the baton of Dimitri Mitropoulos with the New York Philharmonic Symphony. When Tucker appeared in 1952 for the first time as Don José in *Carmen,* staged by Tyrone Guthrie, *Time* (February 11, 1952) reported that the singer "had a triumph of his own . . . his is probably the finest tenor to be heard today." On June 22, 1953 Tucker performed in *Madame Butterfly* before an audience of 22,000 at Robin Hood Dell in Fairmont Park, Philadelphia, Pennsylvania, under the direction of Eugene Ormandy. During the 1953-54 season he was a frequent guest artist on such television shows as Ed Sullivan's *Toast of the Town.*

In the season of 1954–55 Olin Downes of the New York *Times* wrote that Tucker sang the part of Don Carlos "with great beauty and brilliancy of tone." Tucker also portrayed Andrea Chenier for the first time in the opera of the same name. During the summer of 1955 Tucker participated in the third annual musical festival held at Newport, Rhode Island and appeared at the Lewisohn Stadium in New York in a presentation of *La Traviata.* In the summers of 1954 and 1955 he sang at La Scala.

Opening its seventy-first season on November 14, 1955, the Metropolitan offered *Les Contes d'Hoffman* under the baton of Pierre Monteux, with Tucker in the title role. Louis Biancolli of the New York *Telegram and Sun* and Winthrop Sargeant of the *New Yorker* (November 26, 1955) thought Tucker was miscast in the part. *Musical America* (December 1, 1955) wrote that Tucker "was in full command of those ringing full-bodied tones and the fluent, unrestrained lyricism of the most refined quality." On December 8, 1955 he portrayed Mario Cavaradossi in *Tosca,* under the direction of Mitropoulos.

Winthrop Sargeant (*Life,* November 3, 1952) wrote that "meticulous critics might easily point out that Mr. Tucker's eminence is due partly to the mediocrity of his era. He is no Caruso . . . But no tenor now at the Met can equal the combined agility, emotional fervor and power that Tucker's voice possesses."

Almost from the start of his operatic career, Tucker recorded for Columbia and then later RCA. However, measured against the sheer length of his career, Tucker's commercial recordings are proportionately sparse and inadequately convey the power of his voice. However, his recordings with soprano Leontyne Price (especially Madama Butterfly and La Forza del Destino) do illustrate his dramatic presence and fine ringing voice. He also made a famous recording of Aida with Maria Callas, from his Verona debut. Many other commercial recordings, as well as private recordings of his concerts and broadcast performances, have been digitally remastered and are available in CD and online downloadable formats. A number of his national television appearances on "'The Voice of Firestone'" and "'The Bell Telephone Hour'" were preserved in kinescope and videotape form, and have been reissued in VHS and DVD format.

A great number of the complete opera disks issued in collaboration with the Metropolitan featured the singer. Tucker was the first American tenor invited to make official La Scala recordings, and he was alone in being the first to record for both the Metropolitan and La Scala. His La Scala recordings were released by Angel Records. In a statement for *This I Believe,* broadcast over WCBS in 1953, Tucker said, "To me the truth implies that I am willing to face the consequences of my acts." A deeply religious man, he continued his duties as a cantor whenever opportunity permitted. He attributed his success to "energy, singleness of purpose, and unremitting diligence" (*Life,* November 3, 1952). "God blessed me with a good memory and a keen mind," Tucker said.

Personal Life

On February 11, 1936 he married Sara Perelmuth, the sister of the noted tenor, Jan Peerce. The couple had three sons, Barry, David and Henry. Tucker was five feet eight inches in height, and weighed 185 pounds, and had black hair and brown eyes. His hobbies were writing comic verse, golf, photography, baseball, football, handball, swimming, bicycle riding, gardening, and listening to records. In 1952 he received a citation from the National Father's Day Committee.

Richard Tucker died of a heart attack on January 8, 1975 in Kalamazoo, Michigan while he was touring with the baritone Robert Merrill in a series of joint concerts. His funeral was held on the stage of the Metropolitan Opera. (He is the only person whose funeral has been held here.) In tribute to his legacy at the Met, the city of New York designated the park adjacent to Lincoln Center as Richard Tucker Square. After his death, his widows, sons, and friends and colleagues established the Richard Tucker Music Foundation, which holds annual televised concerts and award grants and scholarships to aspiring vocalists. The sopranos Renée Fleming and Deborah Voight and the tenor Richard Leech are among the recipients of grants from the Tucker Foundation.

Further Reading

Drake, J A, *Richard Tucker: A Biography,* Dutton Adult, F 27 '84

Life 33:127+ N 3 '52 pors

Mus Courier 152:6 N 1 '55 pors

N Y Post Mag p27 Ap 18 '49 pors

Opera News 11:16 Ap 7 '47 por

Saleski, G. ed. *Famous Musicians of Jewish Origin* (1949)

Who's Who in America, 1954-55

Sophie Tucker

Singer

Born: January 13, 1887; Tulchyn, Ukraine
Died: February 9, 1966; New York, New York
Primary Field: Jazz
Group Affiliation: Solo Artist; The Five Kings of Syncopation

Introduction

'The "Last of the Red-hot Mamas," Sophie Tucker, boomed her throaty tones for almost three score years: she began her career in 1906 in the heyday of American vaudeville, and through night-club appearances, survived its decline and fall. Endowed with the determination, stamina, and spirit of a good trouper, and with a personality and voice which matched her generous proportions, this vaudevillian won audiences not only in the United States, but in the British Isles and on the Continent. Her autobiography, named for her theme song, "Some of These Days," was published in the spring of 1945 and gave a hearty account of her full life.

Early Life

Sophie Tucker was literally born "on the road." In 1884 her mother was traveling by wagon out of Russia on her way to join her husband in America, when the child was born. The family name was originally Kalish, but on his journey to America, the father took the name of a dead friend. Miss Tucker described the circumstances: "Papa, who had a terror of the Russian authorities reaching out and grabbing him and shipping him to Siberia for life, prudently helped himself to the Italian's papers and moniker. Don't ask me what the United States immigration officers made of an Italian who couldn't speak anything but Russian and Yiddish; but it was as 'Charles Abuza' that Papa got into this country, and found a job in Boston."

Hence, in 1884, at the age of three months, Sophie Abuza arrived in Boston, where the family lived for eight years—Miss Tucker remarked regretfully that nobody ever admired her "Harvard accent." They moved to Hartford when the father bought a restaurant there. With her brothers, Philip and Moses, and her sister, Anna, young Sophie enjoyed the excitement of the city streets near the Connecticut River. The children had to help in the restaurant, which Sophie disliked. She hated especially the endless dish washing but obediently followed her mother's stern orders. Because she rose early to finish kitchen chores before going to school, she sometimes fell asleep in class.

While working at her job at the tables as a young girl, she listened to the talk of the actors who frequented the Abuza Restaurant. She had a strong voice and would often sing popular songs in the restaurant, after which the customers would tip her. Once her mother saved enough money to buy a second-hand piano, but when Sophie neglected her piano practice, the instrument was sold. Hoping to draw customers, the girl began to sing regularly in the restaurant, winning some applause. She went to vaudeville matinees and learned the songs in the shows. But while actors complimented her singing, her parents warned her against show business. Miss Tucker recalled how thrilled she was when she served the great Jewish actors Jacob Adler and Boris Thomashefsky, who had come to eat Mrs. Abuza's cooking. These celebrities urged the girl's family to permit her to join one of the Jewish theatrical companies, but the parents firmly refused. Soon after her graduation from school, when she was sixteen, Sophie Abuza eloped with Louis Tuck. She had hoped to escape the drudgery of the kitchen, but the joy of her own small apartment was short lived. When their son Bert was born, the couple moved back with the Abuza family to ease their financial difficulties. Once more Sophie was back in the restaurant. She started singing there again, and was told her voice was better than before. About this time she was separated from her husband, eventually obtaining a divorce.

The ambitious young woman, determined to get away from restaurant chores, saved all her money and, on the pretext of going on a vacation, left home to become an entertainer. She went first to New Haven to see Willie Howard, who had advised her to try the entertainment field. The comedian told her to go to New York to try her luck. She spent her first weeks in the big city looking for work as a "song plugger" in Tin Pan Alley, with no success. When her money ran low she "sang for her supper" in restaurants. Meanwhile, she continued to frequent the offices of the music publishers, making friends and becoming known to the song writers. In 1906 she changed her name to Tucker.

Life's Work

In November of that year she obtained a job at a popular cafe, the German Village, singing for fifteen dollars a week. She worked herself up to leading entertainer in this place all the while continuing to visit the music publishers for new songs. Throughout her career she was careful about her songs, seeking new tunes continually, especially those suited to her robust style of singing. She auditioned for an amateur show at the 125th Street Theatre and overheard the manager give orders for her to appear in blackface, saying she was "too big and ugly." Thus she started her stage career in disguise, wearing blackface make-up. Joe Woods booked her on a small-time vaudeville circuit, billing her as a "World-renowned Coon Shouter." Later she played on the Park Circuit, performing in the smaller cities of New York, New Jersey, Pennsylvania, and Ohio, where she began to acquire a following. Her first New York date was at the Music Hall on 116th Street on December 9, 1906. Thereafter she played her blackface act on the New England circuit, learning from other performers and developing her technique.

Tony Pastor's Theatre in New York was then one of the city's famous entertainment centers. Miss Tucker obtained an engagement there and made elaborate preparations for her appearance. When he came on the stage, a noisy audience entering the theatre paid little attention to her. She shouted at the audience, won their attention and, soon, their approval. After seeing her act at Pastor's, a burlesque manager offered Miss Tucker a contract. She accepted, having heard that burlesque work was good theatrical training. Her first part in burlesque was a cranky old wife, and although she learned dialogue quickly, she had difficulty with the character. But despite the bad rehearsals, she was a success when the show opened.

One day while playing the burlesque circuit her trunk containing her make-up and costumes was lost, forcing her to perform without blackface. It was a triumphant moment for her when she realized she could hold an audience without the benefit of disguise. In 1909 a talent scout saw Miss Tucker in one of these shows and she was offered a part in the current Ziegfeld *Follies.* Nora Bayes was the star of this particular production, a lavish production with the usual abundance of beautiful girls. During rehearsals nobody seemed to notice Miss Tucker, .who was doubtful until the last minute that she would actually appear in the show.

Finally she was assigned to a jungle scene, and at the time of her first and only rehearsal, a cold prevented her from singing. In this show she was also scheduled to fill in time between acts with songs selected by her old friend Irving Berlin. Opening night was a gala event, with an audience of celebrities including "Diamond Jim" Brady, Lillian Russell, George M. Cohan, and Sam Harris. Miss Tucker stopped the show with her inter-act specialty. The star objected, and Ziegfeld decided that Miss Tucker was to do only the jungle song. Years later Miss Tucker became a close friend of Nora Bayes's, but neither of them ever mentioned this incident. When the *Follies* came to New York, Miss Bayes had left the show and was replaced by Eva Tanguay, who wanted the jungle number herself. So Miss Tucker was fired.

Affiliation: Solo Performer

Miss Tucker delighted in telling of her return in triumph to her home town to headline the show at Poli's Theatre in Hartford. The joy of her return was increased by the presence of her son who was vacationing from military school. (Whenever she was in New York, Miss Tucker always sent for the boy.) During her next engagement she met Frank Westphal, who had a piano act, and the two became a team. In August 1914 she attained the pinnacle of vaudeville success—a date at the Palace Theatre in New York. For this engagement she earned one thousand dollars and the plaudits of both audience and critics. One critic stated, "She just walked out and owned the place." Miss Tucker married Westphal in Chicago, where the wedding party was treated to the *Wedding March* from *Lohengrin* played by Paderewski, who happened to be in the restaurant in which they were celebrating. The couple's strenuous vaudeville schedule, Miss Tucker said, was not exactly conducive to matrimonial harmony—they played two shows daily, six or seven days a week for several seasons of "big-time" vaudeville. During the years of the First World War Miss Tucker introduced the famous song "M-o-t-h-e-r, the Word That Means the World to Me." She was changing her singing style, abandoning "coon shouting." In 1916 she toured in the show *Town Topics.* During her tours she met the great celebrities of the time, as well as many struggling vaudevillians who later rose to fame. On one bill she played with Gus Edwards' school act: among the child actors were Eddie Cantor, George Jessel, and Walter Winchell.

During her trying times with the *Follies,* she was befriended by a Negro maid, Mollie Elkins, who became her lifelong friend.

Back in New York, without work or money, the singer suffered a temporary loss of voice. With Miss Elkins' help she managed to start again after a brief rest. It was then she began her long association with William Morris, whose agency managed her throughout her career. Morris organized his own vaudeville circuit of American Music Halls, for which he brought to America such English entertainers as Sir Harry Lauder and Charlie Chaplin. Miss Tucker played this circuit with great success; she had finally attained a sense of security in her work. In Chicago, where she was especially popular, billed as "The Mary Garden of Ragtime," Ashton Stevens wrote: "Miss Tucker can move an audience or a piano with equal address. Don't miss any of her." During this period of her career, she started to use the double-entendre songs which became closely identified with her style. She explained that she sang "hot numbers" to entertain, not to shock, insisting that all of these songs had as themes something real in people's lives. She said: "The innocents couldn't find a thing in it to object to, and the others would find a belly laugh in every line." (Jack Yellen wrote this type of song for her for over twenty years.) Miss Tucker first saw her name in lights at an Atlantic City theater—she was a headliner at last. She made recordings for the Edison Company and sent the money she earned home to her mother. During all these years, she contributed to her family's support and had sent her brother through college.

When she was booked on the Pantages Circuit, the singer traveled West, increasing her popularity. Once in Dayton she tried a costume publicity stunt which failed because people were more interested in the airplane the Wright brothers were trying out. Back in Chicago in April 1911, after her Western tour, she accepted a part in the show *Merry Mary.* This was a failure, but her next venture, *Louisiana Lou,* was a hit. Her earnings were high but gambling took its toll. However, whenever she was in financial difficulties she would sign for a road tour and wipe out the deficit. In 1911 the Negro composer Shelton Brooks brought her his song "Some of These Days." She made it her trade mark and remained popular for a long time.

When Miss Tucker found her marriage failing she set her husband up in the garage business and continued alone. She organized a jazz band, named it "The Five Kings of Syncopation" and called herself "The Queen of Jazz." The new act was a success; Miss Tucker started dramatizing songs, an innovation which became popular. Then her father's death brought about another change in her style: she began to sing ballads—"tearjerkers"—and discovered that she could sing them effectively. This new act entailed greater responsibility for the singer, charged with the supervision of the men in the band. In December 1916 they opened at Reisenweber's, one of the leading restaurants of the day. That was the beginning of the Jazz Era and Miss Tucker and her band were a smash success. Her "Bohemian Nights" at Reisenweber's became famous; she introduced new songs and new performers. On Sunday nights she sang in concerts at the Winter Garden Theatre, where she was the hit of the 1919 season. That year she also appeared in the show *Hello Alexander.* After a summer at her Freeport (Long Island) home, among theatrical friends, Miss Tucker and Westphal were divorced. Following frequent changes in the personnel of her act, it was disbanded. Miss Tucker hired a new pianist, Ted Schapiro, who remained with her for a long time afterwards. After playing Reisenweber's for five years she decided to try something new. Morris arranged her booking in the British music halls (equivalent of vaudeville in America), and the singer sailed for England on March 25, 1922.

Upon her arrival in England she noted the differences between the technique of the English music hall and American vaudeville and set about adapting her material to her new audience. She slowed her tempo down to British tastes and also changed some of the lyrics to follow British colloquialisms more closely. Overcoming her nervousness and becoming accustomed to the sloping British stages, Miss Tucker was a hit with the English. At a Jewish benefit at the Palladium in London, she used a duo-piano team for the first time and also delighted the audience by her remarks in Yiddish. Her tour included Glasgow, Edinburgh, Cardiff, Nottingham, Manchester, and the provinces. Everywhere she was well received, and Miss Tucker said simply: "The British are just folks, same as those in the U.S.A." Dramatic critic Hanan Swaffer expressed the British view, describing Miss Tucker as "a big, fat blond genius, with a dynamic personality and amazing vitality." While in England the singer played in the show *Round in Fifty* for three months. She made many friends in London, entertaining for "high society" and royalty. But her proudest memory of London was the reception she received at the Rivoli Theatre in Whitechapel from

London's Jewish population. Before returning home, Miss Tucker visited Brussels, Berlin, and Paris.

After a triumphant return to the Palace Theatre in New York, she began a new tour, this time on the Orpheum Circuit. There was a brief stop in Hollywood for work in silent films, which was unsuccessful. The next two years were filled with steady vaudeville work, highlighted by her acquaintance with Helen Keller (who appeared on the stage), and by a performance at San Quentin Prison, where the singer met Tom Mooney. In August 1925 Miss Tucker again sailed for England to fill an engagement at the fashionable Kit-Kat Klub in London. In addition to her night-club performances, the singer played in the music halls and appeared with Beatrice Lillie and Gertrude Lawrence in *Charlot's Revue.* One of her most popular songs in England was "My Yiddisha Mama," which audiences always demanded. Her stay in England was halted by news of her mother's illness. She broke contracts to return home, but during the voyage was notified of her mother's death. It was three months before Miss Tucker was able to sing again. She lost her self-confidence and her desire to be amusing. Finally, with the assistance of Morris, she began to sing again, first at benefits and then in her own cafe, Sophie Tucker's Playground. Eventually, fully restored, Miss Tucker went back to vaudeville. She was offered a part in Earl Carroll's *Vanities,* but after ten days among the "beauties" she left the show. At another appearance at the Palace she was billed as the "Last of the Red-hot Mamas"— and that title stayed with her.

In 1928 Miss Tucker was once more back in London, playing at the Kit-Kat Klub, the music halls and touring the provinces. She was persuaded to take a part opposite Edmund Brean in a Greek play, *Socrates,* which thereby was transformed into an uproarious farce. In 1929, back in America, she made her first talking film, *Honky Tonk,* for Warner Brothers, but found motion pictures a difficult type of work. Returning to London in 1930 she played in a musical comedy, *Follow a Star.* (In the intervening years she had been married to Al Lackey.) After this London engagement Miss Tucker attempted performances for Continental audiences, but the language bar was a handicap. At Ostend the audience did not understand any of her songs; at her Paris opening her only knowledge of French was one chorus of "Some of These Days," which she had had translated. So she returned for a tour in England, after which she and her husband vacationed in Europe. In Vienna she discovered that her records were popular—the best seller was "My Yiddisha Mama." Miss Tucker was invited to broadcast this song in Berlin in 1931; after Hitler came into power her records were ordered smashed and their sale banned in the Third Reich.

The singer returned to the United States to find vaudeville in its last days. The years 1931 and 1932 saw the death of vaudeville—a painful episode for the "oldtimers" who had to step aside for the new motion picture idols. But although her pride suffered, the singer continued her active career. In 1934 she played at the Hollywood Country Club in Florida. (At about this time she was divorced from Al Lackey.) Cafe business was bad; besides films, there was now radio competition. In 1934 Miss Tucker was back in England, performing in the big cities and provinces. That year she gave a command performance for King George V and Queen Mary. On her return to America she was given a gala homecoming party by the American Federation of Actors. During the winter of 1934–35 she played at the Hollywood Restaurant in New York, and at many benefit performances. Next she appeared at the Hollywood Trocadero, making a new bid for motion pictures but without success. In 1936 she returned to London in time to witness the strained weeks leading up to the abdication of King Edward VIII (Duke of Windsor). Miss Tucker was acquainted with the former Prince of Wales and was deeply touched by the entire affair.

In 1937 Miss Tucker was in Hollywood, trying the films again, under contract to MetroGoldwyn-Mayer. Anxious for success in the new medium, she took acting lessons from Laura Hope Crews. In *Broadway Melody* Miss Tucker played with Eleanor Powell, Robert Taylor, and Judy Garland. Then in *Thoroughbreds Don't Cry* she played a straight character part without singing. But she was dissatisfied with her career in motion pictures and left Hollywood. She did not recommend the pictures she made, declaring: "That is not Tucker you see on the screen." From Hollywood she went back to night-club work, appearing in 1938 at Ben Marden's Riviera in New Jersey. In that same year she was elected president of the American Federation of Actors, the first woman to hold that office.

In November 1938 she opened in the musical comedy *Leave It To Me,* which was a success on Broadway and later on tour. While performing in this show she did cafe and radio work, also participating actively in the affairs of the A.F.A. Her next show, in 1941, was George Jessel's *High Kickers.* It received bad critical notices much to Miss Tucker's indignation. In March

1944 "The Durable Tucker" opened as star of a brilliant revue at New York's Copacabana. Discussing the show, the New York *Sun* stated: "Sophie Tucker isn't cooling off any, and for that matter neither is her doting audience . . . Miss Tucker, magnificently turned out, gives utterance to hardy aphorisms and characteristic laments with all of her raucous sincerity, and her audience loves it." In April 1944 *PM* paid tribute to Miss Tucker for canceling a Boston night-club engagement to entertain wounded servicemen at Halloran General Hospital in New York. The singer was as popular with servicemen in the Second World War as she was in the First.

The sixty-one-year-old trouper was given a write-up in *Variety* in October 1945, a report of her engagement at the Mayfair in Boston: "Headlining at $3,500-a-week salary, an accepted invitation to speak at the Boston Book Fair, and sell-out dinner tables every night, Sophie Tucker is doing very well by herself. Time has not changed nor custom withered the marvelous trouper's 'Honey Boy', 'Some of These Days,' and 'How You Gonna Keep 'Em Down on the Farm?' which have the same wow reaction as when Soph was here three years ago . . . She still has the spirit of youth, and now and then carries out the promise of a hit song, 'Red Hot Mama Is a Jitterbug Now.'" *Variety* added that only Miss Tucker could put the rowdy "Tax on Love" across under Boston censorship—and that she did it with a "cosmic bang." On the occasion of her engagement at the Martinique, New York newspaper reviews were equally enthusiastic.

For a number of years Miss Tucker had been writing down her own account of her long life in show business. In March 1945 the finished book, *Some of These Days,* was published. The autobiography, as one might expect, was full of anecdotes of Miss Tucker's famous friends in the entertainment world, as well as being a lively, hearty tale of struggle and success, with no mistake about the success. Stanley Walker described it as one of the "pleasantest, most ingratiating and unpretentious autobiographies ever turned out by anybody in show business." The *Library Journal* called it "frank and racy," written "entertainingly and with engaging honesty." Dissenting opinion was voiced by Bernard Sobel, who wrote in the *Saturday Review of Literature:* "As an autobiographer Sophie Tucker is—to use her own idiom—a 'flop.' But as an entertainer she is still 'tops' . . . international goddess of off-color laughter and song." But *Variety,* the "showbiz" paper, called the book "real, earthy, honest. Soph takes pride in herself, her work, and her profession . . . Her cavalcade of names reads like a who's who out of *Burke's Peerage* and the Ellis Island steerage, with a very imposing array of Equity, NVA, Hollywood, and Côte d'Azur names in between." Jo Ranson in the *New York Times* said pungently, "This is a sharp, honest, and frequently uncorseted tale . . . Sophie herself has gone right on, singing the 'hot numbers' which, she explains, are all very moral because 'they have to do with sex, but not with vice.'" "She does not gloss over or apologize for anything, not even her love life, which she admits 'set her back a million,'" the *Book-of-the-Month Club News* commented. And when Miss Tucker arrived in New York in July 1945 after a run at the Chez Paree in Chicago, *Variety* reported she "sliced a $34,200 melon to theatrical and other charities gained through sales of fifteen hundred of the twenty-five-dollar deluxe editions of her autobiog. Beneficiaries on an even split are Actors Fund, Catholic, Episcopal, and Jewish Theatrical Guilds, Home for the Aged, Hartford, Connecticut, and the Sophie Tucker Playground Camp Fund."

Personal Life

The fair-haired, blue-eyed entertainer was "big in voice, heart and beam." Disarmingly frank about her appearance, Miss Tucker capitalized on her unglamorous aspects in song. When performing she was always elaborately gowned and gorgeously bejeweled. Even when past sixty, the personable performer was still an audience favorite and still "good old Sophie" to the admiring members of her profession. Called by one critic "an institution" in the entertainment world, Miss Tucker had a formula for success in show business: "Above all, the performer must look ahead. You can't grow stale or cling to a period. You must belong to your time." She firmly believed in organization in the theatrical profession; her experiences in unionism formed an interesting part of her autobiography. She stated: "I am convinced that the actor needs his union. But he needs to be an active, vigorous part of it." High-spirited, philanthropic Miss Tucker was proud of her profession and its great tradition. "Show business has been my life. I wouldn't have had any other. It is the life I always wanted."

Sophie Tucker died on February 9, 1966 in New York of a lung ailment and kidney failure. She continued to work until just before her death, playing shows at the Latin Quarter weeks before.

Further Reading
N Y *Post* p20 Mr 24 '44
N Y *World-Telegram* pl3 S 22 '41;p15 Ap 17 '44 pors
International Motion Picture Almanac, 1937-38
Tucker, S. *Some of These Days* (1945)

Mark Turner

Saxophonist

Born: Nov. 10, 1965; Ohio
Primary Field: Jazz
Group Affiliation: Solo performer; Kurt Rosenwinkel

Introduction

The tenor saxophonist and composer Mark Turner has impressed critics and won respect among young jazz musicians for his understated, lyrical, sometimes experimental style, which is influenced by the works of the German classical composer Johann Sebastian Bach as well as the music of the jazz saxophonists John Coltrane and Warne Marsh. Writing for the New York Times *(June 16, 2002), Ben Ratliff called Turner's music "intellectual and rigorously composed, defined by long, flowing, chromatically complex lines that keep their stamina and intensity as they stay dynamically even. He has learned how to play the highest reaches of his instrument . . . with a serene strength, never shouting for the effect that audiences love. The overwhelming sense about Mr. Turner is that he wants to get on with his work." In addition to his own material, Turner has played, on his four albums as a bandleader, music from a wide range of composers—including Broadway, pop, and even rock numbers. Although highly acclaimed, Turner has not become a commercial success; indeed, his record label dropped him in 2001. Nevertheless, he is one of the most influential musicians in jazz today. At a recent Thelonious Monk Institute saxophone competition, Ben Ratliff noted, it was evident that Turner's influence on the young musicians was second only to Coltrane's. "His music is the freshest thing around . . . ," the composer and vocalist Luciana Souza told Ratliff, adding: "It's 'out' music that still sounds very musical and consonant."*

Early Life

Mark Turner was born on November 10, 1965 in Ohio. At the age of four, he moved with his family to California, where he lived in the towns of Cerritos and Palos Verdes, near Los Angeles. In high school Turner played saxophone and was also an enthusiastic break-dancer; he once broke his front teeth in an attempt at a back flip. Talented in the visual arts as well, Turner studied design and illustration at Long Beach State University. Deciding to focus on the tenor saxophone instead, he transferred to the prestigious Berklee College of Music, in Boston, Massachusetts, in the late 1980s. "Obviously the mediums are different, in that music happens in the moment and art doesn't in the same way," he said for the official Web site of B. H. Hopper Management, in Munich, Germany, "but I see a lot of similarities in the creative processes. The connection is not that literal, though. You could be a great bricklayer, or a great chef; if you derive the same feeling from doing something completely different, it's bound to shed light and new meaning." At Berklee, Turner focused intensely on the work of the late John Coltrane. "I was fairly methodical," he told Ben Ratliff. "I almost always wrote out Coltrane's solos, and I'd have a lot of notes on the side." Although when a musician studies another musician so intensely there is the danger of mimicry, Turner was not worried. "I knew I would eventually not be interested in [studying Coltrane] anymore," he told Ratliff. "Also, I noticed that if you looked at someone else who was into [Coltrane], and if you could listen through that person's ear and mind, it would be a slightly different version."

Life's Work

In 1990 Turner moved to New York City, where he worked for several years as a sideman with a wide variety of jazz artists. "I've played in bands that did only standards," he told Bradley Bambarger for *Billboard* (April 11,1998), "or only 1960s Coltrane- type stuff. . . . I'd put myself into a situation that was very free, or by contrast, very structured. Sometimes it would be a situation that would be very uncomfortable for me, musically. Even though I didn't think I could pull it off, I'd find a way to make it work." Turner grew tired of the sound

Affiliation: Kurt Rosenwinkel

Following Ballad Session, Turner toured with Kurt Rosenwinkel, whose album *The Enemies of Energy* (2000) features Turner. The saxophonist was also heard on Rosenwinkel's *The Next Step* (2001), and when Turner recorded *Dharma Days* (2001), he asked Rosenwinkel to be his guitarist for the sessions. Featuring nine Turner originals, *Dharma Days* alternates between post-bop and more experimental pieces. In a review for the *Philadelphia City Paper* (on-line), Nate Chinen wrote that Turner "improvises with the same alluringly elusive quality that distinguishes his compositions." "Sleek but never slick, his compositions are often laced with hip unison passages and intricately designed interludes that trade off between his soulful tenor sax and guitarist Kurt Rosenwinkel's similarly understated guitar lines," Mike Joyce wrote for the *Washington Post* (June 1, 2001). In a dissenting view, Art Lange commented in his review for *Pulse!* (on-line), "Though his themes are sometimes quirky, Turner's tunes just aren't memorable, despite the internal alterations [and] tempo shift here, a change of texture there." In December 2001 Warner Bros, dropped Turner from its roster of artists, noting that his albums were not selling sufficiently. "It's fine," Turner told Ben Ratliff. "I was considering trying to get out of it myself. Nothing against Warner, but I feel relieved and open and free."

of many contemporary tenor saxophonists, who, he told Ratliff, played with "more of an aggressive sound, with a vocabulary that's come to be a bit programmed." By contrast, he was attracted by the sound of the late saxophonist Warne Marsh, "a linear, melodic improviser who managed to merge spontaneity and research, playing nearly Bach-like melodic lines," as Ratliff noted.

Turner released his first album, *Yam Yam* (1994), on the Criss-Cross label. The album featured six original compositions and marked his first recording session with the guitarist Kurt Rosenwinkel, another former Berklee student, and the pianist Brad Mehldau. Writing for All Music Guide (on-line), David R. Adler remarked that the album "reveals much about the evolution of all these players, and is therefore well worth the attention of serious fans." Three years passed before Turner released his next album. Signing with Warner Bros., he was featured on *Warner Jams Vol. 2: The Two Tenors* (1997), along with the noted tenor saxophonist James Moody. "I like to interact with another similar voice," Turner told Bambarger about his collaborations. "It adds more energy, more elements. A little sparring doesn't hurt." In his article for the *Village Voice* (April 14, 1998), Gary Giddins noted that on The Two Tenors, "Turner holds his own fairly well, but he is clearly unnerved at times, and there is no disgrace in that: Moody is imperial throughout." In a change of pace from his first solo release, only one of the songs on Turner's second solo album, *Mark Turner* (1998), was penned by him. Several tracks featured collaborations between Turner and the acclaimed young tenor saxophonist Joshua Redman. Writing about the record for All Music Guide (on-line), Ken Dryden noted that Turner's tune "Mr. Brown" is "a pulsating blues vehicle for the two inspired reed men," while "Lennie Tristano's slippery bop anthem '327 East 22nd Street' is also an excellent showcase for their talent." His only complaint was about a version of Ornette Coleman's "Kathelin Gray," which he found to be "ponderous, dissonant and overlong." Gary Giddins wrote that Turner "has a sound of his own, anomalously cool, and is in the process of working out a style that favors a sober midrange, sinuous phrases, and a penchant for prettily sustained ballads." Later in 1998 Turner released *In This World*, which features Brian Blade on drums and Mehldau on piano. In his review for All Music Guide (on-line), Tim Sheridan noted, "'Mesa,' the album's opening track, meanders from a relaxed melodic path to a switch-back road of surprises," and wrote that Turner's cover of the Beatles' "She Said, She Said" is "a deceptively breezy journey into the unknown." In his review for *All About Jazz* (on-line), David R. Adler characterized the record as "thoughtful" and concluded, "While casual jazz fans might find In This World a difficult listen, anybody who's into Coltrane, Tristano or Marsh should really dig it."

Turner's next album was *Two Tenor Ballads* (2000), which comprises collaborations between Turner and the tenor saxophonist Tad Shull on ballad standards. (The tracks were recorded in December 1994.) Later in 2000 Turner released *Ballad Session*, consisting of his versions of other ballad standards, culled from pop, Broadway, and jazz sources. In his review for All Music Guide (on-line), William Ruhlman wrote that the record "doesn't break any new ground for Turner, but it demonstrates his grasp of jazz history and repertoire." The album was something of a disappointment for Turner, as his record label had ruled against his preference, a selection of slow material from a wider variety of composers, ranging from himself to the classical composer Olivier Messaien to the experimental electronica artist Aphex Twin.

Personal Life

Turner currently lives in New Haven, Connecticut, and commutes to play in New York City. He is married to Helena Hansen, a doctoral candidate in anthropology at Yale University. The couple have two children. Remarking on the New York jazz scene to Bradley Bambarger, Turner noted that it is "vibrant, definitely vibrant. It's easy to find a lot of diverse playing experiences in New York. It's not difficult to get in with the other musicians and start playing; it just takes persistence." Turner is known as being quiet, self-assured, and noncompetitive. He practices Buddhism. He has said that he is no longer interested in fronting a group but would like to form a band whose members would share composing and publishing credits.

Further Reading

Billboard Apr. 11, 1998
New York Times II pi June 16, 2002
Village Voice pll9 Apr. 14, 1998

Tina Turner

Singer

Born: Nov. 25, 1940; Brownsville, Tennessee
Primary Field: Rock and soul
Group Affiliation: Ike and Tina Turner Revue; solo artist

Introduction

Singing professionally since 1956, when she joined Ike Turner and the Kings of Rhythm in a black juke joint in St. Louis, Missouri, Tina Turner has powerfully influenced the whole texture of contemporary rock and soul music. A seminal "crossover" group, the Ike and Tina Turner Revue first brought their irresistibly danceable blend of wailing blues, raw soul, and hip-shaking rock 'n' roll to the attention of white audiences in the late 1960s and enjoyed world-wide fame in the 1970s. Miss Turner's songs of love's sorrows and pleasures, delivered in a voice that combines Otis Redding's husky break and James Brown's growl with some of Aretha Franklin's soaring cadences, went to the heart of 1960s sensibility; her volcanic and erotic stage performance, which has spawned would-be "raunch-and-roll" imitators, was a definitive musical "happening." She broke with Ike Turner in 1976 and has since then toured on her own. Having imprinted the genre for a generation of popular musicians, in her 1984 solo album Private Dancer Tina Turner retains the passionate vocal rhythms of an authentic rock 'n' roller who, in the words of one reviewer, "has come through the fire, cognizant in the ways of the world, her spirit undefeated."

Tina Turner.

Early Life

The daughter of a cotton plantation manager and his wife, Tina Turner was born Anna Mae Bullock on

November 25, 1940 in the country borough of Nutbush, near Brownsville, Tennessee. (Her year of birth is listed in some sources as early as 1938 and as late as 1941.) She has described the borough's ambience in her own composition "Nutbush City Limits" (1973): "Church house/Gin house . . . Schoolhouse/Out-house . . . Just a one-horse town . . . Better watch what you're putting down." In her large family even the young children shared the field work, and Anna Mae quickly learned to hate it. Displaying her musical instinct precociously, as a schoolgirl she sang everything from ballads and operatic selections in class talent shows, to gospel hymns in a Sanctified Church choir and "the low-down dirty" blues—her favorite even then—with rhythm bands at picnics. "And I've always danced," Tina Turner told David Thomas, as quoted in his article for the British publication The *Face* (January 1984). "I never had any training. I just danced." She dreamed of one day transcending the lot of poor rural blacks, as Cheryl Lavin reported in a Chicago Tribune profile (January 30, 1983): "I had an image in my head of how a star was-somebody with a star on the door and a lot of chiffon dresses. I wanted that." She admitted to Miss Lavin that she did not like herself very much as a child.

Following her parents' divorce when she was eleven, Anna Mae Bullock moved in with her grandmother. She and her sister Ailene joined their mother in St. Louis after the grandmother died in the mid-1950s, and the teen-age girls began to frequent such local rhythm-and-blues night spots as the Club Manhattan, where, in 1956, they met Ike Turner and his band, the Kings of Rhythm. After "about a year" of coaxing on her part, one night she was allowed to take the microphone and belt out a B. B. King blues number with the group. Her soulful expressiveness was immediately apparent. "When Ike heard me," Carl Arrington quotes Tina Turner as saying in an article for *People* [December 7, 1981), "he said, 'My God!' He couldn't believe that voice coming out of this frail little body." Soon after, she joined the band for occasional engagements, using the name "Little Anna." Meanwhile she worked days at a St. Louis hospital.

Life's Work

The Turners, who continued to record for the Sue label, hit the rhythm-and-blues singles charts in 1961 with "It's Gonna Work Out Fine," "I Pity the Fool," and "I Idolize You" and the following year with "Poor Fool" and "Tra La La La La." Considered by the music industry to have great potential, the Revue produced several albums in the mid- 1960s, at first for Warner Brothers and later for the Liberty label and its parent company, United Artists. The group's single recordings in the late 1960s, such as "I've Been Lovin' You Too Long," "Bold Soul Sister," and "The Hunter," were produced by Blue Thumb. By 1969, the Ike and Tina Turner Revue had fifteen albums and sixty singles to its credit.

Mainstream stardom in the United States long eluded the Ike and Tina Turner Revue because, as Ike Turner explained for an *Ebony* profile (May 1971), "The black radio stations kept telling [him], 'It's too pop,' and the white stations claimed it was 'too rhythm and blues.'" In Great Britain, however, the Revue's sound provoked considerable excitement, as was the case for a number of black performers in the mid-1960s. When the group's single "River Deep, Mountain High," produced by rock 'n' roll wizard Phil Spector and featuring, in the words of Jon Pareles, Tina Turner's "hurricane alto," was released by London Records in 1966, it jumped straight to the top of the British pop charts and held the number-one spot for many weeks. (Spector later called that cut his "masterpiece.") A stint as the opening act for the Rolling Stones, a preeminent British rock group of the period, on a European tour that year proved to be the turning point for the Revue. "The whole world was changing in '66, remember?" Miss Turner observed to Michael T. Leech in an interview for *After Dark* (December 1971). "I knew the world was going to be different, and us too." During the long tour, the Ike and Tina Turner Revue purveyed its brand of overdrive rhythm-and-blues to wild acclaim, while its members gradually absorbed some of the techniques of white rock bands. By the time the group hit the United States, again with the Rolling Stones, later in the decade, it had evolved into the most explosive rock 'n' roll band white concert-goers had ever seen—"They didn't know what it was, but they liked it," Miss Turner has recalled—and Tina Turner was widely acknowledged to be the "grittiest, most sensual female soul singer around."

The Ike and Tina Turner Revue presented a concert act of seemingly spontaneous ecstasy. It was, in fact, meticulously rehearsed. After the band played several rhythm-and-blues numbers to warm up the house, Ike Turner, looking cool and gaunt with his helmet of slicked-down hair and wearing, typically, a double-breasted yellow-green suit, came onstage and picked up the bass line on his guitar. joined by the provocatively strutting Ikettes, the Revue increased the musical tension until Tina Turner, in the shortest of miniskirts, pounced onstage, as one observer wrote, "in midscream with both legs pumping, hips grinding, long mane whirling, [with] her mouth wrapped around some of the sexiest sounds ever set to music." In such manner, she worked her way through rock and soul standards like the Beatles' "Help" and "With a Little Help from My Friends," the Rolling Stones' "Honky Tonk Woman," Aretha Franklin's "Respect," and Sly and the Family Stone's "I Want to Take You Higher." Concert reviewers competed to find words adequate to convey Miss Turner's kinetic, erotic performance, describing her as a "voodoo doctor's fetish object flung down hard" and a springing "tiger" whose face was "a mask of sensuality."

Miss Turner explained her style of musical interpretation in her introduction to the Revue's single "Proud Mary" (1970), which was first recorded by the group Creedence Clearwater Revival. "We never, ever, do nothin' nice and easy," she intones as the song begins. "So we're gonna do it nice—and *rough.*" That rough yet insistently melodic hard-rock sound took the Ike and Tina Turner Revue to engagements in Japan, Africa, and other spots around the world in the early 1970s, including some of the most prestigious concert halls and music festivals in the United States. Millions of rock 'n' roll devotees who failed to catch the Revue live were treated to Tina Turner's pseudo-orgasmic performance of the number "I've Been Lovin' You Too Long" in *Gimme Shelter* (Cinema V, 1971), the Maysles brothers' documentary film of the Rolling Stones' 1969 United States tour. Although none of the Revue's albums, such as *Workin' Together* (Liberty, 1970), *Blues Roots* (United Artists, 1972), *Nutbush City Limits* (UA, 1973), and *The Gospel* According *to Ike and Tina* (UA, 1974), reached the gold record mark, they were prized for their effervescent synthesis of major trends in black- and white-oriented popular music. In 1971 the Ike and Tina Turner Revue won a Grammy Award for best rhythm-and-blues vocal by a group for their recording of "Proud Mary."

Television appearances on late-night talk shows and variety programs hosted by Ed Sullivan, Pearl Bailey, Andy Williams, and others further confirmed the Turners' arrival as certified superstars. (That hard-won recognition from Middle America led one commentator to theorize that "the new consciousness may be upon us.") Ike and Tina Turner kept a sumptuous home, equipped with a recording studio and Ike Turner's personally designed furniture shaped like musical instruments, in a Los Angeles suburb, and they drove the most expensive cars. Some music critics suggested that the couple's conspicuous commercial success threatened to overwhelm the gutsy vitality of their music with "cellophane packaging," but the pair nevertheless commanded enormous respect from their colleagues in the rock music profession. Janis Joplin, for example, considered Tina Turner the best performer in the business, and Mick Jagger of the Rolling Stones credited her with teaching him how to dance on the concert stage.

Although Tina Turner was the visible and audible dynamo of the Revue's success, behind the scenes Ike Turner engineered every facet of the group's act, picking the songs, directing the band, producing the records, and managing the money. Miss Turner's earnings, it was said, were less a salary than an "allowance." His reputation was that of a brilliant but severe taskmaster, and, as Miss Turner has recalled, by the early 1970s their marriage was irreparably strained. Striking out on her own professionally, she released the solo albums *Let Me Touch Your Mind* [1972), *Tina Turns the Country On* (1974), and, following her much-praised appearance as the wild "Acid Queen" in the motion picture rock-opera *Tommy* (Columbia, 1975), *Acid Queen* (United Artists, 1975).

Throughout the early 1970s, Miss Turner continued to tour with the Revue, but meanwhile her perspective on her career and her life had matured. She had learned the professional ropes from her husband, but then, as she explained to Cheryl Lavin, "There was no room to grow." Under Ike Turner's omnipresent direction, she had come to see herself as a "shadow." "I was living a life of death," she went on. "I didn't exist." She had been considering a split for some time when, in Dallas, Texas in July 1976, Turner physically beat her shortly after their arrival there for a concert date. Later that day she left the tour and Ike Turner and flew to Los Angeles with a ticket bought by a friend. She had only a few cents and a credit card in her pocket, but, she told Carl Arrington, "I felt proud. I felt strong. I felt like Martin Luther King." In an interview with Marion Collings of the *New York Daily News*, (June 1, 1984) Tina Turner described the immediate aftermath of the breakup: "I stopped. I rented a house and second-hand furniture. . . . At night, I'd look at the stars in the sky instead of at concert lights. It was a year before I could even think of going back to work." Fending for herself for the first time in her life, she was slapped with lawsuits because she had walked off a nationwide tour, and she faced her husband's anger. The eventual divorce settlement in 1978 left her, she has claimed, with little to show except her "peace of mind."

Tina Turner rebuilt her career slowly, at first taking on advisers and producers who proved "disastrous." A 1978 solo album, *Rough* (United Artists], sparked little commercial or critical attention, and record companies interested in new wave or disco music deemed her material out-of-date. Miss Turner performed outside the country and, in the United States, concentrated on dates at hotels or small clubs, where she experimented with a slick new show that featured a five-piece band and two backup singers. "I never stopped touring," she pointed out to Carolyn Martin in an interview for *Rockamerica's Videofile* (July 1984), "but as far as the press were concerned it was 'Tina what? Tina who?'" When she appeared in New York City in early 1981 after a five-year absence, pop music critics acknowledged Tina Turner's rock 'n' roll credentials and the theatrical success of her "jungle Aphrodite" characterization, but some agreed with Stephen Holden that her "music suffer[ed] for the sake of that image." "[Miss Turner] pushes her powerful voice to a screeching frenzy that is a caricature . . . ,"Holden wrote in his review for the *New York Times* [May 14, 1981). "The set has gusto but no subtlety."

Confidently impervious to any attempts to dismiss her and irrepressibly hard-working, Tina Turner was the special guest artist with the Rolling Stones on their sold-out United States tour in 1981. Young audiences for whom the Ike and Tina Turner Revue was a grand legend rediscovered her roiling musical intensity and up-front sexual appeal, laced with a knowing good humor. Other major concert bookings followed. Signing on new managers, Miss Turner developed a repertoire that adhered more closely to its blues-roots sound while incorporating synthesized and reggae-influenced music. Stephen Holden withdrew his reservations about Miss Turner's style when he reviewed her 1983 performance at the Ritz in New York City for the *New York Times* (January 30, 1983). "The material she picks", he wrote, "invariably supports [her pushing] her large coarse voice with its frayed edges close to its physical limits. . . . [The song] Proud Mary's central image of a great riverboat has become an exhilarating metaphor for Miss Turner's staying power, and her sprinting hard-rock version of it was magnificent." Her recent appearances have included an internationally televised show with pop-rocker Rod Stewart at the Los Angeles Forum in 1981; a record-breaking European tour in 1983-84; and special-guest billing with the singer Lionel Richie on his 1984 United States tour.

Tina Turner's LP *Private Dancer* (Capitol, 1984), headed solidly for a gold record as of late 1984, drew unanimous high marks from critics, who hailed the "startling scope," "scratchy, luscious sensitivity," and "lucid center inside her raspy coloratura" demonstrated in her diverse offerings. Produced by several contemporary British arrangers, among them Martyn Ware and Greg Walsh of Heaven 17, the album features her interpretation of David Bowie's future-shock ballad "1984," a tear-your-heart-out version of Ann Peebles' "I Can't Stand the Rain," and an upbeat rendering of AI Green's "Let's Stay Together." The last-named song, along with her "What's Love Got to Do With It?", was a number-one single hit for weeks in 1984. Stephen Holden, writing in the *New York Times* (August 26, 1984), judged *Private Dancer*, with its "innovative fusion of old-fashioned soul singing and new wave synth-pop," to be a "landmark . . . in the evolution of soul-pop music."

Turner's success continued when she travelled to Australia to star opposite Mel Gibson in the 1985 post-apocalyptic film *Mad Max Beyond Thunderdome*. The movie provided her with her first acting role in ten years—she portrayed the glamorous Aunty Entity, the ruler of Bartertown. Upon release, critical response to her performance was generally positive, and the film became a global success, making more than $36 million in the United States alone. Turner later received the NAACP Image Award for Outstanding Actress for her role in the film. She also recorded two songs for the film, "We Don't Need Another Hero (Thunderdome)" and "One of the Living"; both became hits, with the latter winning Turner a Grammy Award for Best Female Rock Vocal Performance. In July, Turner performed at Live Aid alongside Mick Jagger. Encouraged by a performance together during Tina's filmed solo concert in England, singer Bryan Adams released their duet single together, "It's Only Love," later resulting in a Grammy nomination for Best Rock Performance by a Duo or Group with Vocal.

Turner followed up *Private Dancer* with *Break Every Rule* in 1986, which sold over four million copies worldwide. Prior to the album's release, Turner published her memoirs, *I, Tina*, which later became a bestseller, and received a star on the Hollywood Walk of Fame. Turner's European *Break Every Rule Tour*, which culminated in March 1987 in Munich, Germany, contributed to record breaking sales and concert attendances. In January 1988, Turner made history alongside Paul McCartney when she performed in front of the largest paying audience (approximately 184,000) to see a solo performer in Maracanã Stadium in Rio de Janeiro, Brazil, earning her a Guinness World Record. The success of Turner's two live tours led to the recording of *Tina Live in Europe* which was released that April. Turner lay low following the end of her *Break Every Rule Tour*, emerging once again with *Foreign Affair* which included one of Turner's signature songs, "The Best." She later embarked on a European tour to promote the album. While *Foreign Affair* went gold in the United States, with its singles "The Best" and "Steamy Windows" becoming Top 40 hits there. It was hugely successful in Europe, where Turner had personally relocated.

Turner returned in 1995 with the U2 composition, "GoldenEye" for the James Bond film of the same name. Its huge success in Europe and modest success in her native United States led Turner to record a new album, releasing the *Wildest Dreams* album in 1996. Though the album itself was not as hugely successful in the United States, thanks to a world tour and a much played Hanes hosiery commercial, the album went gold in the United States. The album reached platinum success in Europe where Turner had hits with "Whatever You Want," "Missing You," which briefly charted in the U.S., "Something Beautiful Remains," and the sensual Barry White duet "In Your Wildest Dreams." Following the tour's end in 1997, Turner took another break before re-emerging again in 1999 appearing on the VH-1 special *Divas Live '99*.

In 1998 the duet with Italian musician Eros Ramazzotti in "Cose della vita" became a European hit. Before celebrating her 60th birthday, Turner released the dance-infused song, "When the Heartache Is Over" and its parent album, *Twenty Four Seven* the following month in Europe, releasing both the song and the album in North America in early 2000. The success of "When the Heartache Is Over" and Turner's tour supporting the album once again helped in the album going gold in the U.S. The *Twenty Four Seven Tour* became her most successful concert tour to date and became the highest-grossing tour of 2000 according to Pollstar grossing over $100 million. Later, Guinness World Records announced that Turner had sold more concert tickets than any other solo

Affiliation: Ike and Tina Turner Revue

Already a seasoned producer and performer when he teamed up with young Anna Mae Bullock, the Mississippi-born Ike Turner had traveled the South's black-music circuit with the Kings of Rhythm for several years, sharing bills with seminal early blues artists like Johnny Ace, Howlin' Wolf, and B. B. King. By all accounts, Turner's combination of management ability-it is reported that he formed his first band at age eleven-and musical sense served him well during the ferment in black music in the 1950s, when the electrified instruments and faster rhythms of urban black musicians were translating the rural blues sound into the beat that would become rock 'n' roll. A "hot" regional band in those days, the Kings of Rhythm had recorded at least one single, Jackie Brenston's "Rocket 88" (1951), which was a "race record" hit on black radio stations.

When the scheduled vocalist failed to appear for a recording session with the Kings of Rhythm in 1959, Anna Mae Bullock filled in at the last moment. The resulting cut for the Sue record label, Ike Turner's "Fool in Love" (1960), sold 800,000 copies in the rhythm-and-blues market and remained on *Billboard's* Hot 100 chart for thirteen weeks. The group's transformation into its slicker, star-class form rapidly followed. Turner chose for his lead singer the name Tina, and later they married; a female dance-and-vocal backup trio, dubbed the Ikettes, joined the act; the instrumental section expanded to comprise trombone, trumpet, two saxophones, two guitars, drums, and organ; and thus, as the Ike and Tina Turner Revue, the troupe embarked on cross-country tours. With Ike Turner's musical composition and scoring adapted to Miss Turner's passionate, wailing delivery, and her own choreography designed to highlight her energetically seductive stage persona, the Revue won renown on the rhythm-and-blues circuit, showcasing the roots of rock 'n' roll, in the words of Irwin Stambler, with the "sounds of the ghetto, raucousness of low-down blues, plaintiveness of country blues, and a gospel fervor." Tina Turner's soul-drenched quaking, pleading, and shaking while she sang, as she once put it, "Baptist and blues" transformed the "chitlin'-belt" auditoriums and ghetto nightclubs that welcomed them into revival meetings flavored as much with a sexual as an evangelical message. Eighteen performances a week, for a reported fee of $450 per night, were not unusual for the ambitious Revue at that time.

concert performer in music history. Afterwards Turner announced a semi-retirement.

In December 2003, Turner was recognized by the Kennedy Center Honors at the John F. Kennedy Center for the Performing Arts in Washington, D.C. and was elected to join an elite group of entertainers. President George W. Bush commented on Turner's "natural skill, the energy and sensuality," and referred to her legs as "the most famous in show business." Several artists paid tribute to her that night including Oprah Winfrey, Melissa Etheridge (performing "River Deep - Mountain High"), Queen Latifah (performing "What's Love Got to Do with It"), Beyoncé (performing "Proud Mary"), and Al Green (performing "Let's Stay Together").

In 2007, Turner gave her first live performance in seven years, headlining a benefit concert for the Cauldwell's Children Charity at London's Natural History Museum. That year, Turner performed a rendition of Joni Mitchell's "Edith and The Kingpin" on Herbie Hancock's Mitchell tribute album, *River: The Joni Letters*. Turner made her public comeback in February 2008 at the Grammy Awards where she performed alongside Beyoncé. In addition, she picked up a Grammy as a featured artist on *River: The Joni Letters*. In October 2008, Turner embarked on her first tour in nearly ten years with the Tina!: 50th Anniversary Tour. In support of the tour, Turner released another hits compilation. The tour became a huge success and culminated in the release of the live album/DVD, *Tina Live*.

Turner appeared on the cover of the German issue of *Vogue* magazine in April 2013, becoming at the age of 73 the oldest person worldwide to feature on the cover of *Vogue*. On February 3, 2014, Parlophone Records released a new compilation titled *Love Songs*. Later in the year, *Beyond 2: Love Within* was released with Turner contributing some gospel

One of the world's best-selling music artists of all time, she has also been referred to as The Queen of Rock 'n' Roll. Turner has been termed the most successful female Rock 'n' Roll artist, receiving eleven Grammy Awards, including eight competitive awards and three Grammy Hall of Fame awards. Turner has also sold more concert tickets than any other solo performer in history. Her combined album and single sales total approximately 180 million copies worldwide, making her one of the biggest selling females in music history. She is noted for her energetic stage presence, powerful vocals, and career longevity. In 2008, Turner returned from semi-retirement to embark on her *Tina!: 50th Anniversary Tour*. Turner's tour became one of the highest selling ticketed shows of 2008–09. *Rolling Stone* ranked her no. 63 on their 100 greatest artists of all time. In 1991, she was inducted into the Rock and Roll Hall of Fame.

Personal Life

A lanky, curvaceously proportioned woman who proudly flaunts her "great legs," Tina Turner has a tawny gold complexion ("the same color as her voice," according to one interviewer), and a mobile, handsome face. When not on the road, she lives alone at her home in Sherman Oaks, California, where her frequent solitary pursuit-reading in occult subjects-belies her semi-manic stage image. "That's my act. That's not who I am. I consider myself a very balanced person," she has said. An adherent since about 1970 of Nichiren Shoshu Buddhism, she chants every day, and she credits that practice with making her "stronger" and revealing "the power of the self." The four sons she raised, Craig, Ike Jr., Michael, and Ronald, now live on their own. She and Ike Turner divorced in 1978. In 1985, Tina met German music executive Erwin Bach. Initially starting out as a friendship, Turner and Bach began dating the following year and have remained together since. In July 2013, after a 27-year romantic partnership, the couple married in a civil ceremony on the banks of Lake Zurich in Küsnacht, northern Switzerland.

Further Reading

After Dark 4:31+ D '71 pars
Chicago Tribune XII p1+ Ja 30 '83 pars
Dial p31+ Jl84 pars
Ebony 26:88+ My '71 pars, 37:66+ Je '82 pars
NY Times II p22 Ag 26 '84 por
Newsweek 74:92+ N 3 '69 por, 104:76 S 10 '84 por
People 16:100+ D 7 '81 pars
Jahn, Michael. *Rock* (1973)
Roxon, Lillian. *Rock Encyclopedia* (1971)
Stambler, Irwin. *Encyclopedia of Pop, Rock, and Soul* (1974)
Who's Who in America, 1982-83
Preston, Kate. *Tina Turner* (1999)

Steve Turre (tuh-RAY)

Trombonist

Born: Dec. 8, 1949; Omaha, Nebraska
Primary Field: Jazz
Group Affiliation: House band, *Saturday Night Live;* Art Blakey and the Jazz Messengers; Woody Shaw; Robin Eubanks

Introduction

One of the most accomplished and well-rounded musicians currently working in any genre, Steve Turre has been the top jazz and freelance trombonist in New York City for more than a decade. Turre, who gained experience in the bands of Rahsaan Roland Kirk, Woody Shaw, Thad Jones/Mel Lewis, and Dizzy Gillespie (to name just a few musical giants), is known by television audiences for his longtime membership in the house band of the popular comedy show Saturday Night Live. *Equally adept at muted and open-horn styles of jazz improvisation, Turre is a skilled composer, arranger, and jazz educator as well as an instrumentalist. Since the mid-1980s he has also led a seashell choir—an assemblage unprecedented in the history of jazz—in which the musicians use seashells as instruments, breathing new life into an ancient Mexican tradition.*

Early Life

Steve Turre was born on December 8, 1949 in Omaha, Nebraska. In early 1950 his father, a gynecologist, moved the family to San Francisco, California. His mother, a Mexican-American and former flamenco dancer, played the piano and castanets. As a child Turre expressed the desire to play the violin, but he was dissuaded from doing so by his father, who compared the sounds of that instrument in the hands of a beginner to "a cat in an alley," as Turre recalled to Bob Bernotas in a 1994 interview published in the *Online Trombone Journal.* Excited by the trombonists that he saw in a parade, Turre began studying the instrument, at about age 10. "The first time I played it, I liked it," he told Bernotas. By age 13 he was playing professional jobs with his older brother, Mike, a saxophonist.

In high school Turre joined the football team to avoid compulsory participation in the marching band. The summer after he graduated from high school, in 1968, he successfully "sat in" with the saxophonist and gifted multi-instrumentalist Rahsaan Roland Kirk at the Jazz Workshop in San Francisco. He told Bob Bernotas, "It felt like we had been playing together all our lives. It clicked immediately. We'd breathe in the same place. We would phrase the same, intuitively. I was just able to tap into his brain waves. . . . We really struck up a wonderful friendship, and every time he would come through San Francisco he would call me for the gig."

Having qualified for a football scholarship to Sacramento State University, in California, Turre was enrolled there briefly, in 1968. After a few months he transferred to North Texas State University, in Denton (now the University of North Texas), which had a respected jazz-education program. After encountering racism from other students because of his Hispanic ancestry, Turre became discouraged and dropped out. Returning to San Francisco in 1970, he rejoined Kirk for a weeklong engagement at the Both/And nightclub.

Life's Work

During the next year Turre worked and recorded with the Irish pop singer Van Morrison. In early 1972 he successfully auditioned in Los Angeles for the big band of the legendary rhythm-and-blues pianist and vocalist Ray Charles. Following a European tour with Charles, Turre returned to San Francisco in late 1972. The jazz trumpeter Woody Shaw, who had recently moved to that area, invited Turre to sit in with Art Blakey's Jazz Messengers at the Keystone Korner jazz club. Shaw was a member of that band, which had enjoyed a reputation since the 1950s as a finishing school for outstanding emerging jazz musicians. Despite being "scared to death," as he put it to Bernotas, Turre played well, and on the spot the eminent drummer and bandleader Blakey invited him to join the band. The next day Turre recorded several performances with the Jazz Messengers that were included on the albums *Anthenagin* and *Buhaina,* on the Prestige label. "Playing with Art Blakey, the things that he'd put on you musically would take you years to realize," Turre told Bernotas. '"Don't play everything you know in your first chorus. Take your time. Tell a story.' You know, all those kinds of things: how to build a solo, not just go out there and start playing. And so that was 'graduate school.' Art Blakey and the Jazz Messengers, that was a degree right there."

After fulfilling engagements in St. Louis, Missouri, and Chicago, Illinois, the band traveled to New York City, where they appeared at the Village Gate. There, Turre met and played alongside one of his key influences, Curtis Fuller, the original Jazz Messengers' trombonist. Although Turre received job offers from the saxophonist Anthony Braxton and others during his first few months in New York, Turre told Bernotas in 1994, "I'm glad I didn't walk away from that school. I've been with everybody now and that training has served me in good stead all these years."

After he left Blakey, toward the end of 1973, Turre joined the Thad Jones-Mel Lewis Jazz Orchestra, the leading big band of the time, co-led by Jones, a trumpeter and composer, and Lewis, a drummer. In the trombone section Turre was seated next to Quentin "Butter" Jackson, who had formerly played with the Duke Ellington Orchestra and was a master of plunger-mute soloing. The plunger mute, used to create vocal effects from a trombone or trumpet, was popular early in jazz history. Its use declined in the bebop era, and by the 1970s, the plunger style was the province of only a few specialists, Jackson and the Count Basie Orchestra trombonist Al Grey chief among them. Turre continued to refine and modernize his plunger concept, and today he ranks with the trombonists Wycliffe Gordon and Art Baron as a leading plunger practitioner.

Although mainly influenced by the linear, melodic style of J.J. Johnson-who is generally considered the first bebop trombonist and who was Curtis Fuller's primary influence—Turre had become a student of the full jazz trombone lineage, having received encouragement from Kirk. "He turned me on to Vic Dickenson and Trummy Young and Dicky Wells and J. C. Higginbotham and Jack Teagarden-the guys from the swing period that were between J.J. and [the early jazz trombonist] Kid Dry," Turre told Bernotas. "You've got to build the house from the foundation on up. Rahsaan stressed this to me and I took it to heart." During the apprenticeship with Jackson, which lasted into early 1974, Turre went far in developing his vibrant, signature sound and perspicacious approach to the jazz trombone tradition.

Affiliation: Seashell Choir

In addition to jazz groups of standard and not-so-standard instrumentation (some of the latter included his wife and other string players), Turre began leading a unique seashell choir. Acting on an idea he had gotten from Rahsaan Roland Kirk in about 1970, he recruited several trombonists and trumpeters to play original compositions, jazz standards, and blues on giant conch shells. Using an ancient technique, he had cut and sanded each conch at one end to form a mouthpiece; with a hand inserted into the side opening of the shell, a player could produce a limited range of notes. "Rahsaan had a shell, and he would just blow one note, and he would do that circular breathing thing, and it would just mesmerize the audience," Turre recalled to Fred Jung. "After the gig I asked him, could I try, and he said, yeah. So I blew the shell, and oh, man, it got to me. . . . I just started experimenting with it, and one thing led to another." During a tour of Mexico with Shaw in 1978, Turre had been astonished to learn from relatives that his Aztec ancestors had made music using the same technique. "These ancient instruments are played the exact same way modern brass instruments are-by vibrating the lips, by blowing through a tube or chamber," he explained to Pat Cole for *Down Beat* (March 1993).

In 1974 Turre joined Woody Shaw's septet, dubbed the Concert Ensemble. In December of that year, Shaw, with Turre, recorded *The Moontrane,* considered a classic of adventurous hard-bop writing and simpatico ensemble playing. In 1975 Shaw signed with Columbia Records, for which he recorded the critically acclaimed *Rosewood* (1978) and two other albums, all with Turre. The trombonist continued to play with the Concert Ensemble from time to time until 1981, when the group disbanded; it later re-formed as a quintet with Turre. Turre received much important musical and business guidance from Shaw, which served him well when he started his music publishing company, Fruit Tree Music (mainly, apparently, to maintain copyrights). From 1974 to 1976 Turre also played trombone and electric bass guitar with the drummer Chico Hamilton's quintet.

In 1976 Turre joined Rahsaan Roland Kirk's last group, the Vibration Society. After Kirk's death, from a stroke, in 1977, Turre played with the Collective Black Artists Ensemble, led by the trombonist and composer Slide Hampton—another prominent J.J. Johnson disciple who had a major stylistic influence on Turre. At about this time Turre worked in addition with the legendary tenor saxophonist Dexter Gordon. Gigs with the drummer Elvin Jones and the pianist Cedar Walton followed, in 1979. That year, after several years of course work, Turre earned a bachelor's degree from the University Without Walls, a division of the University of Massachusetts at Amherst.

The year 1980 saw Turre freelancing in the tenor saxophonist Archie Shepp's big band as well as with the bassist Reggie Workman and the trumpeters Lester Bowie and Jon Faddis. In 1981 Turre worked with Slide Hampton in Hampton's nine-trombone group, the World of Trombones, and with the tenor saxophonist Pharoah Sanders and the South African trumpeter Hugh Masakela. Performing from 1981 to 1987 with Shaw's quintet—an unusual group in that it had no saxophone in the front line—Turre displayed a powerful tone and sure sense of rhythm on such recordings as *Night Music* (1982) and *Imagination* (1987). In 1989 Shaw—widely considered the foremost jazz trumpeter of his generation—died, at the age of 44, two months after an accident in which he had fallen onto subway tracks and was hit by an oncoming train.

Throughout the 1980s Turre had freelanced extensively, deepening his involvement in New York City's Latin music scene. In 1982 he became a founding member of the trumpeter Jerry Gonzalez's progressive Afro-Cuban group, the Fort Apache Band. The next year he was a featured soloist in the Village Gate's "Salsa Meets Jazz" concert series, appearing with such Latin-music heavyweights as Tito Puente, Johnny Ventura, and Ruben Blades. In the mid-1980s he worked with, among others, Manny Oquendo & Libre, one of Turre's favorite groups, and the vocalists Celia Cruz and Jose Alberto. He also played in theater pit bands and in orchestras that backed such rhythm-and-blues singers as Lou Rawls and Gladys Knight. He became a member of Lester Bowie's Brass Fantasy in 1983, pianist McCoy Tyner's big band in 1984, and Cedar Walton's hard-bop sextet in 1985.

In 1986, benefitting from his reputation as a skilled and dependable freelancer, Turre was asked to join the house band for the NBC television network's long-running comedy series *Saturday Night Live.* His new salary was far greater than what he had previously earned as a jazz musician. ("I get more money doing that than playing with Dizzy [Gillespie]." he told Fred Jung for a 2000 interview published on the *Jazz Weekly* Web site. "That is a statement about America right there.") Thanks to his increased income, he moved with his wife, the cellist, composer, and conductor Akua Dixon, from New York City to a large house in suburban New Jersey. He also increased his activity as a bandleader.

In 1987, at the age of 38, Turre released his first album as a leader, *Viewpoint,* on Stash, an independent label. That year he also won the *Down Beat* magazine critics' poll in the category "talent deserving wider recognition." Fast becoming a recognized presence on *Saturday Night Live,* thanks to his distinctive long braid and dark goatee, Turre released his sophomore Stash album, *Fire and Ice* (1988), to critical acclaim. Several tracks on that album feature the jazz string ensemble Quartette Indigo, of which his wife is a member. In the late 1980s Turre performed on trombone with the Art Farmer-Benny Golson Jazztet, and on trombone and seashell with Dizzy Gillespie's United Nations Orchestra. In the 1990 *Down Beat* readers' poll, he was named best trombonist, barely edging out J.J. Johnson. Thereafter, Turre has often ranked first or second among trombonists in the *Down Beat* and *JazzTimes* polls and has frequently topped the list of performers on "miscellaneous instruments" as well.

Meanwhile, with his job at *Saturday Night Live* providing a steady but musically unchallenging source of income, Turre had turned increasingly to recording as a means of self-expression. Together with the trombonist Robin Eubanks, he recorded *Dedication* for JMT, a German label, in 1989. In 1991 Turre signed with Antilles, a division of PolyGram. For the album *Right There* (1991), he assembled a sextet featuring his wife and the jazz violinist John Blake. He recorded the album *Sanctified Shells* (1993) for Antilles, with the shell choir and Dizzy Gillespie as a guest trumpeter. Turre's mother, Carmen, played castanets on the album. Supported by unusually vigorous promotion for a jazz album, *Sanctified Shells* was a modest commercial success. In 1993 and 1994 Turre recorded as a guest soloist on trombone with the Jamaican reggae pioneers the Skatalites.

Turre released a second shell-choir album, *The Rhythm Within,* in 1995. The album *Steve Turre,* recorded in 1996, includes shell music, but its main selling point was the contribution of J.J. Johnson on several tracks. (The following year Johnson featured Turre on his album *The Brass Orchestra.)* Ironically, although it had taken Turre years to persuade a label to approve of his making an entire album of shell music, Verve (a division of PolyGram) now pressed him to record more albums in the *Sanctified Shells* vein—simple melodies laid over hypnotic Latin grooves and spiced with hot jazz solos. His own idea, to further the trombone-and-strings concept explored on *Fire and Ice* and *Right There,* met with resistance from the label. When Turre finally succeeded in getting *Lotus Flower* made, in 1997, Verve delayed its release for more than a year. "They even went so far as to tell me that they thought the shell stuff was a gimmick they could make some money off," he told a writer for the *Jazz Report* (on-line). After *Lotus Flower's* release, in 1999, the label dropped Turre, as he had requested.

Earlier, in 1995, Turre's shell choir had performed at the Monterey Jazz Festival, in California. The following year Turre wrote the score for a French film, *Anna Oz,* directed by Eric Rochant. In 1998 he appeared with Slide Hampton and Curtis Fuller at the Central Park Summerstage, in New York City. His album *In the Spur of the Moment* (2000) was released on Telarc, an independent label; the album features a reunion with Ray Charles, in a collaboration with Peter Turre, Steve's younger brother and Charles's drummer since the late 1970s. That summer Turre appeared on the National Public Radio series *Jazz at the Kennedy Center,* hosted by the pianist Billy Taylor, and he performed with Charles at the JVC Jazz Festival in New York City. In 2001 the trombonist marked his 15th season on *Saturday Night Live.* For his most recent album, *TNT* (2001)—the title is an acronym for "trombone 'n tenor"—Turre collaborated with the front-ranking tenor saxophonists David Sanchez, Dewey Redman, and James Carter. In a review of the record for *Amazon.com,* the jazz pianist Stuart Broomer wrote, "For all the variety, tenor fireworks, and input from two excellent rhythm sections, it's Turre who makes the strongest impression, imparting consistent musical and emotional focus. He's a consummate trombonist, from vocalic mute work to crisp bop articulation and warm balladry, and he feels his material, seemingly concentrating all his attention on the phrase at hand."

Personal Life

In addition to his concertizing and recording activity, Turre has taught at some of the nation's top schools of jazz, including the Manhattan School of Music, in New York City; the Berklee College of Music, in Boston, Massachusetts; the University of Hartford, in Connecticut; and William Paterson University, in New Jersey. "I feel very, very lucky and blessed to be able to make a living playing this music that I love so much," Turre told Bob Bernotas. "It's truly America's classical music and even though we haven't gotten full respect at home, I feel it's coming. And in the meantime, I'm still able to grow and be around people that share the same interest and inspiration and goals as myself. A musician's like a doctor, you're supposed to heal people. You make them feel better. As long as I can keep doing that, I'm a happy man."

Further Reading

All About Jazz (on-line)
Chicago Tribune Arts p14+ Apr. 29, 1990, with photos
Down Beat p28+ Dec. 1987, with photos, p21+ Mar. 1993, with photos, p34+ Aug. 2000, with photo
Down Beat Jazz Weekly (on-line)
Unesco Courier p44 Dec. 1997, with photo

TV on the Radio

Music group

David Sitek
Guitarist; producer
Born: 1972

Tunde Adebimpe
Singer; songwriter; actor
Born: 1974; Nigeria

Kyp Malone
Guitarist; singer; songwriter
Born: 1973(?)

Gerard Smith
Bassist; keyboardist
Born: 1974(?)

Jaleel Bunton
Drummer
Born: 1975(?)-

Primary Field: Fusion
Group Affiliation: TV on the Radio

Introduction

"I was a lover, before this war." Those words, crooned in falsetto by Tunde Adebimpe on the rock group TV on the Radio's critically acclaimed album Return to Cookie Mountain *(2006), represent the simultaneously personal and political nature of the group's songs—which have drawn comparisons to the works of artists as disparate as Brian Eno, Peter Gabriel, Prince, and 1950s-era doo-wop groups. The band formed in 2001, when Adebimpe and the producer/multi-instrumentalist David Sitek became roommates in Brooklyn, New York, and began experimenting with multilayered vocal and electronic tracks. The self-released* OK Calculator *(2002), of which Adebimpe admitted to Matt Bernstein for downhillbattle.org (May 12, 2004), "There's more hiss on some of those songs than there are songs," laid the groundwork for what would become some of the decade's most innovative music.*

Early Lives

Adebimpe, whose full given name is Babatunde, was born in Nigeria in 1974 and grew up mainly in Pittsburgh, Pennsylvania; he also lived in Nigeria for several years. His father, Victor Adebimpe, who died in 2005, was a psychiatrist and social worker noted for battling racial prejudice on the part of mental-health-care providers; he was also a classical pianist, painter, and writer. Speaking with Lauren Mechling for the *Wall Street Journal* (September 20, 2008), Adebimpe described his mother, Folasade Oluremi Ogunlana, who worked as a pharmacist, as "one of the best storytellers I know." His sister is an opera and gospel singer, and his brother, now deceased, was a writer. When Adebimpe was young his parents listened to jazz and classical music as well as the work of Afrobeat artists such as Fela Kuti. As Adebimpe grew into a gawky, shy, and angst-ridden teenager, he found that he preferred music that expressed alienation and aggression. "When I was about 14, my friends introduced me to bands like Dead Kennedys, Bad Brains, The Pixies," he told Phil Meadley for the London *Independent* (July 19, 2006). "Everything else sounded stupid. Suddenly I'd found a vessel for how awkward I felt, and I met people who were in the same boat as me." Adebimpe's social anxiety has followed him to some degree into his adult life; at New York University, where he studied filmmaking, he changed his focus from live-action film to animation because he had trouble directing actors, and, as he told Theodore Hamm for the *Brooklyn Rail* (September 2008), it took him quite some time to introduce himself to band members Malone, Bunton, and Smith because he was intimidated by the thought that "that guy is way cooler than I am-I can't really talk to him." Despite his shyness, the tall, bespectacled Adebimpe has become something of a hipster heartthrob, appearing in half-joking projects such as the magazine *Venus Zine's* "Sexbomb" issue.

After graduating from NYU, Adebimpe supported himself through freelance animation work, including a year-and-a-half-long stint as an animator for the MTV claymation show *Celebrity Deathwatch.* He later animated the video for the Yeah Yeah Yeahs' song "Pin." Adebimpe also won small-scale fame as an actor, starring in his NYU classmate Joel Hopkins's film *Jump Tomorrow* (2001), which received critical acclaim and rotation on the Independent Film Channel.

Like Adebimpe, David Sitek, born in 1972, had felt alienated as a young man growing up in Baltimore, Maryland. A visual artist, he moved to New York in 2000, hoping to sell some paintings and get a fresh start in life. He moved into a loft in the then low-rent neighborhood of Williamsburg, Brooklyn, with his brother, Jason Sitek, and Adebimpe. Adebimpe and Sitek discovered a shared commitment to creative pursuits. While both men had been playing music for some time, neither had envisioned a career in it. Adebimpe had been in a noise-rock band, Strugglepuss, after finishing college. "Our main aim was to pretty much drive everyone out of the room," he told Phil Meadley. Adebimpe, Sitek, and their friends formed an artistic community of sorts, or what Sitek described to Meadley as "a karaoke vodka-energy-drink collective," and Sitek asked Adebimpe to help him experiment with a new multitracking software program, Pro-Tools, by singing on some tracks. "We'd be up way too late painting and drinking too much coffee," Adebimpe told Wayne Bledsoe for knoxnews.com (October 24, 2008). "The music making became an extension of that." Sitek described himself and Adebimpe to Steve Chick for *EQ* (2006) as having been "functionally unemployable" during that period, recalling that they would spend their time coming up with song ideas while hawking their paintings on the street. They recorded their songs at home, and as Sitek told Chick, "a couple came out way better than we imagined they would. It didn't seem like such a big joke anymore.... Finally, we decided, 'okay, we're a band.'" They began playing gigs at the Stinger Club and other local bars, took the name TV on the Radio (suggested by a friend), and continued experimenting with music software.

Lives' Work

The duo's experimentation resulted in a self-released album, *OK Calculator* (2002), whose title is a reference to the electronic group Radiohead's *OK Computer* (1997). "We silk-screened the CD sleeves ourselves and left copies in coffeehouses and bookstores around Brooklyn with nothing more than an e-mail address on them," Adebimpe told Chris Riemenschneider for the *Minneapolis Star-Tribune* (October 6, 2006). Despite its roughness, the homemade record contained the electronic soundscapes and melancholy vocals that would serve as the raw elements of TV on the Radio's later albums. Around that time Sitek also embarked on a parallel career as a producer and engineer, working at a feverish pace on other bands' albums. Chick described Sitek as "a jumble of restless, fitful energy, like he knows time spent talking is time not spent making music." "But he has so much to say," Chick continued, "like the ideas are percolating like lethally strong coffee in his head, and they're going to tumble out of him *somehow.*"

Shortly after *OK Calculator* was completed, Sitek met David Caruso of the independent record label Touch and Go through his friends in the Yeah Yeah Yeahs. Caruso persuaded him and Adebimpe to let the label put out their next record. *The Young Liars* EP (2003) was a further exploration of the motifs of *OK Calculator.* Heather Phares wrote for the All Music Guide: "Elements of electronica, postrock, film music, even spirituals and traditional African vocal music combine and recombine throughout *Young Liars'* five songs so organically that it's clear that TV on the Radio isn't striving to be 'eclectic' or 'atmospheric': the band is simply using their naturally diverse elements and influences to create something wholly distinctive." The buzz generated by the album, as well as Sitek's work as a producer for the Yeah Yeah Yeahs and other members of the exploding Williamsburg music scene, helped the band's star rise quickly. They recruited the guitarist/singer Kyp Malone, a Pittsburgh, Pennsylvania, native, noted for the political consciousness he brought to the band, as well as the drummer Jaleel Bunton, who had also worked as a scenic artist for movies including *Murder* (2000), and the bassist Gerard Smith, a visual artist from Long Island, New York.

TV on the Radio's full-length debut album was *Desperate Youth, Bloodthirsty Babes* (2004). Making use of harmonics and electronic textures, the record demonstrated the band's ever-changing nature. The Yeah Yeah Yeahs guitarist Nick Zinner and Celebration vocalist Katrina Ford also contributed to the album, which was recorded in Sitek's recently established Stay Gold studio. In reviews of the album, Adebimpe's soulful falsetto drew many comparisons to that of Peter Gabriel, but Chris Dahlen, writing for *Pitchfork Media* (March 8, 2004), was quick to point out the difference. Adebimpe "isn't a man who would go on stage dressed like a flower [as Gabriel did]," Dahlen wrote. "Instead, Adebimpe sounds like a superhero-a troubled, Batman-style superhero, who can rescue the girl but frets over whether to take the grateful French kiss when they hit safe ground. Nobody with his talents and forthrightness could also have insecurities, yet that was what the lyrics made us believe."

The album's lyrics also dealt with the issue of race. Although TV on the Radio has balked at being defined as a "black rock band," the Malone-penned lyrics to "The Wrong Way" comment on stereotypes of blacks in America. The song begins with a hypothetical situation: "Wake up in a magic nigger movie I With the bright lights pointed at me I As a metaphor· I Teachin' folks the score I About patience, understanding, agape babe I And sweet sweet amour." Adebimpe then sings the question, "When realized where I was I Did I stand up and testify I Oh, fist up signify I or did I show off my soft shoe?" He expresses regret that "no new Negro politician ... is stirring inside me ... there's nothing inside me I but an angry heartbeat," notes the irony of black entertainers' contributing to exploitation in Africa by supporting that continent's diamond trade ("the bling drips down"), and con. eludes with the album's titular line: "Hey, desperate youth! I Oh; bloodthirsty babes! I Your guns are pointed the wrong way." The band toured in support of the album, released the single "New Health Rock" (with "The Wrong Way" and a cover of the Yeah Yeah Yeahs' "Modern Romance" as B-sides), then returned to the. studio to record *Return to Cookie Mountain* (2006). While recording, the band fielded many offers from major labels, ultimately agreeing to a deal with Interscope. Shortly before the release of *Return to Cookie Mountain,* the band put out a non-album single, "Dry Drunk Emperor," which was inspired by the George W. Bush administration's poor handling of the Hurricane Katrina disaster and the war in Iraq.

As with the band's previous albums, *Return to Cookie Mountain* both revisited previous themes and introduced new ones, employing many different styles in songs that combined the personal and political. The album included contributions from Katrina Ford, Kazu Makino of Blonde Redhead, the Antibalas Afrobeat Orchestra, and David Bowie, who had become a fan of TV on the Radio after Sitek gave recordings of the band's songs to Bowie's doorman to pass along to him. The album was widely hailed as one of the year's best. *Spin* named *Return to Cookie Mountain* album of the year, while the *Village* Voice and *Pitchfork Media* placed it second, and *Rolling Stone,* fourth. Jon Pareles wrote for the *New York Times* (September 11, 2006), "The second full-length album by Brooklyn's best band, it expands TV on the Radio's music in multiple directions. It's more experimental yet catchier, more introspective yet more assertive, by turns gloomier and funnier, and above all richer in both sound and implication, *Return to Cookie Mountain* is simply one of this year's best albums," Following the release of *Return to Cookie Mountain,* the industrial rocker Trent Reznor invited TV on the Radio to accompany his band, Nine Inch Nails, and the post-punk band Bauhaus on a national tour. The tour, as well as Internet buzz and downloading of the band's songs, exposed TV on the Radio to a wider audience than ever before. By the time the band returned home, after nearly two years of touring, to record *Dear Science* (2008), they had the attention and anticipation of many. Adebimpe told Chris Martins for the *A.V. Club* (October 14, 2008, on-line) that the album's recording had gone more smoothly than sessions for previous efforts, which had found band members taking offense and sitting "depressed on a pier" when their ideas were not met with enthusiasm. With *Dear Science,* he said, "we all tried to keep in mind a kind of loving fast-forward button, where you're like, 'This isn't *really* important right now, so let's just skip to the part where you realize no one is trying to hurt you.'"

The album's name came from a note Sitek had jokingly tacked up in the studio, which read, "Dear Science, please fix all the things you keep talking about or shut . . . up." Adebimpe told Martins that the title also referred to "the questionable faith that we put in science. You know, we're allegedly able to live longer because of scientific advancement, but we're doing so in a world that might be getting hurt in the process. Or it's thinking about how quickly vessels for communication have progressed, but how genuine communication on a host of things that are still marring the human race hasn't advanced." The record continued the group's examination of complex issues such as race, technology, and liberalism in America. On the track "Red Dress," Adebimpe laments, "It's a stone cold shame / how they got you tame / and they got me tame," stating his opinion of how liberals (himself included) have behaved in the face of the Iraq war, the existence of prison camps at Guantanamo Bay, and other perceived injustices. However, the record's outlook also includes

Affiliation: Group Evolution

Members of the emergent Brooklyn rock group the Yeah Yeah Yeahs joined Adebimpe and Sitek on the *Young Liars EP* (2003), released by the independent label Touch and Go Records. Though it had limited distribution, Internet buzz over its unique fusion of styles, including African vocal music, post-punk sounds, and electronica, helped garner a cult following. Shortly after its release the band added the guitarist/vocalist Kyp Malone, bassist Gerard Smith, and drummer Jaleel Bunton to the lineup, embarked on their first national tour, and recorded their debut full-length album, *Desperate Youth, Bloodthirsty Babes* (2004), for Touch and Go Records. Heather Phares, writing for the *All Music Guide* Web site, called that album "a deeper, darker, denser version of the band's already ambitious sound . . . an impressive expansion of TV on the Radio's fascinating music." The album won the 2004 Shortlist Music Prize, given by a panel of music-industry professionals to recognize accomplished recordings selling fewer than 100,000 copies. The group signed to a major label, Interscope, for *Return to Cookie Mountain,* which included contributions from the likes of the rock legend David Bowie. Return was widely hailed as one of the best albums of the year, with *Spin* magazine giving it the top spot and the Village Voice and Pitchfork Media placing it at number two. "Evoking Fear of Music Talking Heads, Station to Station David Bowie and Sign 0' the Times Prince," Jonathan Ringen wrote for *Rolling Stone* (September 7, 2006), "the resulting disc might be the most oddly beautiful, psychedelic and ambitious of the year." The band duplicated their 2006 success with *Dear Science* (2008), which incorporates more pop influences and has received great acclaim. In support of their albums, TV on the Radio has toured with bands including Nine Inch Nails, Grizzly Bear, Celebration, and the Fall and has appeared on television shows including *The Tonight Show with Jay Leno* and *The Late Show with David Letterman.*

hope and optimism, especially on the disco-inflected single "Golden Age," written mainly by Malone. "I was trying consciously to create a utopian world inside a pop song," Malone told Jon Pareles for the *New York Times* (September 7, 2008). "I don't think that three minutes of music on a commercial record is going to bring paradise, but I feel like there is power in music and power in our words and power in what we put out into the world." Critics responded favorably to the album. *Rolling Stone, Spin,* and the *Village Voice* named *Dear Science* the best album of 2008.

In April 2009 the band released an EP, *Read Silence,* which consisted of other artists' remixes of three songs from *Dear Science.* In September of that year Adebimpe announced that TV on the Radio would be taking a break from their work together. He told James Montgomery and Kyle Anderson for MTV.com (September 3, 2009), "We've decided to take, well, the going theory is to take about a year off, because you have to go and live a life and change things up."

Personal Lives

The members of TV on the Radio carry on numerous other projects. Sitek has produced records for bands including Liars, Foals, Dragons of Zynth, Celebration, and The Knife, as well as the actress Scarlett Johansson's record *Anywhere I Lay My Head* (2008). In 2008 Adebimpe returned to acting, with a role as the title character's fiancé in the family drama *Rachel Getting Married* (2008). He also released a seven-inch record as a solo act called *FMV* (Fake Male Voice) and has recently collaborated with Mike Patton of Faith No More and Mr. Bungle, among other acts. In 2009 Malone, calling himself Rain Machine, released a solo album on the Anti- label. The eponymously named album, according to the label's Web site, contains 10 "unflinchingly original and emotional songs mixing elements of modern jazz, blue-grass and blistering guitar driven rock."

TV on the Radio, meanwhile, has experienced a level of renown they never thought possible. "If you're going to reach for it, reach all the way for it," Sitek told Pareles in 2008 of the efforts that produced *Dear Science.* "Albums like *Purple Rain* and *Thriller* and those kind of records, you had to reach far above the din of cynicism and modern living to get to that place, against all the odds. The industry used to support that kind of record making, and just because the marketplace of the industry doesn't support it now doesn't mean you shouldn't still try for it."

Further Reading

All Music Web site; *Downhill Battle* (on-line) May 12, 2004

(London) *Independent* p15 July 19, 2006

New York Times Arts & Leisure p61 Sep. 7, 2008

Salon.com Sep. 30, 2008; *Washington Post* Weekend p6 Apr. 13, 2007

Tweet

Singer; songwriter

Born: Jan. 21, 1971; Rochester, New York
Primary Field: "Gumbo soul," a stew of gospel, hip-hop, R&B, soul, and country
Group Affiliation: Sugah; Missy "Misdemeanor" Elliott; solo performer

Introduction

In 2002, after battling deep depression and struggling in vain for years to achieve success in the music world as a member of the group Sugah, the singer/songwriter Tweet fulfilled her long-held dream: with the release of her debut album, Southern Hummingbird, *she earned both critical and popular acclaim. The songs on the album, among them the risqué number-one hit "Oops (Oh My)," range in style from hip-hop to R&B to gospel and showcase Tweet's passionate and heartfelt songwriting and her skills on acoustic guitar. "A lot of my songs come from the bad situations I've been in," the singer said to Dimitri Ehrlich for* Interview *(March 1, 2001). "The best medicine for a broken heart is to write songs. It's better than seeing a psychiatrist; it's like a healing process for me." Tweet has been compared to the folk-influenced singer, songwriter, and acoustic-guitar player Tracy Chapman and the singer Minnie Riperton. Immediately after its release, in April of this year,* Southern

Hummingbird *hit number two on the* Billboard *R&B album charts.*

EARLY LIFE

The youngest of Tom and Shirley Keys's five children, Tweet was born Charlene Keys on January 21, 1971 in Rochester, New York. According to *People* (August 19, 2002), her father was the foreman of a labor union, her mother a missionary minister. Tweet has said that she cannot remember why she was given her nickname. Referring to a Warner Bros, cartoon character, she joked to Shaheem Reid for the MTV Web site, "Maybe I had a big head like the Tweety bird character. I've been Tweet since I was a little girl. It's been a nickname that everybody in my family wants to get credit for. T named her that.' 'No, I named her that.'" Beginning virtually from her birth, Tweet told Kelly L. Carter for the *Detroit Free Press* (July 3, 2002, on-line), her parents exposed her to music. "I watched my mom and dad sing in gospel groups all my life. That influenced me to want to do music some kind of way. . . . I've always watched my cousins, my brothers, my uncle play. I just jumped to the drums one day in church. I started playing the guitar because I got tired of waiting for people's music. And I never took lessons." Her siblings were also musically inclined and played various instruments. "I think coming from a musical family centered me," the singer wrote in an article posted on tweet.330.ca, a Canadian fan site. "I inherited a real passion for music, and a respect for those who dedicate their lives to it as a career." As a teenager, Tweet attended the School of the Arts in Rochester. There, for the first time, she recalled on tweet.330.ca, "I was surrounded by so many creative people who were determined to follow their heart. I allowed myself to dream when I was there."

LIFE'S WORK

After her graduation from high school, in 1988, Tweet set out to succeed in the music world. She spent six years with the all-female trio Sugah, which disbanded in 2000 without ever releasing an album. "I guess I gave a lot of my life over to this producer and to people that I thought would [bring me success]. I was moving around to a lot of different cities but in the end it wasn't right," she told Chris Lamb for the Teenmusic Web site. Adding to her unhappiness was the failure of an eight-year intimate relationship. "For so many years I was stuck," the singer told Gil Kaufman for the MTV Web site. "I couldn't breathe, I was depressed and miserable." After Sugah broke up, Tweet moved to Panama City, Florida, where her parents had taken up residence. There she turned to alcohol and contemplated suicide. She was on the brink of carrying out her plan to kill herself when the hugely successful hip-hop star and music producer Missy "Misdemeanor" Elliott contacted her. Elliott, who had met Tweet in the mid-1990s, before becoming a star herself, asked Tweet to sing background vocals on songs such as "Take Away," a duet by Elliott and Ginuwine, for Elliott's third album, released as *Miss E . . .So Addictive,* in 2001. (Tweet later contributed vocals to three tracks on Elliott's album Under Construction, which was scheduled for release in November 2002.) Elliott then signed Tweet to her label, Gold Mind Records, and since then has served as the young singer's mentor. "I call [Elliott] my guardian angel because she truly rescued me from ending my life," Tweet told *Jet* (April 22, 2002). She said to Dimitri Ehrlich for *Interview* (March 1, 2001), "If it wasn't for Missy I don't know what I would have

Affiliation: Critical Reception

The overall critical response to *Southern Hummingbird* has been positive, with many reviewers praising Tweet's smooth voice and her songwriting. "Tweet's a talented singer, with a warm rich voice that's stuck in the melismatic territory of high octaves," Sterling Clover wrote. "She can't do cold or aloof; even her kiss-off songs sound like come-ons. More than anything else she's got the voice of a woman who's got to stop kissing you and catch her train, and tells you this as she keeps kissing you. Sometimes the voice of a woman who's doing more than kissing." In a review of *Southern Hummingbird* for amazon.com, Rebecca Levine wrote, "Tweet is the classic show-biz story: an overnight sensation 10 years in the making. The sultry singer/songwriter traveled a long and twisted path to success. . . . Fans of intelligent soul music will be glad Tweet stuck it out. *Hummingbird* is the work of an introspective and talented woman." A fair number of industry insiders, however, while not criticizing Tweet's performance, have credited Elliott and Timbaland with a considerable part of her success.

Black Entertainment Television (BET) nominated Tweet as best new artist in 2002. She sang part of the chorus for "Paradise," a song on L.L. Cool J's 2002 album, *Ten.* The soul singer is due to appear on an episode of the UPN television sitcom *The Parkers* in November 2002.

done. I was going through a lot after I left Sugah. . . . I was on the road to self-destruction. I wasn't feeling life at all. If it wasn't for her being concerned and remembering me, I don't know where I would be."

Tweet's album, *Southern Hummingbird,* released in April 2002, debuted at number two on the *Billboard* R&B album chart. Regarding the inspiration for its title, Tweet said to Reid, "I'm the only person in my family that was born in New York. Everybody else is from the South but me. Every summer I go to the South. Everybody thinks I'm Southern because I talk kind of country." Several songs on *Southern Hummingbird* feature Tweet playing acoustic guitar—her instruments also include bass guitar, piano, and drums—creating a sound bridging hip-hop and folk music that has been called alternative soul, or in Tweet's words, "gumbo soul," a stew of gospel, R&B, soul, and country. Tweet wrote most of the songs on Southern Hummingbird herself, and most are about love, heartbreak, and redemption. "The album has three seduction songs, two being-seduced songs, three about being in love, one about regret of lost love, one about not regretting lost love, one about betrayal, one about friendship, and one about self-love," Sterling Clover reported in a review of *Southern Hummingbird* for the British Web site freakytrig-gerco.uk. "Oops (Oh My)," the first single from the album, spent six weeks at number one on Billboard's chart for R&B/hip-hop singles and tracks in the first half of 2002. The song has polished, seductive beats supplied by Timbaland (whose real name is Timothy Mosley), lyrics full of double entendres, and a rap interlude by Elliott, who, along with Timbaland and Tweet herself, produced the songs on *Southern Hummingbird.* (Tweet also contributed vocals to Timbaland's 2001 album, *Indecent Proposal.*) The lyrics to "Oops (Oh My)" include the lines, "Oops there goes my shirt up over my head, oh my. / Oops there goes my skirt dropping to my feet, oh my." When asked by Chris Lamb if, as the lyrics might suggest, the song is about masturbation, Tweet answered, "No, it's not, although everybody thinks it is. But I want people to take my songs and have it mean whatever it means to you. To me it means a woman coming into tune with herself, self-appreciation." "Oops (Oh My)," which enjoyed frequent airplay on the radio, has been nominated by the Soul Train Lady of Soul Awards for best R&B/soul or rap new-artist, solo. According to the Web site tweet.330.ca, Tweet described another song on the record, "Always Will," as one she had written to the man she had dated for eight years. "I know he won't be able to love another like he loved me and I have no problem putting that into a song." *Southern Hummingbird* also includes, among other songs, "Best Friend," a duet with the R&B star Bilal (Bilal Sayeed Oliver), and "Boogie 2nite," a hip-hop dance track.

Personal Life

In her leisure time Tweet enjoys going to the movies, playing billiards, and bowling. From a brief marriage that ended in divorce, she has a daughter, Tashawna, who was 12 years old in mid-2002. She and her daughter live in Atlanta, Georgia.

Further Reading

askmen.com
Ebony p83+ Aug. 2002, with photo
Interview pl34+ Mar. 1, 2001
Jet p57 Apr. 22, 2002, with photo; mtv.com
Rolling Stone p30 May 9, 2002, with photo
tweet.330.ca (on-line)

Tyler the Creator

Rapper; producer

Born: Mar. 6, 1991; Los Angeles
Primary Field: Rap
Group Affiliation: Odd Future

Introduction

"You can't really ignore Odd Future Wolf Gang Kill Them All," Paul Lester wrote for the London Guardian *(May 7, 2011) about the prolific Los Angeles, California-based hip-hop collective. "Well, you could, but you'd have to not use the internet and not read any press. They are everywhere. There's a good reason for the ubiquity: OFWGKTA are astonishing, both on record and live, where they approximate the combined imagined force of the Sex Pistols, Slipknot and NWA."*

The collective (usually referred to as "Odd Future"), consisting of 11 members, has a catalogue of more than a dozen self-produced albums, which first generated a following on-line.

Early Life

The rapper was born Tyler Okonma on March 6, 1991 in Los Angeles. He has a younger sister. His mother was a social worker. His father, who is African, was absent from his life from early on, that absence would later become a recurring subject in his lyrics. In an interview with Kelefa Sanneh for the *New Yorker* (May 23, 2011), Tyler said that his father is Nigerian (he added, "That's what my mom told me—but she also told me she loved me, the other day"); he has publicly divulged few other details about him. When Tyler was 12 he began to make his own beats with the software program Reason, and at age 13 he taught himself to play piano. Some of his early hip-hop influences were staples of the genre, such as Dr. Dre's *Tile Chronic* (2001) and the work of the rock, funk, and hip-hop band N.E.R.D, He later became interested in jazz, punk rock, electronica, and ambient music. He told Lester that some aspects of his own music-specifically, what Lester called "the plaintive atmospheres and mournful violins"—were inspired by "a bunch of French jazz, old soundtracks, library music, [music] … with crazy chord progressions and changes in it."

Tyler's teen years were tumultuous; he was plagued with asthma (from which he still suffers) and took Ritalin for hyperactivity, until he found that it interfered with his asthma medication. He was often disruptive in school and as a result attended a series of public schools in Los Angeles and Sacramento before enrolling at Media Arts Academy, in Hawthorne, California. That charter school, Sanneh wrote, "was also known as Hip-Hop High," a place that "used music facilities to lure students from all over the city who might otherwise have dropped out, or already had." Media Arts Academy allowed Tyler to develop his creative side; there, he made use of the school's music equipment and became skilled at graphic design. A skateboarder, Tyler often went to a skate park near Media Arts Academy, where he began to make friends from around the city. Tyler and his friends soon formed a collective they dubbed Odd Future Wolf Gang Kill Them All, with the intention—at least on Tyler's part—of producing a magazine. Soon, however, they decided to create music instead. While there are said to be members of the group involved in various other creative pursuits, only 11 make music. One of the first members of the collective was the producer known as Left Brain, who shared Tyler's musical tastes. The rapper Hodgy Beats was the next to join. The others now include the 17-year-old rapper known as Earl Sweatshirt, the youngest member (he has not appeared with the collective recently because his mother sent him to a reform school in Samoa, prompting the oft-heard "Free Earl" rallying cry at shows); the rapper Domo Genesis; the R&B singer Frank Ocean, the oldest member at 24; the producer Matt Martian; the rapper Mike G; Taco and Jasper, who contribute little of a musical nature to Odd Future, which is a running joke among the collective; and Syd the Kid (also written as Syd tha Kyd), the group's sound engineer, overall producer, live deejay, and sole female. Tyler, considered the founder of the group and its de facto leader, creates Odd Future's art and videos. The collective began to assemble tracks at the home of Syd the Kid's parents, in Los Angeles, where she had her own recording studio.

Life's Work

Since its formation Odd Future has created more than a dozen albums or "mixtapes," many initially made available as free downloads on the collective's Web site. Some are solo works, others collaborations among several members, still others projects of the full collective. Tyler's *Goblin* is the first to have been released on a label (XL Recordings); *BlackenedWhite* by MellowHype (Hodgy Beats and Left Brain) and Frank Ocean's mixtape, *Nostalgia, ULTRA,* were slated for July 2011 releases on the Fat Possum and Def Jam labels, respectively. Tyler has rapped on, and had a hand in the production of, almost every Odd Future release, including its two full-collective mixtapes *The Odd Future Tape* (2008) and *Radical* (2010). In 2011the collective signed a deal with Sony/RED for the distribution rights to its albums; the label agreed to let Odd Future retain creative control.

Tyler initially drew attention by posting his solo music on-line. With the help of a viral video for his song "French," he and Odd Future became an Internet sensation. His debut solo album, *Bastard* (2009), showcased what would become his signature sound: raspy vocals accompanied by ambient textures, minimal piano, and, occasionally, heavy drums and bass. His lyrics tackled themes of alienation, his absent father, his frustration with the opposite sex and more. Most critics found the album to be both refreshing and unsettling.

Tom Breihan wrote for Pitchfork.com, "*Bastard* is a minor masterpiece of shock art and teenage spleen-vent, a spiritual cousin of some of the most misanthropic tantrums that the L.A. hardcore scene produced 30 years earlier. But it's also a beautifully put-together piece of work, one that lays out its position right away and then does everything it can to keep you uncomfortable. Tyler is smart enough to start things off with the title track, a soul-laid-bare rant about evil thoughts and absent fathers over still, eerie piano plinks. The track works great on its own, but it also creates a context for all the rape jokes and murder talk that follows; no matter how grisly things get, you still stay on this kid's side to at least some extent. And things really do get grisly."

In 2010, thanks to the popularity of *Bastard* and other Odd Future releases, as well as a flurry of articles about Odd Future in the music press, the collective enlisted the former Interscope executives Christian Clancy and David Airaudio as managers. Odd Future toured in the fall of that year and broke into the mainstream with a chaotic performance of Tyler's "Sandwitches" on the TV show *Late Night with Jimmy Fallon* in February 2011. A black-and-white video for the *Goblin* single "Yonkers," in which Tyler eats a live cockroach and then appears to hang himself, added to the buzz when it went viral on the Internet.

Goblin was produced by Tyler and Left Brain. It was generally well-received, although most critics found space in their reviews to condemn the rapper's apparent homophobia and rape fantasies. Jon Caramanica wrote for the *New York Times* (May 8, 2011), "*Goblin* is spiteful, internal, confident, vitriolic, vividly bruised stuff, a shocking—and shockingly good—album that bears little resemblance to contemporary hip-hop. It has more in common with the stark, thick-with-feelings independent rap of the mid-to-late-1990s and also the improbably rich-sounding minimalism of the Neptunes in the early 2000s. For every caustic rhyme about violence there's a pensive, unexpectedly gentle production choice to go with it, Unlike the maximalism of hip-hop radio, you can feel the air in these songs, the gasping for breath."

Not all critics were pleased, however. Eric Harvey wrote for the *Village Voice* (May 11, 2011, on-line), "*Goblin's* highest points and most infuriating moments come from the fact that it's a verite depiction of the worst aspects of American boy culture. You know, hating girls because they don't like you because you're a weirdo, hating any and all authority figures because they try to tell you how not to be such a weirdo. But most importantly (and scarily), there's the part that involves lashing out about being viewed as a weirdo, and being summarily rewarded—i.e. seen as normal for doing so . . . Nobody cares about Tyler the Creator being someone's role model in 2011. Which in a way, is the scariest thing about Goblin—too much of his scary fantasizing, for too many boys, is all

Affiliation: Odd Future

Since it gained recognition in the mainstream music press, in 2010, Odd Future has become one of the most talked-about now groups in hip-hop, praised for its brilliant production work, unique rapping, shocking lyrics, and ability to win over a legion of devoted fans through social-media promotion and free music downloads. Chris Richards described the collective for the *Washington Post* (May 15, 2011) as "the most hyped pop act of 2011, and the most complex: a handful of bratty, sometimes-brilliant rappers, singers and producers who have spent the past year enchanting bloggers while building a feverishly devout fan base. Their vulgar lyrics grabbed the pop world's attention, and their reckless charisma has managed to keep it." The founder and leader of Odd Future is the 20-year-old rapper and producer known as Tyler, the Creator (the comma is an official part of his stage name). Tyler has also become the collective's breakout star, with the success of his self-released solo debut, *Bastard* (2009), and major-label follow-up, *Goblin* (2011). Critics have compared his minimalist production and clever rhyming to those of pioneering 1990s underground rap artists as well as the work of the shock-rapper Eminem. He has also been reviled, due to his penchant for raunchy, violence-obsessed, misogynistic, and homophobic lyrics. Andrew Nosnitsky wrote for *Billboard* (March 11, 2011, on-line) that Tyler is "rap's most buzzed-about new star—and quite possibly an emerging threat to both decency-minded parent groups and the major-label infrastructure." Those who take Tyler and Odd Future's lyrics least seriously may be the members of the collective themselves. Before an Odd Future performance in Washington, D.C., Chris Richards wrote that the group "will rap about murder, rape, kidnapping, arson, torture and necrophilia. It'll also rap about absentee fathers, puppy love crushes and how none of its absurdly violent boasts is actually true."

too normal." The critical reception generated by *Goblin* was overshadowed somewhat by the reaction to its lyrical content. Caramanica wrote, "With imagery depicting rampant drug use, systemic violence against women, and any number of other distasteful things, Odd Future has become the flashpoint for reigniting the culture wars in hip-hop for a generation that hasn't previously experienced them, that didn't realize culture wars were still a possibility. No act in recent memory has engendered so many think pieces about music, think pieces about critics and think pieces about think pieces, Are the group's lyrics reports of literal desires? The goofs of misguided kids? Does the difference matter?" In defense of his music, Tyler has argued that he is not homophobic or ignorant of the realities of sexual violence. In an interview with *NME,* as quoted by Alex Macpherson in the London *Guardian* (May 9, 2011, on-line), he explained that he uses certain taboo words or evokes violent scenarios simply to shock, and that a word such as "f**got"—often used in his rhymes—is meant as a general insult and not a put-down of the gay community. "I'm not homophobic," he said. "I just think 'f**got' hits and hurts people." In defense of her musical collaborator, Syd the Kid, who is openly lesbian, told Lester about Tyler, "He ... isn't necessarily saying, 'I want to rape so-and-so'. They're just sick, twisted fantasies that he's had, based on girls that have hurt him in the past. A lot of people have sick, twisted fantasies, so why not give them something to relate to?" Chris Richards wrote, "As heinous as some of Odd Future's lyrics can be, they still possess an exaggerated, cartoonish quality. They don't feel like a true espousal of violence, misogyny or homophobia so much as a big joke you're not in on. It's just too bad it has to be such an ugly joke."

Odd Future is currently producing a pilot for a series on the cable-television cartoon network Adult Swim, and Tyler is expected to release a third album, *Wolf,* in 2012.

PERSONAL LIFE

Caramanica described the six-foot two-inch, deep-voiced Tyler as "lanky and sinewy and irrepressibly goofy, with a vibrant antisocial streak." The rapper, he added, is "partial to flamboyantly patterned shirts, gym socks pulled up to the knee and desiccated Vans; loves bacon and doughnuts; says he doesn't drink or do drugs; and can barely get a sentence out without a curse." Tyler's goal, according to a post he made on his Formspring account, as quoted by Jeff Weiss in the *Los Angeles Times* (April 10, 2011, on-line), is to "make great music . . . be the leader for the kids who were picked on and called weird, and show the world that being yourself and doing what you want without caring what other people think, is the key to being happy."

FURTHER READING

(London) *Guardian* Guide p6 May 7, 2011;
New York Times Arts and Leisure p1 May 8, 2011;
New Yorker p58 May 23, 2011;
oddfuture.com; *Washington Post* T p1 May 15, 2011

Underworld

Producer; remixer

Karl Hyde
Vocalist; guitarist; songwriter
Born: May 10, 1957(?); Worchester, England

Rick Smith
Keyboardist; songwriter;
Born: May 25, 1959(?); Ammanford, Wales

Primary Field: Production
Group Affiliation: Underworld

Introduction

"There are few production outfits more important to the development of modern electronic dance music than Underworld," Justin Kleinfeld wrote for Remix *magazine (March 1, 2006) about that British electronic group. "The group's importance doesn't lie with the fact that it was able to break through to the mainstream or that it produced countless club hits. Rather, Underworld's stamp on the dance world is marked by its jaw-dropping live show and ability to bring out the beautiful sides of our emotions. There aren't many dance music songs that make people weep the way the beginning of 'Born Slippy' does. While on the other end of the spectrum, there are very few songs that bring the same electricity as the dynamic ending of 'Cowgirl.' Those tracks are classics because they are true songs and not just dance tracks made for a specific setting or mood."*

Early Lives

Karl Hyde was born on May 10 sometime between 1957 and 1961 in Worcester, a town in the West Midlands, England. His attraction to music began early in life. At 11 he started playing the guitar. As a preadolescent Hyde shared an affinity for pop music with his father. During his teens his musical tastes expanded to include film soundtracks, electronic music, and music with avant-garde elements. One of his greatest influences was the British deejay John Peel, whose BBC Radio 1 show was among the first in Great Britain to broadcast nonmainstream music. Peel played recordings by such artists as the British art-rock group Roxy Music and the pioneering German electronic-music band Kraftwerk. "John was a great catalyst, the way he would turn us on to all this great music and connected like-minded people, just because you were tuned into one place-his radio show ... ,"Hyde told Stuart Barrie for the Glasgow, Scotland, *Daily Record* (July 21, 2006). "He opened up dub, German electronica, hardcore metal, African music, and all sorts of strange sounds." Hyde studied art at Cardiff Art College, in Wales, in the latter half of the 1970s. (It is now the Cardiff School of Art and Design, a division of the University of Wales Institute, Cardiff.) During that time he played in several bands, among them the Screen Gemz, a pop group that incorporated elements of German electronica and Jamaican reggae and had a lot of fans in Cardiff. Shortly after completing his art studies, Hyde met Rick Smith by chance when both were working in a Cardiff diner, one during the day and the other at night. (Some sources report that they met at the college.) Richard Smith was born on May 25, 1959 (or 1960) in Ammanford, in Carmarthenshire County, Wales, to a minister and his wife, a piano teacher. He worked in a bank in his hometown before he enrolled at the Cardiff division of the University of Wales, with the intention of pursuing a career as a synthesizer engineer. Smith played the piano and, like Hyde, admired Kraftwerk and enjoyed various experimental forms of music. At Hyde's urging Smith joined the Screen Gemz as their synthesizer player.

The difficulties of touring Great Britain in a crowded transit van led to Smith's departure from the Screen Gemz after a year. The band itself dissolved in 1981. Hyde next joined Smith and the bassist Alfie Thomas to form a New Wave band called Freur. In 1983, after recruiting the drummer Bryn Burrows (from the British New Wave band the Fabulous Poodles) and the keyboardist John Warwicker, Freur landed a recording contract with CBS Records. The title track of Freur's first album, *Doot Doot* (1983), reached number two on the U.K. singles chart. The group released a second album, *Get Us Out of Here* (1985), and scored the soundtrack to the Clive Barker penned horror film *Underworld* (1985; released in the U.S. as *Transmutations)* before disbanding, in 1986.

Lives' Work

Taking inspiration from the Barker film, Hyde, Smith, Thomas, Burrows, and the bassist Baz Allen formed a funk-rock group and named themselves Underworld; the band's earliest incarnation, it is commonly called Underworld Mark 1. After signing with Sire Records, they released the albums *Underneath the Radar* (1988) and *Change the Weather* (1989), neither of which received much attention. In 1989 the group landed the opening slot on the U.S. leg of the farewell tour of the Eurythmics, the British electro-pop duo made up of Annie Lennox and Dave Stewart. "I stood in front of like 30,000 people," Smith told Tamara Palmer for *URBMagazine* (November/December 1999, online), as quoted on enotes.com. "It was nice for five seconds, and after that it was awful." Soon afterward Sire Records dropped the group, which then dissolved.

By that time Hyde and Smith had become fed up with the music industry and dissatisfied with their own musical development. "We were obsessed with Kraftwerk and dub music, yet we were stuck, in the middle of a tour, with a style we realized wasn't something we were interested in anymore," Hyde recalled to Emma Forrest for the London *Independent* (August 23, 1996). "Re-inventing yourself in the music business is anathema to most people—apart from the real innovators like Miles Davis or Frank Zappa. Most musicians are encouraged to stay the way they are." Hyde told Mark Jenkins for the *Washington Post* (April 18, 1999), "There are some things more important than trying to knock out hits. In the 1980s, Rick and I learned that this wasn't in our nature. We felt that if we just carried on, we were in danger of being caught up in a wave that wasn't of our own making."

After the Eurythmics tour Hyde worked in the U.S. as a session guitarist. He later became friendly with Deborah "Debbie" Harry and toured with her band, Blondie. Smith, meanwhile, had moved back to England, settling in Romford, in Greater London, Essex County, where he set up a makeshift recording studio in his bedroom. Through his brother-in-law, he met Darren Emerson (born on April 30, 1971 in Hornchurch, Greater London), then a young futures trader on the London Stock Exchange and a much-in-demand part-time deejay. Emerson was already a fixture in British acid house (a subgenre of house music, a kind of dance music) when Smith suggested to him that they work together. With rave culture spreading throughout England, the two began recording tracks with a strong dance-club sensibility, fusing elements from indie rock, techno, electronica, and even jazz. Hyde soon joined them, and the three named their group Lemon Interrupt. In 1992 they released the singles "Dirty" and "Minneapolis" on one disk and "Bigmouth" and "Eclipse" on another, both on the dance label Junior Boy's Own, a subsidiary of London Records. The next year they readopted the moniker Underworld for the singles "Mmm . . . Skyscraper I Love You" and "Rez." *Dubnobasswithmyheadman* (1993), the first album released by the second incarnation of Underworld (sometimes referred to as Underworld Mark 2), is regarded as "a towering landmark in the techno genre," Graeme Virtue wrote for the London *Sunday Herald* (November 10, 2002); Michael Bodey wrote for the Sydney *Daily Telegraph* (January 9, 2003) that it is "rightfully considered one of electronica's finest moments." With songs including "Dark & Long (Dark Train)," "Mmm ... Skyscraper I Love You," "Dirty Epic," and "Cowgirl," the album "blends acid house, techno, and dub into a refined, epic headrush," Sal Cinquemani wrote for *Slant.com* (November 2, 2002). In a review posted on Amazon.com, Matthew Corwine called the album "a long and seductive hypnosis session, a decadent *film noir* journey through dark impulses and impure thoughts." "Vocalist Karl Hyde provides a monotonous, stream-of-consciousness narrative which, when chopped and rearranged, reveals a quintessentially British reserve that keeps the album mysterious," he wrote. *Dubnobasswithmyheadman* showcased Hyde's unconventional lyrics, which typically include everything from fragmented musings to snippets from found material, such as overheard conversations and answering machine recordings. "It can appear to be just noises, just sounds, disparate words but they're not," Hyde told Graeme Virtue. "They're my particular way of writing my autobiography, the fragments of my day which make up an impression of my state of mind in a particular place. . . . I write about everything I see and hear and overhear. I go to the music with several notebooks in my hand and look through them and see what's on the page that corresponds to how I feel about the music." With *Dubnobasswithmyheadman,* Jason Bracelin wrote for the *Las Vegas (Nevada) Review-Journal* (July 31, 2009), "Underworld gradually began to establish itself as a gateway act for a new form of electronic music, a hybridization of sorts, one that fused techno trademarks with a rock 'n' roll style, big production live show, a jam band's flair for improvisation and a hint of conventional songwriting that harnessed the dance music of the day to a fine, bayonet-sharp point." He added, "It was a deliberately broad sound, impulsive and amorphous, with songs that drifted apart and came together like cloud formations."

For their next album, *Second Toughest in the Infants* (1996), Underworld broadened their progressive sound by including elements from such genres as ambient, breakbeat, jungle, house, and pop. The single "Pearl's Girl" reached number 22 on the U.K. charts; the album received widespread critical praise and was nominated for a Mercury Music Prize (now known as the Barclaycard Mercury Prize), awarded annually to the best album from the United Kingdom or Ireland. In a review for the All Music Guide (on-line), Stephen Thomas Eriewine wrote, *"Second Toughest in the Infants* carries the same knockout punch of their debut, *Dubnobasswithmyheadman,* but it's subtler and more varied, offering proof that the outfit is one of the leading dance collectives of the mid-90s."

Second Toughest enjoyed rare commercial success for a techno album, selling a respectable 87,000 copies in the U.S. alone. Its appeal was attributed largely to Danny Boyle's controversial but critically lauded film *Trainspotting,* which featured the song "Dark & Long (Dark Train)" as well as "Born Slippy .NUXX." The latter, originally released as a B-side and heard over the end credits of the film, has stream-of-consciousness lyrics shouted over a thumping bass line with the now-famous "lager, lager, lager" refrain, which was inspired by Hyde's struggles with alcohol addiction. (It was not included on the original British release of *Second Toughest in the Infants* but was added to other versions and reissues of the album.) "Born Slippy .NUXX" reached number two on the U.K. charts and became a worldwide hit, selling more than a million copies. It served as "a powerful madeleine"—that is, a memory jogger—"for a generation, marking the point in the mid-Nineties when club culture became mass culture," Kitty Empire wrote for the London *Observer* (November 10, 2002). Comparing the electronic opus to one of the rocker Bruce Springsteen's best-known anthems, Empire added, "In many ways it is Underworld's 'Born in the USA'—woefully misunderstood by air-punching men like the 'lager, lager, lager' bit, but a skin-prickling anthem all the same." "Born Slippy .NUXX" has been included on many compilations, mash-up records, and remixes and remains an exceedingly popular dance track.

In early 1999 Underworld released the much-anticipated *Beaucoup Fish.* Its singles included "Moaner," released earlier on the soundtrack to the 1997 Joel Shumacher film *Batman & Robin;* the house track "Shudder/King of Snake," which sampled the bassline from Donna Summer's disco hit "I Feel Love"; "Push Upstairs"; and "Jumbo." Danya Pincavage wrote for the *University Wire* (July 22, 1999) that *Beaucoup Fish* "is not only stunningly good, but also even more musically complex than some of [Underworld's] previous work," with songs that "are more consistently dark and more complex than their earlier works." John Bush, in a review for the All Music Guide (on-line), wrote, "While *Second Toughest in the Infants* showed Underworld were no mere novices at introducing super-tough breakbeats, here the focus is on throwback acid-house and trance [a dance music genre]. The effect is that Underworld have refused to compromise their artistic vision to anyone's view of commercialism; as such the few excesses on *Beaucoup Fish* can be forgiven." Such praise notwithstanding, the album was a commercial disappointment, due to the overall waning interest in electronica at the time.

Emerson left Underworld in 2000 to pursue a solo career as a deejay and producer. He had earlier performed at the show that was recorded for the live album and DVD set *Everything, Everything,* which went on sale later that year. Contrary to speculation that Emerson's departure would mark the end of Underworld,

Affiliation: Origins

Underworld's founders are Karl Hyde, a vocalist and guitarist, and Rick Smith, a keyboardist; both are also songwriters, producers, and remixers. Since 1990 six others have been members of Underworld and its forebears. Only one of the six is still with them: Darren Price, who has served as keyboard player, studio engineer, and assistant since 2005. Hyde and Smith started Underworld as a rock-funk act in the mid-1980s. The pair released two unsuccessful albums before the deejay Darren Emerson joined them, in 1990. With Emerson, Hyde and Smith reinvented themselves as a techno outfit and made the groundbreaking recording *Dubnobasswithmyheadman* (1993). Underworld's Mercury Prize-nominated next album, *Second Toughest in the Infants* (1996), enjoyed commercial success thanks to the chart-topping single "Born Slippy .NUXX," which the filmmaker Danny Boyle included on the soundtrack to *Trainspotting* (1996). Underworld's other studio albums include *Beaucoup Fish, A Hundred Days Off, Oblivion with Bells,* and *Barking.* The band has released a live CD and DVD set, *Everything, Everything;* a greatest-hits compilation, *1992–2002;* and three download only albums, collectively titled *The Riverrun Project.* Hyde and Smith helped to score the soundtracks for Anthony Minghella's *Breaking and Entering* (2006) and Danny Boyle's *Sunshine* (2007). "I'm always surprised that people struggle for creative ideas," Hyde told Craig Mathieson for the *Sydney (Australia) Morning Herald* (June 4, 2010). "The problem I find is that there are too many. The hard work comes from sorting them out and figuring what is worth taking further." Hyde and Smith have remixed work for other artists, including Depeche Mode, Bjiork, St. Etienne, Sven Vath, Simply Red, and Leftfield. The men are also co-founders of Tomato, a self-described "collective of artists, designers, musicians and writers."

Hyde and Smith continued as a duo, often referred to as Underworld Mark 3. Their first effort without Emerson, *A Hundred Days Off* (2002), maintained the group's dance-oriented sound and was generally well received by critics and fans alike; it included the hit song "Two Months Off," which peaked at number 12 on the U.K. singles chart.

Underworld's two-disc anthology, *1992–2002* (2003), included some previously unreleased singles and B-sides. The keyboardist and studio engineer Darren Price joined the band around the time they started recording *The Riverrun Project,* three download-only albums available through their Web site, underworldlive.com. Its three parts were *Lovely Broken Thing* and *Pizza for Eggs* (both made available in 2005) and *I'm a Big Sister, and I'm a Girl, and I'm a Princess, and This Is My Horse* (2006). Hyde noted to Justin Kleinfeld that *The Riverrun Project* "was born out of a desire for change." "Around 2003, we were feeling content and at ease, and that's a lethal place to be for an artist," he added. Also in 2006 Underworld released five limited-edition 12-inch singles that contained remixes of various *Riverrun* tracks, and they collaborated with the Lebanese composer Gabriel Yared on the score for Anthony Minghella's film *Breaking and Entering.*

Underworld's soundtrack accompanied Danny Boyle's science-fiction film *Sunshine* (2007). That year marked the release of the band's seventh studio album, *Oblivion with Bells,* which contains dance and ambient tracks; one song, "To Heal," was used as the central theme in *Sunshine.* Underworld's latest album, *Barking* (2010), includes collaborations with the Welsh drum and bass artist High Contrast, Deep Dish's Dubfire, the Grammy Award-winning trance deejay and producer Paul Van Dyk, and the British house artists Mark Knight and D. Ramirez. The album's lead single, "Scribble," peaked at number 32 on the U.K. dance singles chart. In 2010 Underworld toured Europe, Asia, Australia, and the U.S. to promote *Barking.* Hyde told an interviewer for guestlisted.blogspot.com (May 18, 2010) that when performing live he and Smith try never to repeat themselves. "The music is never fully stationary," he said. "It's already done as a recorded piece of music, so when we play it live, each time it can become something new. Whenever we play, I've already done the show over and over in my mind so that way, when it comes to the actual event, I feel I can be open to exploring ways of deconstructing everything and rebuilding it as it's happening."

In 1991 Hyde, Smith, and John Warwicket launched the design collective Tomato, which has offices in London and Hollywood, California, and, currently, 10 people on staff. According to its Web site, Tomato "has involved itself with hosting workshops, publishing, exhibiting, live performances and public speaking as well as working with clients in the areas of advertising, architecture, fashion, public installations, music, television, film and graphic design." The firm has designed all of Underworld's album covers and has produced all the videos and graphics for the group's live performances. Its outside clients include Microsoft, Nike, Adidas, Chevrolet, Sony, and Pepsi. In the area of art, in 2008 a show called Beautiful Burnout Artjam: The Art of Underworld was held at the Jacobson-Howard Gallery, in New York City. In 2010 an exhibit of paintings and films by Hyde called What's Going On in Your Head When You're Dancing was mounted at the Laforet Museum, in Harajuku, Japan; Smith's new record label, Bungalow with Stairs, made the soundtrack that accompanied the show.

Personal Lives

Hyde and Smith are both married and live in Romford. Each reportedly has one child.

Further Reading

ABC Magazine p4 Nov. 19, 2006
DrownedinSound.com Sep. 29, 2010
(Edinburgh, Scotland) *Scotsman* p16 Feb. 26, 1999
(Glasgow, Scotland) *Daily Record* p36 July 21, 2006
Las Vegas (Nevada) Review-Journal p24 July 31, 2009
(London) *Guardian* p14+ Feb. 26, 1999
(London) *Independent* p6 Aug. 23, 1996
Remix p29+ Mar. 1, 2006
South China Morning Post p3 Nov. 4, 2007
(Tokyo, Japan) *Daily Yomiuri* p12 Oct. 5, 2007
tomato.co.uk
Washington Post G p1+ Apr. 18, 1999

Rudy Vallee

Band leader, radio and night club performer

Born: July 28, 1901; Island Pond, Vermont
Died: July 4, 1986; Hollywood Hills, California
Primary Field: Big band
Group Affiliation: Connecticut Yankees Band

Introduction

Among perennial radio favorites in the United States in the 1940s was Rudy Vallee. Once the matinee idol of the "flapper," Vallee retained his popularity for more than twenty years of radio, stage, and screen performances.

Early Life

Of Irish, French, and English descent, he was born Hubert Prior Vallee, one of the three children of Charles Alphonse and Katherine (Lynch) Vallee. (His brother, William Lynch Vallee, later became a writer for magazines, and his sister, Kathleen Vallee Lenneville, a music teacher.) Hubert Vallee was born at Island Pond, Vermont, on July 28, 1901. Some years later the family moved to Westbrook, Maine, where the elder Vallee, a pharmacist, opened a drugstore. Young Vallee dropped out of the Westbrook High School to join the Navy in 1917 when the United States entered World War I, but was discharged when it was discovered that he was under age.

Returning to his high school classes and to after-hour clerking in his father's store, the former sailor prepared for a pharmacist's career. He also ushered at the local movie house in order to learn how to run the projection machine. Meanwhile, music was becoming of more interest to him than pharmacy, but there was no adequate teacher in the neighborhood for his chosen instrument, the saxophone. He improved his technique by using records of Rudy Wiedoeft's playing as a guide. By practicing five or six hours a day on the saxophone he had rented from the theater's chief electrician, Vallee was able to appear as a soloist at the Strand Theater in Portland in less than a year. While studying at the University of Maine in 1921, the year after his graduation from high school, Vallee continued his practice on the saxophone, and played the trumpet, drums clarinet, and piano. It was at the University of Maine that he was nicknamed "Rudy," because of his admiration for Wiedoeft.

Life's Work

The month of February 1928 marked Vallee's premier American broadcast, over Station WABC, sponsored by Herbert's Blue-White Diamonds. By October of the succeeding year, under the auspices of the Fleischmann Yeast Company, the Connecticut Yankees had begun their Thursday night stint, which remained among the ten top radio programs for ten years. On this hour and his other radio hours, Vallee introduced performers who were later to become stars in their own right: Edgar Bergen, Bob Burns, Alice Faye, Frances Langford, and Joan Davis. The radio variety show, featuring guest stars, was a Vallee innovation in 1932, and his subsequent series of programs over stations WMCA, WOR (of M:BS), and WJZ (of NBC), produced by Sealtest Milk, Standard Brands, Drene Shampoo, and Philip Morris cigarettes, starred Beatrice Lillie, John Barrymore, Helen Hayes, Katharine Hepburn, Fanny Brice. In the meantime Vallee and the Connecticut Yankees filled several stage engagements, appearing first at the Palace Theatre in New York, then for ten weeks at the New York and Brooklyn Paramount theaters in the spring of 1929, to which they returned the following October for a twenty-one-month run. This tour grossed an average of eighteen thousand to twenty thousand dollars a week for Vallee, which was, at that time, an unusually high figure.

Vallee's talents were not, however, limited entirely to radio and night clubs. He made his first motion picture, *The Vagabond Lover,* in 1929. Two years afterward, he appeared in the stage version of George White's *Scandals* which was adapted for the motion pictures in 1934. The 1936 stage production of the *Scandals* also starred Vallee. Other films in which he appeared were *Sweet Music* (1935), *Gold Diggers in Paris* (1938), *Second Fiddle* (1939), *Time Out for Rhythm* and *Too Many Blondes* (1941). *The Palm Beach Story,* which he made in 1942, revealed Vallee as "the picture's biggest surprise," said Bosley Crowther (New York *Times),* in the role of a stuffy millionaire—John D. Hackensacker 3d—which he performs with amusing pomposity." In 1943 Vallee was seen in the film, *Happy Go Lucky.*

Vallee terminated his radio engagements in 1943, a year after his enlistment in the Coast Guard. At first a chief petty officer and later a lieutenant (s.g.), Vallee was conductor of the Eleventh Naval District Coast Guard Band Previous to assuming full-time duties with the auxiliary service, Vallee had donated the salary from his radio program to the Coast Guard Welfare Fund. The service band under his direction appeared at hundreds of war bond rallies and became known as one of the finest military bands in the country. Vallee was placed on the inactive list in 1944, subject to recall to duty.

The singer returned to commercial radio that year. Although obtaining a fairly high Hooper rating for his program *Villa Vallee* in the ranks of the top fifteen programs, Vallee was criticized by *Variety.* His new program, wrote *Variety,* was "poorly produced and written." Later the entertainment trade journal amended this judgment when the Hooper rating rose to 10.1, by explaining that, despite Vallee's two-year absence from the air, he still retained a following and "had garnered consistent fan mail" while in the Coast Guard. The show's average rating for the season was 12, which was not considered unfavorable. An adjunct to Vallee's radio activities was his establishment of the Rudy Vallee Music Company, underwritten by Broadcast Music Incorporated; afterward (in 1945) he formed the Ruval Music Company, affiliated with ASCAP on a nonparticipating basis. In 1945 he also formed Saint Enterprises, Incorporated, with Leslie Charteris, the author of the "Saint" mystery stories.

The *Villa Vallee* broadcast went off the air in August 1946. A succeeding program, inaugurated in September 1946, was discontinued in March 1947, when the radio star entered upon the first personal appearance tour he had made in eight years, booked to appear at a Chicago night club at a salary of seventy-five hundred dollars a week. For release in 1947 he had also made a motion picture, *The Bachelor and the Bobby-Soxer,* co-starring Cary Grant '41, Myrna Loy, and Shirley Temple'45. Earlier motion pictures in which he had appeared after his discharge from the Coast Guard include *Man Alive* (1945), *It's In The Bag* (1945) and *People Are Funny*

Affiliation: Connecticut Yankees Band

Upon transferring to Yale University the following year, Vallee became one of the three saxophonists with the Yale Collegians, an orchestra that toured the vaudeville circuits. For nine months in 1924 the young American played with the Savoy Havana Band at the Hotel Savoy in London; while there, he also made broadcasts and recordings. He returned to Yale in 1925 to continue his major study of Spanish and play with the Yale football band, with which he was soloist. After receiving his Ph.B. degree from Yale in 1927 (Vallee's orchestra engagements had paid for his support while in college), the young man joined Vincent Lopez' orchestra as third saxophonist, but he left the next year to form his own group, the Connecticut Yankees. Using the first "mellow-sax" unit of any American band, the Connecticut Yankees opened at the Heigh-Ho Club in New York early in 1928. The Connecticut Yankee style evolved by Vallee was based on rendering the choruses of each composition in varied tempos and types, without repetition of any chorus, and without playing any two successive tunes in the same key. Since the Heigh-Ho Club was small, the personnel of the band was limited, and it was the emphasis on the band's two violinists, two saxophonists, and one pianist that caught the public's attention. At the club Vallee first used his greeting of "Heigh-ho, everybody" (followed by announcements in the manner of Yale's William Lyon Phelps), and the practice of singing through a megaphone.

(1946). In 1947 Vallee was in the cast of *I Remember Mama,* playing a "straight" role.

Other engagements that Vallee filled in his long career were at various ballrooms and hotels throughout the country, including New York's Hotel Pennsylvania Grill and Roof, the Hotel Astor Roof the Hollywood Restaurant and Los Angeles Cocoanut Grove. In 1937 Vallee and the Connecticut Yankees appeared in a London engagement celebrating Coronation Week. Vallee's autobiography, *Vagabond Dreams Come True,* was published in 1930; the radio star also wrote a series of articles for *Radio Digest* (1937) and for *Radio Stars,* as well as numerous guest columns. His professional affiliations were with the American Federation of Musicians, the American Society of Composers, Authors, and Publishers, the American Federation of Radio Artists, the Academy of Motion Picture Arts and Sciences, the Amateur Cinema League, the National Association of Performing Artists, and the Screen Actors' Guild. In 1937 he was president of the American Federation of Actors. Other organizations to which he belonged were the American Arbitration Association, the American Legion, La Société des 40 Hommes et 8 Chevaux, and the fraternity Sigma Alpha Epsilon. His clubs were the New York Athletic, the Lambs, the Friars, the Elks, and the Yale (New York City). In 1933 the singer served as lieutenant commander on the staff of Governor Brann of Maine. Texas and Kentucky both made him an honorary colonel. From Suffolk Law School, of which he was a trustee, Vallee received the degree of Master of Arts in 1936. He was a Roman Catholic. With other representatives of the entertainment profession, Vallee sponsored the Hospitalized Veterans National Radio Foundation in 1947, for the purpose of supplying patients in veteran's hospitals with bedside and pillow-type radio receivers.

Personal Life

The singer's hobbies were tennis, motoring, and colored motion picture photography. His height was five feet eleven inches and a half, and he weighed 170 pounds and had gray eyes and brown hair. Vallee was married four times; a marriage to Leonia Cauchors ended by annulment, and those to Fay Webb and Jane Greer ended in divorce. His fourth marriage, to Eleanor Norris, lasted from 3 September 1949 until his death in 1986. Vallee greatly enjoyed the legend that pictured him as a Vagabond Lover and a millionaire host with a checkroom. It was said of him that he "worries with the rest of the citizens around the fifteenth of March, is an openhanded host, and an appreciator of the pretty ankle like every normal, unattached male."

Rudy Vallee died of cancer on July 3, 1986 at his home in Hollywood Hills, California. His remains are interred in St. Hyacinth's Cemetery in Westbrook, Maine.

Further Reading

Newsweek 13:31 My 15 '39
America's Young Men, 1938-39
International Motion Picture Almanac 1946-47
Who's Who in America 1946-47
Who's Who in New York, 1938

Steven Van Zandt

Musician; producer; actor; radio host

Born: Nov. 22, 1950; Winthrop, Massachusetts
Primary Field: Rock
Group Affiliation: E Street Band; solo performer

Introduction

Nineteen ninety-nine was a banner year for the multifaceted performer Steven Van Zandt: he released his fifth solo album, Born Again Savage*; he made his debut as an actor, appearing as Silvio Dante, a top adviser, or consigliere, to the ruthless mafia boss Tony Soprano, in HBO's runaway-hit series* The Sopranos*; and he reunited with Bruce Springsteen and the E Street Band on an extended world tour. As the E Street Band's eccentric, bandana-clad guitarist and raspy-voiced backup vocalist, from 1975 to 1984, "Van Zandt emerged—along with saxman Clarence Clemons—as one of the focal points of the band," Lynn Van Matre wrote for the* Chicago Tribune *(January 30, 1983), "whose contributions . . . played an integral part in shaping the E-Street sound." A savvy, streetwise studio hand, "Miami Steve"* *(as he became known to his fans) served as the band's part-time producer during that period of exceptional critical and commercial success, arranging the music to several of Springsteen's brooding tales of working-class angst.*

Early Life

Van Zandt was born Steven Lento on November 22, 1950 in Winthrop, Massachusetts, which is part of the greater Boston area. His father's family came from the Calabria region of southern Italy. When Van Zandt was an infant, his father died; not long afterward his mother remarried, and her new husband adopted young Steven. That explains "how somebody from an Italian family ends up with a Dutch name," Van Zandt told Lynn Van Matre. Van Zandt's younger brother, Billy, has written for such television comedies as *Newhart, Martin,* and *Yes, Dear,* among others. His sister, Kathi, is an executive at Victoria's Secret, a retail marketer of lingerie and women's beauty products.

Before Van Zandt entered middle school, his family moved from Massachusetts to Middletown, New Jersey, in Monmouth County, near the Jersey Shore. He spent the bulk of his childhood and adolescence a stone's throw from the state's beaches and pinball-arcade-lined boardwalks. Raised as a Baptist, Van Zandt described his early religious awakening in an essay that accompanied the release of *Born Again Savage,* which is also posted on his official Web site: "I got very religious as a kid around the age of 10,11, or 12. . . . I remember looking forward to the Easter Sunrise service every year. Waking up when it was still night and gathering at the mountain top was a rare mystical experience that seemed to connect to some dark, mysterious, long-past ritual in my subconscious." That development was soon followed by another epiphany, which occurred as he was listening to the song "Pretty Little Angel Eyes," by Curtis Lee. "A feeling of pure bliss flooded my body," Van Zandt wrote for his Web site. "It was my second epiphany in as many years and this one was even stronger than the first. It wouldn't become my life until two or three years later when the Beatles and the Rolling Stones would reveal my future, but from that moment on what would dominate the emotional part of my spiritual consciousness would be rock and roll. In other words, at that moment, rock and roll became my religion." He then purchased as many singles as he could afford, including "Tears on my Pillow" by Little Anthony and the Imperials, "Duke of Earl" by Gene Chandler, "Twist and Shout" by the Isley Brothers, "Sherry" by the Four Seasons, and "Pretty Little Angel Eyes."

By the time he was 16 years old, Van Zandt had formed his own band, named the Source, for which he played lead guitar and sang lead vocals. He also arranged the Source's music. "We were one of the first bands to break the mold," he explained to Terry Gross, host of the National Public Radio program *Fresh Air* (June 27, 2002). "In those days you had to play the top 40, and my band was one of the first to play FM radio rock type of album cuts. . . . I was playing songs by The Who and Buffalo Spring- field and Youngbloods, people like that, which was a bit strange back then. There wasn't too many of us—there wasn't too many bands back then, actually. It was a very different world. It was not a viable way to make a living yet, so you were considered really one step above a criminal, you know, being in a rock 'n' roll band." Such earlier acts as the Drifters, Little Richard, and Gary "U.S" Bonds also influenced Van Zandt.

As a teenager, Van Zandt met and befriended Bruce Springsteen, a native of Freehold, New Jersey, who would become one of the most popular musicians of his generation. "We just had a thing right from the start," Van Zandt explained to Robert Hilburn for the *Los Angeles Times* (December 19, 1999). "I was one of the two guys in my high school of 3,000 with long hair. He was the only one in his high school with long hair. That meant you didn't really fit in. . . . This was before everyone wanted to be in a band. But we found something in the music that we believed in—even though no one else was supportive and there was no way of realistically thinking you were going to make a living at it. "

Life's Work

After they had both graduated from high school, Van Zandt and Springsteen performed together in various groups in clubs near and around the ocean town of Asbury Park, which is located south of Middletown and east of Freehold. Dr. Zoom and the Sonic Boom, the Bruce Springsteen Band, and the more popular Steel Mill were among the many bands for which the two musicians played. Van Zandt also performed with such rockers as Johnny Lyon and, much later, Jon Bon Jovi on that circuit.

While he loved performing, Van Zandt became disillusioned with the music industry and quit briefly to become a construction worker. He returned to his playing music around 1973, touring as a member of a

Affiliation: "Little Steven" and Solo Career

In 1982 Van Zandt changed his on-stage name to "Little Steven" and embarked on a solo career, teaming up with the Disciples of Soul to release several overtly political albums between 1982 and 1999. "Miami Steve was a sharpie sporting an ever-present fedora or beret and the aura of a small-time slick operator; Little Steven, with his bright headkerchief, black leather and multitude of scarves, has the look of an Italian Gypsy," Van Matre wrote, noting that Van Zandt had called his Little Steven persona "the real me."

Van Zandt is known for his political awareness, having organized Artists United Against Apartheid, which included such icons as Bob Dylan, Miles Davis, and Run-D.M.C. His music is recognized as containing elements of rhythm and blues, doo-wop, soul, and rock. Despite having a reedy Steven Van Zandt singing voice and no training as an actor, he was dubbed "the coolest guy in the entire state of New Jersey" by Jeffrey Goldberg, writing for the *New York Times* (December 26,1999). Among his many achievements in the music industry, Van Zandt "helped create the archetypal Jersey bar-band sound," according to Jay Lustig, writing for *Newhouse News Service* (October 18, 1999). Since 2002 Van Zandt has been the host of the highly successful syndicated radio program *Little Steven's Underground Garage,* heard on more than 200 stations nationwide. Since 2004 Van Zandt has also produced for the subscriber-supported Sirius Satellite Radio two channels—*Underground Garage* and *Outlaw Country*—and one program, *The Wiseguy Show.*

backup band for the Dovells, a Philadelphia-based R&B and dance-music group who had recorded such hits as "Bristol Stomp" and "You Can't Sit Down" in the early 1960s. "The audience was just perfect for being creative because they didn't care if we lived or died," Van Zandt explained to Lynn Van Matre. "So we would do obscure Marvin Gaye things, whatever I felt like. That was where my personal musical identity really came together." Traveling around the country with the Dovells, Van Zandt played at such prominent venues as Madison Square Garden, in New York City, and he also performed with one of the men he had idolized in his youth, a doo-wop sensation named Dion DiMucci (better known to his fans as Dion), who had recorded such hits as "Runaround Sue" and "The Wanderer."

Afterward, in 1974, Van Zandt returned to New Jersey and collaborated with the musician and songwriter Johnny Lyon; together they cofounded Southside Johnny and the Kid. Later, the group changed its name to Southside Johnny & the Asbury Jukes, due in part to its growing membership and increasing popularity on the Jersey Shore's club circuit. Boasting a "horn-heavy, R&B-drenched sound," according to Jay Lustig, the Jukes' original lineup included such musicians as guitarist Billy Rush, keyboardist Kevin Kavanaugh, drummer Kenny Pentifallo, trumpeters Tony Palligrossi and Ricky Gazda, and trombonist Richie "La Bamba" Rosenberg. Van Zandt gained more experience as a songwriter and producer with the group, and he also worked inside a studio for the first time. "I just kept on doing what I had been doing all along," Van Zandt told Lynn Van Matre, "which was taking obscure R&B things and arranging them in more of a rock and roll way." He later served as the Jukes' manager, helping the band sign a contract with Epic Records in 1976, the year they released *I Don't Want to Go Home.* Kit Keifer, writing for the *All Music Guide* Web site, hailed that song as an "R&B Revivalist's delight."

Meanwhile, Van Zandt's friend Springsteen had successfully launched his own career, releasing *Greetings from Asbury Park, N.J.* (1973) and *The Wild, the Innocent & the E Street Shuffle* (1973). Prior to the recording of and release of Springsteen's third album for the Columbia label, *Born to Run* (1975), Van Zandt joined the E Street Band, assisting Springsteen in the studio with horn arrangements for the album's tracks, playing some guitar, and singing backup vocals. He also promised Springsteen that he would perform live with the band for a short period on a promotional tour to promote the album's release. *Born to Run,* which has sold more than six million copies to date, was released on August 25,1975, after Springsteen had "spent everything he had—patience, energy, studio time, the physical endurance of his E Street Band—to ensure that his third album was a masterpiece," according to a reviewer for *Rolling Stone* (November 1, 2003, on-line). *Born to Run* rose to number three on *Billboard's* pop charts, and both *Time* and *Newsweek* magazines put Springsteen on their covers on the same day, October 27, 1975. The album was considered by most reviewers to be Springsteen's best effort thus far.

Van Zandt's enduring and lucrative association with Springsteen was just beginning. Debuting their songs live rather than on the radio, at the suggestion of their agent, Frank Barsalona, Bruce Springsteen and the E Street Band secured a devoted following, playing to packed houses. During that time, Van Zandt became a fixture in the E Street Band, emerging on-stage as the band's effervescent, bandana-clad guitarist, "Miami Steve." Springsteen and the E Street Band followed up *Born to Run* with a string of successful albums, including *Darkness on the Edge of Town* (1978), the double-disc set *The River* (1980)—which Van Zandt co-produced—and *Born in the U.S.A.* (1984), which yielded seven hit singles in the U.S. and reached number one on the *Billboard* charts. By the summer of 1984, Bruce Springsteen and the E Street Band had become one of the most commercially successful and critically adored acts of all time.

Van Zandt, working with Springsteen, coproduced most of the tracks on Gary "U.S." Bonds's comeback albums *Dedication* (1981) and *On the Line* (1982). Van Zandt also produced Bonds's *Standing in the Line of Fire* (1984). But Van Zandt also wanted to become a successful solo artist in his own right. While touring and working tirelessly in the studio for Springsteen and others, he formed a 12-piece band called the Disciples of Soul, which included horn players from the Asbury Jukes and other musicians with whom he had developed close ties over the course of his career. In 1982 Little Steven and the Disciples of Soul released *Men Without Women,* which "in many ways . . . is the finest album the Asbury Jukes never made," Mark Deming wrote for the *All Music Guide* Web site. The name of the album, which appeared on the Razor & Tie label, came from a 1927 collection of short stories by the American writer Ernest Hemingway. *Men Without Women* was the first of six solo efforts released by Van Zandt between 1982 and 1999, and it is considered by most reviewers to be his best. "Van Zandt's guitar (and Jean Beauvior's bass) speak with the sound and fury of a true roots rock rebel. . . . On *Men Without Women, Little Steven & the Disciples* merged the brassy swing of a classic Motown side with the sweaty blare of an amped-up garage band," Deming wrote.

The album was also the first to express Van Zandt's emerging left-leaning political beliefs, which he began to expound with great fervor in his music and in the media. Having traveled overseas in the early 1980s, Van Zandt witnessed South Africa's brutal, government-sanctioned system of racial segregation, known as apartheid. What he saw had a profound impact on his life; his subsequent musical efforts addressed pressing political and social issues. Respectively, *Voices of America* (1984), *Freedom—No Compromise* (1987), *Revolution* (1989), and *Born Again* Savage (1999) explored issues of the family, the state, the economy, and religion. None of those albums brought Van Zandt the sort of mainstream success Springsteen had enjoyed as a solo artist. They sold more copies in Europe than in the U.S.; in Sweden two of the albums reached the Top 10. For the *Artists United Against Apartheid* record, released in 1985, Van Zandt wrote and produced the title song, "Sun City" (1985). The album was described as "certainly the most political of all the charity rock albums of the 1980s," by Stephen Thomas Erlewine, writing for *All Music Guide* Web site. Such acclaimed artists as Miles Davis, U2's Bono, Jackson Browne, Bobby Womack, Lou Reed, Bonnie Raitt, George Clinton, Bob Dylan, and Springsteen joined Van Zandt on the record.

In May 1997 Van Zandt served as the presenter for the induction ceremony of the Rascals—a popular blue-eyed soul group of the 1960s and 1970s—into the Rock and Roll Hall of Fame, in Cleveland, Ohio. Van Zandt's speech caught the attention of David Chase, a television producer and writer, who, at the time, was in the process of creating a weekly series for HBO. Chase later recalled thinking, according to the Montreal *Gazette* (April 15, 2003), that Van Zandt "was the face of New Jersey," which was to be the location of Chase's Mafia-family drama, *The Sopranos*. Though Van Zandt had no professional experience or training as an actor, Chase offered him a part on the show. The musician was initially reluctant to accept; he did not want to take work away from a more capable actor. He accepted the offer, though, when Chase told him he was creating a new character specifically for him. "David and I agreed the character was going to be the . . . throwback to the past, philosophically . . . that he should also reflect that physically," Van Zandt explained to Terry Gross. "We wanted to make sort of a '5Os-looking guy, you know, a guy who never really left the 50s. . . . he's not particularly concerned with being fashionable or taking part in the modern world at all."

On *The Sopranos,* which has aired since 1999, Van Zandt plays Silvio Dante, a loyal adviser, or consigliere, to the New Jersey mob boss Tony Soprano. Silvio is also the proprietor of Bada Bing, a gentlemen's club where the show's sundry characters can often be found. The Sopranos has enjoyed unusual success, gaining widespread popularity and enthusiastic critical acclaim

for its realism in depicting the lives of a contemporary Mafia family. Van Zandt told Robert Hilburn for the *Los Angeles Times* (December 19, 1999), "What I think makes the show connect with so many people is that the problems they have, generally speaking, are the problems that everybody has. Everybody has two families. Everybody has their family at home and their family at work. Everybody has those kind of complicated human relations. That's what a lot of the show is about. It's not just about gangster stuff. Take Silvio for instance .... When it comes to life-threatening situations, he's a very, very cool professional. But he'll completely lose his temper at his daughter's soccer game." *The Sopranos's* sixth season began in March 2006. The following July Van Zandt signed another contract with HBO, according to which he reportedly was to earn $187,000 for each of the final eight episodes of that season.

Earlier, in 1999, Van Zandt joined Springsteen and the E-Street Band on an extremely successful reunion tour that lasted for over a year. Van Zandt performed with the E-Street Band on a long and fruitful tour for the band's studio release entitled *The Rising* (which represented Springsteen's first collaboration with the E-Street Band since the mid- 1980s). The album, recorded in the wake of the September 11, 2001 terrorist attacks in New York City and Washington, D.C., was "one of the very best examples in recent history of how popular art can evoke a time period and all of its confusing and often contradictory notions, feelings, and impulses," according to Thom Jurek, writing for the *All Music Guide* Web site.

Around the same time, Van Zandt began hosting a Sunday-evening syndicated radio program, *Little Steven's Underground Garage*. The immensely popular show debuted from Los Angeles, California, on April 7, 2002, and now airs on more than 200 radio stations nationwide. *Little Steven's Underground Garage* features music spanning several decades of rock and roll and includes popular songs from such "garage rock" genres as rockabilly, British invasion, punk, and psychedelia, to name a few. "I miss those days when the deejay would turn you on to new things and you could develop a relationship with that deejay and a relationship with that station," Van Zandt told Terry Gross. "And that's what I'm trying to do. . . . Quite a bit of what I do is turning people on to, hopefully, new things." He told Valerie Block for *Crain's New York Business* (February 23-29, 2004): "I am a supporting player with *The Sopranos,* and I love it. I am a supporting player in Bruce Springsteen's life, which I am honored to be. This *[Little Steven's Underground Garage]* is my thing. It's become my artistic expression." According to Mark Brown, writing for the *Denver Rocky Mountain News* (April 29, 2006), *Little Steven's Underground Garage* "attract[s] more than 1 million listeners nationwide on 146 stations." Van Zandt also produces VARGAS two channels for Sirius Satellite Radio: *Underground Garage,* a spin-off from Van Zandt's regular radio show, in which a series of rotating disc jockeys air an eclectic selection of little-known music, and *Outlaw Country,* which showcases edgier offerings from the country-music scene. He also produces *The Wiseguy Show,* hosted by the former *Sopranos* cast member Vincent Pastore and described in an Associated Press article (October 8, 2004) as a celebration of "life, the arts and meatballs."

Personal Life

Jeffrey Goldberg described Van Zandt as "the original white boy funk soul brother," who attends a lunch meeting "pretty much the same way he always dresses, which is to say he looks like some kind of purple-paisley snakeskin hippie gypsy pirate." The musician and actor is married to the actress Maureen Van Zandt, who joined the cast of *The Sopranos* as Silvio Dante's wife, Gabriella, during its second season. A classically trained dancer, Maureen Van Zandt was also raised in New Jersey. In 2001 she co-founded the With Out Papers Theatre Company, which has produced such plays as *Golden Boy, Simpatico, Kingdom of Earth,* and *Burn This*. Van Zandt and his wife live in Manhattan.

Further Reading

All Music Guide Web site
Chicago Tribune VI pl7+ Jan. 30, 1983
Little Steven On-line
New York Times XIV pi2 Nov. 7, 1999, VI pl4 Dec. 26, 1999
Newhouse News Service Oct. 18, 1999

Justin Vernon

Singer and songwriter

Born: April 30, 1981; Eau Claire, Wisconsin
Primary Field: Folk
Group Affiliation: Bon Iver

Introduction

Singer-songwriter Justin Vernon is the founder, singer, and front man of the band Bon Iver. Vernon's first album as Bon Iver, For Emma, Forever Ago *(2008), was recorded in his father's cabin in his home state of Wisconsin. Music critics praised the album for its spare, subtle instrumentation, lyrical language, and—most notably—the deep emotion of Vernon's multi-tracked falsetto voice. Many publications nationwide dubbed the album one of the year's best. Vernon's second full-length album,* Bon Iver, Bon Iver *(2011), showed him expanding his musical style while maintaining the emotional depth and sensitive multi-tracked vocals of his debut. Bon Iver has been nominated for four 2012 Grammy Awards: record of the year (for the song "Holocene"), song of the year (also for "Holocene"), best new artist, and best alternative album. At the request of hip-hop megastar Kanye West, Vernon contributed his vocals to nearly half of West's album* My Beautiful Dark Twisted Fantasy *(2010). Vernon and three multi-instrumentalists have been touring extensively as Bon Iver in Europe and North America. Bon Iver has also performed on various TV shows, such as the* Colbert Report *and the* Late Show with David Letterman.

Early Life

The middle of three children, Justin DeYarmond Edison Vernon was born on April 30, 1981 in Eau Claire, Wisconsin. Along with his brother, Nate, and sister, Kim, Vernon was raised in Eau Claire in a musical household. Vernon's parents, Justine and Gil, were supportive of Vernon's varied musical interests. His mother played organ and French horn and would sometimes sing in the car while driving her children. Vernon also listened to his parents' record collection, which included albums by Bob Dylan, Tom Waits, and John Prine. Vernon was also a fan of Jackson Browne, Primus, and the Indigo Girls.

During his teens, while attending Eau Claire Memorial High School, Vernon-by then a tall young man-played on the football team and served as the team's captain. He was also involved in several music projects: playing guitar in his high school's jazz band and playing saxophone in the school's marching band. He also served as the front man for Mount Vernon, a ska-influenced jazz/pop/rock group that at times had as many as ten members. Apparently, even then, Vernon had the ability to touch an audience. His friend Drew Christopherson, speaking to Andrea Swensson for the Minneapolis *City Pages* (31 Aug. 2011), recalled, "It's very easy for him to get people to feel connected. He played our graduation party in high school, and our whole gymnasium filled with the graduating class was practically up in arms watching him play these songs. Everyone was kind of tearing up."

Life's Work

After high school Vernon went on to attend college in his hometown, the University of Wisconsin, Eau Claire, where he majored in world religious studies and minored in women's studies. Speaking to Jon Cararnanica for the *New York Times* (5 June 2011), Vernon explained why he did not want to major in music: "I didn't want to be proficient ... It seemed like other people were valuing things that were more about technical ability and not, like, feel." Vernon continued to make music, this time with a new band named DeYarmond Edison after his two middle names. A four-member band, DeYarmond Edison had elements of Wilco, old blues, indie rock, The Band, acoustic Americana, and folk; Vernon sang in a low voice similar to his actual speaking voice. In 2005, the year after Vernon graduated from the University of Wisconsin, all the band members (and their girlfriends) left Wisconsin and moved to Raleigh, North Carolina, to explore new terrain and make a name for themselves in a new music scene that was somewhat bigger than that of their hometown.

They all lived together in a big house in Raleigh and worked on their music. When they got an opportunity to play multiple shows at the multimedia space known as the Bickett Gallery, they decided to push their music even further by letting each band member focus on exploring his or her own musical and artistic strengths prior to one of the shows: the drummer, for example, focused on free jazz improvisation, and the keyboard player explored early American music. Vernon

asked that everyone in the band sing during one Bickett Gallery concert—they did—and he even sang a song in a falsetto voice, which was new for him at that point.

The four-concert residency at the Bickett Gallery led to the band's breakup, however, as it became evident that Vernon and the rest of the band members had conflicting ideas about the direction DeYarmond Edison should pursue. Speaking to Grayson Currin of the Durham, North Carolina, *Independent Weekly* (27 July 2011), Vernon recalled, "The Bickett residency, ironically, was the most I've ever learned about music and simultaneously the reason we started to break apart. We realized there were so many things we'd never explored as musicians." He went on to say, "I had this intense friendship with all these guys, and it was like we had gotten divorced. We made all these life commitments to each other. I couldn't imagine going through something deeper." Although breaking up with his band was painful, Vernon had more trouble ahead: he was diagnosed with mononucleosis of the liver and mostly stayed in bed for three months. Because he had quit his job at a local restaurant, he had no money; Vernon's situation worsened when he lost a few hundred dollars playing poker online. He also broke up with his girlfriend.

DeYarmond Edison went on to perform without Vernon as a trio called Megafaun. Vernon, meanwhile, recorded a solo EP—as Justin Vernon-titled *Hazelton* (2006), of which he made one hundred copies to sell. He also served as a producer and collaborator for an album by the band The Rosebuds. In the fall of 2006, Vernon left Raleigh, overwhelmed, tired, and broke.

As a kind of tribute to his time in the cabin, Vernon decided to adopt the stage name Bon Iver, which is an intentional misspelling of the French greeting *bon hiver,* "good winter." Vernon, as Bon lver, released *For Emma, Forever Ago* in 2007. He only made a few hundred CDs to sell at con certs and online. But word of his music spread, especially after the album got positive mentions on music review websites such as Pitchfork and BrooklynVegan. As a result of this attention, Bon Iver was asked to perform at the CMJ music marathon festival in New York City, a potentially big opportunity for up-and-coming musicians. Vernon was approached by many record labels eager to sign him. He ultimately went with the record label Jagjaguwar, which officially released *For Emma, Forever Ago* in February 2008. The record received nearly unanimous positive reviews in all sorts of mainstream publications. In an elaborate review for the *Village Voice* (19 Feb. 2008), Melissa Giannini wrote: "Equal parts awe and nostalgia, hearing Vernon's muted strums and granular falsetto fade like spun sugar into breath vapor is like seeing the Grand Canyon for the first time. With idiosyncratic vocals and the simple acoustics of a man alone in this world (plus guitar), the tunes could've easily melted into monotony. But each track folds seamlessly yet distinctively into the next, like imperfect logs split and added to the pile; audible is the intensifying beat of a heart burdened by physical/emotional labor, and the layered echoes of a ghost chorus cascading across a chasm or against the walls of a creaky cabin-turned-cloister."

For Emma, Forever Ago has only nine songs, most of which feature guitar and multiple tracks of Vernon's voice. The latter allowed Vernon to harmonize with himself, creating interesting textures and layers of sound. Also featured on the album are spare drums and horns, all working subtly beneath his voice. The song "Skinny Love" contains a few of his voices (some in falsetto), acoustic guitars, a slide guitar, electric guitars, and quiet drums. The album's opening track, "Flume," opens with a simple, strumming acoustic guitar, which continues to provide the rhythm, but what stands out are the many falsetto voices that soon enter the song, sounding almost choral. Most of the album's lyrics focus less on meaning than on sound and on the emotion conveyed by Vernon's singing. In a profile for the *New Yorker* (12 Jan. 2009), Sasha Frere-Janes wrote, "Sometimes I am surprised by the fragmentary lyrics on *For Emma;* more often, I am moved by the beauty of Vernon's massed voice, and held in place by the force of each careful, dogged song." In yet another positive review, Kitty Empire for the London *Observer* (17 May 2008) called *For Emma* a "very full and emotionally rich record."

The media attention surrounding Vernon's debut album as Bon Iver led to a successful series of tours in 2008, both in the United States and Europe. In the former, his concerts included New York's Bowery Ballroom, as well as the South by Southwest Music Festival in Austin, Texas. Performing live as Bon lver, Vernon usually had two or three musicians (all multi-instrumentalists) with him onstage. The songs—alongside Vernon's now famous voice-usually featured some of the following instruments: drums, guitars, keyboard, bass, and violin; his bandmates also sang backup. In December 2008, the band appeared on the *Late Show with David Letterman,* performing the song "Skinny Love." Bon Iver also contributed a new song to *The Twilight Saga: New Moon Soundtrack* (2009).

Bon Iver's popularity continued to grow with the release of *Blood Bank* (2009), an EP of four new songs. The title track, "Blood Bank," was written and recorded when Vernon was making *For Emma.* The last track on the EP, "Woods," is a quiet, meditative song sung a cappella that builds with multiple voices that have been manipulated in various ways by the pitch-correcting audio processor Auto-Tune. Because *Blood Bank* was only a four-song EP, it did not receive nearly the amount of attention in the mainstream press that *For Emma* did. But the popular rapper Kanye West heard it and was so enthralled with the song "Woods" that he asked Vernon if he could sample it on his album, *My Beautiful Dark Twisted Fantasy* (2010). Vernon agreed and "Woods" ended up as the basis for West's song "Lost in the World." West had something bigger in mind, however: he flew Vernon out to Hawaii, where the album was being recorded, and Vernon ended up singing on almost half of the album's songs. In the spring of 2011, Vernon, as Bon Iver, performed with West, who headlined the Coachella music festival in California. Soon after that, Vernon made the cover of the May 2011 edition of *Billboard* magazine and, according to that article, sales of *For Emma* reached 323,000 copies.

Affiliation: Change in Artistic Direction

After spending some time at his parents' home in Wisconsin, Vernon drove to his father's hunting cabin in Dunn County, northwest of Eau Claire, where he would spend the winter months mostly in solitude. He had no plans to record an album or write songs but just wanted to get away and retrieve some sense of self. He did practical chores like chopping wood, and he even hunted deer. In a revealing interview with Guy Raz for the National Public Radio program *All Things Considered* (3 Jan. 2009), Vernon talked about his time at the cabin, describing it as "an attempt to still my life, I think. I think you can lose track of your inner voice because there are so many people around, there are so many distractions, there are so many voices and influences. And for me, it was really beautiful to sort of reconnect with this person that I felt like I haven't really had that much quiet time with since I was a little boy." And with regard to making music in the cabin, Vernon said: "I brought my musical gear with me because I thought, you know, it would be a smart idea to have it with me. But I think I was so confused; it was at a point in my life that I think everybody goes through where something needs to budge and then something needs to change, and you just—you can't really be aware of that because you're so within it, you're so in the present moment. And that present moment seems to be constantly fleeting at the same time."

After a few weeks of near solitude in the woods, Vernon felt that he had to start making music—so he played his guitar and sang. In his singing he emphasized emotions and feelings, and he began to work on his falsetto; he also experimented with voice-manipulation effects. Some of the songs he played and recorded in the cabin he had already written prior to leaving North Carolina, but his singing and overall approach to how the music should feel and sound was new. Vernon had no idea how popular his cabin recordings would become.

June 2011 saw the release of Bon Iver's second full-length album, *Bon Iver, Bon Iver,* which received mostly positive reviews. It was recorded at April Base, a studio Vernon had built in Fall Creek, Wisconsin. Although the new album features more instruments than *For Emma* and delved into different musical styles (1970s country rock, 1980s synthesizer-driven rock, 1990s art rock, and others), it still has Vernon's voice—falsetto and multiple tracks—as its central musical foundation and emotional force. Once again the lyrics are more focused on sound and feel rather than on concrete meaning. All the song titles are geographic names, some real and some made up. The song "Calgary" transitions from a mellow, acoustic mood to a more rock-centered one. "Perth" features heavy drums and "Lisbon, OH" has synthesizers.

Perhaps the most controversial song on the album is "Beth/Rest," the last track: it has a 1980s soft-rock feel that is very different from Vernon's previous Bon Iver works. The critics who did not like the album singled out this song as a primary example of the record's faults. In a review for the *Chicago Sun-Times* (20 July 2011), Thomas Conner argued that "there's a crucial missing ingredient: soul." Conner called most of the album's songs "claustrophobic and flat compositions." Most critics, however, did not share that view. As Chris Richards wrote for the *Washington Post* (21 June 2011): ''The best album of our halfway-over year proves that rock-and-roll isn't dead—it's only sleeping.

And dreaming. Vividly." Similarly, Dorian Lynskey put *Bon Iver* on the "best albums of 2011" list for the London *Guardian* (12 Dec. 2011), calling the album "rich and expansive without being the least bit grandiose." Writing for the *San Francisco Chronicle* (19 June 2011), Aiclin Vaziri observed, "The music feels as if it's suspended in air, as if getting a taste of mainstream pop only confirmed Vernon's desire to make music that sets a mood but doesn't require motion. The naive charm of the first album has dissipated a bit, but *Bon Iver, Bon Iver* still feels like a shot of integrity in a world of fake."

In February 2012, Bon Iver competed with The Band Perry, Nicki Minaj, J. Cole, and Skrillex to win the Grammy Award for Best New Artist. The band's album, *Bon Iver* also won the Grammy for Best Alternative Album, beating out albums from Death Cab for Cutie, Foster the People, and Radio Head.

Further reading

Braiker, Brian. "Into the Wild with Bon Iver." *Rolling Stone* 19 Feb. *2009:* 19. Print.

Caramanica, Jon. "Kanye's Boy in Eau Claire." *New York Times* 5 June 2011: MM28. Print.

Eells, Josh. "The Sound of Silence." *Rolling Stone* 23 June 2011: 70-73. Print.

Frere-Jones, Sasha. "Into the Woods: The Bon Iver Sound." *New Yorker* 12 Jan. 2009: 70-71. Print.

Greenwald, Andy. "Bon Iver." *Entertainment Weekly* 24 June 2011: 73. Print.

Fats Waller

Jazz musician songwriter

Born: May 21, 1904; New York, New York
Died: December 15, 1943; Kansas City, Missouri
Primary Field: Jazz
Group Affiliation: Ensemble performer

Introduction

As composer, organist, pianist, band leader, and vocalist, Fats Waller achieved great fame, even though many listeners never really got to the music behind his "mugging" and "jivey" humor. Of course, these were important, too. As Mark Schubart expressed it: "He's as much fun to watch as to listen to. He paws the piano lovingly, wags his head, grunts out lyrics in a completely untuneful voice, and keeps up a running fire of gags and comments."

Fats Waller.

Early Life

The "black Horowitz," as Oscar Levant called him, was born in New York City on May 21, 1904, and christened Thomas Wright Waller. His parents were the Rev. Edward Martin and Adeline (Lockett) Waller. At one time his father, an Abyssinian Baptist minister, had one of the largest Protestant congregations in the country, but in spite of this the family did not always have as much money as they needed. Waller's musical talent came from both branches of the family. His grandfather, Adolph Waller, was a violinist; his mother played piano and organ, and sang.

Waller's father considered jazz "music from the devil's workshop" and wanted "Thomas to become a minister." Music won out, undoubtedly through the inspiration of Thomas' mother who died when he was still quite young. By the time he was ten he was playing piano and organ at students' concerts and playing the organ in his father's church. He was a member of the orchestras of his grade and high schools. Playing with them was more important to him than studying, and when he got low marks, especially in mathematics, he claimed it was because he "had a mind-full of music." However, in his leisure moments he read Nick Carter novels as well as books on musical theory. And he ran errands for a grocery store and "pigs' feet stand" to earn his spending money of seventy-five cents a week.

One day in 1918, while attending De Witt Clinton High School, he was asked to play the organ at the Lincoln Theatre during the illness of the regular organist. He recalled as one of the great thrills of his life the first time he sat at the console of that $10,000 Wurlitzer Grand organ. Following this temporary job he was called back to become regular organist at $23 weekly, and his high school studies were cut short by his career. About this time he met James P. Johnson, dean of Harlem piano players. Johnson taught him ragtime and also taught him so much about piano style in general that there were many similarities between the styles of the two pianists.

Life's Work

In Boston in 1919, while on tour with a vaudeville act as pianist, Waller wrote his first tune and called it *Boston Blues.* Later, when he changed its title to *Squeeze Me,* it became one of the best known jazz pieces. The early 1920s were fruitful for the young composer pianist. Under the tutelage of James P. Johnson he became one of the most prominent pianists in Harlem, playing at Harlem parlor socials (rent parties), in cabarets, night clubs, and in vaudeville. He met composers like Irving Berlin and George Gershwin. During this period he cut his first player piano rolls for QRS, getting $100 per roll, and it was not long before he made his first records (he made hundreds since) as accompanist for Sara Martin. He was paid $250 for two sides. He also recorded with Clara and Bessie Smith, and in 1926 he toured in vaudeville with the latter. In 1927 he returned to the Lincoln Theatre, this time with his own band.

While the stout, good-natured composer was developing his talent as entertainer-pianist, he continued his studies. Two of his teachers, Carl Bohm and Leopold Godowski, were well known in the "art music" world. To an early manager, Phil Ponce, Waller gave credit for helping him over rough spots which, however, diminished as his composing talents developed. By 1928 he was already writing show music, and in that year he and James P. Johnson shared composing honors for *Keep Shufflin'.* This began a long period of writing show music, in which Waller usually collaborated with the talented lyricist, Andy Razaf, who was also one of his closest personal friends.

Keep Shufflin' had in it one of Waller's many delightfully melodic tunes, *Willow Tree.* In 1929 he did the score for the *Hot Chocolates* revue, which had among its hit tunes his famous *Ain't Misbehavin'.* This was followed by the production of several shows at Harlem night clubs, notably Connie's Inn. In these years (late 1920's and early 1930's) he wrote such hits as *Honeysuckle Rose, Keepin' Out of Mischief Now,* and *I've Got a Feelin' I'm Fallin'.*

Fats Waller had a nasal baritone voice that fit his entertaining "jive" patter. His piano and band styles were more serious, yet some of his best numbers were those that intrigued the listener with the light, frothy exuberance that made Fats a favorite of the "house-rent" parties. He recorded his organ work and his solo piano and also recorded piano duets with fellow pianists.

"In listening to Fats," states *The Jazz Record Book,* "one feels that his is a simple style of off-beats and notes on the beat, with occasional triplet phrases, plus his dynamic left hand. The uniqueness of the style, though, consists in the way he brings down the off-beats—forcefully, but not suddenly." And Hugues Panassié observed: "There is a symmetry in his solos but it is a symmetry always finally broken at just the right moment, at the precise point necessary to avoid monotony." There was a third characteristic of his piano style described in the first book mentioned. "He likes to heighten tension by 'worrying' a passage by repeating a phrase—a trick passed on to Count Basie and that even Lionel Hampton seems to have picked up somewhere along the way."

In July 1938 Waller left for a second European tour in which he drew record crowds everywhere he appeared. It was a concert tour, and Waller, who was "undoubtedly the only jazz musician who has ever played the organ of Notre Dame de Paris," played classical selections as well as jazz. He visited England, Scotland, Holland, Denmark, and Sweden, was held over for a week at the London Palladium, and in September did a television broadcast from Alexandria Palace. Returning to America, he opened at the Yacht Club in October and left there in January only because the demand for his theatre appearances was so great. In 1939 he again toured England and Scotland. He has since appeared m two films, *Hooray for Love* and *King of Burlesque.*

Waller was completely unaffected in his attitude toward music in general, and especially toward jazz. "I am nobody to get mighty about swing," is the way Fats puts it. "I think it is just a musical phase of our social life." He seemed most at home in that medium

Affiliation: Band Member

In 1932 Fats toured England and the Continent, playing at such internationally known spots as London's Kit Kat Club and the Moulin Rouge in Paris. In 1933 he was in Cincinnati, broadcasting a program over WLW. On this program they called him a "harmful little armful." Later he made his debut over WABC and the Columbia network. His recording activities continued on steadily, both in the United States and in England. He headed several "mixed" recording dates, at which both white and Negro musicians played, and several of his records are still among the most treasured in the jazz collector's library, particularly his small band work. He also played with other groups, sometimes under his own name, as on the Ted Lewis record of *Dallas Blues,* and sometimes under the pseudonym "Maurice," as on the Lee Wiley disc. Maurice is the name of his youngest son.

although he has tried his hand at a piano suite called *London Sketches.*

Personal Life

Fats Waller was five feet, eleven inches tall, has black hair and brown eyes. He once weighed 310 pounds but eventually went down to 285—still enough to warrant the description, "girth full of blues." In 1926 he married Anita Priscilla Rutherford. This was his second marriage. He had two children, both boys.

Waller lived with his family in a modern brick house overlooking a park at St. Albans, Long Island. He had a built-in Hammond Electric organ, an automatic recorder and phonograph with an immense library of records, a Steinway Grand, and a varied library of music that included both classic and swing. He had two Lincolns, but his favorite form of travel was by boat.

Waller's tastes were so extensive and so varied that it would be hard to classify him. He said that his favorite poets were Longfellow and Andy Razaf. His favorite great characters in history were Lincoln, Bach, Theodore Roosevelt, and Gershwin, and modern greats in his opinion included Franklin Roosevelt, Toscanini, Whiteman, and "my wife." He liked to watch baseball but did not play it. When asked what hobbies he had, he replied: "Music, music, music, and more music."

Fats Waller died on December 15, 1943 near Kansas City, Missouri after contracting pneumonia during a cross-country train trip. More than 4,000 people his funeral in Harlem, at which Adam Clayton Powell, Jr. delivered the eulogy. In 1978 the Broadway revue *Ain't Misbehavin',* which highlighted Waller's music, opened at the Longacre Theatre and ran for more than 1600 performances. One of its stars, Nell Carter, won a Tony Award for her part. The show was revived in 1988.

Further Reading

Down Beat 9:3 F 1 '42 pors
N Y *Herald Tribune* p14 Ja 14 '42
N Y *World-Telegram* N 12 '38 pars; p14 Ja 15 '42
PM p57 Ja 11 '42 por; p24 Ja 15 '42
International Motion Picture Almanac 1938-39
Panassie, H. *Hot Jazz* 1936
Smith, C. E. *Jazz Record Book* 1942

Bruno Walter

Symphony and opera conductor

Born: September 15, 1876; Berlin, Germany
Died: February 17, 1962; Beverly Hills, California
Primary Field: Classical
Group Affiliation: Solo conductor

Introduction

Bruno Walter was called "a true German in his solid musicianship, in his enormous knowledge of the musical repertoire, and his sincerely artistic approach." But it was in America, with its great orchestras and with the Metropolitan Opera, that he demonstrated these qualities, for Walter was insufficiently "German" to conform to the standards of Germany and Austria during the Nazi era.

Early Life

This eminent conductor was born Bruno Walter Schlesinger in the city of Berlin, where his father was a poor Jewish shop keeper. When he was only four he excited the attention of an old musician whom his family met on vacation. The child's sense of pitch was uncanny, his feeling for rhythm remarkable, the musician discovered, as he listened to Bruno whistle and hum. Caught up by his enthusiasm, Bruno's mother taught him piano but after less than a year of instruction found that her son had progressed far beyond her. It meant sacrifices, but a teacher was hired. By the time he was eight, young Bruno was applying for a scholarship at Berlin's *Singakademie,* and he got it, too, after a testimonial from the director that stated: "Every inch a musician." By the time he was nine he had made his official debut there, playing at a students' recital, and he had composed a duet for piano and violin as a birthday present for his father.

Getting a musical education was a struggle which meant long stretches accompanying singers at fifty *Pfennige* an hour, hours spent poring over scores in the State library, continual saving and scrimping in order to hear an occasional concert, and hard study under Ehrlich, Bussler, and Radecke at the Stern Conservatory in Berlin. During these years Walter was not only studying the piano; he was preparing himself to become a conductor. He got his first chance in 1893 when he was only seventeen, directing a performance of Lortzing's *Der Waffenschmied* in Cologne. The press was favorable, and Walter's career was launched.

Life's Work

From Cologne Walter went to Hamburg in 1894 as coach of the opera there, then under the leadership of the great conductor and composer, Gustav Mahler. Mahler befriended and encouraged Walter and gave direction to his art, and Walter, in turn, "worshiped Mahler as a personality and as an artist." Walter remained with Mahler for two seasons, learning about conducting, operatic production, staging, lighting, and scene designing, learning how to handle opera singers and choruses. And then he left Mahler to present what he had learned from him in Breslau, in Pressburg and finally, in 1898, in Riga, at the opera where Wagner had conducted in his early years.

Walter remained at Riga until 1900, when he joined the Berlin State Opera. After a year in that post, in 1901 he settled with his newly acquired wife, the former Elsa Wirthschaft, in Vienna, there to remain for ten years. Mahler was head of the Imperial Opera there and Bruno its first conductor, and "during this brilliant decade in Vienna, opera was carried by Mahler and Walter to a height which it had seldom attained in Europe before and never has since." After Mahler's death in 1911 Walter became head of the Imperial Opera, but in 1913 he left to become Felix Mottl's successor at the Munich Opera House. For ten years he conducted a repertoire concentrating on Wagner and Mozart, presenting concerts that created a furore in the musical world. He was responsible, too, for the importance and popularity of the Munich Music Festivals. The First World War interrupted the career of some musicians, but not his, for the Government exempted him from military service as indispensable in his post.

Walter's reputation as a conductor grew during these years, and in the 1920's he was in great demand all over Europe. He conducted in Brussels, Barcelona, Stockholm, Warsaw, Budapest, Moscow, Prague, and every other city where there were great operas and orchestras. In 1922 he made his American debut conducting the old New York Symphony Society, but his stature was not apparent at the time, partly because of a strong current of antagonism toward German conductors. It is reported that he found it hard to maintain discipline and "in spite of himself was compelled to tolerate readings whose standards were lower than those to which he had been accustomed." Nevertheless, Walter was invited back each season until 1926 and at the same time appeared with other American orchestras in Boston, Detroit, and Minneapolis. In the spring of 1924, too, he led the first German season since the War at London's Covent Garden, and he continued to lead German programs there for the eight years following.

Walter had left his position in Munich in 1923, "driven by intrigue and pre-Hitler '42 anti-Semitism," and in 1925 he became director of the Städtische Opera in Berlin. Here, with "incandescent and revitalized recreations of classic German opera and healthy experiments with new operatic expressions," he brought great prestige to the opera house and to himself, transforming it in the four years he was there from a second-rate opera house into one of Europe's first-rank houses. He received further glory from his leadership of the Salzburg Festivals from 1925 until the *Anschluss* of Germany and Austria. In Salzburg, inspired by Mozart traditions and the assistance of great artists, he "surpassed even his own great achievements as a conductor and musician."

It was at Walter's suggestion that Toscanini '42 came to Salzburg, and the two conductors were the guiding spirits of these great musical events.

Disagreements with municipal authorities about programs and about the scale of the productions led to Walter's resignation from the Städtische Opera in Berlin in 1929. Walter went to the United States to conduct the San Francisco Summer Symphony at the Hollywood Bowl and then returned to Germany to take over the leadership of the Leipzig Gewandhaus Orchestra. His concerts there were interspersed with guest-conductorships abroad, with the New York Philharmonic Symphony in 1932 and each year thereafter through the 1934 to 1935 season, and with concerts all over Europe. It was right after Walter's return from eleven weeks of conducting the Philharmonic in 1933 that the German authorities banned his Leipzig concerts on the grounds that they threatened "public order and security."

Walter went to London, where he received tremendous ovations and where one newspaper commented: "Germany, in expelling Walter, has made a present of its greatest conductor to the rest of the world." And then he went to Vienna, where there were "such ovations as are rare, even in Vienna." Here Walter commented, obliquely, on the fate that had driven him from his country. After one concert he observed that in the world of music all men were friends and brothers.

It was in 1938, only a month after his contract had been renewed for three years, that Walter had to resign this position, too, for questionnaires on ancestry were being circulated throughout his orchestra. The French Government immediately asked him to take up his residence in France, and upon his acceptance he was made a French citizen and a commander of the Légion d'Honneur. Holland received him with open arms, too and after his guest-conducting of the Concertgebouw Orchestra he was made a grand officer of the Orange-Nassau Order. While in Holland Walter learned that his younger daughter, Lotte, had been arrested in Vienna for anti-Nazi activities, and his anguish was great until she was finally set free.

On March 11, 1939 Walter conducted the first of many concerts for the NBC Symphony Orchestra, substituting for its regular conductor, Toscanini. His experiences then and later with radio work led him to a number of interesting conclusions. There was no doubt, he felt, that the radio helped the understanding and performances of great music. But there were too many people who thought of radio concerts "as merely a background for conversation," who failed to be "intense and alert every minute." And even when an audience listened well, still radio listening is "the same in music as in love; like talking to a sweetheart by telephone instead of being with her."

In the spring of 1939 Walter was back in Europe, filling an intensive schedule of engagements in various cities. It was while he was conducting a music festival at Lucerne that he received the tragic news of the death of his elder daughter, Marguerite. The tragedy of World War II came soon after, and Walter once more left Europe for America. He came to this country without a regular orchestral or opera post, without even a permanent home, his possessions remaining in a rented house in Switzerland. "But I am never homesick," he explained with dignity, "because my home is in music."

It wasn't long before he was occupied. In November and December 1939 he was conducting the Los Angeles Philharmonic during the illness of Otto Klemperer; in February and March of 1940 he led the NBC Symphony Orchestra; in the fall of that same year he was back in Los Angeles again; and in January and February 1941 he was conducting the New York Philharmonic, after an appearance with the Minneapolis Symphony.

During January 1941, Walter was also busy making his first American recordings for Columbia, increasing the large repertoire of recorded music for which he has long been famous. And in February of that year he made his first long-awaited appearance in the orchestra pit of the Metropolitan Opera. The date was February 14, and the opera was Beethoven's *Fidelio,* a fitting subject, for, as Walter said: "The principal issue of our time is the theme of Beethoven's *Fidelio*. . . Should we live as slaves or should every possible sacrifice be made in order to secure our liberty?" As the opera progressed "the Metropolitan rocked with cheers and bravos, wave upon wave of thunderous applause," and thirteen curtain calls summoned Walter to the stage when it was finished. It was, the critics agreed, "one of the finest performances of Beethoven's *Fidelio* ever given in the Western Hemisphere," and by "one of the great operatic interpreters of our time."

Walter was happy to be at the Metropolitan surrounded by artists with whom he had worked abroad. "It is like coming home again to the world in which I lived as a child in Berlin, the world where I have labored since I was seventeen as a coach in Cologne—the world of opera." These artists, happy to have him there, presented him with a rosewood and silver baton in recognition of his greatness as a conductor and his ability, in the words of Lotte Lehmann, "to develop the essential individuality of the artist with whom he is working."

Walter's second undertaking at the Metropolitan was Mozart's *Don Giovanni,* which Olin Downes found "the finest interpretation of Mozart that the writer has witnessed in this lyric theatre. It made history for the institution and did honor to its traditions." His final performance of that season was Smetana's *Bartered Bride,* and "the sovereign virtue" of the presentation, critics believed, "lay in the orchestra pit, where Mr. Walter conducted with warm feeling and lyricism and evident love of the score."

These operatic performances, after much symphonic conducting, convinced Walter of how much he enjoyed conducting opera. "Opera," he admitted, "bears the. stigmata of non-perfection. But in non-perfection there may be a demoniac attraction and power. The warring elements of drama and music, speech and song, are the very forces which give opera so much of its virility and its possibilities for varied and original achievement." As a conductor, observers have pointed out, "Walter's delight in building up a role or a scene is without precedent. He is essentially a man of the theatre—rich in imagination. He loves to work out new ways . . . He can make opera scenes which have become dull and lifeless through routine repetition . . . vital and new."

A month after his last opera engagement, in April 1941, Bruno Walter, with his wife and daughter, Lotte, applied for American citizenship. He considered the American way of life "the desirable way" for himself and his family, he said. In the fall of 1941 he was conducting the New York Philharmonic in a two weeks' engagement and during the 1941 to 1942 Metropolitan season he was active presenting German opera. In January 1942 he again took over the Philharmonic and in April he re-appeared with it for a two weeks' engagement. He has been engaged to lead the Philharmonic for six weeks in the 1942 to 1943 season and plans to present the Bach *St. Matthew Passion* during that time.

Among musicians and music lovers Bruno Walter is known as a conductor of catholic abilities. His readings of Wagner are "deeply sympathetic and searching"; his Haydn has "balance, precision, euphony, grace, and elegance"; his Mozart is famous for its clarity and understanding; he is one of the foremost interpreters of Bruckner, whom he feels he knows more and more as he gets older; he is probably the greatest conductor of Mahler; he has distinguished himself in the presentation of American music, in the future of which he strongly believes. According to one critic, no matter what he is playing Walter's "performances are notable for their refinement, their subtlety, and precision of tonal balances . . . He never strives for bizarre, startling effects. His readings are marked by their polish, their carefully shaded nuances, their poetry and fidelity to the composer's intention." David Ewen, however, disagrees. "Liberty with tempi, with a preponderance of rubato, exaggeration of dynamics, reconstruction of the melodic phrase are occasional intruders into the performance," he says. But even he concedes Walter's "tremendous vitality and strength" and his sensitivity.

Walter is one of the few conductors extant who omits tantrums, tempers, and vigorous gestures from his leadership of an orchestra. Standing firmly in one spot, "his suggestive and animating power over an orchestra is little short of hypnotic. He leads with the expression of his eyes and facial muscles as well as with his hands, and requires a minimum of gesticulation to achieve a maximum of effect." His memory is astonishing, and even away from an orchestra he can play on the piano any remote theme that crops up in conversation and indicate the proper instrumentation. He is, too, one of the few conductors who dares to play and conduct at the same time, and his performance of Mozart's D Minor Concerto, K. 466; for instance, is famous for that reason.

Walter has never learned to play any other instrument than the piano, which he considers "the most complete of instruments," though he tried. His attempts at the violin, fairly late in life, were unsuccessful. "With the mastery of one instrument to my credit," he

Affiliation: Conductor Vienna State Opera

After serving as guest conductor of the Vienna State Opera following personal negotiations with Chancellor Kurt von Schuschnigg, in 1935 Walter was made artistic adviser and permanent conductor of this opera house. An American reporter, familiar only with the dignified respect and understanding that Walter's conducting had received in the United States, attended one of his performances. He was amazed and excited at the enthusiasm. "Here the town storms the halls at his approach," he wrote.

confessed, "I could not bear the sheer nervous strain of beginning another, with its elementary scratching, and I gave it up." He has composed for instruments other than his own, though, and he is the author of Schiller's *Siegesfest* for chorus, soli, and orchestra as well as of a piano quintet, a string quartet, a piano trio, a violin sonata, and many symphonies and songs.

After relocating to the United States permanently in the early 1940s, he was active in the musical life of his adopted country, especially with the New York Philharmonic. He was offered the post of conductor with that orchestra but declined it, claiming that he was too old for the position. After the end of World War II he also led concerts in Europe. He suffered from heart disease, and after a heart attack in 1957 his concert performances were greatly reduced. His time in America coincided with major changes in recording technology, with the introduction of long-playing vinyl records and later stereophonic recording. Starting in the late 1940s he recorded many major orchestral works, concentrating on the Austro-Germanic repertory. He twice recorded the complete symphonies of Beethoven and Brahms, and made notable recordings of the music of Haydn, Mozart, Wagner, Mahler, and Bruckner. He also made the premiere recording of Samuel Barber's First Symphony.

Personal Life

Dark-haired, dark-eyed, Bruno Walter had a massive head, a sturdy, strong figure. "There is sweetness in his face, a pleasant preoccupation in his eyes, a smile upon his lips," an interviewer once wrote. "His voice is tranquil, even in tone, rather deliberate. He does not punctuate his remarks with his hands, which the nervous conductor is supposed to do. He has a trick of uttering a profound truth in disarmingly simple language." In his spare time he often wrote: he was the author of a biography of Gustav Mahler, published abroad in 1936 and in English in 1941, and of pamphlets and essays, one of the best known of them, published in 1935, called *Von den Moralischen Kräften der Musik* (About the Moral Forces of Music). He also wrote an autobiography, *Theme and Variations,* published in 1946, and *On Music and Music Making,* published in 1961. Outside of writing and reading serious literature and philosophy, he had no hobbies, no idiosyncrasies, no avocations. When an interviewer, familiar with the odder diversions of the usual conductor, expressed surprise, Walter quoted Shaw's epigram: "Happy is the man whose hobby is his profession." Sometimes he added: "Music is magic enough."

Bruno Walter died on February 17, 1962 at his home in Beverley Hills, California of a heart attack. When informing members of the New York Philharmonic of Walter's death, Leonard Bernstein described him as "one of the saints of music—a man all kindness and warmth, goodness, and devotion."

Further Reading

Etude 52:75-6 F '34 por; 56:706 N '38 por
N Y Times VII p8+ 0 8 '33 por
Newsweek 17:52 Ja 20 '41 por
Theatre Arts 26:50-4 Ja '42 il por
Time 37:38+ F 24 '41 por
Armsby, L. W. *Musicians Talk* p28-33,113-23 1935
Ewen, D. *Man with the Baton* p241-69 1936
Ewen D. ed. *Living Musicians* 1940
Kaufmann, H. L. and Hansl, E. E. vom B. *Artists in Music of Today* p109 1933
Thompson, 0. ed. *International Cyclopedia of Music and Musicians* 1939
Who's Who in America 1942-43
Who's Who in American Jewry 1938-39

David S. Ware

Saxophonist

Born: Nov. 7, 1949; Plainfield, New Jersey
Died: October 18, 2012; New Brunswick, New Jersey
Primary Field: Jazz
Group Affiliation: Band leader

Introduction

In an article for the Village Voice *(August 7, 2001), the music critic Gary Giddins called the David S. Ware Quartet "the best small band in jazz today. . . . Every time I see Ware's group or return to the records, it flushes the competition from memory." Ware, who played the saxophone professionally for over 30 years, was recognized since the mid- 1990s as one of the finest musicians in the world of free jazz. Building on the most experimental music of the jazz saxophonists John Coltrane, Sonny Rollins, and Albert Ayler, Ware's fiery, improvised sound was also heavily influenced by his interest in meditation and yoga and, in keeping with his love of free jazz, was unrestricted by traditional concepts of melody, structure, or rhythm.*

EARLY LIFE

David S. Ware was born on November 7, 1949 in Plainfield, New Jersey, and was raised in nearby Scotch Plains. His father owned hundreds of jazz records, which Ware often heard while growing up. When he was around 10 years old, he announced that he wanted to play the drums, whereupon his father, who loved listening to horns, encouraged him to take up the tenor saxophone instead. "I've always felt that rhythm was my primary motivation," Ware told William Sacks for *Perfect Sound Forever* (November 1998), ''the first thing which I seek to represent musically, and I guess it felt that way very early on." Because he learned to play the saxophone, he told Sacks, "I got a better primary musical education than I would have if I'd become a drummer, just because of the attitudes toward drummers in the schools at the time. I mean, the classical basis wasn't there, and it wasn't like modern jazz was even being considered." While most jazz musicians develop mastery of their instruments by learning hundreds of different tunes in different keys, Ware recalled to Glenn Good in an interview for the Evanston-Chicago radio station WNUR (March 11, 1996), "I would pick up the horn and I would just play. Because I didn't have a lot of other musicians to develop with in terms of jazz. In terms of jazz, I had basically myself and one other musician, and that was a drummer. I didn't have the rhythm section and this type of thing to develop the tunes with, to learn the tunes with." Ware did, however, have exposure to many newer jazz pieces through a friend of his father's, a neighbor who had an up-to-date collection from which Ware borrowed the first John Coltrane album he ever heard. "What [Coltrane] did for me was the idea of transcendence, using music as a vehicle for transcendence," Ware told Good. Ware also bought transcriptions of jazz recordings by such legendary saxophonists as Coltrane, Rollins, and Charlie Parker and learned to approximate their solos alongside a drummer. He recalled to Good, "I would hear a concept on the record. I would hear Sonny Rollins' conception on the record, his overall concept, Coltrane's overall concept, and then I would just try to get that concept, that style in the early years. And that's basically how I developed."

At the age of 12, Ware decided that he wanted to focus on music for the rest of his life. "Being committed to this music has enabled my character to develop," he told Good. "The point is, I had to be committed to this ideal life I've had since I was 12 years old, and more or less always knowing that I wanted to do this like this." In his junior high and high schools, he played alto or baritone saxophone in the dance band, the marching band, the concert band, and the orchestra as well as the New Jersey All-State Band. In addition, he took private saxophone lessons. At 17 Ware enrolled at the Berklee School of Music, in Boston, Massachusetts, on a scholarship. His experience there was decidedly mixed, as Berkelee's teachers did not have high regard for his musical heroes, who included Ornette Coleman and Thelonious Monk—men who were pushing the boundaries of jazz. Furthermore, Ware's interest in free jazz ran counter to the school's focus on musical notation. Despite that conflict, he made a personal breakthrough during that time, deciding to focus on the tenor saxophone instead of the alto and baritone; and in spite of his indifference to much of what was taught at Berklee, he made honors during the three semesters he attended the school. In addition, at Berkelee Ware met his first mentors, who gave him practical advice and exposed him to more new music. One of those, Herb Pomeroy, taught musical structure in terms of harmonic tension; another, Joe Hanna (now known as Abdul Hannan), combined his music instruction with an introduction to meditation and yoga, two spiritual practices that have become essential to Ware's life and music and whose importance would be reinforced by his friendship with Sonny Rollins. "When you sit down in meditation, you start with form—you are this person in this position, with this name—and you drop all of that and go from form to the formless back to form again," Ware was quoted as saying on the *Jazz & Blues Loft* (on-line). "Basically this is what the music does. It goes from the finite to the infinite, from boundaries to the boundless, and it's beautiful, man. There's a path you can trace, a release and bliss, and when you come back you bring some of that back with you. It's a state of mind, of course." During the spring semester of 1968, Ware became ill and returned home to recuperate. Also during that spring he formed his first group, a quintet called the

Third World, with two members on saxophone and one each on electric piano, congas, and violin. The group recorded a tape of their music, which was influenced by both free jazz and African- and Latin-inflected jazz. They sent the tape to a magazine owned by a record company, but the magazine's staff, lacking the right equipment to play the tape, never listened to it. Ware returned to Berklee in September 1969 and completed another semester, but before the spring term, he and the faculty both decided that he should not continue at the school. Ware remained in Boston, where he played occasional gigs with his group, Apogee. (Ware had also played some informal practice sessions with Sonny Rollins in the late 1960s.) In 1973 the members of Apogee moved to New York City and became part of the "loft jazz" scene, which found experimental jazz musicians performing and living in cheap Manhattan lofts. "There was incredible energy coming from New York at the time," Ware told William Sacks, "and I knew that I was interested in the flow of the new music, in finding other musicians who shared that interest. So in that sense I knew where things were happening and wanted to be part of it." Ware moved with the rest of Apogee into a house on Canal Street that served as both living quarters and performance space. "I remember this time as being very positive," Ware told Sacks, "the music was being played in some places where you might not have otherwise thought to look for it."

Life's Work

During the early and mid-1970s, Ware toured Europe several times with the legendary free-jazz pianist Cecil Taylor, whose focus at that time was playing one extended, improvised piece of music for each concert or record. Ware played as a member of Taylor's big band at the pianist's famous 1974 concert at Carnegie Hall, in New York, and was heard on Taylor's album *Dark Unto Themselves* (1976). "From Cecil Taylor, I learned this: when you write music, pay attention to its details, deal with it from inside," Ware told Sacks. "Deal with the form, develop it so that it becomes a unique idea in itself, and then when you're playing it, take your cue from the form. Getting to the inner details of a piece was something I remember working on all the time, every time we played in fact." While he found his collaboration with Taylor artistically fulfilling, it did not always satisfy his financial needs; during this time and for much of the 1980s, Ware earned additional money by working as a messenger, delivering food, and driving a cab. He told Glenn Good that he did "whatever I had to do in order to just keep playing the music like I wanted to do it," adding, "I've always known that to do my own thing in the way that I've always wanted to do it, it would take a bit of time. . . . It was like an intuition I had—yeah, you're gonna be involved in music, but in order to really do your own thing, it's going to take some time." Apogee broke up in 1977. In the late 1970s Ware played with the drummer Andrew Cyrille in Cyrilla's group Maono on the albums *Metamusician's Stomp* (1978) and *Special People* (1980). "The style was very rhythmic," Ware told William Sacks, "and I developed ways of playing with the rhythm and being caught in it. . . . Learning to be caught by the rhythm,

Affiliation: Jazz Discipline

Nonetheless, Ware explained, as quoted in a Columbia Records press release, "There's a misunderstanding about the kind of music we play, that there's no discipline, that anything goes. We're fighting to dispel those myths. We're like the Marines coming in to create a platform for the spirit of exploration and freedom in music." "Ware's tenor sound is huge, centered, and multi-hued, all up and down its range," Chris Kelsey wrote for the *All Music Guide* (on-line). "His facility is great, his imagination broad, and his expressive abilities immense. And no saxophonist now active plays with more unadulterated passion. Without question, he is a very, very fine, maybe even great, player." Ware formed his band as a trio in 1988; the two mainstays in the group, whose work was called the most exciting music by a jazz ensemble since that of the John Coltrane Quartet of 1960–65, were the bassist William Parker and pianist Matthew Shipp. Some critics complained that Ware's quartet recorded too many albums in a similar vein, but starting in the 2000s Ware broadened the array of music he recorded, occasionally softening his tone and adding electronic instruments. He described his music to Nils Jacobson for *All About Jazz* (on-line) as "music to travel. If you close your eyes, you can travel with this music. It's moving within oneself. It could be like a moving meditation through music. So it's different functions of music." He added, "The whole message behind what it is I do is that we are part of nature. And realize that, and access that. So there's more true harmony amongst human beings, and in nature. We're not separate from nature."

that's something which I've tried to apply to my own writing as well." Also in the late 1970s, Ware released his first solo albums: *From Silence to Music* (1978), on the Palm label, and *The Birth of a Being* (1979), on Hat Hut. The latter record had been recorded with Apogee in 1977 but was released under Ware's name. In the early 1980s Ware toured Europe with Andrew Cyrilla.

Starting in 1984 Ware began to withdraw from performing and instead worked extensively on rebuilding and developing his own sound. For the first half of the 1980s, he did not perform on any recording. Rather, as he told Glenn Good, "I started paying more attention to my relationship to chords, what I was doing to my relationship to chords, and scales, and [chord] changes. I was starting to pay attention—well, how am I actually moving through this or that? And it makes a difference when you start real slow." While Ware was refining his style, he occasionally performed, putting on a couple of concerts in New York City in 1984 and making a tour to Europe in 1985 with a trio he had formed. Two years later he appeared on the trumpeter Ahmed Abdullah's record *Ahmed Abdullah and the Solomonic Quintet.* At around this time he formed a new trio with the experimental jazz bassist William Parker, who had worked with Ware in Taylor's band, and the drummer Marc Edwards. In 1988 that trio recorded the album *Passage to Music,* consisting entirely of original material by Ware. On most of the record Ware played tenor saxophone, but he also performed one song apiece on the saxello (a rare, reconfigured soprano saxophone) and the stritch (a modified alto saxophone dating from the 1920s). By the time of his next release, *Great Bliss, Volume 1* (1990), his trio had grown to a quartet, with the addition of the pianist Matthew Shipp. Ware displayed his instrumental versatility on this album by playing the flute in addition to the three saxophones he had also played on his previous record. Moving among several styles, the album featured forceful free-jazz pieces, including "Forward Motion" and "Thirds," in addition to the more mainstream "Bliss Theme." The quartet's next release was *Flight of I* (1991), which, while far from mainstream jazz, was more accessible than some of his previous material. The record featured Ware's quartet performing avant-garde interpretations of two jazz standards—"There Will Never Be Another You" and ''Yesterdays"—as well as such complex originals as "Aquarian Sound."

In 1992 Ware and his quartet released *Third Ear Recitation.* Before the album was recorded, Edwards had left Ware's group and was replaced on the drums by Whit Dickey. Prominent on the record were two versions of the standard "Autumn Leaves," one of which was played as composed while the other took a far freer approach. In addition to a version of the standard "Angel Eyes" and a take on Sonny Rollins's "East Broadway Run Down," the album featured several intense originals, such as the nine-minute "The Chase." Writing for the *All Music Guide* (on-line), Thorn Jurek commented that the record "is one of David S. Ware's most notorious, yet well-developed and executed recordings. . . . This is truly a record that should be studied for decades to come." The year 1994 saw the release of *Great Bliss, Volume 2,* which was culled from the same sessions as volume one. Also recorded that year was *Cryptology,* a raw and fierce album that opens with "Panoramic," a piece that according to Collin Berry, writing for *HotWired* (on-line), "kicks off with saxophone and piano, roaring like a bonfire with strings of breathless arpeggios that fades as Parker fans its glowing embers with a gentle pizzicato." The experimental-music magazine *Wire* named the record one of its top 45 albums of the year, and the mainstream rock magazine *Rolling Stone* featured the album as part of its lead review on free jazz in the May 18, 1995 issue. David Fricke praised Ware in the review for his "surprisingly warm, enveloping tone and textural ingenuity." Ware followed with *Earthquation* (1995), which Don Snowden criticized in *All Music Guide* (on-line), noting, "The sound is drastically compressed, which creates much density but makes you want to send out a search party for Parker, who's all but buried between Dickey and Shipp, let alone when Ware comes in.... *Earthquation* is almost certainly a lesser work in the David S. Ware discography but the surest conclusion is that the sonic equation will cheat most listeners out of the chance-or the desire-to find out."

The trio's next album, *Dao* (1996). was received with greater applause. Thorn Jurek wrote for *All* Music *Guide,* "The difference ... between *Dao* and any previous recording by Ware [is that) ... this work unfolds not as a series of pieces with something in common, but as a number of demarcations along the intuitive way. There are no 'tunes' on *Dao* as there are on his other records, there are only intervals, brief rests, and changes in direction that all logically lead to the end of the disc.... This is a stunner, and a beautiful example of four musicians listening intently to one another in the process of discovery." *Dao* was followed later that year by another lauded release, *Oblations and Blessings.* In an impressive and probably exhausting session, Ware barely paused for breath for 54 minutes of the 69-minute disk, performing, as Don Snowden wrote for *All Music Guide,* "interval leaps and [Albert] Ayler shrieks, high harmonics and lower-register honks, buzzsaw-quick runs and scale slurs, wringing every possible melodic permutation out of every theme." In 1997 the Ware quartet released *Wisdom of Uncertainty.* The album featured a new drummer, Susie Ibarra, who provided danceable fills and played a wide range of percussive instruments. Commenting on the album, Mike Joyce wrote for the *Washington Post* (September 5, 1997), "Ware ultimately achieves a certain accessibility on his own terms by pouring so much music through his horn, reaching back as far as ancient blues and gospel refrains for inspiration." The group returned in 1998 with *Godspelized,* which Thorn Jurek, in *All Music Guide,* called "purely spiritual music, inspiring, moving, and deeply affecting. It is also one of the greatest examples of the new jazz to reach outside itself and embrace the traditions of the culture around it, [no] matter how dissonant that embrace may be."

In 1998 the David S. Ware Quartet was signed for the first time by a major label, Columbia, in a deal worked out by the renowned mainstream bop trumpeter Branford Marsalis, who was then the label's artistic director. In the *Village Voice* (June 23, 1998), David Yaffe noted that the signing "was the musical equivalent of [James Joyce's difficult novel] *Finnegan's Wake* being selected by the Book of the Month Club." The quartet's first album for the label was *Go See the World* (1998), which Phil Freeman, in a review of a later album for *Culturevulture* (on-line), called "free in the extreme," consisting "of workouts in what was, by then, the time-honored Ware style: minimal, choppy melodic phrases, repeated mantra-like and serving as the launching pad for epic, valve-bursting, reed-crashing solos. Behind him Shipp, Parker and Ibarra constructed a wall of sound like nothing else in contemporary jazz." Other critics found the record restrained in comparison with some of Ware's previous work. One of the album's highlights was a 15-minute meditation on the standard "The Way We Were." Remarking on his treatment of standards, Ware noted to William Sacks, "There's a level on which they just appeal to me as melodies, and on another level they're suggestive of intervals or motifs which seem to me to flow well within that tune, from which I can build something even more freely flowing-something the tune has always suggested without ever having been made explicit, and which comes forth once its motif has been freed of the original structure." Ware and his quartet returned with *Surrendered* (2000), featuring a new drummer, Guillermo E. Brown, whose background was in funk and rock. The record was much gentler than anything Ware had recorded before and was grounded in swing. Ware had noted in interviews during this time that, having recorded about a dozen albums in a similar manner, he felt it was time to move in a new direction. Included on the album was "Peace Celestial," which Phil Freeman called "one of the most beautiful ballads Ware has ever attempted." At around the time of the release of *Surrendered,* Ware and his quartet performed at each of the four Bell Atlantic Jazz Festivals and at a free outdoor concert at Columbia University, in New York, that drew 10,000 people.

In December 2000 Columbia Records dropped the quartet. Ware and his bandmates returned to an independent label for his next release, *Corridors and Parallels* (2001). That was the first Ware quartet album to include an electronic instrument, in this case a Korg synthesizer, which Shipp and Ware programed with such sounds as organ tones, rhythms from various cultures, and hurricane noises. Breaking from tradition even more, the group did not rehearse for the album. *Corridors and Parallels* was chosen as among the year's best jazz releases by the *Village Voice, Jazz Times,* the *Boston Globe, LA Weekly, Seattle Weekly,* and the *Washington City Paper.* In 2001 the group performed their debut engagement at the famed Blue Note club, in New York City.

In 2002 the organization SFJAZZ invited Ware and his quartet to perform in San Francisco his rearrangement of Sonny Rollins's legendary "Freedom Suite," first recorded in 1958. While Rollins's version was roughly 19 minutes in length, the Ware quartet's rendition was twice as long. The group later performed their version of the work at the Le Weekend Festival, in Stirling, Scotland, a major gathering in the world of experimental music, among other venues. They also recorded "Freedom Suite" in the studio and released it in October 2002, on the AUM Fidelity label. "Where Rollins' original bordered on atonality with restrained tension held by the rhythm section, Ware allows the dissonance free rein, or nearly so," Thorn Jurek wrote for *All Music Guide.* "This does not mean he doesn't follow Rollins' dictations for flow or progression, quite the opposite; it's more that Ware allows the dynamic and rhythmic invention a freer passage." Ware noted, as quoted on the AUM Fidelity Web site, "This is a perfect opportunity to show the link between me and

Sonny, an opportune time to show how one generation is built upon another and how the relationships work in the whole stream of music that's called jazz." In 2003 Ware, as part of the new String Ensemble—featuring Mat Maneri on viola and Daniel Bernard Roumain on violin—released *Threads* (2003), which was anchored by a stronger compositional element than some of his other albums. In the *All Music Guide* (on-line), Thorn Jurek gushed, "*Threads* is easily Ware's classic thus far in that it showcases the musician at the height of all of his powers: improvisational, compositional, and as an arranger and bandleader. This is Ware's masterpiece and the first really new compositional statement in jazz in years; if this record isn't at least nominated for a Grammy as 2003's best jazz record, then the entire category deserves to be struck from the ballot."

Regarding Ware's quartet, the three other members recorded extensively on their own. In addition to playing as a drummer with various groups, Guillermo E. Brown released a solo album, *Soul at the Hands of the Machine,* in 2002. In 1994 William Parker founded the Improvisers Collective, which presented free jazz in association with other forms of spontaneous art. He released some 20 albums as a soloist or group leader since 1990—the latest being *Wood Flute Songs* (2013) and *For Those Who Are, Still* (2015). Shipp made more than 20 albums as a soloist or group leader. His most recent release is *The Conduct of Jazz* (2015).

Personal Life

Ware lived with his wife close to where he grew up, in Scotch Plains, New Jersey. He spent much of his time concertizing in Europe. Although he continued to push boundaries in his music throughout his life, he said that he did not listen to much recorded music later in life. Commenting on his musical explorations of his last three decades, he told Glenn Good, "I've basically come full circle to the point where now I feel that I can deal with tunes that I never had a chance to really play before, not really. So now I can put my pure conceptual idea inside of a musical form, inside of a standard, or inside of this, inside of that, without being overshadowed by the form." At one point, Ware told Nils Jacobson, "I would like to mimic the music of the spheres, you know. Cosmic spheres. That's what I want to more or less mimic. The music of the spheres. Which I have heard, and which is a very real thing. . . . I want people one day to *hear* that. And I want them to lose control of themselves. I want them to . . . just break down and cry. . . . For a whole auditorium full of people to do that. Then I'll know that I'm getting closer to be able to manifest that which goes beyond language. I want to be able to manifest that through music."

David S. Ware was diagnosed with kidney failure in 1999 and received a kidney transplant in 2009. The operation was successful, but it required him to take drugs that suppressed the immune system. He died on October 18, 2012 at Robert Wood Johnson University Hospital in New Brunswick, New Jersey of a blood infection.

Further Reading

All About Jazz (on-line), with photo
Perfect Sound Forever (on-line) Nov. 1998, with photo
Village Voice p64 Aug. 7, 2001, with photo
WNUR Jazz Web (on-line) Mar. 11, 1996

Dionne Warwick

Popular singer

Born: December 12, 1940; East Orange, New Jersey
Primary Field: Popular music
Group Affiliation: Burt Bacharach

Introduction

The distinctive, versatile voice of Dionne Warwick, interpreting the moody songs of Burt Bacharach and Hal David on the Scepter label, has demolished the barriers that used to separate pop, rhythm and blues, jazz, and gospel singing. Miss Warwick began recording for Scepter Records in 1962, when the company was a small enterprise specializing in rhythm and blues aimed largely at the Negro market. Within six years the sales of her LP's reached 5,000,000 and those of her singles 6,500,000. Three of the LP's and one of the singles—"Valley of the Dolls"—earned her Gold Records, awards signifying sales of more than 1,000,000 copies each. Miss Warwick herself summed up the significance of her career when she explained to John S. Wilson in an interview for the New York Times *(May 12, 1968): "I came along in an era when kids were tired of hearing songs that just said, 'Boo-boo-boo.' Until then, any Negro singer—except Ella Fitzgerald or Nat Cole, who were jazz or hip pop—was categorized as R & B no matter what they did. I had a different kind of sound that was accepted by both the R & B audience and the pop audience."*

Early Life

Dionne Warwick's professional name derives from a misspelling in one of her early recording contracts. She was born Marie Dionne Warrick in Orange, New Jersey on December 12, 1940. Her parents are Mancel (spelled Marcel in some sources) Warrick, a chef, and Lee Warrick, who was business manager of the Drinkard Singers, a church choir group composed of members of the family and relatives. The group toured professionally for twenty-seven years and became perhaps the most successful gospel group of its time in the United States. It was the first such group to record for RCA Victor and the first to participate in the Newport Jazz Festival. Miss Warwick has a younger sister, Dee Dee, and a younger brother, Mancel, Jr.

The satin-voiced songstress grew up in modest comfort in a devoutly Methodist home—owned, and still lived in, by her parents—in a racially integrated middle-income section of Orange. In adolescence she began to make appearances with the Drinkard Singers at the New Hope Baptist Church in Newark and elsewhere, playing the organ accompaniment for the group and filling in as a singer when one of the adults was absent. "You just know she's had gospel training," her mother has observed. "She's got that deep soul feeling." In 1954 Miss Warwick, her sister, and their cousin Myrna Utley formed their own group, the Gospelaires, and sang together as a trio for seven years. As the only member who could read music, Dionne was the natural leader of the group.

Intending to become a music teacher, Miss Warwick obtained a scholarship to the Hartt College of Music at the University of Hartford, where she enrolled as a student of piano, theory, and voice in the autumn of 1959. During summers and other vacation periods she continued singing with the Gospelaires, who were then doing choral backgrounds for Sam ("The Man") Taylor, the Drifters, and other featured singers and groups at the Apollo in Harlem and other Negro theatres and in recording sessions.

Life's Work

While continuing her studies at the Hartt College of Music, Miss Warwick cut some of the demonstration records that Bacharach and his lyricist, Hal David, used in presenting their compositions to record companies and singers. In 1962 Florence Greenberg at Scepter Records heard one of them and told Bacharach: "Forget the song. Get the girl." Scepter signed a contract with Bacharach, David, and Miss Warwick and soon afterward released the team's "Don't Make Me Over." When the record hit the top ten on the pop charts, Miss Warwick quit school to concentrate on her career. Following an agenda mapped out by Bacharach and her manager, Paul Cantor, she began a ceaseless round of tours, the first of them in France, where the response of audiences was wildly enthusiastic.

(The feeling was reciprocal. "Paris is a home away from home," she said four years later. I've been to Paris a million times. . . . I never learned how to live until Europe.") Eventually she settled into an annual itinerary that took her to world capitals during four months out of each year. During the other eight months she toured college campuses and the Negro theatrical circuit in the United States.

For Jerry Tallmer in the New York *Post* interview Miss Warwick ran through the first three years of her discography: "From 'Don't Make Me Over' we went on to two bombs, and then 'Anyone Who Had a Heart' and then 'Walk On By' and then 'Who Can I Turn To?' and then 'Here I Am' and then two bombs more and then 'Reach Out for Me' and then 'Message to Michael' and 'Trains, Boats, and Planes' and . . . 'I Just Don't Know What to Do.' "Paul Cantor, who was present at the interview kibitzed: "Bombs? I just want to say that her bombs sell over 100,000 copies each."

The young singer's first appearance in a big-time nightclub was at Basin Street East in New York City in 1964. Approaching that engagement with some trepidation, she fortified her performance with special material. "A man, who shall be nameless, was paid a lot of money to write things for me to say, to pick my songs," she has revealed, as quoted in the *New York Times* (May 12, 1968). "Opening night was disastrous. The man wrote something for somebody else, not me. I didn't know who I was. I was very insecure, very uncertain. The audience was uncomfortable. After that first night I threw out everything the man wrote and put in what I'd been doing at college concerts. There's no booze, no knives and forks. My college act works' because I speak to them, not above them." In the poll conducted by the trade magazine *Cash Box* at the end of 1964, Miss Warwick was rated the top rhythm and blues singer recording in the United States. During the 1964-65 television season she appeared three times on the network musical show *Hullabaloo*, and early in 1965 she sang at the Savoy Hotel in London.

With Bacharach conducting the orchestra, Miss Warwick made her debut at Philharmonic Hall in New York's Lincoln Center in October 1966. Singer and orchestra lost each other briefly during the first number, but the rest of the performance was, as a reviewer in *Newsweek* (October 10, 1966) observed, "straight up, like fireworks." The *Newsweek* critic went on: "All [the songs] came out Warwick, in her restrained gospel style, deliciously phrased, uncontrived, and in a polished, flexible voice that was deep purple below and sky-blue above. Not only does she reach up to E natural comfortably, but she stays there in a dazzling acrobatic display of vocal weightlessness, changing colors and dynamics with chilling impact. Cushioning all her songs is an uncanny rhythmic sense. . . . Her body pulsates and twitches. . . . Her songs . . . leave Dianne limp. . . . Even a standing ovation failed to bring an encore. She had nothing left to give."

In October 1966 Miss Warwick performed on the French television program *he Grand Gala du Disque,* which was transmitted to viewers all over Europe through Eurovision, and in the following months on American television she was a guest on the Red Skelton and *Ed Sullivan* shows. In the 1966 *Cash Box* poll she was rated second, after Petula Clark, among all pop recording artists. By the end of 1966, eight million copies of Miss Warwick's single records and four million of her albums had been sold. In 1967 her recording of "Alfie" outsold the versions of that song done by some forty other singers.

Affiliation: Burt Bacharach

Burt Bacharach, then a relatively unknown composer-arranger for Marlene Dietrich and others, met Miss Warwick in 1960. The occasion of their meeting was a session in which Bacharach conducted the Drifters and, in the background, the Gospelaires in a rendition of his song "Mexican Divorce." Dionne caught the composer's attention immediately. "She was singing louder than everybody else," he has recalled, as quoted in *Ebony* (May, 1968), "so I couldn't help noticing her. Not only was she clearly audible, but Dionne had something. Just the way she carries herself, the way she works, her flow and feeling for the music—it was there when I first met her. She had, and still has, a kind of elegance, a grace that very few other people have." Bacharach was impressed with her "tremendous strong side" combined with her "delicacy when singing softly," but he wanted to write songs for her above all because, as he has explained, she was "no play-safe girl. What emotion I could get away with!"

Bacharach's compositions are brilliant but sometimes difficult to sing or play. Miss Warwick recalled her first experience singing a Bacharach solo, at the Apollo Theatre, in an interview with Jerry Tallmer of the New York *Post* (November 26, 1966): "The musicians said: It's impossible to have a 5/4 bar, then a 4/4 bar, then a 7/8 bar,' I said: 'Speak to Bacharach. It's just as difficult for me as for you.' But I've never had a problem anywhere, except that first night at the Apollo. The musicians appreciate that I'm testing their abilities. They're testing mine too." Tallmer noted that she made the last statement "laughing her good laugh."

During 1967 Miss Warwick's bookings included the supper dub rooms of the Fairmont Hotel in San Francisco and the Shoreham Hotel in Washington, D.C. After witnessing her show at the Shoreham, William Rice wrote in the *Washington Post* (December 22, 1967): "She chooses to use her vocal ability rather than relying on stomping and screaming. . . . She can produce the impression of a 'soul-singer's scream' without raising her voice and so practiced is her vocal control and her technical mastery that she glides from a gospel chant to a torchsinger's moan with disarming ease."

In May 1968 she had her initial booking at the Copacabana in New York City, and the critic for *Variety* (May 15, 1968) reported on her opening night at the Copa thus: "Miss Warwick . . . was surprisingly uptight in her initial brace of tunes (she was winning a nervous race with the band). But in the middle of her third number—a belted ballad—she broke out of the clutch in so dramatic a fashion it could have been part of the act. From then on it was swinging all the way with a lively and varied run-through of her hits and such tunes as "The Impossible Dream" and "Battle Hymn of the Republic." At the Newport Jazz Festival in 1968 she attracted an audience of 19,000, a festival attendance record. In recognition of her 1968 hit "Do You Know the Way to San Jose?" she was made an honorary citizen of San Jose, California.

In the autumn of 1968 Miss Warwick completed work before the cameras in the first independent movie production ever undertaken by the Theatre Guild. The film, entitled *Slaves* and released by the Walter Reade Organization in 1969, is a realistic portrayal of the oppressive servitude suffered by blacks in the United States before the Civil War. Costarring with Ossie Davis and Stephen Boyd, Miss Warwick is cast in the nonsinging role of the slave mistress of a corrupt plantation owner, played by Boyd. The motion picture was produced by Peter Lang and directed by Herbert Biberman, who also coauthored the original script with John Killens and Alida Sherman.

The trim 118-pound singer has, according to Jerry Tailmer, "high cheekbones, poignant mouth, fine-drawn chin and jaw, [and] beautiful eyes. More statuesque than her five feet five inches would suggest, especially when she is on stage in a slinky gown, she looks, in the words of one observer, "tall, elegant, and wickedly curvy." Her gowns, costing upwards of $3,500 each, are designed for her by Sarmi, Dior, Balmain and Balenciaga, and although she regularly gives those she does not intend to wear again to young, struggling singers, there is always an abundant supply of them in her wardrobe at any given time.

Untouched in her own life by the harsher aspects and effects of racial prejudice and discrimination (until she experienced Southern segregation as a young adult), Miss Warwick has compassion for the children growing up in ghetto slums, and in 1968 she set up a college scholarship fund for underprivileged students. "I am not a marcher or a sign-carrier," she has said, "but I am busy with the problems of poverty and race." About young people, including hippies and "flower children" (for whom she once performed in Golden Gate Park in San Francisco), she has said: "Man, I dig that scene. . . . It means peace, just peace. If I could have my way, all of my audiences would be like these kids." She has entertained in Vietnam out of concern for the young men dying there.

Later that same year, Warwick earned her first RIAA Certified Gold Single for U.S. sales of over one million units for the single "I Say a Little Prayer" (from her album *The Windows of the World*). "I Say a Little Prayer" became Warwick's biggest U.S. hit to that point, reaching #4 on the U.S. and Canadian Charts and # 8 on the R & B Charts. The tune was also the first RIAA certified USA million seller for Bacharach-David.

Her follow-up to "I Say a Little Prayer," "(Theme from) Valley of the Dolls," was the "B" side of her "I Say a Little Prayer" single. Warwick performed the song, and when the film became a success in the early weeks of 1968, disc jockeys flipped the single and made the single one of the biggest double-sided hits of the rock era and another million seller. At the time, RIAA rules allowed only one side of a double-sided hit single to be certified as Gold, but Scepter awarded Warwick an "in-house award" to recognize "(Theme from) Valley of the Dolls" as a million selling tune.

The LP *Dionne Warwick in Valley of the Dolls,* released in early 1968 and containing the re-recorded version of the movie theme (#2–4 weeks), "Do You Know the Way to San Jose?" and several new Bacharach-David compositions, hit the #6 position on the Billboard album chart and would remain on the chart for over a year and earned an RIAA Gold certification. The single "Do You Know the Way to San Jose?," an international million seller and a Top 10 hit in several countries, including the UK, Canada, Australia, South Africa, Japan and Mexico, was also a double sided hit with the "B" side "Let Me Be Lonely" charting at #79.

Other LPs certified RIAA Gold include *Dionne Warwick's Golden Hits Part 1* released in 1967 and *The Dionne Warwick Story: A Decade of Gold* released in 1971. By the end of 1971, Dionne Warwick had sold an estimated thirty-five million singles and albums internationally in less than nine years and more than 16 million singles in the USA alone. Exact figures of Warwick's sales are unknown and probably underestimated, due to lax accounting policies and company policy of not submitting recordings for RIAA audit.

In 1971, she signed a $5 million contract, the most lucrative recording contract ever given to a female vocalist up to that time, according to *Variety*. Following her signing with Warners, with Bacharach and David as writers and producers, Dionne returned to New York City's A&R Studios in late 1971 to begin recording her first album for the new label, the self-titled album *Dionne* in January 1972. The album peaked at #57 on the *Billboard* Hot 100 Album Chart. In 1972, Burt Bacharach and Hal David scored and wrote the tunes for the motion picture *Lost Horizon*. But the film was panned by the critics, and in the fallout from the film, the songwriting duo decided to terminate their working relationship. The break-up left Dionne devoid of their services as her producers and songwriters. Dionne was contractually obligated to fulfill her contract with Warners without Bacharach and David and she would team with a variety of producers during her tenure with the label. Faced with the prospect of being sued by Warner Bros. Records due to the breakup of Bacharach/David and their failure to honor their contract with Dionne, she filed a $5.5 million lawsuit against her former partners for breach of contract. The suit was settled out of court in 1979 for $5 million including the rights to all Warwick recordings produced by Bacharach and David.

Without the guidance and songwriting that Bacharach/David had provided, Warwick's career stalled in the 1970s. There were no big hits during the decade aside from 1974's "Then Came You," recorded as a duet with the Spinners and produced by Thom Bell. Bell later noted, "Dionne made a (strange) face when we finished [the song]. She didn't like it much, but I knew we had something. So we ripped a dollar in two, signed each half and exchanged them. I told her, 'If it doesn't go number one, I'll send you my half.' When it took off, Dionne sent hers back. There was an apology on it." It was her first U.S. #1 hit on the *Billboard* Hot 100. Other than this success, Warwick's five years on Warner Bros. Records produced no other major hits. The singer's five-year contract with Warners expired in 1977, and with that, Warwick ended her stay at the label.

With the move to Arista Records and the release of her RIAA certified million seller "I'll Never Love This Way Again" in 1979, Dionne was again enjoying top success on the charts. The song was produced by Barry Manilow. The accompanying album, *Dionne*, was certified Platinum in the United States for sales exceeding one million units. The album peaked at #12 on the Billboard Album Chart and made the Top 10 of the Billboard R&B Albums Chart. Warwick had been personally signed and guided by the label's founder Clive Davis. Dionne's next single release was another major hit for her. "Deja Vu" was co-written by Isaac Hayes and hit #1 Adult Contemporary as well as #15 on Billboard's Hot 100. In 1980, Dionne won the NARAS Grammy Awards for Best Pop Vocal Performance, Female for "I'll Never Love This Way Again" and Best R&B Vocal Performance, Female for "Déjà Vu." Dionne became the first female artist in the history of the awards to win in both categories the same year. Her second Arista album, 1980's *No Night So Long* sold 500,000 U.S. copies and featured the title track which became a major success.

In 1982, Warwick recorded a full-length collaboration with Barry Gibb of the Bee Gees for the album *Heartbreaker*. The song became one of Dionne's biggest international hits, returning her to the Top 10 of Billboard's Hot 100 as well as #1 Adult Contemporary and No. 2 in both Great Britain and Australia. The title track was taken from the album of the same name which sold over 3 million copies internationally and earned Dionne an RIAA USA Gold record award for the album. In Britain, the disc was certified Platinum. Dionne later stated to Wesley Hyatt in his 'Billboard Book of Number One Adult Contemporary Hits' that she was not initially fond of "Heartbreaker" but recorded the tune because she trusted the Bee Gees' judgment that it would be a hit.

In 1983, Dionne released *How Many Times Can We Say Goodbye* produced by Luther Vandross. The album's most successful single was the title track, "How Many Times Can We Say Goodbye," a Warwick/Vandross duet, which peaked at #27 on the *Billboard* Hot 100. It also became a Top 10 hit on the Adult Contemporary and R&B charts. The album peaked at #57 on the *Billboard* album chart. Of note was a reunion with the original Shirelles on Warwick's cover of "Will You (Still) Love Me Tomorrow?" The album *Finder Of Lost Loves* followed in 1984 and reunited her with both Barry Manilow and Burt Bacharach, who was writing with his then current lyricist partner and wife, Carole Bayer Sager. In 1985, Warwick contributed her voice to the multi-Grammy Award winning charity song "We Are the World," along with vocalists like Michael Jackson, Diana Ross, and Ray Charles. The song spent four consecutive weeks at #1 on *Billboard's* Hot 100 chart. It was the year's biggest hit—certified four times Platinum in the United States alone.

In 1985, Warwick recorded the American Foundation for AIDS Research (AmFAR) benefit single "That's What Friends Are For" alongside Gladys Knight, Elton John and Stevie Wonder. The single, credited to "Dionne and Friends" was released in October and eventually raised over three million dollars for that cause. The tune was a triple #1: R&B, Adult Contemporary, and four weeks at the summit on the *Billboard* Hot 100 in early 1986, selling close to two million 45s in the United States alone. The single won the performers the NARAS Grammy Award for Best Pop Performance by a Duo or Group with Vocal, as well as Song of the

Year for its writers, Bacharach and Bayer Sager. It also was ranked by *Billboard* magazine as the most popular song of 1986. With this single Warwick also released her most successful album of the 1980s, titled *Friends*, which reached #12 on *Billboard's* album chart.

In the nineties, Warwick hosted infomercials for the Psychic Friends Network until it filed for bankruptcy in 1998.

On October 16, 2002, Warwick was nominated Goodwill Ambassador of the Food and Agriculture Organization of the United Nations (FAO). In 2004, Dionne Warwick's first Christmas album was released. The CD, entitled *My Favorite Time of the Year* featured jazzy interpretations of many holiday classics. In 2007, Rhino Records re-released the CD with new cover art. In 2005, Warwick was honored by Oprah Winfrey at her Legends Ball. She appeared on the May 24, 2006, fifth-season finale of *American Idol*. Millions of U.S. viewers watched Warwick sing a medley of "Walk On By" and "That's What Friends Are For," with longtime collaborator Burt Bacharach accompanying her on the piano.

In the 2000s, Warwick continued to release reworkings and collaborations with various performers, though these did not chart well. On October 20, 2009, Starlight Children's Foundation and New Gold Music Ltd. released a song that Dionne recorded about 10 years prior called "Starlight." The lyrics had been written by Dean Pitchford, prolific writer of Fame, screenwriter of, and sole or joint lyricist of every song in the soundtrack of, the original 1984 film *Footloose*, and lyricist of the *Solid Gold* theme. The music had been composed by Bill Goldstein, whose versatile career included the original music for NBC's *Fame* TV series. Dionne, Dean, and Bill announced that they were donating 100% of their royalties to Starlight Children's Foundation as a way to raise money to support Starlight's mission to help seriously ill children and their families cope with their pain, fear, and isolation through entertainment, education, and family activities.

Personal Life

Dionne Warwick married Bill Elliott, a drummer who is now studying acting, in September 1967, and the two made their home in a new house they have purchased in Maplewood, New Jersey. On May 30, 1975, the couple separated and Warwick was granted a divorce in December 1975 in Los Angeles. Miss Warwick told reporter Jerry Parker in an interview for *Newsday* (May 12, 1969) of her preference for the suburbs; "If you paid me, I couldn't live in New York. I like air, trees, and houses—that's how I was brought up." She has said she may some day leave show business and teach music in a public school.

In January 1969 she gave birth to her first child, a son. Closely attached to her roots, she often visits her parents in Orange, and keeping in touch with her family by long-distance is one of the contributing factors in a telephone bill that runs into hundreds of dollars per month. Having no weight problem, she is forever munching on snacks, and she is a heavy cigarette smoker.

According to a report in *Newsweek* (October 10, 1966), Dionne is "cheerful, bright, quick to respond to people." The report went on: "Dionne is pleased but relatively unaffected by success. . . . She has her own definition of success: 'Someday I want the kind of loyalty among audiences that Ella Fitzgerald has, so that if I want to stop for two years or ten years I could come back and still be Miss Dionne Warwick. Right now I'd just like people to understand what I try to do—that it's not conjured up, not just style, that I'm pleading the case and you're getting it all, baby, ready or not, here comes all of it."

Further Reading

Ebony 23:37+ My '68 pors
N Y *Post* p64 Ap 20 '65 por; p33 N 26 '66 por
N Y *Sunday News* p129 D 15 '68 por
N Y Times II p17 My 12 '68 por
N Y *World Journal Tribune Mag* p27 S 25 '66 por
Newsday A p40 My 12 '69 por
Newsweek 68:101 O 10 '66 por
Washington (D.C.) Post E p4 D 24 '67 por
Feather, Leonard. *Encyclopedia of Jazz in the Sixties* (1966)
Who's Who of American Women, 1970-71
The Independent on Sunday F 23 '03

Muddy Waters

Blues singer, guitarist, band leader

Born: April 4, 1915; Rolling Fork, Mississippi
Died: April 30, 1983; Westmont, Illinois
Primary Field: Blues
Group Affiliation: The Muddy Waters Blues Band

Muddy Waters.

Introduction

Muddy Waters was the creator and principal exponent of the modern electric blues sound known as Chicago blues. He was the "architect of a new music," which he "firmly stamped with [his] personality and musical thinking" (Phil Hardy, Faber Encyclopedia of Twentieth Century Music). *His influence on modern blues and blues-inspired rock and roll cannot be overstated. According to his biographer at the Rock and Roll Hall of Fame, Waters transformed the soul of the rural South into the sound of the city, electrifying the blues at a pivotal point in the early postwar period. His recorded legacy, particularly the wealth of sides he cut in the Fifties, is one of the great musical treasures of this century. Aside from Robert Johnson, no single figure is more important in the history and development of the blues than Waters. The real question as regards his lasting impact on popular music isn't "Who did he influence?" but—as* Goldmine *magazine asked in 2001—"Who didn't he influence?" ("Muddy Waters Biography," Rock and Roll Hall of Fame)*

"Muddy Waters," writes singer-songwriter Van Morrison, has been "a prime influence for anybody who's ever done anything rock 'n' roll" (Chilton, The Telegraph*).His legacy survives not only in his own body of work but in the music of the Beatles, the Rolling Stones (named after a Waters song), Eric Clapton, Jimi Hendrix, Led Zeppelin, and many other heirs to the Chicago sound, past, present, and still to come.*

Early Life

McKinley Morganfield, soon to be known as Muddy Waters, was born near Rolling Fork, Mississippi, in 1915, to Della Jones and Ollie Morganfield. By 1918, however, McKinley's parents had separated, his mother had died, and he had gone to live with his grandmother on the Stovall plantation near Clarksville, Mississippi. It was his grandmother who began calling him "Muddy Water" (the "s" came later) because that was his favorite place to play (Van Dijk, "Waters, Muddy").

Although Muddy worked full time at Stovall plantation, "he always thought of himself as a musician." At the age of 17, he learned to play guitar by imitating recordings from blues legends such as Robert Johnson and Son House, and by 1940, as Van Dijk explains, "he was well-known in the Clarksdale area, while blues people in Chicago also had heard of, in Waters' own words, 'Stovall's famous guitar picker.'" He would soon be ready to take the blues world by storm.

Life's Work

By 1941-1942, Muddy Waters was still playing for local audiences in Clarksville, Mississippi, when he was recorded by Alan Lomax for the Library of Congress Archive of Folk Song. As Peter Rutkoff and Will Scott explain in an article for *Kenyon Review*, these early recordings are deeply steeped in the "rich and complex" interplay between African-American and West African musical cultures. The song "I Be's Troubled," for instance, "expressed the dream of leaving the Delta, not just for Muddy Waters but for the men and women who worked with him at Stovall, and a hundred other plantations, for those who dreamed of a better life" (Rutkoff and Scott).

At this point in his life, Waters was "a mature Delta blues player" (Rutkoff and Scott). It was only when Waters moved to Chicago in 1943 that he began to realize his destiny as an *urban* blues innovator. In the move itself, he was simply following in the footsteps of the Great Migration in which, as Rutkoff and Scott explain, "one hundred thousand African Americans from the Mississippi Delta who had lived and worked on cotton plantations but juked and shopped on a dozen black business district streets took their experiences with them." And, of course, they also took their music, with its West African and Southern roots.

When Waters arrived in Chicago, he took a job at a paper factory, performed in small venues, and started to build a band—and a sound. That sound, as Ruud Van Dijk explains, consisted of four major elements: a band consisting of a singer, lead guitar, rhythm guitar, harmonica, bass, drums, and piano; a tempo more energetic than a lot of traditional blues; amplification or "electrification" producing not only a louder but also a fuller sound; and, despite all the innovation, a firm grounding in the traditions of the Mississippi Delta, or "country" blues.

From 1947 to 1949, Waters recorded successful singles for Aristocrat records. Interestingly, one of those singles was "I Can't Be Satisfied," a reprise of "I Be's Troubled," which Lomax, the folklorist, had recorded in the thirties. This version, as Rutkoff and Scott point out," reflected Waters' altered perspective from the south to the north, of someone who had already 'skipped off.'"

This was the urban sound that Muddy Waters brought to life in post-war Chicago. Not long after their success with "I Can't Be Satisfied," Aristocrat changed its name to Chess and produced "Like a Rollin' Stone," Waters' signature tune.

Initially, Aristocrat/Chess insisted on recording Waters with studio musicians, but in 1953, the entire working band began to record together. The Muddy Waters band consisted of Little Walter Jacobs on harmonica, Jimmy Rogers on guitar, Elga (Elgin) Edmonds on drums. Otis Spann on piano, and Willie Dixon on bass. Dixon also shared songwriting duties with Waters. The period between 1950 and 1955 represented the height of Waters' creativity, with such groundbreaking hits as "I Just Want to Make Love to You," "Hoochie-Coochie Man," and "Mannish Boy."

As Phil Hardy writes, Muddy Waters was "an extraordinarily potent singer and guitarist, [who] conceived a new kind of band music, gathered the ideal musicians to execute it, and led them with an authority and magnetism unmatched by any of his contemporaries." *Rolling Stone* rated Waters among the 100 greatest guitarists because, as Derek Trucks, of the Tedeschi Trucks Band, writes:

> There was a physicality in the way he played the guitar – percussive, like a drum. When he plays slide, it's not on the high strings. It's lower, guttural, and it sounds like he's about to rip the strings off.

According to Ted Drozdowski of Gibson Guitars, Waters was "arguably the finest of the first generation bluesmen." He "defined the recorded sound of early electric blues: dirty, gritty, stinging, growling, sweet and supremely emotive" with his mastery of the slide and his "dark, rolling, Delta-born, finger picking, single-note style."

Rolling Stone also ranked Waters among the 100 greatest singers: "His baritone always stood out—not only above other blues singers but above all voices and styles of music. . . . It grabs you by the throat." In the 1983 *New York Times* obituary for Waters, Robert Palmer writes:

> He was a great singer of American vernacular music, a vocal artist of astonishing power, range, depth, and subtlety.

Affiliation: Chicago Blues

The Chicago Blues was a product of the Great Migration, an era in which hundreds of thousands of African-Americans left the rural South to escape the poverty of the Great Depression and traveled to the industrial cities of the North. The music that emerged from that great social upheaval was necessarily a kind of cultural amalgamation. In the "Blues and Jazz" section of the *African-American Almanac,* Christopher Brooks explains: "The evolution of Chicago blues hinged on the amplification and rearrangement for small bands of traditional solo Delta blues." The man who, for many, best characterized both the deep Delta roots and the modern, electric sound of the city, was Muddy Waters.

> Among musicians and singers, his remarkable sense of timing, his command of inflection and pitch shading, and his vocabulary of vocal sounds and effects, from the purest falsetto to grainy moaning rasps, were all frequent topics of conversation. And he was able to duplicate many of his singing techniques on electric guitar, using a metal slider to make the instrument "speak" in a quivering, voice-like manner. In a sense, then, his voice and his guitar were two parts of the same instrument, an utterly unique musician whose influence has spread widely over the years.

The second half of the 1950s saw the rise of rock and roll, the 1960s brought soul music and the "British Invasion," and the wellspring of musical innovation moved to the new genres. As Van Dijk explains,

Around 1955 Muddy Waters's rise began to level off. Rock and roll and soul performers scored commercial successes that blues musicians could not even dream of, and it became ever more difficult to score a chart hit. On top of that, Muddy's sound was fully developed by now. It appeared that where the likes of Chuck Berry and James Brown were making great creative strides, Muddy and his colleagues were basically offering the same old fare. But that "same old fare" was something new and exciting for a generation of young British musicians who fell in love with the blues, and Muddy Waters in particular.

Waters toured extensively in the sixties and was a popular performer at jazz festivals. In the seventies, he regained truly widespread popularity when he began to appear with some of the younger blues/rock stars who were so deeply influenced by his music. His relationship with Eric Clapton was especially close. Clapton considered him a father figure and was best man at his wedding in 1979. "His music was the first that got to me," said Clapton, "and it remains some of the most important music in my life today. I love this man so much that I want to do it absolutely perfectly, and, of course, that's not possible." A very productive collaboration with Johnny Winter produced "three strong studio albums, [and] what is probably the most impressive live album of Muddy's career—*Muddy "Mississippi" Waters Live"* (Van Dijk).

Over the expanse of his career, Muddy Waters recorded 61 singles, 23 compilation albums, 7 live albums, and 15 studio albums. He won 8 Grammys for Best Ethnic or Traditional Folk Recording from 1972 to 1980. He was inducted into the Blues Foundation Hall of Fame in 1980 and the Rock and Roll Hall of Fame in 1987. In 1992, he received the Grammy Lifetime Achievement Award, and he was featured on a postage stamp in 1994. The Rock and Roll Hall of Fame rated five of Waters' singles among the 500 Songs That Shaped Rock and Roll: "Rollin' Stone," "Hoochie Coochie Man," "Mannish Boy," and "Got My Mojo Working."

After a long struggle with lung cancer, Muddy Waters suffered a heart attack and passed away in 1983. His *New York Times* obituary, written by Robert Palmer, summed up his unique contribution to modern music:

His blues sounded simple, but it was so deeply rooted in the traditions of the Mississippi Delta that other singers and guitarists found it almost impossible to imitate it convincingly. "My blues looks so simple, so easy to do, but it's not," Mr. Waters said in a 1978 interview. "They say my blues is the hardest blues in the world to play."

"By the time of his death," writes Bill Dahl in *Billboard*, "Waters' exalted place in the history of blues (and 20th century popular music, for that matter) was eternally assured."

Personal Life

Muddy Waters married Mabel Berry in 1932 and Sally Ann Adams in 1942. His third marriage, to Geneva Wade, lasted from 1948 until her death in 1973. He married Marva Jean Brooks in 1979, and Eric Clapton served as his best man. Waters fathered four children outside of his marriages, and according to Van Dijk, "his children remember him as a caring and responsible father."

Further Reading

Brooks, Christopher A. "Blues and Jazz." *African-American Anthology.* Cengage, 2011.

Dahl, Bill. "Muddy Waters." *Billboard.* 2015.

Drozdowski, Ted. "An Insider's Guide to Muddy Waters' Guitar Sound." *Gibson.* Apr. 4, 2011.

Hardy, Phil. "Waters, Muddy." *Faber Encyclopedia of Twentieth-Century Music.*

"Muddy Waters." *The Penguin Biographies.*

"Muddy Waters." *Rock and Roll Hall of Fame*

Palmer, Robert. "Muddy Waters, Blues Performer, Dies." *New York Times.* May 1, 1983.

Trucks, Derek. "Muddy Waters." *Rolling Stone.* Nov. 23, 2011.

Van Dijk, Ruud. "Waters, Muddy." *The Scribner Encyclopedia of American Lives.*

Doc Watson

Folksinger; guitarist

Born: Mar. 3, 1923; Stoney Fork, North Carolina
Died: May 29, 2012; Winston-Salem, North Carolina
Primary Field: Folk
Group Affiliation: Frosty Morn Band; Merle Watson

Introduction

According to Dan Miller, the editor and publisher of Flatpicking Guitar Magazine *(September/October 1998, on-line), the acoustic guitarist and folksinger Doc Watson "has had the deepest, most enduring, and most profound influence on the way the acoustic flat top guitar is played as a lead instrument in folk, traditional, and bluegrass music." Blind since infancy, the North Carolina native has been making music since he was five years old; he began playing the guitar professionally at the age of 30 and recorded his first album* 10 *years later, in 1963. Watson came to national prominence in the 1960s; when folk music experienced a revival, and he has since come to be regarded as the godfather of contemporary folk music.*

Early Life

The sixth of the nine children born to Annie Watson and her husband, whose given name was General Dixon, Arthel Lane Watson was born on March 3, 1923 in Stoney Fork, North Carolina. He was raised in nearby Deep Gap, in the heart of the Blue Ridge Mountains, an area with a rich folk-music tradition. Born with a defect in the blood vessels surrounding his eyes, he lost his sight at the age of one year, after contracting an eye infection. Watson has said that the most important thing his father ever did for him was to set him to work with a cross-cut saw when he was 14. "He made me know that just because I was blind didn't mean I was helpless," he told *Bluegrass Unlimited* (August 1984), as quoted by Miller.

General Watson worked as a part-time farmer and day laborer. For the Watsons-and millions of other rural southerners during the 1920s and 1930s—money was scarce. Doc Watson shared a bed with two of his brothers in the small shack the family called home. "There was no such thing as indoor plumbin'," he told Roger Wolmuth for *People* (August 10, 1987). "In real cold weather you'd wake up in the morning with frost on your pillow. When hard-blowin' snow came, you had to go up in the attic to sweep up the snow and put it out through the shutter window. If you let it go until you got your big fire hot, it would melt and wet everything."

Music played a large role in the lives of the Watsons, and General Watson encouraged Arthel's love of music. "The first music that I can remember hearing was at the little church I went to," Watson told Richard Harrington for the *Washington Post* (January 25, 1988). General Watson led a small choir at church, which sang without benefit of instrumental accompaniment. Annie Watson sang in the church choir and would often sing as she did housework or when she put her children to sleep at night. A grandfather of Watson's future wife lived nearby and taught singing in the brief period just prior to harvest time. Watson recalled to Harrington that the students practiced the "shape note" method of singing, devised for people who could not read music. "After they learned the harmonies, each person would sing his part . . . ," Watson recalled to Harrington. "It was so strange and yet so pretty.... I loved music. When I was little, before I got the five-string banjo, if it was music, I liked it. Didn't make any difference what it was. As a child I was attracted to the sound." Using the family's wind-up phonograph, Watson listened to music by Jimmie Rodgers, Mississippi John Hurt, and Gid Tanner and the Skillet Lickers, among others. As a six-year-old, he received a harmonica as a gift, and every year after that, he was given a new one at Christmastime. When he was 11 his father made a banjo for him, using a cat's hide for the head (the round part of the instrument, which consists of a membrane stretched tightly over a hoop).

Earlier, beginning at age 10, Watson had enrolled at the General Morehead School for the Blind, in Raleigh, North Carolina, where he was a boarding student. When he was 13 a friend of his at the school taught him to play the G, C, and D chords on the guitar. One morning soon afterward, when Watson was home, his father heard him fooling around on a guitar one of his brothers had borrowed from a neighbor. He told Arthel that if he could learn a whole song by the time he, General, came home from work that night, he would help him buy a guitar. Watson did just that, teaching himself the Carter Family's "When the Roses Bloom in Dixieland." That Saturday, Watson (with money from a piggy bank) and his father bought a $12 Stella guitar.

Watson quit school before completing the seventh grade. Afterward he worked on the family farm. He continued his academic education through recorded books that he received from the Library of Congress. He honed his skills on guitar by listening to records: he would slow the speed at which the disks revolved so that he could hear each note the guitarists played; then he would "figure out the lick or the run or get the lyrics, a half or a whole verse, and work on that till I got it down," as he explained to Harrington in 2001. At first he played in the "thumb lead" style, using a thumb pick to play most of the melody parts, while the other fingers played supporting notes in the chords. Later, he adopted flat-picking, a technique associated with Jimmie Rodgers. In about 1940 Watson bought, on the installment plan, a Martin guitar—an instrument far superior to the one he had been using. To pay for it, he began playing on street corners; within four or five months, he had made the last payment. Meanwhile, he had also begun to play at amateur contests and local shows. He came by his nickname at a radio station where he performed one day when he was 18: the announcer had difficulty pronouncing "Arthel," so someone in the audience suggested calling him "Doc" instead.

That same year Watson met his future wife, Rosa Lee Carlton, one of his third cousins. At the time she was only eight years old, and Watson hardly took notice of her. Six years later her family moved into a house half a mile down the road from the Watson family's. Watson recalled to Miller, "I went out to their house and Rosa Lee and a neighbor girl were unpacking dishes. She turned around and said, 'Hello, I haven't seen you in a long time.' Somebody might as well have hit me with a brick. I lost it. I thought, 'Where have I been all these years! There she is!' It was like that, and it still is." One year later, when Watson was about 25 and Rosa Lee about 15, they married. In 1949 they became the parents of a son, named Eddy Merle (and known as Merle), after the country singers Eddy Arnold and Merle Travis. Two years later their daughter, Nancy, was born.

Life's Work

In the early years of their marriage, the Watsons had trouble making ends meet, despite the small government stipend Watson received because of his blindness and the money he earned as a piano tuner. Eager to supplement his income, in 1953 Watson joined a local country-and-western, swing, and rockabilly band called

Affiliation: Folk Style

An acoustic guitarist with a rich baritone voice, Watson blends traditional music from Appalachia with bluegrass, country, gospel, blues, and even jazz. Along with only a few other guitarists, he has been credited with perfecting the flat-picking technique—in which the guitarist holds a plectrum between thumb and forefinger—to play rhythm or lead guitar. The folklorist and musicologist Ralph Rinzler, who "discovered" Watson in 1960, wrote of him, as quoted in the *New York Times* (November 12, 1995), "He is single-handedly responsible for the extraordinary increase in acoustic flat-picking and finger-picking guitar performance. His flat-picking style has no precedent in earlier country music history."

Watson has recorded nearly 50 albums, 20 of them with his son, Merle (who died in 1985), and has earned five Grammy Awards and the National Medal of the Arts. Described as a brilliant storyteller who is unassuming, good-natured, and full of country charm, Watson has an unpretentious philosophy about music. "If a fella can play music on the guitar that shows exactly what he feels inside," he told Richard Harrington for the *Washington Post* (July 6, 2001), "then he's accomplished something." "I really appreciate people's love of what I do with the guitar," he once said, as quoted in a biography of him on the Web site of MerleFest, a North Carolina bluegrass/folk-music festival. "That's an achievement as far as I'm concerned, and I'm proud of it. But I'd rather people remember me as a decent human being than as a flashy guitar player."

Jack Williams and the Country Gentlemen. Soon, by playing area clubs and festivals with the band, Watson was earning enough to support his family comfortably. During his eight-year tenure with the band, he developed the ability to flat-pick, on the guitar, songs meant for the fiddle. Years before, he had tried in vain to learn to play the fiddle. "I had a fiddle for about eighteen months and my bowing hand weren't worth a stink," he told Miller. "I stopped one day and said, 'Heck, I'm going to sell this thing. I can't fiddle.'" His fondness for the sound of the fiddle inspired him to try to replicate on his guitar the rapid single-note runs that a fiddler can produce. That skill proved useful to the Country Gentlemen, which lacked a fiddler but often performed for audiences whose requests included fiddle-oriented square-dance music. Acting upon Jack Williams's suggestion that he play lead on some fiddle tunes with his guitar, Watson learned to play such songs as "Black Mountain Rag," "Old Joe Clark," and "Bill in the Lowground." By then he had sold his acoustic guitar and replaced it with an electric model—a Les Paul Standard—which was more suitable to the style of music the band played. When he was not performing with the Country Gentlemen, Watson increased his repertoire of mountain music, playing with friends and family, including his father-in-law, Gaither Carlton, a fiddler, and the banjoist Clarence "Tom" Ashley.

In 1960 the musicologist Ralph Rinzler—the cofounder of the Newport Folk Festival and the Smithsonian Folklife Festival on the Mall, in Washington, D.C.—and the music historian Eugene Earle came to North Carolina to record Ashley's "old-time" music. Ashley had gathered some local musicians, including Doc Watson, to accompany him on the recording. (Called *Old-Time Music at Clarence Ashley's,* it was released in 1962.) Watson made a deep impression on Rinzler and Earle. "I was completely astonished by him," Rinzler recalled to Harrington (January 25, 1988), "as an intellect, as a personality and as a musician. . . . Doc was the first traditional musician I ever became a close friend of. And what astonished me was that the people who are great musicians in traditional music are as profound as great artists in any kind of art. He is an extraordinarily warm, compassionate and witty human being with an incredible breadth of knowledge."

In 1961, with Rinzler's encouragement, Watson bought a new acoustic guitar and traveled with his father-in-law, Ashley, the vocalist and guitarist Clint Howard, and the fiddler Fred Price to New York City, where they performed at a Friends of Old-Time Music concert. The group were subsequently invited to perform at colleges and folk festivals. A year later Watson gave his debut solo performance, in Gerde's Folk City, a cafe in the Greenwich Village section of New York City. As the folk scene began to flourish, demand grew for Watson's music. In addition to coffeehouses and clubs, he started to appear in concert halls and at music festivals. In 1963 he played at the Newport Folk Festival for the first time, turning in a performance that catapulted him to the forefront of the folk revival. Later that year he released his first solo album, *Doc Watson.* In 1964 he made another now-legendary appearance at Newport. Many parts of his 1963 and 1964 performances are included in the four-CD box set *Doc Watson: The Vanguard Years* (1995), which also contains other Watson recordings from the 1960s and early 1970s.

Although Watson loved concertizing, he did not like being on the road. He often felt lonely, and his blindness made traveling difficult. As he explained to Harrington in 1988, "For a green country man not really used to the city, it was a scary thing to come to New York and wonder, 'Will that guy meet me there at the bus station, and will the bus driver help me change buses?' and all that stuff, people not knowing you're blind and stepping on your feet. It's just scary, the road is." Watson was considering giving up touring when, in 1964, his 15-year-old son joined him as a rhythm guitarist. In the few months since Merle had started playing guitar' he had become remarkably proficient, to the extent that father and son made their first appearance as a musical duo that year, at the Berkeley Folk Festival, in California. Over the next two years, Merle performed with Doc only on weekends and during summers, but after he graduated from high school, the two played together fulltime; In 1965 they released their first album, *Doc Watson and Son.* Merle served as his father's man· ager and driver as well as rhythm guitarist, and his presence alleviated Watson's loneliness. "There's no way I could have done the hard part of the dues paying day without Merle's driving. and help on the road and taking care of the business. Most people don't realize what it come to. He was doing the hard driving and things I could not do as far as the business," he told *Bluegrass Unlimited* (November 1997), as quoted by Miller. As a musician, Merle did not copy his father's style; he had his own interests and was deeply influenced by the blues. In 1973, inspired by the Allman Brothers' lead guitarist, Duane Allman, he began to play slide guitar.

A masterful guitarist whom some considered as skilled as his father, Merle preferred to stay in the background when his father played or spun stories of the rural South for audiences.

In 1972 Watson was invited to take part in the recording of *Will the Circle Be Unbroken,* in collaboration with such celebrated bluegrass musicians or groups as Mother Maybelle Carter, Merle Travis, Earl Scruggs, Jimmy Martin, and the Nitty Gritty Dirt Band. At first Watson refused the offer, because Merle had not been asked to participate. Merle persuaded him to change his mind, predicting—correctly, as it turned out—that the album would expose them to new audiences and would thus benefit their careers greatly. The duo found themselves in great demand following the release of *Will the Circle Be Unbroken.* They subsequently formed the Frosty Morn Band, with the bassist T. Michael Coleman, the guitarist and pianist Bob Lamar Hill, and the guitarist Joe Smothers; the band broke up within a year. In 1974 the Watsons began playing with Coleman. The trio toured in Europe, Japan, and Africa, sometimes appearing at as many as 300 gigs a year.

On the night of October 23, 1985, as Merle Watson was returning home from a neighbor's house (where he had sought help after badly injuring an arm), the tractor he was driving slid into a ditch and overturned, pinning him underneath. The 36-year-old musician died at the scene. Within a week of Merle's funeral, Doc Watson was back on the road; he has explained that Merle had come to him in a dream and, in effect, urged him not to give in to his impulse to stop entertaining. "I don't know if we'll ever get through it," Watson told Wolmuth in 1987. "There's times on the road yet when it's so hard that you wonder, 'Well, can I do this show? Can I go on?' God helped me get to where I am with it, and maybe I can learn to live with it eventually. I don't know." Merle's friend Jack Lawrence, a rhythm guitarist who had occasionally filled in for him before Merle's death, took over as Doc Watson's partner and traveling companion. "If I had to travel by myself again like I did in the early '60s before Merle started, I would have quit a long time ago," Watson told Harrington in 1988.

Between 1965 and 1985 Doc Watson and Merle recorded 20 albums together. Two of them—*Then and Now* (1973) and *Two Days* in *November* (1974)—won Grammy Awards, as did the song "Big Sandy/Leather Britches" from *Live and Pickin'* (1979). "I never was an overlording father in music," Watson told Harrington in 2001. "Merle and I thought about songs and talked about them and figured out how we were going to do it and then just tried to complement each other when we played them. That sound won't ever be again."

Since his son's death Watson has recorded nine albums. He won a fourth Grammy Award for *Rid*ing *the* Midnight *Train* (1986) and a fifth for *On* Praying *Ground* (1990). He has also performed as a guest artist on 20 records. In 1997 President Bill Clinton awarded him the National Medal of the Arts. Watson also holds an honorary doctorate from the University of North Carolina, in Chapel Hill. In April1988 Watson led the first MerleFest, in Wilkesboro, North Carolina. The event started as a one-day tribute to Merle—its official name was the Merle Watson Memorial Festival—with performers entertaining a crowd of 4,000. Now billed as MerleFest—An Americana Music Celebration, it has become an annual four-day event attended by more than 70,000 people; it features workshops, contests, and performances on a dozen stages by some of the brightest names in American roots music, among them Alison Krauss, Willie Nelson, Nanci Griffith, Sam Bush, Dolly Parton, and Earl Scruggs. "You have to perform more at MerleFest than at other festivals, sometimes three or four sets a day," the singer and multi-instrumentalist Tim O'Brien told Ray Waddell for *Billboard* (January 27, 2001). "But nobody complains, because Doc Watson's doing the same damn thing and putting us all to shame." Watson performs at the Festival with Merle's son, Richard, a guitarist who was about 19 when his father died.

Although Doc Watson does not perform as often as he has in the past, he is booked for concerts well into 2004. Music has remained for Watson a matter of the heart. As he explained to Ron Stanford for the introduction to *The Songs of Doc Watson* (1970), as quoted by Miller, "When I play a song, be it on the guitar or banjo, I live that song, whether it is a happy song or a sad song. Music, as a whole, expresses many things to me-everything from beautiful scenery to the tragedies and joys of life. . . . Whether I'm playing for myself or for an enthusiastic audience, I can get the same emotions I had when I found that Dad had seen to it that Santa Claus had brought exactly what I wanted for Christmas. A true entertainer, I think, doesn't ever lose that feeling."

Personal Life

Watson lives in Deep Gap, North Carolina, with his wife, Rosa Lee.

Further Reading
Flatpicking Guitar Magazine (on-line) Oct. 2, 2000, with photo
MerleFest Web site
New York Times II p38+ Nov. 12, 1995i
Washington Post C p1+ Jan. 25, 1988, with photos, WW p6+ July 6, 2001

André Watts

Concert Pianist

Born: June 20, 1946; Nüremberg, Germany
Primary Field: Classical
Group Affiliation: Solo Performer

Introduction

The young pianist André Watts was only sixteen when he substituted for the world-famous Glenn Gould at a New York Philharmonic subscription concert on January 31, 1963. He emerged overnight as a major new talent on the musical scene. Since that appearance, Watts has performed with most major American orchestras, including annual appearances with Josef Krips and the San Francisco Symphony, and has performed with similar success abroad. His technical mastery, poetic impulse, and inflammatory temperament have consistently generated excitement in his listeners. Watts has been unanimously acclaimed by critics for what Raymond Ericson of the New York Times *has called, "the indefinable electric quality that marks the artist who can communicate with his audience."*

André Watts.

Early Life

The son of an American Negro father and a Hungarian mother, André Watts was born on June 20, 1946 in Nüremberg, Germany. His father, Sergeant Herman Watts, a career soldier, was stationed in Germany when he married Maria Alexandra Gusmits, who was living there as a displaced person. After their son's birth, the couple remained in Germany until 1954, when Sergeant Watts completed his tour of duty. Except for one year when his father was assigned to Philadelphia, André spent his first eight years on Army posts in Germany.

When Watts was five, his mother, who comes from a musical family, tried to interest him in the piano, but he failed to respond. At six, however, he began playing a miniature violin and his talent soon became apparent. At seven, while receiving professional instruction on the violin, Watts again began to study the piano with his mother and quickly showed an affinity for that instrument. "Soon I knew I preferred the piano. I had the hands for it and I was more at home at the keyboard," he later recalled. When the family returned from Europe and settled in Philadelphia, Watts was promptly enrolled for piano studies under Genia Robinor, Doris Bawden, and Clement Petrillo at the Philadelphia Musical Academy. His progress was phenomenal and he was soon making his way to the concert stage.

At nine, Watts made his first public appearance, as a substitute soloist, playing a Haydn concerto at one of the Philadelphia Orchestra's Children's Concerts. At ten he performed Mendelssohn's Concerto No. 1 in G Minor with the Philadelphia Orchestra at a Robin Hood Dell summer concert. At fourteen he was again soloist with the Philadelphia Orchestra in César Franck's *Symphonic Variations*. In spite of his obvious musical precocity, however, Watts was not rushed into a childhood career. He spent his early years in piano study, three or four hours of daily practice, and regular schooling. Watts attended both Quaker and Roman Catholic elementary schools, a Roman Catholic high school, and the Lincoln Preparatory School, from which he graduated in June 1963. During those early years Watts' parents separated, obtaining a divorce in 1962, and Watts, an only child, continued to live with his mother in Philadelphia.

Life's Work

In December 1962 Watts won an audition to appear at a Young People's Concert with Leonard Bernstein and the New York Philharmonic. That audition proved to be the beginning of his rapid climb to fame. The concert, which had been videotaped three days earlier, was nationally televised on CBS-TV on January 15, 1963. Watts's first exposure to a national audience was also his first notable success. The response to his performance of Liszt's Concerto No. 1 in E Flat was more than enthusiastic, and ticket requests for his student recital at the Philadelphia Academy of Music the following week were several times that of the hall's capacity. Samuel L. Singer observed in the Philadelphia *Inquirer* (January 24, 1963) that "Only a prodigy could have amassed the technique and musical insight at the age of sixteen as were demonstrated at this recital."

Later in January, when the young Canadian pianist Glenn Gould fell ill two days before his scheduled concert appearance at New York's Philharmonic Hall, Leonard Bernstein, who had been deeply impressed with André Watts's earlier performance, called on him as a substitute soloist. On January 31, 1963 Watts turned his unscheduled debut with the New York Philharmonic into an unqualified triumph and became, according to *Newsweek* (February 11, 1963), the first Negro instrumentalist since the turn of the century to appear as soloist with that orchestra at a regular concert. His brilliant execution of the Liszt E Flat Concerto won him a standing ovation from both audience and orchestra, and, despite the information blackout imposed by New York's newspaper strike, he became an immediate success. National magazines, as well as the Western edition of the *New York Times*, lauded Watts' impressive display of technical brilliance and musical sensitivity. "After the opening display of power there came a ravishing modulation to poetic lyricism. The young man made the ensuing gentle passages sing exquisitely. . . ," wrote *New York Times* reviewer Ross Parmenter (Western Edition, February 2, 1963). "And his playing, perfectly disciplined though it was, seemed wonderfully spontaneous." Watts performed the Liszt concerto three more times before that season's Philharmonic subscription audiences.

His dramatic rise to prominence did not, however, launch Watts on an immediate full-time concert career. Soberly realizing the need for further study and development, he continued to work with renewed discipline and slowly and painstakingly built a repertoire. Accordingly, he limited his engagements that first year.

Appearing at New York's Lewisohn Stadium on July 9, 1963 with Seiji Ozawa and the New York Philharmonic, Watts won acclaim for his animated and musicianly performance of the Saint-Saëns' Concerto No. 2 in G Minor Op. 22. At the Hollywood Bowl in September, he gave another brilliant reading of the Liszt Concerto. On both occasions Watts showed an impressive musicality and an extraordinary gift for bravura pianism. The Liszt and the Saint-Saëns concertos, both rich in bravura passages, afforded Watts ample elbow-room for his impeccable technique and fiery temperament. His performances were marked by spontaneity and excitement. But aside from his technical brilliance, Watts also displayed, according to Robert Riley, "a rewarding penchant for romanticism, a poetic impulse constantly in evidence and well reinforced by technical authority" (*Christian Science Monitor,* September 4, 1963).

Following his graduation from high school in 1963, Watts began to study part-time for a Bachelor of Music degree at the Conservatory of Music of Peabody Institute in Baltimore. During the next two years he again limited his engagements, devoting most of his time to study and practice. In October 1964 he opened the new season with Howard Mitchell and the National Symphony Orchestra in Washington, D.C., and received a "rousing, tumultuous ovation" for his fiery reading of the Saint-Saëns Concerto. On January 21, 1965 he captivated New York audiences with his; performance, with the Philharmonic Orchestra, of Chopin's Concerto No. 2 in F Minor Op. 21. Harriett Johnson of the *New York Post* (January 27, 1965) saw in Watts's performance "the freshness of youth, and the inborn maturity of the greatest talents," although Harold C. Schonberg of the

Times (January 22, 1965) and Alan Rich of the *Herald Tribune* (January 22, 1965) noted some stylistic immaturities. In May 1965 Watts returned to Washington for another concert with the National Symphony.

By the beginning of 1967, Watts could count some eighteen concertos in his repertoire, a substantial increase on the slim portfolio of his early years. His engagements had also multiplied. Early in January he gave a "warmly communicative" performance at his first Toronto, Canada appearance and in February gave a "fire-breathing performance of the first movement" of Brahms's Concerto No. 2 in B Flat Op. 83 at an "Alumni Reunion" Young People's Concert, televised by WCBS-TV on April 19. The highlight for that year, however, was Watts' debut in the land of his birth. On June 19 and 20, around the time of his twenty-first birthday, Watts performed in Berlin in a pair of concerts with the Berlin Philharmonic under the direction of guest conductor Zubin Mehta. Watts' execution of the Brahms B Flat Concerto received high praise from West Berlin critics, including one for *Die Welt,* who wrote that "the chains of trills were never heard so quick-marching and clear, the octaves fell like cataracts but with machine precision."

Returning to the United States after his Berlin debut, Watts appeared in four concerts with the New York Philharmonic and, in August, performed with the Los Angeles Philharmonic Orchestra at the Hollywood Bowl. In September he embarked on a three-month world concert tour, sponsored by the United States Department of State, which took him to sixteen Asian and Western European cities. As part of that tour, Watts returned to West Berlin in October for the 1967 Berlin Festival. There, under the direction of Zubin Mehta and the Los Angeles Philharmonic, Watts again displayed his virtuosity in the Liszt E Flat Concerto. "He tossed off the difficult bravura piece as if it were nothing at all," Everett Helm reported from Berlin for the *Christian Science Monitor* (October 27, 1967). "The runs and passage work were crystal clear, the dynamic control was complete, the coloristic shadings were sensitive."

Watts owes his prodigious technique to a natural gift for the keyboard, that has been disciplined to perfection by many hours of practice. His technical command is complete. His strong, long fingers move with dazzling precision, and his large hands, spanning twelve keys, can execute thundering octaves and intricate, delicate passages with equal facility. "He is completely ambidextrous, with a left hand that lives a life of its own," wrote Ron Eyer for *Newsday* (October 27, 1966), "and

Affiliation: Solo Performer

On June 12, 1966 Watts made his European debut in a successful London appearance with Hans Schmidt-Isserstedt and the London Symphony Orchestra. Shortly thereafter he traveled to Holland, where an Amsterdam audience greeted his performance with Karel Ancerl and that city's Concertgebouw Orchestra with a standing ovation. That same year was marked by other notable successes. In April his performance of the Rachmaninoff Second Piano Concerto evoked enthusiasm from New York critics. In July, under the baton of the Russian conductor Kiril Kondrashin, Watts was again in command of his virtuosity at New York Philharmonic Hall where he played Rimsky-Korsakov's Concerto in C Sharp Minor. And at Carnegie Hall in November, with Leopold Stokowski and the American Symphony Orchestra, Watts reinforced his virtuosity with a "youthful enthusiasm" which, according to one critic, made Edward MacDowel's sometimes flashily performed Concerto No. 2 in D Minor Op. 23 sound "as though it were a message of salvation from the gods" (*New York Times,* November 21, 1966).

On October 26, 1966 Watts made his New York recital debut, opening the Great Performers series at Philharmonic Hall. As in previous performances, his genuine musical gifts and bravura artistry remained undisputed, but in works requiring more sustained lyricism, he met with some criticism. "When it comes to bravura music, few can teach him anything," wrote Harold C. Schonberg (*New York Times,* October 27, 1966). "In more lyric music, on the other hand, he is not exactly sure where to go . . . The Chopin [G Minor Ballade] . . . emerged in a badly mannered way . . . full of overexpressive devices that were continually breaking the line of the music." Alan Rich of the *World Journal Tribune* (October 27, 1966) concurred with Schonberg's observation. Both reviewers, however, directed their criticism at Watts not as a mature artist but as one of great potential with some immaturities yet to overcome. Winthrop Sargent of the *New Yorker* (November 5, 1966) on the other hand, found Watts already "a bravura pianist of stunning achievements and a romantic pianist whose style takes one back to the great days of men like Moriz Rosenthal."

even the most formidable technical difficulties of the keyboard do not phase him."

In May 1964 the National Academy of Recording Arts and Sciences presented André Watts with its annual Grammy Award as "the most promising classical artist for 1963." In the initial years of his career, Watts did not, however, devote much time to recording. "One of the drawbacks to making recordings when you're young . . . is that your style changes so quickly," he said in a *New York Times* interview (October 23, 1966) with Joan Barthel. His only two early recordings are both on the Columbia label. One contains Liszt's Piano Concerto No. 1 in E Flat with Leonard Bernstein and the New York Philharmonic, and Chopin's Concerto No. 2 in F Minor with Thomas Schippers conducting the same orchestra. The other recording is entitled *An André Watts Recital.* With a view to an intensified recording program in the future, Watts, on his twenty-first birthday, signed a long-term contract with Columbia Records. That agreement recently produced a disc containing the Brahms Piano Concerto No. 2 in B Flat with Bernstein and the New York Philharmonic.

By 1969 Watts was on a full-scale concert schedule, booked three years in advance. Watts made his Boston debut in 1969 for the Peabody Mason Concert series. He graduated from the Peabody Institute in 1972. In February 1973, Watts was selected as Musical America's Musician of the Month. Other honors and awards include doctor honoris causa from Albright College and Yale University, the Order of Zaire, and a University of the Arts Medal from the University of the Arts in Philadelphia. By the mid-1970s, Watts was giving 150 concerts, recitals, and chamber performances per season, performing about eight months out of the year. In 1976, at age thirty, he celebrated his tenth consecutive appearance in the Lincoln Center Great Performers Series at Avery Fisher Hall. The PBS Sunday afternoon telecast was the first solo recital presented on Live from Lincoln Center and the first full-length recital to be aired nationally in prime time. In November 2002, Watts suffered a subdural hematoma. He quickly recovered and resumed a full concert schedule. In 2004, Watts joined the faculty at Indiana University as professor at the Jacobs School of Music, through the Jack I. and Dora B. Hamlin Endowed Chair in Music.

Personal Life

As a young concert pianist, André Watts led a severely disciplined life. He studied at the Peabody Conservatory under Leon Fleisher, practicing over six hours per day. This left little time for social engagements. "I can't afford to lose even a weekend or two away from my music," Watts told Joan Barthel in the *New York Times* interview. "I don't have many friends; it's a kind of secluded life." At the time, his mother was his closest and constant companion. When not practicing or performing, Watts spent his time reading and studying languages. To relieve the strain of his many hours at the piano, he relaxes with Yoga exercises.

In 1995, Watts married Joan Brand.

Further Reading

Ebony 18:124+ Ap '63 por
Esquire 61:106+ Mr '64
N Y *Sunday News* mag p16 Jl 7 '63 por
N Y Times p17 O 23 '66 por
N Y Times (Western edition) p3 F 2 '63
Newsweek 61:58 F 11 '63 por
Sat R 46:53+ F 16 '63
Seventeen 23:22 Ja '64 por
Time 81:60 F 8 '63 por

Jeff "Tain" Watts

Drummer, composer, and bandleader

Born: Jan. 20, 1960; Pittsburgh, Pennsylvania
Primary Field: Jazz
Group Affiliation: Various ensembles, including house band for *The Tonight Show*

Introduction

Fans of contemporary "straight-ahead" jazz are likely familiar with the work of Jeff "Tain" Watts, one of the most prominent drummers working in the genre today. After gaining attention as part of the trumpeter and composer Wynton Marsalis's quintet in the early 1980s,

Watts joined the group led by Marsalis's brother Branford, following the saxophonist to the West Coast in 1992 to become part of Jay Leno's Tonight Show *band. He later formed groups of his own, releasing five critically acclaimed recordings to date, while contributing to the award-winning albums of the Marsalis brothers, among the more than 100 albums that feature his work. "Watts forges a colossal sound," John Murph wrote for the* Washington Post *(February 5, 2000). "Never one to simply ride the groove, he constantly shifts tempos and breaks up time, sometimes at lightning speed."*

Early Life

Jeff "Tain" Watts was born on January 20, 1960 in Pittsburgh, Pennsylvania. He has said that his family was not particularly musical; his parents did not collect music or even own a record player, and his older brothers bought mainly the music they heard on the radio, such as albums by Stevie Wonder or Aretha Franklin. He took general-music classes as part of his elementary-school curriculum; in the fourth grade, Watts was asked to choose an instrument to play for class, and he picked the trumpet, "because," as he told R. J. DeLuke for the All About Jazz Web site (July 2002, on-line), "it looked fun and cool. You could play some 'legit' music on it, but you could also jam around and have fun with it." Watts's teacher told him that the formation of his teeth would prevent him from playing the trumpet correctly and suggested that he choose another instrument. (Later, after consulting trumpeters who claimed that his teeth were fine for playing the instrument, Watts reached his own conclusion. "What I suspect was, they ran out of trumpets," he told DeLuke. "So I wouldn't cry, they said my teeth were completely wrong.") It was thus that Watts began playing the drums. In the sixth grade he got his own drum set and began to play along with songs on the radio. In those days he was "still pretty much unaware of classic jazz figures," as he told DeLuke, with the exception of big-band musicians such as the drummer Buddy Rich, because "the Big Band thing is easily marketed to schools." When he was 16 or 17, his brother James expanded Watts's musical horizons, giving him jazz-fusion records by artists and groups such as Return to Forever, the Mahavishnu Orchestra, and Herbie Hancock. Thanks to those influences, Watts said for his Web site, "I began a backtracking process that other musicians in my age group share. I'd check out a Chick Corea album, then find out that Chick Corea played with Miles Davis, who played with Charlie Parker, etcetera."

After Watts graduated from high school, he studied classical percussion at nearby Duquesne University, where he focused on the timpani—also known as the kettledrum—and played in operas, musicals, and orchestra concerts. Soon he began to seek other musical settings. "I wanted to be able to perform authentically and accurately on the classical percussion, but also play different styles on the drum set," Watts told R. J. DeLuke. Discovering the work of Harvey Mason, he learned that that jazz drummer had studied at the New England Conservatory and "was capable of all these different things in a studio setting. So I started trying to be versatile. My thirst to explore jazz was pretty much out of that." That "thirst" led Watts to transfer to the Berklee College of Music, in Boston, Massachusetts. There, his fellow students included a number of other future jazz stars, among them the saxophonists Branford Marsalis and Greg Osby and the guitarist Kevin Eubanks.

Life's Work

During 1981, the year that Watts graduated from Berklee, Wynton Marsalis—Branford's younger brother—was organizing a quintet, which would play many of the trumpeter's original compositions as well as classic jazz tunes. (It was among those musicians that Watts received his nickname, "Tain," short for "Chieftain.") The brothers had recruited Kenny Kirkland on piano; despite the availability of more seasoned drummers, Branford knew that Watts was the type of drummer his younger brother was looking for. "I always felt that Tain was the guy," Branford told Ted Panken for *Down Beat* (November 2002). "I liked how he constructed his [accompanying of) soloists at jam sessions. As opposed to being a complete, thorough historian of the music and playing all the right things at the right time, he played strange things at the right time, imposing his fusion influences on a jazz context. I appreciated that and thought it would be great for Wynton's band." (The Wynton Marsalis Quintet had a number of bassists over the years.) The younger Marsalis spoke with Panken about his impressions of Watts: "My brother liked Tain. There were no auditions. . . . I liked Tain because he was funny, but he has a phenomenal level of talent and intellect. He's a master of form, with perfect pitch and tremendous reflexes. Over the years, he developed a vocabulary that only he plays. All those pieces with time changes and different meters came from playing off of him, because he could do it. It forced me to shape my lines that way, too." Watts told Bob Blumenthal for the *Boston Globe* (April 23, 1999), "Having to interpret a lot of original music from early on, I was able to develop a less derivative approach. Billy Higgins says that every time you sit behind the drums you learn something, and he's right." Watts stayed with the quintet until 1988, performing on three of Wynton Marsalis's Grammy Award-winning albums of the period: *Black Codes (From the Underground]* (1985), *J Mood* (1985), and *Marsalis Standard Time-Volume 1* (1986).

Affiliation: House Musician

In 1992, when Branford Marsalis was invited to be the bandleader for the *Tonight Show with Jay Leno,* he brought his band, including Watts. The gig lasted three years; Watts has said repeatedly that the time he spent in Los Angeles, California, as part of the *Tonight Show* band was very beneficial, as he had the opportunity to play on the program with a number of musical luminaries, including Lou Rawls, Peter Gabriel, and Elton John. Eventually, though, Watts found his work on the *Tonight Show* to be both stagnant and all-encompassing. He told Blumenthal about working on the show: "You're even less than a studio musician, because you play in such a narrow scope. It's more purely entertainment, and I felt that the real world of art was going on somewhere else." It was then that Watts began to think more seriously about composing music.

In 1988 and 1989 Watts worked variously with the guitarist and singer George Benson, the vocalist Harry Connick Jr., and the pianist McCoy Turner. Then Branford Marsalis invited Watts to join his quartet, which included Kirkland and the bassist Bob Hurst. Watts has played with the quartet on and off ever since and performed on both of the band's Grammy Award-winning albums: *I Heard You Twice the First Time* (1992) and *Contemporazy Jazz* (2000). (Watts is the only musician to have appeared on every Grammy-winning album by Wynton and Branford Marsalis, respectively.)

While it is somewhat unusual for a jazz drummer to lead an ensemble (two famous exceptions are Art Blakey and Buddy Rich), Watts decided to try. An early result was the album *Megawatts,* which was recorded in 1991 but not released until 2003; for that reason *Citizen Tain* (1999) is considered his first album as leader. The Marsalis brothers (including Delfeayo, a trombonist) and Kirkland performed on the album, as well as the saxophonist Kenny Garrett and bassist Reginald Veal. For the most part critics commended the playing but were less taken with Watts's original compositions. In a representative review, Mark Stryker wrote for the Alberta, Canada, *Calgazy Herald* (October 14, 1999), "The fierce soloing and lively group interaction make up for Watts' rather thin modal compositions. Watts has a curiously bouncy beat for a post-bop drummer, but his time feel and the aggressive looseness with which he drives a band are recognizable, and that's quite an accomplishment in our homogenized era."

In 2002 Watts released his second album as leader, *Bar Talk,* which featured his band, made up of the saxophonist Ravi Coltrane (son of the sax great John Coltrane), the pianist David Budway, the bassist James Genus, the guitarist Paul Hollenback, and the harmonica player Gregoire Maret; guest musicians on the recording were Branford Marsalis, saxophonist Michael Brecker, guitarist Hiram Bullock, percussionist Robert Thomas Jr., and pianist Joey Calderazzo. Watts spoke with Terry Perkins for the *St. Louis (Missouri) Post-Dispatch* (December 31, 2003) about the new direction signaled by his sophomore release: "Working on *Bar Talk* really was a transitional effort for me. I was trying to move both my writing and my playing into a more open space, and that's definitely a direction I'm trying to pursue with my current band." Reviewers of *Bar Talk* universally recognized improvement in Watts's compositions, which made up eight of the album's 10 tracks. A representative review, for PR Newswire (May 8, 2002), read, *"Bar Talk* elaborates on *Citizen Tain's* strengths—and takes them a step further. Where Watts was once a newcomer to jazz composition and band-leading, these days he is a seasoned veteran. *Bar Talk* investigates a wider array of rhythms, and explores more exotic musical terrain through daring arrangements and scorching solos while preserving the clever melodic style and bold rhythmic assurance that made *Citizen Tain* one of 1999's sleeper hits."

Watts's third album, DeTAINed at the Blue Note, recorded in February 2004 at the famous New York City jazz club of the title, showcased the work of the alto saxophonist Kenny Garrett, the tenor saxophonist Marcus Strickland, the pianist Dave Kikoski, the bassist Eric Revis, and the guitarist Dave Gilmour. Three years passed before Watts released another studio album,

Folk's Songs, as leader. His new group, Tain & the Ebonix, includes Strickland, Kikoski, and the bassist Christian McBride. Watts composed seven of the album's 10 tunes. (He was also a guest on his own album, as vocalist "Juan Tainish," who even has his own MySpace page on the Internet.) Bob Karlovits, writing for the *Pittsburgh Tribune Review* (June 10, 2007), found that "Watts has put together a forward-looking band that doesn't take its work lightly. Throughout ['Sarno'] and the rest of the album, [the band members] create patterns that drive the songs without ever lapsing into ordinary rhythms. That's not surprising from Watts." James Hale, reviewing *Folk's Songs* for *Down Beat* (September 2007), was impressed by the album, though he found fault with Watts's leadership: "Watts has long since established himself as the exemplar of seamless modern drumming. He has an unparalleled ability to introduce rhythmic nuances and maintain a taut time structure behind soloists. Witness the way he keeps a tough edge on 'Laura Elizabeth' and builds intensity behind pianist David Kikoski. As a bandleader and producer, though, he could benefit from a shade less self-indulgence."

In 2008 Watts performed on *Letter to Herbie,* a survey of various Herbie Hancock compositions; the album, by the Los Angeles-based contemporary jazz pianist and composer John Beasley, reached the top spot on the jazz music charts.

Watts has cited the work of the jazz drummers Elvin Jones, Roy Haynes, Art Blakey, Ed Blackwell, and Max Roach as influences on his own music. He was voted best drummer by *Modern Drummer* magazine in 1988 and 1993. Watts played the role of the drummer Rhythm Jones in Spike Lee's 1990 film, *Mo' Better Blues.* It has been reported that he is dating the trumpeter Laura Kahle, who has performed with him and, since 2005, has aided him as a copyist and arranger.

FURTHER READING

(Alberta, Canada) *Calgary Herald* HL p14 Oct. 14, 1999;
All About Jazz Web site July 2002;
Boston Globe C p17 Apr. 23, 1999;
Columbia Records Web site; *Down Beat* p40 Nov. 2002, p70 Sep. 2007;
Jeff "Tain" Watts Web site; PR Newswire May 8, 2002;
St. Louis (Missouri) Post Dispatch p30 Dec. 31, 2003;
Washington Post C p9 Feb. 5, 2000

ANDREW LLOYD WEBBER

Composer

Born: Mar. 22, 1948; London
Primary Field: Musical theater
Group Affiliation: Broadway

INTRODUCTION

Transcending his classical training, Andrew Lloyd Webber is an eclectic composer who has combined elements of folk song, rock 'n' roll, the English music hall, and other musical genres into works of dramatic force and popular appeal for the contemporary musical theatre. Although his two best-known works—the youth-oriented rock opera Jesus Christ Superstar *and the award-winning musical* Evita, *both written in collaboration with lyricist Tim Rice—have provoked controversy, they have made him one of the most widely acclaimed celebrities among younger contemporary composers. In the spring of 1982, two of his creations,* Evita *and his earlier* Joseph and the Amazing Technicolor Dreamcoat, *were being performed on Broadway, and a third production,* Cats, *opened there in October of that year.*

EARLY LIFE

Andrew Lloyd Webber was born in London, England on March 22, 1948 into a musical family. His father, William Southcombe Lloyd Webber, is a composer and the director of the London College of Music. His mother, the former Jean Hermione Johnstone is a teacher of piano, and his younger brother, Julian, is an accomplished cellist. As a child, Lloyd Webber played French horn, Violin, and piano. His fascination with musical theatre began when, at the age of eight, he staged productions of American shows in a toy theatre in his home, and at nine he published a suite of his own composition. His eclecticism was encouraged by his father, a man of wide-ranging musical tastes. "He bought me my first rock and roll record . . . Lloyd Webber told Robert

Palmer of the *New York Times* (February 10, 1982). "I was brought up to believe that music was just music, that the only division within it was between good music and bad." His "absolute idol" was Richard Rodgers, he has recalled.

Life's Work

After attending Westminster School in London, Lloyd Webber went to Magdalen College, Oxford for a year and then transferred in about 1965 to the Royal College of Music.' While still in college, he composed his first full-length dramatic production, "The Likes of Us," about a Victorian philanthropist, Dr. Bernardo, for which Timothy Rice, a record producer, wrote the lyrics. Although their first joint venture was never produced, their second proved more successful. *Joseph and the Amazing Technicolor Dreamcoat,* written in 1967 at the request of a schoolmaster friend, was first performed in March 1968 by the choir of St. Paul's Junior School in London, Unknown to the young collaborators, the father of one of the school's students was a music critic with the London *Sunday Times;* his favorable review led to a public concert version in Westminster Central Hall, and later to other public performances. Eventually the musical was expanded from its original twenty-five minutes into a ninety-minute, two-act production.

If *Joseph* demonstrated that the Lloyd Webber-Rice team could produce an engaging piece of cult theater, their next work, *Jesus Christ Superstar*, proved their commercial potential beyond expectations. A vastly popular and extremely controversial work, it demonstrated that popular music and classical form, far from being incompatible, were capable, in the right combination, of commanding wide public attention.

The "rock opera" began not as a stage play, but as a recording. Unable to interest a stage producer in the work, Lloyd Webber and Rice, put together a demonstration disc for Decca. The company released it in the form of a two-record album, which Lloyd Webber and Rice then publicized in a series of slide-show concerts and in churches. Although the reception in England was lukewarm, the American response, beginning with a November 1970 concert at St. Peter's Lutheran Church in New York City, was overwhelming. As Christian revivalism reinforced the hippie phenomenon among America's young, record sales skyrocketed, and by the time the Broadway staging was ready, the album had sold nearly 3,000,000 copies. Aware of its potential, Robert Stigwood obtained the production rights to *Jesus Christ Superstar* and signed Lloyd Webber and Rice to ten-year contracts. Advance sales for the New York opening were in excess of $1,000,000, prompting Mel Gussow of the New York Times (October 12, 1971), to call *Jesus Christ Superstar* "probably . . . the most presold musical in Broadway history."

Preceded by a successful run in Pittsburgh and by several unauthorized productions around the United States, *Jesus Christ Superstar* opened at Broadway's Mark Hellinger Theatre on October 12, 1971 to mixed reactions. Most reviewers acknowledged the writers' imagination and daring, but many criticized the eclectic musical style, and some found the use of rock idioms in a play about Jesus inherently irritating. Tom O'Horgan's ribald staging came in for special attack: such innovations as having Herod appear as "a drag queen" and having the singers miked for extra volume seemed, to many traditionalists, affronts to both dramatic and religious decorum. Even Hubert Saal, who in a *Newsweek* (November 16, 1970) review of the recording had called Lloyd Webber's musical eloquence "dazzling" and who had praised his "boundless store of melody," conceded that a rock treatment of the Passion might be construed as a "double-barreled provocation."

From its first Broadway performance, the play was attacked by religious groups. Christian pickets expressed dismay that the agnostic version of Jesus' life denied his divinity, that it hinted at a carnal relationship between Jesus and Mary Magdalene, and that it ennobled the treachery of Judas. Jewish groups, on the other hand, alleged that Lloyd Webber and Rice had resurrected the "Christ-killer" image of the Jews. The American Jewish Committee and the Anti-Defamation League of B'nai B'rith were among the influential groups that excoriated the work.

Although Lloyd Webber admitted that he found some of director O'Horgan's effects "vulgar," he was puzzled by the resistance to his presumably "rock-inspired" score. "Actually," he told *Newsday's* Leo Seligsohn (July 12, 1973), "it's no more rock than Stravinsky. What we were trying to do was find a new idiom, a new style we could use to communicate." Even more puzzling, both to Lloyd Webber and to his lyricist, were the religious objections. "Only a moron or a gorilla," Tim Rice told the *New York Times'* Guy Flatley (October 31, 1971), "could say that Christ and Mary had an affair." Both members of the writing team emphasized their Anglican upbringing, and Lloyd Webber, while conceding that he was agnostic, asserted that the point of the play was to raise unanswered questions about "one of the great figures of history." As for the charges of anti-Semitism, Lloyd Webber complained to Flatley: "This whole silly thing just isn't worth talking about. . . . The priests represent the establishment. They're establishment people, not Jewish people."

Before closing on Broadway on June 30, 1973 after 720 performances, *Jesus Christ Superstar* had garnered five Tony nominations and earned Lloyd Webber a Drama Desk Award as the most promising composer of the 1971-72 season. Concurrently with its Broadway run, road company productions, organized by Stigwood, were presented on the West Coast and in Great Britain, France, West Germany, Italy, Denmark, and Australia. Its eight-year London run made it the longest-running musical in British theatre history. Altogether, the show has been presented in twenty-two countries.

In an apparent effort to counteract charges of anti-Semitism, Lloyd Webber and Rice engaged Norman Jewison, the director of *Fiddler on the Roof,* to direct the motion picture version of Jesus Christ Superstar on location in Israel. Released by Universal in the summer of 1973, the movie fared poorly at the box office, and despite some praise for the performances of the black actor Carl Anderson as Judas and of Yvonne Ellman as Mary Magdalene, it was roundly scored by critics for the same supposed "excesses" that had characterized the play. The *Washington Post's* critic Gary Arnold (June 29, 1973) denounced the film as a "pop atrocity" and a "work of kitsch" and claimed that it was based on "one of the worst scores and librettos in the annals of the musical theatre." Writing in New York (July 10, 1973), Judith Crist noted that the musical had been "first-rate as a sixty-five minute record album" but had become "increasingly banal" with its expansion into a two-hour motion picture. But despite the film's failure, the stage version prospered worldwide. By the end of the 1970's the earnings from *Superstar*— including recordings, concerts, stage productions, and the motion picture—had exceeded $150,000,000.

Although he was preoccupied with *Jesus Christ Superstar* in the early 1970's, Lloyd Webber managed to find time to write the scores for two Columbia films-the thrillers *Gumshoe* (1972) and *The Odessa File* (1974) and to create a new musical based on the works of the English humorist P. G. Wodehouse, whose famous character Jeeves is the quintessence of the plucky English butler. After conferring with Wodehouse at his Long Island home in 1973, Lloyd Webber contacted the British playwright Alan Ayckbourn, who agreed to do the lyrics. The result, Jeeves, completed in 1975, was produced in London and had a run of only forty-seven performances.

Collaborating again with Tim Rice, Lloyd Webber next composed *Evita*, a work of great dramatic complexity which surpassed even *Jesus Christ Superstar* in its success. Based on the life of Eva Peron, the actress-courtesan who married Argentine dictator Juan Peron in 1945, the play employed Lloyd Webber's characteristic array of musical forms. Although it was, like *Jesus Christ Superstar*, condemned for mishandling a sensitive theme, it became a smash hit.

The idea for the play came to Tim Rice in 1973, after he had heard part of a documentary about Peron on his car radio. Lloyd Webber, to whom he brought the suggestion, had never even heard of Eva Peron but was impressed by a tape of the program and soon began work on the score. To direct the

Affiliation: Joseph and the Amazing Technicolor Dreamcoat

Based loosely on the Biblical story of Joseph and his brothers, *Joseph and the Amazing Technicolor Dreamcoat* boldly mixed French cafe music, calypso, country, and jazz. Most noticeable, however, was the use of rock music forms, which gave the Biblical tale a fervent, if anachronistic, gusto. Its most popular songs included "One More Angel in Heaven," described by Lloyd Webber as a "new rock Western," and "Song of the King," sung by a rock-idol Pharaoh as a tribute to Elvis Presley.

Since *Joseph* was originally conceived as a school musical, its reputation spread mainly through academic circles. Its first American showing was in May 1970 at the College of the Immaculate Conception in Douglaston, Long Island, and since then it has been often revived in schools throughout the world. Professional productions have included performances by the Young Vic at the 1972 Edinburgh Festival, American runs in Washington, D.C. and at the Brooklyn Academy of Music and, since 1973, traditional Christmas performances in London's West End. A television version was aired in 1972, and in that same year the Music Corporation of America brought out an album of the score, it was not until 1981, however, that the show was presented in its definitive version on the New York stage.

Robert Stigwood production, the two secured the veteran Broadway director Hal Prince, whose interest in directing *Jesus Christ Superstar* had been thwarted years before by a postal error. Musically, Evita went beyond Jesus Christ Superstar because Lloyd Webber was determined to create a more operatic form than he had for the previous work. Evita's richly textured orchestration and the fact that it was "through composed," without spoken dialogue, reflected the composer's classical background as well as his ambition to mount shows in more traditional classical formats.

The show was again preceded by a record release. The American reception was indifferent, but Evita's most winning tune, "Don't Cry for Me, Argentina," sung by Julie Covington, as well as the two-record album itself, became popular in England in the year before the stage premiere. The show opened in London on June 21, 1978 and was an immediate hit. Prince's elaborate staging-employing murals, banners, and parades—matched the score, and when *Evita* came to the United States in 1979, it was already so well known that advance sales for the Broadway version exceeded $2,000,000.

Audiences at the Dorothy Chandler Pavilion in Los Angeles, where it was shown in the spring of 1979, and at the Broadway Theatre in New York, where it opened on September 25 of that year, were as receptive as those in London had been; critics, however, were not so enthusiastic. Although Douglas Watt of the New York *Daily News* (September 26, 1979) found the score "melodic and musically literate," he suggested that it was "about as Latin as steak and kidney pie," while Martin Gottfried of *Cue* (October 26, 1979) observed that the production was rescued only "by Hershy Kay's ingenious orchestrations and two or three noticeable melodies." In his review, Brendan Gill of the *New Yorker* (October 8, 1979) expressed his dismay over the "sunny simplemindedness with which the show addresses itself to its grim subject matter."

Some critics suggested that in its portrayal of the Perons, *Evita* tended to glamorize fascism. The charge was as mystifying to Lloyd Webber as the religious qualms about *Jesus Christ Superstar* had been. The political thrust of the play, he said, was precisely that demagoguery was alluring, and therefore dangerous. "The whole point of *Evita*" he told the *Washington Post's* Megan Rosenfeld (November 15, 1981), "is that what she did could happen here. The democratic way of life is something that can very easily be overthrown by an attractive extremist." To Glenn Loney of *Opera News* (April 4, 1981), he explained that he had tried to make the score undercut the attraction of the main character. "I cannot imagine any intelligent person going to *Evita*," he explained, "and coming away with anything but the idea that she was a fairly grisly piece of work."

Despite the adverse criticism, at the end of its first season on Broadway, Evita had collected the New York Drama Critics Circle award as best musical as well as an astonishing seven Tony awards, including best-of-the-year honors for Prince's direction, Patti LuPone's interpretation of the title role, Rice's lyrics, Lloyd Webber's score, and the musical itself. Its creators were further honored in February 1981, when the National Academy of Recording Arts and Sciences gave the recording of the play the Grammy award for best cast show album of the year. In the late spring of 1981, Paramount Pictures bought the movie rights to *Evita*.

Lloyd Webber's *Variations*, a set of Paganini variations he composed in 1977 for his brother Julian, earned him a gold record in England. In 1980, working with lyricist Don Black, he did the score for *Tell Me on a Sunday,* a "mini-opera" about an English girl living in New York, which was produced first by BBC television and then by New York's Metromedia station. A double bill comprising *Tell Me on a Sunday* and a dance interpretation of *Variations*, under the direction of John Caird, opened with the title *Song and Dance* at London's Palace Theatre for an extended run beginning in the spring of 1982. Meanwhile, a new production of *Joseph and the Amazing Technicolor Dreamcoat* opened to glowing reviews at Off Broadway's Entermedia Theatre in New York's East Village on November 18, 1981. Because of its success there, it was transferred on January 27, 1982 to Broadway, where it had a long run at the Royale Theatre.

A new musical, *Cats*, with Lloyd Webber's music set to lines from T.S. Eliot's volume of children's verse, *Old Possum's Book of Practical Cats*, opened at London's Palace Theatre in May 1981 and was virtually sold out in the months that followed. Directed by Trevor Nunn and designed by John Napier, the production featured seven electronic synthesizers, a full orchestra, and a large cast of singers and dancers dressed in feline costumes. Before it came to the United States, its ballad "Memory," recorded by Barbra Streisand, Judy Collins, and others, had become an international hit.

Probably the most expensive production ever presented on the New York stage, *Cats* opened at Broadway's Winter Garden on October 7, 1982 with advance sales of $6,000,000, but critical opinion was not universally laudatory. Frank Rich, for example, reviewing it in the *New York Times* (October 8, 1982), noted its "excesses" and "banalities" while praising its "purely theatrical magic." Commenting on Lloyd Webber's score in the New York *Post*, Clive Barnes found it "breathtakingly unoriginal yet superbly professional."

Released from the Stigwood contract, Lloyd Webber has formed his own production company and has helped to organize an arts festival. Somewhat chagrined by the attention he has received, in 1981 he admitted to Glenn Loney that when *Jesus Christ Superstar* became a "cult item," he was as much annoyed as gratified. "With all those ludicrous pro and con reactions people had, it's taken a long time for some to realize I'm serious about composing."

Attesting to his seriousness, Lloyd Webber continues to refine his craft. His aim, he has said, is to control the music completely, as an architect controls a building. At the same time, he is acutely aware that for a piece to work as theatre it must be presented in an accessible musical language. "If on first hearing," he told Loney, "a new opera doesn't speak to audiences—not music experts—on some level, forget it." In late 1982 Lloyd Webber was working on a children's musical about American railroad travel, to be called "Starlight Express," and a "sophisticated" show about the "Bloomsbury Group."

Personal Life

Married since 1971, Andrew Lloyd Webber makes his home in Newbury, west of London with his wife, the former Sarah Jane Tudor Hugill, a singer, clarinetist, and pianist, and their children, Nicholas and Imogen. The Lloyd Webbers also maintain a flat in London and a rented hotel suite in New York City. Five feet nine inches tall, Lloyd Webber is, according to Sidney Fields of the New York *Daily News* (September 21, 1979), "reserved, with a round, boyish face and dark eyes that seem sad." Guy Flatley has described him as looking like "a hippie Buster Keaton." Lloyd Webber's extracurricular interests include architecture. His club is the Savile in London.

Further Reading

Chicago Tribune VI pl3 + S 28 *80 por
N Y Times p48 O 12 '71 por, II pi + O 31 *71 por, C p21 F 10 '82 por
Opera N 17:12 + Ap 4 '81 por
Washington Post K pl + N 15 '81 por
International Who's Who, 1982-83
Who's Who, 1982-83
Who's Who in the Theatre (1981)

Alisa Weilerstein

Cellist

Born: April 14, 1982; Rochester, New York
Primary Field: Classical
Group affiliation: Weilerstein Trio

Introduction

American cellist Alisa Weilerstein has been making a name for herself in the classical-music world since her professional debut with the Cleveland Orchestra at age thirteen. Born into an accomplished musical family, Weilerstein picked up her first "cello"—really a toy made from an empty cereal box—when she was two years old and started playing the real thing less than two years later. Though her parents were careful never to push her and to let her learn at her own pace, Weilerstein says she always knew what she wanted to do with her life. "I don't remember a single moment of my life where I ever questioned that I was going to be a cellist," she told Scott Simon in an interview for National Public Radio (27 May 2011).

Early Life

Alisa Weilerstein was born on April 14, 1982, in Rochester, New York, the oldest child of violinist Donald Weilerstein and pianist Vivian Hornik Weilerstein. At the time, Donald was the first violinist of the Cleveland Quartet, which he had helped found in 1969, while Vivian frequently performed as both a soloist and a chamber musician. "I listened to my parents practicing in the house from the time I was just a few days old," Weilerstein told Colin Eatock for the *Houston Chronicle*

(18 May 2011). "My mom is very disciplined: she was practicing again almost immediately after I was born. And I heard my father's quartet in the house until I was seven years old."

Growing up surrounded by music, Weilerstein fell in love with it at an early age. Speaking about her parents to David Abrams for the Internet Cello Society (Apr. 2005), she said, "I loved listening to them practice so much that apparently I'd have terrible tantrums if my mother practiced less than three hours a day. I also was a very precocious concert-goer; apparently I was six weeks old when I first went into a concert hall." Her love affair with the cello began when she was two years old and sick with chicken pox; both her parents were out of town performing, and her grandmother, to cheer her up, made her a toy string quartet (two violins, a viola, and a cello) out of cereal boxes. "The cello, made out of a Rice Krispies box with an old toothbrush for an end pin, was the instrument I immediately fell in love with," Weilerstein told Abrams. "I ignored the others completely. So I was happy when my parents returned to their normal routines of practicing and rehearsing, because now I could participate."

Weilerstein was four years old when she convinced her parents to replace her cereal-box cello with a real one. "Both my parents were reluctant at first because they were sure I was too young, but they soon relented," she told Abrams. "I began lessons a couple of months after that, and I instinctively knew that this was what I wanted to do." At age six, Weilerstein began performing with her parents as the Weilerstein Trio. When she was seven, her family moved to Cleveland, where she began playing in the Cleveland Institute of Music's preparatory recitals. She had had several cello teachers by that time, but her lessons had not been very structured. "My first teachers instilled good habits, but also gave me a wonderful sense of freedom," she said to Abrams, adding, "I really ran wild in my first years." At age nine, Weilerstein began studying with celebrated cello teacher Richard Aaron. "He was the first teacher who told me and my parents that I needed to be much more disciplined in the way that I practiced," she told Abrams. "He told my parents (and eventually he told me) that I was too talented to just run wild. I had to have a structured practice routine. He basically told my parents to listen to me with the same standard that they would use for a talented conservatory student." She began practicing with her father for two hours a day; soon, her practice time increased to four hours.

In 1995, Weilerstein made her professional debut when, at age thirteen, she won a competition to perform with the Cleveland Orchestra. Despite her young age, her performance attracted the attention of management firm ICM Artists. "It built gradually, with not too many concerts at first, so I could still go to high school and have a normal life," she said to Jessica Duchen for the *Jewish Chronicle* (7 Oct. 2010). Also at age thirteen, she entered the Young Artist Program at the Cleveland Institute of Music. "That meant I went to regular public school in the mornings and took conservatory-level classes and practiced in the afternoon," Weilerstein explained to Abrams. She graduated from Cleveland Heights High School in 1999, two years after making her Carnegie Hall debut with the New York Youth Symphony and one year after releasing her debut CD with EMI Records.

After high school, Weilerstein attended Columbia University, where she studied Russian history. "I had dreams of pursuing an academic degree early on—I think as early as middle school," she told Abrams. "I was surrounded by musicians and was taking classes in theory and music history . . . and I realized I wanted something entirely different for my college experience. I had a terrible fear of becoming a very isolated musician who knew nothing of the rest of the world." In 2000, she received an Avery Fisher Career Grant, the majority of which she put toward her tuition. She did not neglect her musical studies, however, taking advantage of Columbia's New York location to work with Joel Krosnick at the Juilliard School. She also continued to perform during this time. "My college life felt like I had about three full-time jobs," she said to Abrams. "When I wasn't playing concerts I was either going to class or writing papers, and vice versa.... I literally wrote papers on planes, trains, buses, and automobiles and e mailed them to my professors, who were (with a couple of exceptions) very understanding of my situation." During her first year at Columbia, Weilerstein lived across the hall from actor and fellow student Julia Stiles. "She said she liked hearing me practice while she was studying, but I don't know whether she was just saying that to be nice," she told Beth Satkin for *Columbia College Today* (May 2002).

Life's Work

Following her graduation in 2004, Weilerstein continued to perform as a soloist, recitalist, and chamber musician, as well as with her parents as the Weilerstein

Trio; the three of them released their first recording in 2006. Also in 2006, Weilerstein was presented with the Leonard Bernstein Award at the Schleswig-Holstein Musik Festival in Germany, the first cellist to receive the honor. The award is given annually to a promising young artist and comes with a prize of ten thousand euros. In 2008, the Lincoln Center named Weilerstein one of two winners of that year's Martin E. Segal Awards, another prize that recognizes outstanding achievements by young artists.

In summer 2007, Weilerstein made her debut at Lincoln Center's annual Mostly Mozart Festival playing Osvaldo Golijov's cello concerto *Azul,* originally performed by world-famous cellist Yo-Yo Ma the year before. Prior to the Mostly Mozart performance, Golijov collaborated with Weilerstein to completely rework the piece. "I was unhappy with some of the music in the concerto," he told Steve Smith for the *New York Times* (31 July 2007). He explained, "Originally the piece was very, very still all the time"—a stillness that did not mesh with Weilerstein's energetic performance style. Describing the experience to Louise Lee for *Strings* magazine (Feb. 2010), Weilerstein said, "I got the final score just two days before the performance.... It was an exhilarating, and kind of scary, process, but it was very natural. It had evolved in a very unselfconscious way." Since then, she has worked directly with several composers, including Lera Auerbach and childhood friend Gabriel Kahane. Weilerstein enjoys the collaborative process, telling Lee, "Each composer has become a friend."

Weilerstein became a celebrity advocate for the Juvenile Diabetes Research Foundation in November 2008. She was diagnosed with juvenile (type 1) diabetes at age nine, and though she did not hide her diagnosis from friends, for a long time she kept it a secret from her professional colleagues—including her manager. "I never even told my manager until three years ago, because the perception of diabetes is that you're on dialysis or going blind or facing amputation," she said to Donna Perlmutter for the *Los Angeles Times* (20 Mar. 2011). "I wanted to prove I could have my music, my career, and encourage other young people who were as scared as I was in the beginning."

In November 2009, Weilerstein was one of four musicians invited by First Lady Michelle Obama to perform at the White House and provide instruction for young musicians. "It was Michelle Obama's initiative, first to have music in the White House, but also to have some seminars," she told Duchen. She continued, "We talked a lot about the state of music education in the US, where there's not much government support for the arts; the National Endowment for the Arts is miniscule. This was a great day for classical music—it attracted the most press attention I've ever seen for classical music in the US."

Weilerstein achieved a major turning point in her career when she performed Edward Elgar's Cello Concerto in E Minor under the conductorship of Daniel Barenboim—the husband of famed late cellist Jacqueline du Pre, whose performance of the concerto had made it a world-famous best seller and whom Weilerstein had idolized from a young age. "I was kind of obsessed with her. I had a poster of her on my wall. I could quote her interviews. I saw every single bit of film footage on her by the time I was ten," Weilerstein told David Patrick Stearns for the *Philadelphia Inquirer* (13 Dec. 2012). "But when I started to learn the concerto on my own, I had to put the recordings away. They were so seductive."

Since du Pre's death in 1987 from multiple sclerosis, Barenboim had conducted the Elgar concerto only once, for Yo-Yo Ma. When Weilerstein first met Barenboim in December 2008, she was initially determined not to play the concerto for him; the following May, conductor Asher Fisch, who had introduced the two, convinced her otherwise. ''He said, Well, I hear that you're playing for Maestro [Barenboim] a lot, you really ought to play the Elgar concerto for him; And I said, 'No way. I can't play the Elgar for him possibly.' And he said, 'No, no one knows the piece the way he does: You'll learn so much from him," Weilerstein recalled to Julie Subrin for the *Tablet Magazine* podcast *Vox Tablet* (20 Nov. 2012). She added, "Probably the hardest thing that I ever did was to play the Elgar for him for the first time."

Nevertheless, her playing impressed Barenboim, and he immediately asked her to play the concerto with him and the Berliner Philharmoniker the following year. ''I was just in complete shock," Weilerstein told Rick Schultz for the *Jewish Journal* (21 Nov. 2012). "Of course, I gave a very enthusiastic yes, but afterward I walked out of Carnegie Hall with my cello and wound up somewhere in Central Park. I was so completely stunned." She made her debut with Barenboim and the Philharmoniker on April 27, 2010.

In October 2010, Weilerstein signed a contract with the prestigious record label Decca Classics, becoming

Affiliation: Classical Music

Weilerstein has performed as a soloist, a recitalist, and a chamber musician. She also per forms with her parents as the Weilerstein Trio; the three first played in concert together when Weilerstein was six years old. Weilerstein, who studied at the Julliard School and graduated from Columbia University in 2004, won the 2006 Leonard Bernstein Award and a 2008 Martin E. Segal Award in recognition of her exceptional talent and promising future. In 2009, she was invited by First Lady Michelle Obama to perform and lead musical seminars at the White House.

In April 2010, Weilerstein performed Edward Elgar's Cello Concerto in E Minor with the Berliner Philharmoniker under the direction of conductor Daniel Barenboim. The performance was a historic one, as it was Barenboim's wife (and Weilerstein's idol), Jacqueline du Pre, who had performed the definitive version of the concerto, and Barenboim had not conducted another female cellist in the role since du Pre's death in 1987. In October 2010, Weilerstein in became the first cellist in over thirty years to sign with renowned music label Decca Classics. The following year, she was one of twenty-two recipients of a MacArthur Fellowship, a $500,000 prize recognizing exceptionally outstanding work in one's field.

the first cellist to be signed by the label in over three decades. Her first recording with Decca, released in fall 2012, features the Elgar concerto as conducted by Barenboim as well as a concerto ·by Elliott Carter, written in 2000. Shortly after the album's release, on November 5, Carter died at age 103. Weilerstein had met with him in summer 2012 to discuss her performance for the album, due to be recorded in September; the meeting, which Weilerstein recorded on video, proved to be the last videotaped interview of the composer and is available online.

Personal Life

In 2011, Weilerstein received her most significant award to date: a MacArthur Fellowship, a no-strings-attached award of $500,000 paid out over five years. Yet she almost did not hear the news, dismissing the MacArthur Foundation's first attempt to contact her, an e-mail from an unfamiliar address promising good news and asking her to call, as spam. "I thought it was one of those, you know, I'm your long-lost Nigerian grandparent who wants to give you a million dollars,' that sort of thing," she told Timothy Mangan for the *Orange County Register* (30 Nov. 2012).

Weilerstein is particularly noted for her physical, passionate performances onstage; Zachary Woolfe, a critic for the *New York Times,* described her as performing "with soulful expression and physical abandon" (2 Oct. 2011).

'When I was first starting out, many people used to say, 'Oh, you move around so much on stage, you make so many faces, you're so expressive.' And I really had no idea," Weilerstein told Simon. She explained, "I try to use the analogy, you know, if you go to, like, a rock concert . . . you see the rock musicians on stage are going crazy. I mean, they're bouncing all over the walls and dancing. It always struck me as sort of surprising that people would find that strange in· classical music."

Weilerstein is dating Venezuelan conductor Rafael Payare; She and her parents, the Weilerstein Trio, have been a trio in residence at the New England Conservatory of Music in Boston, Massachusetts, since 2002. Her brother, Joshua Weilerstein, horn in 1987, studied violin at the New England Conservatory before becoming an assistant conductor with the New York Philharmonic in 2011.

Further Reading

Abrams, David. "Conversation With Alisa Weilerstein." *Internet Cello Society.* Internet Cello Society; Apr. 2005. Web. 17 Dec. 2012. ·

Duchen, Jessica. "The New Jacqueline du Pre? Barenboim Might Just Agree." *Jewish Chronicle Online.* Jewish Chronicle, 7 Oct. 2010. Web. 17 Dec. 2012.

Eatock, Colin. "CellistAlisa Weilerstein on Center Stage with Symphony." *Houston Chronicle.* Hearst Communications, 18 May 2011. Web. 17 Dec. 2012.

Perlmutter, Donna. "Cello Virtuoso Alisa Weilerstein Is Always at the Head of Her Class." *Los Angeles Times.* Los Angeles Times, 20 Mar. 20 H. Web. 17 Dec. 2012.

Schultz, Rick. "Cellist Weilerstein Brings Worldly Depth to SoCal Stages." *Jewish Journal.* Tribe Media, 21 Nov. 2012. Web. 17 Dec. 2012.

Florence Welch

Singer

Born: August 28, 1986; Camberwell, South London, England
Primary Field: Pop/rock
Group Affiliation: Florence and the Machine

Introduction

Florence Welch is the lead singer of the British pop/rock band Florence and the Machine. Her debut album Lungs *(2009) yielded five hit singles and has sold over four million copies worldwide. Her follow-up album* Ceremonials *(2011) has been climbing the charts as Welch tours with her band, which includes key player and Lungs co-creator, Isabella Summers, as well as a four-piece band and string section. Welch, who has no formal musical training, is known for her otherworldly compositions and her booming, soulful voice. She described her unique sound to Tom Lamont for the London* Observer *(30 Oct. 2011), as "big, tribal goth pop." After several musical false starts—a stint as a folk singer and earlier, at the age of thirteen, as the lead in a band called Toxic Cockroaches—Welch found her sound after an emotional breakup with longtime boyfriend Stuart Hammond. Welch and Summers, who was also going through a rough breakup, sequestered themselves in Summers's small London recording studio and created* Lungs, *a record which Lamont deemed "one of the best breakup albums in years."*

Early Life

Florence Leontine Mary Welch was born on August 28, 1986 in Camberwell in South London, England. Her mother, Evelyn Welch, is a professor of Renaissance studies and the dean of arts at the University of London, Queen Mary. Her father, Nick Welch, was formerly in the advertising business. Welch names her mother as an early artistic influence for introducing her to gothic architecture and Renaissance and Egyptian mythology. The gruesomeness of the latter captivated the young Welch's imagination. Her father, on the other hand, introduced her to the punk rock band the Ramones. A self-described "dreamy" child, Welch attended Alleyn's School, located in Dulwich in Southeast London, where she sang in the choir and frequently got in trouble for bursting into song during lessons. Early on, Welch was diagnosed with both dyslexia and dyspraxia. She has suffered from insomnia since she was a child and used to draw crosses on her bed to protect her from lurking werewolves and vampires.

When Welch was ten years old, her parents divorced. Three years later, her mother fell in love with their next-door neighbor, Peter Openshaw, a professor of medicine at Imperial College, London. Evelyn Welch moved in with Openshaw, bringing Florence and her two younger siblings, Grace and John James, with her. Openshaw was a widower with three teenage children of his own. Welch has described early years with her new brothers and sisters as chaotic. To escape the household bickering, she turned to punk rock and a growing fascination with witchcraft.

Around the same time, Welch's grandfather fell ill and died in a coma, and her manic-depressive grandmother died by suicide. She sang at both of their funerals. Welch then took to writing songs. The songs were mostly about breakups, even though she had never had a boyfriend. By the time Welch was sixteen, she was seriously pursuing a musical career and spent a lot of time in London clubs. Her family was supportive; her mother and stepfather read books on the music business while her stepbrother, Nick, drove her and her early bands to gigs. Her father was an early tour manager.

The first of Welch's bands was called Toxic Cockroaches. It began in 1999 when Welch was only thirteen. Another, more recent predecessor to Florence and the Machine was a band called Ashok, which she fronted in her late teens. She signed a music deal with Ashok but decided to walk away from it. In 2006, Welch started playing the drums with her longtime friend and musical collaborator, Isa Summers, a keyboardist. They called themselves Florence Robot and Isa Machine, then later shortened the name to Florence and the Machine. The band played small London venues, and Welch became known for her on-stage antics and crowd surfing. Welch briefly attended Camberwell College of the Arts, though she left after eighteen months to continue her music career. She was officially discovered in December 2006 during a black-tie event. In the restroom, a tipsy Welch cornered Mairead Nash of the indie/pop DJ duo Queens of Noize and sang the Etta James song "Something's Got a Hold on Me." Nash was impressed and asked

Welch to sing at her Christmas party. Weeks later, Nash became Welch's manager.

Life's Work

In 2007, Welch signed with the independent label Moshi Moshi Records, and then with Island Universal Records in 2008. Prior to either deal, Welch and Summers spent time at various London pubs, partying and performing. Welch, who had just ended a tumultuous relationship with literary editor Stuart Hammond, told Gareth Grundy for the *Observer* (20 Dec. 2009) that her life during that period was "spinning out of control." She recalled waking up one morning after a particularly raucous night and finding herself on the roof of a pub wearing a Captain America costume. Nash intervened and told Welch that she needed to make a change. 'Things were very much in the balance," she told Grundy. 'There was a moment when it could have tipped either way and I could have completely gone under. But I resurfaced and life got itself back on track, I think."

For an entire summer, Welch and Summers kept to Summers's London recording studio and wrote most of what would become Florence and the Machine's debut album, *Lungs.* Inspired .by the music of Madonna, among others, the two composed songs on Summers's keyboard and a drum set borrowed from a neighboring band. Welch claims that it was due to these sessions that she found the gothic, thundering pop sound for which she has become famous. For Welch, writing the song "Between Two Lungs," which she recorded pounding the studio walls with her hands in lieu of drums, was a revelation. Armed with their new material, Florence and the Machine attracted the attention of Island Universal Records in 2008. By early 2009, Welch had won a Critic's Choice Brit Award-a new prize within the recording industry given to the year's most promising acts. Though the band's first single, "A Kiss with a Fist," was released in 2008, *Lungs* was officially released in July of 2009.

Lungs, produced by Paul Epworth, debuted at the number two slot on the charts due to the death of pop icon Michael Jackson that year. The album peaked at number one the following year. Critics praised Welch and compared her to musicians like P. J. Harvey, Bjork, David Bowie, and Kate Bush for her mystical, gothic imagery and persona. *Lungs* successfully lived in two worlds; it was considered both macabre ("My Boy Builds Coffins") and euphoric ("Cosmic Love"). The album garnered five singles, including "You've Got the Love," a cover of the 1986 Candi Staton song that became wildly popular in the United Kingdom.

The song "Dog Days Are Over," a heart-pounding crescendo with tribal drums, made Welch a star across the pond. She described the song to Korina Lopez for *USA Today* (9 Aug. 2010) as a symbol of "apocalyptic euphoria, chaotic freedom, and running really, really fast with your eyes closed." Welch was asked to perform "Dog Days Are Over" live for the MTV Video Music Awards in Los Angeles in 2010. She was encouraged to recreate the song's strange and ritualistic music video, which was nominated for Best Video at the awards. The song was also used that year in the film *Eat, Pray, Love,* starring Julia Roberts. Welch attributes the successful performance at the VMA's with her newfound popularity in America. By her own account, the search term "Florence and the Machine" ignited Internet search engines that night following her performance. In a matter of minutes, Welch had gone global.

In 2010, Florence and the Machine returned to the Brit Awards, where they won Best Album. Welch also wrote and recorded a song called "Heavy in Your Arms" for the soundtrack of the film *Twilight: Eclipse* (2010). The song is available on a repackaged edition of *Lungs.* In early 2011, she sang at the Nobel Peace Prize ceremony in Oslo. She was also invited to the Grammys and asked to participate in a tribute to soul singer Aretha Franklin. Standing beside Christina Aguilera, Martina McBride, Jennifer Hudson, and Yolanda Adams, Welch sang part of Franklin's famous song 'Think." Two weeks later, she filled in for pop singer Dido at the 2011 Academy Awards. She performed one of the Best Original Song nominees, *If I Rise,*" written by Indian composer A. R. Rahman for the movie *127 Hours* (2010). Dido, who originally performed the song with Rahman, could not make the event. Rahman called Welch, whom he had seen at the Nobel Prize ceremony in Norway, and asked her to perform the song. At the after- party, Welch sang a duet with Elton John.

After the release of *Lungs,* Welch's fan base expanded to include celebrities such as Beyoncé, who told Welch that the album was an inspiration for her own latest release, to the popular television show *Glee,* whose cast sang "Dog Days Are Over" in a November 2010 episode. For much of the time between 2009 and the release of *Ceremonials* in 2011, Welch was on tour. It was an exhausting schedule, but Welch learned to keep up. Reversing the drunken, crowd-surfing persona associated with her London days, Welch made the decision to no longer drink on the road. Meanwhile, her live performances became famous. "During 'Dog Days Are Over' she invites the crowd to howl like wolves and leap into the air, which they do, spectacularly," a London *Sunday Times* (20 Sep. 2009) reporter wrote of Welch's performance at the Lowlands Festival in Holland in 2009. "By the end of 'Cosmic Love,' a girl at the front is in tears." Before the release of *Ceremonials,* Florence and the Machine toured with the Irish rock band U2.

After the whirlwind of touring, Welch returned to both her childhood home in Camberwell and a small Soho recording studio—the legendary Studio 3 of Abbey Road Studios—where she recorded her follow-up album, *Ceremonials.* She again worked with producer Paul Epworth but also collaborated with writer Francis "Eg" White, who has created songs with popular singers such as Natalie Imbruglia and Adele Adkins. White and Welch co-wrote "What the Water Gave Me," the album's five-minute-long first single. The song and the album as a whole employ imagery associated with death and drowning. "To me, this album is almost like a battle cry," she told Cameron Adams for Australia's *Courier Mail* (27 Oct. 2011). "People thought I might be coming back with something more ethereal and twinkly; I wanted to come back with something tough and heavier." Her original plan was to record the album in Los Angeles in a larger studio, but ultimately she felt more comfortable returning to London. If there were any doubts about Welch's decisions on *Ceremonials,* they were quickly dispelled when the album shot up the UK charts to the number-one spot upon its October 2011 release. After a little more than three months, the album had sold over 1.8 million copies worldwide.

Reviewers have described *Ceremonials* using various synonyms for the word "epic." Welch has said that she wanted the album, in all respects, to be bigger than her first. From the soaring vocals and orchestra backing to lyrics about conquering life and death, *Ceremonials* operates on different scale than *Lungs* in almost every respect-certainly it is a good fit for the larger venues Florence and the Machine continue to sell out. Music critic Jon Pareles for the *New York Times* called *Ceremonials* an "album of anthems" (8 Nov. 2011). He added, however, that "soon after the songs make their initial splash, grandeur turns to grandiosity. In making the songs so monumental, Florence and the Machine have also made them impersonal."

Ceremonials experiments with various styles, including soul, as evidenced on the track "Lover to Lover." Welch also included songs that dealt with her second breakup with Hammond, "Breaking Down" and "No Light, No Light." Although *Ceremonials* has its darker tones, her single "Shake It Out" is an anthem of positivity that draws on American gospel. The song "Spectrum," which prominently features a harp, showcases Welch's voice at its most restrained. The album reached number six on the music charts in the United States.

In July 2012 the group was forced to cancel two European dates after Welch sustained a vocal injury. She did recover quickly and was back on tour in August. In October of 2012, she was featured on Scottish singer-songwriter and producer Calvin Harris's song "Sweet Nothing", which debuted at number one on the UK singles chart, marking Welch's second number one. In

Affiliation: Crossover Appeal

Welch has successfully managed several crossovers that remain a challenge for other musical acts. After performing at the 2010 MTV Video Music Awards in Los Angeles, at which she recreated live the music video for her hit single "Dog Days Are Over," her hype extended well beyond her native England; the song was even used in the film *Eat, Pray, Love* in 2010. She leapt from her status as an "indie" icon to a mainstream music staple—performing a tribute to the "Queen of Soul" Aretha Franklin alongside Christina Aguilera, Martina McBride, Jennifer Hudson, and Yolanda Adams at the 2011 Grammy Awards. She was also asked to write the song "Heavy in Your Arms" for the soundtrack of the *Twilight* film *Eclipse* (2010).

With her bright red hair and gothic vintage flair, Welch has captured the attention of designers, including British retailer Topshop and Chanel director Karl Lagerfeld. While the art and fashion world celebrate Welch's softer, more wraithlike qualities, Welch celebrates dark impulses that drive her personal aesthetic. "I want my music to sound like throwing yourself out of a tree, or off a tall building, or as if you're being sucked down into the ocean and you can't breathe," she says in the "About" section on her website, florenceandthemachine.net. "It's something overwhelming and all-encompassing that fills you up, and you're either going to explode with it, or you're just going to disappear."

November of the same year, Florence joined the Rolling Stones at the O2 Arena in London to sing "Gimme Shelter". Her performance with Mick Jagger was described as "sexy" and "electrifying". Florence + the Machine's third album, *How Big, How Blue, How Beautiful*, was released on June 1, 2015.

Personal Life

A lifelong lover of vintage fashion, Welch is known for elaborate, Victorian-inspired stage costumes. Her free-flowing style and striking bone structure has attracted designers such as Topshop and Chanel director Karl Lagerfeld, whom many consider to be the king of couture. For the latter's "Under the Sea"-themed 2012 Spring/Summer runway show on October 4, 20 II, Welch emerged singing from a giant shell. Lagerfeld also photographed Welch for the cover of her single "Shake it Out."

Welch had a relationship with literary editor Stuart Hammond from 2008 to 2011. Their split in 2009 provided inspiration for the *Lungs* album. Welch says, "He prefers me not to talk about it. It's funny then singing about it. It's easier to hide things talking about them rather than singing about them." The couple broke up again in 2011 because of conflicting career demands, and the break-up provided material for Florence + the Machine's second album, *Ceremonials*.

Welch is in a relationship with events organizer James Nesbitt and lives with her family in Camberwell. Her younger sister, Grace, is her personal handler and travels with her on tour.

Further Reading

Adams, Cameron. "Rise of the Machine." *Courier Mail* [Brisbane] 27 Oct. 2011, first ed.: 44. Print.

Grundy, Gareth. 'The Faces of 2009: Florence Welch." *Observer* [London] 20 Dec. 2009: 4. Print.

Lamont, Tom. "'Do I Want to Be Stuck in Teenage Land, Where Everything Is Free and Easy?"' *Observer* [London] 30 Oct. 2011: 27. Print.

Lopez, Korina. "Fortuitous Bathroom Visit Propels Her Career; A Chance Meeting Led to a Big Musical Break." *USA Today* 9 Aug. 2010, final ed.: D5. Print.

Pareles, Jon. "New Music." *New York Times* 8 Nov. 2011, late ed.: C3. Print.

Howe, Z., *Florence + The Machine: An Almighty Sound*, Omnibus Press, Nov. 1, 2012

Lawrence Welk

Band leader; accordionist; television personality

Born: March 11, 1903; Strasburg, North Dakota
Died: May 17, 1992; Santa Monica, California
Primary Field: Big band
Group Affiliation: Lawrence Welk Orchestra

Introduction

The first dance band in television history to be signed for a full-hour coast-to-coast network program on an every-week basis is the Lawrence Welk band. Welk has two hour length television shows on the ABC-TV network, the Lawrence Welk Show *and* Lawrence Welk's Top Tunes and New Talent. *When the bandleader was booked as a summer replacement in July 1955 the experts were dubious. But as the Nielson rating for his show rose from 7.1 to 32.5 within a year, Welk crowded out four half-hour network favorites on NBC and CBS. Called "Liberace of the accordion," Welk replied that "you have to play what the people understand" (*Time, *May 21, 1956).*

A self-taught musician, Welk formed his first band in 1927. It gained popularity on radio station WNAX, Yankton, South Dakota. He introduced "Champagne Music" (which his band still features) in 1938 while broadcasting over a nation-wide radio network from Pittsburgh, and composed "Bubbles in the Wine," his theme song. His popularity extended to hotels and ballrooms on the West Coast in 1946. From 1951 to 1954 his show was telecast over a local Los Angeles station (KTLA). Over 1,000,000 "Champagne Music" records were sold by Coral Records during 1956.

Early Life

Lawrence Welk was born on March 11, 1903 in Strasburg, a German community in North Dakota, the son of Ludwig Welk, a blacksmith who immigrated to the

United States in 1878 from Alsace-Lorraine. Lawrence was next to the youngest of eight children in the family.

Lawrence's public school education ended in the fourth year, and he went to work in the fields. During winter evenings members of the family entertained themselves by playing various instruments. Lawrence's father taught him to play the accordion and by the time he was thirteen, he was invited to play at weddings and other affairs in the community. He also got a job with a band although unable to read a note of music. Young Welk sometimes took in $150 when he passed the hat at a wedding. On weekends he secured small engagements in surrounding towns until his fifteen-dollar accordion wore out.

On Lawrence's seventeenth birthday, his father gave him a $400 accordion with the new-style piano keyboard. He then had one job after the other with small bands, which dropped him because he played off-key and so loud that he drowned out the other musicians. If he had a band of his own, he reasoned, the members would have to play as he did. There was no money to hire a band, but he got a drummer to accompany his accordion and played on afternoon radio programs free, in exchange for publicity about dance engagements. Welk hired the required number of musicians for each date he secured. WNAX, Yankton, South Dakota engaged Welk for its initial broadcast, and he was heard thereafter on a daily program with a saxophone player and piano player. By 1927 he had a six-piece band known as L.W.'s Hotsy-Totsy Boys.

Life's Work

After he married in 1930, he tried managing in turn a hotel, a restaurant, a music store, and failed in each. He operated a chewing gum business combined with Lawrence Welk's Fruit Gum Orchestra, secured dance hall engagements and gave free gum to the dancers. The customers dropped wads of gum on the floors, ruined them, and Welk was out of business again.

He joined George T. Kelly, a comedian, wore a Spanish costume, and played the accordion in shows put on in small-town vaudeville houses in the Dakotas and neighboring states. After three years he had saved enough money to start a large band—seventeen pieces. As the band grew popular, he added more pieces and played in larger towns.

"His roaring accordion had subsided to a tuneful ripple" when Welk secured a tryout at the Edgewater Beach Hotel in Chicago in 1939 *(American Magazine,* July 1956). It has been related that lack of education and a German accent had made him too shy even to announce dance numbers; so when told that he must "emcee" the show he memorized an opening speech. The band was to play on an outdoor terrace. Welk said only three words and the audience fled. He finished the speech before he realized that a sudden cloudburst had flooded the terrace.

The following week while the band was playing at the Chicago Theater, the manager of a Milwaukee theatre offered Welk $1,750 a week. He was "staggered" by the sum, but said he could not be a master of ceremonies. The manager returned minutes later with the offer of $3,500. "Welk leaped. . . · and shouted: 'For $3,500, I will talk'" *(American Magazine,* July 1956). Now when he makes mistakes the audience laughs and he laughs with them.

While playing at Pittsburgh's William Penn Hotel in 1938 and broadcasting over a radio network, Welk received fan letters calling the band "sparkly and bubbly." The producer suggested "Champagne Music" as the theme featuring the soloist as "Champagne Lady." The plan was adopted as the Welk trademark.

"It goes to your head," *Band Leaders* (August 1943) remarked and added that Welk's style was distinctive— "a compromise people wanted between dance rhythm and flowing melody." When he opened at the Capitol Theatre in New York, *Band Leaders* (May 1944) commenting on Welk's first New York engagement noted, "There's a touch of America in this genial, wholesome maestro's lilting danceable music."

In 1951 the manager of the Aragon Ballroom offered Welk a four-week contract to telecast the band over KTLA, a local Los Angeles station. The show was so successful that Welk stayed on and four years later it was among the top ten of all TV programs in

Affiliation: Band Leader

The band's first engagement at the Aragon Ballroom in Ocean Park, California in 1946 marked the beginning of Welk's success on the West Coast. His records were being played from coast-to-coast on radio networks. The following year when he played at New York's Hotel Roosevelt, *Variety* (June 4, 1947) wrote that the Welk group was musically good and had the "enthusiasm . . . sadly lacking in too many swing bands."

southern California. The Dodge division of the Chrysler Corporation hired Welk for a weekly full-hour network attraction in 1955. Originating "live" from the ABC television studios in Hollywood, *The Lawrence Welk Show* made its coast-to-coast bow on July 2, 1955. The twenty-four piece band included vocalist Alice Lon as "Champagne Lady."

According to the *American Weekly* (August 21, 1955), Welk grosses more than. $1,000,000 a year "with music some sophisticates call 'corn'" and plays a $5,000 handmade accordion. John Crosby (New York *Herald Tribune,* January 15, 1956) wrote that Welk had a "tinkly style of music . . . very easy to dance to" and found "pleasantness the chief characteristic of all members of the band." Jack Gould (*New York Times,* February 10, 1956) observed that some quarters of Tin Pan Alley were "stunned and amazed" when Welk's rating shot to a phenomenal 30.4 in six months. Ticket requests for his personal appearance show on February 11, 1956 in the New York studio exceeded 4,000. *Cue* (May 12, 1956) concluded that Welk's "magical gimmick" was his "happy musicians" who played and sang "pretty for the people."

In a promotion tour for its sponsor (Dodge) the Welk show made a nine-day tour through Texas in January 1956. A similar one in the East was climaxed by the Dodge Show at Madison Square Garden in New York on March 26, 1956. Welk has also appeared in several short motion pictures. On October 8, 1956 *Lawrence Welk's Top Tunes and New Talent* was launched over ABC-TV, an hour-long show sponsored by Dodge and Plymouth. Since 1951 Coral Records, a subsidiary of Decca Records, has made about 500 "Champagne Music" recordings, which include five albums in 1956. *Bubbles in the Wine* and *Sparkling Strings* are among the most popular albums.

Personal Life

Lawrence Welk married Fern Renner, a nurse, in 1930. They have three children—Shirley, Donna Lee, and Lawrence, Jr.—and occupy an eleven-room house of Spanish architecture. The bandleader is five feet nine inches tall, weighs 177 pounds, and has brown hair and blue eyes. His religion is Roman Catholic. He neither smokes nor drinks. For relaxation, he likes to golf, hunt and fish and he sponsors a Little League baseball team.

Welk was the master of ceremonies of his programs and opens each dance number with the old "uh-one—uh-two—uh-three" routine he has always used. The 1956 *Radio-Television Daily* Poll named the Welk program the "musical show of the year." The National Ballroom Operators of America called it "the nation's number one dance band." Welk, himself, was named "musical father of the year" in May 1956.

Further Reading

Am Mag 162:20+ Jl '56 pors
Coronet 40:149+ 0 '56 pors
Newsweek 47:75 My 21 '56 por
Time 67:89 My 21 '56 por
Town J 63:27 Ag '56 pors
Who is Who in Music (1951)

Kanye West (KHAN-yay)

Hip-hop artist; record producer

Born: June 8, 1977; Atlanta, Georgia
Primary Field: Hip-hop
Group Affiliation: Solo performer

Introduction

The hip-hop artist and producer Kanye West came before the public eye in February 2004, with his multi-platinum solo debut, College Dropout *selling more than 400,000 copies in its first week of release and spawning several hit singles, including "Through the Wire," "Slow Jamz," and "Jesus Walks,"* College Dropout *won three Grammy Awards and announced West's arrival as one of hip-hop's wittiest satirists and most flamboyant stars. The album, a mix of edgy beats, soulful hooks, spiritual themes, and smart humor, showcased West's primary musical signature—his artful "sampling," or creative manipulating (and appropriating) of classic tunes for modern musical application. Commenting on West's sampling techniques for* L.A. Weekly *(December 2, 2005), Ernest Hardy wrote, "[West] listens to old music and hears raw data, potential samples waiting to be chiseled from the fat. Unlike many of his peers, however,*

[West] . . . has both a heartfelt appreciation for that music in and of itself, and an intuitive knowledge of how to wield it."

Kanye West.

Early Life

Kanye Omari West was born on June 8, 1977, the only child of Ray West, a former member of the Black Panther Party and currently a professor of sociology at the College of Southern Maryland, and Donda West, a literature professor and the recently retired chairperson of the English Department at Chicago State University. The intellectual energy and political convictions of his parents (who divorced when he was three) and of other family members left an indelible mark on West's consciousness and, later, his rhymes. Donda West's literary pursuits, in particular, helped to foster Kanye's love for language and knack for wordplay, and he has often cited the influence of his grandfather Portwood Williams, who was a civil rights activist in 1950s Oklahoma. By all accounts Kanye West, whose given name means "the only one" in Swahili, possessed a rare self-assuredness even as a young child growing up in the South Shore suburb of Chicago. He "displayed his charisma even in day care," his father noted to Rob Tannenbaum for *Playboy* (March 1, 2006). During his formative years West took art and music lessons and came up with rhymed variations on such children's tales as Dr. Seuss's *Green Eggs and Ham*. As his fascination with hip-hop's subculture grew, so did his abilities; he continued to experiment with rhythms and beats and showed a good ear for syncopation. After graduating from high school, in 1995, he matriculated at a local Chicago art academy, then at Chicago State University, before dropping out altogether to pursue his musical ambitions. His mother was not pleased with that development. "My plan was that he would get at least one degree, if not several," she told Josh Tyrangiel for *Time* (August 29, 2005). But Donda West could not overcome her son's determination. She recalled to Tyrangiel, "He said, 'Mom, I can do this, and I don't need to go to college because I've had a professor in the house with me my whole life.' I'm thinking, This boy is at it again. He always could twirl a word."

Life's Work

West's ascent into hip-hop lore began locally, when he developed a reputation as a crafty beat- maker for several Chicago-area rappers. He recognized the importance of beats early on. "Themes are important to me, but beats are what catches someone's ear and makes a record a hit," he declared to Robert Hilburn for the *Los Angeles Times* (August 28, 2005). West made his first sale—a collection of samples for $8,000—to the Chicago rapper Gravity and also forged a friendship with the city's rap star Common, who told Greg Kot for the *Chicago Tribune* (August 28, 2005), "I loved [West's] confidence, and I always thought he was clever, but he needed to grow as far as his delivery." Craig Bauer, who owned Hinge Studio—where West often recorded in the late 1990s—told Kot about West, "There was always something about the guy, even then, that commanded respect. He knew what he wanted, and he was always striving to make his beats sound like no one else's. He would lift samples and manipulate them—twist them around, turn them up an octave—until he got something fresh out of something that was made 20 or 30 years ago. He never wanted to be like someone else."

In 1998 West turned a professional corner with his contributions to the Atlanta, Georgia-based recording artist Jermaine Dupri's *Life in 1472,* producing the album's introductory track, "Turn It Out." In the wake of the album's release, West journeyed to one of hip-hop's bastions of hit-making— New York City—in search of one of its elder statesman, the rapper Jay-Z. West's next major breakthrough came when Jay-Z commissioned five tracks originally sampled and produced by West for the 2001 album *The Blueprint*, including the single "Izzo (H.O.V.A.)," which recalled 1970s soul with its innovative sampling of the Jackson 5 track "I Want You Back." With his work on *The Blueprint*, West became a star in the world of hip- hop production.

As a result of that exposure, West oversaw production for a roster of other East Coast hip-hop notables, including DMX, Beanie Siegel, Foxy Brown, and the R&B singer Alicia Keys. Eager for greater celebrity of his own, he sought to parlay his reputation as a producer into a role as MC. He tried to enlist the support of Jay-Z and Damon Dash, the co-founders of Roc-A-Fella Records, who responded to West's requests with incredulity. As Dash recalled for Tyrangiel, he and Jay-Z did not consider West "street"—or street-smart—enough to perform good rap music: "We all grew up street guys who had to do whatever we had to do to get by. Then there's Kanye, who to my knowledge has never hustled a day in his life. I didn't see how it could work." Others in the industry reacted similarly. "It was a strike against me that I didn't wear [typical 'gangsta' attire] and that I never hustled, never sold drugs," West said to Tyrangiel. "But for me to have the opportunity to stand in front of a bunch of executives and present myself, I had to hustle in my own way. I can't tell you how frustrating it was that they didn't get that. No joke—I'd leave meetings crying all the time." In the end, West's determination prevailed. Jay-Z explained to Lola Ogunnaike for *Rolling Stone* (February 9, 2006) his and Dash's reasons for taking on West: "We figured if we kept him close, at the very least we'd still have some hot beats."

In late 2001 West began crafting his debut album, *College Dropout*, which coupled his layered beats with self-effacing lyrics, signature highlights of West's style. One day about a year later, following a lengthy recording session, he fell asleep while driving home and crashed his car into another vehicle. For three weeks after that near-fatal episode, West was immobile, his jaw wired shut. He managed to draw inspiration and even humor from his condition and composed "Through the Wire," which became the anchor track for *College Dropout*. Influenced by Lauryn Hill's 1998 Grammy Award-winning album, *The Miseducation of Lauryn Hill,* West framed *College Dropout* in similar thematic terms, setting zany, ironic takes on the subculture of the streets, and suggestions of spirituality, against the soulful background loops of classic 1970s R&B. *College Dropout,* which featured cameos by a roster of former West collaborators—among them Jay-Z, Talib Kweli, and Mos Def—reached record stores on February 10, 2004 to great fanfare and critical praise, selling 400,000 copies in less than a week and peaking at number two on the *Billboard* Top 200 album chart. Describing his album's themes, West said to Renee Graham for the *Boston Globe* (March 21, 2004), "I make my lyrics about stuff people go through every day in the streets. And when I say the streets, I don't mean specifically selling drugs. I mean anybody who has to get up in the morning, get on the bus, or . . . drive to work. I mean any- and everybody." Ken Micallef, writing for *Remix* (February 1, 2004), hailed *College Dropout* as "the most socially responsible hip-hop album since Public Enemy's heyday," while Chris Salmon, in Time Out (February 18, 2004), declared that West's tunes "build from soul foundations, fizzing with inventive flourishes and laden with hooks capable of hauling Pharrell [a rival hip-hop artist] off his perch."

In addition to "Through the Wire," *College Dropout* spawned the hit singles "All Falls Down" and "Slow Jamz," an ode to witty, seductive soul songs, which sampled Luther Vandross's "A House Is Not a Home." The album's crowning achievement was the radio hit "Jesus Walks," a gospel- imbued song with choral arrangements and lyrics that teetered on moral ambiguity: "The only thing that I pray is that my feet don't fail me now / (Jesus Walks) / And I don't think there is nothing I can do now to right my wrongs / (Jesus Walks with me) / I want to talk to God but I'm afraid because we ain't spoke in so long." *College Dropout* went on to sell nearly three million copies, garnered 10 Grammy Award nominations (winning three), and cemented West as rap's newest solo star. The album also represented West's seeming contradictions, both as an artist and a person. Hua Hsu addressed that issue, writing for *Slate* (September 8, 2005, online), "West's expansive empathy and pendulum-like swing between arrogance and insecurity have made him into something more than a rapper. He's become a pop star, in the fullest sense of that term: He's someone whom people use as a guiding light, with whom they identify, and whose experiences and ambitions seem universal."

The success of *College Dropout* allowed West to pursue a number of activities. He started his own record label (Getting Out Our Dreams, or GOOD, Records), created a fashion line (Pastelle Clothing, set to debut in late 2006), and initiated a philanthropic venture (the Kanye West Foundation) that promotes music education in schools. Meanwhile, his first year in the spotlight also exposed his now-legendary egotism. At the November 2004 American Music Awards ceremony, West walked out after being passed over, in favor of Gretchen Wilson, for the favorite-breakthrough-artist award. According to Ed Bumgardner, writing for *JournalNow.com* (November 17, 2005), West declared in a backstage press room, "I was the best new artist this year, so get that other [expletive] out of here."

In 2005 West began work on his highly anticipated follow-up album, *Late Registration*, which saw him move into new territory—undergirding the rhythms of hip-hop with lush pop melodies. He collaborated on the record with the producer Jon Brion, who was best known for his work with the folk-rock artists Aimee Mann and Fiona Apple. Brion saw his teaming with West as odd but promising. "[West's] knowledge and understanding of records across the board is great. That's the reason why we got along: We don't see music as something that happens in one genre," he said to Gail Mitchell for *Billboard* (September 3, 2005). West continued to refine his beats and lyrics, while Brion experimented with orchestrations and percussion. Brion fondly recalled to Kot for the *Chicago Tribune* article, referring to the process of producing the record, "There was [a] kind of lunacy going on. And then there was me conducting an orchestra who had to play these precisely timed phrases. The look of delight—everything from laughter to these shy smiles on some of the more prim members of the string section—while playing along with Kanye's raps in their headphones for the first time is something I'll never forget."

During the buildup to the release of *Late Registration*, West appeared on a promotional spot, "All Eyes on Kanye West," that aired on MTV on August 22, 2005. During the program he addressed the homophobia he saw as prevalent in the black community and elsewhere, referring to his own family experiences—namely, the recent disclosure that a favorite cousin of his was gay. As reported in the *Commercial Appeal* (August 20, 2005), West said that hip-hop had always been about "speaking your mind and about breaking down barriers, but everyone in hip-hop discriminates against gay people. . . . Not just hip-hop, but America just discriminates. And I wanna just, to come on TV and just tell my rappers, just tell my friends, Wo, stop it.'"

Late Registration landed in music stores on August 30, 2005 and became an instant hit, selling nearly 900,000 copies in its first week—more than double the debut sales of *College Dropout*. Hilburn wrote for the *Los Angeles Times* that *Late Registration* "is a 71-minute tour de force that mixes every- man tales with sonic invention—a record that could change the musical framework of rap," while Hua Hsu, in *Slate*, described it as "an amazingly intimate album, at once funny and sad and self-obsessive." Sasha Frere-Jones, the pop-music critic for the *New Yorker* (August 22, 2005), was more measured in his praise, writing, "There are few pop stars as consistently discontent and as obstreperously proud as the rapper and producer Kanye West. . . . listening to his thrilling and frustrating new record, *Late Registration*, is a bit like being chauffeured around in the fanciest car you can imagine by a driver who won't stop complaining about the mileage or the radio reception. You're annoyed, but at the same time you don't want the ride to end."

The album's singles reflected more of West's political and personal views than had his preceding work. "Diamonds from Sierra Leone" deals with Western materialism, citing the illegal diamond trade in Africa, which has funded civil wars throughout the continent; "Crack Music," a song about drug addiction, is critical of the black community; and "Hey Mama" offers a heartfelt tribute to the rapper's mother for the love and support she has given him. The hit track "Gold Digger" showcased, once again, West's ability to integrate classic samples (it opens with the actor Jamie Foxx singing Ray Charles's "I've Got a Woman") with quirky, humorous lyrics to make lightly sardonic commentary—this time about gender differences. West said to Tannenbaum about the process of creating his songs, "I beg for criticism. I'll get 30 opinions on what's wrong with a song and fix all of those things. So when it comes out, you can't tell me [anything]. You can't learn anything from a compliment."

Adding to the already considerable press coverage of West were the controversial remarks he made on September 2, 2005, during NBC's live telecast of *A Concert for Hurricane Relief*, which benefited the victims of Hurricane Katrina and the flooding it caused in and around New Orleans, Louisiana. As quoted in Ogunnaike's *Rolling Stone* article, West deviated from the show's script to voice his opinions about the federal government's slow relief efforts in the largely African-American city and the media's portrayals of the victims:

Affiliation: Sampling and Its Influence

West's follow-up album, *Late Registration* (2005), took his sampling artistry to new heights. With production contributions from the noted folk-rock producer Jon Brion, *Late Registration* highlighted West's trademark samples, this time couched within lush pop arrangements; the hit single "Gold Digger," for example, incorporated Ray Charles's classic "I've Got a Woman," while "Addiction" featured an old Ella Fitzgerald rendition of "My Funny Valentine." West's second album also reflected his growing maturity as a lyricist, boasting such tracks as "Diamonds from Sierra Leone" and "Crack Music," two searing social critiques on materialism and drugs in America's inner cities. By 2006 *Late Registration,* like its predecessor, had reached the three- million mark in total album sales, and it received a Grammy Award for best rap album.

With the success of West's two solo albums, the general public has caught on to what the hip-hop community has acknowledged for years—namely, West's role as a creative force behind the notable records of other artists. Some of West's more substantive production contributions include samples for Jermaine Dupri's *Life in 1472* (1998), Jay-Z's *The Blueprint* (2001), Talib Kweli's *Quality* (2002), and Alicia Keys's *The Diary of Alicia Keys* (2003). But it is West's storied, egotistical, sometimes self-contradictory persona, perhaps more than his work itself, that has drawn the most attention. The product of a middle-class upbringing outside Chicago, Illinois, West eschewed the glamorized "gangsta"- rap image in favor of preppy chic, becoming the rare artist who has successfully bridged the gap between street culture and bourgeois taste. Equally comfortable in Polo T-shirts and overly baggy pants, West is famous, as an artist and a person, for his embodying—perhaps pioneering—of classic-modern, street-suburban, sarcastic-reflective sensibilities. He said to Neil McCormick for the London *Daily Telegraph* (February 18, 2006), "I'm a popular artist but I'm a Pop artist too. Usually Pop art samples things, Andy Warhol taking Marilyn [Monroe] or Kanye West taking Ray Charles and giving it a new form, a new shape and making it something the masses today will connect with."

"I hate the way they portray us in the media. You see a black family, it says they're looting. If you see a white family, it says they're looking for food." He capped his remarks with his widely publicized indictment of the president of the United States: "George Bush doesn't care about black people." Concerning his remarks, West later told Bumgardner, "I said what was on my mind. I had sized up the state of black Americans today, I had watched what was going on in New Orleans, and that was the conclusion I came to. I had no plans to come out and say that. I just listened to my heart. You can't live in fear." On the subject of the wide and varied reaction to his criticism of the president, West said to Ogunnaike, "Does anybody remember the whole thirty seconds I spent talking about how I turned away from the television set [during coverage of the flood damage], how I went shopping? No, all anyone remembers is 'George Bush doesn't care about black people.'"

By early 2006 West's *Late Registration*, like *College Dropout* before it, had gone triple platinum (that is, sold three million copies). It garnered eight Grammy Award nominations and took home three awards, one for best rap album. Meanwhile, West continued to generate controversy. The cover of the February 9, 2006 issue of *Rolling Stone* featured a picture of West, wearing what appeared to be a crown of thorns—an image meant to evoke Jesus—under the headline, "The Passion of Kanye West." In response, Jonah Goldberg wrote for the *National Review Online* (February 3, 2006), "Kanye West . . . sells himself as a victim of a society that can't handle his truth. Four million records sold and saturation adulation in the media suggest that it can handle his truth just fine. The problem is, it ain't the truth. It's just a scam for kids too stupid to recognize they're being played—again." West composed two songs for the soundtrack of the big-budget 2006 film *Mission: Impossible III,* making a fan of the film's star and producer, Tom Cruise. He also recorded *Late Orchestration: Live at Abbey Road Studios,* a collection of his hits performed with a 17-piece string orchestra at the London studios where the Beatles had worked. The album was released only in Europe, with an accompanying DVD. Later in the year West appeared as the opening act at the first three concerts of the *Rolling Stones'* autumn U.S. tour. He continues to oversee the GOOD record label and its slate of recording artists, including Common and the R&B artist John Legend, whose debut, *Get Lifted*, produced by West, won him the prize for best new artist at the 2006 Grammy Awards ceremony.

After spending the previous year touring the world with U2 on their Vertigo Tour, West was inspired to compose anthemic rap songs that could operate more efficiently in large arenas. To do this, West incorporated the synthesizer into his hip-hop production, utilized slower tempos, and experimented with electronic music and influenced by music of the 1980s. In addition to U2, West drew musical inspiration from arena rock bands such as The Rolling Stones and Led Zeppelin. To make his next effort, the third in a planned tetralogy of education-themed studio albums, more introspective and personal in lyricism, West listened to folk and country singer-songwriters Bob Dylan and Johnny Cash in hopes of developing methods to augment his wordplay and storytelling ability.

West's third studio album, *Graduation*, garnered major publicity when its release date pitted West in a sales competition against rapper 50 Cent's *Curtis*. Upon their September 2007 releases, *Graduation* outsold *Curtis* by a large margin, debuting at number one on the U.S. *Billboard* 200 chart and selling 957,000 copies in its first week. *Graduation* once again continued the string of critical and commercial successes by West, and the album's lead single, "Stronger," garnered the rapper his third number-one hit. "Stronger," which samples French house duo Daft Punk, has been accredited to not only encouraging other hip-hop artists to incorporate house and electronica elements into their music, but also for playing a part in the revival of disco and electro-infused music in the late 2000s. Ben Detrick of XXL cited the outcome of the sales competition between 50 Cent's *Curtis* and West's *Graduation* as being responsible for altering the direction of hip-hop and paving the way for new rappers who didn't follow the hardcore-gangster mold, writing, "If there was ever a watershed moment to indicate hip-hop's changing direction, it may have come when 50 Cent competed with Kanye in 2007 to see whose album would claim superior sales."

For his 2008 *Glow in the Dark Tour* West decided to sing using the voice audio processor Auto-Tune, which would become a central part of his next effort because he felt his emotions could not be expressed through rapping. West had previously experimented with the technology on his debut album *The College Dropout* for the background vocals of "Jesus Walks" and "Never Let Me Down." Recorded mostly in Honolulu, Hawaii in three weeks, West announced his fourth album, *808s & Heartbreak,* at the 2008 MTV Video Music Awards, where he performed its lead single, "Love Lockdown." Music audiences were reportedly taken aback by the uncharacteristic production style and the presence of Auto-Tune.

808s & Heartbreak, which features extensive use of the eponymous Roland TR-808 drum machine and contains themes of love, loneliness, and heartache, was released by Island Def Jam to capitalize on Thanksgiving weekend in November 2008. Reviews were positive, though slightly more mixed than his previous efforts. Despite this, the record's singles demonstrated outstanding chart performances. Upon its release, the lead single "Love Lockdown" debuted at number three on the *Billboard* Hot 100 and became a "Hot Shot Debut," while follow-up single "Heartless" performed similarly and became his second consecutive "Hot Shot Debut" by debuting at number four on the *Billboard* Hot 100. While it was criticized prior to release, *808s & Heartbreak* had a significant effect on hip-hop music, encouraging other rappers to take more creative risks with their productions. In 2012, *Rolling Stone* journalist Matthew Trammell asserted that the record was ahead of its time and wrote, "Now that popular music has finally caught up to it, *808s & Heartbreak* has revealed itself to be Kanye's most vulnerable work, and perhaps his most brilliant."

An incident the following year at the 2009 MTV Video Music Awards was arguably his biggest controversy, and led to widespread outrage throughout the music industry. During the ceremony, West crashed the stage and grabbed the microphone from winner Taylor Swift in order to proclaim that, instead, Beyoncé's video for "Single Ladies (Put a Ring on It)," nominated for the same award, was "one of the best videos of all time." He was subsequently withdrawn from the remainder of the show for his actions. West's tour with Lady Gaga was cancelled in response to the controversy, and it was suggested that the incident was partially responsible for *808s & Heartbreak's* lack of nominations at the 52nd Grammy Awards.

Following the highly publicized incident, West took a brief break from music and threw himself into fashion, only to hole up in Hawaii for the next few months writing and recording his next album. Importing his favorite producers and artists to work on and inspire his recording, West kept engineers behind the boards 24 hours a day. A variety of artists contributed to the project, including close friends Jay-Z, Kid Cudi and Pusha T, as well as off-the-wall collaborations, such as with Justin Vernon of Bon Iver.

My Beautiful Dark Twisted Fantasy, West's fifth studio album, was released in November 2010 to rave reviews from critics, many of whom described it as his best work that solidified his comeback. In stark contrast to his previous effort, which featured a minimalist sound, *Dark Fantasy* adopts a maximalist philosophy and deals with themes of celebrity and excess. The record included the international hit "All of the Lights," and Billboard hits "Power," "Monster," and "Runaway," the latter of which accompanied a 35-minute film of the same name. During this time, West initiated the free music program GOOD Fridays through his website, offering a free download of previously unreleased songs each Friday, a portion of which were included on the album. This promotion ran from August 20 to December 17, 2010. *Dark Fantasy* went on to go platinum in the United States, but its omission as a contender for Album of the Year at the 54th Grammy Awards was viewed as a "snub" by several media outlets.

Following a headlining set at Coachella 2011 that was described by *The Hollywood Reporter* as "one of greatest hip-hop sets of all time," West released the collaborative album *Watch the Throne* with Jay-Z. By employing a sales strategy that released the album digitally weeks before its physical counterpart, *Watch the Throne* became one of the few major label albums in the Internet age to avoid a leak. "Niggas in Paris" became the record's highest charting single, peaking at number five on the *Billboard* Hot 100. In 2012, West released the compilation album *Cruel Summer,* a collection of tracks by artists from West's record label GOOD Music. *Cruel Summer* produced four singles, two of which charted within the top twenty of the Hot 100: "Mercy" and "Clique."

Sessions for West's sixth solo effort begin to take shape in early 2013 in his own personal loft's living room at a Paris hotel. Determined to "undermine the commercial," he once again brought together close collaborators and attempted to incorporate Chicago drill, dancehall, acid house, and industrial music. Primarily inspired by architecture, West's perfectionist tendencies led him to contact producer Rick Rubin fifteen days shy of its due date to strip down the record's sound in favor of a more minimalist approach. Initial promotion of his sixth album included worldwide video projections of the album's music and live television performances. Yeezus, West's sixth album, was released June 18, 2013 to rave reviews from critics. It became the rapper's sixth consecutive number one debut, but also marked his lowest solo opening week sales. On September 6, 2013, Kanye West announced he would be headlining his first solo tour in five years, to support Yeezus, with fellow American rapper Kendrick Lamar, accompanying him along the way.

West released a single, "Only One," featuring Paul McCartney, on December 31, 2014. "FourFiveSeconds," a single jointly produced with Rihanna and McCartney, was released on January 23, 2015. West had played the song before radio programmers at the iHeartMedia Music Summit. West also appeared on the *Saturday Night Live 40th Anniversary Special* and performed the songs "Jesus Walks," "Only One" (without Paul McCartney, who also performed at the event) and premiered a new song entitled "Wolves," which features Sia Furler and fellow Chicago rapper, Vic Mensa. "Wolves" is reported to be the first track on West's seventh solo album, titled Swish. On March 2, 2015, West released the second single from the album called "All Day" which features Theophilus London, Allan Kingdom and Paul McCartney. West performed the song at the 2015 BRIT Awards with a number of US rappers and UK grime MC's including: Skepta, Wiley, Novelist, Fekky, Krept & Konan, Stormzy, Allan Kingdom, Theophilus London and Vic Mensa, although McCartney was not present for the performance.

Allmusic editor Jason Birchmeier writes of his impact, "As his career progressed throughout the early 21st century, West shattered certain stereotypes about rappers, becoming a superstar on his own terms without adapting his appearance, his rhetoric, or his music to fit any one musical mold." On the other hand, Jon Caramanica of *The New York Times* said that West has been "a frequent lightning rod for controversy, a bombastic figure who can count rankling two presidents among his achievements, along with being a reliably dyspeptic presence at award shows (when he attends them)."

Personal Life

According to reports that were widely published in the summer of 2006, West was engaged to marry his girlfriend, Alexis, whom he had begun to date before his 2002 car crash but with whom he had not been romantically involved consistently since then. West's life was deeply affected when his mother, Donda West, died of complications from cosmetic surgery involving abdominoplasty and breast reduction in November 2007. Months later, West and fiancée Alexis Phifer ended their engagement and their long-term intermittent relationship, which had begun in 2002.

West began dating reality star and longtime friend Kim Kardashian in April 2012. West and Kardashian became engaged in October 2013, and married on May 24, 2014 at Fort di Belvedere in Florence, Italy. They have two children: daughter North "Nori" West (born June 15, 2013) and son Saint West (born December 5, 2015).

Further Reading

Chicago Tribune C pl+ Aug. 28, 2005
Entertainment Weekly p22+ Feb. 3, 2006
Los Angeles Times E pl+ Aug. 28, 2005
Playboy p49+ Mar. 1, 2006
Rolling Stone p3846 Feb. 9, 2006
Time p54+ Aug. 29, 2005
Bourus, Anthony. *Kanye West: Grammy-Winning Hip-Hop Artist & Producer* (2013)

White Stripes

Rock band

Jack White
Vocalist; guitarist; songwriter
Born: July 9, 1975; Detroit, Michigan

Meg White
Drummer
Born: Dec. 10, 1974; Grosse Pointe, Michigan

Primary Field: Garage rock
Group Affiliation: White Stripes

Introduction

In his review of the White Stripes' Elephant *(2003) for* NME *(March 19, 2003), John Mulvey gushed that the album contained "some of the most obliteratingly brilliant rock'n'roll of our time." Such praise has become nearly commonplace in critical descriptions of the White Stripes, who, since their humble beginnings in Detroit, Michigan, in 1997, have become one of the most celebrated and popular rock bands of the day. Playing the straightforward, feedback-drenched protorock that has come to be known as "garage rock," the White Stripes draw from American folk music, blues, punk, and classic Broadway musicals. The group's combination of grittiness, simplicity, and emotional depth has made them, in the opinions of many, the perfect antidote to the highly produced teen-pop and homogenous alternative rock and metal that dominate current rock-radio playlists.*

Early Lives

Jack White was born John Anthony Gillis in Detroit, Michigan, on July 9, 1975. He has said that he has nine siblings. After teaching himself guitar and drums, Gillis began playing the former with the local garage-rock band the Go and the latter with a country-rock group known as Goober and the Peas. To make ends *meet,* he ran an upholstery business. He recalled to Austin Scaggs for *Rolling Stone* (May 1, 2003) that he became enamored of the blues at the age of 18. "I dabbled in things like Howlin' Wolf, Cream and Led Zeppelin, but when I heard Son House and Robert Johnson, it blew *my* mind. It was something I'd been missing *my* whole life. That music made *me* discard everything else and just get down to the soul and honesty of the blues."

Megan White was born on December 10, 1974 and grew up in Grosse Pointe, Michigan. Before she and Gillis met, in Detroit, she did not play any instrument. When the two married, on September 21, 1996, Gillis took White's surname. One day Megan White, who worked as a cook and a bartender, decided to accompany her husband on drums while he jammed on guitar. The sound pleased Jack, and on July 14, 1997 the White Stripes came into being. (The name was inspired by the look of peppermint candy canes.) Jack and Meg. White both wear red and white outfits on stage. "When we played we decided we wanted to dress up in our Sunday best like a kid would," Jack White told a writer for *BBC News* (August 10, 2001, on-line). "If you tell a kid that they are going to church, they'll always *come* down in a red outfit or something and be told 'No, you can't go to church in that.'"

Lives' Work

In 1997 the White Stripes' first single, "Let's Shake Hands," was released on seven-inch vinyl on the Italy

Records imprint. The disk also contained the pair's version of "Look Me Over Closely," written by Terry Gilkyson in 1952 and made famous by Marlene Dietrich. The White Stripes' first concert was at the Gold Dollar, a Detroit bar. "They had an open-mike night," Jack White recalled to Austin Scaggs, "and there was only, like, ten or fifteen people there. We played three songs, one of which was 'Love Potion Number Nine' [written by Jerry Lieber and Mike Stoller in 1959]. We were shocked that people dug what we were doing."

After releasing their second single, "Lafayette Blues," for Italy Records, the White Stripes spent the next couple of years playing at various venues in the Detroit indie-rock scene, drawing attention with the wide variety of influences reflected in their sound. In 1999 they released their third single, "The Big Three Killed My Baby," on the *Sym*pathy for the Record Industry label. The same label released their eponymous debut album later that year. Writing for the *All* Music *Guide* Web site, Chris Handyside called the album "minimal to the point of sounding monumental" and remarked that the White Stripes "sound like arena rock as handcrafted in the attic." Along with original material, the album contains covers of the blues legend Robert Johnson's "Stop Breakin' Down" and Bob Dylan's "One More Cup of Coffee."

Although the mainstream press in the United States barely noticed the band's debut album, *White Stripes* gained a great deal of media attention in England, where the Whites were featured prominently in such popular music magazines as *NME* and *Melody Maker.* In addition, national British tabloids including the London *Daily Telegraph* and the London *Sun,* and even the somewhat conservative BBC Radio, reported on the group. The influential BBC deejay John Peel compared their importance to that of the rock legend Jimi Hendrix and the punk pioneers the Sex Pistols. In the United States the White Stripes began to receive some national recognition after two tours with the successful indie-rock bands Pavement and Sleater-Kinney in 1999 and 2000.

The White Stripes survived the Whites' divorce, in 2000. That year they released their album *De Stijl;* Dutch for "the style," *De Stijl* is a reference to a Dutch design movement that advocated simplicity and minimalism. The record sold well for an independent release and, like its predecessor, impressed critics. In *Rolling Stone* (on-line), Jenny Eliscu described the album as "feisty and clever, full of scuzzy garage rock. ... Meg White's drumming is so minimal that it's almost funny: It forces a smile because, like everything about the White Stripes, it proves that you don't need bombast to make a blues explosion."

With the release of *White Blood Cells,* in 2001, the music press began to treat the Whites as indie-rock superstars. Both *Rolling Stone* and *Mojo* featured laudatory articles about the band, and *NME* placed a photo of the White Stripes on its front cover, virtually crediting them with the rebirth of rock and roll. On the band's tour to promote *White Blood Cells,* in 2001, several of their shows sold out; indeed, the White Stripes had become so hip that celebrities including the actress Kate Hudson and the Black Crowes' vocalist Chris Robinson attended their shows. The duo's single "Fell in Love with a Girl" became a hit on rock radio; the associated video received play on MTV and Much Music USA. Jack and Meg White reacted to their newfound popularity with both surprise and apprehension. Reflecting the band's discomfort with publicity, the cover of *White Blood Cells* shows the couple against a blood-red background facing silhouetted people in threatening postures. In another photo, on the back of the album notes, the Whites are swarmed by reporters. "A lot of the lyrics are kind of paranoid," Jack White told Benjamin Nugent for *Time* (June 16, 2001, on-line). "It does kind of match all these figures coming at us on the cover." With *White Blood Cells* the duo made a conscious effort to abandon the more overt references to blues in their music. "Before any more of this blues label is thrown on us . . . Meg and I decided to take a break from it," Jack White told Chris Morris for *Billboard* (June 23, 2001). "No slide guitar, no cover songs—just me, Meg, guitar, drums, vocals." Others among their eclectic influences remain evident on the record: Black Sabbath-style heavy metal in the Whites' "Expecting," for example, and classic cinema in "The Union Forever," whose lyrics come exclusively from the script of *Citizen Kane* (1941), Jack White's favorite film. *White Blood Cells* received enthusiastic reviews. In her critique for the *All Music Guide* Web site, Heather Phares wrote that the group "wraps their powerful, deceptively simple style around meditations on fame, love, and betrayal" on an album that sounds "bigger and tighter than their earlier material, but not so polished that it will scare away longtime fans." "The White Stripes have certainly borrowed from rock's past, but each song on this rough-and-ragged mix emerges as a unique and oddly satisfying gem," Joe Heim wrote for the *Washington Post* (July 11, 2001). Heim also noted, "This album's unifying force . . . resides largely in Jack's anguished vocal style and intensely interesting songwriting. His hook-filled songs boast lyrics that are as poppy and accessible as they are fascinating and beguiling."

In November 2001, following complaints from the public that their new album was not readily available in stores, the White Stripes signed with V2 Records, a larger independent label, which reissued *White Blood Cells.* With stronger label backing, the disk rose to number 61 on the *Billboard* album chart. On the strength of *White Blood Cells,* the White Stripes won three MTV Video Music awards, opened twice for the Rolling Stones, and sold out Radio City Music Hall in New York City in a joint concert with the garage-rock band the Strokes.

In their fourth album, *Elephant,* the duo again tinkered with their trademark sound, adding bass guitar. The album was dedicated to the "death of the sweetheart," which, as Jack White explained to Hugo Lindgren for the *New York Times* (March 9, 2003), was a reference to what he sees as a contemporary emphasis on being tough and aloof at the expense of being gentle and kind: "You look at your average teenager with the body piercings and tattoos. You have white kids going around talking in ghetto accents because they think that makes them hard. It's so cool to be hard. We're against that." Meg White added, "The message everywhere is it's OK not to care about anything. Everything can be judged, everything can be trashed." *Elephant* opens with the song "Seven Nation Army," which reached the top spot on *Billboard's* modern-rock singles chart. Another song, "There's No Home for You Here," features some rare studio wizardry from the band: the layered multi-tracking of Jack White's voice to produce harmonies, which drew critical comparisons to the work of the operatic rock band Queen. The album also includes "In the Cold, Cold Night," sung by Meg White accompanied only by an acoustic guitar, and "It's True That We Love One Another," a lighthearted number that plays off the myth that the Whites are siblings.

Elephant received mostly glowing reviews and peaked at number six on *Billboard's* album chart. In a review for that magazine's March 29, 2003 issue, Andrew Katchen called the record "mighty and uncompromising . . . gloriously muddy around the edges and incisively executed." In *Rolling Stone* (April 17, 2003), David Fridge characterized *Elephant* as "a work of pulverizing perfection.... [The duo] finally romp and rattle like a fully armed band. It is a glorious thing to hear. It will be one of the best things you hear all year." The album struck Heather Phares, writing for the *All Music Guide* Web site, as "sound[ing] even more pissed-off, paranoid, and stunning" as well as "darker and more difficult" than the band's previous album. By contrast, Jon Pareles wrote for the *New York Times* (April 6, 2003) that *Elephant* "reverts to posturing and in-jokes" while delivering "less than half an album's worth" of songs.

Affiliation: Garage Rock

In his assessment of *Elephant* for the British magazine *Q* (March 2003, on-line), John Harris characterized the White Stripes' contribution to rock music: "Firstly, in fusing a transparently punk approach with the blues, they spoke a fantastically authentic language—enough to reveal a lot of rock bands as careerist, conformist clowns—without falling prey to tedious history worship. Secondly, they provided a commendably timely reminder of the fact that the best groups live in their own universes, laden with reference points and brimming with mystery."

The White Stripes are a duo: Jack White, who contributes the vocals, lyrics, and guitar accompaniment, and Meg White, who supplies the beats. Writing for the *All Music Guide* Web site, Chris Handyside hailed Jack White's voice as "a singular, evocative combination of punk, metal, blues, and backwoods" and his guitar playing as "grand and banging with just enough lyrical touches of slide and subtle solo work to let you know he means to use the metal-blues riff collisions just so." Equally important to the band's sound is Meg White, who, with powerful strokes, drums simply yet effectively. Except for the rare addition of organ or piano, the White Stripes' music comes from only guitar and drums. The nature of the Whites' personal relationship has provided much fodder for the press. Many in the rock media accepted at face value the Whites' claims to be brother and sister. In reality, as *Time* reported in 2001, Jack White and Meg White are not related and were married for several years before divorcing, in 2000. Nevertheless, Jack White told Tom Sinclair for *Entertainment Weekly* (May 17, 2 002), "We will be brother and sister till the day we die."

Personal Lives

Jack White and Meg White both live in Detroit, where they remain fixtures of the city's club circuit; Jack White produces and collaborates with many local bands, including Green Horns and Whirlwind Heat. With the intention of producing Whirlwind Heat's debut album, Jack White signed a deal with V2 to establish Third Man Records, a V2 subsidiary. The White Stripes' concert schedule was disrupted twice in 2003, when Meg fractured a wrist in March after slipping on a patch of ice in New York City, and again when Jack broke an index finger in a car accident in July. Jack White has said that he idolizes Robert Johnson; Johnny Cash, whose country songs contain elements of rock and roll and blues; and the late classic pop composer Cole Porter. "My real dream is unattainable," he told Tom Sinclair. "I wish I could be a blues musician back in the '20s and '30s, just playing in juke joints in the South by myself. But I'm white and I was born in Detroit in the '70s, so I guess I'll have to settle for this."

Further Reading

BBC News (on-line) Aug. 10, 2001
Billboard p85 June 23, 2001, p1 Apr. 27, 2002
Entertainment Weekly (on-line) May 17, 2002
Interview (on-line) May 2003
New York Observer p20 Feb. 24, 2003
New York Times VI p17 Mar. 9, 2003, with photo
Rolling Stone May 1, 2003, with photo
Time (on-line) June 16, 2001, with photo

Wilco

Music Group

Jeff Tweedy
Singer; songwriter; guitarist
Born: Aug. 25, 1967; Belleville, Illinois

John Stirratt
Bass guitar player
Born: 1967

Nels Cline
Guitarist
Born: Jan. 4, 1956

Glenn Kotche
Drummer
Born: 1970

Pat Sansone
Multi-instrumentalist
Born: June 21, 1969

Mikael Jorgensen
Keyboardist
Born: 1972(?)

Primary Field: Classic rock music performers and recording artists
Group Affiliation: Wilco

Introduction

After the popular "alternative-country" music act Uncle Tupelo disbanded, in 1993, its co-founder Jeff Tweedy launched Wilco, which has earned critical recognition and commercial success and is one of the few contemporary groups that appeal to teenagers, their parents, and the generation in between. Wilco has cultivated its audience through an idiosyncratic mix of "roots" country, experimental yet accessible pop, psychedelia, and classic-style rock. It has won praise from the music press for its seven studio albums, collaborations with Billy Bragg on two collections based on songs by Woody Guthrie, and live album. Tweedy, the band's main vocalist and primary songwriter, is the face of Wilco.

Early Lives

The youngest of four children, Jeffrey Scott Tweedy was born on August 25, 1967 in Belleville, Illinois, a working-class suburb of St. Louis, Missouri. His father, Bob, was a switching-yard supervisor with the Alton & Southern Railroad; his mother, Jo Ann, was a kitchen designer. Tweedy showed an inclination toward music at a very young age. "My mom put records on for me before I could operate the turntable," he told Steven Chean for *USAWeekend.com* (April 7, 2002). "Before I could speak, she says, I would point to it." Tweedy's siblings, Debra Ann, Steven, and Robert, all born in the 1950s, "were more like doting aunts and uncles" to their younger brother, according to Greg Kat, in his book *Wilco: Learning How to Die* (2004). When they left for college, he picked through their record collections, discovering bands including Herman's Hermits and the Beatles. Soon he was also listening to punk rock, absorbing the sounds of X and the Clash. In eighth grade, while confined to his bed for several weeks with a leg injury he suffered in a bicycle accident, Tweedy picked up the acoustic guitar his mother had given him when he was six. "I saw the life my dad had, and I knew I didn't want it," he told Kot. "He had to take care of a family basically since he was seventeen, and the only real outlet he had was a twelve-pack after working all day. I saw the guitar as my outlet."

While a freshman at Belleville Township High School West, Tweedy saw his first live rock show, performed at a junior-high-school dance by the Plebes—a band consisting of Tweedy's classmate Jay Farrar and his older brothers, Wade and Dade. "I just went nuts . . . ," he told Kat. "I was just completely blown away in awe—in awe of Jay, in awe of his brothers, in awe of the idea that this could be happening, that I was part of their inner circle in some way. . . . They were empowered in the way that I imagined myself to be empowered." Tweedy began to spend time with the Farrar brothers and took over on bass guitar when Dade left the band. Before departing Dade had brought in a new drummer, Mike Heidorn, for a lineup that now included Wade on vocals and Jay on guitar. The band changed its name to the Primitives (sometimes spelled "Primatives") and began to play raw, fast-paced covers of garage-rock, punk, and country songs. When Wade became too busy at college to practice regularly, the remaining trio re-formed as Uncle Tupelo, taking its name from two words randomly chosen from two columns of nouns they had written. (Tupelo, Mississippi, is the birthplace of Elvis Presley.) Uncle Tupelo began to write its own material, inspired by such punk bands as Husker Du and the Minutemen and by Neil Young, the Canadian singer-songwriter and guitarist known for his unique brand of acoustic folk and harder, guitar-heavy rock. Richard Byrne, then a music columnist for the St. Louis weekly the *Riverfront Times*, told Kot, "[Uncle Tupelo was] hearing the country and folk stuff that they grew up around, and they were listening to all their . . . punk records, and Neil crystallized it for them."

After high school Tweedy enrolled in courses at Southern Illinois University–Edwardsville and Belleville Area College. Less passionate about school than about playing in the band, however, he failed to graduate. To support themselves the members of Uncle Tupelo worked odd jobs; Tweedy found work as a clerk at a St. Louis music store, Euclid Records. Although the store's manager, Tony Margherita, was unmoved the first time he saw a live performance by Tweedy's band, a later acoustic show—free of the feedback and distortion Uncle Tupelo created during a regular set—so impressed him that he became the band's manager, booking shows and talking the band members into recording a demo tape. Soon Uncle Tupelo was playing regularly at Cicero's, a St. Louis "dive" bar that was quickly becoming the center of a growing independent-music scene. The band developed a small but devoted following.

Lives' Work

In 1989 Uncle Tupelo signed with the independent label asatanka/Rockville/Crepescule, Their debut album, *No Depression* (1990), has been widely credited as the catalyst for "alt-country"—music that merged the energy of punk with traditional Americana and country, Jason Ankeny wrote for the All Music Guide Web site, "The most rock-centric of Uncle Tupelo's releases, its songs were meditations on small-town, small-time life, candid snapshots of days spent working thankless jobs and nights spent in an alcoholic fog."

Uncle Tupelo's sophomore effort, *Still Feel Gone* (1991), expanded on the sound of its predecessor, *March 16-20, 1992*, released the next year, was named for the five days over which it was recorded. Consisting of all-acoustic originals and covers of traditional folk songs, the album was a critical success. Shortly after its release, Heidorn left the band and was replaced by the drummer Ken Coomer. Around that time Tweedy and Farrar recruited Max Johnston to play violin and mandolin at live shows and added John Stirratt (born in 1967) to the road crew, to maintain the conditions of the guitar. Stirratt also played bass for Uncle Tupelo occasionally, freeing Tweedy to play guitar.

Uncle Tupelo signed to Sire Records before the release of *Anodyne* (1993), which is considered to be the band's most accomplished and cohesive work. Ankeny wrote for the All Music Guide that Uncle Tupelo "never struck a finer balance between rock and country than on *Anodyne*." Although the record was not supported by mainstream radio or MTV, it sold more than 150,000 copies and became an alt-country staple. Not long after its release, however, differences between Farrar and Tweedy led Farrar to break up the band. Since the release of Uncle Tupelo's first recording, the two had been vying to have songs included on the albums. "It just seemed like it reached a point where Jeff and I really weren't compatible," Farrar told the alt-country magazine *No Depression*, according to a *Los Angeles Times* article (January 20, 2005) by Randy Lewis. "It had ceased to be a symbiotic songwriting relationship." Tweedy told Kot, "I thought it could go on for a long time, with each of us contributing our six best songs to an album, and I would have been happy to continue on that way, I was nätive."

Intent on continuing to write and record music, Tweedy—with Coomer, Johnston, and Stirratt—formed a new group. After briefly considering the name "National Dust," the band members settled on "Wilco"—short for "will comply," a term used in two-way radio communication. Tweedy told Deborah Solomon for the *New York Times* (July 5,

2009, on-line) that the name "struck me as an ironic name for a rock band, which is historically responsible for not complying." Under Margherita's management, Wilco signed with Reprise, a Warner Bros, subsidiary.

Wilco's debut, *A.M.*, recorded less than a year after Uncle Tupelo dissolved, included the work of the guitarist Brian Henneman of Missouri's Bottle Rockets and the pedal-steel player Lloyd Maines, *A.M.* received generally positive reviews, with some critics noting the continuation of Uncle Tupelo's sound and themes, Holly George-Warren wrote for *Rolling Stone* (February 2, 1998), "The band's back-porch groove is the perfect underpinning for Tweedy's laconic baritone; he leaves wide-open spaces with his laid-back phrasing and the plain-spoken poetry of his lyrics. Maines' lovesick pedal steel and Johnston's nimble offerings on mandolin, banjo, dobra and fiddle add plaintiveness, while Henneman's Neil Young-inspired guitar antics provide muscle."

In 1995 Tweedy married a booking agent, Sue Miller, bought a home in Chicago, Illinois, and became a father, and the emotions stirred by those developments came through in Wilco's next album, *Being There* (1996). "I was a later bloomer," Tweedy told Kat. "I was in my thirties before I even came to terms with the idea that I was making a living as a recording artist. . . . [With Uncle Tupelo] I was a bass player in a band making fifty dollars a night, paying eighty dollars a month in rent . . . and having this näive sense of well-being that I would always do this and never have much more responsibility than that. I went from that to being a dad and a major label-recording artist who had the pressure of supporting a family and also making something I felt good about artistically." A 19-song double album, *Being There* won critical acclaim. It featured the work of a recently recruited second guitarist, Jay Bennett, who replaced Henneman, and the pedal-steel player Bob Egan of the band Freakwater on two tracks. *Being There* was regarded by the music press as a bit of a departure from the alt-country sounds of *A.M.*, as many of the songs had off-the-wall lyrics, improvised moments, and other

Affiliation: Classic Pop Rock Music

Bob Mehr wrote for the *American Way* Web site, "Tweedy has continually challenged both his audience and himself musically. A somewhat reluctant rock star, he's managed to toe the fine line between underground respect and mainstream success and has become one of contemporary music's most compelling and revered figures in the process."

Wilco has gone through several lineup changes, with Tweedy and John Stirratt being the only constant members; the band currently includes, in addition, the guitarist Nels Cline, the multi-instrumentalists Pat Sansone and Mikael Jorgensen, and the drummer Glenn Kotche. Joe Klein wrote for the *New York Times* (June 13, 2004), "Through it all, Tweedy has produced some terrific (and not so terrific) music. Each Wilco album is different from the last. Tweedy is a classic autodidact, inhaling books, constantly pushing himself to grow and change. Over time, he has become a better guitar player and learned how to mess with the computerized gimmickry of the modern recording studio. Most important, he has figured out how to sing in an entirely distinctive and compelling way. Like [Bob] Dylan, Neil Young and others, Tweedy has a scratchy, nasal, good-bad voice, which depends on his emotional intelligence and phrasing, rather than timbre, for its effectiveness. His delivery is purposefully nervous, artfully irresolute. He will bend or slur a phrase, pause uncomfortably, allow a note to shatter in mid-attack; at times, it sounds as if he's very close to a nervous breakdown. There is a terrible sadness to it."

experimental elements. For example, in a portion of the opening track, "Misunderstood," the band members can be heard in the background playing one another's instruments. In an article for the *Chicago Tribune* (October 18, 1996), Kat wrote, "The first sound heard on Wilco's new record, *Being There*, suggests studio meltdown: amplifiers buzzing, violins sawing, noise swelling. It's a cacophonous introduction that says, put away all your preconceptions and enjoy the ride, because the band's friendly Midwestern twang has taken on some new accents." The album fared better than *A.M.* commercially, peaking at number 73 on the *Billboard* 200 album chart and landing on several "best-of-the-year" lists. The single "Outtasite (Outta Mind)" received a moderate amount of play on college radio stations.

Not long after the release of *Being There*, Johnston left Wilco to play music with his sister, Michelle Shocked; he was replaced by Egan. In 1998 Wilco collaborated with the British singer-songwriter Billy Bragg on a collection of songs based on previously unrecorded material by the iconic folk singer Woody Guthrie, who died in 1967. The recording sessions were organized by Guthrie's daughter, Nora, who had approached Bragg in 1995 about recording her father's songs for a new audience. Bragg told Kat that the influence of traditional music on Wilco's sound appealed to him: "With a lot of American roots bands, it doesn't go back much beyond the 1950s, but Wilco gives you the feeling that they go back to the '30s and even into the last century."

Although Wilco and Bragg had creative clashes during the recording sessions, the results—*Mermaid Avenue* (1998) and *Mermaid Avenue*, Vol. 2 (2000)—were critically acclaimed, and *Mermaid Avenue* was nominated for a Grammy Award for best contemporary folk album. On the albums Bragg performed Guthrie's more overtly political material, while Tweedy chose to record the singer's more personal songs. In a 1998 review posted on his Web site, the music critic Robert Christgau wrote of the first release, "It's the music, especially Wilco's music, that transfigures the enterprise. Projecting the present back on the past in an attempt to make the past signify as future, they create an old-time rock and roll that never could have existed. Finally—folk-rock!" Mark Guarino wrote for the *Chicago Daily Herald* (July 10, 1998), "The timeless sound of *Mermaid Avenue* prevents it from being a novelty knock-off and instead surrounds Guthrie's words with lively arrangements and an unholy playfulness. Here, there's the clunky pianos, honking harmonicas, shout-along choruses, wheezy slide guitars and the unpretentious production heard on Wilco's acclaimed double-album *Being There*. Not only demonstrating the breezy interplay between folk and rock styles, the new album clearly links Guthrie to modern times without damaging nor deifying him."

Wilco's *Summerteeth* (1999), recorded prior to the Mermaid Avenue sessions, won rave reviews for songs that largely eschewed country influences in favor of densely layered pop. Jason Ankeny wrote, "While lacking the sheer breadth and ambition of . . . *Being There, Summerteeth* is the most focused Wilco effort yet, honing the lessons of the last record to forge a majestic pop sound almost completely devoid of alt-country elements; the lush string arrangements and gorgeous harmonies of tracks like 'She's a Jar' and 'Pieholden Suite' suggest nothing less than a landlocked Brian Wilson [of the Beach Boys], while more straightforward rockers like the opening 'I Can't Stand It' bear the influence of everything from R&B to psychedelia." Christgau included *Summerteeth* in the Top 10 of his annual "Pazz and Jop Critics Poll" in the *Village Voice*. Nonetheless, *Summerteeth's* failure to sell as well as *Being There* caused strained relations between Wilco and the band's record label.

Wilco recorded its fourth album, *Yankee Hotel Foxtrot*, at a Chicago loft converted into a recording studio. Tweedy tapped the experimental solo musician Jim O'Rourke to serve as producer, added the multi-instrumentalist Leroy Bach to the lineup, and hired the drummer Glenn Kotche (born in 1970) to replace Coomer, whom he had fired. Coomer learned of his dismissal from Margherita and was taken by surprise. "I made a decision to honor inspiration as opposed to honoring loyalty to a friend," Tweedy told Kat. "It was about loyalty to the music and to the band, and making the band better. It's not that Ken wasn't a good drummer. But he wasn't the right drummer anymore." He added, "I should have called him. . . . By the time I did make the call, I don't think he wanted to talk to me." *Yankee Hotel Foxtrot* comprised quirky pop songs with sound textures and collages provided by O'Rourke and Bennett. Despite the album's pop hooks and lush instrumentation, Reprise—under pressure to cut costs—rejected *Yankee Hotel Foxtrot* as uncommercial. Instead of reworking the album, Wilco bought out its $50,000 contract with Reprise and gained the rights to *Yankee Hotel Foxtrot*. While shopping for a new label, Wilco streamed the album on the Internet, generating anticipation among fans and critics and drumming up negative publicity for Warner Bros. and Reprise executives, who were demonized by journalists for seemingly placing profit above artistic integrity. *Yankee Hotel Foxtrot* was released in 2002 by Nonesuch Records, another Warner Music Group subsidiary. It is the biggest popular success of Wilco's career to date, debuting at number 13 on the *Billboard* pop-album chart and selling more than 400,000 copies within two years. It was named the best album of 2002 in the *Village Voice's* annual critics' poll and otherwise lavished with praise. Jeff Gordinier wrote for *Entertainment Weekly* (April 26, 2002) that it was "a subliminal album. Spin it once and it barely registers. Play it five or six times and its vaporous, insinuating, rusty-carousel melodies start to carve out a permanent orbit in your skull." Ben Wener wrote for the Orange County (*California*) *Register* (April 26, 2002), "[*Yankee Hotel Foxtrot*] is entrancing, uplifting rock 'n' roll that embodies the yin and yang of love, the exuberant joy of it all and the inevitable insecurity and tension that brings."

Although Bennett had contributed heavily to the songwriting and production of *Yankee Hotel Foxtrot*, he was asked to leave Wilco shortly after the album's release. Tweedy told Kat that during the sound-mixing process for *Yankee Hotel Foxtrot*, Bennett's controlling approach made for a tense atmosphere and undermined the group's creativity. Although Bennett initially said, as quoted by Kot, that he believed he was fired because "Jeff was threatened by me," he later acknowledged that the band's decision had been the right one. The contentious relationship between Bennett and Tweedy was captured in the 2002 documentary about the making of *Yankee Hotel Foxtrot*, Sam Jones's *I Am Trying to Break Your Heart*.

Wilco's next release, *A Ghost Is Born* (2004), was written and recorded with the help of Mikael Jorgensen, who provided sound manipulation and later joined the band as a keyboardist and live-sound manipulator. The album, like its predecessor, sprinkled Tweedy's idiosyncratic pop songs with experimental flourishes. It was also influenced by Tweedy's longtime struggle with addiction to painkillers, which he developed in an attempt to treat migraine headaches and depression. In a piece for the *New York Times* Web site (March 5, 2008) about the making of the album, Tweedy wrote, "For a lot of that record I was just trying not to be too drugged out and as a result I was suffering from enormous migraine type throbbing pain. Quite a bit of that came out on *A Ghost Is Born*. . . . In particular there's a piece of music—'Less Than You Think'—that ends with a 12-minute drone that was an attempt to express the slow painful rise and dissipation of migraine in music." (Tweedy shook his addiction after a period of rehab in 2004.) The album was a critical success and earned Wilco its first two Grammy Awards—one for best alternative-music album and another for best recording package. It also reached number eight on the *Billboard* 200 chart.

Wilco's next release, *Sky Blue Sky* (2007), included playing by the guitarist Nels Cline (born on January 4, 1956) and the multi-instrumentalist Pat Sansone (born on June 21, 1969). (Bach had left the band, amicably, after *Yankee Hotel Foxtrot*.) *Sky Blue Sky* was a more laid-back and straightforward collection, with songs reminiscent of those written during earlier incarnations of the band. *Wilco (The Album)* (2009) offered experimental tracks such as the dissonant "Bull Black Nova" along with pop-rock fare, such as the George Harrison-inspired "You Never Know," the band's second number-one song on the *Billboard* Triple A (adult album alternative) chart in 12 years. (The first was "Outtasite [Outta Mind]," in 1997.) The album also found the band poking fun at itself and reflecting on its reputation for playing emotionally charged music. For example, the opening track, "Wilco (The Song)," features Tweedy singing the sarcastic lines, "Do you dabble in depression? / Is someone twisting a knife in your back? . . . Wilco will love you, baby." *Wilco (The Album)* received generally positive reviews. David Fricke wrote for *Rolling Stone* June 29, 2009, on-line), "Wilco's seventh studio album is a triumph of determined simplicity by a band that has been running from the obvious for most of this decade."

Tom Breihan, writing for *Pitchfork.com* July 7, 2010), reported that in an interview with an express-nightout.com reporter, Cline revealed that Wilco would be leaving Nonesuch Records and would launch its own label. The following month Wilco organized its own three-day independent festival, the Solid Sound Festival, at the Massachusetts Museum of Contemporary Art (Mass MoCA), in North Adams. The festival included performances by Wilco and each Wilco member's side groups, including the Nels Cline Singers; Glenn Kotche's On Fillmore; the Autumn Defense, with both Stirratt and Sansone; and Mikael Jorgensen's Pronto.

Tweedy has sometimes been criticized for the control he exerts over the band—as when he fired when Bennett. That criticism arose again in May 2009, when Bennett sued Tweedy over royalty payments and non-compensation for his appearance in *I Am Trying to*

Break Your Heart. In statements to the media, Tweedy denied that he owed Bennett money and noted that he was not the producer of the documentary. That same month Bennett died after an accidental overdose of prescription painkillers. Tweedy told Romesh Ratnesar for *Time* (June 30, 2009) about Bennett's death, "It's a real hard thing to talk about. . . . It's been eight years since he's been in the band, and our situation was very tenuous and not very well connected. But it's a tragic end to a brilliant and gifted guy and musician. And that's really sad."

Tweedy described his singing voice to Solomon as being "somewhere between Gordon Lightfoot and a tea kettle. I would not get past the first round of *American Idol*." In addition to Wilco and Loose Fur, Tweedy has performed in the "super group" Golden Smog.

Personal Life

He lives in Chicago with his wife and two young children, Spencer and Sam. When Ratnesar asked him what had inspired the more optimistic songs on *Wilco (The Album)*, Tweedy said, "I don't think there's any reason to feel guilty about having joy in your life, regardless of how bad things are in the world. Even the most dismal and hopeless-sounding Wilco music, to my ears, has always maintained a level of hope and consolation. I think art is a consolation regardless of its content. It has the power to move and make you feel like you're not alone. And ultimately that's what everybody wants to know."

Further Reading

All Music Guide Web site
Rolling Stone Web site
USA Weekend (on-line) Apr. 7, 2002
Kot, Greg. *Wilco: Leaning How to Die*, 2004

Andy Williams

Singer

Born: December 3, 1930; Wall Lake, Iowa
Died: September 15, 2012; Branson, Missouri
Primary Field: American songbook
Group Affiliation: Solo performer

Introduction

Known for his smooth delivery of love ballads and his relaxed and casual manner, Andy Williams has built up a nationwide following through his appearances on television and his best-selling recordings. A seasoned entertainer over radio and in the smarter supper clubs, Williams has been in show business for twenty years. Since he made his TV debut on Steve Allen's Tonight *program in 1954, he has continued to enhance his reputation by a series of successful recordings, well-received summer-replacement shows on television, and video "specials." In November 1959 the Variety Club of Washington, D.C. bypassed celebrated television stars to honor the disarming Williams with its Personality of the Year award.*

Early Life

Andrew Williams was born on December 3, 1930 (some sources cite earlier dates) in Wall Lake, Iowa, a town with a population of under 1,000. His parents, Jay E. and Florence Bell (Finley) Williams, have three older sons, Richard, Robert, and Donald, and a daughter, Jane. Jay Williams, a railway mail clerk and amateur musician, trained his family into a choir to sing at the local Presbyterian Church. "We finally decided we were too good to stay home," Andy has recalled. The four Williams Brothers made their professional debut over radio station WHO in Des Moines, Iowa, when Andy was eight years old.

Until the early part of World War II, the Williams family moved with the engagements of their four singing sons. After Des Moines, they went to Chicago to appear on the *National Barn Dance* program over radio station WLS, then to Cincinnati's radio station WLW. Finally, in Los Angeles, the quartet was signed to a motion-picture contract with Metro-Goldwyn-Mayer Pictures.

The Williams Brothers were obliged to disband, however, when the two oldest brothers were called for military service. Andy, who had attended public schools along the family's route, settled down to finish his secondary education in Los Angeles, graduating in 1947. About this time the Williams Brothers reformed and teamed with comedienne Kay Thompson to create a night club act.

Life's Work

The team of Kay Thompson and the Williams Brothers made its debut in 1947. "They have since spent their time making money hand over fist," wrote a reviewer in *Harper's Magazine* a year later (July 1948). This critic described the brothers as follows: "Four young men, all of equal height and California complexion." Their singing, dancing, and buffoonery amused night club audiences in Europe and the United States for six years, until 1953. The brothers then dissolved their unit: Donald tried acting, Robert went into business, and Richard became a solo singer. "I was the youngest," Andy has said, "And I was in no hurry to do anything."

In 1954 Andy Williams recorded his first song and went to New York to market it. While there, he auditioned for a spot on the Steve Allen *Tonight* show and obtained a commitment for a two-week run. "After that no one said anything and I just reported each week and kept singing and they kept paying me," he has explained. He remained on the show for two and a half years, selecting his own songs and winning admirers with his warm voice and disarming smile. Besides singing, Williams noted, "I was called on to be anything from an Apache dancer to a gangster, from a precocious child to a Russian bartender. And it was great fun as well as a great professional experience."

Shortly after joining the *Tonight* program, Williams signed a contract with Cadence Records. Fans were soon buying discs of his mellow renditions of "Baby Doll," "Butterfly," "I Like Your Kind of Love," "Lips of Wine," "Are You Sincere?" and "Promise Me Love." His recordings of "Canadian Sunset," The Hawaiian Wedding Song," and "The Village of St. Bernadette" sold about 1,000,000 copies each. In 1956 Cadence released his first album, *Andy Williams Sings Steve Allen,* which was followed by *Andy Williams Sings Rodgers and Hammerstein* and *Two Time Winners.*

After leaving the Steve Allen program, Williams shared a minor summer-replacement series with June Valli on NBC-TV in 1957 and made several guest appearances on *The Dinah Shore Chevy Show.* Williams, who favorably impressed Miss Shore's sponsor, was chosen to replace another Chevrolet program, *The Pat Boone Chevy Showroom,* during the summer of 1958. He also impressed John Crosby, who admitted in the New York *Herald Tribune* on July 14, 1958 that he preferred Andy Williams to Pat Boone. "Not that I've got anything against Pat Boone," Crosby hastened to add. "Coming out against Pat Boone would be like coming out against the American flag—but he is just so healthy and wholesome and normal that he puts me to sleep."

In addition to entertaining on TV, Williams in 1959 returned to the night club circuit, appearing, among other places, at the Hotel Roosevelt in New Orleans. He also continued to record for Cadence, which in late 1959 released an album entitled *Lonely Street,* prompted by Williams' best-selling record with the same title. On November 21, 1959 he received the annual Personality of the Year award from the Variety Club of Washington, D.C.

During the 1960s, Williams became one of the most popular vocalists in the country and was signed to what was at that time the biggest recording contract in history. He was primarily an album artist, and at one time he had earned more gold albums than any solo performer except Frank Sinatra, Johnny Mathis and Elvis Presley. By 1973 he had earned as many as 18 gold album awards. Among his hit albums from this period were *Moon River*, *Days of Wine and Roses* (number one for 16 weeks in mid-1963), *The Andy Williams Christmas Album*, *Dear Heart*, *The Shadow of Your Smile*, *Love, Andy*, *Get Together with Andy Williams*, and *Love Story*. These recordings, along with his natural affinity for the music of the 1960s and early 1970s, combined to make him one of the premier easy listening singers of that era.

Williams forged an indirect collaborative relationship with Henry Mancini, although they never recorded together. Williams was asked to sing Mancini and Johnny Mercer's song "Moon River" from the movie *Breakfast at Tiffany's* at the 1962 Oscar Awards. The song won the Oscar and quickly became Williams' theme song; however, because it was never released as a single, "Moon River" was never actually a chart hit for Williams.

On August 5, 1966, the 14-story, 700-room Caesars Palace casino and nightclub opened in Las Vegas, Nevada, with the stage production of "Rome Swings", in which Williams starred. He performed live to a sold-out crowd in the Circus Maximus showroom. He headlined for Caesars for the next twenty years.

On September 17, 1968, Columbia released a 45-rpm record of two songs Williams sang at the funeral of his close friend, Robert F. Kennedy: "The Battle Hymn of the Republic" and Franz Schubert's "Ave Maria."

These were never released on a long-playing record.

Building on his experience with Allen and some short-term variety shows in the 1950s, he became the star of his own weekly television variety show in 1962. This series, *The Andy Williams Show*, won three Emmy Awards for outstanding variety program. Among his series regulars were the Osmond Brothers. He gave up the variety show in 1971 while it was still popular and reduced his show to three specials per year. His Christmas specials, which appeared regularly until 1974 and intermittently from 1982 into the 1990s, were among the most popular of the genre. Williams recorded eight Christmas albums over the years and was known as "Mr. Christmas," due to his perennial Christmas specials and the success of "It's the Most Wonderful Time of the Year."

Williams hosted the most Grammy telecasts—seven consecutive shows—from the 13th Annual Grammy Awards in 1971 through to the 19th Awards in 1977. He returned to television to do a syndicated half-hour series in 1976–77. Williams continued to perform live into his 80s. In a 2007 tour of the UK, Williams said that it was this that kept him vital.

In June 1991, Williams' brother Don invited him to Branson, Missouri, a small town in the Ozarks. Don Williams was the manager for entertainer Ray Stevens, who had just opened a theatre in Branson. While attending Stevens' show, Williams was encouraged by numerous Branson guests to open a venue in the town. This led Williams to build his own theatre in Branson opening on May 1, 1992 as the Moon River Theatre. The name came from his signature song. The theatre was designed to blend with the rough terrain of the Ozark Mountains. It went on to become the first theatre ever to be featured in *Architectural Digest*, and also won the 1992 Conservation Award from the State of Missouri. The theater's auditorium can accommodate 2,054 people and is arranged stadium-style for the best view. The seats and carpets match Williams' Navajo rug collection and are forest green, magenta, gold and blue. When it first opened, it was unique because his was the first non-country act to open in the then-mostly-country music town. It was said he was discouraged by many back home in California from making such a bold move, but that was what he wanted. Other non-country entertainers like Bobby Vinton, Tony Orlando, Wayne Newton and the Osmond Brothers soon followed. In 2007, Williams opened the Moon River Grill adjacent to his theater in Branson.

In his lifetime, Williams recorded forty-four albums, seventeen were Gold-certified and three were Platinum-certified.

Affiliation: Television

For thirteen weeks in 1958 *The Chevy Showroom with Andy Williams* serenaded summer audiences with such established favorites as "You Do Something to Me," "Swinging Down the Lane," and "Alexander's Ragtime Band." "This is perfect summer fare," said a New York *Herald Tribune* reviewer (July 4, 1958). "It is a lazy, good-natured show with an extremely pleasant host in Williams. He sings well in casual style and doesn't attempt to overpower you with personality."

Disappointed in his hope that the show would lead to a permanent commitment, Williams settled for guest appearances until the following summer, when he was signed to substitute for *The Gary Moore Show* on CBS-TV with a one-hour variety program, *The Andy Williams Show.* It was praised for its showmanship, simple but refreshing sets, and judicious selection of guest performers, including Carol Lawrence, the Mills Brothers, and Stan Freberg.

In the autumn of 1959 Williams began to concentrate on one-hour video "specials." The first was *Music from Shubert Alley* over NBCTV on November 13, 1959. The hour's entertainment, with Williams as a vocalist and master of ceremonies, featured dances and songs from Broadway musicals of the last sixty years.

Personal Life

Williams met French-born Claudine Longet when he came to her aid on a Las Vegas road. She was a dancer at the time at the Folies Bergère. They married on December 15, 1961. Over the next eight years they had three children, Noelle, Christian, and Robert. After a lengthy separation, they divorced in 1975. In March 1976, Longet was charged with fatally shooting her boyfriend, alpine ski racer Spider Sabich, in Aspen. Williams played a public role in the subsequent events, escorting her to and from the courtroom, testifying to her character at the trial and providing legal assistance. She claimed the shooting was accidental, and eventually received 30 days in jail.

On May 3, 1991, Williams married Debbie Meyer, they made their homes at Branson, Missouri and La Quinta, California, where he was known as the "honorary mayor."

Williams was an avid golfer and hosted the PGA Tour golf tournament in San Diego from 1968–88 at Torrey Pines. Known then as the "Andy Williams San Diego Open", the tournament continues as the Farmers Insurance Open, usually played in February. He was also a competent ice skater, and occasionally skated as part of his television Christmas shows.

Williams was also a noted collector of Navajo blankets. His collection could be seen hanging in his home, his offices, and the Moon River Theater, and was exhibited at the Saint Louis Art Museum in 1997–1998. Williams collection was valued at over $1 million by Sotheby's, who sold it in May of 2013 for $978,506.

In a surprise appearance at his theater in November 2011, Williams announced that he had been diagnosed with bladder cancer. On September 25, 2012, Williams died of bladder cancer at the age of 84 at his home in Branson, Missouri. He was survived by his wife, Debbie and three children.

FURTHER READING

N Y *Post* Mag p3 N 1 '59 por
N Y Times II p3 Ag 24 '58 por
Wood, C. *TV Personalities vol 3* (1957)
Andy Williams: Moon River and Me, A Memoir, Williams, A., Viking Oct 13, 2008

HANK WILLIAMS, JR.

Singer; songwriter; instrumentalist

Born: May 26, 1949; Shreveport, Louisiana
Primary Field: Country
Group Affiliation: Solo performer

Hank Williams, Jr.

INTRODUCTION

"It's a good thing I was born Gemini / 'Cause I'm living for more than one man," the country musician Hank Williams Jr. sings in "Living Proof," one of the many autobiographical songs he has written. Williams was referring to his astrological sign-the constellation also known as the Twins—and to something he has wrestled with almost since birth: the legend of his father, Hank Williams, who is widely regarded as the father of modern country music songwriting. In the mid-1970s, Hank Williams Jr. decided to follow his own muse, and he distinguished himself as one of country music's "outlaws" by playing a rock-flavored brand of honky-tonk twang that became hugely successful. Thirteen of the 68 albums Williams has recorded have reached the top of the music charts; 20 have been certified gold, seven platinum, and one triple platinum. He has received 16 Broadcast Music Inc. (BMI) awards for his songwriting, and he has been named the "entertainer of the year" by both the Academy of Country Music and the Country Music Association.

Early Life

Hank Williams Jr., who has one sister, was three years old when his father died. He was born Randall Hank Williams in Shreveport, Louisiana, on May 26, 1949, just days before his parents moved to Nashville. His father liked to call him Bocephus, a nickname that many of his fans continue to use. His mother, Audrey Shepard Williams, was the woman who inspired many of Hank Williams's classic hymns to misery. It should also be noted that, by all accounts, without Audrey's strong encouragement, her husband might never have pursued a recording career.

Hank Jr. learned to play guitar and several other instruments in early childhood; he eventually became proficient at more than eight, including fiddle, harmonica, and drums. "I was taught by the best, like [the famed bluegrass banjoist] Earl Scruggs," he told Melvin Shestack in an interview for the *Country Music Encyclopedia* (1974). "He'd come over and show me a couple of things." Hank Jr. was soon performing onstage. "I played my first show at eight, with Grandpa Jones, my sister, and Momma," he told Shestack. "Between the ages of eight and 14, I did about 30 to 50 shows a year." With his name and heritage, it is hardly surprising that Hank Williams Jr. won praise for playing and, in fact, was expected to play-his father's biggest hits. "There was never any resentment about my singing his songs," he told Robert Hilburn of *Coronet* (February 1968). "Everybody thought it was cute to see a kid with a big guitar."

Reportedly, Audrey Williams tried to protect her son from Nashville record executives, who were eager from the start to cash in on Hank Jr.'s unique appeal, and she turned down the many offers of recording contracts that came his way. At the same time, she encouraged her son's development as a performer, and when he was 14, she included him in her traveling revue, the Audrey Williams Musical Caravan of Stars, when he wasn't in school. He began as an opening act, and immediately began working his way toward the top of the bill. Soon Hank Jr. signed a record contract with MGM, and moved with Audrey to California to begin his recording career.

Life's Work

In January 1964, he released his first single, a. version of "Long Gone Lonesome Blues," which became a top-10 country hit. His first album, *Hank Williams Jr. Sings the Songs of Hank Williams,* was released that May. Curious and hopeful country enthusiasts made the record a steady seller. Before the end of the year, Hank Jr. released two more albums, *Great Country Favorites* and *Your Cheatin' Heart,* the latter of which was the soundtrack to the biographical film of the same name, which premiered in 1965 and starred George Hamilton as Hank Williams.

For the better part of the decade that followed, Hank Williams Jr. continued to rely on his father's music. He did not feel satisfied doing this, because, as the *Encyclopedia of Folk, Country & Western Music* reported, "unlike many other sons of famous fathers, Hank Williams Jr. was immensely talented." In 1965, he wrote and recorded his first original song, "Standing in the Shadows," which made obvious autobiographical references to the legacy of a "very famous man." The song was another top- 10 hit, and it earned him a BMI songwriting award. He was the youngest person up to that point to win that award. Williams's restlessness also led him to play rock-'n'-roll concerts in high school, under the name Rockin' Randall, and he often included tunes by such artists as Chuck Berry and Fats Domino in his regular concerts, if he felt the audiences were young enough. A handsome young man with an athletic build; he loved hunting and fishing and executed in varsity football, basketball, and boxing. In addition, he flirted with an acting career; in the MGM film *A Time to Sing* (1968), he starred as a farm boy who becomes a successful country-and-western singer.

To many of the older fans who came to hear him sing, and especially the Nashville music establishment that promoted him, Hank Williams Jr.'s interests and ambitions didn't matter. With the death of Hank Williams Sr., Hank Jr. had inherited a complete career—as long as he was content to be the second coming of Hank Williams. The result was that, at a time when Willie Nelson, Waylon Jennings, and other country musicians were growing impatient with the production-by-committee practices and the worn-out "Nashville sound" of contemporary country music, Hank Jr. was kept on a tighter leash than anyone else. In assessments of Williams's career, the merits of such albums as. *Hank Williams Jr.'s Greatest Hits* (1969) and *Eleven Roses* (1972) are largely ignored, because his later work in the 1970s made clear that the "Nashville sound" was not what Williams truly wanted to produce. Many critics identify a concert given in 1969 by Williams and Johnny Cash at Cobo Hall; in Detroit, Michigan, as a harbinger of his style to come. On the album *Live at Cabo Hall* (1969),

Affiliation: Hank Williams Sr.

Any account of the life of Hank Williams Jr. would be inadequate without at least a brief summary of the life of his father, Hiram Hank Williams. Usually referred to as Hank Williams or Hank Williams Sr., his father was born in Alabama in 1923. He learned to play the organ and the guitar as a child, and was writing songs by the age of 12. In 1946, after years of playing with his band, the Drifting Cowboys, he arrived in Nashville, country music's holy city, to make records. The body of work he produced during his short career has been praised for both its eclecticism—it combined country music with hillbilly and blues traditions—and its depth of feeling. More than virtually arty other performer, Williams is said to have lived the pain and heartache that he wrote about in such songs as "Your Cheatin' Heart," "I'm So Lonesome I Could Cry," and "Long Gone Lonesome Blues." In 1949, in his first appearance at the famed Grand Ole Opry, in Nashville, he played six encores of "Lovesick Blues." Williams's success was unprecedented. But despite his prosperity, he was tortured by his failed marriage and his problems with drugs and alcohol. On January 1, 1953, at the age of 29, Hank Williams died of a heart attack while riding in a car on his way to perform a New Year's Day concert in Ohio. He is still considered by many to be the greatest country-music star of all time.

Williams's music and voice sound rawer than they do on the studio recordings he made earlier.

"I have loved some ladies, and I have loved Jim Beam," Williams sings in his song "Family Tradition," "and they both tried to kill me in 1973." Technically, it was his overdose of the painkiller Darvon that almost did him in that year, but it was depression, brought on by the stress of his career, his failing first marriage, and his problems with alcohol and drugs, that led him to attempt suicide. He has often recalled the strong advice given to him by a psychiatrist during his recovery. "He said, 'You got to get out of this,'" Chet Flippo quoted Williams as saying in *Rolling Stone* (June 1, 1978). '"These people have wanted you to be Hank Williams all your life and they have succeeded, *almost.* You're almost just like him-dead."' The psychiatrist strongly recommended that Williams move away from Nashville and the "vicious triangle" of his mother, his manager, and Nashville itself.

In October 1974, Williams moved to Cullman, Alabama. He paid many visits to recording studios in Muscle Shoals (less than two hours away by car), where he met session musicians who were interested in bridging the gap between rock and country music. Among them were Charlie Daniels, Toy Caldwell of the Marshall Tucker Band, and Chuck Leavell of the Allman Brothers Band. With these country-rock pioneers and other players, Williams recorded the landmark album *Hank Williams Jr. and Friends* (1976). It stands, along with the mid-1970s recordings of Jennings and Nelson, as one of the classic works of the "outlaw" country movement, which changed country music significantly. "I had those songs saved up," Williams told John Morthland of *Newsday* (August 13, 1978). "I wasn't about to waste them on another slick Nashville record." Standouts from the album include "Stoned at the Jukebox," "Clovis," and "Montana Song." The most poignant track is "Living Proof," a virtual manifesto of the "new" Hank Williams Jr. In sentiments that reflected the advice of the psychiatrist, Williams crooned, "I'm gonna quit singin' all these sad songs / 'Cause I can't stand the pain / The life I sing to you about / And the one I live are the same. / When I sing them old songs of Daddy's / Seems every word comes true / Lord please tell me do I have to be / The living proof." In the summer of 1975, after the album had been recorded and before its scheduled date of release, Williams went on vacation. While hunting and hiking in the Rocky Mountains of Montana, he fell 500 feet down the side of Ajaz Mountain, smashing his face, cracking his skull, and breaking many other bones. Doctors did not expect him to live. "I was laying in that hospital with no face and no teeth and no mouth and an eyeball down to here, and I thought at first I'd never go on stage again," he told Morthland. "But I decided I had to go on and finish what I started; when I got out, the doctors were as surprised as I was." Though he was told he would have to remain in the hospital for six weeks, he was released after 15 days. Over the next five months, Williams was in and out of hospitals, undergoing reconstructive and cosmetic facial surgery. Celebrities from both the country and rock communities reached out to him during his recovery, as did a woman named Becky White, who became his second wife.

The music Williams made after his recovery did not gain immediate acceptance. *Hank Williams Jr. and Friends* had baffled many country enthusiasts; his two 1977 releases, *One Night Stands* and *The New South,* for the Warner Bros. label, did so as well. In 1978, Williams played smaller venues than he had previously in his career, and he began to spurn flashy Nashville suits in favor of jeans and plain shirts. He wore sunglasses at all public appearances and grew a beard to hide his scars-a look that he has maintained ever since. He also worked on his autobiography, *Living Proof,* which was published in 1979.

With his next album, *Family Tradition* (1979), recorded on the Elektra label, Williams found his audience. He also converted many critics. "It's heresy," Charles Bell wrote in the *New York Daily News* (June 15, 1979), "but the truth is, the son has matured into a finer singer than the father. . . . The son is also a finer musician." Unsurprisingly, the album's famous title track makes reference to Williams's father, but the attitude conveyed in the song is quite different from the mournfulness of "Living Proof." "I had a smile on my face when I wrote it," Williams told Bell. With such good-time refrains as "Stop and think it over *I* Try to put yourself in my unique position *I* If I get stoned and sing all night long *I* It's a family tradition," "Family Tradition" has inspired many sing-alongs at concerts. The song was a top-10 hit and was nominated for a Grammy Award as country song of the year.

The albums that followed catapulted Williams to country superstardom, even though his music was considered too radical by many Nashville purists. *Whiskey Bent and Hell Bound* (1979) and *Habits Old and New* (1980) both sold well. The first two tracks of *Rowdy* (1981), "Dixie on My Mind" and "Texas Women," both became number-one hits, Williams's first since "Eleven Roses," in 1972. His other 1981 album, *The Pressure Is On,* featured another chart-topper—"All My Rowdy Friends Have Settled Down"—as well as the top-10 single and lifestyle-defining anthem "A Country Boy Can Survive." *High Notes,* which contains the country number-one hit "Hanky Tonkin,"' followed in 1982, as did *Hank Williams Jr.'s Greatest Hits I,* which remains his biggest seller.

In many of his songs, Williams defines a character—some might say a caricature—that many of his listeners have apparently identified with. This figure embodies a rowdy rural masculinity; he spends much of his time drinking, smoking, womanizing, hunting, fishing, and fighting. The chorus of "Texas Women" presents a vivid picture of the man: ''I'm a country plow-boy, not an urban cowboy *I* And I don't ride bulls, but I have fought some men *I* Drive a pickup truck, trust in God and luck *I* And I live to love Texas women." To some observers, his emphasis on that sort of manliness makes Williams the singing equivalent of the American heroes featured in the works of Ernest Hemingway and Robert Ruark (two of his favorite writers). Many critics have remarked that Williams's deep voice belts out such lyrics "unapologetically."

Williams has been called a "sectional chauvinist" for his expressed love of the American South, or "Dixie," and for his attacks on New York City. "I don't hate New York," he told Bill Bell of the *New York Daily News* (June 20, 1982). "I hate all cities—Nashville, Houston, L.A., you name it." For a time, Williams and his fans exhibited their love for Dixie by waving Confederate flags. Some people felt that this gesture had racist overtones, and took it as an apology when, at his concerts, Williams cited black artists whose work he admired, among them Lightnin' Hopkins, Howlin' Wolf, and Robert Johnson. Williams's expressed view of America as a whole is marked by both a distrust of corporations and government and a jingoistic pride.

Although Williams's new identity and career were firmly established by the early 1980s (at one point, he set a record, with nine albums in the country-music top 75), he remained outside the country-music mainstream. In 1985, he entered that mainstream once again, with two albums: *Five-0,* which contained two number-one singles—"I'm for Love" and "Ain't Misbehavin'"—and his collection *Greatest Hits Volume 2.* The two studio albums that followed, *Montana Cafe* (1986) and *Born to Boogie* (1987), each featured a chart-topping single. This time around, the country music establishment did not ignore Williams. He won the 1985 video of the year award from the Country Music Association (CMA), a Nashville organization, and in 1986, the Hollywood-based Academy of Country Music (ACM) named Williams the entertainer of the year. Both organizations chose him as entertainer of the year in 1987 and 1988. His overdubbed version of his father's recording "There's a Tear in My Beer" won Williams his only Grammy, in 1989, and he collected Emmys in four consecutive years, beginning in 1990, for his theme music for the television series *ABC Monday Night Football.*

In 2001, Hank co-wrote his classic hit "A Country Boy Can Survive" after 9/11, renaming it "America Can Survive". In 2004, Williams was featured prominently on CMT Outlaws. In April 2009, Williams released a new single, "Red, White & Pink-Slip Blues", which peaked at number 43 on the country charts. The song was the lead-off single to Williams's album *127 Rose*

Avenue. The album debuted and peaked at number 7 on the *Billboard* Top Country Albums chart. Also in July 2009, *127 Rose Avenue* was announced as his last album for Curb Records. In 2011. Hank, Jr. ended his 22-year-association with Monday Night Football, after ABC officials were critical of comments he made on the Fox & Friends television show.

Personal Life

Williams was married to Gwen Yeargain until 1977. The couple had one son, Shelton Hank Williams, who performs as Hank III. With his second wife, Becky White, Williams had two daughters, Holly and Hilary. Both daughters are also involved in the music business. In 1990, Williams married Mary Jane Thomas; they have two children, Katherine and Samuel. The pair separated in 2007, but later reconciled. On the 1996 release *Three Hanks: Men with Broken Hearts,* Williams sings alongside old recordings of his father, but this time he is joined by a third voice, that of his son Shelton Hank Williams.

Williams divides his time between Paris, Tennessee and Victor, Montana. His interests include fishing, hunting, and collecting guns. He can play multiple instruments including the guitar, banjo, piano, keyboards, harmonica, drums and the fiddle. He has earned five Entertainer of the Year Awards, four Emmys, has had 10 #1 singles, 13 #1 albums, 20 Gold Albums and six Platinum Albums. "I've been a very lucky man," Hank Jr. is fond of saying, but he has made his own luck, and made his own way finding a new song to sing, and a new way to sing it.

Further Reading

Chicago Tribune VI p11 July 18, 1982, with photo, XII p5+ Oct. 16, 1983, with photos
Coronet p91+ Feb. 1968, with photo
New York Daily News Leisure p5 June 20, 1982, with photo
Newsday II p4+ Aug. 13, 1978, with photos
Rolling Stone p8+ June 1, 1978, with photos
Country Music Encyclopedia, 1974
Encyclopedia of Folk, Country & Western Music, 1983
http://www.hankjr.com/

John (Towner) Williams

Composer; conductor

Born: Feb. 8, 1932; Queens, New York City
Primary Field: Cinema; classical; jazz
Group Affiliation: Boston Pops Orchestra

Introduction

On January 10, 1980 the composer John Williams, a superstar in the firmament of movie music, was appointed conductor of the renowned Boston Pops Orchestra, a post that had been left vacant six months earlier by the death of Arthur Fiedler. One of America's most beloved musical personalities, Fiedler had led the Pops to unprecedented popularity during the half century that it performed under his direction. Although Williams, who is equally at home in classical music and jazz, has written some concert pieces as well as music for television, he is best known as the composer of some fifty motion picture scores, including the "music of the spheres" featured in such science fiction spectaculars as Star Wars *and* Close Encounters of the Third Kind. *Along the way he has accumulated a number of honors, including three Oscars, two Emmys, and several Grammy awards. Influenced both by jazz and a modified form of serialism, Williams nevertheless works largely in a traditional idiom.*

Early Life

John Towner Williams was born in the Flushing section of Queens, in New York City, on February 8, 1932, the oldest child of Esther and Johnny Williams. His father, a jazz drummer, had been one of the original members of the Raymond Scott Quintet and later was a percussionist with the CBS Radio Orchestra and NBC's Your Hit Parade. Music played an important part in the lives of John, his brothers Jerry and Don, and his sister Joan. From the age of seven he studied piano, and he also learned to play the trombone, the trumpet, and the clarinet. In 1948 the family moved to Los Angeles, where the father free-lanced with film studio orchestras. After graduating in 1950 from North Hollywood High School, where he played, arranged, and composed for the school band, Williams took courses in piano and composition at UCLA and studied privately with pianist-arranger Bobby Van Eps. He composed his first serious work, a piano sonata, as a nineteen-year-old student.

Drafted in 1952, Williams was assigned to the United States Air Force, and as part of his tour of duty he conducted and arranged music for service bands. After his discharge in 1954, he spent a year at the Juilliard School of Music as a piano student of Rosina Lhevinne. During his stay in New York he also worked at various nightclubs as a jazz pianist. Later he was accompanist and conductor for singer Vic Damone, played for composer Alfred Newman at Twentieth Century-Fox, and was engaged as a pianist with Morris Stoloff's Columbia Pictures staff orchestra in Hollywood, of which his father was then a member. His talent for orchestration was soon recognized and encouraged by the studio · composers. Meanwhile, he continued his serious music studies in Hollywood with Arthur Olaf Anderson and with the noted Italian composer Mario Castelnuovo-Tedesco.

Life's Work

Beginning with· his first screen credit, for *Because They're Young* (Columbia, 1960), Williams' career as a composer of film scores gathered steady momentum. Prized for his versatility, he wrote music for jazz combos, dance bands, and symphony ensembles.

The Academy of Motion Picture Arts and Sciences presented Williams with his first Oscar in April 1972 for his adaptation of the music for the screen version of the Sheldon Harnick-Jerry Bock musical *Fiddler on the Roof* (United Artists, 1971). He received his second Academy Award in March 1976 for his original score for *Jaws* [Universal, 1975), which he wrote as a "sea symphony" with a "Melvillian motif." Its soundtrack recording by MCA also brought him a Grammy award that same year. In April 1978, Williams obtained his third Oscar, winning top honors for the best original score, for director George Lucas' *Star Wars* (Twentieth Century-Fox, 1977), in a competition that included another of his works, the score for *Close Encounters of the Third Kind* (Columbia, 1977), among the year's Oscar nominees.

Star Wars also brought Williams three Grammy awards in 1978. Its music was designated the year's best motion picture or television special score; its main theme was cited as the best instrumental composition; and its London Symphony soundtrack recording, conducted by Williams, won honors as the best pop instrumental recording. In 1979 Williams won Grammy awards for *Close Encounters*, in the best original score and best instrumental composition categories. The Hollywood Foreign Press Association honored Williams with Golden Globe awards for his film scores for *Jaws* in 1976 and *Star Wars* in 1978. The music for *Star Wars* has also been enjoying great popularity as a concert piece. Since the initial *Star Wars* concert by the Los Angeles Philharmonic in the Hollywood Bowl in November 1977, a number of orchestras have featured the music. When the Oregon Orchestra held a *Star Wars* concert in January 1978, it packed 12,000 people into the Portland Coliseum.

Commenting on the soundtrack recording for *Star Wars*, Steve Simels wrote in *High Fidelity* (September 1977): "Williams is no innovator ... , but he has a wonderful ear for the endearingly hackneyed tropes of Hollywood film scoring." John Von Rhein observed in the *Chicago Tribune* (January 27, 1980) that "Williams' scores have the same lushly Romantic flavor that characterizes the work of Dimitri Tiomkin, Franz Waxman, Alfred Newman, and other greats with whom he served his studio apprenticeship." And Charles Gerhardt, who conducted the National Philharmonic's recording of the *Close Encounters* score for RCA Records Classic Film Scores series, called that composition "an excursion into serial writing and almost all forms of tonality of the highest imagination" but noted that its futuristic sounds were "produced by imaginative use of the orchestra ... rather than electronic gadgetry."

In recent years, producers and directors have been growing increasingly aware of the importance of music in films. "Today the film composer is a star," producer Robert Evans told Charles Higham of the *New York Times* (May 25, 1975). "The audience doesn't know it is being turned on by the music, but a good score can grab an audience and hold it. ... Music is the most underrated single contribution to pictures today." In line with that view, director Steven Spielberg adopted an entirely new approach to Williams' score for *Close Encounters*. "In many instances," Spielberg has explained, "John wrote his music first, while I put the scenes to it much later." Williams was thus allowed much more freedom than was usual for a composer, and he enabled Spielberg to use the music as inspiration for certain visual effects. "John became more than just a composer for hire,"

Spielberg pointed out. "He was a creative collaborator in all phases of post-production, spending every day for fifteen weeks in the mixing studio and editing rooms."

John Badham, who directed *Dracula* for Universal (1979), has provided some insight into the way that Williams composed the score for that film. When Williams saw the first rushes of *Dracula,* he confessed to Badham that he had never seen a vampire movie, and the director was delighted that Williams approached his assignment without preconceptions of "the kind of ketchup and thunder music that prevails in the horror film genre." For several weeks Williams worked at the piano, constantly viewing and reviewing *Dracula* as he composed.

Contrasting the writing of film scores with other forms of musical composition, Williams told Charles Higham, as quoted in the *New York Times* (May 25, 1975): "Film scoring may be very rewarding, but it's also agony. Film composers are not their own masters. They are working for corporations. You accept that as part of the job." In an interview with Irwin Bazelon for his book *Knowing the Score*, Williams discussed the positive and negative aspects of record company exploitation of title songs and other film music. "The commercial part of me says something has to do some business, and the music-selling business is not altogether a bad thing," he observed. On the other hand, Williams suggested to Bazelon that one reason why so few composers of serious music work in films might be frustration over the lack of control over the final product, which often includes as little as half of what the composer has written and is seldom a faithful representation of a composer's work.

Williams' recent output for motion pictures includes the scores for *Jaws II* (Universal, 1978), *Superman* (Warner, 1978), *1941* (Universal, 1979), and the *Star Wars* sequel *The Empire Strikes Back* (Twentieth Century-Fox, 1980). The 109-minute Empire score was Williams' longest and most ambitious to date. Williams has been commissioned by Spielberg to write the score for his forthcoming "The Raiders" and for a third film in the Star Wars series.

Beginning in the late 1950's, Williams was also involved in television. He appeared as a jazz pianist in the detective series *Johnny Staccato,* and he both composed and conducted for such shows as M-Squad, Wagon Train, and Chrysler Theater. Other television programs that benefited from his musical talent included the *Kraft Suspense Theatre, Lost in Space, Convoy, Time Tunnel, Checkmate, Playhouse* 90, *Tales of Wells* Fargo, *Gilligan's Island,* and *Land of the Giants*. The Academy of Television Arts and Sciences honored him with two Emmy awards for outstanding achievement in musical composition: for the NBC-TV special *Heidi*, presented in the 1968-69 season; and for *Jane Eyre*, shown on NBC's *Bell System Family Theatre* during 1971-72.

In addition to working for motion pictures and television, Williams made his mark as a composer of serious ·music. His *Essay for Strings* was played by the Pittsburgh Symphony in 1966. In the same year he wrote his *Symphony No. 1*, dedicating it to his long-time Hollywood associate Andre Previn, who gave it its premiere performance with the Houston Symphony in 1968 and its first European performance with the London Symphony in 1972. *A Sinfonietta for Wind Instruments*, composed by Williams in 1968, was played by the Eastman Wind Ensemble in 1972. His works also include several pieces of chamber music, a flute concerto, and a violin concerto. As a songwriter, Williams collaborated with Johnny Mercer on "Beautiful Ball" and "Inamorata," and he has also worked with Leslie Bricusse and with Alan and Marilyn Bergman.

Williams has often conducted orchestras for soundtrack recordings of his own works, and over the years he has also undertaken assignments for conducting light classical music with the symphony orchestras of such cities as Atlanta, Dallas, Pittsburgh, and Los Angeles. His two guest appearances with the Boston Pops in May 1979 were well received. After the death, on July 10, 1979, of the legendary Arthur Fiedler, a Committee for the Future of the Pops embarked on a search to find a new conductor who could build on the Fiedler tradition and maintain the financial strength of the ninety-five-year-old orchestra, which consists of the members of the Boston Symphony without its twelve principal players. As the source of about one-third of its income, the Pops has been a major factor in keeping the Boston Symphony solvent.

By the autumn of 1979 the search for a successor to Fiedler had narrowed down to five candidates. They included, in addition to Williams, the long-time assistant conductor of the Pops, Harry Ellis Dickson, the Cincinnati Orchestra conductor, Erich Kunzel, the orchestra leader and television personality, Mitch Miller, and the conductor of the symphony of Flint, Michigan, John Covelli. On January 10, 1980 the Boston Symphony management announced that it had concluded a three-year contract with John Williams, who became the nineteenth conductor of the Pops. Although it was generally agreed that no one could totally replace the revered Fiedler, the choice of Williams was greeted with enthusiasm. Announcing his plans for the Pops, Williams asserted that Fiedler's legacy would be "carefully nurtured" but indicated that there would also be considerable innovation. "Our country is bursting with· gifted young people," he told Ernest Leogrande of the New York *Daily* News (January 18, 1980). "We ought to try on a once-a-week or a once-a-month basis to introduce a new piece and contemporize the repertoire as much as possible."

Williams' first concert as conductor of the Pops, before a standing-room-only crowd at Carnegie Hall in New York City on January 22, 1980, was hailed by critics, including John Rockwell of the *New York Times*, who observed: "The crisply efficient performances he elicited from the orchestra suggested that the Pops chose wisely." When on April 20, 1980 Williams made his debut at the Boston Symphony Hall, his program—featuring such celebrities as violinist Isaac Stern, actor Burgess Meredith, and the robot C-3PO conducting the Star Wars theme—charmed both audience and critics. With that concert Williams launched the Pops's program for the year, including its regular twelve-week season of concerts from May through July, as well as a series of appearances at the Tanglewood Music Festival and a special Christmas-week program of seven concerts.

Williams has announced plans to continue the live concert series on the Public Broadcasting Service network begun by Fiedler and to expand recording opportunities for the Pops. As permitted by his contract, he intends to continue to compose for motion pictures, but with a reduced output. He also plans to take on guest conducting engagements with other orchestras and to continue composing new orchestral works, including perhaps a march he did not have time to write when Fiedler asked him to do so for his fiftieth anniversary with the Pops. Williams' most recent composition, as of early 1980, was his *Cowboy Overture*, which he wrote for the Boston Pops. Undisturbed by the reduction in

Affiliation: Film Scores

Among the films for which he composed scores were *I Passed for White* (Allied Artists, 1960); *Bachelor Flat* (Twentieth Century-Fox, 1961); *The Secret Ways* (Universal, 1961); *Diamond Head* (Columbia, 1962); *Gidget Goes to Rome* (Columbia, 1963); *John Goldfarb, Please Come Home* (Twentieth Century-Fox, 1964); *The Killers* (Universal, 1964); *None But the Brave* (Warner, 1965); *How to Steal a Million* (Twentieth Century-Fox, 1966); *Not With My Wife You Don't* (Warner, 1966); *The Rare Breed* (Universal, 1966); *The Plainsman* (Universal, 1966); *Penelope* (MGM, 1966); *A Guide for the Married Man* (Twentieth Century-Fox, 1967); and the Dick Van Dyke vehicle *Fitzwilly* (United Artists, 1967), to which he contributed the song "Make Me a Rainbow."

Other films with music by Williams included *Daddy's Gone A-Hunting* (National General, 1969); *The Story of a Woman* (Universal, 1970); *The Cowboys* (Warner, 1972); *Pete 'n' Tillie* (Universal, 1972); *The Paper Chase* (Twentieth Century-Fox, 1973); *The Long Goodbye* (United Artists, 1973); *The Man Who Loved Cat Dancing* (MGM, 1973); *Conrack* (Twentieth Century-Fox, 1974); *Sugarland Express* (Universal, 1974); *Earthquake* (Universal, 1974); *The Eiger Sanction* (Universal, 1975); *Family Plot* (Universal, 1976); *Midway* (Universal, 1976); *The Missouri Breaks* (United Artists, 1976); *Raggedy Ann and Andy* (Twentieth Century-Fox, 1977); *Black Sunday* (Paramount. 1977); *Superman* (Warner, 1978); and *The Fury* (Twentieth Century-Fox, 1978). Critical notice of the scores, although often perfunctory in film reviewing, at times recognized the music's important contribution to the success of a film. For example, Pauline Kael, in her book *When the Lights Go Down* (Holt, 1980) called Williams' music for *The Fury* "as apt and delicately varied a score as any horror movie has ever had, ... otherworldly, seductively frightening." Recognition also came to Williams through the dozen or more Academy Award nominations he garnered for music he wrote or arranged, beginning with the score for *Valley of the Dolls* (Twentieth Century-Fox, 1967), and including those for *Goodbye, Mr. Chips* (MGM, 1969), on which he also served as music director; *The Reivers* (National General, 1969), for which he assembled a pastiche of Stephen Foster tunes; *Cinderella Liberty* (Twentieth Century-Fox, 1973), which featured his song "Nice to Be Around"; *Images* (Columbia, 1972), for which he created eerie, dissonant sound effects appropriate to the psychological theme; *Tom Sawyer* (United Artists, 1973); and the Twentieth Century-Fox disaster movies *Poseidon Adventure* (1973) and *Towering Inferno* (1974).

income that his move from Hollywood to Boston entailed, Williams assured John Von Rhein of the *Chicago Tribune* (January 27, 1980): "My sole motive is musical-to keep the continuity of a great orchestra having a great tradition, and vitalize it as much as I can. I would frankly do it for nothing." Williams was the orchestra's Principal Conductor from 1980-93 and is now the Pops' Laureate Conductor, making several guest conducting appearances per year.

In a career spanning over six decades, Williams composed some of the most recognizable film scores in cinematic history, including *Jaws*, the *Star Wars* series, *Superman*, the *Indiana Jones* series, *E.T. the Extra-Terrestrial*, *Jurassic Park*, and the first three *Harry Potter* films. He has been associated with director Steven Spielberg since 1974.

Other notable works by Williams include theme music for four Olympic Games, NBC Sunday Night Football, the television series *Lost in Space* and *Land of the Giants*, and the original, not-as-well-known, calypso-based theme song to *Gilligan's Island*. Williams composed the soundtrack for eight movies in the Top 20 highest grossing films at the US Box Office (adjusted for inflation). Williams has won five Academy Awards, four Golden Globe Awards, seven British Academy Film Awards, and 22 Grammy Awards. With 50 Academy Award nominations, Williams is the second most-nominated individual, after Walt Disney. In 2005, the American Film Institute selected Williams' score to 1977's *Star Wars* as the greatest American film score of all time. He was inducted into the Hollywood Bowl's Hall of Fame in 2000, and was a recipient of the Kennedy Center Honors in 2004. In 2016 he will receive the AFI Life Achievement Award.

Personal Life

Trimly bearded, tall, and sandy-haired, John Williams is familiar to many as a result of his frequent appearances as an Oscar nominee at the annual televised Academy Award ceremonies. Williams married Barbara Ruick, an American actress and singer, in 1956. Together they had three children: Jennifer, Joseph, who is the lead singer of Toto, and Mark Towner Williams. The two remained married until her death in 1974. Williams was married a second time, on June 9, 1980, to Samantha Winslow, a photographer and interior decorator.

Fond of golf and tennis and of playing chamber music with his friends, he frequently has little time for such diversions. But a heavy work schedule delights Williams. "I know it sounds corny," he explained, as quoted in *Newsweek* (January 21, 1980), "but my life revolves around music."

Further Reading

Chicago Tribune VI p2 + Ja 27 '80 par
N Y Daily News p5+ Ja 18 '80 par
N Y Times C p24 Ja 11 '80
People 14:45+ Je 23 '80 pars
Bazelon, Irwin. Knowing the Score: Notes on Film Music (1975)
Who's Who in America, 1980-81
Audissino, E., *John Williams's Film Music: Jaws, Star Wars, Raiders of the Lost Ark, and the Return of the Classical Hollywood Music Style,* (Je 12, 2014)

Gretchen Wilson

Country-music singer

Born: June 26, 1973; Pocahontas, Illinois
Primary Field: Country music performer and recording artist
Group Affiliation: Solo artist

Introduction

"Unlike most women in country [music] in recent years," Randy Lewis wrote for the Los Angeles Times *(May 22, 2004), the singer Gretchen Wilson "doesn't look like she just stepped off the cover of* Cosmo, *doesn't sing to soccer moms and doesn't pine for champagne and roses. In Wilson's world, a cold beer will do just fine." Wilson has refused to create an image of herself that does not accurately portray who she really is—a "redneck woman," to use the title of her breakout song. "To me, being a redneck woman means being a strong woman," she told Robert Hilburn for the* Los Angeles Times *January 22, 2006) Acknowledging that the term "redneck" once had "other meanings," she added,*

"It's about holding your head up no matter what is happening."

Early Life

Gretchen Frances Wilson was born on June 26, 1973 and raised in the very small town of Pocahontas, Illinois. Her mother, Christine, was 16 at the time of her daughter's birth. Wilson said about Pocahontas to Kevin C. Johnson for the *St. Louis (Missouri) Post-Dispatch* (May 9, 2004), "There's not a lot going on or a lot to do. Everybody is a little backward, but they're really good people. They look out for one another, stick up for one another. And everybody knows everybody's business." Her parents separated when she was a toddler, and her mother later married a man—10 years her senior—who became the father of Wilson's half-brother, Josh. Wilson's stepfather, a self-employed contractor, often cheated his clients by abandoning jobs after he was paid for materials; as a result, the family moved frequently, leaving rent unpaid as they relocated from one trailer to the next in different parts of Illinois, living among pig farms and cornfields. Sometimes the family lived in southern Florida. Wilson has said that during her youth she attended a series of approximately 20 schools, At the beginning of ninth grade, she dropped out of school and started cooking and serving drinks at a bar called Big O's, where her mother was employed. While working there she would go onstage and sing along to songs that were playing on CD. When she was 15 years old, Wilson began living on her own in Illinois. Over the next few years, she became a member of several musical groups, such as Sam A. Lama and the Ding Dongs, Midnight Flyer, and Baywolfe. Her performing was limited to singing and playing tambourine until, joining one band, she was called on to learn guitar—which she accomplished quickly.

Life's Work

In 1996, at 23, "with $500 and no clue about the music business," as Jon Bream wrote for the Minneapolis, Minnesota, Star *Tribune* (September 3, 2004), Wilson moved to Nashville, Tennessee, the center of the country-music world. There, while working at a bar called Printers Alley and singing on demo records, she met the singer-songwriter John Rich, who introduced her to other aspiring musicians; she soon became a member of Muzik Mafia, a group of singer-songwriters who performed in Nashville. During that time Wilson was living in a rented house with her then-boyfriend, Mike Penner, and their young daughter, while struggling to pay her bills. She attempted to land record deals with numerous Nashville labels, all of which turned her down. "I did showcase after showcase and the story was the same," she recalled to Robert Hilburn. "They thought my hair was too dated, that I was too heavy, too old." Then, in 2003, she won a recording contract with Epic Records, which is owned by Sony Music Entertainment, after performing for John Grady, a new executive at Sony—which had already turned Wilson down twice. "When John Grady said he wanted to sign me at Sony, I was shocked," Wilson told Hilburn. "I had given up. He was the first person I met at any label that I felt like he got it. I didn't even have to explain myself to him, I didn't have to change my ain'ts into isn'ts," Grady recalled being struck by the power of Wilson's voice. "She filled up the room," he said to Hilburn. "It was almost like my teeth were rattling. I identified with her right away because I know a lot of people like her. I grew up in a town in Nebraska as small as her hometown."

Early 2004 saw the release of Wilson's debut single, "Redneck Woman," which was the first song by a solo female singer to top the *Billboard* country-singles chart in over two years. Co-written by John Rich, "Redneck Woman" contains lyrics such as, "Cause I'm a redneck woman / And I ain't no high class broad / I'm just a product of my raisin' / And I say 'hey y'all' and 'Yee-Haw' / And I keep my Christmas lights on, on my front porch all year long." Before coming up with the idea for the song, Wilson and Rich were brainstorming while watching Country Music Television. "We watched videos by two or three different females and I said, 'John, I don't know if I'm going to be able to do that," Wilson told Randy Lewis. "'Look at them—they're all so slick. That's not who I am.' And he asked me, 'Who are you?' And I said, 'I guess I'm just a redneck woman.' And that's what inspired it." The song topped the charts faster than any single in the previous decade and spent six weeks at the number-one spot. "When you hear 'Redneck Woman,' there's nothing up the middle about it," Dale Libby, a former senior vice president of sales for Sony Nashville, told Johnson. "Not only was 'Redneck Woman' a song we gravitated to, but when we first heard Gretchen and her vocal range and her command of the material, it was a real attraction." Due to the success of the song, Sony speeded up the release of Wilson's first album, *Here for the Party* (2004), which entered the country-album chart at number one and went on to sell more than five million copies. As described

Affiliation: Country Music

Wilson's disadvantaged upbringing is detailed in her 2006 memoir, *Redneck Woman: Stories from My Life,* which won a place on the *New York Times* best-seller list. Despite the hardships she faced, Wilson worked her way up from bartending high school dropout to Grammy Award–winning country-music star. "I've just learned that throughout the years nothing out there that's good really comes easy," she said in an interview for the CBS TV program the *Early Show* (March 31, 2010), "you have to work for everything." Critics and fans have celebrated not only Wilson's rags-to-riches story but the quality of her voice—which has, in Hilburn's words, "the purity and power of Patsy Cline or Loretta Lynn"—and her faithfulness to country music's roots. Kyle Young, the director of the Country Music Hall of Fame and Museum, in Nashville, Tennessee, told Hilburn that Wilson "sings about her own life, which is what all great country artists have done."

After landing a major recording contract with Epic Records, in 2003, following years of struggle and rejection, Wilson released her debut album, *Here for the Party* (2004). The CD contained her hit single "Redneck Woman," which has been called the quickest-rising country single of all time and sold millions of copies. Since then Wilson has come out with three additional albums, to which she contributed much of the songwriting: *All Jacked Up* (2005), *One of the Boys* (2007), and, most recently, *I Got Your Country Right Here* (2010)—the last-named disk produced and distributed by Redneck Records, a label she established after· leaving Epic Records, in 2009. "I hope I make enough of a mark in country music," she told Michael Rampa for *American Songwriter* (October 18, 2010, online). "I would like to be remembered as the redneck woman that came along just in time to tell the world to heck with everybody else. Be yourself."

by Robert Hilburn for the *Los Angeles Times* (September 25, 2005), "The album [has] some solid barroom tunes, both the rowdy kind that work best just when the bartender can't keep up with all the orders and the melancholy kind that serve as therapy when you're alone at closing time." With the release of *Here for the Party,* Wilson shot to fame.

Wilson's second album, *All Jacked Up* (2005), was also very successful, with singles including "All Jacked Up," "Don't Feel Like Loving You Today," "Politically Uncorrect," and "California Girls." Around the same time she began working on her autobiography, *Redneck Woman: Stories from My Life,* which was co-authored by Allen Rucker and published in 2006. "In a song, you generalize so that listeners can put themselves into the story. But a book is just about you, so it's more detailed," Wilson told Alison Bonaguro for the *Chicago Tribune* (November 12, 2006). "I hope people will read parts and think, 'I know exactly how she felt. I can attach myself to that.'" According to Bonaguro, "Wilson's memoir has all the makings of a good read: disaster, dilemma and drama." In 2007 Wilson released her third album, *One of the Boys,* which is very personal and features more songs written by Wilson. "I'm a singer-songwriter and I write my experiences and the things that I've been through," she said to Ellen Mallemee in an interview for Gibson.com (October 18, 2007). "The best and the worst moments of my life are the things that I put on paper. This last record is my life as it was happening, and I'm really close to it. It's my diary set to music." *One of the Boys* did not sell as well as her previous albums.

In 2008 Wilson earned her GED. "This is something that I promised myself a long time ago that I would do," she told Julie Chen for the *Early Show* on CBS (May 6, 2008). "And I'm sure that having a little girl in school is a big part of it as well, you know, wanting to be able to be there for her and help her with her homework when the time comes."

In 2009 Wilson formed her own label, Redneck Records. "I have the ability to do whatever I want, to record what I want when I want," she said in the interview with Michael Rampa. "I don't have to ask anyone's opinion anymore. I don't need permission to do something on a creative piece of work from some suits that don't have a musical bone in their bodies." She added, "You don't stand over a painter's back when they're painting and say 'Oh! I wouldn't use that color, I'm not sure if it's safe.' A song is a piece of art. If you're not involved in the creation of the music you should just let the artist put it together and then the business people take it from there, but it doesn't work like that at a major label." Redneck Records produced the 2009 single "Work Hard, Play Harder," which Wilson co-wrote with John

Rich and Vicky McGehee. The song is included on *I Got Your Country Right Here,* Wilson's fourth album, which went on sale in 2010. "This record is mainly upbeat, with only a few select tracks to slow down the pace," Jessie Aulis wrote for the *Sherbrooke (Quebec) Record* (April 16, 2010). "With the slower songs, Gretchen Wilson seems to show a different side of her personality. We get to see and hear a more vulnerable side of her on 'I'm Only Human' and 'I'd Like to Be Your Last.'" Described as a combination of country and southern rock, *I Got Your Country Right Here* debuted at number six on the *Billboard* country albums chart.

Wilson's honors include a Horizon Award from the Country Music Association (2004), an American Music Award for favorite new artist (2004), a Grammy Award for best female country vocal performance (2005, for "Redneck Woman"), a *Billboard* Music Award for female country artist of the year (2005), an Academy of Country Music Award for top new artist (2005), a Country Music Television Award for female video of the year (2005, for "When I Think About Cheatin'"), and a Country Music Television Award for breakthrough video of the year (2005, for "Redneck Woman"). Also in 2005 she was named female vocalist of the year by the Country Music Association. After earning her GED, Wilson was given a 2009 National Coalition for Literacy Leadership Award by the Library of Congress. In 2010 her song "I'd Like to Be Your Last" received a Grammy Award nomination for best female country vocal performance.

Personal Life

Wilson purchased a farm near Nashville in 2004. Prior to her relationship with Mike Penner (which ended in 2005), she was married to Larry Rolens, a former bandmate; their union ended in divorce.

Further Reading

Chicago Tribune C p10 Nov. 12, 2006

(Fort Wayne, Indiana) *Journal Gazette* W p3 Feb. 24, 2006

Los Angeles Times E p1 Jan. 22, 2006

(Minneapolis, Minnesota) *Star Tribune* E p1 Sep. 3, 2004

St. Louis (Missouri) Post Dispatch F p1 May 9, 2004

Wilson, Gretchen. *Redneck Woman: Stories from My Life* (with Allen Rucker), 2006

Julia Wolfe

Composer; co-founder of Bang on a Can music festival

Born: Dec. 18, 1958; Philadelphia, Pennsylvania
Primary Field: Classical
Group Affiliation: All-Stars; SPIT Orchestra

Introduction

"It's so great to write music-like singing a thousand times over, like building bridges, like bicycling," Julia Wolfe wrote for the liner notes of her album Arsenal of Democracy. *"Composing is an activity that's full of everything you've ever experienced. It can be so focused and maniacal and at the same time endlessly expansive.... What grabbed my spirit about writing music was the amazing combination of the physicality of making it, the poetry, the ideas."* Amazon.com *lists Wolfe's recordings with classical music, and articles about her life and work have appeared in* Sequenza21/The Contemporary Classical Music Weekly, *which covers what it considers "serious modern music."*

Early Life

Wolfe was born Julia Fink on December 18, 1958 in Philadelphia, Pennsylvania, to Jack Fink, a physician, and Janet Fink, a schoolteacher. (Her mother now works as a tour guide at the Pennsylvania Academy of Fine Arts.) "Fink" was the name that appeared on the passport her father's paternal grandfather used when he emigrated from Russia to the U.S. Her great-grandfather's real surname was Wolfe, and she reclaimed the name when she was in her mid-20s. Along with her twin brother, David, and her older brother, Marc, Wolfe was raised in Lansdowne, Pennsylvania, a suburb of Philadelphia. "I was always musical," she told Deborah Artman during an interview for Red Poppy Music. As a child she studied piano, playing pieces by Beethoven and Debussy "for hours," as she recalled to Artman; later, she took dancing lessons and flute lessons as well. Describing herself as "not from one of these families where people are raised strictly on classical music," she was exposed to a lot of popular music and folk music at home; sometimes her mother would join her at the piano and the two would sing "the most corny show tunes," as Wolfe told Krasnow. She also loved the music of Leonin, one of the earliest composers known by name, and his student Perotin, who lived in 12th-century France and wrote for voice; she was a fan of the influential rock-and-roll group Led Zeppelin, too. During her teens she played with chamber-music ensembles, and as an alto-the voice range midway between soprano and bass-sang in choruses that specialized in madrigals (secular songs from the 16th century). "It's incredible to be in the middle, because you feel a part of the chord, and part of the harmony," she told Krasnow. She recalled to Artman, "I was drawn to the arts that involved direct communications with an audience, and I was drawn to the intensity of that communication." Also as a teenager she started to compose; her first works were folk songs for guitar. "When I started writing music, I knew immediately: this was it," she told Artman. "Music satisfied all these interests. It's intellectually challenging, it's emotional, it's physical. The physical aspect was especially important, I think, initially. You construct music, you play it, you get it through your body. Right away I got the bug."

Wolfe attended the University of Michigan at Ann Arbor, where she studied music and theater, primarily through the school's Residential College program. "I studied with a wonderful woman there named Jane Heirich, who taught me a very wide range of musicianship," she told Current *Biography.* As an undergraduate she returned to the piano and also tried her hand at playing various styles of music on other instruments, among them mountain dulcimer, harmonica, African drums, and bones. In 1980, the year she earned a B.A. degree from the university, she co-founded the Wild Swan Theater, in Ann Arbor, with three other women. Wolfe helped to write plays, directed, and acted in addition to composing music for the ensemble's productions, many of which were based on folk tales and all of which were geared to children as well as adults. "That was a great collaborative experience," she told Krasnow. "I'm a real team player—I love being in situations where you're getting ideas from everybody. But musically I really wanted to do more, to write for big groups of instruments."

After several years Wolfe moved to the East Coast to study composition with Martin Bresnick at Yale University, in New Haven, Connecticut, where she earned a master's degree in music in 1986. "There was something very special about coming out of that atmosphere," she told Frank J. Oteri for *New Music Box* (May 1999, on-line). "It was a very open place. It still was . . . classically oriented. It wasn't like we were listening to rap or funk in class but still, there was no dogma. It wasn't like you had to write like Martin, and I think that was somewhat unique at the time." Wolfe also took graduate courses at Princeton University, in Princeton, New Jersey, which awarded her a fellowship; she studied works by the contemporary Dutch composer Louis Andriessen, whom she has cited among her major influences.

LIFE'S WORK

In 1987, with David Lang and Michael Gordon, both of whom she had met at Yale, Wolfe cofounded the Bang on a Can music festival in New York City. (She and Gordon had married several years earlier.) The inspiration for the event was an all-night music festival, called Sheep's Clothing, organized by Martin Bresnick at Yale during their years there. Bang on a Can features works by established composers (for example, John Cage, Steve Reich, Philip Glass, and Meredith Monk) as well as music by little-known or virtually unknown composers that has seldom if ever been performed and is difficult if not impossible to categorize. (As the Bang on a Can Web site explains, "When you go into the record store, ... all the different kinds of music have their own rooms-rock, techno, classical, world, jazz. The music that interests us has always been the music that doesn't fit well into any of those rooms. Maybe the music belongs between rooms, or in the walls, or on the stairs between the floors.") The goal of the three partners, Wolfe told Oteri, was "to break down barriers within music, not just 'uptown' and 'downtown,' but all kinds of stylistic differences, and what we were aiming for was what [we] considered 'innovation' and an 'adventurous spirit.'" In putting together a festival program, Wolfe, Gordon, and Lang spend two weeks listening to several hundred submissions; the identities of the composers are revealed to them only after they have made their choices, and only works that win the approval of all three partners become finalists. "That process is very hard for me," Wolfe admitted to Krasnow, because she feels "terrible" when she learns that the work of someone she knows has not been chosen.

During the first Bang on a Can festival—a 12- hour marathon that took place on May 10, 1987 at Exit Art, in SoHo—30 compositions were performed, among them Wolfe's *Williamsburg Bridge,* in its world premiere. Since then the festival has been held annually, either as a one-day marathon or a several-day event, at venues ranging from Alice Tully Hall, at Lincoln Center, and Town Hall to La MaMa Experimental Theater and the auditorium of the New York Society for Ethical Culture, all in New York City. In 2000, in addition to a marathon at the Brooklyn Academy of Music (known as BAM), Bang on a Can organized a four-day event as part of the Schleswig-Holstein Festival in Hamburg, Germany. Works by such contemporary composers as Linda Bouchard, Somel Satoh, Michael Maguire, Don Byron,

Affiliation: Composer

The clarinetist and composer Evan Ziporyn, echoing many other aficionados of her compositions, has described her works as "defy[ing] easy categorization." In a short essay that appears on the Web site of the music publisher G. Schirmer Inc., Ziporyn wrote that the word "style" as it is "traditionally used in musical circles simply doesn't apply" to Wolfe's compositions, which include works for orchestra, string quartet, woodwind quintet, piano, chorus, unusual ensembles (such as a sextet of pianos), and unusual instruments (such as a toy piano amplified by a toy boombox). "What her pieces have in common is not any single identifiable element but . . . rather a focus on the act of making sound, sound not for its own sake but as a product of human endeavor, as a beautiful and powerful abstraction that people create, contemplate, imbue with and derive meaning from. Sound is for Wolfe a metaphor for human activity in general, and she approaches it with a care and attention to detail that is both masterful and highly respectful. The result is a music that is, as she herself puts it," according to Ziporyn, "not meant to be 'clever' or 'well-written,' but rather entered into by the listener."

A trained musician who has studied piano, flute, voice, and composition as well as dance and theater, Wolfe has received many commissions, from such sources as the American Composers Orchestra, the Pan American Chamber Players, the Library of Congress, the Next Wave Festival at the Brooklyn Academy of Music, and Netherlands Public Radio, and she has earned two ASCAP Foundation grants and a Fulbright Fellowship, among other honors. Wolfe wrote the music for Anna Deavere Smith's theater piece *House Arrest* (2000) and, with Michael Gordon and David Lang, the score for Ben Katchor's Obie Award-winning opera *The Carbon Copy Building* (1999). The choreographers Doug Varone, Eliot Feld, and Heinz Spoerli have created dances to music by Wolfe, and the Dusseldorf Ballet, the Deutsche Opera Ballet, and the Zurich Opera have danced to works by her. "For me, the boundaries between musics are all blurring ... ," Wolfe told David Krasnow for the interview magazine *Bomb* (Fall 2001), which focuses on the creative process. "Classical music has a great history, but it's a museum piece. . . . A lot of people don't even know what classical music is today. I've been through customs at the airport, where the official asked what I do and I said 'composer.' And he said, 'I thought composers were all dead.' Well, here I am."

With her husband, Michael Gordon, and David Lang, Wolfe is a co-founder of Bang on a Can, which originated in 1987 as a one-day music festival in an art gallery in the SoHo section of New York City and has developed into an organization with international partnerships; in the words of its founders, it is "a full-time home for new ideas." As Bang on a Carr's co-artistic director, Wolfe, along with Lang and Gordon, has contributed enormously to the world of modern music, by commissioning new works and providing venues for the premieres of those and other contemporary compositions as well as for the exposure of hundreds of other pieces that seldom get performed. In addition to its annual festivals, Bang on a Can has spawned two musical groups—the Bang on a Can All-Stars and the SPIT Orchestra—and a summer music institute. In "About Us" on the Web site of Red Poppy Music, Wolfe, Gordon, and Lang wrote, "As composers we are passionate about remaining curious and open to all new music.... Our styles and approaches to music are deeply individual, but we share the same vision-we want to be challenged, we want to expand the borders of what music is going to be." The three friends also run their own music-publishing company (Red Poppy Music), and record label (Cantaloupe).

and Henry Threadgill, as well as by Wolfe, Gordon, and Lang, have premiered during Bang on a Can festivals.

In 2002 Bang on a Can began operating a three-week summer institute for composers, instrumentalists, and conductors at the Massachusetts Museum of Contemporary Art, in North Adams. The annual institute offers classes in such subjects as improvisation; performance coaching; business matters; and, in 2003, gamelan (music from the islands of Southeast Asia, particularly Indonesia, that is played on an array of instruments, also called gamelan). Those attending the institute also perform at public concerts. In 2001 Wolfe, Gordon, and Lang founded the record label Cantaloupe Music, whose catalog currently includes 14 CDs, among them *Bang on a Can: Renegade Heaven, Bang on a Can: Terry Riley in* C, *Evan Ziporyn: This Is Not a Clarinet,* and *Phil Kline: Unsilent Night,* all released in 2001, and *Arnold Dreyblatt: The Adding Machine, Toby Twining: Chrysalid Requiem,* and *Steve Reich: Tehillim/ The Desert Music,* all released in 2002.

Renegade Heaven and *Terry Riley in C* are among the half-dozen recordings made by the Bang on a Can All-Stars, an ensemble that has been described as "part classical ensemble, part rock band, [and] part jazz band." Hand-picked by Wolfe, Gordon, and Lang, the current members of the All-Stars are Robert Black, Mark Stewart, Wendy Sutter, Evan Ziporyn, Lisa Moore, and David Cossin, modern-music specialists who play bass, guitar, cello, clarinet, piano, and percussion, respectively. "The voice of Bang on a Can on the road," as Wolfe characterized them to Oteri, the All-Stars have performed in a dozen countries overseas. The SPIT Orchestra, a pick-up group, is another Bang on a Can offshoot.

The quartet Ethel (Ralph Farris, viola; Dorothy Lawson, cello; Todd Reynolds, violin; and Mary Rowell, violin) performed Wolfe's piece *Dig Deep* for her album *Wolfe: The String Quartets,* released by Cantaloupe in 2003. Also on that record are *Four Marys,* played by the Cassatt String Quartet, and *Early That Summer,* in a rendition by the Lark Quartet. (All three quartets were commissioned *Dig Deep* by the Kronos Quartet, *Four Marys* by the Cassatt, and *Early That Summer* by the Lark-with funds from, respectively, the music lover Nora Norden, the Koussevitzky Foundation, and Meet the Composers, a program of the New York State Council on the Arts.) Allen Gimbel, a reviewer for *American Record Guide* (May/June 2003), wrote of the album, "This is not music to take tea with-it will make your hair stand on end, make your heart race, and send your fuddy-duddy neighbors running to the police. Let 'em run." According to a writer for *Sequenza21.com* (February 10, 2003, online), "Through their relentless high energy and ferocious passion, Wolfe's quartets have become popular repertoire for many of the younger quartets who specialize in contemporary music. Her music conveys an intensity and intimacy, a virtuosity and joy of sound that turns the string quartet into a high voltage vehicle of expression. *Dig Deep* is a hard-charging force of nature; *Four Marys* was inspired by Wolfe's love for playing the Appalachian dulcimer, and *Early That Summer* is perhaps the best known of all of Wolfe's work. As composer Evan Ziporyn writes, 'There are no power chords in the breathtakingly virtuosic string quartet *Early That Summer,* but the vibrancy of rock and roll sears through every moment.'"

The first recording devoted solely to works by Wolfe was *Arsenal of Democracy* (1996), which includes several pieces played by different ensembles drawn from the Orkest de Volharding, from the Netherlands, conducted by Jurjen Hempel. "Ms. Wolfe's work is unconcerned with subtle gradations in texture, color or dynamics; she likes her music dense in texture, dark in color and just plain loud," K. Robert Schwarz wrote in a review of *Arsenal of Democracy* for the *New Y ark Times* (June 30, 1996). "Nor does she care much about melody or harmony; her static, dissonant chords shift slowly, and conventional lyricism is absent. This is music about rhythm, about the clash between primal pulsation and asymmetrical patterns, about repetition and its permutations. . . . Some listeners may find her sonic assault too unrelenting. But the cumulative impact is exhilarating and, on occasion, amusingly self-deprecating, as if Ms. Wolfe were reminding her audience that things may not be so bleak after all."

Wolfe's other works (with dates of publication by Red Poppy Music) include, for orchestra, *Amber Waves of Grain* (1988), *The Vermeer Room* (1989), *Window of Vulnerability* (1991), and *Tell Me Everything* (1994); and, for a full chorus and four instruments, *Lick* (1994), *Steam* (1995), *Believing* (1997), and *Girlfriend* (1998). She has also written pieces for woodwind quintet—On *Seven-Star Shoes* (1985); violin and *piano—Mink Stole* (1997); and piano—Earring (2001) and *Compassion* (2001). Her more unusual instrumentations include those of *My Lips from Speaking* (1993), written for six pianos; *East Broadway* (1996), for toy piano and toy boombox; and *Dark Full Ride* (2002), for four drum sets. *Democracy,* which features cello, percussion, and electric guitar, was composed for the choreographer Doug Varone in 1999; at performances the music is played on tape, not live. Wolfe has collaborated with Gordon and Lang on several works, among them *Haircut* (2000), *Lost Objects* (2000), and the opera *The Carbon Copy Building* (1999). Based on the work of the cartoonist Ben Katchor, *The Carbon Copy Building* was commissioned by the Settembre Musica Festival, in Turin, Italy, and premiered there on September 9, 1999. The Off-Broadway mounting won an Obie Award (Off-Broadway's highest honor) for best new production of the 1999-2000 theater season. "Writing music is always about breaking through," Wolfe told Deborah Artman. "I like to keep challenging myself-new combinations of instruments, working with different media." She told David Krasnow, "When I'm thinking of melody I'm thinking of who's playing it: this is the guitar lick, here's what the flute's gonna do, this is the drums. For me the essence of what a piece is about is connected to the sound of the instruments." Wolfe's awards include a Charles Ives Scholarship, an Academy Award from the American Academy and Institute of Arts and Letters, two ASCAP Foundation grants, residencies at the MacDowell Colony and Djerassi Institute, a Fulbright Fellowship, and a grant from the Foundation for Contemporary Performance Arts.

Personal Life

Wolfe lives with her husband, Michael Gordon, and their two young children in New York City. When Krasnow asked her how often she and Gordon talked about their work, she answered, "All the time."

Further Reading

Bang on a Can Web Site
Bomb Magazine p66+ Fall 2001, with photo
New Music Box (on-line) May 1999
Red Poppy Music Web site

Lee Ann Womack

Country-music singer

Born: August 19, 1966; Jacksonville, Texas
Primary Field: Country music performer and recording artist
Group Affiliation: Solo artist

Introduction

Womack burst onto the country-music scene in 1997 with an eponymous debut album that achieved instant critical and commercial success, and she went on to greater fame with the hit crossover recording I Hope You Dance *(2000), which reached the number-one spot on the* Billboard *country album chart and sold nearly four million copies in the U.S. Womack "is one of the few mainstream female country artists left in Nashville who continues to remain successful by maintaining a traditional influence in her music," Michael A. Capozzoli Jr. wrote for the BPI Entertainment News Wire (June 29, 2000).*

Early Life

The daughter of Aubrey and Ann Womack, Lee Ann Womack was born on August 19, 1966 in Jacksonville, Texas. She has a sister, Judy, who is six years her senior. Her father, who was the principal of an East Texas high school, worked as a part-time country-music disc jockey at KEBE-AM, a local radio station, and her mother, a teacher, loved show tunes. As a child Womack listened to country music on the radio and often accompanied her father to the station, where she helped select the records he played. "My dad had a lot of Ray Price and Bob Wills and Tommy Duncan records," she recalled to Chet Flippo for *Billboard* (April 5, 1997). "And then, of course, Tammy Wynette and Dolly Parton." Womack soon began dreaming of becoming a country-music star. "She always wanted to go to Nashville," Ann Womack told Steve Dougherty for *People* (July 31, 2000). "We never dissuaded her. We wanted her to follow her dreams."

At her parents' suggestion, Womack began taking piano lessons. "At first I hated every minute of it," she explained to Dougherty. "My teacher made me play classical music, and I wanted to play country. I used to sit and play these sad little songs, wishing I was in Nashville." She skipped her high school's senior class trip and used the money for a trip to Nashville, to visit Music Row and other iconic sites.

Affiliation: Country Music

Lee Ann Womack is known for her signature twang and old-fashioned musical style, which have earned her comparisons to such country-music legends as Dolly Parton and Tammy Wynette. Womack is currently putting the finishing touches on her next studio album. The lead single from the album, "There Is a God," was released in late 2009 and debuted at number 60 on the *Billboard* country-singles chart. Womack has since revealed the titles of other songs on the album, including "Talking Behind Your Back" and "You Do Until You Don't." Womack was named best new female vocalist by the Academy of Country Music (ACM), top new artist of the year by *Billboard*, and favorite new country artist at the American Music Awards (AMAs). Additionally, she was nominated for a Horizon Award from the Country Music Association (CMA); that prize ultimately went to the teenage singer LeAnn Rimes.

Womack brought out her sophomore album, *Some Things I Know*, in 1998. The recording, which was also produced by Wright, featured the hit singles "A Little Past Little Rock" and "I'll Think of a Reason," both of which reached the number-two spot on the country-singles chart. *Some Things I Know* peaked at number 20 on the *Billboard* country-album chart and later achieved gold status.

After graduating from Jacksonville High School, in 1984, Womack attended South Plains Junior College, in Levelland, Texas, where she studied music. (The school was one of the first in the nation to offer degrees in bluegrass and country music.) Shortly after entering South Plains, Womack became a vocalist in Country Caravan, a college band that toured the country. She left junior college after a year, however, and moved to Nashville to pursue her musical career. In order to satisfy her parents, Womack entered Nashville's Belmont University, where she studied the commercial aspects of the music industry. During that time she landed a student internship in the A&R department of MCA Records.

Womack remained at Belmont until 1990, when she left to marry her college sweetheart, the country-music artist Jason Sellers. (She was just three courses shy of earning her degree.) The following year she gave birth to her first daughter, Aubrie Lee. While putting in hours as a waitress and childcare worker, Womack remained focused on her music career. Craig Seymour wrote for the *Atlanta Journal-Constitution* (August 25, 2002), "Unable to afford a babysitter, she would stroll down Music Row holding her baby with one hand and a demo tape with the other." Womack's persistence paid off in 1995, when she was offered a songwriting deal at Sony/ATV Music Publishing. As a staffer at the company's subsidiary Tree Publishing, she co-wrote songs with such prominent country-music names as Ed Hill, Bill Anderson, Sam Hogin, and Mark Wright. Ricky Skaggs recorded Womack's composition "I Don't Remember Forgetting" for his 1995 album *Solid Ground*.

Life's Work

In early 1997 Womack's songwriting abilities and strong desire to sing landed her an audition with MCA Nashville's chairman, Bruce Hinton, who quickly signed her to a contract with MCA's sister label, Decca Records. "She came into the office and performed acoustically, and it was a very special moment," Hinton recalled to Chet Flippo. Shortly after signing with Decca, Womack showcased her talents at the Country Radio Seminar, an annual convention held in Nashville that was attended by more than 2,000 industry insiders. That performance helped bolster the release of her debut single, "Never Again, Again," which made the *Billboard* country-singles chart and received heavy radio airplay

In May 1997 Womack released her eponymous debut album, which was produced by Mark Wright and consisted of both original material and songs written by Mark Chesnutt, Ricky Skaggs, and Tony Brown. The traditional style of the album, which included the hit singles "The Fool," "You've Got to Talk to Me," and "Buckaroo," struck a chord with fans; it peaked at number nine on the *Billboard* country-album chart and reached gold status within months. "*Lee Ann Womack* is a rarity in modern Nashville—an authentic honky-tonk debut album," the music critic Geoffrey Himes wrote in a review available on Amazon.com. "Producer Mark Wright has refused to bury Womack's small-town, East Texas drawl under the Hollywood soft rock cloaking that Music Row favors these days. As a result, the young singer's soprano projects an attitude too unsophisticated to hide any emotion. On the first single, 'Never Again, Again,' you can hear in quivering high notes the dilemma of a woman who keeps breaking her own promise to never take her ex-lover back. Not every song is that sharply focused, and the obligatory boot-scootin' dance numbers and string-smothered ballads dilute the album's impact. But you can hear Womack's potential."

In 1999 Decca Records folded, and Womack moved to MCA Records. The following year her third album, *I Hope You Dance*, appeared. The title track, a crossover hit, reached number one on the *Billboard* country-singles chart, topped the adult contemporary chart, and peaked at number 14 on the *Billboard* Hot 100 chart. The recording as a whole debuted at number one on the *Billboard* country-album chart and entered the *Billboard* 200 chart at number 17; it has since sold almost four million copies in the U.S. Womack landed six CMA nominations for the album and won the awards for single of the year and song of the year. She also received two ACM awards, in the same categories, and took home a Grammy Award for best country song.

Because of the uplifting theme of "I Hope You Dance," which includes the lyrics "Promise me you'll give faith a fighting chance / And when you get the choice to sit it out or dance / I hope you dance," Womack was asked to perform at the 2000 Nobel Peace Prize concert (an annual event honoring the year's laureate) and on an installment of the widely watched *Oprah Winfrey Show*. The track has been played at countless proms, graduations, and weddings. "[The song) made me think about my daughters and the different times in their lives," Womack told Chuck Taylor for *Billboard* July 1, 2000, on-line). "But it can be so many things to different people. Certainly, it can represent everything a parent hopes for their child, but it can also be for someone graduating, having a baby, or embarking on a new path. It fits almost every circumstance I can think of."

I Hope You Dance, which also featured the Top 40 country singles "Ashes by Now," "Why They Call It Falling," and "Does My Ring Burn Your Finger," received widespread attention from critics. In a review for the All Music Guide Web site, Maria Konicki Dinola called the recording "one of the finest albums to hit country music [since] Shania Twain" and added, "Womack possesses such a sweet, melodious voice and its distinctiveness graces every one of the 12 tracks like they were chosen just for her vocals." In an assessment for *People* (June 19, 2000), Ralph Novak wrote, "With its rueful tone, evocative songs and emotion-drenched, sweet-voiced vocals, this could have been mistaken for a Dolly Parton album. Who would have guessed it's the erstwhile Texas firebrand Womack in a new mode less suited to honky-tonks than to wedding receptions." In a review featured in the *Quincy (Massachusetts) Patriot Ledger* (June 14, 2000), Ken Rosenbaum expressed untempered praise: "Womack's sweet, crystalline voice blends a wide assortment of country song types into a craftsmanlike, cohesive, and satisfying package. She glides from painful laments and torchy sizzlers to fiddle-drenched waltzes and bouncy honky-tonkers, leaving in her wake a profound feeling that something special has just been heard."

In 2002 Womack's album *Something Worth Leaving Behind* reached stores. Despite reaching number two on the *Billboard* country-music album chart and peaking at number 16 on the *Billboard* 200 chart, the recording failed to produce a Top 10 country hit and received tepid notices from reviewers, who criticized Womack for abandoning her signature sound in favor of a more pop-oriented style and for sporting a new, more glamorous look than before. In a review published in the *Bergen County (New Jersey) Record* (September 6, 2002), Nick Cristiano wrote, "*Something Worth Leaving Behind* contains too many pedestrian songs that are further burdened by schlocky, play-it-safe production. The title track, done in two equally unsatisfying versions, is a prime example. With its inspirational message, it is an obvious attempt to repeat the success of Dance's title song, but it is much triter."

In the summer of 2002, Womack toured with the country legend Willie Nelson, and in October of that year, she released a Christmas album, *The Season for Romance*, featuring a rendition of the popular standard "Baby It's Cold Outside," which she performed with Harry Connick Jr. Womack next collaborated with Nelson on his single "Mendocino County Line," which won a 2003 Grammy Award for best country collaboration. The single also garnered awards from the ACM and the CMA.

In early 2003 Womack made her acting debut, with a small guest role on the CBS drama *The District*. She returned to the record stores in 2004, with the appearance of a greatest-hits collection, which also included two new songs, the Top 40 country hit "The Wrong Girl" and "Time for Me to Go." That year Womack performed "I Hope You Dance" at the Republican National Convention and collaborated with the country band Cross Canadian Ragweed on the song "Sick and Tired," which became a minor hit.

In 2005 Womack released *There's More Where That Came From*. The album, which included a duet with the country icon George Strait called "Good News, Bad News," marked a return to the singer's traditional roots.

The lead single, "I May Hate Myself in the Morning," cracked the Top 10 on the *Billboard* country-singles chart and featured background vocals by Jason Sellers, with whom Womack had split amicably in 1997. Two additional singles, "He Oughta Know That by Now" and "Twenty Years and Two Husbands Ago," became Top 40 country hits. Womack told Mikel Toombs for the *San Diego Union-Tribune* (February 17, 2006), "Everybody has different definitions of what traditional country music is. To me, traditional country music is twin fiddles and steel guitars, and the hardcore country [songs]. There are some people out there who love it. I'm from Texas, and that's where a lot of them are." She also discussed the topic with Michael A. Capozzoli Jr., asserting, "Even though it's been hard to stay grounded in the real traditional music with radio the way it is right now, I love very real country music. . . . That will always be a priority to me."

Critics were almost universally impressed with *There's More Where That Came From*. Anthony Easton wrote for *Stylus* magazine (March 23, 2005, on-line), "The brilliance of this album is that it knows its history, but collapses and expands it into a universe all its own." Making mention of the hazy, vintage-looking portrait of Womack that adorned the album jacket, Stephen Thomas Eriewine wrote for the All Music Guide Web site, "*There's More Where That Came From* . . . is still firmly within the country-pop confines, but there's a notable difference—as the rather brilliant cover art suggests, this hearkens back to the sound and style of early-'70s country-pop albums from the likes of Barbara Mandrell, Loretta Lynn, and Dolly Parton. Not that this is a retro effort, or anything like a stab at neo-traditionalist country. Instead, Womack takes her inspiration from these records, crafting a record that's laidback but never lazy, smooth but never too slick, tuneful without being cloying." He concluded, "All this adds up to an album that's not only the best album that Lee Ann Womack has yet made, but one that does suggest that there is indeed more where this came from." *There's More Where That Came From* was named album of the year by the CMA, and "I May Hate Myself in the Morning" garnered song-of-the-year honors. "Good News, Bad News" also took home the CMA award for best "musical event" of the year. (The association uses the term "event" to refer to a collaboration between artists.)

In the summer of 2006, Womack released the single "Finding My Way Back Home," on the Mercury Nashville label. The single debuted at number 46 on the *Billboard* country-singles chart and peaked at number 37. Womack had intended to include the song on a studio album of the same name, but those plans fell through when she left Mercury and returned to MCA Nashville. In 2008 she released *Call Me Crazy*, which debuted at number four on the *Billboard* country-album chart. Produced by Tony Brown, the Grammy-nominated record included the single "Last Call," which became Womack's first Top 20 hit in nearly three years. Another single, "Solitary Thinkin'," cracked the Top 40 of the country charts. Like its predecessor, the album included a duet with Strait ("Everything but Quits") and also featured a cover of the Strait classic "The King of Broken Hearts."

Call Me Crazy received largely mixed reviews. Expressing sentiments echoed by other critics, Jonathan Keefe wrote for *Slant Magazine* (October 19, 2008, on-line), that *Call Me Crazy* is "characterized by a stylistic diversity and an insistence on playing against her strengths." He added, "Though her voice sounds thin when compared to that of Patty Loveless or Trisha Yearwood, Womack is a first-rate stylist and one of the finest interpretative singers of her generation, so she is able to carry the album even when the production and the songwriting fail her." Christian Hoard wrote for *Rolling Stone* (November 13, 2008, on-line), "The album sounds way more professional than crazy, but tunefulness this pleasant works out just fine."

Personal Life

Womack, who spent the early months of 2010 touring with Strait and Reba McEntire, has been married to the record producer Frank Liddell since November 1999. In addition to Aubrie Lee, her daughter with Sellers, she has one daughter with Liddell, Anna Lise.

Further Reading

Atlanta Journal-Constitution L p1+ Aug. 25, 2002
Billboard p67 Aug. 10, 2002
BPI Entertainment News Wire June 29, 2000
Chicago Tribune C p7 Oct. 1, 2000
Miami Herald G p5 Dec. 2, 2005
People p129 July 31, 2000

Stevie Wonder

Singer; composer

Born: May 13, 1950; Saginaw, Michigan
Primary Field: R&B singer
Group Affiliation: *Innervisions*

Introduction

Probably the most original and popular performer among the pop musicians of the younger generation, Stevie Wonder has made the transition from singing rhythm and blues hits to creating innovative music that has bridged the gap between soul and pop. The blind singer began his career during the early 1960's as Little Stevie Wonder, a precocious child singer and harmonica player for Motown Records, which discovered much of its talent, including Wonder, in the black ghetto of Detroit. After struggling for several years to break away from the stereotyped black soul sound of Motown, Wonder renegotiated his contract with the record company in 1971 and now has complete control over the music he performs. Since then he has brought forth a remarkable series of "one-man" record albums (Music of My Mind, Talking Book, Innervisions, *and* Fulfillingness' First Finale) *that he has produced himself. He has written all of the music and most of the lyrics for those albums, prepared the arrangements, played most of the musical instruments, and sung the vocals. Complex, highly electronic, and ranging from love ballads to funky soul, Wonders music has made him the reigning favorite of pop music critics and the most influential figure in black music. Although his subtleties can best be enjoyed on recordings, he is an exciting performer in concert, where he bounces and jumps from piano to drums to synthesizer projecting what one writer called "the image of a loose, happy child of music." Wonder's hit singles of recent years have included "Superstition," "You Are the Sunshine of My Life," and "Higher Ground." All of his work appears on the Motown or Motown Tamla labels.*

Stevie Wonder.

Early Life

Stevie Wonder was born Steveland Judkins Morris on May 13, 1950 in Saginaw, Michigan. He has two older brothers, Milton and Calvin, a younger brother, Larry, and a younger sister, Renee. Stevie's parents separated when he was small, and he was brought up by his mother, Lula Mae, who moved the family to Detroit. She was subsequently remarried to Paul Hardaway, a black baker who worked in a Jewish bakery. Wonder grew up in Detroit's east side ghetto in what he likes to call "upper-lower-class circumstances."

A premature baby, Wonder has been blind since birth. "I have a dislocated nerve in one eye and a cataract on the other," he explained to Henry Edwards of *New York* (September 16, 1974). "It may have happened from being in the incubator too long and receiving too much oxygen." Despite his disability, the boy had a fairly normal childhood, running, climbing trees, and, with someone to steer, even riding a bicycle. His family was not particularly musical, but Stevie showed his aptitude early. At two he pounded a tin pan with a spoon to the rhythm of music on the radio. At four he began playing the piano, and shortly after that he started to learn the harmonica on a little four-hole instrument given to him by an uncle. Stevie wore out several sets of toy drums until the local Lions club gave him a real set at a Christmas party for blind children. By the age of nine the boy was singing solos at the services of the Whitestone Baptist Church, but he was expelled from the choir after a church member heard him singing and playing rock 'n' roll on a doorstep with some other children.

In 1960, when Stevie Morris was nine years old, a playmate's big brother, who was a member of the singing group, the Miracles, brought him to the studios of Motown Records, the fast-rising black record label then based in Detroit.

The young blind boy began hanging around the recording studio every day after school, playing every instrument he could get his hands on and writing songs (his first was "Lonely Boy"). People started calling him the little boy wonder, and so Motown released his records under the name Little Stevie Wonder. In 1963 he had his first big hit, "Fingertips Part 2," a jumpy, finger-snapping harmonica number punctuated with soul screams and squeals. The "Fingertips" single rose to the top of the charts during the summer of 1963 and sold over 1,000,000 copies, earning Wonder his first gold record. Among Wonder's early albums were *Little Stevie Wonder: the Twelve-Year-Old Genius,* which contained the "Fingertips" cut, and *A Tribute to Uncle Bay,* a vocal salute to Ray Charles, the blind soul singer whose style Wonder imitated during his early years as a performer.

Life's Work

When Little Stevie Wonder became a recording artist for Motown, he became a member of the Motown "family." A court-appointed guardian was secured for him, and the money he earned was put in a trust to await his majority. Motown kept tight control over the music he performed, seeing that it conformed to the slick soul sound that became known as Motown. About two weeks a month Wonder spent touring with the Motown Revue, which traveled by bus to black theatres and night spots around the country. For a time Wonder continued to attend public school, but then he transferred to the Michigan School for the Blind in Lansing. While traveling, he studied for three or four hours a day with a private tutor. Wonder received his diploma from the Michigan School for the Blind around 1969, and according to some sources, went on to study composing and arranging at the University of Southern California. Pie writes and arranges music with the aid of a tape recorder and braille music sheets.

After the smash success of "Fingertips," Little Stevie Wonder recorded a string of hits, including "Uptight," "Blowin' in the Wind," "A Place in the Sun," "I Was Made to Love Her," "Shoo-be-oo-be-oo-be-oo-da-day," "Yester-me, Yester-You, Yesterday," "For Once in My Life," "My Cherie Amour," and "Signed, Sealed and Delivered." His 1970 album, *Signed, Sealed and Delivered,* which was the first that he himself produced, was judged to be one of the best records of the year by many critics.

By the late 1960's Motown had dropped the "Little" from the six-foot singer's billing, and Stevie Wonder was one of the record company's most successful acts. Besides appearing in concerts with such other Motown headliners as the Supremes and Martha and the Vandellas, Wonder began appearing at such clubs as the Cellar Door in Washington, D.C. and the Village Gate in New York City. In September 1969 he made his bow at New York's Philharmonic Hall and a few months later, in April 1970, he filled his first supperclub engagement in New York City at the Copacabana. After hearing him there, Alfred G. Aronowitz of the New York *Post* (March 20, 1970) wrote that Wonder was "an honest prodigy of flawless taste and superb talent. Not only has he developed his own style as a soul singer, but he's one of the world's virtuosos on the chromatic harmonica."

From the beginning of his professional career, Stevie Wonder took such an interest in the creation of the music that he performed that he often collaborated with Motown's lyricists and composers. Most of his material after "Uptight" in 1966 includes his name in the credits. Shortly after *Signed, Sealed and Delivered* he produced an even more ambitious album, *Where I'm Coming From* (1970), written entirely by Wonder and his wife, singer-songwriter, Syreeta Wright. A transitional work, *Where I'm Coming From* struck an uneasy compromise between the Motown Sound and Wonder's own free-wheeling musical explorations.

Chafing under Motown's paternalism and the restrictions of its sound, Wonder decided, when he turned twenty-one in May 1971, to leave the record company. Taking the million dollars that had been held in trust for him, he used a quarter of the money to rent a recording studio in New York, where he taped his experiments on the Moog and ARP synthesizers and poured out the musical ideas he had been storing up for years. Finally he came up with the album, *Music of My Mind,* on which, aided by modern recording techniques, he was able to play most of the instrumental accompaniments on the piano, drums, harmonica, organ, clavichord, clavinet, and synthesizers—and to sing most of the background vocals. "One-man recordings have been tried by other performers . . . but no one has brought off the complicated trick of playing most—or all—of the parts better than Wonder in this collection," wrote *New York Times* music critic Don Heckman on July 30, 1972. Finding it more than a feat of dexterity, he went on to say, "After a few minutes of the first track, one promptly forgets all about the technical legerdemain and settles down to hear a constantly provocative flow of musical ideas, good humor, artistic invention and solid swing."

Wonder returned to Motown with *Music on My Mind* released in 1972, and he negotiated a new and more favorable contract that gave him more money and complete control over his music, production of his records, and bookings for his personal appearances. Early in 1972 he organized Wonderlove, a back-up group of three female singers and several musicians. After touring with his new show for a few months, he accompanied the Rolling Stones on their triumphant North American tour in July and August 1972. As the opening act in their show, Wonder received generally appreciative reviews and exposure to a large, new, mostly white audience. Shortly after the Stones tour, Wonder released "Superstition," an infectiously rhythmic song that became his biggest hit since "Fingertips," and on February 7, 1973 he made a Carnegie Hall debut to a responsive audience and critical acclaim.

"Superstition" was included on Wonder's second one-man album, *Talking Book,* which was released late in 1972 to an even better reception than that encountered by his previous LP. "Every cut is a colorfully multi-tracked sonic canvas making heavy use of the synthesizer," wrote Stephen Holden of the *Saturday Review* (February 3, 1973), who concluded that it was "the most mature, though not the most accessible, album to date by a prodigious figure in pop music." Besides "Superstition," *Talking Book* contained a second hit song, "You Are the Sunshine of My Life."

Wonders latest album, *Fulfillingness' First Finale,* was released in the summer of 1974. By September it was the nation's best-selling LP. More meditative than his previous discs, it was perhaps especially vulnerable to the criticism of having excessively sentimental lyrics, about the only complaint ever leveled at Wonder's music. "Too gushy," was the verdict of Josh Mills, for example, who wrote in the New York *Sunday News* (October 6, 1974), "Stevie Wonder is a genius, but his taste is moving too far into the mystic and the romantic for me." During the fall of 1974 Wonder and his band

Affiliation: Innervisions

Seven months went into the preparation of *Innervisions* which Wonder has called his "most personal album." After its release in the summer of 1973, David Marsh of *Newsday* (August 26, 1973) expressed the consensus of critics when he wrote, "With his last three albums, Stevie has accomplished what few rock musicians ever do. He has made one record after another which not only seems to transcend his previous work, but also reflects a cohesive style, a unity of direction and purpose which renders comparisons of quality among the albums futile." Among the cuts of *Innervisions* are the hit single "Living for the City," a pulsating song about a boy who exchanges the hardships of the country for an even harder life in the city; another hit, "Higher Ground," which begins in gloom and ends on a note of religious affirmation; "Don't You Worry 'Bout a Thing," a humorous tune with a Latin beat; and "All in Love Is Fair," which has been recorded by Barbra Streisand.

While record reviewers and the public were becoming acquainted with Wonder's new album, the blind star's career almost came to a tragic end. On August 6, 1973, in Salisbury, North Carolina, the car in which he was riding to a personal appearance struck the back of a log truck. Logs tumbled through the windshield and hit the singer in the forehead with such force that he lay in a coma for nearly a week. The brain injury that Wonder suffered required him to be hospitalized for several weeks, followed by months of slow recuperation. While he was still recovering his health, he was nominated in January 1974 for six Grammy awards, more than any other recording artist in the sixteen-year history of the awards. That March he won five Grammies, including one for best pop vocal performance by a male singer ("You Are the Sunshine of My Life") and another for best album of the year *(Innervisions).* In 1974 he was also named best-selling male soul artist of the year by the National Association of Recording Merchandisers, and he received the American Music awards for best male soul vocalist and soul single ("Superstition").

toured thirty cities, including Boston, Buffalo, Washington, and Los Angeles.

As of October 1974 over 40,000,000 copies of Wonders records had been sold. He has accumulated fourteen gold singles (sales of over 1,000,000 copies each); four gold albums (sales of more than $1,000,000 worth of copies each); and two platinum albums (sales of more than 1,000,000 copies each). It seems unlikely that his huge output will slacken, since he told a *Newsweek* reporter (October 28, 1974) that he has some 200 recorded songs that he has not yet released. In 1975 Wonder won four Grammy awards, a National Association of Recording Merchandisers presidential award, and a Rock Music award for best male vocalist.

The double album-with-extra-EP *Songs in the Key of Life* was released in September 1976. Sprawling in style, unlimited in ambition, and sometimes lyrically difficult to fathom, the album was hard for some listeners to assimilate, yet is regarded by many as Wonder's crowning achievement and one of the most recognizable and accomplished albums in pop music history. The album became the first by an American artist to debut straight at No. 1 in the *Billboard* charts, where it stood for 14 non-consecutive weeks. Two tracks became No. 1 Pop/R&B hits "I Wish" and "Sir Duke." The baby-celebratory "Isn't She Lovely?" was written about his newborn daughter Aisha, while songs such as "Love's in Need of Love Today" and "Village Ghetto Land" reflected a far more pensive mood. *Songs in the Key of Life* won Album of the Year and two other Grammys. The album ranks 57th on *Rolling Stone's* 500 Greatest Albums of All Time.

In the 1980s Wonder achieved his biggest hits and highest level of fame; he had increased album sales, charity participation, high-profile collaborations, political impact, and television appearances. The 1979 mainly instrumental soundtrack album *Stevie Wonder's Journey Through "The Secret Life of Plants"* was composed using an early music sampler, a Computer Music Melodian. Wonder toured briefly in support of the album, and used a Fairlight CMI sampler on stage. In this year Wonder also wrote and produced the dance hit "Let's Get Serious," performed by Jermaine Jackson and (ranked by *Billboard* as the No. 1 R&B single of 1980). *Hotter than July* (1980) became Wonder's first platinum-selling single album, and its single "Happy Birthday" was a successful vehicle for his campaign to establish Dr. Martin Luther King's birthday as a national holiday. The album also included "Master Blaster (Jammin')," "I Ain't Gonna Stand for It," and the sentimental ballad, "Lately."

In 1982, Wonder released a retrospective of his 1970s work with *Stevie Wonder's Original Musiquarium,* which included four new songs: the ten-minute funk classic "Do I Do" (which featured Dizzy Gillespie), "That Girl" (one of the year's biggest singles to chart on the R&B side), "Front Line," a narrative about a soldier in the Vietnam War that Wonder wrote and sang in the first person, and "Ribbon in the Sky," one of his many classic compositions. He also gained a No. 1 hit that year in collaboration with Paul McCartney in their paean to racial harmony, "Ebony and Ivory."

1984 saw the release of Wonder's soundtrack album for *The Woman in Red.* The lead single, "I Just Called to Say I Love You," was a No. 1 pop and R&B hit in both the United States and the United Kingdom, where it was placed 13th in the list of best-selling singles in the UK published in 2002. It went on to win an Academy award for best song in 1985. Wonder accepted the award in the name of Nelson Mandela and was subsequently banned from all South African radio by the Government of South Africa. The album also featured a guest appearance by Dionne Warwick, singing the duet "It's You" with Stevie and a few songs of her own. The following year's In Square Circle featured the No. 1 pop hit "Part-Time Lover." The album also has a Top 10 Hit with "Go Home." It also featured the ballad "Overjoyed," which was originally written for *Journey Through "The Secret Life of Plants,"* but did not make the album. He performed "Overjoyed" on *Saturday Night Live* when he was the host. He was also featured in Chaka Khan's cover of Prince's "I Feel For You," alongside Melle Mel, playing his signature harmonica. In roughly the same period he was also featured on harmonica on Eurythmics' single, "There Must Be an Angel (Playing with My Heart)" and Elton John's "I Guess That's Why They Call It the Blues."

Wonder was in a featured duet with Bruce Springsteen on the all-star charity single for African Famine Relief, "We Are the World," and he was part of another charity single the following year (1986), the AIDS-inspired "That's What Friends Are For."

After 1987's *Characters* album, Wonder continued to release new material, but at a slower pace. He recorded a soundtrack album for Spike Lee's film *Jungle Fever* in 1991. From this album, singles and videos were released for "Gotta Have You" and "These Three Words." The B-side to the "Gotta Have You" single was

"Feeding Off The Love of the Land," which was played during the end credits of the movie *Jungle Fever* but was not included on the soundtrack. A piano and vocal version of "Feeding Off The Love of the Land" was also released on the *Nobody's Child: Romanian Angel Appeal* compilation. *Conversation Peace* and the live album *Natural Wonder* were released in the 1990s.

Into the 21st century, Wonder continues to record and perform; though mainly occasional appearances and guest performances, he did do two tours, and released one album of new material, 2005's *A Time to Love*. His key appearances include performing at the opening ceremony of the 2002 Winter Paralympics in Salt Lake City, the 2005 Live 8 concert in Philadelphia, the pre-game show for Super Bowl XL in 2006, the Obama Inaugural Celebration in 2009, and the opening ceremony of the 2011 Special Olympics World Summer Games in Athens, Greece. He sang at the Michael Jackson memorial service in 2009, at Etta James' funeral, in 2012, and a month later at Whitney Houston's memorial service.

Wonder's first new album in ten years, *A Time to Love*, was released in October 2005 to lower sales than previous albums, and lukewarm reviews—most reviewers appearing frustrated at the end of the long delay to get an album that mainly copied the style of Wonder's "classic period" without doing anything new.

Wonder did a 13-date tour of North America in 2007, starting in San Diego on August 23; this was his first U.S. tour in over ten years. On September 8, 2008, Wonder started the European leg of his Wonder Summer's Night Tour, the first time he had toured Europe in over a decade. His opening show was at the National Indoor Arena in Birmingham. During the tour, Wonder played eight UK gigs; four at the O2 Arena in London, two in Birmingham and two at the M.E.N. Arena in Manchester. Wonder's other stops in the tour's European leg also found him performing in the Netherlands (Rotterdam), Sweden (Stockholm), Germany (Cologne, Mannheim and Munich), Norway (Hamar), France (Paris), Italy (Milan) and Denmark (Aalborg). Wonder also toured Australia (Perth, Adelaide, Melbourne, Sydney and Brisbane) and New Zealand (Christchurch, Auckland and New Plymouth) in October and November. His 2010 tour included a two-hour set at the Bonnaroo Music Festival in Manchester, Tennessee, a stop at London's "Hard Rock Calling" in Hyde Park, and appearances at England's Glastonbury Festival, Rotterdam's North Sea Jazz Festival, and a concert in Bergen, Norway and a concert in Dublin, Ireland at the O2 Arena on June 24.

A prominent figure in popular music during the latter half of the 20th century, Wonder has recorded more than 30 U.S. top ten hits and won 25 Grammy Awards (the most ever won by a solo artist) as well as a Lifetime Achievement Award. He has also won an Academy Award for Best Song, and been inducted into both the Rock and Roll and Songwriters halls of fame. He has also been awarded the Polar Music Prize. American music magazine *Rolling Stone* named him the ninth greatest singer of all time.

Personal Life

When not on tour Stevie Wonder divides his time between New York, where he has an East Side apartment, and Los Angeles, where he has a house and a magnificently equipped recording studio. Wonder lives with his fiancée Yolanda Simmons, who is his secretary and bookkeeper. His marriage around 1970 to Syreeta Wright, a Motown secretary who developed her own career as a singer-songwriter under his guidance, was dissolved in 1974. Wonder and Miss Wright have continued their musical association, however, and in 1974 he produced her second album, *Stevie Wonder Presents Syreeta,* for which he wrote the music to accompany her lyrics. Wonder drinks only sparingly and uses no drugs, although the way in which he constantly rolls his head back and forth has sometimes been mistaken for a drug-induced "high." He has explained that his head movements are "blindisms," triggered by the energy that sighted people release through the use of their eyes.

Endowed with an incredibly acute sense of hearing, Wonder can pinpoint the position of people in a room and pick up reverberations from solid objects like walls as he approaches them. He uses neither a cane nor a Seeing Eye dog, but he seldom ventures out without one of his aides to guide him. After his near-fatal accident, which has left two scars on his forehead, he had some impairment of the senses of smell and taste, and he still suffers from occasional headaches.

Over six feet tall and slender, Stevie Wonder is infectiously good-natured, soft-spoken, and charismatic. "He really seems to give off a kind of spiritual glow as he talks with his rich voice and eager hands," wrote a *Newsweek* reporter (October 28, 1974) of the singer, who now seems as interested in religion as he always has been in social and racial matters. Wonder has often performed at benefit concerts, especially to help the blind. In 1975 he and Yolanda Simmons became the parents of a daughter, Aisha Zakia, whose name means strength and intelligence. Wonder has nine children with five different mothers. Wonder was introduced to Transcendental Meditation through his marriage to Syreeta Wright. Consistent with that spiritual vision, Wonder became vegetarian, and later a vegan.

Further Reading

N Y *Post* p15 Jl 22 72 por
Newsday II p 17 F 4 73 por
Newsweek 84:59+ O 28 74 pors
Sr Schol 102:20+ Mr 26 73 pors
Brown, Jeremy K. *Stevie Wonder: Musician* (2010)

Zakk Wylde

Guitarist

Born: Jan. 14, 1967; Jersey City, New Jersey
Primary Field: Heavy metal
Group Affiliation: Ozzy Osbourne; Black Label Society

Introduction

"Zakk Wylde live. It's an unforgettable experience. An endless hurricane of sweat-soaked blonde hair whipping around as fast and furious as the ear-bleeding [decibel] riffs this muscular Thor-turned guitar hero churns and burns on his ready and willing audience.... Pure, raw, unapologetic heavy metal thunder. Indeed, Zakk Wylde may not have invented rock and roll ... but, he's doing his damndest to save it." That is how a reviewer for the Web site monstercable.com described Wylde, the hard-driving guitarist for Ozzy Osbourne's band. Wylde is also the leader of his own band, Black Label Society, whose music he has characterized as "alcohol-fueled brewtality [sic] for the next millennium."

Early Life

Zakk Wylde was born in Jersey City, New Jersey, on January 14, 1967. (According to various sources, his name at birth was Jeff Wiedlandt; an article posted on the Web site blacklabelsociety.net reported that he called himself Zakari Wyland when he was a teenager playing with the band Zyris, and, after joining Osbourne's band, changed his name legally to Zachary Phillip Wylde-the "Zachary" inspired by the character Dr. Zachary Smith from the TV show *Lost in Space.)* He took piano lessons as a youngster and again in his early teens, only to quit each time after a few lessons. Some sources state that he played the bass clarinet in school. While in his early teens, he began learning the guitar; by 17 he had formed his first band, Stone Henge, and played with others, performing regularly in bars near the New Jersey shore. Wylde became known for his speed and soulful sounds on the electric guitar.

Life's Work

One night, after a gig in a bar, a patron suggested that Wylde audition for Ozzy Osbourne's band. (Osbourne has been a heavy-metal and rock icon since his days as a singer and songwriter for the seminal British band Black Sabbath, whose fame and popularity date from the 1970s. With the sinister, gothic imagery of his lyrics and his sometimes extreme stage antics, Osbourne was derided by some as a Satanist. He has enjoyed enormous success, however, and is considered one of the most important figures in the heavy-metal, hard-rock genre.) Wylde recorded himself playing guitar and sent the tape to Osbourne, who then invited him to audition. Osbourne liked Wylde's playing style and look and in 1987 hired him to replace Jake E. Lee as the band's lead guitarist. "It was like a dream come true," Wylde said to R. Scott Bolton in an interview posted to the Web site Roughedge.com. "I was a huge [Black] Sabbath fan and we all loved Ozzy when he started his solo career." (In another version of events, which Wylde has occasionally confirmed, Wylde met Osbourne while selling him drugs.)

As Osbourne's stage and studio guitarist and co-songwriter, Wylde contributed to a series of albums that were critical and popular successes, among them the multiplatinum *No Rest for the Wicked* (1988); *Just Say Ozzy* (1990), a live album recorded during one of the band's national tours; *No More Tears* (1991); *Live and Loud* (1993), a double album that won a Grammy Award for best live performance for the song "I Don't Want to Change the World"; and the Grammy-nominated

Ozzmosis (1995), which despite mixed reviews sold three million copies within a year of its release. (''Platinum" indicates that an album has sold at least a million copies.) In a review of *No Rest for the Wicked* that appeared on the Web site artistdirect.com, Steve Huey wrote, "Things start to improve here, as Zakk Wylde replaces Jake E. Lee on guitar and Ozzy comes up with his best set since 1983. Again, it's not quite up to the level of excellence his Blizzard of Ozz band achieved, but Osbourne sounds somewhat rejuvenated, and Wylde is a more consistently interesting guitarist than Lee." Popular songs from the album are "Miracle Man," "Crazy Babies," and "Breaking All the Rules." Regarding *No More Tears,* a *CMJ New Music* review posted on the Web site cdnow.com stated, "[The title song] boasts a sowing [-destruction,] armies-on-the-march rhythm, a haunting chorus and some killer slide work from Zakk Wylde, who doesn't put a finger wrong on the entire album: his tasteful but ferocious mixture of rootsy and futuristic licks marks him as one of the best guitarists of the genre." Wylde co-wrote the above-mentioned title track; it is considered one of the album's better songs.

Wanting to return to his southern-rock roots, Wylde left Osbourne in 1994 and formed the band Pride and Glory with himself as lead guitarist and front man. Pride and Glory's self-titled debut album melded blues and rock in the style of the Allman Brothers and Lynryd Skynyrd. A writer for metal-reviews.com commented, "As the album progresses you'll notice the skillful integration of banjos, harmonicas, and other non-rock standard noise makers into the songs. Nice gruff vocals—which are also performed by [Wylde]." At about the same time, Axl Rose invited Wylde to join his legendary hard-rock band Guns N' Roses, whose members were thinking about attempting a comeback. (Wylde and the Guns N' Roses guitarist Slash had been mutual fans.) The collaboration never came to fruition. In 1996 Wylde released a solo album, *Book of Shadows,* for which he played electric guitar, acoustic guitar, harmonica, piano, keyboards, and bass. In a review of *Book of Shadows* on the Satan Stole My Teddybear Web site, Rog Billerey-Mosier wrote, "Paradoxically, what makes [Wylde] interesting is not his guitar playing, which is good but rather unimpressive.... He is passable as a singer, and one must give him credit for working on his vocals after his first album. . . . But what is interesting is the quality and range of songwriting on this album. The songs are very introspective, often slow and melancholy, and incorporate Wylde's conflicting influences very successfully: country blues, rock, metal and soulful [balladry], among others." In a dissenting opinion, Geoffrey Himes wrote for the *Washington Post* (August 16, 1996), "Wylde's fatal weakness . . . is his tendency to write shameless, humorless, grammarless lyrics along the lines of 'Without you woman by my side / I'm contemplating suicide torn from all my pride' . . . "

In 1998 Wylde, who earlier had disbanded Pride and Glory, formed Black Label Society. "We're out to destroy bands like Third Eye Blind and Blink- 182," Wylde told Richard Bienstock for the *Guitar World* Web site, when asked about Black Label Society's mission. "Since the whole grunge thing died it's like nobody plays guitar anymore unless it's these [expletive] pop songs. It makes you think. Haven't these bands ever heard of Sabbath or Zeppelin or anything that rocks?" The group's debut album, *Sonic Brew,* was released first in Japan and then, in early 1999, in the United States. On the band's second album, *Stronger Than Death* (2000), Wylde played guitar, bass, and piano, handled all of the vocals, and served as the album's producer; the only other performer was the drummer Philth Ondich. Both *Sonic Brew* and *Stronger Than Death* earned praise from heavy-metal fans and critics. Bienstock, for example, wrote, "The album brings together all of the guitarist's musical characteristics-squealing harmonics that have been Wylde's trademark since his years with Ozzy Osbourne, the bluesy, drawling vocal style he developed while fronting the southern-rock band Pride and Glory, the lighter, more melodic aspects explored on his 1996 solo album, *Book of Shadows*—and wraps them up in pummeling, Pantera-esque guitar riffs." (Pantera is a popular heavy-metal group known for its furious, searing music.) The next offering from Black Label Society was *Alcohol Fueled Brewtality Live + Five* (2001), which was given an "explicit" rating. His next album, *1919 Eternal* (2002), a tribute to Wylde's father, Jerome, who was born in 1919, earned positive critical reviews. Referring to his father and others of the World War II generation, Wylde told a writer for the Spitfire Records Web site, "You can beat those suckers down, but they'll always get back up again. It's a mindset, and it's about strength and determination, merciless forever, man. It's the same with [Black Label Society]. . . . You gotta keep on marching. That's why we've got the song 'Berserkers' on there; it sums up this band's whole mentality." In a review of the album that appears on the Web site mfnrocks.com, Bryan Shaw called Wylde "one of America's last true guitar heroes of note" and wrote that on *1919 Eternal* "Wylde continues to showcase his incredible musicianship by handling virtually all the instruments himself." In an interview posted on the Web site monstercable.com, the guitarist stated, "As a musician I like doing different things. I don't like just doing one thing. I don't sit around all day just practicing scales. Black Label is just another extension of the stuff I like, ya know. I'll listen to like Neil Young when I'm kicking back, but when I want to lift weights and get rowdy as hell, I'll put on Pantera. At the end of the day I'm a musician. Period. I don't care about any of that rock star b.s."

Affiliation: Heavy Metal

Wylde came out of obscurity in 1987, when Osbourne named the 20-year-old his lead guitarist. Playing guitar for and writing songs with Osbourne from 1988 to 1994, Wylde contributed to several hugely successful heavy-metal albums, including the multiplatinum *No More Tears* (1991) and the Grammy-nominated, multiplatinum *Ozzmosis* (1995), before leaving to form his own band and pursue a solo career. One of the premier heavy-metal guitarists working today, Wylde—who reunited with Osbourne in 2001—has contributed to the latter's continuing success and the popularity of the annual Ozzfest heavy-metal tours. In both 2003 and 2004, Wylde was voted most valuable player in *Guitar World* magazine's annual readers' poll. Although he is known best as a guitarist, Wylde has also impressed critics and fans with his skill at playing other instruments as well as with his songwriting. He is also known for his plain, candid speech, which tends to be rich in expletives, his disdain for soft music, the bull's-eye designs on his guitars, and his love of beer.

Black Label Society's album *The Blessed Hellride* (2003) further cemented Wylde's status as one of the heroes of heavy-metal music. The album debuted at number 50 on *Billboard* magazine's Top 100 albums chart and was voted the best heavy-metal album of the year in *Guitar World's* readers' poll. Reviewing *The Blessed Hellride* for amazon.com, Dominic Wills praised the music's intensity and Wylde's "crushing riffs and head-spinning solos," especially on the tracks "Blackened Waters," "Suffering Overdue," and "Stillborn," a song that laments lost love and features vocals by Osbourne. The DVD *Black Label Society: Boozed, Bruised & Broken-Boned,* released in 2003, includes footage of a Black Label Society concert held in Detroit, Michigan; a clip from a guitar instruction video that Wylde has released; and the video, directed by Rob Zombie, for the track "Stillborn." Wylde and Black Label Society's fifth studio album, and sixth overall, *Hangover Music Volume VI,* was released in the spring of 2004. While the album features a number of guest musicians, Wylde wrote all of its songs, in addition to singing and playing guitar, bass, and piano. *Hangover Music* offers an interpretation of Procol Harum's hit song "Whiter Shade of Pale" (1967) and the song "Layne," a tribute to the late singer Layne Staley, the front man for the band Alice in Chains. On his personal Web site, Wylde described *Hangover Music* as "darker and heavier than some of our previous CDs.; earlier, Wylde had toured with Black Label Society as part of Ozzfest 2001, a hard-rock and heavy-metal tour of the U.S. and other countries by Ozzy Osbourne's band and many others. Per formed annually since 1996, the Ozzfest tour has featured such bands as Pantera, System of a Down, Marilyn Manson, Megadeath, Motorhead, Slayer, and a reunited Black Sabbath. Wylde, having been asked by Osbourne to return to play with his band, laid down guitar tracks on Osbourne's album *Down to Earth* (2001); the record received fairly positive reviews. Unlike the earlier Osbourne albums on which the two men collaborated, *Down to Earth* did not contain any songs written by Wylde. "I love being in Black Label, but I'll always be around Ozzy, too," the guitarist told a writer for the Spitfire Records Web site. "Ozzy knows all he has to do is call and I'll be there." At Ozzfest 2002 Wylde played two sets in every show—one with Black Label Society and another with Osbourne's group. The demands of the two performances over the course of the tour left Wylde mentally and physically exhausted; his condition led to the cancellation of the final two weeks of the European leg of the tour. Either as the lead guitarist for Osbourne's band or with Black Label Society, Wylde was also an integral part of the Ozzfest tours in 2003 and 2004.

Wylde has named as his major influences the guitarists Jimmy Page, of Led Zeppelin; Randy Rhoads, a member of Osbourne's band who died in a plane crash in 1982; and Al DiMeola. His favorite acts include Van Halen, Neil Young, Black Sabbath, Led Zeppelin, and Pantera. He has played live or in the studio with Mike Inez, Randy Castillo, John Sinclair, Derek Sherinian, James LoMenzo, and the Allman Brothers, among others. Wylde's friends include several professional wrestlers; in 2001 he composed entrance music for the popular Stone Cold Steve Austin of the World Wrestling Federation. In addition to writing and performing much of the music on the soundtrack to the movie *Rock Star* (2001), starring Mark Wahlberg and Jennifer Aniston, Wylde appears in the film as the ferocious guitarist Ghode. He has also appeared on television on *Saturday Night Live, Mad TV,* and the popular cable show *The Osbournes,* which stars Ozzy Osbourne and members of his family.

Personal Life

Wylde is married and has three children, two sons and a daughter, whose godfather is Osbourne. Wylde told R. Scott Bolton, "Somebody was asking me, 'Is that all there is to your life? Beer, music, and that's it?' And I was like, 'Oh, dear God, I hope so.'"

Further Reading

blacklabelsociety.net
electricbasement.com
metal-reviews.com
monstercable.com;
ozzfest.com; roughedge.com
xtrememusician.com
zakkwylde.com

Yehudi Wyner

Composer; teacher; pianist

Born: June 1, 1929; Calgary, Alberta, Canada
Primary Field: Classical
Group Affiliation: Various

Introduction

"I felt at the time that I had hit the jackpot," the pianist Robert Levin told Richard Dyer for the Boston Globe *(April 19, 2006), in recalling his first impression of the concerto written for him by his longtime friend Yehudi Wyner. "And now he has, too," Levin added, referring to the news that Wyner, at the age of 74, had won the 2006 Pulitzer Prize for music. The Pulitzer judges recognized Wyner's concerto, subtitled "Chiavi in Mana" ("Keys in Hand" in Italian), as a "distinguished musical composition by an American that had its first performance or recording in the United States" during the year 2005. At its premiere, Wyner's concerto was performed by Levin and the Boston Symphony Orchestra, which had commissioned the work three years earlier. "To me," Levin told Dyer, "what he delivered is a piece of vintage Wyner, rich in emotional communication, eloquence, and vehemence." "Of all my pieces, this one most comprehensively reflects the various sides of me, both the serious and the absurd," Wyner said to the same reporter.*

Early Life

Yehudi Wyner was born on June 1, 1929 in Calgary, Alberta, Canada, to Lazar Weiner and Sarah Naomi (Shumiatcher) Weiner. (His parents changed the spelling of their sons' surname to avoid mispronunciation by others.) Wyner grew up with his brother, David, in New York City. His mother was a skilled pianist. His father was a celebrated composer of Jewish liturgical music and Yiddish art songs; an immigrant from the Ukraine, he was also the longtime director of music at the Central Synagogue, a prominent New York City house of worship, and he hosted a weekly radio program called *The Message of Israel.* According to an article about Wyner for the Milken Archive of American Jewish Music (2006, on-line), "Throughout his youth, ... [his parents'] home was frequented by literati and artists from the Yiddish cultural orbit." Wyner told the music scholar Richard Dyer that he started composing before he turned five. "My father noticed what I was doing at the piano, and he'd write down the little pieces for me," he recalled. Beginning in early childhood, guided by his father, Wyner practiced the piano two or three hours every day-a routine that increased in difficulty as he got older. "It was a very intense and directed professional track," he told Stephen Heyman for the Brandeis University publication *Justice* (as reprinted by University Wire, May 9, 2006, on-line). He told Judith Wershil Hasan for the *New York Times* (August 2, 1981) that the training was "a very painful experience.... Later on, I had to struggle to reconcile my natural musical impulses with the vestigial resentment that I was forced to give away the normal pursuits and fellowship of childhood." In one example of his successful efforts at such reconciliation, at a concert held in 1988, six years after his father's death, Wyner performed three preludes for piano composed by Weiner in 1932. In a review of that concert for the *Los Angeles Times* (December 20, 1988), Bruce Burroughs wrote that Wyner played the preludes, which "make real virtuoso demands," with "uncompromising energy, deep respect and the love available only from one to whom this work had been dedicated at the age of 3."

At the private high school he attended, Wyner took no courses in science or math, affording him more time for pianistic pursuits. Concurrently, he studied piano at the Juilliard School of Music, in New York City, which awarded him a diploma in 1946. He told Dyer that he decided to become a composer after leaving Juilliard. "I was pretty sure that the career of a virtuoso pianist was not for me—I didn't want all that traveling and repetition. Also I knew I lacked the kind of commanding memory that a touring virtuoso has to have." After his high-school graduation, Wyner enrolled at Yale University, where he studied under the composers Richard Donovan and Paul Hindemith. As an undergraduate he composed one movement of a concerto for piano and orchestra and had an opportunity to attend a rehearsal of it, under the baton of another student (James Yannatos, now a conductor and composer). "I was so horrified by what it sounded like, by my own ignorance, that I didn't write orchestra work for 25 years!" he told Dyer. Wyner earned three degrees at Yale: an A.B. in 1950; a B.Mus. (bachelor's degree in music) in 1951; and an M.Mus. (master's degree in music) in 1953. The last came one year after he had received an M.A. degree in music from Harvard University, in Cambridge, Massachusetts, where he studied under the composers Randall Thompson and Walter Piston. During that period he spent one summer at the Brandeis Arts Institute in Santa Susana, California, where he met well-regarded Jewish composers, some from Israel, and, according to the Milken Archive article, was "profoundly affected by the founder and director of the institute, Shlomo Bardin, whom he credits with instilling in him . . . a fresh appreciation for Jewish cultural identity."

Life's Work

In 1953 Wyner won a Rome Prize in composition, bestowed by the American Academy in Rome, Italy. Supported by his award money, he spent the next three years at the academy, playing piano and composing music; he also traveled in Italy and elsewhere in Europe. According to Martin Brody, Wyner's experience of other cultures influenced him profoundly, by providing him, in Wyner's words, with a "view of other cultures ... a connection with the past"; fostering in him "a tolerance and an acceptance of many other ways of life"; and awakening him to "the possibility for integrating, even in an informal way, ideas from all over the world and ideas from all over one's internal landscape, finding things that would be normally regarded as disparate, disorganized or as simply messy; finding that there were ways to have those live together, to be integrated to result in a new synthesis." By the end of his time in Rome, his compositions included a suite, a partita, and a sonata for piano; two chorale preludes for organ; a set of dance variations for wind octet; and choral music set to Psalm 143, which begins "Hear my prayer, 0 Lord, give ear to my supplications." During the 1950s he and others began to perform some of those works in concerts, in such places as Carnegie Recital Hall, Columbia University, and Town Hall, all in New York City.

In 1957, after his return to the U.S., Wyner began teaching music theory as an instructor at Hebrew Union College, in New York City. He taught at Hofstra College (now University), in Hempstead, New York, in 1959 and at Queens College, a division of the City University of New York, in 1959-60. He served as the music director of the Westchester Reform Temple, a suburban New York synagogue, from 1959 until 1968. In 1960 he won a Guggenheim fellowship and the next year a grant from the American Institute of Arts and Letters. In 1963 he joined the faculty of Yale; he chaired the composition division of the Department of Music there from 1969 until 1973. Wyner left Yale in 1977 and, the next year, became a professor of music at the State University of New York (SUNY) at Purchase. He taught there until1989 and served as the dean of music from 1978 to 1982. He told Judith Wershil Hasan in 1981, "I've had the luck of the Irish really. . . . Because of fellowships and major prizes, I have had the privilege of taking years off to cultivate me. In a sense, I'm repaying that privilege now, with service as a teacher, coach and as a dean." In 1989 Wyner made another move, to Brandeis University, in Waltham, Massachusetts, where he remained until he retired from college teaching, in 2005.

Meanwhile, in 1968, Wyner had joined the nine-member Bach Aria Group as keyboardist and sometime conductor, after the ensemble's then-pianist, Paul Ulanowsky, became ill and recommended Wyner as his successor. Founded in 1946 and made up of five instrumentalists and four singers, the group performs Bach cantatas, arias from the cantatas, and instrumental chamber music. The job gave Wyner the means to devote more time to his own musical interests; as he told Dyer, "The first years of touring . . . brought financial freedom in a way unimaginable for a young composer. My salary from the Bach Aria Group was larger than I earned for an entire year of teaching at Yale." For six summers beginning in 1981, the group held the Bach Aria Festival and Institute at the State University of New York (SUNY) at Stony Brook, on Long Island, offering coaching and lectures as well as concerts. A documentary recorded at the festival in 1983 was broadcast in 1985 on PBS television stations, with the title *In Search of Bach,* to celebrate the 300th anniversary of Bach's birth.

Earlier, in 1967, Wyner's first, 16-year marriage, to the former Nancy Braverman, a mezzo-soprano, had ended in divorce. That same year he married the former Susan M. Davenny, a onetime violinist, who was building a career as a soprano. By his own account, Davenny (who has worked as a conductor in recent years) inspired the composition of a number of his works, among them *Canto Cantabile* (1972), for soprano and concert band; *Memorial* Music (1971–73), for soprano and three flutes; *Intermedio* (1976), for soprano and strings; *Fragments from Antiquity* (1978-81), for soprano and symphony orchestra; five songs set to ancient Chinese and classical romantic poems; and the song cycle *On This Most Voluptuous Night* (1982), for soprano and seven instruments, based on poems by William Carlos Williams.

Affiliation: Classical

Wyner has written more than 70 works for full orchestra, chamber groups, piano, and voice, ranging in length from two minutes (in the cases of such songs as "The Grass Is High" and "Florida Express") to 28 minutes (*Prologue and Narrative* for cello and orchestra). While they are instantly recognizable as 20th/21st-century creations, they reflect, sometimes subtly and other times plainly, Wyner's unusually diverse musical passions and influences, which encompass everything from Christian and Jewish liturgical compositions, Baroque sonatas and cantatas, and 19th-century operas to klezmer, pop, jazz, rock, honky-tonk, torch songs, and 12-tone pieces. As the music professor and composer Martin Brody noted in an essay written in 2004 for Associated Music Publishers (which prints and sells scores of Wyner's compositions), "His oeuvre does not neatly divide into periods, genres, or any other categories." Writing for the Raleigh, North Carolina, *News and Observer* (October 19, 2003), David Perkins characterized Wyner's music as "at once deeply thoughtful and full of nervous energy and impatience."

In his essay "Reflections on the Pulitzer Prize" for the Internet magazine *NewMusicBox* (April 27, 2006), Wyner described his compositions as reflections of "emotional and physical states of mind and motion.... It is music which seeks to embrace as broad a gamut of experience as I am able to organize in a given musical framework. . . . It is music that does not seek to avoid the influence of all the music I have heard and loved and played and conducted and studied. It permits expression of the raunchy as well as the refined, the trivial as well as the tragic. These statements should not suggest that my music is a collage of references and quotations. Far from it. The references are transformed to reveal something new about the material. ... I believe that whatever originality my work may have lies in its process of transformation and the significance of unpredictable juxtapositions."

A highly accomplished, Juilliard-trained pianist who has graduate degrees in music, Wyner taught at the college level from 1959 until his retirement from academia, in 2005. In 2008 he began his fifth decade with the Bach Aria Group, as the ensemble's pianist and occasional conductor. In "Reflections on the Pulitzer Prize," he wrote, "My hope is that the prize will stimulate curiosity, and that the curiosity will lead to active engagement with the music for listeners and performers alike. I want my music to be heard and received with an involvement akin to what I feel and imagine as I write it."

Others among his compositions from the 1960s, 1970s, and 1980s include the Serenade for seven instruments (1958); *Passover Offering* (1959), for flute, clarinet, cello, and trombone; *Friday Evening Service* (1963; orchestrated, 1992), for cantor, chorus, and organ; *Dances of Atonement* (1976), for violin and piano; *All the Rage* (1980), for flute and piano; and 0 *to Be a Dragon* (1989), four songs for women's chorus and piano, set to whimsical poems by Marianne Moore. Wyner also wrote incidental music for two plays: *The Old Glory* (1964), set to a poem by Robert Lowell, which premiered at the American Place Theater, and *The* Mirror (1972-73), set to a fantastical tale by Isaac Bashevis Singer and mounted at the Yale Repertory Theater. *The Mirror* is one of three pieces on an album recorded by Wyner in 2004. Performed by instrumentalists including the flutist Carol Wincenc and the clarinetist Richard Stoltzman, the disk was nominated for two classical-music Grammy Awards, for producer of the year (David Frost) and best small ensemble.

In composing his 28-minute *Prologue and Narrative* for cello and orchestra (1994), Wyner collaborated with the cellist Ralph Kirshbaum, who lives in England. "We would exchange letters, and whenever Ralph came to America for concerts, we would meet and go over passages in detail," Wyner told Richard Dyer (April 11, 1999). "I kept rewriting until both of us were satisfied." The work was introduced to the public in a performance by Kirshbaum and the BBC Philharmonic, which had commissioned it. Another work, *Horntrio* (1997), was written as a sort of appreciation for Brahms's Trio for Horn, Violin, and Piano, one of the rare classical chamber pieces that include the horn. Wyner composed it with the support of the WorldWide Concurrent Premieres and Commissioning Fund, an organization that attempts to generate interest in new music by sponsoring multiple, simultaneous premieres of the works around the around. *Horntrio* debuted at nine locations on December 7, 1997, among them Jordan Hall in Boston, Massachusetts, where it was performed with Wyner on piano, Jean Rife on horn, and James Buswell on violin. "Has any composer since Benjamin Britten played the piano as well as Wyner? How many fulltime professional pianists do?" Dyer wrote for the *Boston Globe* (December 9, 1997) after attending the premiere. In the following months 30 additional concerts included the *Horntrio.* Ellen Pfeifer, writing for the *Boston Herald* (December 9, 1997), described the piece as "an intense, mercurial, brilliant affair written in a charged chromatic idiom." Now one of Wyner's most frequently performed pieces, *Horntrio* was among the finalists for the 1998 Pulitzer Prize in music.

In 1999 a program sponsored by the city of Santa Fe, New Mexico, called 20th Century Unlimited, commissioned Wyner to write a vocal piece for the soprano Dominique Labelle. "I've had a lot of experience writing for the voice and making a great effort to get out of the way, but at the same time providing continuity and support," Wyner told Craig Smith for the *Santa Fe New Mexican* (June 4, 1999). "It's a very neat craft; it's very demanding." The commissioned work is the 24-minute song cycle *The Second Madrigal: Voices of Women* for soprano, violin, viola, cello, double bass, and percussion, a set of musical interpretations of poems by or about women collected by Czelaw Milosz in *A Book of Luminous Things*—in particular, from the section of the anthology entitled "Woman's Skin." *The Second Madrigal* was recorded for a 2003 CD that also includes *Horntrio* and Wyner's Quartet for oboe and string trio.

The debut of Wyner's Piano Concerto: "Chiavi in Mano," in early 2005, marked the first concert in over a dozen years at which a Boston composer's work was performed by the city's symphony orchestra with a Boston-based pianist and Mozart specialist (Robert Levin) as the featured soloist. The subtitle refers both to the keys that physically and symbolically give a person use of a house or a car and to the keys of the piano. "As in many of my compositions, simple, familiar musical ideas are the starting point," Wyner explained in a note posted on schirmer.com (December 13, 2004). "A shape, a melodic fragment, a rhythm, a chord, a texture, or a sonority may ignite the appetite for exploration. How such simple insignificant things can be altered, elaborated, extended, and combined becomes the exciting challenge of composition. I also want the finished work to breathe in a natural way, to progress spontaneously, organically, moving toward a transformation of the musical substance in ways unimaginable to me when I began the journey. Transformation is the goal, with the intention of achieving an altered state of perception and exposure that I am otherwise unable to achieve." Wyner is currently composing a violin concerto for Daniel Stepner, one of the Brandeis University professors who comprise the Lydian String Quartet.

Personal Life

Wyner and his wife live in Medford, Massachusetts. From his first marriage he has two sons, Isaiah and Adam, and a daughter, Cassia. He also has several grandchildren, for whom he wrote a multilyric song called "The Button at the Bottom of the Butt." "I'm not sure it's suitable for all children," he told Stephen Heyman.

Further Reading

Boston Globe N p2 Apr. 11, 1999, C p13 Feb. 18, 2005, F p3 Apr. 19, 2006

Jewish Music WebCenter Nov. 5, 2006

Milken Archive of American Jewish Music

New York Times Westchester section p5 Aug. 2, 1981

Santa Fe New Mexican P p46 June 4, 1999

Schirmer.com

Who's Who in America

Neil Young

Musician; composer; singer

Born: Nov. 12, 1945
Primary Field: Rock; country; folk; heavy metal
Group Affiliation: Buffalo Springfield; Crosby, Stills, Nash and Young; Crazy Horse; solo performer

Introduction

Many critics consider Canadian-born Neil Young to be, after Bob Dylan, the most important rock composer and performer that North America has produced. Young, a "flaky" rebel with a wry wit and a goofy smile that belies a dark seriousness, is an enigmatic artist who mixes folk, country, and pop in an original way, a rock poet with a musical style all his own, midway between "heavy metal" on the one extreme and rockabilly on the other. His lyrics are autobiographical, or at least highly personal, laments, simple in statement and complex in meaning—melancholy dreams tempered by a sense of reality and lightened by a love of life and a touch of irony.

Early Life

A son of Edna ("Rassy") Young, a former Canadian television quiz show panelist, and Scott Young, a *Toronto Sun* sportswriter, Neil Young was born in Toronto, Canada on November 12, 1945. His musical career might be dated from Christmas 1958, when his father gave him, among other presents, an inexpensive ukulele. Soon afterward, his parents separated, and Neil moved with his mother to Winnipeg while his older brother, Bob, remained in Toronto.

In Winnipeg, Young learned to play the banjo and the guitar and gravitated to dances at community clubs and schools where local groups he liked, especially the Reflections, were playing. An apathetic student—except for English classes—he dropped out of Kelvin High in Winnipeg in the fall of 1962 to devote himself to his own band, the Squires. With Young's mother as their aggressive booking agent, the Squires were soon well known to every disc jockey and entertainment writer in Winnipeg.

By 1964 Young was doing his own arrangements for the Squires and had begun to write songs. "He was uncertain of his voice then, an uncertainty that was to last five years until it became a fear that adversely affected his first solo album, Neil Young," his brother recalled in an article in *Maclean's* (May 1971), written with Jon Ruddy. "Only Rassy, working around the house and listening to Neil, sensed that he was finding himself and that the journey that would lead to Carnegie Hall had begun." Mrs. Young herself has said that she was always acutely aware of the "forlorn and desolate undertone" in her younger son's music: "At times I would wonder why his face would light up with a sort of joy when he'd play something he'd composed that was so sad it brought tears to my eyes." Formative influences on Young included Elvis Presley, the Ventures, the Shadows, and, of course, the Beatles and Bob Dylan.

Life's Work

Moving back to Toronto, Young did folk-singing gigs in coffeehouses, accompanying himself on the twelve-string acoustic guitar. On the coffeehouse circuit he met, among others, singer Joni Mitchell and musicians Stephen Stills and Richie Furay. After hearing "Sugar

Mountain," Young's song about growing too old for admission to the local teen club, Miss Mitchell wrote "The Circle Game," one of her most popular works, with him in mind.

In Toronto, Young joined a rock and blues group called Ricky James and the Mynah Birds. As quoted by Cameron Crowe in *Rolling Stone* (February 8, 1979), James remembers Young as "never very healthy—he got bad epileptic fits sometimes ... ," When the Mynah Birds broke up—after cutting a record in Detroit—Young and bassist Bruce Palmer headed £or Los Angeles in an old black hearse that Young had bought. After making a stopover in Albuquerque, New Mexico (where Young was hospitalized for shock and exhaustion following an automobile accident) they reached their destination. In Los Angeles early in 1966 they joined with Stephen Stills, Richie Furay, and Springfield, named after a steamroller parked drummer Dewey Martin to form the Buffalo outside the house they were rehearsing in.

The Buffalo Springfield quickly gained a massive reputation-and an amazingly enduring one, despite its relatively brief existence of less than two years. Although Stills's song "For What It's Worth" (about hippie riots on the Sunset Strip), became a countercultural anthem and made the Buffalo Springfield famous nationwide, Neil Young attracted most, of the attention with his personality and style and the energy he put into his lead-guitar duels with Stills. The ten songs that Young contributed to the four albums the Buffalo Springfield cut on the Atco label included "Nowadays Clancy Can't Even Sing," "Burned," and "Out of My Mind." The four albums were *Buffalo Springfield* (February 1967), *Buffalo Springfield Again* (December 1967), *Last Time Around* (August 1968) and the retrospective *The Best of the Buffalo Springfield* (January 1969).

Observing that "Buffalo Springfield has long been streamlined into the key myth of L.A. rock," Bart Testa wrote in the *Toronto Globe and Mail* (September 30, 1978): "The band produced music crucial to the evolution of L.A. rock. Its legacy anticipated the coincidence of opposites inherent in L.A. rock—a sparkling surface blanketing the melancholy of song writers obsessed with the theme of survival. Young's special contributions, in songs like 'Mr. Soul' and 'Broken Arrow' pushed this theme a bit further: his lyrics were about people who didn't survive. They sank away out of sight to become aliens. Young, the outsider, had caught on; he was already singing about the California secret, the California ghosts, like the American Indian of 'Broken Arrow' whom Young frequently impersonated at the time."

During Buffalo Springfield's short life span, Joni Mitchell introduced Young to her manager, Elliot Roberts, a man whose sensibility was in tune with Young's reputed erraticism and skewed sense of humor, an idiosyncratic commodity that escaped many of Young's associates. The two felt an immediate rapport, and after Buffalo Springfield's demise Roberts launched Young on his solo career.

After the failure of the over-dubbed *Neil Young* (January 1969)—which included the self-portrait "The Loner"—Young set up his own studio, in the garage of his mountain home in Topanga, California. More important, he found the backup band he needed in Crazy Horse (originally the Rockets), consisting of lead guitarist Danny Whitten, bassist Billy Talbot, drummer Ralph Molina, and occasionally, pianist Jack Nitzsche, who also served as producer and arranger. Later, guitarist Nils Lofgrin was added to the group. In recent years the members have been Talbot, Molina, and Frank Sampedro (organ and rhythm guitar).

The first collaboration of Young and Crazy Horse was the "cosmic cowboy" recording *Everybody Knows This Is Nowhere*, released in May 1969 by Warner Brothers' Reprise [Young's solo label ever since]. That album, which included" the "strange songs" (Molina's description) "Cowgirl in the Sand," "Cinnamon Girl," and the big hit "Down by the River," easily earned Young and Crazy Horse a gold record, and it remained on the charts for a year and a half.

Meanwhile, Stephen Stills and David Crosby (formerly of the Byrds) met Graham Nash of the Hollies at the home of Joni Mitchell, and the three formed their supergroup. With the understanding that he would be free to come and go as he pleased, Young was brought into the superstar ensemble in time for the debut of Crosby, Stills, Nash, and Young at the historic Woodstock Festival in August 1969. Young has self-effacingly described his role in the group as "just a guitarist who sang a few songs," but the songs included "Helpless" and "Country Girl," his contributions to Crosby, Stills, Nash, and Young's Atlantic album Deja Vu (March 1970), and "Ohio," which saturated the airwaves during the nationwide student uprisings that followed the Kent State University massacre in May 1970.

Atlantic issued a second Crosby, Stills, Nash, and Young recording, *Four-Way Street*, in April 1971, and the four musicians were temporarily reunited in a

Affiliation: Multiple Styles and Groups

Young delivers them in a fragile voice that is as haunting as the words themselves, an unmistakable, unforgettable high tenor that hovers on the verge of cracking, and he accompanies himself on the electric or acoustic guitar, sometimes with slashing intensity, sometimes in a "laid-back" manner, but always with an underlying urgency. Young first gained recognition in the late 1960's as a member of the legendary Buffalo Springfield, a seminal contributor to the evolution of Los Angeles "hard rock," and in 1970 and 1971 as a member of Crosby, Stills, Nash, and Young, once described in Time magazine as "perhaps the mightiest U.S. super-group of all . . . whose pungent lyrics and soft-edged counterpoint to acid rock made them a primal force in popular music." As a solo artist, Young has toured widely—but preferably in a low-key way, to avoid the superstar trap—often with his backup group, Crazy Horse, and he has made some dozen albums, including the "gold" [million-selling) releases Everybody Knows This Is Nowhere (1969), *After the Goldrush,* (1970), Harvest (1972), and *Comes a Time* (1978). *Rust Never Sleeps* (1979) was number seven on *Rolling Stone*'s Top 100 chart in November 1979, after sixteen weeks on the chart. Among all of his songs, "Heart of Gold" has achieved the widest popularity.

summer tour three years later. Assessing the quartet in his syndicated newspaper column, the late music critic Ralph Gleason as early as 1970 singled out Young as "an extraordinary new songwriter, quite possibly the most important new poet since Bob Dylan."

Young's first screen soundtrack credits were *The Landlord* (United Artists, 1970), *The Strawberry Statement* [MGM, 1970), and *Celebration at Big Sun* (Twentieth Century-Fox, 1971). Young was interested in making films himself, and the actor Dean Stockwell, a friend of his, suggested to him an idea for a screenplay with an apocalyptic theme—about three persons (one a moody musician) caught up in an imagined tidal wave that devastates Topanga Canyon. The film project fell by the wayside, but the idea inspired most of the material for Young's third solo album, *After the Gold Rush* (August 1970), which included the cuts "Southern Man," "Tell Me Why," "Only Love Can Break Your Heart," "Don't Let It Bring You Down," and "I Believe in You." Recorded with various pickup musicians over a period of several months, the recording was released by Reprise in August 1970.

In *Melody Maker*'s international poll *After the Gold Rush* was chosen album of the year, and Robert Hilburn spoke for a legion of reviewers and fans when he wrote in the *Los Angeles Times* (September 29, 1971): "Words like lovely, beautiful and romantic cannot often be applied to rock albums, but there haven't been many rock albums like Neil Young's *After the Gold Rush.* It is a delicate, fragile jewel. ... In the album's best moments, Young's soft, disarming voice and the crisp haunting instrumentation are almost therapeutically gentle in this time of assault rock." A back ailment forced Young to wear a brace and use an acoustic guitar when making a low-key tour following the release of *After the Gold Rush.* During a stopover in Nashville, Tennessee, the capital of country music, he began recording his fourth solo album, with Nashville's Stray Gators and two others who were, like himself, "crossovers" from pop-rock singer Linda Ronstadt and singer-musician James Taylor. (Taylor can be heard playing banjo on "Heart of Gold.") Following operations for. a slipped disk and a long recuperation at his new ranch in northern California, Young finished *Harvest* (February 1972). The album was the biggest seller of 1972, and the cut "Heart of Gold" ["I've been searchin' for a heart of gold/ And I'm growin' old"] remains the number-one single of Young's career. The success (especially that of "Heart of Gold") put Young, as he later wrote in the liner notes for the retrospective album *Decade* (October 1977), "in the middle of the road. Traveling there soon became a bore so I headed for the ditch. A rougher ride, but I saw more interesting people there."

Journey through the Past (November 1972) was the soundtrack for an undistributed movie, a musical fantasy written and directed by and starring Young. The failure of the film project was followed by the drug-related deaths of Danny Whitten and Crazy Horse "roadie" Bruce Berry—and the beginning of what Young calls his "dark period." The acute anguish he felt at that time is evident in the albums *Time Fades Away* (October 1973), *On the Beach* (July 1974), and, above all, *Tonight's the Night* (June 1975). Of the latter, Bart Testa wrote in his *Toronto Globe* and *Mail* article: "This brutally direct evocation of drugs, death, and naked impotence deliberately dispensed with all the niceties associated with L.A. rock. And there was certainly no hint of the cosmic cowboy. On one song, 'Mellow My Mind,' Young sings with vicious irony of a 'situation that can casualize your mind.' Tonight gave new meaning to the phrase, 'bad gestalt.' Before this, Young had always been the affable, if somewhat withdrawn, Canadian kid. Here he tortured his frail voice, made music of raw nerves and blurted out thoughts that no one ever suspected he had."

Teaming up once more with the reorganized Crazy Horse, Young regained an upbeat with Zuma (November 1975), a majestic rock soliloquy about the Aztecs, with "Cortez the Killer" as its centerpiece. *American Stars 'n Bars* (June 1977) was so called, Young has explained, "because one side is about American folk heroes and the other is about getting loose in bars." Before the album was completed he added several songs "written fast and in the spirit of country music," performed with Crazy Horse and the Saddlebags (singers Nicolette Larson and Linda Ronstadt]. One of the songs omitted from the released version of *American Stars 'n Bars*, "Powderfinger," was sent to Ronnie Van Zant of Lynyrd Skynyrd, who was intending to use it in a recording at the time he was killed in a plane crash. (Ultimately the song turned up in *Rust Never Sleeps*.) Regarding one of the late Van Zant's best known compositions, Young has said, "I'd rather play 'Sweet Home Alabama' than 'Southern Man' any time. I first heard it and really liked the way they played their guitars. Then I heard my own name in it and I thought, 'Now this is pretty great.'"

Until word got out and crowds began to converge, Young unwound for several weeks in 1977 by playing in bars around Santa Cruz, California with Ducks, a band that included Johnny C. Craviotto and Bob Mosley. Later in the year he took a leisurely trip across country in his tour bus. Arriving in Nashville again, he cut *Comes a Time* (September 1978) with Nicolette Larson and an orchestra composed of twenty-two pickup musicians. *Comes a Time*, Young's sunniest, most easy-going and calmly philosophical recording in years, evoked comparisons with *After the Gold Rush* and sold better than any of his albums since *Harvest*. Young was one of the guest performers seen in the concert film *The Last Waltz* (United Artists, 1978), Martin Scorsese's documentary of the final reunion of Bob- Dylan and The Band.

Always moving on, Young could barely relate to *Comes a Time* by the time it hit the charts, as he explained to Cameron Crowe: "I'm somewhere else now. I'm into rock 'n' roll. . . . I first knew something was going on when we visited England a year and a half ago. Kids were tired of the rock stars and the limousines and the abusing of stage privileges as stars. There was a new music the kids were listening to. Punk music, New Wave. You can call it what you want. It's rock 'n' roll to me."

It was members of the New Wave group Devo (when working with Young in another of his abortive film projects, the fantasy "Human Highway") who suggested to him "Rust never sleeps," a commercial slogan (for Rustoleum) to which he gave a new meaning, having to do with the death of rock stars like Elvis Presley and Johnny Rotten, the threat of entropy in rock 'n' roll generally (including the threat to himself), and rock's preoccupation with destruction and violence.

Out of a tour with Crazy Horse in the fall of 1978 came the concert film *Rust Never Sleeps* (International Harmony, 1979), with Young credited as director, under the alias Bernard Shakey. The film received mixed notices, leaning to the negative. Joseph McLellan of the *Washington Post* (August 17, 1979) observed that Young "occasionally can be a powerful though somewhat unfocused poet," and Wayne Roberts reported in *Newsday* (August 16, 1979): "In concert Young's gaunt, haggard look gave him a charismatic, if sallow, glow. That look doesn't survive the transformation to film. Young looks edgy and haunted." The critic for *Variety* (July 25, 1979) wrote, "Young's music is hauntingly effective, but he seems determined to translate some kind of message about rock 'n' roll during his performance that is never made clear." The essential message was in clear enough, as expressed in the song "Out of the Blue," written with the Sex Pistols in mind. Its lines included the ironic "My, my, hey, hey / Rock 'n' roll is here to stay" and the darkly philosophical "It is better to burn out than it is to rust."

In his review of the album *Rust Never Sleeps* (June 1979) in the *New York Times* (July 1, 1979), John Rockwell observed that Young's artistic reputation has never reached its due height, perhaps because "he's too obsessed with his loner-wastrel Romantic image." He challenged the prevalent impression that Young is a "hippie-flake, some sort of strange, self-indulgent, anti-social eccentric," asserting: "In fact, he's produced a steadier, higher quality sequence of rock albums than anyone [else] one can think of in the 1970's, balancing the needs of commerciality and conscience with a rare delicacy. One of these days he'll have an album that tops the charts and convinces doubters that he deserves to be ranked right at the center of that mythic rock pantheon."

Young's voice, criticized by others as "a scratchy warble" and "a cracked moan," was earlier described by

Rockwell as ''a quavery poignant tenor whose rawness is itself a metaphor for vulnerability." Young's superb guitar work has "such urgency," a critic for *Newsday* (July 2, 1976) observed, as to make one feel he is "attempting to drive a stake through the heart of a vampire." But the strongest talent of this triple-threat artist is for reflective lyrics, deceptively simple while rich in metaphor and emotional shading.

At the start of the 1980s, distracted by domestic medical concerns relating to his second disabled son, Ben, Young had little time to spend on writing and recording. After providing the incidental music to a 1980 biographical film of Hunter S. Thompson entitled *Where the Buffalo Roam*, Young released *Hawks & Doves* (November 3, 1980), a short record pieced together from sessions going back to 1974.

1981's *Re-ac-tor*, an electric album recorded with Crazy Horse, also included material from the 1970s. Young did not tour in support of either album; in total, he played only one show, a set at the 1980 Bread and Roses Festival in Berkeley, between the end of his 1978 tour with Crazy Horse and the start of his tour with the Trans Band in mid-1982.

The 1982 album *Trans*, which incorporated vocoders, synthesizers, and electronic beats, was Young's first for the new label Geffen Records (distributed at the time by Warner Bros. Records, whose parent Warner Music Group owns most of Young's solo and band catalogue) and represented a distinct stylistic departure. Young later revealed that an inspiration for the album was the theme of technology and communication with his son Ben, who has severe cerebral palsy and cannot speak. An extensive tour preceded the release of the album, and was documented by the video *Neil Young in Berlin*, which saw release in 1986. MTV played the video for "Sample and Hold" in light rotation. The entire song contained "robot vocals" by Neil and Nils Lofgren.

Young's 1989 single "Rockin' in the Free World," which hit No. 2 on the US mainstream-rock charts, and accompanying album, *Freedom*, rocketed him back into the popular consciousness after a decade of sometimes-difficult genre experiments. The album's lyrics were often overtly political; "Rockin' in the Free World" deals with homelessness, terrorism, and environmental degradation, implicitly criticizing the government policies of President George H.W. Bush.

The use of heavy feedback and distortion on several *Freedom* tracks was reminiscent of the *Rust Never Sleeps* (1979) album, and foreshadowed the imminent rise of grunge. The rising stars of the genre, including Nirvana's Kurt Cobain and Pearl Jam's Eddie Vedder, frequently cited Young as a major influence, contributing to his popular revival. A tribute album called *The Bridge: A Tribute to Neil Young* was released in 1989, featuring covers by alternative and grunge acts including Sonic Youth, Nick Cave, Soul Asylum, Dinosaur Jr, and the Pixies.

Young's 1990 album *Ragged Glory*, recorded with Crazy Horse in a barn on his Northern California ranch, continued this distortion-heavy esthetic. Young toured for the album with Orange County, California country-punk band Social Distortion and alternative rock pioneers Sonic Youth as support, much to the consternation of many of his old fans. *Weld*, a two-disc live album documenting the tour, was released in 1991. Sonic Youth's influence was most evident on *Arc*, a 35-minute collage of feedback and distortion spliced together at the suggestion of Sonic Youth's Thurston Moore and originally packaged with some versions of *Weld.*

1992's *Harvest Moon* marked an abrupt return to the country and folk-rock stylings of *Harvest* (1972) and reunited him with some of the musicians from that album, including singers Linda Ronstadt and James Taylor. The title track was a minor hit and the record was well received by critics, winning the Juno Award for Album of the Year in 1994. In 1995 Young was inducted by Eddie Vedder into the Rock and Roll Hall of Fame.

Neil Young continued to release new material at a rapid pace through the last decade of the twentieth century and the first decade of the new millennium. The studio album *Silver & Gold* and live album *Road Rock Vol. 1* were released in 2000 and were both accompanied by live concert films. His 2001 single "Let's Roll" was a tribute to the victims of the September 11 attacks, and the effective action taken by the passengers and crew on Flight 93 in particular. At the "America: A Tribute to Heroes" benefit concert for the victims of the attacks, Young performed John Lennon's "Imagine" and accompanied Eddie Vedder and Mike McCready on "Long Road," a Pearl Jam song that was written with Young during the *Mirrorball* sessions.

Young continues to be socially and politically active. He remains on the board of directors of Farm Aid, an organization he co-founded with Willie Nelson and John Mellencamp in 1985. According to its website, it is the longest running concert benefit series in the USA, and it has raised $43 million since its first benefit concert in 1985. Each year, Young co-hosts and performs with well-known guest performers who include Dave Matthews and producers who include Evelyn Shriver and Mark Rothbaum, at the Farm Aid annual benefit concerts to raise funds and provide grants to family farms and prevent foreclosures, provide a crisis hotline, and create and promote home grown farm food in the United States.

On January 22, 2010, Young performed "Long May You Run" on the final episode of *The Tonight Show with Conan O'Brien*. On the same night, he and Dave Matthews performed the Hank Williams song "Alone and Forsaken," for the *Hope for Haiti Now: A Global Benefit for Earthquake Relief* charity telethon, in response to the 2010 Haiti earthquake. Young also performed "Long May You Run" at the closing ceremony of the 2010 Olympic winter games in Vancouver, British Columbia, Canada.

He has also started his Archives project, having released eight CDs so far in a box set covering his early years through 1972. His autobiography, *Waging Heavy Peace: A Hippie Dream* received both critical praise and commercial success.

PERSONAL LIFE

Neil Young is a gangly man with blue eyes, black hair that is graying, and a slight limp, the residue of a childhood bout with polio, and a manner that most interviewers have found "warm" and "congenial." He "stalks the stage like a slightly seedy James Stewart/ Henry Fonda type-moving in rhythmic bobs and weaves," as Paul Nelson limned him in *Rolling Stone* (July 27, 1978). "Head down, chin tucked into his shoulders like a boxer, he peers out at you with those all-knowing eyes filled with humor and flashes that beatific silly grin." According to Cameron Crowe in his *Rolling Stone* article, "For all his disheveled looks and maybe-I-know-where-I-am-maybe-I-don't stage presence, Young is not a drug case, has never taken acid, and never tried heroin," and he composed "The Needle and the Damage Done" for the late Danny Whitten.

Young lived at his ranch in San Mateo County, California with his second wife, Pegi and his son Zeke, the offspring of his earlier, long relationship with actress Carrie Snodgress. Young, who writes constantly and is fastidious about both the quality and the timing of his recordings, has a trove of unreleased tracks, many of them on the theme of disillusionment in romantic love. ''I think that romance itself is a quest," he has said. "When I sing about that, people see themselves as heading somewhere. They're not there—they're thinking about going there—they're on their way. . . . The music is about the frustration of not being able to attain what you want." As John Rockwell observed, Young is "the quintessential hippie-cowboy loner, struggling to build bridges from himself to women and through them to cosmic archetypes of the past arid of myth." On July 29, 2014, Young filed for divorce after 36 years of marriage.

FURTHER READING

Melody Maker 51:16+ Mr 27 '76 par

N Y Times II p1 + N 27 '77 par

Newsweek 92:118 + N 13 '78 par

Dufrechou, Carole. *Neil Young* (1978)

Logan, Nick and Woffinden, *Bob. The Illustrated Encyclopedia of Rock* (1976)

Stambler, Irwin. *Encyclopedia of Pop, Rock and Soul* (1974)

Who's Who in America, 1978-79

Young, Neil. *Waging Heavy Peace: A Hippie Dream* (2013)

Z

Dolora Zajick (ZAH-chick, duh-LORE-uh)

Opera singer

Born: 1954(?); Reno, Nevada
Primary Field: Opera
Group Affiliation: Solo performer with multiple companies

Dolora Zajick.

Introduction

"When I began, my voice was loud and ugly," the opera singer Dolora Zajick told Anthony Tommasini for the New York Times *(January 11, 1998). "I had no high notes and no low notes. I had to find my voice." The mezzo-soprano's search has led her to the pinnacle of her profession: according to the noted soprano Birgit Nilsson, Zajick's voice is "the only one existing today without any competition "in the world"; the equally renowned mezzosoprano Marilyn Horne, whom Tommasini also quoted, described Zajick herself as "a force of nature." "It's not just her amazing voice," Horne said; "it's what she can do with her voice because of her superb technique and dedication." Zajick is considered a foremost interpreter of mezzo-soprano roles created by the great 19th-century Italian operatic composer Giuseppe Verdi. She has performed three of the best known—Azucena in* Il Trovatore, *Amneris in* Aïda, *and Eboli in* Don Carlo*—with major companies all over the world.*

Early Life

Zajick has revealed little about her personal life to journalists. She was born in about 1954 in Reno, Nevada, the eldest of two sisters and three brothers in a family of Slavic descent. Of limited economic means, the family owned few records; their collection reportedly consisted merely of several pieces of orchestral music—Handel's *Water Music,* Tchaikovsky's *Nutcracker Suite,* and Rimsky-Korsakov's *Scheherazade.* Zajick often sang at home with her brothers, and in eighth grade she joined her school choir. For a short time she played the drums. "Every singer should study percussion—you'd be

Affiliation: Operatic Range and Craftsmanship

That same year Zajick won the $20,000 Richard Tucker Music Foundation Award; she also auditioned for two prestigious companies—the Chicago Lyric Opera and the Houston Opera-and for the prominent conductors Riccardo Muti and Mstislav Rostropovich. Emerging from each of the auditions with an assignment, she traveled all over the world to perform, generally to great acclaim. Critics marveled at her range: while the average mezzo has a range of two octaves, from A flat to A flat, Zajick can hit a stunning high C and then descend to a solid low G. In October 1988 she made her debut with the Metropolitan Opera in New York City, singing Azucena, a role she would also perform at her debut in Vienna, Austria, later that year. In assessing her performance in Austria for the *New York Times* (October 13, 1988), the notoriously exacting opera critic Will Crutchfield wrote, "Her assumption of Azucena was distinguished by certain details of craftsmanship that have long been rare in Verdian mezzo parts." Although he felt that Zajick lacked a sense of drama, he conceded that since this was her Met debut, judging her dramatic skills was premature. At the Met the next season, she appeared as Amneris, the spurned princess in *Ai'da,* a role with which she has become as closely identified as she has with that of Azucena.

Throughout the next decade almost every major opera company sought out Zajick, but she accepted roles selectively, reasoning that her voice would remain healthy longer if she didn't accept every job that came her way. Operas in which she agreed to sing included Tchaikovsky's *Dyeva,* Rimsky Korsakov's little-performed *Mlada,* and Sergei Prokofiev's *Alexander Nevsky.* A meticulous planner, she prepares for each role by writing in a notebook the complete text of the opera, with both a phonetic transcription using the International Phonetic Alphabet and a verbatim translation into English. Zajick has sung in Russian, French, and Italian. (Italian audiences have difficulty pronouncing her name, so she has become known simply as "La Dolora" in Italy.)

Zajick has rarely indulged in the type of dramatic or demanding behavior for which some other divas have become notorious. "A successful production is one that people get wrapped up in. That happens only when everyone works together, when nobody involved-director, conductor, or singer-is out there using 'applaud me' techniques or is on an ego trip," she explained to Phillips. "Oh, celebrities are good, and they should be encouraged, but the important thing is making the piece work, not ego." She continued, "I don't mind being in the background if it's appropriate. Singers, like jewels, work better in a good setting. Who cares about being center stage?"

In addition to avoiding discussions about her personal life, Zajick—unlike many of her colleagues in the competitive world of opera—has refused to discuss her colleagues with interviewers. She is willing to express her peeves about her profession, however. For example, she has bemoaned the trend among directors to update classic pieces-often, she feels, to their detriment-rather than to commission new works. "Opera could handle a lot of social issues with sensitivity, even AIDS. What you don't want is a *Traviata* with Violetta dying of AIDS," she told Phillips. (In Verdi's opera, Violetta dies of what is universally assumed to be consumption.) "There's a real need to do new works, and they don't have to be atonal, unvocal, or unmusical to be contemporary .... There are a lot of composers out there, but they're not being used. The film industry soaks up the good composers, the ones who could give us new works and thereby save us from the old ones done in a bizarre way." She has also voiced her distress about the current lack of emphasis on technical training of opera students. Zajick still studies with Puffer, who joined the faculty of the Manhattan School of Music in 1994, and believes that the greatest artists are oriented toward technique. "When you're connected technically, you empty out all the energy that is in you-that is you," she told Matthew Gurewitsch for *Opera News* (March 1996), as quoted on her Web site. "All the anguish, joy, everything. That's what people pay to see." Zajick has said that she feels a deep affinity for her audience, and despite her apparent lack of ego, she has admitted that she basks in applause. She also enjoys the feedback she receives via the Internet, which she uses extensively as a means of communication as well as a way to research her many interests.

Affilation ontinued on next page

Affiliation: Operatic Range and Craftsmanship (continued)

Zajick's albums include several recordings with the Metropolitan Opera conducted by James Levine, including *Aïda* (1991); *Highlights from Aïda* (1994); *Verdi: Greatest Hits* (1994); *Verdi: Highlights of Don Carlo* (1994); and *James Levine's 25th Anniversary Metropolitan Opera Gala* (1996). Another is Jules Massenet's *Herodiade* (1995), in a live performance by the San Francisco Opera Chorus and Orchestra, conducted by Valery Gergiev, in which Placido Domingo and Renee Fleming also sang.

In 2001 Zajick will be making many appearances in Verdi operas to mark the centennial of the composer's death, on January 27, 1901. The highlight will be a performance in Munich of the Verdi Requiem, conducted by Zubin Mehta.

Marilyn Horne told Anthony Tommasini, "Tenacity has counted for a tremendous amount in Dolora's career and her life." Matthew Gurewitsch wrote, "Willpower, cognition, study, patience: these are the tools of Zajick's craft." Gurewitsch also reported, "There is something sphinxlike about [the singer]. something abstract, withheld .... By her own account, Zajick prefers, in her work and her life, to operate on the intellectual level." Professing to favor solitary pursuits over socializing, Zajick wrote for the *New York Opera Newsletter* (June 1997), "I never feel at a loss after a performance. If anything, I feel relieved that I can go home and let my hair down and read or sleep, because by then I am very tired. Performing takes a lot out of me." According to an unsigned note in the newsletter, "While Ms. Zajick laughingly calls herself a hermit, she is known as a unifying factor in a cast, taking time to make other singers, chorus, and stage hands feel included."

surprised how many don't know the difference between an eighth and a sixteenth note," she told Harvey E. Phillips for *Opera News* (July 1988).

Zajick enrolled at the University of Nevada as a premed major. When journalists express surprise about that choice, she informs them that she has always had many interests other than music. Music won out, however, after she realized that she felt much happier singing with a chorus in her spare time than she did attending her biochemistry classes. After earning a bachelor's degree in music, she began to get small roles with the Nevada Opera. By her own account, the quality of her early performances was far from satisfactory; she has recalled with amusement being referred to as "King Kong" by a young tenor with whom she was to perform in *Trovatore.* "I had the basic vocal material to work with, and an instinctive ability to mimic sound, just the way some visual artists have an almost photographic gift for copying pictures," she told Tommasini. "But I was lucky to run into a teacher who knew how to form this material." That teacher was Ted Puffer, the artistic director of the Nevada Opera, to whom she has credited much of her success. "With him," she said to Tommasini, "I took my voice apart and put it back together." Although she envisioned remaining in her home state under his tutelage, Puffer encouraged her to further her studies in New York City, where he felt she would find greater opportunities to develop her career. Able to afford only a one-way plane ticket, she arrived in the city in 1982 with $200 in cash and one small suitcase. Rejected by the Juilliard School, she was admitted to the Manhattan School of Music, where she studied part-time.

Struggling to support herself, Zajick took odd jobs at the Jewish Guild for the Blind, among other places; her desperate financial straits even drove her to peddle decorated eggs from a stand outside Macy's department store, from which the police often chased her. She shared a one-bedroom apartment with 16 other students until they were evicted for violating rental restrictions. Afterward Zajick endured a period of homelessness. Unable to turn to her cash-strapped family, she sometimes stayed with friends, doing housework in exchange for a bed. Many times she slept in the music school's lounge or on a bench in Central Park. "I could have taken a job and had a stable living, but I probably would not have had my career," she explained to Tommasini. "When the choice was giving up comfort in order to have time for singing, I gave up comfort."

Meanwhile, Zajick's musical studies were going well, and her teachers encouraged her to prepare for the prestigious Tchaikovsky International Competition, held every four years for singers and instrumentalists in Moscow, in what was then the Soviet Union. Although she had no idea how she would raise the money to get there, she followed their advice. When the members of the First Presbyterian Church in Manhattan, where she sang in the choir, learned of her problem, they took up a collection to finance the trip. In addition, a member of the Manhattan School of Music's board of directors gave her $300 to buy suitable clothing. Zajick won a bronze medal in the 1982 competition; she was the only non-Soviet citizen to win that year and the first American to place in the event in 12 years.

LIFE'S WORK

After her performance in Moscow, Manhattan School administrators secured a loan for Zajick, thus enabling her to rent a comfortable apartment while she completed her studies. At about this time, the voice teacher and opera director Lou Galtiero approached Elizabeth Crittenden, a manager who had a reputation for nurturing young talent, and told her, according to Walter Price in the *New York Times* (February 11, 1990), "I've got this big mama with a big voice." Crittenden agreed to represent Zajick professionally, and with her manager's help, she gained admittance into the three-year Merola Opera Program for young artists, at the San Francisco Opera. While in San Francisco, Zajick has said, she turned into a full-fledged Verdi mezzo; punning to Phillips on the word "green" and the name "Verdi," which mean the same thing, she said, "I went in green and came out Verdi." In 1986 Terence McEwen, the general director of the San Francisco Opera, decided she was ready to make her San Francisco debut, and she did so in a major Verdi role, that of the gypsy Azucena in *Il Trovatore.*

PERSONAL LIFE

At her home in Nevada, she reads extensively on such topics as medicine, anthropology, history, and psychology. She also writes poetry and paints, most often pictures of natural subjects. Samples of her poetry and painting are on her Web site. In addition, Zajick is an accomplished gardener, and her home is lavishly landscaped. A self-described expert on frogs and toads, she keeps thousands of these amphibians in a pond on her property. Although she has lost some weight since she began her career, she remains a large, majestic performer, and critics agree that her voice more than matches her physique. Gurewitsch quoted an article from *Die Welt* (May 1995) that stated, "She has a voice on which one could raise whole temple complexes."

FURTHER READING

Classical p12 May 1990, with photo
Dolora Zajick Web site
Metropolitan Opera Web site
New York Times II p39 Jan. 11, 1998, with photos
Opera News p10+ July 1988, with photos

FRANCO ZEFFIRELLI

Theatrical and operatic director

Born: Feb. 12, 1923; Florence, Italy
Primary Field: Theater
Group Affiliation: Various production companies

INTRODUCTION

The Florentine director and designer Franco Zeffirelli has been called "the most authentic genius in the modern theater." Zeffirelli began his career as an actor, worked in the theater and in films as assistant director to Luchino Visconti, and then established a reputation as a stage and costume designer. He became a director in 1954, when he launched a one-man international "crusade against boredom in the opera." His campaign culminated in 1964 with his triumphant Falstaff *at the Metropolitan—a production acclaimed as "a gigantic forward step in the concept of opera." Until now Zeffirelli has worked comparatively little in the legitimate theater, but his Italian production of* Who's Afraid of Virginia Woolf? *took Rome by storm, and his* Old Vic Romeo and Juliet *was praised as "a revelation."*

EARLY LIFE

Franco Zeffirelli Gorsi was born on February 12, 1923 in Florence, Italy, the son of a businessman called Ottorini Corsi and of the former Adelaide Garosi, a fashion designer. He has three stepsisters and a stepbrother. The Corsi family originated in Vinci, near Florence, and has connections with the family of Leonardo da Vinci. Zeffirelli, as he prefers to be called, owes his excellent English to the British governess who was his first teacher. He subsequently enrolled in the Liceo Artistico (the art school) in Florence, graduating in 1941. His father planned a career in architecture for him, and Zeffirelli went on to study at the School of Architecture at the University of Florence. There he became director of the university's theater company and gained his first operatic experience as a director and designer of amateur productions staged in Siena by students of his aunt, the former soprano Ines Alfani Tellini.

In 1943, when he was twenty, Zeffirelli was swept up in the war. Italy was then under German occupation, and he fought against the Nazis for a year as a partisan. Zeffirelli, who later received a silver medal for his work as a partisan, served in 1944-45 as an interpreter attached to the Scots Guards. During this period he met a number of British theater people then serving with the armed forces in Italy, and found his imagination fired. The war ended in 1945 and Zeffirelli, against parental opposition, abandoned his architectural studies and went to Rome. He began his theatrical career in 1945 as a radio actor and in 1946 joined Luchino Visconti's Morelli-Stoppa Company as an actor and stage manager.

Life's Work

Two small roles with the famous stage company were enough to convince Zeffirelli that his future did not lie in acting, and thereafter, for about two years, he worked with Morelli-Stoppa as an assistant director. In 1948, when Visconti took a sabbatical from the company to work on his film *La Terra Trema,* Zeffirelli went with him to Sicily. *La Terra Trema* was acted entirely by the Sicilian fishermen whose harsh lives were its subject, and stands as one of the crowning achievements of Italian neorealism. Zeffirelli subsequently worked on films with de Sica and Rossellini but, as he has acknowledged, it was from Visconti that he learned most. Although he has long since developed his own unique style, Zeffirelli has never lost the perfectionism or the infinite attention to detail that Visconti instilled in him, and he remains an exponent of *verismo*, which Kenneth Tynan has defined as "an unqualified conviction that the roots of art lie in actual human behaviour."

Zeffirelli turned to stage design in 1948, when he assisted Salvador Dali with the extraordinary sets for the Morelli-Stoppa production of *As You Like It.* In 1948-49 he designed Visconti's production of *A Streetcar Named Desire,* and in 1949 the same director's lavish version of Shakespeare's *Troilus and Cressida.* This production, spectacularly staged in the Boboli Gardens in Florence, was Zeffirelli's first great success as a designer. His second came in 1951, when he created sets for a Morelli-Stoppa production of Chekhov's *Three Sisters* that, according to one authority, "are a legend among Italian playgoers."

Troilus and Cressida had brought Zeffirelli to the attention of the director of La Scala, Milan. His first major assignment for the opera house came during 1952-53, when he designed a production of Rossini's *L'Italiana in Algeri.* A year later he served as both director and designer of Rossini's *La Cenerentola* at the same theater, contriving rather stolid sets and costumes that some critics thought inappropriate to the frivolity of the opera. No reservations greeted the "exquisite" production of L'Elisir d'Amore with which Zeffirelli graced La Scala's 1954-55 season. Meanwhile, intent on broadening his experience, he had begun an intensive period of work in Italy's provincial opera houses, where during the next few years he staged most of the standard repertory operas.

His first foreign assignment was at the 1956 Holland Festival, to which he contributed a brilliant *Falstaff.* The following year he made the first of a series of annual visits to the Dallas Civic Opera, where in 1958 he attracted international attention with his unorthodox design and staging of Verdi's *La Traviata.* Violetta, sung by Maria Callas, was revealed at the beginning of the Prelude already close to death. The rest of the opera then unfolded in flashback. Some critics were outraged, but others felt that Zeffirelli had seized upon a conception implicit but previously unrecognized in Verdi's music. In the same year Zeffirelli directed a revival of *Mignon* at La Scala, with sets by his friend Lila de Nobili, which met with only limited success.

In November 1960 Zeffirelli returned to Dallas, where he directed *Alcina* in which Joan Sutherland made her American debut, visualizing it as "a grand musical evening in the noble milieu of Handel's time." He further enriched the Dallas season with sumptuous productions of *Don Giovanni* and *Daughter of the Regiment.* July 1961 found him back in England with a production at Glyndebourne of *L'Elisir d'Amore*. The color, movement, and vivacity of the production were admired, but J. W. Lambert in the *Christian Science Monitor* (July 5, 1961) accused Zeffirelli of "producer's itch," and suggested that the "calculated over-elaboration" of his effects distracted attention from the singers and even, to some extent, from the music. Similar criticisms greeted his 1961 production of Shakespeare's *Othello* at Stratford on Avon. Sir John Gielgud was thought miscast in the lead, and the "gorgeous stage pictures" that

Zeffirelli created as designer tended further, in the opinion of some critics, to submerge Gielgud's rather petulant Othello. It was in 1961 also that Zeffirelli directed a stylish *Falstaff* at Covent Garden and worked for a season with the Lyric Opera of Chicago.

The United States saw Zeffirelli's *Romeo and Juliet* in 1962, when the Old Vic took it on tour. American critics echoed the praises of their British counterparts, but entertained fewer reservations. Zeffirelli spent most of that year repeating various of his operatic successes in a number of European cities, and in March 1963 he opened his production of *The Lady of the Camellias* at the Winter Garden in New York. It was his first genuine failure. A new dramatization by Giles Cooper of the Dumas novel, the play starred Susan Strasberg as the prostitute redeemed by love. Rejecting the tradition that Camille should be played by a mature actress, Zeffirelli conceived of it as a drama about youth thwarted by age. Most critics believed his approach did nothing to redeem a faded and old-fashioned valentine.

Another controversial production followed in May 1963, when Zeffirelli directed *Aida* at La Scala, with Leontyne Price and Carlo Bergonzi singing the leads. It was the director's most expensive and spectacular presentation, crowding the stage with massive pyramids, 200-foot idols, 600 singers and dancers, and ten live horses. "I have tried to give the public the best that Cecil B. De Mille could offer, but in good taste," Zeffirelli said cheerfully. Most critics conceded that he had succeeded in the first part of his intention, but some thought the production's visual opulence overwhelmed the singing. The otherwise unsatisfactory year included at least one major success, however. Zeffirelli directed the first Italian production of *Who's Afraid of Virginia Woolf?* in Rome, winning unanimous acclaim.

Zeffirelli's *Tosca*, which brought Maria Callas back to Covent Garden in January 1964 after a long absence, was greeted with enthusiasm. The director seemed to have disciplined the weakness for overelaboration that had exercised his critics. Philip Hope-Wallace in the *Guardian* (January 23, 1964) wrote that "Zeffirelli . . . does not intrude; there is none of that distraction which in my view mars his Falstaff and Don Giovanni, nor any liberties against the musical planning. . . ." Noting many instances of imaginative thinking, the critic concluded, "Mr. Zeffirelli has done nothing better." A production of *Rigoletto* in the same Covent Garden season earned similar if more subdued praise.

Affiliation: The "Real International Zeffirelli Explosion"

What William Weaver in *High Fidelity* (March 1964) has called the "real international Zeffirelli explosion" followed in 1959. Making his English debut at the Royal Opera House, Covent Garden, Zeffirelli staged rejuvenated productions of *Lucia di Lammermoor, Cavalleria Rusticana,* and *I Pagliacci.* His *Covent Garden Lucia,* establishing him as an operatic director of the first rank, also launched Joan Sutherland's career, and Zeffirelli has been widely credited with helping to develop Miss Sutherland as an actress. One critic called the production "a Victorian period piece, but seen through the eyes of 1959," and it was widely hailed as a "triumph." During the same crowded year Zeffirelli directed *The Barber of Seville at Dallas,* and as director and in some cases as designer also mounted productions in Genoa, Palermo, Siena, and at the Piccola Scala.

If Zeffirelli's *Lucia* won him international recognition as an operatic director, his Old Vic production of *Romeo and Juliet* the following year did as much for his reputation in the legitimate theater. As a foreign director in a Shakespearean stronghold, he might have been expected to treat the play reverently. Instead he staged it as "a passionate story of young love in a rather seedy Italian town." Zeffirelli's own sets created a crumbling, sun-drenched, and turbulent Verona. The young bullies who milled about the piazza resembled today's juvenile delinquents, and they fought with a violence more often found on the screen than on the stage of the Old Vic. Romeo and Juliet themselves were presented as confused and passionate adolescents.

The result, which gained in naturalism what it lost in poetry, divided the British critics. Some regarded Zeffirelli's *Romeo and Juliet* as a misguided nonmusical version of *West Side Story.* Others—by far the majority—shared the view expressed by Kenneth Tynan in the New York *Herald Tribune* (October 16, 1960). He called it "a revelation, even perhaps a revolution. The production evoked a whole town, a whole riotous manner of living; so abundant and compelling was the life on the stage that I could not wait to find out what happened next. The Vic has done nothing better for a decade."

Zeffirelli made his debut at the Metropolitan Opera House on March 6, 1964, handling direction, sets, and costumes in a production of Verdi's *Falstaff* that was a personal triumph. Directing the opera for the fifth time, Zeffirelli set a logical but richly imaginative interpretation of the work against a "rowdily Elizabethan" decor, and with Leonard Bernstein's assistance on the podium achieved what was recognized as "a cohesive unity of words, music and sight." Alan Rich, writing in *The Lively Arts* (March 29, 1964), said: "Zeffirelli's achievement in Falstaff is on a level that perhaps surpasses any operatic production the Metropolitan Opera has ever mounted. . . . What he has done . . . represents a distinct forward step in the whole conception of visual opera . . . he has orchestrated *Falstaff* in terms of light, color and action, and has created an orchestration exactly congruent with the one conceived by Verdi."

Shortly after the triumph of his Metropolitan Opera *Falstaff*, Zeffirelli told a *Time* interviewer (March 13, 1964): "I've spent the ten best years of my life doing opera, and now I will do it only for special events." One such event will be the opening of the new Metropolitan Opera House in Lincoln Center in the fall of 1966. Samuel Barber is writing an opera based on Shakespeare's *Antony and Cleopatra* for the occasion, and Zeffirelli has agreed to direct and design the production and to collaborate with Barber on the libretto.

British critics found his production of Shakespeare's *Hamlet* with the Anna Proclemer-Giorgio Albertazzi Company of Rome at the Old Vic in September 1964 another special event. Using an abstract, semicircular setting, Zeffirelli adopted a subjective approach to Shakespeare's masterpiece, in which all the action is seen through the eyes of Hamlet. Reviewers were impressed by the visual fascination, especially the lighting, and the intellectual gymnastics of the production.

Zeffirelli's first film as director was a version of *The Taming of the Shrew* (1967), originally intended for Sophia Loren and Marcello Mastroianni but finally including the Hollywood stars Elizabeth Taylor and Richard Burton instead. Taylor and Burton helped fund production and took a percentage of the profits rather than their normal salaries. While editing *The Taming of the Shrew*, Zeffirelli's native Florence was devastated by floods. A month later, Zeffirelli released a short documentary, *Florence: Days of Destruction,* to raise funds for the disaster appeal.

Zeffirelli's major breakthrough came the year after when he presented two teenagers as *Romeo and Juliet* (1968). The movie is still immensely popular and was for many years the standard adaptation of the play shown to students. This movie also made Zeffirelli a household name - no other subsequent work by him had the immediate impact of *Romeo and Juliet.*

After two successful film adaptations of Shakespeare, Zeffirelli went on to religious themes, first with a film about the life of St. Francis of Assisi titled *Brother Sun, Sister Moon* (1972), then his extended miniseries *Jesus of Nazareth* (1977) with an all-star cast. The latter was a major success in the ratings and has been frequently shown on television in the years since.

He moved on to contemporary themes with a remake of the boxing picture *The Champ* (1979) and the critically panned *Endless Love* (1981). In the 1980s, he made a series of successful films adapting opera to the screen, with such stars as Plácido Domingo, Teresa Stratas, Juan Pons, and Katia Ricciarelli. He returned to Shakespeare with *Hamlet* (1990), casting the then–action hero Mel Gibson in the lead role. His 1996 adaptation of the Charlotte Brontë novel *Jane Eyre* was a critical success.

In November 2004, he was awarded an honorary knighthood by the United Kingdom.

PERSONAL LIFE

Franco Zeffirelli is unmarried. In 1996, Zeffirelli came out as gay, but has since preferred to be discreet about his personal life. Zeffirelli considers himself "homosexual" rather than gay, he feels the term "gay" is less elegant. Zeffirelli has adopted two adult sons, men he has worked with for years and who now live with him and manage his affairs. He has gray-blue eyes and light-brown hair and has been described as "slight and willowy." Gareth Lloyd Evans in the *Guardian* (October 5, 1961) wrote of him that "his accent is slight, his voice even-toned, his gestures spare. The eyes are restless, but sometimes pause on you with disconcerting acuteness. He slips into first acquaintance easily, and smokes Salems like a furnace." Zeffirelli was born a Roman Catholic; he belongs to no political party. He has a passion for fast cars and enjoys gardening, sea sports, and the company of friends. But, he wrote recently, "I actually take the work in the theatre as my best recreation, particularly the time spent in paint shops, props departments, and wardrobes."

Further Reading
High Fidelity 14:30 Mr '64 por
London Observer pi 3 D 18 '60
Manchester *Guardian* p7 O 5 '61
Mus Am 82:17 N '62 por
Opera p771+ D '59 por
Opera N 27:15 D 15 '62 por
Cole, T. and Chinoy, H. K. *Directors on Directing* (1964)
International Who's Who, 1963-64
Kitchin, L. *Mid-Century Drama* (1962)
Who's Who, 1964
NY Times Ag 8 '09

Eugenia Zukerman (ZOOK-er-man)

Flutist; writer; television journalist

Born: Sep. 25, 1944; Cambridge, Massachusetts
Primary Field: Classical
Group Affiliation: Solo performer

Introduction

Torn as a young adult between choosing a career in music or pursuing one in writing, Eugenia Zukerman did both. Zukerman is a renowned flutist and the author of four books—two novels, a collection of reminiscences by accomplished women, and an account of her ordeal in fighting a life-threatening lung disease. Since 1980 she has also worked as a journalist for the CBS-TV show Sunday Morning, *and since 1998 as the assistant art director of the Bravo! Vail Valley Music Festival, in Colorado. According to Zukerman, her varied vocations have two important elements in common: "structure and form," as she wrote for the Hong Kong Philharmonic Orchestra Web site. "When I look at a piece of music, I look at it in an intellectual way ...," she explained. "When I'm writing, I think that writing has to be musical to be good. Journalism is about listening.... Music is about listening. . . . I use all of the skills I've learned."*

Early Life

The second of the three children of Shirley Cohen Rich and Stanley Rich, Zukerman was born Eugenia Rich on September 25, 1944 in Cambridge, Massachusetts; she grew up in Hartford, Connecticut. Her older sister, now Julie Ingelfinger, is a pediatric nephrologist; her younger sister, Laurie Rich Alban, is a media consultant and writer. Zukerman has credited her mother-a modern dancer and the first woman accepted into the graduate engineering program at the City College of New York-with encouraging her and her two sisters to be guided by the knowledge that life is filled with possibilities. Her father was a nuclear physicist who taught at the Massachusetts Institute of Technology; a prolific inventor and entrepreneur, he developed a scanning sonar device used in submarines during World War II. Zukerman's parents both loved music, and her father played the piano. When Eugenia was 10 years old, the Hartford Symphony Orchestra performed at her grade school. The orchestra's flutist caught her attention immediately. "It was one of the huge moments in my life," she told Richard Duckett for the Worcester, Massachusetts, *Telegram & Gazette* (January 10, 2002). "I just ran home and said I have to do this." She soon began taking flute lessons. During her senior year at William Hall High School, in West Hartford, she began studying with Julius Baker, the principal flutist of the New York Philharmonic.

After she graduated from high school, Zukerman enrolled at Barnard College, in New York City, where she majored in English and struggled to decide which of her passions, writing or music, she would pursue as a career. "Academics told me you will never be a writer if you play the flute. And the musicologists were saying you have to choose something," she told Linda Lehrer for the *Chicago Tribune* (February 13, 1994). Julius Baker, however, encouraged her to study both music and writing; she could get a job in an orchestra to support herself while writing a novel, he told her. After her sophomore year at Barnard, she transferred to the Juilliard School of Music, also in New York City. At Juilliard, where she earned a bachelor's degree, she became friendly with the violinist and violist Pinchas Zukerman, who won the highly prestigious Leventritt Competition in 1967. The two married in 1968. Eugenia Zukerman spent the next several years accompanying her husband on his concert tours. The couple's two daughters, Arianna and Natalia, were born in 1972 and 1975, respectively.

Life's Work

Earlier, on March 9, 1971, shortly after she won a Young Concert Artists competition, Eugenia Zukerman made her solo concert debut, at New York City's Town Hall. Since then she has performed as a soloist with more than 100 orchestras and other musical ensembles, among them the Royal Philharmonic Orchestra (London); the National Symphony Orchestra (Washington, D.C.); the Los Angeles Philharmonic; the Minnesota Orchestra; the Moscow, Prague, Stuttgart, Slovakian, Israel, Denver, and English Chamber Orchestras; the Shanghai Quartet (China); and the Chamber Music Society of Lincoln Center (New York City). She has also collaborated with many other soloists, among them the cellist Yo-Yo Ma and the pianist Emanuel Ax, and, in a recital, with the actress Claire Bloom. In addition, she has performed at many music festivals, including the Aspen festival, in Colorado; Mostly Mozart (New York City); OKMozart (near Tulsa, Oklahoma); Ravinia (near Chicago, Illinois); Tanglewood (Lenox, Massachusetts); Edinburgh (Scotland); South Bank (London); Spoleto (Italy); Schleswig-Holstein (Germany); Gstaad (Switzerland); and Angel Fire (New Mexico).

Zukerman has recorded more than 20 albums, among them *Music for a Sunday Morning* (1995) and *China-Song* (2002, both with the Shanghai Quartet), *Incantation* (1996), *Mozart: Flute Cancertos, Clarinet Concerto* (1996, with the English Chamber Orchestra), *Aria* (1997, with the oboist Allan Vogel and the pianist Dennis Helmrich), and *Lowell Liebermann: Symphony No. 2, Concerto for Flute & Orchestra* (2000, with the Dallas Symphony Orchestra). She has also contributed to various albums, among them *CBS Masterworks Dinner Classics: Sunday Brunch, Volume II* (1991, with the English Chamber Orchestra), *For the Friends of Alec Wilder* (1994, with the Manhattan Chamber Orchestra), *The Essential Classics Collection* (1997), *Engineer's Choice II* (1997), *Music of Alan Hovhaness* (2000), and many compilations of music for children, among them *Heigh-hot Mozart: Favorite Disney Tunes in the Style of Great Classical Composers* (1995), *Bibbidi! Bobbidi! Bach: More Favorite Disney Tunes* (1996), *Baby Needs Mozart* (1998), *Baby Needs Baroque* (1998), *Baby Needs Bach* (1999), *Baby Needs More Mozart* (1999), and *Baby Needs Music* (2002).

Zukerman spent three and a half years, during breaks in her performance schedule, writing her first novel, *Deceptive Cadence* (1981). The story is about a Hungarian pianist who disappears before a major concert. In a review for the *New York Times* (December 28, 1980), Alan Cheuse described *Deceptive Cadence* as an "admirable and entertaining first novel" and "a pleasure to read." Zukerman's second novel, *Taking the Heat*

Affiliation: Classical Music

In a review of *Time Pieces* (1991), for which Zukerman and the harpsichordist Anthony Newman played works by Haydn, Mozart, Hemmel, and Kuhlau, Joseph McLellan wrote for the *Washington Post* (March 17, 1991), "*Time Pieces* is a meeting of minds between two strong musical personalities who do not know how to play a phrase routinely." After attending a performance of Christopher Rouse's Flute Concerto by Zukerman and the Colorado Symphony Orchestra, Kyle MacMillan wrote for the *Denver Post* (May 20, 2001), as quoted on Zukerman's Web site, "Zukerman was quite simply superb throughout. The flutist capably handled all of the many technical challenges, from the twists and jolts of the fourth movement to the minute phrasings necessary in the first, and she did it with a warm, inviting and enveloping tone. But what was more important was the result: a subtle, sensitive and expressive interpretation that revealed the heart and soul of this deeply moving music and made it achingly and movingly vivid." Martha Erwin, reviewing a concert by Zukerman and the harpist Yolanda Kondonassis for the *Richmond [Virginia] Times Dispatch* (October 3, 2002), was impressed by the pair's rendering of Hovhaness's "The Garden of Adonis" and Persichetti's Serenade No. 10. Of the former, Erwin wrote, "Zukerman's flute, sounding a trifle more breathy than usual for this veteran, weaved skillfully through the difficult intervals and echoed the composer's fondness for the music of India and Japan by minimizing the vibrato." Commenting on the latter piece, she wrote, "The scherzando, typically a high-energy movement, pushed the flutist into the extremes of high and low range. Both performers were up to these challenges, and the final movement-marked vivo-was fast, furious, and expressive.... The flutist needs the diaphragm of a long-distance swimmer, and Zukerman sustains long melodic lines with never a gasp."

(1991), focuses on a flutist who leaves her husband to play chamber music near Auschwitz, Poland, the site of an infamous World War II concentration camp. Joseph McLellan wrote that *Taking the Heat* is "a superbly crafted story of suburban family life, adultery, guilt and retribution, peopled with vividly realized characters and weaving music . . . deftly into its fabric." Jack Sullivan, who assessed *Taking the Heat* for the *Washington Post* (March 22, 1991), praised Zukerman's dramatic depiction, in "vivid fictional scenarios," of the "intimate, authoritatively sketched details of a musician's life-the womanizing conductor, the guerrilla warfare of competitive players, the incredible adrenaline level required for a successful performance." Sullivan complained, however, that Zukerman's "characters often exist not as people but as didactic mouthpieces.... Other musician-writers, from E.T.A. Hoffman to Anthony Burgess, have found ways to fuse musical prose with musical form. Here one simply wants to put down this oddly unmusical book and put on one of the author's wonderful recordings."

For her nonfiction book *In My Mother's Closet: An Invitation to Remember* (2003), Zukerman interviewed 42 women, among them her mother and daughters; the actresses Carrie Fisher, Claire Bloom, and Mary-Louise Parker; the singers Judy Collins and Renee Fleming; Joy Behar of the ABC daytime talk show *The View;* and the writer Erica Jong. Colette Bancroft, in a review for the *St. Petersburg [Florida] Times* (May 10, 2003), found the book to be "an affecting and sometimes surprising look at the infinite variety of ways that mothers can be role models for their daughters. From thrifty homemakers who sewed their own clothes . . . to a movie star whose massive closet includes the 'Shrine of the Wigs,' their closets tell their stories."

In her third career, as a television journalist, Zukerman has served since 1980 as the arts correspondent for the CBS show *Sunday Morning,* reporting on theater, music, the visual arts, and film by interviewing noteworthy professionals in those fields. (She had neither seen the program nor had any experience in television journalism before Shad Northshield, one of *Sunday Morning's* co-creators, recruited her.) She told Linda Lehrer that the program "brings people into live performance in a way I don't think any other [network news] show does." Zukerman was nominated for an Emmy Award for her piece on the violinist Itzhak Perlman (whom she has known personally for many years) and received the New York Foundation for the Arts' Champions of the Arts award for her work on *Sunday Morning.* In addition, she has written articles for *Vogue,* the *New York Times,* the *Washington Post,* and *Esquire* and has sold screenplays to three major Hollywood studios.

In 1995 Zukerman was diagnosed with eosinophilic pneumonitis, a rare, occasionally fatal lung disease. Prednisone, the drug she took to combat her illness (which is now in remission), led to side effects—bone loss, mood swings, and panic attacks—that to her seemed almost as difficult to bear as the symptoms of the disease. *Coping with Prednisone* (1997), which she wrote with her sister Julie Ingelfinger, describes her experiences during her illness and with the drug. "With her sister . . . Zukerman has written an empathetic, easy-to-understand, and factually accurate guide that offers suggestions, recipes, and exercises for relieving the drug's unpleasantness," Margaret Norden wrote in a review for *Library Journal* (July 1, 1997). "I feel lucky to be alive but I feel urgently that I have things to do," Zukerman told Richard Duckett.

Zukerman, who currently gives from 40 to 60 concerts a year, has been the artistic director of the six-week Bravo! Vail Valley Music Festival, in Colorado, since 1998. Since her arrival the Dallas Symphony Orchestra, the Rochester Philharmonic, and the Colorado Symphony, among other groups, have served as orchestras in residence. The violinists Pamela Frank and Nadja Salerno-Sonnenberg, the pianists Andre Watts and Garrick Ohlsson, the Shanghai Quartet, and the ensemble eighth blackbird have performed at the festival in recent years. During her travels Zukerman often visits schools to talk about music and a life in music, hoping to inspire young students to pursue careers in the arts. "I'm a real champion of outreach programs, being a musician [myself] because of an outreach program," she told Lehrer. "I remember the feeling of that day, hearing the sound of the flute-which was completely magical-and being transformed. And you have to say to yourself if that happened to me it can happen to other children. I want to make that possible for them."

Zukerman also hopes to change how children and others perceive classical music. "People look at classical music as a dinosaur," she told Lehrer. "Well, dinosaurs became extinct because they failed to adapt to a change in climate. I think it is possible to adapt to a change in the climate in America without compromising the arts." Zukerman believes that because American society has become so visually oriented, she and her colleagues must find new ways to draw audiences and make them want to return. In her own concerts, she often talks about the pieces on her program. "As a flute player, lots of the music I play is not well known. So I find myself . . . giving historical context to the music, and information about the composer," she told Elizabeth Murfee for the *Carnegie Hall Stagebill* (October 1993). "There has been a change in the way concerts are presented today. The concert hall is no longer a 'temple of art' with the audience playing the role of worshiping acolytes. The atmosphere is friendlier, more relaxed. You can see it in the clothing of the audience and even the performers. Talking to the audience is an outgrowth of this."

Personal Life

Zukerman's marriage to Pinchas Zukerman ended in divorce in 1983. In 1988 she married the film writer and director David Seltzer, whose screenwriting credits include *The Omen* and *My Giant*. The couple have homes in Venice, California, and New York City. Zukerman's older daughter, Arianna Zukerman, is a professional soprano who performs regularly with her mother. Her younger daughter, Natalia Zukerman, is a professional guitarist and singer-songwriter. In her free time Eugenia Zukerman enjoys the outdoors, especially hiking on mountain trails. "I feel, as [do] many women my age, that I want to age gracefully," she told Lehrer. "I want to be one of those great old ladies. I want to have young friends, to be able to be supportive of my kids and other kids and play the flute until I can't breathe anymore."

Further Reading

Chicago Tribune VI p8 Feb. 13, 1994, with photo
New York Times XIV p11 Oct. 18, 1998, with photo
People p213 Sep. 15, 1997, with photo
(Worcester, Massachusetts) *Telegram & Gazette* C p1 Jan. 10, 2002, with photo

Appendixes

Music Timeline

Date	Milestone
1936	Electric guitars debut. In 1946 the Fender Electric Instrument Manufacturing Company is founded. In 1950 the Fender Broadcaster is introduced for national distribution.
1942	Bing Crosby releases "White Christmas," from the film *Holiday Inn.* The song goes on to be the all-time, top-selling song from a film.
	RCA Victor sprays gold over Glenn Miller's million-copy-seller *Chattanooga Choo Choo*, creating the first "gold record."
1948	Columbia Records introduces the 33 1/3 LP ("long playing") record at New York's Waldorf-Astoria Hotel. It allows listeners to enjoy an unprecedented 25 minutes of music per side, compared to the four minutes per side of the standard 78 rpm record.
1949	45 rpm records are sold in the U.S.
1951	In an effort to introduce rhythm and blues to a broader white audience, which was hesitant to embrace "black music," disc jockey Alan Freed uses the term rock 'n' roll to describe R&B.
1954	Bill Haley and the Comets begin writing hit songs. As a white band using black-derived forms, they venture into rock 'n' roll.
1956	With many hit singles (including "Heartbreak Hotel"), Elvis Presley emerges as one of the world's first rock stars. The gyrating rocker enjoys fame on the stages of the Milton Berle, Steve Allen and Ed Sullivan shows, as well as in the first of his many movies, *Love Me Tender*.
1957	Leonard Bernstein completes *West Side Story*.
1958	*Billboard* debuts its Hot 100 chart. Ricky Nelson's "Poor Little Fool" boasts the first No. 1 record.
1959	The National Academy of Recording Arts and Sciences sponsors the first Grammy Award ceremony for music recorded in 1958.
	Frank Sinatra wins his first Grammy Award—Best Album for *Come Dance with Me*.
1963	A wave of Beatlemania hits the U.K. The Beatles, a British band composed of John Lennon, George Harrison, Ringo Starr and Paul McCartney, take Britain by storm.
	The Rolling Stones emerge as the anti-Beatles, with an aggressive, blues-derived style.

1964 Folk musician Bob Dylan becomes increasingly popular during this time of social protest with songs expressing objection to the condition of American society.

The Beatles appear on *The Ed Sullivan Show*.

1967 The Beatles release their break-through concept album, *Sergeant Pepper's Lonely Hearts Club Band.*

Psychedelic bands such as The Grateful Dead and Jefferson Airplane enjoy great success during this period with songs celebrating the counterculture of the '60s.

1969 In August, more than half a million people attend the Woodstock music festival in Bethel, N.Y. (near Woodstock, N.Y.) Performers include Janis Joplin; Jimi Hendrix; The Who; Joan Baez; Crosby, Stills, Nash and Young; Jefferson Airplane; and Sly and the Family Stone.

1973 The Jamaican film *The Harder They Come*, starring Jimmy Cliff, launches the popularity of reggae music in the United States.

1974 Patti Smith releases what is considered to be the first punk rock single, "Hey Joe." Punk roars out of Britain during the late-'70s, with bands such as the Sex Pistols and the Clash expressing nihilistic and anarchistic views in response to a lack of opportunity in Britain, boredom, and antipathy for the bland music of the day.

1977 *Saturday Night Fever* sparks the disco inferno.

Elvis Presley dies at Graceland, his Memphis, Tenn. home. He was 42.

1978 Sony introduces the Walkman, the first portable stereo.

1979 The Sugar Hill Gang releases the first commercial rap hit, "Rapper's Delight," bringing rap off the New York streets and into the popular music scene. Rap originated in the mid 1970s as rhyme spoken over an instrumental track provided by snatches of music from records. Over the decades, rap becomes one of the most important commercial and artistic branches of pop music.

1981 MTV goes on the air running around the clock music videos, debuting with "Video Killed the Radio Star."

1982 Michael Jackson releases *Thriller*, which sells more than 25 million copies, becoming the biggest-selling album in history.

1983 With the introduction of noise-free compact discs, the vinyl record begins a steep decline.

1984 Led by Bob Geldof, the band Band Aid releases "Do They Know It's Christmas," with proceeds of the single going to feed the starving in Africa.

1985 Madonna launches her first road show, the Virgin Tour.

Dozens of top-name musicians and bands perform at the Live Aid concerts in Philadelphia and London. The shows benefit African famine victims.

1988 CDs outsell vinyl records for the first time.

1991 Seattle band Nirvana releases the song "Smells Like Teen Spirit" on the LP *Nevermind* and enjoys national success. With Nirvana's hit comes the grunge movement, which is characterized by distorted guitars, dispirited vocals,and lots of flannel.

1992 Compact discs surpass cassette tapes as the preferred medium for recorded music.

1994 Woodstock '94 commemorates the original weekend-long concert. Green Day and Nine Inch Nails join Woodstock veterans including Santana and Joe Cocker.

1995 The Rock and Roll Hall of Fame Museum opens in Cleveland. Renowned architect I. M. Pei designed the ultra-modern, 150,000 square-foot building.

2000 The Internet transforms music scene as companies offer free music over the Internet without paying copyright fees. Music industry executives take the issue to court. A ruling prompts Napster to stop distributing copyrighted music free and team up with industry giant Bertelsmann to provide material for a fee.

2003 Apple Computer introduces Apple iTunes Music Store, which allows people to download songs for 99 cents each.

2013 Vinyl records continue to make a strong comeback. While CD sales decline 14.5% and digital sales decline 2%, vinyl sales increase 33.5% for the year. According to Nielsen SoundScan, for the sixth consecutive year, the music industry sees an increase in vinyl sales. In fact, more vinyl albums are purchased in 2013 than any other year since Nielsen SoundScan started keeping score.

Hall of Fame for Music and Musicians

Alabama Jazz Hall of Fame (1978)
Birmingham, AL
www.jazzhall.com/jazzhalloffame/jazzhalloffame.htm
Inductees listed by year of induction

American Classical Music Hall of Fame and Museum (1996)
Cincinnati, OH
http://classicalwalkoffame.org/
Inductees listed both alphabetically and by year of induction

Blues Foundation Blues Hall of Fame (1980)
Memphis, TN
http://blues.org
Inductees listed alphabetically

Country Music Hall of Fame (1961)
Nashville, TN
http://countrymusichalloffame.org/
Inductees listed by year

Folk Music Hall of Fame (2011)
New York
http://folkmusichalloffame.org/

Hip Hop Hall of Fame (1992–97, relaunched 2013)
New York
http://hiphophof.tv/
No inductees listed on web site

International Bluegrass Music Museum (1991)
Owensboro, KY
www.bluegrassmuseum.org/inductees/
Inductees listed by year

Musicians Hall of Fame and Museum (2011)
Nashville, TN
www.musicianshalloffame.com/
Musicians listed by year of induction

New Jersey Jazz Society/American Jazz Hall of Fame (1983)
New Jersey
http://rockhall.com/visit-the-museum/plan/
www.njjs.org/p/AJHOF_roster.php
Inductees listed alphabetically

Oklahoma Jazz Hall of Fame (1988)
Tulsa, OK
http://okjazz.org
Inductees listed alphabetically

Rhythm and Blues Hall of Fame (2010)
Memphis, TN and Detroit, MI
http://rhythmandblueshof.com/
2013–15 inductees listed

Rock and Roll Hall of Fame (1986)
Cleveland, OH
http://rockhall.com
Musicians listed alphabetically

Music Awards Ceremonies

American Music Awards (AMAs)
http://theamas.com
20 award categories

***Billboard* Music Awards**
www.billboard.com/billboard-music-awards
41 award categories

Gospel Music Awards (GMAs)
www.gmahalloffame.org/

Grammy Awards
www.grammy.com/
33 award categories

MTV Music Awards (VMAs)
http://mtv.com
20 award categories

Indexes

Music Category Index

Soul

Theater

Western

Index